Modern
English Readings

Modern
English Readings

Fifth Edition

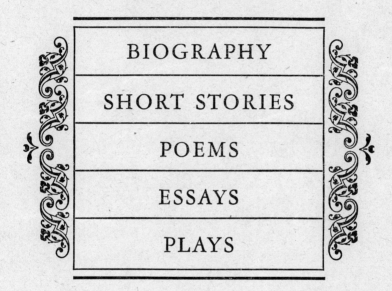

BIOGRAPHY

SHORT STORIES

POEMS

ESSAYS

PLAYS

Edited by

ROGER SHERMAN LOOMIS

and

DONALD LEMEN CLARK

COLUMBIA UNIVERSITY

1 9 4 6

RINEHART & COMPANY, INC., *NEW YORK*

I N this, as in other editions of *Modern English Readings,* the editors have been guided in their selection by three aims: (1) The teaching of vital and correct expression through the study of models. (2) The quickening of the student's interest in literature by giving some of the best fiction, drama, essays, biography, and poetry of the last hundred years to read attentively and to enjoy. (3) An introduction to those problems which, today more than ever, if left unsolved or wrongly solved, mean individual misery and a world in utter chaos.

The end of the second World War has intensified some problems and introduced others. The relation of a college education to the requirements and responsibilities of postgraduate life is discussed in two new and provocative articles, which may be compared and contrasted with Chancellor Hutchins' "Education for Freedom." There is an authoritative discussion of "The Radio Boom and the Public Interest." This and Lilienthal's article on TVA and Crowther's proposal for a "People's Charter" involve the perennial and momentous issue, the merits of public control as against "freedom of enterprise." Three Americans, the financier Lamont, the professor Dobie, and the war correspondent Hersey, contribute to our understanding of the peoples of England and Russia, an understanding on which the peace of the world so largely depends. The limitless possibilities of the atomic age for the easing or the ending of life on this planet are discussed with knowledge and power by Harry M. Davis and Norman Cousins.

To the section entitled Autobiographic Chapters we have added Oliver La Farge's brilliant account of the technique and the thrills of rowing and three extracts from Ernie Pyle's unpretentious masterpiece *Brave Men.* Elizabeth Jackson's familiar essay "Of Goodness" handles with a light touch and catholic wisdom the most difficult of subjects in a self-conscious and anti-Puritan age, a subject, however, which is never out of date. The head of the Human Engineering Laboratory presents in "Vocabulary and Success" his data proving an unexpected correlation between the understanding of words and the management of men. And Langewiesche's article "Why an Airplane Flies" affords a perfect example of the use of words for the most utilitarian purposes.

Continuing our effort to select short stories which bear a close relationship in theme and material to the lives and interests of our students today, we have added Irwin Shaw's new story, "The Veterans Reflect," with its challenge for the entering students who were not in the war as well as for the returning veterans whom we welcome to college classes. With a different setting, but alike in theme and intention, is another new story now included, Howard Fast's "The Day of Victory." We have also added a deceptively simple and very brief story of college life, James Reid Parker's "The First Day," which may do something, we hope, to dispel the notion that students and teachers are natural enemies.

In the third edition we added to our selection of plays MacLeish's poetic radio play, *The Fall of the City,* remarking in our preface on the vast audiences reached by the radio play as compared to the smaller audiences reached by the traditional theater. Since then great progress has been made in the development of dramatic programs on the air, in recognition of which we add the justly famous *Good Heavens* by the acknowledged chief of radio dramatists, Norman Corwin.

In our continuing effort to represent modern poets in ever-increasing number, we have omitted in this edition a number of early nineteenth century poetic classics, easily accessible elsewhere, in order to include new poems by Leonora Speyer, Robert Frost, Franklin P. Adams, Siegfried Sassoon, E. E. Cummings, Stephen Spender, Thomas S. Jones, Jr., José Garcia Villa, Gerard Manley Hopkins, Edith Sitwell, T. S. Eliot, Alfred Kreymborg, Langston Hughes, and George Santayana. Some of these modern poets, as well as some older ones, appear in a new section, *Poems about Liberty,* which like the section, *Poetry of Social Change,* groups together a number of poetic treatments of a theme of vital contemporary interest to young people of all ages.

As in previous editions, the Student Helps and Theme Suggestions at the close offer some guidance to student reading and classroom discussion and furnish possible answers to the question, "What shall I write about?" Brief biographical notes at the end enable one to identify the authors.

We wish to express our thanks to the authors, publishers, and editors who have generously allowed us to use copyright material. Specific indebtedness is acknowledged in our footnotes. Our gratitude is due to the generations of college men and women who have patiently sat in our classes and from whom we have learned most of what we know of the desires and the needs of those for whom we have prepared this book. And there have been kindly critics who have given us their impressions of what could be dispensed with and their suggestions as to what to add. They deserve our all too inadequate thanks.

R. S. L.
D. L. C.

Columbia University
April, 1946

Hiroshima —
Hersey

TABLE OF CONTENTS

Arranged by Forms

BIOGRAPHY

READING, WRITING, AND REVIEWS

EXPOSITION

DISCUSSIONS OF MODERN PROBLEMS

SHORT STORIES

TABLE OF CONTENTS

Arranged by Topics and Purposes [1]

ENJOYING

[1] Since this is not a strictly scientific classification and many of the items lend themselves to different methods of approach, the same title may be found under two or more headings.

SONG

READING

THE GIFT OF AMERICA

UNDERSTANDING

SCIENCE AND ITS APPLICATIONS

NATURE AND MAN

MAN AND GOD

DOING

INTRODUCTORY

ALL writing worthy of the name of literature confers on the sensitive reader a thrill of pleasure. It is out of gratitude for this pleasure that the world has always honored its writers of epic and romance, comedy and tragedy, genial essay and caustic satire. The pleasure varies vastly in kind and degree, and one bit of verse or prose may combine many forms of pleasure. There may be rhythms of phrase or line or stanza that charm the inner ear; there may be music of vowels and consonants; there may be exquisite imagery or faithful portrayal of men and things; there may be emotions of curiosity, humor, indignation, passion, worship, despair, courage, and pity. There may be simply the pleasure of enlightenment, of gaining a clearer insight into questions that perplex and baffle. And always there must be for the sensitive and intelligent reader the pleasing sense of artistry, of a job done with the right tools, with the right technique of verse or prose.

This collection of literature is intended for those college men and women who have learned already to demand honesty, intelligence, and taste in their reading, whose minds have graduated beyond the faked sentimentality of sob-sisters, and the boyish heroisms of Western stories. Between these covers there is literary fare of many flavors, but all of it adapted to mature minds and exacting tastes, and some of it the work of the recognized literary geniuses of the last hundred or more years. Here is a small part of your rich heritage of emotional experience and intellectual insight. It is for you to read, to ponder, to enjoy.

Perhaps you would like to stop there. But it is part of your preparation for life, a requirement for your joining the company of educated men and women, that you should be able to use this same instrument of language yourself. Not that any one expects you to become a Newman or a Poe or a Swinburne. But the ability to write with clarity and correctness, and if possible with some force and charm, is of immense use both in college and after; without it the rest of your education loses much of its efficacy. Your reading in this book, therefore, will form the basis for class discussion and for written papers. You will have an opportunity to learn from the masters of prose how to put your ideas and your experiences on paper. Write always with honesty, saying what you have really felt or what you believe to be true. Work always toward greater and greater clarity of thought and expression. Develop your capacity for seeing the humors, the shams, the ecstasies, the tragedies that give life its enthralling interest. Search for the right word and the telling phrase; build the paragraph or the composition into a reasoned or a shapely whole. In sum, develop in your writing that sincerity, intelligence, and taste which are the earmarks of all good writing. And if you do, some of you will be writing literature; in a modest way, of course, but still literature.

BIOGRAPHY

BIOGRAPHY

It is a good sign, perhaps, that biography and detective fiction have had a special vogue in the United States during the decades just past; for good biography creates and satisfies a craving for realities, and even mediocre detective stories rouse the torpid faculties of observation and reasoning. If we could evolve a species of literature which would render the interpretation of present-day realities as exciting and as clear-cut as the solution of a murder mystery, we might have some hope of emerging from chaos and muddlement into a happier world.

As it is, we have biography. Here are segments of reality as observed by sensitive and acute minds, phases of experience with which most of us have had no direct contact, or phases of experience familiar enough but seen with other and sharper eyes. To read biography with an active imagination is vastly to extend the orbit of one's life; to travel in other times and climes with fascinating companions—and at a minimum of expense. Who does not feel pride and pleasure in making the acquaintance of "Jeb" Stuart, gallant cavalry officer of the Confederacy, whose gold spurs and chivalrous heart were realities of eighty-five years ago? Who can read without fascination the story of the great gawky giant from the Prairie who preserved the Union,—the plain facts of his young manhood, clerking in a store, joking, wrestling with toughs, finding ecstasy and agony in love? Who does not live through those four years with the Curies in a leaky shed in Paris and tingle with excitement when at last radium glows in the darkness? And we venture to question whether any of our own experiences with parents or professors can be more vivid and pleasurable than our vicarious—and hilarious—experiences with the father of Clarence Day and the botany professor of James Thurber.

Reading biography not only multiplies the possibilities of pleasurable and interesting experience, but also provokes thought. Side by side in this volume are portrayed two kinds of war experience, Florence Nightingale's and "Jeb" Stuart's; and two extraordinary characters thrive on that experience. What thoughts arise in the reading as to the effects of war on character, honor in warfare, the role of women? As one makes the acquaintance of Pyle's "Brave Men," what thoughts arise about the last world conflict? Can one read about Elizabeth Arden without some reflections on the beauty business, about Sheean's college days without asking what is the main business of education? Biography extends our acquaintance with the realities of the past and the present, and offers a broader basis for judgment than our own limited lives afford.

Close attention will reveal something of the arts of narrative and character analysis. How is the impression of reality conveyed? What uses may be made of description and background? How are effects of irony, suspense, and humor secured? When is direct quotation from dialogue or letters employed? What are the most impressive passages? What lends them their power?

BIOGRAPHY

Florence Nightingale[1]

by LYTTON STRACHEY

EVERYONE knows the popular conception of Florence Nightingale. The saintly, self-sacrificing woman, the delicate maiden of high degree who threw aside the pleasures of life of ease to succour the afflicted, the Lady with the Lamp, gliding through the horrors of the hospital at Scutari, and consecrating with the radiance of her goodness the dying soldier's couch—the vision is familiar to all. But the truth was different. The Miss Nightingale of fact was not as facile fancy painted her. She worked in another fashion, and towards another end; she moved under the stress of an impetus which finds no place in the popular imagination. A Demon possessed her. Now demons, whatever else they may be, are full of interest. And so it happens that in the real Miss Nightingale there was more that was interesting than in the legendary one; there was also less that was agreeable.

Her family was extremely well-to-do, and connected by marriage with a spreading circle of other well-to-do families. There was a large country house in Derbyshire; there was another in the New Forest; there were Mayfair rooms for the London season and all its finest parties; there were tours on the Continent with even more than the usual number of Italian operas and glimpses at the celebrities of Paris. Brought up among such advantages, it was only natural to suppose that Florence would show a proper appreciation of them by doing her duty in that state of life unto which it had pleased God to call her—in other words, by marrying, after a fitting number of dances and dinner-parties, an eligible gentleman, and living happily ever afterwards. Her sister, her cousins, all the young ladies of her acquaintance, were either getting ready to do this or had already done it. It was inconceivable that Florence should dream of anything else; yet dream she did. Ah! To do her duty in that state of life unto which it had pleased God to call her! Assuredly she would not be behindhand in doing her duty; but unto what state of life *had* it pleased God to call her? That was the question. God's calls are many, and they are strange. Unto what state of life had it pleased Him to call Charlotte Corday, or Elizabeth of Hungary? What was that secret voice in her ear, if it was not a call? Why had she felt, from her earliest years, those mysterious promptings towards . . . she hardly knew what but certainly towards something very different from anything around her? Why, as a child in the nursery, when her sister had shown a healthy pleasure in tearing her dolls to pieces, had *she* shown an almost morbid one in sewing them up again? Why was she driven now to minister to the poor in their cottages, to watch

[1] From Lytton Strachey, *Eminent Victorians* (1918). By permission of Harcourt, Brace and Co.

by sick-beds, to put her dog's wounded paw into elaborate splints as if it was
a human being? Why was her head filled with queer imaginations of the
country house at Embley turned, by some enchantment, into a hospital, with
herself as matron moving about among the beds? Why was even her vision
of heaven itself filled with suffering patients to whom she was being useful?
So she dreamed and wondered, and, taking out her diary, she poured into it
the agitations of her soul. And then the bell rang, and it was time to go and
dress for dinner.

As the years passed, a restlessness began to grow upon her. She was unhappy, and at last she knew it. Mrs. Nightingale, too, began to notice that
there was something wrong. It was very odd; what could be the matter with
dear Flo? Mr. Nightingale suggested that a husband might be advisable;
but the curious thing was that she seemed to take no interest in husbands.
And with her attractions, and her accomplishments, too! There was nothing
in the world to prevent her making a really brilliant match. But no! She
would think of nothing but how to satisfy that singular craving of hers to be
doing something. As if there was not plenty to do in any case, in the
ordinary way, at home. There was the china to look after, and there was
her father to be read to after dinner. Mrs. Nightingale could not understand
it; and then one day her perplexity was changed to consternation and alarm.
Florence announced an extreme desire to go to Salisbury Hospital for several
months as a nurse; and she confessed to some visionary plan of eventually
setting up in a house of her own in a neighboring village, and there founding
"something like a Protestant Sisterhood, without vows, for women of educated
feelings." The whole scheme was summarily brushed aside as preposterous;
and Mrs. Nightingale, after the first shock of terror, was able to settle down
again more or less comfortably to her embroidery. But Florence, who was
now twenty-five and felt that the dream of her life had been shattered, came
near to desperation.

And, indeed, the difficulties in her path were great. For not only was it
an almost unimaginable thing in those days for a woman of means to make
her own way in the world and to live in independence, but the particular
profession for which Florence was clearly marked out both by her instincts
and her capacities was at that time a peculiarly disreputable one. A "nurse"
meant then a coarse old woman, always ignorant, usually dirty, often brutal,
a Mrs. Gamp, in bunched-up sordid garments, tippling at the brandy-bottle
or indulging in worse irregularities. The nurses in the hospitals were especially notorious for immoral conduct; sobriety almost unknown among them;
and they could hardly be trusted to carry out the simplest medical duties. Certainly, things have changed since those days; and that they *have* changed is
due, far more than to any other human being, to Miss Nightingale herself.
It is not to be wondered at that her parents should have shuddered at the
notion of their daughter devoting her life to such an occupation. "It was as
if," she herself said afterward, "I had wanted to be a kitchen-maid." Yet the
want, absurd, impracticable as it was, not only remained fixed immovably in

her heart, but grew in intensity day by day. Her wretchedness deepened into a morbid melancholy. Everything about her was vile, and she herself, it was clear, to have deserved such misery, was even viler than her surroundings. Yes, she had sinned—"standing before God's judgment seat." "No one," she declared, "has so grieved the Holy Spirit"; of that she was quite certain. It was in vain that she prayed to be delivered from vanity and hypocrisy, and she could not bear to smile or to be gay, "because she hated God to hear her laugh, as if she had not repented of her sin."

A weaker spirit would have been overwhelmed by the load of such distresses—would have yielded or snapped. But this extraordinary young woman held firm, and fought her way to victory. With an amazing persistency, during the eight years that followed her rebuff over Salisbury Hospital, she struggled and worked and planned. While superficially she was carrying on the life of a brilliant girl in high society, while internally she was a prey to the tortures of regret and of remorse, she yet possessed the energy to collect the knowledge and to undergo the experience which alone could enable her to do what she had determined she would do in the end. In secret she devoured the reports of medical commissions, the pamphlets of sanitary authorities, the histories of hospitals and homes. She spent the intervals of the London season in ragged schools and workhouses. When she went abroad with her family, she used her spare time so well that there was hardly a great hospital in Europe with which she was not acquainted, hardly a great city whose slums she had not passed through. She managed to spend some days in a convent school in Rome, and some weeks as a "Sœur de Charité" in Paris. Then, while her mother and sister were taking the waters at Carlsbad, she succeeded in slipping off to a nursing institution at Kaiserswerth, where she remained for more than three months. This was the critical event of her life. The experience which she gained as a nurse at Kaiserswerth formed the foundation of all her future action and finally fixed her in her career.

But one other trial awaited her. The allurements of the world she had brushed aside with disdain and loathing; she had resisted the subtler temptation which, in her weariness, had sometimes come upon her, of devoting her baffled energies to art or literature; the last ordeal appeared in the shape of a desirable young man. Hitherto, her lovers had been nothing to her but an added burden and a mockery; but now— For a moment, she wavered. A new feeling swept over her—a feeling which she had never known before, which she was never to know again. The most powerful and the profoundest of all the instincts of humanity laid claim upon her. But it rose before her, that instinct, arrayed—how could it be otherwise?—in the inevitable habiliments of a Victorian marriage; and she had the strength to stamp it underfoot.

I have an intellectual nature which requires satisfaction [she noted], and that would find it in him. I have a passional nature which requires satisfaction, and that would find it in him. I have a moral, an active nature which requires satisfaction, and that would not find it in his life. Sometimes I think that I will satisfy my passional nature at all events. . . .

But no, she knew in her heart that it could not be. "To be nailed to a continuation and exaggeration of my present life . . . to put it out of my power ever to be able to seize the chance of forming for myself a true and rich life" —that would be a suicide. She made her choice, and refused what was at least a certain happiness for a visionary good which might never come to her at all. And so she returned to her old life of waiting and bitterness.

The thoughts and feelings that I have now [she wrote] I can remember since I was six years old. A profession, a trade, a necessary occupation, something to fill and employ all my faculties, I have always felt essential to me, I have always longed for. The first thought I can remember, and the last, was nursing work; and in the absence of this, education work, but more the education of the bad than of the young. . . . Everything has been tried, foreign travel, kind friends, everything. My God! What is to become of me?

A desirable young man? Dust and ashes! What was there desirable in such a thing as that? "In my thirty-first year," she noted in her diary, "I see nothing desirable but death."

Three more years passed, and then at last the pressure of time told; her family seemed to realize that she was old enough and strong enough to have her way; and she became the superintendent of a charitable nursing home in Harley Street. She had gained her independence, though it was in a meagre sphere enough; and her mother was still not quite resigned: surely Florence might at least spend the summer in the country. At times, indeed, among her intimates, Mrs. Nightingale almost wept. "We are ducks," she said with tears in her eyes, "who have hatched a wild swan." But the poor lady was wrong; it was not a swan that they had hatched; it was an eagle.

Miss Nightingale had been a year in her nursing-home in Harley Street, when Fate knocked at the door. The Crimean War broke out; the battle of the Alma was fought; and the terrible condition of our military hospitals at Scutari began to be known in England. It sometimes happens that the plans of Providence are a little difficult to follow, but on this occasion all was plain; there was a perfect co-ordination of events. For years Miss Nightingale had been getting ready; at last she was prepared—experienced, free, mature, yet still young—she was thirty-four—desirous to serve, accustomed to command: at that precise moment the desperate need of a great nation came, and she was there to satisfy it. If the war had fallen a few years earlier, she would have lacked the knowledge, perhaps even the power, for such a work; a few years later and she would, no doubt, have been fixed in the routine of some absorbing task, and, moreover, she would have been growing old. Nor was it only the coincidence of Time that was remarkable. It so fell out that Sidney Herbert was at the War Office and in the Cabinet; and Sidney Herbert was an intimate friend of Miss Nightingale's, convinced, from personal experience in charitable work, of her supreme capacity. After such premises, it seems hardly more than a matter of course that her letter, in which she offered her services for the East, and Sidney Herbert's letter, in which he asked for them, should actually have crossed in the post. Thus it all happened, without a hitch. The appointment was made, and even Mrs. Nightingale, overawed by the magnitude of the venture, could only approve. A pair of faithful friends offered themselves as personal attendants; thirty-eight nurses were collected; and within a week of the crossing of the letters Miss Nightingale, amid a great burst of popular enthusiasm, left for Constantinople.

Among the numerous letters which she received on her departure was one from Dr. Manning, who at that time was working in comparative obscurity as a Catholic priest in Bayswater. "God will keep you," he wrote, "and my prayer for you will be that your one object of Worship, Pattern of Imitation, and source of consolation and strength may be the Sacred Heart of our Divine Lord."

To what extent Dr. Manning's prayer was answered must remain a matter of doubt; but this much is certain, that, if ever a prayer was needed, it was needed then for Florence Nightingale. For dark as had been the picture of the state of affairs at Scutari, revealed to the English public in the despatches of the *Times* correspondent and in a multitude of private letters, yet the reality turned out to be darker still. What had occurred was, in brief, the complete breakdown of our medical arrangements at the seat of war. The origins of this awful failure were complex and manifold; they stretched back through long years of peace and carelessness in England; they could be traced through endless ramifications of administrative incapacity—from the inherent faults of confused systems to the petty bunglings of minor officials, from the inevitable ignorance of Cabinet Ministers to the fatal exactitudes of narrow routine. In the inquiries which followed it was clearly shown that the evil was in reality that worst of all evils—one which has been caused by nothing in particular and for which no one in particular is to blame. The whole organisation of the war machine was incompetent and out of date. The old Duke had sat for a generation at the Horse Guards repressing innovations with an iron hand. There was an extraordinary overlapping of authorities, an almost incredible shifting of responsibilities to and fro. As for such a notion as the creation and the maintenance of a really adequate medical service for the army —in that atmosphere of aged chaos, how could it have entered anybody's head? Before the war, the easy-going officials at Westminster were naturally persuaded that all was well—or at least as well as could be expected; when someone, for instance, actually had the temerity to suggest the formation of a corps of army nurses, he was at once laughed out of court. When the war had begun, the gallant British officers in control of affairs had other things to think about than the petty details of medical organisation. Who had bothered with such trifles in the Peninsula? And surely, on that occasion, we had done pretty well. Thus the most obvious precautions were neglected, the most necessary preparations put off from day to day. The principal medical officer

of the army, Dr. Hall, was summoned from India at a moment's notice, and
was unable to visit England before taking up his duties at the front. And
it was not until after the battle of the Alma, when we had been at war for
many months, that we acquired hospital accommodations at Scutari for more
than a thousand men. Errors, follies, and vices on the part of individuals
there doubtless were; but, in the general reckoning, they were of small
account—insignificant symptoms of the deep disease of the body politic—the
enormous calamity of administrative collapse.

Miss Nightingale arrived at Scutari—a suburb of Constantinople, on the
Asiatic side of the Bosphorus—on November 4th, 1854; it was ten days after
the battle of Balaclava, and the day before the battle of Inkerman. The organisation of the hospitals, which had already given way under the stress of
the battle of the Alma, was now to be subjected to the further pressure which
these two desperate and bloody engagements implied. Great detachments of
wounded were already beginning to pour in. The men, after receiving such
summary treatment as could be given them at the smaller hospitals in the
Crimea itself, were forthwith shipped in batches of two hundred across the
Black Sea to Scutari. This voyage was in normal times one of four days and
a half; but the times were no longer normal, and now the transit often lasted
for a fortnight or three weeks. It received, not without reason, the name of
"the middle passage." Between, and sometimes on the decks, the wounded,
the sick, and the dying were crowded—men who had just undergone the
amputation of limbs, men in the clutches of fever or of frostbite, men in the
last stages of dysentery and cholera—without beds, sometimes without blankets, often hardly clothed. The one or two surgeons on board did what they
could; but medical stores were lacking, and the only form of nursing available
was that provided by a handful of invalid soldiers, who were usually themselves prostrate by the end of the voyage. There was no other food besides
the ordinary salt rations of ship diet; and even the water was sometimes so
stored that it was out of reach of the weak. For many months, the average
of deaths during these voyages was seventy-four in the thousand; the corpses
were shot out into the waters; and who shall say that they were the most unfortunate? At Scutari, the landing-stage, constructed with all the perverseness
of Oriental ingenuity, could only be approached with great difficulty, and, in
rough weather, not at all. When it was reached, what remained of the men
in the ships had first to be disembarked, and then conveyed up a steep slope of
a quarter of a mile to the nearest of the hospitals. The most serious cases
might be put upon stretchers—for there were far too few for all; the rest were
carried or dragged up the hill by such convalescent soldiers as could be got together, who were not too obviously infirm for the work. At last the journey
was accomplished; slowly, one by one, living or dying, the wounded were
carried up into the hospital. And in the hospital what did they find?

Lasciate ogni speranza voi ch'entrate: the delusive doors bore no such inscription; and yet behind them Hell yawned. Want, neglect, confusion,
misery—in every shape and in every degree of intensity—filled the endless

corridors and the vast apartments of the gigantic barrack-house, which, without forethought or preparation, had been hurriedly set aside as the chief shelter for the victims of the war. The very building itself was radically defective. Huge sewers underlay it, and cess-pools loaded with filth wafted their poison into the upper rooms. The floors were in so rotten a condition that many of them could not be scrubbed; the walls were thick with dirt; incredible multitudes of vermin swarmed everywhere. And, enormous as the building was, it was yet too small. It contained four miles of beds, crushed together so close that there was but just room to pass between them. Under such conditions, the most elaborate system of ventilation might well have been at fault; but here there was no ventilation. The stench was indescribable. "I have been well acquainted," said Miss Nightingale, "with the dwellings of the worst parts of most of the great cities in Europe, but have never been in any atmosphere which I could compare with that of the Barrack Hospital at night." The structural defects were equalled by the deficiencies in the commonest objects of hospital use. There were not enough bedsteads; the sheets were of canvas, and so coarse that the wounded men recoiled from them, begging to be left in their blankets; there was no bedroom furniture of any kind, and empty beer-bottles were used for candlesticks. There were no basins, no towels, no soap, no brooms, no mops, no trays, no plates; there were neither slippers nor scissors, neither shoebrushes nor blacking; there were no knives or forks or spoons. The supply of fuel was constantly deficient. The cooking arrangements were preposterously inadequate, and the laundry was a farce. As for purely medical materials, the tale was no better. Stretchers, splints, bandages—all were lacking; and so were the most ordinary drugs.

To replace such wants, to struggle against such difficulties, there was a handful of men overburdened by the strain of ceaseless work, bound down by the traditions of official routine, and enfeebled either by old age or inexperience or sheer incompetence. They had proved utterly unequal to their task. The principal doctor was lost in the imbecilities of a senile optimism. The wretched official whose business it was to provide for the wants of the hospital was tied fast hand and foot by red tape. A few of the younger doctors struggled valiantly, but what could they do? Unprepared, disorganised, with such help only as they could find among the miserable band of convalescent soldiers drafted off to tend their sick comrades, they were faced with disease, mutilation, and death in all their most appalling forms, crowded multitudinously about them in an ever-increasing mass. They were like men in a shipwreck, fighting, not for safety, but for the next moment's bare existence—to gain, by yet another frenzied effort, some brief respite from the waters of destruction.

In these surroundings, those who had been long inured to scenes of human suffering—surgeons with a world-wide knowledge of agonies, soldiers familiar with fields of carnage, missionaries with remembrances of famine and of plague—yet found a depth of horror which they had never known before. There were moments, there were places in the Barrack Hospital at Scutari,

where the strongest hand was struck with trembling, and the boldest eye
would turn away its gaze.

Miss Nightingale came, and she, at any rate, in that Inferno, did not
abandon hope. For one thing, she brought material succour. Before she left
London she had consulted Dr. Andrew Smith, the head of the Army Medical
Board, as to whether it would be useful to take out stores of any kind to
Scutari; and Dr. Andrew Smith had told her that "nothing was needed."
Even Sidney Herbert had given her similar assurances; possibly, owing to an
oversight, there might have been some delay in the delivery of the medical
stores, which, he said, had been sent out from England "in profusion," but
"four days would have remedied this." She preferred to trust her own instincts, and at Marseilles purchased a large quantity of miscellaneous provisions, which were of the utmost use at Scutari. She came, too, amply provided with money—in all, during her stay in the East, about £7000 reached
her from private sources; and, in addition, she was able to avail herself of another valuable means of help. At the same time as herself, Mr. Macdonald, of
the *Times,* had arrived at Scutari, charged with the duty of administering the
large sums of money collected through the agency of that newspaper in aid
of the sick and wounded; and Mr. Macdonald had the sense to see that the
best use he could make of the *Times* Fund was to put it at the disposal of
Miss Nightingale.

I cannot conceive [wrote an eye-witness], as I now calmly look back on the first
three weeks after the arrival of the wounded from Inkerman, how it could have
been possible to have avoided a state of things too disastrous to contemplate, had
not Miss Nightingale been there, with the means placed at her disposal by Mr.
Macdonald.

But the official view was different. What! Was the public service to admit,
by accepting outside charity, that it was unable to discharge its own duties
without the assistance of private and irregular benevolence? Never! And
accordingly when Lord Stratford de Redcliffe, our Ambassador at Constantinople, was asked by Mr. Macdonald to indicate how the *Times* Fund could
best be employed, he answered that there was indeed one object to which it
might very well be devoted—the building of an English Protestant Church
at Pera.

Mr. Macdonald did not waste further time with Lord Stratford, and immediately joined forces with Miss Nightingale. But, with such a frame of mind
in the highest quarters, it is easy to imagine the kind of disgust and alarm
with which the sudden intrusion of a band of amateurs and females must have
filled the minds of the ordinary officers and the ordinary military surgeon.
They could not understand it; what had women to do with war? Honest
Colonels relieved their spleen by the cracking of heavy jokes about "the Bird";
while poor Dr. Hall, a rough terrier of a man, who had worried his way to
the top of his profession, was struck speechless with astonishment, and at last
observed that Miss Nightingale's appointment was extremely droll.

Her position was, indeed, an official one, but it was hardly the easier for that. In the hospitals it was her duty to provide the services of herself and her nurses when they were asked for by the doctors, and not until then. At first some of the surgeons would have nothing to say to her, and, though she was welcomed by others, the majority were hostile and suspicious. But gradually she gained ground. Her good will could not be denied, and her capacity could not be disregarded. With consummate tact, with all the gentleness of supreme strength, she managed at last to impose her personality upon the susceptible, overwrought, discouraged, and helpless group of men in authority who surrounded her. She stood firm; she was a rock in the angry ocean; with her alone was safety, comfort, life. And so it was that hope dawned at Scutari. The reign of chaos and old night began to dwindle; order came upon the scene, and common sense, and forethought, and decision, radiating out from the little room off the great gallery in the Barrack Hospital where, day and night, the Lady Superintendent was at her task. Progress might be slow, but it was sure. The first sign of a great change came with the appearance of some of those necessary objects with which the hospitals had been unprovided for months. The sick men began to enjoy the use of towels and soap, knives and forks, combs and tooth-brushes. Dr. Hall might snort when he heard of it, asking, with a growl, what a soldier wanted with a tooth-brush; but the good work went on. Eventually the whole business of purveying to the hospitals was, in effect, carried out by Miss Nightingale. She alone, it seemed, whatever the contingency, knew where to lay her hands on what was wanted; she alone could dispense her stores with readiness; above all, she alone possessed the art of circumventing the pernicious influences of official etiquette. This was her greatest enemy, and sometimes even she was baffled by it. On one occasion 27,000 shirts, sent out at her instance by the Home Government, arrived, were landed, and were only waiting to be unpacked. But the official "Purveyor" intervened; "he could not unpack them," he said, "without a Board." Miss Nightingale pleaded in vain; the sick and wounded lay half-naked, shivering for want of clothing; and three weeks elapsed before the Board released the shirts. A little later, however, on a similar occasion, Miss Nightingale felt that she could assert her own authority. She ordered a Government consignment to be forcibly opened, while the miserable "Purveyor" stood by, wringing his hands in departmental agony.

Vast quantities of valuable stores sent from England lay, she found, engulfed in the bottomless abyss of the Turkish Customs House. Other shiploads, buried beneath munitions of war destined for Balaclava, passed Scutari without a sign, and thus hospital materials were sometimes carried to and fro three times over the Black Sea, before they reached their destination. The whole system was clearly at fault, and Miss Nightingale suggested to the home authorities that a Government Store House should be instituted at Scutari for the reception and distribution of the consignments. Six months after her arrival this was done.

In the meantime she had reorganized the kitchens and the laundries in the hospitals. The ill-cooked hunks of meat, vilely served at irregular intervals, which had hitherto been the only diet for the sick men, were replaced by punctual meals, well-prepared and appetising, while strengthening extra foods —soups and wines, and jellies ("preposterous luxuries" snarled Dr. Hall)— were distributed to those who needed them. One thing, however, she could not effect. The separation of the bones from the meat was no part of official cookery: the rule was that the food must be divided into equal portions, and if some of the portions were all bone—well, every man must take his chance. The rule, perhaps, was not a very good one; but there it was. "It would require a new Regulation of the Service," she was told, "to bone the meat." As for the washing arrangements, they were revolutionised. Up to the time of Miss Nightingale's arrival the number of shirts which the authorities had succeeded in washing was seven. The hospital bedding, she found, was "washed" in cold water. She took a Turkish house, had boilers installed, and employed soldiers' wives to do the laundry work. The expenses were defrayed from her own funds and that of the *Times;* and henceforward the sick and wounded had the comfort of clean linen.

Then she turned her attention to their clothing. Owing to military exigencies the greater number of the men had abandoned their kits; their knapsacks were lost forever; they possessed nothing but what was on their persons, and that was usually only fit for speedy destruction. The "Purveyor," of course, pointed out that, according to the regulations, all soldiers should bring with them into hospital an adequate supply of clothing, and he declared that it was no business of his to make good their deficiencies. Apparently, it was the business of Miss Nightingale. She procured socks, boots, and shirts in enormous quantities; she had trousers made, she rigged up dressing-gowns. "The fact is," she told Sidney Herbert, "I am now clothing the British Army."

All at once, word came from the Crimea that a great new contingent of sick and wounded might shortly be expected. Where were they to go? Every available inch in the wards was occupied; the affair was serious and pressing, and the authorities stood aghast. There were some dilapidated rooms in the Barrack Hospital, unfit for human habitation, but Miss Nightingale believed that if measures were promptly taken they might be made capable of accommodating several hundred beds. One of the doctors agreed with her; the rest of the officials were irresolute: it would be a very expensive job, they said; it would involve building; and who could take the responsibility? The proper course was that a representation should be made to the Director-General of the Army Medical Department in London; then the Director-General would apply to the Horse Guards, the Horse Guards would move the Ordnance, the Ordnance would lay the matter before the Treasury, and if the Treasury gave its consent, the work might be correctly carried through, several months after the necessity for it had disappeared. Miss Nightingale, however, had made up her mind, and she persuaded Lord Stratford—or thought she had persuaded him—to give his sanction to the required expenditure. A hundred and twenty-five workmen were immediately engaged, and the work was begun.

The workmen struck; whereupon Lord Stratford washed his hands of the whole business. Miss Nightingale engaged two hundred other workmen on her own authority, and paid the bill out of her own resources. The wards were ready by the required date; five hundred sick men were received in them; and all the utensils, including knives, forks, spoons, cans and towels, were supplied by Miss Nightingale.

This remarkable woman was in truth performing the function of an administrative chief. How had this come about? Was she not in reality merely a nurse? Was it not her duty simply to tend to the sick? And indeed, was it not as a ministering angel, a gentle "lady with a lamp" that she actually impressed the minds of her contemporaries? No doubt that was so; and yet it is no less certain that, as she herself said, the specific business of nursing was "the least important of the functions into which she had been forced." It was clear that in the state of disorganisation into which the hospitals at Scutari had fallen the most pressing, the really vital, need was for something more than nursing; it was for the necessary elements of civilised life—the commonest material objects, the most ordinary cleanliness, the rudimentary habits of order and authority. "Oh, dear Miss Nightingale," said one of her party as they were approaching Constantinople, "when we land, let there be no delays, let us get straight to nursing the poor fellows!" "The strongest will be wanted at the wash-tub," was Miss Nightingale's answer. And it was upon the wash-tub, and all that the wash-tub stood for, that she expended her greatest energies. Yet to say that is perhaps to say too much. For to those who watched her at work among the sick, moving day and night from bed to bed, with that unflinching courage, with that indefatigable vigilance, it seemed as if the concentrated force of an undivided and unparalleled devotion could hardly suffice for that portion of her task alone. Wherever, in those vast wards, suffering was at its worst and the need for help was greatest, there, as if by magic, was Miss Nightingale. Her superhuman equanimity would, at the moment of some ghastly operation, nerve the victim to endure and almost to hope. Her sympathy would assuage the pangs of dying and bring back to those still living something of the forgotten charm of life. Over and over again her untiring efforts rescued those whom the surgeons had abandoned as beyond the possibility of cure. Her mere presence brought with it a strange influence. A passionate idolatry spread among the men: they kissed her shadow at it passed. They did more. "Before she came," said a soldier, "there was cussin' and swearin', but after that it was as 'oly as a church." The most cherished privilege of the fighting man was abandoned for the sake of Miss Nightingale. In those "lowest sinks of human misery," as she herself put it, she never heard the use of one expression "which could distress a gentlewoman."

She was heroic; and these were the humble tributes paid by those of grosser mould to that high quality. Certainly, she was heroic. Yet her heroism was not of that simple sort so dear to the readers of novels and the compilers of hagiologies—the romantic sentimental heroism with which mankind loves to invest its chosen darlings: it was made of sterner stuff. To the wounded soldier on his couch of agony she might well appear in the guise of a gracious angel of mercy; but the military surgeons, and the orderlies, and her own nurses, and the "Purveyor," and Dr. Hall, and even Lord Stratford himself could tell a different story. It was not by gentle sweetness and womanly self-abnegation that she had brought order out of chaos in the Scutari Hospitals, that, from her own resources, she had clothed the British Army, that she had spread her dominion over the serried and reluctant powers of the official world; it was by strict method, by stern discipline, by rigid attention to detail, by ceaseless labour, by the fixed determination of an indomitable will. Beneath her cool and calm demeanour lurked fierce and passionate fires. As she passed through the wards in her plain dress, so quiet, so unassuming, she struck the casual observer simply as the pattern of a perfect lady; but the keener eye perceived something more than that—the serenity of high deliberation in the scope of the capacious brow, the sign of power in the dominating curve of the thin nose, and the traces of a harsh and dangerous temper—something peevish, something mocking, and yet something precise—in the small and delicate mouth. There was humour in the face; but the curious watcher might wonder whether it was humour of a very pleasant kind; might ask himself, even as he heard the laughter and marked the jokes with which she cheered the spirits of her patients, what sort of sardonic merriment this same lady might not give vent to, in the privacy of her chamber. As for her voice, it was true of it, even more than her countenance, that it "had that in it one must fain call master." Those clear tones were in no need of emphasis: "I never heard her raise her voice," said one of her companions. Only, when she had spoken, it seemed as if nothing could follow but obedience. Once, when she had given some direction, a doctor ventured to remark that the thing could not be done. "But it must be done," said Miss Nightingale. A chance bystander, who heard the words, never forgot through all his life the irresistible authority of them. And they were spoken quietly—very quietly indeed.

Late at night, when the long miles of beds lay wrapped in darkness, Miss Nightingale would sit at work in her little room, over her correspondence. It was one of the most formidable of all her duties. There were hundreds of letters to be written to the friends and relations of soldiers; there was the enormous mass of official documents to be dealt with; there were her own private letters to be answered; and, most important of all, there was the composition of her long and confidential reports to Sidney Herbert. These were by no means official communications. Her soul, pent up all day in the restraint and reserve of a vast responsibility, now at last poured itself out in these letters with all its natural vehemence, like a swollen torrent through an open sluice. Here, at least, she did not mince matters. Here she painted in her darkest colours the hideous scenes which surrounded her; here she tore away remorselessly the last veils still shrouding the abominable truth. Then she would fill pages with recommendations and suggestions, with criticism of the minutest details of organisation, with elaborate calculations of contingencies, with exhaustive analyses and statistical statements piled up in breathless eagerness one on top of the other. And then her pen, in the virulence of its volubility, would rush on to the discussion of individuals, to the denunciation of an incompetent surgeon or the ridicule of a self-sufficient nurse. Her sarcasm searched the ranks of the officials with the deadly and unsparing precision of a machine-gun. Her nicknames were terrible. She respected no one: Lord Stratford, Lord Raglan, Lady Stratford, Dr. Andrew Smith, Dr. Hall, the Commissary-General, the Purveyor—she fulminated against them all. The intolerable futility of mankind obsessed her like a nightmare, and she gnashed her teeth against it. "I do well to be angry," was the burden of her cry. How many just men were there at Scutari? How many who cared at all for the sick, or had done anything for their relief? Were there ten? Were there five? Was there even one? She could not be sure.

At one time, during several weeks, her vituperations descended upon the head of Sidney Herbert himself. He had misinterpreted her wishes, he had traversed her positive instructions, and it was not until he had admitted his error and apologised in abject terms that he was allowed again into favour. While this misunderstanding was at its height an aristocratic young gentleman arrived at Scutari with a recommendation from the Minister. He had come out from England filled with a romantic desire to render homage to the angelic heroine of his dreams. He had, he said, cast aside his life of ease and luxury; he would devote his days and nights to the service of that gentle lady; he would perform the most menial offices, he would "fag" for her, he would be her footman—and feel requited by a single smile. A single smile, indeed, he had, but it was of an unexpected kind. Miss Nightingale at first refused to see him, and then, when she consented, believing that he was an emissary sent by Sidney Herbert to put her in the wrong over their dispute, she took notes of her conversation with him, and insisted on his signing them at the end of it. The young gentleman returned to England by the next ship.

This quarrel with Sidney Herbert was, however, an exceptional incident. Alike by him, and by Lord Panmure, his successor at the War Office, she was firmly supported; and the fact that during the whole of her stay at Scutari she had the Home Government at her back, was her trump card in her dealings with the hospital authorities. Nor was it only the Government that was behind her: public opinion in England early recognised the high importance of her mission, and its enthusiastic appreciation of her work soon reached an extraordinary height. The Queen herself was deeply moved. She made repeated inquiries as to the welfare of Miss Nightingale; she asked to see her accounts of the wounded, and made her the intermediary between the throne and the troops.

Let Mrs. Herbert know [she wrote to the War Minister] that I wish Miss Nightingale and the ladies would tell these poor noble, wounded, and sick men that *no one* takes a warmer interest or feels *more* for their sufferings or admires their courage and heroism *more* than their Queen. Day and night she thinks of her beloved troops. So does the Prince. Beg Mrs. Herbert to communicate these last words to those ladies, as I know that *our* sympathy is much valued by these noble fellows.

The letter was read aloud in the wards by the Chaplain. "It is a very feeling letter," said the men.

And so the months passed, and that fell winter which had begun with Inkerman and had dragged itself out through the long agony of the invest- ment of Sebastopol, at last was over. In May, 1855, after six months of labour, Miss Nightingale could look with something like satisfaction at the condition of the Scutari hospitals. Had they done nothing more than survive the terrible strain which had been put upon them, it would have been a matter for con- gratulation; but they had done much more than that; they had marvellously improved. The confusion and the pressure in the wards had come to an end: order reigned in them, and cleanliness; the supplies were bountiful and prompt; important sanitary works had been carried out. One simple com- parison of figures was enough to reveal the extraordinary change: the rate of mortality among the cases treated had fallen from 42 per cent. to 22 per thou- sand. But still the indefatigable lady was not satisfied. The main problem had been solved—the physical needs of the men had been provided for; their mental and spiritual needs remained. She set up and furnished reading-rooms and recreation-rooms. She started classes and lectures. Officers were amazed to see her treating their men as if they were human beings, and assured her that she would only end by "spoiling the brutes." But that was not Miss Nightingale's opinion, and she was justified. The private soldier began to drink less, and even—though that seemed impossible—to save his pay. Miss Nightingale became a banker for the army, receiving and sending home large sums of money every month. At last, reluctantly, the Government followed suit, and established machinery of its own for the remission of money. Lord Panmure, however, remained sceptical; "It will do no good," he pronounced; "the British soldier is not a remitting animal." But, in fact, during the next six months, £71,000 was sent home.

Amid all these activities, Miss Nightingale took up the further task of inspecting the hospitals in the Crimea itself. The labour was extreme, and the conditions of life were almost intolerable. She spent whole days in the saddle, or was driven over those bleak and rocky heights in a baggage cart. Sometimes she stood for hours in the heavily falling snow, and would only reach her hut at dead of night after walking for miles through perilous ra- vines. Her powers of resistance seemed incredible, but at last they were ex- hausted. She was attacked by fever, and for a moment came very near to death. Yet she worked on; if she could not move, she could at least write; and write she did until her mind had left her; and after it had left her, in what seemed the delirious trance of death itself, she still wrote. When, after many weeks, she was strong enough to travel, she was to return to England, but she utterly refused. She would not go back, she said, before the last of the soldiers had left Scutari.

This happy moment had almost arrived, when suddenly the smouldering hostilities of the medical authorities burst out into a flame. Dr. Hall's labours had been rewarded by a K.C.B.—letters which, as Miss Nightingale told Sidney Herbert, she could only suppose to mean "Knight of the Crimean Burial-grounds"—and the honour had turned his head. He was Sir John, and he would be thwarted no longer. Disputes had lately arisen between Miss Nightingale and some of the nurses in the Crimean hospitals. The situation had been embittered by rumours of religious dissensions, for, while the Crimean nurses were Roman Catholics, many of those at Scutari were suspected of a regrettable propensity towards the tenets of Dr. Pusey. Miss Nightingale was by no means disturbed by these sectarian differences, but any suggestion that her supreme authority over all the nurses with the Army was in doubt was enough to rouse her to fury; and it appeared that Mrs. Bridgeman, the Reverend Mother in the Crimea, had ventured to call that authority in question. Sir John Hall thought that his opportunity had come, and strongly supported Mrs. Bridgeman—or, as Miss Nightingale preferred to call her, the "Reverend Brickbat." There was a violent struggle; Miss Nighingale's rage was terrible. Dr. Hall, she declared, was doing his best to "root her out of the Crimea." She would bear it no longer; the War Office was playing her false; there was only one thing to be done—Sidney Herbert must move for the production of papers in the House of Commons, so that the public might be able to judge between her and her enemies. Sidney Herbert with great difficulty calmed her down. Orders were immediately dispatched putting her supremacy beyond doubt, and the Reverend Brickbat withdrew from the scene. Sir John, however, was more tenacious. A few weeks later, Miss Nightingale and her nurses visited the Crimea for the last time, and the brilliant idea occurred to him that he could crush her by a very simple expedient—he would starve her into submission; and he actually ordered that no rations of any kind should be supplied to her. He had already tried this plan with great effect upon an unfortunate medical man whose presence in the Crimea he had considered an intrusion; but he was now to learn that such tricks were thrown away upon Miss Nightingale. With extraordinary foresight, she had brought with her a great supply of food; she succeeded in obtaining more at her own expense and by her own exertions; and thus for ten days, in that inhospitable country, she was able to feed herself and twenty-four nurses. Eventually the military authorities intervened in her favour, and Sir John had to confess that he was beaten.

It was not until July, 1856—four months after the Declaration of Peace—that Miss Nightingale left Scutari for England. Her reputation was now enormous, and the enthusiasm of the public was unbounded. The Royal approbation was expressed by the gift of a brooch, accompanied by a private letter.

You are, I know, well aware [wrote Her Majesty] of the high sense I entertain of the Christian devotion which you have displayed during this great and bloody war, and I need hardly repeat to you how warm my admiration is for your services, which are fully equal to those of my dear and brave soldiers, whose sufferings you have had the *privilege* of alleviating in so merciful a manner. I am, however, anxious of marking my feelings in a manner which I trust will be agreeable to you, and therefore send you with this letter a brooch, the form and emblems of which commemorate your great and blessed work, and which I hope you will wear as a mark of the high approbation of your Sovereign!

"It will be a very great satisfaction to me," Her Majesty added, "to make the acquaintance of one who has set so bright an example to our sex."

The brooch, which was designed by the Prince Consort, bore a St. George's cross in red enamel, and the Royal cypher surmounted by diamonds. The whole was encircled by the inscription, "Blessed are the Merciful."

The name of Florence Nightingale lives in the memory of the world by virtue of the lurid and heroic adventure of the Crimea. Had she died—as she nearly did—upon her return to England, her reputation would hardly have been different; her legend would have come down to us almost as we know it to-day—that gentle vision of female virtue which first took shape before the adoring eyes of the sick soldiers at Scutari. Yet, as a matter of fact, she lived for more than half a century after the Crimean War; and during the greater part of that long period all the energy and all the devotion of her extraordinary nature were working at their highest pitch. What she accomplished in those years of unknown labour could, indeed, hardly have been more glorious than her Crimean triumphs; but it was certainly more important. The true history was far stranger even than the myth. In Miss Nightingale's own eyes the adventure of the Crimea was a mere incident—scarcely more than a useful stepping-stone in her career. It was the fulcrum with which she hoped to move the world; but it was only the fulcrum. For more than a generation she was to sit in secret, working her lever: and her real life began at the very moment when, in the popular imagination, it had ended.

She arrived in England in a shattered state of health. The hardships and the ceaseless effort of the last two years had undermined her nervous system; her heart was pronounced to be affected; she suffered constantly from fainting-fits and terrible attacks of utter physical prostration. The doctors declared that one thing alone would save her—a complete and prolonged rest. But that was also the one thing with which she would have nothing to do. She had never been in the habit of resting; why should she begin now? Now, when her opportunity had come at last; now, when the iron was hot, and it was time to strike? No; she had work to do; and, come what might, she would do it. The doctors protested in vain; in vain her family lamented and entreated, in vain her friends pointed out to her the madness of such a course. Madness? Mad—possessed—perhaps she was. A demoniac frenzy had seized upon her. As she lay upon her sofa, gasping, she devoured blue-books, dictated letters, and, in the intervals of her palpitations, cracked her febrile jokes. For months at a stretch she never left her bed. For years she was in daily expectation of Death. But she would not rest. At this rate, the doctors assured her, even if she did not die, she would become an invalid for life. She could not help that; there was the work to be done; and, as for rest, very likely she might rest . . . when she had done it.

Wherever she went, in London or in the country, in the hills of Derbyshire, or among the rhododendrons at Embley, she was haunted by a ghost. It was the spectre of Scutari—the hideous vision of the organisation of a military hospital. She would lay that phantom, or she would perish. The whole system of the Army Medical Department, the education of the Medical Officer, the regulations of hospital procedure . . . *rest?* How could she rest while these things were as they were, while, if the like necessity were to arise again, the like results would follow? And, even in peace and at home, what was the sanitary condition of the Army? The mortality in the barracks was, she found, nearly double the mortality in civil life. "You might as well take 1100 men every year out upon Salisbury Plain and shoot them," she said. After inspecting the hospitals at Chatham, she smiled grimly. "Yes, this is one more symptom of the system which, in the Crimea, put to death 16,000 men." Scutari had given her knowledge; and it had given her power too: her enormous reputation was at her back—an incalculable force. Other works, other duties, might lie before her; but the most urgent, the most obvious of all was to look to the health of the Army.

One of her very first steps was to take advantage of the invitation which Queen Victoria had sent her to the Crimea, together with the commemorative brooch. Within a few weeks of her return, she visited Balmoral, and had several interviews both with the Queen and the Prince Consort. "She put before us," wrote the Prince in his diary, "all the defects of our present military hospital system and the reforms that are needed." She related the whole story of her experiences in the East; and, in addition, she managed to have some long and confidential talks with His Royal Highness on metaphysics and religion. The impression which she created was excellent. "Sie gefällt uns sehr," noted the Prince, "ist sehr bescheiden." Her Majesty's comment was different—"Such a *head!* I wish we had her at the War Office."

But Miss Nightingale was not at the War Office, and for a very simple reason: she was a woman. Lord Panmure, however, *was* (though indeed the reason for that was not quite so simple); and it was upon Lord Panmure that the issue of Miss Nightingale's efforts for reform must primarily depend. That burly Scottish nobleman had not, in spite of his most earnest endeavours, had a very easy time of it as Secretary of State for War. He had come into office in the middle of the Sebastopol campaign, and had felt himself very well fitted for the position, since he had acquired in former days an inside knowledge of the Army—as a Captain of Hussars. It was this inside knowledge which had enabled him to inform Miss Nightingale with such authority that "the British soldier is not a remitting animal." And perhaps it was this same consciousness of a command of his subject which had impelled him to write a dispatch to Lord Raglan, blandly informing the Commander-in-Chief in the Field just how he was neglecting his duties, and pointing out to him that if he would only try he really might do a little better next time. Lord Raglan's reply, calculated as it was to make its recipient sink into the earth, did not quite have that effect upon Lord Panmure, who, whatever might have been his faults, had never been accused of being supersensitive. However, he allowed the matter to drop; and a little later Lord Raglan died—worn out, some people said, by work and anxiety. He was succeeded by an excellent red-nosed old gentleman, General Simpson, whom nobody had ever heard of, and who took Sebastopol. But Lord Panmure's relations with him were hardly more satisfactory than his relations with Lord Raglan; for, while Raglan had been too independent, poor General Simpson erred in the opposite direction, perpetually asked advice, suffered from lumbago, doubted, his nose growing daily redder and redder, whether he was fit for his post, and, by alternate mails, sent in and withdrew his resignation. Then, too, both the General and the Minister suffered acutely from that distressingly useful new invention, the electric telegraph. On one occasion General Simpson felt obliged actually to expostulate.

I think, my Lord [he wrote], that some telegraphic messages reach us that cannot be sent under due authority, and are perhaps unknown to you, although under the protection of your Lordship's name. For instance, I was called up last night, a dragoon having come express with a telegraphic message in these words, "Lord Panmure to General Simpson—Captain Jarvis has been bitten by a centipede. How is he now?"

General Simpson might have put up with this, though to be sure it did seem "rather too trifling an affair to call for a dragoon to ride a couple of miles in the dark that he may knock up the Commander of the Army out of the very small allowance of sleep permitted him"; but what was really more than he could bear was to find "upon sending in the morning another mounted dragoon to inquire after Captain Jarvis, four miles off, that he never has been bitten at all, but has had a boil, from which he is fast recovering." But Lord Panmure had troubles of his own. His favourite nephew, Captain Dowbiggan, was at the front, and to one of his telegrams to the Commander-in-Chief the Minister had taken occasion to append the following carefully qualified sentence—"I recommend Dowbiggan to your notice, should you have a vacancy, and if he is fit." Unfortunately, in those early days, it was left to the discretion of the telegraphist to compress the messages which passed through his hands; so that the result was that Lord Panmure's delicate appeal reached its destination in the laconic form of "Look after Dowb." The Headquarters Staff were at first extremely puzzled; they were at last extremely amused. The story spread; and "Look after Dowb" remained for many years the familiar formula for describing official hints in favour of deserving nephews.

And now that all this was over, now that Sebastopol had been, somehow or another, taken; now that peace was, somehow or another, made; now that the troubles of office might surely be expected to be at an end at last—here was Miss Nightingale breaking in upon the scene, with her talk about the state of the hospitals and the necessity for sanitary reform. It was most irksome; and Lord Panmure almost began to wish that he was engaged upon some more congenial occupation—discussing, perhaps, the constitution of the Free Church of Scotland—a question in which he was profoundly interested. But no; duty was paramount; and he set himself, with a sigh of resignation, to the task of doing as little of it as he possibly could.

"The Bison" his friends called him; and the name fitted both his physical demeanour and his habit of mind. That large low head seemed to have been created for butting rather than for anything else. There he stood, four square and menacing, in the doorway of reform; and it remained to be seen whether the bulky mass, upon whose solid hide even the barbed arrows of Lord Raglan's scorn had made no mark, would prove amenable to the pressure of Miss Nightingale. Nor was he alone in the doorway. There loomed behind him the whole phalanx of professional conservatism, the stubborn supporters of the out-of-date, the worshippers and the victims of War Office routine. Among these it was only natural that Dr. Andrew Smith, the head of the Army Medical Department, should have been pre-eminent—Dr. Andrew Smith, who had assured Miss Nightingale before she felt England that "nothing was wanted at Scutari." Such were her opponents; but she too was not without allies. She had gained the ear of Royalty—which was something; at any moment that she pleased she could gain the ear of the public—which was a great deal. She had a host of admirers and friends; and—to say nothing of her personal qualities—her knowledge, her tenacity, her tact—she possessed, too, one advantage which then, far more even than now, carried an immense weight—she belonged to the highest circle of society. She moved naturally among Peers and Cabinet Ministers—she was one of their own set; and in those days their set was a very narrow one. What kind of attention would such persons have paid to some middle-class woman with whom they were not acquainted, who possessed great experience of army nursing and had decided views upon hospital reform? They would have politely ignored her; but it was impossible to ignore Flo Nightingale. When she spoke, they were obliged to listen; and, when they had once begun to do that—what might not follow? She knew her power, and she used it. She supported her weightiest minutes with familiar witty little notes. The Bison began to look grave. It might be difficult—it might be damned difficult—to put down one's head against the white hand of a lady.

Of Miss Nightingale's friends, the most important was Sidney Herbert. He was a man upon whom the good fairies seemed to have showered, as he lay in his cradle, all their most enviable gifts. Well born, handsome, rich, the master of Wilton—one of those great country-houses, clothed with the glamour of a historic past, which are the peculiar glory of England—he possessed, besides all these advantages, so charming, so lively, so gentle a disposition that no one who had once come near him could ever be his enemy. He was, in fact, a man of whom it was difficult not to say that he was a perfect English gentleman. For his virtues were equal even to his good fortune. He was re-

ligious—deeply religious: "I am more and more convinced every day," he
wrote, when he had been for some years a Cabinet Minister, "that in politics,
as in everything else, nothing can be right which is not in accordance with the
spirit of the Gospel." No one was more unselfish; he was charitable and
benevolent to a remarkable degree; and he devoted the whole of his life with
an unwavering conscientiousness to the public service. With such a character,
with such opportunities, what high hopes must have danced before him, what
radiant visions of accomplished duties, of ever-increasing usefulness, of beneficent power, of the consciousness of disinterested success! Some of those hopes
and visions were, indeed, realised; but, in the end, the career of Sidney Herbert seemed to show that, with all their generosity, there was some gift or
other—what was it?—some essential gift—which the good fairies had withheld, and that even the qualities of a perfect English gentleman may be no
safeguard against anguish, humiliation, and defeat.

That career would certainly have been very different if he had never
known Miss Nightingale. The alliance between them, which had begun with
her appointment to Scutari, which had grown closer and closer while the war
lasted, developed, after her return, into one of the most extraordinary of friendships. It was the friendship of a man and a woman intimately bound together by their devotion to a public cause; mutual affection, of course, played
a part in it, but it was an incidental part; the whole soul of the relationship
was a community of work. Perhaps out of England such an intimacy could
hardly have existed—an intimacy so utterly untinctured not only by passion
itself but by the suspicion of it. For years Sidney Herbert saw Miss Nightingale almost daily, for long hours together, corresponding with her incessantly
when they were apart; and the tongue of scandal was silent; and one of the
most devoted of her admirers was his wife. But what made the connection
still more remarkable was the way in which the parts that were played in it
were divided between the two. The man who acts, decides, and achieves; the
woman who encourages, applauds, and—from a distance—inspires:—the combination is common enough; but Miss Nightingale was neither an Aspasia
nor an Egeria. In her case it is almost true to say that the *rôles* were reversed;
the qualities of pliancy and sympathy fell to the man, those of command and
initiative to the woman. There was one thing only which Miss Nightingale
lacked in her equipment for public life; she had not—she never could have—
the public power and authority which belong to the successful politician.
That power and authority Sidney Herbert possessed; the fact was obvious,
and the conclusion no less so: it was through the man that the woman must
work her will. She took hold of him, taught him, shaped him, absorbed him,
dominated him through and through. He did not resist—he did not wish to
resist; his natural inclination lay along the same path as hers; only that terrific
personality swept him forward at her own fierce pace and with her own
relentless stride. Swept him—where to? Ah! Why had he ever known Miss
Nightingale? If Lord Panmure was a bison, Sidney Herbert, no doubt, was
a stag—a comely, gallant creature springing through the forest; but the forest

is a dangerous place. One has the image of those wide eyes fascinated suddenly by something feline, something strong; there is a pause; and then the tigress has her claws in the quivering haunches; and then—!

Besides Sidney Herbert, she had other friends who, in a more restricted sphere, were hardly less essential to her. If, in her condition of bodily collapse, she were to accomplish what she was determined that she should accomplish, the attentions and the services of others would be absolutely indispensable. Helpers and servers she must have; and accordingly there was soon formed about her a little group of devoted disciples upon whose affections and energies she could implicitly rely. Devoted, indeed, these disciples were, in no ordinary sense of the term; for certainly she was no light task-mistress, and he who set out to be of use to Miss Nightingale was apt to find, before he had gone very far, that he was in truth being made use of in good earnest—to the very limit of his endurance and his capacity. Perhaps, even beyond those limits; why not? Was she asking of others more than she was giving herself? Let them look at her lying there pale and breathless on the couch; could it be said that she spared herself? Why, then, should she spare others? And it was not for her own sake that she made these claims. For her own sake, indeed! No! They all knew it! it was for the sake of the work. And so the little band, bound body and soul in that strange servitude, laboured on ungrudgingly. Among the most faithful was her "Aunt Mai," her father's sister, who from the earliest days had stood beside her, who had helped her to escape from the thraldom of family life, who had been with her at Scutari, and who now acted almost the part of mother to her, watching over her with infinite care in all the movements and uncertainties which her state of health involved. Another constant attendant was her brother-in-law, Sir Harry Verney, whom she found particularly valuable in parliamentary affairs. Arthur Clough, the poet, also a connection by marriage, she used in other ways. Ever since he had lost his faith at the time of the Oxford Movement, Clough had passed his life in a condition of considerable uneasiness, which was increased rather than diminished by the practice of poetry. Unable to decide upon the purpose of an existence whose savour had fled together with his belief in the Resurrection, his spirits lowered still further by ill-health, and his income not all that it should be, he had determined to seek the solution of his difficulties in the United States of America. But, even there, the solution was not forthcoming; and when, a little later, he was offered a post in a government department at home, he accepted it, came to live in London, and immediately fell under the influence of Miss Nightingale. Though the purpose of existence might be still uncertain and its nature still unsavoury, here, at any rate, under the eye of this inspired woman, was something real, something earnest: his only doubt was—could he be of any use? Certainly he could. There were a great number of miscellaneous little jobs which there was nobody handy to do. For instance, when Miss Nightingale was travelling, there were the railway-tickets to be taken; and there were proof-sheets to be corrected; and then there were parcels to be done up in brown paper, and carried to the post. Certainly he could be useful. And so, upon such occupations as these, Arthur Clough was set to work. "This that I see, is not all," he comforted himself by reflecting, "and this that I do is but little! nevertheless it is good, though there is better than it."

As time went on, her "Cabinet," as she called it, grew larger. Officials with whom her work brought her into touch and who sympathised with her objects, were pressed into her service; and old friends of the Crimean days gathered round her when they returned to England. Among these the most indefatigable was Dr. Sutherland, a sanitary expert, who for more than thirty years acted as her confidential private secretary, and surrendered to her purposes literally the whole of his life. Thus sustained and assisted, thus slaved for and adored, she prepared to beard the Bison.

Two facts soon emerged, and all that followed turned upon them. It became clear, in the first place, that that imposing mass was not immovable, and in the second, that its movement, when it did move, would be exceedingly slow. The Bison was no match for the lady. It was in vain that he put down his head and planted his feet in the earth; he could not withstand her; the white hand forced him back. But the process was an extraordinarily gradual one. Dr. Andrew Smith and all his War Office phalanx stood behind, blocking the way; the poor Bison groaned inwardly, and cast a wistful eye towards the happy pastures of the Free Church of Scotland; then slowly, with infinite reluctance, step by step, he retreated, disputing every inch of the ground.

The first great measure, which, supported as it was by the Queen, the Cabinet, and the united opinion of the country, it was impossible to resist, was the appointment of a Royal Commission to report upon the health of the Army. The question of the composition of the Commission then immediately arose; and it was over this matter that the first hand-to-hand encounter between Lord Panmure and Miss Nightingale took place. They met, and Miss Nightingale was victorious; Sidney Herbert was appointed Chairman; and, in the end the only member of the Commission opposed to her views was Dr. Andrew Smith. During the interview, Miss Nightingale made an important discovery: she found that "the Bison was bullyable"—the hide was the hide of a Mexican buffalo, but the spirit was the spirit of an Alderney calf. And there was one thing above all others which the huge creature dreaded— an appeal to public opinion. The faintest hint of such a terrible eventuality made his heart dissolve within him; he would agree to anything—he would cut short his grouse-shooting—he would make a speech in the House of Lords —he would even overrule Dr. Andrew Smith—rather than that. Miss Nightingale held the fearful threat in reserve—she would speak out what she knew; she would publish the truth to the whole world, and let the whole world judge between them. With supreme skill, she kept this sword of Damocles poised above the Bison's head, and more than once she was actually on the point of really dropping it. For his recalcitrancy grew and grew. The *personnel* of the Commission once determined upon, there was a struggle, which lasted for six months, over the nature of its powers. Was it to be an efficient body, armed with the right of full inquiry and wide examination, or was it to be a polite official contrivance for exonerating Dr. Andrew Smith? The War Office phalanx closed its ranks, and fought tooth and nail; but it was defeated: the Bison was bullyable.

Three months from this day [Miss Nightingale had written at last] I publish my experience of the Crimean Campaign, and my suggestions for improvement, unless there has been a fair and tangible pledge by that time for reform.

Who could face that?

And, if the need came, she meant to be as good as her word. For she had now determined, whatever might be the fate of the Commission, to draw up her own report upon the questions at issue. The labour involved was enormous; her health was almost desperate; but she did not flinch, and after six months of incredible industry she had put together and written with her own hand her "Notes affecting the Health, Efficiency, and Hospital Administration of the British Army." This extraordinary composition, filling more than eight hundred closely printed pages, laying down vast principles of far-reaching reform, discussing the minutest details of a multitude of controversial subjects, containing an enormous mass of information of the most varied kinds—military, statistical, sanitary, architectural—was never given to the public, for the need never came; but it formed the basis of the Report of the Royal Commission; and it remains to this day the leading authority on the medical administration of armies.

Before it had been completed the struggle over the powers of the Commission had been brought to a victorious close. Lord Panmure had given way once more; he had immediately hurried to the Queen to obtain her consent; and only then, when her Majesty's initials had been irrevocably affixed to the fatal document, did he dare to tell Dr. Andrew Smith what he had done. The Commission met, and another immense load fell upon Miss Nightingale's shoulders. To-day she would, of course, have been one of the Commission herself; but at that time the idea of a woman appearing in such a capacity was unheard of; and no one even suggested the possibility of Miss Nightingale's doing so. The result was that she was obliged to remain behind the scenes throughout, to coach Sidney Herbert in private at every important juncture, and to convey to him and to her other friends upon the Commission the vast funds of her expert knowledge—so essential in the examination of witnesses— by means of innumerable consultations, letters, and memoranda. It was even doubtful whether the proprieties would admit of her giving evidence; and at last as a compromise, her modesty only allowed her to do so in the form of written answers to written questions. At length the grand affair was finished. The Commission's Report, embodying almost word for word the suggestions of Miss Nightingale, was drawn up by Sidney Herbert. Only one question remained to be answered—would anything, after all, be done? Or would the

Royal Commission, like so many other Royal Commissions before and since, turn out to have achieved nothing but the concoction of a very fat blue-book on a very high shelf?

And so the last and the deadliest struggle with the Bison began. Six months had been spent in coercing him into granting the Commission effective powers; six more months were occupied by the work of the Commission; and now yet another six were to pass in extorting from him the means whereby the recommendations of the Commission might be actually carried out. But, in the end, the thing was done. Miss Nightingale seemed indeed, during these months, to be upon the very brink of death. Accompanied by the faithful Aunt Mai, she moved from place to place—to Hampstead, to Highgate, to Derbyshire, to Malvern—in what appeared to be a last desperate effort to find health somewhere; but she carried that with her which made health impossible. Her desire for work could now scarcely be distinguished from mania. At one moment she was writing a "last letter" to Sidney Herbert; at the next she was offering to go out to India to nurse the sufferers in the Mutiny. When Dr. Sutherland wrote, imploring her to take a holiday, she raved. Rest!—

I am lying without my head, without my claws, and you all peck at me. It is *de rigueur, d'obligation,* like the saying something to one's hat, when one goes into church, to say to me all that has been said to me 110 times a day during the last three months. It is the *obbligato* on the violin, and the twelve violins all practise it together, like the clocks striking 12 o'clock at night all over London, till I say like Xavier de Maistre, *Assez, je le sais, je le sais que trop.* I am not a penitent; but you are like the R. C. confessor, who says what is *de rigueur.* . . .

Her wits began to turn, and there was no holding her. She worked like a slave in a mine. She began to believe, as she had begun to believe at Scutari, that none of her fellow-workers had their hearts in the business; if they had, why did they not work as she did? She could only see slackness and stupidity around her. Dr. Sutherland, of course, was grotesquely muddle-headed; and Arthur Clough incurably lazy. Even Sidney Herbert . . . oh yes, he had simplicity and candour and quickness of perception, no doubt; but he was an eclectic; and what could one hope for from a man who went away to fish in Ireland just when the Bison most needed bullying? As for the Bison himself he had fled to Scotland, where he remained buried for many months. The fate of the vital recommendation in the Commission's Report—the appointment of four Sub-Commissions charged with the duty of determining upon the details of the proposed reforms and of putting them into execution—still hung in the balance. The Bison consented to everything; and then, on a flying visit to London, withdrew his consent and hastily returned to Scotland. Then for many weeks all business was suspended; he had gout—gout in the hands, so that he could not write. "His gout was always handy," remarked Miss Nightingale. But eventually it was clear even to the Bison that the game was up, and the inevitable surrender came.

There was, however, one point in which he triumphed over Miss Nightingale. The building of Netley Hospital had been begun, under his orders, before her return to England. Soon after her arrival she examined the plans, and found that they reproduced all the worst faults of an out-of-date and mischievous system of hospital construction. She therefore urged that the matter should be reconsidered, and in the meantime building stopped. But the Bison was obdurate; it would be very expensive, and in any case it was too late. Unable to make any impression on him, and convinced of the extreme importance of the question, she determined to appeal to a higher authority. Lord Palmerston was Prime Minister; she had known him from her childhood; he was a near neighbour of her father's in the New Forest. She went down to the New Forest, armed with the plans of the proposed hospital and all the relevant information, stayed the night at Lord Palmerston's house, and convinced him of the necessity of rebuilding Netley.

It seems to me [Lord Palmerston wrote to Lord Panmure] that at Netley all consideration of what would best tend to the comfort and recovery of the patients has been sacrificed to the vanity of the architect, whose sole object has been to make a building which should cut a dash when looked at from the Southampton river. . . . Pray, therefore, stop all further progress in the work until the matter can be duly considered.

But the Bison was not to be moved by one peremptory letter, even if it was from the Prime Minister. He put forth all his powers of procrastination, Lord Palmerston lost interest in the subject, and so the chief military hospital in England was triumphantly completed on unsanitary principles, with unventilated rooms, and with all the patients' windows facing northeast.

But now the time had come when the Bison was to trouble and to be troubled no more. A vote in the House of Commons brought about the fall of Lord Palmerston's Government, and Lord Panmure found himself at liberty to devote the rest of his life to the Free Church of Scotland. After a brief interval, Sidney Herbert became Secretary of State for War. Great was the jubilation in the Nightingale Cabinet; the day of achievement had dawned at last. The next two and a half years (1859-61) saw the introduction of the whole system of reforms for which Miss Nightingale had been struggling so fiercely—reforms which make Sidney Herbert's tenure of power at the War Office an important epoch in the history of the British Army. The four Sub-Commissions, firmly established under the immediate control of the Minister, and urged forward by the relentless perseverance of Miss Nightingale, set to work with a will. The barracks and the hospitals were remodelled; they were properly ventilated and warmed and lighted for the first time; they were given a water supply which actually supplied water, and kitchens where, strange to say, it was possible to cook. Then the great question of the Purveyor—that portentous functionary whose powers and whose lack of powers had weighed like a nightmare upon Scutari—was taken in hand, and new regulations were laid down, accurately defining his responsibilities and his duties. One Sub-Commission reorganised the medical statistics of the Army. Another estab-

lished—in spite of the last convulsive efforts of the Department—an Army
Medical School. Finally the Army Medical Department itself was completely
reorganised; an administrative code was drawn up; and the great and novel
principle was established that it was as much a part of the duty of the authorities to look after the soldier's health as to look after his sickness. Besides this,
it was at last officially admitted that he had a moral and intellectual side.
Coffee-rooms and reading-rooms, gymnasiums and workshops were instituted.
A new era did in truth appear to have begun. Already by 1861 the mortality
in the Army had decreased by one half since the days of the Crimea. It was no
wonder that even vaster possibilities began now to open out before Miss Nightingale. One thing was still needed to complete and to assure her triumphs.
The Army Medical Department was indeed reorganised; but the great central
machine was still untouched. The War Office itself—! If she could remould
that nearer to her heart's desire—there indeed would be a victory! And until
that final act was accomplished, how could she be certain that all the rest of
her achievements might not, by some capricious turn of Fortune's wheel—a
change of Ministry, perhaps, replacing Sidney Herbert by some puppet of the
permanent official gang—be swept to limbo in a moment?

Meanwhile, still ravenous for more and yet more work, her activities had
branched out into new directions. The army in India claimed her attention.
A Sanitary Commission, appointed at her suggestion, and working under her
auspices, did for our troops there what the four Sub-Commissions were doing
for those at home. At the same time, these very years which saw her laying
the foundations of the whole modern system of medical work in the army, saw
her also beginning to bring her knowledge, her influence, and her activity into
the service of the country at large. Her *Notes on Hospitals* (1859) revolutionised the theory of hospital construction and hospital management. She was
immediately recognised as the leading expert upon all the questions involved;
her advice flowed unceasingly and in all directions, so that there is no great
hospital to-day which does not bear upon it the impress of her mind. Nor was
this all. With the opening of the Nightingale Training School for Nurses at
St. Thomas's Hospital (1860), she became the founder of modern nursing.

But a terrible crisis was now fast approaching. Sidney Herbert had consented to undertake the root and branch reform of the War Office. He had
sallied forth into that tropical jungle of festooned obstructiveness, of inter-
twisted irresponsibilities, of crouching prejudices, of abuses grown stiff and
rigid with antiquity, which for so many years to come was destined to lure
reforming ministers to their doom.

The War Office [said Miss Nightingale] is a very slow office, an enormously expensive office, and one in which the Minister's intentions can be entirely negatived
by all his sub-departments, and those of each of the sub-departments by every other.

It was true; and, of course, at the first rumour of a change, the old phalanx of
reaction was bristling with its accustomed spears. At its head stood no longer
Dr. Andrew Smith, who, some time since, had followed the Bison into outer

darkness, but a yet more formidable figure, the permanent Under-Secretary himself, Sir Benjamin Hawes—Ben Hawes the Nightingale Cabinet irreverently dubbed him—a man remarkable even among civil servants for adroitness in baffling inconvenient inquiries, resource in raising false issues, and, in short, a consummate command of all the arts of officially sticking in the mud. "Our scheme will probably result in Ben Hawes's resignation," Miss Nightingale said; "and that is another of its advantages." Ben Hawes himself, however, did not quite see it in that light. He set himself to resist the wishes of the Minister by every means in his power. The struggle was long and desperate; and, as it proceeded, it gradually became evident to Miss Nightingale that something was the matter with Sidney Herbert. What was it? His health, never very strong, was, he said, in danger of collapsing under the strain of his work. But, after all, what is illness, when there is a War Office to be reorganised? Then he began to talk of retiring altogether from public life. The doctors were consulted, and declared that, above all things, what was necessary was rest. Rest! She grew seriously alarmed. Was it possible that, at the last moment, the crowning wreath of victory was to be snatched from her grasp? She was not to be put aside by doctors; they were talking nonsense; the necessary thing was not rest but the reform of the War Office; and, besides, she knew very well from her own case what one could do even when one was on the point of death. She expostulated vehemently, passionately: the goal was so near, so very near; he could not turn back now! At any rate, he could not resist Miss Nightingale. A compromise was arranged. Very reluctantly, he exchanged the turmoil of the House of Commons for the dignity of the House of Lords, and he remained at the War Office. She was delighted. "One fight more, the best and the last," she said.

For several more months the fight did indeed go on. But the strain upon him was greater even than she perhaps could realise. Besides the intestine war in his office, he had to face a constant battle in the Cabinet with Mr. Gladstone —a more redoubtable antagonist even than Ben Hawes—over the estimates. His health grew worse and worse. He was attacked by fainting-fits; and there were some days when he could only just keep himself going by gulps of brandy. Miss Nightingale spurred him forward with her encouragements and her admonitions, her zeal and her example. But at last his spirit began to sink as well as his body. He could no longer hope; he could no longer desire; it was useless, all useless; it was utterly impossible. He had failed. The dreadful moment came when the truth was forced upon him: he would never be able to reform the War Office. But a yet more dreadful moment lay behind; he must go to Miss Nightingale and tell her that he was a failure, a beaten man.

Blessed are the merciful! What strange ironic prescience had led Prince Albert, in the simplicity of his heart, to choose that motto for the Crimean brooch? The words hold a double lesson; and, alas!—when she brought herself to realise at length what was indeed the fact and what there was no helping, it was not in mercy that she turned upon her old friend.

Beaten! [she exclaimed]. Can't you see that you've simply thrown away the game? And with all the winning cards in your hands! And so noble a game! Sidney Herbert beaten! And beaten by Ben Hawes! It is a worse disgrace. . . . [her full rage burst out at last] . . . a worse disgrace than the hospitals at Scutari.

He dragged himself away from her, dragged himself to Spa, hoping vainly for a return of health, and then, despairing, back again to England, to Wilton, to the majestic house standing there resplendent in the summer sunshine, among the great cedars, which had lent their shade to Sir Philip Sidney, and all those familiar, darling haunts of beauty which he loved, each one of them, "as if they were persons"; and at Wilton he died. After having received the Eucharist he had become perfectly calm; then, almost unconscious, his lips were seen to be moving. Those about him bent down. "Poor Florence! Poor Florence!" they just caught. ". . . Our joint work . . . unfinished . . . tried to do . . ." and they could hear no more.

When the onward rush of a powerful spirit sweeps a weaker one to its destruction, the commonplaces of the moral judgment are better left unmade. If Miss Nightingale had been less ruthless, Sidney Herbert would not have perished; but then, she would not have been Miss Nightingale. The force that created was the force that destroyed. It was her Demon that was responsible. When the fatal news reached her, she was overcome by agony. In the revulsion of her feelings, she made a worship of the dead man's memory; and the facile instrument which had broken in her hand she spoke of for ever after as her "Master." Then, almost at the same moment, another blow fell upon her. Arthur Clough, worn out by labours very different from those of Sidney Herbert, died too: never more would he tie up her parcels. And yet a third disaster followed. The faithful Aunt Mai did not, to be sure, die; no, she did something almost worse: she left Miss Nightingale. She was growing old, and she felt that she had closer and more imperative duties with her own family. Her niece could hardly forgive her. She poured out, in one of her enormous letters, a passionate diatribe upon the faithlessness, the lack of sympathy, the stupidity, the ineptitude of women. Her doctrines had taken no hold among them; she had never known one who had *appris à apprendre;* she could not even get a woman secretary; "they don't know the names of the Cabinet Ministers—they don't know which of the Churches has Bishops and which not." As for the spirit of self-sacrifice, well—Sidney Herbert and Arthur Clough were men, and they indeed had shown their devotion; but women—! She would mount three widow's caps "for a sign." The first two would be for Clough and for her Master; but the third, "the biggest widow's cap of all"—would be for Aunt Mai. She did well to be angry; she was deserted in her hour of need; and, after all, could she be sure that even the male sex was so impeccable? There was Dr. Sutherland, bungling as usual. Perhaps even he intended to go off, one of these days, too? She gave him a look, and he shivered in his shoes. No!—she grinned sardonically; she would always have Dr. Sutherland. And then she reflected that there was one thing more that she would always have—her work.

Sidney Herbert's death finally put an end to Miss Nightingale's dream of a reformed War Office. For a moment, indeed, in the first agony of her disappointment, she had wildly clutched at a straw; she had written to Mr. Gladstone to beg him to take up the burden of Sidney Herbert's work. And Mr. Gladstone had replied with a sympathetic account of the funeral.

Succeeding Secretaries of State managed between them to undo a good deal of what had been accomplished, but they could not undo it all; and for ten years more (1862-72) Miss Nightingale remained a potent influence at the War Office. After that, her direct connection with the army came to an end, and her energies began to turn more and more completely towards more general objects. Her work upon hospital reform assumed enormous proportions; she was able to improve the conditions in infirmaries and workhouses; and one of her most remarkable papers forestalls the recommendations of the Poor Law Commission of 1909. Her training school for nurses, with all that it involved in initiative, control, responsibility, and combat, would have been enough in itself to have absorbed the whole efforts of at least two lives of ordinary vigour. And at the same time her work in connection with India, which had begun with the Sanitary Commission on the Indian Army, spread and ramified in a multitude of directions. Her tentacles reached the India Office and succeeded in establishing a hold even upon those slippery high places. For many years it was *de rigueur* for the newly appointed Viceroy, before he left England, to pay a visit to Miss Nightingale.

After much hesitation, she had settled down in a small house in South Street, where she remained for the rest of her life. That life was a very long one; the dying woman reached her ninety-first year. Her ill-health gradually diminished; the crises of extreme danger became less frequent, and at last, altogether ceased; she remained an invalid, but an invalid of a curious character— an invalid who was too weak to walk downstairs and who worked far harder than most Cabinet Ministers. Her illness, whatever it may have been, was certainly not inconvenient. It involved seclusion; and an extraordinary, an unparalleled seclusion was, it might almost have been said, the mainspring of Miss Nightingale's life. Lying on her sofa in the little upper room in South Street, she combined the intense vitality of a dominating woman of the world with the mysterious and romantic quality of a myth. She was a legend in her lifetime, and she knew it. She tasted the joys of power, like those Eastern Emperors whose autocratic rule was based upon invisibility, with the mingled satisfactions of obscurity and fame. And she found the machinery of illness hardly less effective as a barrier against the eyes of men than the ceremonial of a palace. Great statesmen and renowned generals were obliged to beg for audiences; admiring princesses from foreign countries found that they must see her at her own time, or not at all; and the ordinary mortal had no hope of ever getting beyond the downstairs sitting-room and Dr. Sutherland. For that indefatigable disciple did, indeed, never desert her. He might be impatient, he might be restless, but he remained. His "incurable looseness of thought," for so she termed it, continued at her service to the end. Once, it is true, he had

actually ventured to take a holiday; but he was recalled, and he did not repeat
the experiment. He was wanted downstairs. There he sat, transacting business, answering correspondence, interviewing callers, and exchanging innumerable notes with the unseen power above. Sometimes word came down
that Miss Nightingale was just well enough to see one of her visitors. The
fortunate man was led up, was ushered, trembling, into the shaded chamber,
and, of course, could never afterwards forget the interview. Very rarely,
indeed, once or twice a year, perhaps, but nobody could be quite certain, in
deadly secrecy, Miss Nightingale went out for a drive in the Park. Unrecog-
nised, the living legend flitted for a moment before the common gaze. And
the precaution was necessary; for there were times when, at some public function, the rumour of her presence was spread abroad; and ladies, mistaken by
the crowd for Miss Nightingale, were followed, pressed upon and vehemently
supplicated—"Let me touch your shawl,"—"Let me stroke your arm"; such
was the strange adoration in the hearts of the people. That vast reserve of
force lay there behind her; she could use it, if she would. But she preferred
never to use it. On occasions, she might hint or threaten; she might balance
the sword of Damocles over the head of the Bison; she might, by a word, by
a glance, remind some refractory minister, some unpersuadable viceroy, sitting
in audience with her in the little upper room, that she was something more
than a mere sick woman, that she had only, so to speak, to go to the window
and wave her handkerchief for . . . dreadful things to follow. But that was
enough; they understood; the myth was there—obvious, portentous, impalpa-
ble; and so it remained to the last.

With statesmen and governors at her beck and call, with her hands on a
hundred strings, with mighty provinces at her feet, with foreign governments
agog for her counsel, building hospitals, training nurses—she still felt that she
had not enough to do. She sighed for more worlds to conquer—more, and yet
more. She looked about her—what was there left? Of course! Philosophy!
After the world of action, the world of thought. Having set right the health
of the British Army, she would now do the same good service for the religious
convictions of mankind. She had long noticed—with regret—the growing
tendency towards free-thinking among artisans. With regret, but not altogether with surprise; the current teaching of Christianity was sadly to seek;
nay, Christianity itself was not without its defects. She would rectify these
errors. She would correct the mistakes of the Churches; she would point out
just where Christianity was wrong; and she would explain to the artisans what
the facts of the case really were. Before her departure for the Crimea, she had
begun this work; and now, in the intervals of her other labours, she completed
it. Her "Suggestions for Thought to the Searchers after Truth among the
Artisans of England" (1860), unravels, in the course of three portly volumes,
the difficulties—hitherto, curiously enough, unsolved—connected with such
matters as Belief in God, the Plan of Creation, the Origin of Evil, the Future
Life, Necessity and Free Will, Law, and the Nature of Morality. The Origin
of Evil, in particular, held no perplexities for Miss Nightingale. "We cannot

conceive," she remarks, "that Omnipotent Righteousness would find satisfaction in *solitary existence.*" This being so, the only question remaining to be asked is, "What beings should we then conceive that God would create?" Now, He cannot create perfect beings, "since, essentially, perfection is one"; if He did so, He would only be adding to Himself. Thus the conclusion is obvious: He *must* create *im*perfect ones. Omnipotent Righteousness, faced by the intolerable *impasse* of a solitary existence, finds itself bound, by the very nature of the case, to create the hospitals at Scutari. Whether this argument would have satisfied the artisans, was never discovered, for only a very few copies of the book were printed for private circulation. One copy was sent to Mr. Mill, who acknowledged it in an extremely polite letter. He felt himself obliged, however, to confess that he had not been altogether convinced by Miss Nightingale's proof of the existence of God. Miss Nightingale was surprised and mortified; she had thought better of Mr. Mill; for surely her proof of the existence of God could hardly be improved upon. "A law," she had pointed out, "implies a lawgiver." Now the Universe is full of laws—the law of gravitation, the law of the excluded middle, and many others; hence it follows that the Universe has a lawgiver—and what would Mr. Mill be satisfied with, if he was not satisfied with that?

Perhaps Mr. Mill might have asked why the argument had not been pushed to its logical conclusion. Clearly, if we are to trust the analogy of human institutions, we must remember that laws are, as a matter of fact, not dispensed by lawgivers, but passed by Act of Parliament. Miss Nightingale, however, with all her experience of public life, never stopped to consider the question whether God might not be a Limited Monarchy.

Yet her conception of God was certainly not orthodox. She felt towards Him as she might have felt towards a glorified sanitary engineer; and in some of her speculations she seems hardly to distinguish between the Deity and the Drains. As one turns over these singular pages, one has the impression that Miss Nightingale has got the Almighty too into her clutches, and that, if He is not careful, she will kill Him with overwork.

Then, suddenly, in the very midst of the ramifying generalities of her metaphysical disquisitions there is an unexpected turn, and the reader is plunged all at once into something particular, something personal, something impregnated with intense experience—a virulent invective upon the position of women in the upper ranks of society. Forgetful alike of her high argument and of the artisans, the bitter creature rails through a hundred pages of close print at the falsities of family life, the ineptitudes of marriage, the emptiness of convention, in the spirit of an Ibsen or a Samuel Butler. Her fierce pen, shaking with intimate anger, depicts in biting sentences the fearful fate of an unmarried girl in a wealthy household. It is a *cri du cœur;* and then, as suddenly, she returns once more to instruct the artisans upon the nature of Omnipotent Righteousness.

Her mind was, indeed, better qualified to dissect the concrete and distasteful fruits of actual life than to construct a coherent system of abstract philos-

ophy. In spite of her respect for Law, she was never at home with a general-
isation. Thus, though the great achievement of her life lay in the immense
impetus which she gave to the scientific treatment of sickness, a true comprehension of the scientific method itself was alien to her spirit. Like most great
men of action—perhaps like all—she was simply an empiricist. She believed
in what she saw, and she acted accordingly; beyond that she would not go.
She had found in Scutari that fresh air and light played an effective part in the
prevention of the maladies with which she had to deal; and that was enough
for her; she would not inquire further; what were the general principles underlying that fact—or even whether there were any—she refused to consider.
Years after the discoveries of Pasteur and Lister, she laughed at what she called
the "germ-fetish." There was no such thing as "infection"; she had never seen
it, therefore it did not exist. But she *had* seen the good effects of fresh air;
therefore there could be no doubt about them; and therefore it was essential
that the bedrooms of patients should be well ventilated. Such was her doctrine; and in those days of hermetically sealed windows it was a very valuable
one. But it was a purely empirical doctrine, and thus it led to some unfortunate results. When, for instance, her influence in India was at its height, she
issued orders that all hospital windows should be invariably kept open. The
authorities, who knew what an open window in the hot weather meant, protested, but in vain; Miss Nightingale was incredulous. She knew nothing of
the hot weather, but she did know the value of fresh air—from personal experience; the authorities were talking nonsense and the windows must be kept
open all the year round. There was a great outcry from all the doctors in
India, but she was firm; and for a moment it seemed possible that her terrible
commands would have to be put into execution. Lord Lawrence, however,
was Viceroy, and he was able to intimate to Miss Nightingale, with sufficient
authority, that he himself had decided upon the question, and that his decision
must stand, even against her own. Upon that, she gave way, but reluctantly
and quite unconvinced; she was only puzzled by the unexpected weakness of
Lord Lawrence. No doubt, if she had lived to-day, and if her experience had
lain, not among cholera cases at Scutari but among yellow-fever cases in Panama, she would have declared fresh air a fetish, and would have maintained
to her dying day that the only really effective way of dealing with disease was
by the destruction of mosquitoes.

Yet her mind, so positive, so realistic, so ultra-practical, had its singular
revulsions, its mysterious moods of mysticism and of doubt. At times, lying
sleepless in the early hours, she fell into long strange agonised meditations, and
then, seizing a pencil, she would commit to paper the confessions of her soul.
The morbid longings of her pre-Crimean days came over her once more; she
filled page after page with self-examination, self-criticism, self-surrender. "O
Father," she wrote, "I submit, I resign myself, I accept with all my heart this
stretching out of Thy hand to save me. . . . O how vain it is, the vanity of
vanities, to live in men's thoughts instead of God's!" She was lonely, she was
miserable. "Thou knowest that through all these horrible twenty years, I have

been supported by the belief that I was working with Thee who wert bringing everyone, even our poor nurses, to perfection,"—and yet, after all, what was the result? Had not even she been an unprofitable servant? One night, waking suddenly, she saw, in the dim light of the night-lamp, tenebrous shapes upon the wall. The past rushed back upon her. "Am I she who once stood on that Crimean height?" she wildly asked—" 'The Lady with a lamp shall stand. . . .' The lamp shows me only my utter shipwreck."

She sought consolation in the writings of the Mystics and in a correspondence with Mr. Jowett. For many years the Master of Balliol acted as her spiritual adviser. He discussed with her in a series of enormous letters the problems of religion and philosophy; he criticised her writings on those subjects with the tactful sympathy of a cleric who was also a man of the world, and he even ventured to attempt at times to instil into her rebellious nature some of his own peculiar suavity. "I sometimes think," he told her, "that you ought seriously to consider how your work may be carried on, not with less energy, but in a calmer spirit. I am not blaming the past. . . . But I want the peace of God to settle on the future." He recommended her to spend her time no longer in "conflicts with Government offices," and to take up some literary work. He urged her to "work out her notion of Divine Perfection," in a series of essays for *Frazer's Magazine*. She did so; and the result was submitted to Mr. Froude, who pronounced the second essay to be "even more pregnant than the first. I cannot tell," he said, "how sanitary, with disordered intellects, the effects of such papers will be." Mr. Carlyle, indeed, used different language, and some remarks of his about a lost lamb bleating on the mountains having been unfortunately repeated to Miss Nightingale, all Mr. Jowett's suavity was required to keep the peace. In a letter of fourteen sheets, he turned her attention from the painful topic towards a discussion of Quietism. "I don't see why," said the Master of Balliol, "active life might not become a sort of passive life too." And then, he added, "I sometimes fancy there are possibilities of human character much greater than have been realised." She found such sentiments helpful, underlining them in blue pencil; and, in return, she assisted her friend with a long series of elaborate comments upon the Dialogues of Plato, most of which he embodied in the second edition of his translation. Gradually her interest became more personal; she told him never to work again after midnight, and he obeyed her. Then she helped him to draw up a special form of daily service for the College Chapel, with selections from the Psalms, under the heads of "God the Lord, God the Judge, God the Father, and God the Friend,"—though, indeed, this project was never realised; for the Bishop of Oxford disallowed the alterations, exercising his legal powers, on the advice of Sir Travers Twiss.

Their relations became intimate. "The spirit of the twenty-third psalm and the spirit of the nineteenth psalm should be united in our lives," Mr. Jowett said. Eventually, she asked him to do her a singular favour. Would he, knowing what he did of her religious views, come to London and administer to her the Holy Sacrament? He did not hesitate, and afterwards declared that he would always regard the occasion as a solemn event in his life. He was devoted to her; though the precise nature of his feelings towards her never quite transpired. Her feelings towards him were more mixed. At first, he was "that great and good man"—"that true saint, Mr. Jowett"; but, as time went on, some gall was mingled with the balm; the acrimony of her nature asserted itself. She felt that she gave more sympathy than she received; she was exhausted, she was annoyed, by his conversation. Her tongue, one day, could not refrain from shooting out at him. "He comes to me, and he talks to me," she said, "as if I were someone else."

At one time she had almost decided to end her life in retirement, as a patient at St. Thomas's Hospital. But partly owing to the persuasions of Mr. Jowett, she changed her mind; for forty-five years she remained in South Street; and in South Street she died. As old age approached, though her influence with the official world gradually diminished, her activities seemed to remain as intense and widespread as before. When hospitals were to be built, when schemes of sanitary reform were in agitation, when wars broke out, she was still the adviser of all Europe. Still, with a characteristic self-assurance, she watched from her Mayfair bedroom over the welfare of India. Still, with an indefatigable enthusiasm, she pushed forward the work, which, perhaps, was nearer to her heart, more completely her own, than all the rest—the training of nurses. In her moments of deepest depression, when her greatest achievements seemed to lose their lustre, she thought of her nurses, and was comforted. The ways of God, she found, were strange indeed. "How inefficient I was in the Crimea," she noted. "Yet He has raised up from it trained nursing."

At other times she was better satisfied. Looking back, she was amazed by the enormous change which, since her early days, had come over the whole treatment of illness, the whole conception of public and domestic health—a change in which, she knew, she had played her part. One of her Indian admirers, the Aga Khan, came to visit her. She expatiated on the marvellous advances she had lived to see in the management of hospitals, in drainage, in ventilation, in sanitary work of every kind. There was a pause; and then, "Do you think you are improving?" asked the Aga Khan. She was a little taken aback, and said, "What do you mean by 'improving'?" He replied, "Believing more in God." She saw that he had a view of God which was different from hers. "A most interesting man," she noted after the interview; "but you could never teach him sanitation."

When old age actually came, something curious happened. Destiny, having waited very patiently, played a queer trick on Miss Nightingale. The benevolence and public spirit of that long life had only been equalled by its acerbity. Her virtue had dwelt in hardness, and she had poured forth her unstinted usefulness with a bitter smile upon her lips. And now the sarcastic years brought the proud woman her punishment. She was not to die as she had lived. The sting was to be taken out of her: she was to be made soft;

she was to be reduced to compliance and complacency. The change came gradually, but at last it was unmistakable. The terrible commander who had driven Sidney Herbert to his death, to whom Mr. Jowett had applied the words of Homer, αμοτον μεμαυια—raging insatiably—now accepted small compliments with gratitude, and indulged in sentimental friendships with young girls. The author of *"Notes on Nursing"*—that classical compendium of the besetting sins of the sisterhood, drawn up with the detailed acrimony, the vindictive relish, of a Swift—now spent long hours in composing sympathetic Addresses to Probationers, whom she petted and wept over in turn. And, at the same time there appeared a corresponding alteration in her physical mould. The thin, angular woman, with her haughty eye and her acrid mouth had vanished; and in her place was the rounded bulky form of a fat old lady, smiling all day long. Then something else became visible. The brain which had been steeled at Scutari was indeed, literally, growing soft. Senility—an ever more and more amiable senility—descended. Towards the end, consciousness itself grew lost in a roseate haze, and melted into nothingness. It was just then, three years before her death, when she was eighty-seven years old (1907), that those in authority bethought them that the opportune moment had come for bestowing a public honour on Florence Nightingale. She was offered the Order of Merit. That Order, whose roll contains, among other distinguished names, those of Sir Laurence Alma Tadema and Sir Edward Elgar, is remarkable chiefly for the fact that, as its title indicates, it is bestowed because its recipient deserves it, and for no other reason. Miss Nightingale's representatives accepted the honour, and her name, after a lapse of many years, once more appeared in the Press. Congratulations from all sides came pouring in. There was a universal burst of enthusiasm—a final revivification of the ancient myth. Among her other admirers, the German Emperor took this opportunity of expressing his feelings towards her. "His Majesty," wrote the German Ambassador, "having just brought to a close a most enjoyable stay in the beautiful neighbourhood of your old home near Romsey, has commanded me to present you with some flowers as a token of his esteem." Then, by Royal command, the Order of Merit was brought to South Street, and there was a little ceremony of presentation. Sir Douglas Dawson, after a short speech, stepped forward, and handed the insignia of the Order to Miss Nightingale. Propped up by pillows, she dimly recognised that some compliment was being paid her. "Too kind—too kind," she murmured; and she was not ironical.

J. E. B. Stuart[1]

by GAMALIEL BRADFORD

STUART was a fighter by nature. When he was at West Point in the early fifties, his distinguishing characteristics, as chronicled by Fitzhugh Lee, were "a strict attendance to his military duties, an erect, soldierly bearing, an immediate and almost thankful acceptance of a challenge from any cadet to fight, who might in any way feel himself aggrieved." The tendency, if not inherited, did not lack paternal encouragement; for the elder Stuart writes to his son, in regard to one of these combats: "I did not consider you so much to blame. An insult should be resented under all circumstances." The young cadet also showed himself to be a fearless and an exceptionally skillful horseman.

These qualities served him well in the Indian warfare to which he was immediately transferred from West Point. His recklessness in taking chances was equaled only by his ingenuity in pulling through. One of his superiors writes: "Lieutenant Stuart was brave and gallant, always prompt in execution of orders and reckless of danger and exposure. I considered him at that time one of the most promising young officers in the United States Army."

Later Stuart took a prominent part in the capture of John Brown. He himself wrote an account of the matter at the time for the newspapers, simply to explain and justify Lee's conduct. He also wrote a letter to his mother, with a characteristic description of his own doings: "I approached the door in the presence of perhaps two thousand spectators, and told *Mr. Smith* that I had a communication for him from Colonel Lee. He opened the door about four inches, and placed his body against the crack, with a cocked carbine in his hand; hence his remark after his capture that he could have wiped me out like a mosquito. . . . When *Smith* first came to the door I recognized old *Osawatomie Brown,* who had given us so much trouble in Kansas. No one present but myself could have performed that service. I got his bowie-knife from his person, and have it yet."

From the very beginning of the war Stuart maintained this fighting reputation. He would attack anything anywhere, and the men who served under him had to do the same; what is more, and marks the born leader, he made them wish to do the same. "How can I eat, sleep, or rest in peace without you upon the outpost?" wrote Joseph Johnston; and a noble enemy, who had been a friend, Sedgwick, is reported to have said that Stuart was "the greatest cavalry officer ever foaled in America."

[1] From Gamaliel Bradford, *Confederate Portraits* (1914). By arrangement with and permission of Houghton Mifflin Company.

Danger he met with more than stolid indifference, a sort of furious bravado, thrusting himself into it with manifest pleasure, and holding back, when he did hold back, with a sigh. And some men's luck! Johnston was wounded a dozen times, was always getting wounded. Yet Stuart, probably far more exposed, was wounded only once in his life, among the Indians; in the war not at all. His clothes were pierced again and again. According to Von Borcke, the general had half of his moustache cut off by a bullet "as neatly as it could have been done by the hand of an experienced barber." Yet nothing ever drew blood till the shot which was mortal. Such an immunity naturally encouraged the sort of fatalism not unusual with great soldiers, and Stuart once said of the proximity of his enemies, "You might have shot a marble at them—but I am not afraid of any ball aimed at me."

In this spirit he got into scores of difficult places—and got out again. Sometimes it was by quick action and a mad rush, as when he left his hat and a few officers behind him. Sometimes it was by stealth and secrecy, as when he hid his whole command all night within a few hundred yards of the marching enemy. "And nothing now remained but to watch and wait and keep quiet. Quiet? Yes, the men kept very quiet, for they realized that even Stuart never before had them in so tight a place. But many a time did we fear that we were betrayed by the weary, hungry, headstrong mules of the ordnance train. Men were stationed at the head of every team; but in spite of all precautions, a discordant bray would every now and then fill the air. Never was the voice of a mule so harsh!"

The men who had watched and tried and tested him on such occasions as these knew what he was and gave him their trust. He asked nothing of them that he would not do himself. Therefore they did what he asked of them. Scheibert says that "he won their confidence and inspired them by his whole bearing and personality, by his kindling speech, his flashing eye, and his cheerfulness which no reverse could overcome." Stuart himself describes his followers' enthusiastic loyalty with a naïveté as winning as it is characteristic. "There was something of the sublime in the implicit confidence and unquestioning trust of the rank and file in a leader guiding them straight, apparently, into the very jaws of the enemy, every step appearing to them to diminish the very faintest hope of extrication." Yet he asked this trust and they gave it simply on the strength of his word. "You are about to engage in an enterprise which, to ensure success, imperatively demands at your hands coolness, decision, and the strictest order and sobriety on the march and in the bivouac. The destination and extent of this expedition had better be kept to myself than known to you."

The men loved him also because, when the strain was removed, he put on no airs, pretense, or remoteness of superiority, but treated them as man to man. "He was the most approachable of major-generals, and jested with the private soldiers of his command as jovially as though he had been one of themselves. The men were perfectly unconstrained in his presence, and treated him more like the chief huntsman of a hunting party than as a major-general."

His officers also loved him, and not only trusted him for war, but enjoyed his company in peace. He was constantly on the watch to do them kindnesses, and would frolic with them—marbles, snowballs, quoits, what not?—like a boy with boys.

And Stuart loved his men as they loved him, did not regard them as mere food for cannon, to be used, and abused, and forgotten. There is something almost pathetic in his neglect of self in praising them. "The horseman who, at his officer's bidding, without question, leaps into unexplored darkness, knowing nothing except that there is danger ahead, possesses the highest attribute of the patriot soldier. It is a great source of pride to me to command a division of such men." Careless of his own danger always, he was far more thoughtful of those about him. In the last battle he was peculiarly reckless, and Major McClellan noticed that the general kept sending him with messages to General Anderson. "At last the thought occurred to me that he was endeavoring to shield me from danger. I said to him: 'General, my horse is weary. You are exposing yourself, and you are alone. Please let me remain with you.' He smiled at me kindly, but bade me go to General Anderson with another message."

Any reflection on his command arouses him at once to its defense. "There seems to be a growing tendency to abuse and underrate the services of that arm of the service [cavalry] by a few officers of infantry, among whom I regret to find General Trimble. Troops should be taught to take pride in other branches of the service than their own."

It is very rare that Stuart has any occasion to address himself directly to the authorities at Richmond. Fighting, not writing, was his business. But when he feels that his men and horses are being starved unnecessarily, he bestirs himself, and sends Seddon a letter which is as interesting for nervous and vigorous expressions as for the character of the writer. "I beg to urge that in no case should persons not connected with the army, and who are amply compensated for all that is taken, be allowed more subsistence per day than the noble veterans who are periling their lives in the cause and at every sacrifice are enduring hardship and exposure in the ranks."

And the general's care and enthusiasm for his officers was as great as for the privates. It is charming to see how earnestly and how specifically he commends them in every report. Particularly, he is anxious to impress upon Lee that no family considerations should prevent the merited advancement of Lee's own son and nephew. Even on his deathbed one of his last wishes was that his faithful followers should have his horses, and he allotted them thoughtfully according to each officer's needs.

The general did not allow his feelings to interfere with subordination, however. His discipline "was as firm as could be with such men as composed the cavalry of General Lee's army," writes Judge Garnett. "He never tolerated nor overlooked disobedience of orders." Even his favorites, Mosby and Fitz Lee, come in for reproof when needed. Of the latter's failure to arrive at Raccoon Ford when expected he writes: "By this failure to comply with instructions not only the movement of the cavalry across the Rapidan was postponed a day, but a fine opportunity was lost to overhaul a body of the enemy's cavalry on a predatory excursion far beyond their lines." His tendency to severity in regard to a certain subordinate calls forth one of Lee's gently tactful cautions: "I am perfectly willing to transfer him to Paxton's brigade, if he desires it; but if he does not, I know of no act of his to justify my doing so. Do not let your judgment be warped." There were officers with whom Stuart could not get along; for instance, "Grumble Jones," who perhaps could get along with no one. Yet, after Stuart's death, Jones said of him: "By G—, Martin! You know I had little love for Stuart, and he had just as little for me; but that is the greatest loss the army has ever sustained except the death of Jackson."

From these various considerations it will be surmised that Stuart was no mere reckless sworder, no Rupert, good with sabre, furious in onset, beyond that signifying nothing. He knew the spirit of the antique maxim, "Be bold, and evermore be bold; be not too bold." He had learned the hardest lesson and the essential corrective for such a temperament, self-control. To me there is an immense pathos in his quiet, almost plaintive explanation to Lee, on one occasion: "The commanding general will, I am sure, appreciate how hard it was to desist from the undertaking, but to any one on the spot there could be but one opinion—its impossibility. I gave it up." On the other hand, no one knew better that in some cases perfect prudence and splendid boldness are one and the same thing. To use again his own language: "Although the expedition was prosecuted further than was contemplated in your instructions, I feel assured that the considerations which actuated me will convince you that I did not depart from their spirit and that the bold development in the subsequent direction of the march was the quintessence of prudence." Lee always found the right words. In one of his reports he says of Stuart [italics mine]: "I take occasion to express to the Department my sense of the boldness, *judgment,* and *prudence* he displayed in its execution."

But one may have self-control without commanding intelligence. Freemantle's description of Stuart's movements does not suggest much of the latter quality. "He seems to roam over the country at his own discretion, and always gives a good account of himself, turning up at the right moment, and hitherto he has not got himself into any serious trouble." Later, more studious observers do not take quite the same view. One should read the whole of the Prussian colonel Scheibert's account of Stuart's thorough planning, his careful calculation, his exact methods of procedure. "Before Stuart undertook any movement, he spared nothing in the way of preparation which might make it succeed. He informed himself as exactly as possible by scouts and spies, himself reconnoitred with his staff, often far beyond the outposts, had his engineer officers constantly fill out and improve the rather inadequate maps and ascertain the practicability of roads, fords, etc. In short, he omitted no precaution and spared no pains or effort to secure the best possible results for such undertakings as he planned; therefore he was in the saddle almost as

long again as his men." Similar testimony can be gathered incidentally everywhere in Stuart's letters and reports, proving that he was no chance roamer,
but went where he planned to go and came back when he intended. For
instance, he writes of the Peninsular operations: "It is proper to remark here
that the commanding general had, on the occasion of my late expedition to
the Pamunkey, imparted to me his design of bringing Jackson down upon
the enemy's right flank and rear, and directed that I should examine the
country with reference to its practicability for such a movement. I therefore
had studied the features of the country very thoroughly and knew exactly
how to conform my movements to Jackson's route."

On the strength of these larger military qualities it has sometimes been
contended that Stuart should have had an even more responsible command
than fell to him and that Lee should have retained him at the head of Jackson's
corps after Jackson's death. Certainly Lee can have expressed no higher opinion of any one: "A more zealous, ardent, brave and devoted soldier than
Stuart the Confederacy cannot have." Johnston called him "calm, firm, acute,
active, and enterprising, I know of no one more competent than he to estimate
occurrences at their true value." Longstreet, hitting Jackson as well as praising
Stuart, said: "His death was possibly a greater loss to the Confederate army
than that of the swift-moving General Stonewall Jackson." Among foreign
authorities Scheibert writes that "General von Schmidt, the regenerator of
our [Prussian] cavalry tactics, has told me that Stuart was the model cavalry
leader of this century and has questioned me very often about his mode of
fighting." And Captain Battine thinks that he should have had Jackson's
place. Finally, Alexander, sanest of Confederate writers, expresses the same
view strongly and definitely: "I always thought it an injustice to Stuart and
a loss to the army that he was not from that moment *continued in command
of Jackson's corps.* He had *won* the right to it. I believe he had all of Jackson's genius and dash and originality, without the eccentricity of character
which sometimes led to disappointment. Jackson's spirit and inspiration were
uneven. Stuart, however, possessed the rare quality of being always *equal to
himself at his very best."*

This is magnificent praise, coming from such a source. Nevertheless, I
find it hard to question Lee's judgment. There was nothing in the world to
prevent his giving Stuart the position, if he thought him qualified. It is not
absolutely certain how Stuart would have carried independent command. I
can hardly imagine Davis, even early in the war, writing of Jackson as he did
of Stuart: "The letter of General Hill painfully impresses me with that which
has before been indicated—a want of vigilance and intelligent observation on
the part of General Stuart." Major Bigelow, who knows the battle of Chancellorsville as well as any one living, does not judge Stuart's action so favorably
as Alexander. And Cooke, who adored Stuart and served constantly under
him, says: "At Chancellorsville, when he succeeded Jackson, the troops,
although quite enthusiastic about him, complained that he led them too recklessly against artillery; and it is hard for those who knew the man to believe

that, as an army commander, he would have consented to a strictly defensive campaign. Fighting was a necessity of his blood, and the slow movements of infantry did not suit his genius."

May it not be also that Lee thought Stuart indispensable where he was and believed it would be as difficult to replace him as Jackson? Most of Stuart's correspondence has perished and we are obliged to gather its tenor from letters written to him, which is much like listening to a one-sided conversation over the telephone. From one of Lee's letters, however, it is fairly evident that neither he nor Stuart himself had seriously considered the latter's taking Jackson's place. Lee writes: "I am obliged to you for your views as to the successor of the great and good Jackson. Unless God in his mercy will raise us up one, I do not know what we shall do. I agree with you on the subject, and have so expressed myself."

In any event, what his countrymen will always remember of Stuart is the fighting figure, the glory of battle, the sudden and tumultuous fury of charge and onset.

And what above all distinguishes him in this is his splendid joy in it. Others fought with clenched fist and set teeth, rejoicing, perhaps, but with deadly determination of lip and brow. He laughed and sang. His blue eye sparkled and his white teeth gleamed. To others it was the valley of the shadow of death. To him it was a picnic and a pleasure party.

He views everything by its picturesque side, catches the theatrical detail which turns terror and death into a scenic surprise. "My arrival could not have been more fortunately timed, for, arriving after dark, the ponderous march, with the rolling artillery, must have impressed the enemy's cavalry, watching their rear, with the idea of an immense army about to cut off their retreat." He rushed gayly into battle, singing, "Old Joe Hooker, won't you come out of the Wilderness?" or his favorite of favorites, "If you want to have a good time, jine the cavalry." When he is riding off, as it were into the mouth of hell, his adjutant asks, "How long?" and he answers, as Touchstone might, with a bit of old ballad, "It may be for years and it may be for ever." His clear laughter, in the sternest crises, echoes through dusty war books, like a silver bell. As he sped back from his Peninsular raid, the Union troops were close upon him and the swollen Chickahominy in front, impassable, it seemed. Stuart thought a moment, pulling at his beard. Then he found the remains of an old bridge and set his men to rebuild it. "While the men were at work upon it, Stuart was lying down on the bank of the stream, in the gayest humor I ever saw, laughing at the prank he had played on McClellan."

It is needless to enlarge on the effect of such a temper, such exuberant confidence and cheerfulness in danger, on subordinates. It lightened labor, banished fatigue, warmed chill limbs and fainting courage. "My men and horses are tired, hungry, jaded, but all right," was the last despatch he ever wrote. So long as he was with them, they were all right. His very voice was like music, says Fitz Lee, "like the silver trumpet of the Archangel." It sounded oblivion of everything but glory. His gayety, his laughter, were infectious and turned a raid into a revel. "That summer night," writes Mosby of the McClellan expedition, "was a carnival of fun I can never forget. Nobody thought of danger or sleep, when champagne bottles were bursting and wine was flowing in copious streams. All had perfect confidence in their leader. . . . The discipline of the soldiers for a while gave way to the wild revelry of Comus."

And this spirit of adventure, of romance, of buoyant optimism and energy, was not merely reserved for occasions of excitement, was not the triumphant outcome of glory and success. It was constant and unfailing. To begin with, Stuart had a magnificent physique. "Nothing seemed strong enough to break down his powerful organization of mind and body," says his biographer; and Mosby, "Although he had been in the saddle two days and nights without sleep, he was as gay as a lark." When exhaustion finally fell upon him, he would drop off his horse by the roadside, anywhere, sleep for an hour, and arise as active as ever. Universal testimony proves that he was overcome and disheartened by no disaster. He would be thoughtful for a moment, pulling at his beard, then seize upon the best decision that presented itself and push on. Dreariness sometimes crushes those who can well resist actual misfortune. Not Stuart. "In the midst of rainstorms, when everybody was riding along grim and cowering beneath the flood pouring down, he would trot on, head up, and singing gayly."

The list of his personal adventures and achievements is endless. He braved capture and death with entire indifference, trusting in his admirable horsemanship, which often saved him, trusting in Providence, trusting in nothing at all but his quick wit and strong arm, curious mainly, perhaps, to see what would happen. On one occasion he is said to have captured forty-four Union soldiers. He was riding absolutely alone and ran into them taking their ease in a field. Instantly he chose his course. "Throw down your arms or you are all dead men." They were green troops and threw down their arms, and Stuart marched the whole squad into camp. When duty forbids a choice adventure, he sighs, as might Don Quixote: "A scouting party of one hundred and fifty lancers had just passed toward Gettysburg. I regretted exceedingly that my march did not admit of the delay necessary to catch them."

I have sometimes asked myself how much of this spirit of romantic adventure, of knight-errantry, as it were, in Stuart was conscious. Did he, like Claverhouse, read Homer and Froissart, and try to realize in modern Virginia the heroic deeds, still more, the heroic spirit, of antique chivalry? In common with all Southerners, he probably knew the prose and poetry of Scott ,and dreamed of the plume of Marmion and the lance of Ivanhoe. He must have felt the weight of his name, also, and believed that "James Stuart" might be aptly fitted with valorous adventure, and knightly deeds, and sudden glory. It is extremely interesting to find him writing to Jackson: "Did you receive the volume of Napoleon and his Maxims I sent you?" I should like to own that volume. And in his newspaper account of Brown's raid he quotes Horace, horribly, but still Horace: *Erant fortes ante Agamemnona.*

Yet I do not gather that he was much of a student. He preferred to live poems rather than read them. The spirit of romance, the instinct of the picturesque, was born in him and would out anywhere and everywhere. Life was a perpetual play, with ever shifting scenes, and gay lime-light, and hurrying incident, and passionate climax. Again and again he reminds me of a boy playing soldiers. His ambition, his love of glory, was of this order, not a bit the ardent, devouring, growing, far-sighted passion of Jackson, but a jovial sense of pleasant things that can be touched and heard and tasted here, to-day. He had a childlike, simple vanity which all his biographers smile at, liked parade display and pomp and gorgeousness, utterly differing in this from Jackson, who was too proud, or Lee, who was too lofty. Stuart rode fine horses, never was seen on an inferior animal. He wore fine clothes, all that his position justified, perhaps a little more. Here is Fitz Lee's picture of him: "His strong figure, his big brown beard, his piercing, laughing blue eyes, the drooping hat and black feather, the 'fighting jacket' as he termed it, the tall cavalry boots, forming one of the most jubilant and striking figures in the war." And Cooke is even more particular: "His fighting jacket shone with dazzling buttons and was covered with gold braid; his hat was looped up with a golden star, and decorated with a black ostrich plume; his fine buff gauntlets reached to the elbow; around his waist was tied a splendid yellow sash, and his spurs were of pure gold." After this, we appreciate the biographer's assertion that Stuart was as fond of colors as a boy or girl, and elsewhere we read that he never moved without his gorgeous red battle-flag which often drew the fire of the enemy.

As to the spurs, they were presented to the general by the ladies of Baltimore and he took great pride in them, signing himself sometimes in his private letters, K.G.S., Knight of the Golden Spurs.

This last touch is perfectly characteristic and the Stuart of the pen is precisely the same as the Stuart of the sword. He could express himself as simply as Napoleon: "Tell General Lee that all is right. Jackson has not advanced, but I have; and I am going to crowd them with artillery." But usually he did not. Indeed, the severe taste of Lee recoiled from his subordinate's fashions of speech: "The general deals in the flowery style, as you will perceive, if you ever see his reports in detail." But I love them, they ring and resound so with the temper of the man, gorgeous scraps of tawdry rhetoric, made charming by their riotous sincerity, as with Scott and Dumas. "Their brave men behaved with coolness and intrepidity in danger, unswerving resolution before difficulties, and stood unappalled before the rushing torrent of the Chickahominy, with the probability of an enemy at their heels armed with the fury of a tigress robbed of her whelps." Could anything be worse from Lee's point of view? But it does put some life into an official report. Or take this Homeric picture of a charge, which rushes like a half-dozen stanzas of "Chevy Chase": "Lieutenant Robbins, handling it in the most skilful manner, managed to clear the way for the march with little delay, and infused by a sudden dash at a picket such a wholesome terror that it never paused to take a second look. . . . On, on dashed Robbins, here skirting a field, there leaping a fence or ditch, and clearing the woods beyond."

When I read these things, I cannot but remember Madame de Sévigné's fascinating comment on the historical novels of her day. "The style of La Calprenède is detestable in a thousand ways: long-winded, romantic phrases, ill-chosen words, I admit it all. I agree that it is detestable; yet it holds me like glue. The beauty of the sentiments, the violence of the passions, the grandeur of the events, and the miraculous success of the hero's redoubtable sword—it sweeps me away as if I were a child."

And Stuart's was a real sword!

Then, too, as in Shakespearean tragedy or modern melodrama, the tension in Stuart's case, is constantly relieved by hearty, wholesome, cheery laughter, which shook his broad shoulders and sparkled in his blue eyes. See what a strange comedy his report makes of this lurid night scene, in which another might have found only shadow and death: "It so far succeeded as to get possession of his [General Bartlett's] headquarters at one o'clock at night, the general having saved himself by precipitate flight in his nether garments. The headquarters flag was brought away. No prisoners were attempted to be taken, the party shooting down every one within reach. Some horses breaking loose near headquarters ran through an adjacent regimental camp, causing the greatest commotion, mid firing and yelling and cries of 'Halt!' 'Rally!' mingling in wild disorder, and ludicrous stampede which beggars description." Can't you hear him laugh?

It must not be concluded from this that Stuart was cruel in his jesting. Where gentleness and sympathy were really called for, all the evidence shows that no man could give more. But he believed that the rough places are made smooth and the hard places soft and the barren places green and smiling by genial laughter. Who shall say that he was wrong? Therefore he would have his jest, with inferior and superior, with friend and enemy. Even the sombre Jackson was not spared. Once he had floundered into winter-quarters oddly decorated. Stuart suggested "that a drawing of the apartment should be made, with the race-horses, gamecocks, and terrier in bold relief, the picture to be labelled: 'View of the winter-quarters of General Jackson, affording an insight into the tastes and character of the individual.'" And Jackson enjoyed it.

When it came to his adversaries, Stuart's fun was unlimited. Everybody knows his telegraphed complaint to the United States Commissary Department that the mules he had been getting lately were most unsatisfactory and he wished they would provide a better quality. Even more amusing is the correspondence that occurred at Lewinsville. One of Stuart's old comrades wrote, addressing him by his West Point nickname. "My dear Beauty,—I am sorry that circumstances are such that I can't have the pleasure of seeing you, although so near you. Griffin says he would like to have you dine with him at Willard's at 5 o'clock on Saturday next. Keep your Black Horse off me, if you please. Yours, etc., Orlando M. Poe." On the back of this was penciled in Stuart's writing: "I have the honor to report that 'circumstances' were such that they could have seen me if they had stopped to look behind, and I answered both at the cannon's mouth. Judging from his speed, Griffin surely left for Washington to hurry up that dinner."

I had an old friend who adored the most violent melodrama. When the curtain and his tears had fallen together, he would sigh and murmur, "Now let's have a little of that snare-drum music." Such was Stuart. "It might almost be said that music was his passion," writes his biographer. I doubt, however, whether he dealt largely in the fugues of Bach. His favorites, in the serious order, are said to have been "The dew is on the blossom," and "Sweet Evelina." But his joy was the uproarious "If you get there before I do"; or his precious "If you want to have a good time, jine the cavalry." He liked to live in the blare of trumpets and the crash of cymbals, liked to have his nerves tingle and his blood leap to a merry hunts-up or a riotous chorus, liked to have the high strain of war's melodrama broken by the sudden crackle of the snare-drum. His banjo-player, Sweeney, was as near to him as an aide-de-camp, followed him everywhere. "Stuart wrote his most important correspondence with the rattle of the gay instrument stunning everybody, and would turn round from his work, burst into a laugh, and join uproariously in Sweeney's chorus."

And dance was as keen a spice to peril as song and laughter. To fight all day and dance all night was a good day's work to this creature of perfect physique and inexhaustible energy. If his staff officers could not keep pace with him and preferred a little sleep, the general did not like it at all. What? Here is—or was—a gay town, and pretty girls. Just because we are here to-day and gone to-morrow, shall we not fleet the time carelessly, as they did in the golden world? And the girls are got together, and a ball is organized, and the fun grows swifter and swifter. Perhaps a fortunate officer picks the prettiest and is about to stand up with her. Stuart whispers in his ear that a hurried message must be carried, laughs his gay laugh, and slips into the vacant place. Then an orderly hurries in, covered with dust. The enemy are upon us. "The officers rushed to their weapons and called for their horses, panic-stricken fathers and mothers endeavored to collect around them their bewildered children, while the young ladies ran to and fro in most admired despair. General Stuart maintained his accustomed coolness and composure. Our horses were immediately saddled, and in less than five minutes we were in rapid gallop to the front." Oh, what a life!

You divine that with such a temperament Stuart would love women. So he did. Not that he let them interfere with duty. He would have heartily accepted the profound doctrine of Enobarbus in regard to the fair: "It were pity to cast them away for nothing; yet between them and a great cause they should be esteemed as nothing." Stuart arrested hundreds of ladies, says his biographer, and remained inexorable to their petitions. Cooke's charming account of one of these arrests should be read in full: how the fair captives first raved, and then listened, and then laughed, and then were charmed by the mellifluous Sweeney and the persuasive general, and at last departed with kissed hands and kindly hearts, leaving Stuart to explain to his puzzled aide, who inquired why he took so much pains: "Don't you understand? When those ladies arrived they were mad enough with me to bite my head off, and I determined to put them in good humor before they left me."

And the women liked Stuart. It was a grand thing to be the first officer in the Confederate cavalry, with a blue eye and a fair beard, and all gold, like Horace's Lydia, from hat to spurs. When he rode singing and laughing into a little town, "by river or seashore," they flocked to meet him, young and old, and touched his garments, and begged his buttons and kissed his gloved hands, until he suggested that his cheeks were available, and then they kissed those, young and old alike. They showered him with flowers also, buried him under nosegays and garlands, till he rode like old god Bacchus or the queen of May. What an odd fashion of making war! And the best I have met with is, that one day Stuart described one of these occurrences to his great chieftain. "I had to wear her garland, till I was out of sight," apologized the young cavalier. "Why aren't you wearing it now?" retorted Lee. Isn't that admirable? I verily believe that if any young woman had had the unimaginable audacity to throw a garland over Lee, he would have worn it through the streets of Richmond itself.

You say, then, this Stuart was dissipated, perhaps, a scapegrace, a rioter, imitating Rupert and Murat in other things than great cavalry charges. That is the curious point. The man was nothing of the sort. With all his instinct of revelry, he had no vices, a very Puritan of laughter. He liked pretty girls everywhere; but when he was charged with libertinism, he answered, in the boldness of innocence, "That person does not live who can say that I ever did anything improper of that description"; and he liked his wife better than any other pretty girl. He married her when he was twenty-two years old and his last wish was that she might reach him before he died. His few letters to her that have been printed are charming in their playful affection. He adored his children also; in short, was a pattern of domesticity. He did, indeed, love his country more, and telegraphed to his wife, when she called him to his dying daughter's bedside, "My duty to the country must be performed before I can give way to the feelings of a father"; but the child's death was a cruel blow to him. With his intimates he constantly referred to her, and when he himself was dying, he whispered, "I shall soon be with my little Flora again."

"I never saw him touch a card," writes one who was very near him, "and he never dreamed of uttering an oath under any provocation, nor would he permit it at his headquarters." We are assured by many that he never drank and an explicit statement of his own on the subject is reported: "I promised my mother in my childhood never to touch ardent spirits and a drop has never passed my lips, except the wine of the communion."

As the last words show, he had religion as well as morals. He joined the

Methodist church when he was fifteen; later the Episcopal. When he was twenty-four, he sent money home to his mother to aid in the building of a church. He carried his Bible with him always. In his reports religion is not obtrusive. When it does occur, it is evidently sincere. "The Lord of Hosts was plainly fighting on our side, and the solid walls of Federal infantry melted away before the straggling, but nevertheless determined, onset of our infantry columns." "Believing that the hand of God was clearly manifested in the signal deliverance of my command from danger, and the crowning success attending it, I ascribe to Him the praise, the honor, and the glory." He inclined to strictness in the observance of Sunday. Captain Colston writes me that when twelve struck of a Saturday night Stuart held up his hand relentlessly and stopped song and dance in their full tide, though youth and beauty begged for just one more. He was equally scrupulous in the field, though, in his feeling of injury because the enemy were not, I seem to detect his habitual touch of humor: "The next morning being the Sabbath, I recognized my obligation to do no duty other than what was absolutely necessary, and determined, so far as possible, to devote it to rest. Not so the enemy, whose guns about 8 A.M. showed that he would not observe it."

I have no doubt that Stuart's religion was inward as well as outward and remoulded his heart. But, after all, he was but little over thirty when he died, and I love to trace in him the occasional working of the old Adam which had such lively play in the bosom of many an officer who was unjustly blamed or missed some well-deserved promotion. Stuart's own letters are too few to afford much insight of this kind. But here again we get that one-sided correspondence with Lee which is so teasingly suggestive. On one occasion Lee writes: "The expression 'appropriated by the Stuart Horse Artillery' was not taken from a report of Colonel Baldwin, nor intended in any objectionable sense, but used for want of a better phrase, without any intention on my part of wounding." And again, after Chancellorsville: "As regards the closing remarks of your note, I am at a loss to understand their reference or to know what has given rise to them. In the management of the difficult operations at Chancellorsville, which you so promptly undertook and creditably performed, I saw no errors to correct, nor has there been a fit opportunity to commend your conduct. I prefer your acts to speak for themselves, nor does your character or reputation require bolstering up by out-of-place expressions of my opinion."

But by far the most interesting human revelation of this kind is one letter of Stuart's own, written to justify himself against some aspersions of General Trimble. With the right or wrong of the case we are not concerned; simply with the fascinating study of Stuart's state of mind. He begins evidently with firm restraint and a Christian moderation: "Human memory is frail I know." But the exposure of his wrongs heats his blood, as he goes on, and spurs him, though he still endeavors to check himself: "It is true I am not in the habit of giving orders, particularly to my seniors in years, in a dictatorial and authoritative manner, and my manner very likely on this occasion was more

restive than imperative; indeed, I may have been content to satisfy myself
that the dispositions which he himself proposed accorded with my own ideas,
without any blustering show of orders to do this or that. . . . General Trimble
says I did not reach the place until seven or eight o'clock. I was in plain view
all the time, and rode through, around, and all about the place soon after its
capture. General Trimble is mistaken." Nay, in his stammering eagerness
to right himself, his phrases, usually so crisp and clear, stumble and fall over
each other: "In the face of General Trimble's positive denial of sending me
such a message, 'that he would prefer waiting until daylight,' or anything
like it, while my recollection is clear that I did receive such a message, and
received it as coming from General Trimble, yet, as he is so positive to not
having sent such a message or anything like it, I feel bound to believe that
either the message was misrepresented or made up by the messenger, or that
it was a message received from General Robertson, whose sharpshooters had
been previously deployed."

A real man, you see, like the rest of us; but a noble one, and lovable.
Fortunate, also, in his death as in his life. For he was not shot down in the
early days, like Jackson and Sidney Johnston, when it seemed as if his great
aid might have changed destiny. He had done all a man in his position
could do. When he went, hope too was going. He was spared the long,
weary days of Petersburg, spared the bitter cup of Appomattox, spared the
cruel domination of the conqueror, spared what was perhaps worst of all,
the harsh words and reproaches which flew too hotly where there should have
been nothing but love and silence. He slept untroubled in his glory, while
his countrymen mourned and Lee "yearned for him." His best epitaph has
been written by a magnanimous opponent: "Deep in the hearts of all true
cavalrymen, North and South, will ever burn a sentiment of admiration
mingled with regret for this knightly soldier and generous man."

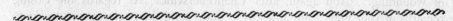

Abraham Lincoln: The First Prairie Years [1]
by CARL SANDBURG

IN THE summer of the year 1831, Abraham Lincoln, twenty-two years old,
floated a canoe down the Sangamon River, going to a new home, laughter
and youth in his bones, in his heart a few pennies of dreams, in his head
a ragbag of thoughts he could never expect to sell.

New Salem, the town on a hill, to which Abraham Lincoln was shunting
his canoe, was a place of promise there in the year 1831, just as all towns in
Illinois then were places of promise. New Salem then had a dozen families

[1] From *The Prairie Years* (1926), by Carl Sandburg. By permission of Harcourt, Brace and
Company.

as its population, just as Chicago in the same year reckoned a dozen families and no more. Both had water transportation, outlets, tributary territory, yet one was to be only a phantom hamlet of memories and ghosts, a wind-swept hilltop kept as cherished haunts are kept.

New Salem stood on a hill, a wrinkle of earth crust, a convulsive knob of rock and sod. The Sangamon River takes a curve as it comes to the foot of that bluff and looks up. It is almost as though the river said, "For such a proud standing hill as this I must make a proud winding curve for it to look at."

Up on the ridge level of that bluff, the buffalo, the wild horse, the wild hog and the Red Indian had competed for occupation a thousand years and more. Herds of shaggy-whiskered buffalo had roamed the Sangamon Valley; deer antlers had been plowed up and arched above doorways where men six feet tall walked under without stooping. Plows had turned up brown and white flint arrowheads of Indian hunters, red men whose learning had included buffalo and snake dances, and a necromancy of animal life unknown to men of the white race. Before the rifle and plow of the white man, the red man in that particular southern region of Illinois had moved off, had, in the words of some who followed, "gone and skedaddled." Yet the red man was still a near enough presence to be spoken of as more than a ghost who had just passed.

At the foot of a bluff where the Sangamon begins its curve, a thousand wagon-loads of gravel had been hauled and packed into the river to make a power-dam and mill-grind. The Rutledges and Camerons who started the mill bought the ridge of land on the bluff above and in 1829 laid out a town, sold lots, put up a log tavern with four rooms, and named the place New Salem.

Farmers came from fifty miles away to have their grain turned into flour and to buy salt, sugar, coffee, handkerchiefs, hardware, and calico prints and bonnets. If people asked, "Has the mud wagon come in?" they referred to the stagecoach driving from Havana to Springfield once a week, and carrying mail to the New Salem post office. The town in its time had a sawmill, fifteen houses, a hundred people, two doctors, a school, a church and Sunday school, a saloon, and a squire and two constables. The Herndon brothers, Rowan and James, kept a store; so did the partnership of Samuel Hill and James McNamar; also one Reuben Radford had a grocery.

And Denton Offut, who had rented the Rutledge and Cameron gristmill, had ordered a stock of goods and was going to open a new store, with A. Lincoln as clerk in charge. When Offut had seen Lincoln handle his flatboat on the New Salem mill-dam so masterfully, Offut had told people he would soon have a regular steamboat running up and down the Sangamon with Lincoln as captain; the boat would run the year round, in all weathers, with rollers for shoals and dams, runners for ice; Offut said that with Lincoln in charge, "By thunder, she'd have to go!"

Election Day was on when Lincoln arrived in New Salem and loafed along the main street. At the voting-place they told him a clerk was wanted and asked if he could write. Of course, he might have answered that where he came from in Indiana he used to write letters for the whole township; instead he answered with an up-and-down of careless inflections, "Oh, I guess I can make a few rabbit tracks." So, with a goose quill, he sat registering ballots that first day in New Salem; and he felt as much at home with the goose quill as he had felt with the ax, the hoe, the flatboat oars, and other instruments he had handled.

The voting was by word of mouth. Each voter told the election judges which candidates he wanted to vote for. Then a judge would bawl out the voter's name and his candidates, which names would be written down by the clerks. Lincoln got acquainted with names and faces of nearly all the men in New Salem on his first day there.

Offut's stock for the new store had not come as yet, so when Dr. Nelson, who was leaving New Salem for Texas, said he wanted a pilot to take his flatboat through the channels of the Sangamon to Beardstown on the Illinois River, Lincoln was willing. When he came back from that little job, he said there were times he ran the flatboat three miles off onto the prairies, but always got back to the main channel of the Sangamon. A genius of drollery was recognized by the New Salem folks as having come among them to live with and be one of them. They were already passing along the lizard story, a yarn spun by the newcomer the first day he arrived. He had said it happened in Indiana and was as strange as many other things that had happened in Indiana.

In a meeting-house far and deep in the tall timbers, a preacher was delivering a sermon, wearing old-fashioned baggy pantaloons fastened with one button and no suspenders, while his shirt was fastened at the collar with one button. In a loud voice he announced his text for the day, "I am the Christ, whom I shall represent today." And about that time a little blue lizard ran up under one of the baggy pantaloons. The preacher went ahead with his sermon, slapping his legs. After a while the lizard came so high that the preacher was desperate, and, going on with his sermon, unbuttoned the one button that held his pantaloons; they dropped down and with a kick were off. By this time the lizard had changed his route and circled around under the shirt at the back, and the preacher, repeating his text, "I am the Christ, whom I shall represent today," loosened his one collar button and with one sweeping movement off came the shirt. The congregation sat in the pews dazed and dazzled; everything was still for a moment; then a dignified elderly lady stood up slowly, and pointing a finger toward the pulpit, called out at the top of her voice, "I just want to say that if you represent Jesus Christ, sir, then I'm done with the Bible."

Men were telling of Lincoln and a crew loading Squire Godbey's hogs onto a flatboat down at Blue Banks; the hogs were slippery and stubborn and the crew couldn't chase them on board. The gossip was that Lincoln said, "Sew their eyes shut." And farmers were "argufyin'" as to whether a hog is easier handled when his eyes are sewed shut.

On a lot Offut bought for ten dollars, he and Lincoln built a cabin of logs; this was to be the new store, and Lincoln started boarding at the home of the Reverend John Cameron, whose eleven daughters ran the house.

Offut's goods arrived; Lincoln stacked shelves and corners with salt, sugar, tea, coffee, molasses, butter and eggs, whisky, tobacco, hardware, stoneware, cups and saucers, plates, dishes, calico prints, hats, bonnets, gloves, socks, shoes. Bill Green, the eighteen-year-old son of Squire Bowling Green, was put in as a helper mainly to tell Lincoln which of the customers were good pay. Offut's enthusiasm about his new clerk ran high: "He knows more than any man in the United States. . . . Some day he will be President of the United States. . . . He can outrun, outlift, outwrestle, and throw down any man in Sangamon County."

And the Clary's Grove Boys, just four miles away, began talking about these claims; what they said mostly was, "Is that so?" Bill Clary, who ran a saloon thirty steps north of the Offut store, put up a bet of ten dollars with Offut that Lincoln couldn't throw Jack Armstrong, the Clary's Grove champion.

Sports from fifty miles around came to a level square next to Offut's store to see the match; bets ran high, from money to jackknives and treats of whisky. Armstrong was short and powerful in build with the muscle haunches of a wild steer; his aim from the first was to get in close with his man where he would have the advantage of his thick muscular strength.

Lincoln held him off with long arms, wore down his strength, got him out of breath and out of temper. Armstrong then fouled by stamping on Lincoln's right foot and instep with his boot heel. This exasperated Lincoln so that he lost his temper, lifted Armstrong up by the throat and off the ground, shook him like a rag, and then slammed him to a hard fall, flat on his back.

As Armstrong lay on the ground, a champion in the dust of defeat, his gang from Clary's Grove started to swarm toward Lincoln, with hot Kentucky and Irish epithets on their lips. Lincoln stepped to where his back was against a wall, braced himself, and told the gang he was ready for 'em.

Then Jack Armstrong broke through the front line of the gang, shook Lincoln's hand and told the gang Lincoln was "fair," had won the match, and, "He's the best feller that ever broke into this settlement."

As the Clary's Grove Boys looked Lincoln over they decided he was one of them; he weighed 180 pounds; he was hard as nails; he outran the foot-racers of the Sangamon County; he threw the maul and crowbar farthest; he told the lizard story; he saved a flatboat that looked like a wreck on the Cameron mill-dam. Yes, he belonged; even though he didn't drink whisky nor play cards, he belonged. They called on him to judge their horse-races and chicken fights, umpire their matches, and settle disputes. Their homes were open to him. He was adopted.

Counting the money a woman paid for dry goods one day, Lincoln found she had paid six and a quarter cents more than her bill; that night he walked six miles to pay it back. Once, finding he weighed tea with a four-ounce weight instead of an eight, he wrapped up another quarter of a pound of tea, took a long walk and delivered to the woman the full order of tea she had paid for. A loafer used the wrong kind of language when women customers were in the store one day; Lincoln had warned him to stop; he talked back. Lincoln took him in front of the store, threw him on the ground and rubbed smartweed in his face. When trade was slack, he split rails for Offut and built a pen to hold a thousand hogs.

The two clerks, Lincoln and young Bill Green, slept together on a narrow cot in the back of the store; "when one turned over, the other had to." When a small gambler tricked Bill, Lincoln told Bill to bet him the best fur hat in the store that he (Lincoln) could lift a barrel of whisky from the floor and hold it while he took a drink from the bunghole. Bill hunted up the gambler, made the bet and won it; Lincoln lifted the barrel off the floor, sat squatting on the floor, rolled the barrel on his knees till the bunghole reached his mouth, drank a mouthful, let the barrel down—and stood up and spat out the whisky.

Wildcat money, "rag money," "shinplasters," came across the counter sometimes. The clerk asked the customer: "What kind of money have you?" Once in a while he told about a Mississippi steamboat captain, short of firewood, who steered to a landing-place and offered the man in charge wildcat money for wood; but the owner of the wood said he could only trade "cord for cord," a cord of money for a cord of wood.

Lincoln and John Brewer acted as seconds for Henry Clark and Ben Wilcox when those two settled a dispute with a stand-up and knockdown fight with bare fists. The seconds had washed the blood off the faces and shoulders of the two fighters, when John Brewer, whose head came about as high as Lincoln's elbows, strutted like a bantam rooster up to Lincoln and broke out, "Abe, my man licked yours and I can lick you." Lincoln searched his challenger with a quizzical look and drawled: "I'll fight you, John, if you'll chalk your size on me. And every blow outside counts foul." In the laugh of the crowd even Brewer joined.

Between times, in spare hours, and in watches of the night when sleep came to the town and river, Lincoln toiled and quested for the inner lights of what was known as education and knowledge. Mentor Graham, the schoolmaster, told him there was a grammar at Vaner's house, six miles off; he walked the six miles, brought back the book, burned pine shavings in the blacksmith shop to light a book with a title page saying it held, "English Grammar in Familiar Lectures accompanied by a Compendium embracing a New Systematick Order of Parsing, a New System of Punctuation, Exercises in False Syntax, and a Key to the Exercises, designed for the Use of Schools and Private Learners. By Samuel Kirkham." As he got farther into the book, he had Bill Green at the store hold it and ask him questions. When Bill asked what adverbs qualify, Lincoln replied, "Adverbs qualify verbs, adjectives and other adverbs." When Bill asked "What is a phrase?" the answer came, "A phrase is an assemblage of words, not constituting an entire proposition, but performing a distinct office in the structure of a sentence or of another phrase."

Geography he studied without knowing he was studying geography. The store had calico prints from Massachusetts, tea from China, coffee from Brazil, hardware and stoneware from New York and Pennsylvania, products and utensils from the hands and machines of men hundreds and thousands of miles away. The feel of other human zones, and a large world to live in, connected with the Offut grocery stock.

A literary and debating society was formed in New Salem, with the educated and accomplished people as members, and all others who wished to "advance" themselves. Lincoln stood up for his first speech one evening. And there was close attention. For they all knew this was a joker, the young husky who brought the lizard story to their town, the lusty buck who grappled Jack Armstrong and slammed him for a fall, the pleasant spinner of yarns. He opened his address in a tone of apology, as though he had been thinking over what he was going to say, but he wasn't sure he could put on the end of his tongue the ideas operating in his head. He went on with facts, traced back and picked up essential facts, and wove them into an argument, apologized again and said he hoped the argument would stand on its own legs and command respect. His hands wandered out of the pockets of his pantaloons and punctuated with loose gestures some of the decisive propositions, after which his hands slowly and easily slid back into the pantaloons pockets.

Then it came to Lincoln through the talk of friends that James Rutledge, the president of the society, was saying there was "more than wit and fun" in Abe's head; he was already a fine speaker; all he lacked was "culture to enable him to reach a high destiny which was in store for him." Lincoln noticed that Mr. Rutledge looked more keenly into his face and was more kindly in manner.

This had a double interest for the young store-clerk, because he had spent afternoons and evenings in the Rutledge tavern, and he had almost trembled and dark waves ran through him as he had looked wholly and surely into the face of the slim girl with corn-silk hair, Ann Rutledge, the eighteen-year-old daughter of James Rutledge.

When all New Salem laughed and wondered at the way he saved his flatboat when it hung over the dam the spring before, he had glimpsed this slim girl with light corn-silk hair, blue-eyed, pink-fair. Since then he had spoken with her as she sat sewing in a hickory splint chair, a quiet soft bud of a woman.

Some mentioned her as "beautiful"; the Clary's Grove Boys said she "wasn't hard to look at." While her two sisters, Nancy and Margaret, helped their mother with the dishes and the baby, Sarah, Ann did the sewing for all the women and showed new stitches to other New Salem girls who came in.

After the first evening in which Lincoln had sat next to her and found that bashful words tumbling from his tongue's end really spelled themselves out into sensible talk, her face, as he went away, kept coming back. So often all else would fade out of his mind and there would be only this riddle of a pink-fair face, a mouth and eyes in a frame of light corn-silk hair. He could ask himself what it meant and search his heart for an answer and no answer would come. A trembling took his body and dark waves ran through him sometimes when she spoke so simple a thing as, "The corn is getting high, isn't it?"

The name "Ann Rutledge" would come to him and he would pronounce it softly to the shadows in the blacksmith shop where he lay burning wood shavings to light the pages of Kirkham's Grammar. He knew the Rutledges branched back out of South Carolina and the Revolutionary War Rutledges, one of whom signed the Declaration of Independence; their names were in high places; her father was a Southern gentleman of the old school; and he, Abe Lincoln, was from the Kentucky "Linkerns" who had a hard time to read and write. His heart would be hurting if he hadn't learned long ago to laugh at himself with a horse laugh.

The Cameron girls, where he boarded, tried to tease him about his long legs, long arms, his horsy ways; and he was always ready to admit he "wasn't much to look at." And as the blue spray from one young woman's eyes haunted him, he felt it was enough to have looked into such a face and to have learned that such an earthly frame as that of Ann Rutledge had been raised out of the breathing dust. He could say, and it was easy to say, "It can't happen that a sucker like me can have a gal like her."

* * *

When the Illinois legislature met at Vandalia in 1834, one of the sitting members was Abraham Lincoln. He was twenty-five years old, holding his first elective political office, and drawing three dollars a day pay, with privileges of ink, quills, and stationery. The four highest candidates from Sangamon County in the voting had stood: Dawson, 1,390; Lincoln, 1,376; Carpenter, 1,170; Stuart, 1,164. On being elected Lincoln went to a friend, Coleman Smoot, who was farming near New Salem, and asked Smoot, "Did you vote for me?" and on Smoot answering, "Yes," he said, "I want to buy some clothes and fix up a little, and I want you to loan me $200.00." Therefore he sat at his desk in the state capitol wearing brand-new blue jeans.

He was now away from New Salem and Ann Rutledge. And the girl Ann Rutledge had been engaged to marry John McNeil, the storekeeper and farmer who had come to New Salem and in five years acquired property worth $12,000.00. In money and looks McNeil was considered a "good catch"; and he and Ann Rutledge were known as betrothed, when McNeil started on a trip East. In a short time, as soon as he could visit his father and relatives in New York, he would come back and claim his bride. This was the promise and understanding.

And it was known to Lincoln, who had helped McNeil on deeds to land holdings, that McNeil's real name was McNamar. This was the name put in the deeds. He said he had come West taking another name in order that he might make his fortune without interference from his family back East. He had, for convenience, kept his name off election poll books, and never voted.

McNamar had been away for months and sent few letters, writing from Ohio that he was delayed by an attack of fever, writing again from New York that his father had died and he could not come West till the estate was settled. Thus letters came, with excuses, from far off. Whisperers talked about it in New Salem. Had his love died down? Or was a truthful love to be expected from a man who would live under a false name?

Days were going hard for the little heart under the face framed in auburn hair over in New Salem, as Lincoln had his thoughts at his desk in the capitol at Vandalia. She had sung to him, clear-voiced, a hymn he liked with a line, "Vain man, thy fond pursuits forbear."

He introduced a bill limiting the jurisdiction of justices of the peace; he introduced a bill to authorize Samuel Musick to build a toll bridge across Salt Creek; he moved to change the rules so that it should not be in order to offer amendments to any bill after the third reading; he offered a resolution relating to a state revenue to be derived from the sale of public lands; he moved to take from the table a report submitted by his committee on public accounts. And he had his thoughts. The line had been sung for him clear-voiced, "Vain man, thy fond pursuits forbear."

Back to New Salem he came in the spring of 1835. And there was refuge for Ann Rutledge, with her hand in a long-fingered hand whose bones told of understanding and a quiet security. She had written McNamar that she expected release from her pledge to him. And no answer had come; letters had stopped coming. Her way was clear. In the fall she was to go to a young ladies' academy in Jacksonville; and Abraham Lincoln, poor in goods and deep in debts, was to get from under his poverty; and they were to marry. They would believe in the days to come; for the present time they had understanding and security.

The cry and the answer of one yellowhammer to another, the wing flash of one bluejay on a home flight to another, the drowsy dreaming of grass and grain coming up with its early green over the moist rolling prairie, these were to be felt that spring together, with the whisper, "Always together."

He was twenty-six, she was twenty-two; the earth was their footstool; the sky was a sheaf of blue dreams; the rise of the blood-gold rim of a full moon in the evening was almost too much to live, see, and remember. . . .

James Rutledge had sold his New Salem tavern to the Onstotts, and taken his family to a farm near Sand Ridge. Lincoln rode back and forth between New Salem and the Rutledge farm when he paid Ann a call. They were talking over their plans. Ann was proud of Lincoln, and believed he had a future and would make a name as a great man. In her father's tavern at

New Salem she had heard men say Abe Lincoln was considerable of a thinker and a politician; he had a way with people; he had an independent mind and yet he wanted to learn. He would go far and she would go with him; she would be to him what other women had been to other men in days gone by, women who were the wives of Rutledges, among whom there had been a signer of the Declaration of Independence, a governor, judges of courts, and other holders of high place.

For a time Ann worked at the farm of James Short and Lincoln rode over there to see her. He could laugh with her over Parthenia Hill, who had married a man who once wanted to marry Ann, saying, "Ann isn't beautiful —to begin with she has red hair."

She and Lincoln talked over the plan for her to go in the following autumn to the Jacksonville Female Academy, while he would register in the Illinois College at Jacksonville. A brother of Bill Green was a student there, some of the school-teachers around Sangamon County had been Illinois College students, and Ann's own brother David was studying there in that spring of 1835. Out of his companionship with Ann Rutledge, Lincoln had taken seriously to plans for a college education. He would have to leave college to sit in legislative sessions, but that could be arranged. . . .

August of that summer came. Corn and grass, fed by rich rains in May and June, stood up stunted of growth, for want of more rain. The red berries on the honeysuckles refused to be glad. The swallows and martins came fewer.

To the homes of the settlers came chills and fever of malaria. Lincoln had been down, and up, and down again with aching bones, taking large spoons of Peruvian bark, boneset tea, jalap, and calomel. One and another of his friends had died; for some, he had helped nail together the burial boxes.

Ann Rutledge lay fever-burned. Days passed; help arrived and was helpless. Moans came from her for the one man of her thoughts. They sent for him. He rode out from New Salem to the Sand Ridge farm. They let him in; they left the two together and alone a last hour in the log house, with slants of light on her face from an open clapboard door. It was two days later that death came.

There was what they called a funeral, a decent burial of the body in the Concord burying ground seven miles away. And Lincoln sat for hours with no words for those who asked him to speak to them. They went away from him knowing he would be alone whether they stayed or went away.

A week after the burial of Ann Rutledge, Bill Green found him rambling in the woods along the Sangamon River, mumbling sentences Bill couldn't make out. They watched him and tried to keep him safe among friends at New Salem. And he rambled darkly and idly past their circle to the burying ground seven miles away, where he lay with an arm across the one grave.

"Vain man, thy fond pursuits forbear." As the autumn weeks passed, and the scarlet runners sent out signals across the honey locust and the sycamore tree where they had sat together on the Salem hilltop, and the sunsets flamed earlier in the shortening afternoons, the watchers saw a man struggling on a brink; he needed help. Dr. Allen said rest would help. They took him to the home of Bowling and Nancy Green, at the foot of a bluff climbed by oak-timber growths. A few days he helped in the field at cornhusking; most of the time Nancy had him cutting wood, picking apples, digging potatoes, doing light chores around the house, once holding the yarn for her as she spun.

In the evenings it was useless to try to talk with him. They asked their questions and then had to go away. He sat by the fire one night as the flames licked up the cordwood and swept up the chimney to pass out into a driving storm-wind. The blowing weather woke some sort of lights in him and he went to the door and looked out into a night of fierce tumbling wind and black horizons. And he came back saying, "I can't bear to think of her out there alone." And he clenched his hands, mumbling, "The rain and the storm shan't beat on her grave."

Four Years in a Shed[1]

by EVE CURIE

A MAN chosen at random from a crowd to read an account of the discovery of radium would not have doubted for one moment that radium existed: beings whose critical sense has not been sharpened and simultaneously deformed by specialized culture keep their imaginations fresh. They are ready to accept an unexpected fact, however extraordinary it may appear, and to wonder at it.

The physicist colleagues of the Curies received the news in slightly different fashion. The special properties of polonium and radium upset fundamental theories in which scientists had believed for centuries. How was one to explain the spontaneous radiation of the radioactive bodies? The discovery upset a world of acquired knowledge and contradicted the most firmly established ideas on the composition of matter. Thus the physicist kept on the reserve. He was violently interested in Pierre and Marie's work, he could perceive its infinite developments, but before being convinced he awaited the acquisition of decisive results.

The attitude of the chemist was even more downright. By definition, a chemist only believes in the existence of a new substance when he has seen the substance, touched it, weighed and examined it, confronted it with acids, bottled it, and when he has determined its "atomic weight."

Now, up to the present, nobody had "seen" radium. Nobody knew the atomic weight of radium. And the chemists, faithful to their principles, con-

[1] From Eve Curie, *Madame Curie: A Biography,* copyright, 1937, by Doubleday & Company, Inc.

cluded: "No atomic weight, no radium. Show us some radium and we will believe you."

To show polonium and radium to the incredulous, to prove to the world the existence of their "children," and to complete their own conviction, M. and Mme Curie were now to labor for four years.

The aim was to obtain pure radium and polonium. In the most strongly radioactive products the scientists had prepared, these substances figured only in imperceptible traces. Pierre and Marie already knew the method by which they could hope to isolate the new metals, but the separation could not be made except by treating very large quantities of crude material.

Here arose three agonizing questions:

How were they to get a sufficient quantity of ore? What premises could they use to effect their treatment? What money was there to pay the inevitable cost of the work?

Pitchblende, in which polonium and radium were hidden, was a costly ore, treated at the St Joachimsthal mines in Bohemia for the extraction of uranium salts used in the manufacture of glass. Tons of pitchblende would cost a great deal: a great deal too much for the Curie household.

Ingenuity was to make up for wealth. According to the expectation of the two scientists, the extraction of uranium should leave, intact in the ore, such traces of polonium and radium as the ore contains. There was no reason why these traces should not be found in the residue. And, whereas crude pitchblende was costly, its residue after treatment had very slight value. By asking an Austrian colleague for a recommendation to the directors of the mine of St Joachimsthal would it not be possible to obtain a considerable quantity of such residue for a reasonable price?

It was simple enough: but somebody had to think of it.

It was necessary, of course, to buy this crude material and pay for its transportation to Paris. Pierre and Marie appropriated the required sum from their very slight savings. They were not so foolish as to ask for official credits. . . . If two physicists on the scent of an immense discovery had asked the University of Paris or the French government for a grant to buy pitchblende residue they would have been laughed at. In any case their letter would have been lost in the files of some office, and they would have had to wait months for a reply, probably unfavorable in the end. Out of the traditions and principles of the French Revolution, which had created the metric system, founded the Normal School, and encouraged science in many circumstances, the State seemed to have retained, after more than a century, only the deplorable words pronounced by Fouquier-Tinville at the trial in which Lavoisier was condemned to the guillotine: "The Republic has no need for scientists."

But at least could there not be found, in the numerous buildings attached to the Sorbonne, some kind of suitable workroom to lend to the Curie couple? Apparently not. After vain attempts, Pierre and Marie staggered back to their point of departure, which is to say to the School of Physics where Pierre taught, to the little room where Marie had done her first experiments. The room gave on a courtyard, and on the other side of the yard there was a wooden shack, an abandoned shed, with a skylight roof in such bad condition that it admitted the rain. The Faculty of Medicine had formerly used the place as a dissecting room, but for a long time now it had not even been considered fit to house the cadavers. No floor: an uncertain layer of bitumen covered the earth. It was furnished with some worn kitchen tables, a blackboard which had landed there for no known reason, and an old cast-iron stove with a rusty pipe.

A workman would not willingly have worked in such a place: Marie and Pierre, nevertheless, resigned themselves to it. The shed had one advantage: it was so untempting, so miserable, that nobody thought of refusing them the use of it. Schutzenberger, the director of the school, had always been very kind to Pierre Curie and no doubt regretted that he had nothing better to offer. However that may be, he offered nothing else; and the couple, very pleased at not being put out into the street with their material, thanked him, saying that "this would do" and that they would "make the best of it."

As they were taking possession of the shed, a reply arrived from Austria. Good news! By extraordinary luck, the residue of recent extractions of uranium had not been scattered. The useless material had been piled up in a no-man's-land planted with pine trees, near the mine of St Joachimsthal. Thanks to the intercession of Professor Suess and the Academy of Science of Vienna, the Austrian government, which was the proprietor of the State factory there, decided to present a ton of residue to the two French lunatics who thought they needed it. If, later on, they wished to be sent a greater quantity of the material, they could obtain it at the mine on the best terms. For the moment the Curies had to pay only the transportation charges on a ton of ore.

One morning a heavy wagon, like those which deliver coal, drew up in the Rue Lhomond before the School of Physics. Pierre and Marie were notified. They hurried bareheaded into the street in their laboratory gowns. Pierre, who was never agitated, kept his calm; but the more exuberant Marie could not contain her joy at the sight of the sacks that were being unloaded. It was pitchblende, *her* pitchblende, for which she had received a notice some days before from the freight station. Full of curiosity and impatience, she wanted to open one of the sacks and contemplate her treasure without further waiting. She cut the strings, undid the coarse sackcloth and plunged her two hands into the dull brown ore, still mixed with pine needles from Bohemia.

There was where radium was hidden. It was from there that Marie must extract it, even if she had to treat a mountain of this inert stuff like dust on the road.

Marya Sklodovska had lived through the most intoxicating moments of her student life in a garret; Marie Curie was to know wonderful joys again in a dilapidated shed. It was a strange sort of beginning over again, in which a sharp subtle happiness (which probably no woman before Marie had ever experienced) twice elected the most miserable setting.

The shed in the Rue Lhomond surpassed the most pessimistic expectations of discomfort. In summer, because of its skylights, it was as stifling as a hot-house. In winter one did not know whether to wish for rain or frost; if it rained, the water fell drop by drop, with a soft, nerve-racking noise, on the ground or on the worktables, in places which the physicists had to mark in order to avoid putting apparatus there. If it froze, one froze. There was no recourse. The stove, even when it was stoked white, was a complete disappointment. If one went near enough to touch it one received a little heat, but two steps away and one was back in the zone of ice.

It was almost better for Marie and Pierre to get used to the cruelty of the outside temperature, since their technical installation—hardly existent—possessed no chimneys to carry off noxious gases, and the greater part of their treatment had to be made in the open air, in the courtyard. When a shower came the physicists hastily moved their apparatus inside: to keep on working without being suffocated they set up draughts between the opened door and windows.

Marie probably did not boast to Dr Vauthier of this very peculiar cure for attacks of tuberculosis.

We had no money, no laboratory and no help in the conduct of this important and difficult task [she was to write later]. It was like creating something out of nothing, and if Casimir Dluski once called my student years "the heroic years of my sister-in-law's life," I may say without exaggeration that this period was, for my husband and myself, the heroic period of our common existence.

. . . And yet it was in this miserable old shed that the best and happiest years of our life were spent, entirely consecrated to work. I sometimes passed the whole day stirring a mass in ebullition, with an iron rod nearly as big as myself. In the evening I was broken with fatigue.

In such conditions M. and Mme Curie worked for four years from 1898 to 1902.

During the first year they busied themselves with the chemical separation of radium and polonium and they studied the radiation of the products (more and more active) thus obtained. Before long they considered it more practical to separate their efforts. Pierre Curie tried to determine the properties of radium, and to know the new metal better. Marie continued those chemical treatments which would permit her to obtain salts of pure radium.

In this division of labor Marie had chosen the "man's job." She accomplished the toil of a day laborer. Inside the shed her husband was absorbed by delicate experiments. In the courtyard, dressed in her old dust-covered and acid-stained smock, her hair blown by the wind, surrounded by smoke which stung her eyes and throat, Marie was a sort of factory all by herself.

I came to treat as many as twenty kilograms of matter at a time [she writes], which had the effect of filling the shed with great jars full of precipitates and liquids. It was killing work to carry the receivers, to pour off the liquids and to stir, for hours at a stretch, the boiling matter in a smelting basin.

Radium showed no intention of allowing itself to be known by human creatures. Where were the days when Marie naïvely expected the radium content of pitchblende to be *one per cent?* The radiation of the new substance was so powerful that a tiny quantity of radium, disseminated through the ore, was the source of striking phenomena which could be easily observed and measured. The difficult, the impossible thing, was to isolate this minute quantity, to separate it from the gangue in which it was so intimately mixed.

The days of work became months and years: Pierre and Marie were not discouraged. This material which resisted them, which defended its secrets, fascinated them. United by their tenderness, united by their intellectual passions, they had, in a wooden shack, the "anti-natural" existence for which they had both been made, she as well as he.

At this period we were entirely absorbed by the new realm that was, thanks to an unhoped-for discovery, opening before us [Marie was to write]. In spite of the difficulties of our working conditions, we felt very happy. Our days were spent at the laboratory. In our poor shed there reigned a great tranquillity: sometimes, as we watched over some operation, we would walk up and down, talking about work in the present and in the future; when we were cold a cup of hot tea taken near the stove comforted us. We lived in our single preoccupation as if in a dream. . . . We saw only very few persons at the laboratory; among the physicists and chemists there were a few who came from time to time, either to see our experiments or to ask for advice from Pierre Curie, whose competence in several branches of physics was well-known. Then took place some conversations before the blackboard—the sort of conversation one remembers well because it acts as a stimulant for scientific interest and the ardor for work without interrupting the course of reflection and without troubling that atmosphere of peace and meditation which is the true atmosphere of a laboratory.

Whenever Pierre and Marie, alone in this poor place, left their apparatus for a moment and quietly let their tongues run on, their talk about their beloved radium passed from the transcendent to the childish.

"I wonder what *It* will be like, what *It* will look like," Marie said one day with the feverish curiosity of a child who has been promised a toy. "Pierre, what form do you imagine *It* will take?"

"I don't know," the physicist answered gently. "I should like it to have a very beautiful color. . . ."

It is odd to observe that in Marie Curie's correspondence we find, upon this prodigious effort, none of the sensitive comments, decked out with imagery, which used to flash suddenly amid the familiarity of her letters. Was it because the years of exile had somewhat relaxed the young woman's intimacy with her people? Was she too pressed by work to find time?

The essential reason for this reserve is perhaps to be sought elsewhere. It was not by chance that Mme Curie's letters ceased to be original at the exact moment when the story of her life became exceptional. As student, teacher or young wife, Marie could tell her story. . . . But now she was isolated by all that was secret and inexpressible in her scientific vocation. Among those she loved there was no longer anybody able to understand, to realize her worries and her difficult design. She could share her obsessions with only one person, Pierre Curie, companion. To him alone could she confide rare thoughts and dreams. Marie, from now on, was to present to all others, however near they might be to her heart, an almost commonplace picture of herself. She was to paint for them only the bourgeois side of her life. She was to find sometimes accents full of contained emotion to express her happiness as a woman. But of her work she was to speak only in laconic, inexpressive little phrases: news in three lines, without even attempting to suggest the wonders that work meant to her.

Here we feel an absolute determination not to illustrate the singular profession she had chosen by literature. Through sutble modesty, and also through horror of vain talk and everything superfluous, Marie concealed herself, dug herself in; or rather, she offered only one of her profiles. Shyness, boredom, or reason, whatever it may have been, the scientist of genius effaced and dissimulated herself behind "a woman like all others."

Marie to Bronya, 1899:
Our life is always the same. We work a lot but we sleep well, so our health does not suffer. The evenings are taken up by caring for the child. In the morning I dress her and give her her food, then I can generally go out at about nine. During the whole of this year we have not been either to the theater or a concert, and we have not paid one visit. For that matter, we feel very well. . . . I miss my family enormously, above all you, my dears, and Father. I often think of my isolation with grief. I cannot complain of anything else, for our health is not bad, the child is growing well, and I have the best husband one could dream of; I could never have imagined finding one like him. He is a true gift of heaven, and the more we live together the more we love each other.

Our work is progressing. I shall soon have a lecture to deliver on the subject. It should have been last Saturday but I was prevented from giving it, so it will no doubt be this Sunday, or else in a fortnight.

This work, which is so dryly mentioned in passing, was in fact progressing magnificently. In the course of the years 1899 and 1900 Pierre and Marie Curie published a report on the discovery of "induced radioactivity" due to radium, another on the effects of radioactivity, and another on the electric charge carried by the rays. And at last they drew up, for the Congress of Physics of 1900, a general report on the radioactive substances, which aroused immense interest among the scientists of Europe.

The development of the new science of radioactivity was rapid, overwhelming—the Curies needed fellow workers. Up to now they had had only the intermittent help of a laboratory assistant named Petit, an honest man who came to work for them outside his hours of service—working out of personal enthusiasm, almost in secret. But they now required technicians of the first order. Their discovery had important extensions in the domain of chemistry, which demanded attentive study. They wished to associate competent research workers with them.

Our work on radioactivity began in solitude [Marie was to write]. But before the breadth of the task it became more and more evident that collaboration would be useful. Already in 1898 one of the laboratory chiefs of the school, G. Bémont, had given us some passing help. Toward 1900 Pierre Curie entered into relations with a young chemist, André Debierne, assistant in the laboratory of Professor Friedel, who esteemed him highly. André Debierne willingly accepted work on radioactivity. He undertook especially the research of a new radio element, the existence of which was suspected in the group of iron and rare clays. He discovered this element, named "actinium." Even though he worked in the physico-chemical laboratory at the Sorbonne directed by Jean Perrin, he frequently came to see us in our shed and soon became a very close friend to us, to Dr. Curie and later on to our children.

Thus, even before radium and polonium were isolated, a French scientist, André Debierne, had discovered a "brother," *actinium*.

At about the same period [Marie tells us], a young physicist, Georges Sagnac, engaged in studying X rays, came frequently to talk to Pierre Curie about the analogies that might exist between these rays, their secondary rays, and the radiation of radioactive bodies. Together they performed a work on the electric charge carried by these secondary rays.

Marie continued to treat, kilogram by kilogram, the tons of pitchblende residue which were sent her on several occasions from St Joachimsthal. With her terrible patience, she was able to be, every day for four years, a physicist, a chemist, a specialized worker, an engineer and a laboring man all at once. Thanks to her brain and muscle, the old tables in the shed held more and more concentrated products—products more and more rich in radium. Mme Curie was approaching the end: she no longer stood in the courtyard, enveloped in bitter smoke, to watch the heavy basins of material in fusion. She was now at the stage of purification and of the "fractional crystallization" of strongly radioactive solutions. But the poverty of her haphazard equipment hindered her work more than ever. It was now that she needed a spotlessly clean workroom and apparatus perfectly protected against cold, heat and dirt. In this shed, open to every wind, iron and coal dust was afloat which, to Marie's despair, mixed itself into the products purified with so much care. Her heart sometimes constricted before these little daily accidents, which took so much of her time and her strength.

Pierre was so tired of the interminable struggle that he would have been quite ready to abandon it. Of course, he did not dream of dropping the study of radium and of radioactivity. But he would willingly have renounced, for the time being, the special operation of preparing pure radium. The obstacles seemed insurmountable. Could they not resume this work later on, under better conditions? More attached to the meaning of natural phenomena than to their material reality, Pierre Curie was exasperated to see the paltry results to which Marie's exhausting effort had led. He advised an armistice.

He counted without his wife's character. Marie wanted to isolate radium and she would isolate it. She scorned fatigue and difficulties, and even the gaps in her own knowledge which complicated her task. After all, she was only a very young scientist: she still had not the certainty and great culture Pierre had acquired by twenty years' work, and sometimes she stumbled across phenomena or methods of calculation which she knew very little, and for which she had to make hasty studies.

So much the worse! With stubborn eyes under her great brow, she clung to her apparatus and her test tubes.

In 1902, forty-five months after the day on which the Curies announced the probable existence of radium, Marie finally carried off the victory in this war of attrition: she succeeded in preparing a decigram of pure radium, and made a first determination of the atomic weight of the new substance, which was 225.

The incredulous chemists—of whom there were still a few—could only bow before the facts, before the superhuman obstinacy of a woman.

Radium officially existed.

It was nine o'clock at night. Pierre and Marie Curie were in their little house at 108 Boulevard Kellermann, where they had been living since 1900. The house suited them well. From the boulevard, where three rows of trees half hid the fortifications, could be seen only a dull wall and a tiny door. But behind the one-story house, hidden from all eyes, there was a narrow provincial garden, rather pretty and very quiet. And from the "barrier" of Gentilly they could escape on their bicycles toward the suburbs and the woods. . . .

Old Dr Curie, who lived with the couple, had retired to his room. Marie had bathed her child and put it to bed, and had stayed for a long time beside the cot. This was a rite. When Irène did not feel her mother near her at night she would call out for her incessantly, with that "Mé!" which was to be our substitute for "Mamma" always. And Marie, yielding to the implacability of the four-year-old baby, climbed the stairs, seated herself beside the child and stayed there in the darkness until the young voice gave way to light, regular breathing. Only then would she go down again to Pierre, who was growing impatient. In spite of his kindness, he was the most possessive and jealous of husbands. He was so used to the constant presence of his wife that her least eclipse kept him from thinking freely. If Marie delayed too long near her daughter, he received her on her return with a reproach so unjust as to be comic:

"You never think of anything but that child!"

Pierre walked slowly about the room. Marie sat down and made some stitches on the hem of Irène's new apron. One of her principles was never to buy ready-made clothes for the child: she thought them too fancy and impractical. In the days when Bronya was in Paris the two sisters cut out their children's dresses together, according to patterns of their own invention. These patterns still served for Marie.

But this evening she could not fix her attention. Nervous, she got up; then, suddenly:

"Suppose we go down there for a moment?"

There was a note of supplication in her voice—altogether superfluous, for Pierre, like herself, longed to go back to the shed they had left two hours before. Radium, fanciful as a living creature, endearing as a love, called them back to its dwelling, to the wretched laboratory.

The day's work had been hard, and it would have been more reasonable for the couple to rest. But Pierre and Marie were not always reasonable. As soon as they had put on their coats and told Dr Curie of their flight, they were in the street. They went on foot, arm in arm, exchanging few words. After the crowded streets of this queer district, with its factory buildings, wastelands and poor tenements, they arrived in the Rue Lhomond and crossed the little courtyard. Pierre put the key in the lock. The door squeaked, as it had squeaked thousands of times, and admitted them to their realm, to their dream.

"Don't light the lamps!" Marie said in the darkness. Then she added with a little laugh:

"Do you remember the day when you said to me 'I should like radium to have a beautiful color'?"

The reality was more entrancing than the simple wish of long ago. Radium had something better than "a beautiful color": it was spontaneously luminous. And in the somber shed where, in the absence of cupboards, the precious particles in their tiny glass receivers were placed on tables or on shelves nailed to the walls, their phosphorescent bluish outlines gleamed, suspended in the night.

"Look . . . Look!" the young woman murmured.

She went forward cautiously, looked for and found a straw-bottomed chair. She sat down in the darkness and silence. Their two faces turned toward the pale glimmering, the mysterious sources of radiation, toward radium—their radium. Her body leaning forward, her head eager, Marie took up again the attitude which had been hers an hour earlier at the bedside of her sleeping child.

Elizabeth Arden, Glamour, Inc.[1]

by MARGARET CASE HARRIMAN

I N ONE day recently, between the hours of nine and six, three hundred and
ninety-four women went through the little red door of Elizabeth Arden's
New York salon at 691 Fifth Avenue to be rolled, massaged, baked,
bathed, and otherwise persuaded into beauty. Two hundred and ninety-four
of them relaxed for facial treatments in booths dreamily accented by a single
white flower which stands in a vase on each dressing-table; the other hundred,
intent upon improving their figures, drifted through the scented corridors
toward the exercise rooms and the baths.

Facial treatments in the Arden salons range from simple massage through
the newer excitements of Sensation salve (which looks like mud applied to
the face, but produces a mad, hygienic glow) and Arden gland cream (described with unassailable simplicity by the operators as "a combination of
hormones") to the costly climax of the Vienna Youth Mask. The Vienna
Youth Mask, perhaps more than any other Arden creation, represents the
accommodation of science to the beauty business. Arden thought it up ten
years ago, in Vienna, when she heard Professor Steinach talk about diathermy
—the application of heat to tissues in the body by means of electrical current
—and the benefits derived from it by soldiers whose muscles and nerves had
been injured in the World War. Physicians for some thirty years have used
this method in treating arthritic and other inflammatory conditions, but it
took Elizabeth Arden to turn it into a beauty treatment. With one Dr. Last
of Vienna, she invented the Youth Mask, a device made of papier-mâché and
lined with tinfoil, which is fitted over the client's face and connected by con-
ducting cords to a diathermy machine. Arden's belief is that electricity so
applied replenishes the cells in a woman's face, which, she says, die first under
the eyes, and next under the chin. Medicine offers no corroboration for the
Arden theory; diathermy does stimulate circulation, but it cannot restore dead
cells. Arden gland cream, said to penetrate the skin and nourish the glands,
is another mild surprise for the medical profession, which has demonstrated
that thyroid extract, for example, is never entirely utilized by the glands, even
when swallowed. Whatever the scientific value of either of these treatments
may be, the fact that patrons of Elizabeth Arden continue contentedly to
absorb gland cream and to pay two hundred dollars for the course of thirty-
two Vienna Youth Mask treatments indicates that their appeal is considerable.

In the departments devoted to improving the figure, the treatments are
simpler. Good circulation and posture are a creed with Arden, who likes to

[1] From The New Yorker, April 6, 1935. By permission of the author.

turn her clients upside down to stir up what she calls their "little insides," and then to set them on their feet again with shoulders and hips classically poised. In the exercise rooms for tap and rhythmic dancing, are a number of slanting boards, made to tip the client's head a good eighteen inches lower than her feet, so that her vitals may slip gently, for a little space, back to where Arden feels they ought to be. Down the hall are cabinet and infra-red light baths, where women drowse and endure—brooding, possibly, upon the Arden diet, which, devised by Dr. Benjamin Gayelord Hauser, is fairly succulent but substitutes brown sugar or honey for white sugar as being purer, and requires all vegetables to be steamed. The Ardena bath—the most elaborate of the body treatments—is a coating, from neck to heels, of paraffin which creates, upon contact with the skin, a vacuum to induce perspiration. Every new client who wants an Ardena bath must wait with other newcomers, shy as sheep, in the reception rooms until Dr. Charles Kemm Good, the staff physician, has examined her heart. Even if her heart action is less than perfect, he may let her have the bath with the paraffin omitted over the heart and that area packed with ice bags; but if there is any real danger of ill effects, she is steered off into the giant roller—a contraption of wooden cylinders which smooth the pounds off—or into a mild massage. The Arden salons have never had an accident, and don't want one. They lose few customers by such precautions. As one operator put it, "There's always some treatment a client can have."

Fashions in beauty began to change with the gradual disappearance of the great beauties of the nineties and early nineteen hundreds—remote, inimitable creatures with naturally flawless features and coloring. Beauty in women then became less a matter of tranquil profiles and violet eyes, and more the combination of health, personality, and grooming which it now is. The average woman, long eclipsed, realized that now was her chance to come into her stride with a new and practical kind of beauty, the product of intelligent care, which could be hers for the asking—and the paying. Elizabeth Arden's first important flash of inspiration, in a long career of lesser ones, came when she chose that moment to go into the business of selling beauty.

She had, when she arrived in New York from Toronto in 1908, no knowledge of the beauty business and little interest in it. Her name was Florence Nightingale Graham, and what she wanted to do was to build up a big mailorder drug business. Born of Scotch-English parents who had emigrated to Canada with the hazy idea of making a living from the soil, she and her family had lived, on the outskirts of Toronto, chiefly upon the small allowance made by a relative in England to each of the five Graham children. When the allowance stopped with the death of the relative, Florence got a job as assistant to a dentist in Toronto. When she wasn't handing him his instruments, she worked on his books, and soon got the idea—a novel one at the time—of bombarding patients with letters racily implying what might happen to their teeth if they didn't come in to see the dentist pretty soon. She doubled her employer's business in a year and, with the success of that mild coup, began to exhibit some of the restlessness and thirst for action which has dominated her ever since. After a brief and inconclusive period as a student nurse in a Toronto hospital, she came to New York and went to work, as bookkeeper and stenographer, for E. R. Squibb & Sons, the chemical manufacturers. Her ambition for a career in the drug industry came to an end, however, when she left Squibb's, after ten days, and got a job with Eleanor Adair, a beauty specialist. At Adair's she learned massage, found that she had the hands for it, picked up the elementary formulas for manufacturing cosmetics, and began to perceive, for the first time, the golden future in the beauty business.

The average woman's dressing-table equipment at that time was a can of talcum powder, a chamois facecloth, and a little rosewater and glycerin; face powder was obtainable only in two shades, pink and white. One or two pioneers like Adair and Helena Rubinstein were beginning to popularize "nourishing" creams and astringent lotions, but for the galaxy of muscle oils, eyeshadows, and youth masks which soon followed women in general had nothing but mild curiosity and enormously open minds. By 1910, Florence Graham had undertaken a partnership with Elizabeth Hubbard in a beauty salon, Elizabeth Hubbard, Inc., at 509 Fifth Avenue, but the engagement was not a success emotionally for either partner, and it was not long before Miss Hubbard vanished from the partnership altogether. Florence Nightingale Graham, continuing business at the same address, began to cast about for a new name for the firm. First she tried to register the name Florence Nightingale, but was unable to do that. She finally took her last name from the poem "Enoch Arden," and retained Elizabeth Hubbard's first name. To make sure that the combination was a happy one, she mailed a letter to herself addressed "Miss Elizabeth Arden." When the envelope reached her next morning, she took one look at it and ceased to regret that she could not be incorporated as Florence Nightingale.

From the first she was autocratic, exacting, and sustained by an unshakable conviction that her own point of view in any situation was the right one. When she decided that the face cream of that day was too hard and slippery, she told the firm of chemists from whom she bought her supplies that she wanted a face cream that was light and fluffy—"like whipped cream," she said. When they told her it was impossible, she looked for another chemist, but it was not until 1914 that she found, in the firm of Stillwell & Gladding, analytical chemists, a young man named A. F. Swanson, who was able to produce the cream she wanted; she named it Cream Amoretta. Her second joint product with Mr. Swanson was the Ardena skin tonic, which he used to bring from the Stillwell and Gladding laboratories uptown to 509 Fifth Avenue on the Third Avenue "L." He carried it in a gallon demijohn at first, but it sold so well that the gallon demijohn became a two-gallon demijohn, and Mr. Swanson, a mild-mannered man, was forced into a row once or twice with the "L" guard because the demijohn got in the way of other passengers' feet. Presently a messenger was engaged to deliver the Amoretta and the skin tonic and, later, the rouges and eyeshadow; and when the delivery at length required an expressman, Miss Arden felt that the time had come for her to move to larger quarters. In 1915, when she was about twenty-four, she opened a salon at 673 Fifth Avenue and, a few doors down the Avenue, at 665, a small wholesale department to supply the growing demand for Arden preparations in stores all over the country. Mr. Swanson, newly installed as chemist, made up the preparations in a little laboratory back of the wholesale offices, with Miss Arden dashing in every now and then to do a little brewing and stirring of her own. One day she created an indelible lipstick and tried it out on Mr. Swanson; it was so indelible that, after forty-eight hours of intermittent wiping and rubbing, he was obliged to take a nailbrush to it.

By her marriage to T. J. Lewis, in that same year, Arden became an American citizen, but she still speaks with a faint burr which might be called Scotch-Canadian. Mr. Lewis, who had a flair for advertising, was manager of the wholesale department throughout the nineteen years of their marriage, but never owned any stock in the business, and was never admitted to partnership. Since the marriage ended, last year, in divorce, and in Mr. Lewis's departure from the firm, Arden is rather wistfully inclined to suspect people of giving her former husband more credit for building up the business than she thinks he deserves.

The growth of the business has been steady since its beginning, twenty-five years ago. With her first profits at 509, she satisfied an innate craving for elegance by buying a genuine Oriental rug and an antique table (authentic) for the salon. Within five years she was able to open a branch salon in Washington, D. C., and not long afterward another in Boston. By 1920 the demand for Arden preparations in department stores and novelty shops had so increased that Mr. Swanson, working away like a gnome in his little laboratory, was unable to supply a sufficient quantity. Arden bought a warehouse at 212 East Fifty-second Street, and turned it into a factory to supply her wholesale market, which had then come to include drugstores. Her wholesale department, once again removed to a more spacious setting, is now a vast organization in itself, occupying three floors at 681 Fifth Avenue and distributing Arden preparations to some five thousand drug and department stores. The factory on Fifty-second Street has absorbed two buildings and part of a third; across the street, Arden owns three brownstone houses, left over from a flyer in real estate, which she has turned into rooming houses for Arden representatives in from the road, giving them food and lodging at reasonable rates. In addition to the New York factory there are five others, in London, Paris, Berlin, and Toronto, and a small branch factory in Mexico. Twenty-six salons in the United States, Canada, and Europe are owned outright by Arden and operated by managers engaged by her; her Paris salon, for example, is managed by Arden's sister, now the Vicomtesse de Maublanc, and the New York salon by Florence Delaney, who joined the organization at 509 Fifth Avenue and spent a considerable part of these early days trying to make Miss Arden drink a glass of milk beetween facials now and then for her own good.

Arden's program of expansion has not abated perceptibly during the depression. Ever since she found that the cosmetic business was going to be one of the few industries to weather hard times with any profit (which it has done), she has followed her own inclination to treat the general financial disaster with what amounts to unconcern. "This depression," she said, in its early days, "is going to make a lot of manufacturers pull in, economize, cut down—and that leaves us a clear field." Her salons in Los Angeles, Palm Springs, and Miami Beach, and four other salons in department stores, have all been opened since 1929; and she has continued to extend her wholesale trade with a zest which causes some conservatives to prophesy gloomily that she will ruin the business by over-expansion. Arden can afford to be indifferent to such predictions. She is the sole stockholder and complete dictator of the business, and in 1929 she refused an offer of fifteen million dollars for it.

It is difficult to distinguish Arden's vitality—which she often mentions, and constantly demonstrates by a little clenching of the hands and a stretching upward of the entire body—from the restlessness which generally impels her. Physically she is small—not much over five feet in height—and slim. Her skin is in good condition and her face youthful, partly because her constant rubbing of it when she tries out new preparations on herself keeps its circulation brisk. Her hands are fairly large—she wears a six-and-a-half glove—and have all the requirements for massage which she demands in her operators: fingers of almost even length placed close together, and without a pronounced cushion at the base of the thumb, which would be apt to drag across a client's face and irritate her. When she talks, Arden's hands are continually in motion, curving in consciously graceful gestures, or fluttering toward her own diaphragm to emphasize some point or other about breathing or posture. Occasionally she is overtaken by a kind of mysterious *joie-de-vivre* which sends her spinning around in a brief dance step, clasping her hands, and uttering little cries of simple well-being. She laughs frequently, sometimes without reason and often simply because a silence has suddenly seemed awkward to her. She is forever, with a docile and flattering air, asking for advice, which she almost never follows. Once it became necessary, in the course of the business, to investigate the record and activities of a certain person whom she had thought of placing in an important position. Arden put a member of her own staff on his trail, and in the meantime privately decided that the man in question was wholly irreproachable. When the investigator reported him as undesirable and dangerous, and showed proofs, Arden's response was typical. She fired the investigator, not only from his temporary job of sleuthing but out of her organization altogether.

Her payroll numbers a thousand employees, of whom she requires a great amount of work. She has trained most of them from the beginning and has so skillfully accustomed them to the special and shining Arden world that they are almost unconscious of any other. With them she is tyrannical and exacting or affectionate and lavish, by turns. Her employees, seldom knowing from one hour to the next whether to expect a calling down or a champagne party, have learned to take what comes with a good deal of serenity.

She tries out all of her preparations on everybody, beginning with herself when she gets up in the morning. Before she gets into her bath, she puts cream on her face and, while she is dressing, puts on a new chin strap, or applies some of the experimental preparations, sent up from the factory, that crowd both her dressing-table and her bureau. If the chin strap is not right, she will take a pair of scissors and slash it, then and there, to the proper pattern. (To women, incidentally, who shrink from greasing and strapping themselves at night when their husbands are around, Arden says that there is always time for these things at some moment during the day, while they are puttering around the house.) Throughout the three floors of her wholesale department at 681 Fifth Avenue, secretaries, stenographers, and file clerks frequently work with one eye made up in gray-brown mascara and the other in straight brown, with each hand colored with a different nail lacquer, waiting for Arden's decisions. A tense moment in the organization was caused one time by Miss O'Leary, who has been in the wholesale department for seventeen years. She began to break out under constant application of experimental lotions, creams, and powders, and, on top of that, got a bad sunburn at the beach in spite of a coating of Arden oil. The boss, brooding, decided that Miss O'Leary had a supersensitive skin. Instantly a new batch of preparations was created, expressly for delicate skin, with Miss O'Leary's face again the proving ground. The O'Leary face became once more as the rose, the wholesale department relaxed, and Arden found herself with a brand-new, and profitable, group of preparations on the market.

Consumers' Research and other critics of modern industrial methods, estimating her probable margin of profit from the manufacture and sale of cosmetics, point out that a bottle of Ardena skin tonic, retailing for eighty-five cents, consists of water, grain alcohol, boric acid, and perfume and costs three cents to manufacture. They also allege that most of her preparations, in common with those of many other leading beauty specialists, are made of the cheapest ingredients obtainable—the muscle oil, as one example, containing nothing but third-grade castor oil and water. To these indictments the Arden organization replies not categorically but in parables. Any of its employees will tell you the proud tales of the two young women who, crashing in an airplane in the African desert without water, drank Ardena skin tonic out of their travelling kit without ill effects; of Mrs. Robert Warwick, who always fed Velva cream to her dog while she was having treatments; and of a client's cook who, mistaking a jar of Orange Skin Cream in the icebox for shortening, made a cake out of it which was eaten by the entire family with relish and impunity. There seems little question but that most Arden creams are made from pure fats, harmless when taken internally in small quantities.

Arden has for nearly thirty years suffered long periods of illness, with, at times, excruciating pain, owing to an injury to her hip. When she was eighteen she slipped and fell while kicking toward a chandelier in an effort to cinch, for all time, her reputation as the highest kicker in her set in Toronto. The fall did something to the sacro-iliac joint of her hip from which she has never quite recovered. About twenty years ago, when she had been bedridden for six months, her doctors wanted to operate; instead, she dragged herself out of bed and went to certain yogis, who at that time were grouped in meditation somewhere on Forty-second Street. When they showed her how they could stand on one another's stomachs, she became converted, and now says that it was only through doing the yogi exercises that she was able to avoid the operation. The exercises prescribed in the Arden salons are much the same as those she learned from the yogis, although she has modified them for women, so as not to produce bulges and knots of muscle.

The pain and weakness in her hip from which she still suffers—although massage and manipulative surgery have corrected it to an extent—have never produced any noticeable languor either in her business routine or in the strenuous social life in which she is known as Mrs. Elizabeth Graham Lewis. Her duplex apartment at 834 Fifth Avenue, decorated two years ago by Remisoff, the Russian artist, has a modernistic drawing room, with a Georgia O'Keefe flower piece, and a crystal chandelier imported from a Russian palace at a cost, one may learn, of two thousand dollars. There is a bar with pink horses prancing around the walls, and there are clusters of plumes painted over the doorways nearly everywhere. The library has a portrait of Elizabeth Arden by Augustus John, and, lying on the hearth, a stuffed otter. Somebody gave her the otter and it has followed her around for years.

The apartment has from ten to two hundred people in it a good deal of the time. Arden loves to give parties with crooners or accordion-players wandering around, and a vast number of friends and acquaintances arriving in great, glittering masses. Last summer, when she turned her country place near Mount Vernon, Maine, into a rest cure for women who wanted to restore their complexions and figures among luxurious though rural surroundings, she gave a Democratic rally there in memory of her friend, the late Elisabeth Marbury, a staunch Democrat. In addition to the local hundreds who attended the rally, thirty-five guests were invited from New York, and their railroad tickets and accommodations delivered to their homes. The private car that took them to Maine carried also an accordion-player for their amusement and a hostess to introduce them to each other, and they were all requested upon arrival not to tip any of the servants. Departing guests, on Monday, were given their choice of transportation by motor, rail, or airplane, prepaid.

About three years ago, feeling the need of something jaunty in the way of a hobby, Arden bought a horse named How High, which in the same year won $1,440 in a race at Aqueduct. Toward her present stable of about ten racehorses, at Belmont, her attitude is emotional rather than practical. She talks baby talk to the entire stable, and frequently startles her trainer by telling him that "this little darling's ankles are hot" or that another horse ought to be blanketed because he is perspiring. Her stable is decorated as tastefully as any drawing-room in her racing colors of crimson and blue, and she is careful to see that her jockey's silks, of the finest taffeta, are sent only to the best cleaners. Once, when a couple of horses came down with colds, Miss Arden instructed the trainer to rub them down with Ardena skin tonic instead of horse liniment, which, she said, smelled terrible. When the trainer protested that such stuff was no good for horses, he was replaced almost immediately by another, more acquiescent.

Arden is planning to open two new beauty salons in Buenos Aires and Rio de Janeiro this year; and is thinking of starting another in Wall Street as well, for working girls. She has a genuine passion for improving women's looks, and is impatient with any woman who is not as beautiful as she might be. A good physical appearance is required of all operators engaged to work in the salons; to one young woman who applied for a job with a gold tooth plainly visible, Arden said that she would engage her if she first got rid of the gold tooth, and advanced her the money to pay the dentist. When she meets a woman who has an unnecessary imperfection in her skin, she tries to keep still about it, but is impelled in the end to bawl her out affectionately. Once, in London, she took a luncheon party of ten women out into the garden and stood them against the wall on their heads (a favorite exercise of hers) because she thought they looked sluggish. She is pleased by the great strides Englishwomen have taken from their former position as the world's dowdiest to their present eminence as sirens who frequently occupy the headlines. It flatters her, too, to know that her beauty aids have taken a firm hold upon France, the home of feminine allure. She is always sticking pins in the great map that hangs on the wall of her office, to indicate the sale of Arden preparations all over Europe, China, Japan, Manchuria, Java, and South Africa. Not long ago a woman came into the wholesale department and asked to see Miss Arden; informed that Miss Arden was busy, she prepared humbly to depart, murmuring that she had only wanted to tell her about the great success she had been having with Arden preparations in her little shop. Her little shop, it turned out, was in Jerusalem.

My Brother Steve [1]

by WILLIAM ROSE BENÉT

ALTHOUGH I am twelve years older than the subject of this sketch, the above title seems to me almost too flippant. It refers to a man who is one of the best writers of our time, a man I esteem too highly to treat lightly or sentimentally. We are, of course, brothers—but perhaps the difference in our ages accounts for the fact that we have never clashed as some brothers do. Or perhaps it is the similarity of our tastes. I think there is something more too. And it is good to see a man you esteem carrying on the battle. The life of a writer is a constant fight for his integrity, for his best and most honest expression. The more successful one becomes, the more pitfalls present themselves, the more false lures attract. I have watched my brother become a first-rate writing man, support a wife and three children, and at the same time save his own soul. Nor has he ever shirked a real assignment.

Those who are called "poets" are of as great variety as any other type of mankind. They emerge from every walk of life. An orphan of a Finsbury hostler whose name chanced to be John Keats—a scion of the moneyed English squirearchy named Percy Bysshe Shelley. Stephen Vincent Benét's forebears happened to have been largely graduates of the West Point Military Academy, including a great-grandfather, William Rose, on his mother's side. Our Benét grandfather was of Spanish descent, from Catalonia by way of the Balearics. He was Stephen Vincent Anastasius originally, the two middle names being Catholic Saints' names. Both he and my father, who was a Kentuckian on his mother's side, had keen senses of humor and a love of literature. Steve was, of course, named for the grandfather, who wrote Army texts and translated admirably. A few years ago, James Thurber, the humorist, presented me with an old book in the back of which was advertised (Redfield, Nassau St., New York, 1855) "The Political and Military History of the Campaign of Waterloo from the French of Gen. Baron Jomini, by Lieut. S. V. Benét, U. S. Ordnance, with a Map, 12, cloth, 75 cents." What wonder that his grandson, through an early study of my father's old Rebellion Records and "Battles and Leaders of the Civil War," became profoundly interested in American military campaigns! As for my father, he had a genuine love for the best in English poetry and was never in the slightest degree ashamed of it. He would, in fact, at the drop of a hat, discuss the more abstruse bards, like Chivers and Beddoes, with a Major-General or a startled Bishop. He read poetry aloud in the bosom of his family. He acquainted us with the best, and aroused our

[1] From *The Saturday Review of Literature*, November 15, 1941. By permission of the editors and the author.

interest in how it was constructed. He was a connoisseur and collector of the worst, also—what he called "Minus Poetry!" His reading voice could crinkle your backbone, and made you astonishedly aware of nobility and hero-ism—a valuable inoculation.

Steve was born in July of the year of the Spanish War, 1898. My father was superintending a Government contract at the then Bethlehem Iron Works in Pennsylvania. My sister and I returned from a visit to my grandmother's in the Cumberland Valley, to find in a rented house on Fountain Hill, South Bethlehem, a new and extremely young member of our family, with a bright red complexion and a penetrating voice. We were not sure that this new acquisition was altogether a good idea. But he clenched his fists and evinced a fighting spirit.

When we moved to Buffalo, N. Y., where his elder brother joined a gang of boys who smoked cubebs and read nickel libraries in a backyard shanty, Steve chiefly distinguished himself by throwing blankets and anything else graspable out of his baby-carriage as he was wheeled along the street, to an accompaniment of cooing noises from the housewives he encountered—for at this period he was quite a personable infant, who, however, chewed capstrings indignantly and wore his bonnet at a rakish angle. His demeanor was, I am sorry to report, that of a dictator. Later still, at Watervliet Arsenal, between Albany and Troy, N. Y., he developed golden curls (though hardly a Lord Fauntleroy!) and a rasping Cockney accent through association with an Eng-lish nurse. He was everybody's favorite—even as was Booth Tarkington at a tender age. His nickname was "Tibbie." This his elder brother adopted, with the Latin spelling of "Tibi," as a pseudonym for sundry writings in his school paper. But, later on, Steve squared matters by adopting a poetical epithet of mine in a certain poem of his. He even admits it!

The earliest instance I recall of Steve's desire to communicate an interest in literature occurred when he was still quite small. He was discovered by my mother seated on the nursery floor with a book upside-down in his lap, reading aloud, although he had not yet learned to read. He was reading aloud to a mouse—or so he informed her. Unfortunately the mouse protruded from an ordinary mouse-trap—and was quite dead.

Army officers never stay long in the same place, so that by the time the boy was of school age, he was living in California, at another Ordnance Arsenal, this time near the town of Benicia which once in years far past just missed being the capital of the State. Here, I remember, Steve possessed a gray donkey, though I have forgotten the donkey's name. The donkey was hitched to a two-wheeled cart, and almost as soon as anyone climbed into the cart, the donkey lay down in the road. The obstructionist aspect of life was thus vividly presented to my brother at an early age.. It was quite impossible to move the donkey.

Steve also possessed a curly brown dog named Prince. Prince usually had something the matter with his ear. I have before me as I write a pencil draw-ing I made of that dog in his more familiar aspect, that is, sound asleep.

And I have a drawing I made at the same time of a small boy in a dark blue sailor suit, sitting in a Chinese wicker chair. His curls have vanished. His short hair falls straight over his forehead. He wears rimless glasses. Constant reading in any dim corner, usually with the feet elevated high above the head, had already taken toll of his eyesight. He developed then a chronic nearsightedness, today only excelled by that of the novelist, John Dos Passos. In my drawing, his hands grasp firmly the arms of the chair, and his attitude suggests the supreme court about to come to a decision. He looks a very little like the youthful Kipling when the latter was known as "Beetle."

The dog Prince was his constant companion and was defended—or would have been—to the death against the constant scorn and criticism of a sweet little elderly aunt of ours who lived with us. She was otherwise as good as gold. Steve was then eight years old, and he denied hotly that Prince had any trace of smell.

Like many a man who has lived to accomplish a great deal (notably the late Theodore Roosevelt) Steve's early constitution was not of the most robust. Consequently, he did not go in very heavily for games, and began to lead an interior life of the mind. At the same time, his taste in books was catholic enough. He easily descended to "Peck's Bad Boy" and an American humorist with the peculiar typographical pseudonym of "M. Quad." He still contends to this day that the incident where Peck's bad boy fed his father white rubber hose for spaghetti revealed a remarkable power of invention on the part of the author. He read Lang, "E. Nesbit," dozens of Henty books (like thousands of other boys), Dumas—and from Howard Pyle's "Men of Iron" and some of William Morris's poetry and prose, he began to gain an idea of how the past could be presented in terms of realistic detail.

At about the age of ten he was sent to the Hitchcock Military Academy in California, where one boy he remembers was the son of the famous early French flier, Moisant. Neither boy, I think, cared for that school. Like so many writers in youth, Steve was bullied a good deal, schoolboy misery preserved for us in such poems from his second book, "Young Adventure," as "Going Back to School" and the sympathetic poem about Shelley at Eton. Not that my brother was a self-pitier. He took what was coming to him from the Nazi-minded of that day, and licked his wounds in secret. He came to know that life was not exactly that of a knight in the days of chivalry, and began to develop the protective integument we all have to assume.

So far as literary taste was concerned, he had already perceived the difference between a work like "The Haystack in the Floods" and such tripe as "The Helmet of Navarre." And then, in our family, you soon saw the necessity for a sense of humor. My father could tease more expertly than anyone I have ever known. He could be merciless if he thought he perceived a joint in your armor. This went along with a great companionableness and kindness. But it was always there, and kept one upon the alert. He now developed a liking for controversy with a small boy, who (thought my sister and myself, now both in college) was allowed many more privileges than had attended our own early years. It was quite usual to observe Steve reclining upon the back of his neck in a certain large familiar leather armchair, drawling his "Maybe so, but—" to some argument of my father's, who sat across from him beyond the book-laden table. What was being argued was, I feel certain, either Socialism or sundry campaigns of Grant or Lee. At this time my brother discovered the old Rebellion Records and the "Battles and Leaders of the Civil War" in the family book-cases.

There were early stories then, composed while the author absorbed some horrifying concoction of a strange and lurid color which he got together in the kitchen from God knows what ingredients! One story was called "The Butcher's Bill," and, for so humdrum a title, was short, crisp, and startling. There were some rather violent poems too—one beginning:

> I have been on the old tramp steamer
> When heads were quickly bashed,
> When dead men rolled in the scuppers
> And revolvers spat and flashed . . .

Such was a crude and early precursor of Steve's later and excellent ballad, "The Hemp: A Virginia Legend," which appeared in *The Century Magazine* while he was still a schoolboy. In those early days he would go riding with us along dusty California roads, mounted upon an old Army mare. In a poem toward the end of "Young Adventure" he reveals a little of what it made him think about:

> A cicada's cry deepens the hot silence.
> The hills open
> To show a slope of poppies,
> Ardent, noble, heroic,
> A flare, a great flame of orange;
> Giving sleepy, brittle scent
> That stings the lungs.
> A creeping wind slips through them like a ferret; they
> bow and dance, answering Beauty's voice . . .

I have put this same small boy into a long poem of my own, telling how he also would offer us his hoarded nickels for lunch in the restaurant of the ferry-boat, *Solano,* which used to carry the Southern Pacific trains across the Carquinez Straits from Benicia to Port Costa. It was a stunt of ours to ride the boat back and forth and examine the new tourists from the East, after stuffing particularly good corn muffins.

By the time I was established in New York as a publisher's reader, Steve was down in Augusta, Georgia, with my father and mother. To the latter he owed much through his early years not only for devoted care but for lively understanding. Just prior to the change of base, at the age of thirteen, he had won a cash prize from the *Saint Nicholas League* with a poem, "The Regret of Dives." It was apparent from this poem that he did not, however, desire to become rich. He has since told us that he was then under the impression that *Dives* rhymed with *hives,* though fortunately the name occurred only in the poem's title. He got three dollars for it and spent it on the train coming East from California. In another poem of the period he stigmatized "The Proud Man," imagining himself sitting in a tower aloof from the world, till at last a glance from a window showed him how all mankind had passed him by and gone beyond him. The execution of these verses leaves something to be desired, but the point-of-view remained characteristic. My brother has never cared much about an ivory tower.

A rare issue of a book-collector's quarterly of eight years ago contains an essay of Steve's called "The Sixth Man," in which he describes our father's influence upon his formative years, the big house in California, and how he came to realize early in life that poetry "was not a dead thing or an alien thing or a dry game of words. I knew there were rules and that you could break the rules but that you must never break them unintentionally. I knew it was always written by the living, even though the date-line said that the man was dead."

Steve entered Yale. The first World War was just coming over the horizon. In his sophomore year my brother was taken on the *Lit,* of which he later became Chairman. Those happened to be great years for writing among undergraduates in the Eastern universities. Yale had Archibald MacLeish, Thornton Wilder, Philip Barry. Harvard could boast Dos Passos, Cummings, and T. S. Eliot. At Princeton were F. Scott Fitzgerald, Edmund Wilson, and John Peale Bishop. It was such a renaissance as has not shone again.

In his Junior Year Steve wrote the Yale University Prize Poem, "The Drug Shop, or, Endymion in Edmonstoun," a poem about Keats; and in the same year, after enlisting and then being rejected from the Army because of defective eyesight, he entered the State Department as a cipher-clerk, a profession also then adorned by Mr. James Thurber, afterward author of "The Seal in the Bedroom." Later on Steve became a clerk in the Office of the Counselor. At that time he roomed in Washington with John Franklin Carter (later well-known under a pseudonym as a writer on political and international subjects), Thornton Wilder, and Bill Taylor. After the war he returned to college for his B.A.; and his second book of poems, "Young Adventure," was published by the Yale University Press.

Subsequent to graduation, Steve worked the next summer in the office of Charles W. Hoyt, Planned Advertising, the only business office in which, to my knowledge, he has ever labored. He went back to the Yale Graduate School to take his M. A. in one year, a possible thing at that time. He presented, in lieu of a thesis, his third book of poems, "Heavens and Earth," and Ex-Governor Wilbur Cross, then head of the Graduate School, accepted the substitution. In that young and enthusiastic volume you will find in the section, "The Tall Town," a poem of the war called "Colloquy of the Statues," and poems about lunch-time on Broadway, the strike pickets on lower Fifth Avenue, morning on 32nd Street, and the red and white flashes by night of the Metropolitan Tower, reflections of my brother's thoughts while pursuing for a brief moment the almighty dollar of national advertising!

By this time Steve had definitely decided to throw in his lot with literature. He spent the summer after leaving Yale in writing his first novel, "The Beginning of Wisdom," and went over to Paris with John Carter, to study, presumably, at the Sorbonne. In Paris he got some reading done, and some drinking, and incidentally met the delightful and talented girl he was soon to marry. She was working for the Paris edition of the Chicago *Tribune* and for the London *Daily Mail*. When they returned to the United States separately, to consult their respective parents and prepare for marriage, Steve turned to and, under high pressure, wrote his second novel, "Young People's Pride," which Carl Brandt serialized for him with Henry Blackman Sell of *Harper's Bazaar*. The book is dedicated to Rosemary Carr with a special delightful poem, and on the first page occurs the name of one of the characters, Johnny Chipman—part of the name of John Chipman Farrar.

The serial money enabled my brother and his wife, after their wedding in Chicago, to return to Paris and begin life together in that city of cities that had early won their hearts. It also marked the beginning of a literary and business association between him as author and Carl Brandt as his literary agent and adviser that has endured for many years. Later Steve and his bride returned to New York, and, after another novel, "Jean Huguenot," he squared away at the magazines as a writer of short stories.

The neophyte thinks that the established writer of short stories and novels has it all his own way. How very pleasant to dash off this or that immediately and receive large sums for it! The experienced know, of course, that the trade of writer is uncertain enough to make strong men break down and cry like babies! "To be a writer," a successful one once said to me, "you need the heart of a lion." Steve could take it. But at length he wrote himself completely out on short stories, and came to that point of desperation all writers know, when the vein of invention begins to run thinner and thinner, and the stories become flimsier and flimsier. Yet now there was a small and growing daughter to be cared for. Taking stock of his gifts, of his literary chance, of the trend of his writing life, my brother decided on a complete break-away and a fresh cast.

Those who think that poets—like the conies—are a feeble folk, might profit by regarding the decision of this one. It was over fifteen years ago that he laid before the board of the Guggenheim Foundation his plan for a long poem of the Civil War. He went abroad, with wife and child, on the stipend they gave him, while almost everybody, including his publishers, seemed to think it a crazy self-indulgence. Today there are not many people in this country who have not read and enjoyed "John Brown's Body."

To a certain extent every writer has to be a gambler; but it takes entrails, with a family to support, to turn away from the lucrative field and embark upon a questionable project. It took the courage of his wife, too, of course— a courage and an admirable commonsense which she has never failed to show in an emergency. The book had to be written. It sprang from inner neces-sity. And, actually, it paid reckonable dividends.

Out at Neuilly, Steve dug in, toted masses of books home from a Paris library, and went to work recreating the American Civil War. Those long armchair discussions with his father, in California and Georgia, must have recurred to him vividly! His utter surprise when the finished book became a best-seller is a story that has often been told. When asked by a ship-news re-porter what it felt like, he characteristically remarked that to him it was as though he had given birth to a grand piano. Prior to this, his longest flight into history had been a novel concerning the Minorcan revolt at New Smyrna, Florida, called "Spanish Bayonet." Then our father had been alive. This time the only shadow on Steve's success was the fact that our father was gone, though he had lived to read portions of the manuscript in its early stages. As for myself, the summer of its completion I was staying with my wife, Elinor Wylie, in the village of Burley in the New Forest in England. I vividly recall Steve coming over from Paris to see us, reading to us one night in our cot-tage from his manuscript, before a glimmering fire of coals. It was an im-mortal evening.

The success of this book enabled him to proceed with his writing more at his own pace. It also brought him the Pulitzer Prize. His short stories grew better and better. Today one of the most famous is being interpreted on the screen by Walter Huston, Edward Arnold, and others. But at first he was loath to collect them. He brought out, instead, a collection of ballads and poems, work of the past fifteen years. Here were, among other excellent things, his earlier *Nation* Prize poem, "King David," the famous "Mountain Whippoorwill," that fine sonnet sequence called "The Golden Corpse," and also a strangely moving earlier poem of untried youth, which he had attempted to revise. But it was now 1930 and the poem had first been written in 1917. So the new last verse reads:

> After the thirteenth year, the water runs as before,
> The gemmed wave in the water, the starlight on the gem,
> All but the crew who sailed there, and they return no more,
> But the words are as they were written. I cannot alter them.

That too I find characteristic of Steve; for one of his virtues is loyalty—not blind, not sentimental, but considered, wise, and final. He has something in his character like a rampart. It cannot be moved. Five or six years later, in "Burning City," which contains his great poem against dictators, he gives us several fiery glimpses of what it is to be a real poet.

He had written his new novel, "James Shore's Daughter," and now at last he launched selected "Stories of Several Worlds" in "Thirteen o'Clock." Among them stands "The Devil and Daniel Webster" (now appearing on the screen), "The King of the Cats," and "Daniel Webster and the Sea Serpent." Already his wife and he had collaborated on a gay book in rhyme concerning historic Americans. In a second volume of short stories came other fantastic masterpieces like "Johnny Pye and the Fool-Killer" and "Doc Mellhorn and the Pearly Gates." But there is moving realism too, concerning the vile tyranny of our time, in "The Blood of the Martyrs" and "Into Egypt." And there is in certain others that deep understanding of youth that made Steve so admirable an editor of the Yale Series of Younger Poets, where his unerring judgment has turned up such fine rebellious talent as Paul Engle's, Muriel Rukeyser's, or that of Joy Davidman. Other critics than I, who am no fit critic of my brother's work, have praised his art in the short story. You have only to read them.

By now I have had to regard my younger brother as by way of becoming an American institution! "Stephen Benét Wins O. Henry Story Prize"— "Roosevelt Medal Awarded Stephen Benét"—"Re-elected Vice President of National Institute"—"Member of the American Academy"—and so on *ad infinitum!* One source of pale envy on my part, incidentally, has been the way Steve has always collected prizes. Every time they put one up, they decide to give it to him! He was always lucky with slot-machines, too, I remember. Frank Morley once organized the "Brothers Club," because his brother Christopher was getting altogether too famous. I am a charter member of that organization—just because of Steve!

There are three children now, an older daughter who is, indeed, no longer a child, but a young lady; a son at Exeter; a younger daughter of highly original gifts. There is Rosemary, Steve's wife, who was born to understand just why he has wished to write exactly as he has written. She lends his household infinite charm, collaborates with him on the portraits of other writers that they do for Irita Van Doren's *Books,* translates Colette from the French, and judges children's books with rare ability. And now there is the Whistler House in the old whaling port of Stonington, Connecticut, where Steve and Rosemary hope to spend years that are sure to be anything but "declining"! In town, there is the large old-fashioned house in the East Sixties, with a more secluded air-conditioned study now, on an upper floor, where work upon a pioneer epic, among other projects, goes steadily forward.

If one has been at one time pretty hard hit by arthritis, one does not stand quite as straight as one has in the past, even though one's spirit may be like a lance. But one does not lose, for all that, the persistent twinkle, the drawlingly American sense of humor, the keen appraisal of the follies and crimes of the times. There is a southern tinge to the hospitality too—a courtesy and kindness at once apparent, a consideration that caused a young in-law of mine once to remark, "Why good Lord, he was asking me *my* opinion!"

Steve has developed in a manner I can thoroughly admire. Perhaps it is true, as he avers, that once I was in a position to read to him most of Bryant's translation of the Iliad, or to write a foreword and draw a cover for an early unpublished work then known as "Poems and Battle Songs." I can, indeed, remember the time when I actually used to tell him stories. Today, how utterly preposterous that seems!

I have said elsewhere and before this that my brother early developed a habit of gritting his teeth and being thrilled by tales of heroic exploits. He will never quite lose that faculty. And he still absorbs pulp-magazines dealing with horror, mystery, and marvel, with as great a relish as he did in his youth. For instance, he was entirely familiar with the work of H. P. Lovecraft long before that little-known master of horror was brought to the attention of the critics. That is one aspect. And then there has been the radio work and there have been the speeches before the National Academy and elsewhere. There has been advisory lecturing in the art of writing. There has been book-reviewing. There was the making of a Lincoln picture with David Wark Griffith, and the making of "The Devil and Daniel Webster" into a light opera, with the aid of his old friend, now head of the Columbia School of Music, Douglas Moore. Steve also collaborated with Mr. Moore on a picture, "Power and the Land," put out by the Rural Electrification Administration, and has prepared for the screen at least one novel by another writer. Life has been rich in effort and opportunity. And sometimes, in spite of that, the driven body has needed badly, and found, what my brother early wrote of as "The Quality of Courage."

Steve has not been spared his full share of the acerbity of contemporary criticism. But he can usually tell exactly what is eating the critics and why. He drawls, "Oh, we-ll—!" He does not take himself too seriously. He has enjoyed his work, and the rewards thereof. He could calculate to a nicety just when he knew he was hitting the ball, and when he wasn't. Lately, it has seemed to one admiring relative, he has hit it pretty consistently right upon the nose. "Wait till you come to forty year!" warned Thackeray. But today we know that that is just when life begins. Steve is three years past, and but only coming into his own. What matters is what he himself has written in "Thanks":

> The metal heats, the flesh grows numb again
> And I can still go muttering down the street
> Not seeing the interminable world
> Nor the ape-faces, only the live coal

—which is, after all, the writer's one permanent reward. That and the skill that was fought for and hard-won, that burns in the hand now, and can reveal the vision.

Life with Father[1]

by CLARENCE DAY

ONE late afternoon when Father came up from downtown, he found his home much upset. Our cook had walked out and left us. I was a child of four, George was two, and there was a new baby besides. Mother was ill. She hadn't been able to leave us to go to an agency. And as she was no hand at cooking herself, the outlook for dinner was poor.

This state of affairs was unprecedented in all Father's experience. In his father's home, they never changed their servants suddenly; they seldom changed them at all; and as his mother was a past mistress of cooking, he had always been doubly protected. Since his marriage, he had had to live a much bumpier life. But this was the worst yet.

He asked Mother, who was lying in bed, what she was going to do about it. There were no telephones then, and she couldn't do anything at all, at the moment; but she said she would try to go to an agency in the morning and see what she could find. "In the morning? Good God!" Father said. "Where is the place, anyhow?" And he clapped on his hat and strode out again, over toward Sixth Avenue.

As I heard the story years afterward, it was late when he got there, and he bounded up the front stoop two or three steps at a time, and went quickly into the little office, where the gaslights were burning. He had never been in such a place before, and to his surprise it was empty, except for a severe-looking woman who sat at a desk at one side. "Where do you keep 'em?" he urgently demanded, his mind on the question of dinner.

She looked at him, got out her pen, and opened a large book deliberately. "I will take your name and address," she informed him, "and then, if you please, you may give me the details as to what kind of person you require and when you would wish her to call."

But Father had no time, he told her, for any damned fol-de-rol. "Where do you keep 'em?" he said again. She was standing in the way of his dinner. I can imagine how his face must have reddened and how his eyes must have blazed at her. "I am asking you where you keep them!" he roared.

"Why, the girls are in there," the lady explained, to calm him, "but clients are not allowed in that room. If you will tell me the kind of position you wish me to fill for you, I will have one come out."

Before she'd half finished, Father had thrown open the door and gone in. There sat a crowd of the girls, young and old, sickly and brawny, of all

[1] Reprinted from *Life with Father* by Clarence Day, by permission of Alfred A. Knopf, Inc. Copyright 1933 by Clarence Day.

shapes and sizes; some ugly, some pretty and trim and stylish, some awkward; nurses, ladies' maids, waitresses, washerwomen, and cooks.

The manager was by now at Father's elbow, trying to make him get out, and insisting that he tell her the position he wished her to fill. But Father was swiftly glancing around at the crowd, and he paid no attention. He noticed a little woman in the corner, with honest gray eyes, who sat there, shrewd-looking and quiet. He pointed his cane over at her and said, "I'll take that one."

The manager was flustered, but still she kept trying to enforce her authority. She protested she didn't yet know the position. . . .

"Cook," Father said, "cook."

"But Margaret doesn't wish to be a cook, she wants—"

"You can cook, can't you?" Father demanded.

Margaret's plain little face was still pink with excitement and pleasure at being chosen above all that roomful by such a masterful gentleman. Father had probably smiled at her, too, for they liked each other at once. Well, she said, she had cooked for one family.

"Of course she can cook," Father said.

The manager didn't like this at all. The discipline of the office was spoiled. "If you are going to take her anyhow," she said acidly, "what day would you wish her to come, and will you please give me your name?"

"Yes, yes," Father said, without giving it. "Come on, Margaret." And he planked down the fee and walked out.

Margaret followed him through the door and trotted over to our home at his heels. He sent her down to the kitchen immediately, while he went upstairs to dress.

"I don't know why you make such a fuss about engaging new servants. It's simple enough," he said comfortably to Mother that evening, after Margaret's first dinner.

It was the first of a long series, for she stayed with us twenty-six years.

* * *

Buttons were Father's worst trial, however, from his point of view. Ripped shirts and socks with holes in them could still be worn, but drawers with their buttons off couldn't. The speed with which he dressed seemed to discourage his buttons and make them desert Father's service. Furthermore, they always gave out suddenly and at the wrong moment.

He wanted help and he wanted it promptly at such times, of course. He would appear at Mother's door with a waistcoat in one hand and a disloyal button in the other, demanding that it be sewn on at once. If she said she couldn't just then, Father would get as indignant as though he had been drowning and a life-guard had informed him he would save him to-morrow.

When his indignation mounted high enough to sweep aside his good judgment, he would say in a stern voice, "Very well, I'll sew it on myself," and demand a needle and thread. Mother knew only too well what it meant. She would beg him to leave his waistcoat in her work basket and let her do it next day. Father was inflexible. Moreover, his decision would be strengthened if he happened to glance at her basket and see how many of his socks were dismally waiting there in that crowded exile.

"I've been looking for those blue polka-dotted socks for a month," he said angrily one night before dinner. "Not a thing is done for a man in this house. I even have to sew on my own buttons. Where is your needle and thread?"

Mother reluctantly gave these implements to him. He marched off, sat on the edge of his sofa in the middle of his bedroom, and got ready to work. The gaslight was better by his bureau, but he couldn't sit on a chair when he sewed. It had no extra room on it. He laid his scissors, the spool of thread, and his waistcoat down on the sofa beside him, wet his fingers, held the needle high up and well out in front, and began poking the thread at the eye.

Like every commander, Father expected instant obedience, and he wished to deal with trained troops. The contrariness of the needle and the limp obstinacy of the thread made him swear. He stuck the needle in the sofa while he wet his fingers and stiffened the thread again. When he came to take up his needle, it had disappeared. He felt around everywhere for it. He got up, holding fast to his thread, and turned around, facing the sofa to see where it was hiding. This jerked the spool off onto the floor, where it rolled away and unwound.

The husbands of two of Mother's friends had had fits of apoplexy and died. It frightened her horribly when this seemed about to happen to Father. At the sound of his roars, she rushed in. There he was on the floor, as she had feared. He was trying to get his head under the sofa and he was yelling at something, and his face was such a dark red and his eyes so bloodshot that Mother was terrified. Pleading with him to stop only made him more apoplectic. He said he'd be damned if he'd stop. He stood up presently, tousled but triumphant, the spool in his hand. Mother ran to get a new needle. She threaded it for him and he at last started sewing.

Father sewed on the button in a violent manner, with vicious haulings and jabs. Mother said she couldn't bear to see him—but she couldn't bear to leave the room, either. She stood watching him, hypnotized and appalled, itching to sew it herself, and they talked at each other with vehemence. Then the inevitable accident happened; the needle came forcibly up through the waist-coat, it struck on the button, Father pushed at it harder, and it burst through the hole and stuck Father's finger.

He sprang up with a howl. To be impaled in this way was not only exasperating, it was an affront. He turned to me, as he strode about on the rug, holding onto his finger, and said wrathfully, "It was your mother."

"Why, Clare!" Mother cried.

"Talking every minute," Father shouted at her, "and distracting a man! How the devil can I sew on a button with this gibbering and buzz in my ears? Now see what you made me do!" he added suddenly. "Blood on my good waistcoat! Here! Take the damned thing. Give me a handkerchief to tie up my finger with. Where's the witch-hazel?"

Early Impressions [1]

by HENRY ADAMS

Boys are wild animals, rich in the treasures of sense, but the New England boy had a wider range of emotions than boys of more equable climates. He felt his nature crudely, as it was meant. To the boy Henry Adams, summer was drunken. Among senses, smell was the strongest —smell of hot pine-woods and sweet-fern in the scorching summer noon; of new-mown hay; of ploughed earth; of box hedges; of peaches, lilacs, syringas; of stables, barns, cow-yards; of salt water and low tide on the marshes; nothing came amiss. Next to smell came taste, and the children knew the taste of everything they saw or touched, from pennyroyal and flagroot to the shell of a pignut and the letters of a spelling-book—the taste of A-B, AB, suddenly revived on the boy's tongue sixty years afterwards. Light, line, and color as sensual pleasures, came later and were as crude as the rest. The New England light is glare, and the atmosphere harshens colors. The boy was a full man before he ever knew what was meant by atmosphere; his idea of pleasure in light was the blaze of a New England sun. His idea of color was a peony, with the dew of early morning on its petals. The intense blue of the sea, as he saw it a mile or two away, from the Quincy hills; the cumuli in a June afternoon sky; the strong reds and greens and purples of colored prints and children's picture-books, as the American colors then ran; these were ideals. The opposites, or antipathies, were the cold grays of November evenings, and the thick, muddy thaws of Boston winter. With such standards, the Bostonian could not but develop a double nature. Life was a double thing. After a January blizzard, the boy who could look with pleasure into the violent snow-glare of the cold white sunshine, with its intense light and shade, scarcely knew what was meant by tone. He could reach it only by education.

Winter and summer, then, were two hostile lives, and bred two separate natures. Winter was always the effort to live; summer was tropical license. Whether the children rolled in the grass, or waded in the brook, or swam in the salt ocean, or sailed in the bay, or fished for smelts in the creeks, or netted minnows in the salt-marshes, or took to the pine-woods and the granite quarries, or chased muskrats and hunted snapping-turtles in the swamps, or mushrooms or nuts on the autumn hills, summer and country were always sensual living, while winter was always compulsory learning. Summer was the multiplicity of nature; winter was school.

The bearing of the two seasons on the education of Henry Adams was no

[1] From Henry Adams, *Education of Henry Adams* (1918). By permission of Houghton Mifflin Company.

fancy; it was the most decisive force he ever knew; it ran through life and made the division between its perplexing, warring, irreconcilable problems irreducible opposites, with growing emphasis to the last year of study. From earliest childhood the boy was accustomed to feel that, for him, life was double. Winter and summer, town and country, law and liberty, were hostile, and the man who pretended they were not, was in his eyes a schoolmaster— that is, a man employed to tell lies to little boys. Though Quincy was but two hours' walk from Beacon Hill, it belonged in a different world. For two hundred years, every Adams, from father to son, had lived within sight of State Street, and sometimes had lived in it, yet none had ever taken kindly to the town, or been taken kindly by it. The boy inherited his double nature. He knew as yet nothing about his great-grandfather, who had died a dozen years before his own birth: he took for granted that any great-grandfather of his must have always been good, and his enemies wicked; but he divined his great-grandfather's character from his own. Never for a moment did he connect the two ideas of Boston and John Adams; they were separate and antagonistic; the idea of John Adams went with Quincy. He knew his grand-father John Quincy Adams only as an old man of seventy-five or eighty who was friendly and gentle with him, but except that he heard his grandfather always called "the President," and his grandmother "the Madam," he had no reason to suppose that his Adams grandfather differed in character from his Brooks grandfather, who was equally kind and benevolent. He liked the Adams side best, but for no other reason than that it reminded him of the country, the summer, and the absence of restraint. Yet he felt also that Quincy was in a way inferior to Boston, and that socially Boston looked down on Quincy. The reason was clear enough even to a five-year-old child. Quincy had no Boston style. Little enough style had either; a simpler manner of life and thought could hardly exist, short of cave-dwelling. The flint-and-steel with which his grandfather Adams used to light his own fires in the early morning was still on the mantel piece of his study. The idea of a livery or even a dress for servants, or of an evening toilette, was next to blasphemy. Bathrooms, water-supplies, lighting, heating, and the whole array of domestic comforts, were unknown at Quincy. Boston had already a bathroom, a water-supply, a furnace, and gas. The superiority of Boston was evident, but a child liked it no better for that. . . .

The Madam was a little more remote than the President, but more decora-tive. She stayed much in her own room with the Dutch tiles, looking out on her garden with the box walks, and seemed a fragile creature to a boy who sometimes brought her a note or a message, and took distinct pleasure in looking at her delicate face under what seemed to him very becoming caps. He liked her refined figure; her gentle voice and manner; her vague effect of not belonging there, but to Washington or to Europe, like her furniture, and writing-desk with little glass doors above and little eighteenth-century volumes in old binding, labelled "Peregrine Pickle" or "Tom Jones" or "Hannah More." Try as she might, the Madam could never be Bostonian, and it was her cross in life, but to the boy it was her charm. Even at that age, he felt drawn to it. The Madam's life had been in truth far from Boston. She was born in London in 1775, daughter of Joshua Johnson, an American merchant, brother of Governor Thomas Johnson of Maryland; and Catherine Nuth, of an English family in London. Driven from England by the Revolutionary War, Joshua Johnson took his family to Nantes, where they remained till the peace. The girl Louisa Catherine was nearly ten years old when brought back to London, and her sense of nationality must have been confused; but the influence of the Johnsons and the services of Joshua obtained for him from President Washington the appointment of Consul in London on the organization of the Government in 1790. In 1794 President Washington appointed John Quincy Adams Minister to The Hague. He was twenty-seven years old when he returned to London, and found the Consul's house a very agreeable haunt. Louisa was then twenty.

At that time, and long afterwards, the Consul's house, far more than the Minister's, was the centre of contact for travelling Americans, either official or other. The Legation was a shifting point, between 1785 and 1815; but the Consulate, far down in the City, near the Tower, was convenient and inviting; so inviting that it proved fatal to young Adams. Louisa was charming, like a Romney portrait, but among her many charms that of being a New England woman was not one. The defect was serious. Her future mother-in-law, Abigail, a famous New England woman whose authority over her turbulent husband, the second President, was hardly so great as that which she exercised over her son, the sixth to be, was troubled by the fear that Louisa might not be made of stuff stern enough, or brought up in conditions severe enough, to suit a New England climate, or to make an efficient wife for her paragon son, and Abigail was right on that point, as on most others where sound judgment was involved; but sound judgment is sometimes a source of weakness rather than of force, and John Quincy already had reason to think that his mother held sound judgments on the subject of daughters-in-law which human nature, since the fall of Eve, made Adams helpless to realize. Being three thousand miles away from his mother, and equally far in love, he married Louisa in London, July 26, 1797, and took her to Berlin to be the head of the United States Legation. During three or four exciting years, the young bride lived in Berlin; whether she was happy or not, whether she was content or not, whether she was socially successful or not, her descendants did not surely know; but in any case she could by no chance have become educated there for a life in Quincy or Boston. In 1801 the overthrow of the Federalist Party drove her and her husband to America, and she became at last a member of the Quincy household, but by that time her children needed all her attention, and she remained there with occasional winters in Boston and Washington, till 1809. Her husband was made Senator in 1803, and in 1809 was appointed Minister to Russia. The life at St. Petersburg was hardly gay for her; they were far too poor to shine in that extravagant society; but she survived it, though her little girl baby did not, and in the winter of 1814-15, alone with the boy of seven years old, crossed Europe from St. Petersburg to Paris, in her travelling-carriage, passing through the armies and reaching Paris in the *Cent Jours* after Napoleon's return from Elba. Her husband next went to England as Minister, and she was for two years at the Court of the Regent. In 1817 her husband came home to be Secretary of State, and she lived for eight years in F Street, doing her work of entertainer for President Monroe's administration. Next she lived four miserable years in the White House. When that chapter was closed in 1829, she had earned the right to be tired and delicate, but she still had fifteen years to serve as wife of a Member of the House, after her husband went back to Congress in 1822. Then it was that little Henry, her grandson, first remembered her, from 1843 to 1848, sitting in her panelled room, at breakfast, with her heavy silver teapot and sugar-bowl and cream-jug, which still exist somewhere as an heirloom of the modern safety-vault. By that time she was seventy years old or more, and thoroughly weary of being beaten about a stormy world. To the boy she seemed singularly peaceful, a vision of silver gray, presiding over her old President and her Queen Anne mahogany; an exotic, like her Sèvres china; an object of deference to every one, and of great affection to her son Charles; but hardly more Bostonian than she had been fifty years before, on her wedding-day, in the shadow of the Tower of London.

Such a figure was even less fitted than that of her old husband, the President, to impress on a boy's mind, the standards of the coming century. She was Louis Seize, like the furniture. The boy knew nothing of her interior life, which had been, as the venerable Abigail, long since at peace, foresaw, one of severe stress and little pure satisfaction. He never dreamed that from her might come some of those doubts and self-questionings, those hesitations, those rebellions against law and discipline, which marked more than one of her descendants; but he might even then have felt some vague instinctive suspicion that he was to inherit from her the seeds of the primal sin, the fall from grace, the curse of Abel, that he was not of pure New England stock, but half exotic. . . .

The boy naturally learned only one lesson from his saturation in such air. He took for granted that this sort of world, more or less the same that had always existed in Boston and Massachusetts Bay, was the world which he was to fit. Had he known Europe he would have learned no better. The Paris of Louis Philippe, Guizot, and de Tocqueville, as well as the London of Robert Peel, Macaulay, and John Stuart Mill, were but varieties of the same upper-class *bourgeoisie* that felt instinctive cousinship with the Boston of Ticknor, Prescott, and Motley. Even the typical grumbler Carlyle, who cast doubts on the real capacity of the middle class, and who at times thought himself eccentric, found friendship and alliances in Boston—still more in Concord. The system had proved so successful that even Germany wanted to try it, and Italy yearned for it. England's middle-class government was the ideal of human progress.

Even the violent reaction after 1848, and the return of all Europe to military practices, never for a moment shook the true faith. No one, except Karl Marx, foresaw radical change. What announced it? The world was producing sixty or seventy million tons of coal, and might be using nearly a million steam-horse-power, just beginning to make itself felt. All experience since the creation of man, all divine revelation or human science, conspired to deceive and betray a twelve-year-old boy who took for granted that his ideas, which were alone respectable, would be alone respected.

Viewed from Mount Vernon Street, the problem of life was as simple as it was classic. Politics offered no difficulties, for there the moral law was a sure guide. Social perfection was also sure, because human nature worked for Good, and three instruments were all she asked—Suffrage, Common Schools, and Press. On these points doubt was forbidden. Education was divine, and man needed only a correct knowledge of facts to reach perfection:

> "Were half the power that fills the world with terror,
> Were half the wealth bestowed on camps and courts,
> Given to redeem the human mind from error,
> There were no need of arsenals nor forts."

Nothing quieted doubt so completely as the mental calm of the Unitarian clergy. In uniform excellence of life and character, moral and intellectual, the score of Unitarian clergymen about Boston, who controlled society and Harvard College, were never excelled. They proclaimed as their merit that they insisted on no doctrine, but taught, or tried to teach, the means of leading a virtuous, useful, unselfish life, which they held to be sufficient for salvation. For them, difficulties might be ignored; doubts were waste of thought; nothing exacted solution. Boston had solved the universe; or had offered and realized the best solution yet tried. The problem was worked out.

Of all the conditions of his youth which afterwards puzzled the grown-up man, this disappearance of religion puzzled him most. The boy went to church twice every Sunday; he was taught to read his Bible, and he learned religious poetry by heart; he believed in a mild deism; he prayed; he went through all the forms; but neither to him nor to his brothers or sisters was religion real. Even the mild discipline of the Unitarian Church was so irksome that they all threw it off at the first possible moment, and never afterwards entered a church. The religious instinct had vanished, and could not be revived, although one made in later life many efforts to recover it. That the most powerful emotion of man, next to the sexual, should disappear, might be a personal defect of his own; but that the most intelligent society, led by the most intelligent clergy, in the most moral conditions he ever knew, should have solved all the problems of the universe so thoroughly as to have quite ceased making itself anxious about past or future, and should have persuaded itself that all the problems which had convulsed human thought from earliest recorded time, were not worth discussing, seemed to him the most curious social phenomenon he had to account for in a long life. The faculty of turning away one's eyes as one approaches a chasm is not unusual, and Boston showed, under the lead of Mr. Webster, how successfully it could be done in politics; but in politics a certain number of men did at least protest. In religion and philosophy no one protested.

Rowing [1]

by OLIVER LA FARGE

No WRITER has told the nature of rowing in an eight-oared shell to landsmen, none who haven't rowed understand what it is we remember, the crash of the oars in the locks, the shell leaping at the catch, the unity and rhythm and the desperate effort, so when we meet we babble with joy.

What is the nature of it? To begin with the setting—the greenbanked river of the Charles Basin ringed by the city, both are beautiful. The shell swinging through open country on a fine spring day is hard to beat. Down on the Basin the water is oily, in the late afternoon it catches the deepening sunset, after dark the advertising signs over the factories are reflected on it, twisting as if the lights were darting snakes, and the swirl of one's oar is shot with colour. There is the slight excitement and the echoing change of sound in shooting under a bridge, there is the fresh day on the river as you carry your shell down to the float. Rural or urban water, rowing is set in beauty to begin with.

There is the nature of the stroke itself, the most perfect combination I have ever known of skill and the full release of one's power. It takes more than a dumb ox to make a fine oarsman, the traditional "weak brain and strong back" won't serve. To my mind it begins with the "recovery" the forward reach to get ready for a stroke. You are sitting on a slide, a seat on rollers, which runs on a track about two feet long, set variously according to the type of stroke your coach favours. Your two hands are on the loom of your twelve-foot oar, balancing it neatly. If you lower them too far, you sky the blade of your oar and the shift of the centre of gravity will make the boat rock and cost you precious headway; if you raise them too high your oar will touch the waves and you may cause a jolt that will throw the whole boat out of time. So your hands are balancing delicately—next time you see a good crew rowing, watch the oars moving together clear of the water on the recovery, see how narrow that long shell is and realize the miracle of balance that keeps it steady while those big men swing aft and the long

[1] From Oliver La Farge, *Raw Material* (1945). By permission of Houghton Mifflin Company.

sweeps reach forward. Or watch a green crew, see the oars at eight different levels and the shell wallowing from side to side.

You are moving your hands, your shoulders and your tail aft (you are facing aft) at three different rates, to bring each to its stopping point at the same time. If you rush your slide to the end of its run, that sharp motion and possibly the abrupt stopping at the end will check the motion of the shell (you can see it happen) and you yourself will fall into the position of your maximum effort with a jerk which will put you out of balance. Hands, shoulders, slide, must move in related time one to another, and in perfect time with the other seven men, so that at the right moment you are leaning forward just far enough for reach and not too far for power, your slide is all the way aft, your legs and knees are ready, your back is arched, not slumped, and your balancing hands are holding firmly to the oar. In the very last part of your swing your outside hand—the one towards the blade—has turned the oar a quarter circle, so that the blade, which was parallel to the water, is perpendicular to it.

CATCH! A slight raising of your hands and arms has dropped your blade into the water, and instantaneously your shoulders take hold. That simple action is not quite so simple. If you have not done it minutely right your oar may skitter out above the water, slice too deeply into the water to help the boat, or you may catch a crab—entangle your oar in water so that you can't get it out. That last is virtual shipwreck, it may knock you out of the boat, and it will almost certainly lose a race. Once you and seven other men are driving with all your forces it is too late to attempt to turn or guide your oar. You must have dropped it into the water so accurately that it will stay with the blade just submerged all the way through your pull and come out willingly. That is part of the turn of your outside hand and the act of slightly raising your arms. This raising of your arms must be neat; you don't let your oar into the water on a diagonal after you have begun to pull (that is you don't and stay on a good crew), nor do you succumb to the natural tendency which you will see in any fisherman's rowing, to let your hands dive slightly as you get ready to catch on hard, causing the blade first to rise slightly in the air and then to hit the water with a spanking motion.

An immeasurably short time after your shoulders, your legs start to drive. Now your arms are merely straps attaching your hands to your body, legs and shoulders and back for all they are worth are pulling on the oar, everything you've got is going into it, but you have taken care that your tail, driven by your legs, will not shoot on the slide ahead of your shoulders.

You have driven through almost to the end of the catch, your slide is almost home, your shoulders are back. Now your arms come in, and just as your knees come down locked, your hands touch your stomach. Here is the prettiest part of the stroke, the shoot of the hands to start the recovery. Remember, your oar is still deep in the water rushing powerfully past your boat; if it becomes caught in that, it turns to a wild machine. As your hands touch your belly they drop, shoot out, in a motion 'as fast and smooth as a billiard ball caroming,' at the same time your inside wrist turns and the blade is once more parallel to the water—feathered. The shoot of your hands and arms brings your shoulders forward and you commence your recovery once more.

All of what I have described happens in a single stroke by a good oarsman. This stroke, its predecessors and successors, is performed in a unison with seven other men which is more perfect than merely being in time, with the balance of the body maintained also in relation to the keel so that the boat shall not roll. At a moderate racing rate it is performed thirty-two to thirty-six times to the minute, all of this, nothing omitted, and in a rhythm which keeps the time of the recovery not less than double that of the catch.

This is not the whole of rowing, but it is the basic part of the individual's job in it. Unite it to another fundamental and you have a crew.

The other fundamental is unison. I have said that a crew does not merely keep time; it does something subtler than that, it becomes one. This it cannot do if there is bad feeling between any of the men in the boat; a single antagonistic personality can keep eight oarsmen accurately following stroke's oar and the coxswain's counting from becoming a crew rowing together. Crews are not made up on a basis of personalities, but according to the coach's estimates of individual capacities; it is after they are rowing together that they become friends. My crews at Harvard contained men with whom I had nothing in common, men by whom I should have been bored or antagonized, and who should have disliked me. As we rowed together we became fond of each other. It had no lasting value, but for the duration of our rowing, we esteemed each other dearly. As this feeling grew, so did our boat shake down and become one, and so did we increasingly care for the foul-mouthed, brilliant little devil who was our cox and in a race the instrument, voice, and control of our unity. . . .

Rowing at School was fun, but rowing at Harvard was magnificent. There was more of it, it was more intense, and it was better rowing. The hundred and fifty pound crews were step-children, born of hesitant concessions by doubting authorities; at first they could hope for no insignia, they accepted cast-off shells and unwanted, used oars and liked them. They were made up of boys who were perfectly willing to row in a soap-box if necessary so long as they could row and count from time to time on a full-fledged race. We won recognition slowly, better boats, decent oars, a minor sports letter. Not until after my time did the light weights get the same breaks in equipment and general treatment that less conservative colleges gave their rivals. We didn't care. For three years we rowed under the brothers, Bert and Bill Haynes, who themselves adored rowing and held it a prime part of their work to make us love them. We consciously rowed for them. We became a crew that could make the real varsity stretch over a short distance, we were made use of to pace the Varsity for starts and sprints, one splendid afternoon we beat the Junior Varsity handily in a regular, two-mile race.

We loved it from the bitter, all-but-winter days when ice formed on the oars to the long, grass-smelling spring afternoons when we went far upriver and then, before turning back, leaned on our oars and made the age-old jokes about going a little farther and seeing if we could stroke the Wellesley crew. The rowing after dark I remember especially; I've tried to describe it a little; I never became entirely used to the beauty of city-ringed water and the mystery of the bridges.

One night in the early spring there were a great many crews out on the Charles River Basin. We were heading upstream for home, taking it easy, and I remember how clearly the voices of coxswains and coaches, the sounds of the oars, came to us from many sides. Our cox was peering ahead a trifle nervously. Presently, to one side of us, we heard a practice race coming downstream, two class crews and the coaching launch behind them, with their coxswains making lots of noise and the coach calling from time to time. To play safe we lay on our oars. It was full dark, the water around us pearly in colour because of the city lights, the distance a very dark-grey haze rather than black, the sky above having the tawny quality so common over cities. A big sign on the Cambridge bank blinked on and off, flashing a red and yellow reflection across the basin almost to the side of the boat. Against it we caught a glimpse of the racing crews, the two long, ruled ink-lines of the shells and the figures in them black, small outlines in motion sliding across the flash of light in an instant. There was some other race going on somewhere, and at a safe distance behind the class crews several more were being given a workout.

It seemed to us that the sounds of boats and of racing were getting too close together in the darkness below us. Then we heard a coach boom out in a new kind of a voice, "Easy all, there! Easy all! Look out, Tech crew! Look out, you there!" And into this the coxswains' voices shouting, and other coaches, commands, "Hold her, Starboard! Hold her, Starboard! Hold her all! Look out, for Crissakes, look out!" There was miscellaneous yelling and then a sound as if someone had jumped on an unusually large bass viol. It was a wonderful crash, and it was almost immediately followed by another.

Like reinforcements coming into battle the second set of Harvard racers swept past us, going full tilt. The shouting broke out again, more tumult even than before, and there was a third crash. Then there were a lot of orders and questions being called in the night.

Someone said, "What the hell?"

"They ran into a bunch of Tech crews coming out from their boathouse."

"Let's go down and pitch in."

Ridiculous of course, but one halfway felt like that. A wind from distant, ancient seas seemed to blow across us, the sound of many oars in their locks, the shouting, the crash of galleys ramming . . .

Cox ordered, "Forward all!" We settled into position. It was time to row home, but the quiet paddle upstream seemed strangely tame.

In the due course of time it is given to you to row a race. Not a practice race against one of your own, but the real article, and the oars of the boat taking position on your port side are painted, not crimson, but a fine, shining blue. The feeling of it starts before then, when you take your shell down and toss her better than you ever did before, and you and the managers are in a different, special communion over the free running of your slide, the grease on your oar where it passes through the lock, the comfort of the stretcher into which your feet are laced. The love you bear each man in the boat is stronger, warmer, than it has ever been; it is positive, almost visible. Each man looks smilingly at his neighbour—a curious combination, already the tension and the earnestness is on their faces, but with it comes affection. You shove off and paddle along to the start taking it easily, perfecting your form, the cox saying just what he always says, everything ordinary, everything calming.

Starting an eight-oared race is a frightful job. There is the current, and then there will be a slight cross-wind, something you wouldn't notice if you weren't trying to hold two or more boats as light as cigar-boxes in perfect line beside each other. You jockey and jockey, the good effect of the paddle wears off. You get into position, the starter has asked "Are you ready Harvard? Are you ready Yale?" and one of the shells swings, and it all has to be done over again.

At last you are set. A racing start is entirely different from the ordinary process of getting a shell under way. This time you want to make her fly at full speed from the first stroke, you want to develop speed just as fast as is humanly possible, and faster. You have practised many times the series of short, hard strokes and the lengthening to the full, rhythmed swing but it remains tricky, a complex set of motions to be done so rapidly and hard that it's unreasonable to think it can happen without something going wrong.

Beyond that lies the race, the test itself. You know what a gut-racking process it is, you are too tense about the outcome, you doubt if you can stand up to it. What's ahead of you is too much. There are many things that can postpone a start and several that can cause a race to be called back within the first ten strokes. You pray for them all to happen. You are so taut inside you twang. You are afraid, not of anything, just afraid.

The pistol cracks. You carry out those first three, scrambling strokes neatly, you begin to form the full, balanced stroke as you go on to complete the ten fast ones. All your fears and tremors are gone and you are racing. Coxswain's voice comes, intentionally soothing, carrying you over into the regular swing and beat of the long-term pace your crew must set, you are eight men and you are one, the boat is going with a sizzle, smoothly through the water, and out of the corner of your eye you can see the blue blades flashing alongside you.

The effort settles down and mounts again. There are races within the race, spurts when one crew tries to pull suddenly ahead, and the other answers, the sustained, increasing efforts, the raised beats of the crew behind, the somehow easier but intense drives of the leader. Cox tells you you are past the halfway mark, he tells you you are near the end. The start tests a good crew, the last stretch proves it. You are tired now, everything is coming to a final settlement very soon, you must row harder, faster, and still row smoothly and well. You have got your second wind and used it up, you are pooped out and you know you are at the end of your strength, you simply have nothing left in you. The beat—the rate of the stroke—goes up. Cox is yelling, pleading, advising, cursing. And you are staying with it. On the recovery the captain grunts out something unintelligible but urgent. Near the end other men may wring out cries intended to be "Come on!" "Let's go!" hardly recognizable. There's not much of that, it's against your training and besides wind is too precious, but the pent-up feeling is so strong that sometimes it must have an outlet. This is a good crew, a real one. As the beat is raised, as the reserve behind the reserves of strength is poured in, each stroke taken as if it were the last you'd ever row on earth, the crew still swings together, it is still one, that awareness of each other and merging together is still present and still effective.

Three-quarters of the way through you could hear them on the referee's launch and whatever others are permitted to follow, shouting, "Come on Harvard!" "Come on Yale!" Now you vaguely know that they are still shouting, but you can't really hear them. There is some sort of sound around the finish line, you do not know that a great many people must be making a lot of noise, but you don't hear either. You are conscious of something arching up from the banks which, without looking at it, you see, and you know it's cheering. Your eyes are fixed on the shoulder of the man in front of you and (I rowed starboard side) the blade of Number Seven's oar, but the one thing you do know is exactly where the other boat is. Then here it comes, the final spurt, and you cease to hear or see anything outside your business. Faint and hardly noticeable the pistol fires, then the cox says, "Easy all," and you loll forward.

Done. Like that, done, over, decided. And now you are through, you are truly empty now, you have poured yourself out and for a while you can hardly stand the effort of your own breathing but your tradition despises a man who fails to sit up in the boat. You have known complete exertion, you have answered every trouble of mind, spirit, and being with skilled violence and guided unrestraint, a complete happiness with eight other men over a short stretch of water has brought you catharsis.

University Days [1]

by JAMES THURBER

I PASSED all the other courses that I took at my university, but I could never pass botany. This was because all botany students had to spend several hours a week in a laboratory looking through a microscope at plant cells, and I could never see through a microscope. I never once saw a cell through a microscope. This used to enrage my instructor. He would wander around the laboratory pleased with the progress all the students were making in drawing the involved and, so I am told, interesting structure of flower cells, until he came to me. I would just be standing there. "I can't see anything," I would say. He would begin patiently enough, explaining how anybody can see through a microscope, but he would always end up in a fury, claiming that I could *too* see through a microscope but just pretended that I couldn't. "It takes away from the beauty of flowers anyway," I used to tell him. "We are not concerned with beauty in this course," he would say. "We are concerned solely with what I may call the *mechanics* of flars." "Well," I'd say, "I can't see anything." "Try it just once again," he'd say, and I would put my eye to the microscope and see nothing at all, except now and again, a nebulous milky substance—a phenomenon of maladjustment. You were supposed to see a vivid, restless clockwork of sharply defined plant cells. "I see what looks like a lot of milk," I would tell him. This, he claimed, was the result of my not having adjusted the microscope properly; so he would readjust it for me, or rather, for himself. And I would look again and see milk.

I finally took a deferred pass, as they called it, and waited a year and tried again. (You had to pass one of the biological sciences or you couldn't graduate.) The professor had come back from vacation brown as a berry, bright-eyed, and eager to explain cell-structure again to his classes. "Well," he said to me, cheerily, when we met in the first laboratory hour of the semester, "we're going to see cells this time, aren't we?" "Yes, sir," I said. Students to right of me and to left of me and in front of me were seeing cells; what's more, they were quietly drawing pictures of them in their notebooks. Of course, I didn't see anything.

"We'll try it," the professor said to me, grimly, "with every adjustment of the microscope known to man. As God is my witness, I'll arrange this glass so that you see cells through it or I'll give up teaching. In twenty-two years of botany, I—" He cut off abruptly for he was beginning to quiver all over, like Lionel Barrymore, and he genuinely wished to hold onto his temper; his scenes with me had taken a great deal out of him.

[1] From James Thurber, *My Life and Hard Times* (1933). By permission of the author.

So we tried it with every adjustment of the microscope known to man. With only one of them did I see anything but blackness or the familiar lacteal opacity, and that time I saw, to my pleasure and amazement, a variegated constellation of flecks, specks, and dots. These I hastily drew. The instructor, noting my activity, came back from an adjoining desk, a smile on his lips and his eyebrows high in hope. He looked at my cell drawing. "What's that?" he demanded, with a hint of a squeal in his voice. "That's what I saw," I said. "You didn't, you didn't, you *did*n't!" he screamed, losing control of his temper instantly, and he bent over and squinted into the microscope. His head snapped up. "That's your eye!" he shouted. "You've fixed the lens so that it reflects! You've drawn your eye!"

Another course that I didn't like, but somehow managed to pass, was economics. I went to that class straight from the botany class, which didn't help me any in understanding either subject. I used to get them mixed up. But not as mixed up as another student in my economics class who came there direct from a physics laboratory. He was a tackle on the football team, named Bolenciecwcz. At that time Ohio State University had one of the best football teams in the country, and Bolenciecwcz was one of its outstanding stars. In order to be eligible to play it was necessary for him to keep up in his studies, a very difficult matter, for while he was not dumber than an ox he was not any smarter. Most of his professors were lenient and helped him along. None gave him more hints, in answering questions, or asked him simpler ones than the economics professor, a thin, timid man named Bassum. One day when we were on the subject of transportation and distribution, it came Bolenciecwcz's turn to answer a question. "Name one means of transportation," the professor said to him. No light came into the big tackle's eyes. "Just any means of transportation," said the professor. Bolenciecwcz sat staring at him. "That is," pursued the professor, "any medium, agency, or method of going from one place to another." Bolenciecwcz had the look of a man who is being led into a trap. "You may choose among steam, horse-drawn, or electrically propelled vehicles," said the instructor. "I might suggest the one which we commonly take in making long journeys across land." There was a profound silence in which everybody stirred uneasily, including Bolenciecwcz and Mr. Bassum. Mr. Bassum abruptly broke this silence in an amazing manner. "Choo-choo-choo," he said, in a low voice, and turned instantly scarlet. He glanced appealingly around the room. All of us, of course, shared Mr. Bassum's desire that Bolenciecwcz should stay abreast of the class in economics, for the Illinois game, one of the hardest and most important of the season, was only a week off. "Toot, toot, too-toooooot!" some student with a deep voice moaned, and we all looked encouragingly at Bolenciecwcz. Somebody else gave a fine imitation of a locomotive letting off steam. Mr. Bassum himself rounded off the little show. "Ding, dong, ding, dong," he said, hopefully. Bolenciecwcz was staring at the floor now, trying to think, his great brow furrowed, his huge hands rubbing together, his face red.

"How did you come to college this year, Mr. Bolenciecwcz?" asked the professor. "*Chuf*fa chuffa, *chuf*fa chuffa."

"M'father sent me," said the football player.

"What on?" asked Bassum.

"I git an 'lowance," said the tackle, in a low, husky voice, obviously embarrassed.

"No, no," said Bassum. "Name a means of transportation. What did you *ride* here on?"

"Train," said Bolenciecwcz.

"Quite right," said the professor. "Now, Mr. Nugent, will you tell us—"

If I went through anguish in botany and economics—for different reasons—gymnasium work was even worse. I don't even like to think about it. They wouldn't let you play games or join in the exercises with your glasses on and I couldn't see with mine off. I bumped into professors, horizontal bars, agricultural students, and swinging iron rings. Not being able to see, I could take it but I couldn't dish it out. Also, in order to pass gymnasium (and you had to pass it to graduate) you had to learn to swim if you didn't know how. I didn't like the swimming pool, I didn't like swimming, and I didn't like the swimming instructor, and after all these years I still don't. I never swam but I passed my gym work anyway, by having another student give my gymnasium number (978) and swim across the pool in my place. He was a quiet, amiable blonde youth, number 473, and he would have seen through a microscope for me if we could have got away with it, but we couldn't get away with it. Another thing I didn't like about gymnasium work was that they made you strip the day you registered. It is impossible for me to be happy when I am stripped and being asked a lot of questions. Still, I did better than a lanky agricultural student who was cross-examined just before I was. They asked each student what college he was in—that is, whether Arts, Engineering, Commerce, or Agriculture. "What college are you in?" the instructor snapped at the youth in front of me. "Ohio State University," he said promptly.

It wasn't that agricultural student but it was another a whole lot like him who decided to take up journalism, possibly on the ground that when farming went to hell he could fall back on newspaper work. He didn't realize, of course, that that would be very much like falling back full-length on a kit of carpenter's tools. Haskins didn't seem cut out for journalism, being too embarrassed to talk to anybody and unable to use a typewriter, but the editor of the college paper assigned him to the cow barns, the sheep house, the horse pavilion, and the animal husbandry department generally. This was a genuinely big "beat," for it took up five times as much ground and got ten times as great a legislative appropriation as the College of Liberal Arts. The agricultural student knew animals, but nevertheless his stories were dull and colorlessly written. He took all afternoon on each of them, because he had to hunt for each letter on the typewriter. Once in a while he had to ask somebody to help him hunt. "C" and "L," in particular, were hard letters for him to find. His editor finally got pretty much annoyed at the farmer-journalist because his pieces were so uninteresting. "See here, Haskins," he snapped at him one day, "why is it we never have anything hot from you on the horse pavilion? Here we have two hundred head of horses on this campus—more than any other university in the Western Conference except Purdue—and yet you never get any real low-down on them. Now shoot over to the horse barns and dig up something lively." Haskins shambled out and came back in about an hour; he said he had something. "Well, start it off snappily," said the editor. "Something people will read." Haskins set to work and in a couple of hours brought a sheet of typewritten paper to the desk; it was a two-hundred word story about some disease that had broken out among the horses. Its opening sentence was simple but arresting. It read: "Who has noticed the sores on the tops of the horses in the animal husbandry building?"

Ohio State was a land grant university and therefore two years of military drill was compulsory. We drilled with old Springfield rifles and studied the tactics of the Civil War even though the World War was going on at the time. At 11 o'clock each morning thousands of freshmen and sophomores used to deploy over the campus, moodily creeping up on the old chemistry building. It was good training for the kind of warfare that was waged at Shiloh but it had no connection with what was going on in Europe. Some people used to think there was German money behind it, but they didn't dare say so or they would have been thrown in jail as German spies. It was a period of muddy thought and marked, I believe, the decline of higher education in the Middle West.

As a soldier I was never any good at all. Most of the cadets were glumly indifferent soldiers, but I was no good at all. Once General Littlefield, who was commandant of the cadet corps, popped up in front of me during regimental drill and snapped, "You are the main trouble with this university!" I think he meant that my type was the main trouble with the university but he may have meant me individually. I was mediocre at drill, certainly— that is, until my senior year. By that time I had drilled longer than anybody else in the Western Conference, having failed at military at the end of each preceding year so that I had to do it all over again. I was the only senior still in uniform. The uniform which, when new, had made me look like an interurban railway conductor, now that it had become faded and too tight, made me look like Bert Williams in his bell-boy act. This had a definitely bad effect on my morale. Even so, I had become by sheer practise little short of wonderful at squad manoeuvres.

One day General Littlefield picked our company out of the whole regiment and tried to get it mixed up by putting it through one movement after another as fast as we could execute them: squads right, squads left, squads on right into line, squads right about, squads left front into line, etc. In about three minutes one hundred and nine men were marching in one direction and I was marching away from them at an angle of forty-five degrees, all alone. "Company, halt!" shouted General Littlefield, "That man is the only man who has it right!" I was made a corporal for my achievement.

The next day General Littlefield summoned me to his office. He was swatting flies when I went in. I was silent and he was silent too, for a long time. I don't think he remembered me or why he had sent for me, but he didn't want to admit it. He swatted some more flies, keeping his eyes on them narrowly before he let go with the swatter. "Button up your coat!" he snapped. Looking back on it now I can see that he meant me although he was looking at a fly, but I just stood there. Another fly came to rest on a paper in front of the general and began rubbing its hind legs together. The general lifted the swatter cautiously. I moved restlessly and the fly flew away. "You startled him!" barked General Littlefield, looking at me severely. I said I was sorry. "That won't help the situation!" snapped the General, with cold military logic. I didn't see what I could do except offer to chase some more flies toward his desk, but I didn't say anything. He stared out the window at the faraway figures of co-eds crossing the campus toward the library. Finally, he told me I could go. So I went. He either didn't know which cadet I was or else he forgot what he wanted to see me about. It may have been that he wished to apologize for having called me the main trouble with the university; or maybe he had decided to compliment me on my brilliant drilling of the day before and then at the last minute decided not to. I don't know. I don't think about it much any more.

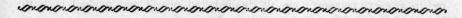

The Modern Gothic [1]

by VINCENT SHEEAN

THE armistice came when I was eighteen. What it meant to the war generation I can only imagine from the stories they tell; to me it meant that we in the University of Chicago, that mountain range of twentieth-century Gothic near the shores of Lake Michigan, went out of uniform and into civilian clothes.

The world has changed so much that it seems downright indecent to tell the truth: I was sorry when the war ended. I fumed with disappointment on the night of the false armistice—the celebrated night when the American newspapers reported the end of the war some days before it happened. We were all patriots then. We knew nothing about that horror and degradation which our elders who had been through the war were to put before us so unremittingly for the next fifteen years. There were millions of us, young

[1] From Vincent Sheean, *Personal History*, copyright 1934, 1935, reprinted by permission of Doubleday & Company, Inc.

Americans between the ages of fifteen or sixteen and eighteen or nineteen, who cursed freely all through the middle weeks of November. We felt cheated. We had been put into uniform with the definite promise that we were to be trained as officers and sent to France. In my case, as in many others, this meant growing up in a hurry, sharing the terrors and excitements of a life so various, free and exalted that it was worth even such hardships as studying trigonometry. So we went into uniform and marched about the place from class to class like students in a military academy; listened to learned professors lecturing about something called "War Aims"; lived in "barracks"; did rifle drill. The rifles were dummies, and the "barracks" were only the old dormitories rechristened, but such details made little difference. We played at being soldiers for a few months with tremendous seriousness, and then the glorious uproar to which we had been preparing our approach suddenly died down. Our part of the war had been a prelude to something that did not take place.

And when demobilization came at last the prospect of returning to the regular life of the University had become repellent to me. I had nobody to persuade but my mother, who was still too thankful for the Armistice to make many objections. Consequently I went job hunting and spent three months as secretary to a millionaire builder and real estate operator in the Chicago financial district. It was there, hanging out a window above the crevasse of LaSalle Street, that I watched the Black Hawk Division come home. Waving flags and the thump of a military march were enough to stir me to any extravagance; we all shouted and waved and winked back the hysterical tears. Those were patriotic days.

My employer was an odious little man who had quarreled with his wife and disinherited his son because the latter wanted to go on the stage. He was a brilliant entrepreneur, the little man: he used to point with pride to the ceilings of the skyscraper in which he had his office, saying, "That ceiling is a good six inches shallower than the law allows. You can always arrange things if you know how. I got eight extra storeys into this building by that little detail." When I inquired if the building was likely to fall down he sniffed contemptuously. "Buildings don't fall down," he said. The building did start to fall down some years later, was condemned and demolished. By an unfortunate accident, its builder was not buried under the ruins.

He sent me on one occasion to collect rents from the impoverished tenants of a village he owned in Indiana. It was a horrible experience from which I escaped as quickly as I could, but the thought of it came back to me for years. The tenants of the wretched little Indiana town worked in a coal mine belonging to my employer when they worked at all, but they had not worked for many months. They lived in houses belonging to him (if you could call such hovels houses) and bought their food from stores belonging to him. I was to collect what I could of the back rent owed on the disgraceful shacks in which they were obliged to live. I was a failure at the job, for the sight of the life into which children were there being born disorganized whatever efficiency I possessed as a secretary. That day in the little mining town was my introduction to capitalism at work, and it filled me, even then, with disgust. I blamed the busy little entrepreneur as well as the system of which he was a part, and it was not long before the idea of continuing to work for him became insupportable. "Business" (if this was business) bored, irked, and revolted me, and I determined to do whatever I could to avoid being involved in it again.

In the spring of 1919, therefore, I went back to the University and stayed on throughout the summer to make up for lost time. My education up to then had been a sorry failure. I had never made any headway with science, mathematics or the classical languages. Of the first two I remembered nothing; of the second I remembered just one Greek sentence, *enteuthen exelaunei* ("and the next day he marched onward")—this not because it had any stirring significance for me, but because it marked the welcome end of nearly every chapter in the *Anabasis*.

I had derived, it was true, considerable pleasure of a low order from some other academic pursuits in my first two years of college. I had come to the University knowing some Italian, German, and French (particularly French), and could easily make a better showing in these subjects than my contemporaries. My favourite trick had been to register for courses in which I was unlikely to encounter anything I did not already know. Such conduct was lazy and dishonest, but you could make out a good case for the theory that young people were all lazy and dishonest when they could be. Certainly what the undergraduates called "snaps" (i. e., courses easy to get through without undue effort) were always crowded in my day at the University. The football players, the social lights, the pretty co-eds, and all the other students who regarded study as an inconvenient detail in college life, rushed to inscribe themselves for "snap" courses. I was in a more advantageous position than some of my fellows for wasting time, since more courses were "snaps" for me. I could go to a series of lectures on Victorian Prose, for example, and be confident of hearing nothing new; similarly, in French, with the novels of Victor Hugo or the plays of Molière. I had read altogether too much in the two languages, thanks to a bookish childhood. There was thus a group of studies open to me at the University in which I could, without working or learning, impress my instructors sufficiently to make a good record.

More than two years of my three and a half at the University of Chicago had already been wasted in this way. It was a kind of confidence game of which the victim was, of course, myself. I did well enough in the subjects I already knew to make up for my failures in the subjects I did not know and was too lazy to study. I was too undisciplined, too indolent, and too dishonest to force myself to learn what did not interest me. And it was not until that summer of 1919 that I began to realize the silliness of such an approach to what ought to be one of the great experiences of a life. The University of Chicago in summer was invaded by hordes of earnest men and women from the smaller colleges and schools of the Middle West, working towards their master's or their doctor's degree. These thin, spectacled myrmidons, humpbacked from carrying armfuls of books up and down academic steps for many years, filled the cool gray corridors and covered the green lawns I had always thought reserved for pretty girls and long-legged youths. The summer school, I discovered, was an altogether different affair from the ordinary academic year. If you tried to talk to a summer student during a lecture, a cold glance through glittering spectacles was the only reply. The brilliant hot sun of a Chicago July threw into merciless relief all the unloveliness of these dank visitors from the provincial colleges of Indiana, Wisconsin, Illinois, Iowa, and Minnesota. Their presence was somehow unbecoming, both to their surroundings and to the general fitness of things. I resented them for two or three weeks, and on the few occasions when I saw my vacationing friends, the undergraduates who had finished their college year in June, we were exceedingly witty about the looks, manners, lives, and minds of the pitiable summer students. There were probably not half a dozen of these book worms, we calculated, who could dance the fox trot decently.

But as the summer study advanced I became more and more uncomfortable about them. They were not beautiful, but neither were they ignorant. They were always putting me to shame, somehow or other. I was not to remember much about most of the studies of that summer; only one was vivid in retrospect. It was a fairly advanced course in French—the poetry of Victor Hugo, all of it, including every pitiless line of *La Légende des Siècles*. The instructor was a visiting bigwig from one of the Eastern universities, a Frenchman with a German name. He used to conduct the course in an informal fashion, lecturing some of the time, reading occasionally, and starting discussions whenever the spirit moved him. It was assumed that students in such a course as this would be mature and educated enough to know something besides the actual subject matter itself. Comparisons were always popping up, were constantly invited. Most of the students—there may have been twelve or fifteen, men and women—were well past thirty, and probably all of them taught French literature somewhere or other. In that company, through July and August, I first began to be ashamed of my evil ways, and no amount of smug scorn for the bookworms could disguise the fact.

"Vous trouverez ici sans doute que Hugo a beaucoup emprunté à Chateaubriand; n'est-ce pas, Mademoiselle?" the professor would inquire innocently, smiling across his desk at an eager spinster from Indiana. And then off she would go, talking about Hugo and Chateaubriand in a French accent that would have been incomprehensible to either of those gentlemen—but talking, just the same, with information and intelligence. The professor would argue with her; others would join in; and it appalled me that I could not even follow their battle from afar. I had never read a word of Chateaubriand; my interest in Christianity was almost nonexistent; I had no real idea why it had ever seemed intellectually important to Victor Hugo or to anybody else. And I looked at the summer students in amazements. Their excitement over such subjects actually brought color to their wan faces; they could smile, make jokes, go through all the movements of living organisms when their attention was aroused.

My salvation was that the instructor was a Frenchman. If he had been an American or an Englishman he would have seen at once that my glibness in French was a sheer accident, and that I actually understood nothing of the turmoil through which Victor Hugo had lived and written. But, being French, the professor had a natural prejudice in favor of hearing his language pronounced correctly. In spite of all their knowledge and interest, most of the students in this course had abominable accents; it seemed to be a rule among American school teachers. I had learned French so young that all the laziness in the world could never rob me of a fairly good pronunciation. Consequently, when I had occasion to read some of Victor Hugo's detested verses aloud, the professor would lean back in his chair with satisfaction. This, combined with a prudent silence when the discussions were out of my depth, gave the good man the idea that I really knew something of the subject, and I finished the course with an unjustifiably handsome record.

But something important happened to me during the summer of 1919, thanks chiefly to the Hugo poems. I had been realizing with increasing clarity, week after week, the superficial character of my own mind. I was nineteen, and I knew nothing. The fact that I could speak a sort of French had nothing to do with me; what credit there might be for that should have gone to the devout and kindly Irish priest who had tutored me in it for years. Of the actual meaning of French literature I knew far less than the scrubbiest high-school teacher from Iowa. The struggles of men's minds—whether of contemporary minds or of those like Chateaubriand's and Hugo's, long gone to dust—meant nothing to me at all. I had existed without realizing that it seriously mattered to anybody what men believed, or under what form of government, in what structure of society, they lived. The summer's study gave me no love for the poetry of Victor Hugo: on the contrary, the mere thought of La Légende des Siècles made me feel slightly uneasy for years to come. But I did derive from it some idea of what the process of literature could be —some hint of the stormy sincerity in which minds like Hugo's sought for the truth. The suggestion, however dim, was sufficient reward for the boredom of reading what then seemed to me an intolerable quantity of pompous, overstuffed verse.

My ideas of what I might get out of the University thereafter submitted to rearrangement. Words could no longer suffice: I understood Hugo's words well enough, the upholstery of his mind, but it was the mind itself that escaped me. If a mind of Hugo's quality was incomprehensible, how could I expect to know anything about the rarer minds that did (even then) seem to me most worth the effort of comprehension: Molière, Racine, Shakespeare? And, even in a world I found tiresome beyond my powers of resistance, the world of the "Victorian Prose Writers," what could I hope to understand by words alone? It was clear, after the Hugo experience, that literature involved something at once more complex and more ordinary, more closely related to the whole life of mankind, than the science of stringing words together in desirable sequences, however fascinating the contemplation of such patterns might seem to a bookish and word-conscious nature.

Nothing could be learned about literature by studying literature: that was what it came to. Courses in literature seldom took on the vitality of that special Hugo course with its special participants. In general, they were either arranged to suit average students with no interest in the subject, or specialists with an interest so minute that it was (in my view) equivalent to no interest at all. I had no desire to count the feminine endings in the lines of the Canterbury Tales. What I wanted to know—in so far as I really wanted to know anything about them—was why the Canterbury Tales were written; what mysterious springs existed in the mind and heart of a man named Geoffrey Chaucer to bring forth such a particular stream of articulated language; what the world was like for which he wrote, in which he lived, and what was his particular struggle with it. Professors did sometimes try to convey this sort of information; but it was obvious that they had obtained it elsewhere and were passing it on in capsule form. Where had they obtained it?

History, perhaps, was the answer; philosophy might be part of it.

That autumn, when the regular academic year began, I switched from the faculties of English literature and Romance languages to those of history and philosophy. And perhaps if this had been the arrangement two years before I might not have wasted quite so much time.

I am not suggesting that I became a model of industry and scholarship promptly at nine o'clock on the morning of registration day in October, 1919. I still frittered away a good three quarters or four fifths of my time, still registered for an occasional course of lectures that could be treated cavalierly as a "snap" (History of Venetian Art, for instance). But at least I was not behaving altogether as if the University were a country club. Both in history and in philosophy I learned something—not much, but something. There was a course in Plato that conveyed meaning to me; another, on the German idealists, I found as exciting as a romantic novel. But perhaps the most interesting of all—the one to be recalled most often in subsequent life—was a term of lectures and reading on the Decline of the Ottoman Empire.

This—an "advanced," and therefore a rather small, class—was in charge of an inspired teacher. I never knew what made the difference between a good and a bad teacher, but I did know that Ferdinand Schevill was a superlatively good one. He was a German, short and rather formidable in appearance, with eyeglasses and a neatly trimmed Vandyke beard. His university was Heidelberg or Bonn, I believe, and yet he had none of that pedantry which is supposed to be the vice of German scholarship. When he led us through the immense and complicated story of the decay that fell upon Suleiman's empire after the seventeenth century he did not try to treat it microscopically as an isolated phenomenon. He talked about the Arabs, the Turks, the Balkan peoples, as if they were alive; and they soon began to come to life for me. Schevill's system was to allow his students to read at will through the whole literature of the subject, and therefrom to choose, halfway through the course, a particular aspect for further reading and a final paper. I began to read everything I could find about the Asiatic empire of the Turks. Almost from the first day that side of the Bosphorus seemed to me of greater interest than this. I extended my researches to the files of newspapers and magazines, and when it came time to choose, I took for my term paper the history of the Wahabite movement.

An odder choice for a nineteen-year-old undergraduate at the University of Chicago would be hard to imagine. Ibn es-Sa'ud was then almost unknown to the Western world, and the literature on the Wahabi was scarce indeed. I read everything I could find in English, French, or German, and performed the best piece of honest work I had ever done. For a few weeks, while I was reading in the library, I nearly persuaded myself that I was living in Arabia, and sometimes the vast cloaks and camel turbans of the Bedawin seemed more real than the swishing skirts of the co-eds going by. Later on I obtained permission to go down into the stacks of that huge library—steel stacks with glass floors running among them, layer upon layer. The world's knowledge lay there like a sunken continent swimming in subaqueous light, and through its fields I ranged more or less at will. My interest in Islam, such as it was, began that year, and what I learned in Schevill's course was never wholly forgotten. If other teachers had been like him, other subjects as vivid to me as the disintegration of Turkey became, I might have learned more in my long sojourn under the sham-Gothic towers.

Flyers Are Inarticulate[1]

by BEIRNE LAY, JR.

A TINY inky shadow lurked there motionless, sitting by itself out in front of the hangar. It was an Army pursuit ship. An open cockpit single-seater—a P-6. A howling bullet, resting bare and silent on the cold ground.

I shivered a bit in the shoulder muscles. *That* was my transportation for the night. I had to take a two hundred and fifty-mile jump through the November darkness in *that* thing before I'd be warm in bed at Langley Field, Virginia. As I stood there eyeing the P-6 warily the palms of my hands were wet; I felt rigid in the stomach and uncomfortable.

I was an Army pilot. Why did I feel that way? Why the wet palms? Perhaps you won't believe me when I tell you. But you might as well know what I'm talking about, so here's the case for the defense.

[1] From Beirne Lay, Jr., *I Wanted Wings* (1937). By permission of Harper & Brothers.

I had flown the P-6 up to Philadelphia earlier in the afternoon with a manuscript and turned it over to a magazine editor. It was an article called "Aerobatics, Thirty Minutes," later published in HARPER's, and was an experiment—an attempt to convey in print the detailed sensations of stunting a P-6.

The first draft of the article had been pretty bad. As I read it over, I realized that it didn't convey anything—didn't capture the sensation of flying. I had not been able to inject imagination into it. So I got a P-6 next morning and went through all the maneuvers I had wanted to describe, including a terminal velocity power dive and pull-out, *with a deliberate eye to perceiving and recording in my brain the sensations I had experienced*. I came down with my imagination alive for the first time since I had learned to fly, and hammered those sensations out on my portable with sweat streaming down my cheeks.

That did two things to me. It released an ordinarily repressed emotional reaction to flight and it ripped away the flyer's defense mechanism against fear of falling and of speed. Fear of falling, although you probably don't remember it, was the first instinct you had as a baby. But it is one which must be suppressed in aviation. From the day flyers first strap themselves in a bucket seat, listen to a good deal of rough language, and learn what to do with a stick, rudder, and throttle, they are forced to forget that there is any hazard connected with plummeting toward the scenery from fifteen thousand feet at three hundred miles per hour. And they become inarticulate where flight sensation is concerned. Why? Because you must imagine, *visualize*, intensely before you can express yourself vividly, either by the spoken or written word. But the flyer has learned *not* to visualize what he is doing. It is a subconscious safety compensation. This explains why it is so hard to get a flyer to describe a harrowing personal experience in more eloquent terms than "the wings came off, so I bailed out."

I didn't realize I had stirred up trouble for myself when I wrote that stunting article, but I knew something was wrong as soon as I took off in the P-6 for Philadelphia, eager to release the masterpiece to a breathless reading public. The ship didn't feel right. It felt too sensitive on the controls. Unstable. I worried unaccountably about a dozen little things. The slightly high oil temperature, the dearth of landing fields sliding past below, the question whether I should be able to get down into one of them without cracking up if the engine cut, the slight changes in note of the six-hundred-horsepower Conqueror engine when we passed over an air bump. I was even a little air sick, and I'd never been nauseated in the air before, except once down at flying school—after I did fifteen slow rolls in succession with gas spraying in my face from the top tank air-vent.

I dismissed my uneasiness with the thought that I wasn't really at home in a Pursuit ship. I was a bombardment pilot. But I hadn't guessed what the trouble was. I didn't realize it fully until I was sitting in the crowded bus, returning to Camden airport. It hit me then in a flash. I knew that the trip back was going to be much worse than the trip up. Call it a delayed reaction.

I saw myself all of a sudden in a queer light. There I sat, an average person with two hands and two feet, rolling along securely in a bus filled with other average people with two hands and two feet. The rest of those sensible people were going to leave the bus and walk up the good solid sidewalk to a cabbage supper and Major Bowes' hour, or they were bound for Camden, where they would let a crack airline take care of them. But what was I going to do? I was going to strap myself into a tiny cockpit and let six hundred detonating horsepower yank me off the ground and up into the sky at one hundred and seventy miles per hour—at night too, when you can't see much —and I was going to try to set myself down on a spot of light two hundred and fifty miles away. I thought of it that way instead of as a routine "night cross country from Camden to Langley." I realized for the first time *exactly what I was going to do,* with all its implications of danger, with *your* eyes.

Naturally I said with my mind: "You know how to fly. You've done this plenty of times before. Don't be a damned fool." But it was no use. I had tampered with the mental machinery just to write an article, and knocked away the bars of a circus cage holding a black leopard. I was a prey to incongruous forebodings that had long ago been buried and forgotten. As I stood there looking down at the P-6 parked in front of that dark hulking hangar, I was positive I wasn't safe to fly. And I *wasn't.* Still it didn't seem "safe" either to send a telegram to the Commanding Officer, Langley Field, and say: "RETURNING BY TRAIN STOP SEND PILOT FERRY P-6 LANGLEY STOP AFRAID FLY BACK STOP LAY."

In the dispatcher's room the weather man turned away from his teletype machines and sputtering radio receivers to give me a weather report. Visibility was good all the way down the line, with ceiling unlimited except for scattered clouds at 3,000 over Washington. So that was that. The weather offered no excuse.

I left a departure message for Langley, via Bolling Field, and walked down to where the P-6 was waiting. Inside the hangar a mechanic unlocked the wooden toolchest in which I had left my flight gear. "I'd warm the ship up for you, Mister," he said, "but I don't know how to *start* one of them peashooters."

Very deliberately, I stripped off my uniform blouse, and, shivering in my shirtsleeves, folded it and handed it to the mechanic. He took it out and stowed it in the baggage compartment behind the pilot's seat in the P-6. I stepped into the warm leather flying trousers, lined with gray fur, and wriggled into the winter flying jacket with the big fur collar. The shivering didn't stop though, even after I'd twined the white silk scarf round my throat and, sitting on the toolchest, pulled on the sheepskin flying moccasins, and stood up, armored in warmth. Those moccasins are great, but just then they didn't seem warm enough.

I removed my flight cap, folded it flat and stuck it in a knee pocket. From the other knee pocket I extracted a pack of cigarettes, lit up, and walked out toward the P-6, carrying the rest of my gear—parachute, radio helmet, fur gloves, map, and flashlight. I tossed the cigarette away after a couple more puffs, swung a leg up over the fuselage, lowered myself into the dark, deep, narrow cockpit, and switched on the cockpit light.

A scattering of radium-coated needles glimmered from behind their glass dials in the black metal instrument board, and countless little gadgets gleamed in the shadows round my knees—cold-metal oil-smelling gadgets. The mechanic stepped up on the wing and tugged at the crank of the inertia starter until he had its whining gears revolving at top speed. "Contact!" he yelled.

I turned on the reserve gas tank, the ignition switch, the starter toggle-switch, and kicked my padded right toe against the starter cable beyond the rudder pedal—all as though someone were leaning over me and telling me what to do.

The Conqueror caught like a short string of firecrackers.

Its 600 H.P. settled down to purring smoothly. I warmed her up slowly for ten minutes, shoved the throttle forward, and let her race wide open, while I tried each ignition switch, noted the R.P.M. (engine revolutions per minute) and the oil pressure, and listened for a sour note. There was none. The thunder of explosions was rhythmic and full-bodied.

I retarded the throttle to idling speed, glanced out at the short-clipped shiny yellow wings, and wiggled the ailerons. I looked back over my shoulder and waggled the rudder and flippers, and, as an extra precaution, climbed out of the ship again and checked the parachute flare, to make doubly sure that it was "armed." The flare is "safetied" in the daytime, so that it will not ignite if accidentally dropped.

I strapped myself in tight with the safety belt, motioned the chocks away, and taxied out toward a dark far corner of the field, where the longest runway into the wind began. The floodlights flowed out, cast the shadow of my head against the side of the windshield and the trailing edge of the top wing, and guided me to the center of the wide, gravelly runway strip, as I swung round and paused, aimed at the floodlights. A "shadow bar" in the center of the lights prevented the glare from blinding me and illuminated the tapering avenue in front of me. I was warm all over now in my heavy flying clothes, but my feet trembled against the rudder pedals with convulsive jerks—enough to jitter the pedals back and forth. Bad business. You can't have your feet jittering in a P-6. Its rudder, in the air, is sensitive and responds quick as thought.

I stamped my feet on the flooring and placed them against the pedals again, but they jittered as before if I relaxed them; and you have to relax them to feel the airplane. All right then, I'd have to push hard against the pedals. I tried it and the trembling stopped. But that meant I'd have to take off mechanically, without feeling the ship, when I skimmed along with my tail up, gathering speed.

I moved the throttle forward and catapulted down the runway, feet braced solidly, weaving badly, as I tried to hold the nose straight mechanically—correcting a swerve only after it had begun, visually, instead of *feeling* it before it started. In my anxiety to get off the ground before a really bad swerve got out of hand, I pulled the stick back and staggered off in a skid, and with a bare minimum of speed, hurtling forward into a vague blare of light, with shadows streaking by close under the wings.

I straightened out of the skid, partly by a desperate glance at the bank-and-turn indicator, climbed in a quivering rush of speed up over the glistening smear of lights that blazed from the congested area of Camden and nearby Philadelphia, and took up the compass course that would lead me down the string of rotating beacons to Bolling Field, Washington. I kept on climbing, far above the necessary altitude, until I was at 7,000 feet. I wanted that extra height to give me lots of time in case anything should happen. But why was I afraid something was going to happen?

Why did it seem like madness to entrust my life to the proper functioning of an engine built and cared for by fallible human hands—to a little stream of sparks flickering from the sparkplugs up front—a little stream of sparks suspending me tenuously above the inky blackness thousands of feet below, but only so long as they continued to flicker? Why did it seem like curious optimism to depend on the weather's not changing its mind and stirring up some nasty concoction between me and Bolling Field? Why, only a few minutes out of Camden, was I already worrying about landing safely at Bolling? I hadn't landed a P-6 at night before, it was true, but I had landed a P-12 several times at night a year before, and there wasn't much difference between a P-6 and a P-12. Why wasn't I all right once in the air, as I'd expected I'd be?

The uneasiness increased with the miles that clicked by. I looked down at the double railroad bridge at Havre de Grace, and farther on, at the car headlights below me on the main highway near Aberdeen—looked down at sensible people with good solid ground under them. The tiny white Capitol Dome of Washington presently rose out of the broad flat glow beyond the nose to the right, and then I could see the red and green boundary lights that outlined Bolling Field, off to the left.

I tightened my belt another notch, broke into a sweat, eased the throttle back, and nosed down in a power glide that would bring me over Bolling at 2,000 feet. As I came over the field, I looked down below the trailing edge of the wing and cussed at what I saw down there—a sprinkling of red lanterns, dotting nearly its entire area, placed there to mark off runways under construction and soft spots from recent rains. I dropped down and circled to have a better look. Apparently there was only one small strip, running along close to the hangar line, available for landings. I thought of going on over to Washington-Hoover airport but decided against it. There was a mess of red tape connected with purchasing gasoline away from Army fields; and besides, Bolling had not been declared unsafe for landings.

I slowed the P-6 down to 90 and circled the field twice more. The floodlights came on. Everything looked wrong. The field was too small. My speed seemed too high—things happened in too rapid sequence—and the motor sounded funny. Height and distance looked wrong. This was going to be a mechanical landing, like the mechanical take-off. Why couldn't I slow the ship down anyway so that I could have time to see what I was doing, instead of barging down into that confusion of red lanterns at 65 miles an hour?

I knew how to make a mechanical landing—the kind those lazy airline pilots make. I flew far downwind of the field and started a long, low, straight-away approach, with a little power on and a little excess speed. "Low and fast" gives you better control and is safer at night than trying to land out of a normal slow glide. The low approach keeps you from over-shooting, and the excess speed keeps you from dropping in if you level off too high.

The blot of the floodlights swelled out in front of the nose close ahead and I could see that I was down to about fifty feet, with the ground skipping by like a jackrabbit. "You're doing 140!" I yelled inwardly. I glanced at the air-speed indicator. Only 85. "Somebody's crazy!" I cut the gun all the way back and nosed down till I was skimming along just above the ground. I kept the nose pointed at a cluster of red lights in the distance. Another glance at the air-speed. It was 70. "You've lost all your speed—you'll spin in before you reach the edge of the light." I gave a quick burst of the gun to carry me fifty yards farther, still holding the ship just off the ground. I reached the edge of the light clearing, eased the stick all the way back into my gut—and waited.

The nose reared up high in front of me in full landing position, obstructing forward vision, so I looked out the side toward the hangar line, feeling helpless and blind and scared. A wing started to drop. Awkwardly I picked it up. I had a sinking feeling—seemed to be sinking into a bottomless pit. Endless seconds passed. I touched bottom. I was "on."

A red flag whipped past under the left wing and then two more, beneath the right wing. Had I landed in a danger area? I wanted to tramp the brakes, but the ground felt soft, and I was afraid of a nose-over. I waited until the P-6 had slowed down to thirty or forty, then eased on the brakes, and came to a stop with the wheels sinking in. It was muddy all right.

I taxied over to where a mechanic on the line was waving his flashlight and rolled to a stop. I clambered out and stretched, glad to be on the old sod again.

"Fill her up," I said, and waited expectantly for the mechanic to comment about my having landed on the worst part of the field. No comment.

"Corporal," I said, "the field looks pretty bad out there. What's the safest part to use?"

"Lieutenant," he said, "you landed on it." I scratched my head.

Ten minutes later I was back at 7,000 feet again, with the big bend in the Potomac River near Dahlgren Naval Air Station creeping in under me. I felt a little better. I had got up and got down again to-night—and off again once more. All I had to do now was get down once more. Yes, I felt reassured, but I was still having a bad time with my nervous system.

A late moon had cut a round white hole in the sky off to the east, shedding enough light so that down below I could see the thin smokelike scattered clouds floating half way between me and the chromium-plated highway of the Potomac. Isolated, huge white cumulus clouds towered up above my altitude a few miles farther down the course—ghostly promontories in a setting of luminous vastness. Grandeur like that would thrill a blind man, and I was beginning to half-enjoy it and relax a little when, without a mite of warning, the Conqueror engine cut cold, the echo of its explosions still seeming to linger in a silence that was like the grave.

I sat there frozen, feeling as if my heart had stopped, listening to the suddenly audible shrill of the wind through the wires, listening to that abrupt awful silence.

Even as I swung my head round toward Dahlgren to see if I could reach it, the Conqueror sputtered and broke out in full cry again and, in amazement, I realized that my fingers were on the gasoline valve. *Without knowing it* I had instantly switched tanks after the engine cut. The faithful habits born of hundreds of hours at the controls had been standing at my elbow all the time to-night, invisible, but on the job. They were stronger than imagination or fear. Suddenly I knew it.

I relaxed—completely—drew a deep breath of relief and let a big grin spread over my face. I was all right. And so, apparently, was the Conqueror, which continued to flog away in a determined manner. A vapor lock in the gas line from the belly tank had probably cut off the gas supply until I changed tanks, but that seemed unimportant now. What was important was that I was in command of myself again.

Of course I sat down at Langley without any more grief, and *of course* I pulled off some night aerobatics on the way, snap-rolling at the moon and tobogganing down a few cloud "snowdrifts." And *of course* flyers are inarticulate. Wouldn't you be?

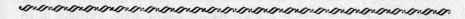

Brave Men [1]

by ERNIE PYLE

ONE OF the most fabulous characters in that war theatre was Lieutenant Rudolf Charles von Ripper. He was so fabulous, a man might have been justified in thinking him a phony until he got to know him. I had known him since the previous summer in Algeria. Most of the other correspondents knew him. One whole fighting infantry division knew him. He was no phony.

[1] From Ernie Pyle, *Brave Men* (1943). By permission of Henry Holt & Co.

Von Ripper was the kind they write books about. He was born in Austria. His father was a general in the Imperial Austrian Army, his mother a baroness. They had money. He could have had a rich, formal, royal type of existence. Instead he ran away from home at fifteen, worked in the sawmills, collected garbage, was a coal miner for a while, and then a clown in a small travelling circus. At nineteen he went into the French Foreign Legion, served two years, and was wounded in action. After that he went back to Europe and studied art. He was first of all an artist.

He travelled continuously. He lived in London and Paris. He lived in Shanghai during 1928. Then he returned to Berlin, joined liberal groups, and did occasional cartoons. Because he helped friends hiding from the Nazis, he was arrested in 1933, accused of high treason, and sent to a concentration camp. Dollfuss of Austria got him out after seven months. Then he went to the Balearic Islands off the coast of Spain and hibernated for a year, doing political, satiric drawing.

During his entire life he had fluctuated between these two extremes of salon intellectualism and the hard, brutal reality of personal participation in war. You don't think of an artist as being tough or worldly; yet Von Ripper had been shot in battle more than twenty times. In 1936 he went to Spain as an aerial gunner in the Loyalist air force. He got sixteen slugs in his leg during that adventure, and barely came out alive.

Back in Austria in 1938, he saw that there was no possibility of organizing even a token resistance against Hitler, so he left for America. He became an American citizen five years later. By that time he was a private in the United States Army.

His army career was a curious one. First he was a hospital laboratory technician. Then he was transferred to the newly formed Army Art Corps, and left for North Africa in May of 1943 to paint battle pictures for the War Department. I happened to meet him a few days after he arrived overseas. He had hardly got started on his art work when Congress abolished the whole program. So he went back to being a regular soldier again, this time as an infantry-man. He was transferred to the Thirty-fourth Division.

In the fall of '43 he was put in a front-line regiment, and in October he was wounded by shell splinters. He didn't seem to mind being shot at all. A month later, while leading a night patrol, he got four machine-pistol slugs in him. One slug split his upper lip just where it joined his nose. Another ripped a deep groove in the back of his hand. Another shot one finger clear off at the first joint. The fourth went through his shoulder. Before all his bandages were off he was back patrolling again.

Up to that time he had been a sergeant, but then he was given a battlefield commission as second lieutenant, and transferred to the division's engineers. Later it was possible for him to resume his art work in his spare time.

When I ran into him again, Lieutenant Von Ripper had a nice little room on the top floor of a Naples apartment building which had been taken over by the Army. There he worked at a huge drawing board, doing water colors and pen-and-ink sketches of war. He slept on a cot in the same room. Around the walls were tacked dozens of his sketches. Now and then he returned to the front with his old outfit. Whenever he did, he was out in front getting shot at before you could say scat.

Von Ripper was quite a guy—a soldier of fortune in a way, yet he didn't look or act like one. He was intelligent, and his manner was simple. He was thirty-nine, but seemed younger. He was medium tall, slightly stooped, and one eye had a cast that made it appear to be looking beyond you. His face was long and thin, and his teeth prominent. His knowledge of the English language was profound and his grammar perfect, but he still pronounced his words with a hissing imperfection. He swore lustily in English. He was as much at home discussing philosophy or political idealism as he was describing the best way to take cover from a machine gun. He was meticulous about his personal appearance, but he didn't seem to care whether he slept between satin sheets or in the freezing mud of the battlefield.

It was hard to reconcile the artist with the soldier in Von Ripper, yet he was obviously professional at both. It may be that being a fine soldier made him a better artist. His long experience at warfare had made him as cunning as a fox. I couldn't conceive of his being rattled in a tight spot; he seemed to have been born without the normal sense of fear that dwells in most men. He was so calm and so bold in battle that he had become a legend at the front. High officers asked his advice in planning attacks.

He would volunteer for anything. Being wounded four times hadn't affected his nerve in the slightest. In fact, he became so famous as an audacious patrol leader that his division finally forbade his going on patrol unless by specific permission.

One night Von Ripper, returning from patrol, was stopped by an itchy-fingered sentry who called, "Who goes there?" The answer came back in a heavy German accent, "Lieutenant Von Ripper." He was wearing lieutenant bars, but his dog tag showed him to be a sergeant. It took an hour to get it straightened out. Some sentries would have shot first and then investigated.

Out of this background as a proven fighting man, Von Ripper was painting the war. He had produced more than a hundred pictures. His work went to the War Department in Washington, but he hoped that an arrangement might be made whereby a book of his drawings could be published.

Von Ripper, like most of us over there, had finally become more interested in the personal, human side of war than in the abstract ideals for which wars are fought. He said that in his paintings he was trying to take the applesauce out of war, trying to eliminate the heroics with which war is too often presented. From what I saw of the work of other artists, Von Ripper was not alone in this sincerity. It's hard to be close enough to war to paint it, and still consider it heroic.

Von Ripper's dead men look awful, as dead men do. His live soldiers in foxholes have that spooky stare of exhaustion. His landscapes are sad and pitifully torn. His sketches aren't photographic at all; they are sometimes distorted and grotesque, and often he goes into pen-and-ink fantasy.

He gave me one of these, labeled "Self-Portrait in Italy," which shows himself and another wounded man, against a background of wrecked walls and starving children, being led downhill by the bony arms of a chortling skeleton.

You get to seeing things like that when you've been a soldier for a long time.

In this war I have known a lot of officers who were loved and respected by the soldiers under them. But never have I crossed the trail of any man as beloved as Captain Henry T. Waskow, of Belton, Texas.

Captain Waskow was a company commander in the Thirty-sixth Division. He had led his company since long before it left the States. He was very young, only in his middle twenties, but he carried in him a sincerity and a gentleness that made people want to be guided by him.

"After my father, he came next," a sergeant told me.

"He always looked after us," a soldier said. "He'd go to bat for us every time."

"I've never known him to do anything unfair," another said.

I was at the foot of the mule trail the night they brought Captain Waskow down. The moon was nearly full, and you could see far up the trail, and even partway across the valley below.

Dead men had been coming down the mountain all evening, lashed onto the backs of mules. They came lying belly-down across the wooden pack-saddles, their stiffened legs sticking out awkwardly from the other, bobbing up and down as the mules walked.

The Italian mule skinners were afraid to walk beside dead men, so Americans had to lead the mules down that night. Even the Americans were reluctant to unlash and lift off the bodies when they got to the bottom, so an officer had to do it himself and ask others to help.

I don't know who that first one was. You feel small in the presence of dead men, and you don't ask silly questions.

They slid him down from the mule, and stood him on his feet for a moment. In the half-light he might have been merely a sick man standing there leaning on the others. Then they laid him on the ground in the shadow of the low stone wall beside the road. We left him there beside the road, that first one, and we all went back into the cowshed and sat on water cans or lay on the straw, waiting for the next batch of mules.

Somebody said the dead soldier had been dead for four days, and then nobody said anything more about it. We talked soldier talk for an hour or more; the dead men lay all alone, outside in the shadow of the wall.

Then a soldier came into the cowshed and said that there were some more bodies outside. We went out into the road. Four mules stood there in the moonlight, in the road where the trail came down off the mountain. The soldiers who led them stood there waiting.

"This one is Captain Waskow," one of them said quietly.

Two men unlashed his body from the mule and lifted it off and laid it in the shadow beside the stone wall. Other men took the other bodies off. Finally, there were five lying end to end in a long row. You don't cover up dead men in the combat zones. They just lie there in the shadows until somebody comes after them.

The unburdened mules moved off to their olive grove. The men in the road seemed reluctant to leave. They stood around, and gradually I could sense them moving, one by one, close to Captain Waskow's body. Not so much to look, I think, as to say something in finality to him, and to themselves. I stood close by and I could hear.

One soldier came and looked down, and he said out loud, "God damn it!" That's all he said, and then he walked away.

Another one came, and he said, "God damn it to hell anyway!" He looked down for a few last moments and then turned and left.

Another man came. I think he was an officer. It was hard to tell officers from men in the dim light, for everybody was bearded and grimy. The man looked down into the dead captain's face and then spoke directly to him, as though he were alive, "I'm sorry, old man."

Then a soldier came and stood beside the officer and bent over, and he too spoke to his dead captain, not in a whisper but awfully tenderly, and he said, "I sure am sorry, sir."

Then the first man squatted down, and he reached down and took the captain's hand, and he sat there for a full five minutes holding the dead hand in his own and looking intently into the dead face. And he never uttered a sound all the time he sat there.

Finally he put the hand down. He reached over and gently straightened the points of the captain's shirt collar, and then he sort of rearranged the tattered edges of the uniform around the wound, and then he got up and walked away down the road in the moonlight, all alone.

The rest of us went back into the cowshed, leaving the five dead men in a line, end to end, in the shadow of the low stone wall. We lay down on the straw in the cowshed, and pretty soon we were all asleep.

In wandering around our far-flung front lines we could always tell how recently the battles had swept ahead of us. We could sense it from the little things even more than from the big things: From the scattered green leaves and the fresh branches of trees still lying in the middle of the road. From the coils of telephone wire, hanging brokenly from high poles and entwining across the roads. From the gray, burned-powder rims of the shell craters in the gravel roads, their edges not yet smoothed by the pounding of military traffic. From the little pools of blood on the roadside, blood that had only begun to congeal and turn black, and the punctured steel helmets lying near by. From the square blocks of building stone still scattered in the village streets, and from the sharp-edged rocks in the roads, still uncrushed by traffic. From the burned-out tanks and broken carts still unremoved from the road. From the cows in the fields, lying grotesquely with their feet to the sky, so newly dead they had not begun to bloat or smell. From the scattered heaps of personal gear around a gun. I don't know why it was, but the Germans always seemed to take off their coats before they fled or died.

From all these things we could tell that the battle had been recent—from these and from the men so newly dead that they seemed to be merely asleep. And also from the inhuman quiet. Usually battles are noisy for miles around. But in the fast warfare after our break-through a battle sometimes left a complete vacuum behind it. The Germans would stand and fight it out until they saw there was no hope. Then some gave up, and the rest pulled out and ran for miles. Shooting stopped. Our fighters moved on after the enemy, and those who did not fight, but moved in the wake of the battles, would not catch up for hours. There was nothing left behind but the remains—the lifeless debris, the sunshine and the flowers, and utter silence. An amateur who wandered in this vacuum at the rear of a battle had a terrible sense of loneliness. Everything was dead—the men, the machines, the animals—and he alone was left alive.

One afternoon we drove in our jeep into a country like that. The little rural villages of gray stone were demolished—heart-breaking heaps of still-smoking rubble. We drove into the tiny town of Le Mesniltore, a sweet old stone village at the "T" of two gravel roads, a rural village in rolling country, a village of not more than fifty buildings. There was not a whole building left. Rubble and broken wire still littered the streets. Blackish-gray stone walls with no roofs still smoldered inside. Dead men still lay in the streets, helmets and broken rifles askew around them. There was not a soul nor a sound in the village; it was lifeless.

We stopped and pondered our way, and with trepidation we drove on out of town for a quarter of a mile or so. The ditches were full of dead men. We drove around one without a head or arms or legs. We stared, and couldn't say anything about it to each other. We asked the driver to go very slowly, for there was an uncertainty in all the silence. There was no live human being, no sign of movement anywhere.

Seeing no one, hearing nothing, I became fearful of going on into the unknown. So we stopped. Just a few feet ahead of us was a brick-red American tank, still smoking, and with its turret knocked off. Near it was a German horse-drawn ammunition cart, upside down. In the road beside them was a shell crater. To our left lay two smashed airplanes in adjoining fields. Neither of them was more than thirty yards from the road. The hedge was low and we could see over. They were both British fighter planes. One lay right side up, the other on its back.

We were just ready to turn around and go back, when I spied a lone soldier at the far side of the field. He was standing there looking across the field at us like an Indian in a picture. I waved and he waved back. We walked toward each other. He turned out to be a second lieutenant—Ed

Sasson, of Los Angeles. He was a graves registration officer for his armored division, and he was out scouring the field, locating the bodies of dead Americans. He was glad to see somebody, for it is a lonely job catering to the dead. As we stood there talking in the lonely field, a soldier in coveralls, with a rifle slung over his shoulder, ran up breathlessly and almost shouted: "Hey, there's a man alive in one of those planes across the road! He's been trapped there for days!"

We ran to the wrecked British plane, lying there upside down, and dropped on our hands and knees to peek through a tiny hole in the side. A man lay on his back in the small space of the upside-down cockpit. His feet disappeared somewhere in the jumble of dials and pedals above him. His shirt was open and his chest was bare to the waist. He was smoking a cigarette, the only immediate relief the two soldiers who had discovered him could offer. The pilot turned his eyes toward me when I peered in, and he said in a typical British manner of offhand friendliness, "Oh, hello."

"Are you all right?" I asked, stupidly.

He answered, "Yes, quite. Now that you fellows are here."

I asked him how long he had been trapped in the wrecked plane. He said he didn't know for sure as he had got mixed up about the passage of time. But he did know the date of the month he was shot down. He told me the date. And I said out loud, "Good God!" For, wounded and trapped, he had been lying there for eight days!

His left leg was broken and punctured by an ack-ack burst. His back was terribly burned by raw gasoline that had spilled. The foot of his injured leg was pinned rigidly under the rudder bar. The space was so small he couldn't squirm around to relieve his own weight from his paining back. He couldn't straighten out his legs, which were bent above him. He couldn't see out of his little prison. He had not had a bite to eat or a drop of water. All this for eight days and nights. Yet when we found him his physical condition was good, and his mind was calm and rational. He was in agony, yet in his correct Oxford accent he even apologized for taking up our time to get him out.

The American soldiers of our rescue party cussed as they worked, cussed with open admiration for this British flier's greatness of heart which had kept him alive and sane through his lonely and gradually hope-dimming ordeal. One of them said, "God, but these Limeys have got guts!"

It took us almost an hour to get him out. While we were ripping the plane open to make a hole, he talked to us. And here is what happened—in the best nutshell I can devise from the conversation of a brave man whom we didn't want to badger with trivial questions: He was an RAF flight lieutenant, piloting a night fighter. Over a certain area the Germans began letting him have it from the ground with machine-gun fire. The first hit knocked out his motor. He was too low to jump, so—foolishly, he said—he turned on his lights to try a crash landing. Then they really poured it on him. The second hit got him in the leg. And a third bullet cut right across his right-hand fingers, clipping every one of them to the bone.

He left his wheels up, and the plane's belly hit the ground going uphill. We could see the groove it had dug for about fifty yards. Then the plane flopped, tail over nose, onto its back. The pilot was absolutely sealed into the upside-down cockpit. "That's all I remember for a while," he told us. "When I came to, they were shelling all around me."

Thus began the eight days. He had crashed right between the Germans and Americans in a sort of pastoral no man's land. For days afterwards the field in which he lay passed back and forth between German hands and ours. The pasture was pocked with hundreds of shell craters. Many of them were only yards away. One was right at the side of his wing. The sides of the plane were speckled with hundreds of shrapnel holes.

He lay there, trapped in the midst of that inferno of explosions. The fields around him gradually became littered with dead. At last American strength pushed the Germans back, and silence came. But no help. Because, you see, he was in that vacuum behind the battle, and only a few people were left. The days passed. He thirsted terribly. He slept some; part of the time he was unconscious; part of the time he undoubtedly was delirious. But he never gave up hope.

After we had finally got him out, he said as he lay on the stretcher under a wing, "Is it possible that I've been out of this plane since I crashed?"

Everybody chuckled. The doctor who had arrived said, "Not the remotest possibility. You were sealed in there and it took men with tools half an hour to make an opening. And your leg was broken and your foot was pinned there."

"I didn't think it was possible," the pilot said, "and yet it seems that I was out once and back in again."

That little suggestion of delirium was the only thing that remarkable man said, during the whole hour of his rescue, that wasn't as dispassionate and matter-of-fact as though he had been sitting comfortably at the end of the day in front of his own fireplace. It was one of the really great demonstrations of courage in this war.

I visited him a month later in England. He would be in bed for a year with his shattered leg. But he was happy. His name was Robert Gordon Fallis Lee, of Shalford, Surrey.

THE PERSONAL ESSAY

THE PERSONAL ESSAY

Though the personal essay has its roots far back in the immemorial past—as does, in fact every form of writing—it was the genius of Lamb and of Hazlitt in the 1820's which created a vogue lasting for a century. The personal essay no longer enjoys its favored position in the "quality magazines," for it tended toward an artificial archness and a cultivated triviality. But it is far from defunct. Without the label and the Lamb-like archaism, it may still be found very much alive in the *New Yorker,* on certain editorial pages, and in certain columns of lighter vein. And there will always be those who chat entertainingly and those who will pause from more serious affairs to listen.

There are often elements of biography in the personal essay, as in *Hunting the Deceitful Turkey* and *From Spargo to Carver to Speaker,* but neither of these essays would belong in a biography. Both Twain and Broun are less concerned with biographic fidelity to fact than with telling a good story. *On Going a Journey* and *Sounds* contain scraps of personal experience, but the experience is subordinated to the meaning of the experience, the fully developed emotions and reflections engendered by it. The essay is under no obligation to stick close to reality; one may touch up, rearrange, exaggerate the facts, the better to entertain.

But the personal essay must be personal. There is no taboo on the pronoun "I" or its inflected forms. Count the "I's" in *On Going a Journey;* even the "you's" in *Codfish Chowder and Sun* are really a subterfuge, for "you" are told to do what "I" or "we" used to find such delight in doing. Such a seemingly objective treatment as *The Gentle Giantess* reveals much of the gentleness and whimsicality of the author.

What are the difficulties of the informal essayist? He cannot attract and hold his readers by the thrill of plot or dramatic situation or by the importance of the subject discussed, and yet he must make his personality and his opinions interesting. Humor, of course, helps—when it does not hinder. Nothing is more rasping than feeble jokes, hoary anecdotes, strained efforts to raise a laugh. Far better to be serious, as Thoreau is serious throughout and as Stevenson is for the most part. But if there is not the piquancy of humor, there should at least be the charm of novelty. Stale platitudes and commonplace observation will not do. Study in the essays which follow the elements of originality in the topic itself, in the introduction and presentation, and in the observation of men and things.

One more essential—style. Few immature writers can achieve the rich sophistication of Stevenson, and should not attempt it. But read him aloud and watch the effect of his rhythms. Try changing the wording in Beerbohm's *How Shall I Word It?* and relish the perfect choice of phrase. The style of the personal essay may vary with mood and purpose and preference, but it is never ponderous and never flat.

The Gentle Giantess[1]
by CHARLES LAMB

THE widow Blacket of Oxford is the largest female I have ever had the pleasure of beholding. There may be her parallel upon the earth, but surely I never saw it. I take her to be lineally descended from the maid's aunt of Brainford, who caused Master Ford such uneasiness. She hath Atlantean shoulders; and, as she stoopeth in her gait—with as few offenses to answer in her own particular as any of Eve's daughters—her back seems broad enough to bear the blame of all the peccadillos that have been committed since Adam. She girdeth her waist—or what she is pleased to esteem as such—nearly up to her shoulders, from beneath which that huge dorsal expanse, in mountainous declivity, emergeth. Respect for her alone preventeth the idle boys, who follow her about in shoals whenever she cometh abroad, from getting up and riding. But her presence infallibly commands a reverence. She is indeed, as the Americans would express it, something awful. Her person is a burthen to herself, no less than the ground which bears her. To her mighty bone she hath a pinguitude withal, which makes the depth of winter to her the most desirable season. Her distress in the warmer solstice is pitiable. During the months of July and August she usually renteth a cool cellar, where ices are kept, whereunto she descendeth when Sirius rageth. She dates from a hot Thursday some twenty-five years ago. Her apartment in summer is pervious to the four winds. Two doors, in north and south direction, and two windows, fronting the rising and the setting sun, never closed, from every cardinal point, catch the contributory breezes. She loves to enjoy what she calls a quadruple draft. That must be a shrewd zephyr that can escape her. I owe a painful face-ache which oppresses me at this moment to a cold caught sitting by her one day in last July at the receipt of coolness. Her fan in ordinary resembleth a banner spread, which she keepeth continually on the alert to detect the least breeze. She possesseth an active and gadding mind totally incommensurate with her person. No one delighteth more than herself in country exercises and pastimes. I have passed many an agreeable holiday with her in her favorite park at Woodstock. She performs her part in those delightful ambulatory excursions by the aid of a portable garden chair. She setteth out with you at a fair foot gallop, which she keepeth up till you are both well breathed, and then she reposeth for a few seconds. Then she is up again for a hundred paces or so and again resteth—her movement on these sprightly occasions being something between walking and flying. Her great weight seemeth to propel her forward ostrich-fashion. In this kind of relieved marching I have traversed with her many scores of acres on these

[1] First published 1822.

well-wooded and well-watered domains. Her delight at Oxford is in the public walks and gardens, where, when the weather is not too oppressive, she passeth much of her valuable time. There is a bench at Maudlin or rather situated between the frontiers of that and ——'s college (some litigation latterly about repairs has vested the property of it finally in ——'s) where at the hour of noon she is ordinarily to be found sitting—so she calls it by courtesy —but in fact pressing and breaking of it down with her enormous settlement as both those Foundations, who however are good-natured enough to wink at it, have found, I believe, to their cost. Here she taketh the fresh air, principally at vacation times, when the walks are freest from interruption from the younger fry of students. Here she passeth her idle hours, not idly, but generally accompanied by a book—blest if she can but intercept some resident Fellow (as usually there are some of that brood left behind at those periods) or stray Master of Arts (to most of them she is better known than their dinner-bell), with whom she may confer on any curious topic of literature. I have seen these shy gownsmen, who truly set but a very slight value on female conversation, cast a hawk's eye upon her from the length of Maudlin grove and verily glide off into another walk—true monks as they are and ungently neglecting the delicacies of her polished converse for their own perverse and uncommunicating solitariness. Within doors her principal diversion is music, vocal and instrumental, in both which she is no mean professor. Her voice is wonderfully fine; but till I got used to it, I confess it staggered me. It is for all the world like that of a piping bullfinch, while from her size and stature you would expect notes to be drawn from a deep organ. The shake, which most fine singers reserve for the close of cadence, by some unaccountable flexibility or tremulousness of pipe, she carrieth quite through the composition; so that her time, to a common air or ballad, keeps double motion like the earth—running the primary circuit of the tune and still revolving upon its own axis. The effect, as I said before, when you get used to it, is as agreeable as it is altogether new and surprising. The spacious apartment of her outward frame lodgeth a soul in all respect disproportionate. Of more than mortal make, she evinceth withal a trembling sensibility, a yielding infirmity of purpose, a quick susceptibility to reproach, and all the train of diffident and blushing virtues, which for their habitation usually seek out a feeble frame and attenuated and meager constitution. With more than man's bulk, her humors and occupations are eminently feminine. She sighs—being six feet high. She languisheth—being two feet wide. She worketh slender sprigs upon the delicate muslin—her fingers being capable of molding a Colossus. She sippeth her wine out of her glass daintily—her capacity being that of a tun of Heidelberg. She goeth mincingly with those feet of hers— whose solidity need not fear the black ox's pressure. Softest and largest of thy sex, adieu! By what parting tribute may I salute thee, last and best of the Titanesses, Ogress, fed with milk instead of blood, not least, or least handsome, among Oxford's stately structures—Oxford, who in its deadest time of vacation, can never properly be said to be empty, having thee to fill it.

On Going a Journey[1]

by WILLIAM HAZLITT

O NE OF the pleasantest things in the world is going a journey; but I like to go by myself. I can enjoy society in a room; but out of doors, nature is company enough for me. I am then never less alone than when alone.

> The fields his study, nature was his book.

I cannot see the wit of walking and talking at the same time. When I am in the country, I wish to vegetate like the country. I am not for criticising hedge-rows and black cattle. I go out of town in order to forget the town and all that is in it. There are those who for this purpose go to watering-places, and carry the metropolis with them. I like more elbow-room, and fewer incumbrances. I like solitude, when I give myself up to it, for the sake of solitude; nor do I ask for

> ———— a friend in my retreat,
> Whom I may whisper, solitude is sweet.

The soul of a journey is liberty, perfect liberty, to think, feel, do just as one pleases. We go a journey chiefly to be free of all impediments and of all conveniences; to leave ourselves behind, much more to get rid of others. It is because I want a little breathing-space to muse on indifferent matters, where Contemplation

> May plume her feathers and let grow her wings,
> That in the various bustle of resort
> Were all too ruffled, and sometimes impaired,

that I absent myself from the town for a while, without feeling at a loss the moment I am left by myself. Instead of a friend in a post-chaise or in a Tilbury, to exchange good things with, and vary the same stale topics over again, for once let me have a truce with impertinence. Give me the clear blue sky over my head, and the green turf beneath my feet, a winding road before me, and a three hours march to dinner, and then to thinking! It is hard if I cannot start some game on these lone heaths. I laugh, I run, I leap. I sing for joy. From the point of yonder rolling cloud, I plunge into my past being, and revel there, as the sunburnt Indian plunges headlong into the wave that wafts him to his native shore. Then long-forgotten things, like "sunken wrack and sunless treasures," burst upon my eager sight, and I begin to feel, think, and be myself again. Instead of an awkward silence, broken by at-

[1] From W. Hazlitt, *Table Talk* (1822).

tempts at wit or dull commonplace, mine is that undisturbed silence of the
heart which alone is perfect eloquence. No one likes puns, alliterations,
antitheses, argument, and analysis better than I do; but I sometimes had rather
be without them. "Leave, oh, leave me to my repose!" I have just now other
business in hand, which would seem idle to you, but is with me "very stuff of
the conscience." Is not this wild rose sweet without a comment? Does not
this daisy leap to my heart set in its coat of emerald? Yet if I were to explain
to you the circumstance that has so endeared it to me, you would only smile.
Had I not better then keep it to myself, and let it serve me to brood over,
from here to yonder craggy point, and from thence onward to the far-distant
horizon? I should be but bad company all that way, and therefore prefer
being alone. I have heard it said that you may, when the moody fit comes on,
walk or ride on by yourself, and indulge your reveries. But this looks like a
breach of manners, a neglect of others, and you are thinking all the time that
you ought to rejoin your party. "Out upon such half-faced fellowship," say I.
I like to be either entirely to myself, or entirely at the disposal of others; to
talk or be silent, to walk or sit still, to be sociable or solitary. I was pleased
with an observation of Mr. Cobbett's, that "he thought it was a bad French
custom to drink our wine with our meal, and that an Englishman ought to
do only one thing at a time." So I cannot talk and think, or indulge in melancholy musing and lively conversation by fits and starts. "Let me have a
companion of my way," says Sterne, "were it but to remark how the shadows
lengthen as the sun declines." It is beautifully said: but in my opinion, this
continual comparing of notes interferes with the involuntary impression of
things upon the mind, and hurts the sentiment. If you only hint what you
feel in a kind of dumb show, it is insipid: if you have to explain it, it is making a toil of a pleasure. You cannot read the book of Nature, without being
perpetually put to the trouble of translating it for the benefit of others. I am
for the synthetical method on a journey, in preference to the analytical. I am
content to lay in a stock of ideas then, and to examine and anatomise them
afterwards. I want to see my vague notions float like the down of the thistle
before the breeze, and not to have them entangled in the briars and thorns of
controversy. For once, I like to have it all my own way; and this is impossible
unless you are alone, or in such company as I do not covet. I have no objection to argue a point with anyone for twenty miles of measured road, but not
for pleasure. If you remark the scent of a beanfield crossing the road, perhaps
your fellow-traveller has no smell. If you point to a distant object, perhaps he
is short-sighted, and has to take out his glass to look at it. There is a feeling
in the air, a tone in the colour of a cloud which hits your fancy, but the effect
of which you are unable to account for. There is then no sympathy, but an
uneasy craving after it, and a dissatisfaction which pursues you on the way,
and in the end probably produces ill humour. Now I never quarrel with
myself, and take all my own conclusions for granted till I find it necessary
to defend them against objections. It is not merely that you may not be of
accord on the objects and circumstances that present themselves before you—

these may recall a number of objects, and lead to associations too delicate and refined to be possibly communicated to others. Yet these I love to cherish, and sometimes still fondly clutch them, when I can escape from the throng to do so. To give way to our feelings before company, seems extravagance or affectation; and on the other hand, to have to unravel this mystery of our being at every turn, and to make others take an equal interest in it (otherwise the end is not answered) is a task to which few are competent. We must "give it an understanding, but no tongue." My old friend Coleridge, however, could do both. He could go on in the most delightful explanatory way over hill and dale, a summer's day, and convert a landscape into a didactic poem or a Pindaric ode. "He talked far above singing." If I could so clothe my ideas in sounding and flowing words, I might perhaps wish to have someone with me to admire the swelling theme; or I could be more content, were it possible for me still to hear his echoing voice in the woods of All-Foxden. They had "that fine madness in them which our first poets had"; and if they could have been caught by some rare instrument, would have breathed such strains as the following.

> ——— Here be woods as green
> As any, air likewise as fresh and sweet
> As when smooth Zephyrus plays on the fleet
> Face of the curled stream, with flow'rs as many
> As the young spring gives, and as choice as any;
> Here be all new delights, cool streams and wells,
> Arbours o'ergrown with woodbine, caves and dells;
> Choose where thou wilt, while I sit by and sing,
> Or gather rushes to make many a ring
> For thy long fingers; tell thee tales of love,
> How the pale Phoebe, hunting in a grove,
> First saw the boy Endymion, from whose eyes
> She took eternal fire that never dies;
> How she conveyed him softly in a sleep,
> His temples bound with poppy, to the steep
> Head of old Latmos, where she stoops each night,
> Gilding the mountain with her brother's light,
> To kiss her sweetest. ———
> *Faithful Shepherdess.*

Had I words and images at command like these, I would attempt to wake the thoughts that lie slumbering on golden ridges in the evening clouds: but at the sight of nature my fancy, poor as it is, droops and closes up its leaves, like flowers at sunset. I can make nothing out on the spot:—I must have time to collect myself.

In general, a good thing spoils out-of-doors prospects: it should be reserved for Table-talk. Lamb is for this reason, I take it, the worst company in the world out of doors; because he is the best within. I grant, there is one subject on which it is pleasant to talk on a journey; and that is, what one shall have for supper when we get to our inn at night. The open air improves this sort of conversation or friendly altercation, by setting a keener edge on appetite. Every mile of the road heightens the flavour of the viands we expect at the end of it. How fine it is to enter some old town, walled and turreted, just at the approach of nightfall, or to come to some straggling village, with the lights streaming through the surrounding gloom; and then after inquiring for the best entertainment that the place affords, to "take one's ease at one's inn!" These eventful moments in our lives' history are too precious, too full of solid, heartfelt happiness to be frittered and dribbled away in imperfect sympathy. I would have them all to myself, and drain them to the last drop: they will do to talk of or to write about afterwards. What a delicate speculation it is, after drinking whole goblets of tea,

The cups that cheer, but not inebriate,

and letting the fumes ascend into the brain, to sit considering what we shall have for supper—eggs and a rasher, a rabbit smothered in onions, or an excellent veal-cutlet! Sancho in such a situation once fixed upon cow-heel; and his choice, though he could not help it, is not to be disparaged. Then in the intervals of pictured scenery and Shandean contemplation, to catch the preparation and the stir in the kitchen—*Procul, O procul este profani!* ("Avaunt! avaunt! ye unhallowed.") These hours are sacred to silence and to musing, to be treasured up in the memory, and to feed the source of smiling thoughts hereafter. I would not waste them in idle talk; or if I must have the integrity of fancy broken in upon, I would rather it were by a stranger than a friend. A stranger takes his hue and character from the time and place; he is a part of the furniture and costume of an inn. If he is a Quaker, or from the West Riding of Yorkshire, so much the better. I do not even try to sympathize with him, and he breaks no squares. I associate nothing with my travelling companion but present objects and passing events. In his ignorance of me and my affairs, I in a manner forget myself. But a friend reminds one of other things, rips up old grievances, and destroys the abstraction of the scene. He comes in ungraciously between us and our imaginary character. Something is dropped in the course of conversation that gives a hint of your profession and pursuits; or from having someone with you that knows the less sublime portions of your history, it seems that other people do. You are no longer a citizen of the world: but your "unhoused free condition is put into circumscription and confine." The incognito of an inn is one of its striking privileges—"lord of one's-self, uncumber'd with a name." Oh! it is great to shake off the trammels of the world and of public opinion—to lose our importunate, tormenting, everlasting personal identity in the elements of nature, and become the creature of the moment, clear of all ties—to hold to the universe only by a dish of sweetbreads, and to owe nothing but the score of the evening—and no longer seeking for applause and meeting with contempt, to be known by no other title than *the Gentleman in the parlour!* One may take one's choice of all characters in this romantic state of uncertainty as to one's real pretensions, and become indefinitely respectable and negatively rightworshipful. We baffle prejudice and disappoint conjecture; and from being so to others, begin to be objects of curiosity and wonder even to ourselves. We are no more those hackneyed commonplaces that we appear in the world: an inn restores us to the level of nature, and quits scores with society! I have certainly spent some enviable hours at inns—sometimes when I have been left entirely to myself, and have tried to solve some metaphysical problem, as once at Witham-common, where I found out the proof that likeness is not a case of the association of ideas— at other times, when there have been pictures in the room, as at St. Neot's (I think it was), where I first met with Gribelin's engravings of the "Cartoons," into which I entered at once, and at a little inn on the borders of Wales, where there happened to be hanging some of Westall's drawings, which I compared triumphantly (for a theory that I had, not for the admired artist) with the figure of a girl who had ferried me over the Severn, standing up in the boat between me and the twilight—at other times I might mention luxuriating in books, with a peculiar interest in this way, as I remember sitting up half the night to read "Paul and Virginia," which I picked up at an inn at Bridgewater, after being drenched in the rain all day; and at the same place I got through two volumes of Madame D'Arblay's "Camilla." It was on the tenth of April, 1798, that I sat down to a volume of the "New Eloise," at the inn at Llangollen, over a bottle of sherry and a cold chicken. The letter I chose was that in which St. Preux describes his feelings as he first caught a glimpse from the heights of the Jura of the Pays de Vaud, which I had brought with me as a *bon bouche* to crown the evening with. It was my birthday, and I had for the first time come from a place in the neighbourhood to visit this delightful spot. The road to Llangollen turns off between Chirk and Wrexham; and on passing a certain point, you come all at once upon the valley, which opens like an amphitheatre, broad, barren hills rising in majestic state on either side, with "green upland swells that echo to the bleat of flocks" below, and the river Dee babbling over its stony bed in the midst of them. The valley at this time "glittered green with sunny showers," and a budding ash-tree dipped its tender branches in the chiding stream. How proud, how glad I was to walk along the high road that overlooks the delicious prospect, repeating the lines which I have just quoted from Mr. Coleridge's poems! But besides the prospect which opened beneath my feet, another also opened to my inward sight, a heavenly vision, on which were written, in letters large as Hope could make them, these four words, LIBERTY, GENIUS, LOVE, VIRTUE; which have since faded into the light of common day, or mock my idle gaze.

The beautiful is vanished, and returns not.

Still I would return some time or other to this enchanted spot; but I would return to it alone. What other self could I find to share that influx of thoughts of regret, and delight, the fragments of which I could hardly conjure up to myself, so much have they been broken and defaced! I could stand on some tall rock, and overlook the precipice of years that separates me from what I then was. I was at that time going shortly to visit the poet whom I have above named. Where is he now? Not only I myself have changed; the world, which was then new to me, has become old and incorrigible. Yet will I turn to thee in thought, O sylvan Dee, in joy, in youth and gladness as thou then wert; and thou shalt always be to me the river of Paradise, where I will drink of the waters of life freely!

~~~~~~

Sounds [1]

by HENRY DAVID THOREAU

A s I sit at my window this summer afternoon, hawks are circling about my clearing; the tantivy of wild pigeons, flying by twos and threes athwart my view, or perching restless on the white-pine boughs behind my house, gives a voice to the air; a fish-hawk dimples the glassy surface of the pond and brings up a fish; a mink steals out of the marsh before my door and seizes a frog by the shore; the sedge is bending under the weight of the reedbirds flitting hither and thither; and for the last half-hour I have heard the rattle of railroad-cars, now dying away and then reviving like the beat of a partridge, conveying travellers from Boston to the country. For I did not live so out of the world as that boy, who, as I hear, was put out to a farmer in the east part of the town, but ere long ran away and came home again, quite down at the heel and home-sick. He had never seen such a dull and out-of-the-way place; the folks were all gone off somewhere; why, you couldn't even hear the whistle! I doubt if there is such a place in Massachusetts now:—

> "In truth, our village has become a butt
> For one of those fleet railroad shafts, and o'er
> Our peaceful plain its soothing sound is—Concord."

The Fitchburg Railroad touches the pond about a hundred rods south of where I dwell. I usually go to the village along its causeway, and am, as it were, related to society by this link. The men on the freight trains, who go over the whole length of the road, bow to me as to an old acquaintance, they pass me so often, and apparently they take me for an employee: and so I am. I too would fain be a track-repairer somewhere in the orbit of the earth.

The whistle of the locomotive penetrates my woods summer and winter, sounding like the scream of a hawk sailing over some farmer's yard, informing me that many restless city merchants are arriving within the circle of the

[1] From *Walden* (1854).

town, or adventurous country traders from the other side. As they come under one horizon, they shout their warning to get off the track to the other, heard sometimes through the circles of two towns. Here come your groceries, country; your rations, countrymen! Nor is there any man so independent on his farm that he cay say them nay. And here's your pay for them! screams the countryman's whistle; timber like long battering-rams going twenty miles an hour against the city walls, and chairs enough to seat all the weary and heavy-laden that dwell within them. With such huge and lumbering civility the country hands a chair to the city. All the Indian huckleberry hills are stripped, all the cranberry meadows are raked into the city. Up comes the cotton, down goes the woven cloth; up comes the silk, down goes the woollen; up come the books, but down goes the wit that writes them.

When I meet the engine with its train of cars moving off with planetary motion,—or rather, like a comet, for the beholder knows not if with that velocity and with that direction it will ever revisit this system, since its orbit does not look like a returning curve,—with its steam-cloud like a banner streaming behind in golden and silver wreaths, like many a downy cloud which I have seen, high in the heavens, unfolding its masses to the light,— as if this travelling demigod, this cloud-compeller, would ere long take the sunset sky for the livery of his train; when I hear the iron horse make the hills echo with his snort like thunder, shaking the earth with his feet, and breathing fire and smoke from his nostrils (what kind of winged horse or fiery dragon they will put into the new Mythology I don't know), it seems as if the earth had got a race now worthy to inhabit it. If all were as it seems, and men made the elements their servants for noble ends! If the cloud that hangs over the engine were the perspiration of heroic deeds, or as beneficent as that which floats over the farmer's fields, then the elements and Nature herself would cheerfully accompany men on their errands and be their escort.

I watch the passage of the morning cars with the same feeling that I do the rising of the sun, which is hardly more regular. Their train of clouds stretching far behind and rising higher and higher, going to heaven while the cars are going to Boston, conceals the sun for a minute and casts my distant field into the shade, a celestial train beside which the petty train of cars which hugs the earth is but the barb of the spear. The stabler of the iron horse was up early this winter morning by the light of the stars amid the mountain, to fodder and harness his steed. Fire, too, was awakened thus early to put the vital heat in him and get him off. If the enterprise were as innocent as it is early! If the snow lies deep, they strap on his snow-shoes, and with the giant plough plough a furrow from the mountains to the seaboard, in which the cars, like a following drill-barrow, sprinkle all the restless men and float-ing merchandise in the country for seed. All day the fire-steed flies over the country, stopping only that his master may rest, and I am awakened by his tramp and defiant snort at midnight, when in some remote glen in the woods he fronts the elements incased in ice and snow; and he will reach his stall only with the morning star, to start once more on his travels without rest or slumber. Or perchance, at evening, I hear him in his stable blowing off the superfluous energy of the day, that he may calm his nerves and cool his liver and brain for a few hours of iron slumber. If the enterprise were as heroic and commanding as it is protracted and unwearied:

Far through unfrequented woods on the confines of towns, where once only the hunter penetrated by day, in the darkest night dart these bright saloons without the knowledge of their inhabitants; this moment stopping at some brilliant station-house in town or city, where a social crowd is gathered, the next in the Dismal Swamp, scaring the owl and fox. The startings and arrivals of the cars are now the epochs in the village day. They go and come with such regularity and precision, and their whistle can be heard so far, that the farmers set their clocks by them, and thus one well-conducted institution regulates a whole country. Have not men improved somewhat in punctuality since the railroad was invented? Do they not talk and think faster in the depôt than they did in the stage-office? There is something electrifying in the atmosphere of the former place. I have been astonished at the miracles it has wrought; and some of my neighbours, who, I should have prophesied, once for all, would never get to Boston by so prompt a conveyance, are on hand when the bell rings. To do things "railroad fashion" is now the by-word; and it is worth the while to be warned so often and so sincerely by any power to get off its track. There is no stopping to read the riot act, no firing over the heads of the mob, in this case. We have constructed a fate, an *Atropos,* that never turns aside. (Let that be the name of your engine.) Men are advertised that at a certain hour and minute these bolts will be shot toward particular points of the compass; yet it interferes with no man's business, and the children go to school on the other track. We live the steadier for it. We are all educated thus to be sons of Tell. The air is full of invisible bolts. Every path but your own is the path of fate. Keep on your own track, then.

What recommends commerce to me is its enterprise and bravery. It does not clasp its hands and pray to Jupiter. I see these men every day go about their business with more or less courage and content, doing more even than they suspect, and perchance better employed than they could have consciously devised. I am less affected by their heroism who stood up for half-an-hour in the front line at Buena Vista, than by the steady and cheerful valour of the men who inhabit the snow-plough for their winter quarters; who have not merely the three o'clock in the morning courage, which Bonaparte thought was the rarest, but whose courage does not go to rest so early, who go to sleep only when the storm sleeps or the sinews of their iron steed are frozen. On this morning of the Great Snow, perchance, which is still raging and chilling men's blood, I hear the muffled tone of their engine bell from out the fog-bank of their chilled breath, which announces that the cars *are coming,* without long delay, notwithstanding the veto of a New England north-east snow-storm, and I behold the ploughmen covered with snow and rime, their heads peering above the mould-board which is turning down other than daisies and the nests of field-mice, like boulders of the Sierra Nevada, that occupy an outside place in the universe.

Commerce is unexpectedly confident and serene, alert, adventurous, and unwearied. It is very natural in its methods, withal, far more so than many fantastic enterprises and sentimental experiments, and hence its singular success. I am refreshed and expanded when the freight train rattles past me, and I smell the stores which go dispensing their odours all the way from Long Wharf to Lake Champlain, reminding me of foreign parts, of coral reefs, and Indian oceans, and tropical climes, and the extent of the globe. I feel more like a citizen of the world at the sight of the palm-leaf which will cover so many flaxen New England heads the next summer, the Manila hemp and cocoa-nut husks, the old junk, gunny bags, scrap iron, and rusty nails. This car-load of torn sails is more legible and interesting now than if they should be wrought into paper and printed books. Who can write so graphically the history of the storms they have weathered as these rents have done? They are proof-sheets which need no correction. Here goes lumber from the Maine woods, which did not go out to sea in the last freshet, risen four dollars on the thousand because of what did go out or was split up; pine, spruce, cedar, —first, second, third, and fourth qualities, so lately all of one quality, to wave over the bear, and moose, and caribou. Next rolls Thomaston lime, a prime lot, which will get far among the hills before it gets slacked. These rags in bales, of all hues and qualities, the lowest condition to which cotton and linen descend, the final result of dress,—of patterns which are now no longer cried up, unless it be in Milwaukie, as those splendid articles, English, French, or American prints, ginghams, muslins, &c.—gathered from all quarters both of fashion and poverty, going to become paper of one colour or a few shades only, on which, forsooth, will be written tales of real life, high and low, and founded on fact! This closed car smells of salt fish, the strong New England and commercial scent, reminding me of the Grand Banks and the fisheries. Who has not seen a salt fish, thoroughly cured for this world, so that nothing can spoil it, and putting the perseverance of the saints to the blush? with which you may sweep or pave the streets, and split your kindlings, and the teamster shelter himself and his lading against sun, wind, and rain behind it, —and the trader, as a Concord trader once did, hang it up by his door for a sign when he commences business, until at last his oldest customer cannot tell surely whether it be animal, vegetable, or mineral, and yet it shall be as pure as a snowflake, and if it be put into a pot and boiled, will come out an excellent dun fish for a Saturday's dinner. Next, Spanish hides, with the tails still preserving their twist and the angle of elevation they had when the oxen that wore them were careering over the pampas of the Spanish main,— a type of all obstinacy, and evincing how almost hopeless and incurable are all constitutional vices. I confess, that practically speaking, when I have learned a man's real disposition, I have no hopes of changing it for the better or worse in this state of existence. As the Orientals say, "A cur's tail may be warmed, and pressed, and bound round with ligatures, and after a twelve years' labour bestowed upon it, still it will retain its natural form." The only effectual cure for such inveteracies as these tails exhibit is to make glue of them, which I believe is what is usually done with them, and then they will stay put and stick. Here is a hogshead of molasses or of brandy directed to John Smith, Cuttingsville, Vermont, some trader among the Green Mountains, who imports for the farmers near his clearing, and now perchance stands over his bulk-head and thinks of the last arrivals on the coast, how they may affect the price for him, telling his customers this moment, as he has told them twenty times before this morning, that he expects some by the next train of prime quality. It is advertised in the *Cuttingsville Times.*

While these things go up other things come down. Warmed by the whizzing sound, I look up from my book and see some tall pine, hewn on far northern hills, which has winged its way over the Green Mountains and the Connecticut, shot like an arrow through the township within ten minutes, and scarce another eye beholds it; going

> "to be the mast
> Of some great ammiral."

And hark! here comes the cattle-train bearing the cattle of a thousand hills, sheepcots, stables, and cow-yards in the air, drovers with their sticks, and shepherd boys in the midst of their flocks, all but the mountain pastures, whirled along like leaves blown from the mountains by the September gales. The air is filled with the bleating of calves and sheep, and the hustling of oxen, as if a pastoral valley were going by. When the old bell-wether at the head rattles his bell, the mountains do indeed skip like rams and the little hills like lambs. A car-load of drovers, too, in the midst, on a level with their droves now, their vocation gone, but still clinging to their useless sticks as their badge of office. But their dogs, where are they? It is a stampede to them; they are quite thrown out; they have lost the scent. Methinks I hear them barking behind the Peterboro' Hills, or panting up the western slope of the Green Mountains. They will not be in at the death. Their vocation, too, is gone. Their fidelity and sagacity are below par now. They will slink back to their kennels in disgrace, or perchance run wild and strike a league with the wolf and the fox. So is your pastoral life whirled past and away. But the bell rings, and I must get off the track and let the cars go by—

> "What's the railroad to me?
> I never go to see
> Where it ends.
> It fills a few hollows,
> And makes banks for the swallows,
> It sets the sand a-blowing,
> And the blackberries a-growing,"

but I cross it like a cart-path in the woods. I will not have my eyes put out and my ears spoiled by its smoke, and steam, and hissing.

Now that the cars are gone by and all the restless world with them, and the fishes in the pond no longer feel their rumbling, I am more alone than ever. For the rest of the long afternoon, perhaps, my meditations are interrupted only by the faint rattle of a carriage or team along the distant highway.

Sometimes, on Sundays, I heard the bells, the Lincoln, Acton, Bedford, or Concord bell, when the wind was favourable, a faint, sweet, and, as it were, natural melody, worth importing into the wilderness. At a sufficient distance over the woods this sound acquires a certain vibratory hum, as if the pine needles in the horizon were the strings of a harp which it swept. All sound heard at the greatest possible distance produces one and the same effect, a vibration of the universal lyre, just as the intervening atmosphere makes a distant ridge of earth interesting to our eyes by the azure tint it imparts to it. There came to me in this case a melody which the air had strained, and which had conversed with every leaf and needle of the wood, that portion of the sound which the elements had taken up and modulated and echoed from vale to vale. The echo is, to some extent, an original sound, and therein is the magic and charm of it. It is not merely a repetition of what was worth repeating in the bell, but partly the voice of the wood; the same trivial words and notes sung by a wood-nymph.

At evening, the distant lowing of some cow in the horizon beyond the woods sounded sweet and melodious, and at first I would mistake it for the voices of certain minstrels by whom I was sometimes serenaded, who might be straying over hill and dale; but soon I was not unpleasantly disappointed when it was prolonged into the cheap and natural music of the cow. I do not mean to be satirical, but to express my appreciation of those youths' singing, when I state that I perceived clearly that it was akin to the music of the cow, and they were at length one articulation of Nature.

Regularly at half-past seven, in one part of the summer, after the evening train had gone by, the whippoorwills chanted their vespers for half-an-hour, sitting on a stump by my door, or upon the ridge pole of the house. They would begin to sing almost with as much precision as a clock, within five minutes of a particular time, referred to the setting of the sun, every evening. I had a rare opportunity to become acquainted with their habits. Sometimes I heard four or five at once in different parts of the wood, by accident one a bar behind another, and so near me that I distinguished not only the cluck after each note, but often that singular buzzing like a fly in a spider's web, only proportionally louder. Sometimes one would circle round and round me in the woods a few feet distant as if tethered by a string, when probably I was near its eggs. They sang at intervals throughout the night, and were again as musical as ever just before and about dawn.

When other birds are still the screech owls take up the strain, like mourning women their ancient u-lu-lu. Their dismal scream is truly Ben Jonsonian. Wise midnight hags! It is no honest and blunt tu-whit to-who of the poets, but, without jesting, a most solemn graveyard ditty, the mutual consolations of suicide lovers remembering the pangs and the delights of supernal love in the infernal groves. Yet I love to hear their wailing, their doleful responses, trilled along the woodside; reminding me sometimes of music and singing birds; as if it were the dark and tearful side of music, the regrets and sighs that would fain be sung. They are the spirits, the low spirits and melancholy forebodings, of fallen souls that once in human shape nightly walked the earth and did the deeds of darkness, now expiating their sins with their wailing hymns or threnodies in the scenery of their transgressions. They give me a new sense of the variety and capacity of that nature which is our common dwelling. *Oh-o-o-o-o that I never had been bor-r-r-r-n!* sighs one on this side of the pond, and circles with the restlessness of despair to some new perch on the grey oaks. Then—*That I never had been bor-r-r-r-n!* echoes another on the farther side with tremulous sincerity, and—*bor-r-r-r-n!* comes faintly from far in the Lincoln woods.

I was also serenaded by a hooting owl. Near at hand you could fancy it the most melancholy sound in Nature, as if she meant by this to stereotype and make permanent in her choir the dying moans of a human being,—some poor weak relic of mortality who has left hope behind, and howls like an animal, yet with human sobs, on entering the dark valley, made more awful by a certain gurgling melodiousness,—I find myself beginning with the letters gl when I try to imitate it,—expressive of a mind which has reached the gelatinous mildewy stage in the mortification of all healthy and courageous thought. It reminded me of ghouls and idiots and insane howlings. But now one answers from far woods in a strain made really melodious by distance,—*Hoo hoo hoo, hoorer hoo!* and indeed, for the most part it suggested only pleasing associations, whether heard by day or night, summer or winter.

I rejoice that there are owls. Let them do the idiotic and maniacal hooting for men. It is a sound admirably suited to swamps and twilight woods which no day illustrates, suggesting a vast and undeveloped nature which men have not recognised. They represent the stark twilight and unsatisfied thoughts which all have. All day the sun has shone on the surface of some savage swamp, where the single spruce stands hung with usnea lichens, and small hawks circulate above, and the chicadee lisps amid the evergreens, and the partridge and rabbit skulk beneath; but now a more dismal and fitting day dawns, and a different race of creatures awakes to express the meaning of Nature there.

Late in the evening I heard the distant rumbling of waggons over bridges, —a sound heard farther than almost any other at night,—the baying of dogs, and sometimes again the lowing of some disconsolate cow in a distant barnyard. In the meanwhile all the shore rang with the trump of bull-frogs, the sturdy spirits of ancient wine-bibbers and wassailers, still unrepentant, trying to sing a catch in their Stygian lake,—if the Walden nymphs will pardon the comparison, for though there are almost no weeds, there are frogs there,— who would fain keep up the hilarious rules of their old festal tables, though their voices have waxed hoarse and solemnly grave, mocking at mirth, and the wine has lost its flavour, and become only liquor to distend their paunches, and sweet intoxication never comes to drown the memory of the past, but mere saturation and water-loggedness and distention. The most aldermanic, with chin upon a heart-leaf, which serves for a napkin to his drooling chaps, under this northern shore quaffs a deep draught of the once scorned water, and passes round a cup with the ejaculation *tr-r-r-oonk, tr-r-r-oonk, tr-r-r-oonk!* and straightway comes over the water from some distant cove the same pass-word repeated, where the next in seniority and girth has gulped down to his mark; and when this observance has made the circuit of the shores, then ejaculates the master of ceremonies, with satisfaction, *tr-r-r-oonk!* and each in his turn repeats the same down to the least distended, leakiest, and flabbiest paunched, that there be no mistake; and then the bowl goes round again and again, until the sun disperses the morning mist, and only the patriarch is not under the pond, but vainly bellowing *troonk* from time to time, and pausing for a reply.

I am not sure that ever I heard the sound of cock-crowing from my clearing, and I thought that it might be worth the while to keep a cockerel for his music merely, as a singing bird. The note of this once wild Indian pheasant is certainly the most remarkable of any bird's, and if they could be naturalised without being domesticated, it would soon become the most famous sound in our woods, surpassing the clangour of the goose and the hooting of the owl; and then imagine the cackling of the hens to fill the pauses when their lords' clarions rested! No wonder that man added this bird to his tame stock, —to say nothing of the eggs and drumsticks. To walk in a winter morning in a wood where these birds abounded, their native woods, and hear the wild cockerels crow on the trees, clear and shrill for miles over the responding earth, drowning the feebler notes of other birds,—think of it! It would put nations on the alert. Who would not be early to rise, and rise earlier and earlier every successive day of his life, till he became unspeakably healthy, wealthy, and wise? This foreign bird's note is celebrated by the poets of all countries along with the notes of their native songsters. All climates agree with brave Chanticleer. He is more indigenous even than the natives. His health is ever good, his lungs are sound, his spirits never flag. Even the sailor on the Atlantic and Pacific is awakened by his voice; but its shrill sound never roused me from my slumbers. I kept neither dog, cat, cow, pig, nor hens, so that you would have said there was a deficiency of domestic sounds; neither the churn, nor the spinning-wheel, nor even the singing of the kettle, nor the hissing of the urn, nor children crying, to comfort one. An old-fashioned man would have lost his senses or died of ennui before this. Not even rats in the wall, for they were starved out, or rather were never baited in,—only squirrels on the roof and under the floor, a whippoorwill on the ridge-pole, a blue-jay screaming beneath the window, a hare or woodchuck under the house, a screech-owl, or a cat-owl behind it, a flock of wild geese or a laughing loon on the pond, and a fox to bark in the night. Not even a lark or an oriole, those mild plantation birds, ever visited my clearing. No cockerels to crow now or hens to cackle in the yard. No yard! but unfenced Nature reaching up to your very sills. A young forest growing up under your windows, and wild sumachs and blackberry vines breaking through your cellar; sturdy pitch-pines rubbing and creaking against the shingles for want of room, their roots reaching quite under the house. . Instead of a scuttle or a blind blown off in the gale,—a pine tree snapped off or torn up by the roots behind your house for fuel. Instead of no path to the front yard gate in the Great Snow,—no gate,—no front yard,—and no path to the civilised world!

Crabbed Age and Youth [1]
by ROBERT LOUIS STEVENSON

> "You know my mother now and then argues very notably; always very warmly at least. I happen often to differ from her; and we both think so well of our own arguments, that we very seldom are so happy as to convince one another. A pretty common case, I believe, in all *vehement* debatings. She says, I am *too witty;* Anglicé, *too pert;* I, that she is *too wise;* that is to say, being likewise put into English, *not so young as she has been*."—Miss Howe to Miss Harlowe, *Clarissa,* vol. ii. Letter xiii.

THERE is a strong feeling in favour of cowardly and prudential proverbs. The sentiments of a man while he is full of ardour and hope are to be received, it is supposed, with some qualification. But when the same person has ignominiously failed and begins to eat up his words, he should be listened to like an oracle. Most of our pocket wisdom is conceived for the use of mediocre people, to discourage them from ambitious attempts, and generally console them in their mediocrity. And since mediocre people constitute the bulk of humanity, this is no doubt very properly so. But it does not follow that the one sort of proposition is any less true than the other, or that Icarus is not to be more praised, and perhaps more envied, than Mr. Samuel Budgett the Successful Merchant. The one is dead, to be sure, while the other is still in his counting-house counting out his money; and doubtless this is a consideration. But we have, on the other hand, some bold and magnanimous sayings common to high races and natures, which set forth the advantage of the losing side, and proclaim it better to be a dead lion than a living dog. It is difficult to fancy how the mediocrities reconcile such sayings with their proverbs. According to the latter, every lad who goes to sea is an egregious ass; never to forget your umbrella through a long life would seem a higher and wiser flight of achievement than to go smiling to the stake; and so long as you are a bit of a coward and inflexible in money matters, you fulfil the whole duty of man.

[1] From *Virginibus Puerisque* (1878).

It is a still more difficult consideration for our average men, that while all their teachers, from Solomon down to Benjamin Franklin and the ungodly Binney, have inculcated the same ideal of manners, caution, and respectability, those characters in history who have most notoriously flown in the face of such precepts are spoken of in hyperbolical terms of praise, and honoured with public monuments in the streets of our commercial centres. This is very bewildering to the moral sense. You have Joan. of Arc, who left a humble but honest and reputable livelihood under the eyes of her parents, to go a-colonelling, in the company of rowdy soldiers, against the enemies of France; surely a melancholy example for one's daughters! And then you have Columbus, who may have pioneered America, but, when all is said, was a most imprudent navigator. His Life is not the kind of thing one would like to put into the hands of young people; rather, one would do one's utmost to keep it from their knowledge, as a red flag of adventure and disintegrating influence in life. The time would fail me if I were to recite all the big names in history whose exploits are perfectly irrational and even shocking to the business mind. The incongruity is speaking; and I imagine it must engender among the mediocrities a very peculiar attitude towards the nobler and showier sides of national life. They will read of the Charge of Balaclava in much the same spirit as they assist at a performance of the *Lyons Mail*. Persons of substance take in the *Times* and sit composedly in pit or boxes according to the degree of their prosperity in business. As for the generals who go galloping up and down among bomb-shells in absurd cocked hats—as for the actors who raddle their faces and demean themselves for hire upon the stage—they must belong, thank God! to a different order of beings, whom we watch as we watch the clouds careering in the windy, bottomless inane, or read about like characters in ancient and rather fabulous annals. Our offspring would no more think of copying their behavior, let us hope, than of doffing their clothes and painting themselves blue in consequence of certain admissions in the first chapter of their school history of England.

Discredited as they are in practice, the cowardly proverbs hold their own in theory; and it is another instance of the same spirit, that the opinions of old men about life have been accepted as final. All sorts of allowances are made for the illusions of youth; and none, or almost none, for the disenchantments of age. It is held to be a good taunt, and somehow or other to clinch the question logically, when an old gentleman waggles his head and says: "Ah, so I thought when I was your age." It is not thought an answer at all, if the young man retorts: "My venerable sir, so I shall most probably think when I am yours." And yet the one is as good as the other: pass for pass, tit for tat, a Roland for an Oliver.

"Opinion in good men," says Milton, "is but knowledge in the making." All opinions, properly so called, are stages on the road to truth. It does not follow that a man will travel any farther; but if he has really considered the world and drawn a conclusion, he has travelled as far. This does not apply to formulæ got by rote, which are stages on the road to nowhere but second childhood and the grave. To have a catchword in your mouth is not the same thing as to hold an opinion; still less is it the same thing to have made one for yourself. There are too many of these catchwords in the world for people to rap out upon you like an oath and by way of an argument. They have a currency as intellectual counters; and many respectable persons pay their way with nothing else. They seem to stand for vague bodies of theory in the background. The imputed virtue of folios full of knockdown arguments is supposed to reside in them, just as some of the majesty of the British Empire dwells in the constable's truncheon. They are used in pure superstition, as old clodhoppers spoil Latin by way of an exorcism. And yet they are vastly serviceable for checking unprofitable discussion and stopping the mouths of babes and sucklings. And when a young man comes to a certain stage of intellectual growth, the examination of these counters forms a gymnastic at once amusing and fortifying to the mind.

Because I have reached Paris, I am not ashamed of having passed through Newhaven and Dieppe. They were very good places to pass through, and I am none the less at my destination. All my old opinions were only stages on the way to the one I now hold, as itself is only a stage on the way to something else. I am no more abashed at having been a red-hot Socialist with a panacea of my own than at having been a suckling infant. Doubtless the world is quite right in a million ways; but you have to be kicked about a little to convince you of the fact. And in the meanwhile you must do something, be something, believe something. It is not possible to keep the mind in a state of accurate balance and blank; and even if you could do so, instead of coming ultimately to the right conclusion, you would be very apt to remain in a state of balance and blank to perpetuity. Even in quite intermediate stages, a dash of enthusiasm is not a thing to be ashamed of in the retrospect; if St. Paul had not been a very zealous Pharisee, he would have been a colder Christian. For my part, I look back to the time when I was a Socialist with something like regret. I have convinced myself (for the moment) that we had better leave these great changes to what we call great blind forces: their blindness being so much more perspicacious than the little, peering, partial eyesight of men. I seem to see that my own scheme would not answer; and all the other schemes I ever heard propounded would depress some elements of goodness just as much as they encouraged others. Now I know that in thus turning Conservative with years, I am going through the normal cycle of change and travelling in the common orbit of men's opinions. I submit to this, as I would submit to gout or grey hair, as a concomitant of growing age or else of failing animal heat; but I do not acknowledge that it is necessarily a change for the better—I daresay it is deplorably for the worse. I have no choice in the business, and can no more resist this tendency of my mind than I could prevent my body from beginning to totter and decay. If I am spared (as the phrase runs) I shall doubtless outlive some troublesome desires; but I am in no hurry about that! nor, when the time comes, shall I plume myself on the immunity. Just in the same way, I do not greatly pride myself on having outlived my belief in the fairy tales of Socialism. Old people have faults of their own; they tend to become cowardly, niggardly, and suspicious. Whether from the growth of experience or the decline of animal heat, I see that age leads to these and certain other faults; and it follows, of course, that while in one sense I hope I am journeying towards the truth, in another I am indubitably posting towards these forms and sources of error.

As we go catching and catching at this or that corner of knowledge, now getting a foresight of generous possibilities, now chilled with a glimpse of prudence, we may compare the headlong course of our years to a swift torrent in which a man is carried away; now he is dashed against a boulder, now he grapples for a moment to a trailing spray; at the end, he is hurled out and overwhelmed in a dark and bottomless ocean. We have no more than glimpses and touches; we are torn away from our theories; we are spun round and round and shown this or the other view of life, until only fools or knaves can hold to their opinions. We take a sight at a condition in life, and say we have studied it; our most elaborate view is no more than an impression. If we had breathing space, we should take the occasion to modify and adjust; but at this breakneck hurry, we are no sooner boys than we are adult, no sooner in love than married or jilted, no sooner one age than we begin to be another, and no sooner in the fulness of our manhood than we begin to decline towards the grave. It is in vain to seek for consistency or expect clear and stable views in a medium so perturbed and fleeting. This is no cabinet science, in which things are tested to a scruple; we theorise with a pistol to our head; we are confronted with a new set of conditions on which we have not only to pass a judgment, but to take action, before the hour is at an end. And we cannot even regard ourselves as a constant; in this flux of things, our identity itself seems in a perpetual variation; and not infrequently we find our own disguise the strangest in the masquerade. In the course of time, we grow to love things we hated and hate things we loved. Milton is not so dull as he once was, nor perhaps Ainsworth so amusing. It is decidedly harder to climb trees, and not nearly so hard to sit still. There is no use pretending; even the thrice royal game of hide-and-seek has somehow lost in zest. All our attributes are modified or changed; and it will be a poor account of us if our views do not modify and change in proportion. To hold the same views at forty as we held at twenty is to have been stupefied for a score of years, and take rank, not as a prophet, but as an unteachable brat, well birched and none the wiser. It is as if a ship captain should sail to India from the Port of London; and having brought a chart of the Thames on deck at his first setting out should obstinately use no other for the whole voyage.

And mark you, it would be no less foolish to begin at Gravesend with a chart of the Red Sea. *Si Jeunesse savait, si Vieillesse pouvait,*[2] is a very pretty sentiment, but not necessarily right. In five cases out of ten, it is not so much that the young people do not know, as that they do not choose. There is

[2] If Youth but knew, if Old Age but could.

something irreverent in the speculation, but perhaps the want of power has more to do with the wise resolutions of age than· we are always willing to admit. It would be an instructive experiment to make an old man young again and leave him all his *savoir*. I scarcely think he would put his money in the Savings Bank after all; I doubt if he would be such an admirable son as we are led to expect; and as for his conduct in love, I believe firmly he would out-Herod Herod, and put the whole of his new compeers to· the blush. Prudence is a wooden Juggernaut, before whom Benjamin Franklin walks with the portly air of a high-priest, and after whom dances many a successful merchant in the character of Atys. But it is not a deity to cultivate in· youth. If a man lives to any considerable age, it cannot be denied that he laments his imprudences, but I notice he often laments his youth a deal more bitterly and with a more genuine intonation.

It is customary to say that age should be considered, because it comes last. It seems just as much to the point, that youth comes first. And the scale fairly kicks the beam, if you go on to add that age, in a majority of cases, never comes at all. Disease and accident make short work of even the most prosperous persons; death costs nothing, and the expense of a headstone is an inconsiderable trifle to the happy heir. To be suddenly snuffed out in the middle of ambitious schemes is tragical enough at best; but when a man has been grudging himself his own life in the meanwhile, and saving up every-thing for the festival that was never to be, it becomes that hysterically moving sort of tragedy which lies on the confines of farce. The victim is dead—and he has cunningly overreached himself; a combination of calamities none the less absurd for being grim. To husband a favourite claret until the batch turns sour, is not at all an artful stroke of policy; and how much more with a whole cellar—a whole bodily existence! People may lay down their lives with cheerfulness in the sure expectation of a blessed immortality; but that is a different affair from giving up youth with all its admirable pleasures, in the hope of a better quality of gruel in a more than problematical, nay, more than improbable, old age. We should not compliment a hungry man, who should refuse a whole dinner and reserve all his appetite for the dessert, before he knew whether there was to be any dessert or not. If there be such a thing as imprudence in the world, we surely have it here. We sail in leaky bottoms and on great and perilous waters; and to take a cue from· the dolorous old naval ballad, we have heard the mermaidens singing, and know that we shall never see dry land any more. Old and young, we are all on our last cruise. If there is a fill of tobacco among the crew, for God's sake pass it round, and let us have a pipe before we go!

Indeed, by the report of our elders, this nervous preparation for old age is only trouble thrown away. We fall on guard, and after all it is a friend who comes to meet us. After the sun is down and the west faded, the heavens begin to fill with shining stars. So, as we grow old, a sort of equable jog-trot of feeling is substituted for the violent ups and downs of passion and disgust; the same influence that restrains our hopes, quiets our apprehensions; if the pleasures are less intense, the troubles are milder and more tolerable; and in a word, this period for which we are asked to hoard up everything as for a time of famine is, in its own right, the richest, easiest, and happiest of life. Nay, by managing its own work and following its own happy inspiration, youth is doing the best it can to endow the leisure of age. A full busy youth is your only prelude to a self-contained and independent age; and the muff inevitably develops into the bore. There are not many Doctor Johnsons, to set forth upon their first romantic voyage at sixty-four. If we wish to scale Mont Blanc or visit a thieves' kitchen in the East End, to go down in a diving-dress or up in a balloon, we must be about it while we are still young. It will not do to delay until we are clogged with prudence and limping with rheumatism, and people begin to ask us: "What does Gravity out of bed?" Youth is the time to go flashing from one end of the world to the other both in mind and body; to try the manners of different nations; to hear the chimes at midnight; to see sunrise in town and country; to be converted at a revival; to circumnavigate the metaphysics, write halting verses, run a mile to see a fire, and wait all day long in the theatre to applaud *Hernani*. There is some meaning in the old theory about wild oats; and a man who has not had his green-sickness and got done with it for good, is as little to be depended on as an unvaccinated infant. "It is extraordinary," said Lord Beaconsfield, one of the brightest and best preserved of youths up to the date of his last novel,[3] "it is extraordinary how hourly and how violently change the feelings of an inexperienced young man." And this mobility is a special talent entrusted to his care; a sort of indestructible virginity; a magic armour, with which he can pass unhurt through great dangers and come unbedaubed out of the miriest passages. Let him voyage, speculate, see all that he can, do all that he may; his soul has as many lives as a cat; he will live in all weathers, and never be a halfpenny the worse. Those who go to the devil in youth, with anything like a fair chance, were probably little worth saving from the first; they must have been feeble fellows—creatures made of putty and packthread, without steel or fire, anger or true joyfulness, in their composition; we may sympathise with their parents, but there is not much cause to go into mourning for themselves; for, to be quite honest, the weak brother is the worst of mankind.

When the old man waggles his head and says, "Ah, so I thought when I was your age," he has proved the youth's case. Doubtless, whether from growth of experience or decline of animal heat, he thinks so no longer; but he thought so while he was young; and all men have thought so while they were young, since there was dew in the morning or hawthorn in May; and here is another young man adding his vote to those of previous generations and riveting another link to the chain of testimony. It is as natural and as right for a young man to be imprudent and exaggerated, to live in swoops and circles, and beat about his cage like any other wild thing newly captured,

[3] *Lothair.*

as it is for old men to turn grey, or mothers to love their offspring, or heroes to die for something worthier than their lives.

By way of an apologue for the aged, when they feel more than usually tempted to offer their advice, let me recommend the following little tale. A child who had been remarkably fond of toys (and in particular of lead soldiers) found himself growing to the level of acknowledged boyhood without any abatement of this childish taste. He was thirteen; already he had been taunted for dallying overlong about the playbox; he had to blush if he was found among his lead soldiers; the shades of the prison-house were closing about him with a vengeance. There is nothing more difficult than to put the thoughts of children into the language of their elders; but this is the effect of his meditations at this juncture: "Plainly," he said, "I must give up my playthings in the meanwhile, since I am not in a position to secure myself against idle jeers. At the same time, I am sure that playthings are the very pick of life; all people give them up out of the same pusillanimous respect for those who are a little older; and if they do not return to them as soon as they can, it is only because they grow stupid and forget. I shall be wiser; I shall conform for a little to the ways of their foolish world; but so soon as I have made enough money, I shall retire and shut myself up among my playthings until the day I die." Nay, as he was passing in the train along the Esterel mountains between Cannes and Fréjus, he remarked a pretty house in an orange garden at the angle of a bay, and decided that this should be his Happy Valley. Astrea Redux; childhood was to come again! The idea has an air of simple nobility to me, not unworthy of Cincinnatus. And yet, as the reader has probably anticipated, it is never likely to be carried into effect. There was a worm i' the bud, a fatal error in the premises. Childhood must pass away, and then youth, as surely as age approaches. The true wisdom is to be always seasonable, and to change with a good grace in changing circumstances. To love playthings well as a child, to lead an adventurous and honourable youth, and to settle, when the time arrives, into a green and smiling age, is to be a good artist in life and deserve well of yourself and your neighbour.

You need repent none of your youthful vagaries. They may have been over the score on one side, just as those of age are probably over the score on the other. But they had a point; they not only befitted your age and expressed its attitude and passions, but they had a relation to what was outside of you, and implied criticisms on the existing state of things, which you need not allow to have been undeserved, because you now see that they were partial. All error, not merely verbal, is a strong way of stating that the current truth is incomplete. The follies of youth have a basis in sound reason, just as much as the embarrassing questions put by babes and sucklings. Their most anti-social acts indicate the defects of our society. When the torrent sweeps the man against a boulder, you must expect him to scream, and you need not be surprised if the scream is sometimes a theory. Shelley, chafing at the Church of England, discovered the cure of all evils in universal atheism. Generous lads, irritated at the injustices of society, see nothing for it but the abolishment of everything and Kingdom Come of anarchy. Shelley was a young fool; so are these cock-sparrow revolutionaries. But it is better to be a fool than to be dead. It is better to emit a scream in the shape of a theory than to be entirely insensible to the jars and incongruities of life and take everything as it comes in a forlorn stupidity. Some people swallow the universe like a pill; they travel on through the world, like smiling images pushed from behind. For God's sake give me the young man who has brains enough to make a fool of himself! As for the others, the irony of facts shall take it out of their hands, and make fools of them in downright earnest, ere the farce be over. There shall be such a mopping and a mowing at the last day, and such blushing and confusion of countenance for all those who have been wise in their own esteem, and have not learnt the rough lessons that youth hands on to age. If we are indeed to perfect and complete our own natures, and grow larger, stronger, and more sympathetic against some nobler career in the future, we had all best bestir ourselves to the utmost while we have the time. To equip a dull, respectable person with wings would be but to make a parody of an angel.

In short, if youth is not quite right in its opinions, there is a strong probability that age is not much more so. Undying hope is co-ruler of the human bosom with infallible credulity. A man finds he has been wrong at every preceding stage of his career, only to deduce the astonishing conclusion that he is at last entirely right. Mankind, after centuries of failure, are still upon the eve of a thoroughly constitutional millennium. Since we have explored the maze so long without result, it follows, for poor human reason, that we cannot have to explore much longer; close by must be the centre, with a champagne luncheon and a piece of ornamental water. How if there were no centre at all, but just one alley after another, and the whole world a labyrinth without end or issue?

I overheard the other day a scrap of conversation, which I take the liberty to reproduce. "What I advance is true," said one. "But not the whole truth," answered the other. "Sir," returned the first (and it seemed to me there was a smack of Dr. Johnson in the speech), "Sir, there is no such thing as the whole truth!" Indeed, there is nothing so evident in life as that there are two sides to a question. History is one long illustration. The forces of nature are engaged day by day, cudgelling it into our backward intelligences. We never pause for a moment's consideration, but we admit it as an axiom. An enthusiast sways humanity exactly by disregarding this great truth, and dinning it into our ears that this or that question has only one possible solution; and your enthusiast is a fine florid fellow, dominates things for a while and shakes the world out of a doze; but when once he is gone, an army of quiet and uninfluential people set to work to remind us of the other side and demolish the generous imposture. While Calvin is putting everybody exactly right in his *Institutes,* and hot-headed Knox is thundering in the pulpit, Montaigne is already looking at the other side in his library in Périgord, and predicting that they will find as much to quarrel about in the Bible as they had found already in the Church. Age may have one side, but assuredly Youth has the other. There is nothing more certain than that both are right, except perhaps that both are wrong. Let them agree to differ; for who knows but what agreeing to differ may not be a form of agreement rather than a form of difference?

I suppose it is written that anyone who sets up for a bit of a philosopher must contradict himself to his very face. For here have I fairly talked myself into thinking that we have the whole thing before us at last; that there is no answer to the mystery, except that there are as many as you please; that there is no centre to the maze because, like the famous sphere, its centre is everywhere; and that agreeing to differ with every ceremony of politeness, is the only "one undisturbed song of pure concent" to which we are ever likely to lend our musical voices.

Hunting the Deceitful Turkey [1]
by MARK TWAIN

WHEN I was a boy my uncle and his big boys hunted with the rifle, the youngest boy Fred and I with a shotgun—a small single-barrelled shotgun which was properly suited to our size and strength; it was not much heavier than a broom. We carried it turn about, half an hour at a time. I was not able to hit anything with it, but I liked to try. Fred and I hunted feathered small game, the others hunted deer, squirrel, wild turkeys, and such things. My uncle and the big boys were good shots. They killed hawks and wild geese and such like on the wing; and they didn't wound or kill squirrels, they *stunned* them. When the dogs treed a squirrel, the squirrel would scamper aloft and run out on a limb and flatten himself along it, hoping to make himself invisible in that way—and not quite succeeding. You could see his wee little ears sticking up. You couldn't see his nose, but you knew where it was. Then the hunter, despising a "rest" for his rifle, stood up and took offhand aim at the limb and sent a bullet into it immediately under the squirrel's nose, and down tumbled the animal, unwounded but unconscious; the dogs gave him a shake and he was dead. Sometimes when the distance was great and the wind was not accurately allowed for, the bullet would hit the squirrel's head; the dogs could do as they pleased with that one—the hunter's pride was hurt, and he wouldn't allow it to go into the gamebag.

In the first faint gray of the dawn the stately wild turkeys would be stalk-

[1] From Mark Twain, *The Mysterious Stranger*. By permission of Harper & Brothers. First published in 1906.

ing around in great flocks, and ready to be sociable and answer invitations to come and converse with other excursionists of their kind. The hunter concealed himself and imitated the turkey-call by sucking the air through the legbone of a turkey which had previously answered the call like that and lived only just long enough to regret it. There is nothing that furnishes a perfect turkey-call except that bone. Another of Nature's treacheries, you see. She is full of them; half the time she doesn't know which she likes best—to betray her child or protect it. In the case of the turkey she is badly mixed: she gives it a bone to be used in getting it into trouble, and she also furnishes it with a trick for getting itself out of the trouble again. When a mamma-turkey answers an invitation and finds she has made a mistake in accepting it, she does as the mamma-partridge does—remembers a previous engagement and goes limping and scrambling away, pretending to be very lame; and at the same time she is saying to her not-visible children, "Lie low, keep still, don't expose yourselves; I shall be back as soon as I have beguiled this shabby swindler out of the country."

When a person is ignorant and confiding, this immoral device can have tiresome results. I followed an ostensibly lame turkey over a considerable part of the United States one morning, because I believed in her and could not think she would deceive a mere boy, and one who was trusting her and considering her honest. I had the single-barrelled shotgun, but my idea was to catch her alive. I often got within rushing distance of her, and then made my rush; but always, just as I made my final plunge and put my hand down where her back had been, it wasn't there; it was only two or three inches from there and I brushed the tail-feathers as I landed on my stomach—a very close call, but still not quite close enough; that is, not close enough for success, but just close enough to convince me that I could do it next time. She always waited for me, a little piece away, and let on to be resting and greatly fatigued; which was a lie, but I believed it, for I still thought her honest long after I ought to have begun to doubt her, suspecting that this was no way for a high-minded bird to be acting. I followed, and followed, and followed, making my periodical rushes, and getting up and brushing the dust off, and resuming the voyage with patient confidence; indeed, with a confidence which grew, for I could see by the change of climate and vegetation that we were getting up into the high latitudes, and as she always looked a little tireder and a little more discouraged after each rush, I judged that I saw safe to win, in the end, the competition being purely a matter of staying power and the advantage lying with me from the start because she was lame.

Along in the afternoon I began to feel fatigued myself. Neither of us had had any rest since we first started on the excursion, which was upwards of ten hours before, though latterly we had paused awhile after rushes, I letting on to be thinking about something else; but neither of us sincere, and both of us waiting for the other to call game but in no real hurry about it, for indeed those little evanescent snatches of rest were very grateful to the feelings of us both; it would naturally be so, skirmishing along like that ever

since dawn and not a bite in the meantime; at least for me, though sometimes as she lay on her side fanning herself with a wing and praying for
strength to get out of this difficulty a grasshopper happened along whose time
had come, and that was well for her, and fortunate, but I had nothing—
nothing the whole day.

More than once, after I was very tired, I gave up taking her alive, and
was going to shoot her, but I never did it, although it was my right, for I
did not believe I could hit her; and besides, she always stopped and posed,
when I raised the gun, and this made me suspicious that she knew about me
and my marksmanship, and so I did not care to expose myself to remarks.

I did not get her, at all. When she got tired of the game at last, she rose
from almost under my hand and flew aloft with the rush and whir of a shell
and lit on the highest limb of a great tree and sat down and crossed her legs
and smiled down at me, and seemed gratified to see me so astonished.

I was ashamed, and also lost; and it was while wandering the woods
hunting for myself that I found a deserted log cabin and had one of the best
meals there that in my life-days I have eaten. The weed-grown garden was
full of ripe tomatoes, and I ate them ravenously, though I had never liked
them before. Not more than two or three times since have I tasted anything
that was so delicious as those tomatoes. I surfeited myself with them, and
did not taste another one until I was in middle life. I can eat them now,
but I do not like the look of them. I suppose we have all experienced a sur-
feit at one time or another. Once, in stress of circumstances, I ate part of a
barrel of sardines, there being nothing else at hand, but since then I have
always been able to get along without sardines.

How Shall I Word It?[1]

by MAX BEERBOHM

IT would seem that I am one of those travellers for whom the railway
bookstall does not cater. Whenever I start on a journey, I find that my
choice lies between well-printed books which I have no wish to read, and
well-written books which I could not read without permanent injury to my
eyesight. The keeper of the bookstall, seeing me gaze vaguely along his
shelves, suggests that I should take 'Fen Country Fanny' or else 'The Track
of Blood' and have done with it. Not wishing to hurt his feelings, I refuse
these works on the plea that I have read them. Whereon he, divining despite
me that I am a superior person, says 'Here is a nice little handy edition of

[1] From Max Beerbohm, *And Even Now* (1920), published and copyrighted by E. P. Dutton &
Co., Inc., New York.

More's "Utopia"' or 'Carlyle's "French Revolution"' and again I make some excuse. What pleasure could I get from trying to cope with a masterpiece printed in diminutive grey-ish type on a semi-transparent little grey-ish page? I relieve the bookstall of nothing but a newspaper or two.

The other day, however, my eye and fancy were caught by a book entitled 'How Shall I Word It?' and sub-entitled 'A Complete Letter Writer for Men and Women.' I had never read one of these manuals, but had often heard that there was a great and constant 'demand' for them. So I demanded this one. It is no great fun in itself. The writer is no fool. He has evidently a natural talent for writing letters. His style is, for the most part, discreet and easy. If you were a young man writing 'to Father of Girl he wishes to Marry' or 'thanking Fiancée for Present' or 'reproaching Fiancée for being a Flirt,' or if you were a mother 'asking Governess her Qualifications' or 'replying to Undesirable Invitation for her Child,' or indeed if you were in any other one of the crises which this book is designed to alleviate, you might copy out and post the specially-provided letter without making yourself ridiculous in the eyes of its receiver—unless, of course, he or she also possessed a copy of the book. But—well, can you conceive any one copying out and posting one of these letters, or even taking it as the basis for composition? You cannot. That shows how little you know of your fellow-creatures. Not you nor I can plumb the abyss at the bottom of which such humility is possible. Nevertheless, as we know by that great and constant 'demand,' there the abyss is, and there multitudes are at the bottom of it. Let's peer down . . . No, all is darkness. But faintly, if we listen hard, is borne up to us a sound of the scratching of innumerable pens—pens whose wielders are all trying, as the author of this handbook urges them, to 'be original, fresh, and interesting' by dint of more or less strict adherence to sample.

Giddily you draw back from the edge of the abyss. Come!—here is a thought to steady you. The mysterious great masses of helpless folk for whom 'How Shall I Word It' is written are sound at heart, delicate in feeling, anxious to please, most loth to wound. For it must be presumed that the author's style of letter-writing is informed as much by a desire to give his public what it needs, and will pay for, as by his own beautiful nature; and in the course of all the letters that he dictates you will find not one harsh word, not one ignoble thought or unkind insinuation. In all of them, though so many are for the use of persons placed in the most trying circumstances, and some of them are for persons writhing under a sense of intolerable injury, sweetness and light do ever reign. Even 'yours truly, Jacob Langton,' in his 'letter to his Daughter's Mercenary Fiancé,' mitigates the sternness of his tone by the remark that his 'task is inexpressibly painful.' And he, Mr. Langton, is the one writer who lets the post go out on his wrath. When Horace Masterton, of Thorpe Road, Putney, receives from Miss Jessica Weir, of Fir Villa, Blackheath, a letter 'declaring her Change of Feelings,' does he upbraid her? No; 'it was honest and brave of you to write to me so straightforwardly and at the back of my mind I know you have done what is best. . . . I give you back your freedom only at your desire. God bless you, dear.' Not less admirable is the behaviour, in similar case, of Cecil Grant (14, Glover Street, Streatham). Suddenly, as a bolt from the blue, comes a letter from Miss Louie Hawke (Elm View, Deerhurst), breaking off her betrothal to him. Haggard, he sits down to his desk; his pen traverses the note-paper—calling down curses on Louie and on all her sex? No; 'one cannot say good-bye for ever without deep regret to days that have been so full of happiness. I must thank you sincerely for all your great kindness to me. . . . With every sincere wish for your future happiness,' he bestows complete freedom on Miss Hawke. And do not imagine that in the matter of self-control and sympathy, of power to understand all and pardon all, the men are lagged behind by the women. Miss Leila Johnson (The Manse, Carlyle) has observed in Leonard Wace (Dover Street, Saltburn) a certain coldness of demeanour; yet 'I do not blame you; it is probably your nature'; and Leila in her sweet forbearance is typical of all the other pained women in these pages: she is but one of a crowd of heroines.

Face to face with all this perfection, the not perfect reader begins to crave some little outburst of wrath, of hatred or malice, from one of these imaginary ladies and gentlemen. He longs for—how shall he word it?—a glimpse of some bad motive, of some little lapse from dignity. Often, passing by a pillar-box, I have wished I could unlock it and carry away its contents, to be studied at my leisure. I have always thought such a haul would abound in things fascinating to a student of human nature. One night, not long ago, I took a waxen impression of the lock of the pillar-box nearest to my house, and had a key made. This implement I have as yet lacked either the courage or the opportunity to use. And now I think I shall throw it away . . . No, I shan't. I refuse, after all, to draw my inference that the bulk of the British public writes always in the manner of this handbook. Even if they all have beautiful natures they must sometimes be sent slightly astray by inferior impulses, just as are you and I.

And, if err they must, surely it were well they should know how to do it correctly and forcibly. I suggest to our author that he should sprinkle his next edition with a few less righteous examples, thereby both purging his book of its monotony and somewhat justifying its sub-title. Like most people who are in the habit of writing things to be printed, I have not the knack of writing really good letters. But let me crudely indicate the sort of thing that our manual needs. . . .

LETTER FROM POOR MAN TO OBTAIN MONEY FROM RICH ONE

(The English law is particularly hard on what is called blackmail. It is therefore essential that the applicant should write nothing that might afterwards be twisted to incriminate him.—Ed.)

Dear Sir,

To-day, as I was turning out a drawer in my attic, I came across a letter which by a curious chance fell into my hands some years ago, and which, in the stress of grave pecuniary embarrassment, had escaped my memory. It is a letter written by yourself to a lady, and the date shows it to have been written shortly after your marriage. It is of a confidential nature, and might, I fear, if it fell into the wrong hands, be cruelly misconstrued. I would wish you to have the satisfaction of destroying it in person. At first I thought of sending it on to you by post. But I know how happy you are in your domestic life; and probably your wife and you, in your perfect mutual trust, are in the habit of opening each other's letters. Therefore, to avoid risk, I would prefer to hand the document to you personally. I will not ask you to come to my attic, where I could not offer you such hospitality as is due to a man of your wealth and position. You will be so good as to meet me at 3.0 A.M. (sharp) to-morrow (Thursday) beside the tenth lamp-post to the left on the Surrey side of Waterloo Bridge; at which hour and place we shall not be disturbed.

I am, dear Sir,
Yours respectfully
James Gridge.

LETTER FROM YOUNG MAN REFUSING TO PAY HIS TAILOR'S BILL

Mr. Eustace Davenant has received the half-servile, half-insolent screed which Mr. Yardley has addressed to him. Let Mr. Yardley cease from crawling on his knees and shaking his fist. Neither this posture nor this gesture can wring one bent farthing from the pockets of Mr. Davenant, who was a minor at the time when that series of ill-made suits was supplied to him and will hereafter, as in the past, shout (without prejudice) from the housetops that of all the tailors in London Mr. Yardley is at once the most grasping and the least competent.

LETTER TO THANK AUTHOR FOR INSCRIBED COPY OF BOOK

Dear Mr. Emanuel Flower,

It was kind of you to think of sending me a copy of your new book. It would have been kinder still to think again and abandon that project. I am a man of gentle instincts, and do not like to tell you that 'A Flight into Arcady' (of which I have skimmed a few pages, thus wasting two or three minutes of my not altogether worthless time) is trash. On the other hand, I am determined that you shall not be able to go around boasting to your friends, if you have any, that this work was not condemned, derided, and dismissed by your sincere well-wisher, *Wrexford Cripps.*

LETTER TO MEMBER OF PARLIAMENT UNSEATED AT GENERAL ELECTION

Dear Mr. Pobsby-Burford,

Though I am myself an ardent Tory, I cannot but rejoice in the crushing defeat you have just suffered in West Odgetown. There are moments when political conviction is overborne by personal sentiment; and this is one of them. Your loss of the seat that you held is the more striking by reason of the splendid manner in which the northern and eastern divisions of Odgetown have been wrested from the Liberal Party. The great bulk of the newspaper-reading public will be puzzled by your extinction in the midst of our party's triumph. But then, the great mass of the newspaper-reading public has not met you. I have. You will probably not remember me. You are the sort of man who would not remember anybody who might not be of some definite use to him. Such, at least, was one of the impressions you made on me when I met you last summer at a dinner given by our friends the Pelhams. Among the other things in you that struck me were the blatant pomposity of your manner, your appalling flow of cheap platitudes, and your hoggish lack of ideas. It is such men as you that lower the tone of public life. And I am sure that in writing to you thus I am but expressing what is felt, without distinction of party, by all who sat with you in the late Parliament.

The one person in whose behalf I regret your withdrawal into private life is your wife, whom I had the pleasure of taking in to the aforesaid dinner. It was evident to me that she was a woman whose spirit was well-nigh broken by her conjunction with you. Such remnants of cheerfulness as were in her I attributed to the Parliamentary duties which kept you out of her sight for so very many hours daily. I do not like to think of the fate to which the free and independent electors of West Odgetown have just condemned her. Only, remember this: chattel of yours though she is, and timid and humble, she despises you in her heart.

I am, dear Mr. Pobsby-Burford,
Yours very truly,
Harold Thistlake.

LETTER FROM YOUNG LADY IN ANSWER TO INVITATION FROM OLD SCHOOLMISTRESS

My dear Miss Price,

How awfully sweet of you to ask me to stay with you for a few days but how *can* you think I may have forgotten you for of course I think of you so very often and of the three years I spent at your school because it is such a joy not to be there any longer and if one is at all down it bucks one up directly to remember that *thats* all over atanyrate and that one has enough food to nurrish one and not that awful monottany of life and not the petty fogging daily tirrany you went in for and I can imagin no greater thrill and luxury in a way than to come and see the whole dismal grind still going on but without me being in it but this would be rather beastly of me wouldnt it so please dear Miss Price dont expect me and do excuse mistakes of English Composition and Spelling and etcetra in your affectionate old pupil,

Emily Therese Lynn-Royston.

ps, I often rite to people telling them where I was edducated and highly reckomending you.

LETTER IN ACKNOWLEDGMENT OF WEDDING PRESENT

Dear Lady Amblesham,

Who gives quickly, says the old proverb, gives twice. For this reason I have purposely delayed writing to you, lest I should appear to thank you more than once for the small, cheap, hideous present you sent me on the occasion of my recent wedding. Were you a poor woman, that little bowl of ill-imitated Dresden china would convict you of tastelessness merely; were you a blind woman, of nothing but an odious parsimony. As you have normal eyesight and more than normal wealth, your gift to me proclaims you at once a Philistine and a miser (or rather did so proclaim you until, less than ten seconds after I had unpacked it from its wrappings of tissue paper, I took it to the open window and had the satisfaction of seeing it shattered to atoms on the pavement). But stay! I perceive a possible flaw in my argument. Perhaps you were guided in your choice by a definite wish to insult me. I am sure, on reflection, that this was so. I *shall not forget.*

Yours, etc.,

Cynthia Beaumarsh.

PS. My husband asked me to tell you to warn Lord Amblesham to keep out of his way or to assume some disguise so complete that he will not be recognized by him and horsewhipped.

PPS. I am sending copies of this letter to the principal London and provincial newspapers.

LETTER FROM . . .

But enough! I never thought I should be so strong in this line. I had not foreseen such copiousness and fatal fluency. Never again will I tap these deep dark reservoirs in a character that had always seemed to me, on the whole, so amiable.

Mr. Dooley on the Education of the Young [1]
by FINLEY PETER DUNNE

"If ye had a boy wud ye sind him to colledge?" asked Mr. Hennessy.
"Well," said Mr. Dooley, "at th' age whin a boy is fit to be in colledge I
wudden't have him around th' house."

THE troubled Mr. Hennessy had been telling Mr. Dooley about the difficulty of making a choice of schools for Packy Hennessy, who at the age
of six was at the point where the family must decide his career.
" 'Tis a big question," said Mr. Dooley, "an' wan that seems to be worryin' th' people more thin it used to whin ivry boy was designed f'r th' priesthood, with a full understandin' be his parents that th' chances was in favor
iv a brick yard. Nowadays they talk about th' edycation iv th' child befure
they choose th' name. 'Tis: 'Th' kid talks in his sleep. 'Tis th' fine lawyer
he'll make.' Or, 'Did ye notice him admirin' that photygraph? H'ell be a
gr-reat journalist.' Or, 'Look at him fishin' in Uncle Tim's watch pocket.
We must thrain him f'r a banker.' Or, 'I'm afraid he'll niver be sthrong
enough to wurruk. He must go into th' church.' Befure he's baptized too,
d'ye mind. 'Twill not be long befure th' time comes whin th' soggarth'll
christen th' infant: 'Judge Pathrick Aloysius Hinnissy, iv th' Northern District iv Illinye,' or 'Professor P. Aloysius Hinnissy, LL.D., S.T.D., P.G.N., iv
th' faculty iv Nothre Dame.' Th' innocent child in his cradle, wondherin'
what ails th' mist iv him an' where he got such funny lookin' parents fr'm,
has thim to blame that brought him into the wurruld if he dayvilops into a
sicond story man befure he's twinty-wan an' is took up be th' polis. Why
don't you lade Packy down to th' occylist an' have him fitted with a pair iv
eye-glasses? Why don't ye put goloshes on him, give him a blue umbrelly an'
call him a doctor at wanst an' be done with it?
"To my mind, Hinnissy, we're wastin' too much time thinkin' iv th'
future iv our young, an' thryin' to larn thim early what they outghn't to
know till they've growed up. We sind th' childher to school, as if 'twas a
summer garden where they go to be amused instead iv a pinitinchry where
they're sint f'r th' original sin. Whin I was a la-ad I was put at me ah-bee
abs, th' first day I set fut in th' school behind th' hedge an' me head was sore
inside an' out befure I wint home. Now th' first thing we larn th' future
Mark Hannas an' Jawn D. Gateses iv our naytion is waltzin', singin', an'
cuttin' pitchers out iv a book. We'd be much betther teachin' thim th'
sthrangle hold, f'r that's what they need in life.

[1] From *Mr. Dooley at His Best*, ed. by Elmer Ellis. By permission of Charles Scribner's Sons.
Essay first published in *Harper's Weekly*, Oct. 20, 1900.

"I know what'll happen. Ye'll sind Packy to what th' Germans call a Kindygarten, an' 'tis a good thing f'r Germany, because all a German knows is what some wan tells him, and his grajation papers is a certyficate that he don't need to think annymore. But we've inthrajooced it into this country, an' whin I was down seein' if I cud injooce Rafferty, th' Janitor iv th' Isaac Muggs Grammar School, f'r to vote f'r Riordan—an' he's goin to—I dhropped in on Cassidy's daughter, Mary Ellen, an' see her kindygartnin'. Th' childher was settin' ar-round on th' flure an' some was moldin' dachshunds out iv mud an' wipin' their hands on their hair, an' some was carvin' figures iv a goat out iv paste-board an some was singin' an some was sleepin' an' a few was dancin' an' wan la-ad was pullin' another la-ad's hair. 'Why don't ye take th' coal shovel to that little barbaryan, Mary Ellen?' says I. 'We don't believe in corporeal punishment,' says she. 'School shud be made pleasant f'r th' childher,' she says. 'Th' child who's hair is bein' pulled is larnin' patience,' she says, 'an' th' child that's pullin' the' hair is discoverin' th' footility iv human indeavor,' says she. 'Well, oh, well,' says I, 'times has changed since I was a boy,' I says. 'Put thim through their exercises,' says I. 'Tommy,' says I, 'spell cat,' I says. 'Go to th' divvle,' says th' cheerub. 'Very smartly answered,' says Mary Ellen. 'Ye shud not ask thim to spell,' she says. 'They don't larn that till they get to colledge,' she says, 'an',' she says, 'sometimes not even thin,' she says. 'An' what do they larn?' says I. 'Rompin',' she says, 'an' dancin',' she says, 'an' indepindance iv speech, an' beauty songs, an' sweet thoughts, an' how to make home home-like,' she says. 'Well,' says I, 'I didn't take anny iv thim things at colledge, so ye needn't unblanket thim,' I says. 'I won't put thim through anny exercise to-day,' I says. 'But whisper, Mary Ellen,' says I, 'don't ye niver feel like bastin' the seeraphims?' 'Th' teachin's iv Freebull and Pitzotly is conthrary to that,' she says. 'But I'm goin' to be marrid an' lave th' school on Choosdah, th' twinty-sicond iv Janooary,' she says, 'an' on Mondah, th' twinty-first, I'm goin' to ask a few iv th' little darlin's to th' house an',' she says, 'stew thim over a slow fire,' she says. Mary Ellen is not a German, Hinnissy.

"Well, afther they have larned in school what they ar're licked f'r larnin' in th' back yard—that is squashin' mud with their hands—they're conducted up through a channel iv free an' beautiful thought till they're r-ready f'r colledge. Mamma packs a few doylies an' tidies into son's bag, an' some silver to be used in case iv throuble with th' landlord, an' th' la-ad throts off to th' siminary. If he's not sthrong enough to look f'r high honors as a middleweight pugilist he goes into th' thought departmint. Th' prisident takes him into a Turkish room, gives him a cigareet an' says: 'Me dear boy, what special branch iv larnin' wud ye like to have studied f'r ye be our compitint profissors? We have a chair iv Beauty an' wan iv Puns an' wan iv Pothry on th' Changin' Hues iv th' Settin' Sun, an' wan on Platonic Love, an' wan on Non-sense Rhymes, an' wan on Sweet Thoughts, an' wan on How Green Grows th' Grass, an' wan on th' Relation iv Ice to th' Greek Idee iv God,' he says. 'This is all ye'll need to equip ye f'r th' perfect life,

onless,' he says, 'ye intind bein' a dintist, in which case,' he says, 'we won't
think much iv ye, but we have a good school where ye can learn that disgraceful thrade,' he says. An' th' la-ad makes his choice, an' ivry mornin'
whin he's up in time he takes a whiff iv hasheesh an' goes off to hear Pro-
fissor Maryanna tell him that 'if th' dates iv human knowledge must be
rejicted as subjictive, how much more must they be subjicted as rejictive if,
as I think, we keep our thoughts fixed upon th' inanity iv th' finite in comparison with th' onthinkable truth with th' ondivided an' inimaginable reality.
Boys, ar're ye with me?' . . ."

"I don't undherstand a wurrud iv what ye'r sayin','" said Mr. Hennessy.

"No more do I," said Mr. Dooley. "But I believe 'tis as Father Kelly says:
'Childher shuddn't be sint to school to larn, but to larn how to larn. I don't
care what ye larn thim so long as 'tis onpleasant to thim.' 'Tis thrainin' they
need, Hinnissy. That's all. I niver cud make use iv what I larned in colledge about thrigojoomethry an'—an'—grammar an' th' welts I got on th'
skull fr'm th' schoolmasther's cane I have niver been able to turn to anny
account in th' business, but 'twas th' bein' there an' havin' to get things to
heart without askin' th' meanin' iv thim an' goin' to school cold an' comin'
home hungry, that made th' man iv me ye see befure ye."

"That's why th' good woman's throubled about Packy," said Hennessy.

"Go home," said Mr. Dooley.

Codfish Chowder and Sun[1]

by ROBERT P. TRISTRAM COFFIN

THERE are many kinds of picnics; but my kind is the only kind that satisfies so well that it lasts me through a whole year.

To begin with, you must have the Maine coast; but more than that,
a particular part of the Maine coast, Casco Bay with its islands, a new one
for every day in the year, ranging in size from Great Chebeague and Great
Island, each capable of supporting far-flung villages, to the Chunk o' Pork
and the Pound o' Tea and Jello with its bushel of soil. And you must have
my kind of a family—one in which there are enough babies sprinkled in
among the grownups to keep a panoramic camera busy. A picnic without
a dozen yards of grandchildren would be only half a picnic for my mother.
Not any children at all will do, either; they must be babies who take life as a
sunrise or a circus or both together even when they still go on all fours.

Then you must have islands with fir trees packed so closely that you might
walk along their tops, if you were spry, and you must have the myrrh of the

[1] From R. P. T. Coffin, *An Attic Room* (1929). By permission of Doubleday & Company, Inc.

balsams in your nose along with the smell of the sea on a summer's day. It must be a day in August and one of the kind that you will find nowhere else on this round earth save Maine; northwest wind blowing the sky as clean and clear as a bell, a blue sky that you can fairly hear ring, and white galleons of clouds with flat keels, which sail over by thousands and yet never get in the way of the sun. The sunshine turns everything to amber and crystal and pours over the world like a tide. You can hear it lapping the granite coasts. The whole world is very hot yet airy; you can smell the tar in the caulking of the boats. Your face turns into a russet banner. Your brain turns into sunlight. The ocean grows darker and deeper blue between the white crests that are coming in from far Spain. The sea and the sun get in under your soul.

I cannot begin to tell you all the ingredients you mix together to make this day of bliss. Somewhere at the beginning you stir in a motor boat of the sort that is wide in the beam, good to hold a small army. You add spray all over everybody, especially the children; for my picnic would lack spice if all of us were not well drenched down with brine and salted down till our eyes were a fast blue. To have the best spray you need a flooding tide to kick up a chop against the wind. Throw into the picnic all the sandwiches, ginger ale, coffee, salads, fruit, cakes, and doughnuts if you please, for nothing can spoil the mess. You have the safe *sine qua non* [2] in the baskets at the bottom of the boat. Nothing could kill the flavor of the clams and lobsters you are carrying with you alive. The codfish are alive and waiting, too, out in the ocean you are heading into.

After the many islands, all white with granite and dark green with spruces and cedars, all looking as bright and new as they looked on the morning of creation, you must have the island where you are to land. I am the last person to be finicky, but this island should be absolutely like Pond Island. Now Pond Island has always been in the family along with my mother's ladderback chairs and melodeon. When they were young and quite brand-new to each other, Mother and Father lived one summer upon this jewel they had acquired soon after marriage. It was before most of us were born or "thought of," as Maine folks delicately put the matter of generation. Pond Island is the last place between Maine and Spain. There isn't a tree on it; the twelve winds from the twelve corners of the sky use it for their play-ground. The spray of a sou'easter salts the springs that bubble up in its very centre. The sheep that bite its grasses have to be thickset and low to the earth; they carry their heads raked like the stacks and masts of ocean craft. They are adopted cousins of the gales and the surf. The island can be smelt miles to the lee, since it is one mass of bayberry and juniper.

Pond Island has its name from the many ponds which pit its slopes. Years ago a lobsterman found a crock full of Spanish doubloons in a cleft of its rocks. That was enough to bring searchers for the treasure of Captain Kidd hither to dig in droves. All Maine fishermen believe in buried treasure

[2] Indispensable.

Why shouldn't they when any lobster pot may bring fortune flapping and kicking to the surface? But pirate legends are one of Maine's richest crops. So you can judge the number of pits on the island. Yet richer than any jeweled crucifix any freebooter hoarded are the pools far out in the ledges where rock-crabs slide like great emeralds through crystal. All the shores slant down into deep water so clear that you can see great fish and more mysterious things fathoms down moving beautifully like thoughts one has in the starlight of a winter night. Mystery comes close up to the island, ribboned kelp and jellyfish that shine like dim moons. But one place, open to the ocean and the White Bull, the reef which bellows and whitens forever with the surf on the rim of the horizon, is the holy of holies of all the island's windy beauty. It is Shell Cove, and it is heaped with the petals of flowers that blossomed in the sea, white with shells of living things that flourished aeons ago and that will go on flourishing for aeons to come, God being willing and God being the lover of sheer, delicate, pearly things that He was of old. Upon this floor the long breakers curl over through the nights and the days, the years and the ages, over and over in arcs that are flawless and complete, patterns of rhythm akin to the rhythm of the circling stars. The tremendous whisper of the things the sea tries to tell to men runs through and through the hours like peace. The air is snowed with seagulls leaning their white breasts on the wind and holding it in the symmetry of their wings. Foam takes flight, and the clouds go over; the place is like Gilead and the cedars of Lebanon. Bones of ships are bleaching among the shells to be your firewood. It is here the feast must be spread. No, no other island will ever do.

The first thing to do is to put most of the babies, with suitable chaperons equipped to feed them, ashore on Pond Island. Those who can run can chase butterflies, which grow bigger out here and fly over like flakes of the clouds and the sky; and those that can only creep can wallow in the sand. The landlubber uncles are best dropped along with the infants and women. But the hardier picnickers are off for the heaving ridges of Lumbo Ledges and the cod which graze there. I shall not dwell on the angling for the savory ladings of the kettles. Deep-sea fishing is a means to an end; it has no beauty or sufficiency in itself. I have crossed the Atlantic a modest number of times, and in such rolling timber as the Beata Marta, of cursed memory, built to ferry bananas and yams on the Caribbean Sea but launched on greater waters without ballast in the desperate times of the War; but I have been seasick only once. That was deep-sea fishing in a motor launch that rolled in a scorching July sun on oily swells off Pond Island. The smell of the fish, the agony of the inexorable anchor, the double movement of the boat—it was such a combination of unspeakable things that undid me. When they put me ashore in their wrath on the island and went back to their fishing, I sat on the solid earth but was not aware of its solidity. The island kept tipping up and sliding off just the way the boat had done. But I won't spoil the picnic by remembering melancholy things.

Nor are the fish one catches in the ocean exciting things. If a twenty-

pound cod had the fight of a trout in his inches, there would be few dories
left over here to tell the tale; they would all be over by Spain. The bite of a
haddock is like the bump of a sluggish automobile in the dark against a wall.
There is no piquancy it it. Suppose a hake should take hold of your line
like a bass! There is no blue lightning in salt-water fishing this side of
whales. The fish you catch, though, are satisfactory things. They flop over
the boat bottom with belated surprise, bulge-eyed and plump with their tooth-
someness. They have bronze spots on their sleek sides, and deep in their
eyes shines the winter moon. They are ripe for the picnic.

The cod taken, you are for the shore and a fire. It is easy to get a cradle
of coals as big as a bed with so much old timber frosty with salt lying about.
You fetch the big iron kettle that was cast to feed a family of the pioneer age.
Sling it on a green fir-bole and put it over the blaze. Now begins the ritual
of your chowder. First you cut salt pork into ribbons and throw it in. When
it begins to seethe, throw in halved onions and fry them till they squirm like
hissing adders. Dowse in half a jugful of water on the blue fumes. Cut up
the codfish and throw them in, heads and fins and all. Throw in salt by
the fistful, pepper by the pound. Slice potatoes, and in with them. Keep the
mess stirred. Give everybody a stick. Let everybody stir. Too many cooks
are the making of this broth. The more cinders and sparks you can get into
the kettle, the tastier the pottage. You stir in everything you can find: the
spray from the sea, the iodine of the kelp, the smell of bayberry bushes
scorching in the sun. Even the wind and the blue day get into the chowder
sooner or later. It is a wedding of sun and sea.

From Spargo to Carver to Speaker[1]

by HEYWOOD BROUN

"TELL me, Mr. Broun," said the young lady to my right, "how did you
happen to become a Red?"

Assuming that her question was sincere, I proceeded to tell her in
my own words, which, by a fortunate coincidence, happened to be just sufficient to fill one page of *The New Republic* when printed in this type.

The first person to tempt me to the left was a Vermont Republican named
John Spargo, who wrote mildly Marxian tracts years ago when I was very
young. Had there been more violence in his views or in his presentation, I
might have scurried home, but he was as soft spoken as any curate and he
succeeded in sneaking up on me. Later, in college, Lippmann asked me to

1 From *The New Republic*. Nov. 17, 1937, p. 41. By permission of the editor and the author.

join the Socialist Club, and as I had failed to make either Gas House or Fly, I yielded to his blandishments.

But commitment was not yet complete. The way of retreat still lay open. It was Professor Carver of the Harvard faculty and Tris Speaker, center fielder of the Boston Red Sox, who closed the door and left me locked in the hall of heresy. Possibly an assist should be scored for a particularly salubrious spring which came to New England in 1908. The good bald economist gave a course which might be roughly described as "radical panaceas and their underlying fallacies." Professor Carver introduced these crack-brained notions in the fall and winter semesters and then proceeded to demolish them in the spring and early summer.

Faithful to the Harvard tradition of fair play, the Professor gave the revolutionaries an ample amount of rope. Indeed, he did not undertake to state the case himself for the various aberrant philosophies, but invited a leader of each school of thought to tell all from his particular point of view. The soap boxes were carried openly into the class room and mounted by the orators. Men with burning causes are generally more eloquent than cloistered dons and there was not a single visitor who could not talk rings around Professor Carver.

We had an anarchist, a socialist, a syndicalist, a single-taxer and a few other theorists whose special lines escape me now with the passing of the years. The single-taxer was a little on the dull side, but all the others sparkled. It may be that I was more susceptible than my fellow students, for I must report that I hit the sawdust trail at each and every lecture in the creation of a united front against the capitalist system.

In other courses it was my custom to draw starfish in my notebook and jot down reminders such as: "Be sure and get Osmond Fraenkel for the poker game tonight." But under Carver I took notes as long as the cavalcade of visiting firemen was on. Later I would peruse the book and find entries such as "Born 1839—died 1897," "unearned increase in land values," "P. J. Proudhon." "Five dollars ($5) with Horseface McCarthy Dartmouth doesn't beat us by two touchdowns." And I used to wonder what some of the notations could possibly mean. But I paid closer attention than ever until the last galoot had reached the shore and Carver went up into the pilot house.

At this point spring broke through. It had been a tough winter. Dartmouth did beat us by two touchdowns and Osmond Fraenkel, who was a mathematical shark, had just become wise to the fact that it doesn't pay to draw to inside straights. I had failed to make *The Harvard Crimson* after my third try. But gone was the winter of our discontent, and now it was Professor Carver's turn to haul us back from the pie counter of the sky and put our feet again upon the good earth and the law of supply and demand.

Carver was at bat, but, as luck would have it, so was Tris Speaker. Spring can come up like thunder in Massachusetts. One day all the elms of the yard may be cased in ice and the next you read that the Boston Red Sox are opening the season against the Athletics. Tris Speaker, just up from the Texas League, was the particular star of the greatest outfield trio that has ever been gathered together. Speaker and Duffy Lewis and Harry Hooper—that was a united front. For a little while I tried to give Professor Carver an even break. Naturally I missed his first blast for the cause of conservatism because that particular lecture conflicted with the opening game. Still I did ask a fellow scholar what went on and he lent me his notebook. He seemed to have boiled the discourse down to the bone because all he had written was, "Adam Smith was Scotch and died before the industrial revolution—look this up in the library. He approached economics from the side of ethics and believed in laissez-faire, which means 'anything goes.' 'Has anybody here seen Kelly?'"

I decided that in all fairness to my parents, who were paying for my education, I should attend some of the lectures myself, and so in the beginning I made it a rigorous rule to give only three afternoons a week to the Red Sox and the other three to Professor Carver. But on a certain Wednesday, which was a baseball afternoon, Tris Speaker made a home run, two triples, and a double. In addition he went all the way back to the flagpole in center field and speared a drive with his gloved hand while still on the dead run. Two innings later he charged in for a low liner and made the catch by sliding the last twenty feet on his stomach. Professor Carver couldn't do that. I had seen him stand on his head in the class room but never did he slide on his stomach. Even at such times as he got to base it was my impression that he had profited by an error or made a lucky-handle hit. Tris Speaker was batting .348 and Carver wasn't hitting the size of his hat. At times he did dig his toes in and take his full cut at the ball, but never when I was around did he succeed in knocking socialism over the fence.

Adam Smith had died in 1790 and Professor Carver wasn't getting any younger. I got hold of *The Wealth of Nations* and learned that to Smith laissez-faire meant "the obvious and simple system of natural liberty." And so in the books I read no more then, and not very much later.

I just went completely laissez-faire and never missed any of the remaining games. The arguments for the radical theories I had heard, but I never got around to hearing the answers. Tris Speaker had thrown Carver out at the plate because the Professor forgot to slide. And I went out into the world the fervent follower of all things red, including the Boston Red Sox.

A Garland of Ibids[1]

by FRANK SULLIVAN

I HAVE just finished reading a book[2] which struck me as being one of the finest books I have read since I read "The Flowering of New England," by the same author.[3] But there is a fly in the ointment. I have been rendered cockeyed by the footnotes. There seem to be too many of them, even for a book largely about Boston.[4] I do not know why the author had to have so many footnotes. Maybe he had a reason for each one, but I suspect the footnote habit has crept up on him, for I got out his book on Emerson,[5] published in 1932, and he used practically no footnotes in it.

You read along in "New England: Indian Summer," interested to the hilt in what Van Wyck Brooks is telling you about Longfellow,[6] Thoreau,[7]

---

[1] From *The New Yorker*, April 19, 1941. By permission of the author.

[2] "New England: Indian Summer."

[3] Van Wyck Brooks, author of "New England: Indian Summer," "The Flowering of New England," "The Life of Emerson," "The Ordeal of Mark Twain," and other books.

[4] Sometimes referred to as The Hub. Capital and chief city of Massachusetts. Scene of the Boston Tea Party and the arrest of Henry L. Mencken. Bostonians are traditionally noted for their civic pride, or, as an envious New York critic once termed it, their parochial outlook. It is related that on an occasion when Saltonstall Boylston learned that his friend L. Cabot Lowell was leaving for a trip around the world, he inquired of Lowell, "Which route shall you take, L.C.?" "Oh, I shall go by way of Dedham, of course," replied Mr. Lowell. On another occasion, the old Back Bay aristocrat Ralph Waldo Mulcahy said to Oliver Wendell Rooney, "By the way, Rooney, did your ancestors come over on the Mayflower?" "Oh, no," replied Mr. Rooney. "They arrived on the next boat. They sent the servants over on the Mayflower."

[5] Ralph Waldo Emerson, Sage of Concord and famous transcendentalist philosopher, not to be confused with Ralph McAllister Ingersoll, editor of *P.M.*

[6] Henry Wadsworth Longfellow, Good Gray Poet. Longfellow was no footnote addict. He preferred foot*prints*. Cf. his "Psalm of Life":
>   And, departing, leave behind us
>   Footprints on the sands of time.

[7] Henry David Thoreau, philosopher who lived at Walden Pond for two years on carrots, twigs, nuts, minnows, creek water, and, as Margaret Fuller suspected (booming it out at Brook Farm in that full, rich voice of hers, to the dismay of William Ellery Channing, Henry Wadsworth Longfellow, Edward Everett Hale, John Lothrop Motley, Charles Eliot Norton, and William Lloyd Garrison), sirloin steaks and creamery butter smuggled to him by Emerson. Suffering as he did from a vitamin deficiency, the result of too much moss in his diet, Thoreau became somewhat of a misanthrope and would often creep up behind members of the Saturday Club and shout "Boo!," or, as some authorities maintain, "Pooh." The matter is not clarified very much, one must admit, by a letter Mrs. Harriet Beecher Stowe wrote to her son, Harriet Beecher Stowe, Jr. (not to be confused with Herbert Bayard Swope), on June 7, 1854, in which she states: "Not much to write home about, as the saying goes. Dave Thoreau here for supper last nite [*sic*]. He got into an argument with John Greenleaf Whittier, the Good Gray Poet, as to whether snow is really ermine too dear for an earl, and Greenleaf called him a Communist. Dave then crept up behind Greenleaf and shouted either 'Boo!' [*sic*] or 'Pooh!' [*sic*], I couldn't make out wich [*sic*]. All well here except F. Marion Crawford, Sarah Orne Jewett, Charles Dudley Warner, Thomas Wentworth Higginson, and William Dean Howells, who complain of feeling sic [*sic*]. Your aff. mother, H. B. Stowe, Sr."

Phillips,[8] James,[9] Alcott,[10] Lowell,[11] Adams,[12] and other great figures of the Periclean Age of The Hub,[13] when suddenly there is a footnote.

The text is in fine, clear type. The footnotes are in small type. So it is quite a chore to keep focussing up and down the page, especially if you have old eyes or a touch of astigmatism.[14] By and by you say to yourself, "I be damn if I look down at any more footnotes!," but you do, because the book is so interesting you don't want to miss even the footnotes.[15]

When you get to the footnote at the bottom of the page, like as not all you find is *ibid*. *Ibid* is a great favorite of footnote-mad authors.[16] It was a great favorite with Gibbon.[17] How come writers of fiction do not need footnotes? Take Edna Ferber.[18] She doesn't use footnotes. Suppose Edna

[8] Wendell Phillips. He was about the only Bostonian of his time who wore no middle name and he was therefore considered half naked. Even Mark Twain, when he went to visit Howells in Boston, registered as Samuel Langhorne Clemens.

[9] Probably not Jesse James. Probably is either William James, deviser of Pragmatic Sanctions, or his brother Henry, the novelist. It was about this time that Henry James was going through his transition period, and could not make up his mind whether he was in England living in America or in America living in England.

[10] Amos Bronson Alcott, educator and bad provider. The Mr. Micawber of his day. Not to be confused with Novelist Bus Bronson of Yale or Mrs. Chauncey Olcott.

[11] James Russell Lowell, poet, essayist, and kinfolk of late rotund, cigar-smoking Back Bay Poetess Amy Lowell, no rhymester she.

[12] Henry Adams, author of "The Education of Henry Adams," by Henry Adams. Not to be confused with Henry Adams, Samuel Adams, John Adams, John Quincy Adams, Abigail Adams, Charles Edward Adams (not to be confused with Charles Francis Adams, Charles Henry Adams, or Henry Adams), Maude Adams, Franklin Pierce Adams, Samuel Hopkins Adams, Bristow Adams, George Matthew Adams, James Truslow Adams, Adams Express, Adams & Flanagan, Horace Flanagan, or Louis Adamic.

[13] Sometimes referred to as Boston. One is reminded of the famous quatrain:
Here's to the City of Boston,
The home of Filene and the Card.,
Where the Rileys speak only to Cabots
And the Cabots speak only to God!

[14] In this connection, it is interesting to note that Louisa May Alcott had a touch of astigmatism, if we are to accept the word of Charles Eliot Norton. Edward Everett Hale states in his Letters, Vol. XV, Ch. 8, pp. 297 *et seq.*, that William Cullen Bryant told Oliver Wendell Holmes that on one occasion when the fun was running high at Thomas Wentworth Higginson's home and all barriers were down, Thomas Bailey Aldrich had put the question bluntly to Charles Eliot Norton, saying, "Now listen, has Louisa May Alcott got astigmatism or hasn't she?" Charles Eliot Norton answered, perhaps unwisely, "Yes." Cf. the famous dictum of General William Tecumseh Sherman, sometimes erroneously ascribed to General Ulysses Simpson Grant: "Never bring up a lady's name in the mess."

[15] Ah there, Van Wyck!

[16] So is cf.

[17] Edward Gibbon, English historian, not to be confused with Cedric Gibbons, Hollywood art director. Edward Gibbon was a great hand for footnotes, especially if they gave him a chance to show off his Latin. He would come sniffing up to a nice, spicy morsel of scandal about the Romans and then, just as the reader expected him to dish the dirt, he'd go into his Latin routine, somewhat as follows: "In those days vice reached depths not plumbed since the reign of Caligula and it was an open secret that the notorious Empress Theodora *in tres partes divisa erat* and that she was also addicted to the *argumentum ad hominem!*" Gibbon, prissy little fat man that he was, did that just to tease readers who had flunked Caesar.

[18] Edna Cabot Ferber, contemporary New England novelist. It is related of Edna Ferber that she once met Oliver Herford in Gramercy Park and recoiled at the sight of an extremely loud necktie he was wearing. "Heavens above, Oliver Herford!" exclaimed Miss Ferber, never one not to speak her mind. "That is a terrible cravat. Why do you wear it?" "Because it is my wife's whim that I wear it," explained Oliver Herford. "Well, land sakes alive, before I'd wear a tie like that just on account of a wife's whim!" jeered Miss Ferber. "You don't know my wife," said Oliver Herford. "She's got a whim of iron." Miss Ferber later made this incident the basis for the dramatic battle between the husband and wife in her novel "The Cravat."

Herford [19] took to writing her novels in this manner: "Cicely Ticklepaw *
sat at her dressing table in a brown study. She had 'a very strange feeling
she'd ne'er felt before, a kind of a grind of depression.' † Could it be love? ‡
If so, why had she sent him § away? She sighed, and a soft cry of 'Aye me!' ||
escaped her. Seizing a nail file desperately, she commenced hacking away at
her fingernails, when a voice behind her said, 'O! that I were a glove upon
that hand, that I might touch that cheek!' $ Cicely reddened, turned. It was
Cleon Bel Murphy! Softly, she told him, 'What man art thou, that, thus
bescreen'd in night, so stumblest on my counsel?' " &

What would Van Wyck Brooks say if Enda Ferber wrote like that? [20]
Yes. Exactly. Now, where were we? [21] No, I was not. I know what I
was saying. You keep out of this. You're a footnote! [22] Yeah? Well, just
for that, no more footnotes. Out you go! [23] I am, that's who.[24] See what
I mean, Van Wyck? Give a footnote an inch and it'll take a foot.[25] I give
up. They got me. And they'll get you too in the end, Van Wyck. You may
think you're strong enough to keep 'em under control; you may think you
can take a footnote or leave it. All I say it, remember Dr. Jekyll! Lay off
'em, Van. I'm telling you for your own good.

—Uneasy Brooks Fan [26]

---

[19] No, no, no, not Edna Herford! Edna *Ferber:* Edna Herford is the fellow who had the
wife with the iron whim.

* Blonde, lovely, and twenty-one.

† See "I'm Falling in Love with Someone"—Victor Herbert.

‡ Sure.

§ Cleon Bel Murphy, the man she loves.

|| "Romeo and Juliet," Act II, Scene 2.

$ *Ibid.*

& *Ibid.*

[20] And what would Edna Ferber say if Edna Ferber wrote like that?

[21] You were saying Louisa May Alcott had astigmatism.

[22] Yeah? And how far would you have got in this article without footnotes?

[23] Who's gonna put me out?

[24] Yeah? You and who else?

[25] Yoo-hoo! Footnote!

[26] Frank Saltonstall Sullivan.

Spring Comes to the Farm [1]

by BETTY FIBLE MARTIN

Vienna, Virginia.

OURS is a back road spilling off U. S. Highway No. 50—one small farm after another. We do not need to be told what is happening. We know. We hear the "peepers" chorusing their high overture to spring from every marsh and pond. We see the cows and horses shedding their heavy winter coats. We find the broody hens clucking over a nest of eggs. We smell the earth again after weeks of odorless snow and ice. In the quiet of the night we hear the rabbits drumming on the ground, calling to their mates.

Our world is being born anew. Out of the darkness of winter has emerged a fresh, bright land of opportunity returned, ours to do with as we will. Last year's failures and mistakes are somehow wiped away, gone with the winter's snow, and here we have a whole new season inviting new adventure. It has been thus since time began, but there is always a wonder, a happy mystery, about the land when spring returns. The land endures, year after turning year; yet it is ever changing, and spring itself is the very epitome of change.

It is time to prune the grapevines, cut out the dead apple wood, clean the fence rows, and burn over the fields of weeds and broom sedge. Columns of smoke dot the horizon—bonfires here, grass fires there "a-poppin' an' a-hissin' "—spreading in the wind until the rolling countryside is enveloped in a dense screen of peaceful smoke.

We turn out the restless stock, anxious to graze on the green fuzz of pasture grass, to roam free from confining stanchions and stalls. We hitch up the horses, lazy after the long idle winter, and devote hours to the heavy task of hauling manure piles from barnyards out into the fields. We watch the warm winds dry the mud in which man, beast, and machine have mired after each successive thaw and rain.

Rusty plows cut through the sod of old fields and garden patches, followed by streams of chickens gorging on grubs and "fishin' worms," and come up glistening at the end of the first long furrow. The air is pungent with the cleanliness of turned earth.

Lights shine early from kitchen windows. There is no "lyin' in the bed" of a morning. Men, women, and children breakfast before dawn, in order to get on with the work clamoring for attention after the paralyzing months of winter inactivity. Trucks of the hay, grain, and fertilizer store rumble

[1] From the New York Times Magazine for April 21, 1940. By permission of the author.

down the road piled high with sacks. Everyone wants his order of lime and fertilizer at one and the same moment. The drivers work early and late. Each sack of fertilizer weighs 160 pounds. Each bag of ground limestone is just so much concentrated dead weight, the moving of each bag of hydrated lime a choking operation. The boys puff and blow and declare quite cheerfully they will be ready to eat their "beans come supper time."

Plans frozen in each mind during the winter thaw into action. One field must be made ready for early oats, grass, and clover, a patch near the house for potatoes, peas, onions, and all the rest of the spring vegetables. This field must be plowed for corn, the next for soy beans.

And there is the livestock. Every creature has babies, from horses to hogs, ducks to barn cats—to the wonder and delight of the children, the satisfaction or sometimes consternation of the grown-ups.

If we want eggs in the fall, we must raise chickens in the spring. Our women start the fires in the brooder houses, tend them, watch thermometers and thermostats preparatory to the arrival of the mail carrier's car noisily filled with boxes of from twenty-five to one hundred day-old chickens, peeping like mad for a warm hover, a drink, and something to eat.

Leggy colts appear in pastures, nuzzling their mothers hungrily, frisking with sheer delight over being here and then lying out flat in the good warm sun to sleep off food and play. Wabbly calves butt at the cows, gambol about after feeding, and inadvertently bring milk, butter, and cheese to larders lean after the long winter.

As the fresh spring weather settles into a steadier warmth, we travel the five miles to the freight station. The freight room, ordinarily housing a scanty array of milk cans, gates, and an occasional piece of farm machinery, is a jam of orders—great bundles of fruit trees, small bundles of cane fruits and grapevines, sack after sack of seed: oats, grass, clover, potatoes, vegetable, soy bean, and corn. We help the bewildered agent search for our order, note his sigh of relief to be rid of a few sacks of responsibility.

We go from there to the post office, alive with peeping chickens, a motley assortment of strawberry plants, perennial flowers and small fruits peeking out from bundles and baskets, even orders of swarms of bees done up neatly in screened packages.

In the village, drug, feed, grocery, and hardware establishment—all save the filling station—display packets of seed, bags of seed, a wealth of rose bushes and mountains of bug and fungus poisons and repellents.

All our ready cash is consumed in futures—the future of the seeds, baby chickens, turkeys, and ducks we have purchased—the future of the colts, calves, and satiny little pigs newly arrived after a long investment in feed and housing for their parent stock. The net gain—if any—will not be reckoned until harvest and market time.

These are our problems, and, if we are less intent on the affairs of Europe and the troubles of a distant world than on them, it is perhaps understandable. We harvested our soy beans and cut our corn in the torrid September days with an ear cocked toward Poland. We roamed up knoll and down bottom under the sparkling fall skies, half a mind on the "beadles" jumping the rabbits, the other half on Finland. But now we are knee-deep in spring, and the echoes from each new danger zone come more faintly over the hills.

It must be so on every farm lying in a nation at peace, this time of year, when soil is turned for other crops than forts and bomb shelters, and fence posts are set for peaceful fences, not barbed-wire entanglements. Ours is a peaceful scene, and our minds are filled with affairs of peace, which somehow fit the season.

Our harrows go up and down the plowed fields, breaking and combing the clods into smooth beauty, clean soil from fence to fence, a virgin bed for our livelihood during the year to come. Fields are small along our road, horse-drawn seeders scarce. So, up and down, across and back, the farmer marches, bucket of seed under his left arm, his right a piston of driving regularity, tossing seed up and out. He watches it fly and settle on the "loomy" soil, then harrows it in.

On porches and in the lee of sheds, wherever the sun is warm, the women pass the time of day. Their hands have not been idle, cutting potatoes into seed, the small children too young for school twittering about their feet. The following morning they were out in the garden with their menfolk, dropping seed potatoes into the straight deep furrows.

Day by day, brown fields green under the tender warmth of spring rain and sun. Hard by the farmhouses—the freshly painted and gray tumbledown shack alike—the bloom comes on the fruit: plums, cherries, peaches, pears, and apples burst forth in all their white and pink glory.

And after the preventive spraying, there is a lull in the work, the breather between seeding and cultivating. We walk over our acres more leisurely. We see the potatoes, up hand-high, alive with potato bugs feeding like gourmands on the young leaves. We linger outside at dusk long enough to hear the whippoorwills calling in the woods and the first bass duets of the bullfrogs in the pond. Bugs, whippoorwills, and bullfrogs—then we know spring has been "tippin' out" and summer "creepin' in."

Of Goodness[1]

by ELIZABETH JACKSON

And what doth the Lord require of thee, but to do justly, and to love mercy, and to walk humbly with thy God?

MICAH

Let us now praise famous men and our fathers that begot us.

ECCLESIASTICUS

"Let us now praise famous men"—
Men of little showing—
For their work continueth,
And their work continueth,
Broad and deep continueth,
Greater than their knowing!

RUDYARD KIPLING, A School Song

His was no lonely mountain-peak of mind,
Thrusting to thin air o'er our cloudy bars,
A sea-mark now, now lost in vapors blind;
Broad prairie rather, genial, level-lined,
Fruitful and friendly for all human kind,
Yet also nigh to heaven and loved of loftiest stars. . . .

Our children shall behold his fame,
The kindly-earnest, brave, foreseeing man,
Sagacious, patient, dreading praise, not blame,
New birth of our new soil, the first American.

JAMES RUSSELL LOWELL'S DESCRIPTION OF LINCOLN, in
Ode Recited at the Harvard Commemoration

Our yeoman should be equal to his home
Set in the fair, green valleys, purple walled,
A man to match his mountains, not to creep
Dwarfed and abased below them.

JOHN GREENLEAF WHITTIER, Among the Hills

Love virtue, she alone is free,
She can teach ye how to climb
Higher than the sphery chime;
Or if virtue feeble were,
Heaven itself would stoop to her.

JOHN MILTON, Comus

[1] From Elizabeth Jackson, *The Faith and Fire within Us* (1944). By permission of the University of Minnesota Press.

"NONE CAN love freedom heartily but good men; the rest love not freedom, but license." That was Milton's opinion, and he had thought much about both freedom and goodness. It is reasonable also to say that none but good men can constitute a free society or, perhaps more accurately, that a free society can succeed only when a considerable number of its citizens are good men. In a study of any democracy it is pertinent to consider both its theories and its habits of goodness.

Here in America it would be interesting if we could have a poll that would show how we estimate the relative importance of different virtues. Of the four so-called cardinal virtues—prudence, temperance, justice, and fortitude—I imagine that fortitude would rank highest and temperance lowest. Justice would be pretty well up. Of the three Christian virtues—faith, hope, and charity—I should guess that the last would be first and the middle one still middle. Some of the virtues of the Beatitudes might not come out very well. Meekness, for instance. "Blessed are the meek" has never been a favorite American text. The stock of the peacemakers has fluctuated a good deal lately. On the whole, perhaps, we incline to be dubious about the people who hunger and thirst after righteousness. I remember that as a child I took *after* in the temporal sense and imagined that the people of the Fourth Beatitude had been righteous so strenuously that they needed a good square meal afterward. Many other people, I have observed, regard righteousness as somewhat exhausting and not to be practiced too freely. And how do we feel about the pure in heart?

As for simple goodness, I should not be surprised if we got quite a substantial negative vote. Of course a lot depends on how you word your question. It has been pointed out that you could get a vote in favor of the common cold by asking, "Would you be willing to catch cold to kiss Hedy Lamarr?" You could get a vote against butter by asking, "Would you eat butter to please Hitler?" If you asked baldly, "Do you believe in goodness?" I firmly believe that many people would say no. Then they would make speeches. One man would start on a diatribe against self-righteousness. Another would say that goodness was lackadaisical, that he liked somebody with guts enough, to be a good sinner. He might quote the epitaph for Mary Jones—"no hits, no runs, no errors"—which, after all, is only a twentieth-century rendering of Milton's great sentence, "I cannot praise a fugitive and cloistered virtue, unexercised and unbreathed, that never sallies out and sees her adversary." A third man would be purely personal. "I've had enough goodness for a lifetime. X was a good man, and of all the dirty, double-crossing skunks . . . !" I think all these responses are American, and I'm not at all sure that they do not indicate rather healthy states of mind.

One thing we obviously need is a definition of goodness. We might look at Bacon's essay "Of Goodness and Goodness of Nature." "I take Goodness," he says, "in this sense, the affecting [we should say *aiming at* or *desiring*] of the weal of men, which is that the Grecians call *Philanthropia*. . . . Goodness answers to the theological virtue Charity, and admits no excess." "Admits no excess"; that is to say, cannot be had in too great quantities. That was the meaning of goodness that you were likely to find in Bacon's century. There was a distinction between righteousness, which consisted in doing right, and goodness, which consisted in doing good. The Son of Man went about doing good. Goodness was active, positive, practical, and kind. Righteousness might be cold and dead, but goodness was warm, human, alive. We have come to use the word goodness today for a negative quality that is even less attractive than righteousness, and we have not added any new word to take the place of the one we have spoiled. Maybe we shall some day, when we realize that we need it.

You still hear the old usage sometimes. We say, "Isn't that good of him!" when we mean that somebody, out of the goodness of his heart (we still use that phrase, though we often use it ironically) has done something positively and practically and perhaps unnecessarily kind. When I was a child there was an elderly gentleman in my town of whom I knew only two things, that he was rich and that he was good. How he got his money I never thought to inquire. I rather think he inherited it. He never seemed to do anything with it except spend it. He made up the deficit in the minister's salary and paid for the janitor's wife's operation. He paid back the money that somebody's boy stole from the butcher and got the boy another job and kept him straight. Some of our nice old ladies let him pay for the little comforts that their economies could never have managed. (They promised not to tell.) People in trouble went to him. When he died, families who had never asked for help in their lives said to each other, "Who shall we go to now? We always knew he was there if we needed him."

One of the deacons of our most strait-laced congregation walked home with my father after the funeral. He shook his head sorrowfully. It was a pity, he said, that such a good man as Mr. Gates should have to go to Hell. "Yes," said my father, "it *would* be."

Now that kind of goodness, at any rate, I think we believe in. If we believe in Heaven, we believe that Mr. Gates is the sort of person who goes there. If we believe in the Gospels, we like reading the explicit statement in the twenty-fifth chapter of Matthew, when the King says to those on his right hand, "Come, ye blessed of my Father, inherit the kingdom prepared for you from the foundation of the world."

For I was hungry, and ye gave me to eat; I was thirsty, and ye gave me drink; I was a stranger, and ye took me in; naked, and ye clothed me, . . .

Then shall the righteous answer him, saying, Lord, when saw we thee hungry, and fed thee? or athirst, and gave thee drink? . . .

And the King shall answer and say unto them, Verily I say unto you, Inasmuch as ye did it unto one of these my brethren, even these least, ye did it unto me.

Do you know "A Lyke-Wake Dirge"? I met it first in *The Oxford Book of English Verse*. It can't very well be quoted except in the old spelling.

This ae nighte, this ae nighte,
   —*Every nighte and alle,*
Fire and sleet and candle-lighte,
   And Christe receive thy saule.

When thou from hence away art past,
   —*Every nighte and alle,*
To Whinny-muir thou com'st at last;
   And Christe receive thy saule.

If ever thou gavest hosen and shoon,
   —*Every nighte and alle,*
Sit thee down and put them on:
   And Christe receive thy saule.

If hosen and shoon thou ne'er gav'st nane
   —*Every nighte and alle,*
The whinnes sall prick thee to the bare bane;
   And Christe receive thy saule.

. . . .

If ever thou gavest meat or drink,
   —*Every nighte and alle,*
The fire sall never make thee shrink;
   And Christe receive thy saule.

. . . .

This ae nighte, this ae nighte,
   —*Every nighte and alle,*
Fire and sleet and candle-lighte,
   And Christe receive thy saule.

It isn't a question of being good in order to get to heaven. One kind of goodness that Americans tend to distrust is the kind that seems to have one eye always on rewards in the hereafter. No; it is simply that in this world there are some people who do good because they *are* good and then find out, often to their own surprise, that the Lord is pleased with them. I always like to hear Marian Anderson sing "All God's Chillun Got Wings." The amount of meaning that she can put into "Ev'rybody talkin' 'bout heaven ain't goin' there" is worth ten sermons. Deep in your stomach you have a sudden conviction about the kind of goodness that counts.

I can see that this belief of ours, like so many others, has a varied ancestry. It belongs to us partly, as I suggested before, because it comes out of the Bible and Christian teaching. It is one of those Christian doctrines widely accepted also by people who do not profess and call themselves Christians. It belongs to us, too, because in the nineteenth century it went hand in hand with the doctrine of liberty. It may sound absurd to cite Byron as an apostle of virtue when his ordinary reputation is that of devil's disciple, yet actually one of the things Byron preached was the goodness of doing good.

It is typical of Byron's age that it chose Prometheus for a hero in a double role: he defied the tyranny of Jove, and he did good to men.

> Thy Godlike crime was to be kind,
> To render with thy precepts less
> The sum of human wretchedness,
> And strengthen Man with his own mind.

The *fraternité* of *liberté, égalité, fraternité* became *brotherhood* in English, which somehow seems to carry greater implications of practical kindliness. What Longfellow said of Burns is true of all the liberty-loving poets.

> But still the music of his song
> Rises o'er all, elate and strong;
> Its master-chords
> Are Manhood, Freedom, Brotherhood.

There were various points of morality on which Burns and Byron differed from the New Englanders, but on the combination of freedom and brotherly goodness they were in perfect accord.

I think this kind of goodness is characteristically American; it throve naturally on the frontier, and it has kept on flourishing in places that the frontier has left behind. In a new community, cut off from the machinery of organized society, practical goodness becomes a necessary part of existence. Moreover, the natural impulses toward kindness and generosity are less inhibited by self-consciousness and custom. The frontier gave men, and more especially women, opportunities for indulging in the pleasures of goodness. I realize that, technically speaking, the frontier has been closed since 1890, but in many ways it still seems to lie round about us. I rather think that the so-called inconveniences of rationing have revived some of the relationships of earlier days and have afforded real comfort to people who like being good to each other.

Suppose we agree that Americans on the whole approve of goodness of this sort. If we went further, though, I imagine that we should find much greater uncertainty; there would be an increased percentage of votes in the category "No opinion." Let me go back to Spenser and *The Faerie Queene.* Spenser wasn't telling a young man how to *do* anything—how to succeed, how to get rich, how to make friends and influence people. He wasn't telling his readers what to do but what to be. Now we may say off-hand that this is one of the silly things about the poem. It is un-American; Americans are doers. That is quite true. "Faith without works is dead" is a good American text, and the American faith in work and works demands a chapter to itself. On the other hand, maybe we are closer to Spenser than we realize. Maybe unconsciously we value achievements less than we think, and qualities of goodness more. We admit as much in our casual, half-slangy estimates of people. We say that So-and-so is a good egg, a good scout, a right guy, a guy you can trust, somebody to tie to. More than we think, we admire people, as Spenser did, for being what they are. It may be one of the deficiencies of the literature of this century that it hasn't made us see clearly enough what kind of people we believe in.

Why shouldn't someone write a modern *Faerie Queene* and call it *What Makes a Good Egg?* Which brings up another sense in which we use the word *good*. We speak of things as being good all the way through. It is notorious that there is no such thing as a partially good egg. An apple, to be sure, may be good in the spots where the worm hasn't yet arrived, but we still maintain a distinction between a good apple and a wormy one. There is a comparable quality in people, and I think we recognize it. This is what Bacon called "goodness of nature" in the essay I have quoted. There are men who by their natural make-up are good in all the senses of the word, and we like them that way. They do right and not wrong because their whole nature is averse to wrongdoing. There is in them a kind of substantial goodness that is satisfying, like good food or good weather.

We find a great deal of this intrinsic goodness in the literature of nineteenth-century America. In recent years it has been customary to disparage American writers, and the New Englanders in particular, for this very reason. We ascribe to them a narrow-minded morality that the best minds escaped entirely. The people who wrote stories of moral instruction for school readers were perhaps responsible for our present strong tendency to demand wickedness in literature and to assume that if a book is full of virtuous people, it must be bad. To be sure, it is both bad art and bad ethics to deny the existence of sins and sinners. No picture of life is complete that leaves out its manifold sins and wickedness, to say nothing of its hypocrisies and affectations. On the other hand I see no artistic objection to accurate representations of goodness when goodness is what you see before you. A great deal of our nineteenth-century literature was pretty poor; nobody can deny it. But much of what these men wrote was better than we realize, and one of its qualities of excellence, I believe, is this very representation of goodness in people.

Emerson, Whittier, and Hawthorne, for instance, give us a consistent sense of their own goodness. Not intentionally, not with any self-righteousness; rather because their words are so clearly the voices of their souls and their souls are so clearly single and clean. There is a kind of primordial innocence about them, "still quiring to the young-eyed cherubins."

> So nigh is grandeur to our dust,
> So near is God to man . . .

Emerson seems to be talking about personal experience. He was conscious, too, of the goodness of men about him, of people like Longfellow. "The gentleman whose funeral we have been attending was a sweet and beautiful soul," he said in the vagueness that came upon him in old age, "but—I have forgotten his name."

In Longfellow's own poetry you get a constant sense of the friendship and followship of good men. He found them in his books and in real life. He was no Chaucer, don't mistake me. Even for good people he lacked some of Chaucer's zest, and of course he had no genius for creating a Nun's Priest or a Wife of Bath. It is no kindness to him to put the Prelude to the *Tales of a Wayside Inn* next to Chaucer's Prologue. The landlord, "known in all Sudbury as 'The Squire'" seems pale beside Harry Baillie. The student, who is compounded of Chaucer's clerk and one of Longfellow's friends and Longfellow himself, is a rather ethereal figure, but still worth putting into a poem.

> A youth was there, of quiet ways,
> A Student of old books and days,
> To whom all tongues and lands were known,
> And yet a lover of his own.
>
> . . . .
>
> Books were his passion and delight,
> And in his upper room at home
> Stood many a rare and sumptuous tome,
> In vellum bound, with gold bedight,
> Great volumes garmented in white,
> Recalling Florence, Pisa, Rome.

The young Sicilian, the Spanish Jew from Alicant, the Poet, all carry with them the breath of virtue. The Musician (Ole Bull, Longfellow said) had not only a Norwegian beauty of face but "a radiance streaming from within." And the Theologian, Wales or Channing or whoever he was in real life, would have been no unworthy friend of Chaucer's parson.

> Skilful alike with tongue and pen,
> He preached to all men everywhere
> The Gospel of the Golden Rule.
>
> . . . .
>
> With reverent feet the earth he trod,
> Nor banished nature from his plan,
> But studied still with deep research
> To build the Universal Church,
> Lofty as is the love of God,
> And ample as the wants of man.

If Longfellow lacked what Kittredge calls Chaucer's "stupendous luck in always meeting nonpareils," he had his own luck in meeting the pure in heart.

Certainly we have had later poets, too, who have maintained this same faith in good men. The growing list of poems on Lincoln, as well as Carl Sandburg's great volumes of prose, bear testimony to this faith. Vachel Lindsay and Edwin Arlington Robinson and Robert Frost, to name only three, have put their trust in human goodness. In fact, I wonder if one great source of Frost's popularity does not lie in a feeling he gives his readers that the poet himself is good to the core.

Yes, I suspect that America has produced even more than its fair share of good men, "the noble living and the noble dead" of Wordsworth's phrase. We have had our great good men in the grand manner, and along with them a nameless host whose simple, matter-of-fact goodness is also part of our heritage.

In fact, I am convinced that we take goodness too much for granted and that one of our national deficiencies is ignorance of evil. If, as I suggested earlier, our ideas of goodness are inconsistent and uncertain, in our theories of evil we are in a state of downright confusion.

I can make myself clearer if I turn once more to Milton, about whose theory of evil there was never any doubt. It is the backbone of *Paradise Lost*. Too many people today know the poem only from the first two books and have the mistaken notion that Satan is Milton's hero. On the contrary, for Milton the heart of the poem was in Books IV and IX, in which Satan was the unmistakable villain.

Let me say quite simply that the theme of *Paradise Lost* is the losing of Paradise, "Of Man's first disobedience, and the fruit of that forbidden tree. . . . " The hero of the poem is Adam. It was the eating of the fruit of the forbidden tree that "brought death into the world and all our woe." That is to say, the poem is about the fall of man and the origin of evil. If Satan is in the poem, he is there to explain evil, to explain why Adam fell and why Adam's descendants suffer. He invades the Garden of Eden in Book IV, he tempts Eve and thereby Adam in Book IX, he returns triumphant to Hell in Book X, to find that his triumph is a hissing and an abomination. From start to finish, Satan is the enemy, the arch plotter, the invader of neutral territory, the first political liar, the first anti-Semite, the first Nazi.

Let us see more precisely what Milton set out to say. In the first place, Satan was cast out of Heaven for pride and ambition. He was the first Fuehrer. He said to his angels, "We are the Herrenvolk. We are destined to rule." So instead of living peaceably with his neighbors, he got his armies together and started a war—and lost it. Cast into Hell, his pride exacerbated by his defeat, he vowed vengeance. Should he fight by force or by guile? Should he re-arm, supplying his munitions factories out of the apparently inexhaustible resources of Hell? Or should he sneak over an unfortified frontier, attacking a powerful God first through his weaker allies?

It was the latter plan that Satan put into effect. In Book II he appears as a practical politician, ingenious and not too scrupulous. He presides over the Council in Pandemonium and leaves the proposals of policy to the Number 2 Nazi, Beelzebub. Then when his plan is adopted he takes credit for it and goes his way, partly as a hero and partly as a liar. He is not only Hitler and Goering but Goebbels and to a certain extent von Ribbentrop. He will tell any lie and make any promise that will win a friend. He hasn't yet perfected any system of propaganda, however. He simply lies instinctively as occasion arises; evil, however splendid in its origins, must always do its business with falsehood and fraud.

In Book IV Satan invades neutral territory. The two human creatures in Paradise are harmless; in fact, Satan would never have suffered from their existence if he had not hunted them out and asked for trouble. Clearly Adam and Eve are the prototypes of all the gentle peoples whom Hitler has accused of aggression and warmongering. Finding them, Satan hates them and envies them, for the simple reason that they are peacefully minding their own business and enjoying, to a lesser degree, the comforts that he would still possess himself if he hadn't started the first of all world wars. He had once been happier than they and had thrown away happiness for ambition and a vain war of conquest. Now he hates all the peaceful ancestors of the Belgians and Norwegians who milk their cows and mind their gardens— hates them and envies them. Satan's pride in Book I may be noble; not so his envy and hatred in Book IV. It is easy enough for him to explain the invasion of Eden as a matter of military necessity and unfortified frontiers. I have read that Hitler surveyed the ruins of Warsaw and said, "How wicked people were to force me to do this!"

Shelley discovered in Satan "the taints of ambition, envy, revenge, and a desire for personal aggrandizement." He thought Milton had erred in letting these faults creep into the character of his hero. On the contrary, the faults are an integral part of the characterization of a villain. Pride goes with cruelty and cruelty with lust, in a perfectly correct Freudian pattern, and after them come all the petty vices of covetousness, envy, fraud, and malice. It is only in Book I that Satan is heroic, with splendid speeches about the unconquerable will and courage never to submit or yield. From that point on Milton charts the degradation of Satan, step by step.

Evil, as Milton understood it, is not a static but an active thing, and it becomes progressively more villainous and less and less heroic. The process has its outward and visible signs. In Book I, to be sure, Satan is still splendid, not "less than Archangel ruined," with "the excess of glory obscured." As the books go on, the glory disappears; the face and form are distorted so that Uriel can recognize the tokens a sun's distance away. Satan sits at the ear of Eve "squat like a toad," and in Book X, when he returns to Hell to report his triumphs, he feels his legs intertwining and falls prone to the ground, hissing, a serpent. That is Milton's ultimate comment on Satan and evil.

Milton once spoke of writing a poem "doctrinal to a nation." *Paradise Lost* was doctrinal to his nation and his century, not to ours. It analyzed the problem of evil for a generation to whom evil was omnipresent and of terrific importance. As I said before, we have lost that conviction. I am not exaggerating when I say that a lack of Milton's comprehension of evil was one of our most serious unpreparednesses in the years when war was coming closer, and this same lack, I believe, is going to tempt us into ways of un- wisdom when we come to make terms of peace.

Speaking as a student of literature, I have found three main currents of thought that have robbed us of a working theory of evil. I will take them up in the chronological order in which they entered the English-American mind. The first I shall call the sentimental theory, or the theory of the beautiful soul. It is a theory that identifies virtue with emotion, with beautiful impulses, with spontaneous outpourings of feeling. We can find the doctrine in some of our wisest teachers and loftiest poets—Wordsworth, Shelley, and Emerson, to name only three. The phrase *beautiful soul* was originally German, *schöne*

Seele, and comes from the teachings of Friedrich Schiller, who we all agree belongs in the category of good, and also liberty-loving, Germans. "The beautiful soul we call a state where the moral sentiment has taken possession of all the emotions to such a degree that it may unhesitatingly commit the guidance of life to instinct." Or as a Frenchman put it, "Be beautiful and then do at each moment whatever your heart may inspire you to do."

Being on the whole goodhearted and sentimental, we have a natural inclination toward this theory. We like Wordsworth's couplet about

> Glad Hearts! without reproach or blot
> Who do thy work, and know it not.

There is nothing wrong in liking the idea of spontaneous goodness. The trouble comes when we lay the emphasis on the spontaneousness and don't inquire too carefully about the goodness. This is the catch—that delight in emotion may completely paralyze the critical intelligence. "I feel beautiful; I am beautiful; whatever I do is beautiful." Yet in practice, the things that that person does may be very ugly. Nobody doubts that beautiful impulses are good in themselves, but we Americans are inclined to trust them too exclusively.

The late Irving Babbitt dedicated himself to a lifelong assault on this theory. He loved to collect instances of beautiful souls doing unbeautiful things. He loved to read out a passage in which Rousseau dilates on his "warmth of heart," his "keenness of sensibility," and "the melting feeling, the lively and sweet emotion" that he experiences at the sight of everything that is virtuous, generous, and lovely. Then Babbitt would roll his eyes at his audience (of which I was one) and read the concluding sentence of Rousseau's paragraph: "And so my third child was put into the foundling hospital."

A quotation that is even more pertinent at the present moment comes from Robespierre. This is from a speech made before the National Convention at the very height of the Reign of Terror. The tumbrils were rolling up to the guillotine with their loads of victims, and it seemed that there was no limit to the blood that might be shed. In the midst of the blood, and while demanding still more blood, Robespierre could dilate on the beauty of virtue! "That tender, irresistible, imperious passion, torment and delight of magnanimous hearts, that profound horror of tyranny, that compassionate zeal for the oppressed, that sacred love of one's country, that still more sacred and sublime love for humanity." He could talk of finding "a celestial voluptuousness in the calm of a pure conscience and the ravishing spectacle of public happiness."

As Americans we are not likely to be fooled by anything so hifalutin, but as Americans we do let ourselves be fooled into trusting emotional and beautiful souls without looking to see whether there are any reigns of terror in the background. To take a trivial instance, we are likely to put our trust in people who are kind to animals. Not long ago the *New Republic* had a charming little sketch of the entire office and editorial staff in a dither over the domestic life of a nesting pigeon. The whole episode was very virtuous and delightful, and if I had been there I should have been hanging out the window with everybody else. The sketch ended with an inference; namely, that this was evidence of the happy state of life in America.

That, as Babbitt would have said, is a false and Rousseauistic conclusion. I understand that Hitler is very kind to squirrels. Kindness to animals and kindness to human beings may go together and they often do. On the other hand, the beautiful soul may be feeding the squirrels with one hand and robbing widows and orphans or wiping out Lidice with the other. We should learn to beware of our instinctive confidence in beautiful emotions. We must be on guard against a reformed enemy who comes to us in virtuous tears.

Another kind of thinking that has confused our vision of evil I shall call the romantic theory. It is this theory that has transformed Satan from villain to hero. It runs this way. Energy is admirable; wickedness is energetic. "The tigers of wrath are wiser than the horses of instruction," said Blake. "Better to live as a lion for a day than for a hundred years as a sheep," said Mussolini. Quietness is contemptible; goodness is quiet. Therefore it follows that evil is good and good is bad. Q.E.D.

As is usual in any romantic theory, we find the name of Byron conspicuous. The Byronic hero in his successive metamorphoses has filled—and also written—more books than tongue can tell. He is volcanic, extreme in all things, magnificent in sin. He is adored of woman (or, conversely, he is misunderstood and betrayed by women and retires into lofty isolation and the pageant of his bleeding heart). With the help of modern psychology he has developed complexes and neuroses. At times, to be sure, he evinces a spasmodic and spectacular goodness, but this is a manifestation of his superb energy and must never, according to the theory, be confused with the goodness of good people.

Early in the nineteenth century this theory got tangled up with Napoleon and also, with far-reaching consequences, with German philosophy. Students of the history of philosophy point to the doctrines of Fichte. From this source come the Superman, the Master Race, Prussianism, and Hitler. Until there was an actual outbreak in war, we did not resent this kind of thing because the ideas were not very different from ones that we had been brought up on. Not that many of us were fooled by Hitler as a person. A bad egg if ever there was one. Yet there was something comic about him, and we are such a good-natured people that we find it hard to realize that funny things can be dangerous.

Furthermore, we saw that Hitler and his friends had energy, and we rather admired them for it. We didn't blame them for not wanting to be bullied. We were inclined to discount the stories of domestic terrorism. Even after the war began in Europe, we felt a certain respect for Prussian competence and efficiency. We were genuinely confused by the romantic theory of evil. The thing that woke us up was not the badness of the egg but the terrific consequences of the things that particular egg did. When the war is over, unless I miss my guess, we are likely to be again misled into the same confusion of values.

There is still a third modern theory of evil, and this I shall call the scientific theory. According to this there is no such thing as sin. Human beings are merely very complicated mechanisms, and they are what they are because of the regular operation of heredity and environment, economic law, vitamin deficiency, hypertrophy of the glands, or whatever else you happen to believe in. Hitler is a paranoiac, and the whole German nation is suffering from a secondary, or induced, paranoia. Exponents of this theory remind us that science doesn't judge; it only explains. You can't blame Hitler for being a paranoiac any more than you blame poison ivy for being poisonous. Some day science will tell us what to do about it, but what if that day doesn't come soon enough?

Here are three ways of looking at the evil in human nature—the sentimental, the romantic, and the scientific. Each one of them has qualities that commend it to the American temperament. Our goodheartedness makes us like the first; our energy and independence incline us to the second; everything that is scientific in our education and training prepares us for the third. The fact that they are often contradictory doesn't worry us. Whatever our characteristic American virtues are, logic isn't one of them. We share with the other English-speaking peoples a genius for living happily with contradictions, anomalies, and compromises. And where does it all get us?

Let me return momentarily to Milton. Far be it from me to say that he knew all the answers, but he knew some of them. He knew that ambition leads to cruelty and terror; he knew that the human race can be saved only by goodness, the goodness of God in man. He knew that the forces of Hell are real and are everywhere and always. He saw them in his imagination, surging and seething and boiling up onto this earth. Theologies, to be sure, are transitory, far more transitory than poetry. So far as *Paradise Lost* is purely theological, it may be obsolete, but as an analysis of good and evil, it teaches a lesson that we still need to learn. Over the theology of the poem towers Satan, incarnate evil, the arch fiend, the destroyer, and on his head sits Horror plumed.

I should like to finish this chapter with a noble peroration on the splendors of American goodness, secure in its native right and triumphant over evil in all its forms; but I shall be on much safer ground if I merely sum up what I have said already. Taking us by and large, we have a considerable faith in goodness and good people. That faith is probably greater than we realize, and in this respect we are lucky, because a faith in the goodness of men is the one thing that democracy cannot do without. Beyond that we are entangled in a lot of familiar notions about good and evil, accepting now one and now another, never following any of them to their logical conclusions. We can get through this war, I am sure, on our faith in ourselves and our native goodness. It is after the war that we are going to run into trouble. Shall we look at Germany as a nation of beautiful souls, temporarily misled in their emotions but presently to return to an idyllic existence of Beethoven, beer, and Grimm's fairy tales? Or as a Byronic hero-nation, magnificent in sin, romantic in its defiant energy, and then tragic in its defeat? Or as the victim of an unfortunate environment, needing merely a treatment in international economic therapy?

Or shall we really get down to the roots of good and evil and wrestle with our theories until we bring them into some kind of working conformity, not only with one another but with fact?

READING, WRITING, AND REVIEWS

READING, WRITING, AND REVIEWS

The following selections about the arts of reading and writing say what they have to say with such brilliance and clarity that any comments from the editors would be surely superfluous and probably impertinent. At the same time, no student needs to feel that he must share the tastes of Professor Lowes in reading or the judgments of Mr. Maugham about writing. Literature is not a science in which all the experts agree as to what is right and what is wrong. There is no court of critics or professors who can impose penalties on the culprit who differs with the late Mrs. Woolf about Hardy's novels or with Mr. Sheean about Pyle's *Brave Men*. There is no absolute formula for writing well. These essays in criticism deserve respect and study because they are the outgrowth of a rich experience with books, and represent the mature reflections of men and women who have made them.

Of Reading Books[1]

by JOHN LIVINGSTON LOWES

THE text (if I may call it so) of what I mean to say is this: "I hope, y-wis, to rede . . . som day." Which, translated into the vernacular, means: "I hope to Heaven that some day I'll get a chance to *read*." That pious hope is part of a line of Chaucer, and unless I much mistake, it finds an ardent response in the minds of scores of us to-day, who find ourselves caught in the toils of a more restless and exigent century than his. And what I propose to say about reading—whether it be for delight, or for information, or for something deeper still—must, if it is to have any value, take into account conditions which all save a few happy mortals are destined to meet.

For we live in an age and a land above all things marked by hurried motion. I happened to come from Pittsburgh to New York the other day, at the rate of fifty miles an hour. Every few minutes another train flashed by in the opposite direction. On a hundred thousand miles of rails the same flying shuttles were hurtling back and forth. The taxi which took me from one station to another in New York was numbered (they know better now) one million seven hundred thousand and odd, and the other million or two were trying simultaneously to hurl themselves along the streets. And under the street, packed trains, a couple of minutes or so apart, were crashing back and forth in the din of steel on steel flung back from walls of stone. My neighbour in the smoking-car that morning was manfully ploughing his way through a Gargantuan Sunday paper. My eye caught a page-wide head-line in one of those instructive sections which temper the comic supplement to the inquiring spirit: "Power enough in a glass of water to drive an ocean liner." And I wondered how far and how fast, when science had done its worst, our harmless necessary glass of water in the morning might one day drive us! A sip before breakfast here in Boston, and in an instant, if we will it, we are catapulted to Chicago. Why not? That is the logical goal of our endeavours. The word of the hour is the word of my headline—"drive." To carry on the business of college, church, or hospital, we initiate a "drive." Even in religion, education, and philanthropy we tend to think and act in terms of energy translated into tense and often fevered motion. The thing meets us everywhere. "In a weekly paper not very long ago"—and now I am quoting William James—"I remember reading a story in which, after describing the beauty and interest of the heroine's personality, the author summed up her charms by saying that to all who looked upon her an impression as of 'bottled

[1] Published 1929. Reprinted by permission of and arrangement with Houghton Mifflin Company.

lightning' was irresistibly conveyed. Bottled lightning, in truth," William James goes on, "is one of our American ideals, even of a young girl's character!" That was twenty-five years ago. To-day, be they masculine or feminine, we dub such persons dynamos. And the human dynamo is fast becoming our ideal.

Matthew Arnold saw all this coming—saw it, indeed, already well under way—much more than fifty years ago. "O born in days when wits were fresh and clear," he cries in his *Scholar-Gipsy*,

> And life ran gaily as the sparkling Thames;
> Before *this strange disease of modern life,*
> *With its sick hurry, its divided aims,*
> *Its heads o'ertax'd, its palsied hearts,* was rife—
> Fly hence, our contact fear! . . .

And he continues:

> But fly our paths, our feverish contact fly!
> For strong is the infection of our mental strife.

And in these last lines Arnold puts his finger on the core of the malady, so far as we are concerned. For this tension in which to-day we live and move and have our being is contagious. And there Matthew Arnold is at one with William James, in that wise discourse on which I have already drawn—his talk to students on "The Gospel of Relaxation": "The American overtension and jerkiness and breathlessness and intensity," he declares, "are primarily social . . . phenomena. They are *bad habits* . . . bred of custom and example." And you know, and I know, that high tension *is* contagious, and that we move in an atmosphere charged with energy driving at action, which sets us driving too, whether we are geared to anything or not. And we are helpless, unless —but that is to anticipate. And now I come back for a moment to Arnold again:

> But we, brought forth and rear'd in hours
> Of change, alarm, surprise—
> What shelter to grow ripe is ours?
> What leisure to grow wise?
>
> Like children bathing on the shore,
> Buried a wave beneath,
> The second wave succeeds, before
> We have had time to breathe.
>
> Too fast we live, too much are tried,
> Too harass'd, to attain
> Wordsworth's sweet calm, or Goethe's wide
> And luminous view to gain.

And that brings us within sight of our theme.

For one of the consequences of this modern malady of ours is that the gracious things which lend to life and human intercourse the beauty of serenity and comeliness are gone, or on the wane. "The wisdom of a learned man," wrote the author of *Ecclesiasticus* long centuries ago, "cometh by opportunity of leisure," and not wisdom only, but grace, and gentle breeding, and amenity, and poise come so, and only so. And leisure (which is not to be confused with empty time, but which is time through which free, life-enhancing currents flow)—leisure in these days is something to be sought and cherished as a rare and priceless boon; leisure to think, and talk, and write, and read—lost arts else, all of them. "John Wesley's conversation is good," said Dr. Johnson to Boswell once, "but he is never at leisure. He is always obliged to go at a certain hour. This is very disagreeable to a man who loves to fold his legs and have out his talk, as I do." The sainted John Wesley in the rôle of a modern "hustler" is a little humorous, and Samuel Johnson did a certain amount of work himself. But an age that loved, on occasion, to fold its legs, and have its talk out, and its book out, and its delightful familiar letters out, may not have been one hundred per cent. efficient (in our devastating modern phrase), but it did have shelter to grow ripe, and it did have leisure to grow wise, and more than our own driving, restless period, it did possess its soul. "He hasteth well," wrote Chaucer, whom business could not make dull, "who wisely can abide," and we first learn to live when we

> . . . claim not every laughing Hour
> For handmaid to (our) striding power . . .
> To usher for a destined space
> (Her own sweet errands all forgone)
> The too imperious traveller on.

"We are great fools," says Montaigne: " 'He spends his life in idleness,' we say, 'I've done nothing to-day.' What! Have you not *lived?* That is not only the most fundamental, but the most illustrious of your occupations."

Our salvation, then, lies in the refusal to be for ever hurried with the crowd, and in our resolution to step out of it at intervals, and drink from deeper wells. "Il se faut reserver une arrière boutique, toute nostre, toute franche"—"we ought to reserve for ourselves an *arrière boutique,* a back-shop, all our own, all free, in which we may set up our own true liberty and principal retreat and solitude." That is Montaigne's ripe, leisured wisdom, and in that *arrière boutique* the wish: "I hope, y-wis, to rede . . . som day," may find accomplishment. And so I mean to talk for a little while, most informally and most unacademically, about reading—a subject which, partly through our fault, I fear, some of you have come to think of in terms of courses and degrees, but which is infinitely bigger than all that. It is not even scholarship that I shall have in mind. It is simply reading, as men and women have always read, for the delight of it, and for the consequent enriching and enhancement of one's life. I have put delight deliberately first, for the rest, I believe, is contingent upon that. "In general," said Goethe once, "we learn from what we love." And I propose first of all to exhibit some lovable readers—not a Professor or even a Doctor in the lot, I think—and allow them to speak for themselves. And first, then, reading for the sheer delight of it.

"In anything fit to be called by the name of reading," says Stevenson in his delectable *Gossip on Romance,*

the process itself should be absorbing and voluptuous; we should gloat over a book, be rapt clean out of ourselves, and rise from the perusal, our mind filled with the busiest, kaleidoscopic dance of images, incapable of sleep or of continuous thought. It was for this . . . that we read so closely, and loved our books so dearly, in the bright, troubled period of boyhood. . . . We dug blithely after a certain sort of incident, like a pig for truffles. For my part, I liked a story to begin with an old wayside inn where, toward the close of the "year 17—," several gentlemen in three-cocked hats were playing bowls. A friend of mine preferred the Malabar coast in a storm, with a ship beating to windward, and a scowling fellow of Herculean proportions striding along the beach—

and so on delightfully. Now it is that unquenchable, bubbling zest on which I wish for the moment to insist, and Stevenson's is the gusto of "the bright, troubled period of boyhood." Let us set beside it, as is fitting, its companion piece. "But, my dearest Catherine"—and need I say that it is the immortal and adorable Jane Austen who is speaking—

"But, my dearest Catherine, what have you been doing with yourself all this morning? Have you gone on with 'Udolpho'?"

"Yes, I have been reading it ever since I woke; and I am got to the black veil."

"Are you indeed? How delightful! Oh, I would not tell you what is behind the black veil for the world! Are you not wild to know?"

"Oh! yes, quite; what can it be? But do not tell me. I would not be told upon any account. I know it must be a skeleton; I am sure it is Laurentina's skeleton. Oh, I am delighted with the book! I should like to spend my whole life in reading it, I assure you; if it had not been to meet you, I would not have come away from it for all the world."

"Dear creature, how much I am obliged to you! and when you have finished 'Udolpho,' we will read 'The Italian' together; and I have made out a list of ten or twelve more of the same kind for you."

"Have you indeed? How glad I am! What are they all?"

"I will read you their names directly. Here they are, in my pocket-book: 'Castle of Wolfenbach,' 'Clermont,' 'Mysterious Warnings,' 'Necromancer of the Black Forest,' 'Midnight Bell,' 'Orphan of the Rhine,' and 'Horrid Mysteries.' Those will last us some time."

"Yes, pretty well; but are they all horrid? Are you sure they are all horrid?"

"Yes, quite sure; for a particular friend of mine, a Miss Andrews, a sweet girl, one of the sweetest creatures in the world, has read every one of them."

Well, that is the meat upon which your inveterate readers are apt to have fed in childhood, and happy are you, if you have been caught at it young. For romances, and stories of giants, magicians, and genii, read with a child's quick and plastic imagination, are stepping-stones to later, deeper, if no more enduring loves. "I read through all gilt-cover little books that could be had at that time," wrote Coleridge to Tom Poole in those precious fragments of an autobiography,

and likewise all the uncovered tales of Tom Hickathrift, Jack the Giant Killer, and the like. And I used to lie by the wall, and mope; and my spirits used to come upon me suddenly and in a flood—and then I was accustomed to run up and down the churchyard, and act over again all that I had been reading on the docks, the nettles, and the rank grass. At six years of age . . . I found the *Arabian Nights' Entertainments,* . . . and I distinctly recollect the anxious and fearful eagerness with which I used to watch the window where the book lay, and when the sun came upon it, I would seize it, carry it by the wall, and bask, and read. . . . My whole being was, with eyes closed to every object of present sense, to crumble myself up in a sunny corner, and read, read, read.

I know there are those to whom all this is heresy, and who would feed children pedagogically desiccated food. There have always been such earnest and misguided souls. Charles Lamb has a gloriously volcanic outburst, in a letter to Coleridge, about Mrs. Barbauld's edifying books for children—Mrs. Barbauld, who objected to *The Ancient Mariner* because it was improbable, and who rushed in where angels fear to tread with *An Address to the Deity:*

I am glad (he writes) the snuff and Pi-pos's books please. "Goody Two Shoes" is almost out of print. Mrs. Barbauld's stuff has banished all the old classics of the nursery. . . . Knowledge insignificant and vapid as Mrs. B's books convey, it seems, must come to a child in the *shape of knowledge,* and his empty noddle must be turned with conceit of his own powers when he has learnt that a Horse is an animal, and Billy is better than a Horse, and such like: instead of that beautiful Interest in wild tales which made the child a man, while all the time he suspected himself to be no bigger than a child. Science has succeeded to Poetry no less in the little walks of children than with men. Is there no possibility of averting this sore evil? Think what you would have been now, if instead of being fed with Tales and old wives' fables in childhood, you had been crammed with geography and natural history!
Damn them! (The Bowdlerizing editors print "Hang them"—but Lamb was righteously indignant, and did *not* write "Hang")—I mean the cursed Barbauld Crew, those Blights and Blasts of all that is Human in man and child.

That at least cannot be charged with ambiguity, but Lamb expressed himself again—this time with reference to a girl's reading:

She was tumbled early (he is writing of Bridget Elia, who was Mary Lamb), by accident or design, into a spacious closet of good old English reading, without much selection or prohibition, and browsed at will upon that fair and wholesome pasturage. Had I twenty girls, they should be brought up exactly in this fashion. I know not whether their chance in wedlock might not be diminished by it; but I can answer for it that it makes (if the worst come to the worst) most incomparable old maids.

On that point I venture no opinion, but the doctrine of the rest is sound.
Now I have dwelt on this seemingly irrelevant theme of early reading, because the element of delight is the point I wish just now to emphasize, and

that eager, childlike zest, once caught, is seldom lost. There is no essential difference, for example, between Coleridge's absorption in the "Arabian Nights," and the irrepressible gusto with which John Keats read Shakespeare. Here is a bit of a letter which Keats wrote from Burford Bridge, one moonlit night, while he was deep in the composition of *Endymion:*

One of the three books I have with me is Shakespeare's Poems: I never found so many beauties in the Sonnets—they seem to be full of fine things said unintentionally—in the intensity of working out conceits. Is this to be borne? Hark ye!

> When lofty trees I see barren of leaves,
> Which erst from heat did canopy the head,
> And Summer's green all girded up in sheaves,
> Borne on the bier with white and bristly head.

He has left nothing to say about nothing or anything: for look at snails—you know what he says about Snails—you know when he talks about "cockled Snails"—well, in one of these sonnets, he says—the chap slips into—no! I lie! this is in the *Venus and Adonis:* the simile brought it to my Mind.

> As the snail, whose tender horns being hit,
> Shrinks back into his shelly cave with pain. . . .

He overwhelms a genuine Lover of poesy with all manner of abuse, talking about—

> "a poet's rage
> And stretched metre of an antique song."

Which, by the bye, will be a capital motto for my poem, won't it? . . . By the Whim-King! I'll give you a stanza—

and at once he is off creating! That is Keats through and through—the Keats who went "ramping" (as Cowden Clarke put it) through *The Faerie Queene;* who "hoisted himself up, and looked burly and dominant, as he said, 'What an image that is—*sea-shouldering whales'* "; who wrote, the night he first opened Chapman's Homer: "Then felt I like some watcher of the skies when a new planet swims into his ken." I always think, when I read in Keats's letters the things he says about his books, of those lines in *Ruth:*

> Before me shone a glorious world—
> Fresh as a banner bright, unfurled
> To music suddenly.

I have known, *you* know, men and women—busy men and women, too—to whom a book still means that. It is the very spirit of Miranda's cry:

> O wonder!
> How many goodly creatures are there here!
> How beauteous mankind is! O brave new world,
> That has such people in't!

And I envy any one to whom for the first time—or for the hundredth time—the brave new world of books is opening, that world which has such people in it: Cleopatra, Mr. Pickwick, Helen of Troy, Samuel Pepys, the Wife of Bath, Sir John Falstaff, Mrs. Proudie, Sir Willoughby Patterne, Becky Sharp, Perdita, Pantagruel, Mephistopheles, Launcelot, Dido, and a thousand others more alive than you and I. "I doe nothing without blithenesse," wrote Montaigne in his essay on "Books"—and if I were going to that famous desert island for which we are periodically asked to select our five-foot shelf, Montaigne in his pithy, sinewy, succulent French would be almost the first whom I should pick—"Je ne fais rien sans gayeté"; and no mortal ever went adventuring more blithely among books than Michael, Lord of Montaigne, or brought home richer treasure-trove.

"But," you will say to me, "we haven't time." I know it; very few of us these days have time—those least, I sometimes think, who have it most. But even if, being modern, and ambitious, and efficient, and all that, we are whirled along with our fellow atoms in the rush, we shall not be losing time if now and then we pause, and loaf (I wish the fine phrase had not been worn so trite), loaf, and invite our souls. And if you worship in the temple of efficiency, don't forget—and again I am drawing on the wise humanity of William James—that "just as a bicycle chain may be too tight, so may one's carefulness and conscientiousness be so tense as to hinder the running of one's mind." And after all, the smooth, free running of one's mind is fairly important to the precious efficiency of whatever machinery it be that your particular intelligence helps to run. Even as a business proposition (to fall again into the jargon of the day), time spent in unclamping our mental processes is time won, and not time lost.

And the thing is possible. Here is part of a letter which Matthew Arnold wrote to his sister. And Arnold, being a hard-driven public official, knew whereof he spoke.

> If I were you, my dear Fan, I should now take to some regular reading, if it were only an hour a day. It is the best thing in the world to have something of this sort as a point in the day, and far too few people know and use this secret. You would have your district still, and all your business as usual, but you would have this hour in your day in the midst of it all, and it would soon become of the greatest solace to you.

Here is a passage in which William Hazlitt is talking of luxuriating in books:

> I remember sitting up half the night to read *Paul and Virginia,* which I picked up at an inn at Bridgewater, after being drenched in the rain all day; and at the same place I got through two volumes of Madame D'Arblay's *Camilla.* It was on the 10th of April, 1798, that I sat down to a volume of the *New Eloise,* at the inn at Llangollen, over a bottle of sherry and a cold chicken.

And that delectable epicureanism is one of the marks of your true reader for delight—he remains a human being while he reads.

And here is Charles Lamb to Coleridge:

Observe, there comes to you, by the Kendal waggon to-morrow, . . . a box, containing the Miltons, the strange American Bible . . . Baxter's *Holy Commonwealth,* for which you stand indebted to me 3s. 6d.; an odd volume of Montaigne, being of no use to me, I have the whole; certain books belonging to Wordsworth, as do also the strange thick-hoofed shoes, which are very much admired at in London—

and there I must pause for a moment. For those thick-hoofed shoes are uncanny in their rich suggestiveness. They are Simon Lee and Goody Blake and the Idiot Boy and Peter Bell in a nutshell. And one of the fascinations of the letters—of Gray's inimitable raciness, of "the divine chit-chat of Cowper," as Coleridge calls it, of Lamb, Byron, Keats, Fitzgerald, Stevenson—one of the quintessential pleasures of the letters lies in their wealth of unexpected flashes: "fine things said unintentionally," as Keats said of the Sonnets. And now I return to Lamb and his box of books:

If you find the Miltons in certain parts dirtied and soiled with a crumb of right Gloucester blacked in the candle (my usual supper), or peradventure, a stray ash of tobacco wafted into the crevices, look to that passage more especially: depend upon it, it contains good matter.

Crumbs of toasted cheese and the ash of a pipe suggest, however, concomitant delights perhaps of scant appeal to certain readers. Well, then, here is Dorothy Wordsworth:

Worked hard, and read *Midsummer Night's Dream,* and ballads. Sauntered a little in the garden. The blackbird sate quietly in its nest, rocked by the wind, and beaten by the rain. . . . Sauntered a good deal in the garden, bound carpets, mended old clothes, read *Timon of Athens,* dried linen. . . . In the afternoon we sate by the fire; I read Chaucer aloud, and Mary read the first canto of the *Faerie Queene.* . . . We spent the morning in the orchard reading the *Epithalamium* of Spenser; walked backwards and forwards. . . . We sowed the scarlet beans in the orchard, and read *Henry V* there. After dinner William added one to the orchard steps. . . . A sunshiny morning, I walked to the top of the hill and sate under a wall . . . facing the sun. I read a scene or two in *As You Like It.* . . . Read part of *The Knight's Tale* with exquisite delight.

The Faerie Queene, the *Epithalamium, Henry V, As You Like It, The Knight's Tale:* those are the things that you "take," as if they were some academic whooping-cough or measles. And there, under no compulsion, is a woman reading them as if they'd actually been written to be *read*—reading them by the fire, in the orchard, on a hill-top under a wall in the sun—reading with exquisite delight. Heaven help us who teach, if through well-meant but sometimes misguided efforts to instruct, we have rubbed the bloom off the great books, and blunted the keen edge of pleasure such as that!

I have not the slightest intention in all this of implying that only the hundred best books, so to speak, will serve our purposes. Some of the most bewitching, completely captivating things in life lie buried in forgotten, relatively worthless books, if one has eyes to see them. An enterprising young

friend of mine suggested in a letter that I had from him not long ago the
alluring enterprise of an anthology of the *worst* poetry. I hope he will make
it! For your true adventurer in "the wide, wild wilderness of books" knows
that often, as Browning has it, "the worst turns best for the brave." "I am
going to repeat my old experiment," Stevenson wrote in a letter to Sidney
Colvin, "after buckling to a while to write more correctly, lie down and have
a wallow." That is not elegant, but it is precise. And after one has wound
up one's faculties, like Mrs. Battle, over serious things, one may indulge with
propriety in what I suppose one may designate as a slumming expedition
among books. I do not recommend it as a practice, but for occasional indulgence there are distinguished precedents. Macaulay, for instance, besides
knowing the romances of a certain prolific Mrs. Meeke almost by heart, was
devoted to the literary efforts of a Mrs. Kitty Cuthbertson—*Santo Sebastiano,
or, the Young Protector, The Forest of Montalbano, The Romance of the
Pyrenees, Adelaide, or, the Countercharm.* And on the last page of his edition of *Santo Sebastiano* appears an elaborate computation of the number of
fainting fits that occur in the course of the five volumes. Here they are:

Julia de Clifford	11
Lady Delamore	4
Lady Theodosia	4
Lord Glenbrook	2
Lord Delamore	2
Lady Enderfield	1
Lord Ashgrove	1
Lord St. Orville	1
Henry Mildmay	1

a total of 27. And here is a specimen of one of these catastrophes: "One of
the sweetest smiles that ever animated the face of mortal now diffused itself
over the countenance of Lord St. Orville, as he fell at the feet of Julia in a
death-like swoon."

There is a volume entitled *A Spiritual Diary and Soliloquies* by a certain
John Ruttey, M.D., which, Boswell informs us, diverted Dr. Johnson vastly
—one of these priceless things on which one stumbles now and then and
which reward excursions off the beaten path. Here are a few of the worthy
Quaker's entries:

Tenth month, 1753.
23. Indulgence in bed an hour too long.
Twelfth month, 17. An hypochondriac obnubilation from wind and indigestion.
Ninth month, 28. An over-dose of whiskey.
29. (Which was the day after the over-dose) A dull, cross, choleric day.
First month, 22. A little swinish at dinner and repast.
31. Dogged on provocation.
Second month, 5. Very dogged or snappish. . . .
23. Dogged again.
Fourth month, 29. Mechanically and sinfully dogged.

I am not, as you see, submitting a bibliography, or suggesting learned apparatus. For the moment we are concerned with reading for the sheer delight of it, when the world is all before us where to choose. But with delight there may be coupled something else. For one also reads to learn. And about that and one thing more, I shall be very brief.

Let me begin with a remark of Oliver Wendell Holmes:

> There are about as many twins in the births of thought as of children. For the first time in your lives you learn some fact or come across some idea. Within an hour, a day, a week, that same fact or idea strikes you from another quarter. . . . Yet no possible connection exists between the two channels by which the thought or the fact arrived. . . . And so it has happened to me and to every person, often and often, to be hit in rapid succession by these twinned facts or thoughts, as if they were linked like chain-shot.

Now all of us have had that experience, and it is apt to give us a curious sensation. "Here," we say, "we've gone all our life without seeing that, and now all at once we see it at every turn. What does it mean?" Not long ago, for example, my attention was called for the first time, in a letter, to an international society of writers; two days later my eye caught a reference to it in a daily paper. Soon afterward I heard, for the first time to my knowledge, the name of a certain breed of terriers. Within a week I had come across the name in two different novels I was reading. What had happened? Simply this. I had doubtless seen both names time and again before, but nothing had ever stamped them on my memory, and so when they turned up again, they wakened no response. Then, all at once, something did fix them in my mind, and when they met my eye once more, they were there behind it, so to speak, to recognize themselves when they appeared. There had been set up in my brain, as it were, by each of them, a magnetic centre, ready to catch and attract its like.

Now one of the things which the process we call education ought to do, and by no means always does, is to establish in the mind as many as possible of these magnetic centres—live spots, which thrust out tentacles of association and catch and draw to themselves their kind. For there are few joys in reading like the joy of the chase. And the joy of the chase comes largely through the action of these centres of association in your brain. Let me illustrate what I mean, and since first-hand experience imparts a certain vividness which abstract theorizing lacks, let me use myself as a *corpus vile,* and draw for a moment upon that.

Years ago, like everybody who was interested in Chaucer, I was puzzled by a mysterious reference to "the dry sea and the Carrenar." There was no Carrenar that anybody knew—nor, for that matter, any assured dry sea. One day, as I was reading in an old battered volume of *Purchas his Pilgrimes,* which is one of my choicest treasures, I was struck by the recurrence in a number of Central-Asian place-names, of the prefix *Kara.* But none of them had the termination *nar.* Might they offer, however, a possible clue? So I asked that one among my colleagues who is an adept in all outlandish tongues, what the combination Kara-nar would mean in any language which he knew. The instant answer was: Black Lake. The rest of the long tale I shall not tell. Suffice it to say that there was and is a lake called Kara-nor; that it lay and lies on the great ancient trade-route between Orient and Occident, travelled in Chaucer's time; and that the lake is at the edge of a vast and terrible desert which was and is, in name and character, a veritable dry sea. And the sole reason of my mention of the business here is this: Had the crux of the Car-renar not been very much alive in my head, I might have seen a thousand Kara's in the travel-books without a thrill, and so have missed the most fascinating exploration—barring two—I ever undertook. And these other two came about in precisely the same way: through the recognition as I read of something which suggested, through a likeness recognized, the solution of a puzzle which had found a lodgment in my mind, and which was there, once more, to recognize its like, when, without warning, its like turned up. I cannot lay too strong an emphasis upon the sort of pleasure which results from the constant recognition in what one reads of things which link themselves, often in endlessly suggestive fashion, with things one has already read, till old friends with new faces meet us at every turn, and flash sudden light, and waken old associations, and quicken the zest for fresh adventures. To read with alert intellectual curiosity is one of the keenest joys of life, and it is pleasure which too many of us needlessly forgo.

And that leads me to say two things. In the first place, one cannot begin too soon to buy one's own books, if for no other reason (and there are many more) than the freedom which they give you to use their fly-leaves for your own private index of those matters in their pages which are particularly yours, whether for interest, or information, or what not—those things which the index-makers never by any possibility include. To be able to turn at will, in a book of your own, to those passages which count for *you*, is to have your wealth at instant command, and your books become a record of your intellectual adventures, and a source of endless pleasure when you want, as you will, to turn back to the things which have given delight, or stirred imagination, or opened windows, in the past.

That is one point. The other is this. Goethe observed to Eckermann one day, in those *Conversations* which constitute one of the most thought-provoking volumes in the world: "You know, Saul the son of Kish went out one day to find his father's asses, and found a kingdom." Which is a parable. For it is when you are looking for one thing as you read—it may be some utterly trivial affair—that ten to one you come upon the unexpected thing, the big or thrilling thing, which opens up new worlds of possibilities. Most of our discoveries—even if, as usually happens, they are discoveries only to us— are made when we are hot on the trail of something else. For because we are looking, we see, and we see more than we look for, because the eye which scans the page is actively alert to everything. And the more you *have*—the more live cluster-points of association there are in your brain—the more you see, and reading becomes a *cumulative* delight. "The dear good people," said Goethe once, "don't know how long it takes to learn to read. I've been at it eighty years, and can't say yet that I've reached the goal." One never does. There are always, as one goes on reading, unpath'd waters, undream'd shores ahead. And that is the secret of its perennial delight.

One reads for the sheer enjoyment of it; one reads to learn; and there is a yet more excellent way. "Man *lernt* nichts," said Goethe of Winckelmann, "wenn man ihn liest, aber man *wird* etwas"—"you don't *learn* anything when you read him, but you *become* something." That strikes to the very root of things, for it puts into one pregnant phrase the supreme creative influence in the world—the contagious touch of great personalities. And if a good book is, in truth, as Milton in a noble passage once declared, "the precious life-blood of a master-spirit, embalmed and treasured up on purpose to a life beyond life," then that creative influence of life on life is in the book, and as we read, our spirit is enriched and grows, and we *become* something. We are just a little ashamed these days, I know, in our reaction from a certain sort of cant, to read for our soul's sake, or our spirit's sake, or for edification, in the fine old sense of a sadly misused word. We feel, somehow, that it isn't quite the thing. Well, I don't care at all what terms you use; but we are more than intellect, and more than sense, and the deepest-lying springs of life are touched by life alone. And the men who have lived, and learned through living, and won through life a wide and luminous view—these men have the imperishable creative power of broadening, deepening, and enhancing life. They are the true humanists, and humanism, as I take it, is the development, not of scholars, not of philosophers, or scientists, or specialists in this or that, but of human beings. Goethe was such a humanist, and Goethe, by practice, not by precept, has pointed out the way.

"I read every year," he said, "a few plays of Molière, just as I also, from time to time, look over the engravings of the great Italian masters. For we little men aren't capable of maintaining within us the greatness of such things, and we have always to keep turning back to them from time to time, in order to quicken within us our impressions." "Today after dinner," wrote Ecker-mann—and this sort of thing happened again and again—"Goethe went through the portfolio of Raphael with me. He busies himself with Raphael very often, in order to keep himself always in touch with the best, and to exercise himself continually in thinking the thoughts of a great spirit after him." And this, mind you, was not a preacher, or a teacher, or a reformer, but the most puissant, richly endowed spirit of the modern world. Beyond delight, and beyond intellectual adventure, there is the spiritual contagion of great books.

And again I should like to be very practical, for we live in a busy world. Matthew Arnold once wrote in a letter, while he was off inspecting schools: "I enjoy my time here very much. I read five pages of Greek anthology every day, looking out all the words I do not know"—a very comforting remark, that last, for some of us. "This," he goes on, "is what I shall always understand by *education,* and it does me good, and gives me great pleasure." And the secret of his practice comes out in another letter, written this time to a British working man: "As to useful knowledge, a single line of poetry, working in the mind, may produce more thoughts and lead to more light, which is what man wants, than the fullest acquaintance (to take your own instance) with the processes of digestion." I am not sure, indeed, that anything which Arnold left is of more worth than his little, narrow, vestpocket notebooks, which extend over a period of thirty-seven years. They served, not only for his record of engagements, but also as a repository for those passages of his daily reading which, in his own words, were "working in his mind"—those passages through pondering on which (to use Montaigne's phrase) he *forged,* instead of merely *furnishing,* his soul. The entries for a dozen years have been printed, in a precious volume, by his daughter, and they exemplify, as nothing else I know can do, the sort of reading which I now have in mind— that reading through which "man *wird* etwas." I take nothing back of what I have said of reading as a delightful intellectual adventure. But this is different—yet not so different after all. "I had an idea," wrote Keats in one of his letters,

that a Man might pass a very pleasant life in this manner—let him on a certain day read a certain Page of full Poesy or distilled Prose, and let him wander with it, and muse upon it, and reflect upon it, and bring home to it, and prophesy upon it, and dream upon it, until it becomes stale—but when will it do so? Never. When Man has arrived at a certain ripeness in intellect, any one grand and spiritual passage serves him as a starting-point towards all "the two-and-thirty Palaces."

Well, there before you are the palaces and the road thereto. I don't know where, for you, they are; I only know they are there.

We have no shrines, most of us, any more—we Protestant-Puritan-Pagan-Anglo-Saxon Occidentals—no tranquil Buddhas or symbols of the Passion by the roadside, no solemn temples, few cool, silent churches, always open and inviting to withdrawal for a moment from the hurly-burly of the world. It is not my business to determine whether that means loss or gain. But one thing it is always in our power to do—to withdraw now and then from the periphery to the centre, from the ceaseless whirl of the life that streams and eddies round us to the deep serenity of those great souls of better centuries ("ces grandes âmes des meilleurs siècles"), who give—and the lines sum up the antidote to the sick hurry of today—who give

> Authentic tidings of invisible things;
> Of ebb and flow, and ever-during power;
> And central peace, subsisting at the heart
> Of endless agitation.

The Pursuit of Values in Fiction[1]

by DOROTHY BREWSTER and ANGUS BURRELL

I

ANATOLE FRANCE, speaking once of the books he had written for children, said he was always afraid of not succeeding: "It is much easier to write for men than for the little monkeys. One persuades men that it is the proper thing to read such and such a book. And they read it and praise it. When a child is bored, he tears the page and makes a paper doll or a boat."

The child's attitude is an honest one. Some adults retain this attitude, reading what pleases them, flinging aside what doesn't, and not concerning themselves with the tastes of others or the reasons for their own likes and dislikes. But most of us by the time we are grown up have had a little training in ethics and esthetics. We feel an obligation to appreciate what is considered good, morally or artistically, and to give our reasons. So we talk of plot and characterization, or what is "convincing" and what is "unreal," of "significance" and "sound psychology," of "message" and "local color" and "truth to life." One praises a book, another damns the same book; to the first the characters are convincing and the plot beautifully proportioned, to the second the same characters are unreal and the same plot badly constructed. These sharply contradictory judgments are expressed in the same technical phrases of criticism that we have been taught to use by teachers, critics, and reviewers. But under the shop-worn formulas lurk intimate personal responses to the book of which we are often unaware. The circumstances under which we read it may predispose us to approval or disapproval; a half forgotten experience may be at work, unlocking our imagination or bolting the door; some unacknowledged prejudice is obscurely active; or some psychological need, proceeding from the unsatisfied impulses that every human being has or the deep-seated inner conflicts that few escape, makes us love or hate the book with a fervor difficult for us to understand. It is no easy matter to trace these intimate personal relations with a book. We need a Socrates to conduct the inquiry, with our favorite psychologist at his elbow to prompt him. Instead we have a few teachers and critics and a few hundred student readers of varying ages, willing but not always able to explore their preferences in fiction.

There was an intelligent young man in a University Extension course whose academic training had been interrupted by the War, but it had left in his mind a débris of critical phrases which he automatically used when asked

[1] Adapted from *Adventure or Experience* (1930), Columbia University Press. By permission of the authors.

his opinion of a novel. He picked out Jack London's *Valley of the Moon* as the best novel he had ever read. It took a couple of weeks to discover why he really liked that book: "Last summer," he ultimately wrote, "when recovering from an accident, I sat out in the park while a young lady read the story aloud. A cool breeze ruffled the leaves of the tree under which we sat, the birds sang, the flowers were in bloom, and the lady had a voice that was pleasant to hear. Row-boats floated on the lagoon near-by, and further off I could see tennis players hopping about after a little ball, while I sat next to the charming young lady. I liked the book for the struggles of the hero. I am very fond of struggles, provided they are someone else's. The tennis players, the boaters, the children playing tag, the motorists, and the hero of the book—all were struggling. So you see I was very happy. It really is a good book, though."

A reader who deeply enjoyed Hamsun's *Growth of the Soil,* because it revived for her the delightful memory of her childhood summers on a Vermont farm, was repelled by Nexö's labor-epic, *Pelle the Conqueror.* "The word strike recalls to my mind my mother's face as the riot call sounded in Lawrence one Friday in 1912." Her father was a mill official, sympathetic with the strike, but bound to protect the mill property at the risk of his life. "I remember the militia camped in the basement of the mill, the soldiers forcing us to move on in the streets, the broken street car windows, the soup kitchens, my hungry schoolmates, many of them fed in our home, and over and over again my father's haggard face. Nexö's picture of economic complexities is too well-drawn. Unless I can act, I had rather not consider it."

Psycho-analysts assure us that we cannot discover our own complexes. They tell us that if we are fascinated by a writer who has a certain psychosis, we ourselves probably share that psychosis, and that is why the "release" he has achieved for himself in art gives us also satisfaction. But some romantically-minded readers, so illumined, begin to detect in themselves all sorts of delightful perversities. A young woman read *Crime and Punishment* and in its murky light inspected her own past; for she was disturbed at her own enthusiasm over the murder and surprised at the profound sense of relief at the close of the reading. Had she always longed to see a murder—or was it possible she had craved to commit one? There had been a time some years before when she had been "very morbid"; she had wanted to be alone all the time, when not wandering about the streets; "I remembered that when I saw a dog or a cat, I would kick it, throw stones at it, torture it." Convinced that she must have been a budding Raskolnikov, she expressed her gratitude to Dostoevsky for relieving her of the heavy burden resting on what she brilliantly called her "subconscientious" mind.

The repression that counts, in these hidden dramas of personality, is of course the one of which we are truly unconscious. But there are many aspects of our relation to a novel that we can detect after some reflection. One reader enjoyed *If Winter Comes* and declared the author a master of character portrayal; later she realized that she read it when she was feeling "a total failure," it made her "quite fond of herself." Her self-satisfaction was disguised as praise of the author.

In a discussion about Somerset Maugham's *Of Human Bondage,* one disputant argued effectively enough that it was in this, that, and the other respect a poor novel; to every point made in its favor, she had a good answer. But presently the real reason for her attitude to the book flashed upon her; her name was Mildred; the odiously genteel, anæmic waitress who holds the hero in degrading bondage is named Mildred. Somewhere below the threshold of her grown-up mind she resented the identification of these Mildreds. But no grown-up mind would acknowledge so childish a reason for taking a dislike to a book, until its rational defenses had been captured one after the other in the argument. Tracking down these personal secrets may open the way to a more impersonal contemplation of values.

It is worth while to set down some of the simpler conclusions to be drawn from these reading experiences of people of diverse temperaments, varying ages, different backgrounds; people who exhibit every kind of psychological need; yet who all desire to be discriminating in their reading and critical in at least a rudimentary fashion. A few complain that the effort at analysis destroys their naïve pleasure in reading; not a few find it destroying their equally naïve pleasure in themselves; some discover in it a new and delightful way of talking about themselves—they love the confessional and their confessions have to be scrutinized carefully before one erects theories of criticism upon them. Others find it interesting and often illuminating.

The experience of the young man with Jack London shows that the circumstances under which one happens to read a book may account for the impression it makes. That sounds utterly obvious. But it is often ignored or forgotten when the reader turns critic. A woman who prefers sophisticated books responded warmly to *The Growth of the Soil* because she happened to read it on her return to New York from wide-open spaces somewhere; and the rush of the city made life seem a meaningless jumble; so that the simple strength, order and purpose in Isak's life satisfied a need. A nurse, taking a correspondence course in fiction, found herself having to read *The Ambassadors* "to the tune of the psychopathic ward" in the hospital. "Strether's complicated brain-storms over Chad Newsome's morals were frequently interrupted by the would-be suicide who tried to tear the bandages from the throat he had failed to cut efficiently; and there was a slender-pale-faced woman of forty who washed her hands and washed her hands ceaselessly." All this variety of the "real" made what the nurse called James's delicate flicking of butterflies from petals seem artificial and absurd. She criticized him for writing about unimportant experiences and not about the "roots of things." But to another woman who had just suffered a pronounced change of attitude towards life, James in *The Ambassadors* was a profoundly satisfying novelist because he pictured men and women in the throes of facing about: "I emerged refreshed and happy. It is just as when one has been trying to spell out a book in the twilight, and suddenly the lamp comes in."

We have been led on into more complicated aspects of the reader's relation to the novel, where interpretation becomes more hazardous. Whenever a comment reveals intense dislike of a book or character, some obsession or complex may be at work, unsuspected by its owner; and we have to read between the lines and risk a guess that by a lucky chance may receive confirmation later. A young man criticized Sudermann's *Dame Care* as a third-rate novel, but he could muster few reasons for the opinion that stood their ground under questioning. It turned out that he hated Sudermann's portrait of Paul's father—as fool, or villain, or both. He realized that his attitude to the book was determined by the similarity between Paul's father and his own; he went on talking about his father, gradually warming to a kind of resentful defence. The father had become very like Paul's father in the end—vindictive and suffering from a sense of inferiority. Why did he hate Sudermann's portrayal so much? Because he loved his father? Or because he had subconsciously passed the same judgment on him that Sudermann passes on Paul's father and resented being made aware of it? Or possibly because he was conscious of his own resemblance to his father? At any rate, a detached judgment on the book's merits could scarcely be expected from him. He was studying to be a librarian and would, no doubt, often be asked to give advice to readers. Yet he disliked having the personal and psychological factors in criticism insisted upon; he wanted a few firmly fixed standards. His confusion about himself and *Dame Care* is in interesting contrast with the clarity of a Chinese student, who preferred it above all others in a reading-list, chiefly because it supported his own inherited conception of life: "It has a theme, and that theme is that extreme sacrifice is necessary in order to attain any great object. It has much the same theme that most of our Chinese novels have. The Chinese novel is predominantly ethical in tone. The hero is always made to undergo all kinds of hardships and sometimes death to attain his object. That object might be the salvation of other persons, the betterment of society, the rescuing of one's family, or the elevation of one's nation. *Dame Care* develops its theme adequately, since every scene contains some misfortune for the hero."

II

The discussion so far has suggested some of the very personal considerations that must be recognized and dealt with, before the neat categories of criticism can be used—or discarded—with intelligence. But there are questions concerning the effects of fiction on the reader that are still more important for the growth of any sound theories of criticism. Is fiction escape or solution, adventure or experience, for the reader?

The escapes furnished by fiction from certain moods and situations are often obvious enough. The young woman of cheerful temperament adores the more melancholy of Chekhov's stories, because it is so "refreshing" to experience a gloomy mood. The only daughter of elderly parents, in her longing for a brother or sister and "intimate family incidents" almost wore the covers off the Alcott books, and later delighted in *Pride and Prejudice,* becoming "absorbed in the family problems of Mrs. Bennett." But it won't do to offer family chronicles to all only children. For here is another only child—and only grandchild, with "five maiden aunts and uncles"—who always felt the Alcott families too prolific: "their sharing of experiences didn't appeal to me, who knew at all times the joy of the limelight. All large families in my childhood's list of fiction excited the sympathy that made me grateful I was not like one of these." The feeling has persisted in her adult life and she is bored with family histories, like Mann's *Buddenbrooks.* Another reader recognized, as she looked back, that she had always read to escape the thing at hand, whatever it was; that she had been an adept at camouflaging her own dreary feelings with the local color of another's painting, and had thus avoided an analysis that might have led to a less boring environment. Years of illness had made her feel neglected and misunderstood, and she liked to read of characters who suffered and were not appreciated, but through keen intelligence finally won out. The fairy-tale of the Ugly Duckling—only slightly disguised in much grown-up fiction—is the archetype of innumerable novels that solace the ugly ducklings of life.

A college boy reads and re-reads *Cyrano de Bergerac, Peter Pan,* and tales by Lord Dunsany; he thinks the ideal world would be peopled with children, that the greatest tragedy is that children grow up, and the next greatest that they want to grow up. "As for me, I shall never grow up." His favorite fiction either idealizes the child or creates a fairy-tale world, of beauty or horror; for he likes horrible tales, too, like *The Seven Who Were Hanged,* tales so far beyond the limits of his own life that he doesn't have to believe in them, not really, any more than a child believes in witches.

To one young man *The Return of the Native* afforded the most complete escape. It revived the impressions of fairy stories read in childhood: "Those in particular which were brought back to me were of the giant who locked all the men he caught in the tower of the castle, or of Jack who had just time enough to get to the bottom of the beanstalk and chop it down before his colossal pursuer arrived. In many places in Hardy's book I felt in the same position as in those nightmares where, try as one may, one is neither able to move forward or to call to one's friends, who are disappearing over the crest of the hill. In the stories and dreams just mentioned one was convinced of the inevitability of certain forces more powerful than one's self; and it was in the return to that sort of fatalism which was so terrifying in one's youth that I found satisfaction and inspiration. It was an escape from the theories of self-sufficient adulthood to the superstitious religions and fears of the old world. His use of coincidences is to some readers a fault, but for me, they make the tragedy more poignant and make me live all the more vitally in the land of dreams and illusions."

A slightly different form of escape is noted in another student's comment on Hardy. She found in his fatalism the beginning of her release from the Catholic fatalism in which she had been taught to believe and which she had come increasingly to dread. "Disaster overtakes Hardy's characters as a matter of course; the world of itself is unfriendly to them. But the machinery that dooms them is impersonal. In Catholic fatalism, a personal God punishes His subjects through His magic. Hardy's kind of fatalism seems as relentless in its movements as the Catholic sort, but far broader and more comfortable to accept."

The fiction of failure may be as satisfying an escape as that of success. Successful people take pleasure in vicariously living through a few failures. Or people who have felt the sting of defeat but in some drab, dish-washing, adding-machine atmosphere, can derive delight from really splendid failures—spectacular ones like Ivan Karamazov's, exquisite ones like Strether's in *The Ambassadors,* romantic ones like Decoud's in *Nostromo.* The dream of a splendid failure might be consoling and congenial in moods when one of blatant success would only disgust.

III

To justify oneself is more permanently satisfactory than merely to escape into an imaginary self and more congenial surroundings. Intentionally or not, readers reveal how this or that novel has made their own actions seem reasonable or inevitable, their own temperaments interesting or excusable; it has made it more possible or more delightful for them to live with themselves. Perhaps it has justified vicious attitudes as well as fine ones and confirmed unpleasant traits as well as admirable ones, though naturally the material readers offer for inspection only inadvertently discloses this reverse side.

A young man who was forced to study medicine, hated it, and abandoned it, read *The Way of All Flesh* and saw his problem in Ernest's, and his justification in Ernest's behavior. Ernest found the Church full of hypocrites —he found the medical world the same. Philip, in *Of Human Bondage,* is one of the most consoling of heroes; he makes so many false starts, suffers so frequently what the world calls failure. Yet his failures all appear to the intimate view justified and valuable. What, asks Philip's uncle, had he got from the years devoted to that art of painting he was now abandoning for medicine? And Philip, with his ironically superior air, makes precisely the response we wish we could always summon when similarly challenged. "Philip," writes a young man, "lives for me because our experiences and thoughts parallel in many instances. His ceaseless and fruitless groping for his niche in life and a satisfactory career leads him into several experiments I have already attempted. I have left college because I believed it would not lead me to any adequate occupation in after life; I have studied art in Paris and discovered my mistake; I have played with the idea of an infinite number of careers and found that my enthusiasm did not survive the realization stage, but exhausted itself in planning and expectation; just as Philip's did about going into the Church. The fact that Philip survived so many failures and finally discovered a path of comparative contentment makes me a little less hopeless on my own account."

Proportionate to our satisfaction in the book that vindicates us is our violent and often obscure resentment of the book that topples over some carefully built-up structure in which we are living comfortably. *Of Human Bondage*—which provides so many readers with satisfying emotional escapes and justifications—made one reader suffer "mentally and physically." "It sickened and angered and ate into me with its red petticoat, dirty smock, crooked teeth, corn-y toes and what-not. The Philips and Miss Prices became unending nightmares. I hate ugliness. It is possible for me to accept it. Without at all understanding it, I am able to sympathize with it. But I refuse to take it to me, to make it part of my life. I have the grained-in English respect for wholesomeness and human dignity. Maugham not only destroyed my illusions regarding the world but gnawed at some of the illusions I had regarding myself. I found myself revaluing almost everything I had previously read. I have never reached a final decision. I am able to see the nobility which grows out of bondage, of human suffering. In that light, I cannot be noble; I have been so utterly free, I can hardly say I have suffered —at least not sufficiently. But must I go looking for suffering? There is so much joy in the world. And I do not believe that a knowledge of the meagreness of life heightens one's appreciation of its goodness. For my own part, I cannot say that I have known a fuller ecstasy of being since I became aware of life's sordidness, than I knew when I raced with my dogs." There was a Social Service worker who had great enthusiasm for her vocation. She was about to marry an engineer whose work was in a coal-mining town where there were plenty of poor people on whom she could try out, as she put it, all the pet theories she had paid for at college. She traced some of her social-service enthusiasm to her early reading of *Pollyanna* books and *Mrs. Wiggs of the Cabbage Patch* and *The Re-creation of Brian Kent* (by Harold Bell Wright), and other books that dealt with broken-down lives, prostitution, desertion, and poor orphans. Now she herself was going to work with Cabbage Patch people. Her favorite fiction in the course she was taking dealt with situations and people that needed the services of a social-service diagnostician: novels by Galsworthy, Hardy, George Eliot. "I love to diagnose in fiction, from any chapter 3 on." But when the Russian novelists came on the scene, she had a severe shock. She felt hatred and contempt for all the characters in *The Brothers Karamazov;* she loathed Gorky; she shuddered at the very mention of murder, insanity, radical, gendarme. She was able to endure *War and Peace* by regarding it as a sociological treatise against war. Now one would have thought that some of the people in these Russian novels so needed the help of a social service expert that she would have responded with alacrity. Probably the trouble was this: she felt equal to a Galsworthy or a Hardy problem, with the equipment of her theories; but Dostoevsky was so much more searching and profound that she felt unable to cope with his situations and his characters, and sought to defend herself by hating them.

IV

There are some glimpses of the interaction between fiction and living in the experiences we have been dealing with. But they have not been those of the actively experimental readers who are likely to try out a suggestion furnished by a novel just as they would other suggestions that come to them. Such readers were not content as children to lose themselves in the delightful dream. If they have been reading *The Arabian Nights,* they prowl about the neighborhood looking for a magic door; and finding a large round stone in the ground, with an iron ring, they lift it up, thrill at the glimpse of a mysterious cave, start to explore it, and have to be rescued from a fall into a disused well. A young man remembers vividly how Edward Stratemeyer's Dave Porter books inspired him to imitation. "When Dave's eyes flashed fire, I used to stand in front of the mirror to see whether I could discover any scintillations. In one of Dave's fights with the school bully, our hero banged the bully's head against the boat-house and made him see stars. I tried this at school one day, banging a fellow's head against the blackboard, but neither the victim, the teacher, nor my parents seemed to approve." He became an ardent Yale rooter, because of Frank Merriwell and Dink Stover; but never risked any money on football games—"not that I had the slightest fear of losing, for I had read so often of what a glorious thing it was to be a good loser; but because neither Stover nor Merriwell nor Dave ever gambled or smoked or drank. Nor did I—then." Inspired to swimming feats by one hero, he built himself up from a delicate boy into a record-breaker. *Black Beauty* made him a lover of horses and Uncle Tom a liker of negroes.

Another young man gave an account of the effect upon him of boys' stories and college tales that is very similar, but the ending is strikingly different. Realizing how suggestible he was, he refrained from exposing himself to "suggestive" novels, fearing they might make him do "something wild," and that would be regrettable, since he was most satisfactorily engaged to a fine girl. Probably the thought of his potential wildness was as satisfying an imaginative experience as any novel would be. Few readers can recall as definite a history of imitation as these young men. The more usual experience is one of perpetual interaction between literature and life; literature now giving some impulse to living, again an actual experience leading us to literature for interpretation or justification. The interplay appears in all possible combinations and the whole process is obscure and difficult to trace as we look back upon it. Yet the moralist and the censor would like to sum it all up in the simple question: will people act upon the suggestions of fiction? And they often risk an affirmative answer, relying on a few instances that furnish no basis for generalization, and on some convenient rough-and-ready psychological theory.

Most of the purposes served by novels in the lives of readers are suggested in these personal analyses: their value as a statement of our own confusedly realized experience; as a dream of what we should like to be—and may possibly be encouraged to become; as an outlet for moods; as an excuse for self-pity, a device for evasion, an instrument for the clarification of conflicts and problems.

And the conclusion of this search for values? No dogmatic conclusion about critical standards has been reached. The purpose of this chapter is to encourage a distrust of arbitrary dogmas in criticism. It is only when a reader—and the reader may be even a "classicist" or an "impressionist" critic —has discovered his own intimate and personal responses to a book, has seen how his hitherto hidden prejudices have been treacherously at work, and has stripped himself of self-deceptions, that he is in a position to make intelligent, rather than emotionally twisted, evaluations of his reading experiences.

The Novels of Thomas Hardy[1]

by VIRGINIA WOOLF

WHEN we say that the death of Thomas Hardy leaves English fiction without a leader, we mean that there is no other writer whose supremacy would be generally accepted, none to whom it seems so fitting and natural to pay homage. Nobody of course claimed it less. The unworldly and simple old man would have been painfully embarrassed by the rhetoric that flourishes on such occasions as this. Yet it is no less than the truth to say that while he lived there was one novelist at all events who made the art of fiction seem an honourable calling; while Hardy lived there was no excuse for thinking meanly of the art he practised. Nor was this solely the result of his peculiar genius. Something of it sprang from his character in its modesty and integrity, from his life, lived simply down in Dorsetshire without self-seeking or self-advertisement. For both reasons, because of his genius and because of the dignity with which his gift was used, it was impossible not to honour him as an artist and to feel respect and affection for the man. But it is of the work that we must speak, of the novels that were written so long ago that they seem as detached from the fiction of the moment as Hardy himself was remote from the stir of the present and its littleness.

We have to go back more than a generation if we are to trace the career of Hardy as a novelist. In the year 1871 he was a man of thirty-one; he had written a novel, *Desperate Remedies,* but he was by no means an assured craftsman. He "was feeling his way to a method," he said himself; as if he were conscious that he possessed all sorts of gifts, yet did not know their

[1] From Virginia Woolf, *The Common Reader, Second Series* (1932). By permission of Harcourt, Brace and Company.

nature, or how to use them to advantage. To read that first novel is to share in the perplexity of its author. The imagination of the writer is powerful and sardonic; he is book-learned in a home-made way; he can create characters but he cannot control them; he is obviously hampered by the difficulties of his technique and, what is more singular, he is driven by some sense that human beings are the sport of forces outside themselves, to make use of an extreme and even melodramatic use of coincidence. He is already possessed of the conviction that a novel is not a toy, nor an argument; it is a means of giving truthful if harsh and violent impressions of the lives of men and women. But perhaps the most remarkable quality in the book is the sound that echoes and booms through its pages of a waterfall. It is the first manifestation of the power that was to assume such vast proportions in the later books. He already proves himself a minute and skilled observer of nature; the rain, he knows, falls differently as it falls upon roots or arable; he knows that the wind sounds differently as it passes through the branches of different trees. But he is aware in a larger sense of Nature as a force; he feels in it a spirit that can sympathise or mock or remain the indifferent spectator of human fortunes. Already that sense was his; and the crude story of Miss Aldclyffe and Cytherea is memorable because it is watched by the eyes of the gods, and worked out in the presence of Nature.

That he was a poet should have been obvious; that he was a novelist might still have been held uncertain. But the year after, when *Under the Greenwood Tree* appeared, it was clear that much of the effort of "feeling for a method" had been overcome. Something of the stubborn originality of the earlier book was lost. The second is accomplished, charming, idyllic compared with the first. The writer, it seems, may well develop into one of our English landscape painters, whose pictures are all of cottage gardens and old peasant women, who lingers to collect and preserve from oblivion the old-fashioned ways and words which are rapidly falling into disuse. And yet what kindly lover of antiquity, what naturalist with a microscope in his pocket, what scholar solicitous for the changing shapes of language, ever heard the cry of a small bird killed in the next wood by an owl with such intensity? The cry "passed into the silence without mingling with it." Again we hear, very far away, like the sound of a gun out at sea on a calm summer's morning, a strange and ominous echo. But as we read these early books there is a sense of waste. There is a feeling that Hardy's genius was obstinate and perverse; first one gift would have its way with him and then another. They would not consent to run together easily in harness. Such indeed was likely to be the fate of a writer who was at once poet and realist, a faithful son of field and down, yet tormented by the doubts and despondencies bred of book-learning; a lover of old ways and plain countrymen, yet doomed to see the faith and flesh of his forefathers turn into thin and spectral transparencies before his eyes.

To this contradiction Nature had added another element likely to disorder a symmetrical development. Some writers are born conscious of everything;

others are unconscious of many things. Some, like Henry James and Flaubert, are able not merely to make the best use of the spoil their gifts bring in, but control their genius in the act of creation; they are aware of all the possibilities of every situation, and are never taken by surprise. The unconscious writers, on the other hand, like Dickens and Scott, seem suddenly and without their own consent to be lifted up and swept onwards. The wave sinks and they cannot say what has happened or why. Among them—it is the source of his strength and of his weakness—we must place Hardy. His own word, "moments of vision," exactly describes those passages of astonishing beauty and force which are to be found in every book that he wrote. With a sudden quickening of power which we cannot foretell, nor he, it seems, control, a single scene breaks off from the rest. We see, as if it existed alone and for all time, the wagon with Fanny's dead body inside travelling along the road under the dripping trees; we see the bloated sheep struggling among the clover; we see Troy flashing his sword round Bathsheba where she stands motionless, cutting the lock off her head and spitting the caterpillar on her breast. Vivid to the eye, but not to the eye alone, for every sense participates, such scenes dawn upon us and their splendour remains. But the power goes as it comes. The moment of vision is succeeded by long stretches of plain daylight, nor can we believe that any craft or skill could have caught the wild power and turned it to a better use. The novels therefore are full of inequalities; they are lumpish and dull and inexpressive; but they are never arid; there is always about them a little blur of unconsciousness, that halo of freshness and margin of the unexpressed which often produce the most profound sense of satisfaction. It is as if Hardy himself were not quite aware of what he did, as if his consciousness held more than he could produce, and he left it for his readers to make out his full meaning and to supplement it from their own experience.

For these reasons Hardy's genius was uncertain in development, uneven in accomplishment, but, when the moment came, magnificent in achievement. The moment came, completely and fully, in *Far from the Madding Crowd*. The subject was right; the method was right; the poet and the countryman, the sensual man, the sombre reflective man, the man of learning, all enlisted to produce a book which, however fashions may chop and change, must hold its place among the great English novels. There is, in the first place, that sense of the physical world which Hardy more than any novelist can bring before us; the sense that the little prospect of man's existence is ringed by a landscape which, while it exists apart, yet confers a deep and solemn beauty upon his drama. The dark downland, marked by the barrows of the dead and the huts of shepherds, rises against the sky, smooth as a wave of the sea, but solid and eternal; rolling away to the infinite distance, but sheltering in its folds quiet villages whose smoke rises in frail columns by day, whose lamps burn in the immense darkness by night. Gabriel Oak tending his sheep up there on the back of the world is the eternal shepherd; the stars are ancient beacons; and for ages he has watched beside his sheep.

But down in the valley the earth is full of warmth and life; the farms are busy, the barns stored, the fields loud with the lowing of cattle and the bleating of sheep. Nature is prolific, splendid, and lustful; not yet malignant and still the Great Mother of labouring men. And now for the first time Hardy gives full play to his humour, where it is freest and most rich, upon the lips of country men. Jan Coggan and Henry Fray and Joseph Poorgrass gather in the malthouse when the day's work is over and give vent to that half-shrewd, half-poetic humour which has been brewing in their brains and finding expression over their beer since the pilgrims tramped the Pilgrims' Way; which Shakespeare and Scott and George Eliot all loved to overhear, but none loved better or heard with greater understanding than Hardy. But it is not the part of the peasants in the Wessex novels to stand out as individuals. They compose a pool of common wisdom, of common humour, a fund of perpetual life. They comment upon the actions of the hero and heroine, but while Troy or Oak or Fanny or Bathsheba come in and out and pass away, Jan Coggan and Henry Fray and Joseph Poorgrass remain. They drink by night and they plough the fields by day. They are eternal. We meet them over and over again in the novels, and they always have something typical about them, more of the character that marks a race than of the features which belong to an individual. The peasants are the great sanctuary of sanity, the country the last stronghold of happiness. When they disappear, there is no hope for the race.

With Oak and Troy and Bathsheba and Fanny Robin we come to the men and women of the novels at their full stature. In every book three or four figures predominate, and stand up like lightning conductors to attract the force of the elements. Oak and Troy and Bathsheba; Eustacia, Wildeve, and Venn; Henchard, Lucetta, and Farfrae; Jude, Sue Bridehead, and Phillotson. There is even a certain likeness between the different groups. They live as individuals and they differ as individuals; but they also live as types and have a likeness as types. Bathsheba is Bathsheba, but she is a woman and sister to Eustacia and Lucetta and Sue; Gabriel Oak is Gabriel Oak, but he is man and brother to Henchard, Venn, and Jude. However lovable and charming Bathsheba may be, she is still weak; however stubborn and ill-guided Henchard may be, still he is strong. This is a fundamental part of Hardy's vision; the staple of many of his books. The woman is the weaker and the fleshlier, and she clings to the stronger and obscures his vision. How freely, nevertheless, in his greater books life is poured over the unalterable frame-work! When Bathsheba sits in the wagon among her plants, smiling at her own loveliness in the little looking-glass, we may know, and it is proof of Hardy's power that we do know, how severely she will suffer and cause others to suffer before the end. But the moment has all the bloom and beauty of life. And so it is, time and time again. His characters, both men and women, were creatures to him of an infinite attraction. For the women he shows a more tender solicitude than for the men, and in them, perhaps, he takes a keener interest. Vain might their beauty be and terrible their fate, but while the glow of life is in them their step is free, their laughter sweet, and theirs is the power to sink into the breast of Nature and become part of her silence and solemnity, or to rise and put on them the movement of the clouds and the wildness of the flowering woodlands. The men who suffer, not like the women through dependence upon other human beings, but through conflict with fate, enlist our sterner sympathies. For such a man as Gabriel Oak we need have no passing fears. Honour him we must, though it is not granted us to love him quite so freely. He is firmly set upon his feet and can give as shrewd a blow, to men at least, as any he is likely to receive. He has a prevision of what is to be expected that springs from character rather than from education. He is stable in his temperament, steadfast in his affections, and capable of open-eyed endurance without flinching. But he, too, is no puppet. He is a homely, humdrum fellow on ordinary occasions. He can walk the street without making people turn to stare at him. In short, nobody can deny Hardy's power—the true novelist's power—to make us believe that his characters are fellow-beings driven by their own passions and idiosyncrasies, while they have—and this is the poet's gift—something symbolical about them which is common to us all.

And it is when we are considering Hardy's power of creating men and women that we become most conscious of the profound differences that distinguish him from his peers. We look back at a number of these characters and ask ourselves what it is that we remember them for. We recall their passions. We remember how deeply they have loved each other and often with what tragic results. We remember the faithful love of Oak for Bathsheba; the tumultuous but fleeting passion of men like Wildeve, Troy, and Fitzpiers; we remember the filial love of Clym for his mother, the jealous paternal passion of Henchard for Elizabeth Jane. But we do not remember how they have loved. We do not remember how they talked and changed and got to know each other, finely, gradually, from step to step and from stage to stage. Their relationship is not composed of those intellectual apprehensions and subtleties of perception which seem so slight yet are so profound. In all the books love is one of the great facts that mould human life. But it is a catastrophe; it happens suddenly and overwhelmingly, and there is little to be said about it. The talk between the lovers when it is not passionate is practical or philosophic, as though the discharge of their daily duties left them with more desire to question life and its purpose than to investigate each other's sensibilities. Even if it were in their power to analyse their emotions, life is too stirring to give them time. They need all their strength to deal with the downright blows, the freakish ingenuity, the gradually increasing malignity of fate. They have none to spend upon the subtleties and delicacies of the human comedy.

Thus there comes a time when we can say with certainty that we shall not find in Hardy some of the qualities that have given us most delight in the works of other novelists. He has not the perfection of Jane Austen, or the wit of Meredith, or the range of Thackeray, or Tolstoy's amazing intellectual power. There is in the work of the great classical writers a finality of effect which places certain of their scenes, apart from the story, beyond the reach of change. We do not ask what bearing they have upon the narrative, nor do we make use of them to interpret problems which lie on the outskirts of the scene. A laugh, a blush, half a dozen words of dialogue, and it is enough; the source of our delight is perennial. But Hardy has none of this concentration and completeness. His light does not fall directly upon the human heart. It passes over it and out on to the darkness of the heath and upon the trees swaying in the storm. When we look back into the room the group by the fireside is dispersed. Each man or woman is battling with the storm, alone, revealing himself most when he is least under the observation of other human beings. We do not know them as we know Pierre or Natasha or Becky Sharp. We do not know them in and out and all round as they are revealed to the casual caller, to the Government official, to the great lady, to the general on the battlefield. We do not know the complication and involvement and turmoil of their thoughts. Geographically, too, they remain fixed to the same stretch of the English countryside. It is seldom, and always with unhappy results, that Hardy leaves the yeoman or farmer to describe the class above theirs in the social scale. In the drawing-room and clubroom and ballroom, where people of leisure and education come together, where comedy is bred and shades of character revealed, he is awkward and ill at ease. But the opposite is equally true. If we do not know his men and women in their relations to each other, we know them in their relations to time, death, and fate. If we do not see them in quick agitation against the lights and crowds of cities, we see them against the earth, the storm, and the seasons. We know their attitude towards some of the most tremendous problems that can confront mankind. They take on a more than mortal size in memory. We see them, not in detail but enlarged and dignified. We see Tess reading the baptismal service in her nightgown "with an impress of dignity that was almost regal." We see Marty South, "like a being who had rejected with indifference the attribute of sex for the loftier quality of abstract humanism," laying the flowers on Winterbourne's grave. Their speech has a Biblical dignity and poetry. They have a force in them which cannot be defined, a force of love or of hate, a force which in the men is the cause of rebellion against life, and in the women implies an illimitable capacity for suffering, and it is this which dominates the character and makes it unnecessary that we should see the finer features that lie hid. This is the tragic power; and, if we are to place Hardy among his fellows, we must call him the greatest tragic writer among English novelists.

But let us, as we approach the danger-zone of Hardy's philosophy, be on our guard. Nothing is more necessary, in reading an imaginative writer, than to keep at the right distance above his page. Nothing is easier, especially with a writer of marked idiosyncrasy, than to fasten on opinions, convict him of a creed, tether him to a consistent point of view. Nor was Hardy any exception to the rule that the mind which is most capable of receiving impressions is very often the least capable of drawing conclusions. It is for the reader, steeped in the impression, to supply the comment. It is his part to know when to put aside the writer's conscious intention in favour of some deeper intention of which perhaps he may be unconscious. Hardy himself was aware of this. A novel "is an impression, not an argument," he has warned us, and again:

Unadjusted impressions have their value, and the road to a true philosophy of life seems to lie in humbly recording diverse readings of its phenomena as they are forced upon us by chance and change.

Certainly it is true to say of him that, at his greatest, he gives us impressions; at his weakest, arguments. *In the Woodlanders, The Return of The Native, Far from the Madding Crowd,* and above all, in *The Mayor of Caster-bridge,* we have Hardy's impression of life as it came to him without conscious ordering. Let him once begin to tamper with his direct intuitions and his power is gone. "Did you say the stars were worlds, Tess?" asks little Abraham as they drive to market with their beehives. Tess replies that they are like "the apples on our stubbard-tree, most of them splendid and sound—a few blighted." "Which do we live on—a splendid or a blighted one?" "A blighted one," she replies, or rather the mournful thinker who has assumed her mask speaks for her. The words protrude, cold and raw, like the springs of a machine where we had seen only flesh and blood. We are crudely jolted out of that mood of sympathy which is renewed a moment later when the little cart is run down and we have a concrete instance of the ironical methods which rule our planet.

That is the reason why *Jude the Obscure* is the most painful of all Hardy's books, and the only one against which we can fairly bring the charge of pessimism. In *Jude the Obscure* argument is allowed to dominate impression, with the result that though the misery of the book is overwhelming it is not tragic. As calamity succeeds calamity we feel that the case against society is not being argued fairly or with profound understanding of the facts. Here is nothing of that width and force and knowledge of mankind which, when Tolstoy criticises society, makes his indictment formidable. Here we have revealed to us the petty cruelty of men, not the large injustice of the gods. It is only necessary to compare *Jude the Obscure* with *The Mayor of Caster-bridge* to see where Hardy's true power lay. Jude carries on his miserable contest against the deans of colleges and the conventions of sophisticated society. Henchard is pitted, not against another man, but against something outside himself which is opposed to men of his ambition and power. No human being wishes him ill. Even Farfrae and Newson and Elizabeth Jane, whom he has wronged, all come to pity him, and even to admire his strength of character. He is standing up to fate, and in backing the old Mayor whose ruin has been largely his own fault, Hardy makes us feel that we are backing human nature in an unequal contest. There is no pessimism here. Throughout the book we are aware of the sublimity of the issue, and yet it is presented to us in the most concrete form. From the opening scene in which Henchard sells his wife to the sailor at the fair to his death on Egdon Heath the vigour of the story is superb, its humour rich and racy, its movement large-limbed and free. The skimmity ride, the fight between Farfrae and Henchard in the loft, Mrs. Cuxsom's speech upon the death of Mrs. Henchard, the talk of the ruffians at Peter's Finger with Nature present in the background or mysteriously dominating the foreground, are among the glories of English fiction. Brief and scanty, it may be, is the measure of happiness allowed to each, but so long as the struggle is, as Henchard's was, with the decrees of fate and not with the laws of man, so long as it is in the open air and calls for activity of the body rather than of the brain, there is greatness in the contest, there is pride and pleasure in it, and the death of the broken corn merchant in his cottage on Egdon Heath is comparable to the death of Ajax lord of Salamis. The true tragic emotion is ours.

Before such power as this we are made to feel that the ordinary tests which we apply to fiction are futile enough. Do we insist that a great novelist shall be a master of melodious prose? Hardy was no such thing. He feels his way by dint of sagacity and uncompromising sincerity to the phrase he wants, and it is often of unforgettable pungency. Failing it, he will make do with any homely or clumsy or old-fashioned turn of speech, now of the utmost angularity, now of a bookish elaboration. No style in literature, save Scott's, is so difficult to analyse; it is on the face of it so bad, yet it achieves its aim so unmistakably. As well might one attempt to rationalise the charm of a muddy country road, or of a plain field of roots in winter. And then, like Dorsetshire itself, out of these very elements of stiffness and angularity his prose will put on greatness; will roll with a Latin sonority; will shape itself in a massive and monumental symmetry like that of his own bare downs. Then again, do we require that a novelist shall observe the probabilities and keep close to reality? To find anything approaching the violence and convolution of Hardy's plots one must go back to the Elizabethan drama. Yet we accept his story completely as we read it; more than that, it becomes obvious that his violence and his melodrama, when they are not due to a curious peasant-like love of the monstrous for its own sake, are part of that wild spirit of poetry which saw with intense irony and grimness that no reading of life can possibly outdo the strangeness of life itself, no symbol of caprice and unreason be too extreme to represent the astonishing circumstances of our existence.

But as we consider the great structure of the Wessex novels it seems irrelevant to fasten on little points—this character, that scene, this phrase of deep and poetic beauty. It is something larger that Hardy has bequeathed to us. The Wessex novels are not one book, but many. They cover an immense stretch; inevitably they are full of imperfections—some are failures, and others exhibit only the wrong side of their maker's genius. But undoubtedly, when we have submitted ourselves fully to them, when we come to take stock of our impressions of the whole, the effect is commanding and satisfactory. We have been freed from the cramp and pettiness imposed by life. Our imaginations have been stretched and heightened; our humour has been made to laugh out; we have drunk deep of the beauty of the earth. Also we have been made to enter the shade of a sorrowful and brooding spirit which, even in its saddest mood, bore itself with a grave uprightness and never, even when most moved to anger, lost its deep compassion for the sufferings of men and women. Thus it is no mere transcript of life at a certain time and place that Hardy has given us. It is a vision of the world and of man's lot as they revealed themselves to a powerful imagination, a profound and poetic genius, a gentle and humane soul.

Outline for a Defense of Poetry [1]

by EARL DANIELS

SOMETHING is wrong, somewhere! That is the obvious thing to say about poetry in America today. Poetry is still being written, perhaps by more people, in larger quantities than ever. Mushroom magazines, countless numbers of them, spring up, to die for the independence of verse. Few read them except the contributors, more often than not unpaid for their contributions save in the doubtful satisfaction of seeing their names in print. In the general magazines, space for verse has been consistently shrinking; many either carry none at all, or carry it only as a space filler, where important fiction or an article happens to end in the middle of a page. Something as attention-compelling as a Pulitzer prize is almost necessary if a poet is to become a best seller and earn a decent living from his work. And publishers' feelings about sales possibilities are summarized in that terse phrase at the end of a statement of manuscript needs—"No poetry."

A member of a faculty in a liberal arts college recently put the common reader's attitude in a question to a friend who was teaching, or trying to teach, poetry in the college. "Do you mean to tell me," he asked, "you would turn to poetry for fun, as you would turn to novels and short stories; that if it weren't part of your job you would read it, of your own accord, for pleasure?" For anyone who knows poetry, the answer to this incredulity is a *yes* loud and emphatic enough to call for italics and boldface type. We do read poetry for pleasure. We do go to it from the same motive we go to fiction. Poetry does not fail us, or turn bitter on the tongue oftener than novels, short stories, or any other kind of reading. If we had to make comparisons, most of us would probably say that more of the time poetry is more

[1] From *The Art of Reading Poetry*, by Earl Daniels (1941). By permission of Rinehart & Company, Inc., publishers.

fun than all other kinds of literature put together. But not until a man has discovered that there is pleasure in it—this before anything else—has he any valid reason for bothering his head about poetry. A young friend, who has · found that pleasure, writes me this in a long letter: "The other morning, before going to work, I went to the bookcase to spend my usual five minutes pondering what I should take with me to read. Looking at *Selections* from Wordsworth, the small *Oxford Classics* edition, I almost felt remorse, and putting the book in my pocket hurried out of the house before I could change my mind. That began it. And last night, when the rest of the family went to the Fair, I stayed home, with the baby and Wordsworth. I began to read at nine-fifteen and went to bed at twelve, only because my eyes dropped shut while I was reading." The rest of the letter is about the discovery of Wordsworth, which came in those quiet evening hours. Like Keats upon his first exposure to *The Faerie Queene,* my friend went through Wordsworth like "a horse through a spring meadow—*ramping";* like Keats on another occasion, he must have felt

> . . . like some watcher of the skies
> When a new planet swims into his ken.

as he went on to quote passage after passage which had stirred his heart.

Great passages are in all poets, to stir the hearts of all readers. No discoverer can forget a first encounter with them, or fail to taste the joys of subsequent, repetitive returns. For example, there is Chaucer's line about the Canon, in the prologue to "The Canon's Yeoman's Tale." On a warm April morning, in fourteenth-century England, he has ridden hard to overtake the pilgrim party, traveling to the shrine of Thomas à Becket at Canterbury. Chaucer says it looked as if he had spurred his horse for three miles, and notes that he had covered his head, as farmers still do, with a large dock leaf, as shade against the sun. Fat and out of breath, he stands there, hot and uncomfortable, puffing from his exertions. As he looks at him, all Chaucer's love for even the meanest commonplace of human nature, and, incidentally, all the abiding humanity of the Canon, is condensed into a single, unforgettable line:

> But it was joye for to seen hym swete! *sweat*

Or, once he has read, who can fail to remember always, Christopher Marlowe's evocation of Helen of Troy, the symbol of woman's glory and beauty? Summoned from the shades by the magic of Mephistophilis, she appears before Faustus in the loveliness of youth which cannot die. He gazes in awed wonder on the vision, remembering what Helen has been in legend, what she has meant to the dreams of men. He can only murmur, under his breath, words which are an epitome of Helen and her power; epitome, too, of that heroic struggle when, for ten years, Greece laid siege against the walls of Troy.

> Was this the face that launch'd a thousand ships
> And burnt the topless towers of Ilium?

The Greek fleet sails through those lines. Greek and Trojan heroes are there —Hector, Patroclus, Achilles, and all the rest. There is a defeated city, wrapped in smoke and flame, resonant with the din of hand-to-hand combat in the narrow streets, dusty with confusion. These things and more were there for Faustus. And these things and more, the words still mean for imaginations capable of being quickened by their implications.

To think of Helen of Troy is also to remember Cleopatra of Egypt, whose face was likewise the doom of a world. Once more a poet has said it best; this time, Shakespeare, in the words of Enobarbus, who has seen and is reporting Cleopatra's journey down the Nile to meet Antony.

> The barge she sat in, like a burnish'd throne,
> Burn'd on the water. The poop was beaten gold;
> Purple the sails, and so perfumèd that
> The winds were lovesick with them. The oars were silver,
> Which to the tune of flutes kept stroke, and made
> The water which they beat to follow faster,
> As amorous of their strokes. For her own person,
> It beggar'd all description: she did lie
> In her pavilion—cloth-of-gold of tissue—
> O'er-picturing that Venus where we see
> The fancy outwork nature. On each side her
> Stood pretty dimpled boys, like smiling Cupids,
> With divers-colour'd fans, whose wind did seem
> To glow the delicate cheeks which they did cool,
> And what they undid did . . .
>
> Her gentlewomen, like the Nereides,
> So many mermaids, tended her i' the eyes,
> And made their bends adornings. At the helm
> A seeming mermaid steers; the silken tackle
> Swell with the touches of those flower-soft hands,
> That yarely frame the office. From the barge
> A strange invisible perfume hits the sense
> Of the adjacent wharfs. The city cast
> Her people out upon her; and Antony,
> Enthron'd i' the marketplace, did sit alone,
> Whistling to the air, which, but for vacancy,
> Had gone to gaze on Cleopatra too
> And made a gap in nature.

If you have not done it already, go back now, after your first reading, and read this aloud, just for the sound. *Listen!*

But these are only fragments; their pleasure is the pleasure only of the part. And the same kind of pleasure is discoverable in prose, if one tears passages from context, to hold them up for admiration in isolation.[2] More

---

[2] Although it cannot be demonstrated at this elementary stage of the discussion, it must be insisted that in the passages cited, the pleasure is a pleasure of poetry, not a pleasure of prose: that their satisfaction is inherent in the poetry, foreign to prose except as it approaches or becomes, essentially, poetry.

important, much more important, is that greater pleasure of the whole, to which parts and fragments are at best subsidiary. For the good poem is unified and organic; we have not read it until we have seen and felt it *as a whole,* even though its power may be manifest in the very way fragments will go singing through the mind long after we are through with the poem. The pounding rhythms of Vachel Lindsay's "The Congo" keep up their music for hours; the "fat black bucks in a wine-barrel room" continue to sag, and reel, and "beat an empty barrel with the handle of a broom" because the totality of the poem moved us, though we remember just a bit here and there, once the mind has relaxed into inattentiveness. Because Chaucer spoke eloquently to him, a publisher's representative, traveling among the colleges, has learned the "Prologue" to *The Canterbury Tales*—all 858 lines of it—simply for the pleasure in reciting it to himself. I remember another striking instance of Chaucer's appeal, this time to a college student. He had been enthusiastic about Chaucer during the final semester of his senior year. Immediately after commencement, he had married, acquiring a dog and a cat as part of the beginnings of housekeeping. That summer he wrote me. Because of dominant traits, revealed in relations with neighborhood cats, he had called the cat Alisoun, after Chaucer's irrepressible Wife of Bath, and he wanted a name for the dog, a name also out of Chaucer. I forget what I suggested. The actual naming makes little difference. What counts is that Geoffrey Chaucer could speak out of medieval England so tellingly and persuasively to a twentieth-century American college student that he wanted his first family possessions named in his honor. Chaucer is always doing that sort of thing to people who will take the time to learn to read him.

Not long ago I was walking home behind a crowd of children, just out of school. They might have been sixth-graders; they couldn't have been older than that. They were shouting, in chorus, at the top of their lungs, not the words of the latest popular song, but the echoing rhythms of *The Ancient Mariner:*

> Water, water, everywhere,
> And all the boards did shrink;
> Water, water everywhere,
> Nor any drop to drink.

It would be silly to suggest that their chanting showed any understanding of the poetry in the words, or of Coleridge's poem as a whole. Probably, most of it went over their heads. They simply reacted to the magic of sound, as many of us react to "The Congo." On a very elementary level, they were demonstrating the validity of poetry, that it does things to people when it is given a chance; and they prove that something is wrong today. For if, as sixth-graders, poetry could bring them a joy insistent on expression, could enliven their way home, exactly like any game they might play along the street, why, as adults, will most of them stop reading poetry "for fun"? Why aren't there more traveling men who learn the "Prologue" to *The Canterbury*

Tales, more college graduates who name their dogs and cats in Chaucer's honor? Why is poetry not only not a best seller, but usually not any kind of seller at all? Why do men and women not continue to read it, treasuring it as an enhancement and enrichment of living, a possession time cannot wither, nor depressions take away?

Whatever may be wrong, it is not the poetry. Not the poetry, but we, potential readers, are wrong, for we have somehow failed to realize our potentialities. And the depth of our wrongness is implicit in that faculty member's wondering that anyone could ready poetry for the fun of it. It is wrong that an educated man—unfortunately, too many are like him—could be so wrong about poetry, so wrongly educated that he could ask so appalling a question. The same kind of wrong is in another remark, more frequently made, and running something like this: "It's all right, I suppose, for those who like it, but why can't a man say what he wants to say, and get it over with? Why can't he say it right out, say it just as well in prose?" An old story tells of two college roommates, one a major in English literature, the other, in science and mathematics. The science man had a curiosity about poetry, and his friend volunteered to show him. For a beginning he would take something easy: a narrative with strong, masculine rhythm. So he selected "The Charge of the Light Brigade," and, wise enough to know poetry should be heard to be enjoyed, he began to read aloud, asking of his friend only that he listen.

> Half a league, half a league,
> Half a league onward,

he read, and he was interrupted. "There!" said the other. "You see! That's what I mean. That's the trouble. If the fool means a league and a half, why doesn't he say so?" Probably the first lesson ended in confusion there. But it is to be hoped the English major persisted in his efforts, until he had shown his roommate something of what poetry may do for a man's mind and spirit.

For poetry—this is an elemental fact about it—cannot be said just as well, cannot be said at all in prose! In prose it would not be the poem; it cannot be translated into any other form without becoming something different. What the poetry of a poem is, what gives a poem its peculiar quality, responsible for the peculiar pleasure of poetry—that is what, primarily, learning to read poetry ought to teach us. Moreover—and this is another elemental fact—poetry does not ask for a particular type of mind, as so many seem to think, if it is to be enjoyed. Like music, like all the arts, it is for all who can and will find time to take it seriously, and a "special soul" may turn out to be more of a hindrance than a help.

This cult of "the special soul" has a good deal to do with the situation. For though poetry is not meant for special souls, being a normal, healthy activity of healthy and normal men and women, too many have, for too long, been busy trying to inculcate the idea of its specialness. Most of us, most of the time, are suspicious of special souls. We shy away from them and are uncomfortably embarrassed in their presence. And the poets themselves are less helpful than they should be, for they have contributed to the mystery in which poetry is mistakenly shrouded, insisting too often on the difference between the poet and other men, on his *apartness,* which calls for similar apartness in a reader. Plato, a poet though he did not use verse, who said much that was bad for poets and poetry, though he may have intended it for praise, wrote this:

A poet is indeed a thing ethereally light, winged, and sacred, nor can he compose anything worth calling poetry until he becomes inspired, and, as it were, mad, or whilst any reason remains in him. . . . Poets are the interpreters of the divinities.[3]

Such ideas are not isolated in the history of literature. They range from Plato all the way to Ezra Pound and the Dadaists of contemporary France. Springing from a sinister belief that poetry, somehow, needs defense, they have turned out to be an insidious kind of attack, and poets, who would be defenders, are much to blame for the defeat of what they thought they were fighting for. Poets and other self-appointed advocates are one reason why poetry is not read today nearly as much as it should be, for they have fostered the belief that poetry is like the Eleusinian mysteries of ancient Greece, open only to a select, a very select, body of initiates, not to be profaned by the touch of a common hand. They have forgotten the wiser, truer word of John Keats, one of the wisest, most human, most sensible of poets: "That if Poetry comes not as naturally as the Leaves to a tree it had better not come at all."[4] They have insisted on the divinity of the poet at the expense of his humanity, have insisted that he writes for a special audience, different from the ordinary run of men and women, whose distinction is their broad and understanding humanity. They have tried to build a cultist's temple, and have wondered why the rest of us have shown them little sympathy. Tennyson tells us that

> The poet in a golden clime was born,
> With golden stars above.

Shelley says: "A poet participates in the eternal, the infinite, and the one; as far as relates to his conceptions, time and place and number are not. . . . A poet is a nightingale, who sits in the darkness and sings to cheer its own solitude with sweet sounds." And after that, he seems to expect us to take him seriously when he asserts, "Poets are the unacknowledged legislators of the world."[5] After all, legislation, even unacknowledged, has a practicality, a reality about it not consonant with the very special soul who has just been pictured.

Despite many vagaries, Wordsworth was closer to truth in his belief that a poet was just "a man speaking to men"; a man whose difference from

---

[3] *Ion* 534.
[4] Letter to John Taylor, 27 February 1818.
[5] The Shelley quotations are from *A Defence of Poetry.*

other men was only in degree, not in kind. Unless we are convinced of the "man-ness" of the poet, we are not likely to be much concerned about poetry. Poets who have written about themselves and their work have not been very much help to the cause in which they believed themselves to be earnestly enlisted.

Posing as priests, they have been discouragers of our hesitancy, turning uncertainty as to whether poetry was worth bothering about into assurance that it wasn't. Better to do without poetry than be obliged to breathe the incense-heavy air in which poetry's articulate advocates seem to prefer to live. And all this when emphasis ought to be put on the simple truth that poetry, most of the time, is a natural activity of the human spirit, a necessity, not a luxury; rightly understood, its appeal is to healthy and red-blooded men and women as a part of the necessary pleasures of a normal life.

If the poet as priest or prophet is bad for poetry, the poet as puzzle-maker has been no less efficient in turning readers away. Often with the best intentions, the puzzle-makers would transform poetry into a riddle, a highly refined acrostic, or a crossword puzzle. An average reader hasn't time for that sort of high jinks. When he wants puzzles, he wants them under their own name; he wants to know what he is getting.

What, for example, is our average reader, even one of trained intelligence, to make of either of these?

ONE X

death is more than
certain a hundred these
sounds crowds odours it
is in a hurry
beyond that any this
taxi smile or angle we do

not sell and buy
things so necessary as
is death and unlike shirts
neckties trousers
we cannot wear it out
no sir which is why
granted who discovered
America ether the movies
may claim general importance

to me you nothing is
what particularly
matters hence in a

little sunlight and less
moonlight ourselves against the worms

hate laugh shimmy

—E. E. CUMMINGS

PAPYRUS

Spring . . .
Too long . . .
Gongula . . .

—EZRA POUND

For the first puzzle, I have no solution adequate for the intricate confusion of the composition. For the second, an answer—by no means a sure one—is fairly easy, implicit in the title. What is here is only a fragment, a part of a poem. It has survived on a small bit of ancient papyrus, worn and torn, buried, it may be, for centuries in desert sand. The rest of the poem is lost with the other part of the papyrus on which it was written. Or these lines may be only notes for a poem, never written out in full. Perhaps a reader is expected to respond to "the spell of the incomplete," to feel his imagination stretch its wings, intrigued by what might have been and once was! But if, instead of concern about the philosophy of parts and wholes, the reader abandons poetry for good and all, he is, though mistaken, hardly to be blamed. When he took time to try to work out a solution, the result was so little worth the effort. The so-called poem had nothing to say to merit attention.

Closely allied to puzzle-makers are poets who may be described as militant independents. Absorbed in the private and, usually, highly complex matters of their own secret thoughts, they have signed, with a John Hancock flourish, a declaration of independence from any responsibility to a prospective reader. They wrap the mantle of indifference about them with an attention-compelling gesture which is an invitation to suspicion. Now a reader has, as reader, a fundamental right to expect results from poetry as from any form of writing, from any art; a right to expect intelligibility to follow earnest effort to understand. The poet who says, "I have spoken, it is enough for me; I have no responsibility to be clear that you may know what I am talking about"—that poet rejects the requirement of all important art. Unless there be communication, there cannot be aesthetic pleasure. Art, not expression *for someone,* poetry, not communication *with someone,* not written for an audience, is less than art, less than poetry. Art has seldom flourished on the desert island of a solitary castaway!

Of course, poets who talk to themselves sometimes transform their solitude into beautiful and significant poetry. Examples of illustrious remoteness from the world readily occur to anyone. Emily Dickinson is one of our choicest spirits in American poetry. Yet all her life, it would seem she wrote only to herself, and for herself, setting down her fragile lyrics on the odds and ends of scraps of paper, guarding them from the eyes of all except the intimates of her family circle. She would not publish them during her lifetime; she wanted them destroyed after her death. Because they were written in that spirit, Emily Dickinson's poems are marked by a sincerity and intimacy often embarrassing to a sensitive reader, who feels that he is listening in on a privacy never intended for his ears. . . .

Yes, poets can talk to themselves. But not when they are self-conscious, boastful about their own self-sufficiency, attitudinizing to alienate a reader. When good poets write to themselves, they do it without a declaration of independence. They write as though with an obligation upon themselves, as poets, to be clear in communicating with their other selves, as readers. And because they are careful about being clear to themselves as readers—selves very much like you and me—they write, without pose, poetry which speaks meaningfully to other people.

Cultists, puzzle-makers, militant independents: these do not include all categories of poets who have talked badly about poetry, but they will serve as examples to show how the poets have themselves contributed to misunderstandings making for its contemporary ill-repute. Those who try to teach what poets have written—and this must be taken to include a wider range than teachers in the technical sense of the word, for the voice of the lecturer is abroad in the land—must also be held responsible for some of the trouble and confusion. It would be foolish to deny that there is good teaching of poetry, as there is good teaching of everything else, and that good teaching is powerfully effective in right directions. But still too many sixth-graders do stop singing *The Ancient Mariner,* and too few adults learn the "Prologue" to *The Canterbury Tales.* Year after year, students crowd into college with ideas about poetry so distorted and wrong that they must be forcibly eradicated if there is to be progress toward enjoyment, so that the reading of poetry shall not cease abruptly, as soon as the compulsion of academic prescription is removed. If any generalization about poetry is valid, it is that at best college students read poetry badly. Most of them cannot read it at all. Unless they learn to perform major surgical operations on their own habits of mind, they will never read effectively, with enjoyment to themselves. For this situation, bad teaching must be in some measure to blame, teaching so bad, so pervasive, as to strike at the roots of a valid, continuing interest and pleasure with poetry.

I should accuse teachers of poetry of at least three great heresies: the heresy of facile talk about appreciation; the heresy of too great concern with peripheral things; the heresy of preoccupation with morals and the meaning of life.

I. THE HERESY OF FACILE TALK ABOUT APPRECIATION

Facile talk about appreciation fosters the rapt expression, the starry eye, and the throbbing heart. Manifest in *oohs* and *ahs,* it is the inarticulate expression of what is thought to be pleasure when it is only lack of understanding. This gush school of poetry readers will always take the easy road of indolence, impatient of the hard work and concentration essential to comprehension. Probably the trouble is in a common misinterpretation of the word *appreciation,* which has nothing facile or effortless about it. Etymologically, it comes from two Latin words: *ad,* meaning *to* or *at,* and *pretium,* meaning *price* or *value.* Thus, as its simplest, *to appreciate* is to put an accurate value on something. *Appreciation* is a synonym for *criticism,* an ugly word for most of the appreciation school, and both words call for the strenuous intel-lectual activity of analysis in order that a sound estimate of value may be reached. Without analysis, without work, there can be no pleasure in read-ing, no appreciation. Moreover, appreciation has little about it that is secret or mysterious. It does not come as a gift of God, by grace of any English department. Only those who seek early, persistently, with assiduity, ever find it; and only those who find enter into the joy of reading poetry. Appre-ciation does not come in the watches of the night as one sleeps; it is a daytime activity of the alert mind and the taut muscle. What Mr. Adler says in *How to Read a Book* applies to poetry as much as to the most difficult, abstract philosophic prose:

a) The most direct sign that you have done the work of reading is *fatigue.* Reading that is reading involves the most intense mental activity. . . . To read books passively does not feed a mind. It makes blotting-paper out of it.
b) . . . nothing helps those who will not keep awake while reading.[6]

The kind of reading Mr. Adler is talking about is an elementary spading-process, a necessary and sweat-provocative preparation of the ground, a *sine qua non* of appreciation.

2. THE HERESY OF TOO GREAT CONCERN WITH PERIPHERAL THINGS

Peripheral things are "off at the side," away from the center; they are extracurricular. Interesting and important when kept in their proper, sub-ordinate position, they are a hindrance to understanding if they are over-emphasized. For them we miss what is central, sacrifice first things for what are at best secondary. Among these second-rate matters in which discussion of poetry often wanders and loses itself, the Bog of Technique is perhaps most dangerous. John Bunyan's Slough of Despond was not blacker or more en-gulfing, and it takes a stout heart to win through this morass. Technique may be, it *is,* important; but not at the beginning of the game. Yet for a majority of students it seems to be all the game. They have been taught to put on labels, like "blank verse," or "heroic couplet," with deadly accuracy, but they cannot read fifty lines of Shakespeare with enjoying understanding, or feel the dancing glamour of *The Rape of the Lock.* They know the names for verse meters, and can mechanically chop lines into so-called feet, but beyond an awareness that Milton's "On the Late Massacre in Piedmont" and Keats' "When I Have Fears That I May Cease to Be" are in the Italian and the English sonnet form, respectively, they have no feeling for differences in the poems, far more important than these superficialities. They can divide Keats' "On First Looking into Chapman's Homer," one of the finest poems in the language, into octave and sestet, and proudly catalogue the rime scheme;

[6] Mortimer J. Adler, *How to Read a Book,* Simon and Schuster (New York: 1940), pp. 110, 218.

but they have never felt the glow which ought to result from intelligent reading, their hearts have never been warmed at the fire of Keats' record of intellectual adventure. And with a new and a different point of departure, their hearts never will be warmed at poetry's flame; they will grow up to wonder how anyone, in his right mind, can bother about poetry. Better they should never in their lives hear of one of the labels they now learn early to recite so glibly.

Technique at best—and this best is at long remove from the academic and mechanic concern for labels—technique at best ought not to come for a long time. It is like dessert, proper, in any well-regulated meal, after the solidities of meat and potatoes, vegetables, and bread and butter. To use the food figure another way, technique is for the adulthood of appreciation, not for its infancy and adolescence. No one ought to think of feeding a six-month-old baby with corned beef and cabbage; no one who cares for poetry ought to confuse beginners with what are the arcana, the mysteries of the craft, proper only to one who has learned already to read, and read well. The general reader doesn't need to know the name of a single verse foot, need never scan, in the word's accepted sense, a line of verse, in order to enjoy poetry as it was meant to be enjoyed.

3. THE HERESY OF PREOCCUPATION WITH MORALS AND THE MEANING OF LIFE

The heresy of preoccupation with morals and the meaning of life is really another aspect of the heresy about peripheral things, but it is so pervasive, so deeply rooted with those who have listened to misinformed talk about poetry, that it deserves the dignity of a place apart to itself. Youth are probably the most moral people in the world. At no other time does the meaning of life burden our shoulders as it does in adolescence. And at that time, of all times, to encourage the pursuit of morals and philosophy, of the personal application in what is read, is likely to turn out to be only too successful. Someone has said that to look for pictures in music we are listening to is to be on the road to perdition as far as the appreciation of music is concerned. To look for morals and philosophy in poetry is to set one's feet in the same broad path. Poetry is devoid neither of morals nor of philosophy; Dante and Milton would rise to confound anyone stupid enough to say that. But he who would enjoy poetry must not look, *primarily,* for morals and a way of life.

That is precisely what too many students do. From "Rabbi Ben Ezra" they copy into their notebooks glib memory gems, like "Grow old along with me, the best is yet to be," and the memory gem, usually a facile platitude, is all they know of what is at best often only a second-rate poem. They come to associate poetry with the inculcation of a lesson for themselves, than which few things could be harder on the vitality of poetry. Concern for ethics is likely to mean that bad poems—"Rabbi Ben Ezra" or "Abou ben Adhem"— are read to the exclusion of better poems. "The Bishop Orders His Tomb at St. Praxed's Church" is a better poem than "Rabbi Ben Ezra," though the

Bishop is not a very moral man. What is more vital, he is human; placed
in a human and a dramatic situation, he should be allowed to speak, and he
will if he is given an opportunity—like that other scoundrel of the "Soliloquy
of the Spanish Cloister," or the lady-villain of "The Laboratory"—speak effectively to the heart of any normal person, anywhere, at any time.

It would be difficult to find memory gem or message in Waller's "Go,
Lovely Rose." Yet it is one of the purest lyrics in English, and a justification
of Emerson's phrase, "Beauty is its own excuse for being." It ought to be
part of the poetry equipment, the mental furniture of everyone, to be learned
by heart for the joy which comes from saying, over and over, the beautiful
words. Read them slowly, aloud; surrender to the pictures and to the sound.
What a pity it would be to look for a lesson, to try to derive personal application to one's own way of living!

SONG

Go, lovely rose!
Tell her that wastes her time and me
That now she knows,
When I resemble her to thee,
How sweet and fair she seems to be.

Tell her that's young
And shuns to have her graces spied,
That hadst thou sprung
In deserts where no men abide,
Thou must have uncommended died.

Small is the worth
Of beauty from the light retired;
Bid her come forth,
Suffer herself to be desired,
And not blush so to be admired.

Then die, that she
The common fate of all things rare
May read in thee;
How small a part of time they share
That are so wondrous sweet and fair!

——EDMUND WALLER

There are many such poems in English literature, and they are one reason
why everybody should learn to read poetry. It does make a difference what
a mind has in the way of furniture. Wordsworth wrote of his ideal for his
sister, Dorothy, to be attained as a result of her closeness to the landscape of
the English Lake Country:

Therefore let the Moon
Shine on thee in thy solitary walk;
And let the misty mountain-winds be free

To blow against thee: and, in after years,
When these wild ecstasies shall be matured
Into a sober pleasure; when thy mind
Shall be a mansion for all lovely forms,
Thy memory be as a dwelling-place
For all sweet sounds and harmonies: . . .

Surely something may be said, simply in terms of potential pleasure to one's self, for the difference in the mind furnished with, as a random example, "Shoot the sherbet to me, Herbert," and one equipped with the haunting loveliness of "Go, Lovely Rose."

If you are one of those taught to approach the presence of the poem in quest of vital lesson, of profound comment on man and the universe, the answer is, *Don't.* Here should be no halfway measures, no reducing the urge to philosophy by half, no gradual tapering-off. You may, after all, rest comfortable in the assurance that if philosophy and morals are present in any vital way, they will make themselves felt without your conscious searching for them, insistent on their share in your awareness of the complete poem.

The way of a group of college freshmen with a poem of Robert Frost illustrates how deadly this concern about morals may be. Here is the poem.

STOPPING BY WOODS ON A SNOWY EVENING

Whose woods these are I think I know.
His house is in the village though;
He will not see me stopping here
To watch his woods fill up with snow.

My little horse must think it queer
To stop without a farmhouse near
Between the woods and frozen lake
The darkest evening of the year.

He gives his harness bells a shake
To ask if there is some mistake.
The only other sound's the sweep
Of easy wind and downy flake.

The woods are lovely, dark and deep.
But I have promises to keep,
And miles to go before I sleep,
And miles to go before I sleep.
—ROBERT FROST

Here are some interpretations by freshmen who were supposed to be better-than-average students.

a) In this poem the underlying thought seems to be that of suicide. . . . The last four lines of the poem indicate that the person decides he has more work to do on earth before he dies in order to fulfill a promise of some kind.

b) A man who has promised to leave town after committing some crime, and has been told "to get going and don't stop." The line, "The darkest evening of the year," might mean the disgrace he has brought on himself; and, "I have promises to keep," may mean he has promised to get out of the country.

c) If he didn't mention that the owner of the woods lived in the village, I would say he was talking about the life he has yet to live before he meets his Maker.

d) It deals with the thought of eternal rest. . . . But then the subject is brought back to reality with the thought of the things he has yet to do, and the rest of his life he has yet to spend.

e) It may represent one who is tired of life's hardships, and is tempted to drop by the wayside in some secluded retreat, but who must press on since he has many years of work ahead and many obligations to fulfill before such rest may be his.

f) Almost every day we find ourselves faced with the lures of temptation. We realize that we ought to keep on our way, yet the temptation to stay where all is peaceful and quiet is often too great for us to resist. While we are here in college we are often tempted to do the easiest thing. That is, to neglect our studies and to run around and have a good time. However we know that there are promises to be kept and obligations to be filled. We have been sent here by our parents for the purpose of receiving an education, and there is no doubt that our duty is to do all in our power to take advantage of this opportunity.

g) I am a college man. I am taking a pre-med course. I am away from home. I am open to temptations that college may offer me. Am I to take advantage of their owner's absence to sit and gaze in his woods—to take advantage of being away from my parents to stop by the wayside and admire the beautiful sirens? Or, am I to be a second Ulysses and have sufficient will power to overcome these temptations? Am I to stop where there is "easy wind and downy flake"—to sit back in my chair, just to dream and forget all hardships? Or am I to heed the impatience of the horse and the warning of the harness bell—to awaken to my will calling for me to go on? True, it is dark now, and I cannot see well, but do I not remember the vows that I have made—to go through at all costs? Yes, I must go through those long miles of roads rougher than *I* can imagine, before *I* call for time out.

Comments *f* and *g* are especially nauseous misunderstandings, and they represent the cardinal sin of personal application. To make a poem mean privately, to ourselves alone, to look first for directions about *our* life and *our* problems—no going wrong can be more abysmally bad. Like the old hocus-pocus magic-formula way in which the Bible used to be consulted, you put your question, open the book at random, drop an equally random finger on the page, and there you are—provided you are ingenious enough in twisting words to meet special situations and personal needs. The method is equally unintelligent with the Bible and with poetry, and to resort to it is to proclaim oneself part of an intellectual underworld of superstition and ignorance. The poet's message, so far as he has a message for the individual, is a message to the individual not in his private and peculiar selfhood, but in his representative capacity as a normal human being. as a man; it is part of the universality of the poet's speaking.

If facile talk about appreciation, concern with peripheral things, and pre-occupation with morals and the meaning of life are heresies, what is sound doctrine in the reading of poetry? What is orthodox? What is a right approach to Frost's poem, or to any poem? The simple, natural approach, the easiest way. What is obvious in "Stopping by Woods on a Snowy Evening" is that the poet has had a perfectly everyday experience. On a snow-filled winter's afternoon, he has come to a patch of woodland; for no reason, save that he simply and unashamedly likes to, he has stopped, just to watch the woods fill up with snow. That is the experience, the start of the poem, which, from such an unassuming start, got itself written because *the poet enjoyed the experience,* remembered it, and something made him want to try to put it in words, *just for fun: the poem is a record of experience to be shared with a reader,* who must take it at this simple face value if he is to read the poem as it should be read. Most poems probably begin much like this. And if someone says, "It may never have happened to Frost; he may have imagined it all," the answer is that in literature and the arts there is no essential difference between experience in actuality and experience in imagination; both are the stuff of poems, in the broadest sense of the term, *experience.* It is really very little a reader's business whether a writer is using memory or imagination, so long as the reality of the result is not affected. Frost may, indeed, have imagined it all, so far as we have a right to know, or care.

But why should a poet want to share experience, if he has nothing "important" to say, no "lesson" to teach, if he is not intent on "improving society," and "bettering the conditions of the human race"? Like so many facts, this is a mystery, hid in elemental human nature. Men do act this way: human nature prompts them to want to tell others what has happened to them. All conversation is built on that ancient formula, "Have you heard this one?" The questioner hopes "this one" has not been heard, so that he can go on and tell his story, enjoy sharing his experience.

The woman in the parable is a case in point. She had lost her money. It is not significant that she went on an orgy of spring cleaning, turning the house upside down, or that she found her money. But when she found it, and this is the important thing, her next move was to give a party, inviting friends and neighbors for miles around, just that they might rejoice with her because she had found what had been lost: in other words, that they might share her experience. So the poet, though tangibilities like money may not be involved. Something emotionally stirring has happened, and he makes a poem, which is his invitation to his friends and neighbors to rejoice with him. How ungracious of the friends and neighbors of the woman, if they had hunted for lessons in the experience, emphasized, perhaps, the moral that in the future she must be more careful about her money, suggested it was all an illustration of the guidance of a good providence, enabling her to recover her fortune—or any other testimony a dyed-in-the-wool moralist might strain to discover. They had been invited to a party; the woman didn't want lessons; she wanted them to have a good time with her. No less ungracious is the reader who would deduce moral teaching from "Stopping by Woods on a Snowy Evening," and from many other poems, when what the poet wants is that we should have a good time at his party, along with him, because he, in the first place, had a good time with his experience. Such sharing is the request every good poet makes of his readers, and it leads straight to an idea at the heart of all poetry, the irrefragable cornerstone on which poetry rests. That idea, the center of this book, is that *poetry, reduced to its simplest, is only experience.* Experience moved the poet, he enjoyed it, and wanted to put it down on paper, as experience and nothing else, partly because writing is a self-contained action which is fun for the writer, partly because he wanted the reader to enjoy the experience with him. If we are to learn to read, we must begin with elemental, irreducible facts like this.

Of course poetry can be, often is, profound and philosophical, probing below surfaces, reaching far down to the depths of the spirit, anxious about Life, and Death, what is before Life, and after Death. In his *De Rerum Natura* (Of the Nature of Things), Lucretius wrote thousands of lines devoted to the origin of the universe, to man's nature and his place within his world. He wrote a poem, which has lived for more than nineteen hundred years, admittedly one of the great things of all literatures. Milton set himself, in *Paradise Lost,* to

> assert eternal Providence,
> And justify the ways of God to men.

And whatever we may think of the success with which he resolved his problem, his poem is one of the few supremely great poems so far given to the world.

Lucretius and Milton are difficult poets. And there are many difficult, extraordinarily difficult poems; poems difficult enough to task the best efforts of best minds for their understanding and enjoyment. They are full of message, philosophy, and morals. But they are not for the neophyte, and we shall never learn to like or understand them if we begin with their complexities. A start must be made where the going is easier and simpler. Failure to start there, traceable in large part to the poets themselves, and to those who have tried, with honest but mistaken zeal, to teach poetry when they did not understand it themselves, is a principal reason why there are not more, and more intelligent, readers of poetry today, why people in increasing numbers do not turn to it in leisure hours, just for fun, without conscious concern for culture, or the higher things of life, or philosophy, or morals, or any of the other wrong motives assigned for the study of literature. It is right to like right things. But to like right things for wrong reasons is hardly a mark of an educated man or woman.

Levels are important. When we are children, we should think and speak as children, and there is a childhood of the mind and spirit as truly as there is a physical, a chronological childhood. If, in poetry, we are to advance beyond seeing through a glass darkly, our sight muddy and confused, we must leave poets like Lucretius and Milton and Dante, content for a while with the simplest simplicities. Nor can we all, variously endowed as we are, expect ever to attain to the heights of Milton and Dante. For some of us, those mountain peaks are too high and difficult of ascent. But we can find ample space for breathing on a lower level; for ourselves, supreme pleasure on the highest level of our own capabilities. Only, we must go as high as possible, stretch to the full measure of our stature and strength. Then, we shall be content to let those things go which for us are unattainable, since, on our own level, *for us,* there is bound to be God's plenty for enjoyment as long as we shall live. The man who has advanced from Edgar Guest and Robert W. Service to Longfellow has made progress; better yet if he can go to Masefield or Kipling. And beyond are so many more: Tennyson and Browning, Wordsworth, Shelley—it would be futile to try to catalogue them, or to arrange them at exact levels. Somewhere, at the end of arduous journeyings among the regions of poetry, are the lofty tablelands and mountain summits, where the masters dwell—Homer, Virgil, Dante, Chaucer, Shakespeare, Milton, and the rest, who are God's noblest voices. Are they reserved for specialists and experts—poets' poets? I should hardly want to say that, though it is certain that the air of their world is too rarefied for many of us, much of the time. And then, too, we are unwilling to discipline ourselves by the hard labor necessary for understanding their voices. If we do not, for one reason or another, attain to fellowship with these saints and giants, it is hardly cause for weeping, since so much remains besides, so many, to speak persuasively to us, in our own tongue. Only—and this is important—we must be sure that we proceed to the highest point we are capable of standing on with comfort and pleasure to ourselves.

To enable a reader to find this "highest point," at which he can read poetry with honest enjoyment to himself—that ought to be the goal of any course in poetry, of any talking about it. Winning to the goal can come only by beginning with simple things, by ridding our minds of corrupting confusions, of mistaken notions, which are barriers to understanding what poetry is all about. This chapter has considered some of those confusions and notions, to clear the ground, as a preliminary to progress in the way of poetry. It has tried to show that for the present despised state of poetry poets and teachers must bear a good deal of the burden of responsibility. For poets have made a cult of poetry, and most of us are suspicious of cults: they have emphasized mystery, they have offered puzzles, where a reader looked for poems; they have frightened us away by their assertive declarations of their independence of any responsibility to us, by their insistence on talking to themselves only, for themselves, in their own way. And teaching has set us wrong by fostering three great heresies: facile talk about appreciation; excessive concern with peripheral things; and too much preoccupation with morals and philosophy. Our consideration of these heresies has led us to two orthodox articles of a right belief about poetry:

1. Poetry exists principally that the reader may find pleasure where the poet had found pleasure before him.

2. Poetry is, fundamentally, a record of pleasurable experience which the poet set down for the fun of it, that the reader might have fun in turn.

At this point, the reader would do well to examine his own experience of poetry. If nowhere in his memory he finds poems which have been fun, if none of the poems quoted in this chapter have made him feel a little pleasanter inside, then, probably, poetry is not for him. He is one of those rarest men for whom it has no word, and he should abandon poetry and this book, for they will prove little more than wasted time and effort. But if he does remember poems pleasantly, no matter how few; even if there be only one, among those quoted here, which he has in the slightest degree liked, he is invited to continue in our common adventure after the peculiar pleasure of poetry, assured, in advance, of fun, and, I hope, of discovering in his experience

life and food
For future years.

Writing Prose [1]

by W. SOMERSET MAUGHAM

I HAVE never had more than two English lessons in my life, for though I wrote essays at school, I do not remember that I ever received any instruction on how to put sentences together. The two lessons I have had were given me so late in life that I am afraid I cannot hope greatly to profit by them. The first was only a few years ago. I was spending some weeks in London and had engaged as temporary secretary a young woman. She was shy, rather pretty, and absorbed in a love affair with a married man. I had written a book called *Cakes and Ale,* and, the typescript arriving one Saturday morning, I asked her if she would be good enough to take it home and correct it over the week-end. I meant her only to make a note of mistakes in spelling that the typist might have made and point out errors occasioned by a handwriting that is not always easy to decipher. But she was a conscientious young person and she took me more literally than I intended. When she brought back the typescript on Monday morning it was accompanied by four foolscap sheets of corrections. I must confess that at the first glance I was a trifle vexed; but then I thought that it would be silly of me not to profit, if I could, by the trouble she had taken and so sat me down to examine them. I suppose the young woman had taken a course at a secretarial college and she had gone through my novel in the same methodical way as her masters had gone through her essays. The remarks that filled the four neat pages of foolscap were incisive and severe. I could not but surmise that the professor of English at the secretarial college did not mince matters. He took a marked line, there could be no doubt about that; and he did not allow that there might be two opinions about anything. His apt pupil would have nothing to do with a preposition at the end of a sentence. A mark of exclamation betokened her disapproval of a colloquial phrase. She had a feeling that you must not use the same word twice on a page and she was ready every time with a synonym to put in its place. If I had indulged myself in the luxury of a sentence of ten lines, she wrote: "Clarify this. Better break it up into two or more periods." When I had availed myself of the pleasant pause that is indicated by a semicolon, she noted: "A full stop"; and if I had ventured upon a colon she remarked stingingly: "Obsolete." But the harshest stroke of all was her comment on what I thought was rather a good joke: "Are you sure of your facts?" Taking it all in all I am bound to conclude that the professor at her college would not have given me very high marks.

[1] From W. S. Maugham, *The Summing Up* (1938). By permission of Doubleday & Company, Inc.

The second lesson I had was given me by a don, both intelligent and charming, who happened to be staying with me when I was myself correcting the typescript of another book. He was good enough to offer to read it. I hesitated, because I knew that he judged from a standpoint of excellence that is hard to attain; and though I was aware that he had a profound knowledge of Elizabethan literature, his inordinate admiration for *Esther Waters* made me doubtful of his discernment in the productions of our own day: no one could attach so great a value to that work who had an intimate knowledge of the French novel during the nineteenth century. But I was anxious to make my book as good as I could and I hoped to benefit by his criticisms. They were in point of fact lenient. They interested me peculiarly because I inferred that this was the way in which he dealt with the compositions of undergraduates. My don had, I think, a natural gift for language, which it has been his business to cultivate; his taste appeared to me faultless. I was much struck by his insistence on the force of individual words. He liked the stronger word rather than the euphonious. To give an example, I had written that a statue would be placed in a certain square and he suggested that I should write: the statue will stand. I had not done that because my ear was offended by the alliteration. I noticed also that he had a feeling that words should be used not only to balance a sentence but to balance an idea. This is sound, for an idea may lose its effect if it is delivered abruptly; but it is a matter of delicacy, since it may well lead to verbiage. Here a knowledge of stage dialogue should help. An actor will sometimes say to an author: "Couldn't you give me a word or two more in this speech? It seems to take away all the point of my line if I have nothing else to say." As I listened to my don's remarks I could not but think how much better I should write now if in my youth I had had the advantage of such sensible, broad-minded and kindly advice.

As it is, I have had to teach myself. I have looked at the stories I wrote when I was very young in order to discover what natural aptitude I had, my original stock-in-trade, before I developed it by taking thought. The manner had a superciliousness that perhaps my years excused and an irascibility that was a defect of nature; but I am speaking now only of the way in which I expressed myself. It seems to me that I had a natural lucidity and a knack for writing easy dialogue.

When Henry Arthur Jones, then a well-known playwright, read my first novel, he told a friend that in due course I should be one of the most successful dramatists of the day. I suppose he saw in it directness and an effective way of presenting a scene that suggested a sense of the theatre. My language was commonplace, my vocabulary limited, my grammar shaky, and my phrases hackneyed. But to write was an instinct that seemed as natural to me as to breathe, and I did not stop to consider if I wrote well or badly. It was not till some years later that it dawned upon me that it was a delicate art that must be painfully acquired. The discovery was forced upon me by the difficulty I found in getting my meaning down on paper. I wrote dialogue

fluently, but when it came to a page of description I found myself entangled
in all sorts of quandaries. I would struggle for a couple of hours over two
or three sentences that I could in no way manage to straighten out. I made
up my mind to teach myself how to write. Unfortunately I had no one to
help me. I made many mistakes. If I had had someone to guide me like the
charming don of whom I spoke just now, I might have been saved much
time. Such a one might have told me that such gifts as I had lay in one
direction and that they must be cultivated in that direction; it was useless to
try to do something for which I had no aptitude. But at that time a florid
prose was admired. Richness of texture was sought by means of a jeweled
phrase and sentences stiff with exotic epithets; the ideal was a brocade so
heavy with gold that it stood up by itself. The intelligent young read Walter
Pater with enthusiasm. My common sense suggested to me that it was anae-
mic stuff; behind those elaborate, gracious periods I was conscious of a tired,
wan personality. I was young, lusty, and energetic; I wanted fresh air, action,
violence, and I found it hard to breathe that dead, heavily scented atmosphere
and sit in those hushed rooms in which it was indecorous to speak above a
whisper. But I would not listen to my common sense. I persuaded myself
that this was the height of culture and turned a scornful shoulder on the
outside world where men shouted and swore, played the fool, wenched and
got drunk. I read *Intentions* and *The Picture of Dorian Gray*. I was intoxicated by the colour and rareness of the fantastic words that thickly stud the
pages of *Salome*. Shocked by the poverty of my own vocabulary, I went to
the British Museum with pencil and paper and noted down the names of
curious jewels, the Byzantine hues of old enamels, the sensual feel of textiles,
and made elaborate sentences to bring them in. Fortunately I could never
find an opportunity to use them and they lie there yet in an old notebook
ready for anyone who has a mind to write nonsense. It was generally thought
then that the Authorized Version of the Bible was the greatest piece of prose
that the English language has produced. I read it diligently, especially the
Song of Solomon, jotting down for future use turns of phrase that struck me
and making lists of unusual or beautiful words. I studied Jeremy Taylor's
Holy Dying. In order to assimilate his style I copied out passages and then
tried to write them down from memory.

The first fruit of this labour was a little book about Andalusia called
The Land of the Blessed Virgin. I had occasion to read parts of it the other
day. I know Andalusia a great deal better now than I knew it then, and I
have changed my mind about a good many things of which I wrote. Since
it has continued in America to have a small sale, it occurred to me that it
might be worth while to revise it. I soon saw that this was impossible. The
book was written by someone I have completely forgotten. It bored me to
distraction. But what I am concerned with is the prose, for it was as an
exercise in style that I wrote it. It is wistful, allusive, and elaborate. It has
neither ease nor spontaneity. It smells of hothouse plants and Sunday dinner
like the air in the greenhouse that leads out of the dining-room of a big house

in Bayswater. There are a great many melodious adjectives. The vocabulary is sentimental. It does not remind one of an Italian brocade, with its rich pattern of gold, but of a curtain material designed by Burne-Jones and reproduced by Morris.

I do not know whether it was a subconscious feeling that this sort of writing was contrary to my bent or a naturally methodical cast of mind that led me then to turn my attention to the writers of the Augustan Period. The prose of Swift enchanted me. I made up my mind that this was the perfect way to write and I started to work on him in the same way as I had done with Jeremy Taylor. I chose *The Tale of a Tub*. It is said that when the Dean re-read it in his old age he cried: "What genius I had then!" To my mind his genius was better shown in other works. It is a tiresome allegory and the irony is facile. But the style is admirable. I cannot imagine that English can be better written. Here are no flowery periods, fantastic turns of phrase or high-flown images. It is a civilized prose, natural, discreet, and pointed. There is no attempt to surprise by an extravagant vocabulary. It looks as though Swift made do with the first word that came to hand, but since he had an acute and logical brain it was always the right one, and he put it in the right place. The strength and balance of his sentences are due to an exquisite taste. As I had done before I copied passages and then tried to write them out again from memory. I tried altering words or the order in which they were set. I found that the only possible words were those Swift had used and that the order in which he had placed them was the only possible order. It is an impeccable prose.

But perfection has one grave defect: it is apt to be dull. Swift's prose is like a French canal, bordered with poplars, that runs through a gracious and undulating country. Its tranquil charm fills you with satisfaction, but it neither excites the emotions nor stimulates the imagination. You go on and on and presently you are a trifle bored. So, much as you may admire Swift's wonderful lucidity, his terseness, his naturalness, his lack of affectation, you find your attention wandering after a while unless his matter peculiarly interests you. I think if I had my time over again I would give to the prose of Dryden the close study I gave to that of Swift. I did not come across it till I had lost the inclination to take so much pains. The prose of Dryden is delicious. It has not the perfection of Swift nor the easy elegance of Addison, but it has a springtime gaiety, a conversational ease, a blithe spontaneousness that are enchanting. Dryden was a very good poet, but it is not the general opinion that he had a lyrical quality; it is strange that it is just this that sings in his softly sparkling prose. Prose had never been written in England like that before; it has seldom been written like that since. Dryden flourished at a happy moment. He had in his bones the sonorous periods and the baroque massiveness of Jacobean language and under the influence of the nimble and well-bred felicity that he learnt from the French he turned it into an instrument that was fit not only for solemn themes but also to express the light thought of the passing moment. He was the first of the

rococo artists. If Swift reminds you of a French canal Dryden recalls an
English river winding its cheerful way round hills, through quietly busy
towns and by nestling villages, pausing now in a noble reach and then running powerfully through a woodland country. It is alive, varied, windswept;
and it has the pleasant-open-air smell of England.

The work I did was certainly very good for me. I began to write better;
I did not write well. I wrote stiffly and self-consciously. I tried to get a pattern into my sentences, but did not see that the pattern was evident. I took
care how I placed my words, but did not reflect that an order that was natural
at the beginning of the eighteenth century was most unnatural at the beginning of ours. My attempt to write in the manner of Swift made it impossible
for me to achieve the effect of inevitable rightness that was just what I so
much admired in him. I then wrote a number of plays and ceased to occupy
myself with anything but dialogue. It was not till five years had passed that
I set out again to write a novel. By then I no longer had any ambition to
be a stylist; I put aside all thought of fine writing. I wanted to write without any frills of language, in as bare and unaffected a manner as I could. I
had so much to say that I could afford to waste no words. I wanted merely
to set down the facts. I began with the impossible aim of using no adjectives at all. I thought that if you could find the exact term a qualifying
epithet could be dispensed with. As I saw it in my mind's eye my book
would have the appearance of an immensely long telegram in which for
economy's sake you had left out every word that was not necessary to make
the sense clear. I have not read it since I corrected the proofs and do not
know how near I came to doing what I tried. My impression is that it is
written at least more naturally than anything I had written before; but I am
sure that is often slipshod and I daresay there are in it a good many mistakes
in grammar.

Since then I have written many other books; and though ceasing my
methodical study of the old masters (for though the spirit is willing, the flesh
is weak), I have continued with increasing assiduity to try to write better. I
discovered my limitations and it seemed to me that the only sensible thing was
to aim at what excellence I could within them. I knew that I had no lyrical
quality. I had a small vocabulary and no efforts that I could make to enlarge
it much availed me. I had little gift of metaphor; the original and striking
simile seldom occurred to me. Poetic flights and the great imaginative sweep
were beyond my powers. I could admire them in others as I could admire
their far-fetched tropes and the unusual but suggestive language in which
they clothed their thoughts, but my own invention never presented me with
such embellishments; and I was tired of trying to do what did not come easily
to me. On the other hand, I had an acute power of observation and it seemed
to me that I could see a great many things that other people missed. I could
put down in clear terms what I saw. I had a logical sense, and if no great
feeling for the richness and strangeness of words, at all events a lively appreciation of their sound. I knew that I should never write as well as I could

wish, but I thought with pains I could arrive at writing as well as my natural defects allowed. On taking thought it seemed to me that I must aim at lucidity, simplicity and euphony. I have put these three qualities in the order of the importance I assigned to them.

I have never had much patience with the writers who claim from the reader an effort to understand their meaning. You have only to go to the great philosophers to see that it is possible to express with lucidity the most subtle reflections. You may find it difficult to understand the thought of Hume, and if you have no philosophical training its implications will doubtless escape you; but no one with any education at all can fail to understand exactly what the meaning of each sentence is. Few people have written English with more grace than Berkeley. There are two sorts of obscurity that you find in writers. One is due to negligence and the other to wilfulness. People often write obscurely because they have never taken the trouble to learn to write clearly. This sort of obscurity you find too often in modern philosophers, in men of science, and even in literary critics. Here it is indeed strange. You would have thought that men who passed their lives in the study of the great masters of literature would be sufficiently sensitive to the beauty of language to write if not beautifully at least with perspicuity. Yet you will find in their works sentence after sentence that you must read twice to discover the sense. Often you can only guess at it, for the writers have evidently not said what they intended.

Another cause of obscurity is that the writer is himself not quite sure of his meaning. He has a vague impression of what he wants to say, but has not, either from lack of mental power or from laziness, exactly formulated it in his mind and it is natural enough that he should not find a precise expression for a confused idea. This is due largely to the fact that many writers think, not before, but as they write. The pen originates the thought. The disadvantage of this, and indeed it is a danger against which the author must be always on his guard, is that there is a sort of magic in the written word. The idea acquires substance by taking on a visible nature, and then stands in the way of its own clarification. But this sort of obscurity merges very easily into the wilful. Some writers who do not think clearly are inclined to suppose that their thoughts have a significance greater than at first sight appears. It is flattering to believe that they are too profound to be expressed so clearly that all who run may read, and very naturally it does not occur to such writers that the fault is with their own minds which have not the faculty of precise reflection. Here again the magic of the written word obtains. It is very easy to persuade oneself that a phrase that one does not quite understand may mean a great deal more than one realizes. From this there is only a little way to go to fall into the habit of setting down one's impressions in all their original vagueness. Fools can always be found to discover a hidden sense in them. There is another form of wilful obscurity that masquerades as aristocratic exclusiveness. The author wraps his meaning in mystery so that the vulgar shall not participate in it. His soul is a secret garden into which the elect may penetrate only after overcoming a number of perilous obstacles. But this kind of obscurity is not only pretentious; it is shortsighted. For time plays it an odd trick. If the sense is meagre, time reduces it to a meaningless verbiage that no one thinks of reading. This is the fate that has befallen the lucubrations of those French writers who were seduced by the example of Guillaume Apollinaire. But occasionally it throws a sharp cold light on what had seemed profound and thus discloses the fact that these contortions of language disguised very commonplace notions. There are few of Mallarmé's poems now that are not clear; one cannot fail to notice that his thought singularly lacked originality. Some of his phrases were beautiful; the materials of his verse were the poetic platitudes of his day.

Simplicity is not such an obvious merit as lucidity. I have aimed at it because I have no gift for richness. Within limits I admire richness in others, though I find it difficult to digest in quantity. I can read one page of Ruskin with delight, but twenty only with weariness. The rolling period, the stately epithet, the noun rich in poetic associations, the subordinate clauses that give the sentence weight and magnificence, the grandeur like that of wave following wave in the open sea; there is no doubt that in all this there is something inspiring. Words thus strung together fall on the ear like music. The appeal is sensuous rather than intellectual, and the beauty of the sound leads you easily to conclude that you need not bother about the meaning. But words are tyrannical things, they exist for their meanings, and if you will not pay attention to these, you cannot pay attention at all. Your mind wanders. This kind of writing demands a subject that will suit it. It is surely out of place to write in the grand style of inconsiderable things. No one wrote in this manner with greater success than Sir Thomas Browne, but even he did not always escape this pitfall. In the last chapter of *Hydriotaphia* the matter, which is the destiny of man, wonderfully fits the baroque splendour of the language, and here the Norwich doctor produced a piece of prose that has never been surpassed in our literature; but when he describes the finding of his urns in the same splendid manner the effect (at least to my taste) is less happy.

But if richness needs gifts with which everyone is not endowed, simplicity by no means comes by nature. To achieve it needs rigid discipline. So far as I know ours is the only language in which it has been found necessary to give a name to the piece of prose which is described as the purple patch; it would not have been necessary to do so unless it were characteristic. English prose is elaborate rather than simple. It was not always so. Nothing could be more racy, straightforward and alive than the prose of Shakespeare; but it must be remembered that this was dialogue written to be spoken. We do not know how he would have written if like Corneille he had composed prefaces to his plays. It may be that they would have been as euphuistic as the letters of Queen Elizabeth. But earlier prose, the prose of Sir Thomas More, for instance, is neither ponderous, flowery nor oratorical. It smacks of the English soil. To my mind King James's Bible has been a very harmful influence on English prose. I am not so stupid as to deny its great beauty.

It is majestical. But the Bible is an oriental book. Its alien imagery has nothing to do with us. Those hyperboles, those luscious metaphors, are foreign to our genius. I cannot but think that not the least of the misfortunes that the Secession from Rome brought upon the spiritual life of our country is that this work for so long a period became the daily, and with many the only, reading of our people. Those rhythms, that powerful vocabulary, that grandiloquence, became part and parcel of the national sensibility. The plain, honest English speech was overwhelmed with ornament. Blunt Englishmen twisted their tongues to speak like Hebrew prophets. There was evidently something in the English temper to which this was congenial, perhaps a native lack of precision in thought, perhaps a naive delight in fine words for their own sake, an innate eccentricity and love of embroidery, I do not know; but the fact remains that ever since, English prose has had to struggle against the tendency to luxuriance. When from time to time the spirit of the language has reasserted itself, as it did with Dryden and the writers of Queen Anne, it was only to be submerged once more by the pomposities of Gibbon and Dr. Johnson. When English prose recovered simplicity with Hazlitt, the Shelley of the letters, and Charles Lamb at his best, it lost it again with De Quincey, Carlyle, Meredith, and Walter Pater. It is obvious that the grand style is more striking than the plain. Indeed many people think that a style that does not attract notice is not style. They will admire Walter Pater's, but will read an essay by Matthew Arnold without giving a moment's attention to the elegance, distinction and sobriety with which he set down what he had to say.

The dictum that the style is the man is well known. It is one of those aphorisms that say too much to mean a great deal. Where is the man in Goethe, in his birdlike lyrics or in his clumsy prose? And Hazlitt? But I suppose that if a man has a confused mind he will write in a confused way, if his temper is capricious his prose will be fantastical, and if he has a quick, darting intelligence that is reminded by the matter in hand of a hundred things, he will, unless he has great self-control, load his pages with metaphor and simile. There is a great difference between the magniloquence of the Jacobean writers, who were intoxicated with the new wealth that had lately been brought into the language, and the turgidity of Gibbon and Dr. Johnson, who were the victims of bad theories. I can read every word that Dr. Johnson wrote with delight, for he had good sense, charm, and wit. No one could have written better if he had not wilfully set himself to write in the grand style. He knew good English when he saw it. No critic has praised Dryden's prose more aptly. He said of him that he appeared to have no art other than that of expressing with clearness what he thought with vigour. And one of his *Lives* he finished with the words: "Whoever wishes to attain an English style, familiar but not coarse, and elegant but not ostentatious, must give his days and nights to the volumes of Addison." But when he himself sat down to write, it was with a very different aim. He mistook the orotund for the

dignified. He had not the good breeding to see that simplicity and naturalness are the truest marks of distinction.

Whether you ascribe importance to euphony, the last of the three characteristics that I mentioned, must depend on the sensitiveness of your ear. A
great many readers, and many admirable writers, are devoid of this quality.
Poets as we know have always made a great use of alliteration. They are
persuaded that the repetition of a sound gives an effect of beauty. I do not
think it does so in prose. It seems to me that in prose alliteration should be
used only for a special reason; when used by accident it falls on the ear very
disagreeably. But its accidental use is so common that one can only suppose
that the sound of it is not universally offensive. Many writers without distress
will put two rhyming words together, join a monstrous long adjective to a
monstrous long noun, or between the end of one word and the beginning
of another have a conjunction of consonants that almost breaks your jaw.
These are trivial and obvious instances. I mention them only to prove that
if careful writers can do such things, it is only because they have no ear.
Words have weight, sound, and appearance; it is only by considering these
that you can write a sentence that is good to look at and good to listen to.

If you could write lucidly, simply, euphoniously and yet with liveliness you
would write perfectly: you would write like Voltaire. And yet we know how
fatal the pursuit of liveliness may be: it may result in the tiresome acrobatics
of Meredith. Macaulay and Carlyle were in their different ways arresting;
but at the heavy cost of naturalness. Their flashy effects distract the mind.
They destroy their persuasiveness; you would not believe a man was very
intent on ploughing a furrow if he carried a hoop with him and jumped
through it at every other step. A good style should show no sign of effort.
What is written should seem a happy accident. I think no one in France
now writes more admirably than Colette, and such is the ease of her expression that you cannot bring yourself to believe that she takes any trouble over
it. I am told that there are pianists who have a natural technique so that
they can play in a manner that most executants can achieve only as the result
of unremitting toil, and I am willing to believe that there are writers who
are equally fortunate. Among them I was much inclined to place Colette.
I asked her. I was exceedingly surprised to hear that she wrote everything
over and over again. She told me that she would often spend a whole morning working upon a single page. But it does not matter how one gets the
effect of ease. For my part, if I get it at all, it is only by strenuous effort.
Nature seldom provides me with the word, the turn of phrase, that is appropriate without being far-fetched or commonplace.

I have read that Anatole France tried to use only the constructions and
the vocabulary of the writers of the seventeenth century whom he so greatly
admired. I do not know if it is true. If so, it may explain why there is some
lack of vitality in his beautiful and simple French. But simplicity is false
when you do not say a thing that you should say because you cannot say it
in a certain way. One should write in the manner of one's period. The

language is alive and constantly changing; to try to write like the authors of a distant past can only give rise to artificiality. I should not hesitate to use the common phrases of the day, knowing that their vogue was ephemeral, or slang, though aware that in ten years it might be incomprehensible, if they gave vividness and actuality. If the style has a classical form it can support the discreet use of a phraseology that has only a local and temporary aptness. I would sooner a writer were vulgar than mincing; for life is vulgar, and it is life he seeks.

I think that we English authors have much to learn from our fellow authors in America. For American writing has escaped the tyranny of King James's Bible and American writers have been less affected by the old masters whose mode of writing is part of our culture. They have formed their style, unconsciously perhaps, more directly from the living speech that surrounds them; and at its best it has a directness, a vitality, and a drive that give our more urbane manner an air of languor. It has been an advantage to American writers, many of whom at one time or another have been reporters, that their journalism has been written in a more trenchant, nervous, graphic English than ours. For we read the newspaper as our ancestors read the Bible. Not without profit either; for the newspaper, especially when it is of the popular sort, offers us a part of experience that we writers cannot afford to miss. It is raw material straight from the knacker's yard, and we are stupid if we turn up our noses because it smells of blood and sweat. We cannot, however willingly we would, escape the influence of this workaday prose. But the journalism of a period has very much the same style; it might all have been written by the same hand; it is impersonal. It is well to counteract its effect by reading of another kind. One can do this only by keeping constantly in touch with the writing of an age not too remote from one's own. So can one have a standard by which to test one's own style and an ideal which in one's modern way one can aim at. For my part the two writers I have found most useful to study for this purpose are Hazlitt and Cardinal Newman. I would try to imitate neither. Hazlitt can be unduly rhetorical; and sometimes his decoration is as fussy as Victorian Gothic. Newman can be a trifle flowery. But at their best both are admirable. Time has little touched their style; it is almost contemporary. Hazlitt is vivid, bracing, and energetic; he has strength and liveliness. You feel the man in his phrases, not the mean, querulous, disagreeable man that he appeared to the world that knew him, but the man within of his own ideal vision. (And the man within us is as true in reality as the man, pitiful and halting, of our outward seeming.) Newman had an exquisite grace, music, playful sometimes and sometimes grave, a woodland beauty of phrase, dignity and mellowness. Both wrote with extreme lucidity. Neither is quite as simple as the purest taste demands. Here I think Matthew Arnold excels them. Both had a wonderful balance of phrase and both knew how to write sentences pleasing to the eye. Both had an ear of extreme sensitiveness.

If anyone could combine their merits in the manner of writing of the present day, he would write as well as it is possible for anyone to write.

Vocabulary and Success [1]

by JOHNSON O'CONNOR

W HAT is success? And how is it gained? Whether one thinks of success as financial reward, or as assured social position, or as satisfaction in able work accomplished and recognized, or as a combination of the three and something more, many factors contribute. Most of them elude our understanding and remain intangibly beyond definition. A vital force drives some persons over every obstacle. With others that great generalization, character, adds strength of a different sort. Neither may ever be restricted to a hard and fast formula; certainly, at the moment, neither can be measured. But other more concrete constituents of success have been isolated and studied in the laboratory. One of these is a large English vocabulary.

An extensive knowledge of the exact meanings of English words accompanies outstanding success in this country more often than any other single characteristic which the Human Engineering Laboratory has been able to isolate and measure.

What is mean by vocabulary? Just what the word signifies. Does ENERVATING mean SOOTHING, EXCITING, DISTRESSING, INVIGORATING, or WEAKENING? For most well-educated persons the choice is between INVIGORATING and WEAKENING. Fifty-two per cent of the college graduates measured by the Laboratory choose INVIGORATING as the synonym; only sixteen per cent choose WEAKENING, the dictionary definition. Does STILTED, in the phrase: 'his STILTED manner,' mean IRRESOLUTE, IMPROPER, CORDIAL, STIFFLY FORMAL, or VICIOUS? A majority of educated persons mark STIFFLY FORMAL, but more than a third select IRRESOLUTE. Answers to the meaning of SCURRILOUS, in the phrase: 'SCURRILOUS rogue,' divide themselves more or less evenly between HURRYING, DESPERATE, ABUSIVE, FRANTIC, and DISEASED, with DESPERATE the most popular. For PEREMPTORY, a majority mark DECISIVE, but many choose PERSUASIVE, UNCERTAIN, and ANGRY. PLEASANT, the fifth choice, is not so popular. LINGUIST and GLUTTON are equally enticing as synonyms for POLYGLOT. For REFULGENT, in 'a REFULGENT smile,' REPELLENT is most alluring, and VERY BRIGHT next, with MISCHIEVOUS, FLATTERING, and SOUR, all following closely in popularity. For MONOGRAPH forty per cent choose SOLILOQUY and less than twenty per cent TREATISE and EPITAPH each.

The word VOCABULARY, as used in this book, signifies a knowledge of the dictionary meaning of just such words as ENERVATING, STILTED, SCURRILOUS,

---

[1] From the *Atlantic Monthly*, February, 1934; reprinted in J. O'Connor, *English Vocabulary Builder*, Human Engineering Laboratory. By permission of the author.

PEREMPTORY, POLYGLOT, REFULGENT, and MONOGRAPH. One may like the sound of a word and use it in a picturesque way without being accurate in its meaning. Not until one attempts to pick an exact synonym does one realize the difficulty.

To measure the vocabulary of an individual the Laboratory uses a list of one hundred and fifty test words. Each is printed in a short phrase and is followed by five choices, all of which fit the phrase but only one of which is a synonym of the test word. The instructions are: 'Underline that one of the five choices which is nearest in meaning to the word in the phrase.' The first selection of words to be defined was made by Alexander Inglis of the Graduate School of Education, Harvard University. His intention was to include words which appear once or twice in 100,000 words of printed matter; and to limit the selection to the general reader's vocabulary, excluding technical terms. Another selection has been made, by Mr. Bartlett Boyden of Deerfield Academy, of words encountered by the preparatory-school student.

The test words vary from some which are easy, such as UNTIDY in the item: his UNTIDY room. BEAUTIFUL DISORDERLY NEAT GORGEOUS HIGH-CEILINGED, to others which are more difficult, such as ANFRACTUOUS in the item: ANFRACTOUS lines. CONTINUOUS DOTTED STRAIGHT DOUBLE WINDING, which only twenty per cent of college graduates mark correctly. Since one fifth, or twenty per cent, should guess the correct answer, the meaning of ANFRACTUOUS is practically unknown. The test measures knowledge of words one recognizes, not necessarily of those one uses. The words one uses accurately are, no doubt, fewer than those one recognizes, but there is probably a relation between the two.

Three hundred high-school freshmen average 76 errors in the list of 150 words. Seven hundred college freshmen average 42 errors. One thousand college graduates, from a wide variety of colleges, average 27 errors, and vary from one person in a thousand who achieves a perfect score to the one who knows less than 50 of the 150 items. College professors, measured by the Laboratory, average 8 errors; major executives average 7 errors. Major executives score higher in this English vocabulary test than any other selected group with which the Laboratory has experimented.

By the term MAJOR EXECUTIVES is meant all persons who, for ten years or longer, have held the position of president or vice president in a business organization. Such a definition includes both successful and unsuccessful executives, provided only that they have survived ten years; it includes alike forceful personalities and figureheads; but it has the great advantage of excluding personal judgment from the process of selection. Major executives as thus defined average in the top ten per cent of college graduates.

Although it is impossible to define success rigidly, a large vocabulary seems to be typical, not exclusively of executives, but of successful persons. It happens that in the business world successful men and women are designated by this special appellation, EXECUTIVE. The successful lawyer or doctor is marked by no such name. But if, to the best of one's ability, one selects successful persons in the professions, they also score high in vocabulary.

For one meaning of success the Century dictionary gives: 'A high degree of worldly prosperity.' The measured English vocabularies of executives correlate with their salaries. This does not mean that every high-vocabulary person receives a large salary, but the relation is sufficiently close to show that a large vocabulary is one element of success, and seemingly an important one.

Furthermore, the executive level which a man or woman reaches is determined to some extent by vocabulary. In many manufacturing organizations the first step in the executive ladder is the leading hand, called sometimes the working foreman. This man is in charge of half a dozen others. He works at the bench or at a machine as they do, but is the executive of the group. The next step is the foreman, who may be in charge of as many as a hundred or more workers. He does no bench work, he is not a producer, but devotes full time to his executive duties, to the keeping of records and to the handling of the personnel. The next step in many large organizations is the department head or superintendent or manager, who ordinarily does not come in direct contact with the workers, but handles them through his foremen. The final step is the major executive or official, the vice president or president.

These four executive ranks represent four degrees of success, in one sense in which that word is used. One is advanced from leading hand to foreman, from foreman to manager, from manager to president. As far as the Laboratory can determine by measurements, the leading hand and the official have much the same inherent aptitudes. They differ primarily in vocabulary. Typical non-college-graduate shop foremen average, as a group, about as high as college graduates. Department heads score higher, roughly fifteen errors, and major executives the highest of all, averaging only seven errors. Whether the word EXECUTIVE refers only to the major group or is used in the broader sense to mean anyone in charge of other workers, it is still true that the executive scores higher than those under him and higher than other persons of similar age and education.

An interesting sidelight on the high vocabulary scores of executives is that they were unforeseen. When a scientist expects a result and finally achieves it there is always the feeling that, regardless of the care he has taken, personal bias may have entered. Six or eight years ago the Human Engineering Laboratory tested forty major executives of the Telephone Company who had offered themselves as victims to be experimented upon in a search for executive characteristics. At the same time the Laboratory was also revising the vocabulary test, not with the notion of using it with executives, but with the hope that it might prove of value in education. One day, with no thought of the consequences, it was given to an executive, and from then on was asked for regularly because of the interest it aroused. The Laboratory paid little heed to the results until one executive refused to take the test. He had been obliged by lack of money to leave school at fourteen. With no further formal education he had worked his way to a major position. He had taken the aptitude tests without hesitation, but vocabulary seemed to him so directly the result of schooling that he knew in advance he would fail. His own words were that he had made his way without being found out and he was not willing to give himself away. But in scientific work one cannot test only those who think they will do well, and he was finally persuaded to try the vocabulary test. He made two errors where the average college graduate makes twenty-seven.

Was it luck? Or was it significant of something not recognized? The Laboratory listed the vocabulary scores of one hundred executives and, parallel with them, the scores of one hundred miscellaneous college graduates. The difference between the two arrays was striking. Only nine per cent of the college graduates scored as high as the average major executive.

Why do large vocabularies characterize executives and possibly outstanding men and women in other fields? The final answer seems to be that words are the instruments by means of which men and women grasp the thoughts of others and with which they do much of their own thinking. They are the tools of thought.

On Jargon[1]

by SIR ARTHUR QUILLER-COUCH

WE PARTED, Gentlemen, upon a promise to discuss the capital difficulty of Prose, as we have discussed the capital difficulty of Verse. But, although we shall come to it, on second thoughts I ask leave to break the order of my argument and to interpose some words upon a kind of writing which, from a superficial likeness, commonly passes for prose in these days, and by lazy folk is commonly written for prose, yet actually is not prose at all; my excuse being the simple practical one that, by first clearing this sham prose out of the way, we shall the better deal with honest prose when we come to it. The proper difficulties of prose will remain; but we shall be agreed in understanding what it is, or at any rate what it is not, that we talk about. I remember to have heard somewhere of a religious body in the United States of America which had reason to suspect one of its churches of accepting spiritual consolation from a coloured preacher—an offence against the laws of the Synod—and despatched a Disciplinary Committee with power to act; and of the Committee's returning to report itself unable to take any action under its terms of reference, for that while a person undoubtedly coloured

[1] From *On the Art of Writing* (1916). Copyright, by G. P. Putnam's Sons, publishers.

had undoubtedly occupied the pulpit, and had audibly spoken from it in the Committee's presence, the performance could be brought within no definition of preaching known or discoverable. So it is with that infirmity of speech—that flux, that determination of words to the mouth, or to the pen,—which, though it be familiar to you in parliamentary debates, in newspapers, and as the staple language of Blue Books, Committees, Official Reports, I take leave to introduce to you as prose which is not prose and under its real name of Jargon.

You must not confuse this Jargon with what is called Journalese. The two overlap, indeed, and have a knack of assimilating each other's vices. But Jargon finds, maybe, the most of its votaries among good douce people who have never written to or for a newspaper in their life, who would never talk of "adverse climatic conditions" when they mean "bad weather"; who have never trifled with verbs such as "obsess," "recrudesce," "envisage," "adum-brate," or with phrases, such as "the psychological moment," "the true inward-ness," "it gives furiously to think." It dallies with Latinity,—"sub silentio," "de die in diem," "cui bono?" (always in the sense unsuspected by Cicero, of "What is the profit?")—but not for the sake of style. Your journalist at the worst is an artist in his way; he daubs paint of this kind upon the lily with professional zeal; the more fragrant (or, to use his own word, arresting) the pigment, the happier is his soul. Like the Babu he is trying all the while to embellish our poor language, to make it more floriferous, more poetical—like the Babu, for example, who, reporting his mother's death wrote, "Regret to in-form you, the hand that rocked the cradle has kicked the bucket."

There is metaphor; *there* is ornament; *there* is a sense of poetry, though as yet groping in a world unrealised. No such gusto marks—no such zeal, artistic or professional, animates—the practitioners of Jargon, who are, most of them (I repeat), douce respectable persons. Caution is its father; the instinct to save everything and especially trouble; its mother, Indolence. It looks precise, but is not. It is, in these times, safe: a thousand men have said it before and not one to your knowledge had been prosecuted for it. And so, like respectability in Chicago, Jargon stalks unchecked in our midst. It is be-coming the language of Parliament; it has become the medium through which Boards of Government, County Councils, Syndicates, Committees, Commercial Firms express the processes as well as the conclusions of their thought and so voice the reason of their being.

Has a Minister to say "No" in the House of Commons? Some men are constitutionally incapable of saying no; but the Minister conveys it thus: "The answer to the question is in the negative." That means "No." Can you dis-cover it to mean anything less, or anything more except that the speaker is a pompous person?—which was no part of the information demanded.

That is Jargon, and it happens to be accurate. But as a rule Jargon is by no means accurate, its method being to walk circumspectly around its target; and its faith, that having done so it has either hit the bull's-eye or at least achieved something equivalent, and safer.

Thus the clerk of a Board of Guardians will minute that—

In the case of John Jenkins deceased the coffin provided was of the usual character.

Now this is not accurate. "In the case of John Jenkins deceased," for whom a coffin was supplied, it is wholly superfluous to tell us that he is deceased. But actually John Jenkins never had more than one case, and that was the coffin. The clerk says he had two,—a coffin in a case; but I suspect the clerk to be mistaken, and I am sure he errs in telling us that the coffin was of the usual character; for coffins have no character, usual or unusual.

For another example (I shall not tell you whence derived)—

In the case of every candidate who is placed in the first class [So you see the lucky fellow gets a case as well as a first-class. He might be a stuffed animal: perhaps he is]—In the case of every candidate who is placed in the first class the class-list will show by some convenient mark (1) the Section or Sections for proficiency in which he is placed in the first class and (2) the Section or Sections (if any) in which he has passed with special distinction.

"The Section or Sections (if any)"—But how, if they are not any, could they be indicated by a mark however convenient?

The Examiners will have regard to the style and method of the candidate's answers, and will give credit for excellence in *these respects.*

Have you begun to detect the two main vices of Jargon? The first is that it uses circumlocution rather than short straight speech. It says: "In the case of John Jenkins deceased the coffin" when it means "John Jenkins's coffin"; and its yea is not yea, neither is its nay nay; but its answer is in the affirmative or in the negative, as the foolish and superfluous "case" may be. The second vice is that it habitually chooses vague woolly abstract nouns rather than concrete ones. I shall have something to say by-and-by about the concrete noun, and how you should ever be struggling for it whether in prose or in verse. For the moment I content myself with advising you, if you would write masculine English, never to forget the old tag of your Latin Grammar—

> Masculine will only be
> Things that you can touch and see.

But since these lectures are meant to be a course in First Aid to writing, I will content myself with one or two extremely rough rules; yet I shall be disappointed if you do not find them serviceable.

The first is: Whenever in your reading you come across one of these words, *case, instance, character, nature, condition, persuasion, degree,* whenever in writing your pen betrays you to one or another of them—pull yourself up and take thought. If it be "case" (I choose it as Jargon's dearest child—"in Heaven yclept Metonymy") turn to the dictionary, if you will, and seek out what meaning can be derived from *casus,* its Latin ancestor, then try how, with a little trouble, you can extricate yourself from that case. The odds are, you will feel like a butterfly who has discarded his chrysalis.

Here are some specimens to try your hand on:

(1) All those tears which inundated Lord Hugh Cecil's head were dry in the case of Mr. Harold Cox.

Poor Mr. Cox! left gasping in his aquarium!

(2) [From a cigar-merchant.] In any case, let us send you a case on approval.
(3) It is contended that Consols have fallen in consequence; but such is by no means the case.

"Such," by the way, is another spoilt child of Jargon, especially in Committee's Rules—"Co-opted members may be eligible as such; such members to continue to serve for such time as"—and so on.

(4) Even in the purely Celtic areas only in two or three cases do the Bishops bear Celtic names.

For "cases" read "dioceses."

Instance. In most instances the players were below their form.

But what were they playing at? Instances?

Character—Nature. There can be no doubt that the accident was caused through the dangerous nature of the spot, the hidden character of the by-road, and the utter absence of any warning or danger signal.

Mark the foggy wording of it all! And yet the man hit something and broke his neck! Contrast that explanation with the verdict of a coroner's jury in the west of England on a drowned postman: "We find that deceased met his death by an act of God, caused by sudden overflowing of the river Walkham and helped out by the scandalous neglect of the way-wardens."

The Aintree course is notoriously of a trying nature.
On account of its light character, purity, and age, Usher's whiskey is a whiskey that will agree with you.
Order. The mésalliance was of a pronounced order.
Condition. He was conveyed to his place of residence in an intoxicated condition.

"He was carried home drunk."

Quality and Section. Mr. ——, exhibiting no less than five works, all of a superior quality, figures prominently in the oil section.

—This was written of an exhibition of pictures.

Degree. A singular degree of rarity prevails in the earlier editions of this romance.

That is Jargon. In prose it runs simply "The earlier editions of this romance are rare"—or "are very rare"—or, even (if you believe what I take leave to doubt), "are singularly rare"; which should mean that they are rarer than the editions of any other work in the world.

Now what I ask you to consider about these quotations is that in each the writer was using Jargon to shirk prose, palming off periphrases upon us when with a little trouble he could have gone straight to the point. "A singular degree of rarity prevails," "the accident was caused through the dangerous nature of the spot," "but such is by no means the case." We may not be capable of much; but we can all write better than that, if we take a little trouble. In place of, "the Aintree course is of a trying nature" we can surely say "Aintree is a trying course" or "the Aintree course is a trying one"—just that and nothing more. . . .

For another rule—just as rough and ready, but just as useful: Train your suspicions to bristle up whenever you come upon "as regards," "with regard to," "in respect of," "in connection with," "according as to whether," and the like. They are all dodges of Jargon, circumlocutions for evading this or that simple statement; and I say that it is not enough to avoid them nine times out of ten, or nine-and-ninety times out of a hundred. You should never use them. That is positive enough, I hope? Though I cannot admire his style, I admire the man who wrote to me, "Re Tennyson—your remarks anent his *In Memoriam* make me sick"; for though *re* is not a preposition of the first water, and "anent" has enjoyed its day, the finish crowned the work. But here are a few specimens far, very far, worse:—

The special difficulty in Professor Minocelsi's case [our old friend "case" again] arose *in connexion with* the view he holds *relative* to the historical value of the opening pages of Genesis.

That is Jargon. In prose, even taking the miserable sentence as it stands constructed, we should write "the difficulty arose over the views he holds about the historical value," etc.

From a popular novelist:—

I was entirely indifferent *as to* the results of the game, caring nothing at all *as to* whether *I had losses or gains*—

Cut out the first "as" in "as to," and the second "as to" altogether, and the sentence begins to be prose—"I was indifferent to the results of the game, caring nothing whether I had losses or gains."

But why, like Dogberry, have "had losses"? Why not simply "lost"? Let us try again. "I was entirely indifferent to the results of the game, caring nothing at all whether I won or lost."

Still the sentence remains absurd; for the second clause but repeats the first without adding one jot. For if you care not at all whether you win or lose, you must be entirely indifferent to the results of the game. So why not say, "I was careless if I won or lost," and have done with it?

A man of simple and charming character, he was fitly *associated with* the distinction of the Order of Merit.

I take this gem with some others from a collection made three years ago, by the *Oxford Magazine;* and I hope you admire it as one beyond price. "He was associated with the distinction of the Order of Merit" means "he was given the Order of Merit." If the members of that Order make a society then he was associated with them; but you cannot associate a man with a distinction. The inventor of such fine writing would doubtless have answered Canning's Needy Knife-grinder with:—

I associate thee with sixpence! I will see thee in another association first!

But let us close our *florilegium* and attempt to illustrate jargon by the converse method of taking a famous piece of English (say Hamlet's soliloquy) and remoulding a few lines of it in this fashion:—

To be, or the contrary? Whether the former or the latter be preferable would seem to admit of some difference of opinion; the answer in the present case being of an affirmative or of a negative character according as to whether one elects on the one hand to mentally suffer the disfavour of fortune, albeit in an extreme degree, or on the other to boldly envisage adverse conditions in the prospect of eventually bringing them to a conclusion. The condition of sleep is similar to, if not indistinguishable from that of death; and with the addition of finality the former might be considered identical with the latter: so that in this connection it might be argued with regard to sleep that, could the addition be effected, a termination would be put to the endurance of a multiplicity of inconveniences, not to mention a number of downright evils incidental to our fallen humanity, and thus a consummation achieved of a most gratifying nature.

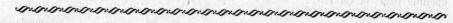

The Cliché Expert[1]

by FRANK SULLIVAN

JOHN B. SMITH takes the stand.

Q. Mr. Smith, are you familiar with the clichés used in football?

A. Naturally, as a football fan.

Q. What kind of football fan are you, may I ask?

A. I am a rabid footfall fan, sir.

Q. In that case, I suppose you attend a great many football games.

A. I go to a great many grid tilts, if that's what you mean.

Q. I see. Who attend these grid tilts?

A. Record crowds, or throngs.

[1] From *The Atlantic Monthly,* November, 1938. By permission of the author and the editor.

Q. And what does a record crowd provide?

A. A colorful spectacle, particularly if it is the Army-Navy game.

Q. Mr. Smith, how do you know when the football season is about to start?

A. When there is a tang of autumn in the air I know that football will soon be king.

Q. Is there any other portent that helps you?

A. About September first, when the newsreels start showing pictures of coaches putting their charges through early practice, I know that football will soon hold sway—*undisputed* sway—over the hearts of sports lovers.

Q. Describe these pictures.

A. The candidates sit around on their haunches looking a little sheepish, while the coach stands in the middle holding a football—pardon *me,* a pigskin—and an announcer states that an atmosphere of optimism prevails in the Gopher camp despite a heavy schedule and the loss of several of their best men through graduation. Then the coach makes a short talk, the gist of which is that, while he will make no predictions, he *will* say that any team that comes up against the Gophers this fall will know they've been in a battle—how about it, men? Then the men line up and tackle a flying dummy.

Q. A shrewd summing up, Mr. Smith. Speaking of "up," what do football teams roll up?

A. A score.

Q. lt they don't roll up a score, what do they do?

A. They battle to a scoreless tie.

Q. What do they hang up?

A. A victory. Or, they pull down a victory.

Q. Which means that they do what to the opposing team?

A. They take the measure of the opposing team, or take it into camp.

Q. And the opposing team?

A. Drops a game, or bows in defeat.

Q. This dropping, or bowing, constitutes what kind of blow for the losing team?

A. It is a crushing blow to its hopes of annexing the Eastern championship. Visions of the Rose Bowl fade.

Q. So what follows as a result of the defeat?

A. A drastic shakeup follows as a result of the shellacking at the hands of Cornell last Saturday.

Q. And what is developed?

A. A new line of attack.

Q. Mr. Smith, how is the first quarter of a football game commonly referred to?

A. As the initial period.

Q. What kind of quarterbacks do you prefer?

A. Elusive quarterbacks.

Q. Who traditionally comprise the membership of Notre Dame's football team, the Fighting Irish?

A. Woszianko, Rumplemeyer, Kozlowski, Goldsmith, Ponzaneri, and so on.

Q. And who play on the Harvard team?

A. Mahoney, Grady, O'Halloran, Dolan, and Cabot.

Q. Very good. Now then, what does a young football player show?

A. An embryo football player? He shows great promise in high school.

Q. Why?

A. Because he is husky, powerful, sturdy, stout-hearted, fast on his feet, a tough man in a scrimmage, and tips the scales at two hundred pounds.

Q. Which makes him?

A. A magnificent physical specimen.

Q. What happens after the magnificent physical specimen shows great promise?

A. He goes to college.

Q. How?

A. On funds donated by wealthy alumni who are rabid football fans.

Q. And who are?

A. And who are dissatisfied with the coach, it is rumored.

Q. Once in college, what does the magnificent physical specimen become?

A. Promising football material.

Q. So he joins the candidates who are trying for positions on the football team, eh?

A. I wouldn't put it that way. I'd just say he goes out for football. By the way, Mr. Sullivan, now that I have amended your statement, how do you stand?

Q. I stand corrected.

A. Good. A bit of a cliché fancier yourself, eh?

Q. Oh, I dabble, I dabble. Now then, Mr. Smith, I suppose that in the course of time—the *due* course of time, to be exact—the magnificent physical specimen is appointed to a place on the regular team.

A. You waste so many words. He makes the varsity eleven.

Q. What kind of practice is he put through?

A. Hard, grueling practice.

Q. Where?

A. Under the eye of the coach.

Q. What kind of eye?

A. Watchful eye.

Q. So that he is?

A. In fine fettle, and a veritable human fighting machine.

Q. What does he shovel?

A. Passes.

Q. What kind of threats is he partial to?

A. Triple threats.

Q. What does he nurse?

A. Bruises.

Q. What does he break?

A. Training.

Q. What does he stave off?

A. Defeat.

Q. What kind of prowess does he boast?

A. Vaunted.

Q. What is a good football captain called?

A. An able field general.

Q. And the able field general leads his team through an unbroken series of victories, does he not?

A. He does unless he is declared ineligible.

Q. Where is he when he is declared ineligible?

A. He is behind in his studies.

Q. Now, Mr. Smith, what, according to tradition, does the coach call the players?

A. He calls them "men."

Q. And what does the captain call his teammates?

A. He calls them "fellows."

Q. What does the coach say in the locker room just before the game?

A. He says, "Well, men, I guess that's about all. Now, get in there and fight!"

Q. What does the captain say?

A. He says, "Come on, fellows, let's go!"

Q. So they go out there?

A. Determined to win.

Q. What for?

A. For the honor of the school; for dear old Alma Mater; for the glory of old Crimson; for God, for country, and for Yale; for dear old Rutgers; for good old coach; for Dad and Mother, and for A Certain Girl.

Q. For anything else?

A. For Delta Kappa Epsilon and good old Sigma Phi, for Scroll & Key and Skull & Bones, and Theta Delta Chi.

Q. Why, you're quite a poet, Mr. Smith!

A. Oh, I dabble, I dabble.

Q. Where is A Certain Girl during the game?

A. Up there in the stands, her heart glowing with pride.

Q. What is she wearing?

A. A chrysanthemum.

Q. Where are Mother and Dad?

A. Up there too, *their* hearts glowing with pride.

Q. When Son drops the punt, do Dad's and Mother's hearts cease glowing with pride?

A. Dad's sinks, but not Mother's.

Q. Why not?

A. Because she thinks he has scored a point.

Q. Why else is Son determined to win?

A. Because he wants to emerge from that game as the greatest end since Larry Kelly.

Q. Why does he wish to be the greatest end?

A. So he can get his letter, and be a candidate for the All-American team.

Q. Why?

A. So that he can get a bid from a big pro team.

Q. Pro team?

A. Professional football.

Q. Why does he want to play pro football?

A. Because that may bring a bid from the movies to play magnificent physical specimen parts, such as Tarzan.

Q. Does he get his letter?

A. Yes.

Q. How?

A. By snatching victory from the jaws of defeat.

Q. How?

A. By carrying the ball seventy-five yards for a touchdown.

Q. When?

A. In the last minute of play.

Q. What was the crowd yelling?

A. "Hold that line!"

Q. What else does the crowd yell?

A. "Block that kick!"

Q. What does the rabid football fan sitting behind you do?

A. He jams my hat down over my head in his excitement.

Q. Why?

A. Because he is an old grad, and he is a little the worse for wear.

Q. You mean?

A. He is feeling good. He's in his cups.

Q. By the way, Mr. Smith, what would you call the annual game between Yale and Harvard?

A. It is a grid classic.

Q. And what is the Yale Bowl—or the Harvard Stadium—on the day of this grid classic?

A. A Mecca for football fans throughout the East.

Q. And the fans?

A. Jam the Bowl to its utmost capacity. Reporters estimate the crowd at 75,000.

Q. Just 75,000?

A. No. Pardon me. *Fully* 75,000.

Q. Do Yale or Harvard care whether they bow to any other eleven prior to their grid classic with each other?

A. Oh, no. They point to each other.

Q. Point?

A. Yes. Train for each other.

Q. Why?

A. Because of their age-old rivalry.

Q. Are they the only two colleges that have an age-old rivalry?

A. Good heavens, no! Every college worthy of the name has an age-old rivalry. Army and Navy. Cornell and Syracuse—you know.

Q. I see. What is it the rooters want Yale to hold?

A. " 'Em." You know—"Hold 'em, Yale!"

Q. If Harvard emerges triumphant over Yale, what does that constitute?

A. A moral victory for Yale.

Q. And the game itself?

A. It was a good game from the spectators' point of view.

Q. Why?

A. Because there were plenty of thrills.

Q. What happens after a football game?

A. The undergraduates tear down the goal posts.

Q. What reigns on the campus of the winning team that night?

A. Joy, or pandemonium.

Q. And the cops?

A. The cops wink.

Q. Mr. Smith, as an expert, what lesson do you draw from the game of football?

A. Life is a game of football, Mr. Sullivan, and we the players. Some of us are only cheerleaders. Some of us are coaches and some of us are old grads, slightly the worse for wear, up in the stands. Some of us thump the people in front of us on the head in our excitement, some of us are the people who always get thumped. But the important thing to remember is—Play the Game!

A. How true!

Stabilizing the Language through Popular Songs[1]

by SIGMUND SPAETH

I F YOU want to write a really popular song, one that will fall naturally from the lips of millions, be sure that somewhere in your chorus you assault the English language in no uncertain terms. With even one reasonably atrocious error in English grammar included in your words, you may find yourself with a hit on your hands.

[1] From *The New Yorker*, July 7, 1934. By permission of the editor and the author.

The tradition of bad grammar is of long standing with the lyric-writers of popular music. (Why "lyric," incidentally?) Their efforts in this direction have been so consistent over a number of years that they have actually succeeded in stabilizing the language in certain details on which the dictionaries and the scholars would never have surrendered.

There is that troublesome word "like," for instance. It is generally agreed that it is not a conjunction but a preposition to be followed by a noun or pronoun in the objective case, not by a complete clause. But your song-writer blithely says "Let's all sing *like* the birdies sing," or "I don't know why I love you *like* I do," and straightway "like" becomes a conjunction, whether you like it or not.

Actually those titles would sound pretty stilted and artificial if you sang "*as* the birdies sing" or "*as* I do," and so good a writer as the late William Bolitho doggedly stuck to the same error. The usage was thoroughly established back in the nineties by Miss Imogen Comer when she sang, at Koster & Bial's music hall:

> I love you *like* a copper loves to sleep,
> And *like* a little newsboy loves a pie.
> I love you *like* a baby loves to creep,
> Well, if I don't love you, Mame, I hope to die.
> I love you *like* the kids love street pianos,
> I love you *like* a gambler loves a game;
> Just *like* the Reuben loves the Tenderloin I love you,
> Well, say, kid, that's how I love you, Mame.

Just to make assurance doubly sure, Joe McCarthy drove it home some years later in one of those Feist songs with which you can't go wrong. He managed to start practically every line with an improper "like," which is a record of some sort. Here is his chorus:

> *Like* the roses need their fragrance,
>   *Like* a sweetheart needs a kiss,
> *Like* the summer needs the sunshine,
>   *Like* a laddie needs a miss,
> *Like* a broken heart needs gladness,
>   *Like* the flowers need the dew,
> *Like* a baby needs its mother,
>   That's how I need you.

The lyric authority for this avalanche of incorrect "likes" came from that ungrammatical classic, "Frankie and Johnnie," which contains the deathless lines "this woman simply dropped her man *like* a hunter drops a bird." After that, the reiterated accusation, "He done her wrong," sounds inevitably right.

Back in 1908 they sang "Love me *like* I like to be loved" and liked it. Gene Austin brought in the touch of nature with his poetic line "*like* the whippoorwill sings in the valley," and Paul Dresser drew tears with "I'll be brave, just *like* father was." It was this same brother of Theodore Dreiser who made the supreme grammatic sacrifice when he wrote "Remember I was once a girl like *she*." It takes courage to disregard so obvious a preposition and so compulsory an objective case for the following pronoun.

Curiously enough, Dresser allowed the girl in "Just tell them that you saw me" to speak correct English when she sent the message to her mother, "I love her *as* I did long, long ago." Jim Thornton also deserves a medal for writing "I love you *as* I never did before," and ex-Mayor Walker a replica for "Will you love me in December *as* you do in May?"

Dresser's "like she" may have been a mere prejudice against the objective case, which is common among songwriters and many other people as well. Those who customarily say "between you and I" would hardly object to the line from that recent hit, "When We're Alone" (generally called the Penthouse Serenade): "A sweet slice of heaven for just you and *I*." H. P. Danks, of "Silver Threads Among the Gold," sanctioned this use of the nominative in a song called "Allie Darling," for which his lyricist, J. T. Rutledge, gave him both "Allie, dear, for you and *I*." Frank Crumit supplies a modern instance in his "Return of Abdul" when he has one of the combatants ejaculate, " 'Twas foolish for *we* two to fight."

This matter of nominative and objective cases reaches a climax in the long-standing "who or whom" controversy, which F. P. A. has pursued so indefatigably. A songwriter would hardly dare to use "whom" in a sentence, even if he knew it was correct. Such things are just unsingable. "Who are you with tonight, tonight?" sounds both proper and provocative, and the song could not possibly have achieved popularity with the burden of a "whom" on its neck. Similarly the oft-reiterated phrase "Who do you love?" would lose all its enticing quality if it were made grammatically correct. Even the famous "Who" song of Jerome Kern slips occasionally, so far as the librettist is concerned.

Adverbs are frankly a puzzle to the lyric-writers. Their instincts tell them to hesitate before becoming involved in the suffix "ly." So it is with a sincere regard for his colleagues' feelings that Rudy Vallee sings "Don't take it serious." And he has an honorable model in the old motto song "Always take Mother's advice," which admonishes us never to "speak hasty or rude."

Irving Berlin's popular "Easter Parade" commits a pardonable error with "never saw you dressed quite so lovely," perhaps on the theory that one "ly" is enough for anybody. But that wail of the outraged moron, "Was that the human thing to do?" (pronounced "youman"), managed to cram several bits of questionable English into a single couplet:

> Never thought that anyone in *their* right mind
> Could ever treat another human so *unkind*.

After that, one hesitates to mention so slight an aberration as the common use of "don't" for the third person singular (literally, he, she, or it "do not"). The popular-song literature is full of it, mostly for reasons of metre, and occasionally in the spirit of deliberate dialect.

"The name of the lady *don't* matter," says the recent "Louisville Lady," in the manner of Robert Service, and there is intentional colloquialism in the Nassau folk-song, "Mamma *don't* want no peas an' rice an' cocoanut oil." "The world *don't* seem the same," wrote Irving Berlin not so long ago, and a still later hit proclaims, "It *don't* mean a thing if you ain't got that swing." (There is no use in arguing about "ain't" because that is now an accepted part of the American language.) An obscure song which gave the melody to "There's Yes, Yes in Your Eyes" had the title "Without You the World *Don't* Seem the same," and there are plenty of other instances of this harmless abbreviation in song, both legitimate and illegitimate.

The popular songwriters, however, have only scratched the surface in their stabilization of bad grammar. The possibilities of the English language as actually spoken are enormous in their opportunities for a really consistent rule-breaker. These possibilities have thus far been realized in only one song, from the pen of Baron Ireland, whose real name is Nate Salsbury.

He has written an ungrammatical song to end ungrammatical songs, and its title is "If I Had of Knew What I'd Ought to of Knew, I'd Never of Did What I Done." With the permission of its publishers, the E. B. Marks Music Company, it is given here as the final word on this whole subject:

> All my to-days is days of sorrow,
> There ain't no dawn to my to-morrow;
> Just one more fool for that thing they call love,
> Acted like I should never of.

CHORUS

> If I had of knew what I'd ought to of knew,
> I'd never of did what I done,
> If I had of saw we was breaking God's law,
> I'd never of kissed you in fun.
> I thought love was glad, didn't mean to be bad,
> But the passions we had druv the both of us mad.
> But if I had of knew what a fool would of knew,
> I'd never of did what I done.

Excerpts from "A Dictionary of Modern English Usage"[1]

by H. W. FOWLER

HAZINESS. What is meant by this is a writer's failure to make a clear line between different members of a sentence or clause, so that they run into one another; if he does not know the exact content of what he has set down or is about to set down, the word or words that he is now writing will naturally not fit without overlapping, or a gap will be left between them. This sounds so obvious that it may seem hardly worth while to devote an article to the matter and find a heading for it; but even the more flagrant transgressions of the principle are so numerous as to make it plain that a warning is called for. Those more flagrant transgressions are illustrated first.

The effect of the tax is not likely to be productive of much real damage (overlapping; part of *be productive of* has been anticipated in *effect;* omit either *the effect of* or *productive of*). / *It is a pity that an account of Amercan activities in aircraft production cannot yet be described* (overlapping; *account* is contained in *described;* omit *an account of,* or change *described* to *given*). / *A full account of this explosion and how it was brought about was narrated in LAND AND WATER of April 11th* (like the last, but not quite so indefensible). / *The need of some effort, a joint effort if possible, is an urgent necessity for all the interests concerned* (*need* and *necessity* overlap). / *They have accounted for three times as many enemy casualties as they themselves have suffered* (cause enemy casualties; account for enemies). *The welfare of the poor and needy was a duty that devolved especially on those who had a seat in that House* (gap; it is not the welfare, but the securing of the welfare, that is a duty). / *Hitherto the only way of tackling the evil was by means of prohibiting the exportation from certain places* (*way* and *means* overlap; the only way of tackling was to prohibit; it could only be tackled by means of). / *With the one exception of Sir Alfred Lyall, who chequers praise with somewhat tentative criticism, all these tributes are naturally eulogistic* (gap; Sir Alfred is not a tribute).

Certain words seem to lend themselves especially to this sort of haziness, as AGO (*It is five years ago since I saw him*); REASON with BECAUSE (*The only reason his wages have not been higher is because*—i.e., that—*the profits of the industry have been miserably low*), OF with DUE (*The reasons of his success were due not only to . . .*); the illogical TOO (*We need not attach too much*

[1] First edition, 1926. By permission of Humphrey Milford, publishers.

importance to . . .); PREFERABLE with MORE (*the former alternative being, in our view, on every ground the more preferable*); BUT with superfluous negatives (*Who knows but what this memorial exhibition may not prove the starting point?*); THAT conjunction with questions or commands (*Crises arise so rapidly in these days that who can say what a few years may bring forth? / Your correspondent suggests that if we lend money let us send it to . . .*); REMAIN with CONTINUE (*and yet through it all I continue to remain cheerful*); SEEM with APPEAR (*These conclusions, it seems to me, appear to be reached naturally*).

ILLITERACIES. There is a kind of offence against the literary idiom that is not easily named. The usual dictionary label for some specimens of it at least is vulg.; but the word vulgar is now so imbued on the one hand with social prejudices and on the other with moral condemnation as to be unsuitable; the property common to these lapses seems to be that people accustomed to reading good literature do not commit them and are repelled by them, while those not so accustomed neither refrain from nor condemn them; they may be more accurately as well as politely called illiteracies rather than vulgarisms; their chief habitat is in the correspondence columns of the press. A few familiar types may be here collected for comparison, with just enough in the way of illustration to enable each usage to be recognized:

Like as conjunction (*if I could think like you do*).

However, whatever, whoever, etc., interrogative (*However did you find out?; Whatever can this mean?*).

Same, such, and *various*, as pronouns (*Will submit same, or the same, for approval; Have no dealings with such; Various have stated*).

Frequent use of split infinitives (*Am ready to categorically affirm*).

Think to=remember to (*I did not think to tell them when I was there*).

Negative after *should not wonder* (*I shouldn't wonder if it didn't come true yet*).

Present tense etc. after *as if* and *as though* (*It looks as if we are winning or shall win*).

Me etc. for *my* etc. in gerund construction (*Instead of me being dismissed*).

Between . . . or for *between . . . and* (*The choice is between glorious death or shameful life*).

Rather unique, more preferable.

Aggravating for *annoying*.

Individual for *person*.

Rev. Jones; the hon. Smith.

ILLOGICALITIES. The spread of education adds to the writer's burden by multiplying that pestilent fellow, the critical reader. No longer can we depend on an audience that will be satisfied with catching the general drift and obvious intention of a sentence and not trouble itself to pick holes in our wording; the words used must nowadays actually yield on scrutiny the desired sense; to plead that anyone could see what you meant, or so to write as to need that plea, is not now permissible; all our pet illogicalities will have to be cleared away by degrees.

If Milton might be excused or even commended for calling Eve fairest of her daughters, the modern newspaper man must not expect pardon for similar conduct. *Sir Edmund Cassel's gift to the hospital of £50,000 is only the latest of many acts of splendid munificence by which he has benefited his fellows before now.* If it is the latest of them, says the pestilent fellow, it is one of them; if one of them, it was given before now; but it is in fact given now, not before now; which is absurd.

Take, again, the following comment on a quotation the commentator thinks unjustified: *Were ever finer lines perverted to a meaner use?* We know well enough what he is trying to do—to emphasize the meanness of the use—; it is in expressing the emphasis that he has gone wrong; it has escaped him that *Never were lines perverted to a meaner use* is made weaker, not stronger, if changed to, *never were finer lines* etc., and that again it is further weakened, not strengthened, by a change of *fine* to *finer;* everything that narrows the field of rivals for the distinction of meanest perversion, as *fine* and *finer* do progressively, has an effect contrary to what was intended; it may be worth while to insert *fine* in spite of that, since it adds a qualifica‑ tion of importance; but the change to *finer* weakens the force without adding to the accuracy. Richard III says *Was ever woman in this humour won?;* to have said *Princess,* or *prouder Princess,* instead of *woman* would have made the marvel less and not greater.

Another common, and more conspicuous, illogicality is the unintended anticlimax. *Masters, it is already proved that you are little better than false knaves, and it will go near to be thought so shortly.* Dogberry felt no un‑ easiness about putting it that way, and some writers seem to agree with him:— *A skepticism about the result of military operations which must have had and probably has had a damping effect upon the soldier* (If it must have had, it certainly, not probably, has had). / *It will, I think, delight the reader as if it were something told by Meadows Taylor; indeed the mysterious 'sadhu' who figures in it, and the account of the flight with the yellow leopard, are not unworthy of the suggested comparison* (Not unworthy, quotha? but *indeed* led us to expect *more than worthy,* a climax instead of an anticlimax).

The abandonment of blind confidence in *much less* is another compliment that will have to be paid to the modern reader's logic. It is still usual to give no hearing to *much more* before deciding for its more popular rival; some‑ times a loose but illogical excuse is to be found in the general effect of the context, sometimes even that is wanting; these two varieties appear in the quotations:—*The machine must be crushed before any real reforms can be initiated, much less carried. / It is a full day's work even to open, much less to acknowledge, all the presents.*

METAPHOR. 1. Live and dead metaphor. In all discussion of metaphor it must be borne in mind that some metaphors are living, i.e., are offered and accepted with a consciousness of their nature as a substitute for their literal equivalents, while others are dead, i.e., have been so often used that speaker and hearer have ceased to be aware that the words used are not literal; but the line of distinction between the live and the dead is a shifting one, the dead being sometimes liable, under the stimulus of an affinity or a repulsion, to galvanic stirrings indistinguishable from life. Thus in *The men were sifting meal* we have a literal use of sift; in *Satan hath desired to have you that he may sift you as wheat, sift* is a live metaphor; in *the sifting of evidence,* the metaphor is so familiar that it is about equal chances whether *sifting* or *examination* will be used, and that a sieve is not present to the thought— unless indeed someone conjures it up by saying *All the evidence must first be sifted with acid tests,* or *with the microscope*—; under such a stimulus our metaphor turns out to have been not dead but dormant; the other word, *examine,* will do well enough as an example of the real stone-dead metaphor; the Latin *examino,* being from *examen* the tongue of a balance, meant originally to weigh; but though weighing is not done with acid tests or microscopes any more than sifting, *examine* gives no convulsive twitches, like *sift,* at finding itself in their company; *examine,* then, is dead metaphor, and *sift* only half dead, or three-quarters.

2. A. Unsustained metaphor. *He was still in the middle of those twenty years of neglect which only began to lift in 1868.* The plunge into metaphor at *lift,* which presupposes a mist, is too sudden after the too literal twenty years of neglect; years, even gloomy years, do not lift./ *The* means of education *at the disposal of the Protestants and Presbyterians of the North were* stunted and sterilized. *The means at disposal* names something too little vegetable or animal to consort with the metaphorical verbs. Education (personified) may be stunted, but means may not./ *The* measure *of Mr. Asquith's shame does not* consist *in the mere* fact *that he has announced his intention to* . . . Metaphorical measuring, like literal, requires a more accommodating instrument than a stubborn fact.

2. B. Overdone metaphor. The days are perhaps past when a figure was deliberately chosen that could be worked out with line upon line of relentless detail, and the following well known specimen is from Richardson:—*Tost to and fro by the high winds of passionate control, I behold the desired port, the single state, into which I would fain steer; but am kept off by the foaming billows of a brother's and sister's envy, and by the raging winds of a supposed invaded authority; while I see in Lovelace, the rocks on one hand, and in Solmes, the sands on the other; and tremble lest I should split upon the former or strike upon the latter.*

2. C. Spoilt metaphor. The essential merit of real or live metaphor being to add vividness to what is to be conveyed, it need hardly be said that accuracy of detail is even more needed in metaphorical than in literal expressions; the habit of metaphor, however, and the habit of accuracy do

not always go together:—*Yet Jaurès was the* Samson *who* upheld the pillars
*of the Bloc./ Yet what more distinguished names does the Anglican Church
of the last reign boast than those of F. D. Maurice, Kingsley, Stanley, Robertson of Brighton, and even, if we will* draw *our* net *a little* wider, *the great
Arnold?/ He was the very essence of cunning and the very* incarnation *of
a* bookthief. Samson's way with pillars was not to uphold them; we draw
nets closer, but cast them wider; and what is the incarnation of a thief? too,
too solid flesh indeed!

2. D. Battles of dead metaphors. In *The Covenanters took up arms*
there is no metaphor; in *The Covenanters flew to arms* there is one only—
flew to for quickly took up—; in *She flew to arms in defence of her darling*
there are two, the arms being now metaphorical as well as the flying; moreover, the two metaphors are separate ones; but, being dead ones, and also
not inconsistent with each other, they lie together quietly enough. But dead
metaphors will not lie quietly together if there was repugnance between them
in life; e'en in their ashes live their wonted fires, and they get up and fight:—
It is impossible to crush *the Government's* aim *to restore the means of living
and working freely. Crush* for baffle, *aim* for purpose, are both dead metaphors so long as they are kept apart; but the juxtaposition forces on us the
thought that you cannot crush an aim./ *National military training is the*
bedrock *on which alone we can hope to* carry through *the great struggles
which the future may have in store for us. Bedrock* and *carry through* are
both moribund or dormant, but not stone-dead./ *The vogue of the motor-car
seems destined to help forward the provision of good road communication, a*
feature *which is sadly* in arrear. Good road communication may be a feature,
and it may be in arrear; things that are equal to the same thing may be
equal to each other in geometry, but language is not geometry./ *They are*
cyphers *living* under the shadow of *a great man.*

2. E. Mixed metaphors. For the examples given in D, tasteless word-
selection is a fitter description than mixed metaphor, since each of the words
that conflict with others is not intended as a metaphor at all. Mixed metaphor is more appropriate when one or both of the terms can only be consciously metaphorical. Little warning is needed against it; it is so conspicuous
as seldom to get into speech or print undetected. *This is not the time to* throw
up the sponge, *when the enemy, already weakened, are* on the run to a new
defensive position. A mixture of prize-ring and battle-field.

In the following extract from a speech, it is difficult to be sure how many
times metaphors are mixed; readers versed in the mysteries of oscillation
may be able to decide:—*No society, no community, can place its house in
such a condition that it is always on a rock,* oscillating *between solvency and
insolvency. What I have to do is to see that our house is* built upon a solid
foundation, *never allowing the possibility of the Society's* life-blood being
sapped. *Just in proportion as you are careful in looking after the condition
of your income, just in proportion as you deal with them carefully, will the
solidarity of the Society's financial condition remain intact. Immediately you*

begin to play fast and loose *with your income* the first blow *at your financial stability* will have been struck.

3. Self-consciousness and mixed metaphor. Writers who are on the defensive apologize for change and mixture of metaphors as though one was as bad as the other; the two things are in fact entirely different; a man may change his metaphors as often as he likes; it is for him to judge whether the result will or will not be unpleasantly florid; but he should not ask our leave to do it; if the result is bad, his apology will not mend matters, and if it is not bad, no apology was called for. On the other hand, to mix metaphors, if the mixture is real, is an offence that should not have been apologized for, but avoided. Whichever the phrase, the motive is the same—mortal fear of being accused of mixed metaphor:—

Certainly we cannot detect the suggested lack of warmth in the speech as it is printed, for in his speech, as in the Prime Minister's, it seems to us that (if we may change the metaphor) exactly the right note was struck. Certainly, gentlemen, you may change your metaphors, if it seems good to you; but you may also be pretty sure that, if you feel the necessity of proclaiming the change, you had better have abstained from it./ *Two of the trump cards played against the Bill are (1) that 'it makes every woman who pays a tax-collector in her own house', and (2) that 'it will destroy happy domestic relations in hundreds of thousands of homes'; if we may at once change our metaphor, these are the notes which are most constantly struck in the stream of letters, now printed day by day for our edification in the Mail.* This writer need not have asked our leave to change from cards to music; he is within his rights, anyhow, and the odds are, indeed, that if he had not reminded us of the cards we should have forgotten them in the three intervening lines; but how did a person so sensitive to change of metaphor fail to reflect that it is ill playing the piano in the water? a stream of letters, it is true, is only a picturesque way of saying many letters, and ordinarily a dead metaphor; but once put your seemingly dead yet picturesque metaphor close to a piano that is being played, and its notes wake the dead—at any rate for readers who have just had the word metaphor called to their memories.

WORTH WHILE. In certain uses great confusion prevails, which can be cleared up with the aid of grammar. The important fact is that the adjective *worth* requires what is most easily described as an object; it is meaningless to say *This is worth,* but sense to say *This is worth sixpence,* or *This is worth saying* (i.e. the necessary expenditure of words), or *This is worth while* (i.e. the necessary expenditure of time); but one such object satisfies the requirements, so that *This is worth while saying,* with the separate objects *while* and *saying,* is ungrammatical.

WORTH-WHILE. This attributive-adjective compound recently extracted from the phrase 'is worth while' (*a worth-while experiment* from *the experi-*

ment was worth while) is at best of doubtful value; and, having been seized upon as a vogue-word, it is fast losing all precision of meaning: *That motherhood is a full-time job all worth-while mothers will readily admit.* An attractive programme of worth-while topics has been arranged for discussion.

The Daily Theme Eye [1]

by WALTER PRICHARD EATON

WHEN I was an undergraduate at Harvard our instructors in English composition endeavored to cultivate in us a something they termed "The daily theme eye." This peculiar variety of optic, I fear, always remained a mystery to a majority of the toilers after clearness, force, and elegance. Clearness, force, and even a certain degree of elegance, may be acquired; but the daily theme eye, like the eye for the sights of a rifle, may be discovered, developed, trained—but not acquired. It comes by the grace of Heaven, not of the Harvard or any other English department, and its possession is often one of the marks of the man whose destiny compels him to write. The Harvard English department has but given it a name; it has no local habitation. It is found in Henry James and the police reporter of the New York *Sun;* it illuminates the pages of *The Harvard Monthly* (sometimes) and of George Moore. It winks at you in Heine and peers solemnly in Mrs. Humphry Ward. And it flashes and beams in a little lady I know who has written nothing save sprightly letters all the days of her life and never opened Hill's *Rhetoric* under the shade of the Washington Elm.

The fairy who stood over my cradle, though he forgot the gold spoon and much else besides, at least bestowed the gift of this wonderful optic. It brought me my college degree; for when other courses failed—which means when I failed in other courses—there was always English; it has brought me a living since; but more than all else it has brought me enjoyment, it has clothed the daily walk with interest, the teeming, noisy town with color and beauty, "the society of my contemporaries," to use Emerson's big phrase for my little purpose, with stimulating excitement. It has turned the panorama of existence into a play, or rather a thousand plays, and brought after sorrow or pain the great comfort of composition.

Daily themes in my day had to be short, not over a page of handwriting. They had to be deposited in a box at the professor's door not later than ten five in the morning. A classmate of mine, when an epigram was called for once wrote, "An epigram is a lazy man's daily theme written at ten-three A.M."

[1] From *Essays and Essay-Writing,* by W. M. Tanner. An Atlantic Monthly Press Publication published by Little, Brown & Company. Reprinted by permission. Essay first published in 1907.

And because of this brevity, and the necessity of writing one every day whether the mood was on you or not, it was not always easy—to be quite modest—to make these themes literature, which, we were told by our instructors, is the transmission through the written word, from writer to reader, of a mood, an emotion, a picture, an idea. I hate to think how few, in fact, of all the thousands that were poured into that yawning box were literature, how seldom the poor instructors could dip their pens into their pots of red ink and write the magic "A" on the back. Their sarcastic comments were surely excusable. I have even forgiven the young man with hair like yellow corn-tassels, who scrawled on verses of mine, required to be written in imitation of some poet, "This may be O'Shaughnessy, it isn't poetry." Did.he think thus to kill two song birds with one stone? Well, the effort of those of us who were sincere and comprehending in our pursuit of the elusive power to write was to make our themes literature as often as possible; and to do this the first essential was the choice of a subject. Not everything one sees or does or thinks can take shape on a page of paper and reproduce itself for the reader. Selection was the first requirement.

It became needful, then, to watch for and treasure incidents that were sharply dramatic or poignant, moods that were clear and definite, pictures that created a single clean impression. The tower of Memorial seen across the quiet marshes against the cool pink sky of evening; the sweep of a shell under the bridge and the rush of the spectators to the other rail to watch the needle-bow emerge, and the bent, brown backs of the crew; the chorus girls, still rubbing the paint from their cheeks with a tiny handkerchief wrapped over the forefinger, coming out of a stage entrance into the snow; the first sharp impression of a book just read or a play just seen,—these were the things we cherished, for these we could put on a page of paper with a beginning, a middle, and an end, and with some show of vividness. What we came to do, then, was to keep a note-book of our impressions, and when in June our themes were returned to us we had a precious record for the year. By training the daily theme eye, we watched for and found in the surroundings of our life, as it passed, a heightened picturesqueness, a constant wonder, an added significance. That hardened cynic, the professional writer, will smile and say, "You saw copy." Yes, we saw copy; but to see copy is to see the significant, to clarify what the ear and heart and eye receive, to add light and shadow to the monochrome of life.

My college roommate, a blessed boy full of good humor and serious purpose, was as incapable of acquiring the daily theme eye as a cat of obeying the eighth commandment. His idea of a daily theme was a task, not a pleasure. If there was no chance to write a political editorial, he supplied an anecdote of his summer vacation. Once he described a cliff he had seen in Newfoundland, and, determined to be pictorial, he added, "tumbling water-falls" and "sighing pines." Unfortunately, the instructor who read it had also been in Newfoundland, and he pointed out that his investigations of the cliff in question had failed to disclose either "tumbling waterfalls" or "sighing pines." My roommate treated the matter as a joke; he could not see that he had been guilty of any fault. And yet he is a much more moral man than I, with a far more troublesome conscience. Truth to his principles he would die for. But truth to the picture his mind retained and his hand tried to portray in the medium of literature, to him so trivial and unimportant, he could not grasp. What did it matter? So it would never occur to him to record in his themes the fleeting impressions of his daily life, to sit up half the night trying to pack into the clumsy frame of words the recollection of a strangely innocent face seen suddenly in the flash of an opened door down a dark, evil alley where the gusts of winter swirled. He went to bed and never knew a headache or jumpy nerve. Yet I could not help thinking then that there was something in life he was missing besides the ultimate mark in our composition course. And I cannot help thinking that there is something in life he misses still.

But perhaps that is only my fancy. George Moore says that happiness is no more than a faculty for being surprised; and it is the sudden vista, the beauty of a city square seen through falling snow, a street-car drama, the face of a passing woman, the dialogue of friends, which make the surprises for the man with the eye for copy. George Moore himself has a daily theme eye of preternatural keenness, and he may be speaking only for a class. Happiness for my roommate lies, I suspect, rather in his faculty for not being surprised. A sudden accession of emotion at the sight of an unexpected view, for instance, would probably be immensely disconcerting. And if he should go into an art museum, as I did the other day, and see a little marble boy with a slightly parted mouth wet his lips with his tongue, I truly believe he would rush off to the doctor's at once, very unhappy, instead of rushing joyfully home to try to put the illusion into a sonnet! Well, every class has its Pharisaism, which in reality isn't a form of priggishness, at all, but merely a recognition of difference. He thinks I am unpractical, a bit odd, not quite a grown man. I think he is—a charming fellow. We are about quits on that!

Letters to the Editor[1]

ANONYMOUS

ONE SOOTHING opportunity offered to everybody is the privilege of writing to the editor. This is a right as inalienable as free speech itself; it requires only a stamp, or for the laconic and economical, a postcard.

[1] From "Topics of the Times" column, New York *Times*, Sept. 13, 1943. By permission of the editor.

Some people are so constituted as to be always poised for the literary flight that the letter to a newspaper entails. Others are prodded into it by choler or unusual circumstance. An editorial may make a subscriber so angry that he must pen his reply before he can go sanely about his business. Or again he may be so well pleased with the views stated that his day is not complete until he has risen to be counted as a parliamentary second.

For others a mere event recorded in the news columns is the spring that touches off action. Or deep dissatisfaction with the regime that happens at any given time to be in power in Washington may come bubbling up to bursting point and insist on expression before interior damage is done.

No two letter writers are the same, of course, and their variety is refreshing.

There is the professorial type, for a beginning. This letter is profound, well rounded in its sentences, carefully documented, and tending, as might be expected, to length. It commonly takes off with comment on an editorial, but quickly diverges to exposition of independent ideas. If it attacks, it does so courteously and by indirection, as a guest expressing a contrary opinion in a home which he may wish to revisit later. There is much meat and, indeed, not infrequently, nourishment sufficient to support another editorial based on the letter itself.

Such letters may be a little heavy, but so are some editorials. They are good, solid substance, applying to current problems the lessons of what has been thought and said in the past. Every newspaper would be the poorer without them.

Some use the letter columns simply as a forum for correcting social or governmental wrongs, and effectively too. Of the lesser evils having to do with administration of a village, city or State nothing might be heard unless some reader wrote indignantly to his newspaper about it. The editorial page offers, for this reader, a platform from which he can be heard and for which, perhaps, there is no ready substitute. Here he can have his say, in public, and not suffer the indignity of having his letter tossed into an official wastebasket to go unheeded. It is one place where the taxpayer can put his elected official on the griddle and make him fry until he corrects the abuse.

It was inevitable under the circumstances that some people would virtually make a career out of writing to the editor. Charles Hooper may be remembered as one such. When he died at 57 on the West Coast, he had written 78,000 letters to editors, representing an average of five a day for forty years. He once described himself as "possibly the only man in the world who does nothing but write letters to newspapers."

The *World-Telegram* a few days ago told us of a New Yorker who makes writing to the editor an avocation. Milton M. Hermanson, an advertising copy writer, has only been at it for a year and a half but he is going strong. When he gets a good idea he "sends it nationwide," and has had hundreds of letters printed all over the country. It is his method of helping win the war.

Of course writing to the editor is a pleasure, or people wouldn't do it. But it happens to be one form of self-satisfaction that benefits others as well. It is very hard for a newspaper to make a mistake of fact in the news or editorial columns without having at least one subscriber—and frequently it is a dozen—write in to point it out in emphatic and gleeful or disgruntled terms. This is as it should be. It helps to keep the record straight; it serves the interests of truth.

But the letter to the editor serves a broader purpose. It tells a newspaper day in and day out what the people are thinking. The newspaper need not necessarily follow the crowd; the majority may sometimes be wrong. But it helps to know.

A Review of *Madame Curie*

(Eve Curie)[1]

by CLIFTON FADIMAN

ESCARTES was unheroic, Leibnitz a fawning courtier, Willard Gibbs a recluse, Gauss cold and secretive. For all his nobility, Pasteur was tainted with chauvinism and race hatred. An infantile religiosity clouded to the end the magnificent minds of Newton and Pascal. Indeed, it is hard to think of many first-rate scientific careers in which some major flaw of character does not show itself, confounding our natural desire for wholehearted hero worship. But the lives of Marie and Pierre Curie, two of the most beautiful lives, I suppose, that have ever been lived, provide an exception. It was almost theatrically apt that this man and woman, with characters of shining purity, should have built their careers around a physical element recognizable by its indestructible and essential radiance.

The life of Madame Curie, who died in 1934, has now been written by Eve, her younger daughter, and sensitively translated by Vincent Sheean. One can give "Madame Curie" no higher praise than to say it is almost worthy of its subject. It is not, I think, as solid a biography as it might be. It does not have that wonderful density of technical information, for example, which made Vallery-Radot's "Pasteur" a classic. It tells you just enough about radium to make you understand the great achievement of the Curies. But the biography of a scientist should do more. One can only regret that Irène Joliot-Curie (the elder daughter, co-winner of the Nobel Prize) did not collaborate with her sister on the scientific chapters. But aside from this defect, here is a noble and moving biography, which takes due advantage of the fact that the life of Marie Curie might have been conceived not by the accidents of nature but by the patterning brain of a tragic dramatist of genius.

One looks at the frontispiece, a photograph of Marie taken in 1929, when she was sixty-two. The face is lined. From underneath the white and casually arranged hair arcs an abnormally spacious brow. She is dressed in a simple black dress that looks like a laboratory smock. The face is that of a truly beautiful woman, the beauty lying in the bones and in the brain that sends its clear signals through the deep, penetrating eyes. What can Hollywood, when it films this book, do with such a face?

The story of Marie Curie is not merely that of a poor Polish governess who struggled against adversity and became a triumphant success. The story of Marie Curie lies precisely in the fact that she was happiest during her

[1] A review from *The New Yorker*, November 27, 1937, entitled "She Did Not Know How To Be Famous." By permission of the author and *The New Yorker*.

struggles and least happy when a vulgar world acclaimed her. Hers is a success story with an ironic twist. Einstein has said, "Marie Curie is, of all celebrated beings, the only one whom fame has not corrupted." "She did not know how to be famous," says Eve Curie. In one deliberate sentence of her perfectly composed introduction, she strikes to the heart of the secret: "I hope that the reader may constantly feel, across the ephemeral movement of one existence, what in Marie Curie was even more rare than her work or her life: the immovable structure of a character; the stubborn effort of an intelligence; the free immolation of a human being that could give all and take nothing, could even receive nothing; and above all the quality of a soul in which neither fame nor adversity could change the exceptional purity."

Recall that unbelievably dramatic life. She is born Manya Sklodowska, youngest child of a Warsaw physicist and a sensitive, tubercular mother. The childhood is unhappy, torn by the death of mother and eldest sister, rendered over-serious by poverty, given a certain tenseness by the fact that she is a member of a subject race, the Poles. She grows up, becomes the conventional intellectual rebel of her time, like "all the little Polish girls who had gone mad for culture." She is intelligent, but nothing yet reveals that "immovable structure" of which her daughter speaks. She becomes a governess, a bit of a bluestocking touched with Tolstoyan sentimentality. Now "the eternal student" begins to rise up in her. The little child who at five stood in rapt awe before her father's case containing the "phys-ics ap-pa-ra-tus" reawakens in the girl of eighteen. Her duties as a governess do not prevent her from studying. She has no money, not even for stamps so that she may write to her brother. But "I am learning chemistry from a book." Back in Warsaw, she is allowed to perform elementary chemical experiments in a real laboratory, and at last, after inconceivable setbacks and economies, after years of weary waiting, she goes to Paris to study at the Sorbonne.

On forty rubles a month Manya (now Marie) Sklodowska lives, studies, learns. Solitude, near-starvation, an unheated garret—none of these things matters, as long as at least a part of her day is spent in the laboratory. Now even the miserable forty rubles cease. She is about to return in despair to Warsaw when she is given a six-hundred-ruble scholarship. A few years afterward, with the first money she earns as a scientist, she returns the amount of the scholarship so that some other poor student may be assisted by it.

In 1894 she meets Pierre Curie, already a physicist of note, a mind "both powerful and noble." In an atmosphere of garrets and laboratories, these two, very grave and serious, conduct their love affair. They marry. On her wedding day, to the generous friend who wishes to give her a bridal dress, she writes, "I have no dress except the one I wear every day. If you are going to be kind enough to give me one, please let it be practical and dark so that I can put it on afterwards to go to the laboratory."

It is a perfect marriage, the marriage not merely of two people who love each other but, what is incomparably more interesting and important, of two great physicists who can help each other. It is Marie, attracted by the uranium researches of Becquerel, who starts herself and her husband on the long, tedious, glorious path at the end of which lies radium. They know that radium and polonium (named by Marie to commemorate her beloved native land) exist, but they must prove it. From 1898 to 1902, in a dilapidated, leaking, freezing shed, with primitive apparatus, with little or no help, unaided by the scientific bureaucracy or by the State, these two gentle fanatics work in an absorption that is like a dream. The government is too busy spending money on armament to buy them the few tons of pitchblende they need. Somehow they get their pitchblende, paying for its transportation themselves out of their insufficient salaries. With "her terrible patience," Marie, doing the work of four strong men, pounds away at her chemical masses, boils, separates, refines, stirs, strains. Somewhere in this inert brown stuff lies radium. Marie loses fifteen pounds during these five years. At last they isolate the element.

All this time they have been bringing up a family. They have had sorrows, family illnesses. Pierre's mother has died of the very disease against which radium is soon to prove a beneficent weapon. All this time no provision is made for these selfless geniuses. The State, as always, cares nothing. Recognition comes first from other countries, from Switzerland, England. "With great merit and even greater modesty," says Montaigne, "one can remain unknown for a long time."

Now the full implications of their work begin to appear. The immovable atom moves; matter is touched with a mysterious life; physics revises its nineteenth-century conceptions of the indestructibility of matter and the conservation of energy. The Curies are triumphant; and their first major decision is to refrain from patenting their radium-extraction process. They give it freely to the world. This gesture alone—or rather the inevitable expression of their characters—is enough to lend their lives a depth that can never attach to a commercial career like that of Edison. The difference between a Curie and an Edison is not merely one of scientific genius, it is a difference of order. The Curies are one kind of human being, Edison was another.

In 1903 the Curies, with Becquerel, receive the Nobel Prize for Physics. The world pursues them. Now they must flee the world. "In science we must be interested in things, not in persons," says Marie, who was never to be interested in herself. One evening, at the height of their fame, as they are about to leave for a banquet, Pierre looks at his wife, with her ash-gray eyes, her ash-blond hair, her exquisite wrists and ankles, and he murmurs, "It's a pity. Evening dress becomes you." Then, with a sigh, he adds, "But there it is, we haven't got time."

They are offered the slimy vulgarity of decorations, ribbons, rosettes. But no laboratory. (Pierre eventually died without getting his laboratory, without being allowed to work properly.) The life of the Curies will remain, forever terrible, as a sombre reminder of the stupidity, the greed, even the sadism of the French ruling class of the period.

Then on April 19, 1906, Aeschylean tragedy, cutting Marie's life in two, giving it at the same time a new emotional dimension. Pierre's head is crushed by a van in a street accident, and Marie becomes "a pitiful and incurably lonely woman." She refuses a pension (always the State makes its generous offers too late); she proceeds with the education of her daughter; she takes over Pierre's teaching post and, in a dry, monotonous voice, without making any reference to her predecessor, resumes the lectures at the exact point at which Pierre had left off.

The rest of her life is the story of her marriage with radium. For her laboratory, for science, she will do anything, even try to be "famous." In 1911 she receives the Nobel Prize for Chemistry. During the war she equips, with superhuman energy, a fleet of radiological cars so that the wounded may be helped by X-rays. She is no rotogravure ministering angel, no Queen Marie of Rumania. She actually works—works for the State which had done its best in those dark years to prevent her from working. Later, again for the sake of science, she comes to America to receive a gram of radium from the hand of an amiable poker player who could not possibly have understood even the most trivial of the thoughts in Marie Curie's mind. Then, applauded by all America, she goes back to France, and all America turns to the next celebrity, Carpentier, to lavish an identical adulation upon him. Almost blind, her hands and arms scarred, pitted, and burned by thirty years of radium emanations, she continues her work almost to the day of her death, caused in part by that very element which she had released for the use of mankind.

Rarely—increasingly rarely—a book appears which reconciles us to belonging to the human race. Here is one.

A Review of *Abraham Lincoln, The Prairie Years*

(CARL SANDBURG)[1]

by STUART PRATT SHERMAN

LINCOLN, unlike the Father of his Country, left no classicized image for our iconoclastic and Rodinesque biographers to shatter. One has always been able to say of him that his hair was rumpled, his feet large, his mouth crooked or his stock ill-adjusted without ruffling the feelings of his admirers or raising suspicion of treasonable designs again the Republic.

When his Virginian grandfather and his neighbors followed Boone into Kentucky and took to wearing moccasins and buckskin shirts, eighteenth-

[1] From *Books*, February 7, 1926. By permission of the New York *Herald Tribune*.

century decorum was doomed and the Roman dignity of the Washingtons and Adamses went glimmering. Old Hickory Jackson smoked a corncob pipe in the White House. Zachary Taylor's rough-necked soldiers, tanned in Texas and Mexico, called him Old Rough-and-Ready. Lincoln was a relatively late arrival in the new school of Western statesmen. While he was callousing his palms with rail-splitting, horny hands were already *de rigueur* for the leaders of a people who were blazing their way westward. In 1855 Whitman's "Shun delicatesse" was a maxim collected from practice and "Leaves of Grass" was a record, not a prophecy, of pioneers.

The traditional Lincoln may be reshaded at discretion, but in the main features he requires little revision. For he registered himself firmly and deeply upon modern realistic minds, supplemented by a photography which had not yet developed the "touching up" process. When Southern gentlemen declared that democracy was played out in Europe and in America, his own partner saw the six-foot-four rawboned Illinoisan pull his long legs off from his desk in the Springfield law office and, picking up his stovepipe hat and his faded umbrella, go out and save the Union and emancipate the slaves. Observers on the spot—Nicolay, Hay, and Herndon—set him down in his black-and-white habit as he lived, or in his shirttail, if they caught him mournfully mooning around the executive mansion at midnight. They emphasized rather than softened the angularity of his physical make and the trenchant and ineffaceable carving with which nature in tragic mood had delineated his character in his face.

As for the inward beauty of the man, his almost flawless exemplification of the Pauline *caritas,* his contemporaries saw him as clear and high—the clear-eyed of them—as we see him now. It was on the day of his death that Garfield declared him "the noblest and most generous spirit that ever put down a rebellion on this earth." And it was in the same year that a Cambridge Brahmin called him "the first American" and a Manhattanese chanted his dirge as "the sweetest, wisest soul of all my days and lands."

Perhaps nobody has read—certainly I have not—all the 2,680 books and pamphlets on Lincoln which are now listed in the Fish-Oakleaf bibliography. But the chief biographers speak respectfully of one another. The later ones gratefully acknowledge the substructure of Nicolay and Hay and Herndon, with some reservations regarding the latter's defective memory and his malice toward Mrs. Lincoln and a certain taste that he had for melodramatizing a situation. And my guess is that the general effect of at least 2,600 of these additions has been corroborative and cumulative, so that a reader who undertook to digest them all would be in a mood to appreciate the colossal Barnard statue, showing the familiar traits—the physical grotesqueness, the humor, the sadness, the gentleness and the strength—enormously magnified by the concurrence of many hands, yet right enough in the total impression of a home-grown national figure against the sky.

In recent years we heard a good deal, however, of a "Lincoln myth." When people use that phrase they ordinarily mean one of two things. They may mean to discredit democracy by intimating that Lincoln does not belong where Lord Charnwood recently ranked him, "among the great men of the earth." They may mean to insinuate that he was a vastly overrated man who was elected to the Presidency because of the deficiencies which he shared with the electorate. The idea inevitably attracts the paradoxer, but it is too thin to make a nourishing meal, like the ethereal soup made of the shadow of a pigeon which had died of starvation. It might be compared with the attempt of political enemies of Lincoln's lifetime to persuade the world that he was a third-rate country lawyer, a human gorilla, and a Uriah Heep. But I shall not discuss this notion because I hold with Lincoln that when a man shows himself wholly insensible to the force of facts there is nothing for it but to stop his mouth with a corncob.

The second and quite discussible sense in which people speak of a "Lincoln myth" is that the popular imagination conceives of him as far more uncouth, untutored and destitute of social advantages than he actually was. The notion that he was not an ill-cultivated man is supported by a generation of research, which has disclosed among other things his membership on a dance committee.

In 1896 and again in 1900 Ida M. Tarbell published the results of a wide and timely inquiry for fresh facts among hundreds of Lincoln's surviving contemporaries. Since that time there has been a vast and continuous interrogation of witnesses and a ransacking of newspapers and state and national archives by the Illinois State and the Chicago Historical societies and by countless individuals who have been producing detailed and critical studies of Lincoln's paternity and ancestry, his homes and his travels, his readings and education, his relations with women, his attitude on all subjects, his speaking tours in New England and elsewhere, the Lincoln-Douglas debates, the story-telling, the law practice, the record in the Illinois Legislature and in Congress, the national statesmanship, the warcraft, and the literary style.

Recent biographers—Lord Charnwood in his critical study of the statesman, 1916; Stephenson in his somewhat mystical "Lincoln" of 1922; Miss Tarbell in her fresh harvest of 1924, "In the Footsteps of Lincoln"; William E. Barton in his third considerable contribution, his two-volume "Life" of 1925, and Mr. Sandburg in 1926—concur in abandoning the attempt to enumerate all their sources; but all of them contribute fresh facts or stimulating interpretation or both, and all of them tend strongly toward the destruction of the second form of the "myth."

To put the matter briefly, Lincoln was not half so plain and simple and humble as he is made out when his encouraging rise from the log cabin is pictured to the Russian peasantry. It is only in a figurative sense that he can be considered a new man created of "sweet clay from the breast of the unexhausted West." Genealogical investigation has confirmed what his physiognomy revealed: that he was not of "poor white" stock. The strong sculpture of his head denoted "race," however derived; and now we are to think of his leadership of a company in the Black Hawk War as the expectable result of his "race," since he was the fifth captain in a line of Lincolns which runs back in seventeenth century Massachusetts.

His education may have lacked trimmings, what though he dabbled in poetry and at least looked into a Greek grammar; but he had disciplined himself long and strenuously in a masculine curriculum. He mastered grammar, logic, mathematics, surveying, oratory, debate and the law, not to speak of the Gospel, Shakespeare, Bunyan and Burns. From early manhood he was both politically and socially ambitious; he was early accepted in the best political society of the state; he married a wife with a temper, to be sure, but intelligent, ambitious and socially fit for cotillions and the Governor's ball.

By straight, hard thinking, square dealing, and a disposition admirably controlled yet eminently companionable and entertaining, he was a notable man twenty years before he was President. He was in excellent odor among his own people. He had done effective work in the Legislature and had made much more impression in Congress than used to be thought. Mr. Sandburg gives a lively account of his congressional terms. The dark horse that ran so hard in 1860 was less obscure than the schoolboy conceives. Well-informed persons knew him for a shrewd, cautious, conservative politician who had followed closely in the footsteps of Henry Clay; for the foremost lawyer in the West; for the ablest debater in the Whig party, tested in a contest with another Springfield lawyer who happened to be leading the Democratic party.

Carl Sandburg's big biography is wholly devoted to showing Lincoln in his times before he went to the White House. It may be considered as the latest synthesis after a generation of research. It is thoroughly well nourished on the enormous new Lincoln literature. It incorporates the new facts and includes the new lights and shadings. In addition Mr. Sandburg furnishes adequately the technical justification or "apology" for another book; he has had access to a long, quaint letter from Mrs. Lincoln to her husband; he has met with sixty-five unpublished letters and papers in Lincoln's handwriting; he has been able to illustrate copiously from rich collections of photographs, maps, etc.—and besides all that he was born in Lincoln's country and for thirty years or more, he tells us, he has had it in his heart to make "a certain portrait" of him.

The effect of this portrait is vital and stimulating. The composition of it is of an interesting complexity. One easily distinguishes certain dominant features of the treatment; an extraordinarily vivid and sympathetic account of Lincoln's early youth, the cabin life, the first school days, trips down the Mississippi, the humors of the grocery store period; full attention to Ann Rutledge, Mary Owens, and Mary Todd; a most elaborate collection of Lincoln's stories and the stories about Lincoln; and a very extensive study of Lincoln's law practice, bringing to our attention scores of the cases and the litigants whom he dealt with in Springfield or on circuit or in Chicago. It is a book, in the first place, full of people—though not to confusion.

But Mr. Sandburg has not taken his life work lightly, nor confined himself to the pictorial and narrative aspects of the biographical art. He has desired, I surmise, to make a book to "live in," and with that in mind he has gone back to 1809 and lived his way down to 1861, as concretely as possible, yet as responsively as possible with reference to all the economic, social, ethical, religious and political forces in all parts of the country which were driving toward the irrepressible conflict. Macaulay would have reveled in Mr. Sandburg's details.

Here are lists of the clothing for sale in a Springfield general store, bills of fare from western hotels, names of the principal varieties of whisky and other liquors available to guests, analysis of the fees received in a law office in the course of a year, analysis of advertising in a Springfield newspaper, enumeration of ox-carts and wagons moving towards the western border, market prices of slaves, value of the cotton crop, value of the negro population, value of New England manufactories, account of the way the millionaires of New York made their fortunes, analysis of Biblical, legal and constitutional arguments on the sacredness of property composition, the circulation of "Uncle Tom's Cabin," death of John Quincy Adams, reading of "Leaves of Grass" by Lincoln, the contents of Herndon's scientific library, Emerson's visit to Springfield. There are some big standing pools in this biography. There are times when one feels the drag of the years pretty heavily, but on the whole it is astonishing how well the streaming processional effect of crowded time is maintained.

The idea underlying this comprehensive study of Lincoln in "the prairie years" is, as it appears to me, rationalistic and liberal. To Mr. Sandburg, Lincoln is a hero, but he is a hero with a rational explanation. He was intelligibly and inevitably "produced" by his own times and circumstances and people. He was the resultant of their benigner impulses, happily disengaged from their baser ones. Lincoln was the man that "our people" are rather blindly and unconsciously striving to become. He is a hero, but a true folk hero; and the Great Mother who brought him forth is lovable, too.

Here, at any rate, is an opportunity to become better acquainted with Carl Sandburg as well as with Abraham Lincoln. They are good companions, the two of them, and mutually illuminating—Illinoisans both, plain people, admirable story tellers, rationalists, Jeffersonian democrats both, both nonprofessing Christians—Lincoln perhaps the completest specimen that has appeared in the Western hemisphere, and both poets withal, made melancholy at times and gentle-hearted by asking themselves what folk remember . . . "in the dust, in the cool tombs."

I am glad Carl Sandburg wrote this book. I like Lincoln the better for it and Carl Sandburg and myself and my neighbor. And that result, when all the ado about free territory and squatter sovereignty is forgotten smoke, that result is the living virtue that streams out of Lincoln forever.

A Review of *Brave Men*

(ERNIE PYLE)[1]

by VINCENT SHEEAN

"EVERYONE by now knows what I feel about the infantry," says Ernie. "I'm a rabid one-man movement bent on tracking down and stamping out everybody in the world who doesn't fully appreciate the common front-line soldier."

In that spirit he takes us with him on the invasion of Sicily, the Italian campaign and the invasion of France. It may be said that he pounds too hard on the one note—indeed it would be hard to find anybody on earth who does not fully appreciate the common front-line soldier. What Ernie really means, I think, is that he himself loves the front-line G.I. so passionately that he doubts if anybody else can attain the same intense feeling; and in this he may be either right or wrong, since that kind of polemic could have no possible conclusion.

At any rate, love is what he feels, and it is what he expresses. The phenomenon is national, because it is also love which reads him—the love of millions of mothers, fathers, loving and beloved objects of all sorts, separated from their sons and lovers, unable even to imagine the conditions under which those young men are giving battle on so many far-off fields. Ernie tells them what they want, more than anything else in the world, to know—that is, how is Joe? How does he eat, sleep, talk, live and fight?

With the utmost simplicity and directness Ernie tells them and suffuses the telling, somehow, with just that glow of tenderness and pathos in which all these millions of hearts at home awaited his coming. The inarticulate soldier is truly not able to write a letter home, although he spends his life trying; I have had to read large numbers of soldiers' letters at various times, and it was amazing to me to find out how even the cleverest and brightest of them were flummoxed by pen, ink and paper.

In one of our squadrons in Italy there was a man who wrote to his wife three or four times a day, and the letters were so nearly alike, and so totally inexpressive, that they could have been interchangeable. If his wife really wants to know anything about him, she has to read Ernie's column; and this is true of millions throughout the United States. Consequently Ernie has become the answer to a real national problem on the home front.

On the other front—the dangerous one—he occupies a position which is *sui generis* and not to be compared with any other, military or civil. Everybody above the rank of sergeant is a little bit afraid of him, because his fierce

[1] From the New York *Post*. By permission of the author and the *Post*.

protective passion for the enlisted man has made him quick to detect (or even to imagine) coldness or indifference to the efforts and conditions of the soldiers.

Among the soldiers themselves he is not only the most popular writer, but I think quite probably the most popular man, in the world today. This is not based upon his writing at all—for months at a time the army may not see what he writes, except as sent from home—but upon, first, his unique role as the living link with family and friends in the United States, and, second, his truly extraordinary personality. The boys became aware of him in Africa during the winter of 1942-1943, even if they had never read anything of his, because their letters from home began to be full of references to his column or clippings from it.

Then, when they asked "Who is this Ernie Pyle?", there he was—right beside them, with them in their ditches, next to them in the mess line, a shy and gentle soul who treated the least among them with a kind of deference. Other war correspondents, constantly rushing about after news, flitting in and out of places in airplanes, never staying anywhere very long—"following the story," as they say—were in a totally different category. Ernie was not interested in news; he was interested in the boys; and his time was completely his own. Thus he could spend weeks in a single infantry company if he chose to do so, and by doing precisely that kind of thing he has left behind him, through the whole army, units of every description to whom he is an object of unique affection and esteem.

This is a perfectly sincere and quintessentially true phenomenon. Ernie has not done this to make money or for any other extrinsic reason; he has done it because it is the law of his nature, because he was moved by—indeed created by—the love of this country for its sons.

What he writes is no more open to ordinary literary criticism than are the *Fioretti* of St. Francis of Assisi, whom, indeed, he also resembles in other ways. Those *Fioretti*, if you remember, were made up by the followers of St. Francis, and tell the stories which enchanted the mind of the Middle Ages —simple, touching stories of how the rich young man espoused My Lady Poverty, and "loved and rejoiced in all God's creatures." Condensed and hardened into concentrated art, they make a notable part of the eleventh canto of Dante's *Paradiso,* but in themselves they have no more to do with literature than has the song of the woodthrush or a cradlesong hummed at twilight.

Ernie's columns are of this kind, and go straight to the hearts of millions of people at the present moment. What they may be five years from now, when all the reverse-of-the-shield writing and thinking may be expected, it is impossible to say. I think that out of so much love something will remain, even at a period when these boys themselves, who are its object, will be carrying their world into the inevitable anti-sentimental, anti-romantic disillusionment.

Certainly nobody up to now has conveyed more exactly what the conditions of our men in these campaigns have been. And there are flashes, throughout, of a much larger comprehension: of something Ernie does not even want to write about now but understands just the same. Such a moment comes early in this book, as he is describing the convoy to Sicily.

"Then darkness enveloped the whole American armada," he says. "Not a pinpoint of light showed from those hundreds of ships as they surged on through the night toward their destiny, carrying across the ageless and indifferent sea tens of thousands of young men, fighting for . . . for . . . well, at least for each other."

A Review of the Film—
Story of GI Joe [1]
by MANNY FARBER

"STORY of GI Joe" is a long, hard, relentless fiction film based on Ernie Pyle's reports of the fighting in North Africa and Italy. Its aim is to show life in the infantry with all the integrity it can—the physical discomfort, the stupor induced by the killing and wounding, the hopelessness, and the malevolence against the conditions of a life that keeps the infantryman constantly humiliated and wretched. It is firmer about its feeling and its concept than any other Hollywood movie has been about anything in years. It has assimilated the whole lesson of the war documentary, which has shown the advantages of truth and some of the techniques for making the truth eloquent in a movie; and as a consequence differs vitally from any recent Hollywood movie. It is very intelligent about the kind of working-class Americans it deals with. Its director, William Wellman ("Public Enemy," "Wild Boys of the Road," "Oxbow Incident") is very able at getting this American's surface hardness, withdrawal, pride, harshness and independence; and he is especially good when he has a group of men in close contact and speech.

The writing, as well as the direction, constantly shuns the romanticisms that have colored almost every other war film. Nobody talks about the war, either as an aim, or as a matter of beating an enemy; in general they seem too tired to talk, and when they do (about rain, mud, work, sex, discomfort) it is in shorthand, avoiding the obvious, which includes every great question like the danger of death and the separation from everybody they love. The men cast as these soldiers (Robert Mitchum, Freddie Steele and Wally Cassell have the principal roles as Captain, Sergeant and Italian-American private) look literally tough enough to have got through the war and don't look any-

[1] From *The New Republic*, August 13, 1945. By permission of the author.

thing like actors. Instead of entertaining you with heroic battle action, the script skips most of the battles in order to show the effects on the men of the stupefying exhaustion, of the death of friends, of the maddening consciousness that nothing they personally endure in battle is going to help their personal situation. One important scene is shown—that in which two Americans adroitly maneuver a victory from two Nazis in a church—and it is so managed that killing is made a hard, real physical fact, and killing in a church made to hold the entire question of war.

The movie has no plot in the sense of a novel or play or the usual movie, but produces an effect like that of a string of newspaper reports on the career of one company of soldiers during the time they were accompanied by Ernie Pyle (who is played by Burgess Meredith). It is the only Hollywood biography I know that presents the hero in a believable relationship to the events and the other characters. Pyle appears as little as possible, and is shown as a self-effacing unparticipating observer, who talks like the soldiers and as little as they do. Besides his humility the movie manages to convey beautifully his iron-cast refusal to trespass on other lives and especially on the tragic parts of those lives; it also conveys some of Pyle's horror of war (most eloquently expressed in his hostile, exploding manner of typing), and starts to express his fatalism but unfortunately doesn't drive it home. The most moving part of Meredith's acting is his projection of the slight, narrow movements of a frail man who seems by temperament utterly unsuited to infantry life—this is done best during a muddy march when Pyle is shown helplessly sitting in a pool of water, conscious of his own weakness and with his fastidiousness overwhelmed. Meredith on the whole seems to me too cuddly and puppyish, the photography makes him look too cute and toylike, and there is a synthetic note in every word of his slow drawl. Freddie Steele's acting seems to me as good as it could possibly be; I liked the casting and acting of Robert Mitchum and of Dorothy Cooney as a nurse; the characterization of the Italian-American is inspired on all counts, including Wellman's and Cassell's.

"GI Joe" is actually a story-film version of "San Pietro," which was a deeper and more moving film. The first third of "GI Joe" is contrived and synthetic and not very well done, and only in the stretch showing the first activity in a just-conquered village does it achieve the breathtaking reality, fullness of detail and sharp effect from shot to shot that all of "San Pietro" has.

But whatever it lacks in grandeur, depth and tragedy and formal beauty, Wellman's is one of the only movies in years that says just about all it has to say, and drives it home with real cinematic strength.

A Review of the Film—*The Grapes of Wrath* [1]
by JOHN MOSHER

Out from California now comes "The Grapes of Wrath," the epic of starvation. With a majesty never before so constantly sustained on any screen, the film never for an instant falters. Its beauty is of the sort found in the art of Burchfeld, Benton, and Curry, as the landscape and people involved belong to the world of these painters. Its visual qualities, too, can be traced back through the history of the movies; the best of the past has been used, every lesson learned. Thus there are moments when we see a long figure silhouetted against the horizon as in the old films which aspired to impress. It was a stunt that was impressive then, and it is still impressive. Again there are moments in "The Grapes of Wrath" so direct and simple that they are like excerpts from a fine newsreel. That, too, is right. Or again, the camera seems to pause in the style of the Russian films, and we are given what is almost a series of stills. Faces are brought forward, out from the huge panorama, and held a moment, close and enlarged—the faces of hungry children, work-racked old men and women—silent and unmoving before us. Such a method, as here employed, does not slow down the film as it has often done in Soviet pictures. John Ford has kept his pace swift, and when familiar approaches to his subject have been essential, he has made them as fresh as though he had been the first to note the dramatic value of that man placed against the sky. He showed what he could do in "The Informer," and he has gone beyond that in "The Grapes of Wrath."

The script he had to work from is in itself a tremendous success. Nunnally Johnson must have found the Steinbeck novel no kindergarten job to adapt for the movies. It was long, outspoken, and, being a best-seller, something sacred. Its scandalized, delighted, and authoritative readers, many of whom refused to find even any monotony in the original discursive and iterative chronicle, were loyally ready to jump on a digression. From the moment it was heard that the book was to be screened, appreciative admirers wondered how the true force of the dialogue could be handled with the propriety requisite for screen delicacy, and, above all, how the odd dietary incident which Steinbeck devised as the shock of his conclusion could be managed. The hegira of the Joads has been abbreviated, of course, but the story of it is fully given. From the first glimpse we have of Tom coming down the dusty Oklahoma road, we are moved straight to the world of the Okies; though without reference to either digestive or procreative processes, the language manages to be virile; Mr. Johnson keeps his characters buttoned up but human. And,

[1] From *The New Yorker*, February 3, 1940. By permission of the editor and the author.

perhaps with more force than the book, the film closes on Ma Joad's words: "We're the people that live. Can't nobody wipe us out. Can't nobody lick us. We'll go on forever. We're the people."

Ma was the great characterization in the book. Holding together her whole family in her desperate effort to survive, she was most definitely a clarified personality—not a mere type, not, so to speak, a social problem. She alone might be called Steinbeck's creation in the novel. Jane Darwell, who plays Ma, has been long in the theatre and in pictures, and now she suffers from the very experience she has had. Here her expertness does not stand her in good stead. Competent she is, yet she never quite frees her performance from the suggestion of the theatre. Actually this does not matter in an appraisal of the film as much as might be thought. This is no scenario for stars. Individuals are lost against the grandeur of the landscape or in the huge mass movements of many people. The extras count as much as the feature players.

Henry Fonda's Tom Joad stands out at times in the vast assemblage, and occasional specific gestures or exclamations draw our eyes and ears to the Grampa or Granma of Charley Grapewin and Zeffie Tilbury, to the Rosasharn of Dorris Bowdon, the Connie of Eddie Quinlan, the Casy of John Carradine, the Pa Joad of Russell Simpson, and the Muley of John Qualen. Mostly, though, we think of the film in terms of groups, the family on the truck, the family gathered around Grampa's grave, the children in the store in front of the candy, the other children staring at food—something to eat—in the camp. It is a great film of the dust plains, the highways, the camps, of the sky above, and of a nameless, evicted people.

EXPOSITION

EXPOSITION

Exposition, as you doubtless know, means "explaining." If it is good exposition, it gives pleasure to the reader—the pleasure of understanding something that was more or less obscure before, or of understanding another person's view on the matter. Even when the information is false or the interpretation doubtful, the clarity, sincerity, and taste of its presentation may give pleasure. One may not agree with President Hutchins on football gate-receipts and what to do about them, or with Newman on the infallibility of the pope, but here are the views of two eminent minds presented with great clarity and force. The main purpose of exposition is practical: to widen the reader's knowledge and understanding. Narrative, description, humor may be introduced to give flavor, or to illustrate a point, but solid information or trenchant interpretation there must be. Whether we have a recipe for broiling chicken, a definition of fascism, a complete report on Boulder Dam, or a textbook on philosophy, no matter how charmingly written, it must be judged largely by its practical value, its fidelity to fact, and its clarity.

Of the expositions which follow, some are rich in literary flavor, some less so. But all have value as the presentation of stimulating facts and ideas, and all afford examples of clarity and system. There are three things you may do with them: read them for the pleasure which any intelligent creature takes in absorbing fresh information and significant ideas; examine them to see whether the information and the ideas are sound and applicable to your own intellectual and practical life; study the literary expression as a model for your own writing. Here is the most practical type of literature, for it should have appreciable consequences in your own action and it is the simplest instrument for influencing the actions of others.

You will do well to observe not only the clarity and vigor of expression, but also the logical organization of the material. In connection with certain addresses and articles, such as those of Robinson, Meiklejohn, and Huxley, it will be profitable to study the divisions of the topic, the introduction, the transitions, the conclusion, the paragraphing. This study of structure, which the rapid reader misses, is essential for the full appreciation of the expository art and its successful practice.

Riveters [1]

by THE EDITORS OF FORTUNE

THE MOST curious fact about a riveter's skill is that he is not one man but four: "heater," "catcher," "bucker-up," and "gun-man." The gang is the unit. Riveters are hired and fired as gangs, work in gangs, and learn in gangs. If one member of a gang is absent on a given morning, the entire gang is replaced. A gang may continue to exist after its original members have all succumbed to slippery girders or the business end of a pneumatic hammer or to a foreman's zeal or merely to the temptations of life on earth, and the skill of the gang will continue with it. Men overlap each other in service and teach each other what they know. The difference between a gang which can drive 525 inch-and-an-eighth rivets in a working day and a gang which can drive 250 is a difference of coördination and smoothness. You learn how not to make mistakes and how not to waste time. You learn how to heat a rivet and how not to overheat it, how to throw it accurately but not too hard, how to drive it and when to stop driving it, and precisely how much you can drink in a cold wind or a July sun without losing your sense of the width and balance of a wooden plank. And all these things, or most of them, an older hand can tell you. . . .

The actual process of riveting is simple enough—in description. Rivets are carried to the job by the rivet boy, a riveter's apprentice whose ambition is to replace one of the members of the gang—which one, he leaves to luck. The rivets are dumped into a keg beside a small coke furnace. The furnace stands on a platform of loose boards roped to steel girders which may or may not have been riveted. If they have not been riveted there will be a certain amount of play in the temporary bolts. The furnace is tended by the heater or passer. He wears heavy clothes and gloves to protect him from the flying sparks and intense heat of his work, and he holds a pair of tongs about a foot-and-a-half long in his right hand. When a rivet is needed, he whirls the furnace blower until the coke is white-hot, picks up a rivet with his tongs, and drives it into the coals. His skill as a heater appears in his knowledge of the exact time necessary to heat the steel. If he overheats it, it will flake, and the flakes will permit the rivet to turn in its hole. And a rivet which gives in its hole is condemned by the inspectors.

When the heater judges that his rivet is right, he turns to face the catcher, who may be above or below him or fifty or sixty feet away on the same floor level with the naked girders between. There is no means of handing the rivet over. It must be thrown. And if the floor beams of the floor above have

[1] Reprinted from *Fortune*, Oct. 1930. Copyright, *Time*, Inc., 1930.

been laid so that a flat trajectory is essential, it must be thrown with considerable force. The catcher is therefore armed with a smallish, battered tin can, called a cup, with which to catch the red-hot steel. Various patented cups have been put upon the market from time to time but they have made little headway. Catchers prefer the ancient can.

The catcher's position is not exactly one which a sportsman catching rivets for pleasure would choose. He stands upon a narrow platform of loose planks laid over needle beams and roped to a girder near the connection upon which the gang is at work. There are live coils of pneumatic tubing for the rivet gun around his feet. If he moves more than a step or two in any direction, he is gone, and if he loses his balance backward he is apt to end up at street level without time to walk. And the object is to catch a red-hot iron rivet weighing anywhere from a pound to a pound and a half and capable, if he lets it pass, of drilling an automobile radiator or a man's skull 500 feet below as neatly as a shank of shrapnel. Why more rivets do not fall is the great mystery of skyscraper construction. The only reasonable explanation offered to date is the reply of an erector's foreman who was asked what would happen if a catcher on the Forty Wall Street job let a rivet go by him around the lunch hour. "Well," said the foreman, "he's not supposed to."

There is practically no exchange of words among riveters. Not only are they averse to conversation, which would be reasonable enough in view of the effect they have on the conversation of others, but they are averse to speech in any form. The catcher faces the heater. He holds his tin can up. The heater swings his tongs, releasing one handle. The red iron arcs through the air in one of those parabolas so much admired by the stenographers in the neighboring windows. And the tin can clanks.

Meanwhile the gun-man and the bucker-up have prepared the connection —aligning the two holes, if necessary, with a drift pin driven by a sledge or by a pneumatic hammer—and removed the temporary bolts. They, too, stand on loose-roped boards with the column or the beam between them. When the rivet strikes the catcher's can, he picks it out with a pair of tongs held in his right hand, knocks it sharply against the steel to shake off the glowing flakes, and rams it into the hole, an operation which is responsible for his alternative title of sticker. Once the rivet is in place, the bucker-up braces himself with his dolly bar, a short heavy bar of steel, against the capped end of the rivet. On outside wall work he is sometimes obliged to hold on by one elbow with his weight out over the street and the jar of the riveting shaking his precarious balance, and the gun-man lifts his pneumatic hammer to the rivet's other end.

The gun-man's work is the hardest work, physically, done by the gang. The hammers in use for steel construction are supposed to weigh around thirty pounds and actually weigh about thirty-five. They must not only be held against the rivet end but held there with the gun-man's entire strength, and for a period of forty to fifty seconds. (A rivet driven too long will develop a collar inside the new head.) And the concussion to the ears and the arms during that period is very great. The whole platform shakes and the vibration can be felt down the column thirty stories below. It is common practice for the catcher to push with the gun-man and for the gun-man and the bucker-up to pass the gun back and forth between them when the angle is difficult.

The weight of the guns is one cause, though indirect, of accidents. The rivet set, which is the actual hammer at the point of the gun, is held in place, when the gun leaves the factory, by clips. Since the clips increase the weight of the hammer, it is good riveting practice to knock them off against the nearest column and replace them with a hank of wire. But wire has a way of breaking, and when it breaks, there is nothing to keep the rivet set and the pneumatic piston itself from taking the bucker-up or the catcher on the belt and knocking him into the next block.

Riveters work ordinarily eight hours a day at a wage of $15.40 a day. They are not employed in bad or slippery weather, and they are not usually on the regular pay roll of the erectors, but go from job to job following a foreman whom they like. There is no great future for a riveter. . . . It would perhaps be more accurate to say that a riveter's future is not bright at all. The rates charged for compensation insurance are generally accepted as the best barometer of risk. Starrett Brothers and Eken fix, in their insurance department, a rate of $23.45 per $100 of pay for erecting and painting steel structures. Rates of other companies run to $30 per $100 of pay. The only higher rate is for wrecking work. The next lower rate ($15.08) is for building raising. Masonry is $6.07 and carpentry $4.39. Figures on industrial accidents published by the United States Department of Labor bear the same connotation. In one year the frequency of accidents, per 1,000,000 hours' exposure, was 228.9 for fabricators and erectors as against 54 for general building.

๛๛๛๛๛๛๛๛๛๛๛๛๛๛๛๛๛๛๛๛๛

Three Kinds of Hash[1]

by WILLIAM RHODE

H ASH DOES not just grow like Topsy; on the contrary, if its preparation is not a careful blending of ingredients you will have nothing more than a mess.

When it comes to hash, the first thought is: Corned beef hash. For that let us turn to Mr. Charles Ranhofer, who as kitchen dictator at the old "Delmonico's" in New York should be considered the best authority on one, of the finest culinary delights of the United States.

[1] From William Rhode, *Of Cabbages and Kings* (1938). By permission of the author.

CORNED BEEF HASH

To two pounds of cold corned beef finely minced, one pound and a half of freshly boiled diced potatoes are added. The corned beef should not be chopped in the meat grinder and the potatoes should not be mashed. Sauté two finely chopped onions and one green pepper in butter, and mix with the corned beef and the potatoes. Season generously with pepper and sparingly with salt. As additional seasoning use one teaspoon of English mustard, stirred to a paste with a few drops of water, and two soupspoons of the juice from pickled watermelon rind. Moisten the whole with sufficient corned beef broth to be able to form the hash into the shape of a pointed bread loaf. In a very hot cast iron pan heat two soupspoons of good lard, fry the hash loaf quickly on all sides to a deep, good brown, and finally place the pan in a moderate oven for half an hour. Serve with tomato ketchup or black walnut ketchup.

So much for the maestro's instructions. I have had excellent results by merely frying the hash in the pan without finishing it in the oven, but that is just one man's opinion.

For many years there existed in Paris a combination which was predestined to produce really good hash. In a "Russian" restaurant which was owned by a German, Armenian food was served almost exclusively. All the food was prepared under the guidance of an amazing character who claimed to be a Turk and also claimed to have been personal chef de cuisine of Amanullah, the former Emir of Afghanistan. Every Wednesday a small group of gourmets would gather to enjoy the former "royal" chef's masterpiece and listen to his weird tales of that strange country beyond the Khyber Pass, because he could cook the best

LAMB HASH

The left overs of a roast leg of lamb are cut into two inch dice and put into a heavy skillet with one tablespoon of lard. Add to this two soupspoons of the lamb gravy per pound of meat, one teaspoon of the mint sauce and one soupspoon of port wine. Heat the whole over a very small fire without actually boiling it. Cut some sour apples into quarters, peel, remove the core and seeds, place in a small pan, sprinkle with brown sugar, and cook them in a medium oven till soft. When everything is ready arrange the meat on a hot platter, place the apples on top of the meat, and pour the port wine gravy over all. Try this some time with stewed corn and you will agree that it doesn't make any difference whether the "royal" chef's stories were true or not.

Another delicious version of lamb hash, although entirely different from the above, is that grand Scotch dish called "Shepherd's pie." Many seem to be the ways of preparing it, and surely the great clans of Scotland must have feuded over the supremacy of their womenfolks' prowess in making Shepherd's pie. If they didn't they should have. It's a worthy cause.

The following recipe hails from one of the chefs of the "Royal Squadron," the world's most exclusive Yacht Club; but what's much more important, it is excellent.

SHEPHERD'S PIE

Have your butcher grind up together one pound of boned shoulder of lamb and one half pound of not too lean pork. In a skillet that has a well fitting cover, heat one soupspoon of lard and sauté one chopped onion. Add the ground meat and two cut up tomatoes. Cut the tomatoes right over the skillet so as not to lose any juice. Season with salt, pepper, and a pinch of cayenne pepper. Turn the flame low, cover the skillet, and let stew in its own juice for 40 minutes. Do not add water. In a separate pot boil a generous handful of finely diced carrots. While these two are busy bubbling, you will have to mess up a third pot by boiling eight large potatoes and mashing them. Butter a large or two small fireproof deep dishes —glass or earthenware are the best—and line with a thin layer of the mashed potatoes like a lower pie crust; now fill the pie with the meat and the boiled carrots, and cover with a top layer of mashed potatoes. Place this in the oven (400) and let the top brown. Remove from the oven and with a thin knife cut into the top a small hole deep enough for a funnel to be thrust through to the meat filling. Pour through the funnel the contents of a two ounce glass of sherry, reseal the hole, and return the dish to the oven, where it remains for 5 minutes with the fire still on, and for another 5 minutes with the fire extinguished. If you have a coal stove just open the oven door for the last five minutes.

Why an Airplane Flies [1]

by WOLFGANG LANGEWIESCHE

WHAT makes an airplane fly is not its engine nor its propeller. Nor is it, as many people think, some mysterious knack of the pilot, nor some ingenious gadget inside. What makes an airplane fly is simply its shape. This may sound absurd, but gliders do fly without engines and model airplanes do fly without pilots. As for the insides of an airplane, they are disappointing for they are mostly hollow. No, what keeps an airplane up is its shape—the impact of the air upon its shape. Whittle that shape out of wood, or cast it out of iron, or fashion it, for that matter, out of chocolate and throw the thing into the air. It will behave like an airplane. It will *be* an airplane.

This—that its shape is what counts—is what makes the airplane so beautiful. It also makes it easy to understand. You don't have to open it up and look at "the works" inside as one has to do with a watch, a refrigerator or an automobile. An airplane's outside appearance is its "works." If you want to understand it, simply have a look.

Look at the wing. It holds the airplane up entirely by its shape. A wing is nothing but an air deflector, curved so and set at such an angle that it will catch the air and push it down. The air, resisting, pushes back up against the wing's bottom surface and that gives it some lift. At the same time— and this is more important—the wing also creates a lack of air on its top surface because of the way it is curved there. Thus it sucks air down from

[1] From *Life*, May 17, 1943. Courtesy of *Life Magazine*. Copyright, *Time*, Inc.

above. That air, resisting, sucks back upward on the wing's top surface and this is what gives the wing most of its lift.

And that's all there is to a wing! Man's greatest invention since the wheel and the boat—the thing that carries weights through thin air—is just a shape. As for the exact shape that will make the best wing, a whole science is concerned with that—aerodynamics. What counts most is the wing's cross section—what you would see if you sawed off the tips. Some 15,000 different shapes have been tested in the world's laboratories. It has been found that the wing with the highly arched top surface and a concave, scooped-out under surface will carry the most weight. The early airplanes had that kind of wing. But a more nearly streamlined cross section will carry good weight too and slide through the air more easily. Hence modern fast airplanes' wings don't have that hollowed-out under surface. But all such engineering refinements don't change the main idea of the wing: a wing is a shape that holds itself up by acting on the air.

It is simple. If flight seems just the same a little miraculous and, to many people, still a little unsound, it is not because the natural law involved is at all strange. The law is the old one of action and reaction: if you push against *anything,* that thing resists and pushes back against you. As the gun pushes the bullet forward, the bullet kicks the gun backward making it recoil. What seems so strange about flying is merely that the thing we work against is air. And air is strange stuff. Because we cannot see it, we think of it as a nothing. Because we cannot pinch it between our fingers, we think of it as empty space. And thus an airplane seems to sit up there in empty space, held up by nothing.

Actually, air is real stuff, just as real as water. It has density and body. It is a thick and slightly sticky fluid, molasses-like, though very thin molasses. Its tendency to stick to the skin of an airplane causes much headache to the engineers. It has weight. A cubic yard of air (a bathtubful) weighs about 2 lb. Thus if we could only see the air, all the mystery would go out of flying at once. We could then see the fierce attack with which the wing smashes into that stuff. We could see the terrific downward wallop which the wing gives to thousands of pounds of air every minute. And we could see that everywhere in the wake of an airplane, the air is in downward flow and keeps swirling and eddying for many minutes when the airplane itself is already miles farther on.

The magic shape of the wing can't have effect, of course, unless it keeps continually attacking new air. If an airplane is to keep flying, it must keep moving. It can't ever stop or even slow down much. If it slows down it sinks; if it slows down too much it sinks too fast. The wings then can no longer catch the air at the proper angle. The lift goes out of the wings like air out of a punctured tire; the airplane drops. That is what is called a stall. A "tailspin" is nothing but a fancy stall. One wing makes lift and wants to fly, the other wing is stalled and keeps dropping. Between them they twist the airplane down in a corkscrew motion. Normally, pulling back on the stick makes the airplane go up. But in the spin or stall, the harder the pilot pulls back, the more obstinately the airplane goes down. The more it goes down, the harder the pilot's self-preservation instinct makes him pull back on the stick. The way to recover from a stall or spin is to get the stick forward, diving at the ground to pick up new speed. But that takes courage. A stall or spin means quite a drop—dozens of feet in a Cub, thousands of feet in a bomber. It is because a wing needs speed that airplanes need big airports. They can't fly until they have gathered speed, and they dare not slow up again until they are firmly on the ground. It is because a wing needs speed that the first rule of the art of piloting, contrary to all common sense, is this: keep your speed. If you want to be safe, *don't* go slow, go fast. When in doubt, speed up. . . .

There are many ways to keep an airplane going. A motor and propeller are not the only way. The gliders, for instance, are pulled by a rope, the rope in turn being pulled by another airplane or by an automobile, or even (as was done in Russia) by galloping horses. Any airplane can also always maintain its speed simply by nosing down a little and coasting. This is called a glide and is the reason why an airplane doesn't crash simply because its engine quits. But a glide means a steady loss of altitude and the airplane must eventually land. Sometimes an airplane can glide in an updraft of air and, though it noses downward, the updraft may at the same time carry it up, much as a piece of paper is sometimes lifted high above the roofs. This sort of gliding is called soaring and is the most delightful of all types of flight. But updrafts are hard to find and unreliable and it takes a slow, light glider to stay in them. The sensible and businesslike way to keep the airplane going is to give it its own source of power, an engine and propeller.

Propellers are weird, doubly so, because at work they become invisible. They whirl too fast. Hence many people don't understand what a propeller really does. Some think that the propeller pulls the airplane always upward as well as forward and that this is really what keeps an airplane up. This is not true. The propeller drives the airplane forward, the wings take care of the lift. In a blimp the propeller drives the ship forward and the balloon takes care of the lift. Again, some people think that the propeller's purpose is to blow air against the wings and that this is how the wings develop lift. That isn't true either. The propeller does throw a blast of air backward, but the engineers would be only too happy to keep that air from hitting any part of the airplane. It is a nuisance. Moreover, the wings don't need a blast of air. If the airplane keeps moving they get plenty of air to work on.

And that's what the propeller does: it keeps the airplane moving forward. It doesn't lift, it drives. Mount one on a sled and it will drive the sled; mount one on a hydroplane and it will drive the hydroplane. And if you mounted one on a trolley car, it would run the trolley car.

The propeller, just like the wing, works upon the air by shape. Each propeller blade is nothing but an "air foil," a shape much like an airplane wing to catch and make use of the air. In fact, a propeller blade's cross section has exactly the same curves as a wing's cross section. The propeller blade catches the air and throws it backward and by so doing gets a forward force.

Because the propeller is driven by a motor, it is almost the same thing as an electric fan; the two look slightly different only because they are used differently. In the propeller you don't use the backward blast of air, but you use the kick and you allow it to make plenty of noise. The electric fan is designed not to make too much noise; you use the blast of air and you don't use the "kick-back.' In fact, most people don't know that an electric fan has a kick just like a propeller. But just set your electric fan on a toy wagon and watch it propel.

How big a propeller, how powerful an engine does it take to keep the airplane going fast enough so that it will fly? The amazing, the at first quite incredible thing is that it takes very little force. A one-man glider weighing 500 lb. can be pulled through the air by a force of only 25 lb. A child in the rumble seat of the tow car could easily hold the tow rope in his hand and keep it flying. For ordinary airplanes, the figures are only a little less favorable; to keep a 10,000-lb. airplane flying takes only about 1,000 lb. of propeller pull.

The force that holds an airplane back, the force which the propeller has to overcome to keep the airplane going is called the drag. Like everything else about the airplane it depends on the shape, and hence you can see it, if you know where to look.

The wing itself makes a drag: the plowing down of air requires force. This drag—the price which we must pay for lift—is called the induced drag, and it depends much on the shape of the wing. A narrow wing of long span catches much air, gives it a gentle push and requires little force. A broad wing of short span catches less air, gives it more of a push and requires more force. This is why patrol bombers and other long-distance airplanes have long narrow wings; they get more miles per gallon that way. That is also why gliders have long narrow wings; they glide more easily. Wingtip shape, too, has much to do with this induced drag: on a square wing, the tip plows too hard, and some of the rest not hard enough, a tapered wing works more easily, slides more easily.

Another drag is skin friction: the air, molasses-like, clings to the skin, and the airplane can't move without dragging a lot of air around. An airplane actually won't dust itself off in flight; if it goes up dusty, it comes down still dusty. The reason is that next to the skin, the air hardly slides at all.

That's why it is important that the shape of an airplane be absolutely smooth: in an airliner or bomber even the tiny roughness of the rivet heads on the skin causes a drag force of a couple of hundred pounds. Racers and soaring gliders are polished with a cloth before each flight. Skin friction is the reason why some airplanes are of odd shape. In very fast airplanes, the

designer sometimes will rather have a less efficient shape simply because it
will give him less total skin surface and hence less friction.

But the biggest thing that holds the airplane back is so obvious that one
doesn't think of it: the many parts of the airplane that are not wing. The
wing is the airplane's essential part—it makes the lift. Yet an airplane also
needs space for passengers and cargo, a pilot seat with windshield, a radiator,
a radio mast. It needs a landing gear, perhaps struts and wires to stiffen the
wings. It needs tail fins.

Each of these parts causes a drag. It takes definite force to push each
of them through the air, for the air, sticky dense stuff, resists their passage.
But unlike the drag of the wings, drag of those parts is not associated with
the making of lift. It is pure evil. It is useless and bears the contemptuous
name of parasite drag.

The airplane is shaped to keep parasite drag small. Hence, that shark-
like look—sharks, too, are shaped to move through a dense fluid fast. And
hence all the little things that aren't there. The most remarkable thing about
a modern airplane is what you *don't* see, and what in older airplanes you used
to see. The engine is hidden under a smooth cowl, pilot and passengers are
inside, the landing gear is tucked away in flight, the wings stick out without
any struts and wires. Just as those things are out of your sight, so they are
out of the way of the air, and can cause no drag. The dream ship of aero-
nautical engineers is the Flying Wing, the all-wing airplane that hasn't even
a fuselage any more. Everything has been pulled into the wing, and the
wing is all there is.

Those then, as every student pilot learns, are the four forces that act on
an airplane in flight: 1) weight pulls it down, but 2) lift of its wings holds
it up; 3) drag holds it back, but 4) pull of the propeller keeps it going. In
steady flight, the four forces balance and all is serene.

So wonderfully is the airplane shaped that in flight it will largely take
care of itself. It always wants to do the right thing, whatever is necessary
to keep itself flying. Many people think that piloting is a balancing stunt,
much like walking a tightrope. Actually, the art of piloting consists of about
nine-tenths of doing nothing and trusting the airplane. Many people think
that on the slightest lapse of the pilot's attention an airplane will go into a
spin. Actually, a stall or a spin is brought on only by heavy misuse of the
controls. Generally speaking, an airplane left to itself does not want to drop,
it wants to fly. A careless pilot sometimes leaves his airplane standing on the
airport with the engine idling while he goes for a cup of coffee—and it has
happened that such an airplane has run away, taken off and flown itself,
pilotless, for a couple of hours.

This uncanny stability is simply a matter of shape. Whenever anything
is wrong, the airplane by that very fact presents a different side of itself to
the onrushing air. Since its shape is designed with just that idea in mind,
the air will create on the new shape a new force, and the new force rights
the airplane.

One such stabilizing shape is the vertical fin on the tail. If a gust turns the airplane crosswise to its line of flight, so that it begins to move in the manner of a skidding car, the vertical fin thereby is turned broadside to the onrushing air and the tail is blown right back where it belongs.

Another such stabilizing refinement of shape is the dihedral angle, that V-like uptilt of the wings as viewed from in front. Let a gust of air try to capsize the airplane, say to the left. The moment it begins to slide off side-wise, the air begins to blow harder against its left side because the designer has tilted the wings at that angle. The air immediately lifts harder on the left wing, less hard on the right wing, and the airplane tries to right itself.

Of all the things that a well-shaped airplane will do, the cleverest is the way it keeps itself going forward, maintains that all-important speed. Suppose that the engine should suddenly quit. If the airplane then wanted to stop it would be dangerous, for without speed there can be no lift, and the ship would stall or spin. But the airplane does not want to stop. It wants to keep going. It noses down slightly and thus by coasting maintains its speed. The shapes that do this are the two horizontal fins on the tail. At first glance, they look like a pair of little wings holding up the small end of the fuselage while the big wings hold up the big end. Actually the horizontal tail fins hold the tail down. They do so partly because of the angle at which they are set, and partly because they are always flying in the down-wash of the air that comes from the wings. The wings themselves are set on the fuselage fairly far back so that the airplane is always a little nose heavy and always wants to go into a dive; and the only thing that keeps the airplane out of that dive is the down force on the tail fins. If the airplane slows up even by only a few m.p.h., the air rushes less hard against the tail fins. The down force fades out, the tail comes up, the nose goes down—and the airplane picks up new speed. The contrary is also true. If the airplane ever gathers speed because the nose drops, the excessive speed puts a powerful force on the tail fins. The tail goes down, the nose comes up and the airplane comes out of the descent all by itself.

Even the airplane's controls work by shape. When the pilot presses against stick or pedals, what he really does thereby is to bend his airplane's wings and tail out of shape. Then the air, hitting the new shape, creates a new force that makes the nose go up or down, or swings it right or left, or banks the wings. In the Wrights' early airplanes this was done by literally bending the structure. Today it is done by moving hinged rudderlike surfaces on the tail, known as the flippers and the rudder, and similar surfaces on the wings, called the ailerons. By putting backward pressure against his stick, the pilot deflects his flippers slightly upward. The air, hitting this sloping surface, blows the tail down and the nose comes up. By putting forward pressure on the stick, the pilot deflects the flippers downward. The air blows the tail up and the nose goes down. By pressing against the right pedal, the pilot deflects the rudder slightly to the right. The air hitting the rudder blows the tail to the left and the nose swings to the right. By holding the stick to the left, the pilot deflects both ailerons—one on each wing. The air then blows the right wing up and the left wing down, and the airplane banks to the left.

Because they work by shape, by the impact of flowing air on shape, an airplane's controls are not mechanical and positive like a car's, but fluid and soft; and they are full of little tricks. As every flying cadet soon finds out, smooth accurate control of an airplane is quite an art. The feel and the effectiveness of each control vary according to the airplane's speed. In fast flight, they feel firm and stiff and the airplane responds promptly. In a slow glide, they feel soft and "mushy" and the airplane is slow to respond. In a stall, the stick feels dead as if it were disconnected. And always, each control produces not only the desired main effect, but all sorts of annoying little by-effects as well. It is as if the gremlins had got at your car and had connected up the controls so that each time you stepped on the gas, the car wanted to turn left; each time you turned right, the brakes went on; each time you blew your horn, something threw out your clutch. Each time the pilot uses one control he thus must make small corrections also with some other control. If he holds the stick to the left, for instance, the air will blow the left wing down and the right wing up and the ship will bank to the left, as it should. But at the same time, the nose slews around to the right, as it should not. This is because the air, blowing against the slightly distorted wings, blows the right wing back and lets the left wing slide forward. Thus the pilot must accompany his hand work on the stick with just the right amount of corrective foot work on his pedals, or else the ship will slip or skid.

Many hours are spent at flying schools practicing this "coordination" between the controls. More cadets are washed out for inability to coordinate smoothly enough than for any other cause. It is true that the shape of an airplane will keep it up, keep it going forward, and keep it right side up. But flying simply by its own shape, it will fly errantly, staggering through the sky in random swoops, and to no purpose. If it is to fly purposefully, the pilot must make it go where he wants it to go—and that is the art of flying. The less spectacular a flight may look, the more skillful it probably is. Simply to make an airplane come down from the mile-high, mile-wide spaces and settle down precisely on a few yards of runway is a feat that requires endless hours of practice and training. It is actually much easier to loop the loop.

Among expert pilots, simply to fly straight and level through jumpy air and flowing winds is considered one of the most telling tests of a man's flying ability. The airplane that moves in a long straight line across your sky does so not by its own will, but only because a skilled pilot keeps it flying straight by a finely coordinated play of his controls, making small, almost imperceptible changes in his airplane's shape, that are much like the small steadying motions of the tail and the wing of the sea gull as it soars.

How to Mark a Book [1]

by MORTIMER J. ADLER

You know you have to read "between the lines" to get the most out of anything. I want to persuade you to do something equally important in the course of your reading. I want to persuade you to "write between the lines." Unless you do, you are not likely to do the most efficient kind of reading.

I contend, quite bluntly, that marking up a book is not an act of mutilation but of love.

You shouldn't mark up a book which isn't yours. Librarians (or your friends) who lend you books expect you to keep them clean, and you should. If you decide that I am right about the usefulness of marking books, you will have to buy them. Most of the world's great books are available today, in reprint editions, at less than a dollar.

There are two ways in which one can own a book. The first is the property right you establish by paying for it, just as you pay for clothes and furniture. But this act of purchase is only the prelude to possession. Full ownership comes only when you have made it a part of yourself, and the best way to make yourself a part of it is by writing in it. An illustration may make the point clear. You buy a beefsteak and transfer it from the butcher's icebox to your own. But you do not own the beefsteak in the most important sense until you consume it and get it into your bloodstream. I am arguing that books, too, must be absorbed in your bloodstream to do you any good.

Confusion about what it means to *own* a book leads people to a false reverence for paper, binding, and type—a respect for the physical thing—the craft of the printer rather than the genius of the author. They forget that it is possible for a man to acquire the idea, to possess the beauty, which a great book contains, without staking his claim by pasting his bookplate inside the cover. Having a fine library doesn't prove that its owner has a mind enriched by books; it proves nothing more than that he, his father, or his wife, was rich enough to buy them.

There are three kinds of book owners. The first has all the standard sets and best-sellers—unread, untouched. (This deluded individual owns woodpulp and ink, not books.) The second has a great many books—a few of them read through, most of them dipped into, but all of them as clean and shiny as the day they were bought. (This person would probably like to make books his own, but is restrained by a false respect for their physical appearance.) The third has a few books or many—every one of them dog-

[1] From *The Saturday Review of Literature*, July 6, 1941. By permission of the author.

eared and dilapidated, shaken and loosened by continual use, marked and scribbled in from front to back. (This man owns books.)

Is it false respect, you may ask, to preserve intact and unblemished a beautifully printed book, an elegantly bound edition? Of course not. I'd no more scribble all over a first edition of "Paradise Lost" than I'd give my baby a set of crayons and an original Rembrandt! I wouldn't mark up a painting or a statue. Its soul, so to speak, is inseparable from its body. And the beauty of a rare edition or of a richly manufactured volume is like that of a painting or a statue.

But the soul of a book *can* be separated from its body. A book is more like the score of a piece of music than it is like a painting. No great musician confuses a symphony with the printed sheets of music. Arturo Toscanini reveres Brahms, but Toscanini's score of the C-minor Symphony is so thoroughly marked up that no one but the maestro himself can read it. The reason why a great conductor makes notations on his musical scores—marks them up again and again each time he returns to study them—is the reason why you should mark your books. If your respect for magnificent binding or typography gets in the way, buy yourself a cheap edition and pay your respects to the author.

Why is marking up a book indispensable to reading? First, it keeps you awake. (And I don't mean merely conscious; I mean wide awake.) In the second place, reading, if it is active, is thinking, and thinking tends to express itself in words, spoken or written. The marked book is usually the thought-through book. Finally, writing helps you remember the thoughts you had, or the thoughts the author expressed. Let me develop these three points.

If reading is to accomplish anything more than passing time, it must be active. You can't let your eyes glide across the lines of a book and come up with an understanding of what you have read. Now an ordinary piece of light fiction, like, say, "Gone with the Wind," doesn't require the most active kind of reading. The books you read for pleasure can be read in a state of relaxation, and nothing is lost. But a great book, rich in ideas and beauty, a book that raises and tries to answer great fundamental questions, demands the most active reading of which you are capable. You don't absorb the ideas of John Dewey the way you absorb the crooning of Mr. Vallee. You have to reach for them. That you cannot do while you're asleep.

If, when you've finished reading a book, the pages are filled with your notes, you know that you read actively. The most famous *active* reader of great books I know is President Hutchins, of the University of Chicago. He also has the hardest schedule of business activities of any man I know. He invariably reads with a pencil, and sometimes, when he picks up a book and pencil in the evening, he finds himself, instead of making intelligent notes, drawing what he calls "caviar factories" on the margins. When that happens, he puts the book down. He knows he's too tired to read, and he's just wasting time.

But, you may ask, why is writing necessary? Well, the physical act of writing, with your own hand, brings words and sentences more sharply before your mind and preserves them better in your memory. To set down your reaction to important words and sentences you have read, and the questions they have raised in your mind, is to preserve those reactions and sharpen those questions.

Even if you wrote on a scratch pad, and threw the paper away when you had finished writing, your grasp of the book would be surer. But you don't have to throw the paper away. The margins (top and bottom, as well as side), the end-papers, the very space between the lines, are all available. They aren't sacred. And, best of all, your marks and notes become an integral part of the book and stay there forever. You can pick up the book the following week or year, and there are all your points of agreement, disagreement, doubt, and inquiry. It's like resuming an interrupted conversation with the advantage of being able to pick up where you left off.

And that is exactly what reading a book should be: a conversation between you and the author. Presumably he knows more about the subject than you do; naturally, you'll have the proper humility as you approach him. But don't let anybody tell you that a reader is supposed to be solely on the receiving end. Understanding is a two-way operation; learning doesn't consist in being an empty receptacle. The learner has to question himself and question the teacher. He even has to argue with the teacher, once he understands what the teacher is saying. And marking a book is literally an expression of your differences, or agreements of opinion, with the author.

There are all kinds of devices for marking a book intelligently and fruitfully. Here's the way I do it:

1. *Underlining:* of major points, of important or forceful statements.

2. *Vertical lines at the margin:* to emphasize a statement already underlined.

3. *Star, asterisk, or other doo-dad at the margin:* to be used sparingly, to emphasize the ten or twenty most important statements in the book. (You may want to fold the bottom corner of each page on which you use such marks. It won't hurt the sturdy paper on which most modern books are printed, and you will be able to take the book off the shelf at any time and, by opening it at the folded-corner page, refresh your recollection of the book.)

4. *Numbers in the margin:* to indicate the sequence of points the author makes in developing a single argument.

5. *Numbers of other pages in the margin:* to indicate where else in the book the author made points relevant to the point marked; to tie up the ideas in a book, which, though they may be separated by many pages, belong together.

6. *Circling of key words or phrases.*

7. *Writing in the margin, or at the top or bottom of the page, for the sake of:* recording questions (and perhaps answers) which a passage raised in your mind; reducing a complicated discussion to a simple statement; record-

ing the sequence of major points right through the books. I use the end-papers at the back of the book to make a personal index of the author's points in the order of their appearance.

The front end-papers are, to me, the most important. Some people reserve them for a fancy bookplate. I reserve them for fancy thinking. After I have finished reading the book and making my personal index on the back end-papers, I turn to the front and try to outline the book, not page by page, or point by point (I've already done that at the back), but as an integrated structure, with a basic unity and an order of parts. This outline is, to me, the measure of my understanding of the work.

If you're a die-hard anti-book-marker, you may object that the margins, the space between the lines, and the end-papers don't give you room enough. All right. How about using a scratch pad slightly smaller than the page-size of the book—so that the edges of the sheets won't protrude? Make your index, outlines, and even your notes on the pad, and then insert these sheets permanently inside the front and back covers of the book.

Or, you may say that this business of marking books is going to slow up your reading. It probably will. That's one of the reasons for doing it. Most of us have been taken in by the notion that speed of reading is a measure of our intelligence. There is no such thing as the right speed for intelligent reading. Some things should be read quickly and effortlessly, and some should be read slowly and even laboriously. The sign of intelligence in reading is the ability to read different things differently according to their worth. In the case of good books, the point is not to see how many of them you can get through, but rather how many can get through you—how many you can make your own. A few friends are better than a thousand acquaintances. If this be your aim, as it should be, you will not be impatient if it takes more time and effort to read a great book than it does a newspaper.

You may have one final objection to marking books. You can't lend them to your friends because nobody else can read them without being distracted by your notes. Furthermore, you won't want to lend them because a marked copy is a kind of intellectual diary, and lending it is almost like giving your mind away.

If your friend wishes to read your "Plutarch's Lives," "Shakespeare," or "The Federalist Papers," tell him gently but firmly, to buy a copy. You will lend him your car or your coat—but your books are as much a part of you as your head or your heart.

The Yankee School[*]

by GEORGE LYMAN KITTREDGE

I N 1834 Miss Harriet Martineau came to America in search of mental re-
freshment and change of scene. She spent a couple of years in this
country and has left a record of her experiences and impressions in two
books which have won a respectable place in the great class of miscellaneous
literature,—*Society in America,* and *Retrospect of Western Travel,*—besides
the minute account of her connection with the anti-slavery movement which
she gives in her Autobiography. With the mass of these writings we have
at this moment no particular concern, but one incident must not pass without notice. In an idle hour,—or let us say rather in a moment of peculiar
inspiration,—Miss Martineau had recourse to a certain "old almanack," where
she discovered something to point an excellent moral. Here is her account
of the discovery:—

All young people in these [New England] villages are more or less instructed.
Schooling is considered a necessary of life. I happened to be looking over an old
almanack one day, when I found, among the directions relating to the preparations
for winter on a farm, the following: "Secure your cellars from frost. Fasten loose
clap-boards and shingles. Secure a good school-master." It seemed doubtful, at
the first glance, whether some new farming utensil had not been thus whimsically
named; as the brass plate which hooks upon the fender, or upper bar of the grate,
is called "the footman"; but the context clearly showed that a man with learning
in his head was the article required to be provided before the winter.[1]

It must be admitted, even by Miss Martineau's warmest admirers, that she
did not always comprehend the American character. Indeed, she had the
good sense not to suppose that she could comprehend it. Just before she
sailed for the United States, James Mill asked her, quizzically, whether she
"expected to understand the Americans" in two years. "He was glad to
find," writes Miss Martineau, "that I had no such idea, and told me that
five-and-twenty years before, he had believed that he understood the Scotch:
and that in another five-and-twenty, he should no doubt understand the
English; but that now he was quite certain that he understood neither the
one nor the other."[2] It was hardly this warning that sent Miss Martineau
to the old almanac, but rather her own sagacity, or perhaps a happy accident.
At all events, she lighted upon a highly characteristic passage, and it is to her
credit that she did not fail to perceive what it signifies,—that to procure a

[*] From G. L. Kittredge, *The Old Farmer and His Almanack* (1904, 1920). By permission of
the Harvard University Press.
[1] *Society in America,* London, 1837, I, 264.
[2] *Autobiography,* Boston, 1877, I, 329.

schoolmaster is as much a matter of course to a Yankee farmer as any other provision for the winter season. To his mind there is nothing incongruous between attention to loose shingles and solicitude for primary education.

It does not appear what almanac Miss Martineau consulted. Very possibly it was that of Mr. R. B. Thomas. The precise passage, to be sure, has not been discovered in the sayings of the Old Farmer; but she may have been quoting from memory, and the form and the sentiment both suggest the admonitions of the Farmer's Calendar. That column contains, along with its precepts of practical agriculture, much exhortation on the subject of schools and scholmasters. Some of the entries are characteristic enough to deserve reproduction. Besides, they are not without value as bits of country life at the end of the eighteenth and the beginning of the nineteenth century.

A passage which comes very near to Miss Martineau's quotation occurs in the Farmer's Calendar for November, 1804:—

Now let the noise of your flail awake your drowsy neighbours.
Bank up your cellars.
Now hire a good schoolmaster, and send your children to school as much as possible.

In November, 1810, there is also a near approach to what Miss Martineau read:—

Bank your cellars unless your underpinning is such as renders it unneedful. Drive all your loose nails; and if the boys have broken any glass during the summer in the windows, you find it more comfortable to have the hole stopped up, than to let it go over winter. Send your children to school. Every boy should have a chance to prepare himself to do common town business.

In December, 1801, we have a good piece of proverbial philosophy:—

"*A cheap school-master makes a dear school*," says Common Sense. As this is the season for opening schools in the country, the above adage may be worthy of attention. Experience teaches, that the master, who will keep for 8 dollars per month, is not worth keeping: yet some towns, to save 2 dollars, give away 10.

Again, in December, 1803 and 1805:—

It is hoped that every town and village is now supplied with a wise and virtuous school-master; not ten dollar men—such pitiful pedants are too plenty. (1803.)
Attend to your schools. Hire not what neighbor Simpkins calls a *four dollar master* to instruct your children; it will be throwing away money. He who deprives his children of education, at once robs himself and society. (1805.)

But the liveliest passage of the kind is in the Calendar for November, 1820, where we have not only a full account of the acquirements of a five-dollar master, but also an eloquent speech from one of the advocates of ill-judged economy:—

This is the last month of Autumn, and it is now the business of the prudent man to be making his calculations about winter matters. I have often mentioned the importance of schooling to the rising generation. Few, if any countries, are blest like New-England, with public school establishments. No stinginess about the business. See that you have an able master, and pay him well. Here my neighbour Hugpurse and I can never agree; for he says, "So much of this here larnin is altogether useless and expensive. There is Joe Simple is good enough for our school. He has cyphered through compound interest, and that's fur enough for any man. He knows nothing about Jogrify and Grammar and such stuff; but he can write as good a hand as I can; and as for reading, he is far better than Squire Puff. In spelling they say he is curious. I have often heard that when a boy he could spell *Nebuchadnezzar* quicker than any one in school. I move, Mr. cheersman, that we hire Joe Simple to keep our school this winter. Give him five dollars a month and board himself, which is all he axes."

Mr. Thomas knew what he was talking about. He had been a country pedagogue himself; and, though he did not fall in love with the profession —in fact, he tells that he grew heartily tired of it—he had always been successful in his schoolmastering. He felt a proper contempt for the shortsighted stinginess of ignorant committeemen, and cherished no illusions as to the quality of the cheap pretenders to learning whose services they secured for little or nothing. He must have known many Ichabod Cranes and Joe Simples in his day. But schoolmasters like Joe Simple were not the only pretenders whom Mr. Thomas satirized. He was equally severe on those who aped the follies of fine gentlemen. Thus in December, 1815, we read:—

It is all important now that you send your children to school; but take care that you have a good instructor for them. It is not everyone who apes the gentleman that is fit for this undertaking. To strut in white top boots, brandish a cane, drink brandy, and smoke segars, are not the most essential qualifications for a schoolmaster. It is a serious misfortune that in many parts our country schools are exceedingly neglected; and it would seem that were it not for the law's obliging them to have at least the appearance of schools, there would be no provision at all for this purpose made for years! What better estate can you give your off-spring than a good education? I would not urge you to send them to college—neither to an academy; but see that you have the best of teachers· in your town schools; be not stingy about the price—let not your children suffer for shoes and other clothing to make them comfortable and decent—Town schools are of the first importance, for here and in the family at home is laid the foundation of the future man, whether he be great, or mean, an honest man, or a scoundrel.

A lesson for parents, as apposite now as it ever was, may be found in the December Calendar for 1807. Here also Mr. Thomas was speaking from experience:—

Let your children go to school as much as possible; and do not interfere with the orders and regulations of the master. When your little darling Jemmy is whipt at school it is a miserable way to give him gingerbread, and call the master puppy, rascal, &c.&c.

And again, in February, 1809:—

Keep the boys at school as much as possible, and take care not to rail against the master in their presence. Some people are eternally complaining about the schoolmaster or mistress. Let the school be never so well kept, they will be dissatisfied.

Another kind of admonition, in the Calendar for December, 1812, sounds strange to modern ears:—

Now you have an opportunity for schooling your children; and what can you give them to more profit? Riches and honors will fly away, but a good education, with habitual improvement, will abide by them, and be a source of pleasure and profit, when business and money, and friends fail them. But do not let them be prevented from going to school for want of shoes, &c. They should have been well shod before this time.

We may close our series of extracts with two eloquent utterances of a generally admonitory character:—

Let your children go to school. No country in the world is so blest with schooling as New-England; then neglect not to improve this excellent advantage. (December, 1806.)

It is a duty to educate our children in the ways of frugality and economy, as well as industry. In some it is owing to inattention, in others to parsimony that their children are kept from school. The heedless man who can just write his name and pick out a chapter or two in his bible and perhaps find the changes of the moon in his almanack, thinks that his children and his children's children are to go on the same way with himself, and so is regardless of their education; but the penurious man, if it cost a cent, will see them hanged before they shall be taught to spell *Caleb*. (March, 1813.)

A generation ago there was a stock question which used to be asked of school children: "What is the chief glory of New England?" And the reply was a matter of clockwork: "The chief glory of New England is in her public schools." The children had their doubts, but they answered dutifully. This kind of catechising is out of fashion now, and the mere thought of it provokes a smile among educational theorists; but it had its uses. In the case in hand, it called attention to the fact that schools do not spring up of themselves; and it may now and then have reminded the rising generation of certain items of indebtedness to the Puritan past. This whole subject of New England schooling is not easy to discuss without losing one's equilibrium. On the one hand, we are habituated to a good deal of undiscriminating eulogy of our ancestors, as if they never faltered in their zeal for education. On the other, there are the iconoclasts, who make much of the difficulty there was in enforcing the school laws.[3] There is evidence of such difficulty. A Massachusetts Act of 1701 declares that the previous statute "is shamefully neglected by divers Towns." In an Election Sermon for 1709 the Rev. Grindal Rawson, of Mendon, exclaims: "How little care is there generally taken, especially in Country Towns, to promote the Liberal Education of Children? How much is it become the Practice of many Towns, to Study Tricks and Shifts whereby the Law of the Land obliging to the upholding and main-

[3] The Massachusetts laws which particularly concern us are those of 1647 (Mass. Colony Records, II, 203), 1692 (4 Wm. and Mary, ch. xi), 1701 (13 Wm. III, ch. xx), 1789 (Acts, ch. xix), and 1824 (Acts, ch. cxi, amending the Act of 1789).

taining of Schools, may be wholly evaded and lose its Efficacy? And is not this Provoking to God, and disserviceable to the interest of Posterity?"[4]   In 1713 Cotton Mather, in one of his innumerable jeremiads,—called *Advice from the Watch Tower, in a Testimony against Evil Customs,*—censures the evasion of this law:—"To Elude the Law about *Schools,* is too Customary. It argues, that a due sense of that Grand Concern, the *Education of Children,* is too much laid aside among us.—Tis *Wonderful!* Tis *Wonderful!* That a People of our Profession would seem so unconcerned, Lest the next Generation be miserably Uncultivated, and have hideous *Barbarity* grow upon it!"

All this, however, should not mislead us. The facts are clear enough and the anxiety of the preachers is really a favorable symptom. The significant thing is not that the laws were not always obeyed, but that the colonial and provincial authorities made an honest attempt to enforce them, and that the outcome of their efforts was, when time was ripe, a public school system which, though not perfect, is at all events a remarkable achievement. We should regard the general tendency and the final results. We have a good many diaries kept by soldiers in the Revolutionary War. Most of these are rudely spelled and not very exact in point of grammar. They show that the rank and file were not highly educated, and they have often been cited as proof that the schools and schoolmasters of the eighteenth century were poor things. What they really prove, however, is that almost every New Englander could read and write, and this, after all, is a pretty creditable showing. When John Adams was in England in 1786, he fell in with a Virginian, Major Langbourne, who had "taken the whim of walking all over Europe, after having walked over most of America." The Major lamented "the difference of character between Virginia and New England." "I offered," writes Adams, "to give him a receipt for making a New England in Virginia. He desired it; and I recommended to him town meetings, training days, town schools, and ministers, giving him a short explanation of each article. The meeting-house and school-house and training field are the scenes where New England men were formed. Colonel Trumbull, who was present, agreed that these are the ingredients. In all countries and in all companies, for several years, I have, in conversation and in writing, enumerated the towns, militia, schools, and churches, as the four causes of the growth and defence of New England. The virtues and talents of the people are there formed; their temperance, patience, fortitude, prudence, and justice, as well as their sagacity, knowledge, judgment, taste, skill, ingenuity, dexterity, and industry."[5]

Here is an uncommonly interesting bit of autobiography from the middle of the eighteenth century. The writer, Rufus Putnam, was an officer of distinction, whom Washington pronounced the best engineer on the American side in the Revolution. No one can doubt that the New England spirit finds

[4] *The Necessity of a Speedy and Thorough Reformation,* Boston, 1709, p. 36.
[5] Diary, July 21, 1786, *Works,* ed. C. F. Adams, III, 400.

a truer expression in the boy's struggles to learn something than in the nonchalance of his guardians.

In Sept 1747, I went to live with my Step Father, Capt John Sadler (at Upton) and continued with him untill his death (in September or october 1753)

during the six year I lived with Capt Sadler, I never Saw the inside of a School house, except about three weeks. he was very illiterate himself, and took no care for the education of his family; but this was not all I was made a ridecule of, and otherwise abused for my attention to books, and attempting to write, and learn Arethmatic, however, amidst all those discouragements I made Some advances in writeing and Arethmatic, that is I could make Letters that could be under stood, and had gon as far in Arethmatic as to work the rule of three (without any teacher but the book)—Oh! my Children beware you neglect not the education of any under your care as I was neglected.—

In March 1754 I was bound apprentice to Daniel Matthews of Brokfield, to the Millw[r]ights trade; by him my education was as much neglected, as by Capt Sadler, except that he did not deny me the use of a Light for Study in the winter evenings—

I turned my attention chiefly to Arethmatic, Geography, and history; had I ben as much engaged in Learning to write well, with Spelling, and Grammar, I might have ben much better qualified to fulfill the duties of the Succeeding Scenes of Life, which In providence I have ben called to pass through. I was zealous to obtain knowledge, but having no guide I knew not where to begin nor what course to pursue,—hence neglecting Spelling and gramer when young I have Suffered much through life on that account.[6]

The Constitution of Massachusetts, adopted in 1781, laid special emphasis on the duty of the Commonwealth with regard to education. In the same year the legislature passed an elaborate law providing for both elementary and grammar schools.[7] By grammar schools, we should remember, was always meant what we now call Latin or High schools. If we compare this act of 1789 with the original law of 1647, we shall find that it is less exacting. Instead of requiring a grammar school in every town of one hundred families, it raises the limit to two hundred. This change is estimated to have released one hundred and twenty towns from an obligation under which they had lain for many years.[8] Doubtless, however, it was as rigorous a rule as the country could bear. What had seemed possible in the compact and homogeneous Colony was no longer practicable in the growing State.

This act of 1789 brings us down to the time of the *Farmer's Almanack*. It defines the conditions which Mr. Thomas had in mind in his constant exhortations.[9] In the lower schools the master was "to teach children to read and write, and to instruct them in the English language, as well as in arithmetic, orthography, and decent behaviour." The higher schools were to be provided with "a grammar schoolmaster of good morals, well instructed in the Latin, Greek and English languages."

[6] *Memoirs of Rufus Putnam,* ed. by Miss Rowena Buell, Boston, 1903, pp. 9-11.
[7] Acts of 1789, ch. xix.
[8] G. H. Martin, *The Evolution of the Massachusetts Public School System,* New York, 1894, lecture iii.
[9] There was no further law until 1824: Acts of 1824, ch. cxi (amending the act of 1789).

An idea of the impression which the schools of New England made upon a highly cultivated and philosophical foreigner may be got from a passage in Rochefoucauld's *Travels in North America.* The distinguished Frenchman, who belonged to the school of Arthur Young, is speaking of Connecticut in 1795:—

There is . . . no instance of a town or parish, remaining, negligently, without a school. Many communities maintain their schools for a greater part of the year, than they are, by law, obliged to do. The select-men and the deputations from the communities manage the farms and other revenues of the schools.

The teachers are commonly young men from the colleges, students of law or theology. Their salaries are at the pleasure of the different parishes, from two to three hundred dollars. Almost all those who now act a distinguished part in the political business of New England, began their careers as teachers in these schools; a situation that is accounted exceedingly honourable. Sometimes, where the salary is small, women are chosen to be the teachers. Even these must, in this case, be well qualified to teach reading, writing, and arithmetic.

Every county must have a school for Greek and Latin. A fine of three dollars is exacted from parents neglecting to send their children to school. The select-men have authority to levy it.[10]

No account of our schools, however brief and incidental, can ignore the Academy,—that peculiarly New England institution which has played so important a part in the social and educational life of America. The smaller towns had found it impossible to support classical schools; but there was no actual falling-off in the zeal for education. Academies were founded, partly by bequests from public-spirited citizens, partly by voluntary contributions from subscribers. These multiplied exceedingly in the late eighteenth and the early nineteenth century, and many of them were subsidized by the States. Most of them have gone out of existence, becoming unnecessary as wealth increased and the towns were able once more to assume the duty of maintaining high schools. But the stronger institutions of the kind, which are also among the oldest, have survived and flourished. They are a distinctive feature of the educational system of the whole United States. Their importance is no longer merely local; it is national.

Mr. Thomas makes an amusing remark about academies in the Farmer's Calendar for December, 1808:—

Now let your boys and girls attend school. Send them to the common town school, rather than to an academy. Fun, frolick, and filigree are too much practised at the academies for the benefit of a farmer's boy. Let them have a solid and useful education.

This should not be misunderstood. It is not an assault on the academy as an institution. It is merely a caution against sending a boy to an inappropriate school. Academies, in Mr. Thomas's opinion, were not meant for

10 *Travels through the United States of North America,* English translation, London, 1799, I, 530.

those who were to spend their lives on the farm. He was no enemy to ambition, but he wished to see it intelligently guided.

It will be noticed that Mr. Thomas mentions girls as well as boys in this last exhortation. The education of girls was neglected in the early days. In 1782 the Rev. John Eliot wrote from Boston to Jeremy Belknap, then minister at Dover, New Hampshire:—

We don't pretend to teach ye female part of ye town anything more than dancing, or a little music perhaps, (and these accomplishmt. must necessarily be confined to a very few,) except ye private schools for writing, which enables them to write a copy, sign their name, &c., which they might not be able to do without such a priviledge, & with it I will venture to say that a lady is a rarity among us who can write a page of commonplace sentiment, the words being well spelt, & ye style & language kept up with purity & elegance.[11]

Two years later Caleb Bingham opened a private school for girls, commonly said to have been the first girls' school ever known in Boston. The letter just quoted shows that this idea is not strictly correct. Yet Bingham's establishment was so far in advance of the mere writing classes which Mr. Eliot mentions that it deserves its reputation. "He taught not only writing and arithmetic, but reading, spelling, and English grammar," thus meeting precisely the needs which Mr. Eliot refers to. Bingham's successful experiment soon led the town to make some provision for the education of girls. This was in 1789, and Bingham was employed in one of these new public schools. He was the author of several text-books which rivalled those of Noah Webster in popularity. His *American Preceptor,* published in 1794, had by 1832 sold to the number of nearly six hundred and fifty thousand copies, and his *Columbian Orator,* published in 1797, to the number of more than two hundred thousand. He also prepared, for his private school, a little English grammar, *The Young Lady's Accidence,* of which a hundred thousand copies were sold by 1832. It was the first English grammar used in the schools of Boston.[12] Several other private schools for girls were established toward the end of the eighteenth century. In 1784 Dr. Jedediah Morse, the well-known geographer, opened such a school at New Haven, and in 1790 a Mr. Woodbridge, who gave himself the grandiloquent title of "the Columbus of female education," followed his example. Three years before, the Moravian brethren had founded a "female seminary" at Bethlehem, Pennsylvania. The opposition to any kind of higher education for women is amusingly illustrated by the experience of Miss Emma Willard, who opened a seminary for girls at Troy, New York, in 1821. She had previously conducted what she called a "female academy" at Waterford, in the same state. A friendly minister, who felt it his duty to mention this institution in his public prayers, styled it a "seminary," not wishing to offend his hearers by speaking of it as an "acad-

---

[11] Feb. 1, 1782. *Coll. Mass. Hist. Soc.,* 6th Series, IV, 223.
[12] See G. E. Littlefield, *Early Schools and School-Books of New England,* 1904, pp. 156, 158, 229-30.

emy" or a "college." Bradford Academy, in Massachusetts, which still flourishes, was founded in 1803.[13]

But chronology is dull work. Let us revert to anecdote, and, in so doing,
to the old-fashioned grammar school. The Rev. John Barnard of Marblehead (who was born at Boston in 1681), after attending the instruction of
a school mistress in the town and another in the country, was sent to the Latin
School in his eighth year, where he was under the tuition of "the aged,
venerable, and justly famous Mr. Ezekiel Cheever," one of the most noted of
New England preceptors. In his autobiography, written when he was eighty-
five years old, Mr. Barnard tells a pretty little story of "an odd accident"
which "drove him from the school after a few weeks":—"There was," he says,
"an older lad entered the school the same week with me; we strove who
should outdo; and he beat me by the help of a brother in the upper class, who
stood behind master with the accidence open for him to read out off; by
which means he could recite his [MS. illegible] three and four times in a
forenoon, and the same in the afternoon; but I who had no such help, and
was obliged to commit all to memory, could not keep pace with him; so that
he would be always one lesson before me. My ambition could not bear to
be outdone, and in such a fraudulent manner, and therefore I left the
school." [14]

But he soon returned and got on very well in his studies, notwithstanding
he was, as he confesses, "a very naughty boy, much given to play." At
length Mr. Cheever resorted to an ingenious device. "You, Barnard," said
he, "I know you can do well enough if you will; but you are so full of play
that you hinder your classmates from getting their lessons; and therefore,
if any of them cannot perform their duty, I shall correct you for it." "One unlucky day, one of my classmates did not look into his book, and therefore
could not say his lesson, though I called upon him once and again to mind
his book; upon which our master beat me. I told master the reason why
he could not say his lesson was, his declaring he would beat me if any of the
class were wanting in their duty; since which this boy would not look into
his book, though I called upon him to mind his book, as the class could
witness. The boy was pleased with my being corrected, and persisted in his
neglect, for which I was still corrected, and that for several days. I thought,
in justice, I ought to correct the boy, and compel him to a better temper;
and therefore, after school was done, I went up to him, and told him I had
been beaten several times for his neglect; and since master would not correct
him I would, and I should do so as often as I was corrected for him; and then
drubbed him heartily. The boy never came to school any more, and so that
unhappy affair ended." [15]

The temptation to go on with Mr. Barnard's delightful anecdotes of his
boyhood is great, but must be resisted. Still, we may indulge ourselves in

[13] See a paper on "The Early History of Schools and School-Books," by R. N. Meriam,
Collections of the Worcester Society of Antiquity, IX, no. 27, pp. 93 f.
[14] *Coll. Mass. Hist. Soc.,* 3d Series, V, 178.
[15] *Ibid.,* 179-80.

one more extract, which is very brief, and gives a charming picture of the little boy and the veteran schoolmaster:—

I remember once, in making a piece of Latin, my master found fault with the syntax of one word, which was not so used by me heedlessly, but designedly, and therefore I told him there was a plain grammar rule for it. He angrily replied, there was no such rule. I took the grammar and showed the rule to him. Then he smilingly said, "Thou art a brave boy; I had forgot it." And no wonder; for he was then above eighty years old.[16]

Mr. Cheever was master of the Boston Latin School for nearly forty years. He died in 1708, at the age of ninety-three, and was honored with a singular poetical tribute from the pen of Benjamin Thompson, "the renowned poet of New England." [17] It bore a title prophetic of Browning, "The Grammarian's Funeral," and was printed as a broadside.[18] It begins:—

> Eight Parts of *Speech* this Day wear *Mourning Gowns*
> Declin'd *Verbs, Pronouns, Participles, Nouns.*
> And not declined, *Adverbs* and *Conjunctions,*
> In *Lillies* Porch they stand to do their functions.
> With *Preposition;* but the most affection
> Was still observed in the *Interjection.*

The chapter may close with a bit from the *Almanac* for 1807 (July), which will serve as a fitting epilogue to our pedagogical miscellany:—

I have more pork in my cellar, said neighbor Braggadocia, *than all the Almanack makers in christendom. Fie on your larnin, and all that stuff; I wants none of your nonsense. No man shall teach me, faith.* Now I forebore to dispute with this great man; for the proverb says, *you cannot make a silken purse of a sow's ear.*

BIBLIOGRAPHY

Adams, John. *Works,* ed. Charles Francis Adams (Boston, 1850–56).
Green, Samuel A. *Ten Facsimile Reproductions* (Boston, 1902).
La Rochefoucault Liancourt, François Alexandre Frédéric, Duc de. *Travels through the United States of North America,* English translation (London, 1799).
Littlefield, G. E. *Early Schools and Schoolbooks of New England* (Boston, 1904).
Martin, G. H. *The Evolution of the Massachusetts Public School System* (New York, 1894).
Martineau, Harriet. *Autobiography,* ed. Maria Weston Chapman (Boston, 1877).
—— *Society in America* (London, 1837).
Massachusetts Historical Society, Collections of (Boston, 1792–   ).
Putnam, Rufus. *Memoirs,* ed. Rowena Buell (Boston, 1903).
Rawson, Grindal. *The Necessity of a Speedy and Thorough Reformation* (Boston, 1709).
Worcester Society of Antiquity, Collections of (Worcester, Mass., 1881–1899).

[16] *Coll. Mass. Hist. Soc.,* 3d Series, V, p. 180.
[17] See pp. 356 f., below.
[18] Reproduced by Dr. Samuel A. Green in his *Ten Fac-Simile Reproductions,* Boston, 19—, No. III.

Propaganda Techniques of German Fascism[1]

by CLYDE R. MILLER AND OTHERS

"WHAT is truly vicious," observed *The New York Times* in an editorial, September 1, 1937, "is not propaganda but a monopoly of it." This monopoly is seen most clearly in totalitarian states where all channels of communication are controlled by the government. The extent to which the propaganda machinery of a country has been brought under the control of one organization or a group of related organizations is a useful measure of the degree to which absolutism dominates it, of the extent to which democracy has been eliminated.

In democratic countries this monopoly aspect of propaganda is held in check by rivalries between competing organizations. Political, economic, educational, and religious spokesmen are able to and actually do disseminate rival propagandas. This gives those at whom the rival propagandas are directed some freedom of choice among the alternatives offered them.

The ability of individuals and organizations in democracies to enter their special viewpoints into the rivalry of propagandas is restricted chiefly by economic considerations.[2] In buying radio time and newspaper space, in the outright purchase of radio stations and newspapers, in securing the expert services of professional propagandists and public relations counselors, individuals and groups with large financial resources have an advantage over those with small resources. Producers of goods, for instance, have greater propaganda power than either consumers or labor.[3]

The power of propaganda increases as its control becomes more centralized, as the trend to monopoly increases. In democratic countries this takes place when competing propagandists resolve their differences and agree upon one propaganda. This maneuver can be seen in amalgamations or agreements within political, economic, educational, and religious groups. As various groups come to collaborate in terms of common interests, their propaganda programs tend to coincide and to increase in power. This process is stimulated by the centralization of the control of the economic structure of a country. A tendency toward a monopoly of wealth is accompanied by a corresponding tendency toward a monopoly of propaganda.

Contrasted with the relative freedom for the dissemination of propaganda in democracies is the complete or nearly complete elimination of this freedom in totalitarian countries. Fascist Germany illustrates how propaganda is used

---

[1] From *Propaganda Analysis*. By permission of the Institute for Propaganda Analysis.

[2] See A. M. Lee, "Freedom of the Press: Services of a Catch Phrase," in *Studies in the Science of Society*, G. P. Murdock, editor (New Haven: Yale University Press, 1937), pp. 355-75.

[3] See A. M. Lee, *The Daily Newspaper in America* (New York: The Macmillan Company, 1937), chapters on "Advertising" (esp. pp. 370-3) and "Labor" (esp. pp. 152-63).

both to bring a dictator into power and to aid him in maintaining that power. In Germany the propaganda which helped convince the people of the efficiency of the National Socialist [4] solution for the country's political and economic problems was reinforced by an army of storm troops that weakened opposition through terrorism. Such methods made difficult and dangerous the promulgation of competing propagandas. The power of the Nazi propaganda was increased further by the financial support of certain business men and by the political intrigues of Colonel Franz von Papen and other officials of the Weimar Republic.

With the establishment of the National Socialist régime its monopoly of propaganda was rapidly achieved. Suppression of opposition was thorough. Every source of public information and nearly every instrument capable of affecting public opinion came under its control. Although some of the church groups were difficult to dominate, in general the National Socialist propaganda drive went forward with a thoroughness which exceeded that of World War propaganda.[5]

To understand how this monopoly of propaganda was effected, it is necessary to review the conditions under which German Fascism was established.

In Germany, as elsewhere, Fascism is the outcome of economic and political instability. It is an undemocratic means for dealing with the mass unemployment of city workers, the economic distress of the middle classes, the impoverishment of farmers, and the efforts of these groups for economic reforms. So long as democratic realities continue to exist, with freedom of speech, press, and assembly, such efforts for reform can obtain a public hearing, and various programs to relieve and prevent distress stand a chance of enactment into law. Thus, representative democracy provides a means for reconciling conflicts through the expression of opinions and propagandas for different solutions, from which an enlightened public can make its choice. In Germany this means of mitigating the abuses of the economic system was feared by influential politicians, industrialists, financiers, and great landowners. After the worldwide depression of the late 1920's these individuals and groups felt that they could maintain their status only through the abolition of representative democratic government. Their opportunity came in Adolf Hitler, master propagandist.

Had there been no depression and no unemployment in Germany, there doubtless would have been no Nazi party in control of Germany today. But the depression was more than another business crisis. It brought back vividly the hardships of the inflation period, the distress at the end of the war. It caused millions of Germans to lose faith in the ability of the Weimar Republic to prevent such recurring disasters. This major crisis was utilized

[4] The official name of the political party which brought Fascism to German is the *National-sozialistische Deutsche Arbeiterpartei* (National Socialist German Workers' Party). For brevity's sake it is commonly referred to as the Nationalist Socialist party or by its initials, NSDAP. A short abbreviation much used in America is Nazi. As shown later, it is not actually a "socialist" or a "workers'" party.

[5] See H. D. Lasswell, *Propaganda Technique in the World War* (New York: Alfred A. Knopf, 1927).

by Hitler to convince growing numbers of Germans, particularly in the middle classes, that the Republic offered no future, no work, no promise, no hope for themselves or for their children. The social strain created by this condition made possible an audience highly susceptible to the propaganda of demagogues and cliques of demagogues.

Sometimes a demagogue is sincere in his propaganda; usually he is confused. Typically, a demagogic clique is corrupt in whole or in part. The corrupt elements are usually successful in proportion to their astuteness and unscrupulousness. They will agitate for a fee; they will exact for their services all that the traffic will bear; they will serve or pretend to serve many interests. The extent to which Hitler and his Nazi clique were sincere, astute, or unscrupulous may never be fully known. At the critical moment the NSDAP did receive the secret financial backing of a small group of Germans who wanted a government which would abolish freedom of speech, press, and assembly; which would eliminate labor unions; and which would deal effectively with expressed opposition. Such a government was established in Germany in 1933 under the leadership of Adolf Hitler.[6]

Germany's defeat in the World War and her humiliation in the Treaty of Versailles had become less significant in the reconstruction period of the Weimar Republic; but at the end of the Twenties the world depression struck the German people another crushing blow and brought unemployment and impoverishment to increasing millions. Anger and unrest filled the land. In such a period it was natural in Germany, as anywhere, that a large section of the population would lend a favorable ear to anyone who offered himself as a savior. The Socialists and Communists attributed the depression and its consequences to the inherent weaknesses of a system of production for private profit. This they sought to replace by a system of public ownership. Their program made a rational appeal; as propaganda, however, it was much less effective than the emotionally charged propaganda of the Nazis.

The program and, more particularly, the actions of the National Socialist party have reflected the frustrations and despairs of the German workers, farmers, and middle class. Hitler's life actually epitomized and dramatized the experiences of the German people. Until his final overwhelming political victory, Hitler had known only failure. He wanted to be an artist and failed; an architect, and became a house painter; he went into the war with all possible enthusiasm and returned from it a physical wreck with no hope and no future in the country which had lost. Some excuse, some outlet, had to be found.

[6] In spite of, or partly because of, the terrorism which accompanied Nazi propaganda, and because of a slight economic upturn in the autumn of 1932, public opinion began to react against Hitler. This was shown by a sharp decline in votes polled by the National Socialist party in the Reichstag election of November 6, 1932. Because the democratic realities of the Weimar Republic still permitted considerable free play of public opinion, a few of Hitler's most influential supporters decided at this juncture to urge his appointment as Chancellor. See Frederick L. Schuman, *The Nazi Dictatorship* (2nd ed., revised; New York: Alfred A. Knopf, 1936), chapter on "Victory by Default," for details of the victory of the National Socialists and of President von Hindenburg's appointment of Hitler as Chancellor on January 30, 1933.

The middle class, one of the most politically important sections of the population, had been neglected. After the war this class in particular suffered from Germany's failure, defeat, and humiliation. It suffered from the failure of the Weimar Republic to cope effectively with the economic crisis. It distrusted communism. It feared violent change, but it wanted such change as would give a sense of security. Then came Adolf Hitler, a leader, who promised the people all that they wanted. Most Germans felt that conditions were too bad even to question how all that he offered could be achieved. The few who did raise their voices in protest or doubt were silenced by argument, by force, or by honest conviction that this new scheme, this new hope, must be tried. Everything was promised to everyone: socialism to the laborer and to the more liberal *Kleinbürger;* partition of the great estates to the peasant; dissolution of trusts and economic security to the middle class citizen; salvation from communism to the upper bourgeois; and to every one elimination of the Jews, rearmament of the Reich, and "national liberation." This was the appeal of the "National Socialist German Labor Party." A mass following was the result. Power, however, could come only by persuading the industrialists, the financiers, and the feudal military caste to support the Nazi movement. Hitler united them, organized them, and won their support with his promises that they should not fear his labor-winning social program. It was understood that they could retain control behind the scenes if Hitler were left free to manage the political show.

It is difficult to estimate the support or strength of the industrialists. As in most countries many business leaders contributed to all the major parties. Despite its socialism, the growing following of the NSDAP made it a useful tool to crush Marxism, democracy, and the German labor movement. The list of industrialists and aristocratic contributors expanded rapidly between 1925 and 1933, especially after 1930. The most powerful figure [7] was the Ruhr magnate, Chairman Fritz Thyssen of the Vereinigte Stahlwerke A.G. The importance of this financial backing, however, should not be overemphasized. So far as present records show, these men did not determine the policies of the party. Those had been decided before their support was elicited. "Socialism" was a Glittering Generality privately admitted by the party leaders. They had no plan and no intention of changing the existing economic system. Capitalism was all they knew and all they wanted. But once in power, political control dominated economic control. "Capitalism," as free enterprise, became a Glittering Generality. Virgil Jordan,[8] president of the National Industrial Conference Board, Inc., writes:

. . . The National-Socialist régime has established a rigid system of planned economy. The aim of the government is to conduct the operation of the economic system in the interest of general welfare, as the government conceives it. All pri-

---

[7] See John T. Flynn, "The Steel Master Behind Hitler's Drive for Power," *The New York World-Telegram,* March 16, 1938 (NEA Service, Inc.). "He [Thyssen] is the man who made Hitler's regime possible and mobilizes big business in Germany behind him now."

[8] *Economic Development of Germany under National Socialism* (New York: National Industrial Conference Board, Inc., 1937), pp. ix-xi.

vate interests may be sacrificed to the national interest. No difference of opinion is allowed as to what constitutes the national interest. That question is decided by the leader of the National-Socialist Party, Chancellor Adolf Hitler, in consultation with party members and with the representatives of industry and trade. Economic planning was found to be impossible without putting labor and industry in a strait-jacket. The government determines the tasks that private industry must fulfill in order to promote national welfare and, through the exercise of dictatorial political power, it tries to create the conditions under which those tasks can be accomplished. . . .

By fixing wage rates, hours of work, prices, profits, and interest rates; by controlling imports and subsidizing exports; by regulating expansion of plant and equipment, the supply and distribution of raw materials, and new security issues; and by spending billions of marks on public works and rearmament—the National-Socialist régime has been successful in providing the available working force of the country with regular employment at a rate of wages sufficient to provide the basic necessities of life, but which does not permit an appreciable increase in the standard of living. . . . Once the government embarked on the program of rearmament and economic self-sufficiency, the freedom of enterprise had to be sacrificed.[9]

To win their way to power the National Socialists used all the techniques of propaganda, all the avenues for its dissemination which modern science and invention have made possible, and all the old appeals and shibboleths. Professor Schuman[10] gives a vivid picture of one of the thousands of carefully planned great mass meetings: the waiting, the expectancy, the late hour when people's resistance is low, the decorations, the company of storm troopers drilling, the dramatic torchlight parade, the bands, the singing, finally the hush, a crash of drums and trumpets, the slow solemn entrance of a well disciplined procession to stirring martial music or perhaps Richard Wagner's "Entry of the Gods into Valhalla"; at the end a special bodyguard, the uniformed party leaders, and then, "the centre of all eyes, Der Führer—in his tan raincoat, hatless, smiling, and affably greetings those to right and left. A man of the people! Germany's Savior!" "Heil! Heil!" and the third "HEIL!" swells into a great ovation. Speeches, spotlights, cheers, waving of arms. The audience responds at the end with an overwhelming chorus, "Heil! Heil! Heil! Hitler!" The bands blare forth, and the multitude chants the "Horst Wessel Lied."

Vernon McKenzie,[11] director of the School of Journalism of the University of Washington, reports such a meeting in September, 1932, when he sat on the platform within ten feet of the Führer.

A Canadian friend who has heard Hitler speak many times expresses succinctly the power of the Leader's eloquence or demagogy, whatever you may call it.

"I could listen to Hitler talk for an hour on one side of a subject," he says, "and then if he turned around and for the next hour directly contradicted everything he had previously said, I would follow him and believe him. That is what I think of

---

[9] See also the articles by Otto D. Tolischus, Berlin correspondent of *The New York Times*, for September 2-7, 1937.

[10] *Op. cit.*, pp. 91 ff.

[11] *Through Turbulent Years* (New York: Robert M. McBride and Company, 1938), pp. 37-8.

Hitler's persuasive powers! If he can get me that way, how much more can he get the German audiences?

"This evening Hitler . . . swayed that audience as I have never seen any audience swayed before or since He did not mention Hindenburg by name, but one of his perorations went something like this:

" 'Certain parties are contending for the right to guide the destinies of the German people. Certain leaders . . . one of them is eighty-six; the other is forty-three. Which do you think is likely to survive to guide the destinies of our race?'

" . . . He could play with that audience just as he wished. As I looked down at the sea of faces from the platform, the 30,000 in the auditorium seemed to be subjects of mass hypnotism."

The evidence of Mr. McKenzie's Canadian friend is borne out by comments of American newspaper correspondents who point out that Hitler's addresses are often unintelligible. Large numbers of his listeners apparently listen with their emotions. When their tension becomes high, they intercept the speech by emotional outbursts at seemingly inappropriate times. Here we see the force of language with or without meaning as a molder of public opinion. Only intelligent citizens skilled in analysis of propaganda and immunized against the wiles of the orator were unaffected by Hitler. Among such doubtless were editors, writers, teachers, clergymen, and others who later were to be killed, imprisoned, or forced to acquiesce in silence to a régime they disapproved.

Hitler, the master propagandist, knew that propaganda, to be effective, must be keyed to the desires, hopes, hatreds, loves, fears, and prejudices of the people; he knew that most human beings crave a scapegoat to take the blame of disaster and to bolster their own pride. The Jews were made the scapegoat. He blamed them not only for the existing unemployment and impoverishment but also for the loss of the war and the Treaty of Versailles. But the anti-Jewish propaganda had even greater value to Nazism than the mere creation of a scapegoat. Through the Jews Hitler was able to strike at anyone, Jew or non-Jew, opposed to Nazism, and to discredit any plan which aimed at the peaceful rehabilitation of Germany. Hitler's objective was to create in the minds of Germans an ugly image of "Jew." The word "Jew" was deliberately made synonymous with everything the Germans resented and hated or could be led to resent and hate. Once that was done, Nazi agitators revived or manufactured for circulation notorious forgeries, which branded all those persons as Jews who did or said anything not in accord with Nazi ideas. To attack the Dawes Plan, for example, it became necessary to label Dawes as a Jew and so, according to Der Stürmer, Dawes was portrayed to its readers as a full-blooded Jew, originally named Davidson. The banking house of J. P. Morgan, which acted as a house of issue for a German government loan opposed by Hitler, was promptly branded a Jewish banking house and the Morgan name given as an abridgment of the more Jewish-sounding Morgenstern. Similarly the entire French nation, whom the Nazis consider to be Germany's natural enemy, was described as a nation of Jews.

The Germans, Hitler said, were the world's greatest race, supreme in the arts of peace and unconquerable in war unless betrayed by the Jews. Thus, he was able to give to the National Socialist program the driving power of strong nationalism, coupled with the emotional appeal of racial superiority, intensified by hatred of the despised Jews. At the same time he inveighed against the great bankers, industrialists, and landowners as vigorously as did the Communists and Socialists. He proclaimed himself the savior of the farmers, the small business men, and the workers. As early as 1920 Hitler's newly created National Socialist party made promises identical with those of the Socialists and Communists. The NSDAP platform adopted in Munich, February 24, 1920, included these demands: abolition of unearned incomes, nationalization of all trusts, abolition of interest on land loans, the enactment of a law for confiscation without compensation of land for public purposes. In May, 1926, the party decided that this program was never to be changed. Two years later, April, 1928, Adolf Hitler signed a statement which in effect held invalid the phrase "confiscation without compensation." Since the National Socialists hold to the view of private property, he claimed, it was "self-evident" that this phrase referred "only to the creation of legal means whereby land which was acquired in illegal ways or which is not being administered to the best interests of the nation's welfare might be expropriated if necessary. This is directed primarily against Jewish land-speculation companies." [12] The official name of the party is a perfect example of the Glittering Generalities device—*Nationalsozialistische Deutsche Arbeiterpartei* (National Socialist German Workers Party). In Germany the great pre-Nazi program of public housing and public works and the higher living standards achieved through labor unions had given the word "socialist" favorable connotations. Hitler took full advantage of these connotations, though later his actual program drove socialists into concentration camps and abolished labor unions.

But spellbinding, emotional meetings were not the only Nazi techniques of propaganda which helped bring the party to power. With its mysterious swastika, its parades, its officers, its "Third Reich," its esoteric "wisdom," its solidarity achieved by familiar symbols and uniforms, the party was and is actually a secret society. It is elaborately organized with a women's auxiliary, children's groups, youth divisions—a place for every one. Subtle suggestions run the gamut of emotions: prestige, love, fear, security, pride, hate. Hitler himself is said to have invented the *Hakenkreuz* flag and much of the elaborate military insignia of the brown-uniformed *Sturm-Abteilung,* or storm troops organized on strictly military lines to combat other parties, and of the black-uniformed *Schutzstaffel,* originally the personal bodyguard of Hitler, now a small army of full-time, well paid mercenaries.

Promises, circuses, societies, banners, slogans, hate, fear, hope, pride—all swept the unsatisfied, discouraged Germans into the crowd on the band wagon behind the swastika. Since the advent of the National Socialists the power of

---

[12] Quoted by Henri Lichtenberger, *The Third Reich* (New York: The Greystone Press, 1937), p. 302.

the agencies of propaganda has been intensified and coördinated so that all avenues of communication—press, school, radio, motion picture, and even the church—must carry but one propaganda to the public mind, must express one will, one voice, one opinion. Hence the Hitler régime has, in common with other fascist countries, established a system wherein authority flows from the top down; and from the people comes blind, instant, unquestioning obedience. In the pages that follow, the propaganda which aided the National Socialists in winning support, which helps them keep the support of a majority of the people today, is analyzed under the seven common propaganda devices suggested in the November letter of the Institute for Propaganda Analysis.

Name Calling

"Name Calling" is a device to make us form a judgment without examining the evidence on which it should be based. Here the propagandist appeals to our hate and fear.

In as much as the first task of the National Socialists was to destroy simultaneously all trade unions as well as all liberal democratic institutions, it was necessary to make the people believe that these were devilish inventions, cleverly designed by malicious persons to ruin the German people. This they sought to accomplish by asserting with endless repetition that these institutions were similar in structure and mood to those of communism. They then painted communism in terms so lurid as to horrify even the skeptical. With people convinced that communism (often used by the Nazis as synonymous with the Weimar Republic) had been forced on them by a "degenerate" and "malicious" cabal of "alien enemies" to create their misery, they could then rally all good Germans around the Führer, who promised to protect his people by waging relentless war on these "enemies of Germany." This picture was widely accepted and was supported by a complete mythology in which the Jews, communism, and liberalism or democracy were held to be the major evil influences from which the National Socialists saved Germany.

Prominent in this campaign is Julius Streicher's newspaper *Der Stürmer,* which, in addition to its regular anti-Semitism, has recently published *A Story Book for Young and Old Alike,* in which Jews are pilloried and "Aryan" Germans warned against them. The seventeen "folk tales" are illustrated by grotesque caricatures of alleged Semitic types with the title "A Poisonous Mushroom."[13] Koppel S. Pinson,[14] editor of the American edition of Professor Lichtenberger's *The Third Reich,* quotes from the *Berliner Tageblatt's* account of a speech by Dr. Goebbels, Minister of People's Enlightenment and Propaganda, on Tempelhof Field in Berlin, June 30, 1935:

"Does one believe that we have buttons instead of eyes not to see how certain counter movements in the capital city are once again attempting to spread out? (Applause) And how the bourgeois intellectuals once again are ready to give them

[13] *New York Herald Tribune,* April 4, 1938.
[14] Lichtenberger, *op. cit.,* p. 153.

brotherly aid with that stupid and inane phrase that the Jew is also a human being. True he is, but what kind of a human being! A flea is also an animal, yet not a very pleasing animal. We do not want the Jew any more! He has no place any longer in the German community!"

"Liberals" are classified as weak, insipid, vacillating, temporizing, and unprincipled. To be a "liberal" or to believe in the "stupid doctrine of equality" fostered by "Jewish-invented democracy" is to be a lily-livered "red." "Jewish democracy" is opposed to the "true democracy," which Hitler claims to have established.

Nazi propagandists supercharge words with feeling and emotion in order to give them greater force in Name Calling. The same supercharging is applied to the "virtue words" which they employ in the Glittering Generalities device. Many of these words derive their virtue from the immense reservoir of honesty, decency, good workmanship, good will, fine imagination, and rich emotionalism of the German people. Others are given significant new meanings.

Glittering Generalities

"Glittering Generalities" is a device by which the propagandist identifies his program with virtue by use of "virtue words." Here he appeals to our emotions of love, generosity, and brotherhood.

Much that is to the interest of those who control the régime is praised in terms of the "community good" and "comradeliness." To the same end there is considerable talk about subjecting all "narrow" and "selfish" interests to the "welfare of the community." Such words as "labor" and "sacrifice" are given additional "virtue" by ceremonials and dramatic awards.[15] As was previously indicated, the virtue that the word "socialist" had come to connote in Germany was the reason for its inclusion in the official name of the National Socialist party. Many Germans who believed in socialism were thus led to vote for a party whose leadership was committed to destroy socialism.

The most sweeping generality is that conveyed by the word *Volk* (folk or people). The *Volk,* after purging itself of Jewish blood, is to return to the true Germanic tradition of the Middle Ages. To lend authority to this theory a "biological mythology" has had to be invented, and is now proclaimed by professors appointed to university chairs for that purpose. Thus, we see the Card Stacking and Testimonial devices used to strengthen an application of the Glittering Generalities device. The régime utilizes the word "science" to sanction practices, policies, beliefs, and races which it wants approved. By "science" it obtains approval for the destruction of all opposition and of all "Marxist liberal culture."

Other generalities are effective in appealing to special groups. The farmers

---

[15] This is one of the many examples of how two or more of the common propaganda devices can be used in combination. Here the Glittering Generalities device is combined with the Band Wagon and Transfer devices.

have been heartened to endure the poor return from their toil by a whole magnificat, written on the theme of *Blut und Boden* (blood and soil). They are told that they are of the "glorious peasant state," and each householder is given the honored title of *Bauer*. (The translation of this word, "peasant" or "farmer," does not convey the same connotation which the original does to National Socialist Germany, where the meaning is more that of a "creative builder.") The title is secured to the *Bauer* if he can prove freedom from Jewish blood after January 1, 1800. "*Bauer* honor" ties him to the land and prevents him from changing his occupation or residence. By way of compensation he has the "honor" of having his name placed on an "Estate Roll," which entitles him to use special insignia—something like a coat of arms.

The flattery, the insignia, and the verbal consolations offered to workers on the land have their parallels in those offered to industrial laborers. Nazi propagandists praise the "dignity of labor" and organize festivals in its honor. Labor, they assert, is filled with a new spirit; and to guard this spirit is the task, or mission, of *Die Treuhänder der Arbeit* (the trustees of labor). These "trustees" are government officials in the organizations controlled by the Nationalist Socialist party. It is their duty to see that labor disputes do not arise, or, having arisen, are settled as totalitarian expediency may determine.

Particularly important in any totalitarian state is the *Gleichschaltung* or coördination of all the activities of the people. The German Labor Front, administered from the Central Office in Berlin by Dr. Robert Ley, staff leader of the political organization of the party, has fourteen sections. These, according to the National Industrial Conference Board,[16] "deal with practically every aspect of economic and social life of German labor." The Department of *Kraft durch Freude* or "Strength through Joy"[17] is designed to employ all of the laborer's leisure activities and to see that in these his "spirit" is coördinated with the "common" good. This makes it possible to check the way he spends his leisure hours and to prevent his developing and expressing opposition to the régime.

As pointed out above, by using such Glittering Generalities as "national honor" and "public interest" the National Socialists sought to justify the *Gleichschaltung* of industry described thus by the National Industrial Conference Board:[18]

The state can dismiss the owner of an enterprise from the position of leadership, if his behavior offends against social honor. For the same reason, it can deprive an employee of the position which he occupies. The state can prohibit investment of capital in certain industries if their growth is not desirable and if capital is more urgently needed in some other branch of the national economy. The state can determine the amount of profits that can be paid out and control the employment

---

[16] *Op. cit.*, p. 20.

[17] See Robert A. Brady, *The Spirit and Structure of German Fascism* (New York: The Viking Press, 1937), pp. 149-157.

[18] *Op. cit.*, p. 32. See also Calvin B. Hoover, *Dictators and Democracies* (New York: The Macmillan Company, 1937), Essay on "Dictatorship and Property."

of the amount retained as surplus. The state determines the amount of raw materials placed at the disposal of the various industries and individual enterprises. In the final analysis, the state fixes prices, wages, rates of interest, and the volume and distribution of credit.

Glittering Generalities are given additional power through the deliberate exploitation and perversion of humane feelings and impulses. This technique, much used by the warring nations in the World War, has made it possible for German Fascists to make the German people serve ends which, in the absence of force or fraud, would not have been respected or tolerated. Examples of such perversion utilize the Transfer device.

Transfer

"Transfer" is a device by which the propagandist carries over the authority, sanction, and prestige of something we respect and revere to something he would have us accept.

Something approaching deification of Chancellor Hitler is an outstanding example of this device. Nazi propagandists seek to establish him as a quasi-divinity and to transfer to him the religious feelings of the German people; then to transfer from him the "divine" sanction of the policies, practices, beliefs, and hatreds which he espouses. Some party spokesmen and supporters refer to Hitler in terms like those applied to Christ. However, the pressure exerted to force the acceptance of the Führer as a modern savior has been resisted by those church leaders who have recognized in the Nazi movement a conflict with Christianity, a conflict admitted by the more outspoken National Socialists. Despite this opposition Nazi leaders have had great success in capturing religious feeling and in establishing Hitler as a divinity embodying the traditions of the old German folklore. The Evangelical Church Letter [19] submitted to Chancellor Hitler in June, 1936, makes these observations:

In this connection we must make known to the Führer and Chancellor our uneasiness over the fact that he is often revered in form that is due to God alone. It is only a few years ago that the Führer himself disapproved of his picture being placed on Evangelical altars. His judgment is taken to be the standard unrestrainedly today not only in political decisions, but also in regard to morality and justice in our people, and he himself is vested with the dignity of the national priest, and even of the mediator between God and the people.

(N.B.: Dr. Goebbels on April 19, 1936: "When the Führer addressed his last appeal to the people of March 28, it was as if a profound agitation went through the whole nation; one felt that Germany was transformed into one single House of God, in which its intercessor stood before the throne of the Almighty to bear witness. . . . It seemed to us that this cry to heaven of a people for freedom and peace could not die away unheard. That was religion in its profoundest and most mystical sense. A nation then acknowledged God through its spokesman, and laid its destiny and its life with full confidence in His hand." See also Göring's speeches.)

[19] *International Conciliation* (Carnegie Endowment for International Peace, No. 324), November, 1936, p. 567.

Pope Pius XI [20] in his encyclical on Germany, March 14, 1937, stressed the same point when he wrote:

Beware, Venerable Brethren, of the growing abuse in speech and writing, of using the thrice holy name of God as a meaningless label for a more or less capricious form of human search and longing.

When members of the Roman Catholic Church and of the Protestant churches are not sufficiently influenced by the attempt to transfer their allegiance from the church beliefs which have held to the beliefs "coördinated" with those of the state, more direct means of persuasion are used. Of these the Pope [21] wrote:

Among the spokesmen there are many who, by reason of their official position, seek to create the impression that leaving the Church, and the disloyalty to Christ the King which it entails, is a particularly convincing and meritorious form of profession of loyalty to the present State. With cloaked and with manifest methods of coercion, by intimidation, by holding out the prospect of economic, professional, civic and other advantages, the loyalty of Catholics and especially of certain classes of Catholic officials to their faith is put under a pressure that is as unlawful as it is unworthy of human beings. All Our fatherly sympathy and deepest condolence We offer to those who pay so high a price for their fidelity to Christ and the Church.

Baldur von Schirach, Nazi youth leader, wrote for the youth of Germany this prayer: [22]

"Adolf Hitler, we believe in Thee. Without Thee we would be alone. Through Thee we are a people. Thou hast given us the great experience of our youth, comradeship. Thou hast laid upon us the task, the duty, and the responsibility. Thou has given us Thy Name [Hitler Jugend], the most beloved Name that Germany has ever possessed. We speak it with reverence, we bear it with faith and loyalty. Thou canst depend upon us, Adolf Hitler, Leader and Standard-Bearer. The Youth is Thy Name. Thy Name is the Youth. Thou and the young millions can never be sundered."

Effective in transferring the sanction of the Almighty to his program are Hitler's public prayers. For example, in his address to the Reichstag, February 20, 1938,[23] in which the Nazi aggression against Austria, Czechoslovakia and other nations was forecast, Hitler used this device to give his acts divine approval in advance. He closed that address with these words:

At this hour I should only like to pray the Lord God also in years to come to bestow His blessing upon our work, our acts, our insight and our resolution to preserve us from overbearing as well as cowardly subservience, guiding us on the right path which His providence mapped out for the German people and that He always will give us the courage to do what is right and never waver or shrink before any violence or any danger. Long live Germany and the German nation.

[20] Reprinted in Lichtenberger, *op. cit.*, p. 348.
[21] *Ibid.*, p. 353.
[22] Brady, *op. cit.*, pp. 196-7.
[23] *The New York Herald Tribune*, February 21, 1938.

That the attempt to give divine sanction to Hitler and the Nazis has been successful is attested by a petition presented to the Chancellor by the chaplains of the armed forces in the autumn of 1937.[24] From it these excerpts are taken:

The one half believes enthusiastically everything that is officially announced; the other half holds that it is all a lie. . . . The repeated promises that the rights of the church would be recognized and that full liberty would be given to it to regulate its own affairs have not been forgotten. . . . The State and the party combat today not only the churches, let alone merely political activities of the churches. They combat Christianity. This fact is repeatedly denied. It is true nevertheless. . . . In the training camps of the party it is repeatedly explained that National Socialism has three enemies: Judaism, Masonry and Christianity. Public acceptance of Christianity is regarded, when a new position is to be filled, as a tie that unfits the candidate for service to the State or the party. . . . Of the 18,000 Protestant pastors in Germany approximately 1,300 have been in prison or under police arrest since 1934. That the pastor should be arrested has become a routine affair for Protestant parishes. . . . The type of men who have become famous by combating Christianity and who employ all their power to defile other men's holy things will display when matters become really serious their moral worthlessness. A keen observer can already see the signs. Bolshevism will easily find followers among some of those who today shout "Heil Hitler!"

The prestige and authority of God are used to sanction the National Socialist party, its foreign policy of military expansion,[25] and its domestic policy of bending to its will labor, agriculture, business, and all ideals, including those of Christianity.

Attempts are made to divert the attention of the industrial worker from the declining purchasing power of his labor and from the facts of his exploitation by transferring the feelings aroused in his breast by songs, processions, and rituals to a sense of pride in the "dignity of labor." [26] The prestige, sanction, and authority of previous traditions of labor solidarity are transferred to the politically controlled labor organizations of the National Socialists, who have taken over the ritual and symbolism built up by the pre-Nazi labor unions and by the Social Democrats. May Day has been made the "Day of National Labor." All the "virtue" of the German *Volk* is transferred to labor. Workers are "honored" and "ennobled" with the "spiritual values" of the German *Volk*. This virtue is symbolized by the swastika, which here is the "symbol of German creative power." [27]

Love of the home and motherhood are similarly exploited to encourage women to accept the form of living which the National Socialist program

[24] *The New York Times,* November 28, 1937.

[25] Note Hitler's reference in his speech at Linz, Upper Austria (*The New York Times,* March 13, 1938), to the taking of Austria as a "divine commission" and this quotation from his Vienna speech (*ibid.,* April 10, 1938): "I believe it was God's will to send this Austrian boy to the Reich and to permit him to return as a mature man to reunite the two great sections of the German people.

"Within three days the Lord struck the former rulers of this country. Everything that has happened must have been pre-ordained by Divine Will."

[26] Albert Förster, in *Kalender der deutschen Arbeit* (Berlin: Verlag der deutschen Arbeitsfront, 1934), p. 195.

[27] Rolf Dreves, in *Kalender, op. cit.,* p. 57.

requires of them. Children are made responsive to military ideals by transferring to these ideals the child's love of adventure. The peasant's love of the land is stimulated and transferred to an acceptance of his place in the present régime by such pronouncements as this:[28]

The peasant, sticking to his soil, tilling all the time, knows what it means to own the ground. There is a higher value besides the one registered in the Hall of Records. Men of the big cities, the heaps of stones, of the fountain pen, of the ledger, of the sewing needle . . . do not know any more what Mother Earth should mean to them.

For children the Transfer device most frequently employed is the symbol of the Nazi hero—especially in his rôle of soldier. Manliness is identified with the glory of the party and is used as a means of encouraging in German boys an attitude of superiority toward women and a belief in the doctrines of militarism and anti-Semitism. Words and symbols appertaining to war have been endowed with a glorious sense to make war appear heroic and thrilling. Little children know and give the Hitler salute. Toy soldiers, tanks, machine guns, and simplified battle instructions abound everywhere—symbols to transfer sanction to the later use of real tanks and machine guns. During special "children's evenings" boys and girls read books like *Horst Wants to Be a Soldier, A Child Goes to War, The Battle of Tannenberg,* and *Two Lads in the Navy.*[29] Problems in some arithmetic books deal with such questions as the quantity of gas bombs that would be necessary, if dropped from an altitude of ten thousand feet, to destroy a town of five thousand inhabitants.

Testimonial

The "Testimonial" is a device to make us accept anything from a patent medicine or a cigarette to a program of national policy.

From the fact that "the Führer knows the goal and knows the direction," it follows that his is the supreme testimonial. No authority and no judgment which does not follow from or accord with his can be right. No specialist knows better than he, no recommendation can be better than his. He can deny even the authority of science. Only the conclusions of "German science" as approved by the Führer may be accepted. When the conclusions of science do not accord with his wishes, as in genetics, a new science has to be invented (Card Stacking); its prestige then has to be established by his testimonial.[30] So along with the arts. Only that art which is approved by the Führer and his subordinates as German art may be accepted by the German people.[31] So also does he decree how men and women shall live their lives. The kind of

---

[28] Kurt Biging, in *Kalender, op. cit.,* p. 138.
[29] Cf. Ralph Thurston. "Under the Nazi Christmas Tree," *The New Republic,* December 25, 1935, pp. 193-4. See also Schuman, *op. cit.,* pp. 370-374.
[30] See Brady, *op. cit.,* "The New Nazi Sciences," pp. 46-52.
[31] See Olin Downes in *The New York Times,* April 3, 1938. ". . . it remains a fact that an absolute dictatorship of the sort now practiced in such extensive areas of the world overseas [Germany, Italy, and Russia] is nothing but destructive to creative thought in any field.

life which has the Führer's approval is that which is surrendered to the state. In this Hitler is the arbiter; his approval is the supreme testimonial.

By the same leadership principle the attempted deification of Hitler is used to justify all actions at the top of the National Socialist pyramid. Delegation of power down through the party hierarchy is made to justify the actions of every "leader." There are no elections in the democratic sense of the word and no free discussions. "Leaders" hold office indefinitely and at the discretion of their immediate superiors.

Plain Folks

"Plain Folks" is a device used by politicians, labor leaders, business men, and even by ministers and educators to win our confidence by appearing to be people like ourselves—"just plain folks among the neighbors."

At the same time that the Führer is canonized, an attempt is made to transform him into a "man of the people." In this, the propagandists are greatly assisted by his habits; for he affects ordinary clothes, wears no medals other than his simple Iron Cross, eats plain food and that sparingly, and leads a quiet, secluded life. He is pictured as a man of the people meeting plain folks in their ordinary walks of life, enjoying with them their simple work and pleasures. But as previously indicated, Hitler wields an almost hypnotic power over an audience as he rushes excitedly through a speech. The simplest peasant and the most untutored servant girl feel that he is talking directly to them. As he speaks, they seem to relive with him his terrible war experiences and his poverty-stricken post-war days. Just as one of the most powerful appeals of the figure of Christ for the poor of all ages is his lowly origin and his expressions of sympathy for humble people, so the National Socialists attempt to capitalize on Hitler's early career. Jesus, a carpenter, is the Messiah of the Christian world; Hitler, a house painter, is the savior of Germany. However, to judge by what Hitler has written in his book, Mein Kampf, he appears to have little sympathy but much contempt for the broad masses. Miriam Beard [32] says:

He [Hitler] will not be squeamish about his methods: "Whenever people fight for their existence all questions of humanity or esthetics fall away to nothing." Mercy is a vain illusion, he informs us on page 267 of the original, cut from the translation, "in a world . . . in which Force is forever mistress over the weak" and in which "Nature does not know" it.
The real sting is taken from his [Hitler's] remarks on labor. His intention to "free economic life from the influences of the mass" is omitted.

In this case, as in that of the other propaganda devices discussed in this paper, the element of misrepresentation of fact is considerable, although it is not always predominant. The device which plays the most important part in National Socialist propaganda is, therefore, "stacking the cards" for or

[32] "Hitler Unexpurgated: Deletions from 'Mein Kampf,'" in Nazism: An Assault on Civilization, Pierre van Paassen, editor (New York: Harrison Smith and Robert Haas, 1934), pp. 268, 272.

against beliefs or facts which the National Socialists wish either to encourage or to suppress.

Card Stacking

"Card Stacking" is a device in which the propagandist employs all the arts of deception to win our support for himself, his group, nation, race, policy, practice, belief, or ideal. He stacks the cards against the truth. He uses under-emphasis and over-emphasis to dodge issues and evade facts.

The misrepresentation of facts works in two ways. On the one hand there is a rigorously enforced censorship, backed by an elaborate spy system and the constant threat of concentration camps. By this means the régime can suppress facts, prevent discussion and expression of discontent and opposition. This largely accounts for the fact that many visitors on returning from Germany report that they heard no expression of discontent. On the other hand the régime has freedom to give publicity to falsehoods. Hitler [33] approves such publicity in *Mein Kampf* (deleted from the English translation) when he writes:

"Propaganda . . . does not have to seek objectively for the truth so far as it favors an opponent . . . but exclusively has to serve our interests." It must adopt every device of slander that ingenuity can suggest: "whenever our propaganda permits for a single moment the shimmer of an appearance of right on the other side, it has laid a foundation for doubt in the right of our cause . . . especially among a people that so suffers from objectivity-mania as the German!"

The Reichstag fire [34] on February 27, 1933, one week before the last free election in the Weimar Republic, affords an example of effective Card Stacking. The records of the trial following the fire establish clearly that the firing was planned and executed with finesse, that Communists were immediately accused of the act, that preparations had been made for the arrest of Communists before the fire-calls had been sounded, and that the evidence submitted by the National Socialists against the accused Communists did not stand in court. But none of the significant facts behind the fire was submitted, although foreign observers were convinced that both the National Socialists and the court knew what they were. The falsity of the charge that the Communists burned the Reichstag buildings was never told the German people.

Similar Card Stacking techniques were utilized at the Olympic Games in Berlin and at the fifth centenary anniversary of Heidelberg University. In connection with the latter the celebrations were taken out of the hands of the regular university authorities. The foreign scholars who attended witnessed a series of National Socialist political speeches, storm troop parades, and demonstrations intended to show the German people that the scientific and educational world approved of the Nazi system. Nothing was said of the fact

[33] Quoted by Beard, *op. cit.*, p. 269.
[34] See Schuman, *op. cit.*, "The Sign from Heaven," pp. 201-212.

that the leading universities of the world, including three of the oldest—Paris, Oxford, and Cambridge—declined to attend. Nor was any publicity given to the letters sent by these universities, in which they declined the invitations and deplored the loss of academic freedom in the country which gave *Lehrfreiheit* to the world.

The spirit of the Reichstag trial and the Heidelberg celebration is reflected in the announcements of foreign policy from Wilhelmstrasse. Treaties and pronouncements are often regarded as instruments useful to placate, appease, or even deceive other governments. After categorical denials of German interference in Spain, official recognition was given Franco, and Hitler made the statement that German troops were in Spain not only to "protect" her from "communism" but also to keep open for Germany access to ores and other raw materials.

In line with this policy is the destruction of books and papers which contain what the Japanese call "dangerous thoughts." Public and private libraries, bookstores, offices, and reference files are searched for "red," "communist," "Jewish" literature—literature which includes the works of Helen Keller, Émile Zola, Marcel Proust, H. G. Wells, Thomas and Heinrich Mann, Arnold Zweig, Albert Einstein, Jacob Wassermann, along with Karl Marx, Friedrich Engels, Lenin, and Stalin. Such books feed great fires in public squares throughout the country. Quotations from some of these works are taken out of their context and presented to the public as examples of how these authors have been "poisoning the community" with "filth" and "lies."

Even long accepted classics are not immune. In a letter [35] to the *Neue Tagebuch* (Prague, Czechoslovakia, April 24, 1937) Dr. Emil Ludwig recounted his abortive attempt to purchase a copy of the only complete edition of *Goethe's Conversations* edited by Baron von Biedermann. The reply which his Zurich bookstore received from Leipzig read, "Biedermann Gespräche mit Goethe destroyed." When he learned that the Third Reich was preparing a new and purged "Selection" of this famous German classic, Dr. Ludwig wrote: "Here are a few examples why *Goethe's Conversations* need to be purged for use in present-day Germany.

"They are Prussians, my friend, so beware! Prussians always claim to know everything better than anyone else."—To Grüner, 1822.

"Patriotism depraves history. Jews, Greeks, and Romans depraved their own history and the history of other peoples by not telling it impartially. The Germans do it, too, with their own history and that of other nations."—To Riemer, 1817.

"He was infuriated by Wurm's efforts to make the Jews an object of ridicule on the stage, and he said, 'It is despicable to pillory a nation which possesses such remarkable talents in art and science. As long as I am in charge of the theatre, this type of play will never be produced.'"—Biedermann Edition, Vol. II, p. 385.

Miriam Beard [36] has shown how the English edition of *Mein Kampf* was purged of remarks which might offend foreigners. Eliminated are the more

---

[35] Translated by Marvin Lowenthal in a letter to *The New York Times,* July 12, 1937.
[36] *Op. cit.,* pp. 257-279.

vitriolic attacks on France and democratic institutions, many of the eulogies of the Germans as a "master race," the more scurrilous references to Jews and to the "stupid masses," and the more blatant advocacy of militarism, force, violence, and war. Hitler says, for example in words deleted from the translation,[37] that he adopted Feder's anti-usury cry for its drawing power, with no intention of keeping his promise, since a great politician "has to bother himself less with means that with the goal."

An analysis of parallel news reports in German and foreign papers offers examples of the effective use of Card Stacking by a controlled press. For instance, during the trial of Pastor Niemoeller the only news carried by the German papers was a brief attack upon him as one who advocated a policy of love to Jews and traitors and preached from the Old Testament. His release by the court was announced but his rearrest by the secret police was not. Convictions of Roman Catholics for "immoral practices" were published; acquittals were "played down." Although the Minister for Church Affairs, Herr Hans Kerrl, announced that more than 8,000 Catholic religious leaders were or had been under arrest, he did not publish the fact that only about forty-nine had been convicted of immoral actions. Similarly, many crimes of individual Jews are publicized, but no publicity is given to ways in which German Jews have served their country. No intimation, for example, is made of the fact that 12,000 Jews died for Germany in the World War; or that, despite official discouragement, approximately the same proportion of Jews as of Gentiles served in the German army and navy.[38]

In addition to influencing the German people in the direction desired by the dictator, the falsehoods inherent in Card Stacking arouse hatreds which have the effect of rallying the people against the supposed enemy or peril.

Band Wagon

The "Band Wagon" is a device to make us follow the crowd, to accept the propagandist's program *en masse*. Here his theme is: "Everybody's doing it." His techniques range from those of medicine show to dramatic spectacle.

One of the great unifying principles adopted by the National Socialists is that of hate. Among the passages deleted from the English version of *Mein Kampf*, Hitler has written: [39]

"Hate is more lasting than dislike, and the thrusting power for the mightiest upheavals on this earth has at all times come less from scientific recognition than from a fanaticism that fills the souls of the masses and in a forward driving hysteria" (*vorwärtsjagenden Hysterie*).

In accordance with this principle Jews, communists, liberals, and democrats, became objects of hatred and scapegoats which could be made to suffer for

---

[37] *Ibid.*, p. 268.
[38] For a summary of statistics relating to the number and positions of Jews in Germany, see Schuman, *op. cit.*, pp. 316-8; and Mildred Wertheimer, "The Jews in the Third Reich," *Foreign Policy Association Reports*, IX (1933), pp. 174-184. According to German census figures in 1925, professing Judaists constituted 0.9 per cent of the total population of 62,410,619.
[39] Beard, *op. cit.*, p. 267.

the people's distress. Unity is further encouraged by patriotic demonstrations. Typical in these are gigan:ic crowds of people, massed ranks of uniformed troops, bands playing patriotic and martial airs, voices declaiming from a hundred mechanical mouths, ecstatic marchers carrying flickering torches, their resinous smoke blending into the darkness, flags and swastikas everywhere. This is the National Socialist equivalent of "bread and circuses." To bring all Germans upon the National Socialist band wagon, the party propagandists play continuously upon the common fears, hatreds, prejudices, aspirations and traditions. All propaganda devices culminate in this one. Not to get on the German fascist band wagon is the gravest heresy, tantamount to treason. This largely accounts for reports of nearly 100 percent "Yes" votes in all Nazi plebiscites.

To What End All This Propaganda?

Prophecies are hazardous. We do not know the future of German Fascism. When Hitler wrote his book, *Mein Kampf,* he stated as objectives so many goals which since have been attained that the book often is called the blueprint of German Fascism. Hitler has written: "A State which . . . devotedly fosters its best racial elements is bound one day to become Master of the Earth (*Herr der Erde*)."[40]

Preparation for war is today the major activity of the National Socialists. Hitler's program for expansion is as impressive as the Berlin-to-Bagdad objective of the former Kaiser. If expansion can be obtained without fighting, as in the case of Austria, by mere threat of military attack with acquiescence, support or approval of politicians, statesmen, and groups in other states, there will be no war—simply the peaceful yielding to German Fascist occupation or domination. Lands so occupied or dominated probably would experience almost immediately five major phenomena characteristic of Fascism in Germany itself:

1. The destruction of labor unions.
2. The destruction of "free enterprise" to bring business under the absolute control of the Führer.
3. The destruction of "free enterprise" in agriculture.
4. The destruction or silencing of members of the intellectual class—editors, professors, teachers, clergymen and others who by reason of native gifts, training, education, and experience are among the best equipped to analyze and appraise the policies and acts of the Führer and the hierarchy of Nazi officials.
5. A monopoly of propaganda, accompanied by coercion, to keep all the people subservient to the authoritarian will.

Preceding such occupation or domination one may expect subversive or open propaganda to make the people receptive to Fascism. This will have the support of those groups and individuals, including high public officials, who expect advantages from German Fascism. In this connection, however,

---

[40] Quoted by Beard, *op. cit.,* p. 258.

a word of warning: We must guard against assuming that German Fascism or any other variety of Fascism arises from propaganda alone. German Fascism come into being not primarily because of Hitler's masterful skill as a propagandist but because conditions of unemployment, impoverishment, despair, anger, and resentment were such in Germany that any person or group offering salvation in terms sufficiently appealing could have influenced profoundly the political and economic decisions of the German people. Hitler was sufficiently appealing. With the financial support of certain individuals and the intrigues and incompetencies of men like von Papen and Hindenburg, Fascism became a reality.

It was a combination of economic breakdown, governmental weakness, and propaganda which made pre-Nazi Germany ready for Fascism. A similar combination could bring Fascism elsewhere.

SUGGESTED READINGS

The foregoing analysis of National Socialist propaganda can do little more than suggest the techniques used in bringing about and maintaining German Fascism. For those who wish detailed accounts, the following books are suggested:

Adolf Hitler's autobiography, *Mein Kampf* (Munich: Verlag Franz Eher Nachfolger, 1933), was begun when he was thirty-five while imprisoned in the fortress of Landsberg am Lech following the abortive *Putsch* of November, 1923. It contains his program and political theories. An English edition, considerably abridged, translated by E. T. S. Dugdale, has been published under the title of *My Battle* (New York: Houghton Mifflin Company, 1937. Pp. viii + 297. $2.50).

Robert A. Brady's *The Spirit and Structure of German Fascism* (New York: The Viking Press, 1937. Pp. xix + 420. $3.00) gives a vivid picture of conditions in Germany under the National Socialists.

Frederick L. Schuman's *The Nazi Dictatorship* (2nd ed., revised; New York: Alfred A. Knopf, 1936. Pp. xiii + 516. $3.50) presents a clear account of the early history and propaganda of the Nazis.

Henri Lichtenberger's *The Third Reich,* translated from the French and edited by Koppel S. Pinson (New York: The Greystone Press, 1937. Pp. xi + 392. $3.00) reviews objectively the functioning of National Socialism. The appendix, containing material not readily available, and the excellent bibliography are particularly valuable.

Stephen H. Roberts' *The House that Hitler Built* (New York: Harper and Brothers, 1938. Pp. xii + 380. $3.00) is a dispassionate judgment of the Hitler régime. The author, an Australian, devotes much attention to the army.

Vaso Trivanovitch's *Economic Development of Germany under National Socialism* (New York: National Industrial Conference Board, Inc., 1937. Pp. xvii + 141. $3.50) contains valuable material on such subjects as the organization and the economic position of labor and industry, foreign trade, and public finance.

Five Years of Hitler (New York: American Council on Public Affairs, 1938. Pp. 46. 15c) sets forth in headline form an account of what has happened in National Socialist Germany. The editor is M. B. Schnapper; the contributors are Frederick L. Schuman, Henry Smith Leiper, Robert A. Brady, Alice Hamilton, Charles A. Beard, and H. C. Engelbrecht.

Calvin B. Hoover's *Dictators and Democracies* (New York: The Macmillan

Company, 1937. Pp. xi + 110. $1.50), while not devoted solely to National Socialism, is an interpretation of developments in Germany, Italy, and Soviet Russia as illustrations of totalitarian states.

Mildred S. Wertheimer's *Germany Under Hitler* (New York: Foreign Policy Association and World Peace Foundation, 1935. Pp. 48. 25c) gives a brief, concise account of the rise of Hitler to power and of his first two years as Chancellor of the German Reich.

The New York Times, New York Herald Tribune, and *Christian Science Monitor* have carried particularly significant day-by-day accounts which reveal all of the common propaganda devices used by the German Fascists. These newspapers should be followed for contemporary evaluation of Nazi propaganda.

The American Observer, a weekly review of social thought and action (Civic Education Service, 744 Jackson Place, Washington, D. C., $2.00 a year), is convenient for those who lack the time to follow the day-by-day accounts in the better daily newspapers.

Vienna: March, 1938—A Footnote for Historians is "a verbatim record of the Austrian crisis, exactly as it came to CBS listeners." Free single copies may be secured by addressing the Columbia Broadcasting System, 485 Madison Avenue, New York, N. Y.

ᴓᴓᴓᴓᴓᴓᴓᴓᴓᴓᴓᴓᴓᴓᴓᴓᴓᴓᴓᴓᴓᴓᴓᴓᴓᴓᴓᴓᴓ

Marco Polo [1]

by EILEEN POWER

LET us go back in mind—as would that we could go back in body—to the year 1268. It is a year which makes no great stir in the history books, but it will serve us well. In those days, as in our own, Venice lay upon her lagoons, a city like a sea-bird's nest afloat on the shallow waves, a city like a ship, moored to the land but only at home upon the seas, the proudest city in all the Western world. For only consider her position. Lying at the head of the Adriatic, half-way between East and West, on the one great sea thoroughfare of medieval commerce, a Mediterranean seaport, yet set so far north that she was almost in the heart of Europe, Venice gathered into her harbour all the trade routes overland and overseas, on which packhorses could travel or ships sail. Merchants bringing silk and spices, camphor and ivory, pearls and scents and carpets from the Levant and from the hot lands beyond it, all came to port in Venice. For whether they came by way of Egypt sailing between the low banks of the Nile and jolting on camels to Alexandria, or whether they came through the rich and pleasant land of Persia and the Syrian desert to Antioch and Tyre, or whether they slowly pushed their way in a long, thin caravan across the highlands of Central Asia and south of the Caspian Sea to Trebizond, and so sailed through the Black Sea

---

[1] Condensed from *Medieval People* (1924). By permission of and arrangement with Houghton Mifflin Company.

and the Dardanelles, Venice was their natural focus. Only Constantinople might have rivalled her, and Constantinople she conquered. To Venice, therefore, as if drawn by a magnet, came the spoils of the East, and from Venice they went by horse across the Alps by the Brenner and St. Gothard passes to Germany and France, or in galleys by way of the Straits of Gibraltar to England and Flanders; and the galleys and pack-horses came back again to Venice, laden with the metals of Germany, the furs of Scandinavia, the fine wool of England, the cloth of Flanders, and the wine of France.

Is it not true to say that Venice was the proudest city on earth, *la noble cite que l'en apele Venise, qui est orendroit la plus bele dou siecle?* [2] Life was a fair and splendid thing for those merchant princes who held the gorgeous East in fee in the year of grace 1268. In that year traders in great stone counting-houses, lapped by the waters of the canals, were checking, book in hand, their sacks of cloves, mace and nutmegs, cinnamon and ginger from the Indies, ebony chessmen from Indo China, ambergris from Madagascar, and musk from Tibet. In that year the dealers in jewels were setting prices upon diamonds from Golconda, rubies and lapis lazuli from Badakhshan, and pearls from the fisheries of Ceylon; and the silk merchants were stacking up bales of silk and muslin and brocade from Bagdad and Yezd and Malabar and China. In that year young gallants on the Rialto (scented gallants, but each, like Shakespeare's Antonio, with a ship venturing into port somewhere in the Levant) rubbed elbows with men of all nations, heard travellers' tales of all lands, and at dawn slipped along the canals in gondolas (not black in those days, but painted and slung with silk), saluting the morning with songs; and the red-haired ladies of Venice, whom centuries later Titian loved to paint, went trailing up and down the marble steps of their palaces, with all the brocades of Persia on their backs and all the perfumes of Arabia to sweeten their little hands.

It was in that year, too, that one Martino da Canale, a clerk in the customs house, began to busy himself (like Chaucer after him) less with his accounts than with writing in the delectable French language ("por ce que lengue franceise cort parmi le monde, et est la plus delitable a lire et a oir que nule autre") a chronicle of Venice. It is of the water, watery, Canale's chronicle, like Ariel's dirge; he has indeed, "that intenseness of feeling which seems to resolve itself into the elements which it contemplates." Here is nothing indeed, of "the surge and thunder of the Odyssey," but the lovely words sparkle like the sun on the waters of the Mediterranean, and like a refrain, singing itself in and out of the narrative, the phrase recurs, "Li tens estoit clers et biaus . . . et lors quant il furent en mer, li mariniers drecerent les voiles au vent, et lesserent core a ploine voiles les nes parmi la mer a la force dou vent"; [3] for so much of the history of Venice was enacted upon deck. It is a

---

[2] Canale, *Cronique,* p. 270.

[3] "The weather was clear and fine . . . and when they were at sea, the mariners let out the sails to the wind, and let the ships run with spread sails before the wind over the sea." See, for instance, Canale, *op. cit.,* pp. 320, 326.

passing proud chronicle, too, for Canale was, and well he knew it, a citizen of no mean city.

Now would I [he says] that every one and all know for ever the works of the Venetians, who they were and whence they came and what they are, and how they made the noble city which is called Venice, which is this day the fairest in the world. And I would that all those who are now living and those who are to come know how the noble city is builded and how all good things abound in her, and how the sire of the Venetians, the noble Doge, is powerful, and what nobility is found therein and the prowess of the Venetian people, and how they are all perfect in the faith of Jesu Christ and obedient to holy Church, and how they never disobey the commandment of holy Church. Within this noble Venice there dares to dwell neither heretic, nor usurer, murderer, thief nor robber. And I will tell you the names of all the Doges that have been in Venice, one after the other, and what they did to the honour of holy Church and of their noble City. And I will tell you the names of the noble captains whom the noble Doges sent in their time to lay low their enemies, and concerning the victories that they won I will have you know, for it is fitting. . . . In the year of the incarnation of our Lord Jesu Christ MCCLXVII years, in the time of Milord Renier Zeno, the high Doge of Venice, I laboured and strove until I found the ancient history of the Venetians, whence they came first and how they builded the noble city called Venice, which is to-day the fairest and the pleasantest in the world, full of beauty and of all good things. Merchandise flows through this noble city even as water flows from the fountains, and the salt water runs through it and round it and in all places save in the houses and the streets; and when the citizens go abroad they can return to their houses by land or by water, as they will. From all parts there come merchandise and merchants, who buy merchandise as they will and take it back to their own countries. Within this town is found food in great plenty, bread and wine, land fowl and river fowl, fresh meat and salt, and sea fish and river fish. . . . You may find within this fair town many men of gentle birth, both old men and young *damoisaus* in plenty, and merchants with them, who buy and sell, and money changers and citizens of all crafts, and therewith mariners of all sorts, and ships to carry them to all lands and galleys to lay low their enemies. And in this fair town is also great plenty of ladies and damsels and maidens, very richly apparelled.[4]

It happened that there was a new Doge that year, our year 1268, Lorenzo Tiepolo by name, and a great procession of the gilds took place before the palace on the Piazza of St. Mary to welcome his accession. Martino da Canale was watching it and wrote it all down in his chronicle. First came the navy sailing past in the harbour, fifty galleys and other ships, with their crews cheering and shouting on deck. Then came the gilds on foot: first the master smiths, with garlands on their heads and banners and trumpets; then the furriers apparelled in samite and scarlet silk, with mantles of ermine and vair; then the weavers richly bedight, and the ten master tailors in white with crimson stars. Then the master clothworkers passed, carrying boughs of olive and wearing crowns of olive on their heads; then the fustian makers in furred robes of their own weaving, and the quilt makers with garlands of gilt beads and white cloaks sewn with fleurs-de-lis, marching two by two, with little children singing *chansonettes* and *cobles* before them. Then came the makers

4 Canale, *op. cit.*, pp. 268-7*

of cloth of gold, all in cloth of gold, and their servants in cloth of gold or of purple, followed by the mercers in silk and the butchers in scarlet, the fish sellers robed and furred and garlanded, and the master barbers, having with them two riders attired as knights-errant, and four captive damsels, strangely garbed. Then came the glass-workers in scarlet furred with vair, and gold-fringed hoods, and rich garlands of pearls, carrying flasks and goblets of the famous Venetian glass before them, and the comb and lantern makers, with a lantern full of birds to let loose in the Doge's presence, and the goldsmiths wearing wreaths and necklaces of gold and silver beads and sapphires, emer-alds, diamonds, topazes, jacinths, amethysts, rubies, jasper, and carbuncles. Masters and servants alike were sumptuously clad, and almost all wore gold fringes on their hoods and garlands of gilded beads. Each craft was accom-panied by its band of divers instruments, and bore with it silver cups and flagons of wine, and all marched in fair order, singing ballads and songs of greeting, and saluted the Doge and Dogaressa in turn, crying "Long live our lord, the noble Doge Lorenzo Tiepolo!" Gild after gild they marched in their splendour, lovely alike to ear and eye; and a week fled before the rejoic-ings were ended and all had passed in procession. Canale surpasses himself here, for he loved State ceremonies; he gives a paragraph to the advance of each gild, its salutation and withdrawal, and the cumulative effect of all the paragraphs is enchanting, like a prose ballade, with a repeated refrain at the end of every verse.[5]

What, they lived once thus in Venice, where the merchants were the kings,
Where St. Mark's is, where the Doges used to wed the sea with rings?

Listening to the magnificent salutation of the Doge by the priests of St. Mark's, "Criste vince, Criste regne, Criste impere. Notre signor Laurens Teuples, Des gracie, inclit Dus de Venise, Dalmace atque Groace, et domi-nator de la quarte partie et demi de tot l'enmire de Romanie, sauvement, honor, vie, et victorie. Saint Marc, tu le aie," [6] who, hearing, could have doubted that Venice, defier of Rome and conqueror of Constantinople, was the finest, richest, most beautiful, and most powerful city in the world?

But was she? Listen and judge. Thousands of miles away from Venice, across the lands and seas of Asia, a little south of the Yangtze River and close to the sea stood the city of Kinsai or Hangchow, the capital of the Sung emperors, who ruled Southern China, not yet (in 1268) conquered by the Tartars.[7] Like Venice, Kinsai stood upon lagoons of water and was inter-sected by innumerable canals. It was a hundred miles in circuit, not counting the suburbs which stretched round it, and there was not a span of ground which was not well peopled. It had twelve great gates, and each of the twelve quarters which lay within the gates was greater than the whole of Venice.

[5] Canale, op. cit., pp. 602-26.
[6] Ibid., p. 600.
[7] This account of Hangchow is taken partly from Marco Polo, Travels, bk. II, ch. LXVIII, and partly from Odoric Pordenone, Yule, Cathay and the Way Thither, pp. 113-20.

Its main street was two hundred feet wide, and ran from end to end of the city, broken every four miles by a great square, lined with houses, gardens, palaces, and the shops of the artisans, who were ruled by its twelve great craft gilds. Parallel with the main street was the chief canal, beside which stood the stone warehouses of the merchants who traded with India. Twelve thousand stone bridges spanned its waterways, and those over the principal canals were high enough to allow ships with their tapering masts to pass below, while the carts and horses passed overhead. In its marketplaces men chaffered for game and peaches, sea-fish, and wine made of rice and spices; and in the lower part of the surrounding houses were shops, where spices and drugs and silk, pearls and every sort of manufactured article were sold. Up and down the streets of Kinsai moved lords and merchants clad in silk, and the most beautiful ladies in the world swayed languidly past in embroidered litters, with jade pins in their black hair and jewelled earrings swinging against their smooth cheeks.

On one side of this city lay a beautiful lake (famous in Chinese history, and still one of the fairest prospects upon earth), studded with wooded islands, on which stood pavilions with charming names: "Lake Prospect," "Bamboo Chambers," "The House of the Eight Genii," and "Pure Delight." Here, like the Venetians, the men of Kinsai came for pleasure parties in barges, nobly hung and furnished, the cabins painted with flowers and mountain landscapes, and looking out they saw on one side the whole expanse of the city, its palaces, temples, convents, and gardens, and on the other the stretch of clear water, crowded with coloured pleasure boats, over which came echoing the high, clear voices and the tinkling instruments of the revellers. There is no space in which to tell of the King's palace, with its gardens and orchards, its painted pavilions, and the groves where the palace ladies coursed the game with dogs, and, tired of the pastime, flung off their robes and ran to the lake, where they disported themselves like a shoal of silver fishes. But a word must be said of the junks, which came sailing into the harbour four and twenty miles away, and up the river to the city; and of the greatest concourse of ships which came to Zaiton (perhaps the modern Amoy), the port of the province. Here every year came a hundred times more pepper than came to the whole of Christendom through the Levantine ports. Here from Indo China and the Indies came spices and aloes and sandalwood, nutmegs, spikenard and ebony, and riches beyond mention. Big junks laded these things, together with musk from Tibet, and bales of silk from all the cities of Mansi,[8] and sailed away in and out of the East India Archipelago, with its spice-laden breezes billowing their sails, to Ceylon. There merchants from Malabar and the great trading cities of Southern India took aboard their cargoes and sold them in turn to Arab merchants, who in their turn sold them to the Venetians in one or other of the Levantine ports. Europeans who saw Zaiton and the other Chinese seaports in after years were wont to say that no one, not even a Venetian, could picture to himself the multitude of trading vessels which sailed upon

[8] Mansi or Manji was Southern China and Cathay was Northern China.

those Eastern seas and crowded into those Chinese harbours. They said also with one accord that Kinsai was without doubt the finest and richest and noblest city in the world. To the men of Kinsai, Venice would have been a little suburb and the Levant a backyard. The whole of the East was their trading field, and their wealth and civilization were already old when Venice was a handful of mud huts peopled by fishermen.

Nor was Kinsai alone and unmatched in all its wonder and beauty, for a three days' journey from it stood Sugui, which to-day we call Suchow, lying also on the great canal, with its circumference of twenty miles, its prodigious multitudes swarming the streets, its physicians, philosophers, and magicians; Sugui, with the ginger which was so common that forty pounds of it might be bought for the price of a Venetian silver groat, the silk which was manufactured in such vast quantities that all the citizens were dressed in it and still ships laden with it sailed away; Sugui under whose jurisdiction were sixteen wealthy cities, where trade and the arts flourished. If you had not seen Hangchow, you would have said that there was no city in the world, not Venice nor Constantinople nor another worthy to be named in the same breath with Sugui. The Chinese indeed, seeing the riches and beauty of these two cities, doubted whether even the pleasant courts of heaven could show their equal and proudly quoted the proverb:

> There's Paradise above, 'tis true
> But here below we've Hang and Su.[9]

Kinsai seems far enough away in all conscience from Venice in the year 1268, and Venice was all unwitting of its existence, far beyond the sunrise. Yet there was in the city of the lagoons that year, watching the same procession of the gilds which Canale watched, a boy who was destined to link them for ever in the minds of men—a lean lad of fourteen, Marco Polo, by name, who was always kicking his heels on the quay and bothering foreign sailors for tales of distant lands. He heard all they had to tell him very willingly, storing it up in that active brain of his, for his curiosity was insatiable; but always the tales that he heard most willingly were about the Tartars.

At this time the Tartars were at the height of their power in the West and the East. Tartars ruled at Peking all over Northern China, Corea, Mongolia, Manchuria, and Tibet, and took tribute from Indo China and Java. Tartars were spread over Central Asia, holding sway in Turkestan and Afghanistan. The Golden Horde ruled the Caucasus, a large part of Russia, and a piece of Siberia. Tartars held sway in Persia, Georgia, Armenia, and a part of Asia Minor. When the great Mangu Khan died in 1259, one empire lay spread across Asia and Europe, from the Yellow River to the Danube. There had been nothing like it in the world before, and there was nothing like it again, until the Russian Empire of modern times. By 1268 it was beginning to split up into the four kingdoms of China, Central Asia, Russia, and Persia, but

[9] Yule, *Book of Ser Marco Polo*, II, p. 184.

still it was one people. Now, the attitude of the West to the Tartars at this time was very interesting. At first it feared them as a new scourge of God, like Attila and his Huns; they overran Poland, ravaged Hungary, and seemed about to break like a great flood upon the West, and overwhelm it utterly. Then the tide rolled back. Gradually the West lost its first stupefaction and terror and began to look hopefully towards the Tartars as a possible ally against its age-old foe, the Moslem. The Christians of the West knew that the Tartars had laid the Moslem power low through the length and breadth of Asia, and they knew too, that the Tartars had no very sharply defined faith and were curious of all beliefs that came their way. Gradually the West became convinced that the Tartars might be converted to Christianity, and fight side by side beneath the Cross against the hated Crescent. There grew up the strange legend of Prester John, a Christian priest-king, ruling some-where in the heart of Asia; and indeed little groups of Nestorian Christians did still survive in Eastern Asia at this time.[10] Embassies began to pass between Tartar khans and Western monarchs, and there began also a great series of missions of Franciscan friars to Tartary, men who were ethnologists and geographers at heart as well as missionaries, and have left us priceless accounts of the lands which they ·visited. In the year of grace 1268, much was known about Central Asia, for in 1245 the Pope had sent the Italian friar John of Plano Carpini thither, and in 1253 another friar, William of Rubruck, a French Fleming, had been sent by the saintly Louis, King of France. Both got as far as Karakorum, the Tartar camp on the borders of Northern China, though they did not enter China itself. They had brought back innumerable stories about the nomad conquerors, who carried their tents on carts, and drank fermented mares' milk, about the greatness of the khan and his welcome to the strangers from the West, and the interest with which he listened to their preaching.[11] These tales were common property now, and Marco Polo must have listened to them.

Marco Polo was always talking of the Tartars, always asking about them. Indeed, he had reason to be interested in them. This (as we have said) was the year of grace 1268, and eight years before (some, indeed, say fifteen years) his father, Nicolo Polo, and his uncle Maffeo had vanished into Tartary. They were rich merchants, trading with their own ship to Constantinople, and there they had decided to go on a commercial venture into the lands of the Golden Horde, which lay to the north of the Black Sea. So they had sailed over to the Crimea, where they had a counting-house at Soldaia, and taking with them a store of costly jewels, for they were jewel merchants, they had set off on horseback to visit the Khan of the West Tartars. So much the Venetians knew, for word had come back from Soldaia of their venture; but they had never returned. And so Marco, kicking his heels upon the quay, caught sailor-men by the sleeve and asked them about those wild horsemen

---

[10] For Prester John see *Encyclopædia Britannica,* and Lynn Thorndike, *History of Magic and Experimental Science,* II, 236-45.
[11] See *Journal of William de Rubruck to the Eastern Parts,* tr. W. W. Rockhill.

with their mares' milk and their magicians and their droves of cattle; and as he asked he wondered about his father and his uncle, and whether they were dead and lost for ever in the wilds of Tartary. But even while he asked and wondered and kicked his heels on the quay, while the Doge Tiepolo was watching the procession of the gilds and the clerk Canale was adding up customs dues or writing the ancient history of the Venetians, at that very moment the two Polos were slowly and wearily making their way across the heights of Central Asia with a caravan of mules and camels, drawing near to golden Samarcand with its teeming bazaars, coming nearer and nearer to the West; and in the following year, 1269, they reached Acre, and took ship there for Venice, and so at last came home.

They had a strange story to tell, stranger and better than anything the lean, inquisitive boy had heard upon the quays. They had soon disposed of their jewels and they had spent a year at the camp of the khan of the Golden Horde of Kipchak on the mighty River Volga. Then war broke out between that ruler and the Khan who ruled the Persian Khanate, and it cut off their way back. But Marco's curiosity was inherited; and no Venetian was ever averse to seeing strange lands and seeking out now opportunities for trade; so the Polos decided to go on and visit the Khan of Central Asia or Chagatai, and perhaps make their way back to Constantinople by some unfrequented route. They struggled over plains peopled only by tent-dwelling Tartars and their herds, until at last they reached the noble city of Bokhara. They must have followed the line of the Oxus River, and if we reverse the marvellous description which Matthew Arnold wrote of that river's course in *Sohrab and Rustum,* we still have a picture of the Polos' journey:

> But the majestic River floated on,
> Out of the mist and hum of that low land,
> Into the frosty starlight, and there moved,
> Rejoicing, through the hush'd Chorasmian waste
> Under the solitary moon; he flow'd
> Right for the Polar Star, past Orgunjè,
> Brimming and bright and large: then sands begin
> To hem his watery march, and dam his streams,
> And split his currents; that for many a league
> The shorn and parcell'd Oxus strains along
> Through beds of sand and matted rushy isles—
> Oxus, forgetting the bright speed he had
> In his high mountain cradle in Pamere,
> A foil'd circuitous wanderer:—till at last
> The long'd-for dash of waves is heard, and wide
> His luminous home of waters open, bright
> And tranquil, from whose floor the new-bathed stars
> Emerge and shine upon the Aral Sea.

For three years the Polos remained at Bokhara, until one day it happened that an embassy came to the city, on its way back from the khan in Persia to the great Khan Kublai, who ruled in far-off China, and to whom all the

Tartar rulers owed allegiance. The chief ambassador was struck with the talents and charm of the brothers, who had now become proficient in the Tartar language, and persuaded them to accompany him on his journey to the presence of the Great Khan, who had never yet set eyes on a man of the West, and would, he assured them, receive them honourably. They would not have been Venetians had they refused such an opportunity, and, taking their Venetian servants with them, they journeyed for a year with the Tartar embassy across the heart of Asia, and so reached the great Kublai Khan. Many years later Marco himself described their reception, as they had told it to him:

Being introduced to the presence of the Grand Khan Kublai, the travellers were received by him with the condescension and affability that belonged to his character, and as they were the first Latins who had made their appearance in that country, they were entertained with feasts and honoured with other marks of distinction. Entering graciously into conversation with them, he made earnest inquiries on the subject of the western parts of the world, of the Emperor of the Romans, and of other Christian kings and princes . . . and above all he questioned them particularly respecting the Pope, the affairs of the Church, and the religious worship and doctrine of the Christians. Being well instructed and discreet men, they gave appropriate answers upon all these points, and as they were perfectly acquainted with the Tartar language, they expressed themselves always in becoming terms; insomuch that the Grand Khan, holding them in high estimation, frequently commanded their attendance.[12]

The Great Khan finally decided to send these two intelligent strangers back to their own land on a mission from himself to the Pope, asking for a hundred men of learning to be sent to teach and preach to his Tartars, and for some holy oil from the lamp which burned over Christ's sepulchre in Jerusalem. He provided them with a golden tablet of honour, which acted as a passport and secured that they should be entertained and their journey facilitated from city to city in all its dominions, and so they set forth once more upon their homeward journey. But they were delayed by the dangers and difficulties of travel, "the extreme cold, the snow, the ice, and the flooding of the rivers," and it was three years before they at last reached Acre in the April of 1269, and finding that the Pope had died the year before, and that no election had yet been made, so that they could not immediately accomplish their mission, they decided to visit their home again, and so went back to Venice. There Nicolo found that his wife, who had been with child at his departure, was dead, leaving behind her a son Marco, our young haunter of quays.

This was the marvellous tale which the same Marco drank in from the lips of his new-found father and uncle. But more marvels were to come. For two years the Venetians remained at home, awaiting the election of a Pope in order to deliver the Great Khan's letters; but no election was made, and at last, fearing that Kublai might suspect them of playing him false, they decided to return to the East, and this time they took with them Marco, now

[12] Marco Polo, *Travels*, ch. I.

a well-grown lad of sixteen or seventeen years with a bright eye that looked everywhere and took in everything, observant and sober beyond his age. But when they got as far as Ayas on the Gulf of Scanderoon, news was brought them of the election of Tebaldo di Piacenza as Pope Gregory X, and as Tebaldo had already interested himself in their mission, they returned with all speed to Acre, and obtained from him letters to the Khan (they had already visited Jerusalem and provided themselves with some of the holy oil), and two Dominican friars, "men of letters and science as well as profound theologians," though not the hundred men of learning for whom the Khan had asked; and so they set out again from Acre in November, 1271. The Dominicans may have been profound theologians, but they were somewhat chicken-hearted adventurers, and when rumours reached them of wars in the district of Armenia, through which they had to pass, they hastily handed over their letters to the Venetians, put themselves under the protection of the Knights Templars, and scuttled back to the coast and safety as fast as they could go, leaving the Polos, "undismayed by perils and difficulties to which they had long been inured," to proceed alone. Assuredly, St. Francis crows over St. Dominick somewhere in the courts of Heaven; his friars never feared for their skins, as they travelled blithely into the heat of India and the cold of Central Asia; and it is easy to imagine the comments of fat William of Rubruck upon the flight of the profound theologians.

The account of this second journey of the Polos may be read in the wonderful book which Marco afterwards wrote to describe the wonders of the world. They went from Lajazzo through Turcomania, past Mount Ararat, where Marco heard tell that Noah's ark rested, and where he first heard also of the oil wells of Baku and the great inland sea of Caspian. Past Mosul and Bagdad they went, through Persia, where brocades are woven and merchants bring caravan after caravan of treasures, to Hormuz, on the Persian Gulf, into which port put the ships from India, laden with spices, drugs, scented woods, and jewels, gold tissues and elephants' teeth. Here they meant to take ship, but they desisted, perhaps because they feared to trust themselves to the flimsy nailless vessels in which the Arabs braved the dangers of the Indian Ocean. So they turned north again and prepared to make the journey by land. They traversed the salt desert of Kerman, through Balk and Khorassan to Badakhshan, where there are horses bred from Alexander the Great's steed Bucephalus, and ruby mines and lapis lazuli. It is a land of beautiful mountains and wide plains, of trout streams and good hunting, and here the brothers sojourned for nearly a year, for young Marco had fallen ill in the hot plains: a breath of mountain air blows through the page in which he describes how amid the clean winds his health came back to him. When he was well, they went on again, and ascended the upper Oxus to the highlands of Pamir, "the roof of the world" as it has been called in our own time, a land of icy cold, where Marco saw and described the great horned sheep which hunters and naturalists still call after him the *Ovis Poli,* a land which no traveller (save Benedict Goës, about 1604) described again, until Lieutenant John Wood of the Indian Navy went there in 1838. Thence they descended upon Kashgar, Yarkand, and Khotan, where jade is found, regions which no one visited again until 1860. From Khotan they pushed on to the vicinity of Lake Lob, never to be reached again until a Russian explorer got there in 1871. They halted there to load asses and camels with provisions, and then, with sinking hearts, they began the terrible thirty days' journey across the Gobi Desert. Marco gives a vivid description of its terrors, voices which seem to call the traveller by name, the march of phantom cavalcades, which lures them off the road at night, spirits which fill the air with sounds of music, drums and gongs and the clash of arms—all those illusions which human beings have heard and seen and feared in every desert and in every age.

> What might this be? A thousand fantasies
> Begin to throng into my memory,
> Of calling shapes, and beckoning shadows dire,
> And airy tongues that syllable men's names
> On sands and shores and desert wilderness.

At last they arrived safely at Tangut in the extreme north-west of China, and, skirting the frontier across the great steppes of Mongolia, they were greeted by the Khan's people, who had been sent forward to meet them at the distance of forty days' journey, and so at last they reached his presence in the May of 1275, having journeyed for three years and a half.

The Great Khan received the Polos kindly, listened attentively to the account which they gave of their mission, commended them for their zeal and fidelity, and received the holy oil and the Pope's gifts with reverence. He then observed the boy Marco, now a "young gallant" and personable enough, no doubt, and inquired who he was, and Nicolo made answer, "Sire, this is your servant, and my son," to which the Khan replied, "He is welcome, and much it pleases me," and enrolled Marco among his own attendants. It was the beginning of a long and close association, for Kublai Khan soon found that Marco Polo was both discreet and intelligent, and began to employ him on various missions. Moreover, Marco, for his part, found that the Great Khan was always desirous of learning the manners and customs of the many tribes over whom he ruled. Kublai had to the full that noble curiosity which is the beginning of wisdom, and it irked him exceedingly that his envoys, good conscientious men, followed their noses upon his business, looking neither to right nor to left, and as like as not never even noticed that among the aboriginal hill tribes of the interior called Miaotzu there prevailed the peculiar and entertaining custom of the *couvade,* wherein

> Chineses go to bed
> And lie in, in their ladies' stead.

"The Prince, in consequence," says Marco, "held them for no better than fools and dolts and would say, 'I had far liever hearken about the strange things and the manners of the different countries you have seen than merely be told of the business you went upon.'"

Very different was the habit of the Venetian, who as a lad had lent ear so readily to swarthy sailors on the Rialto. He quickly picked up several of the languages current in the Great Khan's empire, and here is his account of his proceedings when on a mission to foreign parts:

Perceiving that the Great Khan took a pleasure in hearing accounts of whatever was new to him respecting the customs and manners of people, and the peculiar circumstances of distant countries, he endeavoured, wherever he went, to obtain correct information on these subjects and made notes of all he saw and heard, in order to gratify the curiosity of his master. In short, during seventeen years that he continued in his service, he rendered himself so useful, that he was employed on confidential missions to every part of the empire and its dependencies; and sometimes also he travelled on his own private account, but always with the consent and sanctioned by the authority of the Grand Khan. In such circumstances it was that Marco Polo had the opportunity of acquiring a knowledge, either by his own observation or by what he collected from others, of so many things until his time unknown, respecting the Eastern parts of the world, and these he diligently and regularly committed to writing. . . . And by this means he obtained so much honour that he provoked the jealousy of other officers of the court.[13]

It is small wonder that when first the lad came back with his reports the Great Khan and his courtiers marvelled and exclaimed, "If this young man live he will assuredly be a person of great worth and ability."

It was while on these various public missions that Marco Polo journeyed through the provinces of Shansi, Shensi, and Szechuen, and skirted the edge of Tibet to Yunnan, and entered Northern Burma, lands unknown again to the West until after 1860. For three years he was himself governor of the great city of Yangchow, which had twenty-four towns under its jurisdiction, and was full of traders and makers of arms and military accoutrements. He visited Karakorum in Mongolia, the old Tartar capital, and with his uncle Maffeo spent three years in Tangut. On another occasion he went on a mission to Cochin China, and by sea to the southern states of India, and he has left a vivid picture of the great trading cities of Malabar. He might indeed have pondered with Ulysses,

> I am become a name
> For always roaming, with a hungry heart,
> Much have I seen and known, cities of men,
> And manners, climates, countries, governments,
> Myself not least, but honoured of them all.

He describes the great capital Cambaluc (Peking) in the north, and the beautiful Kinsai (Hangchow) in the south. He describes the Khan's summer palace at Shandu, with its woods and gardens, its marble palace, its bamboo pavilion swung like a tent from two hundred silken cords, its stud of white mares, and its wonder-working magicians. Indeed his description of the

13 Marco Polo, *Travels,* pp. 21-22.

summer palace is better known to Englishmen than any other part of his work, for Shandu is Xanadu, which Coleridge saw in a dream after he had been reading Marco's book and wove into wonderful verse:

> In Xanadu did Kubla Khan
> A stately pleasure dome decree,
> Where Alph the sacred river ran,
> Through caverns measureless to man,
> Down to a sunless sea.
>
> And here were gardens bright with sinuous rills,
> Where blossomed many an incense bearing tree,
> And here were forests, ancient as the hills,
> Enfolding sunny spots of greenery.

Nor is it only palaces which Marco Polo describes, for he tells of the great canal and inland river trade of China, the exports and imports at its harbours, the paper money, the system of posts and caravanserais, which linked it together. He gives an unsurpassed picture of that huge, rich, peaceful empire, full of wealth and commerce and learned men and beautiful things, and of its ruler Kublai Khan, one of the noblest monarchs who ever sat upon a throne, who, since "China is a sea that salts all the rivers that flow into it," was far more than a barbarous Mongol khan, was in very truth a Chinese emperor, whose house, called by the Chinese the "Yuan Dynasty," takes its place among the great dynasties of China.

Even more than Marco Polo tells us he must, indeed, have seen. The impersonality of the greater part of the book is its one blemish, for we would fain know more of how he lived in China. There is some evidence that he consorted with the Mongol conquerors rather than with the Chinese, and that Chinese was not one of the languages which he learned. He makes no mention of several characteristic Chinese customs, such as the compressed feet of the women, and fishing with cormorants (both of which are described by Odoric of Pordenone after him); he travelled through the tea districts of Fo-kien, but he never mentions tea-drinking, and he has no word to say even of the great Wall.[14] And how typical a European he is, in some ways, for all his keen interest in new and strange things. "They are," he says of the peaceful merchants and scholars of Suchow, "a pusillanimous race and solely occupied with their trade and manufactures. In these indeed they display considerable ability, and if they were as enterprising, manly, and warlike as they are ingenious, so prodigious is their number that they might not only subdue the whole of the province, but carry their rule further still."[15] Nearly five hundred years later we find the same judgment expressed in different words: "Better fifty years of Europe than a cycle of Cathay." The answer is a question: Would you rather be the pusillanimous Chinese who painted the landscape roll of which a portion is reproduced opposite page 46, or the

---

[14] On Marco Polo's omissions see Yule, *Book of Ser Marco Polo*, I, Introduction, p. 110.
[15] Marco Polo, *Travels*, p. 288.

enterprising, manly, and warlike European of the same period, whose highest achievement in pictorial art is the picture of Marco Polo's embarkation, reproduced opposite page 40? What is civilization and what progress? Yet Marco Polo shows himself throughout his book far from unable to appreciate other standards than those of his own land and religion, for of Sakya-muni Buddha he says that, "had he been a Christian he would have been a great saint of our Lord Jesus Christ," and he could honour Kublai as that great Khan deserved.

But we must return to the history of the Polos in China. From time to time in Marco's book we hear also of his father and uncle, travelling about the empire, growing rich by trade, and amassing a store of those jewels, in the value of which they are so skilled, even helping the Khan to reduce a rebel town, by constructing siege engines for him on the European model, handy Venetians that they were, who could lay their hands to anything.[16] Without doubt they were proud of their Marco, who from an inquisitive lad had grown to so wise and observant a man, and had risen to so high a position. So for seventeen years the three Polos abode in the Khan's service in China. The long months slipped by; and at last they began to feel upon them a longing to see Venice and the lagoons again, and to hear Mass once more beneath the majestic roof of St. Mark's before they died. Moreover, Kublai Khan was growing old himself, and the favour which he had always shown to them had excited some jealousy among his own people, and they feared what might happen when he died. But the old Khan was adamant to all their prayers; wealth and honours were theirs for the asking, but he would not let them go. They might, indeed, have died in China, and we of the West might never have heard of Marco Polo or of Kublai Khan, but for a mere accident, a stroke of fate, which gave them their chance. In 1286 Arghun, the Khan of Persia, lost by death his favourite wife Bolgana, and, according to her dying wish, he sent ambassadors to the Court of Peking to ask for another bride from her own Mongol tribe. Their overland route home again was endangered by a war, and they therefore proposed to return by sea. Just at that moment, Marco Polo happened to return from a voyage on which he had been sent, and spoke with such assurance of the ease with which it had been accomplished, that the three ambassadors conceived a strong desire to take with them all three of these ingenious Venetians, who seemed to know so much about ships. Thus it was that the great Khan was prevailed upon, very reluctantly, to let them go.

Early in 1292 they set sail from the busy port of Zaiton in fourteen big Chinese junks (of which Marco, writing of the shipping of the Indian and China seas, has left an excellent description),[17] with the three envoys, the princess, a beautiful girl of seventeen, "moult bele dame et avenant," says Marco, who had an eye for pretty ladies, and a large suite of attendants. One version of Marco's book says that they took with them also the daughter of the king of Mansi, one of those Sung princesses who in happier days had wan-

16 *Ibid.*, pp. 281 f.
17 *Ibid.*, pp. 321-23.

dered beside the lake in Hangchow, and who had no doubt been brought up
at Cambaluc by the care of Kublai Khan's favourite queen, the Lady Jamui.
The voyage was a long and difficult one; they suffered lengthy delays in
Sumatra, Ceylon, and Southern India, occupied by Marco in studying the sea
charts of the coast of India which the Arab pilots showed him, and adding
to his knowledge of these parts, which he had already visited. Thus it was
over two years before the junks reached Persia, and two of the three envoys
and a large number of their suite had died by the way. When at last they
landed, it was found that Arghun, the prospective bridegroom, had meanwhile
died too, leaving his throne in the charge of a regent for his young son. But
on the regent's advice a convenient solution of the difficulty was found by
handing the princess over to this prince, and Marco and his uncles duly conducted her to him in the province of Timochain, where Marco Polo noticed
that the women were "in my opinion the most beautiful in the world," where
stood the famed and solitary *arbor secco,* and where men still told tales of
great Alexander and Darius. There they took leave of their princess, who had
come on the long voyage to love them like fathers, so Marco says, and wept
sorely when they parted. It was while they were still in Persia, where they
stayed for nine months after handing over the princess, that the Polos received
news of the death of the Great Khan whom they had served so faithfully for
so many years. He died at the ripe age of eighty, and with his death a shadow
fell over Central Asia, darkening the shining yellow roofs of Cambaluc,

> the barren plains
> Of Sericana, where Chineses drive
> With sails and wind their cany waggons light,

the minarets of Persia, and the tents of wild Kipchak Tartars, galloping over
the Russian steppes. So wide had been the sway of Kublai Khan. A shadow
fell also upon the heart of Marco Polo. It was as though a door had clanged to
behind him, never to open again. "In the course of their journey," he says,
"our travellers received intelligence of the Great Khan having departed this
life, which entirely put an end to all prospects of their revisiting those regions."
So he and his elders went on by way of Tabriz, Trebizond, and Constantinople to Venice, and sailed up to the city of the lagoons at long last at the end
of 1295.

A strange fairy-tale legend has come down to us about the return of the
Polos. "When they got thither," says Ramusio, who edited Marco's book in
the fifteenth century, "the same fate befell them as befell Ulysses, who when he
returned after his twenty years' wanderings to his native Ithaca was recognized
by nobody." When, clad in their uncouth Tartar garb, the three Polos
knocked at the doors of the Ca' Polo, no one recognized them, and they had
the greatest difficulty in persuading their relatives and fellow-Venetians that
they were indeed those Polos who had been believed dead for so many years.
The story goes that they satisfactorily established their identity by inviting all

their kinsmen to a great banquet, for each course of which they put on a garment more magnificent than the last, and finally bringing in their coarse Tartar coats, they ripped open the seams and the lining thereof, "upon which there poured forth a great quantity of precious stones, rubies, sapphires, carbuncles, diamonds, and emeralds, which had been sewn into each coat with great care, so that nobody could have suspected that anything was there. . . . The exhibition of such an extraordinary and infinite treasure of jewels and precious stones, which covered the table, once more filled all present with such astonishment that they were dumb and almost beside themselves with surprise: and they at once recognized these honoured and venerated gentlemen in the Ca' Polo, whom at first they had doubted, and received them with the greatest honour and reverence."[18] Human nature has changed little since the thirteenth century. The precious stones are a legend, but no doubt the Polos brought many with them, for they were jewel merchants by trade; they had had ample opportunities for business in China, and the Great Khan had loaded them with "rubies and other handsome jewels of great value" to boot. Jewels were the most convenient form in which they could have brought home their wealth. But the inquiring Marco brought other things also to tickle the curiosity of the Venetians, as he lets fall from time to time in his book. He brought, for example, specimens of the silky hair of the Tangut yak, which his countrymen much admired, the dried head and feet of a musk deer, and the seeds of a dye plant (probably indigo) from Sumatra, which he sowed in Venice, but which never came up, because the climate was not sufficiently warm.[19] He brought presents also for the Doge; for an inventory made in 1351 of things found in the palace of Marino Faliero includes among others a ring given by Kublai Khan, a Tartar collar, a three-bladed sword, an Indian brocade, and a book "written by the hand of the aforsesaid Marco," called *De locis mirabilibus Tartarorum*.[20]

The rest of Marco Polo's life is quickly told. The legend goes that all the youth of Venice used to resort to the Ca' Polo in order to hear his stories, for not even among the foreign sailors on the quays, where once the boy Marco had wandered and asked about the Tartars, were stories the like of his to be heard. And because he was always talking of the greatness of Kublai Khan's dominions, the millions of revenue, the millions of junks, the millions of riders, the millions of towns and cities, they gave him a nickname and jestingly called him Marco *Milione,* or *Il Milione* which, is being interpreted, "Million Marco"; and the name even crept into the public documents of the Republic, while the courtyard of his house became known as the *Corte Milione.* To return from legend to history, the ancient rivalry between Venice and Genoa had been growing during Marco Polo's absence; nor had Venice always prevailed. Often as her galleys sailed,

[18] Yule, *Book of Ser Marco Polo,* I, Introd., pp. 4-8.
[19] Marco Polo, *op. cit.,* pp. 136, 138, 344.
[20] Yule, *op. cit.,* I, Introd., p. 70.

> dipping deep
> For Famagusta and the hidden sun
> That rings black Cyprus with a lake of fire, . . .
> Questing brown slaves or Syrian oranges,
> The pirate Genoese
> Hell raked them till they rolled
> Blood, water, fruit, and corpses up the hold.

At last in 1298, three years after Marco's return, a Genoese fleet under Lamba Doria sailed for the Adriatic, to bate the pride of Venice in her own sea. The Venetians fitted out a great fleet to meet it, and Marco Polo, the handy man who knew so much about navigation, albeit more skilled with Chinese junks than with Western ships, went with it as gentleman commander of a galley. The result of the encounter was a shattering victory for the Genoese off Curzola. Sixty-eight Venetian galleys were burnt, and seven thousand prisoners were haled off to Genoa, among them Marco Polo, who had now a taste of the results of that enterprise, manliness, and warfare, whose absence he so deprecated in the men of Suchow.

But soon there began to run through the streets and courtyards of Genoa a rumour that in prison there lay a certain Venetian captain, with tales so wonderful to beguile the passing hour that none could tire of hearing them; and anon the gallants and sages and the bold ladies of Genoa were flocking, just as the men of the Rialto, had flocked before, to hear his stories of Kublai Khan,

> Lord of the fruits of Tartary
>   Her rivers silver-pale,
> Lord of the hills of Tartary,
>   Glen, thicket, wood, and dale,
> Her flashing stars, her scented breeze,
> Her trembling lakes, like foamless seas,
> Her bird-delighting citron-trees
>   In every purple vale.

"Messer Marco," so runs Ramusio's account of the tradition which lingered in Venice in his day, "finding himself in this position, and witnessing the general eagerness to hear all about Cathay and the Great Khan, which indeed compelled him daily to repeat his story till he was weary, was advised to put the matter in writing; so he found means to get a letter written to his father in Venice, in which he desired the latter to send those notes and memoranda, which he had brought home with him."

It happened that in prison with Marco Polo there lay a certain Pisan writer of romances, Rusticiano by name,[21] who had probably been taken prisoner before at the battle of Melaria (1284), when so many Pisan captives had been carried to Genoa, that the saying arose "He who would see Pisa let him go to Genoa." Rusticiano was skilled in the writing of French, the language *par excellence* of romances, in which he had written versions of the Round Table Tales, and in him Marco Polo found a ready scribe, who took down the stories

---

21 On Rusticiano see *Ibid.,* Introd., pp. 56 ff.

as he told them, in the midst of the crowd of Venetian prisoners and Genoese gentlemen, raptly drinking in all the wonders of Kublai Khan. It was by a just instinct that, when all was written, Rusticiano prefixed to the tale that same address to the lords and gentlemen of the world, bidding them to take heed and listen, which he had been wont to set at the beginning of his tales of Tristan and Lancelot and King Arthur: "Ye Lords, Emperors and Kings, Dukes and Marquises, Counts, Knights and Burgesses and all ye men who desire to know the divers races of men and the diversities of the different regions of the world, take ye this book and cause it to be read, and here shall ye find the greatest marvels." But he adds, "Marco Polo, a wise and learned citizen of Venice, states distinctly what things he saw and what things he heard from others, for this book will be a truthful one." Marco Polo's truthful marvels were more wonderful even than the exploits of Arthur's knights, and were possibly better suited to the respectable Rusticiano's pen, for his only other claim to distinction in the eyes of posterity seems to be that in his abridgment of the Romance of Lancelot he entirely omits the episode (if episode it can be called) of the loves of Lancelot and Guinevere. "Alas," remarks his French editor, "that the copy of *Lancelot* which fell into the hands of poor Francesca of Rimini was not one of those expurgated by Rusticiano!" [22]

Marco Polo was released from prison (there must have been mourning in the palaces of Genoa) and returned to Venice at the end of a year. Sometimes hereafter his name occurs in the records of Venice, as he moves about on his lawful occasions.[23] In 1305 we find "Nobilis Marchus Polo Milioni" standing surety for a wine smuggler; in 1311 he is suing a dishonest agent who owes him money on the sale of musk (he, Marco, had seen the musk deer in its lair); and in 1323 he is concerned in a dispute about a party wall. We know, too, from his will, that he had a wife named Donata, and three daughters, Fantina, Bellela, and Moreta. Had he loved before, under the alien skies where his youth was spent, some languid exquisite lady of China, or hardy Tartar maid? Had he profited himself from the strange marriage customs of Tibet, of which he remarks (with one of his very rare gleams of humour), "En cele contree aurent bien aler les jeune de seize anz en vingt quatre"? Had Fantina, Bellela, and Moreta half-brothers, flying their gerfalcons at the quails by the shores of the "White Lake" where the Khan hunted, and telling tales of the half legendary father, who sailed away for ever when they were boys in the days of Kublai Khan? These things we cannot know, nor can we even guess whether he regretted that only daughters sprang from his loins in the city of the lagoons, and no Venetian son to go venturing again to the far-distant country where assuredly he had left a good half of his heart. Perhaps he talked of it sometimes to Peter, his Tartar servant, whom he freed at his death "from all bondage as completely as I pray God to release mine own soul from all sin and guilt." Some have thought that he brought Peter the Tartar with him from the East, and the thought is a pleasant one; but it is more likely

[22] *Ibid.*, Introd., p. 61.
[23] *Ibid.*, Introd., pp. 67-73.

that he bought him in Italy, for the Venetians were inveterate slave-owners, and captive Tartars were held of all the slaves the strongest and best. So his life passed; and in 1324 Marco Polo died, honoured much by his fellow-citizens, after making a will which is still preserved in the library of St. Mark's.

A characteristic story of his death-bed is related by a Dominican friar, one Jacopo of Acqui, who wrote some time later. "What he told in the book," says Jacopo, "was not as much as he had really seen, because of the tongues of detractors, who being ready to impose their own lies on others are over hasty to set down as lies what they in their perversity disbelieve or do not understand. And because there are many great and strange things in that book, which are reckoned past all credence, he was asked by his friends on his death-bed to correct the book, by removing everything that went beyond the facts. To which his reply was that he had not told *one half* of what he had really seen." [24] How well one can see that last indignant flash of the dying observer, who in the long years of his youth had taken notes of strange tribes and customs for the wise and gracious Kublai Khan, and whom little men now dared to doubt. Indeed, modern discovery has entirely confirmed the exactitude of Marco Polo's observation. It is true that he sometimes repeated some very tall stories which had been told to him, of dog-faced men in the Andaman Islands and of the "male and female islands" so beloved of medieval geographers. These were sailors' yarns, and where Marco Polo reports what he has seen with his own eyes, he reports with complete accuracy, nor does he ever pretend to have seen a place which he had not visited. The explorers of our own day, Aurel Stein, Ellsworth Huntington, and Sven Hedin, travelling in Central Asia, have triumphantly vindicated him. "It is," says an eminent French historian, "as though the originals of very old photographs had been suddenly rediscovered: the old descriptions of things which were unchanged could be perfectly superimposed upon present reality," [25] and Huntington and Aurel Stein took with them to the inaccessible districts of Central Asia as guide-books the book of the Chinese pilgrim Hiwen Thsang (seventh century) and the book of Marco Polo, and over and over again found how accurate were their descriptions.

The knowledge which Marco Polo had thus brought to Europe, the intercourse between East and West which his experience had shown to be so desirable, continued to grow after him. Merchants and missionaries alike travelled by land or sea eastward to Cathay.[26] Another of those indomitable Franciscan friars, John of Monte Corvino, went out at the age of fifty and became Archbishop of Peking. Churches and houses of friars were founded in some of the Chinese cities. Odoric of Pordenone, another friar, and a very good observer too, set forth in 1316 and sailed around India and through the Spice Islands by the same sea route by which the Polos had brought their

---

[24] On Rusticiano, see *Ibid.*, Introd., p. 54.
[25] Ch. V. Langlois in *Histoire Littéraire de la France*, xxxv, p. 259.
[26] Yule, *Cathay and the Way Thither*, Introd., pp. cxxxii-iv.

Tartar princess back to Persia, and so reached Canton, "a city as big as three Venices . . . and all Italy hath not the amount of craft that this one city hath." He left a wonderful account of his travels in China, including descriptions of Peking and Hangchow, and ends his stories with the words, "As for me, from day to day I prepare myself to return to those countries, in which I am content to die, if it pleaseth Him from whom all good things do come"—no doubt where he had left his heart, but he died at Udine in Italy. Later there went out another friar, John Marignolli, who was Papal Legate to Peking from 1342 to 1346.

Nor was it only missionaries who went to Cathay. Odoric, speaking of the wonders of Hangchow, refers for confirmation to Venetian traders who have visited it: "'Tis the greatest city in the whole world, so great indeed that I should scarcely venture to tell of it, but that I have met at Venice people in plenty who have been there"; John of Monte Corvino was accompanied by Master Peter of Lucolongo, "a great merchant," and John Marignolli mentions a *fondaco* for the use of Christian merchants, which was attached to one of the Franciscan convents at Zaiton. Above all, there is Francis Balducci Pegolotti, that intrepid factor who served the great commercial house of the Bardi of Florence, and who wrote a priceless handbook for the use of merchants about 1340. In this he gives detailed instructions for the guidance of a merchant, who wishes to proceed from Tana on the Black Sea by the overland route across Asia to Cathay and back again with £1,200 worth silk in his caravan, and remarks casually, in passing, "The road you travel from Tana to Cathay is perfectly safe, whether by day or night, according to what merchants say who have used it"—"il chanmino dandare dalla Tana al Ghattajo è sichuris-simo!" [27] Think only of what it all means. Marco Polo travelling where no man set foot again till the twentieth century. The bells of the Christian church ringing sweetly in the ears of the Great Khan in Peking. The long road across Central Asia perfectly safe for merchants. The "many persons at Venice" who have walked in the streets of Hangchow. This is in the late thirteenth and early fourteenth centuries, in the despised and hidebound Middle Ages. È *sichurissimo!* It takes some of the gift off Columbus and Vasco da Gama and the age (forsooth) of "discovery."

But a change came over everything in the middle of the fourteenth century. Darkness fell again and swallowed up Peking and Hangchow, the great ports, the crowding junks, the noble civilization. No longer was the great trade route *sichurissimo,* and no longer did Christian friars chant their masses in Zaiton. The Tartar dynasty fell and the new rulers of China reverted to the old anti-foreign policy; moreover, Islam spread its conquests all over Central Asia and lay like a rampart between the Far East and the West, a great wall of intolerance and hatred stronger by far than the great wall of stone which the Chinese had once built to keep out the Tartars. All Marco Polo's marvels became no more than a legend, a traveller's tale.

But that great adventurer was not done for yet. Nearly a century and a

27 *Ibid.,* II, p. 292; and App., p. lxv.

half after Marco's death a Genoese sea captain sat poring over one of the new printed books, which men were beginning to buy and to hand about among themselves. The book which he was reading was the Latin version of Marco Polo's travels. He was reading it with intentness and indeed with passion. As he read he made notes in the margin; on over seventy pages he made his notes.[28] From time to time he frowned and turned back and read again the tale of those great ports of Cathay and the gold-roofed palaces of Cipangu; and always he wondered how those lands might be reached, now that the wall of darkness covered Central Asia and anarchy blocked the road to the Persian Gulf. One day (may we not see him?) he lifted his head and smote his hand upon the table. "I will sail West," he said. "Maybe I shall find the lost island of Antilha in the western ocean, but maybe on its far rim I shall indeed come to Cipangu, for the world is round, and somewhere in those great seas beyond the coast of Europe must lie Marco Polo's rich Cathay. I will beseech the kings of England and of Spain for a ship and a ship's company, and the silk and the spices and the wealth shall be theirs. I will sail West," said the Genoese sea captain, and he smote his thigh. "I will sail West, West, West!" And this was the last of Messer Marco's marvels; he discovered China in the thirteenth century, when he was alive, and in the fifteenth, when he was dead, he discovered America!

BIBLIOGRAPHY

A. *Original Sources.*

The Book of Ser Marco Polo the Venetian Concerning the Kingdoms and Marvels of the East, trans. and ed. with notes by Sir Henry Yule (3rd edition, revised by Henri Cordier, 2 vols., Hakluyt Society, 1903). The best edition of the French text is *Le Livre de Marco Polo,* ed. G. Pauthier (Paris, 1865). The most convenient edition for readers is *The Travels of Marco Polo,* with Introduction by John Masefield, Everyman Library.

La Chronique des Veneciens de Maistre Martin de Canal. In *Archivo Storico Italiano,* Ser. I, vol. VIII (Florence, 1845).

B. *Modern Works.*

F. C. Hodgson, *The Early History of Venice* (1901).

F. C. Hodgson, *Venice in the Thirteenth and Fourteenth Centuries* (1910).

P. G. Molmenti, *Venice, its Growth till the Fall of the Republic,* vols. I, II. trans. H. F. Brown (1906).

H. F. Brown, *Studies in the History of Venice,* vol. I (1907).

Henry Yule, *Cathay and the Way Thither* (Hakluyt Soc., 1866).

R. Beazley, *The Dawn of Modern Geography,* vols. II, III (1897-1906).

H. Howarth, *History of the Mongols* (1876).

28 Yule, *Book of Ser Marco Polo,* II, App. H, p. 558.

Four Kinds of Thinking[1]

by JAMES HARVEY ROBINSON

WE DO not think enough about thinking, and much of our confusion is the result of current illusions in regard to it. Let us forget for the moment any impressions we may have derived from the philosophers, and see what seems to happen in ourselves. The first thing that we notice is that our thought moves with such incredible rapidity that it is almost impossible to arrest any specimen of it long enough to have a look at it. When we are offered a penny for our thoughts we always find that we have recently had so many things in mind that we can easily make a selection which will not compromise us too nakedly. On inspection we shall find that even if we are not downright ashamed of a great part of our spontaneous thinking it is far too intimate, personal, ignoble or trivial to permit us to reveal more than a small part of it. I believe this must be true of everyone. We do not, of course, know what goes on in other people's heads. They tell us very little and we tell them very little. The spigot of speech, rarely fully opened, could never emit more than driblets of the ever renewed hogshead of thought—*noch grösser wie's Heidelberger Fass*. We find it hard to believe that other people's thoughts are as silly as our own, but they probably are.

We all appear to ourselves to be thinking all the time during our waking hours, and most of us are aware that we go on thinking while we are asleep, even more foolishly than when awake. When uninterrupted by some practical issue we are engaged in what is now known as a *reverie*. This is our spontaneous and favorite kind of thinking. We allow our ideas to take their own course and this course is determined by our hopes and fears, our spontaneous desires, their fulfillment or frustration; by our likes and dislikes, our loves and hates and resentments. There is nothing else anything like so interesting to ourselves as ourselves. All thought that is not more or less laboriously controlled and directed will inevitably circle about the beloved Ego. It is amusing and pathetic to observe this tendency in ourselves and in others. We learn politely and generously to overlook this truth, but if we dare to think of it, it blazes forth like the noontide sun.

The reverie or "free association of ideas" has of late become the subject of scientific research. While investigators are not yet agreed on the results, or at least on the proper interpretation to be given to them, there can be no doubt that our reveries form the chief index to our fundamental character. They are a reflection of our nature as modified by often hidden and forgotten

[1] From *The Mind in the Making* (1921). Copyright, by Harper & Brothers, publishers.

experiences. We need not go into the matter further here, for it is only necessary to observe that the reverie is at all times a potent and in many cases an omnipotent rival to every other kind of thinking. It doubtless influences all our speculations in its persistent tendency to self-magnification and self-justification, which are its chief preoccupations, but it is the last thing to make directly or indirectly for honest increase of knowledge. Philosophers usually talk as if such thinking did not exist or were in some way negligible. This is what makes their speculations so unreal and often worthless.

The reverie, as any of us can see for himself, is frequently broken and interrupted by the necessity of a second kind of thinking. We have to make practical decisions. Shall we write a letter or no? Shall we take the subway or a bus? Shall we have dinner at seven or half past? Shall we buy U. S. Rubber or a Liberty Bond? Decisions are easily distinguishable from the free flow of the reverie. Sometimes they demand a good deal of careful pondering and the recollection of pertinent facts; often, however, they are made impulsively. They are a more difficult and laborious thing than the reverie, and we resent having to "make up our mind" when we are tired, or absorbed in a congenial reverie. Weighing a decision, it should be noted, does not necessarily add anything to our knowledge, although we may, of course, seek further information before making it.

A third kind of thinking is stimulated when anyone questions our beliefs and opinions. We sometimes find ourselves changing our minds without any resistance or heavy emotion, but if we are told that we are wrong we resent the imputation and harden our hearts. We are incredibly heedless in the formation of our beliefs, but find ourselves filled with an illicit passion for them when anyone proposes to rob us of their companionship. It is obviously not the ideas themselves that are dear to us, but our self-esteem, which is threatened. We are by nature stubbornly pledged to defend our own from attack, whether it be our person, our family, our property, or our opinion. A United States Senator once remarked to a friend of mine that God Almighty could not make him change his mind on our Latin-American Policy. We may surrender, but rarely confess ourselves vanquished. In the intellectual world at least peace is without victory.

Few of us take the pains to study the origin of our cherished convictions; indeed, we have a natural repugnance to so doing. We like to continue to believe what we have been accustomed to accept as true, and the resentment aroused when doubt is cast upon any of our assumptions leads us to seek every manner of excuse for clinging to them. *The result is that most of our so-called reasoning consists in finding arguments for going on believing as we already do.*

I remember years ago attending a public dinner to which the Governor of the state was bidden. The chairman explained that His Excellency could not be present for certain "good" reasons; what the "real" reasons were the presiding officer said he would leave us to conjecture. This distinction between "good" and "real" reasons is one of the most clarifying and essential in the whole realm of thought. We can readily give what seem to us "good" reasons for being a Catholic or a Mason, a Republican or a Democrat, an adherent or opponent of the League of Nations. But the "real" reasons are usually on quite a different plane. Of course the importance of this distinction is popularly, if somewhat obscurely, recognized. The Baptist missionary is ready enough to see that the Buddhist is not such because his doctrines would bear careful inspection, but because he happened to be born in a Buddhist family in Tokio. But it would be treason to his faith to acknowledge that his own partiality for certain doctrines is due to the fact that his mother was a member of the First Baptist church of Oak Ridge. A savage can give all sorts of reasons for his belief that it is dangerous to step on a man's shadow, and a newspaper editor can advance plenty of arguments against the Bolsheviki. But neither of them may realize why he happens to be defending his particular opinion.

The "real" reasons for our beliefs are concealed from ourselves as well as from others. As we grow up we simply adopt the ideas presented to us in regard to such matters as religion, family relations, property, business, our country, and the state. We unconsciously absorb them from our environment. They are persistently whispered in our ear by the group in which we happen to live. Moreover, as Mr. Trotter has pointed out, these judgments, being the product of suggestion and not of reasoning, have the quality of perfect obviousness, so that to question them

. . . is to the believer to carry skepticism to an insane degree, and will be met by contempt, disapproval, or condemnation, according to the nature of the belief in question. When, therefore, we find ourselves entertaining an opinion about the basis of which there is a quality of feeling which tells us that to inquire into it would be absurd, obviously unnecessary, unprofitable, undesirable, bad form, or wicked, we may know that that opinion is a nonrational one, and probably, therefore, founded upon inadequate evidence.

Opinions, on the other hand, which are the result of experience or of honest reasoning do not have this quality of "primary certitude." I remember when as a youth I heard a group of business men discussing the question of the immortality of the soul, I was outraged by the sentiment of doubt expressed by one of the party. As I look back now I see that I had at the time no interest in the matter, and certainly no least argument to urge in favor of the belief in which I had been reared. But neither my personal indifference to the issue, nor the fact that I had previously given it no attention, served to prevent an angry resentment when I heard *my* ideas questioned.

This spontaneous and loyal support of our preconceptions—this process of finding "good" reasons to justify our routine beliefs—is known to modern psychologists as "rationalizing"—clearly only a new name for a very ancient thing. Our "good" reasons ordinarily have no value in promoting honest enlightenment, because, no matter how solemnly they may be marshaled, they are at bottom the result of personal preference or prejudice, and not of an honest desire to seek or accept new knowledge.

In our reveries we are frequently engaged in self-justification, for we cannot bear to think ourselves wrong, and yet have constant illustrations of our weaknesses and mistakes. So we spend much time finding fault with circumstances and the conduct of others, and shifting on to them with great ingenuity the onus of our own failures and disappointments. *Rationalizing is the self-exculpation which occurs when we feel ourselves, or our group, accused of misapprehension or error.*

The little word *my* is the most important one in all human affairs, and properly to reckon with it is the beginning of wisdom. It has the same force whether is is *my* dinner, *my* dog, and *my* house, or *my* faith, *my* country, and *my* God. We not only resent the imputation that our watch is wrong, or our car shabby, but that our conception of the canals of Mars, of the pronunciation of "Epictetus," of the medicinal value of salicine, or the date of Sargon I, are subject to revision.

Philosophers, scholars, and men of science exhibit a common sensitiveness in all decisions in which their *amour propre* is involved. Thousands of argumentative works have been written to vent a grudge. However stately their reasoning, it may be nothing but rationalizing, stimulated by the most commonplace of all motives. A history of philosophy and theology could be written in terms of grouches, wounded pride, and aversions, and it would be far more instructive than the usual treatments of these themes. Sometimes, under Providence, the lowly impulse of resentment leads to great achievements. Milton wrote his treatise on divorce as a result of his troubles with his seventeen-year-old wife, and when he was accused of being the leading spirit in a new sect, the Divorcers, he wrote his noble *Areopagitica* to prove his right to say what he thought fit, and incidentally to establish the advantage of a free press in the promotion of Truth.

All mankind, high and low, thinks in all the ways which have been described. The reverie goes on all the time not only in the mind of the mill hand and the Broadway flapper, but equally in weighty judges and godly bishops. It has gone on in all the philosphers, scientists, poets, and theologians that have ever lived. Aristotle's most abstruse speculations were doubtless tempered by highly irrelevant reflections. He is reported to have had very thin legs and small eyes, for which he doubtless had to find excuses, and he was wont to indulge in very conspicuous dress and rings and was accustomed to arrange his hair carefully. Diogenes the Cynic exhibited the impudence of a touchy soul. His tub was his distinction. Tennyson in beginning his *Maud* could not forget his chagrin over losing his patrimony years before as the result of an unhappy investment in the Patent Decorative Carving Company. These facts are not recalled here as a gratuitous disparagement of the truly great, but to insure a full realization of the tremendous competition, which all really exacting thought has to face, even in the minds of the most highly endowed mortals.

And now the astonishing and perturbing suspicion emerges that perhaps almost all that has passed for social science, political economy, politics, and ethics in the past may be brushed aside by future generations as mainly rationalizing. John Dewey has already reached this conclusion in regard to philosophy. Veblen and other writers have revealed the various unperceived presuppositions of the traditional political economy, and now comes an Italian sociologist, Vilfredo Pareto, who, in his huge treatise on general sociology, devotes hundreds of pages to substantiating a similar thesis affecting all the social sciences. This conclusion may be ranked by students of a hundred years hence as one of the several great discoveries of our age. It is by no means fully worked out, and it is so opposed to nature that it will be very slowly accepted by the great mass of those who consider themselves thoughtful. As a historical student I am personally fully reconciled to this newer view. Indeed, it seems to me inevitable that just as the various sciences of nature were, before the opening of the seventeenth century, largely masses of rationalizations to suit the religious sentiments of the period, so the social sciences have continued even to our own day to be rationalizations of uncritically accepted beliefs and customs.

It will become apparent as we proceed that the fact that an idea is ancient and that it has been widely received is no argument in its favor, but should immediately suggest the necessity of carefully testing it as a probable instance of rationalization.

This brings us to another kind of thought which can fairly easily be distinguished from the three kinds described above. It has not the usual qualities of the reverie, for it does not hover about our personal complacencies and humiliations. It is not made up of the homely decisions forced upon us by everyday needs, when we review our little stock of existing information, consult our conventional preferences and obligations, and make a choice of action. It is not the defense of our own cherished beliefs and prejudices just because they are our own—mere plausible excuses for remaining of the same mind. On the contrary, it is that peculiar species of thought which leads us to *change* our mind.

It is this kind of thought that has raised man from his pristine, subsavage ignorance and squalor to the degree of knowledge and comfort which he now possesses. On his capacity to continue and greatly extend this kind of thinking depends his chance of groping his way out of the plight in which the most highly civilized peoples of the world now find themselves. In the past this type of thinking has been called Reason. But so many misapprehensions have grown up around the word that some of us have become very suspicious of it. I suggest, therefore, that we substitute a recent name and speak of "creative thought" rather than of Reason. *For this kind of medita-*

tion begets knowledge, and knowledge is really creative inasmuch as it makes things look different from what they seemed before and may indeed work for their reconstruction.

In certain moods some of us realize that we are observing things or making reflections with a seeming disregard of our personal preoccupations. We are not preening or defending ourselves; we are not faced by the necessity of any practical decision, nor are we apologizing for believing this or that. We are just wondering and looking and mayhap seeing what we never perceived before.

Curiosity is as clear and definite as any of our urges. We wonder what is in a sealed telegram or in a letter in which some one else is absorbed, or what is being said in the telephone booth or in low conversation. This inquisitiveness is vastly stimulated by jealousy, suspicion, or any hint that we ourselves are directly or indirectly involved. But there appears to be a fair amount of personal interest in other people's affairs even when they do not concern us except as a mystery to be unraveled or a tale to be told. The reports of a divorce suit will have "news value" for many weeks. They constitute a story like a novel or play or moving picture. This is not an example of pure curiosity, however, since we readily identify ourselves with others, and their joys and despairs then become our own.

We also take note of, or "observe," as Sherlock Holmes says, things which have nothing to do with our personal interests and make no personal appeal either direct or by way of sympathy. This is what Veblen so well calls "idle curiosity." And it is usually idle enough. Some of us when we face the line of people opposite us in a subway train impulsively consider them in detail and engage in rapid inferences and form theories in regard to them. On entering a room there are those who will perceive at a glance the degree of preciousness of the rugs, the character of the pictures, and the personality revealed by the books. But there are many, it would seem, who are so absorbed in their personal reverie or in some definite purpose that they have no bright-eyed energy for idle curiosity. The tendency to miscellaneous observation we come by honestly enough, for we note it in many of our animal relatives.

Veblen, however, uses the term "idle curiosity" somewhat ironically, as is his wont. It is idle only to those who fail to realize that it may be a very rare and indispensable thing from which almost all distinguished human achievement proceeds, since it may lead to systematic examination and seeking for things hitherto undiscovered. For research is but diligent search which enjoys the high flavor of primitive hunting. Occasionally and fitfully idle curiosity thus leads to creative thought, which alters and broadens our own views and aspirations and may in turn, under highly favorable circumstances, affect the views and lives of others, even for generations to follow. An example or two will make this unique human process clear.

Galileo was a thoughtful youth and doubtless carried on a rich and varied reverie. He had artistic ability and might have turned out to be a musician or painter. When he had dwelt among the monks at Vallombrosa he had been tempted to lead the life of a religious. As a boy he busied himself with toy machines and he inherited a fondness for mathematics. All these facts are of record. We may safely assume also that, along with many other subjects of contemplation, the Pisan maidens found a vivid place in his thoughts.

One day when seventeen years old he wandered into the cathedral of his native town. In the midst of his reverie he looked up at the lamps hanging by long chains from the high ceiling of the church. Then something very difficult to explain occurred. He found himself no longer thinking of the building, worshipers, or the services; of his artistic or religious interests; of his reluctance to become a physician as his father wished. He forgot the question of a career and even the *graziosissime donne.* As he watched the swinging lamps he was suddenly wondering if mayhap their oscillations, whether long or short, did not occupy the same time. Then he tested this hypothesis by counting his pulse, for that was the only timepiece he had with him.

This observation, however remarkable in itself, was not enough to produce a really creative thought. Others may have noticed the same thing and yet nothing came of it. Most of our observations have no assignable results. Galileo may have seen that the warts on a peasant's face formed a perfect isosceles triangle, or he may have noticed with boyish glee that just as the officiating priest was uttering the solemn words, *ecce agnus Dei,* a fly lit on the end of his nose. To be really creative, ideas have to be worked up and then "put over," so that they become a part of man's social heritage. The highly accurate pendulum clock was one of the later results of Galileo's discovery. He himself was led to reconsider and successfully to refute the old notions of falling bodies. It remained for Newton to prove that the moon was falling, and presumably all the heavenly bodies. This quite upset all the consecrated views of the heavens as managed by angelic engineers. The universality of the laws of gravitation stimulated the attempt to seek other and equally important natural laws and cast grave doubts on the miracles in which mankind had hitherto believed. In short, those who dared to include in their thoughts the discoveries of Galileo and his successors found themselves in a new earth surrounded by new heavens.

On the 28th of October, 1831, three hundred and fifty years after Galileo had noticed the isochronous vibrations of the lamps, creative thought and its currency had so far increased that Faraday was wondering what would happen if he mounted a disk of copper between the poles of a horseshoe magnet. As the disk revolved an electric current was produced. This would doubtless have seemed the idlest kind of an experiment to the stanch business men of the time, who, it happened, were just then denouncing the child-labor bills in their anxiety to avail themselves to the full of the results of earlier idle curiosity. But should the dynamos and motors which have come into being as the outcome of Faraday's experiment be stopped this evening, the business man of to-day, agitated over labor troubles, might, as he trudged home past lines of "dead" cars, through dark streets to an unlighted house, engage in a little creative thought of his own and perceive that he and his laborers would have no modern factories and mines to quarrel about had it not been for the strange practical effects of the idle curiosity of scientists, inventors, and engineers.

The examples of creative intelligence given above belong to the realm of modern scientific achievement, which furnishes the most striking instances of the effects of scrupulous, objective thinking. But there are, of course, other great realms in which the recording and embodiment of acute observation and insight have wrought themselves into the higher life of man. The great poets and dramatists and our modern story-tellers have found themselves engaged in productive reveries, noting and artistically presenting their discoveries for the delight and instruction of those who have the ability to appreciate them.

The process by which a fresh and original poem or drama comes into being is doubtless analogous to that which originates and elaborates so-called scientific discoveries; but there is clearly a temperamental difference. The genesis and advance of painting, sculpture, and music offer still other problems. We really as yet know shockingly little about these matters, and indeed very few people have the least curiosity about them. Nevertheless, creative intelligence in its various forms and activities is what makes man. Were it not for its slow, painful, and constantly discouraged operations through the ages man would be no more than a species of primate living on seeds, fruits, roots, and uncooked flesh, and wandering naked through the woods and over the plains like a chimpanzee.

The origin and progress and future promotion of civilization are ill understood and misconceived. These should be made the chief theme of education, but much hard work is necessary before we can reconstruct our ideas of man and his capacities and free ourselves from innumerable persistent misapprehensions. There have been obstructionists in all times, not merely the lethargic masses, but the moralists, the rationalizing theologians, and most of the philosophers, all busily if unconsciously engaged in ratifying existing ignorance and mistakes and discouraging creative thought. Naturally, those who reassure us seem worthy of honor and respect. Equally naturally those who puzzle us with disturbing criticisms and invite us to change our ways are objects of suspicion and readily discredited. Our personal discontent does not ordinarily extend to any critical questioning of the general situation in which we find ourselves. In every age the prevailing conditions of civilization have appeared quite natural and inevitable to those who grew up in them. The cow asks no questions as to how it happens to have a dry stall and a supply of hay. The kitten laps its warm milk from a china saucer, without knowing anything about porcelain; the dog nestles in the corner of a divan with no sense of obligation to the inventors of upholstery and the manufacturers of down pillows. So we humans accept our breakfasts, our trains and telephones and orchestras and movies, our national Constitution, our moral code and standards of manners, with the simplicity and innocence of a pet rabbit. We have absolutely inexhaustible capacities for appropriating what others do for us with no thought of a "thank you." We do not feel called upon to make any least contribution to the merry game ourselves. Indeed, we are usually quite unaware that a game is being played at all.

~~~~~~

Gate Receipts and Glory [1]

by ROBERT M. HUTCHINS

THE football season is about to release the nation's colleges to the pursuit of education, more or less. Soon the last nickel will be rung up at the gate, the last halfback will receive his check, and the last alumnus will try to pay off those bets he can recall. Most of the students have cheered themselves into insensibility long ago.

This has been going on for almost fifty years. It is called "overemphasis on athletics," and everybody deplores it. It has been the subject of scores of reports, all of them shocking. It has been held to be crass professionalism, all the more shameful because it masquerades as higher education. But nobody has done anything about it. Why? I think it is because nobody wants to. Nobody wants, or dares, to defy the public, dishearten the students, or deprive alma mater of the loyalty of the alumni. Most emphatically of all, nobody wants to give up the gate receipts. The trouble with football is the money that is in it, and every code of amateurism ever written has failed for this reason.

Money is the cause of athleticism in the American colleges. Athleticism is not athletics. Athletics is physical education, a proper function of the college if carried on for the welfare of the students. Athleticism is not physical education but sports promotion, and it is carried on for the monetary profit of the colleges through the entertainment of the public. This article deals with athleticism, its cause, its symptoms and its cure.

Of all the crimes committed by athleticism under the guise of athletics, the most heinous is the confusion of the country about the primary purpose of higher education. The primary purpose of higher education is the development of the mind. This does not mean that colleges and universities should neglect the health of their students or should fail to provide them with every opportunity for physical development. The question is a question of emphasis. Colleges and universities are the only institutions which are dedicated

[1] From *The Saturday Evening Post*, December 3, 1938. By permission of the editor and the author.

to the training of the mind. In these institutions, the development of the body is important, but secondary.

The apologists of athleticism have created a collection of myths to convince the public that biceps is a substitute for brains. Athletics, we are told, produces well-rounded men, filled with the spirit of fair play. Athletics is good for the health of the players; it is also good for the morals of the spectators. Leadership on the playing fields means leadership in life. The Duke of Wellington said so. Athletes are red-blooded Americans, and athletic colleges are bulwarks against Communism. Gate receipts are used to build laboratories and to pay for those sports that can't pay for themselves. Football is purely a supplement to study. And without a winning team a college cannot hope to attract the students or the gifts which its work requires.

These myths have about them a certain air of plausibility. They are widely accepted. But they are myths. As the Carnegie Foundation has said, "The fact that all these supposed advantages are tinged at one point or another with the color of money casts over every relaxation of standards a mercenary shadow." The myths are designed consciously or unconsciously, to conceal the color of money and to surround a financial enterprise with the rosy glow of Health, Manhood, Public Spirit and Education.

Since the primary task of colleges and universities is the development of the mind, young people who are more interested in their bodies than in their minds should not go to college. Institutions devoted to the development of the body are numerous and inexpensive. They do not pretend to be institutions of learning, and there is no faculty of learned men to consume their assets or interfere with their objectives.

Athleticism attracts boys and girls to college who do not want and cannot use a college education. They come to college for "fun." They would be just as happy in the grandstand at the Yankee Stadium, and at less expense to their parents. They drop out of college after a while, but they are a sizable fraction of many freshman classes, and, while they last, they make it harder for the college to educate the rest. Even the earnest boys and girls who come to college for an education find it difficult, around the middle of November, to concentrate on the physiology of the frog or the mechanics of the price structure.

Worse yet, athleticism gives the student a mistaken notion of the qualities that make for leadership in later life. The ambition of the average student who grew up reading Stover at Yale is to imitate as closely as possible the attitude and manners of the current football hero. Since this country, like all others, needs brains more than brawn at the moment, proposing football heroes as models for the rising generation can hardly have a beneficial effect on the national future.

The exponents of athleticism tell us that athletics is good for a boy. They are right. But athleticism focuses its attention on doing good for the boys who least need it. Less than half of the undergraduate males—800 out of 1900 at the University of Chicago, for instance—are eligible for intercollegiate competition. But where athleticism reigns, as happily it does not at Chicago, 75 per cent of the attention of the physical-education staff must be lavished on that fraction of the student body who make varsity squads. The Carnegie Foundation found that 37 per cent of all undergraduates engage in no athletic activity, not even in intramural games. Since graduate and professional students are also eliminated from competition, we have more than half the college and university population of the country neglected because we devote ourselves, on the pretext that athletics is good for a boy, to overdeveloping a handful of stars.

And athletics, as it is conducted in many colleges today, is not even good for the handful. Since the fate of the coach sometimes depends on victory, players have sometimes been filled with college spirit through caffein tablets and strychnine. At least one case reached the public in which a coach removed a plaster cast from a star's ankle and sent him in "to win." The Carnegie Foundation found that 17.6 per cent of all football players in twenty-two colleges suffered serious injuries. The same report asserts that college athletes have about the same life expectancy as the average college man and not so good an expectancy as men of high scholarship rank.

Most athletes will admit that the combination of weariness and nervousness after a hard practice is not conducive to study. We can thus understand why athleticism does not contribute to the production of well-rounded men destined for leadership after graduation. In many American colleges it is possible for a boy to win twelve letters without learning how to write one. I need only suggest that you conjure up the name of the greatest college football star of fifteen years ago and ask yourself, "Where is he now?" Many of his contemporaries who made no ninety-yard runs enjoy at least as good health as our hero and considerably more esteem. The cheers that rock the stadium have a rapid depreciation rate.

The alleged connection between athletic experience and moral principles is highly dubious. At worst, the college athlete is led to believe that whatever he does, including slugging, is done for the sake of alma mater. He does not learn that it is sometimes better, both on and off the playing field, to lose than to win. At best, the college athlete acquires habits of fair play, but there is no evidence that he needs to join the football squad to acquire them; he can get them from the studies he pursues and from living in a college community which, since it is a community of comparatively idealistic people, is less tolerant of meanness than most. The football players who threw the campus "radicals" into the lake at the University of Wisconsin knew little of fair play, and incidents in which free speech in the colleges is suppressed have frequently shown the athletic group lined up on the side of suppression.

Even if it were true that athletics developed courage, prudence, tolerance and justice, the commercialism that characterizes amateur sport today would be sufficient to harden the purest young man. He is made to feel that his primary function in college is to win football games. The coach demands it, because the coach wants to hold his job. The college demands it, because the college wants the gate receipts. And the alumni demand it, because the test of a college is the success of its teams and they want to be alumni of a good college.

The university with which I am connected has a different kind of college and a different kind of alumni. I can make this statement because I am in no way responsible for its happy condition. When John D. Rockefeller founded the University of Chicago forty-five years ago, he told William Rainey Harper to run it as he pleased. It pleased Mr. Harper to appoint men of character and distinction. One of the men he appointed was Amos Alonzo Stagg. To the amazement of the country, Mr. Harper made Mr. Stagg a professor on life appointment. It was the first time such a thing had happened.

Secure in his position, whether he produced winning teams or not, Mr. Stagg for forty years kept Chicago an amateur university. Some of his teams were champions. Chicago still has the second best won-and-lost record in the Big Ten, although we are using it up pretty fast. But through all those years Chicago students learned that athletics is only one aspect, and a secondary one, of college education. The result is that today Chicago's alumni are loyal to their university and generous with their moral and financial support.

The prestige that winning teams confer upon a university, and the profits that are alleged to accompany prestige, are the most serious obstacles to reform. Alumni whose sole interest in their alma mater is its athletic standing lose their interest when its teams run on bad years. The result, which horrifies college presidents, is that the alumni do not encourage their children or their neighbors' children to attend the old college. The American public believes that there is a correlation between muscle and manliness. Poor teams at any college are supposed to mean that the character of its student body is in decay.

The myth that donors, like alumni and the public, are impressed by football victories collapses on examination of the report recently issued by the John Price Jones Corporation, showing gifts and bequests to colleges and universities between 1920 and 1937. Among the universities, Harvard, Yale and Chicago led the list, each having received more than $50,000,000. The records of these universities on the gridiron were highly irregular, to say the least; that of one of them was positively bad. Among the colleges, Williams, Wesleyan and Bowdoin led the list, each having received more than $5,000,000. Men of wealth were undeterred by the inconsequential athletic status of these colleges; it does not appear that philanthropists were attracted to their rivals by the glorious victories they scored over them.

If athleticism is bad for students, players, alumni and the public, it is even worse for the colleges and universities themselves. They want to be educational institutions, but they can't. The story of the famous halfback whose only regret, when he bade his coach farewell, was that he hadn't learned to read and write is probably exaggerated. But we must admit that pressure from trustees, graduates, "friends," presidents, and even professors has tended to relax academic standards. These gentry often overlook the fact that a college should not be interested in a fullback who is a half-wit. Recruiting, subsidizing and the double educational standard cannot exist without the knowledge and the tacit approval, at least, of the colleges and universities themselves. Certain institutions encourage susceptible professors to be nice to athletes now admitted by paying them for serving as "faculty representatives" on the college athletic board.

We have the word of the famous Carnegie Report that the maxim "every athlete is a needy athlete" is applied up and down the land. Hard times have reduced the price of football players in conformity with the stock-market index. But when we get back to prosperity we may hope to see the resurrection of that phenomenon of the Golden Era, a corporation which tried to corner the market by signing up high-school athletes and auctioning them off to the highest bidder. The promoter of this interesting venture came to a bad end, and I regretted his fate, for he was a man of imagination and a friend of the football tramp, who has always been a victim of cutthroat competition.

Enthusiastic alumni find it hard to understand why a fine young man who can play football should be deprived of a college education just because he is poor. No young man should be deprived of an education just because he is poor. We need more scholarships, but athletic ability should have nothing to do with their award. Frequently the fine young man the alumnus has in mind can do nothing but play football. The alumnus should try hiring the young man and turning him loose in his factory. From the damage that would result he could gain some insight into the damage done his alma mater through admitting students without intellectual interests or capacity.

If the colleges and universities are to commend themselves to the public chiefly through their athletic accomplishments, it seems to me that they ought to be reorganized with that aim in view. Instead of looking for college presidents among educators, we should find them among those gentlemen who have a solid record of sports promotion behind them. Consider what Tex Rickard could have done for Harvard. I am rapidly approaching the retirement age, and I can think of no worthier successor, from the standpoint of athleticism, than Mr. Mike Jacobs, the sage of the prize ring. Mr. Jacobs has demonstrated his genius at selecting young men and developing them in such a way as to gather both gold and glory for the profession of which he is the principal ornament.

Another suggestion for elevating Chicago to the level of some of its sister institutions was advanced last year by Mr. William McNeill, editor of the student paper. Mr. McNeill proposed that instead of buying football players, the colleges should buy race horses. Alumni could show their devotion to alma mater by giving their stables to alma mater. For the time being, Yale would be way out in front, for both Mr. Jock Whitney and Mr. Cornelius Vanderbilt Whitney graduated there. But by a judicious distribution of honorary degrees horse fanciers who never went to college might be induced to come to the assistance of institutions which had not attracted students who had become prosperous enough to indulge in the sport of kings. Chicago could, for instance, confer the doctorate of letters upon that prominent turfman, Alderman Bathhouse John Coughlin, and persuade The Bath to change the color of his silks from green to maroon. The alumni could place their money on Chicago across the board. The students could cheer. Most important of all, the horses would not have to pass examinations.

The center of football strength has been moving, since the turn of the century, from the East to the Middle West, from the Middle West to the Pacific Coast, and from the Pacific Coast to the South and Southwest. According to a recent analysis by Professor Eells, of Stanford, the leading educational institutions of the country are, in order of their eminence, Harvard, Chicago, Columbia, Yale, California, Johns Hopkins, Princeton, Michigan and Wisconsin. None of these universities, except California, is close to the top of Professor Dickinson's annual athletic ranking, and California's success has something to do with the fact that it has a male undergraduate enrollment of 7500 compared with Harvard's 3700 and Chicago's 1900. We used to say that Harvard enjoyed its greatest years as an educational institution when Ted Coy was playing at Yale. If football continues to move to the poorer colleges, the good ones may be saved. Meanwhile it is only fair to say that some inferior colleges are going broke attempting to get rich—and famous—at football.

Athleticism, like crime, does not pay. Last summer St. Mary's College, home of the Galloping Gaels, was sold at auction and bought in by a bondholders' committee. This was the country's most sensational football college. Since 1924 it has won eighty-six and tied seven of its 114 games. Its academic efforts were inexpensive and its gate receipts immense. The bondholders were surprised to learn that it was running $72,000 a year behind in its budget. They were even more surprised to find that football expenses were almost equal to football income.

To make big money in athletics you have to spend big money. Winning coaches come high. The head coaches in our larger colleges and universities receive, on the average $611 a year more than the highest-ranking professors in the same institutions. One famous coach of a small college was found, not long ago, receiving $25,000 in a year, between his salary and his percentage of the receipts. This situation is not without its advantages to the members of my hard-pressed profession. The president of one celebrated university was paid $8000 a year. A coach qualified to direct the football destinies of the institution could not be found for less than $15,000. Since the trustees had to have the coach, and since they couldn't pay the president less than the coach, they raised the president's salary to $15,000 too.

Subsidizing is expensive. Equipment, travel, advertising and publicity are expensive. These things have been known to run to $10,000 or $15,000, even in the smaller colleges, for football alone. Some of the more glorious teams carry a Pullman full of newspapermen across the country with them, paying the reporters' expenses.

The myth that football receipts support research, education, or even other sports has just been exploded by President Wilkins, of Oberlin. His analysis of football costs in twenty-two typical colleges shows that only two have a surplus of football income over football expense. The twenty others spend on football all they get from football and $1743 apiece a year additional. This is the income on $45,000 of their endowment.

President Wilkins' investigation of the colleges raises an interesting question. If most of the colleges lose money at football, is it not likely that most of the universities, with their proportionately heavy expense, are also playing a losing game? I know of only one university that ever claimed to have built a laboratory out of excess gate receipts, but many of our larger institutions claim that football finances their so-called minor sports. Perhaps it does in a few universities and in the years of their great teams. But I should like to see a study made of the universities along the lines of President Wilkins' investigation of the colleges; and I might suggest to those who make the study that they scrutinize the accounting methods of some of our educators to see if they are charging up coaches and even trainers as "professors," the purchase of players to "contingent expense," and the debt on the stadium to "real estate."

In 1925 the American Association of University Professors expressed the hope that colleges would in time publish the cost of their stadiums. This hope has not been fulfilled, and for the most part the cost of stadiums remains one of the dark secrets of the athletic underworld. I understand that there are only two stadiums in the Big Ten which were not built with borrowed money, and that two have not yet been paid for. One cost $1,700,000.

Last fall I met a university president the day before his team was to play its opening game. All he could say was, "We've got to win tomorrow. We've got to pay off that $35,000 on the stadium this year." The necessity of packing these arenas has led colleges to schedule as many big games as possible. In order to establish the team's value as a spectacle as soon as possible, a big game must be played to open the season. The old scheme of playing easy games until the team is in shape has had to be abandoned. Consequently, practice must begin earlier to get the team in shape earlier. Harvard and Princeton have just extended pre-season practice and have given a bad example to the country.

The reason that college stadiums can't be paid off is plain. They are built for one sport, football. A great team year after year might, in fifteen or twenty years, pay off the bond issue. But there are no great teams year after year. Athletic eminence is cyclical. College A has a great team and decides to build a great stadium, so that the entire population can watch it. But the alumni of College B, which is the traditional rival of College A, are irritated because their alma mater is being beaten by those thugs across the river.

So the alumni go out and buy a great team for College B. Colleges C and D also have alumni who also like to win.

In a few years College A is being beaten regularly and the stadium, except for those local citizens who can't afford to get away to watch B, C, and D, is empty. Then College B builds a great new stadium to cash in on its great new record, and goes through the same routine.

There are several factors already operating to reduce athleticism, whether or not we decide to do anything about it. The rise of the junior colleges, which educate freshmen and sophomores only, is reducing the supply of athletic material for the four-year colleges and universities.

Professional football, which is attracting larger and larger crowds, may ultimately do for college football what professional baseball has done for college baseball. And the United States Supreme Court, in a case involving the taxation of gate receipts, has clarified the national mind to some extent by indicating that intercollegiate football is business.

But neither the Supreme Court, nor professional football, nor the junior colleges can be depended upon to reform us. We must reform ourselves. How?

The committees which have studied the subject—and their name is legion—have suggested stricter eligibility rules, reduction of training periods, elimination of recruiting and subsidizing, easier schedules, limitation of each student's participation to one sport, and abandonment of the double scholastic standard for athletes. President-Emeritus Lowell, of Harvard, once proposed the Oxford and Cambridge system of limiting each sport to one game a season, and that one with the college's natural rival. Mr. Lowell's scheme might have the merit of enabling students and the public to work off their seasonal frenzy in one big saturnalia.

These reforms will never achieve reform. They may serve to offset athleticism at those few institutions which are already trying to be colleges instead of football teams. But it is too much to hope that they will affect the colleges and universities at large.

Since money is the cause of athleticism, the cure is to take the money out of athletics. This can be done only in defiance of the students, the alumni, the public, and, in many cases, the colleges themselves. The majority of the colleges and universities will not do it, because in the aggregate they dare not. Johns Hopkins, in Maryland, and Reed College, in Oregon, have dared, but nobody cares, athletically speaking, what Johns Hopkins or Reed does.

The task of taking the money out of athletics must be undertaken by those institutions which are leaders, institutions which can afford the loss of prestige and popularity involved. I suggest that a group of colleges and of universities composed, say, of Amberst, Williams, Dartmouth, Harvard, Yale, Chicago, Michigan, Stanford and California agree to take the following steps, to take them in unison and to take them at once:

1. Reduce admission to ten cents. This will cover the handling costs. For years prominent educators, all the way from Harper, of Chicago, to Butler, of Columbia, have insisted that college athletics should be supported from endowment like any other educational activity. Colleges should support athletics out of their budgets, or get out of athletics, or get out of education.

2. Give the director of athletics and the major coaches some kind of academic tenure, so that their jobs depend on their ability as instructors and their character as men and not on the gates they draw.

While these two steps are being taken, it might be well, for the sake of once more putting students instead of athletes on the college playing fields, to try to stimulate the urge to play for fun and health, instead of the urge to win at any cost. There are two ways to do this, and many colleges and universities are trying both with considerable satisfaction to their students:

1. Broaden the base of athletic participation, so that all students, graduate and undergraduate, big fellows and little fellows, can play. The development of intramural athletics, which costs less than the maintenance of present programs, is a step in this direction. The English system of selecting a varsity from the intramural teams toward the end of the season and then playing a limited number of intercollegiate games suggests itself at this point.

2. Emphasize games which students will play in later life, when they need recreation and physical fitness as much as in college. Such sports are tennis, handball, skating, swimming, softball, bowling, rackets, golf and touch football. Few college graduates are able to use football, baseball or basketball, except as topics of conversation.

In a word: More athletics, less athleticism.

I think that after the steps I have suggested have been taken by the colleges and universities I have named, the rest of the country's educational institutions will not long be able to ignore their example.

Nor will the public, once the break has been made, attempt for long to prevent reform. The public, in the last analysis, pays for the colleges and the universities. It wants something for its money. It has been taught to accept football. It can, I am confident, be taught to accept education.

The public will not like ten-cent football, because ten-cent football will not be great football. The task of the colleges and the universities, then, is to show the country a substitute for athleticism.

That substitute is light and learning. The colleges and universities, which taught the country football, can teach the country that the effort to discover truth, to transmit the wisdom of the race, and to preserve civilization is exciting and perhaps important too.

ᘐᘐᘐᘐᘐᘐᘐᘐᘐᘐᘐᘐᘐᘐᘐᘐᘐᘐᘐᘐᘐᘐᘐᘐᘐᘐᘐᘐᘐᘐᘐ

The American Student as I See Him [1]

by GILBERT HIGHET

THE American scholar I have long known and long respected. The American student I met first as an ambitious but depressed graduate working in the hard Scottish medical schools; then as an exotic graft on Oxford's gnarled trunk (like Vergil's tree, "admiring strange new leaves and fruit unlike her own"); and finally in several of the great universities of his own country. I like studying him, and he, by now inured to the fads

[1] From *The American Scholar*, Autumn, 1941. By permission of the editor and the author.

of his preceptors, supports with surprising affability the endless process of being studied.

As far as I can judge, he is unlike any other student in the whole world. For one thing, he often works three or four hours a day at some job which is at least extra-curricular, if not extra-mural. My friends at St. Andrews and Glasgow were often poor—much poorer than the freshmen whom I see cheerfully filing clippings or toting luncheon trays—but in term-time they never worked at anything outside their studies. The vast mythology of Scottish education is full of stories about the crofter's son who lived all term in half a room on a barrel of oatmeal and a barrel of herrings brought from home, and then walked a hundred miles back to Inverquharity with the gold medal. And that ideal still persists. Occasionally British and French undergraduates do a little tutoring, and a dozen or two are book shifters in the libraries or demonstrators in the labs; but they don't *work*. James Joyce's miserable Stephen Dedalus in Dublin, drinking watery tea and eating fried bread while he fingered his parents' pawn tickets, would have been far better for a decent meal earned by honest work.

But it is not, or seldom, done. The feeling is that it would interfere with real work and equally real play: that it would keep the undergraduate from having his full share in the life of the university. And there is some truth in this. To spend three or four hours a day on something wholly unacademic nearly always narrows the student's interest in his academic work. He is apt to feel that it too can be done in the same way: two lectures, four hours at his job, four hours' study, and then stop. This therefore is one of the reasons why so few undergraduates in the universities here aspire to honors, compete for prizes, carry their interest in their courses further than the term paper. In France and Britain, on the other hand, it is common for lecturers to get notes from their undergraduate hearers questioning some statement, seeking a reference, asking for extended treatment of some difficulty. A not very intelligent pupil of my own at Oxford handed me a verse translation of six idylls of Theocritus, which he had made in his spare time during the two winter terms; in Jules Romains's *Les Hommes de Bonne Volonté* a student at the École Normale Supérieure translates and annotates the choric odes of Sophocles, just for fun; and, at all the British universities, essay and poem competitions are nearly always burdensome to mark, there are so many competitors. But they would not have the energy, or even the interest, to do all that, if they had to manage a laundry agency for four hours a day.

The American student himself feels this; for when he becomes a graduate student, a radical change comes over him—a change far greater than the corresponding change in other countries. He will doggedly set himself to read and classify every Elizabethan sonnet, or memorize every decision arising out of the Snite Act; he will plunge into labyrinthine bibliographies, from whose depths he can he heard faintly crying, as if he battled with unseen monsters, and from which he emerges through the gate of ivory, pale but uplifted, like Aeneas from the world of the dead; and when you and I make jokes to him, he will copy them and write "laughter" in the margin. It is scarcely too much to say that he then feels himself for the first time to be a whole-time student; and the only thing to be regretted about this metamorphosis is that it often keeps him from being a whole-time member of the university, that he is so often debarred by it from games and societies and other junior academic activities. He feels, not without a certain justice, that he is paying for the comparative diffuseness of his undergraduate days.

There is another way of putting this. No European country thinks that education is, or ought to be, wholly democratic. Not even the United States does, in the last resort—for, in awarding fellowships and scholarships, its universities base their distribution not on *need* but on *achievement*. The principle of competition, thus tacitly acknowledged, is carried much further in Europe. In France [2] the A.B. examination is a national contest, whose winners are rewarded not only with the civic tributes which the French know so well how to dispense, but with prizes, money, trips to Cambodia and certainty of a favorable start in their careers. The bad side of this is obvious—suicides are not at all uncommon among disappointed or overworked candidates, and a man's whole life can be darkened by a sense of his own inescapable inferiority, publicly and competitvely demonstrated. But it makes the students read, and read hard. All scholarships in Britain (except a very few assigned to localities or family names) are awarded on the basis of a long and difficult competitive examination. And there are very many more scholarships there than there are in this country: scholarships are endowed and awarded by cities, counties, prep schools, "public" schools, colleges, universities, alumni societies, guilds and national associations. Besides those, there are hundreds upon hundreds of rich scholarships dependent on the wills of long-dead benefactors. I went through one university on money left by a thread manufacturer who died about 1850, and through another on the rentals of farms bequeathed for the purpose by a Court official of King James the First. It would not be too much to say that the rich man who, in the United States, gives $50,000 for cancer research, gives £10,000 in Britain to support "a student who desires to enter the medical profession, said student to be selected by an examination on the fundamentals of . . . " The University of Oxford is thought to be full of the leisure class. Yet in 1937 60 per cent of its students were wholly or partially supported by scholarships; and all those scholarships had to be won by keen and difficult competition. From a certain Scots university there is one, and only one, scholarship which will take you to Oxford; and it is competed for by every student who wants it: pre-lawyers, chemists, historians, economists, mathematicians, philologists, they all sit there glowering at one another in the same examination room, and furiously laboring at the twelve three-hour papers on which their future depends. It is a painful ordeal; but it makes you study! Not only in France but in Britain too, enormous empha-

[2] This refers of course to France before it was invaded by the Germans, and before its government determined to assist its conqueror in attaining his own ideal, *die Vernichtung Frankreichs,* "the destruction of France."

sis is laid on the exact position of a student in his class. Those who simply collect their grades and their clubs and leave are little regarded; must, practically speaking, have jobs waiting for them; find the higher careers closed. Those who try for honors find themselves arranged into a natural hierarchy, which, *ceteris paribus,* represents their comparative chances of getting a good position when they graduate.

The American student, if I know him, would not care for this system. He would, I think, feel that it too highly rewarded the "grind' and undervalued the character-building and social qualities of college life; he would conclude it was unfair to boys who happened to attend schools which gave them less careful preparation for academic competition; ultimately he would think that, by subjecting him to a constant implied pressure, it deprived him of a good deal of his liberty. And yet, it seems to me that it would do him good, and improve the service of schools and universities to individuals and to the state.

Take only one broad consideration. The development of government all over the world, in the democracies as well as in the despotisms, is towards a more numerous, more elaborate, and more highly trained bureaucracy. For good or bad, every national government now interests itself in the lives of its citizens far more closely than at any time since the Byzantine empire. Therefore it is necessary, year by year, for it to command a great supply of diverse and well-trained officials, mostly specialists of one kind or another. In the despotisms these officials are produced by the Party machine, selected and trained by a system which is at least methodically similar to education. In the democracies they are at present produced and trained by no system, except in a few fields like jurisprudence and public health. In Great Britain the diplomatic service, the higher branches of the civil service, and certain other administrative departments are recruited by rigorous competitive examinations for which, in practice, candidates prepare throughout the universities and even during their last years at school. That system is thought to work well, although it is limited in extent. But many educators feel that the bureaucracies, both local and national, ought to be wholly staffed by men and women trained *on purpose,* and that in the democracies the schools and universities ought to be the organizations which produce and train them. Many a large store will not engage salesmen and saleswomen unless they are college graduates with noticeably good records; it is ludicrous that states and colleges should be less careful about choosing their executives. If we are to have a mandarinate, let us be as sensible as the Chinese in selecting our mandarins. If we want intelligent officials let us train them and discipline them and sift them by competitive examination and reward them with good, appropriate jobs, instead of letting our universities annually pour out a huge undifferentiated mass of graduates, from which only luck or exceptional perseverance will direct the right man to the right place in the social machine.

However, at present that is not done; and the American student, except in a few eccentric universities, estimates his achievement by time spent, which is quantitative, rather than by competitive achievement, which is qualitative. And yet he is at heart emulous. If it is presented civilly and winningly to him, he will welcome authority. He would welcome it still more if it were organized: if he felt that in school and at college its consistent purpose was to make him fit for a career which depended not entirely on his own whim, but on a long series of tests of his abilities and a constructive estimate of his character and capacity.

Another unique attribute characterizes the American student: his huge numbers. Can four real universities exist in one city? Can it be possible that in one state fifty or sixty thousand youths and maidens are capable of the activity required to absorb a university education? Are the inhabitants of California (whose very name derives from a romance describing the Earthly Paradise) so talented that they can every year produce a myriad of university graduates? And what educators could be at once so inspiring and so industrious as to teach, effectively, this enormous horde? Or, finally, can the vast multitudes of adolescents in the United States all be so much more talented than their coevals in Canada, in France, in Sweden?

The paradox, of course, conceals a dichotomy. To put it bluntly and generally, the American student who is not preparing for a profession does not often go to the university in pursuit of higher education. He goes to complete the education which his school left incomplete. He has been badly schooled. It is not his fault, and not wholly the fault of the school. But it is a pity. It sometimes strikes me with a sense of pathos to read the grave works on education, ranging all the way from Mortimer Adler's *How to Read a Book* to the bulletins of the Carnegie Institute for Educational Research, which treat the American school system in total detachment from all others, as if it could learn nothing from Europe, and teach Europe nothing—still less other continents. Mr. Adler, in his efforts to teach his patients how to read books, makes one or two cursory references to the situation in Europe, and throughout the rest of his prescription treats the American student as a chimera bombinating in the void. But of course he finds it difficult to read Locke or Dante when he gets to college. He has seldom been compelled to read anything difficult in school. And a comparison, however invidious, would demonstrate that. I went to a perfectly ordinary school in Scotland, P.S. 93 as it were. In my last three years (ages 15-18) we were forced to read and understand *Hamlet, Macbeth, Henry IV,* Chaucer's *Prologue* and *Knight's Tale, Polyeucte, Le Cid, Le Misanthrope, Eugénie Grandet, Seven Against Thebes, The Persians, Iliad* XVI and XVIII, *Aeneid* II, IV, and VI, Livy IX and several other books. And we read them. (Dickens and Scott and Thackeray and so on, we had read long before.) We had to, under that stringent discipline. We could write a character of Macduff or Célimène, we could reproduce the various explanations and emendations of the "dram of eale" in *Hamlet,* we could compare the shields of Achilles and Aeneas, we could write little essays on Balzac's idea of realism. They were not very good; but they proved that we had read the books. And we were not alone.

In Edinburgh they were doing the same. Bristol Grammar School was doing even more. Sheffield and Manchester and London and Newcastle were doing at least as much. French schools are still more arduous, although they concentrate more closely on the classics of their own tongue; and so, in a more limited way, were Scandinavian and Dutch schools, and even German schools before the despotism.

Now why does the average American student need to learn how to read a book? Why does he approach *Hamlet* or *Crime and Punishment* with a mixture of awe and bravado, and usually look up from it with such puzzled delight and half-understood emotion? Manifestly because he has been ill taught at school. And, so far, that is nobody's fault: certainly not his; but there are two main reasons for the fact.

For one thing, the system of mass-education has nowhere else been applied to a population so huge and so various. Only a nation so gallant and so confident as the United States would have dreamt of administering approximately the same education to the children of long-settled western Europeans, recent central European immigrants, and many millions of emancipated Negroes, of whom Bigger Thomas with his revolt and his tragedy may well be partially symbolic. Whenever I ask my pupils about their schooling they invariably say, if they went to public school, that they were held back by the size of the classes or by lazy and recalcitrant classmates. One of the best students I have ever had praised the history master at his public school most highly, but added that he was forced to devote himself almost wholly to the upper one third of his class. In one of his more frankly autobiographical essays Mr. James Thurber describes a tough school in Columbus, Ohio, as it was a generation ago; and even if we allow for humorous exaggeration there is still the ring of truth in the sentence about his enormous Negro protector, Floyd: "I was one of the ten or fifteen male pupils in Sullivant School who always, or almost always, knew their lessons, and I believe Floyd admired the mental prowess of a youngster who knew how many continents there were and whether or not the sun was inhabited." And the problem is complicated by the almost inevitable rigidity of the school system. It is true that many high schools have recently endeavored to work out special courses of study for pupils who are more intelligent than the average; but such readjustments are not yet common, are nearly everywhere tentative, and often meet with opposition. It is a task of almost inconceivable difficulty to raise the educational standards of an entire population; for at least two thirds of the boys and girls now leaving American schools are much more highly educated than their parents were. This difficulty does not exist in western European countries, and it fills me with admiration to see the courage and tenacity with which it is being faced here. But, in education more than in other things, each generation stands on the shoulders of its predecessor, and in another decade or so a great part of this difficulty will have been removed.

The other reason is the comparatively lax discipline of schools in the United States. High school pupils spend appreciably less time in school here than they do in Britain, and much less than they do in France. In school they spend less time on actual study, because of the surprising amount of attention paid to extra-curricular activities. They spend far less time on preparation at home. And there is much less *drive* behind their learning than there is in western European schools. In the last two years at an ordinary British city school, corresponding to a good high school here, the ordinary pupil averages at least five and a half hours of actual classroom work in school and three hours' preparation at home, with a minimum of six hours' preparation at week ends. The working hours of two good provincial lycées in France, where friends of mine taught during the early '30s, are literally almost double those of an American high school. Any extra-curricular occupation, like producing the school magazine, or football practice, or rehearsing in the school orchestra, takes place outside working hours. And there is a constant disciplinary pressure to keep the pupils at work, to keep them actively attentive, to pull up the laggards and push on the leaders. Attendances are rigidly kept: an incident such as that reported in the New York papers in 1940, when a squad of policemen and truant officers "combed" the cinemas on two different mornings and rounded up nearly two thousand school children A.W.O.L., is frankly inconceivable. If anything like it occurred in Europe it would be instantly followed by the discharge or demotion of dozens of school teachers. It may not be unfair to suggest that some of the laxity observable in American schools is due to the much higher proportion of women acting as teachers. Adolescent boys cannot be properly disciplined by women, and adolescent girls only with much difficulty. But there are other reasons, which are too well known or too controversial to be discussed here. The fact remains. The American high school student has a far better time, but he does far less work than his European counterpart.

Accordingly the American student, when he reaches college, is not so well prepared as the average European freshman. He has not read so much, and he does not know how to read and write so well. He does not buy nearly so many books for his own enjoyment, if indeed he buys any at all. One distinction seems to me particularly significant. English and French undergraduates are apt to publish little magazines in which they practise fine writing: the first sonnet, the first political manifesto, chapters from the first autobiographical novel and so on. The American student hardly ever produces an imitation literary review. Instead, he produces an imitation of a daily newspaper, or occasionally an imitation of a comic weekly. Almost every distinguished contemporary French and British writer wrote his first publishable work when he was an undergraduate; almost no distinguished American writer wrote anything at college which in any way prefigured his later work.

If I have not misunderstood the fairly widespread movement towards establishing "junior colleges" and the frequently emphasized distinction between the first biennium of college work and the second, they are based on this same fact: that some fairly intensive work is required to make up the deficiencies of the schools. Viewed in this light, the multitudinousness of the

American student becomes (although still a little bewildering) intelligible and sympathetic.

The third quality which forces itself on the observer of the American student is his freedom. He will, without great heart-searching, move from one university to another—a thing almost never done in France or Britain, and in Germany chiefly by very earnest undergraduates in search of a particular kind of specialized teaching or even of a particular professor. He will give up college altogether with a facility which still amazes me, although the dean's office usually knows exactly what proportion of the student body can be expected to drop out annually. He will in college drop subjects on which he spent four years in school; and he will take eccentric subjects or anomalous combinations of subjects with complete nonchalance. He is infinitely less cut to pattern (even allowing for his numbers) than the European student. In an English university it is often possible to tell what particular college an undergraduate attends, and even what school he came from, after five minutes' general conversation; but seldom in the United States.

This has its good side and its bad. It makes the American student far more self-reliant—one of my chief difficulties in Oxford was handling the timid, sheltered, hampered boy who might prove to be brilliant and might almost equally well be defeated and crushed; such difficulties hardly ever present themselves here. But, on the other hand, it makes him rather irresponsible, and even restless and discontented. Far too much is left to his own choice, at a time when he is scarcely capable of making a choice. Thanks to the kindly laxity initiated by President Eliot, he is free to take astronomy 17, comparative religion 1, government 33, Spanish drama in translation 21 and hygiene 2A (hygiene 2A is compulsory). A semester of that would, at best, produce a healthy cross between Sir Isaac Newton and the Duke of Plaza-Toro. It is no wonder that the mixture sometimes fails to act, and discourages him that gives and him that takes. The opposite extreme is seen in the English "public" schools, where a schoolboy good at history will be tutored from the age of fifteen till the age of eighteen to win a history scholarship at a good college specializing in history, will spend three or four years reading history for a first class in the final examinations, and then take history at his examination for entrance to the home civil service. (Usually, he will spend most of his time on the same period of history—e.g. medieval history, with special emphasis on the 12th century.) Both extremes are dangerous. The British extreme is often as narrowing as the other is bewildering: it needs, as an offset, the manifold external interests which only a great university and experienced tutors can give. But it has one merit in itself: it sets a premium on unremitting hard work and the long view. The other extreme broadens the student's mind; but it often broadens it without deepening it.

Thus it is that the American student in his last two years at school does not often know what he is going to be, and still less often knows what he will learn in his university; and in the first two years at the university (if he is not firmly steered by his parents into a profession) seldom knows how he will spend his junior and senior years, and how they will dovetail into his future. From one point of view, this shows a genuine, disinterested love of learning, a magnificent belief in the virtues of the university; but from another it means waste of good effort, waste of priceless time, waste of irreplaceable enthusiasm. The task of the university is to cast such a light on a man's youth as will illuminate him through his life, and yet to keep the light unblurred by the shadows of the temporary and the inessential. This task is always supremely difficult, but its difficulty is here enhanced by the inadequacy of the liaison between schools and universities and the lack of emphasis on the essentials of education. The schools have more than enough to do. They cannot tackle this job. It is for the American universities to look, like the wise man, before and after: to induce the student to surrender most of his freedom of choice for a more stable set of patterns in education. Wherever such compulsory patterns have been introduced he needs little persuasion to accept them; at Columbia he looks back on the arduous humanities course with feelings of pleasure and gratitude, not unmingled with surprise. He is a good fellow, the American student: he is energetic and ambitious; but he lacks direction, as the young do everywhere. "For," says Thomas Burton, "as he that plays for nothing will not heed his game; no more will voluntary employment so thoroughly affect a student, except he be very intent of himself." And, in these bad days, few of us are very intent of ourselves.

Education for Freedom [1]

by ROBERT MAYNARD HUTCHINS

THE free community aims at the happiness of its members. Its laws and its education have this aim. They are directed to showing the citizen how to lead a good life, the life which helps him toward happiness and the state toward stability and improvement.

The rulers of a slave state or a bad state do not want their subjects to be happy in any human sense. They do not want them to lead a good life. That would require them to have good moral habits—you cannot be just to a Jew in Germany—and good intellectual habits—you may study only "Aryan science" in Germany. A slave state does not want free minds. It wants instruments of war and instruments of production.

In America we think we have the rudiments, at least, of a free community and a good state. We look to education to give us free minds which will join in our struggle toward a better life for all the people. We need human instru-

[1] Condensed from *Harper's Magazine*, October, 1941. By permission of the editors and the author.

ments of production; we may even need human instruments of war. But aside from the fact that human dignity forbids us to look upon any human being solely as an instrument, we have another need that is far more urgent —we need men and women capable of freedom.

The task of fashioning human instruments of production is easy and is getting easier all the time. If there are jobs to be found they call for little or no preparation. Compare the technical knowledge required in skilled trades to-day with that demanded five hundred years ago. The weaver, the iron-worker, and the glassmaker had to command technics of a complexity that would startle the modern machine operator. We are rapidly becoming a nation of button-pushers. Earning a living in industry is no longer a matter of training; it is a matter of getting a job when the demand for jobs outruns the supply. Going through the simplest mechanical motions forty hours a week will take care of the business of earning a living.

But the business of citizenship in a free community is growing more complicated every day. The disappearance of the frontier, the advance of indus-trialization, the growth of great cities have presented the American citizen with problems the like of which he never knew before. The whirlwind of labor-saving devices which has descended upon us has created more difficul-ties than it has removed. What shall we do with our gadgets? What shall we do with our free time? What shall we do with ourselves? As R. H. Tawney has put it, "If the Kingdom of Heaven is not eating and drinking, but righteousness and peace, neither is civilization the multiplication of motor cars and cinemas or of any other of the innumerable devices by which men accumulate means of ever increasing intricacy to the attainment of ends which are not worth attaining."

The war has made us think about other questions, whether we like to think about them or not. What is a state? What is it for? What is a good state? How can we get one? These questions lead to further questions. How do you tell right from wrong and good from bad? What is the aim of life? How does man differ from the other animals? Does God exist? Is the soul immortal?

These questions have always been there. But up to the time of the great depression we never bothered very much about them. They were the preserve of the professional philosophers. We understood, if we thought about it at all, that American philosophy held that whatever succeeded was O.K. We were doing very well up to 1929. We were living in a New Era. The envi-ronment was wonderful, and all education had to do was to adjust the young to it. Anybody who thought the environment was not wonderful needed a psychiatrist. It was in this period that colleges and universities appointed psychiatrists to look after "maladjusted" students. . . .

We can see now that our faith that science would sooner or later answer all our questions has been misplaced. Everything that goes by the name of science does not deserve the reverence we pay it. Take, for example, the striking conclusions of the paper read at the last meeting of the American

Association for the Advancement of Science by Henry I. Baldwin of the New Hampshire Forestry and Recreation Department. According to *Science,* Dr. Baldwin found that early in the winter trees prevent snow from reaching the ground. He also discovered that snow in the forest lasts from one to three weeks longer than it does in the open.

Our most disturbing questions, moreover, are questions about ends. Science is about means. We cannot rely on science to tell us how to get a better society unless we know what is good. If we know where we want to go, science will help us get there. If our problem is where to go, science cannot help us. When we don't know where we ought to go we shall find, as we are finding to-day, that science makes our wild lunges in all directions more dangerous to ourselves and to our neighbors than they would be if we were ignorant of it.

Education has been turned upside down. Understanding the environment requires experience with the environment. Those studies which do not demand such experience should come first. As Aristotle said, "While young men become geometricians and mathematicians and wise in matters like these, it is thought that a young man of practical wisdom cannot be found. The cause is that such wisdom is concerned not only with universals, but with particulars, which become familiar from experience, but a young man has no experience; for it is length of time that gives experience; indeed one might ask this question, too, why a boy may become a mathematician, but not a philosopher. . . . Is it because the objects of mathematics exist by abstraction, while the first principles of these other subjects come from experience, and because *young men have no conviction about the latter but merely use the proper language,* while the essence of mathematical objects is plain enough to them?"

Those studies which do not demand experience are the necessary tools for understanding those which do. Reading, writing, and figuring are instruments which make intelligible the heterogeneous, undigested, apparently unrelated impressions presented to us by the environment.

· Since education is upside down, the acquisition of these instruments is postponed, slighted, and never completed. It is common knowledge that our professional students and candidates for the Ph.D. are illiterate. One thing you learn very quickly in teaching students at the loftiest levels of education is that they cannot read; and President Conant of Harvard in his report for 1938-39 said, "From all sides, academic and non-academic, we hear complaints of the inability of the average Harvard undergraduate to write either correctly or fluently." Frederick E. Crane, when Chief Judge of the highest court of New York, plaintively remarked to the alumni of the Columbia Law School, "I do wish that the Law School had an effectual way of doing that which the previous college experience has failed to do for so many students—teach them to speak the English language clearly." And he added, "I should say that not one lawyer out of fifty in my court can state clearly the facts of his case and his legal position concerning them."

So the growing mind is deprived of those instruments which enable its members to understand it and is presented instead with a kaleidoscope through which the environment remains meaningless because both experience and the instruments to appraise experience are lacking. In another of Mr. Kandel's papers he has written, "In a period when the trend of educational theory is to discard content in favor of activities and problems, when education must be contemporaneous, modernistic, streamlined, and even futuristic, it is not surprising that education is assuming some of the characteristics of the moving picture, which recreate rather than resolve William James's great, big, buzzing Confusion."

A good example of all the popular fallacies about education is the theory and practice of vocational education. Here society casts on the school the burden of making the population self-supporting, and industry presents it with the task of training its hands. Because we do not see what the proper task of the educational system is, and even deny that it has any, we find nothing incongruous in placing these demands upon it.

These demands have become more and more insistent as the age for going into industry has been forced upward by laws, economic conditions, and technological change. The years formerly devoted to apprenticeship or to learning a trade or gaining experience in it are now spent in school. Thomas Jefferson thought that three years in the grades should be compulsory for every child. Even this was sensational, for in that day the youth of the country could get jobs as soon as they could walk. Adam Smith, writing in 1776, said that marriage to a widow with four children was the best investment an American could make.

I am opposed to child labor. I am in favor of giving everybody as much education as he can stand. But I should prefer to have the length of education determined by the needs and capacities of the young rather than by the fluctuations of economic conditions and the vagaries of social reform. . . . Our notion that the young must go to school until they can go to work, which makes the school a time-killer or waiting room, is simply an aspect of our general view that if anything needs to be done we will let the school do it.

Since the years our forefathers devoted to learning a trade are now spent in school, we naturally look to the school to teach our children a trade. We do not want them to be less "successful" than their ancestors. The situation in Nebraska is typical. The greatest shift in the enrolments in the high schools of that State has occurred in the "practical" arts. In 1904 only 13.4 per cent of the pupils in these schools were studying the practical arts. In 1941 almost all the pupils—96.05 per cent, to be exact—were studying them.

If it could be shown that young people could learn industrial pursuits only in school, or if they could learn them better there than anywhere else, we might be able to defend the elaborate program of vocational training upon which we have embarked. The reverse, however, is true. The school is the worst of all possible places in which to prepare the young for industry. The more rapid the advance of technology the worse place the school becomes. It cannot change its buildings, its curriculum, and its teachers to meet the alterations in manufacturing that take place every day. Its methods, facilities, and staff are always obsolescent. They may have the effect of actually maladjusting the pupil to his economic environment. The motions he has gone through to train him to go through motions in a factory may be just the wrong motions in that factory now.

John Dewey has made this point by saying, "Very often the courses which are called practical are not really practical except in their label. Some of these courses try to teach things which can only be learned in the actual business or calling itself, while they do not take sufficient account of the rapid changes that are going on, since the teachers are out of contact with industry and teach the way things were done five or ten years ago rather than the way they are done now in the actual callings of life. And they are still less in contact with the way things are going to be done five years from now. In consequence, even the so-called practical courses in the long run are often not very practical."

If a boy wants to go to work for Henry Ford he will be better prepared if he has had no vocational training at all. Mr. Ford will not then have to untrain him. Mr. Ford can teach him more in a month about working for Ford than a vocational school can in a year. As the late L. A. Downs, President of the Illinois Central, put it, "The only practical vocational training for any specific business, except where special professional talent is required, is experience."

Years of vocational training may be swept away by a single invention. A university in California has introduced courses in what is called cosmetology, saying that what is called the profession of beautician is the fastest growing in that State. Think of the fate of California's beauticians if self-beautification for ladies becomes as simple a matter as it is for men. Or think of what will happen in that great State when the university has trained so many beauticians that they are all starving to death. Or reflect on the fate of one of these university-trained beauticians who for one reason or another has to return to the remote paternal acres and there languish with nobody to beautify but the domestic animals. Unless she has also taken the course in cosmetology in the agricultural college she will be quite unfitted for any useful occupation.

The Secretary of the Association of Medical Colleges has stated the case accurately. "The moving belt of industry has been adopted by education. The result is the same in both instances. The nut will fit only one kind of bolt. It cannot be used for any other purpose than to fit that certain bolt. It is a purely industrial robot. Those who come through the 'pre'-courses and vocational courses, the product of the educational moving belt, are often educational robots—fit for just one thing and a poor fit at that."

But suppose that none of these objections was valid. Suppose the schools could supply the skill needed to earn a living. Where and how would their benighted graduates learn to use the living they had earned? The mechanical motions they had gone through would not help them after five o'clock. They might have money in their pockets, but nothing in their heads. Having a regular job and getting paid for it may seem like an adequate ideal in early adolescence. When you have achieved it you understand that it is merely a necessary condition of life, not life itself. The problem of the purpose and meaning of life remains, and if your education has not helped you solve it it has been no education at all. It has not been the kind of education that can help you toward happiness. It has not been the kind that can make you capable of freedom. . . .

The aims of education in a democracy must be the same for all the people. Education must aim at making them all capable of freedom, for they are all to be free. Whatever education will achieve this aim must be given to every person in proportion to his capacity to receive it. If, for example, we were to decide that the way to make a person capable of freedom was to try to teach him how to earn a living, then we should try to teach everybody how to earn a living. Everybody has to live. Why should the privilege of learning how to support life be denied the bright and become the exclusive franchise of the dull? What if the dull were all to get rich because of their training and exploit the untrained bright through their dull use of economic power? If any education is necessary for the citizen it must be necessary for all the citizens. Only in this way can we hope to prevent the exploitation of one group by another. Only in this way can we develop a true community.

Learning how to sustain life is very important. Since the school cannot give this learning well, since it can, if it will, do some even more important things better, since the pupil can learn how to sustain life better outside the school than he can in it, it follows that vocational training can be most effectively carried on outside the school.

The best type of vocational training is that given on the job. But any type which does not interfere with education for freedom must be acceptable to those who believe that such education is the primary function of the American school. Part-time work, summer work, night schools, continuation schools, apprenticeship schemes, the co-operative plan at Antioch and in engineering at Cincinnati—all these may help the student learn to earn a living without getting in the way of education. Careful organization of the curriculum might permit the ordinary school to give education for freedom and some vocational experience too. But the heart of any educational program for free men must be education for membership in a free community.

A community depends on communication. The citizens must be able to understand one another. This means more than that they must be able to effect a ready translation of the dialects of the country. They must have a common culture. They must have the intellectual training needed to comprehend it and to communicate with those who share it. What happens when this is lacking is set forth by Mr. Walter Lippmann in describing contemporary education: "There is no common faith, no common body of principle, no common moral and intellectual discipline. Yet the graduates of these modern schools are expected to form a civilized community. They are expected to govern themselves. They are expected to have a social conscience. They are expected to arrive by discussion at common purposes. When one realizes that they have no common culture is it astounding that they have no common purpose? That they worship false gods? That only in war do they unite? That in the fierce struggle for existence they are tearing western society apart?"

The cultural heritage of America is the civilization of Western Europe. The means of understanding it is the liberal arts, the arts of reading, writing, speaking, and calculating. Education for freedom consists in transmitting to the rising generation the civilization they have inherited, together with the technics by which it may be understood. No man or women is equipped to be a ruler in America without this education.

This education, if we can work it out and if we can discover the methods appropriate to it, answers the fundamental questions. It gives us a community; for those who have had this education will be able to communicate with one another. It gives us freedom, because it gives the trained intelligence free play. It gives us adjustment to the environment, because the sights and sounds of the environment take on meaning in and through the tradition in which we live. It gives us adjustment to the environment of 1951, because the liberally educated man is prepared for any world that comes. It gives us the answer to the question what shall we do with ourselves, for it shows us the aim of life and the path to happiness.

Hearken to the moving appeal of the Cornell Alumni Fund "The longer we live the more we need mooring to something that is as lasting as the years, something that gives us a sense of place in the world, of stability of purpose and significance in life. We face all through the years the threat of the sense of futility—the feeling that life doesn't mean anything; that it is all motion, that there is no progress toward something better. If you have a chance to tie up to something lasting, something effectively representing the effort of mankind to ennoble human experience, you had better get a firm hold on it without delay. You will need something of that sort before you are through with life. . . . So I say to any Cornellian, if you really want to get the most out of life, get next to Cornell and stay there."

I am in entire accord with these sentiments. I think every Cornellian should get next to Cornell and stay there. But I think too that Cornell, and all other universities, schools, and colleges, should offer something more to combat the feeling that life doesn't mean anything than the chance to contribute to the Alumni Fund. The natural thing for them to offer is an education.

As a liberal education helps us to establish a free community, so it helps us to preserve it. As Thomas F. Woodlock has lately said in the *Wall Street Journal*, "Democracy rests ultimately upon 'public opinion' as its base. Public opinion follows upon free speech, free interchange of *ideas,* of *judgments,* of *opinions;* it is generated by these things. Men interchange these things by *words.* . . . Sound logic it was that put grammar, logic, and rhetoric as preliminary to geometry, arithmetic, music, and astronomy in the scheme of the seven liberal arts in an age which was notable for the clearness of its thinking and the exactitude of its expression. Both these things are absolutely necessary to the functioning of democracy as the best form of government. If we are going to 'educate for democracy,' we had better find the right way to teach them."

Mr. Woodlock might have added that the ability to read and write is the best defense against anti-democratic propaganda. The reiteration of slogans—now advocated by many American educators under the name of "indoctrination for democracy"—is not much better than the reiteration of lies as practiced by the Nazis. When a person equipped with the liberal arts has critically studied the tradition of the Western world and faced the basic theoretical questions, he is proof against the seductions of the New Order. The reason why we may justly fear foreign propaganda to-day is that we are uneducated.

In addition to all the merits I have listed, liberal education has another: it is the best vocational training. This must be so unless a trained mind is of no advantage in earning a living. Vocational training of the usual sort trains hands. Apart from the educational deficiencies of such a program, we have seen that it has deficiencies as a training program resulting from the rapid changes in industry. Hands are trained to do something that is not wanted when it is time for them to go to work. But the trained mind is by definition a mind that is able to operate well in all spheres and under all conditions.

I do not advocate liberal education because it is the best vocational training. I say only that if you are interested in educating people to earn a living you will find that a liberal education represents the maximum contribution which the school can make to the achievement of your purpose. A liberal education, at least, has never handicapped anybody in earning a living. Vocational training has.

I must admit that liberal education may interfere with getting rich. Two basic theoretical questions are what is good and what is the order of goods. One who has faced these questions intelligently will hardly conclude that he should devote his life to the unremitting pursuit of the Almighty Dollar. I cannot regard a diminution of American selfishness and greed as unfortunate. The solution of many of our most distressing problems may lie just here. Aristotle may have been right again when he said, "For it is not the possessions but the desires of mankind which require to be equalized, and this is impossible, unless a sufficient education is provided by the state."

But, you may say, suppose we grant all you have said about liberal education. What difference does it make if half the youth of America cannot profit by it? We have admitted everybody to citizenship. We must have, you say, the same education for everybody. Yet you have shown yourself that candidates for the Ph.D. cannot read and write to-day. How can an education which even Ph.D.'s do not now possess ever be given to the whole population?

The objection is a good one. Unless I can show that liberal education can be acquired by the mass of the people I must stand convicted as a fabricator of pipe dreams.

Let me first make a few remarks about young people. I think any candid teacher will agree that the most hopeful element in any academic community is the students. They have ability. When they enter an educational institution they show signs of being eager to learn. If I were asked which had the greater effect in slowing down their educational progress, their own dullness or that of the curriculum, I should unhesitatingly blame the curriculum. The first step in communicating an education to the young is to work out an educational program that makes sense.

We have a fatal habit of underrating the capacity of our juniors. For fifty years university presidents, and especially Mr. Lowell of Harvard, have been deploring the constant extension of the period of education and the constant postponement of entrance into active life. The anachronisms in our educational organization, such as an eight-year elementary school, and the multiplication of the educational units through which the pupil must pass, with duplication and overlapping at every stage, bring him to each of these stages two or three years too late. Students at fifteen or sixteen are just as capable of dealing with college work as those of eighteen or nineteen. Students at twenty are fully as capable of attacking law or medicine as those of twenty-two.

We cannot believe that the human race has deteriorated since the Middle Ages. In that dark and backward time young men went to universities at fourteen. They read books and studied subjects that are far too hard for university professors to-day. They did it because it was expected of them. The university was not a nursery school, or a club, or a body-building institute. It was a place for the training of the mind. At fourteen you are presumably ready to train your mind. Our assumption is that young persons of eighteen have very little mind, that they don't want to train what they have, and that it doesn't make very much difference whether it is trained or not. Our object is to keep them out of harm's way for four years, to let them learn how to get along with people, and then obtain contributions from them to the Alumni Fund for the rest of their lives. Since our students have lived up to our expectations, we have succeeded in postponing maturity to a date undreamed of in the Middle Ages, or even in Europe to-day. The American college senior is two or three years less grown up than his French or British contemporary. In ability to use his mother tongue and the other instruments of intellectual operation he does not at all compare with them.

Young Americans are not inherently immature. Industry has successfully made demands on them—such as eight hours' work a day—which no university would think of exacting. Mere boys have gone to work and risen at an early age to positions of great responsibility. Young Americans can and will do what is expected of them. Ten years ago the University of Chicago decided to treat freshmen like adults. It worked out what looked to it like a coherent program for the freshman and sophomore years. It printed syllabi of its courses. It printed and circulated its examinations. It then announced that the student did not have to attend classes; he did not have to accumulate credits; if he passed the examinations he would graduate from the work of the sophomore year; he could prepare himself for the examinations in any way he chose and present himself for them when in his opinion he was ready to take them.

It was freely predicted that Chicago freshmen would be found lying in the gutter while those of other colleges were attending classes, if only because they were compelled to. Actually when freshmen were treated like adults they behaved like adults, or rather in the way adults ought to behave. They got the idea that the University was an educational institution, that education was important, and that whether or not they got an education depended on themselves. The University would not stand in their way. Ten years of the Chicago Plan convinces me that if students are given a chance they will display qualities of energy, independence, and maturity which we never suspected. An educational program based on the assumption that they are dull will make them so.

There are of course wide differences among individuals. It is often said that these differences are so great that no single course of study can be given to all individuals. Some Progressive leaders have gone so far as to say there should be no such thing as a curriculum. If there is no curriculum there can be no community. Without a common education we get only a group of people wrestling with one another in the same geographical region.

Specialization may begin when education for citizenship is completed. We do not want technicians who are without a conception of the objects and traditions of the community. We want men and women who are citizens first and technicians afterward. With a coherent educational program and a rational educational organization we shall have no difficulty in giving every citizen an education for freedom plus technical or professional training in less time than it takes to go through college and do graduate or professional work to-day.

The problem of producing specialists is, therefore, one of order and organization. The problem of dealing with real differences in ability is largely one of method. Some pupils, for example, have a hard time learning to read. Should we say that they do not have to learn to read, or that they should read poor books because good ones are too hard for them? Should we limit Shakespeare to those who like to read him or who can read him readily, and have the others read James Whitcomb Riley, or nothing at all?

If Shakespeare is important in understanding the tradition in which we live—and I think he is—then every citizen should read some of his works. We shall have to find the way to teach them to those who have trouble with them. We must remember that educational technology has made great advances in recent years. American educators, like Americans generally, have been preoccupied with means, and it would have been remarkable if their efforts had been wholly without success. Such studies as those of Gray and Buswell have shown us how to teach pupils to read with an ease and rapidity unheard of in an earlier generation. If you know what you want to do, educational engineering will help you do it far more effectively than you could have done it forty years ago. We should not despair of communicating a liberal education to all the young merely because we have failed with many of them in the past. Forty years ago there was no such thing as educational engineering.

Educational engineering will not solve the educational problem. It cannot tell us what we should aim at, and hence cannot answer our fundamental question: What should education be? We shall be grossly misled, and sadly disappointed, if we rely on technics to educate. But when we know what education we want to give we may get some help in giving it from the educational technicians.

The ideal education for freedom, then, is a liberal education, an education in the liberal arts and the cultural heritage of the Western world. Since it is the ideal, we must aim at it for every citizen. If, with the best teachers and the best methods, we find that we cannot give the overwhelming majority of our people a liberal education then we must admit, not that education is a failure, but that democracy is. For unless the citizen can master the liberal arts and the fundamental principles of a free society he cannot function as a member of a free community. He cannot help to keep the community a community or help to keep it free.

The precise method of transmitting a liberal education is of course immaterial. Different methods may be successful with different students. I have myself a prejudice in favor of books and of the best books there are. They form in the early stages the natural field for learning the liberal arts. As education proceeds, they constitute the mine from which the cultural heritage of the race is dug. They can be read in such an order as to show the development of thought and civilization. But I do not greatly care in what order the books are read, or even how many. In the hands of a great teacher the Bible and Shakespeare can give a boy a liberal education, even a liberal education in natural science. But we are talking about all teachers, including many who would not be able to derive much instruction in astronomy from the story of Joshua's interference with the solar system. We have to have enough books to bring out in the hands of a teacher who is not a Socrates the basic principles in history, philosophy, politics, mathematics, the fine arts, and science.

Our citizens will have to study science. Science is the distinguishing characteristic of the modern world. But since we are educating our students to be citizens, rather than scientists, we should direct their attention primarily to the principles of science. We want them to know what science can and cannot do. We want them to know what it is and what it is not. We want them particularly to understand that it is not a substitute for philosophy or theology. A knowledge of the limitations of science is just as important as a knowledge of its possibilities.

Our citizens will have to study social science. But not only will the present order of learning be reversed so that the study of society comes at the end, rather than at the beginning, of education, but also the content of the subject will be drastically altered. The facts and data of social science will be used to illustrate the principles on which society is founded. The great questions about society: what is it, why is it, and what of it? are philosophical rather than scientific. Hence the social studies must be taught in the setting of moral and political philosophy. Professor Frank Knight concludes his impressive discussion of social science by saying, "But the social problem is not one of fact—except as values are also facts—nor is it one of means and end. It is a problem of values. And the content of social science must correspond with the problem of action in character and scope."

Our citizens will have to learn at least one foreign language. The reason is not so that they can sell things to the Brazilians, or study German medical books, or appreciate those beauties of Homer which are lost in translation. Nor is it because they will gain satisfaction in recognizing the Latin root of the word satisfaction. It is not even because grubbing for roots is good discipline. It is because they cannot understand their own language unless they have studied another. The native of any country is immersed in his own language and never sees it as a linguistic structure. He cannot learn what he ought to know about language from talking about his own.

But you keep telling me it can't be done. I say it can. All the evidence suggests it can. Experience with raw Marylanders at St. John's, raw Middle Westerners at Chicago, and raw New Yorkers at Columbia shows it can. The teachers who have tried it at Annapolis, Chicago, and New York have not been geniuses. The students have been average. Their complaint is not that the work is too hard, but that there is not more of it.

The only comprehensive scheme of this variety has been in operation at St. John's College for four years. This is the only college where the entire time of all the students is given to a coherent plan of liberal education. There, where students must learn not one foreign language, but four; where the amount of mathematics seems to me excessive; where all the difficulties of recalling a very old college to its ancient task have been experienced, a young faculty has shown that this kind of curriculum is interesting and important to ordinary young Americans, and that they can and will master it. So much is this the case that I should like to see the St. John's program tried with students two years younger. I am confident that juniors in high school could enter upon it with pleasure and profit. They would then be ready to specialize, to embark upon professional study, or to engage in the duties of earning a living and being a citizen at the end of the present sophomore year in college, or at the age of twenty instead of at twenty-two.

If we cannot give a liberal education to every citizen in proportion to his capacity to receive it we might as well give up our hopes of achieving a democratic community. We cannot insist on free men and at the same time say that we cannot educate our population for freedom. We cannot insist on a community and at the same time say that it is impossible to lay the basis of communication among our people.

Individual happiness, good citizenship, and the improvement of society all depend on our success in helping the people to achieve a liberal education. They do not depend on our success in training them to earn a living or in adjusting them to their environment. What the world needs, what this country must have, is free minds. This does not mean minds loaded with archaic information or equipped with obsolescent technics. It means minds committed to the good by good moral and intellectual habits. It means minds informed by principles derived from human experience through the ages, minds that will operate well no matter what waves of change beat upon them.

If we are to admit everybody to citizenship we must try to give everybody this education. In so far as men are men they must have this education. Since in our society all men are politically equal, since all men are ruler and ruled, they must all be educated to be ruler and ruled. If we cannot give them all this education we may as well drop the pretense of democracy. We may as well admit that, though it was a good idea, it would not work.

Even A.B.'s Must Eat[1]
by ERNEST EARNEST

THERE is considerable current alarm about the future of the Liberal Arts College. Naturally this emotion is felt most keenly by persons whose livelihood depends upon the continued existence of that type of institution. They usually defend their bread and butter by eloquent pleas for the nonmaterial values. Thus the many articles in academic journals are likely to be labeled "A Defense of Humanism," or "The Humanities and the Opportunity of Peace." And the discussions are filled with phrases like: "stimulating . . . a critical and aesthetic taste"; "an appreciative love for what is truly and enduringly beautiful"; "teach hope, love, and courage"; "recognize or retrieve those eternal truths which are above the stream of evolution and change"; ". . . true education is but a continuous process of re-examining, re-appraising, and re-vitalizing the interrelationships of existence." And of course there is always the old standby: "education for democracy."

Now I have no quarrel with any or all of these objectives except, perhaps, with their vagueness. There is always the suspicion that when a use cannot be found for something, it will be asserted to have "higher values"—like an impractical coffee urn kept in the china closet as an *objet d'art*. Our Victorian ancestors were more prone to that sort of thing than we are—though the whatnot has come back in decorator-designed interiors. The magazines are beginning to speak of the revival of the style of "a more leisurely and comfortable age." There is a suspicious parallel between the advertising of Vic-

[1] From *The American Scholar*, Autumn, 1944. By permission of the author and the editor.

torian reproductions of furniture and the arguments of the humanists. Please don't ask for a definition of humanist or humanity; there seems to be no agreement on that point. A working definition might be *humanist:* a person who teaches some subject other than science or a vocation; and *humanity:* a subject that students must be required to take along with the ones they really want.

Now I, for one, do not believe that a college course in Lunchroom Management or Clothing Selection is preferable to one in aesthetics or Greek history. I am not at all sure that the first two are the more practical. But I do not believe that any number of eloquent pleas for recapturing the "lost soul" of society is going to entice students into the Colleges of Liberal Arts. In fact any students who are attracted by the grandiloquent phrases are likely to be aesthetes, impractical idealists, or potential school teachers. Boys and girls from wealthy homes may come also, but they come for very practical reasons: four years of pleasant life, social polish, and a certificate of culture useful in certain social circles. As a rule the Liberal Arts College is very efficient in supplying these requirements. Certainly more efficient than a school offering training in lunchroom management or methods of teaching shorthand.

It is quite another matter to educate one to appreciate "what is truly and enduringly beautiful" or to "recognize or retrieve . . . eternal truths." Too often it is assumed that these things can be taught as entities unrelated to other considerations—that there is a world in which morality, truth, and beauty exist apart from the ethics of business, or the truth of a scientific or social theory, or the beauty of a particular poem or office building.

The advocates of liberal arts training will deny this. They will argue that a knowledge of philosophy helps one to understand the values in contemporary life (or more often the alleged lack of values); that mathematics trains the accurate use of the reason (an idea long since exploded by psychologists); that history helps in an understanding of today's politics; and that literature and art give one standards of judgment to apply to contemporary literature or art, or that they do something or other for one's personality—something very fine, of course.

Students often pay lip service to these doctrines: they say that they want college to give them "culture." But that is almost always a secondary aim. The vast majority of students are in college to become engineers, accountants, physicians, social workers, teachers—or even chiropodists and undertakers. If at the same time they can acquire the mystic quality called culture by taking a few courses in language, history, and literature they are willing to spare a little time from their real purpose. But few pre-meds will elect Fine Arts 1 if it conflicts with Biology 127; and fewer civil engineers will study Chaucer when they can get Strength of Materials instead.

All this may be simply an indication of mistaken values, the symptoms of a materialistic national culture, the worship of false gods. I believe that it is rather an indication of faulty methods. Two deeply religious men may both desire the kingdom of heaven; one may try to reach it by praying continually, wearing a hair shirt, and refusing to bathe; the other by ministering to the sick. It is quite possible that the second man will find very little time to examine his soul or clarify points of theology. He therefore spends less time on his "specialty" than does the ascetic, but he may be more fully obtaining his objective.

The analogy may apply to a liberal education. It is quite possible that extreme specialization is not the best preparation of most professions or intellectual occupations. It is impossible in a paper of this sort to support this point of view in detail. But it is a point of view almost universal among believers in a liberal education.

However, I venture upon two assertions: one, that the liberal arts colleges fail to implement this point of view; and two, that they fail to demonstrate its validity. To put the case more specifically: I believe that the liberal arts college fails to relate its work to the world the students must face, and that it fails to make the student understand its aims. In colloquial phraseology, the liberal arts college high-hats the vocational phases of education, and it fails to sell itself to its customers.

Almost all the defenders of a liberal education use a tone of moral superiority. The phrases quoted at the beginning of this essay suggest an out-of-this-world point of view. Yet if the liberal arts college is to survive, it must function in this world and must make that function clear. In a democratic society, the primary function demanded of a college or university is that it prepare its students to earn a living. The point of view stated by Jacques Barzun: "Vocational training has nothing to do with education," implies that education is only for a leisure class or a scholarly elite. Only at their peril can liberal arts colleges cater to a Brahmin caste. Most students and parents are certainly not going to be less materialistic about their bread and butter than are the defenders of a liberal education.

It may seem that this promise denies any possibility of preserving the liberal arts. Not at all. I have already pointed out that the arts colleges insist on the superior value of their training as preparation for an intellectual vocation or profession. I agree with this point of view. In the rapidly changing world of business, technology, and social order, a narrowly specialized training is often obsolete before the student graduates. Many of my former college mates are in fields of activity which did not exist twenty years ago. No vocational training then offered could have helped them. A contemporary radio news analyst would certainly find his college work in European history more valuable than his course in News Story Write-up. History, language, literature, philosophy have vocational value. More obvious is the vocational aspect of social science and psychology. All these are elements in a liberal arts program.

Specifically I suggest that the liberal arts colleges integrate their programs with vocational fields. For instance: what courses should be elected by a student interested in entering the diplomatic field, or social security, or a host of other governmental activities for which the A.B. course is the best preparation? Few faculty advisers have this information. Students them-selves are often unaware that certain of these fields exist; more have no idea how to prepare for them. So, instead, they take a degree in marketing or dentistry or advertising—anything with a label indicating possible usefulness. Students are often amazed to find that they can enter law school with an A.B. in history and literature instead of a B.S. in "pre-law."

This brings us to my second recommendation; a better publicizing of the vocational usefulness of a liberal arts education. Bulletins and catalogs of vocational schools often have much to say about opportunities in the fields they train for; those of liberal arts colleges are extremely reticent on this point. Except for occasional listing of requirements for medical school or teaching, there is almost no discussion of so crass a topic as preparing for a job. For instance, in a recent study of training for the field of social security, Karl de Schweinitz states that the best possible background is the academic dis-cipline and a cultural education. It is significant that this study was made for the Social Security Board and not under the auspices of the colleges.

All this may seem to imply that the liberal arts colleges should turn them-selves into vocational schools. The answer is that they are vocational schools and always have been. Harvard College was founded specifically to train ministers of the gospel. The classical education of the nineteenth century was regarded as the best possible training for the law and the church. Today students in liberal arts colleges are preparing to become biologists, psychol-ogists, sociologists, teachers, and lawyers.

What I suggest, then, is not a revision of the curriculum: no addition of gadget courses to attract uncritical customers. It is simply that the colleges intelligently accept the fact that they have a vocational function. That means vocational guidance for students, not in a haphazard way, but by trained counselors with adequate budgets for research; it means well run placement bureaus; it means making vocational information readily available to stu-dents; and it means a constant and intelligent study of the changing needs of the community. It is shortsighted if not unethical to turn out thousands more pre-meds than the medical schools will accept; to produce English teach-ers far in excess of demand, and at the same time to ignore fields where ed-ucated people are desperately needed.

But what happens to "culture" in all this? Does it mean that we forget all about the permanently true and beautiful? My answer is that "culture" is always a by-product of something else. Shakespeare's plays are now studied chiefly for their cultural value; they were written to attract patrons to the box office. Architects have always designed their buildings for specific utili-tarian purposes. Stiegel produced his famous glass for a market; he went bankrupt when he overestimated the market. The arts have always been closely linked with the business of living. It is only when they become art for art's sake that they wither. Similarly, culture for culture's sake becomes exotic and unreal. If literature and history and philosophy cannot be related to the life of the community, they have no very important values. In other words, if a psychologist is not a better psychologist because he knows something about the development of human nature through art, then there is little hope for philosophy, history, and literature.

Many of the defenders of a liberal education emphasize its broader social values: the making of intelligent citizens; the training for life rather than making a living; the understanding of ethical and moral values. But a member of a democratic society functions in that society chiefly through his occupation. A man's contribution to his age is above all his contribution as a physician, a manufacturer, a chemist, a writer, a publisher. A physician's knowledge or lack of knowledge of sociology will appear during dinner table conversations and at the polls. But it is vastly more important in his work as a physician and member of a medical association. It is there that his knowledge or lack of knowledge chiefly affects society.

Culture does not function in a vacuum. The "lost soul" of society will be found not in college courses, but in the market place and the laboratory and the court of law. The liberal arts college cannot educate some sort of mythical men of vision; it must educate chemists and sociologists and journalists with vision. When it fully accepts this function, it will no longer be troubled by falling enrollments. The professors can cease to worry about their own bread and butter when they recognize that even an A.B. must eat.

Alumni and Civic Responsibility [1]

by C. ROBERT PACE

EFFECTIVE citizenship and concern for the social good are broad educational objectives especially pertinent to and significant for the continued growth of American democracy. If large numbers of university graduates do not, as young adults, give evidence of responsible citizenship, democracy will suffer. If men and women who have been exposed to the teachings and experiences offered by free public education and have further extended their educational experiences to the college and university level do not emerge from such training prepared and willing to undertake the duties of citizenship, the schools must assume part of the responsibility for this failure.

The general public certainly expects the products of its educational system to be responsible citizens. College teachers and educational leaders likewise recognize the importance of social and civic affairs in adult life and express publicly their belief that the schools should make a positive contribution to the

[1] From C. Robert Pace, *They Went to College, A Study of 951 Former University Students* (1941). By permission of the University of Minnesota Press, publishers.

production of an informed citizenry. The growing emphasis on education for democracy testifies to this interest. Then too the activities of many pressure groups of laymen advocating the use or restriction of certain social science textbooks, the application of loyalty oaths to teachers, the circulation of specially prepared pamphlets or motion pictures—all these efforts arise from a concern, however misguided some of its applications may be, with the kind and quality of citizens the schools produce. Since college students are drawn largely from the upper social, intellectual, cultural, and economic levels of society, they should be expected as adults to assume responsibility for active participation, if not for leadership, on these particular levels.

Social and civic affairs represent, too, the climax of the ever-widening circle of relationships that have been studied in these former college students. One's existence as an individual, different from all other individuals; one's position in the family group; one's relationship to his fellow workers; one's place in the community, the nation, and the world—these are progressively widening aspects of adult life. The extent to which people see these various areas of living as parts of an interrelated whole, the extent to which they appreciate the fact that social, political, and economic developments, over which they as citizens in a political democracy can exercise some measure of influence, affect their jobs, their families, and their personal lives, constitute one crucial measure of their insight into the contemporary world in which they live.

WHAT THEY DO ABOUT, SAY ABOUT, AND WANT TO KNOW ABOUT SOCIAL AND CIVIC AFFAIRS

As a starting point for presenting the findings in the social and civic area of life, the activities, discussion topics, and needs for information checked by fifty per cent or more of the adults in any one of the eight basic groups are listed in Table 1.[2] The figure following each item indicates the percentage for the total sample of adults—all eight groups combined—and thus provides a rough index to the characteristics of the whole group. The headings in the following outline correspond to the headings of the various sections in the socio-civic area of the questionnaire.

Although many of these adults appeared highly interested in certain very significant social problems and felt a need for more information about them, their interests were directed mostly toward large national issues rather than toward specific local or community problems. Their participation in social and civic affairs was, by and large, limited to quite routine matters and except for voting gave little evidence of political activity.

DIFFERENCES AMONG VARIOUS GROUPS

A study of the differences between the social and political activities of the men and of the women reveals two clear trends. First, the men participated

[2] The statistics cited are based on questionnaires filled out in 1938 and 1939 by 951 former students of the University of Minnesota who had entered in the years 1924, 1925, 1928, and 1929. The eight groups were made on the basis of occupation. [Editor's note.]

TABLE 1. SOCIO-CIVIC AFFAIRS

	Percentage of Responses
Characteristic activities	
Gave aid to Community Fun, Red Cross, etc.	88
Discussed social, political problems with guests	85
Voted	82
Deposited money in a bank	78
Carried life insurance	77
Listened to Roosevelt's speeches	70
Borrowed books from public library	70
Discussed social, political, economic problems with family	69
Discussed social, political, economic problems with job associates	63
Visited national or state parks	59
Attended public musical concerts	54
Belonged to a church organization	47
Carried property and liability auto insurance	45
Filed an income tax return	38
Bought goods on installment plan	37
Inquired for information from a government office	36
Characteristic discussion topics	
Relief	80
Roosevelt	76
New Deal	72
Rising cost of living	71
Can America remain neutral in next war?	66
C. I. O.	64
Main issues in fight between capital and labor	55
National debt	53
Motion pictures and public morals	48
Extent of crime wave	43
Characteristic needs for more information	
Related to government	
How to judge qualifications of candidates	65
What foods are government inspected and how reliable is this inspection	52
Where to obtain reliable information about events in Washington	46
What improvements on the city administration are needed	44
What goods are affected in price by U. S. tariff policy	38
What valid distinctions are there between platforms of major political parties	37
Where to obtain reliable information about foreign governments	35
Related to the community	
What dangers to health exist in the community	39
Related to laws and courts	
What are one's legal rights and obligations as renter or home owner	52
What are one's legal rights and obligations in auto accidents	46
Related to economics	
What financial provisions to make for old age	45
What to watch for in contracts in buying car on installments	42

TABLE 1. SOCIO-CIVIC AFFAIRS (*Continued*)

Characteristic needs for more information

Percentage of Responses

Related to economics—*Contd.*

Where to obtain information about insurance companies and
policies 42

What factors contribute to recurring business depressions...... 41

What advantages are there in joining a consumer's or credit
cooperative 29

more actively than the women. Second, the men differed from the women
in the types of activities they engaged in. The men were chiefly concerned
with government—for example, banking, insurance, legal affairs, and taxes.
The women were more frequently interested in such activities as use of the
public library and attending concerts and church.

In discussion topics a similar pattern of differences was clear. The men
talked more about topics related to business; the women talked more about
the movies, church, school, democracy, and crime. In enumerating needs
for more information the women showed a predominance of interest in all
four areas—government, community, laws and courts, and economics. It is
interesting to note, however, that the items checked more frequently by the
men than by the women seemed to be related to actual experiences that men
as a group have probably had in governmental, economic, and legal affairs.
The items checked more frequently by the women did not, on the whole,
seem very clearly related to their own experiences. Yet in community affairs,
the predominance of the women's desires for more information about schools,
art projects, musical events, libraries, and health standards probably arose
from genuine experiences. Except for community affairs it seems reasonable
to suspect that many women checked items because of general curiosity and a
feeling that they ought to know more rather than because of experienced needs
for more information. Evidence from personal interviews tends to confirm this
suspicion.

Almost all the activities in which there were significant differences between
the older and younger adults showed that the older adults participated more
frequently than the younger in social and civic affairs. Most of these activities were related to business matters—stocks, banks, insurance, and taxes—
but some indicated participation in political affairs—signing petitions, trying
to influence the passage of laws, and dealing with government officials. Discussion topics were also checked more frequently by the older adults, particularly topics relating to government and business. Items indicating needs
or problems were checked about as frequently by the younger as by the older
adults, and no consistent or logical pattern was apparent in the kinds of needs
checked more often by one group than by the other.

Almost no activities, discussion topics, or needs were checked more frequently by the nongraduates than by the graduates. While some of the
activities that the graduates engaged in more frequently may be explained

partly by their higher income and economic status, graduates were also more active in inquiring for information from government offices, making speeches, attending public concerts, and lectures, using the library, visiting schools— differences that cannot be so readily explained by superior economic status. Graduates also checked more frequently than did the nongraduates many discussion topics, such as those that can be grouped under the general headings of war, democracy, and fascism. The graduates also revealed more needs for information than the nongraduates—needs for more reliable sources of information about current events; needs for more information about such community problems as utility rates, housing, newspaper editorial policies, and schools; and needs in legal and economic affairs, such as where to obtain information on legal matters, what factors to consider in purchasing insurance and annuities, and what one's rights and obligations and liabilities are regarding taxes, social security, and automobile accidents.

SOCIAL, POLITICAL, AND ECONOMIC ATTITUDES

Information concerning the attitudes of these young adults was obtained from a scale designed to measure liberal and conservative opinions on a wide variety of contemporary issues, such as government and business, taxes, cooperatives, labor unions, free speech, and war. The test consisted of thirty statements, each followed by five degrees of opinion labeled "strongly agree," "agree," "uncertain," "disagree," and "strongly disagree." The test was scored to yield a general index of liberalism—the higher the score, the greater the degree of liberalism. Liberalism was defined as general agreement with the broad social and economic objectives of the Roosevelt New Deal, and the editorial opinions of such magazines as the *Nation* and the *New Republic*. Thus liberalism means favorable attitudes toward labor unions, opposition to sales taxes, encouragement of cooperatives, approval of governmental attempts to regulate business, and so forth. Conservatism was defined as agreement with ideas expressed by former Republican President Hoover, industrialists such as Henry Ford and Ernest Weir, and similar individuals or groups. These definitions are of course arbitrary; but it is necessary to mention them briefly so that the words used here will be properly understood.

The average scores for the various groups of adults fell almost exactly at the theoretical neutral point on the scale, and the distributions of scores were such that about two thirds of the adults fell between the limits of what may be described as moderate liberalism (similar to the New-Deal Democrats) and moderate conservatism (similar to the younger Republicans). On the whole the graduates tended to be more liberal than the nongraduates, the women to be slightly more liberal than the men; and the younger adults to be slightly more liberal than the older adults. Furthermore the men and women who made high scores on the college aptitude test tended to be somewhat more liberal than those who made low scores. Single men and women were somewhat more liberal than married men and women. Finally, the men in the professions were slightly more liberal than men in other occupational groups.

Except for those between the graduates and nongraduates, none of these differences were consistently significant but rather represented a barely perceptible trend. By and large, the average scores of all the groups reflected generally neutral and middle-of-the-road attitudes. There was but a handful of radicals at one end of the scale and a handful of reactionaries at the other end, although the number of extreme conservatives was somewhat greater than the number of extreme liberals.

These neutral attitudes revealed by the total scores did not result from a summation of neutral attitudes on the separate items of the scale but from liberal attitudes on some issues balanced by conservative attitudes on others. Analysis of the responses to separate items revealed the particular issues on which adults were most liberal or most conservative. These young adults were predominantly liberal in their endorsement of consumers' cooperatives, of cooperative and government housing developments, in their disapproval of sales taxes and irregular business practices; and in their belief that approval of unions or socialistic ideas does not constitute just grounds for dismissing school teachers.

They were predominantly conservative, on the other hand, in their approval of citizens' law-and-order leagues to help employers prevent property damage and violence in strikes, in their disapproval of sit-down strikes, in their belief that ministers in churches should not talk about economics or condemn high profits or speculation and in their belief that the government should not regulate or limit business profits. The inconsistency among some of these attitudes is apparent. They disapproved of chiseling in business, yet they objected to the government's attempts to regulate it. They approved of consumers' attempts to better their lot and of the government's attempts to improve housing, but they exhibited an almost vigilante-like disapproval of labor's attempts to better its lot. Yet teachers of social studies agree that these are all related issues. Such inconsistencies lead one to suspect that these young adults, by and large, reacted to social, political, and economic problems as being specific rather than as interrelated. They might or might not be aware of the fundamentally collective or integrated nature of modern society and its problems. Their attitudes, at any rate, were not consistent with such a recognition.

THEIR DEGREE OF EFFECTIVE CITIZENSHIP

In a broad sense, effective citizenship means more than participation in the political processes of democracy, such as voting and listening to political speeches. It means also having attitudes of tolerance and respect for civil liberties; it means seeking information about social and economic problems; it means supporting those public and private agencies in society that encourage cultural and educational growth by means of symphony orchestras, forums, libraries, schools, art galleries, and charities; and it means, further, taking an interest in and gaining information about local community problems as well as broad issues of national importance.

To form a basis for judging the extent to which these former college students had become good citizens, the members of the General College staff who were working in the social studies, together with other interested persons, examined items from all sections of the questionnaire and listed those they felt would provide clues to judging effective citizenship. They asked themselves, "What are the activities which an effective citizen should engage in? What are some of the problems about which he should be concerned? What attitudes should he hold? What interests should he have?"

Because individuals differ widely in their interests and talents it was not assumed that all of them should engage in all the activities deemed indicators of good citizenship, nor was it assumed that all of them should be concerned about all the social, political, and economic problems that beset the world. Indeed it would probably be an unpleasant, and certainly an unnerving, experience to live in a world all of whose citizens were hypersensitive to every violation of civil liberties and agitated over every failure of the social, political, and economic mechanism to function with 100 per cent efficiency. On the other hand, democratic machinery cannot function in an atmosphere of public lethargy. There are only two ways of solving local, national, and world problems. One is the totalitarian way, by turning for aid to a Hitler, a Mussolini, or a Stalin; the second is the democratic way, which can succeed only if large numbers of informed citizens continually work together, seeking acceptable solutions to the problems that confront them.

Thus in a democracy every problem demands the interest and support of some of the people. Generally speaking, the more competent members of society, both intellectually and culturally, should be interested in more of its problems than the less talented members and should contribute toward the ultimate solution of such problems in accordance with their greater abilities.

One phase of citizenship centers around participation in the political processes of democracy. What do these young adults do to make their opinions on social, political, and economic issues felt? More fundamentally, what do they do to keep informed about the problems and progress of their government? The only direct political activity engaged in by a large number of these adults was voting. Four fifths of them said they had voted during the last year. Less than one third of them had signed petitions, and less than one fourth had campaigned for candidates, written letters to government officials, held elective offices, attended meetings of a political club, tried to influence the passage of a law, or attended meetings of a lawmaking body. *Among most of these former college students, therefore, direct political activity was limited to the mere process of voting for various candidates and issues on election day.*

Since their political activity was largely restricted to the one act of voting, the question of whether or not their ballots were marked on the basis of an informed and intelligent judgment becomes doubly important. What did they do to keep informed about the activities of their government? More than three fourths of them frequently discussed social, political, and economic problems, regularly read foreign news in the daily papers, and enjoyed seeing newsreels, especially March of Time releases. More than two thirds of them listened to Roosevelt's speeches, regularly read foreign news in their papers, and enjoyed listening to radio editorial commentators. Approximately half of them enjoyed listening to narrated broadcasts of events while they were happening. About one third regularly read newspaper editorials or political comment columns. *It appears therefore, that most of these adults did quite a number of things to keep informed about current affairs.* How much of the information they gathered was reliable or how well they absorbed the informa tion and used it as a basis for making decisions, it is not possible to say. But at least they deserve credit for rather actively engaging in the search.

Some insight into the quality of their search may be gained from an analysis of the magazines they subscribed to—magazines that may be considered sources of information and opinion on current social, political, and economic issues. For the purpose of this analysis several well-known magazines have been classified into three types. The first group consists of those that competent observers believe make a genuine attempt to be objective and impartial and to include articles on both sides of controversial issues—*Fortune, Forum, Harpers, Life, Time,* and *Newsweek.* Among the 951 adults in this survey these magazines, especially *Life* and *Time,* accounted for 569 subscriptions. Another group of magazines was classified as being relatively less objective and impartial, tending to include a predominant number of articles and editorials that contained facts, opinions, and propaganda designed to support the status quo, to support a business, or conservative, or Republican, point of view—*American, American Mercury, Collier's, Liberty, Nation's Business, Saturday Evening Post,* and *Business Week.* There was a total of 675 subscriptions to these magazines—chiefly to the *Saturday Evening Post, Collier's,* and *American.* A third group of magazines, while in general more reliable and objective than the second group, nevertheless included a predominant number of articles and editorials that contained facts, opinions and propaganda designed to support a liberal, or New Deal, point of view, was composed of the *Nation, New Republic,* and *Survey.* There was a total of 29 subscriptions to these magazines. These figures speak for themselves. Five hundred sixty-nine subscriptions to magazines which by and large try to be impartial and objective; 675 subscriptions to magazines supporting a predominantly anti-New-Deal philosophy; and 29 subscriptions to magazines supporting a predominantly pro-New-Deal philosophy. Even if one grants that such magazines as the *Nation, New Republic,* and *Survey* are more expensive than the *Saturday Evening Post, Collier's,* and *American,* and granting further that many adults may read the latter magazines for their stories rather than for their editorials and articles, there was still an overwhelming preference for the conservative and anti-New-Deal magazines. If one multiplied by ten the number of subscriptions to liberal magazines this increased number would still be less than half the number of subscriptions to the conservative journals. *While many adults professed a desire for more reliable sources of information about current affairs, and while many of them made use of a variety of sources of information, the magazines to which an overwhelming majority of them subscribed were neither disinterested nor wholly reliable.*

Another clue to the extent of effective citizenship and concern for social welfare among these young adults was obtained from an examination of the problems about which they were sufficiently interested and concerned to feel the need for more information. In general, two thirds of them wanted to know more about how to judge the qualifications of candidates for elective offices. About half wanted to know more about what major improvements were needed in their city's administration, what confidence could be placed in the government's inspection of foods, and what sources of information concerning activities in Washington and concerning foreign relations were valid and reliable.

But there were many problems about which relatively small numbers of the men and women expressed a desire for more information. A third of them wanted to know more about what valid differences existed between the programs of the major political parties and where they could obtain reliable information regarding the activities of foreign governments, the extent of unemployment and what to do about it, trade balances, tariffs, juvenile delinquency, consumer's cooperatives, inflation, factors causing depressions, and government protection against drugs and patent medicines. Only about one fourth wanted more information about the extent of bad housing, the problems of such federal agencies as the FHA, TVA, and RFC, the organization of state and local governments, the cost of national defense, population trends, the adequacy of local milk and water supplies, and federal protection of bank deposits.

It is clear from these data that *although many of the adults seemed to be genuinely interested in major social problems, relatively few of them expressed a desire for more information about the specific attacks being made by government and other agencies upon the solution of these problems.* A general interest that is not transferred and applied to specific problems and situations has little practical or useful effect. There is a need, therefore, to develop appreciation and understanding of the close relationships between government and common affairs of everyday living, so that the increasing scope of government functions will not be accompanied by a loss of interest in government policies, or by an attitude of resignation toward the effectiveness of action and the consequent abandonment of democratic for totalitarian processes.

It is also evident that *these adults exhibited a general lack of participation and interest in local and community affairs and problems.* This fact again emphasizes the need to relate general interests to specific problems that are sufficiently within the range of individuals to be attacked and coped with and that can furnish a sense of the importance of individual and group participation in the determination of policies and the solution of problems—a feeling so necessary in a democratic society. The marble colonnades of Washington may inspire more interest and attract more attention than the grass roots of a local community, but in these young people they apparently provoked a verbalized and abstract interest accompanied by such a sense of awe at the magnificence and enormity of it all that their interest in more ordinary local problems was dulled by contrast. At least, so it might be argued. But the foundations of democratic government rest still in the town hall. As intelligent adults ignore opportunities for participation in the affairs of their own neighborhoods, by just so much do they forfeit their stake in representative government, for if national government is to be representative it must be built upon, and emerge from, grass roots.

Another aspect of citizenship involves interest in, and support of, the many public and private agencies in society that foster educational and cultural development—the nongovernmental agencies contributing to individual and group welfare. What was the status of these young adults in relation to this aspect of citizenship? Nearly nine tenths of them contributed to such charities as the Community Fund and the Red Cross. About two thirds used the public library. Roughly half of them went to church, attended public musical concerts, and enjoyed listening to symphonic music. About one third visited the public schools, belonged to fraternal lodges, and enjoyed operatic music. About one fourth wanted to know more about the services of the Community Fund and of private philanthropies and about the work of the public schools. Less than one fourth suggested improvements to the local schools, attended community forums, and less than one fourth felt a need for more information about community forums and their programs, art projects, museums, or about services provided by the public libraries in addition to book lending. Less than a tenth belonged to labor unions or employers' organizations, or engaged in volunteer social service work. Apparently, then, *the interest of a majority of these adults in many nongovernmental agencies that contribute to individual and group welfare was limited* to *supporting charities, using the public libraries, and attending churches and concerts.*

All the aspects of effective citizenship discussed so far have revealed striking inconsistencies between the activities and the professed interests of these young adults. The evidence leads to a highly important generalization, the implications of which have significance for teaching in all areas of general education. *By and large, these young adults failed to appreciate or understand the interrelationships among contemporary problems and the integrated nature of modern society.*

Their attitudes toward fundamentally related social issues were markedly inconsistent. They exhibited concern about governmental policies, but except for voting they failed to make use of the political processes through which public opinion in a democracy is expressed. They were interested in national problems but not in specific attempts being made to solve national problems. They expressed a desire for more reliable sources of information about current affairs, but they read biased magazines. They failed to take an active interest in community affairs. They acted, apparently, as if they believed that there were in the contemporary world such things as isolated facts.

This unawareness of the interrelationships of society is a serious matter; for it leads to that acceptance of simple solutions for complex problems that is the essence of totalitarian compliance. To overcome this apparent blindness is an obligation not only of social science instructors but of all faculty members in any college. Instructors should continually stress the impact of particular situations, issues, and problems on larger, more universal matters. For example, much vital and living art is an expression of social problems. But how can people be really interested in any such expression of current problems when they are not much concerned about the problems themselves? If people do not understand that art and music are vitally related to the pressing issues of their own time, it is only natural that art and music will not seem very important to them. Until people can see that the arts have something significant to offer they will tend to leave their support to more and more limited groups. Yet if a society is to have a rich, vital culture, the public must support the arts.

Other examples can be drawn from other areas. A large proportion of these young adults were dissatisfied with their incomes, although these were considerably larger than the average family incomes in the United States. Moreover, among the life satisfactions most frequently desired by these adults were a comfortable and pleasant standard of living and financial security for their old age. No individual and no family can achieve these satisfactions outside the framework of organized society. The achievement of either a pleasant standard of living or security in old age cannot be divorced from economic, political, and social matters. Helping students understand and appreciate these interrelationships must be one of the major concerns of general education.

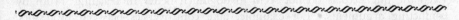

Free Speech in America[1]

by ZECHARIAH CHAFEE, JR.

My God, there is need today of people who can say straight things in a straight way, and not all coated over with sugar.—An Englishwoman's letter written in January 1941 between air-raids.

SPEECH should be fruitful as well as free. Our experience introduces this qualification into the classical argument of Milton and John Stuart Mill: that only through open discussion is truth discovered and spread. In their simpler times, they thought it enough to remove legal obstacles, like the censorship and sedition prosecutions. Mill assumed that if men were

[1] From Z. Chafee, Jr., *Free Speech in the United States* (1941). By permission of the Harvard University Press.

only left alone, their reasoning powers would eventually impel them to choose the best ideas and the wisest course of action. To us this policy is too exclusively negative. For example, what is the use of telling an unpopular speaker that he will incur no criminal penalties by his proposed address, so long as every hall owner in the city declines to rent him space for his meeting, and there are no vacant lots available? There should be municipal auditoriums, schoolhouses out of school hours, church forums, parks in summer, all open to thresh out every question of public importance, with just as few restrictions as possible; for otherwise the subjects that most need to be discussed will be the very subjects that will be ruled out as unsuitable for discussion.

We must do more than remove the discouragements to open discussion. We must exert ourselves to supply active encouragements.

Physical space and lack of interference alone will not make discussion fruitful. We must take affirmative steps to improve the methods by which discussion is carried on. Of late years the argument of Milton and Mill has been questioned, because truth does not seem to emerge from controversy in the automatic way their logic would lead us to expect. For one thing, reason is less praised nowadays than a century ago; instead, emotions conscious and unconscious, are commonly said to dominate the conduct of men.

Is it any longer possible to discover truth amid the clashing blares of advertisements, loud speakers, gigantic billboards, party programs, propaganda of a hundred kinds? To sift the truth from all these half-truths seems to demand a statistical investigation beyond the limits of anybody's time and money. So some modern thinkers despairingly conclude that the great mass of voters cannot be trusted to detect the fallacies in emotional arguments by communists and others, and hence must be prevented from hearing them. Even the intellectuals do not seem to do much better in reaching Truth by conflicting arguments. For example, take controversies between professors. They talk and talk, and at the end, each sticks to his initial position. On which side does Truth stand? We still do not know. Then, too, the emergencies seem greater and more pressing than of yore. We are less willing to await the outcome of prolonged verbal contests. Perhaps Truth will win in the long run; but in the long run, as Walter Lippmann says, we shall all be dead—and perhaps not peacefully in our beds. Debating is only fiddling while Rome burns. Away with all this talk; let's have action—now.

Nevertheless, the main argument of Milton and Mill still holds good. All that this disappointment means is that friction is a much bigger drag on the progress of Truth than they supposed. Efforts to lessen that friction are essential to the success of freedom of speech. It is a problem, not for law, but for education in the wide sense, that includes much more than schools and youngsters. The conflict of oral evidence and arguments can be made increasingly profitable by wise improvements in technique. Anybody who has attended a forum knows how much depends on an able chairman and on sensible rules enforced by him. Journalists and other writers value accuracy of facts far more than formerly—we can expect even more from them in the future. None of us can get rid of our emotions, but we can learn to drive them in harness. As for blazing propaganda on both sides, young Americans can be trained to keep alive the gumption which comes down to us from Colonial farmers; this will make them distrust all men who conceal greed or a lust for power behind any flag, whether red or red-white-and-blue.

Reason is more imperfect than we used to believe. Yet it remains the best guide we have, better than our emotions, better even than patriotism, better than any single human guide, however exalted his position.

A second point deserves renewed emphasis. The effect of suppression extends far beyond the agitators actually put in jail, far beyond the pamphlets physically destroyed. A favorite argument against free speech is that the men who are thus conspicuously silenced had little to say that was worth hearing. Concede for the moment that the public would suffer no serious loss if every communist leaflet were burned, or if some prominent pacifist were imprisoned for discouraging drafted men by talk about plowing under every fourth boy, as perhaps he might be under the loose language of the unprecedented federal sedition law passed last year. Even so, my contention is that those pertinacious orators and writers who are hauled up are merely extremist spokesmen for a mass of more thoughtful and more retiring men and women, who share in varying degrees the same critical attitude toward prevailing policies and institutions. When you put the hotheads in jail, these cooler people do not get arrested—they just keep quiet. And so we lose much they could tell us, which would be advantageous for the future course of the nation. Once the prosecutions begin, then the hush-hush begins too. Discussion becomes one-sided and artificial. Questions that need to be threshed out do not get threshed out. . . .

Suppose Hitler is gone, what then? What is to be done with the Germans? Are they to be exterminated, or split into little duchies like Weimar and Saxe-Coburg-Gotha, or made equal partners in an association of free peoples? Who is to rule Italy in place of Mussolini? How about totalitarian Russia? Are Czechoslovakia and Poland to be set up again? It is going to be ever so much harder to answer these questions than it was to write the Treaty of Versailles. In 1919, there was some chance of sorting out the odd pieces and making a go of it. After all, the League came very near success. If Stresemann had lived a few years longer, if Hindenburg had died a few years sooner, if there had been no Ruhr invasion and resultant inflation to ruin the German middle class, it might have worked. But in 1942 there will be no old pieces. New materials will have to be laboriously fashioned.

In this tremendous task of the day after tomorrow, the United States will be forced to take a major share. We cannot afford to turn away from it in disgust, as in 1920, and let Europe plunge eventually into a third and still more frightful disaster by 1960. The Atlantic will then be more easily crossed by bombers than the English Channel is now. The American arsenal of munitions will be the first objective of the enemy. In short, so long as we permit Europe to be divided into competing armed groups, we shall inevitably be obliged to save the British Empire every twenty years, at increasing cost to ourselves in money and blood. Adequate national defense under such conditions will absorb most of the national life. . . .

The Supreme Court, though much more anxious to support liberty of speech than it was twenty years ago, can do nothing to keep discussion open during an emergency. Cases of suppression will reach Washington long after the emergency is over. What counts is what is done by the local United States judges. Still more important is the attitude of the prosecutors and the police, because they can stifle free speech by breaking up meetings by arrests and by confiscating pamphlets, yet neglecting to bring many persons to trial. Above all, the maintenance of open discussion depends on the great body of unofficial citizens. If a community does not respect liberty for unpopular ideas, it can easily drive such ideas underground, by persistent discouragement and sneers, by social ostracism, by the boycotting of newspapers and magazines, by refusal to rent halls, by objections to the use of municipal auditoriums and schoolhouses, by discharging teachers and professors and journalists, by mobs, and threats of lynching. On the other hand, an atmosphere of open and unimpeded controversy may be made as fully a part of the life of a community as any other American tradition. The law plays only a small part in either suppression or freedom. In the long run the public gets just as much freedom of speech as it really wants.

This brings me to my final argument for freedom of speech. It creates the happiest kind of country. It is the best way to make men and women love their country. Mill says:

A State which dwarfs its men, in order that they may be more docile instruments in its hands even for beneficial purposes, will find that with small men no great thing can really be accomplished.

And Arthur Garfield Hays tells the story of a liberated slave who met his former master on the street. The master asked, "Are you as well off as before you were free?" The Negro admitted that his clothes were frayed, his house leaked, and his meals were nothing like the food on the old plantation. "Well, wouldn't you rather be a slave again?" "No, massa. There's a sort of a looseness about this here freedom that I likes."

Doubtless it is inspiring to see the Piazza Venezia in Rome full of well-drilled blackshirts in serried ranks cheering Mussolini, or to watch Nuremberg thronged with hundreds of thousands of Nazis raising their arms in perfect unison at the first glimpse of Hitler. In contrast, our easy-going crowds seem sloppy and purposeless. But we do not have the other side of the picture—the knock on the door that may mean the father of the family is to be dragged off to a concentration camp from which no words returns; great newspapers reduced to mere echoes of the master's voice; the professorships of universities that once led the world filled as we fill third-class postmasterships; the devoted love of young men and women broken up by racial hatreds; the exiles; the boycotts, and what is perhaps worst of all, the men who conform to the will of those in power in order to avoid financial ruin or worse, and yet, even while holding their jobs, live days and nights in the uneasy fear of calamity and the shame-faced consciousness that they have sold their minds and souls. Once commit ourselves to the ideal of enforced national unanimity, and all this logically and easily follows.

Behind the dozens of sedition bills before Congress last session, behind teachers' oaths, and compulsory flag salutes, is a desire to make our citizens loyal to their government. Loyalty is a beautiful idea, but you cannot create it by law or by force at bottom. A government is the officials who carry it on: legislators and prosecutors, school superintendents, and police. If it is composed of legislators who pass short-sighted sedition laws, of narrow-minded school superintendents, who oust thoughtful teachers of American history, or eight-year-old children whose rooted religious convictions prevent them from sharing in a brief ceremony—a government of snoopers and spies and secret police—how can you expect love and loyalty? You make men love their government and their country by giving them the kind of government and the kind of country that inspire respect and love: a country that is free and unafraid, a country that lets the discontented talk, in order to learn the causes of their discontent and remove them; that refuses to impel men to spy on their neighbors; that protects its citizens vigorously from harmful acts, while it leaves the remedies for objectionable ideas to counter-argument and time.

"Plutarch's Lives" was the favorite reading of the men who framed and ratified our Constitution. There they found the story of Timoleon, who as a youth had saved his native city of Syracuse from the Carthaginian tyrants. In later years young hotheads used to get up in the public assembly and abuse Timoleon as on old fossil. His friends urged him just to say one word, and they would silence his detractors. But Timoleon insisted that the vituperative youngsters should have their say. "He had taken all the extreme pains and had passed so many dangers, in order that every citizen and inhabitant of Syracuse might frankly use the liberty of their laws. He thanked the gods that they had granted him the thing he had so oft requested of them in his prayers, which was, that he might some day see the Syracusans have full power and liberty to say what they pleased."

It is such a spirit that makes us love the United States of America. With all the shortcomings of economic organization, with all the narrowness and ignorance of politicians, we know that we are still immeasurably freer to say what we think and write what we believe and do what we want than we should be in Italy, Germany, or Russia. "There's a looseness about this here freedom that I likes."

The Radio Boom and the Public Interest
by BERNARD B. SMITH [1]

I

DURING 1944 thirty-two radio stations sold for a total of more than ten million dollars. Most of them were small stations. Most of them sold at prices which represented fantastically high profits—so high, indeed, that the Federal Communications Commission got worried and asked Congress what to do about it.

Here are some typical cases:

Station WINX in Washington, a little five-year-old 250-watt station the net value of whose assets at the time was—according to records filed with the FCC—about $75,000, sold for $500,000.

WCOP, Boston, a 500-watt station which was bought in 1936 for $57,000, sold for $225,000

KECA, Los Angeles, a 5,000-watt station, the book value of whose tangible broadcast property was no more than $70,000, went for $800,000.

The reason for these high prices is clear enough. The sale of radio time to advertisers and others is big business, and has been getting bigger and bigger. In 1927 the gross time sales of all broadcasters were less than $5 million; in 1932 (in spite of the depression) they were nearly $62 million; in 1937 they had jumped to more than $144 million; and in 1942 they totaled almost $200 million. From 1942 to 1944 they almost doubled, jumping the figure to nearly $400 million last year.

If these increases in sales had been accompanied by a corresponding increase in the number of stations, there would be no problem. The fact is, however, that few if any new stations were built between 1942 and 1944. What is more, almost all of the standard broadcasting frequencies (in the centers of population where broadcasting is profitable) are now assigned. There are practically no good frequencies left to apply for. The consequence is that anyone who wants to acquire a standard frequency in order to get in on the profitable radio business has to buy a station which already exists. In other words, *he has to buy a frequency from someone who already has a license to broadcast.* It is the value of the frequency, then, which (allowing something for such intangible assets as good will) accounts for most of the difference between the value of a station's assets and the price for which it can be sold.

But radio frequencies cannot be sold. The Supreme Court has held that

[1] From *Harper's Magazine*, March, 1945. Reprinted by permission of the author.

a license to broadcast on a radio frequency does not constitute property. Congress, by the Federal Communications Act of 1934, set up the Federal Communications Commission specifically "to maintain the control of the United States over all the channels of interstate and foreign radio transmission; and to provide for the use of such channels, *but not the ownership thereof,* by persons for limited periods of time, under licenses granted by Federal authority." (Italics ours.)

Congress provided that licenses to broadcast were to be granted free by the FCC "if public convenience, interest, or necessity will be served thereby," but not for a longer term than three years. It further provided that such licenses could not be transferred without FCC approval and could not be renewed except on the same terms which apply to the granting of original applications.

But the purchasers of radio stations know what they are doing when they pay huge prices for a frequency which cost the original licensee not a penny. They know that, whatever the law may be, the FCC almost invariably renews radio station licenses; that out of 9,000 renewal applications, 98 per cent have been granted without so much as a hearing and only a handful of the others have been denied. They know, in other words, that for all practical purposes the purchase of a radio station gives them a perpetual right to a channel of radio transmission which in fact and in law belongs to the people of the United States.

II

Two members of the FCC, Commissioners Clifford Durr and Paul Walker, have in the past year expressed increasing concern over the immensely profitable traffic in these nationally owned frequencies. Finally, last July, after Mr. Durr bitterly dissented from the Commission's approval of three station sales, FCC Chairman Fly appealed to Senator Wheeler and Representative Lea (chairmen respectively of the Senate and House Committees on Commerce) for guidance.

Under the present state of the law [he wrote] it is not clear that the Commission has either the duty or the power to disapprove of a transfer merely because the price is inordinately high—even though it may well be deduced that a substantial value is placed on the frequency. In the absence of a clear Congressional policy on this subject, we thought best to draw the matter to the attention of your Committee. . .

As a result of this appeal, both the Senate and House Committees are preparing to conduct hearings to determine whether legislation is needed to curb station sales prices. The proposal has even been made that Congress enact a law providing for a system of annual, graduated charges to be paid to the government by station owners for the right to use a broadcasting frequency. Such a law would, of course, reduce broadcasting profits and thus undoubtedly bring about a cut in station values and sales prices. But this sort of approach misses the real point at issue.

The fact is that the problem of inordinately high prices for stations need never have arisen if the FCC had, as the law provides, from the beginning revoked or refused to renew licenses "because of conditions . . . which would warrant the Commission in refusing to grant a license on an original application, or for failure to operate substantially as set forth in the license."

Every broadcaster knows, from the form of application he files when he originally seeks his license, that the FCC is directly concerned with the class or type of programs he will broadcast. The applicant is required to "describe fully and in detail the character and types of program service proposed (e.g., entertainment, educational, religious, agricultural, fraternal, news, etc.), showing the total average weekly time to be devoted to each type of program, and the sources of each," and, further, to state the number of hours and percentage of time per month to be devoted to commercial programs and to sustaining programs. The same information is again required when the broadcaster applies for a renewal.

Some there are who like to insist that the FCC has no right to regulate the character or type of broadcast programs. They claim that such regulation is censorship, or an interference with the right of free speech, both of which are expressly forbidden in the act which set up the FCC.

The Supreme Court of the United States, however, in upholding the right of the FCC to control the conditions under which individual stations may contract for network service, said that the Federal Communications Act "does not restrict the Commission merely to supervision of the traffic. It puts upon the Commission the burden of determining the composition of that traffic."

Though some people argue that the Court's use of the words "composition of that traffic" does not necessarily refer to classes or types of radio programs, the heads of the two principal networks—who are presumably advised by the best of legal counsel—disagree.

William S. Paley, president of the Columbia Broadcasting System, testifying before the Senate interstate Commerce Committee in November, 1943, and referring to the Supreme Court decision, said:

I hardly need to add that "the composition of that traffic" in radio means the programs which go over the air waves and can mean nothing else.

Niles Trammell, president of the National Broadcasting Company, testifying before the same Committee a month later, said:

The Supreme Court has declared that Congress placed upon the Federal Communications Commission the burden of determining "the composition of the traffic" —that means programs to us.

Yet the FCC has never made any attempt to require a licensee to provide the "public interest" sustaining programs which he promised when he asked for a handout of one of the nation's radio frequencies. The only station to which it has ever denied a renewal upon anything remotely resembling programmatic grounds was, in the words of the then chairman of the FCC, "engaged in constant and repeated broadcasting of false, fraudulent, and misleading medical advertising, the sale of worthless stocks over the air, etc. The principal owner of the station was one of the chief advertisers of spurious stock-selling schemes." According to the FCC, apparently, any station serves "the public convenience, interest, and necessity" as long as it conforms with the Commission's technical and engineering requirements and its programs are not fraudulent.

Take, for example, the case of Station WIBC, Indianapolis. Six years ago 51 per cent of its stock was sold for $10,000. Soon thereafter its broadcasting time was extended and its power increased. Last year, when the net value of its assets, according to records filed with the FCC, was approximately $75,000, the station was sold for $440,000.

Obviously, if a new frequency had been available in the radio spectrum, no one would have paid $440,000 for WIBC. He would simply have applied for the new frequency (which the government would have given him free), spent $100,000 or so to build and equip a station, and saved $340,000. Making the most liberal allowances for good will and other intangible assets, something like $300,000 of the sale price of WIBC must have represented the value of WIBC's license.

In order to obtain that license in the first place, the original owner of the station stated, under oath, that he would provide certain types of programs. His statements are contained in his application and in the FCC's decision, dated May 4, 1937, granting a license. Let's look for a moment at this decision:

The applicant offered in evidence a tentative program schedule which appears to be well balanced, entertaining, and instructive. . . . It will be the policy of the applicant to furnish ample time free of charge on the proposed station for broadcasting of educational, religious, civic, and agricultural programs. . . . The applicant proposes to form a community radio council composed of representatives of the Chamber of Commerce, Better Business Bureaus, Service Clubs, Public Schools, Parent-Teacher Associations, Department of Conservation of Indiana and other organizations the purpose of which would be to co-ordinate service clubs employing radio facilities, to determine civic programs best suited to meet the needs of the community and to secure the best talent available for the production of such programs. . . .

The applicant also proposes to establish an educational schedule in connection with the subjects currently taught in the schools and will broadcast such programs for two one-half hour periods five days each week for the benefit of the pupils of these schools. The enrollment of the schools of Indianapolis is approximately 60,000 and there are 89 school buildings in the city, a large percentage of which are equipped with radio receiving apparatus. The Parent-Teacher Association will be assisted through the use of a 15 minute broadcast period each day. Time will also be assigned to the University of Indiana, Butler University, the Indiana Central College, and other educational institutions. The applicant will also broadcast religious programs for the Church Federation of Indianapolis which has a membership of approximately 175 churches. . . . It was contended in behalf of the applicant that since the two stations now situated in Indianapolis each have chain affiliations they are unable to devote a sufficient amount of time to the broadcast of programs of purely local interest to satisfy the listeners. . . .

To accomplish all this the licensee, according to his application, promised to devote 10 per cent of free sustaining time to the broadcast of educational programs, 5 per cent to religious programs, 5 per cent to agricultural programs, and 10 per cent to civic programs.

On January 28, 1944, however, when Station WIBC filed its application for renewal, it stated that at that time it was providing not 10 per cent of free sustaining time to educational programs, but four-tenths of one per cent. While it had sold a good deal of commercial time for religious programs, it was providing not 5 per cent of free sustaining time for such programs, but only 1.1 per cent, and 1.5 per cent instead of 10 per cent for civic programs. For agricultural programs it was providing none whatsoever.

It does not appear that in the renewal proceedings WIBC was asked why it was no longer providing any free time for agricultural programs, or what had happened to the two half-hour periods five days a week during which it was going to broadcast programs "for the benefit of the pupils of the schools of Indianapolis," or to the fifteen minutes each day that was to be assigned to the Parent-Teacher Association. Nor were any questions raised about the fact that although this station originally applied for its license on the ground that both the others in Indianapolis were chain affiliates and hence unable to devote a sufficient amount of time to programs of purely local interest, WIBC itself is now a member of the Mutual Broadcasting System. The license was renewed.

III

The case of WIBC is not unique. Few, if any, stations provide the percentage of free public service sustaining programs which they promised when they were applying for a frequency. If they did, it is unlikely that stations would sell for the inordinately high prices which have been troubling the FCC and Congress. For the plain truth is that the enormous increase in revenue from radio time sales—from $200 million to $400 million in two years —was brought about mainly not by charging higher prices for radio time but by dropping public service programs in favor of commercially sponsored ones. One by one the sustaining public service programs disappear or are shifted to undesirable hours when few listeners are on hand. In the typical week ending November 20, 1944, during the peak listening hours from 8:00 to 10:30 P.M., not a single program of this type was broadcast over either of the two principal networks.

Consider the history of the programs which CBS has broadcast from 7 to 9 o'clock on Sunday evenings. For a number of years they were sustaining programs, chiefly because advertisers were reluctant to spend their money on programs which had to compete for listeners with NBC's Jack Benny and

Charlie McCarthy. During those years CBS presented shows like "The Columbia Workshop," "Hello, Americans," and others which by almost anyone's definition would be accepted as in the public interest. Now, however, Kate Smith broadcasts over CBS at 7 o'clock for Jello and Sanka, and at 8 o'clock "Blondie" goes on the air for Super-Suds.

I have nothing against Kate Smith or Blondie (or Jello or Super-Suds, for that matter). Nevertheless, entertaining as Kate and Blondie may be, I am not convinced that the public interest was served when they displaced programs like "The Columbia Workshop." Yet, so long as stations are not required, by law or by FCC regulation, to devote *any* time to sustaining public service programs, it would be silly to expect CBS or any other broadcaster to pass up a commercial.

As a matter of fact, the networks sometimes find that the only way they can keep a worthy program on the air is to find a commercial sponsor for it. Last year the Blue Network developed a program called "The Baby Health Institute," designed to provide sound advice on the care of small children. For a time the H. J. Heinz Company sponsored the program and it was broadcast over virtually the entire Blue Network. Even after Heinz dropped the program, the Blue continued, in the public interest, to make it available on a sustaining basis to all of its stations. Almost at once, however, the vast majority of the stations jettisoned the program, so that last June, when it was finally withdrawn from the air, it was being broadcast by only 30 of the 194 stations affiliated with the Blue.

The same sort of situation threatened the program called "Town Meeting of the Air." It will be recalled that there was a good deal of opposition to the sponsorship by the *Reader's Digest* of this program, which had been broadcast on a sustaining basis for almost ten years. Here is what George V. Denny, Jr., moderator of the program and president of Town Hall, Inc., said in an article in the *New York Times* as justification for seeking commercial sponsorship:

Since local stations are not obligated to carry [sustaining] programs offered by the network, a number of local stations on the Blue began to drop Town Meeting for local commercials, while others sold this time to a competitive network. A tabulation early last fall revealed that while the Blue Network had 168 affiliated stations at that time, Town Meeting was being carried by only 120. It was pointed out to us that this situation was likely to grow worse rather than better in the months ahead.

Once a sponsor was obtained, the program was carried by almost all the stations. Nevertheless, not too much reliance should be placed upon commercial sponsorship as a means for rescuing the few public service programs which remain on the air. At the present time there are a great many companies who look on the sponsorship of radio programs almost entirely as institutional, or prestige, advertising. For the time being they are content if they can build up some good will (and, incidentally, reduce their excess profits taxes). But once the war boom is over, and especially if there is a business slump, it will be a rare corporation which spends money on a program that doesn't show results in dollars and cents.

As Commissioner Durr said recently, in an article in the *Public Opinion Quarterly:*

The only barriers to the complete occupation of the air by advertisers, and the consequent total elimination of public-service programs, are self-restraint on the part of the broadcasters and networks themselves—somewhat fortified, perhaps, by the complaints of their listeners—and the public-interest provisions of the Communications Act. . . .

IV

Thus far, however, the FCC has failed to set up anything like a clear-cut standard of public interest with respect to programs. The indirect result, as we have seen, has been something approaching a scandal in the sales of radio stations. What, then, is the solution?

It is perfectly clear, as the networks have agreed, that the Supreme Court has unequivocally supported the FCC's power and duty to regulate the types of radio programs. This has absolutely nothing to do with censorship or infringement of the right of free speech. It simply means that the Commission has the right, and the obligation, to insist that the radio frequencies it assigns shall be used, as the applicants promise, in the public interest.

At no time in history has an informed public opinion been more necessary than it is today, and the radio could be a powerful vehicle for public education and information. Surely the nation has a right to insist that those who are licensed to use its radio frequencies shall contribute to this end.

Before going further, however, let us remind ourselves that if radio is to retain its vast audiences, *it must serve principally as a means of mass entertainment.* It has been demonstrated, beyond any reasonable doubt, that this can best be achieved through advertiser-supported radio broadcasting. It is essential, therefore, that the major portion of radio time be devoted to commercially sponsored programs.

At the same time, however, it is essential that a reasonable proportion of the programs broadcast should directly serve the public interest.

The proposal I make, therefore, is that the FCC require, as a condition in granting or renewing a broadcasting license, that each station devote a specified half-hour in the morning, afternoon, and evening (a total of an hour and a half a day) to the broadcast of free public service sustaining programs. These might be defined as programs of education, information, or enlightenment—*specifically including the presentation of controversial issues and problems, national and local.*

For example, the FCC could require that between the hours of 11:00 and 11:30 in the morning, 4:00 and 4:30 in the afternoon, and 9:00 and 9:30 in the evening, every one of the 950-odd radio stations in the United States should broadcast sustaining public service programs. Under such a plan no station or network would need to fear that while it was devoting itself to the public service its competitors would be lining up an advertiser-sponsored show. Competition under the proposed plan would be for listeners, on the basis of program quality, rather than for advertisers, and it might well turn out that public service programs at fixed times which the listener could count on would attract a whole new group of listeners. (After all, there is no single half-hour under the present system when more than 35 per cent of the nation's set-owners are listening to the radio.) The networks would provide programs on matters of national interest, and their affiliated stations could either broadcast the network program or provide a public service program of purely local interest, whichever they chose.

There is a reasonable chance that the networks and station owners would welcome such a solution to the vexed question of what to do about radio licenses. Most broadcasters already provide at least a half-hour of public service in the morning and another half-hour in the afternoon; it is only the half-hour in the evening (when radio time is much more valuable) that would cause them any pain. But to counterbalance this, they would at last know the minimum programmatic requirements with which they must comply in order that they might be deemed to be operating "in the public convenience, interest, and necessity."

Nor would the listeners need to fear that these public service programs would be dull or boring. No one could be compelled to listen to them, anyway; and I never discovered anybody who enjoyed every half-hour of radio fare under the present exclusively advertiser-regulated system. It is worth pointing out, further, that the networks and the stations would be subject to powerful economic pressures—from the advertisers who would be sponsoring programs before and after the public service programs—to make these programs so interesting that people would want to listen to them. For the audience that a good program creates spills over onto the programs which precede and follow it.

During election campaigns these half-hours should be employed for political speeches. Today candidates, or the parties behind them, are obliged to pay full station and network rates, without discounts, for radio time, and in addition pay the salaries of the radio artists whose programs they displace. Accordingly, a party, or any minority group within a party, which isn't backed up by a moneyed interest such as organized business or organized labor, is licked before it starts. There is no use standing on a street corner hollering your lungs out to a tiny group on a cold, rainy evening in November while your well-heeled adversary—from a microphone in a comfortable studio—is reaching into the living rooms of vast numbers of the electorate.

v

Some segments of the radio industry argue that, since the licensing of FM stations will create many new problems, there is little point in the FCC attempting at this time to establish programmatic standards of public service for the standard stations. Others argue in a similar vein about television. But it will probably be some years before there are enough FM sets to make it possible for FM to compete with standard broadcasting for advertiser support, and it is increasingly apparent that a truly national system of television may not be with us for a decade.

Whatever the truth about this may be, it seems clear that if we establish sound programmatic public service standards for standard broadcasting now, those standards will be carried over into FM and television. If the FCC would adopt the plan here outlined it would no longer need to concern itself with the prices paid for stations. If the owners of radio stations were required by a vigorous and watchful FCC to observe the proposed minimum standards of "public interest, convenience, and necessity" in programming, the profits from radio would not be likely to get out of hand. and the sale prices of stations would bear a more reasonable relation to the value of their property.

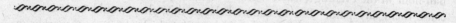

Liberty—For What? [1]

by ALEXANDER MEIKLEJOHN

THE principle of liberty, as we Americans interpret it, forbids interference with certain of our activities. But it also requires or implies that we do not interfere with certain other activities. And the major problem of the defining of freedom, both in theory and in practice, is that of separating these two fields of human action. Our fundamental question is, "To what human enterprises does the demand for liberty apply: in which of our ventures is the demand for it preposterous, contrary to all good social policy?"

At this point we encounter one of the strangest vagaries of our national mind. In the course of three hundred years many Americans have come to believe that the liberty which we love is the liberty to buy and sell without hindrance. In recent years a great array of practical men and scholars have interpreted for us the Spirit of America. And their conclusion can be summed up very briefly. The freedom which Americans worship, in terms of which they live, for the sake of which they are willing to die, is, these men tell us, the freedom to manage their own property without interference from their fellows. The freedom of the spirit is the freedom of the marketplace.

The interpretation, as it stands, is so grotesquely untrue, so contradictory to the human intentions which it explains, that one can deal with it only by taking account of the peculiarities and the aberrations of the mind that makes it. In that mind, something has broken loose. Some fundamental ideas have

[1] From *Harper's Magazine*, August, 1935.

gone wrong. Nonsense has taken the place of sense. Let me try then to break down the interpretation to show its falsity.

The distinction which I have in mind is clearly suggested if we place side by side two familiar provisions of the Constitution. In the Bill of Rights, two sets of "liberties" are dealt with; but they are dealt with in exactly opposite ways. One of them is declared to be outside the field of interference or con-trol by the government. The other is deliberately subjected to control and to interference. Under the term "liberty" then as the Constitution uses it, there are covered two very different kinds of liberty. It is that difference of kind to which I wish to call attention.

The First Amendment to the Constitution reads as follows:

"Congress shall make no law respecting an establishment of religion, or prohibiting the free exercise thereof: or abridging the freedom of speech or of the press: or the right of the people peaceably to assemble, and to petition the government for a redress of grievances."

The Fifth Amendment, adopted at the same time, reads in part as follows:

No person shall "be deprived of life, liberty, or property without due proc-ess of law: nor shall private property be taken without due process of law."

Now the significance of these statements for our argument lies in the sharp-ness of the difference which they establish between two sets of human inter-ests. We are trying in our defining of liberty to separate those activities which may properly be hindered and restrained from those which, in our judgment, brook no interference. And the Amendments to the Constitution which I have quoted tell us, in clear words, what, in the structure of our government, that separation is. On the one hand, Religion, Speech, the Press, Assemblage, Protest—these the Federal Congress may not touch. They are free. On the other hand, Life, Liberty, and Property—these are to be regulated and re-strained by Congress: they may even be taken away provided that the action by which this is done is justly and properly performed.

Our constituted authorities are forbidden—they forbid themselves—to lay hands upon a man's religion. They may, however, deprive him of his life— by due process of law. No authority, public or private, may take from a citizen his freedom of speech. But the liberty of his body, his freedom of external physical action, may be limited and controlled as the public welfare may re-quire. The unhindered integrity of the press is one of the highest ideals of our civilization: the Federal government may not limit it, may not subordi-nate it to other purposes. But as for the holding and managing of property— the regulation and restraint of these is the primary and engrossing occupation of every established governing body. Nothing could be further from the in-tention of the Constitution than to say that with respect to these restraint and limitation by the State are improper and unjustified, contrary to our ideals.

This is, if I am not mistaken, the division of human interests upon which a proper understanding of liberty in America rests. In the field of Religion, Speech, Press, Assemblage a government finds itself facing activities which are beyond, above the level of its authority. It is their servant. It owes them allegiance. In relation to them its one legitimate activity is to see that they are kept free from interference, that no agency, public or private, shall establish control over them. Here the law reads, "Congress shall make no law . . . prohibiting . . . or abridging . . ."

But in the other field, that of external possessions and purposes and actions, a radically different dictum is enacted. Here our government says, in effect, "Men desire life: they crave liberty of external action: they fight and strive for property. No State can allow them to pursue without hindrance or control these multifarious and conflicting desires. It is, however, essential that any government which exercises such control shall do so with justice, with due regard for all men, in ways which will deserve the confidence and respect of all who are affected by the decisions made." Over against the "Congress shall make no law" of the first field, stands the "not without due process of law" of the second field. And these two phrases mark off for us, on the one hand, the field of spiritual activities in which our institutions provide that men shall be free and, on the other hand, the field of external activities in which men must be regulated and restrained.

Here, then, are two sets of liberties, one of which is granted, the other of which is, under our government, denied. Men are free to worship or not to worship. They are not under the law, free in the management of their property. And the argument which concludes that freedom of external action is guaranteed by the Constitution is sheer confusion as between these two differing spheres of liberty. I do not like the phrase "wishful thinking" but, if ever it should be applied, it is applicable here. The American mind has, in terms of its desires, a powerful predisposition toward free competition in business. For three hundred years we have been busily engaged in taking possession of the resources, the opportunities of a new country, a new industry. Out of the rush of these external activities, out of our driven and, at times, frantic preoccupation with them, we have developed habits of mind, forms of belief, judgments of expediency as to the ways in which the getting and distributing of wealth may best be carried on. But these beliefs and impulses are not our spiritual love of liberty. They express desires rather than admirations, expedients rather than principles. No one can doubt their strength; but one may challenge their meaning. And when that is done, the guarantees of the Constitution are, I think, clear and unmistakable. The Fifth and, with it, the Fourteenth Amendment, dealing with the ownership and management of external possessions, give assurance in that field, not of freedom from restraint, but of justice and regularity in the imposing of restraints. They tell us, not that the State is bound, as in the case of freedom of speech, to withhold all regulation, but that, in the making of its regulations, the State must do so justly, by orderly and trustworthy procedure. Justice, rather than liberty, is the principle by which the regulation of property transactions is determined. And justice is not freedom. There is a close and necessary relation between these two, but they are not identical.

The appeal to historical documents is not, however, decisive for our argument. And from this it follows that we must not press too hard even an argument for the Constitution of the United States. This point becomes all too clear if, for example, we compare with the provisions quoted from the Bill of Rights the corresponding statements from the Declaration of Independence. The two documents are on the question at issue so flatly contradictory of each other that the situation is almost ludicrous. The Constitution provides that the rights of life, liberty, and property are to be kept within regulation by orderly and just procedure. The Declaration proclaims that men are "endowed by their creator with certain inalienable rights: that among these are life, liberty and the pursuit of happiness." Now it is of course dangerous to interpret any statement of "natural rights" too literally. When the decrees of a Creator are introduced into discussion of the meaning of laws which men are themselves making, there is abundant room for misunderstanding. And yet, as they stand, the two statements do seem to be in direct opposition to each other. For one of them life, property, and liberty of action are inalienable: no government may take them away. For the other, the explicit task of government is that of determining in what ways and under what conditions life and liberty and property may be alienated, may be limited or taken away. One cannot help suspecting that many of those who interpret the Constitution as in favor of free competition in business are deriving their conviction, not from the Constitution itself, but from the Declaration, which is quite at variance with it. They have mistaken the highly emotional and unclear proclamation with which thirteen colonies flung themselves into a war of revolution for the deliberate and reasoned formulation of principles with which a new nation prepared itself for the organization of the activities of a society at peace.

It is time, however, that we turn from the interpretation of documents to the examination of the actual procedures and attitudes which those documents were attempting to formulate. Here we shall find a sounder basis for deciding as between the Declaration and the Constitution. Here, if anywhere, we shall be able to tell whether or not it is true that our American scheme of life requires and provides that the management of property shall be free from interference by the government.

First, it is very clear that in the actual procedure of our government we do regulate and control the holding and management of property. Ever since the first group of Americans settled in the wilderness there has poured out from every village, district, county, town, city, State, as well as from the Federal authority itself, an increasing stream of ordinances, laws, statutes, regulations, codes which have told men what they may and may not do with respect to their property and that of their fellows. Thus in recent years we have regulated the railroads. We have fixed the hours and conditions and wages of labor. We have taken from men and corporations whatever part of their annual income we deemed just and necessary. We have, by changing the currency, determined what part of his debt a borrower need not pay when the time of settlement comes. We have seized for public use a share of the inheritance of the widow and the orphan. In these and in a multitude of other ways we have hindered the free use by a man of his own possessions. In the face of these actions, what can it mean to say that the Spirit of America is committed to the view that the public control of business is a denial of rightful freedom? To say that is to say that liberty and government are opposites. Do we mean to say that? The makers of our Constitution did not intend to say it. Nor do we.

And, second, when we examine our own motives it is clear that we do intend to regulate the buying and selling of goods. Why should we not regulate them? Why, if a business practice is deemed to be harmful to the general welfare, should we allow it to go on? If a trader in seeking for profit is causing loss to his fellows there is, so far as I can see, no reason why they should allow him to continue doing so. Why in this field should we let a man do as he likes if we do not like what he does? The truth is, I fear, that some of us are trying by appeal to the general principle of liberty to find settlement of a current issue to which that principle does not apply. America is at present, like every other industrial society, facing the issue as between individualism and collectivism in the management of business. With respect to that issue there are, with us as elsewhere, two sets of opposing opinions. Some of us believe that the methods of free competition are more promising than those of its rival. The business freedom of each, we say, is to the advantage of all. Others of us, however, are persuaded that the system of free competition will not work. We are convinced that if the stronger, the more fortunate, the more unscrupulous are left unhindered in their pursuit of wealth, other men will be enslaved and impoverished rather than helped by their successes.

As between these two sets of opinions America is just now trying to make up her mind. What decision she may make no one can yet tell. She may go back to the ways of relatively free enterprise. She may move on into expedients of corporate control. In the latter case we face the practical problem as to whether the activities of regulation and control shall be given to the Federal government or whether they shall be reserved to State and municipal authorities. But in either case the essential point is that the spiritual liberty of America does not mean the freedom of its property holding. In the conflict between individualism and collectivism in business, the issue of the freedom of the human spirit is not at stake. In our scheme of life and government it is agreed, it is established, both in theory and in practice, that the management of business shall so far as needful be regulated and controlled. But to say that is not to say that the activities of the spirit are to be limited and restrained.

To identify the freedom of the human spirit with the absence of legislative control of commerce and industry is then to deny both the theory and the practice of our institutions. As seen in the light of our history, in the face of our obligations and commitments, such an identification is absurd. Only a social system which has built up the external view of human living to the exclusion of the inner view, which has identified business activity with spiritual activity, which has come to regard the creation and distribution of wealth as the primary concern of a society, could create such an illusion as that. I know no deeper ground of reproach against our present social order than that so many of its leaders in scholarship and in affairs have fallen, have led their followers, into that blunder. With the blind thus leading the blind it is little wonder that we totter on the edge of the ditch. With the realms of freedom and justice thus confused, there is little hope for either of them.

To many of our scholars and practical men of affairs, this economic view of liberty has made strong appeal. These are the men who especially think of themselves as "realists," as hard-headed, as rising above sentimentalities and popular illusions. I should like now to point out how disastrously these men are cutting at the roots of the convictions by which our common life is nourished. They are bringing us to such confusion about the nature of freedom that no issue can be clearly seen, no practical situation clearly dealt with.

It is commonly said in our current discussions of social policy that if the principle of liberty is accepted by us then the principles of equality and fraternity must be abandoned. "Liberty and equality," we have many times been told, "are incompatible." We must choose between them. And in fact, as the argument commonly runs, we have already chosen. As a people, our preference is registered for liberty. Therefore, it would be well if we would stop talking of such demands as those of equality and fraternity. These demands are outworn and outmoded. They do not fit into our "free" scheme of life. We moderns take our freedom straight. We ask only for liberty. Let each man be himself. Let each man take and keep what he can get. As for the belief that men are equal, the aspiration that men shall live like brothers, these are the yearnings of dreamers, of "idealists." They have no place in daily planning. It is better to leave them, either to private virtue or to some "Fate" which is so just and kind that free and independent men need not concern themselves with justice or with kindness.

Now the revolutionary drift of this argument will be seen if we recall that the notion of liberty, when first accepted by us, was inextricably bound up with the ideas of equality and fraternity. These three demands were, in fact, so closely linked together that they were in effect parts of a single idea—that of democracy. Here again liberty was seen as only a fragment of a meaning. We did not take it alone. It was the liberty of equals and brothers which we established as the guiding formula of our society. And so damaging is this attempt to tear liberty out of its setting that I am tempted once more to resort to epithets—to use the terms "revolutionary" and "un-American" in describing it. I would protest that except as men are regarded as "equals," except as they are treated as "brothers," the attempt to make them free, even to think of them as free, is a hopeless and futile one. If it has been found true that for the sake of liberty we must give up equality and fraternity, then that constitutes a radical revolution in the theory and practice of American life. To say that is to deny the beliefs and intentions out of which our scheme of life and of government sprang. In my opinion it denies what are at present our

deepest and most cherished convictions. These three principles are still for
us, I am sure, three different aspects of one mode of life which we choose as
our own. To tear them apart is to tear our spirit to shreds. It is such violence as this that sets us at war with ourselves, that brings upon us the tragic
sense of disloyalty to our own integrity. It is essential then that we examine
closely this view of liberty which, once accepted, makes equality impossible
and fraternity ridiculous. I am sure that we shall find that it is both untrue
in principle and disastrous in its consequences.

The arguments by which liberty as a principle has been seen to drive
equality and fraternity out of our tradition are not hard to follow. They are
distinctly of the rough and ready type. Their essence is the interpretation of
all three principles as economic in meaning.

Those who would give up equality as a principle incompatible with liberty
argue from two premises. First, it is observed that men are not equal in
capacity. That this is true in every phase of human living, no one can sensibly
deny. To say that all men are equal in their abilities is not democracy: it is
plain nonsense, plain disregard of obvious fact. Just as men differ in height,
in speed, in digestion, in color of eyes, so do they differ in ability to think,
ability to appreciate, ability to act, ability to lead and dominate their fellows.
And, this being true, it is idle to build a social theory on the assumption that
men are, or can be made, equal in business capacity. Some men are more
shrewd than others. Men differ much in industriousness and perseverance;
and even in such qualities as unscrupulousness, the passionate, overbearing
desire to get a bigger share of worldly goods and power, we human beings
are not all alike. There are diversities of gifts among us.

Second, it is asserted, liberty and equality are economic principles. They
refer to the getting and having of material things. By liberty we mean that,
just so far as possible, men shall be unhindered in their business affairs. The
principle of freedom is the principle of free competition in financial and industrial life. So too, equality is, for this argument, economic in meaning.
Equality would mean—if it were not too nonsensical to mean anything—that
all the members of a society share equally in the having of goods. It is equality of getting, of possessing what one wants.

Now when these two premises are combined, the conclusion in question
follows from them as inevitably as does four from two plus two. If in an
open market men are free to compete with one another, each being free to
get and keep what he can, and if these competitors are different in the capacity for getting and keeping, it follows, by a logic which no one can deny, that
liberty will and must destroy equality. If unequals strive in conflict, the
stronger must win, the weaker must lose. And so—*Quod erat demonstran-
dum*—if men are free they are not equal. A social order must choose between
these two. And we Americans, the argument says, have chosen liberty.
Therefore, we have abandoned equality.

The expulsion of fraternity, on grounds of liberty, has been far less consciously done. We have not argued brotherhood away. Rather, under heavy

pressure, it has drifted out of sight. Few men have spoken against it, except perhaps in the form of vague and uneasy deductions from "liberty" as seen in the process of "the survival of the fittest." In fact, the fate of fraternity has been very much like that of the Devil in modern Protestant theology. No one has demonstrated its non-existence. We have simply ceased to think about it seriously. How can we think of it if the principle of free economic competition holds true? What, in a world defined by that principle, can the Brotherhood of Man mean? On the docks of San Francisco, in the summer of 1934, who was so silly as to make appeal to fraternity as between longshoremen and ship-owners? Are makers of munitions of war called to their trade by the love of their fellow-men? Do they play with governments, contrive and scheme for the national murder of peoples because all men are brothers? No, that is not the theory. The theory of liberty which we are now discussing is very simple. It is that men are free to seek for profits. Under that principle each man is justified in getting what he can, as other men are doing. Our human living is a conflict. Men are not brothers. Liberty, as we construe it, has put an end to our fraternity. We are "free." Therefore fraternity is meaningless.

Now the trouble with this double argument is that the conclusion at which it arrives is false. By a process of shrewd, logical deduction from its premise, it discovers that Americans do not care about equality or fraternity. But that statement is not true. It denies two of our deepest convictions. It contravenes two of our deepest passions. We will not have it as an account of ourselves. And this being the case, an equally savage logic will drive us to the only solution of which the situation admits. It is that the premise from which we started must be abandoned.

Any belief which, directly or by implication, tells us that we have no interest in treating our fellows as equals and brothers we repudiate as denying the things of which we are most certain. Liberty, in its primary sense, is not then the liberty to buy and sell. That liberty we will restrain and diminish whenever the demands of our social order require it. It is our servant, not our master. It is one of our devices, not one of our principles. We find it a sorry substitute for the liberty on which the foundations of our individual and social living are established. The liberty for which we care is that of a fellowship of equals and brothers.

But here, I know, I shall be sharply challenged on the question of fact. What evidence is there, I shall be asked, that Americans have loved, and still love, equality and fraternity? In reply may I say that the evidence, though not of the "laboratory" type, seems to me strong and convincing. I will try at least to suggest what it has been and is.

In the days when the nation was being formed, our devotion to equality found characteristic expression in the Declaration of Independence. The first sentence in that document, after the preamble, begins as follows: "We hold these truths to be self-evident: that all men are created equal; . . ." I suppose that among the great sentences which have determined human destiny no one was ever more muddled than this. At every turn of its meaning one's mind gasps at its unclearness. And yet, as registering a nation's commitment to the cause of equality, its import is clear and unmistakable. Our first pronouncement, as a united people, unanimously made by our representatives was: "All men are created equal." We meant it then as, I am sure, we mean it now.

The evidence of our early commitment to fraternity is not to be found primarily in political documents. It appears rather in the influence of the Christian Church during our early history. "Thou shalt love they neighbor as thyself" was a principle which was recognized as basic to all our documents. And this was true of men who attacked the Church as well as of those who defended it. Strong and bitter assaults were, it is true, directed against the Church. But these were brought not against its principles but against its failures as an institution to hold and to manifest its loyalty to those principles. It seems to me idle to deny that, in its beginnings, ours was a Christian civilization, that it planned for human society in terms of the Brotherhood of Man.

The contemporary evidence of our loyalty to equality and fraternity is not to be found either in political documents or in religious formulas. Our documents are to-day very equivocal and our formulas of belief vague and uncertain. And yet the evidence seems to me vast and sure. One finds it in a prevalent demand for social justice so widespread and powerful that no phase of our common life escapes its influence. In private conversation, in public discussion, in magazines and books, in painting and poetry and music, in theaters and churches, that theme is dominant and engrossing. We are, it is true, bewildered as to ways in which social justice may be done. But we are to an amazing degree united in the conviction that the doing of it is the primary issue of current American life. When, for example, through the breakdown of our economic machinery, millions of families are brought to destitution, no theory of economic liberty can hold us to the view that these men and women and children shall be consigned to the care of natural economic laws. They are our equals, our brothers, and we will deal with them as such.

It is true that we can hide our intentions under formulas of business self-interest. Men tell us that only as these indigents are given the power of purchasing will our markets be restored. They warn us too that if large masses of people are left to starve they will break out into violence, will bring down about our ears the whole economic structure which shelters all of us. But these external arguments are poor and shoddy as compared with the present spirit of our people. One has only to put them side by side with Whitman's "By God! I will accept nothing which all men cannot have the counterpart of on the same terms" to see how poor and superficial they are. And we, as a people, are taking our stand with Whitman. We are not clear as to ways and means, but we are resolute in purpose.

The man who does not see that is, in my opinion, blind to the most powerful forces now at work in the American scene. We have been hoping that an existing economic order which talks much of "liberty" would serve our purpose. Now we are ready to modify that order. And if mere modifying is not enough, we will transform it to suit our needs. Economic disaster and calamity have revealed us to ourselves, have shown us our own purposes. We are a just and friendly people. To say that we love liberty without regard for justice and kindness, to say that liberty, once accepted, has driven equality and fraternity out of our scheme of life, is simply to say that liberty is un-American. The men who think those thoughts have slipped. They do not know themselves nor us. The liberty which we demand is the liberty of equals and of brothers.

I have dwelt at length upon this argument because it reveals so clearly the spiritual tragedy which has come upon America. Here again, our "practical men of affairs" have with an unfailing inaccuracy missed the point when dealing with essential things. They have taken the most fundamental motive in our social life and twisted it into a meaning which is hostile, not only to itself but to all the other deeper principles to which we are committed. They do not tell us—perhaps they have not noticed—that justice too must go the way of equality and fraternity if once their logic is admitted. What can justice mean in a social order defined in terms of free and unrestricted competition? The liberty of such an order is the liberty of men to prey one upon another. And in that conflict, justice is simply what a man can get. Liberty, as so defined, becomes, not the reasonable principle of a free society, but an all-devouring dogma which destroys other meanings or drives them out. It has become, not a principle, but a fetish of the economic mind.

And the human tragedy which has ensued from the worship of that fetish is all too clear in the mind of present-day America. It is often urged to-day that our unrest of spirit is due to the fact that we have tried to keep in a new and changing world old ideals which no longer serve our purposes. Our major task, it is said, is that of creating new ideals to replace those which, though good enough in their own day, can no longer serve our changing purposes. There is something of truth in this statement, and yet it seems to me to be comparatively a minor truth. Far more important is a statement which is almost its exact opposite. Our deepest tragedy lies in the fact that our current institutions, our current beliefs, our current practices fail to give recognition to old ideals which are still the essential and fundamental cravings of the American spirit. Our trouble is that we still believe in equality, however much we may deny it. Our agony comes from the fact that the social world which we are making is false to a fraternity of men to which we are still committed with a passionate devotion. The truth is not that old ideals have disappeared. It is rather that in spite of our mistakes about them they are still within us.

Underneath all the superficialities and externalities of our thinking and practice, the demands that men shall live together on equal terms, that they shall be friends to one another, still dominate us, still hold us fast. And it is the torture of thus finding ourselves holding beliefs which deny our most cherished truths, the agony of seeing our own acts, our own behavior bringing to destruction the causes for which we care—it is that cleavage, that contradition within ourselves which has brought us into such bewilderment and self-condemnation. And the way of escape from this tragedy lies not in the framing of new ideals for a new world, but in the bringing of that new world under the control of principles which have always been the primary spiritual forces in the life of the American people—the principles of liberty, equality, fraternity, and justice.

ᴐᴪ

America [1]

by DOROTHY THOMPSON

As I came across this country, yesterday and the day before that, and the day before that, the incredible wonder, the perennial miracle of the country came home to me again freshly, newly, as it repeatedly does. Suddenly one opens one's eyes and sees it, and is again, as one has been always, amazed and astonished. I thought of a great line from the most representative of all American poets, Walt Whitman, who wrote a hundred years ahead of his time, seeing with prophetic vision the America that has been, and was, and is, and would be.

In the preface to the 1855 edition of "Leaves of Grass," which is one of the greatest essays ever written in this country, on the poet and America, and the poet's relation to America, he said: "The largeness of Nature and of this nation were *monstrous* without a corresponding largeness and generosity of the spirit of the citizen." And without a breed of men full-sized, capable of universal sympathy, full of pride and affection and generosity, this country would indeed be monstrous. Here it lies in the center of the world, looking out on the two great oceans, looking out on the east to the old world, the cradle of white western civilization, looking out here on the west to a still older world, of still older races, out of which have come all the great religions and the deepest of human wisdoms. Its very position makes it sensitive and perceptive to whatever happens anywhere in the world. Its composition makes it sensitive and susceptible. Its geography makes it sensitive and susceptible. Here live no race, but a race of races—a new kind of man bred out of many old kinds of men—in a climate more fierce, more radioactive, less temperate than that of Europe—in a climate that encompasses all climates. Here is no nation, but a nation of nations, a continent enclosing many different kinds of cultures and slowly making them into one culture.

When I think of America, I see it in a series of pictures—of moving pictures. I see the tight white and green farms of Vermont; the quick lush summers knee-deep in fern and field flowers; the narrow faces and the ironic grins

[1] An address to the *Modern Forum*, Los Angeles, California. By permission of the author.

of the Vermonters; the love of thrift and the strange inhibited hospitality of the people; the deep quiet lakes, the hills that are never too high for cattle to graze on them, the long, long bitter winters; small friendly communities where free, independent farmers still help build each other's barns and cut each other's wood; where the hired man calls the farmer by his first name; where the women from the farms and villages will come to cook for you "to help out," but where you never can find anyone with the spirit or attitude of a servant.

I think of the incredible city of Manhattan—sometimes I think it too incredible to last—where the languages of a dozen nations are heard on the streets; where there are more Italians than in any Italian city except Rome; more Jews than there are in Jerusalem or in any other town on earth; where there are more Irish than there are in Dublin; a city which has—shall I call him "the late" Jimmie Hines?—and which also has room for Robert Moses.

I think of the temperate and civilized—and uncivilized Carolinas; of Annapolis, the most beautiful eighteenth-century town in the whole English-speaking world; of the long quays of Savannah and the opulent laziness of the South, and the queer intellectual vigor that has always come up in the South whenever people thought that it was dead—from the South that has repeatedly given us our greatest statesmen.

I think of the great Southwest with a climate in which it is almost impossible to die. Texas, where you could settle a whole nation—yes, even now, when they say our frontiers are exhausted. And here, California, the earth's Eldorado, bigger than all of Italy, with a population only one-seventh that of Italy; great glittery beaches out of which rise the towers of oil wells. The finest fruits on earth. The most enchanting American city: San Francisco.

Yes, this country would be monstrous without a corresponding largeness and generosity of the spirit of its citizens.

This country is only five generations old. In the days of our great-great-great-grandfathers it was still a howling wilderness, still unexplored. Today it is the most powerful single nation on the face of the earth.

This country has seven million farms valued at thirty-three billion dollars. It produces three and a half times as much corn as any other nation in the world. It produces more wheat than any other nation on earth except Soviet Russia. In the great industrial towns of the East and the Middle West—in twenty-six counties of this vast nation—it produces almost as much steel and four times as many automobiles as all the rest of the world combined.

It is so enormous and so powerful that gigantic public works are lost in it; they are done casually without any ballyhoo. We have the greatest roads ever built since the Romans, and they were built without Fascism and without forced labor. In our lifetimes we have undertaken one of the greatest reclamation jobs ever done in the history of mankind. We have taken the Columbia and the Colorado Rivers and bent them, diverted them, stopped them, and pushed them around to create a whole new province in which men can settle and live, to create a lake so vast that it is an internal sea—and most people in the United States don't even know about it.

Always this country has had poets—and epic poets—moved by the grandeur of the country itself, its history, its possibilities, its titanism. Longfellow, who celebrated the trek of the Acadians; the philosopher-poet Emerson, seeking to find this country's over-soul; the anonymous ballad-makers of the ranges and the mountains; Vachel Lindsay trying to catch this country's broad rhythms; the great poets of the contemporary day: your own Robinson Jeffers, who finds in Monterey the sombre grandeur that the Greeks knew; the Benét brothers continuing the great epic; Archibald MacLeish finding the frontiers of poetical stuff not exhausted by modern technology and industry, and creating new rhythms to correspond to new rhythms of work and life, and the titan of all of them, Walt Whitman, who wrote: "The United States themselves are essentially the greatest poem. In the history of the earth hitherto the largest and most stirring appear tame and orderly to their ampler largeness and stir. Here at last is something in the doings of man that corresponds with the broadcast doings of the day and night. Here is not merely a nation, but a teeming nation of nations. Here is action untied from strings, necessarily blind to particulars and details, magnificently moving in vast masses. Here is the hospitality which forever indicates heroes. . . ."

Here is the imagination which could conceive Wilson's dream of a world-state. Is it so fantastic? Is it more fantastic than what this country is? Here is the imagination which could conceive a frontier on another nation, three thousand miles long and at all places vulnerable, and without a single fort. You think that is not something to have accomplished in history? Maybe it is the greatest thing that we have accomplished in history: the idea that two continental nations could live in permanent friendship.

And because of our geography, our position between two oceans, the largeness of the nation, the necessary wideness of sympathy and imagination, this country is of all countries in the world the most susceptible to what happens outside its own boundaries. Throughout our history, we have counseled isolation. Never in our history have we been isolationists. Upon this country beat all the ideas and all the conflicts of the whole world—for in this country are the peoples of the whole world, and in this country is a certain type of mind, which is impatient of boundaries; which is able to contemplate things near and very far—nothing too far.

This country is itself the synthesis of many cultures. Its founders were Anglo-Saxons—one of the most remarkable groups of men that history ever produced at the right moment. It is still incomprehensible to me how, at one critical moment in history, it should happen that in a sparsely populated, remote colony, there should be men of the genius, of the stature, the vision, and the world culture of Washington, and Jefferson, and Hamilton, and Madison, and Benjamin Franklin, and John Jay, and the two Adamses. These men were Anglo-Saxons, but the inspiration for the constitution of the new world did not come only from English traditions.

On the contrary, when in 1910 the Union of South Africa was formed, the British framers of that constitution copied ours and nothing specifically British. For ours remains the first great federal government in history. And the men who designed this government, which has lasted through a terrific civil war and through a world war without the necessity of fundamental change, drew their ideas from two thousand years of history. They were indebted to Aristotle, and to the Frenchman Montesquieu. And I am absolutely convinced that the future organization of the world will draw its greatest inspiration from this constitution which demonstrates that there can be diversity and still unity, that there can be authority and still no concentration of naked power.

I follow the new thought that is going on in the world, and I see that in this new thought there is much that was already known to the founders of this country. They knew that the worst of all governments is a government of naked power. They knew that all power corrupts, and absolute power corrupts absolutely. They knew that it is possible to integrate order and freedom. They knew that it is possible for many forms of activity to exist side by side, provided the areas are defined and do not compete with each other, except under commonly accepted rules. It is my belief that many of the political ideas embodied in this constitution and above all, of the division of power, will one day be applied to our economic life, in an orderly manner and under the regulation of the law; and when that time comes we shall have an unparalleled period of prosperity and expansion.

But these Anglo-Saxons who framed the Constitution did not make America. They broke loose from their old ties; they broke loose, I might even say, from their own race, in order to make a new world and a new race. And they did not build this nation. This nation was built by Germans, Swedes, Russians, Negroes, and Bohunks—men from the Danubian Basin— by Wops, by Anglo-Saxons, and by Jews. It was built by people who came here with a dream. For five generations people have been coming here with a dream. Sometimes the dream was grandiose. The men who built New England came here with a dream of religious freedom. They came here as refugees, persecuted because they wouldn't bend their consciences. Acadians trekked to Louisiana also to find a world in which they could be themselves. And some came here hoping to find gold in the streets. And some came because they were herded up in Hungarian and Slavic villages and brought over here like cattle under false pretensions, full of false hopes. But in all of their minds there was something common. For all of them there was a magnet. And the magnet was that they thought that here, in their own way, they could stand up, and look their neighbors in the face, and call themselves men, and not slaves.

And in five generations we have produced on this continent a race. You think there's not an American race? It's funny. Here we are made up of every stock in the world, and yet you can tell an American if you see him on the streets in Berlin, or Vienna, or Paris. What is an American? A typical American? I don't mean the people who live in the more fashionable suburbs and have their pedigrees framed on the wall to show they go back to one of the Norman conquerors. (If everybody who claims Norman conqueror ancestry really has one, William's army was the largest in history.) An American is a fellow whose grandfather was a German forty-eighter who settled in Wisconsin and married a Swede, whose mother's father married an Englishwoman, whose son met a girl at college, whose mother was an Austrian and whose father was a Hungarian Jew and their son in the twentieth century right now is six feet tall—we are perhaps the tallest race on earth—goes to a state college, plays football, can't speak a word of any known language except American, and is doubtful whether he ever had a grandfather.

This American has several characteristics. He doesn't like to take orders. If you speak to him in a friendly way, he will do almost anything you ask him —inside reason. If you once get him into a war, he is a very good fighter, but he has a very low opinion of war, and, except when he is dressed up for a festival of the Elks or the American Legion, a pretty low opinion of uniforms. He doesn't like to commit himself to stay forever in one place. He is restless, and an inveterate traveler in his own country or elsewhere if he can afford it. He is incredibly ingenious. He can devise more ways to save himself work than any other known race of human beings; that's probably why he has invented so many gadgets. He will wear himself out playing golf, or tennis, or football, but he won't walk to get to the golf links. He is gregarious, but not at all herd-minded. He is not servile. He is enormously inventive. This is one of the greatest races of inventors ever produced. He was born free and he shows it by the way he moves. He is the best-nourished human being on the face of the earth. I know all about Mississippi, Arkansas, and Alabama. I've been there, and it's bad. It's got to be made better. But just the same the per capita consumption of food in the United States is higher than it is anywhere else, and the food that is consumed is more expensive and more various than it is anywhere else, taken for the country as a whole.

Now, what I am saying is this: we have got as far as we have, not only because we have a continent rich in resources—there are other continents rich in resources—we have got as far as we have because we produced a certain kind of human being and a certain type of mind. That human being is, first of all, a fellow with his eye on the future and not on the past. He is skeptical, and yet he has eternal faith. He constantly tries to think why something doesn't work as well as it should and how you can make it better. He is the kind of human being who likes to go off on his own and start something. If anyone wants to come with him, that's all right, too. He's a born democrat—and democrats are born, not made. He hates a stuffed shirt and he doesn't like to be high-hatted. He is suspicious of anybody who pretends to be better than he is. Nobody except the Scot and the Jew has such a passion for education as has the American.

I say all this because I hope that we are going to keep this kind of race alive. This race has emerged out of the concept of equality. Now don't misunderstand this word "equality." Equality does not mean that everybody is as good as everybody else. You can't go into any classroom in a public school and keep that illusion for ten minutes. The child with an IQ of 80 isn't the equal of a child with an IQ of 157—here or anywhere else. The youngster, deformed by Nature, is not the equal of that little boy over there with straight legs, a well-shaped head, sound teeth, and clear eyes. Maybe the child deformed by Nature, though, has something that that youngster hasn't, and the American attitude is to see whether maybe that isn't true. But the American concept of equality is that every person has a right to a break. Every human being shall be judged by what he is and does, and not by any purely arbitrary rule. As a matter of fact, the American concept is a profoundly religious one. It is based on the belief in the sanctity of the human personality, on the immense value of every individual, and the right of every individual to make out of himself the very best human being that he can. The questions that Americans naturally ask concerning other human beings are: "What does he do?" and, "What sort of a guy is he?" and, "Does he know his stuff?"

The attitude of Americans toward themselves and toward all other human beings, the fact that we are a race of races, and a nation of nations, the fact of our outlook upon two oceans—and the miracle of the creation of this country out of stock that for such a large part represents the frustrations of European dreams and the rejection of human material—all these combine to make us a messianic people, with a feeling of mission not only for ourselves but for the world. This has been true from our very beginnings. Our whole political literature, which is one of the greatest possessed by any nation, reiterates the conception that the values that we cherish are of universal validity. The inscription on the Plymouth Rock Monument is addressed, not merely to Americans, but to all the world. Since I prepared this speech on the train, I am having to quote from memory and I may twist a word or two, but surely not the sense:

This spot marks the final resting-place of the Pilgrims of the Mayflower. In weariness and hunger and in cold, fighting the wilderness and burying their dead in common graves that the Indians should not know how many had perished, they here laid the foundations of a state in which all men for countless ages should have liberty to worship God in their own way. All ye who pass by and see this stone remember, and dedicate yourselves anew to the resolution that you will not rest until this lofty ideal shall have been realized *throughout the earth.*

And the Declaration of Independence contains these words:

We hold these truths to be self-evident, that all *men* are created equal—[not all Americans]—and that they are endowed by their Creator with certain unalienable rights, among them life, liberty, and the pursuit of happiness.

And when we wrote the Constitution, we made one which is not confined to any geographic area, but is infinitely expandable.

In all the great speeches of Lincoln, there is the same sense of the American mission. In his farewell speech at Springfield, he spoke of the United States as "the last great hope of earth." And he closed the Gettysburg Address, that great apostrophe to popular government, with the words, "shall not perish from the earth." He did not say "from this soil." He, like all great Americans, and above all the poets, conceived that there was some cosmic significance about this country and about this great experiment. And that feeling is still in the American heart. It is expressed in our reaction, our spontaneous reaction, to all assaults against human rights, to the degradation of personality, to all crimes against human freedom, to all persecutions and bigotries, and, above all, to all tyranny wherever it raises its head, in the most remote quarters of the globe. And since we are a free people, and are not inhibited in our expression, all such crimes have been protested by the American people as individuals long in advance of the protests of their government. Time and again in our history we have broken off diplomatic relations with countries because they have persecuted Jews or Armenians, or any other branch of the human race. We have been told that it is none of our business; but in some undefined way, we know it is some of our business; that the sense and meaning of our life is that we should be sensitive to such things.

And I, for one, believe that if ever the time comes that the antennae of this country are not sensitive to assaults on liberty, wherever these assaults may occur, then this country will have degenerated into an unvirtuous and defeatist senility. Like it or not, that is the way we are. . . .

From this country today should come comfort, and hope, and new strength to everyone, everywhere, who still loves freedom and still believes in a future for the common human being. That message has been written for us to give, time and again, by the great spokesmen of this people. I began with a quotation from Walt Whitman. I will end this with one from the same poet. Like the first, it is written in Walt Whitman's "Mein Kampf," his great essay on the sense and meaning of America:

Come near and you shall learn the faithful American lesson. Liberty is poorly served by men whose good intent is quelled from one failure or two failures or any number of failures, or from the casual indifference or ingratitude of the people, or from the sharp show of the tushes of power, or the bringing to bear soldiers and cannon or any penal statutes. Liberty relies upon itself, invites no one, promises nothing, sits in calmness and light, is positive and composed, and knows no discouragement. The battle rages with many a loud alarm and frequent advance and retreat—the enemy triumphs—the prison, the handcuffs, the iron necklace and anklet, the scaffold, and leadballs do their work . . . the cause is asleep . . . the strong throats are choked in their own blood, the young men drop their eyelashes toward the ground when they pass each other . . . and is liberty gone out of that place? No, never. When liberty goes it is not the first to go nor the second nor third to go, it waits for all the rest to go . . . it is the last. When the memory of the old martyrs is faded utterly away . . . when the large names of patriots are laughed at . . . when the boys are no more christened after them but christened after tyrants and traitors instead . . . when the laws of the free are grudgingly permitted and laws for informers and spies are sweet to the taste of the people . . . when you and I walk abroad upon the earth stung with compassion at the sight of numberless brothers answering our equal friendship and calling no man master, and when we are elated with noble joy at the sight of slaves . . . when the soul has ecstasy over the word and deed that put back a helpless innocent person into any cruel inferiority . . . when the swarms of cringers, suckers, doughfaces, lice of politics, planners of sly involution for their own preferment obtain a response of love and deference from the people . . . when it is better to be a bound booby and a rogue in office at a high salary than the poorest free mechanic or farmer with his hat unmoved from his head and firm eyes and a candid and generous heart . . . and when servility and oppression on a large scale or a small scale can be tried on without its punishment following duly after . . . or rather when all life and all the souls of men and women are discharged from any part of the earth—then only shall the instinct of liberty be discharged from that part of the earth.

The Citizen's Charter[1]

by GEOFFREY CROWTHER

WHAT is this democracy for which we fight? On the political side we all know the answer—by instinct perhaps, rather than by definition. We know a democracy when we see one. We have earned in our earliest years the magnificent slogans and phrases that enshrine democracy's essence. Magna Charta and Habeas Corpus. Government of Laws, not of men. Freedom of Speech. Bill of Rights. Life, Liberty, and the Pursuit of Happiness. Government of the People, by the People, for the People.

Political democracy, then, is a familiar and tolerably precise conception. But what about economic democracy? The totalitarians have a plan and a purpose in economic matters. What is democracy's plan? What is the democratic economic faith? There is general agreement that Adolf Hitler's New Order is unacceptable (and would be, even if it were not Hitler's). But what is the alternate? A very substantial portion of humanity believes that economic security and social welfare can be bought only at the price of freedom and are worth the price. Democracy will never admit this proposition; but what is the reply to the challenge?

No one is very clear about the answers to these questions. But answer there must be, and soon. It is high time that a beginning was made with thinking out again, from the start, what sort of economy it would be that carried over into the economic sphere the fundamental beliefs and the characteristic methods of democracy.

[1] From *Fortune*, October, 1941. By permission of the author.

The system of government that we know as political democracy is, basically, a balance between Freedom and Order. It is certainly not all Freedom. A democracy is capable of discipline, capable of imposing heavy obligations on its members, capable of coercing its minorities. The obligation to pay taxes, or to perform military service, may be as inescapable and as severely enforced in a democracy as in a despotism. Few dictatorships have cribbed, cabined, and confined the lives of their citizens as strictly as the Puritan democracy of New England did. But if there are sectors of its political life in which a democracy follows the principle of Order, there are equally sectors where it follows the principle of Freedom. The system works because, over the centuries, the people have made a free choice of the appropriate spheres for Freedom and for Order, and a working balance has been achieved.

Let us follow the parallel into the economic sphere. The opposing principles of Freedom and Order are clearly visible. Each of them has its contenders for the economic soul of democracy. Mr. Wendell Willkie, for example, is a very sincere and persuasive champion of Economic-Democracy-by-Freedom. American democracy and free private enterprise are inseparable, he maintains, and unless the community liberates the springs of enterprise, democracy will either continue to limp along or cease to be democracy.

There are others who are equally sincere believers in Economic-Democracy-by-Order. Unless democracy can learn to direct its economic affairs by a consistent plan, overseen by a democratically elected government, it will either bump from crisis to worse crisis or turn itself into a fascistic oligarchy.

Should we perhaps side with one or other of these schools of thought in drawing up our sketch of a democratic economy? Whatever our personal predilections, we might as well dismiss the notion that either alternative, as a consistent policy, would be acceptable. Let us list, in simple tabular form, two overriding reasons against either policy:

Reasons why a democratic electorate is unlikely to accept FREEDOM *as the dominant principle of a democratic economy:*

1. A regime of free private enterprise results in the existence of great masses of underprivileged persons. The state must intervene to assert the dogma of humanitarianism.
2. An uncontrolled system has shown itself to be subject to swings of boom and slump far more violent than a democracy, in the twentieth century, can tolerate without interference.

Reasons why a democratic electorate is unlikely to accept ORDER *as the dominant principle of a democratic economy:*

1. No centrally controlled system, working through a vast bureaucracy, can be as efficient in the production of goods as a freely competitive system. The standard of living depends on productive efficiency.
2. There is a natural right for a man to follow his inventive genius and his enterprising spirit wherever they lead. A state in which the government controls all economic activity approaches the totalitarian. And the democratic election of

the central government is an inadequate safeguard while there are fanatics, machine bosses, demagogues, and adventurers.

These arguments are not exhaustive, but they are enough to reveal the dilemma. The democratic economy, like the democratic polity, must have elements of both Freedom and Order.

But there is a world of difference between a mixture of Freedom and Order and a balance between them. It is the difference between having two spigots, hot and cold, and having only a tepid one. It is the difference between painting a house black and white and painting it gray all over. In the particular case with which we are here concerned, it is the difference between a system that works and one that does not. The one overriding test that the electorate will apply to any economic system is whether it avoids mass unemployment or not. If it does, it will be accepted as a working system; if it does not, sooner or later it will be rejected. The very considerable prestige that Hitler's economic system was acquiring even in the democracies when the war broke out was due to nothing so much as to the belief (untrue, if the record be examined) that the Nazi system was more successful than the democratic in providing employment. Judged by this test, our present *mixture* of Freedom and Order does not work very successfully. But a *balance* of Freedom and Order could be contrived that would show a much better record.

Very largely, it is a matter of incentives. Every form of economic activity requires an entrepreneur—someone to hire the labor, to borrow the capital, to buy the materials, to take the inherent risks. Private individuals and corporations can undertake entrepreneurial functions only if they see the possibility of a profit, or at least the avoidance of loss. This is the profit incentive, though it could just as well be called the avoidance-of-loss incentive. Governments, because of their control of the machinery of taxation and credit creation, do not need to trouble about the avoidance of loss. Most of their activities, notably defense and education, are in fact run at a loss (and quite rightly so). Governments act by what we may call the social incentive—because they think their action is in the interests of society. With unimportant exceptions there will be no productive activity unless either an individual is motivated by the profit incentive or the government is motivated by the social incentive to initiate it.

What has been happening in recent decades is that the two incentives have been used to blunt and offset each other. The public has not liked the results of leaving the profit motive unchecked and uncontrolled. It has demanded a greater injection of Order into a system that was previously very largely one of Freedom. In so doing it has checked, controlled, licensed, investigated, and taxed the profit motive, with the result that the entrepreneurial opportunities for private individuals have been substantially reduced. But when the government itself has tried to expand the scope of its own economic activities in pursuit of the social motive, it has been assailed by a barrage of sound and unsound argument and by sincere and insincere political opposition. Unemployment has been the result of the conflict and an outstanding example of the danger of mixing motives.

In the political sphere the democratic formula is one of balance, not of mixture. Taxes are wholly compulsory, not partly voluntary. Religion is wholly free, not partly compulsory. So it should be in the economic sphere. There are parts of the economy where the social motive should be paramount; let it not be clogged up by the prejudices of Victorian laissez faire. There are parts of the economy where the government cannot, will not, or should not take the entrepreneur's responsibility; in these cases let the profit motive have its head. In both cases what is needed is the removal of the impeding, prohibitive, negative influences if the rapid march of material progress is to be resumed.

By far the strongest urge toward the principle of Order comes from the humanitarian desire to remedy the inequities to which a free economy seems to be so distressingly prone. It is not the logic of Karl Marx or the compelling force of the materialist interpretation of history or innate love of the bureaucrat that makes men Communists, Socialists, Radicals, Liberals, New Dealers, or that leads them to embrace any of the other creeds that would attempt to bring Order into a free system. It is simply the spectacle of poverty in a rich community, of starvation next door to bulging granaries, of idleness in the middle of so much unfinished work.

It follows that the proper province of Order is with everything necessary to assure to every citizen of a democracy the essentials of a decent life. In England this policy has come to be known as the National Minimum. But it is an ungainly and a prejudicial phrase and it would be far better to rechristen the doctrine "The Citizen's Charter." The thought is simple and familiar. Just as political democracy gives the citizen his Bill of Rights—his charter of privileges inherent in him as a human being, enjoyed as of right and without proof of individual merit—so an economic democracy should assure to every citizen the essential economic substance of a decent life. The citizen of a democracy should be guaranteed, as of right, enough food to maintain him in health. He should be assured of a minimum standard of shelter, clothing, and fuel. He should be given full and equal opportunities of education. He should have leisure and facilities for enjoying it. He should be secured against the risks of unemployment, ill health, and old age. Above all, the presence of children should not be allowed to bring with it misery for the parents, deprivation for the children, and poverty for all. All these things inhere in the individual as his citizen's rights.

Both in Great Britain and in the U.S. considerable progress has been made in the past three decades toward such a Citizen's Charter. The various provisions are haphazard, scattered, inconsistent, uncoordinated, incomplete, illogical; but they reach a fair way and it would not take a very much greater effort to pull them together into a rounded whole.

But a Democratic Order needs to be something far more dramatic and inspiring than a mere tidying up of social security. Indeed, there are two ways in which the idea far transcends this limited horizon. For one thing, social security has never yet been more than something grafted onto a fundamentally alien system. For example, the whole food industry, from seed to table, is moved by the incentive of private profit; social security merely provides (when it does anything about it at all) that the underprivileged shall have enough money to pay the prices set by private profit in free competition. Education, which in the U.S. is no inconsiderable industry, is not organized to make profits; it is organized to provide education. What is here proposed is that the provision of enough food for the people, instead of being a last-minute modification of a system whose main motive is quite different, should become the chief and deliberate object with which the whole food industry, from the farmer to the retailer, is organized. . . .

Already, in peacetime, governments all over the world have interfered with the free play of the profit motive in the food industries. There is hardly a country in the world where the farmer is not paid, out of the public treasury, something more than the market price of what he grows. And in a large number of countries—the U.S. and Great Britain among them—various measures have been taken to reduce the cost of food to the poor. In short, it has already been recognized that free profit-motivated enterprise is not a satisfactory formula in this largest of all industries. Why not get the full advantages of the alternative formula? Why not frankly recognize that the feeding of the people is by far the most important element of economic activity, that the government must assume responsibility for it? Why not reorganize it according to the principles of Order, following some incentive other than the earning of profits?

Food has here been taken only as an example—though perhaps as the largest possible example—of what is involved in the deliberate construction of a Democratic Order. The plea is not immediate and wholesale socialization— far from it; even with the complete control of the food supply that is exercised by the British Government today, wholesalers and retailers still operate by their accustomed methods. The plea is simply that the community should openly and deliberately admit what it has in fact practiced for decades past: namely, that there are certain forms of economic activity so important that it is not prepared to allow the motive of profit to have the deciding voice in them. One incentive being blunted or removed, another must be provided, if the machinery is to run at all. The incentive of Freedom having been abandoned, the incentive of Order—that is, deliberate purposeful organization by the community—should be substituted.

This, then, is the first reason why a Democratic Order should differ from a mere glorification of social security. It should stand by itself as a deliberately chosen method of organizing one great area of the community's economic life; it should not be a mere outgrowth of the poor farm, a charitable provision for unfortunates, a sort of bargain basement in a competitive structure.

But there is a second reason for distinguishing Democratic Order from the existing forms of social security. There is a strong element of charity in most schemes of social security. Millions of people are being taught to believe that the benefits of security, of cheap food, of cheap housing, and the rest fall like manna from Heaven. They are provided by "the government" or "the rich" or "the bosses." Who pays for them? "Well, anyway, we don't," say the people. "They," the great anonymous "they," bear the burdens: "we" merely cash in.

This is not the spirit of democracy. And it is an urgent and essential task to convince the masses of the people that if social security is to blossom out into the Citizen's Charter, it is a task far greater than can be loaded onto the shoulders of the "rich." We have gone too far already toward the Santa Claus state. But the state is no magic cornucopia; it is only a mechanism of co-operation. If the people want the Citizen's Charter (as there is every indication that they do), it is something they must do for themselves.

In this respect both the Nazis and the Communists have been better democrats than we. The Communists have their motto: "To each according to his needs, from each according to his means." We have acted as if the second half of the slogan were fulfilled by the payment of graduated income taxes. In remembering how great are the differences between the money possessions of different men, we have forgotten that no man has more, and few have less, than two arms, two legs, one brain and twenty-four hours a day. The Nazis have revealed, and exploited, the undoubted psychological fact that the average individual does not wish to be on the receiving end only in his relationship to the community. They have grown powerful on the passionate devotion with which a whole people will embrace an opportunity to give service to their community. It is only in wartime that we democrats provide an opportunity for service; and then we are surprised afresh each time by the eagerness with which it is taken. In England, since the war began, the government has been criticized in every home, not for demanding service, but for taking so little. The same spirit is rising in the U.S. How many American visitors to England in the past twelve months have marveled at the sudden ennobling of the smug and indifferent English character when the people took up the burden of their self-defense? How many have wondered at the fanatical selflessness with which a whole generation of young Germans serves the Reich? All these examples point in the same direction. Give the people the opportunity—no, the obligation—to give their individual, personal, bodily service to a cause they deem worth while, and you will have fired that cause with all the dynamism of the people's will.

Thus if Democratic Order is to be something more than a slow decline into the demoralization of *panem et circenses,*[2] it must be truly and openly cooperative. If there is to be an extended Bill of Rights there should equally be an extended Bill of Duties. The rights could be generalized by saying that every citizen is guaranteed the essentials of the decent life. The duties

[2] Bread and circuses.

could be generalized by saying that every citizen owes to the community, say, a year of his life and two weeks out of every year. What is more, a deliberate effort should be made to integrate the specific rights with specific duties. Is there to be a communal health service? Let it be run, so far as possible, by the community service of those with medical or nursing experience. Is there to be an extension of educational facilities? Let them be provided by the community service of those who have already enjoyed the benefits of education. Is there to be an attempt to endow the leisure of the people? Let them be served by those with skill in entertainment. Are the natural resources of the country to be conserved? Let the work be done by those who have little but brawn to offer. Is there to be an attempt to lift some of the burdens of large families? Let the young unmarried women give their community service in this way.

There must be some forms of service, such as military defense, that would fall on every citizen at one time or another. But in general the object should be to set up the obligation of service, to list the many varieties of acceptable services and as far as possible let each individual choose the way in which he can best serve. During his service he and his dependents would, of course, be maintained by the community; but he would neither receive nor expect any further reward than the very real privilege of doing his duty. In this way, the financial cost of the Citizen's Charter could be very substantially reduced. And just as the medical, nursing, educational, and technical skills required would be provided by those who had them, so also the money needed would be found by those who have it.

Is this a remote and fantastic dream? Why should it be? A democracy at war approaches it quite closely—though with a temporarily distorted objective. Indeed, both sides of the great equation of rights and duties can be seen emerging in Great Britain under the pressures of war. The need for cutting down the consumption of the whole people has brought with it a clearer realization than ever existed before of the need to buttress the consumption of the very poorest. Milk rationing is combined with a scheme of free or cheap milk for all children. The sudden appearance of a grave new peril that threatens every individual, in the shape of bombing from the air, has led to the free provision by the state of shelters and other defenses, in the use of which there are no distinctions of wealth, rank, or personal merit. The citizen has a new right to shelter. But he also has a multifarious collection of new duties, of armed service, of labor, of fire fighting, of receiving evacuees, and the rest. In wartime the citizen of the British democracy has learned that some of his most vital needs, be he rich or poor, can only be provided by the organizing power of the community. He has learned that, if it is to provide these benefits, the community must be able to call on the services of all its members. And he has also learned that the whole process is neither onerous nor unpopular, but charged with the inspiration of a high duty.

Is it fantastic to suggest that what is done in war might be done in peace?

The scale of operations would be smaller rather than larger. At present something like 60 per cent of the economic activity of the British community is controlled and financed by the government. But the Citizen's Charter, even if every particle of it had to be paid for by the government and paid for at list prices and standard wages, could easily be provided out of one-half of the national income of a community like the British or American, and, for the reasons stated, this is a wild overestimate of the actual cost. There is nothing impossible about the Citizen's Charter. If it is considered as desirable as military victory, it can be more easily attained.

Over approximately half the economy of the nation the social incentive is destined to become dominant, and if private business remains in this sector (as it undoubtedly will), it must expect to conform to the promptings of that incentive. But conversely, in the remaining half or more of the economy, the mainspring of activity will remain the profit motive. Over all this sector of Freedom the government naturally has a watching brief as trustee for the community, to protect the rights of labor, to prevent fraud, to foster public health, to check excess. But it cannot provide the mainspring of action. The government of a democracy will neither wish nor be allowed, in any foreseeable time, to take over the initiating responsibility for making automobiles or women's fashions, for publishing news or fiction, for producing moving pictures, for shining shoes or lifting faces. That responsibility should continue—not merely for an interval of transition but forever—to rest with free individuals. And since individuals have neither taxing powers nor unlimited credit-creating facilities, they cannot afford to lose money on their ventures. That is, they will respond, and can only respond, to the profit incentive.

The basic argument of this article is that the incentives of economic action should be, first, distinguished from one another and then liberated from the forces that are now clogging them. "Take off the brakes" must be the slogan for any community that wishes to realize the full fruit of its potentialities. Just as it was argued in the previous section that the brakes should be taken off the social incentive in the sphere that is appropriate to Order, so here the prescription is that the profit motive be liberated from its present handicaps and left free to stimulate the maximum of activity in the sphere of Freedom. Then the appeal was to the Right to abandon its prejudices; now the appeal must be to the Left.

The rehabilitation of profits can hardly be expected to be a popular slogan, the climate of opinion in the democracies being what it now is. There is a task of reeducation here, for there is certainly nothing more necessary for the welfare of all sections of the public than to reconvince the people that the earnings of profits is, by and large, a praiseworthy and a beneficial achievement. The basic reason is the very simplest. The avoidance of chronic unemployment is the first command of any economic system. The way to avoid unemployment is to see that more economic activity is initiated, and wherever the government cannot, will not, or does not take the initiative, it can be taken only by those who foresee the possibility of profit or at least of not losing.

This is, of course, a vastly oversimplified version of the basic argument. Perhaps the argument can be made more palatable by two distinctions of language. First, as has already been suggested, the so-called "profit" motive could better be called the "avoidance of loss" motive. It is not that the capitalist entrepreneur needs a fat yield to tempt his greed before he will move. It is not that employers will close their plants and refuse to play if their profits fall below a satisfactory figure. Indeed, once a plant is built and a firm established, it will continue to do all the business it can, even if the average return is low or an actual loss is being incurred. But the balance and equilibrium of the economic structure depend—and this is one point on which all schools of economists are agreed—on the smoothness and regularity with which the savings of the public are put into *new* capital equipment. The more difficult the earning of profits on existing investments is made, the greater will be the risk of loss on new investments and the smaller will be the part that anybody except the government can play in avoiding unemployment.

Second, the rehabilitation of profits does not mean the rehabilitation of the profiteer. There is no reason why it should not be combined with heavy taxation on rich individuals. This is a point that is almost always misunderstood. There is a most important difference between preventing the emergence of large incomes by throttling profits and taxing them away when they have emerged. The first method increases the risk of loss that faces every entrepreneurial enterprise and therefore diminishes the amount of enterprise that will be shown. The second method neither increases nor diminishes the risk of loss; it merely taxes the reward of success. Both methods diminish the reward of enterprise, but the first also reduces the incentive. It is a perfectly legitimate aim for a democracy to attempt, if it wishes to do so, to abolish gross inequality of wealth. Nothing that is said here seriously conflicts with that aim. It is merely pleaded that if the method chosen for reducing inequality is such as to increase the risks of engaging in legitimate business, the community must not be surprised by the emergence of chronic unemployment.

In this increasingly erratic world the profit motive has been in need of assistance for some decades past. The risks are much greater than they used to be. There is the risk of severe depression, of war, of restrictive legislation. Each of these risks is either new or greater than it used to be. And it was inevitable that they would curtail the volume of new enterprise. A rational community would have asked itself whether it wished to have any part of its economy run by non-governmental enterprise. Having answered yes (as any democracy must do), it would then have set about assisting the earnings of profits by the various devices open to it. This does not, of course, mean that there are never times when the general rate of profits is dangerously excessive; the period 1927-29 is an excellent example of a time when a policy of deliberately limiting and reducing the general rate of profits would have been in the general interest and even in the particular interest of the profit receivers.

Wartime profits provide another example of a period when the necessity is to check rather than to stimulate the volume of new investment undertaken by private enterprise. But in the modern world booms are exceptions, and the more representative state of economic health is one in which there is a tendency to general unemployment. By the same token the *usual* basis of the government's economic policy should be in favor of increasing the rate of profit that can be earned on legitimate competitive enterprise.

Instead of this, however, the earning of competitive profits has been the object of pressure from every side. One strong attack has come in every democratic country from the ranks of labor, with the greater or less backing or approval of the government of the day. Here again it is necessary to guard against misunderstanding. There can be no denying that, all through the nineteenth century, the wage earner was the Cinderella of the industrial system. There can be no denying that he started the twentieth century with an enormous leeway to make up in status and in material reward. There can be no denying that the proper object of all economic activity is to increase the material welfare of the ordinary man. But when all this is admitted, it is still possible for labor's demands to go too far. If labor succeeds in reducing the profit margin in an industry to such an extent that the risk of loss impedes new investment, then labor will suffer unemployment.

Another attack on profits has come from the tax collector. It is not that taxes on wealth are too high or that the rich man is being taxed more than he can bear. On the contrary, there is nothing to prevent a workable system of private enterprise being devised with still higher taxes on wealth. The point is that present tax methods all over the democratic world discriminate against enterprise and in favor of mere passive ownership, against profits and in favor of the rentiers' interest. If a man ventures his capital of $1 million in business enterprise and makes an average return of $30,000 a year, he is taxed more heavily than if he merely put the money into tax-exempt government bonds. Is it to be wondered at that there is an increasing tendency to turn away from the risks of enterprise and to leave the problem of keeping the system going to the government? In fiscal policy, as in labor policy, it is self-defeating to make enterprise unattractive.

Third, there is the attack on competitive enterprise that comes from monopolies, cartels, trusts, rings, combines, trade associations, and other euphemisms for restraint of trade. It cannot be too strongly emphasized that profits made in this way are not the profits with which we are here concerned. The case for private enterprise rests on its efficiency in increasing the total volume of activity. The case is largely thrown away when there is a restraint of the volume of trade. In this, as in the other respects, the guiding principle must be the removal of restraints, the increase of incentives to activity, the liberation of human ambitions to build and expand. This should be the more easily done when the system of private enterprise runs in double harness with cooperative collectivism, each on its own side of the pole—when freedom is teamed with order. For the great urge to the restraint of trade is not greed so much as fear of insecurity. It is the desire to protect existing businesses, existing markets, existing employment that leads one industry after another to try to "stabilize" its own section of the economy. To the extent that security is provided by other means, it will be possible in the sphere of freedom to insist on a return to the full competitive ruthlessness that is inseparable from rapid progress.

With an economic system, as with an individual, it is only when the basic hungers have been met and the strongest fears removed that the human spirit can develop its full powers. When those conditions are met, there are no limits to the new frontiers that the ingenuity of the free man can conquer.

It would be the height of arrogance to claim that in these few paragraphs the problem has been solved, or even that all its aspects have been touched upon. But it is believed that the ideas here sketched, if properly developed, show the way in which the present dilemma could be resolved. There is at present no democratic economy to set up against Hitler's New Order because the democrats have not made up their minds whether they wish to point onward to Order or backward to Freedom. To point to both at once, each in its proper sphere, would enable the democrats to close their ranks and to speak with one voice, not with two quarrelsome jargons.

It should be fully possible for both Right and Left to accept a balance between Freedom and Order. The Right (save for its fanatics) should have no objection to a deliberate intervention by the state to provide the fundamental necessities of a decent life, once it were established that the intervention would not cripple or obstruct the functioning of free enterprise in the remaining part of the national economy. The Left (save for its fanatics) is driven by the humanitarian desire to benefit the underprivileged. Once the Citizen's Charter were established effectively, the fire would go out of the Left's attack on the institution of private property.

But there is no inspiration in compromises and this sketch of a democratic economy is not put forward merely as a dead mean, a soulless average. It is only by some such proposition that democracy can recapture the sense of going forward, that it can leave behind the frustrations of patchwork modifications in which we have been caught for a whole generation, that it can begin once again to forge for itself a positive and dynamic faith. And what a magnificent reply such a policy would be to the specious claims of the despotisms. "What," we could then proclaim, "have the dictators to offer that is even a fraction as attractive? We offer employment without war, security without impoverishment, service without slavery—all this, and freedom too."

The Lessons of TVA[1]

by DAVID E. LILIENTHAL

A NEW CHAPTER in American public policy was written when Congress in May of 1933 passed the law creating the TVA. For the first time since the trees fell before the settlers' ax, America set out to command nature not by defying her, as in that wasteful past, but by understanding and acting upon her first law—the oneness of men and natural resources, the unity that binds together land, streams, forests, minerals, farming, industry, mankind.

This, of course, is not what the creation of TVA meant to most people who read in their newspapers of the action of Congress. For TVA was then ordinarily thought of simply as a "power" project, a venture in public ownership of hydro-electricity. And even today, in spite of its wide range of activities, it is as a "power" project that many people still regard the TVA. Why there has been this limited picture of the scope and purpose of the Authority is wholly understandable.

For fifteen years before TVA came into being Congressional and public debate centered largely on a single potential resource of the Tennessee River, hydro-electric power. For long years there had been determined efforts to dispose of the government dam and power plant at Muscle Shoals in Alabama, built with the public funds for World War I, as if it were like any other of the flotsam left over from that war—the trucks and shoes and trench shovels to be knocked down to the highest bidder. It was simply regarded as a power plant, either to be dealt with as such a plant in the hands of a private operator would be, or, if continued under public control, to be limited to the sale of generated power for distribution at a profit by private industry.

How those power facilities were to be used, that was the major question which attracted public discussion down the years. That question was settled by the passage of the Act creating TVA. But it was not settled on the narrow issue of "public ownership" of power. The message of President Roosevelt urging approval of the Norris bill (which became a law with his signature on May 18, 1933) boldly proposed a new and fundamental change in the development of our country's resources. The words of the President's message were not only eloquent; there was in them a creativeness and an insight born of his New York State experience in establishing regional planning as a political reality. That understanding was matured at his Georgia home, in

[1] From David Lilienthal, *TVA—Democracy on the March* (1944). By permission of Harper & Brothers, publishers.

long days of thinking of the problems of the South and its relation to the whole nation.

It is clear (the message read) that the Muscle Shoals development is but a small part of the potential public usefulness of the entire Tennessee River. Such use, if envisioned in its entirety, transcends mere power development: it enters the wide fields of flood control, soil erosion, afforestation, elimination from agricultural use of marginal lands, and distribution and diversification of industry. In short, this power development of war days leads logically to national planning for a complete river watershed involving many states and the future lives and welfare of millions. It touches and gives life to all forms of human concerns.

The President then suggested

legislation to create a Tennessee Valley Authority—a corporation clothed with the power of government but possessed of the flexibility and initiative of a private enterprise. It should be charged with the broadest duty of planning for the proper use, conservation, and development of the natural resources of the Tennessee River drainage basin and its adjoining territory for the general social and economic welware of the Nation. This authority should also be clothed with the necessary power to carry these plans into effect. Its duty should be the rehabilitation of the Muscle Shoals development and the co-ordination of it with the wider plan.

Many hard lessons have taught us the human waste that results from lack of planning. Here and there a few wise cities and countries have looked ahead and planned. But our nation has "just grown." It is time to extend planning to a wider field, in this instance comprehending in one great project many States directly concerned with the basin of one of our greatest rivers.

The TVA Act was nothing inadvertent or impromptu. It was rather the deliberate and well-considered creation of a new national policy. For the first time in the history of the nation, the resources of a river were not only to be "envisioned in their entirety"; they were to be developed in that unity with which nature herself regards her resources—the waters, the land, and the forests together, a "seamless web"—just as Maitland saw "the unity of all history," of which one strand cannot be touched without affecting every other strand for good or ill.

Under this new policy, the opportunity of creating wealth for the people from the resources of this valley was to be faced as a single problem. To integrate the many parts of that problem into a unified whole was to be the responsibility of one agency. The Tennessee Valley's resources were not to be dissected into separate bits that would fit into the jurisdictional pigeonholes into which the instrumentalities of government had by custom become divided.

It was not conceded that at the hour of Creation the Lord had divided and classified natural resources to conform to the organization chart of the federal government. The particular and limited concerns of private individuals or agencies in the development of this or that resource were disregarded and rejected in favor of the principle of unity. What God had made one, man was to develop as one.

"Envisioned in its entirety" this river, like every river in the world, had many potential assets. It could yield hydro-electric power for the comfort of the people in their homes, could promote prosperity on their farms and foster the development of industry. But the same river by the very same dams, if they were wisely designed, could be made to provide a channel for navigation. The river could also be made to provide fun for fishermen and fish for food, pleasure from boating and swimming, a water supply for homes and factories. But the river also presented an account of liabilities. It threatened the welfare of the people by its recurrent floods; pollution from industrial wastes and public sewage diminished its value as a source of water supply and for recreation; its current carried to the sea the soil of the hills and fields to be lost there to men forever.

To a single agency, the TVA, these potentialities of the river for good and evil were entrusted. But the river was seen as part of a larger pattern of the region, one asset of the many that in nature are interwoven: the land, the minerals, the waters, the forests—and all of these as one—in their relation to the lives of the valley's people. It was the total benefit to all that was to be the common goal and the new agency's responsibility.

That is not the way public resource development had heretofore been undertaken in this country. Congress in creating TVA broke with the past. No single agency had in this way ever been assigned the unitary task of developing a river so as to release the total benefit from its waters for the people. Not far from where I write are other rivers developed by private interests or public agencies. They will serve to illustrate the contrast. On these rivers it is the common practice in public projects as well as private to build a single dam without first having fixed upon a general plan that will ultimately insure the full use of the whole river as a unit. There are dams built for the single purpose of power development. Such individual dams, in order to yield an immediate return in power, impair or destroy the river's full development of power at other sites, for they were not designed or built with the whole river thought of as it is in nature, a unit. These power dams are not built or operated to control floods, and do not provide a continuous navigable channel. The full usefulness of that river is lessened. Similarly, hundreds of millions of dollars in public funds have been expended for the single purpose of navigation on some of our rivers, but most of the dams constructed will not control the rivers' floods or create electric energy. They now stand as massive barriers against the erection of multi-purpose structures.

Over a long period of years scores of millions of dollars have been spent for levees to hold the waters back on the lower reaches of some of our rivers, but at the head-waters there were no reservoir dams that could make local levee protection effective.

And through the long years there has been a continuing disregard of nature's truth: that in any valley of the world what happens on the river is largely determined by what happens on the land—by the kind of crops that the farmers plant and harvest, by the number of trees they cut down. The full benefits of stream and of soil cannot be realized by the people if the water and the land are not developed in harmony.

If the soil is exposed, unprotected from the rains by cover and by roots the people will be poor and the river will be muddy, heavy with the best soil of the fields. And as a consequence each year the farmers will be forced more and more to use their land in ways that speed up this cycle of ruin, until the cover and then the top soil itself are wholly gone. When that day comes, as in the great reaches of China's sorrowful Yellow River Valley, then rains run off the land almost as rapidly as water runs from the pavements. Even a moderate rainfall forces the river from its banks, and every downpour brings disastrous floods, destroying crops and homes and bridges and highways, not only where the land is poor, but down the river's length, down in the areas where people are more prosperous, where the soil is still protected and factories have been built at the river's bend. Industries and railroads will be interrupted, farms flooded out, towns and villages destroyed, while heavy silt deposits fill the power reservoirs and stop up the channels of navigation.

It is otherwise where land is covered with sod or trees, and cultivated each season with the purpose of holding the rain where it falls. Such land literally serves as a water reservoir, a part of a system of flood control and river development, quite as directly as dams that stretch from bank to bank to hold the waters back. In many locations, after such proper land-use programs have been rather fully developed, the results should make it possible to reduce the magnitude and cost of engineering structures required for water control.

The farmers' new pastures and meadows themselves are reservoirs. If the changed farming practices now in use on many tens of thousands of Tennessee Valley farms were applied to all the agricultural area of our watershed (as some day I am confident they will be), the soil might absorb as much as half the customary twelve-inch surface run-off of rain each year; this storage of water on the farms would equal the capacity of two reservoirs as great as the one behind the Norris Dam, which stands 267 feet above the Clinch River.

This is of course nothing new, nothing discovered by the TVA. That a river could offer many benefits and a variety of hazards, that its improvement through engineering structures is inseparable from the development and use of the land as a watershed, has been recognized for many years by scientists and engineers.

For over a generation a distinguished line of conservationists had seen this truth and written and spoken of it with great force. And as a matter of fact almost any farmer, standing in his barn door while he watches a torrential rain beat upon his land and fill his creek, could see that much. The point is that knowledge of this inseparability of land and streams has only once, here on this river, been carried into our national action. On every other watershed we turn our rivers over to engineers of one agency to develop while farm experts of other agencies concern themselves with the land.

Thus far it is only in the Valley of the Tennessee that Congress has directed that these resources be dealt with as a whole, not separately.

The principles of unity whereby this valley has gone about the restoration of its land and the multiplication of the land's usefulness are, of course, the same as those that governed turning the river to man's account. The development of soil and its increased productivity are not simply problems of land, of farming, and of agricultural science, any more than the development of a river is only water control, dams, and engineering techniques. The restoration of land fertility, the healing of gullies, the reforestation of hillsides, these are no more ends in themselves than are flood control, navigation, and power. As the river is not separable from the land, so the land is inseparable from the forests and minerals, from the factories and shops, from the people making their living from their resources.

Here, too, the methods this valley has followed to achieve its purposes break sharply with those long prevailing. The methods differ because to think of resources as a unity compels the use of different ways. The idea of unity makes it inescapable that each man's farm must also be seen as one operating unit. The farm, too, is a "seamless web."

To the farmer on his land the problems do not fit into neat cubicles labeled "forestry" or "soil chemistry" or "mechanical engineering," nor to him is soil erosion or holding water on the land separate from the whole business of making a living on the land. And so in the way TVA goes about its responsibilities there are no "jurisdictional" lines, no excluding of the chemical engineer, say, because this is a "farm" problem, or of the businessman or the inventor because soil erosion is a "public issue," or of a county or state expert because agriculture is a "national" question. The invention by this valley's technicians of a new kind of machine and the decision of a businessman to produce and market it may be as important in land restoration as check dams in the gullies, if it thereby enables the farmer to make a living by raising soil-conserving crops. The invention here of a quick-freezing machine, a portable thresher, or a furrow seeder, all designed to overcome specific economic obstacles in the farmer's path toward land conservation, we see as just as real factors in land restoration as the terracing of the slopes.

Because they sinned against the unity of nature, because they developed some one resource without regard to its relation to every other resource in the life of man, ancient civilizations have fallen into decay and lie buried in oblivion. Everywhere in the world the trail of unbalanced resource development is marked by poverty, where prosperity seemed assured; by ugliness and desolation, with towns now dying that once were thriving; by land that once supported gracious living now eroded and bare, and over wide areas the chill of death to the ambitions of the enterprising young and to the security of the mature.

How industry came to Ducktown in the mountains of eastern Tennessee a generation ago is one such story. Copper ore was discovered; mining began; a smeltery was built. One of the resources of this remote region was being developed; it meant new jobs, income to supplement farming and forestry. But the developers had only copper in their plans. The magnificent hardwood forests to a distance of seven miles were cut and burned as fuel for the smelter's roasting. The sulphur fumes from the stacks destroyed the thin cover that remained; not only the trees but every sign of living vegetation was killed and the soil became poison to life.

The dead land, shorn of its cover of grass and trees, was torn mercilessly by the rains; and the once lovely and fruitful earth was cut into deep gullies that widened into desolate canyons twenty and more feet deep. No one can look upon this horror as it is today without a shudder. Silt, swept from unprotected slopes, filled the streams and destroyed fish life. The water was robbed of its value for men, for animals, and for industry, while farther down the stream a reservoir of a private power company was filling with silt. One of Ducktown's resources, copper, had been developed. But all its other resources had been destroyed in the process. The people and their institutions suffered in the end.

All this desolation caused as much pain to the officials of the copper company as it did to the lovers of nature. For balanced resource development is not, as the naive appear to believe, a simple moral tale of "bad men" versus "good men." It is much more than that. It is the reflection of our national thinking. In fact, in this case, the early operators came to see the point better than most people, for they had to pay cash in damages for some of this destruction, after long and bitter lawsuits by the injured landowners.

The fumes from Ducktown's copper smelteries are harmless now. Indeed, in the hands of a successor company a new technical process that makes the fumes harmless yields a by-product—sulphuric acid—now more valuable than the copper itself. The copper company itself is co-operating actively with the TVA in an extensive, though still experimental, reforestation program on the area the fumes destroyed. What it has already cost and what it ultimately will cost, in manpower, materials, and the dollars of taxpayers, because copper was developed rather than the resources of Ducktown as a unity, has never been calculated. But the bill will be high.

This case seems to be extreme only because the accounting came quickly and was so clearly evident to the eye. It often takes time before the balance shows that more is being subtracted than added from the assets of a region. But there is no escape from the arithmetic. The fall in the "water table," the sub-surface level of water, threatens industry's water supply in the Ohio Valley. The forest areas of northern Wisconsin and Michigan are dotted with towns that are dying and people who are stranded and poor. Lumber was "developed" from the wealth of the forests; there was prosperity for a time. But farming and fish and game were destroyed, and eventually the forests. Now in some areas there is next to nothing to support the towns, the highways and the schools and human beings. Unless the benefit of the people is the purpose, and the principle of the unified development of resources is the method, the harvest in the end is only such bitter fruits as these.

The "played-out" farmlands of the South, now in the process of rebuilding, were "mined" to grow a single crop of cotton: they are one more illustration of the remorseless arithmetic of nature. Here once lovely manor houses stand seedy and deserted because their foundation, the soil, has been exhausted, romantic monuments to a national tragedy of waste. And the great towers of Manhattan and Chicago, the modern business streets of Omaha on the prairies, all rest on the same foundations as the old plantation manor— the land, the waters, the minerals, and the forests. We are all in this together, cities and countryside.

The TVA experience in resource development is being earnestly examined for the lessons it may hold for a battered world facing the giant contours of a historic period of reconstruction. For it is coming to be recognized ever more widely that our hope of future peace or the certainty of new wars rests to an important degree upon the wisdom the world can summon to the task of resource development. This is not the whole story of course; the effect of racial antagonisms and conflicting cultures on political systems goes deep. But at the root of much of the world's turbulence lies the way we deal with the physical base of every man's and hence every nation's livelihood.

The subject has the broadest ramifications; to pursue them is outside the scope of this book. It is obvious, however, that the pressure of people upon resources that do not adequately support them has long nourished a spirit of armed aggression against other nations. It is a commonplace that the development of one people's land and forests and minerals for the sole benefit of another people has started many a fire of hatred that later exploded into war. It has not, however, been quite so apparent that methods of unified development to create sustained productivity rather than quick exhaustion, that technical advance which makes low-grade ores, for example, as useful as the scarce higher grades, or that expert skills which can restore now wasted land and greatly increase its productivity, relieve war-creating tensions of impoverishment and may be the foundation stones upon which peace in a modern world can be slowly built. It is the light which this valley's experience throws on such matters—the brass tacks of world reconstruction—that has made it a center of interest to foreign visitors.

The TVA has come to be thought of (here and abroad) as a symbol of man's capacity to create and to build not only for war and death but for peace and life. This is of great importance in the post-war period. For despair and cynicism in our own ranks will be a deadly enemy after Japan and Germany surrender. The immediate task of fighting keeps us tense. Once that tension is relaxed we must be prepared for a let-down, a bitter loss of faith and hope. When that time comes it will be desperately important as a matter of mental antisepsis that there be, in this country and abroad, many living proofs, of which the TVA is one, of the creative powers of mankind and of democracy's demonstrated and practical concern for the everyday aspirations of people.

The value of TVA as a symbol of what man can do to change his physical environment is increased by the knowledge that in this valley we have had to face so many of those same problems which plague other regions of the world: low income, resignation to the *status quo* as inevitable, complacency on the part of other more favored areas. A demonstration that such gains can be made without forcible changes in social status or property rights, without liquidating all those who do not agree completely with one's plans, will be evidenced to support the conviction of those who have no faith in catastrophe as an instrument of human social improvement.

What I have said in the preceding chapter on "planning" on the importance of starting from where you are and taking a step at a time, *one change promoting the next,* applies with peculiar force to our economic and political thinking about the post-war world. What is dumfounding to me, however, is that men who show they understand this as applied to our own affairs, when they consider the future of world society will abruptly slip these hawsers of experience and reality. They would be quick to condemn TVA if it had sought to make this valley over according to a pattern of TVA's own design. Yet they seem quite eager that America try the even more quixotic task of building a world order on the same kind of undemocratic foundation.

There is yet another way the TVA may throw the light of experience on the conditions for a lasting peace. For TVA is a demonstration, and one that can be readily understood, of this truth: *in any perspective of time, unified resource development anywhere helps everyone everywhere.* A stronger, more productive Tennessee Valley region has benefited the whole American nation and all its regions. So it will be when any region of the world strengthens the basis of its livelihood. Regional economic developments, whether within the nation or the family of nations, are not something to fear but to encourage.

When people of the more developed regions of the earth cease their fear that resource development and greater productiveness elsewhere injure them, and realize instead that they are benefited by them, then international political co-operation will be on the way to full realization. For it is that fear which nourishes extreme nationalism, with its harvest of hatred between peoples, tariff barriers, restrictive trade, autarchy, and finally—war. The physical shrinking of the world only multiplies the opportunities for inflaming these deep anxieties.

It is upon a wide popular comprehension and practice of the economics of the Golden Rule—and particularly among our fellow Americans—that it seems to me the prospects for world peace largely rest. The essential structure of political co-operation between nations will be weakened, may indeed begin to crack the day it is set up, unless those political arrangements rest upon increasingly effective economic co-operation.

The experience of the Tennessee Valley helps to make these matters

clearer to American public opinion, and thus serves a useful educational purpose in world reconstruction. It was a favorite argument against the TVA
in its earliest years that the development of this valley would endanger the
prosperity of people elsewhere—in Ohio and Connecticut and New York. If
an additional factory is built in Alabama—so the oft-repeated story ran—that
will mean less factory employment in Ohio; if Tennessee produces more dairy
products, that means a loss to the dairying business in Wisconsin. Such ideas,
seriously put forward in editorials and speeches about the TVA, rested upon
the assumption that there is a market for just so much goods, and that
America had now reached its highest level of production and of consumption.

Until the falseness of such ideas *within our own country* is understood at
the grass roots, it is politically naive to expect American public opinion to
support the idea of encouraging world-wide economic co-operation in the interest of lasting peace. That many of us would prefer that such a policy be
adopted primarily upon ethical grounds, and would favor it even if it hurt
us economically, is quite irrelevant.

These things can be best understood by demonstrations that are close to
us. Therein lies the value of TVA. For many people in Ohio, for example,
or Connecticut, or New York, have come to see that increased productivity in
the Tennessee Valley has not endangered their own standard of living as they
were repeatedly told it would. The millions of people in this region who
have been producing more, who thereby have been able to buy and enjoy
more automobiles, radios, refrigerators, and clothes, make for a more prosperous nation and a stronger Ohio, Connecticut, New York.

Ten years ago the Tennessee Valley was regarded in the electrical appli-
ance industry as the "zero" market of the entire country; a few years later it
was the leading market of the entire country. The men in the General Electric shops at Schenectady, New York, or at the Westinghouse Company in
Mansfield, Ohio, who produced many of those additional tens of thousands
of electric ranges, water pumps, and refrigerators, now can see that it was in
their interest that this valley had become productive enough to buy and pay
for the products of their shops. This meant that men in Schenectady would
buy overalls and aluminum goods made in this valley; could perhaps afford a
fishing vacation on one of the new TVA lakes.

There was at the outset bitter opposition to the TVA from the coal industry, an opposition which further illustrates how mistaken it is to cling
to the ideal of restricted development. The argument was made that by
developing electricity from the water of the river TVA would rob the coal
industry of its existing market for coal for steam-generated electricity. Actually, of course, sound development of one asset, water power, and a rate
policy that increased its use enormously, inevitably stimulated the use of
other resources, coal included. The valley market for coal for industrial and
other purposes rose to heights never before experienced. Even the use of the
region's coal for power generation has exceeded all records, as TVA's electric

rate example multiplied power use over wide areas where coal is the principal source of electricity.

Never has as much coal been used for the generation of electricity, as since the river has been developed. TVA itself has built and acquired steam-electric plants to supplement the river's power; in 1940 TVA purchased 574,-000 tons of coal; in 1941, 693,000 tons; in 1942, 1,319,000 tons, chiefly for power production.

This is the way—by one object lesson after another—we learn that the dangers to us of economic development elsewhere in the world are imaginary. When Americans see that it has helped, not hurt, the people of Ohio, say, to have this southern valley more productive, we shall see that much the same thing will be true if, in their own way, Mexicans and Brazilians and Russians and Chinese develop their resources and trade with us and with each other. That comprehension can best be learned at first hand.

It is folly to expect Americans clearly to see the tragedy, for the world, of an intense nationalism until restrictive sectionalism within the nation is also seen as a self-defeating policy. A demand for an end of a colonial system far from home is not nearly so important as an understanding of the colonial system within the United States, and the reasons why it is so injurious to this nation's interest. And colonialism, or exploiting the hinterland, is substantially the basis upon which the South and the West have been so long predominantly a raw materials source for the dominant manufacturing regions of the North and Northeast.

American public opinion on world co-operation will not be strengthened by the kind of double talk that displays fervid concern for self-development for India along with lack of interest, even hostility, toward industrial development for undeveloped American regions. Such a cynical attitude will justify the suspicion that far-off China's cause is espoused and that of near-by Georgia and Arkansas ignored because there are fewer American vested interests— political and economic—to be antagonized. Equality of opportunity for all the nations of the world will yield few benefits to the average man if that great principle is dissociated from specific issues of equality of opportunity for regions within our own country. . . .

To what extent and under what terms should private investors or the government of this country finance the development of resources in other parts of the world as a means of buttressing the pillars of peace? A complete discussion of this is obviously beyond the scope of this book. The point I seek to make is simply this: the issue ought not be thought of in terms of fear of "creating competition against our own businessmen and farmers." This fear has as little general validity in the international field as it has between regions here at home. The policy of reciprocal trade for example, takes on meaning only when there is trade, i.e., productiveness, to reciprocate. The flourishing regions and nations can only remain vigorous and strong by encouraging the regions and nations that are less productive.

Whether we encourage or discourage it, or are foolish enough to regard it with indiscriminate fear, world-wide development of natural resources and industrialization will go forward rapidly after the war. The United States can in some ways speed the process and influence its course. But it is nonsense to believe that we hold a broad veto over what other great nations decide to do in developing their rivers or their other resources.

To accept such shallow talk as this is to close our eyes to the central fact that sets our time off from all that went before—the drive, the world over, toward resource development through the machine and science.

There are, however, questions that are still open: what course the development will take, both here and abroad; the methods that will be used; for whose benefit the development will be carried out. Unless the people demand a course that will benefit them, one that will exhaust their resources wastefully, the old exploitative methods of the elite few are likely to be followed.

It is for this reason that the TVA experience ought to be known. For a knowledge of the methods followed in this valley's development will enable the people to be critical, to demand answers to their questions—questions such as these: Will economic development be unified, seen as a whole? Will resources be regarded as a means of benefiting the human beings who depend upon them, or will the development of each resource be deemed as an end in itself, its benefits drained off by a few with no recognition of broad ethical purpose? Will resource development be treated as merely a physical task for technicians and businessmen; or will it be seen to be a democratic opportunity as well, the acceptance of their evolving ideas of what is good, of what it is they want?

Will these new projects be administered by the methods of remote control and extreme centralization, invitations to tyranny; or will decentralized administration of central policies be the general principle? Will these developments be energized and directed by modern tools for getting things done; or by archaic methods of administration, crusted with tradition and fortified by bureaucratic "rights"? Unless the decisions are to go by default to those who always watch out for their own selfish interests, these are some of the questions that should be faced by the people, in our country and in others, as the time draws ever closer when action can take the place of plans for post-war development.

When Can the Atom Be Put to Work?[1]

by HARRY M. DAVIS

THE world of the future is very much present these days in the background of popular thought. Somewhere ahead on the road for humanity, it is widely believed, somewhere past the pitfall of mutual destruction by atomic weapons, beckons an age of atomic abundance.

This new atomic age has been portrayed rather thoroughly in word pictures and quite graphically in the imaginative comic strips. A few well-chosen atoms will drive the Queen Mary across the Atlantic and back. Atomic power plants will make electricity so cheap it won't pay to read your meter. No gas stations along the road—just an annual refill of your automobile's atomic fuel tank. Colonies on the Moon, Mars, Venus and Jupiter will be reached on regular schedule by atomic space ships.

The more responsible sources don't paint such detailed portraits of things to come, but they still leave plenty of scope for the imagination. The three-power declaration on atomic energy stressed its development "for the benefit of mankind." Our House of Representatives is considering a bill to create an Atomic Energy Commission to work not only for national defense but also for "the enrichment of the national life, the promotion of the general welfare." And President Truman has told Congress that atomic energy "may some day prove to be more revolutionary in the development of human society than the invention of the wheel, the use of metals, or the steam or internal combustion engine."

On the other hand, several leading scientists and statesmen have warned us not to expect a new industrial revolution overnight. Wall Street shows no panic in oil or utility stocks. Detroit, strikes excepted, is getting back into its old business, and it looks as if the automobile is here to stay for a while before people begin to shout, "Git an atom."

Why, in the face of the overwhelming display of atomic energy at Hiroshima and Nagasaki, can there be any hesitation as to the imminence of an atomic age? What has been achieved toward that end, and what has not? What remains to be done?

Essentially we have already entered the age of atomic energy. That came when science found the key to unlock the tremendous energies that exist in the nucleus of the atom. The materials that made up the super-bombs can also serve as super-fuel. But at the moment the industrial prospects are somewhat limited. The main reason is that so far, on a scale large enough to pro-

[1] From the New York *Times Magazine*, December 9, 1945. Reprinted by permission of the author and the *Times*.

vide bombs or power plants, nuclear energy has become available from only two kinds of atoms, both of them rare, costly and hard to come by.

One of these energy releasing elements is a rare variety of a rare metal. The rare metal is uranium, and uranium-235 (U-235 for short) is its rare variety. To obtain it, pitchblende ore must be mined at sub-zero temperatures from one of the world's few important deposits at Great Bear Lake only a few miles below the Arctic Circle in Canada's Northwest Territories. The ore has to be shipped during the short season of thaw, or flown across the frozen wastes, to latitudes where refineries operate. Uranium metal must be extracted from it. Then, either under huge electromagnets or by other difficult processes, the small portion which is energy-yielding U-235 must be separated. At last we have a precious metal of which an ounce will yield more heat than a hundred tons of coal. But pound for pound, it probably costs more than a thousand times as much as coal.

The only other mass-produced element that yields atomic energy is plutonium. It is created synthetically out of uranium by a process of atom-building—a modern form of alchemy that actually works, but that requires very special conditions. This process, invented at the University of Chicago, multiplies our resources of energy-yielding atoms, but the resources are still limited. Recently, knowing what to look for, scientists found that some plutonium does exist in nature, but in quantities so minute that for practical purposes it will still have to be made alchemically from uranium, which gets us back again to that frozen and far-away deposit at Great Bear Lake.

Both plutonium and U-235 can be used to run industrial power plants. We know this, even though it has never yet been done for industrial purposes, because the controlled conversion of atomic energy into heat was demonstrated in the early days, before the Government invested its billions for bombs, to prove that the whole things was not a wild dream.

There is no record of when man first used fire, nor of when the first wheel turned. Only with a vagueness of centuries or millenniums can we date man's transition from the Stone Age to the Iron Age. But it can be stated definitely that the Age of Atomic Energy began on Dec. 2, 1942. On that day the first energy-yielding "pile" of contagiously splitting uranium atoms began to simmer in a hiding place on the floor of a squash court under the stands of the University of Chicago's Stagg Field.

From the very beginning, this energy was well harnessed. With control strips in the "retard" position to prevent a premature domestic bomb-blast, the energy release was held at half a watt, almost the minimum measurable rate. After a few days the experimenters let it step up to 200 watts, more than enough to light your living room. Within a year, in Tennessee, a cube of graphite containing slugs of uranium was running day and night with a continuous output of 500,000 watts, and in 1944 it was generating 1,800,000 watts and more.

All this heat energy was wasted in the air, for this was merely an experiment. But it could have been used to boil water into steam, and the experiment showed that atomic-energy processes on a large scale could be controlled.

Even the process of turning uranium into plutonium yields tremendous quantities of heat as a by-product, and the Government's plutonium plant was located where it is in the State of Washington so that the cold water of the Columbia River could be diverted to carry off the heat. So much of it had to be disposed of that the designers actually worried about whether the warmer water downstream would injure the salmon; it didn't, and the heat drained harmlessly but wastefully into the Pacific. The Manhattan Project was in a hurry, and the problem of extracting plutonium for bombs was enough to handle without trying to run electric-power plants from the generated heat. But under peacetime conditions, this can be done.

Aside from the time and effort required to build such plants, there is the commercial consideration that a certain minimum amount of U-235 or plutonium would be needed for each individual installation. As in the case of the bomb, there is a certain "critical size" below which the chain reaction, by which one splitting atom triggers another, will not work. Just how big that critical size is has not been revealed, because it would also tell something about the bombs, but published figures indicate in general that it is measured not in ounces, not in tons, but in pounds.

A plant could operate safely, releasing energy at a controlled rate, with considerably more than the critical quantity of splitable atoms, since control strips of metal can be inserted in the mass of material to slow down the chain of atomic events. But below that critical quantity, nothing would happen. Therefore each atomic-power plant would require a fairly substantial investment from our precious stock of energy material, and for the immediate future a plant would have to be rather sizable to justify it. It might be worth while for an ocean liner—certainly not for a motor-boat.

Another difficulty in applying atomic energy industrially is the matter of safety. This refers not so much to the danger of explosions, which can be forestalled quite effectively by the method of control just described, but rather to the unhealthy rays that are given out in the process of atom-splitting. Without special precautions, people near an operating atom-power source would suffer burns and other ailments like those due to an overdose of radium or X-rays. To stop the powerful rays, thick metal shields must be used. The weight of these shields runs to tons. This automatically excludes, for the immediate future, the atomic automobile.

The most obvious application of atomic energy, and one that could be undertaken tomorrow, would be in large electric central power plants, such as those which light the lamps and drive the subway trains of New York.

In these plants, as now operated, burning coal turns water into steam which spins turbines that drive electric generators. The water could be turned into steam just as well by a pile of plutonium, and the rest of the plant would utilize this steam in the usual way. In a big power plant of today you see very few men at work anyway—the boilers, turbines and generators are run through remote control by a few engineers—so the safety problem could be taken care of simply.

However, what with the cost of the change-over and the high cost of atomic fuel, it is not clear that it would be worth doing—at least in the present centers of population and industry, which by and large have grown up in places where coal or hydro-electric power are conveniently at hand. But when we think of building new cities, new industries, it's another story. Vast areas, even within the United States and certainly in other parts of the world, have remained industrially barren for the very reason that they are too far from coal mines or harnessable rivers.

Starting afresh, atomic-power plants could revitalize entire regions. They might eventually make it possible, for example, to establish new livable communities in the Arctic and the Antarctic, with well-heated homes, offices and factories, to exploit the mineral resources of those regions. For example, Great Bear Lake, where the uranium comes from, might be a highly eligible customer for electric power and steam heat generated by atomic energy.

A more speculative use of atomic energy would be to drive huge aircraft, bigger than any now on the drawing boards. It would be possible to drive such planes by steam engines, the steam being heated by atomic energy. A more likely approach, however, would be to combine atomic energy with the jetpropulsion principle, along which the future of flying seems to be. Jet aircraft employ the direct application of heat to a mass of air, and atomic energy is ideally suited to supply that heat. The saving of fuel weight would be so enormous that, as aircraft got bigger, it would more than make up for the added weight of the shielding. Initially, there might be trials with unmanned freighters of the air, controlled by radio from the ground and delivering huge cargoes to any point on earth. The safety problem would be simplified, because the shielding would only have to be good enough to keep the cargo from getting too radioactive.

Entirely different applications of our present atomic-energy sources have been suggested. One would be to utilize the very explosive forces that blasted the Japanese. Explosives are important in peacetime. They blast the foundations for city skyscrapers, they loosen the coal and ore in our mines, they make it possible to tunnel through mountains, to dig canals which join oceans and irrigate deserts. If one small atomic bomb could flatten a city, what about using atomic explosives to blast the long-sought sea-level canal across Panama, or to improve the climate of the Sahara Desert by letting in the waters of the Mediterranean Sea? Such things may be possible, but it remains to be shown that an atomic explosion in the earth would be as effective as the bombs that burst in air.

A use of the heat from atom-splitting which has some fairly sound scientific support would be its employment at temperatures hotter than the hottest flame to melt materials which resist our ordinary furnaces. The industries which produce our metal, ceramic and plastic materials are limited by the temperatures they can attain with available fuels. The village blacksmith depended on his charcoal fire to make the iron malleable enough to take new shape under his hammer. Atomic furnaces, running at temperatures never before possible, might make other materials malleable. Hard rocks might be melted and fused into new and useful objects. New materials, new alloys of old metals, might emerge.

Here, then, are some of the things that can or may be done with the atomic-energy sources we have now—U-235 and plutonium. What it all adds up to may seem a trifle disappointing. It is not quite revolutionary. It doesn't have nearly the impact on our economy that the atomic bomb has had on war. This, however, does not mean that the long-range possibilities of atomic energy in general should be discounted.

We are only in the primitive beginnings of the atomic age, somewhat like those natives of Tierra del Fuego whom Darwin saw tending their bonfires day and night because they did not know how to start a new flame. The industrial applications are somewhat limited because we are so far able to obtain this new kind of energy in quantity from only two kinds of atoms, both of them rare, costly and hard to handle. Really important industrial energy will come when it can be obtained from the atoms of more common elements which can be obtained cheaply and in abundance.

The most likely road to the fullness of industrial atomic energy will not be through the technological exploitation of uranium and plutonium, but rather through further research in basic nuclear physics that will find the key to the energies known to reside in other atoms. Enough is known about these energies to permit fairly accurate calculation of how much would be released through any given process of atom splitting or atom building. Some of the processes absorb energy, others release it, and for practical purposes we are interested in the latter.

The professors of physics, when they tell the facts of nuclear science, usually start by drawing a curve which shows the energies residing in the various atoms from hydrogen to plutonium. This shows very definitely that energy can be released in two different ways. One is by splitting the heaviest atoms. The other is by combining the smaller atoms. The splitting process takes place in the atomic bombs, and heavy elements other than uranium and plutonium should be susceptible to it.

The combining process takes place in the sun, where hydrogen atoms join to form helium and meanwhile get rid of some surplus weight by giving out the energy we call sunshine—the energy that is captured in coal, oil and all growing things. Hydrogen is plentiful on earth (it can be obtained from water) and if our scientists should learn the secret of the sun's know-how on this source of atomic energy, or some other process using an abundant element, then the lid will really be off.

If we want to arrive at really unlimited atomic energy, therefore, the conditions must be provided that will encourage a flourishing of basic scientific research. What are these conditions?

The first is a condition of peace. Not merely an armed truce, during which nations build up competitive stockpiles of atomic armament, but a true peace based on trust, good-will and global organization. Little fundamental research was done on the bomb project; we capitalized on pre-war science. And so long as there is real fear of being bombed, there will be hesitation about bringing even the technical know-how into the open, for the same materials that release useful atomic energy can also blow up cities. At the moment, our stock of splittable atoms is probably too valuable as a military reserve to be used for generating power for the consumer.

The hopeful thought has been voiced that the universal use of atomic energy should make obsolete the distinction between the have and have-not nations and thus remove a cause of war. But the trouble is with the time scale. The bombs are here first, and the likelihood is that other nations will have similar bombs before we have enough useful atomic energy to make much difference in our own or the world's economy. The lure of a golden atomic era may be tantalizing, but the scientists who brought it within sight are more worried with the fear of destruction.

A second condition, partly predicated on the first, is a measure of freedom of research, discussion and publication of scientific data. The scientists on whom we count for the research are human beings, and perhaps more sensitive than most—because their monetary reward is not great—to such things as morale and esprit de corps. They have to be able to discuss their perplexities and their discoveries, verbally and in print, with their fellow-scientists. They must be permitted to follow curiosity and hunch, for the most fruitful exploration is in the regions of the unknown with no blazed trails.

The third necessary condition is a proper Government agency to sponsor, subsidize, and for purposes of safety to control the arduous tasks of research and development that lie ahead. It is not the peacetime business of the Army, and the Secretary of War has so stated, to run the development of industrial atomic energy. Yet until some new agency is established the Army retains its monopoly.

We need a Government-sponsored program of untrammeled scientific research in a world at peace. If we can attain these conditions, then men can hope to survive into an amazing world of the future. A few well-chosen atoms *will* drive some successor to the Queen Mary across the Atlantic and back. Atomic-power plants *will* make electricity so cheap it won't pay to read your meter. Space ships *will* permit us to cruise to the moon and planets and decide whether they are worth colonizing. Somewhere ahead on the road for humanity, somewhere past the pitfall of mutual destruction by atomic weapons, beckons the age of atomic abundance.

Modern Man Is Obsolete [1]

by NORMAN COUSINS

IN THE most primitive sense, war in man is an expression of his extreme competitive impulses. Like everything else in nature, he has had to fight for existence; but the battle against other animals, once won, gave way in his evolution to battle against his own kind. Darwin called it natural selection; Spencer called it the survival of the fittest; and its most over-stretched interpretation is to be found in *Mein Kampf,* with the naked glorification of brute force and the complete worship of might makes right. In the political and national sense, it has been the attempt of the "have-nots" to take from the "haves," or the attempt of the "haves" to add further to their lot at the expense of the "have-nots." Not always was property at stake; comparative advantages were measured in terms of power, and in terms of tribal or national superiority. The good luck of one nation became the hard luck of another. The good fortune of the Western powers in obtaining "concessions" in China at the turn of the century was the ill fortune of the Chinese. The power that Germany stripped from Austria, Czechoslovakia, Poland, and France at the beginning of World War II she added to her own.

What does it matter, then, if war is not in the nature of man so long as man continues through the expression of his nature to be a viciously competitive animal? The effect is the same, and therefore the result must be as conclusive—war being the effect, and complete obliteration of the human species being the ultimate result.

If this reasoning is correct, then modern man is obsolete, a self-made anachronism becoming more incongruous by the minute. He has exalted change in everything but himself. He has leaped centuries ahead in inventing a new world to live in, but he knows little or nothing about his own part in that world. He has surrounded and confounded himself with gaps—gaps between revolutionary technology and evolutionary man, between cosmic gadgets and human wisdom, between intellect and conscience. The struggle between science and morals that Henry Thomas Buckle foresaw a century ago has been all but won by science.

Given ample time, man might be expected eventually to span those gaps normally; but by his own hand, he is destroying even time. Decision and execution in the modern world are becoming virtually synchronous. Thus, whatever gaps man has to span he will have to span immediately.

This involves both biology and will. If he lacks the actual and potential biological equipment to build those bridges, then the birth certificate of the atomic age is in reality a *memento mori*.[2] But even if he possesses the necessary biological equipment, he must still make the decision which says that he is to apply himself to the challenge. Capability without decision is inaction and inconsequence.

Man is left, then, with a crisis in decision. The main test before him involves his *will* to change rather than his *ability* to change. That he is capable of change is certain. For there is no more mutable or adaptable animal in the world. We have seen him migrate from one extreme clime to another. We have seen him step out of backward societies and join advanced groups within the space of a single generation. This is not to imply that the changes were necessarily always for the better; only that change was and is possible. But change requires stimulus; and mankind today need look no further for stimulus than its own desire to stay alive. The critical power of change, says Spengler, is directly linked to the survival drive. Once the instinct for survival is stimulated, the basic condition for change can be met.

That is why the power of total destruction as potentially represented by modern science must be dramatized and kept in the forefront of public opinion. The full dimensions of the peril must be seen and recognized. Only then will man realize that the first order of business is the question of continued existence. Only then will he be prepared to make the decisions necessary to assure that survival. . . .

At present he is a world warrior; it is time for him to grow up and to become a world citizen. This is not vaporous idealism, but sheer driving necessity. It bears directly on the prospects of his own survival. He will have to recognize the flat truth that the greatest obsolescence of all in the Atomic Age is national sovereignty. Even back in the old-fashioned Rocket Age before August 6, 1945, strict national sovereignty was an anomalous hold-over from the tribal instinct in nations. If it was anomalous then, it is preposterous now.

It is preposterous because we have invested it with non-existent powers. We assume that national sovereignty is still the same as it always was, that it still offers security and freedom of national decision. We assume it still means national independence, the right to get into war or stay out of it. We even debate the question of "surrendering" some of our sovereignty—as though there is still something to surrender. There is nothing left to surrender. There is only something to gain. A common world sovereignty.

At the heart of sovereignty throughout history there has been security based on the advantages of geography or military might. For sovereignty has been inseparable from power. But by the end of World War I, the validity of national sovereignty had sharply changed. The development of air power alone, apart from all other aspects of the world's inexorable trend toward close interrelationship, outdated traditional concepts of independence among na-

[2] Reminder of death.

,tions. Yet we preferred to believe that there was no connection between a world being locked into a single piece and its over-all organization. Unfortunately, our unreadiness or unwillingness to see this connection did not cause the connection to disappear.

So much did this connection exist that it led to World War II. Despite six years of that new war, despite jet planes, rocket planes, despite the abrupt telescoping of a thousand years of human history in the release of atomic energy, despite the loss of millions of lives, still active as though sovereignty can function as it did two thousand years ago.

Can it be that we do not realize that in an age of atomic energy and rocket planes the foundations of the old sovereignties have been shattered? That no longer is security to be found in armies and navies, however large and mighty? That no longer is there security based on size and size alone? That any nation, however small, with atomic energy, is potentially as powerful as any other nation, however large? That in an Atomic Age all nations are now directly accessible to each other—for better or worse? That in the erasure of man-made barriers and boundaries all the peoples of the world stand virtually unarmed in the presence of one another? That they are at the mercy of one another, and will have to devise a common security or suffer a common cataclysm? That the only really effective influence between peoples is such influence as they are able to exert morally, politically, ideologically upon each other? That the use of disproportionate wealth and abundance of resources by any nation, when applied for bargaining purposes, does not constitute influence but the type of coercion against which severe reaction is inevitable?

All these questions have been in the making for centuries, but the triumph over the invisible and mighty atom has given them an exactness and an immediacy about which there can be no mistake. The need for world government was clear long before August 6, 1945, but Hiroshima and Nagasaki raised that need to such dimensions that it can no longer be ignored. And in the glare brighter than sunlight produced by the assault on the atom, we have all the light we need with which to examine this new world that has come into being with such clicking abruptness. Thus examined, the old sovereignties are seen for what they are—vestigial obstructions in the circulatory system of the world.

Much of the attachment to old concepts of sovereignty, as well as the reluctance to face squarely its severe limitations in the modern world, grows out of apprehension over the control a world authority might have over the internal affairs of the individual state. There is the fear, for example, that the individual Constitutions would be subject to central control. There is the fear that institutions built up over centuries would exist only at the pleasure and discretion of a super-state.

Natural and understandable though these concerns may be, they have their source in confusion over a distinction that should be made between world *sovereignty* and state *jurisdiction*. A common world sovereignty would mean that no state could act unilaterally in its foreign affairs. It would mean that no state could have the instruments of power to aggress against other states. It would mean that no state could withdraw from the central authority as a method of achieving its aims. But it would *not* mean that the individual state would lose its *jurisdiction* over its internal affairs. It would *not* mean the arbitrary establishment of a uniform ideology all over the world. It would not mean the forcible imposition of non-democratic systems on democratic states, any more than it would mean the forcible imposition of democratic systems on non-democratic states.

Though the idea of bestowing democracy on all other peoples throughout the world seems both magnanimous and attractive, the fact remains that democracy is not to be had just for the giving or the taking. It cannot be donated or imposed from without. It is an intricate and highly advanced mechanism capable of existing, like man himself, under certain conditions. It depends not only on the love of freedom, but on the ability to carry the responsibilities of freedom. It requires enduring respect for numberless principles, not all of them incorporated into formal law. It requires adherence to the principle of majority rule with preservation of minority rights. It is as much a way of living and a philosophy of life as it is a form of political organization.

This does not mean, however, that peoples not now democratic must be restrained from moving toward democracy. Nor does it mean that the conditions under which democracy can come into being cannot be nurtured and developed. So far as a central authority is concerned, one way to help in that development can be by providing a greater external harmony that will permit a greater internal harmony. . . .

The world has at last become a geographic unit, if we measure geographic units not according to absolute size but according to access and proximity. All peoples are members of this related group, just as the thirteen American colonies belonged to a related group, and just as the city-states of Greece belonged to a related group. The extent of this relationship need only be measured by the direct access nations have to each other for purposes of war. And the consequences of disunion are as applicable to the world group today as they were to individual groupings of states in the past. The unorganized geographic units of the past have given way to the unorganized unit of the present. It is a unit without unity, an order without any order.

In a world where it takes less time to get from New York to Chungking than it took to get from New York to Philadelphia in 1787, the nature and extent of this geographic entity becomes apparent. All natural distances and barriers vanish. Never before in history has the phrase, the human family, had such a precise meaning. This much all of us—American, European, African, Asiatic, Australian—have in common: Whether we like it or not, we have been brought together or thrust together as members of a world unit, albeit an unorganized world unit. Within that unit, to be sure, are divisions and subdivisions, but they are all heavily interdependent. There is little point in musing or speculating whether this unit is desirable or whether it deserves our support. The fact is that it exists.

Here we must meet the argument that even though the world may be a geographical unit, it is too large, too unwieldy, for the creation and operation of a governmental unit. But size alone does not limit the area in which government can function. Unwieldiness is entirely relative to the instruments of control. For harmony among states depends upon relationships; and relationships among states depend upon law and respect for law.

No less an authority on international organization than *The Federalist* tells us that "the larger the society, provided it be within a practical sphere, the more duly capable will it be of self-government." By "practical," *The Federalist* meant both necessity and workability. Thus a state could be as large as the need behind it, so long as it possesses effective machinery for its administration. And two thousand years before *The Federalist,* Aristotle considered the limitations upon the size of a state and decided that it could be determined by the range of a man's voice. Accessibility seemed to Aristotle to be the prime requisite of a governmental unit. According to this definition, radio has converted the entire world into a small enclosure capable of central government. But radio is only one of the instruments available for drawing the peoples of the world together under a common sovereignty. The revolution in transportation can give them a mutuality such as even the people of any one nation a hundred or more years ago never knew among themselves.

This mutuality—a mutuality built on present and future needs—is more important than physical dimensions. A common ground of destiny is not too large a site for the founding of any community.

But reject all other arguments for world government—reject the geographic, economic, the ideological, the sociological, the humanitarian arguments, valid though they may be. Consider only the towering job of policing the atom— the job of keeping the smallest particle of matter from destroying all matter. This means control. But control is no natural phenomenon. It does not operate of and by itself. Control is impossible without power—the power of investigation, the power of injunction, the power of arrest, the power of punishment.

But power, like control, cannot be isolated, nor is it desirable except under carefully defined circumstances. Power must be subordinate to law, unless it is to take the form of brute, irresponsible force. Here, too, we are involved in an important interrelationship, because law can be derived only through government. Law is a product of moral, judicial, executive, legislative, and administrative sanction—all of which adds up to government. And government means what it says: the process of governing. It is not decentralization, it is not informal organization, it is not the right of veto or the right of secession by any state or states. It is a central body none of whose members has the right or the means of aggression or withdrawal. It is the source of legitimate action and legitimate redress.

Approach the problem in reverse. We are all agreed that war must be "outlawed." If that is what we really mean, then we shall have to apply law. Law based on what? On general agreement? With or without sanctions? With or without protective as well as punitive power? With or without a judiciary? To the extent that the answers to these questions are subtractive, we shall fail in our agreed purpose. Outlawry of war is a noble phrase but its translation into tangible effectiveness requires, by its very nature, the existence of the basis and the instruments of legality, by which we mean government.

We are left, then, with three basic principles necessarily related to an effective system of international control:

No control without power.
No power without law.
No law without government.

Are there no other practicable methods of control? Is atomic power such a menace that nothing less than world government may be able to deal with it? What less drastic plans have been suggested?

Before examining these questions, bear in mind that the atom bomb dropped on Nagasaki represented a substantial improvement over the Hiroshima model. Bear in mind that the first atomic bomb, admittedly still in the experimental stage and said to weigh only a few pounds, was the equivalent of 20,000 tons of the most effective TNT explosive ever previously developed. Bear in mind that more than eighty per cent of the world's supply of uranium is located outside the United States, Canada, and Great Britain, which share the distinction and the responsibility for unleashing atomic energy. Bear in mind that other nations, Japan included, have already experimented successfully with plutonium, a derivative of uranium.

Bear in mind that United States territory is no longer safe from bombing attack. Bear in mind that more than four hundred Japanese balloons carrying not atomic but incendiary bombs were able to perform their explosive missions over the western portion of the United States, some being carried as far east as Michigan—although only a small number caused effective damage. Bear in mind that Japan was getting ready to launch long-range, one-way, heavy bombers for a direct attack on the United States when the atomic bombs ended the war. Bear in mind that it is possible *today* to develop pilotless rocket planes, carrying huge explosive atomic cargoes; and that these planes, from their launching stations, will be capable of hitting any specified target area in the world within the radius of a single mile.

Bear in mind that it would require only an infinitesimal percentage of the number of bombing missions in World War II for rocket planes to lay waste every city in the world—not in a matter of months or weeks or even days, but hours. Bear in mind that most military experts predict that within three years—five years at the most—knowledge of utilization of atomic energy may be as commonplace as present-day knowledge of aviation itself.

Bear all this in mind and then consider what would be required to safeguard the world from destructive atomic energy. Consider various suggestions advanced as possible methods of control. Begin by considering the fairly popular theory that every weapon produces a counter-weapon, and that in the course of time the atomic bomb will meet its match in some sort of super-atomic defense. This is by far the coziest, most convenient, approach to the problem. It requires almost no physical and mental exertion and doubtless has its origin in the pleasant belief that everything will come out all right in the end—atomic bombs and rocket planes not excluded. Absurd as the theory seems, it nevertheless requires a sober and serious answer; every shred of hope must be fully and carefully appraised at a time when all hope sorely needs definition and direction.

The obvious answer to the counter-weapon argument is that we can take nothing for granted. We cannot assume the automatic development of such a device, and among those who are the least sanguine in this respect are the scientists themselves. Nor is it true that every new weapon in history has been equated by another weapon. Air power was far ahead of anti-aircraft not only after World War I but after World War II. The only effective answer to air power was more air power, but this did not prevent cities from being leveled during the struggle for air supremacy. Nor did it prevent robots and rocket bombs from taking lives until the invasion of the European Continent overran the launching stations. But the cardinal fallacy of the counter-weapon theory is that it assumes there may be enough time in which to bring the negating devices into play—even granting the possibility of their development.

Modern warfare's only effective counter-weapon is retaliation, and there may not even be time for that, once an attack begins, for the beginning may be the ending as well.

It is said that man can go underground in an atomic war, that he can carve out large cities under the surface of the earth and at the first sign of danger can retire to subterranean shelters and stay there indefinitely if need be. Ingenious cut-away and cross-section sketches have been published, revealing vast improvements over the crude World War II underground shelters. The new shelters will have all conveniences, including hot and cold running water, refrigeration, and moving-picture theaters. But the sketches failed to explain how it would be possible to burrow far enough into the earth to avoid the shattering concussive power of atomic violence. They failed to tell what would happen to those underground cities once the exploded atom left an inextinguishable fire on the crust of the earth. If any imaginative sketches are in order at all, let us see some which can speculate upon the amount of fire and bombarding and atom-splitting a weary planet can absorb without being thrown off its axis or without reverting to its original incandescent mass blazing at millions of degrees. . . .

This is the multiple nature of the challenge to modern man—to bring about world government and to keep it pure; to keep his social, economic, and political institutions apace with his scientific achievements; to make whatever adjustments are needed in his own make-up, conditioning, and outlook on life in order to exist in an Atomic Age.

This is a large order, perhaps the largest order man has had to fill in his fifty thousand-odd years on earth, but he himself has set up the conditions which have made the order necessary. We can put on blinders; we can laugh it all off as just a false alarm; we can claim that talk of an Atomic Age is sheer fancy; we can protest that the threat of the destructive use of atomic energy is exaggeration, overstatement, hysteria, panic.

But all the manufactured calm and scorn in the world cannot alter the precise fact that the atomic bomb plus another war equals global disaster. Nor that the crisis is fast approaching and may be upon us within a few years unless we act now to avert it. Nor that this crisis is created not only by the explosive atom but by inadequate means of controlling international lawlessness. Nor that control is inoperative without power, that power is dangerous without law, and that law is impossible without government.

And if we reject the multiple challenge before us? And if we decide that we are not yet ready for world government? What then? Then there is yet another way, an alternative to world government, an alternative to change in man. This way is the second course. Absurd as this second course may seem, we describe it in all seriousness, for it is possible that through it man may find a way to stay alive—which is the central problem before us.

This second course is fairly simple. It requires that man eliminate the source of the trouble. Let him dissociate himself, carefully and completely, from civilization and all its works. Let him systematically abolish science and the tools of science. Let him destroy all machines and the knowledge which can build or operate those machines. Let him raze his cities, smash his laboratories, dismantle his factories, tear down his universities and schools, burn his libraries, rip apart his art. Let him murder his scientists, his lawmakers, his statesmen, his doctors, his teachers, his mechanics, his merchants, and anyone who has anything to do with the machinery of knowledge or progress. Let him punish literacy by death. Let him eradicate nations and set up the tribe as sovereign. Let him, in short, revert to his condition in society in 10,000 B.C. Thus emancipated from science, from progress, from government, from knowledge, from thought, he can be reasonably certain of prolonging his existence on this planet.

This can be a way out—if "modern" man is looking for a way out from the modern world.

Walt Whitman and the Peace[1]

by ROBERT A. HUME

LITERATURE is not, of course, simply a refined form of propaganda. To cite extreme examples, it would be shocking and mistaken to teach that the DIVINE COMEDY is an apology for Roman Catholicism, with nothing to offer the Protestant or non-believer, and that Plato's REPUBLIC is a classical hornbook for fascists, which democrats should at all costs avoid. Authors must be studied, books must be read, not narrowly for one special revelation but for their total message.

If this observation is distressingly obvious, I am willing to have it so in order to forestall the accusation that in what follows I am counseling teachers to present Walt Whitman as a special pleader for the democratic way of life, as one whose LEAVES OF GRASS is useful solely as a political counterpoise to IL PRINCIPE.[2] As almost any reader is aware, Whitman's book has a multitude of non-political values which the conscientious teacher cannot fail to point out. At the same time it is inescapable, I believe, that, besides being a work of strictly literary importance, LEAVES OF GRASS is in a sense one of the vital documents of democracy; and we are being recreant rather than scholarly if, fearing the unjust title of propagandists, we do not encourage students to be alert to its significance in this regard. In short, if Whitman can help this generation toward a rational and secure world peace, we must insist that he be consulted.

What was the basis of Walt Whitman's democratic belief? Part of it was, inevitably, his native inheritance as an American. He accepted the democratic principle with the same unquestioning exultation that he accepted life itself, and he could scarcely contemplate the deprivation of democracy and liberty except as being somehow proof of their vitality, much as he regarded death as proof of life.

Revolt! and the downfall of tyrants! . . .
The infidel triumphs—or supposes he triumphs,
Then the prison, scaffold, garrote, handcuffs, iron necklace and anklet, do their
    work,
The named and unnamed heroes pass to other spheres,
The great speakers and writers are exiled—they lie sick in distant lands,
The cause is asleep—the strongest throats are still, choked with their own blood,
The young men droop their eyelashes toward the ground when they meet;
—But for all this, liberty has not gone out of the place, nor the infidel entered into
    full possession.

[1] From *College English*, official organ of the National Council of Teachers of English, March, 1945. By permission.
[2] Machiavelli's *Prince*.

When liberty goes out of a place, it is not the first to go, nor the second or third
    to go,
It waits for all the rest to go—it is the last. . .

Revolt! and the bullet for tyrants!
Did we think victory great?
So it is—But now it seems to me, when it cannot be help'd, that defeat is great,
And that death and dismay are great.

Yet there is ample evidence that Whitman's democratic belief was not only
inherent and impulsive but deliberate. It had partly the practical, almost
cynical, basis that one discovers in DEMOCRATIC VISTAS:

We do not (at any rate I do not) put it either on the ground that the People,
the masses, even the best of them, are, in their latent or exhibited qualities, essentially sensible and good—nor on the ground of their rights; but that good and bad,
rights or no rights, the democratic formula is the only safe and preservative one
for coming times.

In this matter, as in many others, he is not particularly consistent. If in one
mood he can thus refuse to grant even guarded praise to the people, in another
mood (and in the same essay) he can cry:

Grand, common stock! to me the accomplish'd and convincing growth, prophetic
of the future; proof undeniable to sharpest sense, of perfect beauty, tenderness, and
pluck, that never feudal lord, nor Greek, nor Roman breed, yet rival'd. Let no
tongue ever speak in disparagement of the American races, north or south. . . .

Such a tribute as this is not unreasoned, for Whitman leads up to it by recalling the heroism with which his countrymen faced and fought the Civil
War. He is being more than patriotic, however; the tribute is tinged with
an emotional insistence that is, perhaps, in a sense religious.

Democracy for him [writes Canby] was also ultimately a religion, based upon
the spiritual worth of the individual soul, upon what he called identity, which lay
beyond analysis and had to be accepted by faith. It is this faith which gives passion
to his prophecies, and this faith which may very possibly account for the truth of
his intuitions.

To whatever extent this passionate element in Walt's democratic belief was indeed religious, one is tempted to agree with Canby that it is superrational and
that little can be gained by an attempt to explain its source. Certain aspects
of this "faith," however, seem amenable to analysis; and I propose briefly to
attempt that analysis here, not confident of full success but hopeful that even
the attempt may prove helpful to some who might be more willing to share
Whitman's high enthusiasm for democracy if only they could discover that the
enthusiasm had a "reasonable" as well as a mystical basis.

The analysis involves both practical observation and poetic realization.
Whitman not only recognized but deeply felt the inevitable physical distinctness of every object and every experience in the universe. Each grain of sand,

each leaf of grass—to take the familiar instances—is individual. It has its own conformation which presumably no other grain or leaf will quite match. Even should a miracle reveal a second specimen identical in composition and form to the first, an essential difference would persist: the two specimens could not possibly occupy the same position in space and time; and what is true of objects is also true of experiences, to whatever degree the two classifications are separable. To say all this is, no doubt, to tolerate a truism boring to the average person. Certainly the poet we are considering never got over a fresh, childlike excitement at Nature's refusal to repeat herself. As each object, and each experience, in the universe is distinct, so it has its distinctive significance and message. To the poet each item is itself a poem. It probably never even occurred to Whitman that a mere listing, a "catalogue" of items, might not appear appropriately again and again in his book, often in what would seem to be very little context:

The blab of the pave, the tires of carts, sluff of boot-soles, talk of the promenaders;
The heavy omnibus, the driver with his interrogating thumb, the clank of the shod
    horses on the granite floor;
The snow-sleighs, the clinking, shouted jokes, pelts of snow-balls;
The hurrahs for popular favorites, the fury of rous'd mobs;
The flap of the curtain'd litter, a sick man inside, borne to the hospital;
The meeting of enemies, the sudden oath, the blows and fall;
The excited crowd, the policeman with his star, quickly working his passage to the
    centre of the crowd;
The impassive stones that receive and return so many echoes. . . .

To Whitman each of these items is individual and important. "I mind them," he says in the same passage, "or the show or resonance of them." And the reader scarcely needs reminding that Walt likewise feels the distinctive significance of a host of other items, animate and inanimate—humble ones like fish eggs, moths, brown ants, mossy scabs of the worm fence, heaped stones, elder, mullein, pokeweed, fog, beetles rolling balls of dung, the quahog, the pismire, the tree toad, gneiss, long-threaded moss, the buzzard, the rattlesnake, the bat, the bull and the bug, dung and dirt.

Frequently, to be sure, Whitman pauses to assert his poet's comprehension of what he sees and hears. As he watches, for example, the circling flight of the wood drake and wood duck, he exclaims:

I believe in those wing'd purposes,
And acknowledge red, yellow, white, playing within me,
And consider green and violet, and the tufted crown, intentional;
And do not call the tortoise unworthy, because she is not something else;
And the jay in the woods never studied the gamut, yet trills pretty well to me;
And the look of the bay mare shames silliness out of me.

The sharp-hoofed moose of the north, the cat on the house-sill, the chickadee, the prairie dog, the litter of the grunting sow, the brood of the turkey hen— in all of these and in himself he sees "the same old law."

Do you guess I have some intricate purpose?
Well, I have—for the Fourth-month showers have, and the mica on the side of the
    rock has.

Thus, by suggesting a natural process of endless itemization and endless ac-
cumulation, Whitman leads toward the conclusion that the infinite universe
itself is a democracy. The items within it have each that same extraordinary
brand of generic individuality and equality that (to seek a parallel in theology)
we may attribute to the angels, each of whom, averred Aquinas, constitutes a
full species unto itself. As far as I can discern, Whitman does not contend that
men are more important than animals or plants or insects or even stones; he
writes mostly of men because, being himself a man, he must. And it is because each man is supremely significant that each can comprehend the supreme significance of another man and understand that the inevitable concomitant of universal individuality is universal equality:

    . . . What I assume you shall assume;
For every atom belonging to me, as good belongs to you. . . .
Whoever degrades another degrades me. . . .

This seems plain enough, but if one has doubts, let him go to the Preface of
the first edition of the LEAVES, where the doctrine is laid down in prose:

    The messages of great poets to each man and woman are, Come to us on equal
terms, only then can you understand us. We are no better than you, what we
inclose you inclose, what we enjoy you may enjoy. Did you suppose there could
be only one Supreme? We affirm there can be unnumber'd Supremes, and that
one does not countervail another any more than one eyesight countervails another—
and that men can be good or grand only of [in?] the consciousness of their
supremacy within them.

    We have thus, in the LEAVES OF GRASS, a book whose assertion of democracy
is not only an act òf faith, so to speak, but also an exercise in reason; and
hence we may doubly trust it as we turn to it, if not only with specific questions, then with those larger ones of right and wrong, of good and evil, of
vision and blindness, to which we in our generation must find correct answers
or perish. By such a book let each "plan for peace" be tested.

    The testing will not always be easy. Yet for each plan the questions to be
asked are the same: What attitude underlies it, and is it an attitude to which
our poet of democracy pays tribute? Very briefly, let me refer to four of the
many general suggestions now being proposed in the press and over the air
which may be developed into actual working plans for peace; and let me
indicate how, in the opinion of one person at least, they fare when tested by
Walt Whitman's poetic message.

    First, there is being suggested what I should call the peace of hatred. Ac-
cording to this suggestion, the Germans and the Japanese have proved themselves incurably evil and should be exterminated. If extermination proves tc
be not feasible, let us do the next best thing: let us annihilate their pretensions

to human significance by subjecting them to peonage or slavery. This peace of hatred is no doubt the kind that they would have liked to impose upon us, but that fact alone should convince us how bad it is. It fails under the test. In the pursuit of a false faith such as the fascism of some Italians, the naziism of some Germans, and the less vicious but still dangerous snobbery of some Americans, it is possible to turn one's eyes from the plain fact of human brotherhood as set forth by Walt Whitman; but the fact persists. Yes, even Germans and Japanese are people, though one does not flatter the human race by conceding that. We must treat them, certainly, as our defeated enemies, meting out to them the discipline which cruel human beings earn for themselves at the hands of their outraged fellows; we must disarm them and deprive them of what they have stolen; and we must insist that they do not start building for another war. But if we talk of their future in terms of wholesale massacre, of sterilization, and of serfdom, we are betraying our own best principles. Whitman has described in ironic terms the kind of world that hatred may be expected to fashion:

Let freedom prove no man's inalienable right! every one who can tyrannize, let him tyrannize, let him tyrannize to his satisfaction!
Let none but infidels be countenanced!
Let the eminence of meanness, treachery, sarcasm, hate, greed, indecency, impotence, lust, be taken for granted above all! let writers, judges, governments, households, religions, philosophies, take such for granted above all!
Let the worst men beget children out of the worst women!
Let death be inaugurated!
Let nothing remain but the ashes of teachers, artists, moralists, lawyers, and learn'd and polite persons!

Second, there is the peace of expediency. This contrasts in some ways to the peace of hatred, for it implies not the angry annihilation of our former enemies but their careful preservation—not for love, to be sure, but for what they may do for us. It seems to ignore the obvious point that if one wants to get things done for him, he is wiser to apply to those who like him than to those who hate him. Nevertheless, in the course of the war we have paid much tribute to expediency. In its name we have dealt politely at times with such long-standing contemners of democracy as Franco of Spain, Pétain of France, and Victor Emmanuel of Italy. We have conversed and jockeyed with these unsavory gentlemen while their respective peoples have undergone the ordeals of hunger and bloody death without even the comfort of knowing that the people of America are their friends. This policy has been a means of asserting, whether we have meant to or not, that under some circumstances we respect power and order more than fairness and humanity. Some Americans, both official and unofficial, seem easily persuaded that this repeated compromise with tyranny has brought us impressive practical rewards, and they become self-righteously vocal in defending it. They should read Walt Whitman and be ashamed:

I sit and look out upon all the sorrows of the world, and upon all oppression and
    shame; . . .
I see the workings of battle, pestilence, tyranny—I see martyrs and prisoners; . . .
I observe the slights and degradations cast by arrogant persons upon laborers, the
    poor, and upon Negroes, and the like;
All these—All the meanness and agony without end, I sitting, look out upon,
See, hear, and am silent.

Third, there is being suggested by implication what I shall call the peace of
good business, and perhaps I should link with it something that might called
the peace of commercialized science. The attitude underlying this suggested
peace is to be seen figured forth in expensive full-page advertising, some of
the cost of which might be more decently given to the Red Cross. The
message of these displays is, in effect: "See what *we* have done to win the
war! And see, too, what a wonderful life we shall enable you to lead once the
emergency is over! The genius of American business and American invention will join to produce every conceivable modern convenience: you will have
television, private airplanes, one-piece houses, shirts and dresses of fine-spun
glass, rocket-driven baby carriages, and robot seeing-eye dogs." Now few
of us are opposed to having our daily living made more convenient, but we
can be deeply disgusted with the assumption seeming to underlie these advertisements—that boys have serenely died on the battlefied so that you and
I may have a host of new machines and gadgets. We can be annoyed, further,
by the persistently implied notion that machines and gadgets are the test of
human improvement. Long after the present chaos has become order, if it
does, the complicated and appalling problem of making a third world war
impossible will still face us, no matter how rapturously new may seem our
streamlined daily existences and no matter how big an economic boom the
country may be enjoying. The immediate danger is, naturally, that we shall
spend our energies planning for our own physical comfort and neglect planning for peace. We shall think of ourselves and not of the other peoples of
the earth with whom we must live; or, if we do think of them, we shall do so
only in terms of the raw materials they can provide and the cheap labor they
can constitute. We shall not be able to think of them as Whitman did:

This moment, yearning and thoughtful, sitting alone,
It seems to me there are other men in other lands, yearning and thoughtful;
It seems to me I can look over and behold them, in Germany, Italy, France, Spain
    —or far, far away, in China, or in Russia or India—talking other dialects;
And it seems to me, if I could know those men, I should become attached to them,
    as I do to men in my own lands. . . .

Definitely, the concept of peace in terms of monetary profit and a more luxurious American standard of living fails under the test. We must determine
to live in mutual respect and comradeship with the other nations of the earth
even if doing so should mean that our standard of living must fall instead of
rise.

Fourth, and finally, let me consider what might be called the peace of isolation or of nationalism. According to this concept, instead of violently taking charge of our late enemies, we should turn our backs upon them, and upon our friends too, much as we did after the first World War. We should live to ourselves, with an important exception: most isolationists insist, hardly with sweet reasonableness, that, while we refuse to be on speaking terms with other peoples, they should continue doing business with us; that they should provide us with air bases and other desiderata; in short, that they should perform numerous favors for us but expect none. This plan would not be worth the tribute of mention except that it exists; it simply will not die. There are large city newspapers, there are senators of the United States, still engaged in a tedious, noisy endeavor to make us resign from the human race, to make us detest and suspect all other peoples—our allies no less than our enemies. Surely we realize at last that the course of isolation is the death-beset highway that we formerly traveled until we collided with a large object labeled "World War II"; and surely we are aware at last not only of the practical impossibility of such a policy but also of how it betrays democracy. Once more, let us turn to Walt Whitman for guidance that is not cheap and hasty and smug. From him we must learn again that democracy is an earth-embracing principle, not for Americans alone (though no one has ever loved America more than he), but for all peoples. As we plan and initiate the peace, we must each be able to say with Walt:

. . . I salute all the inhabitants of the earth. . . .

You, whoever you are! . . .
Health to you! Good will to you all—from me and America sent.

Petty Anglo-American Differences [1]
by THOMAS W. LAMONT

SEVERAL months ago, at a time when the differences in economic and religious views between Americans and the Soviet Government seemed perhaps a damper on complete cooperation on our part, THE NEW YORK TIMES was good enough to print a letter from me urging that, as Russia had again become our ally, as in World War I, it was vital for our own sake that we should render her all possible support. Our public no longer needs exhortation to work with Russia. The valor and unparalleled achievements of their armies, their indomitable leadership, have done that job.

Today the scene shifts. Now I am being asked whether I am not con-

[1] From The New York Times, February 14, 1943. By permission of the author.

cerned about a reported deterioration of good-will between America and Britain. My answer is—No. Under the pressure of great events, petty differences of opinion and approach are sure to arise. And we cannot expect two great and independent nations like the British and ourselves, both reared in the tradition of the utmost freedom of thought and of speech, to live together in a perpetual honeymoon. But on the fundamental issues we think and act alike. Because, however, a stable post-war world will depend vitally upon a consistent Anglo-American relationship, suppose we examine the situation.

Our first complaint seems to be about the British Empire. Its American critics strangely enough overlook entirely such aggregations of territories and peoples as, for example, the French, the Belgian and the Portuguese Empires, with their vast reaches and conglomerate peoples in Asia, the South Seas and the Indian Ocean, in Northern and Equatorial Africa. It is the British Empire that our American reformers wish to wrench apart.

In this connection Ambassador Hugh Gibson is letting me quote what he said only the other day: "The only trouble in Anglo-American relations is a question of definitions—in fact, the definition of one word—namely, 'empire.' In the minds of most Americans this word connotes a predatory government bearing down upon helpless peoples; whereas the British definition of the word is entirely different. In their minds it means 'a school of government that inevitably leads to self-government.'"

Now, like most of my countrymen, I am a regular Fourth-of-July American. I hold no brief for the British. They frequently, like ourselves, make grievous mistakes in judgment and sometimes in action. Yet can any fair-minded person gainsay this: wherever overseas either their flag or ours is carried does not the world find civil law and order existent, and also over the years a steady improvement in hygienic and living standards, a quickening in political self-consciousness, and progress in the Anglo-Saxon conception of justice for all?

In the history of the human race few peoples have shown an aptitude for the art of government. Let me add that over the last thirty years I have traversed the international highways somewhat, on one errand or another, and, though always on the watch for the "outs," I have ever been impressed with the intelligence and devotion shown by the British civil servants in handling vast native populations in bad climates and in good; the efforts for better health conditions; the diligence and sympathy shown in study of language and local tradition; the encouragement given to democratic procedures of administration.

Certainly it is not necessary to point out that the growth of the British Empire has over two or three centuries been a matter not of aggression but of gradual evolution. On this point let me commend to interested persons not only the late Lord Lothian's notable utterances, but particularly Sir Alfred Zimmern's volume, "The Third British Empire," a careful analysis of the growth and of recent years the rapid progress in self-government that the nations under the British flag have made.

It is merely the A B C of history to say that as far back as the time of Queen Elizabeth it was clear that the enterprising, fearless, yet on the whole peace-loving British people had to gain their livelihood largely through overseas trade. And because Britain has generally been able to maintain freedom of the seas, all the other trading nations of the world, including preeminently ourselves since 1815, have reaped the benefit of that policy.

So to those friends who, with seeming good-will, have suggested that the British slough off many of their dependencies and strategic outposts, may I ask these questions:

Where would the world be today if, in September, 1939, Gibraltar had belonged to Spain, Malta to Italy, Suez to Egypt, Ceylon to some Eastern power, the Falkland Islands to Argentina, and so on through the whole list of strategic outposts that are the pressure points of great empire? Where should we be without the bases England turned over to us in Newfoundland, Bermuda and Trinidad? The critics of the British are tireless in their denunciation of British laxity at Singapore and Hong Kong. But what they lament is not that Great Britain possessed these bases, but that she failed to defend them successfully.

If America herself has no intention—which God forbid—to take over by herself the safeguarding of all these critical points here, there and everywhere; if we realize that most of the local peoples are wholly without the means to defend their lands; if we know, as we do, that those strategic points are among the chief ends that bloodthirsty Germany and Japan have for years been striving to secure; then why in the world do any of us suggest the dissolution of the British Empire?—that empire for whose survival we prayed so fervently in the black days of 1940-41.

Yet, even in that dark twelvemonth when Germany's bombs blew Britain's cities to bits and invasion seemed imminent, how many of us Americans understood what would befall us if the British Isles fell to the barbaric invader? Not only would the strategic outposts have fallen, but Australia, New Zealand and South Africa—no one of them could have held out by itself. For today they constitute, in Sir Norman Angell's words, part of "an association which alone has enabled them to survive." Each part is dependent on the whole. That is why each one of that great union is today fighting with such loyalty and desperation.

And what plan do our anti-British friends offer for the preservation of our world interests and our own land, as an alternative to ever closer and friendlier cooperation with the great Anglo-Saxon nation across the Atlantic? If Britain were to be crippled, can we then lean securely on Russia? on China? on the other United Nations?

Certainly with Russia and with China we and the British must have the closest collaboration. Our only hope for a stable post-war world is for these, the four greatest potential powers on the globe, to work in harmony together with the United Nations. Both America and Britain are already committed to that course. But veritable continents, vast and resourceful, as both Russia and China are, neither has the sea power to give great aid in maintaining the freedom of the ocean highways. Of course that is true, too, of the other United Nations, courageous and determined as they have shown themselves to be.

No, at this critical juncture in world affairs, we are driven back to the lesson of history as we have read it for centuries. That lesson is: Without the power there can be no authority. It would be the act of madmen to demand that all backward peoples be promptly cut loose from their present moorings, and directed each respectively to construct a democratic state of its own, to fare as best it could in a world from which aggression has, through some unique form of gigantic international machinery—as yet existing only in the imagination—been banished, and the world thus set free from the thing it loathes.

When almost three years ago General Smuts wrote to me predicting that the war would "become world-wide and reach to the uttermost points of the earth," he added: "This is a gigantic struggle, a war in the souls of men, an immense conflict between light and darkness. Evil incarnate trying to subdue the divine principle in the hearts of men." (Then he added: "Much will in the end depend on the attitude and the action of the United States. The last reserves of our human causes are in your great country, whose fine inner impulses are known to me.")

If we visualize in those terms this great turning point in the history of the world, this crisis of war and peace that is confronting America and all civilization; if we understand the vital necessity of our taking the right turn and avoiding the wrong one; then we shall be the readier to overlook the lesser annoyances furnished by our allies, the ineptitudes or even the wrongheadedness at times of some of our English friends; remembering that we have our own idiosyncrasies and that our world policies for the twenty years following World War I were little to be proud of.

Further, let me emphasize that our British friends must realize that for such present-day surface differences as exist between us we here are not alone responsible. Let them search their own hearts. Let their public men and our own, let the private citizens of good-will of both our countries, seek out the causes of existing misunderstandings and find a way to correct them. Let the British also, if you please, have more faith—even if they feel that by past events it may not be fully justified—in our post-war intentions and in our effective cooperation.

At this present day of writing there must be upward of 1,000,000 of our Americans soldiers in training all over England, in Northern Ireland, and fighting side by side with the British forces. When they have fought the good fight and have returned home, can we imagine serious cleavages between our boys and those British Tommies? No, all such differences will surely have been left behind, forgotten in the great crusade to put an end once for all to Germany's century-old dream to rule the world. And those young Americans, those British, Scotch and Irish troops, will feel that they have all had a common and a glorious heritage, be it in the anguish and sacrifices of a Valley Forge or on the rain-soaked fields of Waterloo.

The American people have almost always been fighting in behalf of liberty —first, to gain our own freedom in 1775, then again in 1812 to keep it, to free the slaves in 1861-65, to liberate Cuba in 1898, to repel the Teutonic onslaught in 1917, and now again to preserve ourselves from German and Japanese conquest over us. As we look back over this century and a half, we can see the long muster roll of those countrymen of ours who in all these wars fought and died to keep men free.

Today in serried ranks they are standing behind our fighting lines. And who can deny that the invisible spirit of those brave and eager souls yet lives, that it is with our own soldiers and sailors and airmen today as they face the foe on land and sea and in the air? So, we Americans of all others can never forget that in the darkest days of 1940 and 1941 it was only British courage and the blind faith of free men that saved the world from a Hitler-ruled Europe, and a convulsion of our own American structure to its very foundations. Nor that England, already hard pressed and unprepared for armed conflict in the Far East, nevertheless declared war on Japan the moment Japan made war on us.

So I end on the same note on which I began: In the conduct of this war, of course, and equally in the post-war world, America's only salvation is to work in close collaboration with our British friends. Such policy is no new thing for us. In the last century, it was the British Government that, after the first enunciation of the Monroe Doctrine in 1823, stood firmly by us in the maintenance of that declaration of ours for the Western Hemisphere; then again later, in the face of the German Kaiser's promises and threats. Witness too the German squadron's attempt to interfere with Admiral Dewey at Manila Bay in 1898. It was a British admiral who quietly moved his own squadron in between and thwarted that effort.

Thus, whenever the outer world has turned against either of us, America and Britain have stood together. It was not chance, it was nobody's choosing, but an inevitability that in the great peril of Britain in 1917, and again in 1941 we finally were found fighting side by side.

Have we now learned the lesson? Or shall we insist on some other Pearl Harbor in another quarter century? Whether we like or dislike individual Englishmen, whether we think they are inclined to high-hat us or not, whether we look upon ourselves as innocents abroad and easy marks for the English trader—or, on the other hand, monarchs of all we survey; nevertheless let us remember that as long as the British and we pull together, not in a political union, nor necessarily with formal treaties; always with the collaboration of Russia and China and with a due regard for the equal rights of all other nations; with the earnest endeavor that at every point they should work as fellow-partners in our enterprise, that, I say, is our only chance of avoiding a repetition of today's tragic events.

And on neither side of the water let us take ourselves too seriously when

occasional differences arise between us. The mutual respect, the forbearance
and the understanding that we have for each other spring from common roots
deep in the past; roots so intimately interwoven and united in history that no
man can sunder them. We can work together because of our common acceptance of certain fundamentals—our instinct for justice and fair play, our preference for an orderly world where each branch of the human family may
work out its own salvation in its own way, our convictions that individual
enterprise and democracy are inextricably dependent each upon the other.

Finally, the English are the people with whom we share our fundamental
religious convictions. These beliefs of ours were brought to the New World
with our forebears at Jamestown and Massachusetts Bay. We have followed
the way as they followed it. We have looked forward, as they looked, to a
city not built with hands. We, like them, through all our vicissitudes, have
had this faith of the spirit that in building our own great nation of free men
we can help create out of the world's tragic present a noble future.

A Texan in England[1]

by J. FRANK DOBIE

I

SAILING west from the British Isles, I cabined with an English civilian who
told me this about himself: "I am sixty-one years old. I was born and
reared in Pennsylvania. My parents were German, with a touch of
Irish. I grew up in an atmosphere hostile to the English. In 1914, at the
age of thirty-one, I went to England, spent a night in London in the old
Morley Hotel on Trafalgar Square, and when I woke up in the morning
realized that for the first time in my life I was at home. I have lived in
England, never far from London, ever since."

I understood him. The impact of England was gradual upon my own
consciousness. I have known, in broken spells, harmony with my own en-
vironments the greater part of my life. I have known it best when I was
doing the kind of work I wanted to do in the way I wanted to do it; I have
known it with individual human beings; I have known it with nature—
more jubilantly perhaps in the vast and unpeopled mountains of western
Mexico than anywhere else. Before I went to England I never knew any
consistent harmony with what is called "civilization"—American civilization
as it is realized in cities, expressed in newspapers, blared out over the radio,
and otherwise proclaimed. I have never felt harmony with that civilization as

[1] From J. Frank Dobie, *A Texan in England* (1945), Little, Brown & Company. By permission of the author and the publishers.

it tries to flower, but generally balls, in American universities. Now, however, that the humanities are cutting loose from the German Ph.D. strait jacket, they may enjoy some freedom. To find harmony, I have had to flee the stridencies, not the strenuousness, the insincerities and blatancies of much that passes for Americanism. The ways of life that I have been in harmony with in my own country have not been typical of the vaunted "American way."

Many times I have thought that the greatest happiness possible to a man— probably not to a woman—is to become civilized, to know the pageant of the past, to love the beautiful, to have just ideas of values and proportions, and then, retaining his animal spirits and appetites, to live in a wilderness where nature is congenial, with a few barbarians to afford picturesqueness and human relations. The young Englishman Frederick Ruxton camping in the Rocky Mountains a hundred years ago with his pack mules, his Pancho horse and a lobo wolf, now and then seeing trappers and Taos Mexicans, while guarding his scalp from Indians, satisfies this ideal. According to it, civilization is necessary to give a man perspective; but is otherwise either a mere substitute for primitiveness or else a background to flee from.

Such an ideal was never practicable except to a few individuals who in retreating from society substituted camp fire for ivory tower. In this shrinking world, it becomes less and less practicable. It precludes the idea of a civilized democracy—though any democracy will be tolerant of nonconformists who draw off to one side as well as of those who march in the ranks.

Some thoughtful Englishmen fear lest civilization, accepting the popular American conception of civilization, will destroy their culture. By culture here I mean not only traditions but traditional outlook derived from the cultivation of mind, body and spirit. American culture is derived largely from frontier life, from space. Population, wealth, mechanical comforts and luxuries and urban living have already largely destroyed that frontier culture. Among tens of millions of Americans, civilization has come to mean the diffusion of manufactured contrivances. The disciplines that created old civilizations have certainly been in retreat against the advance of machine civilization. Machine civilization has not yet had time to demonstrate whether it can create a culture that gives graciousness, charm, depth and tolerance to human life.

In England I was for the first time in my life really confined to civilization—in the old sense of the word. Barring some inconveniences, I liked it. If at times I grew hungry for spaces, I readily found that cultivated nature gave me freedom and joy. Life in an old English college is subject to certain formulas. Yet that life came to me to seem freer of rigidities than much American life, either in or out of a college. This sense of at-easeness, of freedom, is hard for me to explain. Perhaps it depends on the presence of a tolerance made modest by centuries of custom. I believe that it depends also on the absence of propaganda and other forms of controls that big business in America has come to exercise or to try to exercise on all mediums of expression—an unannounced but pervasive fascism, reaching down into primers for infants and up into popular magazines too holy to accept advertisements. The absence of sinister designs, like the absence of noise, contributes to peace of mind.

At any rate, while England gave me serenity and a sense of freedom, it gave me a more critical attitude towards life. I suppose this is a concomitant of civilization. Matthew Arnold defined poetry as "criticism of life."

Under bombs both piloted and pilotless I have felt more serene than I can feel under the everlasting bombing by American avarice wanting to sell me not only goods but a dependence upon goods and calling its business "service," seeking to hinder the spread of truth and the play of ideas and calling its conduct "free enterprise." It is no wonder that young Americans, especially young soldiers, have become as distrustful of the motives behind truth as they are of the motives behind axe-grinders. Little in their training, either pre-military or military, has conduced to the process of clear thinking. Their "opiate" has been not the religion of a church but that of the National Association of Manufacturers. When their distrust brings to them more confusion than enlightenment, it serves their manipulators as well as ignorant trust serves.

"The trail is counter, you false Danish dogs," who restrict your fear of regimentation to government bureaus. We Americans have a promoted mass movement for loving our mothers—promoted by the sellers of gifts; another mass promotion for appreciation of dads, and yet another for remembering the dead. We have proclamations for clean-up week, for garden-planting week, for go-to-church week, for cutting-ragweeds week, for careful-driving week, and proclaiming governors, with the brains of adding machines, alone know how many other special weeks. Not alone our physical acts but our ethics and our very emotions are to be channeled, standardized, mass-formulated.

England, even among its crowded millions receiving war as well as making it, renewed in me a feeling for the individual. I go to a football game at home, and while I hear and look at the organized cheering, I remember the casualness with which a crowd in bleachers viewed a game of rugby between Oxford and Cambridge teams. Each of the loosely massed spectators seemed to feel as easy with himself as if he were fishing alone on a sunlit riverbank. The crowd applauded good plays on either side—without orders from any cheer leader to goose-step.

England gave me a fresh realization of proportions. At the American football game I have just spoken of, two bands paraded the field between halves—a truly colorful spectacle; but each played two local college tunes at which the crowds were expected to rise and stand with as much reverence as if the national anthem were being played. I like to stand for the national anthem; the music and the standing both make me proud and give me noble feelings and bring long memories. Every time one goes through the motions of saluting a bed sheet, the dignity of the salute to the country's flag is lowered.

One early morning I was in a Red Cross club at a bomber base in East Anglia where I had talked the night before. The only people in it were the Red Cross woman, three or four servants scrubbing the floors and washing dishes, and a big good-natured sergeant from Oregon. He wouldn't dance, the Red Cross woman charged him, but she thanked him for always helping decorate for the dances.

Presently he said, "Before the thundering herd comes in I'm going to practise at the piano." He spoke of how it would be possible to keep the British Broadcasting Corporation radio on all day without being driven mad by the advertisements and the "murder of silence" palmed off on the public as music. He said that a good many soldiers had come to prefer British news broadcasts because they are generally more direct than the American broadcasts, which often "seem to be trying to sell the news as well as something that the sponsor of the broadcast has to sell." He wondered whether the American people really want to be constanly "sold" on something. He said that he could make a clock strike twelve times every hour but that noon would still come only once a day and midnight only once between sunset and dawn, yet the radio people often try to make the clock strike twelve even on the quarter hours.

He might have added that if he listened to the B. B. C. clear around the clock he would be unable to hear a syllable from some brass-lined, steel-headed, metal-voiced, hollow-tile-hearted, data-manufacturing, conclusion-prefabricated commentator. In the name of free speech and free enterprise, Americans will stand more propaganda than any other people outside of Russia and Germany. A great many of them have sense enough to be impervious to it. It is probably good taste as much as good sense that saves the British from such sluices of not only sterile but fertility-choking lava.

II

"He valued 'suffrages' at a most low figure," Carlyle said of his boyhood schoolmaster, a Scot. Few Englishmen have the "you-be-damned sort of attitude" of one of Kipling's characters, but their national motto is not "We Aim to Please." "The Irish and the Welsh are difficult people for the English and the Scotch to know or to understand," says Margot Asquith in her wise little book *Off the Record*. "Their desire to please—though a lovable desire— does not commend itself to candid and simple people. You either please or you do not please; in any case, it is not of paramount importance."

It is of paramount importance that a person be candid, be what he is. Contrasting the two countries, Henry Steele Commager said that political democracy is farther advanced in England and social democracy in America. In agreeing, I would add that the working of social democracy in America has made an enormous number of Americans expend an enormous amount of energy and endure an enormous amount of uneasiness within themselves, subjecting themselves to constant financial strain, in order to keep up with the Joneses. More than once I have been embarrassed in England by the apology of some American sergeant or other enlisted man for not being an officer. I remember in particular a gunner whose chief contribution to the conversation at dinner was explaining how at his bomber base he did not have to salute officers. You would have to go a long way to find an English or a Scotch noncommissioned officer apologizing for his rank. In the realm of naturalness a solid red cow does not apologize for not having a white face.

The English belong in the realm of naturalness. I doubt if between the sexes one tenth as much effort is exerted by one sex to impress the other as in America. America has never coined an Americanism more expressive of the country's modern spirit than the special use of "sell" in such phrases as "sell himself," "sold on the idea," and so on. The average Englishman would shrink from the idea of selling himself; on the other hand, because you do not want to buy the article, he will not discount it a penny.

It is pleasant to dwell in the realm of naturalness. George Borrow did not want to wash in a basin inside the house. "I am a primitive sort of man," he said to Jenny at the pump, and doused his head under the stream that she pumped. Too much has, I think, been said of English bluntness. You will during one day in New York encounter more harshness—from elevator operators in public buildings, bus conductors, keepers of newsstands and other folk—than during a whole year in London. After a sojourn in wartime regimented England, Americans upon returning to these democratic shores note the incivilities of civil servants. The natural courtesy and unaffected kindness of the English made a far deeper impression on me than traditional bluntness.

"The way to get along with the British," a much-traveled friend counseled as I was leaving for England, "is to tell them to go to hell." I found no occasion for that procedure. The way to get along with the British is their own way of getting along with each other: Be yourself. The "go to hell" attitude is a holdover from the age that prompted James Russell Lowell to write (1869) "On a Certain Condescension in Foreigners." "It will," he said, "take England a great while to get over her airs of patronage toward us, or even passably to conceal them."

I doubt if any people can conceal "airs of patronage." An English attempt, on a national scale, to practise deception would be as ridiculous as Malvolio's assumption of the courtier's smile and cross-gartered yellow stockings. The fact is that the English in general have gotten over their patronizing ways. In *The American Language,* Mr. H. L. Mencken—himself probably America's largest contributor among sneerers—amasses all the evidence of colonial and succeeding times to show British contempt for and patronization of American diversions from the King's English. What George III's court said about the independence of the United States of America would represent current British respect for this mighty nation about as well as most of the Mencken evidence represents the modern British attitude. In British eyes America is full grown. The English do not relish domination by American economic power, but they have in their realistic way accepted the fact. They prefer their own slang to American slang; yet they constantly adopt vigorous, picturesque American expressions. They consider that they have a right to pronounce their own language in their own way. No newspaper, magazine or individual in their realm has become distinguished for being anti-American. They are in a position where they have to play second fiddle to America in many ways, but—considering anti-British feeling and talk among Americans— their tolerance and dignity are astounding. No, they are not shaking "that rattle" in American faces any longer. Of course, there are always exceptions to any rule. A few Southerners are still fighting the Civil War.

III

The leaders of a country may or may not be typical; when they are ample, they are representative. Lincoln was not typical of lawyers or of the citizens who elected him; he was vastly representative, compassing in himself many types and individuals. Harding was merely typical. The English have a way of electing to their government men more representative than typical. Individuals often drop out of the so-called "governing class"; individuals enter it from other classes. The "class" maintains itself only by virtue of the fact that the people composing it are trained in the science of government, are competent, and are responsible. One would have to read far into Hansard's full reports of Parliamentary debates to find an example of the moronic puerility exemplified in the *Congressional Record* almost daily. The English educational system is not equalitarian in the manner of the American system; it does not recognize every boy as a possible prime minister; yet it certainly does train leaders.

The Evening News recently printed a protest against a move on the part of London cabmen to elect one of their number to Parliament to represent cabby interests. A Member of the House of Commons, the protestor pointed out, should be larger than a "delegate sent by a sectional interest to plug that interest." In America we are used to two kinds of lobbyists; one paid by special interests to work on Congress and legislatures from the outside, and one elected—largely by special interests—to work inside. Parliament may have a few such members; they are not in the tradition of the British government.

Such legislators might at times be useful in performing limited governmental functions. They could never lead a government. They could never advance the civilization of a country and contribute to its culture. Yet the tradition of English statesmanship is the tradition of advancers of civilization and of contributors to culture. The amplitude of Churchill's nature, the prodigality of his wit and the compass of his imagination are hardly realized in his paintings or in his fiction, but they are suggested. Disraeli's epigrams may keep his name alive longer than his career as prime minister. Macaulay's work as historian and man of letters have already overshadowed his useful Parliamentary career. It was Burke's great mind operating in conversation, not in his sublime eloquence, that "called forth" all of Doctor Johnson's powers. The many-sidedness of Thomas Jefferson sets him increasingly apart from traditional American statesmen. Theodore Roosevelt has been the only president who might have written a book like Viscount Grey of Fallodon's *The Charm of Birds*—the kind of book one expects from the ranks of English statesmen.

Emerson observed in Walter Savage Landor "a wonderful brain, despotic, violent and inexhaustible, meant for a soldier, by what chance converted to letters; in which there is not a style nor a tint not known to him, yet with an English appetite for action and heroes." Byron was, in effect, a warrior; Shakespeare managed a theater. The soldier and man of action, Field Marshal Wavell, whose brilliant accomplishments in Africa, achieved with such slender means, were built upon by General Montgomery and the Allied armies, brings out with commentaries of pith an anthology of memorized poetry entitled *Other Men's Flowers*. Lawrence of Arabia translated action into spirit-riven prose. In or out of government, this mixture of the elements in Englishmen is constant. Whether it is owing to something racial, to long-absorbed Greek ideal of balance, to both, or to other elements, I do not know. I know that it both reflects and engenders richness of life. It is civilized.

It is the very antipodes of the powerful and persistent American doctrine that businessmen should run the government, also education, and that a poet like Archibald MacLeish is to be distrusted even in a minor government post. William Randolph Hearst buys art in wholesale lots, but somehow he has never melted the beautiful and the free into his own soul. The people running the British government have for centuries stood steadfast on the idea that government should secure capital; they have not been capitalists themselves, though many of them have been men of capital. They have never confused humanism with unfitness for active life, or liberalism with anarchy. John Locke, who died two hundred and forty years ago, perhaps best formulated the idea that it is the function of government to secure property. He had an immense influence on Jefferson, but when Jefferson nominated the unalienable rights of man to "life, liberty and the pursuit of happiness," he emphatically omitted *property*. In the Warren G. Harding prayer for "more business in government" flowered Jacksonian democracy's denial of the Jefferson idea of a civilization fostering liberal thought and humanism. The stark passion for stark business in charge of government will have nothing to do with the thinking and imagining class. Nor have the thinkers and imaginers of America compounded much action within themselves. No country has ever had more of idealism in government, but idealism flows in one stream and materialism in another, not confluently. The businessman's government, instead of adding sweetness and warmth and grace to national life, making it more fluid, has added barrenness and constricted it. This, even while democratizing material prosperity and manufactured goods.

It takes the human race a long time to adjust itself to revolutionary physical changes; the World Wars might be traced to the Industrial Revolution inaugurated a century and a half ago. It usually takes even longer for revolutionary thoughts to work home. Charles Darwin published *The Origin of Species* in 1859. Before that civilized man could look—historically—for perfection only in the receding past. There had been a paradise on earth, in the Garden of Eden—though the earth was very sparsely populated at the time. Profane historians conspired with biblical to place the ideal life far back, beyond recall.

> Then none was for a party;
>   Then all were for the State;
> Then the great man helped the poor,
>   And the poor man loved the great;
> Then lands were fairly portioned;
> Then spoils were fairly sold;
> The Romans were like brothers
> In the brave days of old.

The theory of evolution implied, in Darwin's own words, a belief that "man in the distant future will be a far more perfect creature than he now is, . . . after long-continued slow progress." At first common men regarded this theory, if they regarded it at all, with hostility, because it apparently contradicted something in their religion. Even after the theory became commonly accepted, it was accepted merely as theory, only remotely connected with man's daily life on earth. At last, however, the import of evolution is coming home. Better ways of living lie ahead, not behind. By taking thought, by employing science in its widest meaning, man can add more than one cubit unto his stature.

Few Englishmen, rich or poor, expect to go back to normalcy. Normalcy was ugly, like the word. Normal life ahead comprises something beyond what electrical fixtures can supply. The economy of the nation did not just happen. Man brought it about. Man can manage it so as to benefit from it in a more democratic way. Yet management does not imply a Russian break with the long continuity of English tradition. To find hope, English people need not migrate to a new world. They have the intelligence and the power to renew their own world. In other words, the British, the conservative English especially, have comprehended the meaning of evolution.

This deduction did not come to me from reading Parliamentary debates, though some debates on the Education bill, the Beveridge Plan and other subjects warrant it. It did not define itself to me anywhere in the multitudinous plans for rebuilding demolished cities and better utilizing the lovely country; yet many plans imply it. I probably base it more on the facts and enthusiasms encountered in youth conferences all over the land and on the spirit of promoting and receiving ABCA (Army Bureau of Current Affairs) among the young men and young women of the British armed forces. The air in England is not static.

IV

Thought is the weariest of all the Titans. Love has many times been explained away; I doubt if ever once it has been explained in. I did not come to like the English because of expositions about them. My liking must have sprung from English literature—and in the long run nothing else so represents the life and spirit of a people as their literature. There is no literature apart from imagination and the emotions. English people on their own good land and in their own mutilated cities were increasingly, so long as I dwelt among them, personifying for me English literature. In a way not intended by the paradoxer, nature followed art.

In a British port I stood on the deck of a lighter carrying many young English wives of American soldiers to the great ship soon to take them to unknown homes. The solemnity of saying good-by, perhaps forever, to their native soil and the wonder, with something of fear, of what might lie ahead were deep in their eyes and on the strained features of their faces. One very young wife said to me, in her low voice, "I know something about American men. I am married to one. This baby is his as well as mine. But I do not understand American women. I have never talked to them. Their voices seem so loud." Voices from a group of young American women on deck pierced the air. Surely the culture, or control, of vitality does not wither it. All sounds of nature—the source of vitality—give a normal human being feelings of harmony. A panther's squall is a lullaby compared with woman's shrillness. I recall often the soothing nature in voices of certain American women. I think that modern party-going has intensified the stridency of many feminine voices in America. At constant parties and conventions they raise and raise their voices to be heard over other voices. I cannot conceive of a more alarming sound than the blend coming out of a big room full of talking American women.

"Their voices seem so loud," the young English wife of the American soldier said, very low. Then, all at once, the representative tone of the voices of Englishwomen came to me. "She left an echo in the sense." But before I heard voices of Englishwomen in their native land, I knew, without particular realization, of their quality. Now on the deck of the lighter, what I knew came really home. Standing over dead Cordelia's body, the wheel at last having "come full circle" for him, spent King Lear said—and it was the last fine truth of life he spoke:—

Her voice was ever soft,
Gentle, and low, an excellent thing in woman.

Twenty years ago on the plaza in Santa Fe I bought an earthen jar from a Pueblo Indian woman. I bought it because it made me feel pleasant. It has a bird painted on it. After I had paid the woman her dollar, just at which time her husband came up, I asked her what bird the picture represents. She looked at the bird, she looked at her benign-featured husband, she looked at me, and then with a laugh that rippled into the sunshine she said, "*Es un pájaro que canta*"—"It is a bird that sings." I don't believe that any ornithologist, or any anthropologist either, could give the Latin name for that bird. But the Pueblo Indian was dead right, and likely she didn't know why.

It is a long way from Santa Fe plaza to a plane tree in a college garden in Cambridge, to Dartmouth House on Charles Street in London, to a certain cheer-lit home down in Suffolk—to forty dozen particular English places that gleam in my memory. The one thing that I really know about England is that it made whatever it is that is inside me respond in the manner of the bird on the Pueblo jar.

Dialogue on Gorki Street[1]

by JOHN HERSEY

YOU ARE sitting on a blue couch. A grand piano crowds you at your left. Before you there is a table holding a plate of dry mass-produced cookies, a plate of chocolates whose cups are decorated with insipid flowers, and a pot of tea now grown cold. A shallow black cardboard cone dangles from the wall in one corner: it is a speaker channeled by direct wire to Radio Moscow. The floor is good polished parquet. There is no rug. A huge cabinet for clothes stands in another corner of the room and a heavy wooden bed lies by the door. On a side table by the bed there is a devilish gnome made of painted glass: his red eyes and red tongue are lit up by little bulbs inside.

At the other side of the tea table sits a Russian writer of about thirty-five— Boris Semyonovitch Petrov, who already has behind him several successful novels and one smash-hit play. He is small, quick in his movements, with a round warm face, big eyes, high forehead crisscrossed by little wrinkles that gather around his eyes. He is animated, deep voiced in his speech, and often jumps up and waves his arms to act out a narrative, or stands silent to let a sentence simmer in your mind.

You have been talking for two hours on this winter evening. And now you ask this Russian writer something that has been on your mind ever since you arrived in Moscow: "Tell me. What do you think Russia wants? I don't mean politically; I don't mean the boys in the Kremlin. I mean what do the people want of their lives? How do you Russians feel now that the war is surely won? What do *you* want?"

[1] From *Fortune*, January, 1944. Copyright, *Time*, Inc.

Boris Semyonovitch, nibbling a cookie and apparently thinking hard, answers, "Let us talk about my play. Do you remember the rats in my play?"

"Yes."

"Here is why they were in the play: One night when I was writing it I was sitting on some packing cases in a little hut in the village of Chistopol. The Germans were advancing, it was 1941. The only light I had was from a crude wick in oil. I looked down in the great holes on the floor and there I saw sixteen pearls. I was fascinated. I went over to pick them up. They moved, they were rats' eyes. The rats lived with me all the time I was writing, so I put them in the play.

"I like peaceful life. My literary career has kept me very busy—I'm no exception; every Russian, no matter what his career, has been very busy during the war. After each play or book I write I am lifted up or thrown down: I become 'obscurantist' or 'a representative of socialist realism.' I am a farmer at heart. I would like to grow vegetables on a large plot of land."

You cannot see what he is getting at; so you ask in the direct American way, "But what do the Russian people want?"

He sits down and looks at you as if wondering about you. He says, "Have you ever been to the public baths in Moscow? No? Well, if you want to know the Russian soul you must go to the baths. Public baths are like social gatherings, like entertainments even, especially for simple people who do not go to theatres or read books and who in any case could never get enough entertainment. And there is something about getting absolutely clean which is very pleasing to our people. Some of us by the nature of our trade have to lead dirty lives. It is nice to get warm and clean at the baths, and to argue and laugh."

"What are these baths like?"

"Well, you go in and buy a ticket. Then you check your outer clothes at a booth just as if at a theatre. Then you go in a big room with rows of benches and undress and wrap your clothes up in a bundle. You go in another room with rows of basins and faucets and you wash yourself. Beyond that there are smaller rooms, very steamy and hot. In one of these hot rooms you take birch switches in your hand and you beat yourself until you tingle all over. There are devils in the public baths," he added. "Have you met any Russian devils?"

"Not yet."

"They are old men, very small and bent. Some are regular goblins, like the ones in Pieter Breughel's paintings. Some look like my favorite devil over there on the table. They make you slip on your soap—if you are lucky enough to have soap. They make your switches break off and hit other men in embarrassing places. They provoke quarrels between Russians."

All this time Boris Semyonovitch, eyes sparkling, face red, has been acting, hopping around the room alternately impersonating various devils and a man switching himself in a steamy room. He breaks off suddenly and asks, "Do you have any such devils? I think not. I think your devil in America wears very good clothes, looks like a prosperous businessman, very pompous, and is given an air-conditioned office in hell, I imagine."

"It is true that we had a moving picture recently called *Heaven Can Wait,* in which the devil was pictured much as you describe. But then the Allied air forces have gnarled little devils who upset the mechanisms of their planes and tease pilots. They are called gremlins."

"I am glad to hear you have such devils. That is very important for the future of the world. Such devils provoke quarrels but they also make people laugh. We are all going to need a sense of humor."

He sits down a moment, long-faced and silent. You wonder whether to ask him your question again, or whether perhaps he really is answering it in his own very Russian way. Finally he asks, deadly serious, "Have you ever worked in close intimacy with eight rats?"

"No, I can't say that I have."

He shudders and says, "I never want to do that again. You asked what I want. I want never to work near rats during a war." He pauses. "You must go to the public baths. In America you do not have public baths, do you?"

"Very few. They are mostly for men with hangovers."

"You have a tub and shower in most homes, I believe." He thinks again. "We will be like that some time. It will be a pity to lose the happiness and the devils of our public baths, but I guess it will be better. Yes, definitely we are determined to have a porcelain tub in every home. As well as a thing of which you can pull the chain."

Again Boris Semyonovitch suddenly changes the subject: "I am proud of being a Russian. The war has made me especially so. It has shown the inner qualities of the Russian man."

"That is true. All admire the men of the Red Army."

"I don't mean just fighting qualities. The world knows now for instance of the great progress Russian science has made. Your public may not know of our great Russian scientists, but your technical journals often run articles by and about Bogoraz, Kapitza, Burdenko, Krylov, and others. Russia is a force in the world of the mind. Every Russian is proud of that."

Boris Semyonovitch reaches forward and puts his hand on the teapot. He says, "Let's have some hot tea." He takes the pot to the side table by the bed. Beside the illuminated gnome there is a *pleetka*—a little round electric burner. He puts the pot on it. "Do you cook with *pleetkas* in America?"

"Usually not. In cities most people use kitchen gas stoves."

"Eventually we will cook on big electric stoves in kitchens. Yes, that is another hope I have—every housewife to have a kitchen with her own big oven and several burners."

He comes back and sits down. "Food will be better after the war," he says. "You and I sit here eating these nice cultural cookies, but for some it is not so easy. You have seen the little mesh bags that look like little pieces of fish net with which women go marketing? There is a slang name for

them. The women laughingly call them *avosska*. That means 'maybe bag.'
Maybe it will bring something home and maybe it won't. I want that there
should never be an element of perhaps in the market place. And I want
kiosks on street corners to sell something more substantial than the extraordinary trifles now sold in the open market—a little square of chocolate broken
from a big bar, a single cigarette. I want such abundance for the common
people that these trifles would no longer be salable."

He gets the teapot and pours. "What do you write with?"

"A fountain pen, usually."

"Let me see it." You hand your pen to him. He takes it and admires it.
"What a cultural pen! You know during the first five-year plan it was very
hard. Not only were there no fountain pens; the simplest things were lacking. And now again during the war it is not easy to get little things. After
the war we will have much more. This beautiful pen is guaranteed to last
you a lifetime, is it not?"

"They say some such thing in advertisements."

"I will have a fountain pen which I will give to my son and he will give
it to his son and it will still write."

The radio speaker in the corner begins to tinkle. As if reminded of the
war by it, Boris Semyonovitch says, "The other evening at the theatre I saw
a pretty girl with a maybe bag on her head—a snood you'd call it. I thought:
maybe she wants to catch a man in it. That was funny, and yet not funny.
She may not catch a man. Whole men are more scarce now."

"I know. I have seen men on crutches and armless in the streets in
numbers that shocked me when I arrived here."

"Our best men went into the Army. That affects our future in two
ways. The ones among them who remain will come home soon and put
some life in our bureaus and offices. But many will never come home. We
have a way of calling our apartments 'lucky houses' or 'unlucky houses.'
This one happens to be a lucky one. Out of sixteen apartments we have
lost only eleven men at the front."

Suddenly the radio tinkling stops and a deep, urgent, confident voice
booms out on the speaker: "Moscow speaks! Listen. Listen, citizens. Order
of Supreme Commander . . ." and the voice goes on to announce another
city captured, and that in ten minutes there will be a salute of twenty salvos
from 224 guns.

"Four nights in a row now," Boris Semyonovitch says. "These salutes
are a great tonic. We know our strength from them. It is a wonderful, unfamiliar feeling. For ten years we have been like a family living in a house
with an open door. On the threshold we could see the shadow of a hostile
man with a gun."

You say: "Many people in America have the idea that this new feeling,
this new sense of security, is making your country more conservative; that
your revolution has mellowed during the war. People point to such things
as restoration of some of the church's privileges, revival of historical pride

in Russia, strengthening of the family by the new divorce laws, and so forth, to prove that Russia is not so revolutionary as formerly. Do you think that is right?"

"That is all nonsense. Russia is still a revolutionary country and still a communist country. What is your idea of a ballerina? You think of her as a beautiful girl with twinkle toes and a dim mind, don't you? Do you know that the ballerinas of the Bolshoi Theatre have periodic individual chats which are called 'heart-to-heart conversations' with members of the party and they read and discuss Stalin's book, *On Dialectical and Historical Materialism?* Does that sound like reaction?"

As you are thinking that one over, there is a cracking sound outdoors, then a heavy boom which shakes the windows. Boris Semyonovitch says, "The salute." He goes to the window and draws the blackout curtain back. Snow is falling. At the next cracking sound the valley of Gorki Street before you is lit up by an eerie greenish light, and by craning toward the right you can see the splashing, arching light of scores of red and green flares. As they die away the rumble of 200-odd guns rolls against the window. The sight and sound are awesome. You say, "That makes even me—an American—feel elated and proud."

Across the street through the filter of green-tinted snow you can see a *gastronome, a mostorg,* a bookstore, a wineshop—bright modern stores with huge plate-glass windows, and behind the windows displays of many good things; you see also a building half repainted in clean yellow and white; and you see in the street a line of dimmed-out trucks and cars running through the snow and several bent-over women bundled up in padded cotton coats, cleaning away the snow as it falls.

Boris Semyonovitch says, "Look at that old woman stopping her work and looking in the *gastronome* window. Those hams and chickens and geese and roast beef in the window are wax, but in the light of the flares they look pretty delicious. You know this street gives a Russian plenty to think about. In the daytime on that corner over there a woman with a white apron around her overcoat sells ice cream out of a box slung over her shoulder. Red Army men and others stop in the freezing weather and buy chunks of ice cream from her for thirty-six rubles, and they stand right there, eating them very happily."

"Thirty-six rubles—that's more than six dollars!"

"Yes, but you know very well as soon as we can get more goods on the market those prices will come down. We have seen your drugstores in the movies and we are determined to have ice cream for all at fifty kopeks. And our drugstores will be like palaces. You have seen our metro. We will have icecream palaces like the metro. That is another hope I have."

"Aren't more practical things bound to come first?"

"I don't know. Maybe. In the daytime I see rows of trucks go by this window. First there will be a Russian truck—Zys. Then there will be a General Motors truck. I can't help seeing the difference: the Zys is square and chunky, and the other so streamlined and fancy. Zys is a wartime truck, urgently built square so the stamping machines could be hastily made, and partly of wood to save steel for guns. But after the war we will have nice cultural trucks as good as yours if not better."

Boris Semyonovitch lets the curtain drop and you return to the chairs. You say, "You have used the word cultural three times, applied it to things we would never use it with—cookies, fountain pens, trucks. What do you mean by it?"

"Our Russian culture is very important to us. I think perhaps it is more important than anything else. With us culture embraces much more than with you. It is more than Pushkin, Tchaikovsky, and Pavlova, much more. It is a good suit of clothes, it is cookies, fountain pens, and streamlined trucks. It is not spitting on the floor and not jostling old ladies in the metro. Nowadays it is kissing ladies' hands."

"You want to raise the level of this broad culture?"

"Of course. We are an ambitious people." He goes over to the piano and picks up a copy of *Pravda*. "Let me read you at random one of today's headlines: *Let us develop all-union emulation for fulfillment of the plan for grain deliveries ahead of time and for deliveries in excess of the plan to the Red Army fund*. 'Socialist emulation' is competition in the name of socialism —competition between man and man, between plant and plant. Usually emulation reaches its peak at the time of the holidays like the October Revolution and Red Army Day."

"Is there ever criticism of work badly done?"

"I should say. Look. Here is a wonderful article about a hospital for women called the 'Third Birth House named for Sechenov.' The other day a woman had a baby. Her husband was naturally very nervous. He called up and gave his name. The nurse answered very indifferently, 'A child has been born.' The father said, 'Of course it is a child. What is it? Boy or girl?' The nurse said, 'Such information we do not give out over the telephone.' The distraught father called a doctor of the same hospital. The doctor said, 'Your wife and child . . .' The father asked, 'What is it?' The doctor said, 'We do not give out information over the telephone.' Many hours later the frantic father applied to the Department of Public Health and they made inquiries, and by the next day he learned he had a daughter. The article ends with a single word: 'Why?' You can wager that hospital will change its tactics."

"Sounds as if you had some bureaucrats here, too."

"Oh, I think the worst Russian devils live in the files and telephone receivers of our bureaucrats. We will change that."

"But surely not everybody is fired with ambition for Russia?"

"You would be surprised how many. Of course, like any country we have some lazy people who don't want to do anything, and some fools too. But it is quite wonderful how many people want to make this the best country in the world."

"Is this all unselfish and purely for the common good?"

"Surely there is some selfishness. That is only human. I have a little *dacha* near Moscow. It is a little wooden house two stories high with nice carving around the roof. I have read in novels about marble mansions in your city called Newport. All right, of course I would like my *dacha* to be somewhat nicer so I could invite my friends to stay with me. But really I am much more ambitious that every woman in Russia should have one of your machines for washing clothes than I am for my *dacha*—and you could hardly call that a selfish ambition."

"Do you think we will be able to sell washing machines to you after the war?"

"We have great esteem for America. We admire your washing machines, your movies, your cars, your astronomical observatories, your architecture— and your spirit and frankness too. But it would be better if we made our own washing machines."

You say, "But surely America could help you start making washing machines by selling you heavy machinery."

Boris Semyonovitch says in a musing way, "You know we Russians hardly know you Americans. What we know we like but we know very little about you. We have a saying that you must eat a pood of salt before judging a man."

"Let's see, that's about forty pounds, isn't it? It takes a long time for one person to eat that much salt."

"It takes a long time for us to judge a person—or a country. It is all very well for you Americans to be openhanded and generous and unsuspecting. Do not forget that for many years our enemies have been right here"—and he leans forward and pounds with his hand on the back of his neck.

"Yes, you have had nice wide oceans on either side of you. We have had enemies very close to us. We have been like a ship in dangerous waters—the crew ceaselessly tense and mobilized." He says more calmly, "You see we have had to be pretty sure of our friends in Britain and America."

You say, "For our part we too feel we would like to know more about you. Don't you think that for a really permanent understanding we must have a free flow of ideas between our countries? We must have no secrets from each other. When you have eaten your pood of salt we hope you will be wholly frank with us and we certainly will be with you."

He says, "The Soviet Union has no things for which it is fighting which are necessary to hide. What we are fighting for and want for the future is that there should be no more wars like this one. If we now have to hide some small things it is only because of the cruel disorganization of the world. That's all.

"The world is before an era of knowledge. We will have great and terrible developments in science: we are on the eve of learning the secret of energy of the atom. We are learning the awful secrets of physical power. The world must be reconstructed on the principles of thought before these secrets fall into the hands of the wrong people. The riches and science of the world must be used for the good of man, not for the evil of man. We must go very fast to a rational world. I believe in Russia for such a world. That does not mean that all the world must be a Soviet power. Not at all, not at all. But all must think. All must realize how small the world has become. Every father in the world must realize that somehow he is the father of every child. I don't say all Russians realize this yet; I say they must and I hope they will. There are many roads to a rational world. I esteem other peoples' roads—but they must all lead to the same place and we must travel quickly on them."

Boris Semyonovitch smiles at you over the cultural cookies. "That," he says, "is most of what I believe and want."

Apology for Man [1]

by EARNEST A. HOOTON

ANTHROPOLOGY is the science of man. However, after nearly a quarter of a century of study of that science, I have decided that the proper functions of the anthropologist is to apologize for man. To some, indeed, it may never have occurred that an apology in behalf of man is required; to others, more thoughtful, it may seem that for man no apology is possible. Man usually either considers himself a self-made animal and consequently adores his maker, or he assumes himself to be the creation of a supreme intelligence, for which the latter is alternately congratulated and blamed. An attitude of humility, abasement, contrition, and apology for his shortcomings is thoroughly uncharacteristic of Homo sapiens, except as a manifestation of religion. This most salutary of religious attitudes should be carried over into science. Man should confess his evolutionary deficiencies and resolve that in future he will try to be a better animal.

I propose to offer two apologies for our species, the one defensive, the other penitential. The defensive apology in behalf of man pertains to his appearance, physique, and biological habits. The only proper recipients of such an apology would be the anthropoid apes, whom man sometimes claims as his nearest relatives. The second and penitential apology is offered for man's behavior—for his use of the gift of articulate speech, for his attempts to control nature, for his social habits and his systems of ethics. It is owed to man himself, to Nature, and to the universe.

[1] From E. A. Hooton, *Apes, Men, and Morons* (1937). Courtesy of G. P. Putnam's Sons.

APOLOGY FOR MAN'S PHYSIQUE: HIS NAKEDNESS

If you were a respectable anthropoid ape catching your first glimpse of a specimen of man, your modesty would be shocked by the spectacle of his obscene nakedness. Indeed, even to man himself it is a well-nigh insupportable sight, unless he be a savage devoid of culture or a nudist devoid of sensibility. For here is a mammalian anomaly which lacks the customary covering of fur or hair and displays only clumps and tufts disgustingly sprouting from inappropriate areas. What strange capillary blight has afflicted this animal so as to denude his body of the hairy coat which protects the tender skin from bruises and abrasions, insulates the vital organs, and prevents too rapid loss of heat or scorching of the tissues by the actinic rays of the sun? Why has man retained abundant hair only in places where it is relatively useless—such as the brain case, which is already adequately protected by a thick shell of bone, and the face, where whiskers merely interfere with feeding?

To cover his bodily nakedness, man has been forced to slay more fortunate mammals so that he may array himself in their furs or to weave fabrics from their shorn hair or from vegetable fibers, wherewith to make inconvenient, unhygienic, and generally ridiculous garments. On the other hand, in order to get rid of the superfluous and entangling hair on his face and head, man has been driven to invent many contrivances for eradicating, cutting, and shaving. The adult male White has experimented unhappily through several millennia, trying everything from a flint flake to an electric lawn mower in order to clear his face from hirsute entanglement without flaying himself. Each morning he immolates himself for ten minutes on the altar of evolutionary inefficiency, until, at the age of threescore and ten, he has paid his full tribute of some 3,047 hours of suffering—physical torture, if self-inflicted; both physical and mental, if he has patronized a barber. And even this staggering total is exclusive of haircuts.

We may dismiss summarily the naïve supposition that parts of the body have been denuded of hair by the friction of clothing. The least amount of body hair growth is found, on the one hand, in Negroid stocks which have gone naked for, presumably, at least 30,000 years and, on the other hand, in Mongoloids, who have probably sewed themselves up for the winter during a considerable part of that period. I do not recall the origin of the suggestion that human hairlessness was evolved in the tropics to enable man to rid himself of the external parasites commonly called lice. It need be remarked only that, if such was the case, the evolutionary device has been singularly unsuccessful.

Darwin noted that the female in man and among the anthropoid apes is less hairy than the male and suggested that denudation began earlier in the former sex. He imagined that the process was completed by the incipiently hairless mothers' transmitting the new characteristic to the offspring of both sexes and exercising, both for themselves and for their comparatively naked daughters, a discriminatory choice of mates. The smooth-skinned suitor would be preferred to the shaggy and hirsute. Thus Darwin, like Adam, blamed it on the woman. But abundant body hair in the male is traditionally and probably physiologically associated with an excess of strength and virility, and the prehuman female probably liked her man hairy. In any case, zoological studies of the habits of contemporary subhuman primates indicate that the female is not asked but taken, that she is passive and devoid of aesthetic perception. She does not choose but only stands and waits. There are other theories to account for this deplorably glabrous human condition, but none which would satisfy a critical anthropoid ape.

HIS BODY BUILD AND POSTURE

The second aspect of man which would revolt the gazing anthropoid is the monstrous elongation of his legs; his deformed feet, with their misshapen and useless toes; his feeble and abbreviated arms; and his extraordinary posture and gait. Beginning with the juncture of the lower limbs and trunk and avoiding indelicate details, a scrutinizing anthropoid would comment unfavorably on the excessive protrusion of the human buttocks. He would judge the architecture of man's rear elevation to be inept, bizarre, and rococo. The anthropoid gaze, hastily lowered to the thighs, would be further offended by monstrous bulges of muscles; knobby kneepans; razor-crested shinbones, insufficiently covered in front and unduly padded behind; hammer-like heels; humped insteps terminating in vestigial digits—a gross, spatulate great toe devoid of grasping power, lesser toes successively smaller and more misshapen, until the acme of degeneracy is reached in the little toe, a sort of external vermiform appendix.

Planting these mutilated slabs flat on the ground, man advances upon his grotesque hind legs, protruding his thorax, his belly, and those organs which in quadrupeds are modestly suspended beneath a concealing body bulk. It devolves on me to attempt a defense of these human deviations from the norms of mammalian posture and proportions.

Seven millions of years ago the common ancestors of man were already giant primates, perhaps as large as they are today. They were tree dwellers, who progressed from bough to bough by the method of arm swinging. Their arms were elongated and overdeveloped by this method of locomotion. Their legs were comparatively short and weak, equipped with mobile, grasping feet. When on the ground, these generalized anthropoids moved on all fours. At this critical juncture of prehuman and anthropoid affairs, man's forebears seem to have abandoned arboreal life and taken to the ground.

Tree dwelling is advantageous and safe only for small and agile animals. The newly terrestrial protohumans were now confronted with two alternatives of posture and gait: either to go down on all fours like baboons or to attempt an erect stance and progression on the precarious support of their hind limbs. The former offers greater possibilities of speed and stability, but it sentences its users to the fate of earth-bound quadrupeds, nosing through life. Bipedal gait and erect posture, on the contrary provide the inestimable advantages of increased stature, the ability to see wider horizons, and an emancipated pair of prehensile limbs. Here, forsooth, the ape with human destiny was at the very crossroads of evolution. He took the right turning.

Almost all of man's anomalies of gait and proportion were necessitated by that supremely intelligent choice. The quadruped had to be remade by dint of all sorts of organic shifts and compromises. The axis of the trunk had to be changed from the horizontal to the vertical by a sharp bending of the spine. The pelvis underwent a process of flattening and other changes necessary to adapt it for the transmission of the entire body weight to the legs. The whole lower limb became enormously hypertrophied in response to its amplified function. However, the most profound modifications were effected in the foot—at that time a loose-jointed, prehensile member, with a great toe stuck out like a thumb; long, recurving outer digits; a small heel; and a flat instep. The great toe was brought into line with the long axis of the foot; the lesser toes, no longer needed for grasping, began to shrink; the loose, mobile bones of the instep were consolidated into a strong but elastic vault; the heel was enlarged and extended backward to afford more leverage for the great calf muscles which lift the body weight in walking. Thus a mobile, prehensile foot was transformed into a stable, supporting organ.

Further, the seemingly grotesque abbreviation of man's arms becomes intelligible if one considers the disadvantages of elongated, trailing arms to an animal with upright stance and gait. The creature would be in continual danger of stepping on his own fingers, and, in order to feed himself, would be forced to move the segments of his upper extremity through vast arcs. Lifting his hand to scratch his nose would involve a major gymnastic effort.

HIS FACE, HIS TEETH, HIS BRAIN

Doubtless, to the superior anthropoid ape, man's most unsightly deformity would be his head. Wherefore the swollen brain case and the dwarfed face receding beneath bulging brows, with a fleshy excrescence protruded in the middle and with degenerative hairy growth pendant from feeble jowls? What of the charnel house exposed when man opens his mouth—the inadequately whited sepulcher of a decaying dentition?

Plausible, if somewhat rationalized, explanations of these features are offered by students of the evolution of the primate brain. The early primates were diminutive, long-snouted, small-brained creatures which ran along the boughs on all fours. The first step toward higher evolution took place when some of the more progressive forms began to sit up in the trees, thus specializing their hind limbs for support and emancipating the upper pair of prehensile limbs. These, equipped with their pentadactyl hands, could be used for plucking food, conveying it to the mouth, bringing objects before the eyes for examination, and general tactile exploration.

The greater the demands made on an organ, the larger it becomes. The movements of the hands are controlled by motor areas in the nervous covering of the forebrain. These areas expand in response to increasing use and complexity of the movements of the members which they direct. Greater use of the brain demands a larger blood supply, which in turn promotes growth. By tactile exploration and visual examination there grow up, adjacent to the respective motor areas in the cortical surface of the brain, areas which picture the movements of the parts concerned, so that the animal is enabled to visualize actions which are to be carried out and to recall those which have been performed. In short, this functional theory of the evolution of the primate brain assumes a sort of physiological perpetual motion, in which emancipated hands continually call for more nervous surface of the brain to govern their increasing movements and to store up their multiplying impressions, while the expanding and active brain, on its part, devises ever more mischief still for idle hands to do.

But what of our shrunken face, the remnant of a once projecting mammalian snout? The elongate muzzle of the lower animals is useful for "feeling," smelling, grazing, and fighting—mainly because the eyes are set well back of the biting or business end, thus allowing the brute to see what it is doing with its jaws. Now the emancipation of the prehensile forelimbs from the duties of support and locomotion permits them to be used for hand feeding and for developing weapons, thus relieving the snout of its grazing and fighting functions.

Just as increased function of a bodily part results in its development, so diminished use causes shrinkage. Consequently, the new utilization of the liberated hands results in a recession of the jaws. The dental arches grow smaller; the outthrust facial skeleton is bent down beneath the expanding brain case; the nose, still a respiratory organ and the seat of the sense of smell, is left—a forlorn, fleshy promontory overhanging the reduced mouth cavity.

However, some doubting Thomases among our ape critics may regard as futile man's attempt to correlate with superior intelligence that vast malignancy which surmounts his spinal cord.

APOLOGY FOR MAN'S BEHAVIOR: HIS GIFT OF ARTICULATE SPEECH

For at least 30,000 years, and quite probably for thrice that period of time, man has existed at his modern anatomical status. With this superior evolutionary endowment, what has been the achievement of Homo sapiens?

Man frequently distinguishes himself from other animals by what he proudly calls the gift of articulate speech. To an anthropoid ape the range, quality, and volume of human vocalization would not be remarkable. A gorilla, for example, can both outscream a woman and roar in a deep bass roll, like distant thunder, which can be heard for miles. Even the small gibbon has a voice described by a musician as much more powerful than that of any singer he had ever heard. In fact, one might conclude that an anthropoid ape would regard a Metropolitan opera star as next door to dumb.

The ape, unimpressed with the range and volume of the human voice, would nevertheless be appalled at its incessant utilization. Lacking himself, presumably, the ability to fabricate lofty and complicated thoughts, he would not understand man's unintermittent compulsion to communicate these results of his cerebration to his fellows, whether or not they care to listen. In fact, it would probably not occur to an ape that the ceaseless waves of humanly vocalized sound vibrating against his eardrums are intended to convey thoughts and ideas. Nor would he be altogether wrong. Man's human wants are not radically dissimilar to those of other animals. He wakes and sleeps; eats, digests, and eliminates; makes love and fights; sickens and dies in a thoroughly mammalian fashion. Why, then, does he eternally discuss his animalistic affairs, preserving a decent silence but once a year, for two minutes, on Armistice Day?

"But," I say (in my role of apologist), "human culture is based on the communication of knowledge through the medium of speech." Many competent anatomists who have examined the various fragmentary skulls and brain cases of the earliest known fossil men—undoubtedly the fabricators of some of the more advanced types of Pleistocene stone tools—have questioned their ability to employ articulate speech. I myself disagree with this view and think that man originated from an irrepressibly noisy and baffling type of ape. However, it seems possible that most of the transmission of culture was effected through watching and through imitation, in the early days of human evolution, rather than by language.

Although language is the universal possession of all races of Homo sapiens, the diversification of speech has been so rapid that the world's population from prehistoric times has consisted of many groups whose articulate and written communications are, for the most part, mutually unintelligible. Thus, whereas the common possession of speech might be expected to unite all men, the reverse is the case. Language erects more barriers than bridges. There is in man a deep-rooted tendency to dislike, to distrust, and to adjudge inferior the individual or group speaking a language unintelligible to him, just as he considers the apes lower animals because they have no language at all. Culture is now transmitted largely by language; and, the more groups differ in the former, the further they are likely to be apart in the latter.

Larger and more powerful groups attempt to impose their languages on alien folk with whom they come into contact. The consequent linguistic servitude not only awakens hatred in the vanquished but tends to destroy their native culture without giving them in exchange an understanding of or participation in that of the conquerors. Possibly, then, language has destroyed as much of culture as it has produced.

HIS ATTEMPTS TO CONTROL NATURE

Man is pre-eminently an animal good at gadgets. However, there is reason for doubting his good judgment in their utilization.

Perhaps the first chemical process which man employed for his own service was combustion. First utilized to warm naked and chilled bodies, it was then discovered to be effective for scaring off nocturnal beasts of prey and an admirable agent for the preparation and preservation of food. Much later came the discovery that fire could be used in extracting and working metals and last of all that it could be employed to generate power. In ancient times man began to use fire as a weapon, beginning with incendiary torches and arrows and proceeding to explosives, which have been developed principally for the destruction of human beings and their works.

In the control and utilization of gases, the achievements of our species have not been commendable. One might begin with air, which man breathes in common with other terrestrial vertebrates. He differs from other animals in that he seems incapable of selecting the right kind of air for breathing. Man is forever doing things which foul the air and poisoning himself by his own stupidity. He pens himself up in a limited air space and suffocates; he manufactures noxious gases which accidentally or intentionally displace the air and remove him from the ranks of the living; he has been completely unable to filter the air of the disease germs, which he breathes to his detriment; he and all his works are powerless to prevent a hurricane or to withstand its force. Man has indeed been able to utilize the power of moving air currents to a limited extent and to imitate the flight of birds, with the certainty of eventually breaking his neck if he tries it.

Man uses water much in the same way as other animals; he has to drink it constantly, washes in it frequently, and drowns in it occasionally—probably oftener than other terrestrial vertebrates. Without water, he dies as miserably as any other beast and, with too much of it, as in floods, he is equally unable to cope. However, he excels other animals in that he has learned to utilize water power.

But it is rather man's lack of judgment in the exercise of control of natural resources which would disgust critics of higher intelligence, although it would not surprise the apes. Man observes that the wood of trees is serviceable for constructing habitations and other buildings. He straightway and recklessly denudes the earth of forests in so far as he is able. He finds that the meat and skins of the bison are valuable and immediately goes to work to exterminate the bison. He allows his grazing animals to strip the turf from the soil so that it is blown away and fertile places become deserts. He clears for cultivation and exhausts the rich land by stupid planting. He goes into wholesale production of food, cereals, fruit, and livestock and allows the fruits of his labors to rot or to starve because he has not provided any adequate method of distributing them or because no one can pay for them. He invents machines which do the work of many men, and is perplexed by the many men who are out of work. It would be hard to convince judges of human conduct that man is not an economic fool.

HIS ATTEMPTS TO CONTROL HIMSELF

Man's efforts to control himself, individually and in society, might impel a gorilla to thump his chest and roar with laughter. Let us consider the probable reactions of the chimpanzee to familial functions as performed by modern man.

The ape child begins to fend for itself at an early age. An anthropoid would not understand the domestic custom whereby the young are maintained as economic parasites by their parents for two decades or more of their lives, long after they have reached sexual maturity and adult size.

In ape society a young male does not acquire a mate until he is able to take her by beating off his rivals and to make good his possession. The female is, of course, always self-supporting. The situation of the young man who could not marry his girl because they couldn't live with her folks because her folks were still living with their folks, would not arise in anthropoid society. Apes appear to manage the number of their progeny with such discretion that no mother produces new offspring while she is still burdened with the care of previous infants. Furthermore, the size of any ape group seems to be restricted by the ability of its members to gain a livelihood, whereas, in human society, the less economically capable the group, the more numerous the offspring.

Again, the weak, sickly, and constitutionally unfit among the anthropoid apes are eliminated, either through neglect or deliberately. This is doubtless because our cousins are insufficiently intelligent to have developed those humanitarian sentiments which demand the preservation of life, however painful it is to its possessors and however useless to society.

A critic who had surveyed the great advances which man has made in his material culture might examine with high expectation the extent to which he has applied his intelligence to the improvement of his health and biological status.

The ordinary animal tries to protract his individual existence only by eating, running away, and hiding and his species' existence by breeding and by some exercise of parental care. Primitive man has added another preservative—medical care. The medical science of the savage is, however, compounded of magic and superstition and includes few remedies of actual value. The doctor at the primitive stage of culture kills oftener than he cures. He merely adds to the strain, on a long-suffering organism, exerted by the pressure of a ruthless natural selection.

Medical skill was a negligible factor in the increase of human populations up to the last century, even in the most civilized societies. Now, however, advance in medical knowledge, together with public hygiene and sanitation, has radically reduced the mortality at the beginning of the life span and literally has taken the graves out from under the feet of the aging. In the United States the death rate during the first year of males born alive has been reduced from 12.7 per cent to 6.2 per cent in 30 years, and the expectation of life has increased since the beginning of the century from 48 to 59 years for males and from 51 to 63 years for females. Short of homicide, a man has practically no chance of outliving his wife; females, after attaining a certain age, become almost immortal.

Now it is perfectly obvious to intelligent judges of man's behavior that this preservation and prolongation of life largely increases the proportion among the living population of the constitutionally inferior—the lame, the halt, and the blind. It also makes for a world peopled increasingly with the immature and the senile—those who have not yet developed their mental powers and their judgment and those who are in process of losing both. If medical science were able to make whole the bodies and minds it preserves, one might find little to criticize in the age shift in the composition of the population. But it is unfortunately true that we have succeeded all too well in keeping the engine running but have been quite unable to repair the steering gear. Since the immature are not granted a voice in the government and the decrepit are not denied it, we may expect ever-increasing social ructions, as a result of senile decay dominating dementia praecox in a world of diminishing average intelligence.

One of the human institutions for which apology is required is government. Undoubtedly an anthropoid ape would appreciate and understand government by dictatorship; he might even realize the advantages of a communistic regime. But a superhuman critic of man's affairs would be puzzled by a democracy. He would have to be informed that democracy involves the essential principle that all law-abiding adults have equal rights and privileges and an equal voice in government. Such a democratic government should imply an approximate parity of intelligence in the electorate or a majority of individuals of superior intelligence, if it is to function capably and successfully. There can be no miracle whereby the group intelligence transcends the possibly moronic mean of its constituent members.

Now, on the whole, there is a marked positive association between bodily health and mental health. A ten-year study of American criminals and insane has convinced me that there is an even stronger correlation between mental and social inadequacy and biological inferiority. Since civilized men are preserving the unfit in body, it follows that they are depreciating their intelligence currency.

Judges of human behavior, examining modern warfare, would probably reason as follows "Men are too soft-hearted to keep their populations down to the right numbers by birth control or infanticide. Therefore, when the weak, the unfit, and the useless grow to adult years and become a menace to the common good, nations conspire mutually to start patriotic crusades, whereby their superfluous and inferior populations destroy each other in a high atmosphere of heroism and devotion to public duty."

As the protagonist of the human race, I must admit that in warfare, on the contrary, we select as the victims not the bodily and mentally unfit but those adjudged to be the flower of each nation. Nor do I know how to answer the retort that man's right hand certainly does not know what his left hand is doing, when with the one he preserves the worst of his kind and with the other destroys the best.

I ought probably to try to divert attention from this issue by descanting on the grandeur of human conceptions of justice, the sanctity of the law, and the efficiency of the police systems organized to prevent its infraction; how we regard the criminal not as a vicious brute to be exterminated but as a wayward or sick child to be rehabilitated and cured by patient and loving care. I ought to tell how, at each Christmas season, our wise and noble governors bestow on their happy States the priceless gift of a goodly parcel of liberated murderers, thieves, and other convicted felons.

Such a plea would nauseate an ape. For no animal society tolerates the outlaw. The anti-social animal is killed or driven out. Judges of superior intelligence, however, would put some pertinent questions:

"Is it not true that a liberal education at the public expense has long been extended to nearly every class of person in the United States?

"Is it true that the noble-spirited, who formerly concerned themselves with the salvation of men's souls, are now no longer attempting to prepare men for heaven but rather to rescue them from a very present hell?

"Has not the treatment of the delinquent been improved until now it almost may be said that the convicted felon receives more social consideration than the law-abiding working man?

"Does not crime still increase enormously, and the discharged convict continue to return to his crime like a dog to his vomit?

"Is it not therefore apparent, in the light of the evidence you have presented, that modern man is selling his biological birthright for a mess of morons, that the voice may be the voice of democracy but the hands are the hands of apes?"

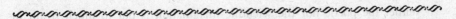

Evolution and Ethics[1]

by THOMAS HENRY HUXLEY

T HERE is a delightful child's story, known by the title of "Jack and the Bean-stalk," with which my contemporaries who are present will be familiar. But so many of our grave and reverend juniors have been brought up on severer intellectual diet, and, perhaps, have become acquainted with fairyland only through primers of comparative mythology, that it may be needful to give an outline of the tale. It is a legend of a bean-plant, which grows and grows until it reaches the high heavens and there spreads out into a vast canopy of foliage. The hero, being moved to climb the stalk, discovers that the leafy expanse supports a world composed of the same elements as that below, but yet strangely new; and his adventures there, on which I may not dwell, must have completely changed his views of the nature of things; though the story, not having been composed by, or for, philosophers, has nothing to say about views.

My present enterprise has a certain analogy to that of the daring adven-

---

[1] From T. H. Huxley, *Evolution and Ethics* (1893). By permission of D. Appleton-Century Co.

turer. I beg you to accompany me in an attempt to reach a world which, to many, is probably strange, by the help of a bean. It is, as you know, a simple, inert-looking thing. Yet, if planted under proper conditions, of which sufficient warmth is one of the most important, it manifests active powers of a very remarkable kind. A small green seedling emerges, rises to the surface of the soil, rapidly increases in size and, at the same time, undergoes a series of metamorphoses which do not excite our wonder as much as those which meet us in legendary history, merely because they are to be seen every day and all day long.

By insensible steps, the plant builds itself up into a large and various fabric of root, stem, leaves, flowers, and fruit, every one moulded within and without in accordance with an extremely complex but, at the same time, minutely defined pattern. In each of these complicated structures, as in their smallest constituents, there is an immanent energy which, in harmony with that resident in all the others, incessantly works towards the maintenance of the whole and the efficient performance of the part which it has to play in the economy of nature. But no sooner has the edifice, reared with such exact elaboration, attained completeness, than it begins to crumble. By degrees, the plant withers and disappears from view, leaving behind more or fewer apparently inert and simple bodies, just like the bean from which it sprang; and, like it, endowed with the potentiality of giving rise to a similar cycle of manifestations.

Neither the poetic nor the scientific imagination is put to much strain in the search after analogies with this process of going forth and, as it were, returning to the starting-point. It may be likened to the ascent and descent of a slung stone, or the course of an arrow along its trajectory. Or we may say that the living energy takes first an upward and then a downward road. Or it may seem preferable to compare the expansion of the germ into the full-grown plant, to the unfolding of a fan, or to the rolling forth and widening of a stream; and thus to arrive at the conception of "development," or "evolution." Here, as elsewhere, names are "noise and smoke"; the important point is to have a clear and adequate conception of the fact signified by a name. And, in this case, the fact is the Sisyphæan process, in the course of which, the living and growing plant passes from the relative simplicity and latent potentiality of the seed to the full epiphany of a highly differentiated type, thence to fall back to simplicity and potentiality.

The value of a strong intellectual grasp of the nature of this process lies in the circumstance that what is true of the bean is true of living things in general. From very low forms up to the highest—in the animal no less than in the vegetable kingdom—the process of life presents the same appearance of cyclical evolution. Nay, we have but to cast our eyes over the rest of the world and cyclical change presents itself on all sides. It meets us in the water that flows to the sea and returns to the springs; in the heavenly bodies that wax and wane, go and return to their places; in the inexorable sequence of the ages of man's life; in that successive rise, apogee, and fall of dynasties and of states which is the most prominent topic of civil history.

As no man fording a swift stream can dip his foot twice into the same water, so no man can, with exactness, affirm of anything in the sensible world that it is. As he utters the words, nay, as he thinks them, the predicate ceases to be applicable; the present has become the past; the "is" should be "was." And the more we learn of the nature of things, the more evident is it that what we call rest is only unperceived activity; that seeming peace is silent but strenuous battle. In every part, at every moment, the state of the cosmos is the expression of a transitory adjustment of contending forces; a scene of strife, in which all the combatants fall in turn. What is true of each part, is true of the whole. Natural knowledge tends more and more to the conclusion that "all the choir of heaven and furniture of the earth" are the transitory forms of parcels of cosmic substance wending along the road of evolution, from nebulous potentiality, through endless growths of sun and planet and satellite; through all varieties of matter; through infinite diversities of life and thought; possibly, through modes of being of which we neither have a conception, nor are competent to form any, back to the indefinable latency from which they arose. Thus the most obvious attribute of the cosmos is its impermanence. It assumes the aspect not so much of a permanent entity as of a changeful process in which naught endures save the flow of energy and the rational order which pervades it.

We have climbed our bean-stalk and have reached a wonderland in which the common and the familiar become things new and strange. In the exploration of the cosmic process thus typified, the highest intelligence of man finds inexhaustible employment; giants are subdued to our service; and the spiritual affections of the contemplative philosopher are engaged by beauties worthy of eternal constancy.

But there is another aspect of the cosmic process, so perfect as a mechanism, so beautiful as a work of art. Where the cosmopoietic energy works through sentient beings, there arises, among its other manifestations, that which we call pain or suffering. This baleful product of evolution increases in quantity and in intensity, with advancing grades of animal organization, until it attains its highest level in man. Further, the consummation is not reached in man, the mere animal; nor in man, the whole or half savage; but only in man, the member of an organized polity. And it is a necessary consequence of his attempt to live in this way; that is, under those conditions which are essential to the full development of his noblest powers.

Man, the animal, in fact, has worked his way to the headship of the sentient world, and has become the superb animal which he is, in virtue of his success in the struggle for existence. The conditions having been of a certain order, man's organization has adjusted itself to them better than that of his competitors in the cosmic strife. In the case of mankind, the self-assertion, the unscrupulous seizing upon all that can be grasped, the tenacious holding of all that can be kept, which constitute the essence of the struggle for exist-ence, have answered. For his successful progress, through the savage state, man has been largely indebted to those qualities which he shares with the ape and the tiger; his exceptional physical organization; his cunning, his sociabil-ity, his curiosity, and his imitativeness; his ruthless and ferocious destructive-ness when his anger is roused by opposition.

But, in proportion as men have passed from anarchy to social organization, and in proportion as civilization has grown in worth, these deeply ingrained serviceable qualities have become defects. After the manner of successful persons, civilized man would gladly kick down the ladder by which he has climbed. He would be only too pleased to see "the ape and tiger die." But they decline to suit his convenience; and the unwelcome intrusion of these boon companions of his hot youth into the ranged existence of civil life adds pains and griefs, innumerable and immeasurably great, to those which the cosmic process necessarily brings on the mere animal. In fact, civilized man brands all these ape and tiger promptings with the name of sins; he punishes many of the acts which flow from them as crimes; and, in extreme cases, he does his best to put an end to the survival of the fittest of former days by axe and rope.

I have said that civilized man has reached this point; the assertion is perhaps too broad and general; I had better put it that ethical man has attained thereto. The science of ethics professes to furnish us with a reasoned rule of life; to tell us what is right action and why it is so. Whatever differences of opinion may exist among experts there is a general consensus that the ape and tiger methods of the struggle for existence are not reconcilable with sound ethical principles.

The hero of our story descended the bean-stalk, and came back to the common world, where fare and work were alike hard; where ugly competitors were much commoner than beautiful princesses; and where the everlasting battle with self was much less sure to be crowned with victory than a turn-to with a giant. We have done the like. Thousands upon thousands of our fellows, thousands of years ago, have preceded us in finding themselves face to face with the same dread problem of evil. They also have seen that the cosmic process is evolution; that it is full of wonder, full of beauty, and, at the same time, full of pain. They have sought to discover the bearing of these great facts on ethics; to find out whether there is, or is not, a sanction for morality in the ways of the cosmos.

Theories of the universe, in which the conception of evolution plays a leading part, were extant at least six centuries before our era. Certain knowl-edge of them, in the fifth century, reaches us from localities as distant as the valley of the Ganges and the Asiatic coasts of the Ægean. To the early philosophers of Hindostan, no less than to those of Ionia, the salient and characteristic feature of the phenomenal world was its changefulness; the unresting flow of all things, through birth to visible being and thence to not being, in which they could discern no sign of a beginning and for which they saw no prospect of an ending. It was no less plain to some of these antique forerunners of modern philosophy that suffering is the badge of all the tribe of sentient things; that it is no accidental accompaniment, but an essential constituent of the cosmic process. The energetic Greek might find fierce joys in a world in which "strife is father and king"; but the old Aryan spirit was subdued to quietism in the Indian sage; the mist of suffering which spread over humanity hid everything else from his view; to him life was one with suffering, and suffering with life.

In Hindostan, as in Ionia, a period of relatively high and tolerably stable civilization had succeeded long ages of semi-barbarism and struggle. Out of wealth and security had come leisure and refinement, and, close at their heels, had followed the malady of thought. To the struggle for bare existence, which never ends, though it may be alleviated and partially disguised for a fortunate few, succeeded the struggle to make existence intelligible and to bring the order of things into harmony with the moral sense of man, which also never ends, but, for the thinking few, becomes keener with every increase of knowledge and with every step towards the realization of a worthy ideal of life.

Two thousand five hundred years ago, the value of civilization was as apparent as it is now; then, as now, it was obvious that only in the garden of an orderly polity can the finest fruits humanity is capable of bearing be produced. But it had also become evident that the blessings of culture were not unmixed. The garden was apt to turn into a hothouse. The stimulation of the senses, the pampering of the emotions, endlessly multiplied the sources of pleasure. The constant widening of the intellectual field indefinitely extended the range of that especially human faculty of looking before and after, which adds to the fleeting present those old and new worlds of the past and the future, wherein men dwell the more the higher their culture. But that very sharpening of the sense and that subtle refinement of emotion, which brought such a wealth of pleasures, were fatally attended by a proportional enlargement of the capacity for suffering; and the divine faculty of imagination, while it created new heavens and new earths, provided them with the corresponding hells of futile regret for the past and morbid anxiety for the future. Finally, the inevitable penalty of over-stimulation, exhaustion, opened the gates of civilization to its great enemy, ennui; the stale and flat weariness when man delights not, nor woman neither; when all things are vanity and vexation; and life seems not worth living except to escape the bore of dying.

Even purely intellectual progress brings about its revenges. Problems settled in a rough and ready way by rude men, absorbed in action, demand renewed attention and show themselves to be still unread riddles when men have time to think. The beneficent demon, doubt, whose name is Legion, and who dwells amongst the tombs of old faiths, enters into mankind and thenceforth refuses to be cast out. Sacred customs, venerable dooms of ancestral wisdom, hallowed by tradition and professing to hold good for all time, are put to the question. Cultured reflection asks for their credentials; judges them by its own standards; finally, gathers those of which it approves into ethical systems, in which the reasoning is rarely much more than a decent pretext for the adoption of foregone conclusions.

One of the oldest and most important elements in such systems is the conception of justice. Society is impossible unless those who are associated agree to observe certain rules of conduct towards one another; its stability depends on the steadiness with which they abide by that agreement; and, so far as they waver, that mutual trust which is the bond of society is weakened or destroyed. Wolves could not hunt in packs except for the real, though unexpressed, understanding that they should not attack one another during the chase. The most rudimentary polity is a pack of men living under the like tacit, or expressed, understanding; and having made the very important advance upon wolf society, that they agree to use the force of the whole body against individuals who violate it and in favour of those who observe it. This observance of a common understanding, with the consequent distribution of punishments and rewards according to accepted rules, received the name of justice, while the contrary was called injustice. Early ethics did not take much note of the animus of the violator of the rules. But civilization could not advance far, without the establishment of a capital distinction between the case of involuntary and that of wilful misdeed; between a merely wrong action and a guilty one. And, with increasing refinement of moral appreciation, the problem of desert, which arises out of this distinction, acquired more and more theoretical and practical importance. If life must be given for life, yet it was recognized that the unintentional slayer did not altogether deserve death; and, by a sort of compromise between the public and the private conception of justice, a sanctuary was provided in which he might take refuge from the avenger of blood.

The idea of justice thus underwent a gradual sublimation from punishment and reward according to acts, to punishment and reward according to desert, or, in other words, according to motive. Righteousness, that is, action from right motive, not only became synonymous with justice, but the positive constituent of innocence and the very heart of goodness.

Now when the ancient sage, whether Indian or Greek, who had attained to this conception of goodness, looked the world, and especially human life, in the face, he found it as hard as we do to bring the course of evolution into harmony with even the elementary requirements of the ethical ideal of the just and the good.

If there is one thing plainer than another, it is that neither the pleasures nor the pains of life, in the merely animal world, are distributed according to desert; for it is admittedly impossible for the lower orders of sentient beings to deserve either the one or the other. If there is a generalization from the facts of human life which has the assent of thoughtful men in every age and country, it is that the violator of ethical rules constantly escapes the punishment which he deserves; that the wicked flourishes like a green bay tree, while the righteous begs his bread; that the sins of the fathers are visited upon the children; that, in the realm of nature, ignorance is punished just as severely as wilful wrong; and that thousands upon thousands of innocent beings suffer for the crime, or the unintentional trespass of one.

Greek and Semite and Indian are agreed upon this subject. The book of Job is at one with the "Works and Days" and the Buddhist Sutras; the Psalmist and the Preacher of Israel, with the Tragic Poets of Greece. What is a more common motive of the ancient tragedy in fact, than the unfathomable injustice of the nature of things; what is more deeply felt to be true than its presentation of the destruction of the blameless by the work of his own hands, or by the fatal operation of the sins of others? Surely Œdipus was pure of heart; it was the natural sequence of events—the cosmic process—which drove him, in all innocence, to slay his father and become the husband of his mother, to the desolation of his people and his own headlong ruin. Or to step, for a moment, beyond the chronological limits I have set myself, what constitutes the sempiternal attraction of Hamlet but the appeal to deepest experience of that history of a no less blameless dreamer, dragged, in spite of himself, into a world out of joint; involved in a tangle of crime and misery, created by one of the prime agents of the cosmic process as it works in and through man?

Thus, brought before the tribunal of ethics, the cosmos might well seem to stand condemned. The conscience of man revolted against the moral indifference of nature, and the microcosmic atom should have found the illimitable macrocosm guilty. But few, or none, ventured to record that verdict.

In the great Semitic trial of this issue, Job takes refuge in silence and submission; the Indian and the Greek, less wise perhaps, attempt to reconcile the irreconcilable and plead for the defendant. To this end, the Greeks invented Theodicies; while the Indians devised what, in its ultimate form, must rather be termed a Cosmodicy. For, although Buddhism recognizes gods many and lords many, they are products of the cosmic process; and transitory, however long enduring, manifestations of its eternal activity. In the doctrine of transmigration, whatever its origin, Brahminical and Buddhist speculation found, ready to hand, the means of constructing a plausible vindication of the ways of the cosmos to man. If this world is full of pain and sorrow; if grief and evil fall, like the rain, upon both the just and the unjust; it is because, like the rain, they are links in the endless chain of natural causation by which past, present, and future are indissolubly connected; and there is no more injustice in the one case than in the other. Every sentient being is reaping as it has sown; if not in this life, then in one or other of the infinite series of antecedent existences of which it is the latest term. The present distribution of good and evil is, therefore, the algebraical sum of accumulated positive and negative deserts; or, rather, it depends on the floating balance of the account. For it was not thought necessary that a complete settlement should ever take place. Arrears might stand over as a sort of "hanging gale"; a period of celestial happiness just earned might be succeeded by ages of torment in a hideous nether world, the balance still overdue for some remote ancestral error.

Whether the cosmic process looks any more moral than at first, after such a vindication, may perhaps be questioned. Yet this plea of justification is not less plausible than others; and none but very hasty thinkers will reject it on the ground of inherent absurdity. Like the doctrine of evolution itself, that of transmigration has its roots in the world of reality; and it may claim such support as the great argument from analogy is capable of supplying.

* * *

Let us now set our faces westwards, towards Asia Minor and Greece and Italy, to view the rise and progress of another philosophy, apparently independent, but no less pervaded by the conception of evolution.

The sages of Miletus were pronounced evolutionists; and, however dark may be some of the sayings of Heracleitus of Ephesus, who was probably a contemporary of Gautama, no better expressions of the essence of the modern doctrine of evolution can be found than are presented by some of his pithy aphorisms and striking metaphors. Indeed, many of my present auditors must have observed that, more than once, I have borrowed from him in the brief exposition of the theory of evolution with which this discourse commenced.

But when the focus of Greek intellectual activity shifted to Athens, the leading minds concentrated their attention upon ethical problems. Forsaking the study of the macrocosm for that of the microcosm, they lost the key to the thought of the great Ephesian, which, I imagine, is more intellible to us than it was to Socrates or to Plato. Socrates, more especially, set the fashion of a kind of inverse agnosticism, by teaching that the problems of physics lie beyond the reach of the human intellect; that the attempt to solve them is essentially vain; that the one worthy object of investigation is the problem of ethical life; and his example was followed by the Cynics and the later Stoics. Even the comprehensive knowledge and the penetrating intellect of Aristotle failed to suggest to him that in holding the eternity of the world, within its present range of mutation, he was making a retrogressive step. The scientific heritage of Heracleitus passed into the hands neither of Plato nor of Aristotle, but into those of Democritus. But the world was not yet ready to receive the great conceptions of the philosopher of Abdera. It was reserved for the Stoics to return to the track marked out by the earlier philosophers; and, professing themselves disciples of Heracleitus, to develop the idea of evolution systematically. In doing this, they not only omitted some characteristic features of their master's teaching, but they made additions altogether foreign to it. One of the most influential of these importations was the transcendental theism which had come into vogue. The restless, fiery energy, operating according to law, out of which all things emerge and into which they return, in the endless successive cycles of the great year; which creates and destroys worlds as a wanton child builds up, and anon levels, sand castles on the seashore; was metamorphosed into a material world-soul and decked out with all the attributes of ideal Divinity; not merely with infinite power and transcendent wisdom, but with absolute goodness.

The consequences of this step were momentous. For if the cosmos is the effect of an immanent, omnipotent, and infinitely beneficent cause, the existence in it of real evil, still less of necessarily inherent evil, is plainly inadmissible. Yet the universal experience of mankind testified then, as now, that, whether we look within us or without us, evil stares us in the face on all sides; that if anything is real, pain and sorrow and wrong are realities.

It would be a new thing in history if *a priori* philosophers were daunted by the factious opposition of experience; and the Stoics were the last men to allow themselves to be beaten by mere facts. "Give me a doctrine and I will find the reasons for it," said Chrysippus. So they perfected, if they did not invent, that ingenious and plausible form of pleading, the Theodicy; for the purpose of showing firstly, that there is no such thing as evil; secondly, that if there is, it is the necessary correlate of good; and, moreover, that it is either due to our own fault, or inflicted for our benefit. Theodicies have been very popular in their time, and I believe that a numerous, though somewhat dwarfed, progeny of them still survives. So far as I know, they are all variations of the theme set forth in those famous six lines of the "Essay on Man," in which Pope sums up Bolingbroke's reminiscences of stoical and other speculations of this kind—

> "All nature is but art, unknown to thee;
> All chance, direction which thou canst not see;
> All discord, harmony not understood;
> All partial evil, universal good;
> And spite of pride, in erring reason's spite,
> One truth is clear: whatever is is right."

Yet, surely, if there are few more important truths than those enunciated in the first triad, the second is open to very grave objections. That there is a "soul of good in things evil" is unquestionable; nor will any wise man deny the disciplinary value of pain and sorrow. But these considerations do not help us to see why the immense multitude of irresponsible sentient beings, which cannot profit by such discipline, should suffer; nor why, among the endless possibilities open to omnipotence—that of sinless, happy existence among the rest—the actuality in which sin and misery abound should be that selected. Surely it is mere cheap rhetoric to call arguments which have never yet been answered by even the meekest and the least rational of Optimists, suggestions of the pride of reason. As to the concluding aphorism, its fittest place would be as an inscription in letters of mud over the portal of some "stye of Epicurus"; for that is where the logical application of it to practice would land men, with every aspiration stifled and every effort paralyzed.

Why try to set right what is right already? Why strive to improve the best of all possible worlds? Let us eat and drink, for as to-day all is right, so to-morrow all will be.

*   *   *

Modern thought is making a fresh start from the base whence Indian and Greek philosophy set out; and, the human mind being very much what it was six-and-twenty centuries ago, there is no ground for wonder if it presents indications of a tendency to move along the old lines to the same results.

We are more than sufficiently familiar with modern pessimism, at least as a speculation; for I cannot call to mind that any of its present votaries have sealed their faith by assuming the rags and the bowl of the mendicant Bhikku, or the cloak and the wallet of the Cynic. The obstacles placed in the way of sturdy vagrancy by an unphilosophical police have, perhaps, proved too formidable for philosophical consistency. We also know modern speculative optimism, with its perfectibility of the species, reign of peace, and lion and lamb transformation scenes; but one does not hear so much of it as one did forty years ago; indeed, I imagine it is to be met with more commonly at the tables of the healthy and wealthy, than in the congregations of the wise. The majority of us, I apprehend, profess neither pessimism nor optimism. We hold that the world is neither so good, nor so bad, as it conceivably might be; and, as most of us have reason, now and again, to discover that it can be. Those who have failed to experience the joys that make life worth living are, probably, in as small a minority as those who have never known the griefs that rob existence of its savour and turn its richest fruits into mere dust and ashes.

Further, I think I do not err in assuming that, however diverse their views on philosophical and religious matters, most men are agreed that the proportion of good and evil in life may be very sensibly affected by human action. I never heard anybody doubt that the evil may be thus increased, or diminished; and it would seem to follow that good must be similarly susceptible of addition or subtraction. Finally, to my knowledge, nobody professes to doubt that, so far forth as we possess a power of bettering things, it is our paramount duty to use it and to train all our intellect and energy to this supreme service of our kind.

Hence the pressing interest of the question, to what extent modern progress in natural knowledge, and, more especially, the general outcome of that progress in the doctrine of evolution, is competent to help us in the great work of helping one another?

The propounders of what are called the "ethics of evolution," when the "evolution of ethics" would usually better express the object of their speculations, adduce a number of more or less interesting facts and more or less sound arguments in favour of the origin of the moral sentiments, in the same way as other natural phenomena, by a process of evolution. I have little doubt, for my own part, that they are on the right track, but as the immoral sentiments have no less been evolved, there is, so far, as much natural sanction for the one as the other. The thief and the murderer follow nature just as much as the philanthropist. Cosmic evolution may teach us how the good and the evil tendencies of man may have come about; but, in itself, it is incompetent to furnish any better reason why what we call good is preferable to what we call evil than we had before. Some day, I doubt not, we shall arrive at an understanding of the evolution of the æsthetic faculty; but all the understanding in the world will neither increase nor diminish the force of the intuition that this is beautiful and that is ugly.

There is another fallacy which appears to me to pervade the so-called "ethics of evolution." It is the notion that because, on the whole, animals and plants have advanced in perfection of organization by means of the struggle for existence and the consequent "survival of the fittest"; therefore men in society, men as ethical beings, must look to the same process to help them towards perfection. I suspect that this fallacy has arisen out of the unfortunate ambiguity of the phrase "survival of the fittest." "Fittest" has a connotation of "best"; and about "best" there hangs a moral flavour. In cosmic nature, however, what is "fittest" depends upon the conditions. Long since, I ventured to point out that if our hemisphere were to cool again, the survival of the fittest might bring about, in the vegetable kingdom, a population of more and more stunted and humbler and humbler organisms, until the "fittest" that survived might be nothing but lichens, diatoms, and such microscopic organisms as those which give red snow its colour; while, if it become hotter, the pleasant valleys of the Thames and Isis might be uninhabitable by any animated beings save those that flourish in a tropical jungle. They, as the fittest, the best adapted to the changed conditions, would survive.

Men in society are undoubtedly subject to the cosmic process. As among other animals, multiplication goes on without cessation, and involves severe competition for the means of support. The struggle for existence tends to eliminate those less fitted to adapt themselves to the circumstances of their existence. The strongest, the most self-assertive, tend to tread down the weaker. But the influence of the cosmic process on the evolution of society is the greater the more rudimentary its civilization. Social progress means a checking of the cosmic process at every step and the substitution for it of another, which may be called the ethical process; the end of which is not the survival of those who may happen to be the fittest, in respect of the whole of the conditions which obtain, but of those who are ethically the best.

As I have already urged, the practice of that which is ethically best—what we call goodness or virtue—involves a course of conduct which, in all respects, is opposed to that which leads to success in the cosmic struggle for existence. In place of ruthless self-assertion it demands self-restraint; in place of thrusting aside, or treading down, all competitors, it requires that the individual shall not merely respect, but shall help his fellows; its influence is directed, not so much to the survival of the fittest, as to the fitting of as many as possible to survive. It repudiates the gladiatorial theory of existence. It demands that each man who enters into the enjoyment of the advantages of a polity shall be mindful of his debt to those who have laboriously constructed it; and shall take heed that no act of his weakens the fabric in which he has been permitted to live. Laws and moral precepts are directed to the end of curbing the cosmic process and reminding the individual of his duty to the community, to the protection and influence of which he owes, if not existence itself, at least the life of something better than a brutal savage.

It is from neglect of these plain considerations that the fanatical individualism of our time attempts to apply the analogy of cosmic nature to society. Once more we have a misapplication of the stoical injunction to follow nature; the duties of the individual to the state are forgotten, and his tendencies to self-assertion are dignified by the name of rights. It is seriously debated whether the members of a community are justified in using their combined strength to constrain one of their number to contribute his share to the maintenance of it; or even to prevent him from doing his best to destroy it. The struggle for existence which has done such admirable work in cosmic nature, must, it appears, be equally beneficent in the ethical sphere. Yet if that which I have insisted upon is true; if the cosmic process has no sort of relation to moral ends; if the imitation of it by man is inconsistent with the first principles of ethics; what becomes of this surprising theory?

Let us understand, once for all, that the ethical progress of society depends, not on imitating the cosmic process, still less in running away from it, but in combating it. It may seem an audacious proposal thus to pit the microcosm against the macroscosm and to set man to subdue nature to his higher ends; but I venture to think that the great intellectual difference between the ancient times with which we have been occupied and our day, lies in the solid foundation we have acquired for the hope that such an enterprise may meet with a certain measure of success.

The history of civilization details the steps by which men have succeeded in building up an artificial world within the cosmos. Fragile reed as he may be, man, as Pascal says, is a thinking reed: there lies within him a fund of energy operating intelligently and so far akin to that which pervades the universe, that it is competent to influence and modify the cosmic process. In virtue of his intelligence, the dwarf bends the Titan to his will. In every family, in every polity that has been established, the cosmic process in man has been restrained and otherwise modified by law and custom; in surrounding nature, it has been similarly influenced by the art of the shepherd, the agriculturist, the artisan. As civilization has advanced, so has the extent of this interference increased; until the organized and highly developed sciences and arts of the present day have endowed man with a command over the course of non-human nature greater than that once attributed to the magicians. The most impressive, I might say startling, of these changes have been brought about in the course of the last two centuries; while a right comprehension of the process of life and of the means of influencing its manifestations is only just dawning upon us. We do not yet see our way beyond generalities; and we are befogged by the obtrusion of false analogies and crude anticipations. But Astronomy, Physics, Chemistry, have all had to pass through similar phases, before they reached the stage at which their influence became an important factor in human affairs. Physiology, Psychology, Ethics, Political Science, must submit to the same ordeal. Yet it seems to me irrational to doubt that, at no distant period, they will work as great a revolution in the sphere of practice.

The theory of evolution encourages no millennial anticipations. If, for millions of years, our globe has taken the upward road, yet, some time, the summit will be reached and the downward route will be commenced. The most daring imagination will hardly venture upon the suggestion that the power and the intelligence of man can ever arrest the procession of the great year.

Moreover, the cosmic nature born with us and, to a large extent, necessary for our maintenance, is the outcome of millions of years of severe training, and it would be folly to imagine that a few centuries will suffice to subdue its masterfulness to purely ethical ends. Ethical nature may count upon having to reckon with a tenacious and powerful enemy as long as the world lasts. But, on the other hand, I see no limit to the extent to which intelligence and will, guided by sound principles of investigation, and organized in common effort, may modify the conditions of existence, for a period longer than that now covered by history. And much may be done to change the nature of man himself. The intelligence which has converted the brother of the wolf into the faithful guardian of the flock ought to be able to do something towards curbing the instincts of savagery in civilized men.

But if we may permit ourselves a larger hope of abatement of the essential evil of the world than was possible to those who, in the infancy of exact knowledge, faced the problem of existence more than a score of centuries ago, I deem it an essential condition of the realization of that hope that we should cast aside the notion that the escape from pain and sorrow is the proper object of life.

We have long since emerged from the heroic childhood of our race, when good and evil could be met with the same "frolic welcome"; the attempts to escape from evil, whether Indian or Greek, have ended in flight from the battle-field; it remains to us to throw aside the youthful over-confidence and the no less youthful discouragement of nonage. We are grown men, and must play the man

strong in will
To strive, to seek, to find, and not to yield,

cherishing the good that falls in our way, and bearing the evil, in and around us, with stout hearts set on diminishing it. So far, we all may strive in one faith towards one hope:

It may be that the gulfs will wash us down,
It may be we shall touch the Happy Isles,

. . . but something ere the end,
Some work of noble note may yet be done.

Why Is God Silent While Evil Rages?[1]

by HARRY EMERSON FOSDICK

No THOUGHTFUL person can live through an era like this without asking searching questions about God. With no desire and no intention to be atheists, still, questions rise within us and among them inevitably this: Why is God so silent in a world filled with noisy evil? We hear, as though it were a lovely truth, that amid earthquake, wind, and fire ravaging the world, God moves like a still, small voice, but far from being a lovely truth, that is what often troubles us. Why, in a world of turbulent evil, can God the Almighty do no better than be a still, small voice? Why does he not speak up, and make a noise in the interest of righteousness? So Carlyle, earnest believer though he was, exclaimed once, "God sits in heaven and does nothing," and long before Carlyle the writer of the eighty-third Psalm cried,

> O God, keep not thou silence:
> Hold not thy peace, and be not still, O God.
> For, lo, thine enemies make a tumult.

This contrast between the blatant violence of evil and the quietness of those spiritual forces in which goodness dwells is a mystery. In what contrast stand a thunderstorm and a mother's love—the one obtrusive, boisterous, the other inaudible, imperceptible, save as one quietly listens! Why should evil have thus the advantage of noise, and goodness always be a still, small voice?

This question gains added difficulty when, believing that these spiritual forces have behind them the might and majesty of the Eternal, we bring God in. Why should the sovereign God of all this universe be so shy? Long ago, during the Hebrew Exile, when proud Babylon violently ruled the earth, the Great Isaiah cried, "Verily thou art a God that hidest thyself, O God of Israel, the Saviour."

No one can crowd the explanation of an infinite universe into a finite head, and the full answer to this question we have asked has depths no human plummet fathoms, but surely some things can be said about it. This, I ask of you, to start with, that when I use the word "God" you will not have in your imagination some human picture of him, like a king seated on a throne. Let us begin with something more realistic and indubitable than that! In one sense of the word no one doubts the existence of God, not even one who calls himself an atheist. There is, behind and in this universe, crea-

[1] From H. E. Fosdick, *A Great Time To Be Alive* (1944). By permission of Harper & Brothers.

tive power. That is fact, not theory. This world and we within it are the consequence of creative power. In what terms we shall think of that creative power, whether in terms material or spiritual, is a further and momentous question, but it is certain that creative power itself is here. From it, all that is came. In it, all that is exists. Without it, nothing is at all. It is the sovereign, basic, original, indubitable fact.

Yet, strangely enough, we have never heard it. It makes no noise. Upon its cosmic loom it weaves millions of solar systems and swings stars and planets in their courses, but as the nineteenth Psalm says,

> There is no speech nor language;
> Their voice is not heard.

Here, surely, is the place for our thought to start. Theists and atheists alike, we all are in the same boat here: We face a universe whose sovereign creative power is silent.

Today consider some facts about this mysteriously quiet power from which all things come, that, so it seems to me, lead us straight to the truth of our Christian faith.

For example, we face at once a stern and ominous fact: This silent power does do something rigorous and austere—it works inevitable retribution upon evil. Like it or not, in this universe there is what the ancient Greeks called Nemesis—the doom that, however long delayed, falls upon arrogance and cruelty and braggart pride. In our days we shall see that Nemesis again, and when Hitler's nazidom breaks down, old texts will come to mind:

> He hath made a pit, and digged it,
> And is fallen into the ditch which he made.

Just as in the physical realm the noiseless force of gravitation brings inevitable consequence on those who disobey its laws, so the law-abiding nature of the cosmos silently reveals itself in the moral realm. "Whatsoever a man soweth, that shall he also reap"—that is a metaphor of silence. The processes of growth are quiet; no one can hear that harvest of retribution grow, but grow it does. So, while it is true that God is silent, it is not true that he "sits in heaven and does nothing."

These are highly emotional days, and among the emotions that naturally roil our spirits is the rebellious mood, resentment and complaint directed often against the very things that once we trusted most. Is anyone here so placid and saintly, so little stirred by the brutal evils of our time, that he has felt no rebellion against God himself? Is not God sovereign? Why does he not speak up? See the blatant wrongs that curse the earth. So we complain, as Dr. Moffatt translates our text,

> Keep not still, O God,
> speak, stir, O God!
> Here are thy foes in uproar.

Nevertheless, any way we look at it, the determining creative forces in this universe are silent, and one major thing they do is noiselessly to work inevitable retribution. Recall the Bible's dramatic presentation of this truth! The Jewish Exile was at its climax. Babylon ruled the world. Then Belshazzar, the king, made a great feast to a thousand of his lords, where they drank wine and praised the gods of gold and of silver, of brass, of iron, of wood and of stone, until upon that scene of insolent evil a sudden silence fell. For out of the unseen and the unheard there "came forth the fingers of a man's hand, and wrote over against the candlestick upon the plaster of the wall of the king's palace: . . . MENE, MENE, TEKEL, UPHARSIN" —weighed, weighed in the balances and found wanting. "Then the king's countenance was changed . . . and his thoughts troubled him; and the joints of his loins were loosed, and his knees smote one against another."

As Theodor Mommsen, the historian, wrote: "History has a Nemesis for every sin." God does not sit in heaven and do nothing. We frail human beings are not alone the originators, improvisers, and backers of goodness in this world. There is, as Matthew Arnold said, a "power, not ourselves, which makes for righteousness." Today we deeply need to believe that. Evil towers so high, seems so strong, makes such a tumult, that we could easily despair were not our hope still where the great souls of other days have found it. Long ago a valiant warrior against a tyrant cried, "The stars in their courses fought against Sisera," and on the threshold of our own era a modern echoed him:

> And for the everlasting right
> The silent stars are strong.

Come further, now, and consider that despite our complaints about God's silence, these spiritual forces making no noise reach deeper, take hold harder, and last longer than any others. We human beings are naturally sensitive to noise. Loud things claim our attention. Yet, when we go deeply within ourselves to note what means most to us, how soon we enter a quiet realm where great thoughts walk with still feet, and great loves feel what they cannot say, and great faiths lift their noiseless aspirations! The creative factors in our lives dwell in the realm of silence. It is there that personally we meet the Eternal. In these days, filled with the din of man's brutality, we need to renew our insight into the reality, the creative power, the abiding persistence, the ultimate dominance of these quiet spiritual forces that are God's still, small voice.

Even as cold-blooded history reveals the truth, what is it that lasts? All that made a noise in ancient Greece is gone, but the *Iliad*, the *Odyssey*, the *Dialogues of Plato*, the dream of beauty and the love of truth—these have not gone. All that made a noise in ancient Israel has vanished, even the Temple with not one stone left upon another; but the faiths of the psalmists and the insights of the prophets—they have not vanished. How will the atheist handle this realistic fact, that, not because of anything man alone plans to do or is capable of doing, but because of the nature of things, there is a power here that, dropping out the stentorian, vociferous things that split the eardrums of contemporaries, preserves the quiet, spiritual forces, so that while empires rise and fall, truths that hardly lift their voices go on and on.

> Egypt's might is tumbled down
>   Down a-down the deeps of thought;
> Greece is fallen and Troy town,
> Glorious Rome hath lost her crown,
>   Venice' pride is nought.
>
> But the dreams their children dreamed
>   Fleeting, unsubstantial, vain,
> Shadowy as the shadows seemed,
> Airy nothing, as they deemed,
>   These remain.

Moreover, far from being merely a historic matter, this truth has important applications to our times. We are dreadfully tempted now to trust the noisy, outward, violent forces to achieve our end. Many, for example, discussing a new society of nations, say, This time we will have an international police force and that will keep order and make the thing go. Now, I agree that some form of internationally used force is necessary, but if we trust that to hold a society of nations together, we have lost our game before we start. An expert on police affairs recently said that in the United States with our 135,000,000 citizens we have about 150,000 policemen all told, and that no more than 50,000 of them are on duty at any one time. Is it 50,000 policemen who keep this nation a nation and preserve order among 135,000,000 citizens? Granted the necessity of police to handle the fringes of criminal disorder, what keeps us together, makes of us a loyal, devoted, and on the whole united nation is not something you can put in uniform and arm with a gun. These coherent forces that make of our communities decent places to live in and of America a cooperative people are spiritual. Quiet as the sun that when it rises makes no noise, but that is still the light of all our seeing and the creator of all that grows strong and beautiful, some spiritual faiths and hopes, loves and loyalties, have shined upon us here to make possible our national family. Do we think an international family is possible without that? Any decent world we ever get must be grounded in, buttressed by, and held together with, intelligent, undiscourageable goodwill.

This is not poetry but political realism. Harold Butler was for years Director of the International Labor Office in Geneva under the League of Nations. Listen, then, as he sums up what he regards as the cause of the League's failure: "More than for any other reason the peace was lost because the policies of nations were empty of charity towards each other." All history is a running commentary on that.

How can the atheist handle this fact that the most powerful, creative, persistent forces in human life are spiritual, and that always when the earth-quake, wind and fire have spent their force the still, small voice is there?

Come a step further now and note that God may be silent but that he or someone mighty like him does do marvelous things in this world. Alike the ultimate mystery and glory of human life is great personality, and you cannot get that out of noisy things. At the age of forty-three Louis Pasteur was a humiliated wreck. One whole side paralyzed, he looked impotently on while war ravaged France, and his fellow-townsmen taunted him with being a use-less mouth eating needed food, so that once, grown man though he was, he came home weeping with the sting of their jibes. Yet now when all that made the big noise is gone, Pasteur towers higher every year. Even on that day when he wept for shame he said to his wife, "I have something to give France that men with swords cannot give." Well, inwardly sustained by the disinterested love of truth, he gave it, and years afterwards, he himself ex-plained his own experience as he understood it: "Christ," he said, "made me what I am." How does an atheist deal with such facts—this indubitable presence of silent spiritual power, transforming, sustaining, illumining, the builder and maker of great souls? Believe me, God does not sit in heaven and do nothing!

Moreover, this is not merely an individual matter. These souls, from Elijah to Pasteur, nourished on the still, small voice, lift the world. Even in the physical cosmos the silent force of gravitation is a deep mystery, but not so deep a mystery as the gravitation by which strong souls lift the world. Long ago on Calvary the violent forces of the age successfully engineered a crucifixion. They finished him off, the Man of Nazareth who troubled them, and Pilate and Caiaphas and all the noisy crowd that had cried "Crucify him" went home content, while there he hung, a man condemned, dying a felon's death. In any world whose creative power is merely materialistic, would not that have been indeed the end, that man extinguished like a blown-out candle, his light forever gone? Instead, Pilate and Caiaphas and the shouting crowds are dead and buried in reproach and shame, and that man they crucified is lifting still, with a silent gravitation that will outlast the noisiest earthquakes that ever shake the world.

To be sure, this does present a problem. The least important and least valuable things are the noisiest and thus the most easily perceived and proved, while the most important and most valuable things are hardest to be abso-lutely sure about. One cannot doubt a thunderstorm; one cannot doubt a war —see the noise they make! But love and liberty and truth and the pro-foundest meanings and values of our souls—men can doubt them. One can-not doubt an air raid siren—what a blare it makes! But one can doubt God, for he is a still, small voice. This is a mystery and a problem, but thus to state the problem frankly is in part to solve it. Think of being a man who goes through life believing in only the least important and least valuable things because they are obvious and noisy! Fish, they say, in a quiet lake do not recognize the existence of water because they live and move and have their being in it. Shall we, like them, be so insensitive and not perceive that the silent forces of the Eternal Spirit, whose noiseless presence is the life of all our being, are real?

I do not pretend to understand the full reason why God so hides himself in quietness. Perhaps it is because if he should speak out with all the thundering compulsion of his power, making himself as terribly evident as we sometimes wish he would, we would be utterly overborne, helpless automatons with no freedom to make our doing of his will a voluntary choice. But whatever the reason for his silent method, it does not mean that he is doing nothing. Everything in this universe that does most is silent.

> What tho', in solemn silence, all
> Move round the dark terrestrial ball?
> What tho' no real voice nor sound
> Amidst their radiant orbs be found?
> In reason's ear they all rejoice,
> And utter forth a glorious voice,
> Forever singing as they shine,
> "The hand that made us is divine."

As for the personal conclusion of the matter, that surely is evident. In days like these we need the inward reinforcement of spiritual power, and nothing noisy can supply it. There are families here whose anxious thought follow their deepest loves to the ends of the earth today. There are homes here where already the War Department's fateful announcement has arrived with news more difficult to meet than any that they ever faced before. And all of us, tossed by the turbulence and wearied with the din of this violent time, need to have our souls restored. But thundering airplanes and falling bombs do not restore the soul, no, nor clanging subways, shouting crowds, and all the blaring noises of our busy days. As God lives his deepest life in silence, so do we. It is when our quiet responds to his quiet that we find him. Only when he leads us in green pastures and beside still waters can he restore our souls.

And when from that silent place one who knows its secret goes out again to face the world, not all its din can overawe his spirit. The destiny of creation is in the hand of forces that make no noise. So, from the complaint of one psalmist we turn to the insight of another who heard the Eternal say, "Be still, and know that I am God."

Infallibility [1]

by JOHN HENRY NEWMAN

STARTING then with the being of a God (which, as I have said, is as certain to me as the certainty of my own existence, though when I try to put the grounds of that certainty into logical shape I find a difficulty in doing so in mood and figure to my satisfaction), I look out of myself into the world of men, and there I see a sight which fills me with unspeakable distress. The world seems simply to give the lie to that great truth of which my whole being is so full; and the effect upon me is, in consequence, as a matter of necessity as confusing as if it denied that I am in existence myself. If I looked into a mirror and did not see my face, I should have the sort of feeling which actually comes upon me when I look into this living busy world and see no reflection of its Creator. This is, to me, one of the great difficulties of this absolute primary truth to which I referred just now. Were it not for this voice, speaking so clearly in my conscience and my heart, I should be an atheist, or a pantheist, or a polytheist when I looked into the world. I am speaking for myself only; and I am far from denying the real force of the arguments in proof of a God, drawn from the general facts of human society, but these do not warm me or enlighten me; they do not take away the winter of my desolation, or make the buds unfold and the leaves grow within me, and my moral being rejoice. The sight of the world is nothing else than the prophet's scroll, full of "lamentations, and mourning, and woe."

To consider the world in its length and breadth, its various history, the many races of man, their starts, their fortunes, their mutual alienation, their conflicts; and then their ways, habits, governments, forms of worship; their enterprises, their aimless courses, their random achievements and acquirements, the impotent conclusion of long-standing facts, the tokens so faint and broken of a superintending design, the blind evolution of what turn out to be great powers or truths, the progress of things, as if from unreasoning elements, not towards final causes, the greatness and littleness of man, his far-reaching aims, his short duration, the curtain hung over his futurity, the disappointments of life, the defeat of good, the success of evil, physical pain, mental anguish, the prevalence and intensity of sin, the pervading idolatries, the corruptions, the dreary hopeless irreligion, that condition of the whole race so fearfully yet exactly described in the Apostle's words: "having no hope and without God in the world"—all this is a vision to dizzy and appal, and inflicts

---

[1] From J. H. Newman, *Apologia pro Vita Sua* (1864).

upon the mind the sense of a profound mystery which is absolutely beyond human solution.

What shall be said to this heart-piercing, reason-bewildering fact? I can only answer that either there is no Creator or this living society of men is in a true sense discarded from His presence. Did I see a boy of good make and mind, with the tokens on him of a refined nature, cast upon the world without provision, unable to say whence he came, his birthplace or his family connections, I should conclude that there was some mystery connected with his history and that he was one of whom, from one cause or other, his parents were ashamed. Thus only should I be able to account for the contrast between the promise and condition of his being. And so I argue about the world: *if* there be a God, *since* there is a God, the human race is implicated in some terrible aboriginal calamity. It is out of joint with the purposes of its Creator. This is a fact, a fact as true as the fact of its existence; and thus the doctrine of what is theologically called original sin becomes to me almost as certain as that the world exists and as the existence of God.

And now, supposing it were the blessed and loving will of the Creator to interfere in this anarchical condition of things, what are we to suppose would be the methods which might be necessarily or naturally involved in His object of mercy? Since the world is in so abnormal a state, surely it would be no surprise to me if the interposition were of necessity equally extraordinary—or what is called miraculous. But that subject does not directly come into the scope of my present remarks. Miracles as evidence involve an argument; and of course I am thinking of some means which does not immediately run into argument. I am rather asking what must be the face-to-face antagonist by which to withstand and baffle the fierce energy of passion and the all-corroding, all-dissolving skepticism of the intellect in religious inquiries. I have no intention at all to deny that truth is the real object of our reason, and that, if it does not attain to truth, either the premise or the process is in fault; but I am not speaking of right reason, but of reason as it acts in fact and concretely in fallen man. I know that even the unaided reason, when correctly exercised, leads to a belief in God, in the immortality of the soul, and in a future retribution; but I am considering it actually and historically; and in this point of view I do not think I am wrong in saying that its tendency is toward a simple unbelief in matters of religion. No truth, however sacred, can stand against it, in the long run; and hence it is that in the pagan world, when our Lord came, the last traces of the religious knowledge of former times were all but disappearing from those portions of the world in which the intellect had been active and had had a career.

And in these latter days, in like manner, outside the Catholic Church things are tending, with far greater rapidity than in that old time from the circumstance of the age, to atheism in one shape or other. What a scene, what a prospect, does the whole of Europe present at this day! and not only Europe, but every government and every civilization through the world which is under the influence of the European mind! Especially, for it most concerns us, how sorrowful, in the view of religion, even taken in its most elementary, most attenuated form, is the spectacle presented to us by the educated intellect of England, France, and Germany! Lovers of their country and of their race, religious men, external to the Catholic Church, have attempted various expedients to arrest fierce wilful human nature in its onward course and to bring it into subjection. The necessity of some form of religion for the interests of humanity has been generally acknowledged; but where was the concrete representative of things invisible which would have the force and toughness necessary to be a breakwater against the deluge? Three centuries ago the establishment of religion, material, legal, and social, was generally adopted as the best expedient for the purpose in those countries which separated from the Catholic Church; and for a long time it was successful; but now the crevices of those establishments are admitting the enemy. Thirty years ago education was relied upon; ten years ago there was a hope that wars would cease forever, under the influence of commercial enterprise and the reign of the useful and fine arts; but will anyone venture to say that there is anything anywhere on this earth which will afford a fulcrum for us whereby to keep the earth from moving onwards?

The judgment which experience passes on establishments or education as a means of maintaining religious truth in this anarchical world must be extended even to Scripture, though Scripture be divine. Experience proves surely that the Bible does not answer a purpose for which it was never intended. It may be accidentally the means of the conversion of individuals; but a book, after all, cannot make a stand against the wild living intellect of man, and in this day it begins to testify, as regards its own structure and contents, to the power of that universal solvent which is so successfully acting upon religious establishments.

Supposing then it to be the Will of the Creator to interfere in human affairs and to make provisions for retaining in the world a knowledge of Himself so definite and distinct as to be proof against the energy of human skepticism, in such a case—I am far from saying that there was no other way—but there is nothing to surprise the mind, if He should think fit to introduce a power into the world invested with the prerogative of infalibility in religious matters. Such a provision would be a direct, immediate, active, and prompt means of withstanding the difficulty; it would be an instrument suited to the need; and when I find that this is the very claim of the Catholic Church, not only do I feel no difficulty in admitting the idea, but there is a fitness in it which recommends it to my mind. And thus I am brought to speak of the Church's infallibility as a provision adapted by the mercy of the Creator to preserve religion in the world, and to restrain that freedom of though which of course in itself is one of the greatest of our natural gifts, and to rescue it from its own suicidal excesses. And let it be observed that, neither here nor in what follows, shall I have occasion to speak directly of the revealed body of truths, but only as they bear upon the defense of natural religion. I say that a power possessed of infallibity in religious teaching is happily adapted to be a working instrument for smiting hard and throwing back the immense energy of the aggressive intellect; and in saying this, as in the other things that I have to say, it must still be recollected that I am all along bearing in mind my main purpose, which is a defense of myself.

I am defending myself here from a plausible charge brought against Catholics, as will be seen better as I proceed. The charge is this: that I, as a Catholic, not only make profession to hold doctrines which I cannot possibly believe in my heart but that I also believe in the existence of a power on earth which at its own will imposes upon men any new set of *credenda*,[1] when it pleases, by a claim to infallibility; in consequence, that my own thoughts are not my own property; that I cannot tell that tomorrow I may not have to give up what I hold today, and that the necessary effect of such a condition of mind must be a degrading bondage, or a bitter inward rebellion relieving itself in secret infidelity, or the necessity of ignoring the whole subject of religion in a sort of disgust, and of mechanically saying everything that the Church says and leaving to others the defense of it. As then I have above spoken of the relation of my mind toward the Catholic Creed, so now I shall speak of the attitude which it takes up in the view of the Church's infallibility.

And first, the initial doctrine of the infallible teacher must be an emphatic protest against the existing state of mankind. Man had rebelled against his Maker. It was this that caused the divine interposition; and the first act of the divinely accredited messenger must be to proclaim it. The Church must denounce rebellion as of all possible evils the greatest. She must have no terms with it; if she would be true to her Master, she must ban and anathematize it. This is the meaning of a statement which has furnished matter for one of those special accusations to which I am at present replying. I have, however, no fault at all to confess in regard to it; I have nothing to withdraw, and in consequence I here deliberately repeat it. I said, "The Catholic Church holds it better for the sun and moon to drop from heaven, for the earth to fail, and for all the many millions on it to die of starvation in extremest agony, as far as temporal affliction goes, than that one soul, I will not say should be lost, but should commit one single venial sin, should tell one wilful untruth, or should steal one poor farthing without excuse." I think the principle here enunciated to be the mere preamble in the formal credentials of the Catholic Church, as an Act of Parliament might begin with a *"Whereas."* It is because of the intensity of the evil which has possession of mankind that a suitable antagonist has been provided against it; and the intial act of that divinely commissioned power is of course to deliver her challenge and to defy the enemy. Such a preamble then gives a meaning to her position in the world and an interpretation to her whole course of teaching and action.

In like manner she has ever put forth with most energetic distinctness those

[1] Articles of faith.

other great elementary truths which either are an explanation of her mission or give a character to her work. She does not teach that human nature
is irreclaimable, else wherefore should she be sent? not that it is to be shattered
and reversed, but to be extricated, purified, and restored; not that it is a mere
mass of evil, but that it has the promise of great things, and even now has a
virtue and a praise proper to itself. But in the next place she knows and she
preaches that such a restoration as she aims at effecting in it must be brought
about, not simply through any outward provision of preaching and teaching,
even though it be her own, but from a certain inward spiritual power of grace
imparted directly from above and which is in her keeping. She has it in
charge to rescue human nature from its misery, but not simply by raising
it upon its own level, but by lifting it up to a higher level than its own. She
recognizes in it real moral excellence though degraded, but she cannot set it
free from earth except by exalting it toward heaven. It was for this end
that a renovating grace was put into her hands, and therefore from the
nature of the gift, as well as from the reasonableness of the case, she goes
on, as a further point, to insist that all true conversion must begin with the
first springs of thought, and to teach that each individual man must be in
his own person one whole and perfect temple of God while he is also one of
the living stones which build up a visible religious community. And thus
the distinctions between nature and grace, and between outward and inward
religion, become two further articles in what I have called the preamble of
her divine commission.

Such truths as these she vigorously reiterates and pertinaciously inflicts
upon mankind; as to such she observes no half-measures, no economical
reserve, no delicacy or prudence. "Ye must be born again," is the simple,
direct form of words which she uses after her Divine Master; "your whole
nature must be reborn, your passions, and your affections, and your aims, and
your conscience, and your will must all be bathed in a new element, and
reconsecrated to your Maker, and, the last not the least, your intellect." It was
for repeating these points of her teaching in my own way that certain passages of one of my volumes have been brought into the general accusation
which has been made against my religious opinions. The writer has said
that I was demented if I believed, and unprincipled if I did not believe, in my
statement that a lazy, ragged, filthy, story-telling beggar-woman, if chaste,
sober, cheerful, and religious, had a prospect of heaven which was absolutely closed to an accomplished statesman, or lawyer, or noble, be he ever
so just, upright, generous, honorable, and conscientious, unless he had also
some portion of the divine Christian grace; yet I should have thought myself defended from criticism by the words which our Lord used to the chief
priests: "The publicans and harlots go into the kingdom of God before you."
And I was subjected again to the same alternative of imputations for having
ventured to say that consent to an unchaste wish was infinitely more
heinous than any lie viewed apart from its causes, its motives, and its consequences; though a lie, viewed under the limitation of these conditions, is a

random utterance, an almost outward act, not directly from the heart, however disgraceful it may be, whereas we have the express words of our Lord to the doctrine that "whoso looketh on a woman to lust after her hath committed adultery with her already in his heart." On the strength of these texts I have surely as much right to believe in these doctrines as to believe in the doctrine of original sin, or that there is a supernatural revelation, or that a Divine Person suffered, or that punishment is eternal.

Passing now from what I have called the preamble of that grant of power with which the Church is invested, to that power itself, Infallibility, I make two brief remarks: on the one hand, I am not here determining anything about the essential seat of that power, because that is a question doctrinal, not historical and practical; nor, on the other hand, am I extending the direct subject-matter over which that power has jurisdiction, beyond religious opinion—and now as to the power itself.

This power, viewed in its fullness, is as tremendous as the giant evil which has called for it. It claims, when brought into exercise in the legitimate manner, for otherwise of course it is but dormant, to have for itself a sure guidance into the very meaning of every portion of the divine message in detail which was committed by our Lord to His apostles. It claims to know its own limits and to decide what it can determine absolutely and what it cannot. It claims, moreover, to have a hold upon statements not directly religious, so far as this, to determine whether they indirectly relate to religion and, according to its own definitive judgment, to pronounce whether or not, in a particular case, they are consistent with revealed truth. It claims to decide magisterially, whether infallibly or not, that such and such statements are or are not prejudicial to the apostolic *depositum* of faith,[2] in their spirit or in their consequences, and to allow them, or condemn and forbid them, accordingly. It claims to impose silence at will on any matters, or controversies, of doctrine, which on its own *ipse dixit*[3] it pronounces to be dangerous, or inexpedient, or inopportune. It claims that whatever may be the judgment of Catholics upon such acts, these acts should be received by them with those outward marks of reverence, submission, and loyalty, which Englishmen, for instance, pay to the presence of their sovereign without public crticism on them, as being in their matter inexpedient or in their manner violent or harsh. And lastly, it claims to have the right of inflicting spiritual punishment, of cutting off from the ordinary channels of the divine life, and of simply excommunicating, those who refuse to submit themselves to its formal declarations. Such is the infallibility lodged in the Catholic Church, viewed in the concrete, as clothed and surrounded by the appendages of its high sovereignty; it is, to repeat what I said above, a supereminent prodigious power sent upon earth to encounter and master a giant evil.

2 Faith entrusted to the Christian religion.
3 Authority

SHORT STORIES

SHORT STORIES

A STORY tells what did happen or what might have happened. What did happen is history. What might have happened is fiction. Biography and autobiography, aspects of history, narrate the occurrences in the lives of actual people. Strachey tells what actually happened to an historical person, Florence Nightingale. Poe, in *The Tell-Tale Heart,* tells what might have happened by the laws of probability and necessity, to a mentally unbalanced person in an imagined situation. Stevenson, in *A Lodging for the Night,* tells what might have happened to an historical character in an imagined situation.

A fictitious story may be just as true, in the sense of "true to life," as an historical story. When we say "Truth is stranger than fiction," we can only mean that actual occurrences may be strange—nay, incredible. But fiction must be true to life as we know it or as we accept it. It must be probable. Even the fabulous must be true to our notions of the fabulous.

The term, short story, has come to be applied to a brief piece of fiction. Brevity distinguishes the short story from the novel. Because it is brief the short story necessarily has a sharper focus on one episode, one moment in time, one character, one mood than has a novel. An artistically written short story is just long enough to get itself told—no longer.

We are all so much in the habit of reading magazine stories for entertainment that this habit may stand in the way of our studying stories as forms of literary art. The stories in this collection will furnish entertainment even to the unsophisticated reader, but they will yield even more enjoyment to the reader who reflects upon them and devotes some thought to the artistic problems the authors have set themselves to solve.

The stories have been selected, not as the "best" in modern English and American literature, nor as representative of the best known names. They have been chosen to present as great a variety of literary experience as possible within the space allowed by the scope of the book. Here the reader will find a variety of themes: revenge, love, adventure, social thesis, satire, the supernatural, romance, realism, humor, tragedy. He will find a wide spread, from the conventional well constructed and carefully plotted story, through impressionism to stream of consciousness. He will find a great variety of literary method and the use of various angles of narration: first person story by principal actor, detached third person story with omniscient viewpoint, third person story from the angle of one of the characters, diary.

But the experience of reading the stories is more valuable than that of theorizing. Read a story first and then think about the questions raised in the study material. Then reread the story. A second reading will show you much that you missed on your first reading.

The Tell-Tale Heart[1]

by EDGAR ALLAN POE

TRUE!—nervous—very, very dreadfully nervous I had been and am! but why *will* you say that I am mad? The disease had sharpened my senses—not destroyed—not dulled them. Above all was the sense of hearing acute. I heard all things in the heaven and in the earth. I heard many things in hell. How, then, am I mad? Hearken! and observe how healthily—how calmly I can tell you the whole story.

It is impossible to tell how first the idea entered my brain; but once conceived, it haunted me day and night. Object there was none. Passion there was none. I loved the old man. He had never wronged me. He had never given me insult. For his gold I had no desire. I think it was his eye! Yes, it was this! One of his eyes resembled that of a vulture—a pale blue eye, with a film over it. Whenever it fell upon me, my blood ran cold; and so by degrees—very gradually—I made up my mind to take the life of the old man, and thus rid myself of the eye forever.

Now this is the point. You fancy me mad. Madmen know nothing. But you should have seen *me*. You should have seen how wisely I proceeded—with what caution—with what foresight—with what dissimulation I went to work!

I was never kinder to the old man than during the whole week before I killed him. And every night, about midnight, I turned the latch of his door and opened it—oh, so gently! And then, when I had made an opening sufficient for my head, I put in a dark lantern, all closed, closed, so that no light shone out, and then I thrust in my head. Oh, you would have laughed to see how cunningly I thrust it in! I moved it slowly—very, very slowly, so that I might not disturb the old man's sleep. It took me an hour to place my whole head within the opening so far that I could see him as he lay upon his bed. Ha!—would a madman have been so wise as this? And then, when my head was well in the room, I undid the lantern cautiously—oh, so cautiously—cautiously (for the hinges creaked)—I undid it just so much that a single thin ray fell upon the vulture eye. And this I did for seven long nights—every night just at midnight—but I found the eye always closed; and so it was impossible to do the work; for it was not the old man who vexed me, but his Evil Eye. And every morning, when the day broke, I went boldly into the chamber, and spoke courageously to him, calling him by name in a hearty tone, and inquiring how he had passed the night. So you see he would have been a very profound old man, indeed, to suspect that every night, just at twelve, I looked in upon him while he slept.

[1] First published in *Pioneer*, January, 1843.

Upon the eighth night I was more than usually cautious in opening the door. A watch's minute hand moves more quickly than did mine. Never before that night had I *felt* the extent of my own powers—of my sagacity. I could scarcely contain my feelings of triumph. To think that there I was, opening the door, little by little, and he not even to dream of my secret deeds or thoughts. I fairly chuckled at the idea; and perhaps he heard me; for he moved on the bed suddenly, as if startled. Now you may think that I drew back—but no. His room was as black as pitch with the thick darkness (for the shutters were close fastened, through fear of robbers), and so I knew that he could not see the opening of the door, and I kept pushing it on steadily, steadily.

I had my head in, and was about to open the lantern, when my thumb slipped upon the tin fastening, and the old man sprang up in bed, crying out: "Who's there?"

I kept quite still and said nothing. For a whole hour I did not move a muscle, and in the meantime I did not hear him lie down. He was still sitting up in the bed listening;—just as I have done, night after night, hearkening to the death watches in the wall.

Presently I heard a slight groan, and I knew it was the groan of mortal terror. It was not a groan of pain or grief—oh no!—it was the low stifled sound that arises from the bottom of the soul when overcharged with awe. I knew the sound well. Many a night, just at midnight, when all the world slept, it has welled up from my own bosom, deepening, with its dreadful echo, the terrors that distracted me. I say I knew it well. I knew what the old man felt, and pitied him, although I chuckled at heart. I knew that he had been lying awake ever since the first slight noise, when he had turned in the bed. His fears had been ever since growing upon him. He had been trying to fancy them causeless, but could not. He had been saying to himself: "It is nothing but the wind in the chimney—it is only a mouse crossing the floor," or "it is merely a cricket which has made a single chirp." Yes, he has been trying to comfort himself with these suppositions; but he had found all in vain. *All in vain;* because Death, in approaching him, had stalked with his black shadow before him, and enveloped the victim. And it was the mournful influence of the unperceived shadow that caused him to feel—although he neither saw nor heard—to *feel* the presence of my head within the room.

When I had waited a long time, very patiently, without hearing him lie down, I resolved to open a little—a very, very little crevice in the lantern. So I opened it—you cannot imagine how stealthily, stealthily—until, at length, a single dim ray, like the thread of the spider, shot from out the crevice and full upon the vulture eye.

It was open—wide, wide open—and I grew furious as I gazed upon it. I saw it with perfect distinctness—all a dull blue, with a hideous veil over it that chilled the very marrow in my bones; but I could see nothing else of the old man's face or person: for I had directed the ray, as if by instinct, precisely upon the damned spot.

And now—have I not told you that what you mistake for madness is but over-acuteness of the senses?—now, I say, there came to my ears a low, dull, quick sound, such as a watch makes when enveloped in cotton. I knew *that* sound well too. It was the beating of the old man's heart. It increased my fury, as the beating of a drum stimulates the soldier into courage.

But even yet I refrained and kept still. I scarcely breathed. I held the lantern motionless. I tried how steadily I could maintain the ray upon the eye. Meantime the hellish tattoo of the heart increased. It grew quicker and quicker, and louder and louder every instant. The old man's terror *must* have been extreme! It grew louder, I say, louder every moment!—do you mark me well? I have told you that I am nervous: so I am. And now at the dead hour of night, amid the dreadful silence of that old house, so strange a noise as this excited me to uncontrollable terror. Yet, for some minutes longer I refrained and stood still. But the beating grew louder, louder! I thought the heart must burst. And now a new anxiety seized me—the sound would be heard by a neighbor! The old man's hour had come! With a loud yell, I threw open the lantern and leaped into the room. He shrieked once—once only. In an instant I dragged him to the floor, and pulled the heavy bed over him. I then smiled gaily, to find the deed so far done. But, for many minutes, the heart beat on with a muffled sound. This, however, did not vex me; it would not be heard through the wall. At length it ceased. The old man was dead. I removed the bed and examined the corpse. Yes, he was stone, stone dead. I placed my hand upon the heart and held it there many minutes. There was no pulsation. He was stone dead. His eye would trouble me no more.

If still you think me mad, you will think so no longer when I describe the wise precautions I took for the concealment of the body. The night waned, and I worked hastily, but in silence. First of all I dismembered the corpse. I cut off the head and the arms and the legs.

I then took up three planks from the flooring of the chamber, and deposited all between the scantlings. I then replaced the boards so cleverly, so cunningly, that no human eye—not even *his*—could have detected anything wrong. There was nothing to wash out—no stain of any kind—no blood-spot whatever. I had been too wary for that. A tub had caught all—ha! ha!

When I had made an end of these labors, it was four o'clock—still dark as midnight. As the bell sounded the hour, there came a knocking at the street door. I went down to open it with a light heart—for what had I *now* to fear? There entered three men, who introduced themselves, with perfect suavity, as officers of the police. A shriek had been heard by a neighbor during the night: suspicion of foul play had been aroused; information had been lodged at the police office, and they (the officers) had been deputed to search the premises.

I smiled—for *what* had I to fear? I bade the gentlemen welcome. The shriek, I said, was my own in a dream. The old man, I mentioned, was absent in the country. I took my visitors all over the house. I bade them search—search *well*. I led them, at length, to *his* chamber. I showed them his treasures, secure, undisturbed. In the enthusiasm of my confidence, I brought chairs into the room, and desired them *here* to rest from their fatigues, while I myself, in the wild audacity of my perfect triumph, placed my own seat upon the very spot beneath which reposed the corpse of the victim.

The officers were satisfied. My *manner* had convinced them. I was singularly at ease. They sat, and while I answered cheerily, they chatted familiar things. But, ere long, I felt myself getting pale and wished them gone. My head ached, and I fancied a ringing in my ears: but still they sat and still chatted. The ringing became more distinct:—it continued and became more distinct: I talked more freely to get rid of the feeling: but it continued and gained definiteness—until, at length, I found that the noise was *not* within my ears.

No doubt I now grew *very* pale;—but I talked more fluently, and with a heightened voice. Yet the sound increased—and what could I do? It was *a low, dull, quick sound—much such a sound as a watch makes when enveloped in cotton.* I gasped for breath—and yet the officers heard it not. I talked more quickly—more vehemently; but the noise steadily increased. Why *would* they not be gone? I paced the floor to and fro with heavy strides, as if excited to fury by the observation of the men—but the noise steadily increased. Oh, God; what *could* I do? I foamed—I raved—I swore! I swung the chair upon which I had been sitting, and grated it upon the boards, but the noise arose over all and continually increased. It grew louder—louder—*louder!* And still the men chatted pleasantly, and smiled. Was it possible they heard not? Almighty God!—no, no! They heard!—they suspected—they *knew!*—they were making a *mockery* of my horror!—this I thought, and this I think. But anything was better than this agony! Anything was more tolerable than this derision! I could bear those hypocritical smiles no longer! I felt that I must scream or die!—and now—again!—hark! louder! louder! *louder!*—

"Villains!" I shrieked, "dissemble no more! I admit the deed!—tear up the planks!—here, here!—it is the beating of his hideous heart!"

A Lodging for the Night[1]

by ROBERT LOUIS STEVENSON

It was late in November, 1456. The snow fell over Paris with rigorous, relentless persistence; sometimes the wind made a sally and scattered it in flying vortices; sometimes there was a lull, and flake after flake descended out of the black night air, silent, circuitous, interminable. To poor people, looking up under moist eyebrows, it seemed a wonder where it all came from. Master Francis Villon had propounded an alternative that afternoon, at a tavern window: was it only Pagan Jupiter plucking geese upon Olympus? or were the holy angels moulting? He was only a poor Master of Arts, he went on; and as the question somewhat touched upon divinity, he durst not venture to conclude. A silly old priest from Montargis, who was among the company, treated the young rascal to a bottle of wine in honour of the jest and grimaces with which it was accompanied, and swore on his own white beard that he had been just such another irreverent dog when he was Villon's age.

The air was raw and pointed, but not far below freezing; and the flakes were large, damp, and adhesive. The whole city was sheeted up. An army might have marched from end to end and not a footfall given the alarm. If there were any belated birds in heaven, they saw the island like a large white patch, and the bridges like slim white spars, on the black ground of the river. High up overhead the snow settled among the tracery of the cathedral towers. Many a niche was drifted full; many a statue wore a long white bonnet on its grotesque or sainted head. The gargoyles had been transformed into great false noses, drooping towards the point. The crockets were like upright pillows swollen on one side. In the intervals of the wind, there was a dull sound of dripping about the precincts of the church.

The cemetery of St. John had taken its own share of the snow. All the graves were decently covered; tall white housetops stood around in grave array; worthy burghers were long ago in bed, benightcapped like their domiciles; there was no light in all the neighbourhood but a little peep from a lamp that hung swinging in the church choir, and tossed the shadows to and fro in time to its oscillations. The clock was hard on ten when the patrol went by with halberds and a lantern, beating their hands; and they saw nothing suspicious about the cemetery of St. John.

Yet there was a small house, backed up against the cemetery wall, which was still awake, and awake to evil purpose, in the snoring district. There was not much to betray it from without; only a stream of warm vapour from the

[1] From *New Arabian Nights.* Charles Scribner's Sons, 1887.

chimney-top, a patch where the snow melted on the roof, and a few half-obliterated footprints at the door. But within, behind the shuttered windows, Master Francis Villon the poet, and some of the thievish crew with whom he consorted, were keeping the night alive and passing round the bottle.

A great pile of living embers diffused a strong and ruddy glow from the arched chimney. Before this straddled Dom Nicolas, the Picardy monk, with his skirts picked up and his fat legs bared to the comfortable warmth. His dilated shadow cut the room in half; and the firelight only escaped on either side of his broad person, and in a little pool between his outspread feet. His face had the beery, bruised appearance of the continual drinker's; it was covered with a network of congested veins, purple in ordinary circumstances, but now pale violet, for even with his back to the fire the cold pinched him on the other side. His cowl had half fallen back, and made a strange excrescence on either side of his bull neck. So he straddled, grumbling, and cut the room in half with the shadow of his portly frame.

On the right, Villon and Guy Tabary were huddled together over a scrap of parchment; Villon making a ballade which he was to call the "Ballade of Roast Fish," and Tabary spluttering admiration at his shoulder. The poet was a rag of a man, dark, little, and lean, with hollow cheeks and thin black locks. He carried his four-and-twenty years with feverish animation. Greed had made folds about his eyes, evil smiles had puckered his mouth. The wolf and pig struggled together in his face. It was an eloquent, sharp, ugly, earthly countenance. His hands were small and prehensile, with fingers knotted like a cord; and they were continually flickering in front of him in violent and expressive pantomine. As for Tabary, a broad, complacent, admiring imbecility breathed from his squash nose and slobbering lips: he had become a thief, just as he might have become the most decent of burgesses, by the imperious chance that rules the lives of human geese and human donkeys.

At the monk's other hand, Montigny and Thevenin Pensete played a game of chance. About the first there clung some flavour of good birth and training, as about a fallen angel; something long, lithe, and courtly in the person; something aquiline and darkling in the face. Thevenin, poor soul, was in great feather: he had done a good stroke of knavery that afternoon in the Faubourg St. Jacques, and all night he had been gaining from Montigny. A flat smile illuminated his face; his bald head shone rosily in a garland of red curls; his little protuberant stomach shook with silent chucklings as he swept in his gains.

"Doubles or quits?" said Thevenin.

Montigny nodded grimly.

"*Some may prefer to dine in state,*" wrote Villon, "On bread and cheese on silver plate. Or, or—help me out, Guido!"

Tabary giggled.

"*Or parsley on a golden dish,*" scribbled the poet.

The wind was freshening without; it drove the snow before it, and sometimes raised its voice in a victorious whoop, and made sepulchral grumblings in the chimney. The cold was growing sharper as the night went on. Villon, protruding his lips, imitated the gust with something between a whistle and a groan. It was an eerie, uncomfortable talent of the poet's, much detested by the Picardy monk.

"Can't you hear it rattle in the gibbet?" said Villon. "They are all dancing the devil's jig on nothing, up there. You may dance, my gallants, you'll be none the warmer! Whew! what a gust! Down went somebody just now! A medlar the fewer on the three-legged medlar-tree!—I say, Dom Nicolas, it'll be cold to-night on the St. Denis Road?" he asked.

Dom Nicolas winked both his big eyes, and seemed to choke upon his Adam's apple. Montfaucon, the great Grisly Paris gibbet, stood hard by the St. Denis Road, and the pleasantry touched him on the raw. As for Tabary, he laughed immoderately over the medlars; he had never heard anything more light-hearted; and he held his sides and crowed. Villon fetched him a fillip on the nose, which turned his mirth into an attack of coughing.

"Oh, stop that row," said Villon, "and think of rhymes to 'fish.'"

"Doubles or quits," said Montigny doggedly.

"With all my heart," quoth Thevenin.

"Is there any more in that bottle?" asked the monk.

"Open another," said Villon. "How do you ever hope to fill that big hogshead, your body, with little things like bottles? And how do you expect to get to heaven? How many angels, do you fancy, can be spared to carry up a single monk from Picardy? Or do you think yourself another Elias—and they'll send the coach for you?"

"*Hominibus impossible*," replied the monk as he filled his glass.

Tabary was in ecstasies.

Villon filliped his nose again.

"Laugh at my jokes, if you like," he said.

"It was very good," objected Tabary.

Villon made a face at him. "Think of rhymes to 'fish,'" he said. "What have you to do with Latin? You'll wish you knew none of it at the great assizes, when the devil calls for Guido Tabary, clericus—the devil with the hump-back and red-hot finger-nails. Talking of the devil," he added in a whisper, "look at Montigny!"

All three peered covertly at the gamester. He did not seem to be enjoying his luck. His mouth was a little to a side; one nostril nearly shut, and the other much inflated. The black dog was on his back, as people say, in terrifying nursery metaphor; and he breathed hard under the gruesome burthen.

"He looks as if he could knife him," whispered Tabary, with round eyes.

The monk shuddered, and turned his face and spread his open hands to the red embers. It was the cold that thus affected Dom Nicolas, and not any excess of moral sensibility.

"Come now," said Villon—"about this ballade. How does it run so far?" And beating time with his hand, he read it aloud to Tabary.

They were interrupted at the fourth rhyme by a brief and fatal movement among the gamesters. The round was completed, and Thevenin was just opening his mouth to claim another victory, when Montigny leaped up, swift as an adder, and stabbed him to the heart. The blow took effect before he had time to utter a cry, before he had time to move. A tremor or two convulsed his frame; his hands opened and shut, his heels rattled on the floor; then his head rolled backward over one shoulder with the eyes wide open; and Thevenin Pensete's spirit had returned to Him who made it.

Every one sprang to his feet; but the business was over in two twos. The four living fellows looked at each other in rather a ghastly fashion; the dead man contemplating a corner of the roof with a singular and ugly leer.

"My God!" said Tabary; and he began to pray in Latin.

Villon broke out into hysterical laughter. He came a step forward and ducked a ridiculous bow at Thevenin, and laughed still louder. Then he sat down suddenly, all of a heap, upon a stool, and continued laughing bitterly, as though he would shake himself to pieces.

Montigny recovered his composure first.

"Let's see what he has about him," he remarked, and he picked the dead man's pockets with a practised hand, and divided the money into four equal portions on the table. "There's for you," he said.

The monk received his share with a deep sigh, and a single stealthy glance at the dead Thevenin, who was beginning to sink into himself and topple sideways off the chair.

"We're all in for it," cried Villon, swallowing his mirth. "It's a hanging job for every man jack of us that's here—not to speak of those who aren't." He made a shocking gesture in the air with his raised right hand, and put out his tongue and threw his head on one side, so as to counterfeit the appearance of one who has been hanged. Then he pocketed his share of the spoil, and executed a shuffle with his feet as if to restore the circulation.

Tabary was the last to help himself; he made a dash at the money, and retired to the other end of the apartment.

Montigny stuck Thevenin upright in the chair, and drew out the dagger, which was followed by a jet of blood.

"You fellows had better be moving," he said, as he wiped the blade on his victim's doublet.

"I think we had," returned Villon, with a gulp. "Damn his fat head!" he broke out. "It sticks in my throat like phlegm. What right has a man to have red hair when he is dead?" And he fell all of a heap again upon the stool, and fairly covered his face with his hands.

Montigny and Dom Nicolas laughed aloud, even Tabary feebly chiming in.

"Cry baby," said the monk.

"I always said he was a woman," added Montigny, with a sneer. "Sit up, can't you?" he went on, giving another shake to the murdered body. "Tread out that fire, Nick!"

But Nick was better employed; he was quietly taking Villon's purse, as the poet sat, limp and trembling, on the stool where he had been making a ballade not three minutes before. Montigny and Tabary dumbly demanded a share of the booty, which the monk silently promised as he passed the little bag into the bosom of his gown. In many ways an artistic nature unfits a man for practical existence.

No sooner had the theft been accomplished than Villon shook himself, jumped to his feet, and began helping to scatter and extinguish the embers. Meanwhile Montigny opened the door and cautiously peered into the street. The coast was clear; there was no meddlesome patrol in sight. Still it was judged wiser to slip out severally; and as Villon was himself in a hurry to escape from the neighbourhood of the dead Thevenin, and the rest were in a still greater hurry to get rid of him before he should discover the loss of his money, he was the first by general consent to issue forth into the street.

The wind had triumphed and swept all the clouds from heaven. Only a few vapours, as thin as moonlight, fleeted rapidly across the stars. It was bitter cold; and by a common optical effect, things seemed almost more definite than in the broadest daylight. The sleeping city was absolutely still; a company of white hoods, a field full of little alps, below the twinkling stars. Villon cursed his fortune. Would it were still snowing! Now, wherever the glittering streets; wherever he went he was still tethered to the house by the cemetery of St. John; wherever he went he must weave, with his own plodding feet, the rope that bound him to the crime and would bind him to the gallows. The leer of the dead man came back to him with a new significance. He snapped his fingers as if to pluck up his own spirits, and choosing a street at random, stepped boldly forward in the snow.

Two things preoccupied him as he went: the aspect of the gallows at Montfaucon in this bright, windy phase of the night's existence, for one; and for another, the look of the dead man with his bald head and garland of red curls. Both struck cold upon his heart, and he kept quickening his pace as if he could escape from unpleasant thoughts by mere fleetness of foot. Sometimes he looked back over his shoulder with a sudden nervous jerk; but he was the only moving thing in the white streets, except when the wind swooped round a corner and threw up the snow, which was beginning to freeze, in spouts of glittering dust.

Suddenly he saw, a long way before him, a black clump and a couple of lanterns. The clump was in motion, and the lanterns swung as though carried by men walking. It was a patrol. And though it was merely crossing his line of march he judged it wiser to get out of eyeshot as speedily as he could. He was not in the humour to be challenged, and he was conscious of making a very conspicuous mark upon the snow. Just on his left hand there stood a great hotel, with some turrets and a large porch before the door; it was half ruinous, he remembered, and had long stood empty; and so he made three steps of it, and jumped into the shelter of the porch. It was pretty dark inside, after the glimmer of the snowy streets, and he was groping forward with outspread hands, when he stumbled over some substance which offered an indescribable mixture of resistances, hard and soft, firm and loose.

His heart gave a leap, and he sprang two steps back and stared dreadfully at the obstacle. Then he gave a little laugh of relief. It was only a woman, and she dead. He knelt beside her to make sure upon this latter point. She was freezing cold, and rigid like a stick. A little ragged finery fluttered in the wind about her hair, and her cheeks had been heavily rouged that same afternoon. Her pockets were quite empty; but in her stocking, underneath the garter, Villon found two of the small coins that went by the name of whites. It was little enough; but it was always something; and the poet was moved with a deep sense of pathos that she should have died before she had spent her money. That seemed to him a dark and pitiable mystery; and he looked from the coins in his hand to the dead woman, and back again to the coins, shaking his head over the riddle of man's life. Henry V. of England, dying at Vincennes just after he had conquered France, and this poor jade cut off by a cold draught in a great man's doorway, before she had time to spend her couple of whites—it seemed a cruel way to carry on the world. Two whites would have taken such a little while to squander; and yet it would have been one more good taste in the mouth, one more smack of the lips, before the devil got the soul, and the body was left to birds and vermin. He would like to use all his tallow before the light was blown out and the lantern broken.

While these thoughts were passing through his mind, he was feeling, half mechanically, for his purse. Suddenly his heart stopped beating; a feeling of cold scales passed up the back of his legs, and a cold blow seemed to fall upon his scalp. He stood petrified for a moment; then he felt again with one feverish movement; and then his loss burst upon him, and he was covered at once with perspiration. To spendthrifts money is so living and actual—it is such a thin veil between them and their pleasure! There is only one limit to their fortune—that of time; and a spendthrift with only a few crowns is the Emperor of Rome until they are spent. For such a person to lose his money is to suffer the most shocking reverse, and fall from heaven to hell, from all to nothing, in a breath. And all the more if he has put his head in the halter for it; if he may be hanged to-morrow for that same purse, so dearly earned, so foolishly departed! Villon stood and cursed; he threw the two whites into the street; he shook his fist at heaven; he stamped, and was not horrified to find himself trampling the poor corpse. Then he began rapidly to retrace his steps towards the house beside the cemetery. He had forgotten all fear of the patrol, which was long gone by at any rate, and had no idea but that of his lost purse. It was in vain that he looked right and left upon the snow: nothing was to be seen. He had not dropped it in the streets. Had it fallen in the house? He would have liked dearly to go in and see; but the idea of the grisly occupant unmanned him. And he saw besides, as he drew near, that their efforts to put out the fire had been unsuccessful; on the contrary, it had broken into a blaze, and a changeful light played in the chinks of door and window, and revived his terror for the authorities and Paris gibbet.

He returned to the hotel with the porch, and groped about upon the snow for the money he had thrown away in his childish passion. But he could only find one white; the other had probably struck sideways and sunk deeply in. With a single white in his pocket, all his projects for a rousing night in some wild tavern vanished utterly away. And it was not only pleasure that fled laughing from his grasp; positive discomfort, positive pain, attacked him as he stood ruefully before the porch. His perspiration had dried upon him; and although the wind had now fallen, a binding frost was setting in stronger with every hour, and he felt benumbed and sick at heart. What was to be done? Late as was the hour, improbable as was success, he would try the house of his adopted father, the chaplain of St. Benoît.

He ran there all the way, and knocked timidly. There was no answer. He knocked again and again, taking heart with every stroke; and at last steps were heard approaching from within. A barred wicket fell open in the iron-studded door, and emitted a gush of yellow light.

"Hold up your face to the wicket," said the chaplain from within.

"It's only me," whimpered Villon.

"Oh, it's only you, is it?" returned the chaplain; and he cursed him with foul unpriestly oaths for disturbing him at such an hour, and bade him be off to hell, where he came from.

"My hands are blue to the wrist," pleaded Villon; "my feet are dead and full of twinges; my nose aches with the sharp air; the cold lies at my heart. I may be dead before morning. Only this once, father, and before God, I will never ask again!"

"You should have come earlier," said the ecclesiastic coolly. "Young men require a lesson now and then." He shut the wicket and retired deliberately into the interior of the house.

Villon was beside himself; he beat upon the door with his hands and feet, and shouted hoarsely after the chaplain.

"Wormy old fox!" he cried. "If I had my hand under your twist, I would send you flying headlong into the bottomless pit."

A door shut in the interior, faintly audible to the poet down long passages. He passed his hand over his mouth with an oath. And then the humour of the situation struck him, and he laughed and looked lightly up to heaven, where the stars seemed to be winking over his discomfiture.

What was to be done? It looked very like a night in the frosty streets. The idea of the dead woman popped into his imagination, and gave him a hearty fright; what had happened to her in the early night might very well happen to him before morning. And he so young! and with such immense possibilities of disorderly amusement before him! He felt quite pathetic over the notion of his own fate, as if it had been some one else's, and made a little imaginative vignette of the scene in the morning when they should find his body.

He passed all his chances under review, turning the white between his thumb and forefinger. Unfortunately he was on bad terms with some old friends who would once have taken pity on him in such a plight. He had lampooned them in verses; he had beaten and cheated them; and yet now, when he was in so close a pinch, he thought there was at least one who might perhaps relent. It was a chance. It was worth trying at least, and he would go and see.

On the way, two little accidents happened to him which coloured his musings in a very different manner. For, first, he fell in with the track of a patrol, and walked in it for some hundred yards, although it lay out of his direction. And this spirited him up; at least he had confused his trail; for he was still possessed with the idea of people tracking him all about Paris over the snow, and collaring him next morning before he was awake. The other matter affected him quite differently. He passed a street corner, where, not so long before, a woman and her child had been devoured by wolves. This was just the kind of weather, he reflected, when wolves might take it into their heads to enter Paris again; and a lone man in these deserted streets would run the chance of something worse than a mere scare. He stopped and looked upon the place with an unpleasant interest—it was a centre where several lanes intersected each other; and he looked down them all, one after another, and held his breath to listen, lest he should detect some galloping black things on the snow or hear the sound of howling between him and the river. He remembered his mother telling him the story and pointing out the spot, while he was yet a child. His mother! If he only knew where she lived, he might make sure at least of shelter. He determined he would inquire upon the morrow; nay, he would go and see her too, poor old girl! So thinking, he arrived at his destination—his last hope for the night.

The house was quite dark, like its neighbours; and yet after a few taps, he heard a movement overhead, a door opening, and a cautious voice asking who was there. The poet named himself in a loud whisper, and waited, not without some trepidation, the result. Nor had he to wait long. A window was suddenly opened, and a pailful of slops splashed down upon the doorsteps. Villon had not been unprepared for something of the sort, and had put himself as much in shelter as the nature of the porch admitted; but for all that, he was deplorably drenched below the waist. His hose began to freeze almost at once. Death from cold and exposure stared him in the face; he remembered he was of phthisical tendency, and began coughing tentatively. But the gravity of the danger steadied his nerves. He stopped a few hundred yards from the door where he had been so rudely used, and reflected with his finger to his nose. He could only see one way of getting a lodging, and that was to take it. He had noticed a house not far away, which looked as if it might be easily broken into, and thither he betook himself promptly, entertaining himself on the way with the idea of a room still hot, with a table still loaded with the remains of supper, where he might pass the rest of the black hours and whence he should issue, on the morrow, with an armful of valuable plate. He even considered on what viands and what wines he should prefer; and as he was calling the roll of his favourite dainties, roast fish presented itself to his mind with an odd mixture of amusement and horror.

"I shall never finish that ballade," he though to himself; and then, with another shudder at the recollection, "Oh, damn his fat head!" he repeated fervently, and spat upon the snow.

The house in question looked dark at first sight; but as Villon made a preliminary inspection in search of the handiest point of attack, a little twinkle of light caught his eye from behind a curtained window.

"The devil!" he thought. "People awake! Some student or some saint, confound the crew! Can't they get drunk and lie in bed snoring like their neighbours? What's the good of curfew, and poor devils of bell-ringers jumping at a rope's end in bell-towers? What's the use of day, if people sit up all night? The gripes to them!" He grinned as he saw where his logic was leading him. "Every man to his business, after all," added he, "and if they're awake, by the Lord, I may come by a supper honestly for once, and cheat the devil."

He went boldly to the door and knocked with an assured hand. On both previous occasions, he had knocked timidly and with some dread of attracting notice; but now when he had just discarded the thought of a burglarious entry, knocking at a door seemed a mighty simple and innocent proceeding. The sound of his blows echoed through the house with thin, phantasmal reverberations, as though it were quite empty; but these had scarcely died away before a measured tread drew near, a couple of bolts were withdrawn, and one wing was opened broadly, as though no guile or fear of guile were known to those within. A tall figure of a man, muscular and spare, but a little bent, confronted Villon. The head was massive in bulk, but finely sculptured; the nose blunt at the bottom, but refining upward to where it joined a pair of strong and honest eyebrows; the mouth and eyes surrounded with delicate markings, and the whole face based upon a thick white beard, boldly and squarely trimmed. Seen as it was by the light of a flickering hand-lamp, it looked perhaps nobler than it had a right to do; but it was a fine face, honourable rather than intelligent, strong, simple, and righteous.

"You knock late, sir," said the old man in resonant, courteous tones.

Villon cringed and brought up many servile words of apology; at a crisis of this sort the beggar was uppermost in him, and the man of genius hid his head with confusion.

"You are cold," repeated the old man, "and hungry? Well, step in." And he ordered him into the house with a noble enough gesture.

"Some great seigneur," thought Villon, as his host, setting down the lamp on the flagged pavement of the entry, shot the bolts once more into their places.

"You will pardon me if I go in front," he said, when this was done; and he preceded the poet up-stairs into a large apartment, warmed with a pan of charcoal and lit by a great lamp hanging from the roof. It was very bare of furniture: only some gold plate on a sideboard; some folios; and a stand of armour between the windows. Some smart tapestry hung upon the walls, representing the crucifixion of our Lord in one piece, and in another a scene of shepherds and shepherdesses by a running stream. Over the chimney was a shield of arms.

"Will you seat yourself," said the old man, "and forgive me if I leave you? I am alone in my house to-night, and if you are to eat I must forage for you myself."

No sooner was his host gone than Villon leaped from the chair on which he had just seated himself, and began examining the room, with the stealth and passion of a cat. He weighed the gold flagons in his hand, opened all the folios, and investigated the arms upon the shield, and the stuff with which the seats were lined. He raised the window curtains, and saw that the windows were set with rich stained glass in figures, so far as he could see, of martial import. Then he stood in the middle of the room, drew a long breath, and retaining it with puffed cheeks, looked round and round him, turning on his heels, as if to impress every feature of the apartment on his memory.

"Seven pieces of plate," he said. "If there had been ten, I would have risked it. A fine house, and a fine old master, so help me all the saints!"

And just then, hearing the old man's tread returning along the corridor, he stole back to his chair, and began humbly toasting his wet legs before the charcoal pan.

His entertainer had a plate of meat in one hand and a jug of wine in the other. He set down the plate upon the table, motioning Villon to draw in his chair, and going to the sideboard, brought back two goblets which he filled.

"I drink your better fortune," he said, gravely touching Villon's cup with his own.

"To our better acquaintance," said the poet, growing bold. A mere man of the people would have been awed by the courtesy of the old seigneur, but Villon was hardened in that matter; he had made mirth for great lords before now, and found them as black rascals as himself. And so he devoted himself to the viands with a ravenous gusto, while the old man, leaning backward, watched him with steady, curious eyes.

"You have blood on your shoulder, my man," he said.

Montigny must have laid his wet right hand upon him as he left the house. He cursed Montigny in his heart.

"It was none of my shedding," he stammered.

"I had not supposed so," returned his host quietly. "A brawl?"

"Well, something of that sort," Villon admitted with a quaver.

"Perhaps a fellow murdered?"

"Oh, no, not murdered," said the poet, more and more confused. "It was all fair play—murdered by accident. I had no hand in it, God strike me dead!" he added fervently.

"One rogue the fewer, I dare say," observed the master of the house.

"You may dare to say that," agreed Villon, infinitely relieved. "As big a rogue as there is between here and Jerusalem. He turned up his toes like a lamb. But it was a nasty thing to look at. I dare say you've seen dead men in your time, my lord?" he added, glancing at the armour.

"Many," said the old man. "I have followed the wars, as you imagine."

Villon laid down his knife and fork, which he had just taken up again.

"Were any of them bald?" he asked.

"Oh, yes, and with hair as white as mine."

"I don't think I should mind the white so much," said Villon. "His was red." And he had a return of his shuddering and tendency to laughter, which he drowned with a great draught of wine. "I'm a little put out when I think of it," he went on. "I knew him—damn him! And then the cold gives a man fancies—or the fancies give a man cold, I don't know which."

"Have you any money?" asked the old man.

"I have one white," returned the poet, laughing. "I got it out of a dead jade's stocking in a porch. She was as dead as Cæsar, poor wench, and as cold as a church, with bits of ribbon sticking in her hair. This is a hard world in winter for wolves and wenches and poor rogues like me."

"I," said the old man, "am Enguerrand de la Feuillée, seigneur de Brisetout, bailly du Patatrac. Who and what may you be?"

Villon rose and made a suitable reverence. "I am called Francis Villon," he said, "a poor Master of Arts of this university. I know some Latin, and a deal of vice. I can make chansons, ballades, lais, virelais, and roundels, and I am very fond of wine. I was born in a garret, and I shall not improbably die upon the gallows. I may add, my lord, that from this night forward I am your lordship's very obsequious servant to command."

"No servant of mine," said the knight; "my guest for this evening, and no more."

"A very grateful guest," said Villon politely, and he drank in dumb show to his entertainer.

"You are shrewd," began the old man, tapping his forehead, "very shrewd; you have learning; you are a clerk; and yet you take a small piece of money off a dead woman in the street. Is it not a kind of theft?"

"It is a kind of theft much practised in the wars, my lord."

"The wars are the field of honour," returned the old man proudly. "There a man plays his life upon the cast; he fights in the name of his lord the king, his Lord God, and all their lordships the holy saints and angels."

"Put it," said Villon, "that I were really a thief, should I not play my life also, and against heavier odds?"

"For gain but not for honour."

"Gain?" repeated Villon with a shrug. "Gain! The poor fellow wants supper, and takes it. So does the soldier in a campaign. Why, what are all these requisitions we hear so much about? If they are not gain to those who take them, they are loss enough to the others. The men-at-arms drink by a good fire, while the burgher bites his nails to buy them wine and wood. I have seen a good many ploughmen swinging on trees about the country; ay, I have seen thirty on one elm, and a very poor figure they made; and when I asked some one how all these came to be hanged, I was told it was because they could not scrape together enough crowns to satisfy the men-at-arms."

"These things are a necessity of war, which the low-born must endure with constancy. It is true that some captains drive overhard; there are spirits in every rank not easily moved by pity; and indeed many follow arms who are no better than brigands."

"You see," said the poet, "you cannot separate the soldier from the brigand; and what is a thief but an isolated brigand with circumspect manners? I steal a couple of mutton chops, without so much as disturbing people's sleep; the farmer grumbles a bit, but sups none the less wholesomely on what remains. You come up blowing gloriously on a trumpet, take away the whole sheep, and beat the farmer pitifully into the bargain. I have no trumpet; I am only Tom, Dick, or Harry; I am a rogue and a dog, and hanging's too good for me—with all my heart; but just ask the farmer which of us he prefers, just find out which of us he lies awake to curse on cold nights."

"Look at us two," said his lordship. "I am old, strong, and honoured. If I were turned from my house to-morrow, hundreds would be proud to shelter me. Poor people would go out and pass the night in the streets with their children, if I merely hinted that I wished to be alone. And I find you up, wandering homeless, and picking farthings off dead women by the wayside! I fear no man and nothing; I have seen you tremble and lose countenance at a word. I wait God's summons contentedly in my own house, or, if it please the king to call me out again, upon the field of battle. You look for the gallows; a rough, swift death, without hope or honour. Is there no difference between these two?"

"As far as to the moon," Villon acquiesced. "But if I had been born lord of Brisetout, and you had been the poor scholar Francis, would the difference have been any the less? Should not I have been warming my knees at this charcoal pan, and would not you have been groping for farthings in the snow? Should not I have been the soldier, and you the thief?"

"A thief?" cried the old man. "I a thief! If you understood your words, you would repent them."

Villon turned out his hands with a gesture of inimitable impudence. "If your lordship had done me the honour to follow my argument!" he said.

"I do you too much honour in submitting to your presence," said the knight. "Learn to curb your tongue when you speak with old and honourable men, or some one hastier than I may reprove you in a sharper fashion." And he rose and paced the lower end of the apartment, struggling with anger and antipathy. Villon surreptitiously refilled his cup, and settled himself more comfortably in the chair, crossing his knees and leaning his head upon one hand and the elbow against the back of the chair. He was now replete and warm; and he was in nowise frightened for his host, having gauged him as justly as was possible between two such different characters. The night was far spent, and in a very comfortable fashion after all; and he felt morally certain of a safe departure on the morrow.

"Tell me one thing," said the old man, pausing in his walk. "Are you really a thief?"

"I claim the sacred rights of hospitality," returned the poet. "My lord, I am."

"You are very young," the knight continued.

"I should never have been so old," replied Villon, showing his fingers, "if I had not helped myself with these ten talents. They have been my nursing mothers and my nursing fathers."

"You may still repent and change."

"I repent daily," said the poet. "There are few people more given to repentance than poor Francis. As for change, let somebody change my circumstances. A man must continue to eat, if it were only that he may continue to repent."

"The change must begin in the heart," returned the old man solemnly.

"My dear lord," answered Villon, "do you really fancy that I steal for pleasure? I hate stealing, like any other piece of work or of danger. My teeth chatter when I see a gallows. But I must eat, I must drink, I must mix in society of some sort. What the devil! Man is not a solitary animal—*Cui Deus fœminam tradit*. Make me king's pantler—make me abbot of St. Denis; make me bailly of the Patatrac; and then I shall be changed indeed. But as long as you leave me the poor scholar Francis Villon, without a farthing, why, of course, I remain the same."

"The grace of God is all-powerful."

"I should be a heretic to question it," said Francis. "It has made you lord of Brisetout and bailly of the Patatrac; it has given me nothing but the quick wits under my hat and these ten toes upon my hands. May I help myself to wine? I thank you respectfully. By God's grace, you have a very superior vintage."

The lord of Brisetout walked to and fro with his hands behind his back. Perhaps he was not yet quite settled in his mind about the parallel between thieves and soldiers; perhaps Villon had interested him by some cross-thread of sympathy; perhaps his wits were simply muddled by so much unfamiliar reasoning; but whatever the cause, he somehow yearned to convert the young man to a better way of thinking, and could not make up his mind to drive him forth again into the street.

"There is something more than I can understand in this," he said at length. "Your mouth is full of subtleties, and the devil has led you very far astray; but the devil is only a very weak spirit before God's truth, and all his subtleties vanish at a word of true honour, like darkness at morning. Listen to me once more. I learned long ago that a gentleman should live chivalrously and lovingly to God, and the king, and his lady; and though I have seen many strange things done, I have still striven to command my ways upon that rule. It is not only written in all noble histories, but in every man's heart, if he will take care to read. You speak of food and wine, and I know very well that hunger is a difficult trial to endure; but you do not speak of other wants; you say nothing of honour, of faith to God and other men, of courtesy, of love without reproach. It may be that I am not very wise—and yet I think I am—but you seem to me like one who has lost his way and made a great error in life. You are attending to the little wants, and you have totally forgotten the great and only real ones, like a man who should be doctoring toothache on the Judgment Day. For such things as honour and love and faith are not only nobler than food and drink, but indeed I think we desire them more, and suffer more sharply for their absence. I speak to you as I think you will most easily understand me. Are you not, while careful to fill your belly, disregarding another appetite in your heart, which spoils the pleasure of your life and keeps you continually wretched?"

Villon was sensibly nettled under all this sermonising. "You think I have no sense of honour!" he cried. "I'm poor enough, God knows! It's hard to see rich people with their gloves, and you blowing in your hands. An empty belly is a bitter thing, although you speak so lightly of it. If you had had as many as I, perhaps you would change your tune. Anyway I'm a thief—make the most of that—but I'm not a devil from hell, God strike me dead. I would have you to know I've an honour of my own, as good as yours, though I don't prate about it all day long, as if it was a God's miracle to have any. It seems quite natural to me; I keep it in its box till it's wanted. Why now, look you here, how long have I been in this room with you? Did you not tell me you were alone in the house? Look at your gold plate! You're strong, if you like, but you're old and unarmed, and I have my knife. What did I want but a jerk of the elbow and here would have been you with the cold steel in your bowels, and there would have been me, linking in the streets, with an armful of golden cups! Did you suppose I hadn't wit enough to see that? And I scorned the action. There are your damned goblets, as safe as in a church; there are you, with your heart ticking as good as new; and here am I, ready to go out again as poor as I came in, with my one white that you threw in my teeth! And you think I have no sense of honour—God strike me dead!"

The old man stretched out his right arm. "I will tell you what you are," he said. "You are a rogue, my man, an impudent and black-hearted rogue and vagabond. I have passed an hour with you. Oh! believe me, I feel myself disgraced! And you have eaten and drunk at my table. But now I am sick at your presence; the day has come, and the night-bird should be off to his roost. Will you go before, or after?"

"Which you please," returned the poet, rising. "I believe you to be strictly honourable." He thoughtfully emptied his cup. "I wish I could add you were intelligent," he went on, knocking on his head with his knuckles. "Age! age! the brains stiff and rheumatic."

The old man preceded him from a point of self-respect. Villon followed, whistling, with his thumbs in his girdle.

"God pity you," said the lord of Brisetout at the door.

"Good-bye, papa," returned Villon with a yawn. "Many thanks for the cold mutton."

The door closed behind him. The dawn was breaking over the white roofs. A chill, uncomfortable morning ushered in the day. Villon stood and heartily stretched himself in the middle of the road.

"A very dull old gentleman," he thought. "I wonder what his goblets may be worth."

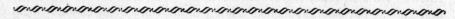

Night Club [1]

by KATHARINE BRUSH

PROMPTLY at quarter of ten P.M. Mrs. Brady descended the steps of the Elevated. She purchased from the newsdealer in the cubbyhole beneath them a next month's magazine and a to-morrow morning's paper and with these tucked under one plump arm, she walked. She walked two blocks north on Sixth Avenue; turned and went west. But not far west. Westward half a block only, to the place where the gay green awning marked *Club Français* paints a stripe of shade across the glimmering sidewalk. Under this awning Mrs. Brady halted briefly, to remark to the six-foot doorman that it looked like rain and to await his performance of his professional duty. When the small green door yawned open she sighed deeply and plodded in.

The foyer was a blackness, an airless velvet blackness like the inside of a jeweler's box. Four drum-shaped lamps of golden silk suspended from the ceiling gave it light (a very little) and formed the jewels: gold signets, those, or cuff-links for a giant. At the far end of the foyer there were black stairs, faintly dusty, rippling upward toward an amber radiance. Mrs. Brady approached and ponderously mounted the stairs, clinging with one fist to the mangy velvet rope that railed their edge.

From the top, Miss Lena Levin observed the ascent. Miss Levin was the checkroom girl. She had dark-at-the-roots blond hair and slender hips upon which, in moments of leisure she wore her hands, like buckles of ivory loosely attached. This was a moment of leisure. Miss Levin waited behind her counter. Row upon row of hooks, empty as yet, and seeming to beckon—wee curved fingers of iron—waited behind her.

"Late," said Miss Levin, "again."

"Go wan!" said Mrs. Brady. "It's only ten to ten. *Whew!* Them *stairs!*"

She leaned heavily, sideways, against Miss Levin's counter and, applying

[1] From *Harper's Magazine*, 1927. By permission of the author.

one palm to the region of her heart, appeared at once to listen and to count. "Feel!" she cried then in a pleased voice.

Miss Levin obediently felt.

"Them stairs," continued Mrs. Brady darkly, "with my bad heart, will be the death of me. Whew! Well, dearie! What's the news?"

"You got a paper," Miss Levin languidly reminded her.

"Yeah!" agreed Mrs. Brady with sudden vehemence. "I got a paper!" She slapped it upon the counter. "An' a lot of time I'll get to *read* my paper, won't I now? On a Saturday night!" she moaned. "Other nights is bad enough, dear knows—but *Saturday* nights! How I dread 'em! Every Saturday night I say to my daughter, I say, 'Geraldine, I can't,' I say, 'I can't go through it again, an' that's all there is to it,' I say. 'I'll *quit*,' I say, An' I *will*, too!" added Mrs. Brady firmly, if indefinitely.

Miss Levin, in defense of Saturday nights, mumbled some vague something about tips.

"Tips!" Mrs. Brady hissed it. She almost spat it. Plainly money was nothing, nothing at all, to this lady. "I just wish," said Mrs. Brady and glared at Miss Levin, "I just wish *you* had to spend one Saturday night, just one, in that dressing room! Bein' pushed an' stepped on and near knocked down by that gang of hussies, an' them orderin' an' bossin' you 'round like you was *black*, an' usin' your things an' then sayin' they're sorry, they got no change, they'll be back. Yah! They *never* come back!"

"There's Mr. Costello," whispered Miss Levin through lips that, like a ventriloquist's, scarcely stirred.

"An' as I was sayin'," Mrs. Brady said at once brightly, "I got to leave you. Ten to ten, time I was on the job."

She smirked at Miss Levin, nodded, and right-about-faced. There, indeed, Mr. Costello was. Mr. Billy Costello, manager, proprietor, monarch of all he surveyed. From the doorway of the big room, where the little tables herded in a ring around the waxen floor, he surveyed Mrs. Brady, and in such a way that Mrs. Brady, momentarily forgetting her bad heart, walked fast, scurried faster, almost ran.

The door of her domain was set politely in an alcove, beyond silken curtains looped up at the sides. Mrs. Brady reached it breathless, shouldered it open, and groped for the electric switch. Lights sprang up, a bright white blaze, intolerable for an instant to the eyes, like sun on snow. Blinking, Mrs. Brady shut the door.

The room was a spotless, white-tiled place, half beauty shop, half dressing room. Along one wall stood washstands, sturdy triplets in a row, with pale-green liquid soap in glass balloons afloat above them. Against the opposite wall there was a couch. A third wall backed an elongated glass-topped dressing table; and over the dressing table and over the washstands long rectangular sheets of mirror reflected lights, doors, glossy tiles, lights multiplied. . . .

Mrs. Brady moved across this glitter like a thick dark cloud in a hurry. At the dressing table she came to a halt, and upon it she laid her newspaper, her magazine, and her purse—a black purse worn gray with much clutching. She divested herself of a rusty black coat and a hat of the mushroom persuasion, and hung both up in a corner cupboard which she opened by means of one of a quite preposterous bunch of keys. From a nook in the cupboard she took down a lace-edged handkerchief with long streamers. She untied the streamers and tied them again around her chunky black alpaca waist. The handkerchief became an apron's baby cousin.

Mrs. Brady relocked the cupboard door, fumbled her keyring over, and unlocked a capacious drawer of the dressing table. She spread a fresh towel on the plate-glass top, in the geometrical center, and upon the towel she arranged with care a procession of things fished from the drawer. Things for the hair. Things for the complexion. Things for the eyes, the lashes, the brows, the lips, and the finger nails. Things in boxes and things in jars and things in tubes and tins. Also, an ash tray, matches, pins, a tiny sewing kit. a pair of scissors. Last of all, a hand-printed sign, a nudging sort of sign:

NOTICE!

These articles, placed here for your convenience, are the property of the *maid*.

And directly beneath the sign, propping it up against the looking-glass, a china saucer, in which Mrs. Brady now slyly laid decoy money: two quarters and two dimes, in four-leaf-clover formation.

Another drawer of the dressing table yielded a bottle of bromo seltzer, a bottle of aromatic spirits of ammonia, a tin of sodium bicarbonate, and a teaspoon. These were lined up on a shelf above the couch.

Mrs. Brady was now ready for anything. And (from the grim, thin pucker of her mouth) expecting it.

Music came to her ears. Rather, the beat of music, muffled, rhythmic, remote. *Umpa-um, umpa-um, umpa-um-mm*— Mr. "Fiddle" Baer and his band, hard at work on the first fox-trot of the night. It was teasing, foot-tapping music; but the large solemn feet of Mrs. Brady were still. She sat on the couch and opened her newspaper; and for some moments she read uninterruptedly, with special attention to the murders, the divorces, the breaches of promise, the funnies.

Then the door swung inward, admitting a blast of Mr. "Fiddle" Baer's best, a whiff of perfume, and a girl.

Mrs. Brady put her paper away.

The girl was *petite* and darkly beautiful; wrapped in fur and mounted on tall jeweled heels. She entered humming the ragtime song the orchestra was playing, and while she stood near the dressing table, stripping off her gloves, she continued to hum it softly to herself:

"Oh, I know my baby loves me,
I can tell my baby loves me."

Here the dark little girl got the left glove off, and Mrs. Brady glimpsed a platinum wedding ring.

> "Cause there ain't no maybe
> In my baby's
> Eyes."

The right glove came off. The dark little girl sat down in one of the chairs that faced the dressing table. She doffed her wrap, casting it carelessly over the chair-back. It had a cloth-of-gold lining, and "Paris" was embroidered in curlicues on the label. Mrs. Brady hovered solicitously near.

The dark little girl, still humming, looked over the articles "placed here for your convenience," and picked up the scissors. Having cut off a very small hangnail with the air of one performing a perilous major operation, she seized and used the manicure buffer, and after that the eyebrow pencil. Mrs. Brady's mind, hopefully calculating the tip, jumped and jumped again like a taximeter.

> "Oh, I know my baby loves me. . . ."

The dark little girl applied powder and lipstick belonging to herself. She examined the result searchingly in the mirror and sat back, satisfied. She cast some silver *Klink! Klink!* into Mrs. Brady's saucer, and half rose. Then,, remembering something, she settled down again.

The ensuing thirty seconds were spent by her in pulling off her platinum wedding ring, tying it in a corner of a lace handkerchief, and tucking the handkerchief down the bodice of her tight white-velvet gown.

"There!" she said.

She swooped up her wrap and trotted toward the door, jeweled heels merrily twinkling.

> "Cause there ain't no maybe—"

The door fell shut.

Almost instantly it opened again, and another girl came in. A blonde, this. She was pretty in a round-eyed babyish way; but Mrs. Brady, regarding her, mentally grabbed the spirits of ammonia bottle. For she looked terribly ill. The round eyes were dull, the pretty, silly little face was drawn. The thin hands, picking at the fastenings of a spacious bag, trembled and twitched.

Mrs. Brady cleared her throat. "Can I do something for you, Miss?"

Evidently the blonde girl had believed herself alone in the dressing room. Panic, and something else. Something very like murderous hate—but for an instant only, so that Mrs. Brady, whose perceptions were never quick, missed it altogether.

"A glass of water?" suggested Mrs. Brady.

"No," said the girl, "no." She had one hand in the beaded bag now. Mrs. Brady could see it moving, causing the bag to squirm like a live thing, and the fringe to shiver. "Yes!" she cried abruptly. "A glass of water— please—you get it for me."

She dropped onto the couch. Mrs. Brady scurried to the water cooler in the corner, pressed the spigot with a determined thumb. Water trickled out thinly. Mrs. Brady pressed harder, and scowled, and thought, "Something's wrong with this thing. I mustn't forget, next time I see Mr. Costello—"

When again she faced her patient, the patient was sitting erect. She was thrusting her clenched hand back into the beaded bag again.

She took only a sip of the water, but it seemed to help her quite miraculously. Almost at once color came to her cheeks, life to her eyes. She grew young again—as young as she was. She smiled up at Mrs. Brady.

"Well!" she exclaimed. "What do you know about that!" She shook her honey-colored head. "I can't imagine what came over me."

"Are you better now?" inquired Mrs. Brady.

"Yes. Oh, yes, I'm better now. You see," said the blonde girl confidentially, "we were at the theater, my boy friend and I, and it was hot and stuffy—I guess that must have been the trouble." She paused, and the ghost of her recent distress crossed her face. "God! I thought that last act *never* would end!" she said.

While she attended to her hair and complexion she chattered gayly to Mrs. Brady, chattered on with scarcely a stop for breath, and laughed much. She said, among other things, that she and her "boy friend" had not known one another very long, but that she was "ga-ga" about him. "He is about me, too," she confessed. "He thinks I'm grand."

She fell silent then, and in the looking-glass her eyes were shadowed, haunted. But Mrs. Brady, from where she stood, could not see the looking-glass; and half a minute later the blonde girl laughed and began again. When she went out she seemed to dance out on little winged feet; and Mrs. Brady, sighing, thought it must be nice to be young . . . and happy like that.

The next arrivals were two. A tall, extremely smart young woman in black chiffon entered first, and held the door open for her companion; and the instant the door was shut, she said, as though it had been on the tip of her tongue for hours, "Amy, what under the sun *happened?*"

Amy, who was brown-eyed, brown-bobbed-haired, and patently annoyed with something, crossed to the dressing table and flopped into a chair before she made reply.

"Nothing," she said wearily then.

"That's nonsense!" snorted the other. "Tell me. Was it something she said? She's a tactless ass, of course. Always was."

"No, not anything she said. It was—" Amy bit her lip. "All right! I'll tell you. Before we left your apartment I just happened to notice that Tom had disappeared. So I went to look for him—I wanted to ask him if he'd remembered to tell the maid where we were going—Skippy's subject to croup, you know, and we always leave word. Well, so I went into the kitchen, thinking Tom might be there mixing cocktails—and there he was—and there *she* was!"

The full red mouth of the other young woman pursed itself slightly. Her arched brows lifted. "Well?"

Her matter-of-factness appeared to infuriate Amy. "He was *kissing* her!" she flung out.

"Well?" said the other again. She chuckled softly and patted Amy's shoulder, as if it were the shoulder of a child. "You're surely not going to let *that* spoil your whole evening? Amy *dear!* Kissing may once have been serious and significant—but it isn't nowadays. Nowadays, it's like shaking hands. It means nothing."

But Amy was not consoled. "I hate her!" she cried desperately. "Red-headed *thing!* Calling me 'darling' and 'honey,' and s-sending me handkerchiefs for C-Christmas—and then sneaking off behind closed doors and k-kissing my h-h-husband. . . ."

At this point Amy quite broke down, but she recovered herself sufficiently to add with venom, "I'd like to slap her!"

"Oh, oh, oh," smiled the tall young woman, "I wouldn't do that!"

Amy wiped her eyes with what might have been one of the Christmas handkerchiefs, and confronted her friend. "Well, what *would* you do, Claire? If you were I?"

"I'd forget it," said Clare, "and have a good time. I'd kiss somebody myself. You've no idea how much better you'd feel!"

"I don't do—" Amy began indignantly; but as the door behind her opened and a third young woman—red-headed, earringed, exquisite—lilted in, she changed her tone. "Oh, hello!" she called sweetly, beaming at the newcomer via the mirror. "We were wondering what had become of you!"

The red-headed girl, smiling easily back, dropped her cigarette on the floor and crushed it out with a silver-shod toe. "Tom and I were talking to 'Fiddle' Baer," she explained. "He's going to play 'Clap Yo' Hands' next, because it's my favorite. Lend me a comb, will you, somebody?"

"There's a comb there," said Clare, indicating Mrs. Brady's business comb.

"But imagine using it!" murmured the red-headed girl. "Amy darling, haven't you one?"

Amy produced a tiny comb from her rhinestone purse. "Don't forget to bring it when you come," she said, and stood up. "I'm going on out; I want to tell Tom something."

She went.

The red-headed young woman and the tall black-chiffon one were alone, except for Mrs. Brady. The red-headed one beaded her incredible lashes. The tall one, the one called Claire, sat watching her. Presently she said, "Sylvia, look here." And Sylvia looked. Anybody, addressed in that tone, would have.

"There is one thing," Claire went on quietly, holding the other's eyes, "that I want understood. And that is, *'Hands off!'* Do you hear me?"

"I don't know what you mean."

"You do know what I mean!"

The red-headed girl shrugged her shoulders. "Amy told you she saw us, I suppose."

"Precisely. And," went on Claire, gathering up her possessions and rising, "as I said before, you're to keep away." Her eyes blazed sudden white-hot rage. "Because, as you very well know, he belongs to me," she said and departed, slamming the door.

Between eleven o'clock and one Mrs. Brady was very busy indeed. Never for more than a moment during those two hours was the dressing room empty. Often it was jammed, full to overflowing with curled cropped heads, with ivory arms and shoulders, with silk and lace and chiffon, with legs. The door flapped in and back, in and back. The mirrors caught and held—and lost— a hundred different faces. Powder veiled the dressing table with a thin white dust; cigarette stubs, scarlet at the tips, choked the ash-receiver. Dimes and quarters clattered into Mrs. Brady's saucer—and were transferred to Mrs. Brady's purse. The original seventy cents remained. That much, and no more, would Mrs. Brady gamble on the integrity of womankind.

She earned her money. She threaded needles and took stitches. She powdered the backs of necks. She supplied towels for soapy, dripping hands. She removed a speck from a teary blue eye and pounded the heel on a slipper. She curled the straggling ends of a black bob and a gray bob, pinned a velvet flower on a lithe round waist, mixed three doses of bicarbonate of soda, took charge of a shed pink-satin girdle, collected, on hands and knees, several dozen fake pearls that had wept from a broken string.

She served chorus girls and school girls, gay young matrons and gayer young mistresses, a lady who had divorced four husbands, and a lady who had poisoned one, the secret (more or less) sweetheart of a Most Distinguished Name, and the Brains of a bootleg gang—She saw things. She saw a yellow check, with the ink hardly dry. She saw four tiny bruises, such as fingers might make, on an arm. She saw a girl strike another girl, not playfully. She saw a bundle of letters some man wished he had not written, safe and deep in a brocaded handbag.

About midnight the door flew open and at once was pushed shut, and a gray-eyed, lovely child stood backed against it, her palms flattened on the panels at her sides, the draperies of her white chiffon gown settling lightly to rest around her.

There were already five damsels of varying ages in the dressing room. The latest arrival marked their presence with a flick of her eyes, and, standing just where she was, she called peremptorily, "Maid!"

Mrs. Brady, standing just where *she* was, said, "Yes, Miss?"

"Please come here," said the girl.

Mrs. Brady, as slowly as she dared, did so.

The girl lowered her voice to a tense half-whisper. "Listen! Is there any way I can get out of here except through this door I came in?"

Mrs. Brady stared at her stupidly.

"Any window?" persisted the girl. "Or anything?"

Here they were interrupted by the exodus of two of the damsels-of-varying ages. Mrs. Brady opened the door for them—and in so doing caught a glimpse of a man who waited in the hall outside, a debonair, old-young man with a girl's furry wrap hung over his arm, and his hat in his hand.

The door clicked. The gray-eyed girl moved out from the wall, against which she had flattened herself—for all the world like one eluding pursuit in a cinema.

"What about that window?" she demanded, pointing.

"That's all the farther it opens," said Mrs. Brady.

"Oh! And it's the only one—isn't it?"

"It is."

"Damn," said the girl. "Then there's *no* way out?"

"No way but the door," said Mrs. Brady testily.

The girl looked at the door. She seemed to look *through* the door, and to despise and to fear what she saw. Then she looked at Mrs. Brady. "Well," she said, "then I s'pose the only thing to do is to stay in here."

She stayed. Minutes ticked by. Jazz crooned distantly, stopped, struck up again. Other girls came and went. Still the gray-eyed girl sat on the couch, with her back to the wall and her shapely legs crossed, smoking cigarettes, one from the stub of another.

After a long while she said, "Maid!"

"Yes, Miss?"

"Peek out that door, will you, and see if there's anyone standing there."

Mrs. Brady peeked, and reported that there was. There was a gentleman with a little bit of a black mustache standing there. The same gentleman, in fact, who was standing there "just after you come in."

"Oh, Lord," sighed the gray-eyed girl. "Well . . . I can't stay here all *night,* that's one sure thing."

She slid off the couch, and went listlessly to the dressing table. There she occupied herself for a minute or two. Suddenly, without a word, she darted out.

Thirty seconds later Mrs. Brady was elated to find two crumpled one-dollar bills lying in her saucer. Her joy, however, died a premature death. For she made an almost simultaneous second discovery. A saddening one. Above all, a puzzling one.

"Now what for," marveled Mrs. Brady, "did she want to walk off with them *scissors?*"

This at twelve-twenty-five.

At twelve-thirty a quartette of excited young things burst in, babbling madly. All of them had their evening wraps with them; all talked at once. One of them, a Dresden-china girl with a heart-shaped face, was the center of attention. Around her the rest fluttered like monstrous butterflies; to her they addressed their shill exclamatory cries. "Babe," they called her.

Mrs. Brady heard snatches: "Not in this state unless. . . ." "Well, you can in Maryland, Jimmy says." "Oh, there must be some place nearer than. . . ." "Isn't this *marvelous?*" "When did it happen, Baby? When did you decide?"

"Just now," the girl with the heart-shaped face sang softly, "when we were dancing."

The babble resumed. "But listen, Babe, what'll your mother and father? . . ." "Oh, never mind, let's hurry." "Shall we be warm enough with just these thin wraps, do you think? Babe, will you be warm enough? Sure?"

Powder flew and little pocket combs marched through bright marcels. Flushed cheeks were painted pinker still.

"My pearls," said Babe, "are *old*. And my dress and my slippers are *new*. Now let's see—what can I *borrow?*"

A lace handkerchief, a diamond bar-pin, a pair of earrings were proffered. She chose the bar-pin, and its owner unpinned it proudly, gladly.

"I've got blue garters!" exclaimed another girl.

"Give me one, then," directed Babe. "I'll trade with you. . . . There! That fixes that."

More babbling, "Hurry! Hurry up!" . . . "Listen, are you *sure* we'll be warm enough? Because we can stop at my house, there's nobody home." "Give me that puff, Babe, I'll powder your back." "And just to think a week ago you'd never even met each other!" "Oh, hurry *up,* let's get *started!*" "I'm ready." "So'm I." "Ready, Babe? You look adorable." "Come on, everybody."

They were gone again, and the dressing room seemed twice as still and vacant as before.

A minute of grace, during which Mrs. Brady wiped the spilled powder away with a damp gray rag. Then the door jumped open again. Two evening gowns appeared and made for the dressing table in a bee line. Slim tubular gowns they were, one silver, one palest yellow. Yellow hair went with the silver gown, brown hair with the yellow. The silver-gowned, yellow-haired girl wore orchids on her shoulder, three of them, and a flashing bracelet on each fragile wrist. The other girl looked less prosperous; still, you would rather have looked at her.

Both ignored Mrs. Brady's cosmetic display as utterly as they ignored Mrs. Brady, producing full filled equipment of their own.

"Well," said the girl with the orchids, rouging energetically, "how do you like him?"

"Oh-h—all right."

"Meaning, 'Not any,' hmm? I suspected as much!" The girl with the orchids turned in her chair and scanned her companion's profile with disapproval. "See here, Marilee," she drawled, "are you going to be a damn fool *all* your life?"

"He's fat," said Marilee dreamily. "Fat, and—greasy, sort of. I mean, greasy in his mind. Don't you know what I mean?"

"I know one thing," declared the girl with orchids. "I know Who He Is! And if I were you, that's all I'd need to know. *Under the circumstances.*"

The last three words, stressed meaningly, affected the girl called Marilee curiously. She grew grave. Her lips and lashes drooped. For some seconds she sat frowning a little, breaking a black-sheathed lipstick in two and fitting it together again.

"She's worse," she said finally, low.

"Worse?"

Marilee nodded.

"Well," said the girl with orchids, "there you are. It's the climate. She'll never be anything *but* worse, if she doesn't get away. Out West, or somewhere."

"I know," murmured Marilee.

The other girl opened a tin of eye shadow. "Of course," she said dryly, "suit yourself. She's not *my* sister."

Marilee said nothing. Quiet she sat, breaking the lipstick, mending it, breaking it.

"Oh, well," she breathed finally, wearily, and straightened up. She propped her elbows on the plate-glass dressing-table top and leaned toward the mirror, and with the lipstick she began to make her coral-pink mouth very red and gay and reckless and alluring.

Nightly at one o'clock Vane and Moreno dance for the *Club Français*. They dance a tango, they dance a waltz; then, by way of encore, they do a Black Bottom, and a trick of their own called the Wheel. They dance for twenty, thirty minutes. And while they dance you do not leave your table— for this is what you came to see. Vane and Moreno. The new New York thrill. The sole justification for the five-dollar couvert extorted by Billy Costello.

From one until half past, then, was Mrs. Brady's recess. She had been looking forward to it all the evening long. When it began—when the opening chords of the tango music sounded stirringly from the room outside— Mrs. Brady brightened. With a right good will she sped the parting guests.

Alone, she unlocked her cupboard and took out her magazine—the magazine she had bought three hours before. Heaving a great breath of relief and satisfaction, she plumped herself on the couch and fingered the pages. Immediately she was absorbed, her eyes drinking up printed lines, her lips moving soundlessly.

The magazine was Mrs. Brady's favorite. Its stories were true stories, taken from life (so the Editor said); and to Mrs. Brady they were live, vivid threads in the dull, drab pattern of her night.

Paul's Case [1]

by WILLA CATHER

I⎯T was Paul's afternoon to appear before the faculty of the Pittsburgh High School to account for his various misdemeanors. He had been suspended a week ago, and his father had called at the Principal's office and confessed his perplexity about his son. Paul entered the faculty room suave and smiling. His clothes were a trifle outgrown, and the tan velvet on the collar of his open overcoat was frayed and worn; but for all that there was something of the dandy about him, and he wore an opal pin in his neatly knotted black four-in-hand, and a red carnation in his buttonhole. This latter adornment the faculty somehow felt was not properly significant of the contrite spirit befitting a boy under the ban of suspension.

Paul was tall for his age and very thin, with high, cramped shoulders and a narrow chest. His eyes were remarkable for a certain hysterical brilliancy, and he continually used them in a conscious, theatrical sort of way, peculiarly offensive in a boy. The pupils' were abnormally large, as though he were addicted to belladonna, but there was a glassy glitter about them which that drug does not produce.

When questioned by the Principal as to why he was there, Paul stated, politely enough, that he wanted to come back to school. This was a lie, but Paul was quite accustomed to lying; found it, indeed, indispensable for overcoming friction. His teachers were asked to state their respective charges against him, which they did with such a rancour and aggrievedness as evinced that this was not a usual case. Disorder and impertinence were among the offenses named, yet each of his instructors felt that it was scarcely possible to put into words the real cause of the trouble, which lay in a sort of hysterically defiant manner of the boy's; in the contempt which they all knew he felt for them, and which he seemingly made not the least effort to conceal. Once, when he had been making a synopsis of a paragraph at the blackboard, his English teacher had stepped to his side and attempted to guide his hand. Paul had started back with a shudder and thrust his hands violently behind him. The astonished woman could scarcely have been more hurt and embarrassed had he struck at her. The insult was so involuntary and definitely personal as to be unforgettable. In one way and another, he had made all his teachers, men and women alike, conscious of the same feeling of physical aversion. In one class he habitually sat with his hand shading his eyes; in

---

[1] Reprinted from *Youth and the Bright Medusa* by Willa Cather, by permission of Alfred A. Knopf, Inc. Copyright 1920 by Willa Cather.

another he always looked out of the window during the recitation; in another he made a running commentary on the lecture, with humorous intent.

His teachers felt this afternoon that his whole attitude was symbolized by his shrug and his flippantly red carnation flower, and they fell upon him without mercy, his English teacher leading the pack. He stood through it smiling, his pale lips parted over his white teeth. (His lips were continually twitching, and he had a habit of raising his eyebrows that was contemptuous and irritating to the last degree.) Older boys than Paul had broken down and shed tears under that ordeal, but his set smile did not once desert him, and his only sign of discomfort was the nervous trembling of the fingers that toyed with the buttons of his overcoat, and an occasional jerking of the other hand which held his hat. Paul was always smiling, always glancing about him, seeming to feel that people might be watching him and trying to detect something. This conscious expression, since it was as far as possible from boyish mirthfulness, was usually attributed to insolence or "smartness."

As the inquisition proceeded, one of his instructors repeated an impertinent remark of the boy's, and the Principal asked him whether he thought that a courteous speech to make to a woman. Paul shrugged his shoulders slightly and his eyebrows twitched.

"I don't know," he replied. "I didn't mean to be polite or impolite, either. I guess it's a sort of way I have of saying things regardless."

The Principal asked him whether he didn't think that a way it would be well to get rid of. Paul grinned and said he guessed so. When he was told that he could go, he bowed gracefully and went out. His bow was like a repetition of the scandalous red carnation.

His teachers were in despair, and his drawing master voiced the feeling of them all when he declared there was something about the boy which none of them understood. He added: "I don't believe that smile of his comes altogether from insolence; there's something sort of haunted about it. The boy is not strong, for one thing. There is something wrong about the fellow."

The drawing master had come to realize that, in looking at Paul, one saw only his white teeth and the forced animation of his eyes. One warm afternoon the boy had gone to sleep at his drawing-board, and his master had noted with amazement what a white, blue-veined face it was; drawn and wrinkled like an old man's about the eyes, the lips twitching even in his sleep.

His teachers left the building dissatisfied and unhappy; humiliated to have felt so vindictive toward a mere boy, to have uttered this feeling in cutting terms, and to have set each other on, as it were, in the gruesome game of intemperate reproach. One of them remembered having seen a miserable street cat set at bay by a ring of tormentors.

As for Paul, he ran down the hill whistling the Soldiers' Chorus from *Faust,* looking wildly behind him now and then to see whether some of his teachers were not there to witness his light-heartedness. As it was now late in the afternoon and Paul was on duty that evening as usher at Carnegie Hall, he decided that he would not go home to supper.

When he reached the concert hall the doors were not yet open. It was chilly outside, and he decided to go up into the picture gallery—always deserted at this hour—where there were some of Raffelli's gay studies of Paris streets and an airy blue Venetian scene or two that always exhilarated him. He was delighted to find no one in the gallery but the old guard, who sat in the corner, a newspaper on his knee, a black patch over one eye and the other closed. Paul possessed himself of the place and walked confidently up and down, whistling under his breath. After a while he sat down before a blue Rico and lost himself. When he bethought him to look at his watch, it was after seven o'clock, and he rose with a start and ran downstairs, making a face at Augustus Cæsar, peering out from the cast-room, and an evil gesture at the Venus of Milo as he passed her on the stairway.

When Paul reached the ushers' dressing-room half-a-dozen boys were there already, and he began excitedly to tumble into his uniform. It was one of the few that at all approached fitting, and Paul thought it very becoming—though he knew the tight, straight coat accentuated his narrow chest, about which he was exceedingly sensitive. He was always excited while he dressed, twanging all over to the tuning of the strings and the preliminary flourishes of the horns in the music-room; but tonight he seemed quite beside himself, and he teased and plagued the boys until, telling him that he was crazy, they put him down on the floor and sat on him.

Somewhat calmed by his suppression, Paul dashed out to the front of the house to seat the early comers. He was a model usher. Gracious and smiling he ran up and down the aisles. Nothing was too much trouble for him; he carried messages and brought programs as though it were his greatest pleasure in life, and all the people in his section thought him a charming boy, feeling that he remembered and admired them. As the house filled, he grew more and more vivacious and animated, and the colour came to his cheeks and lips. It was very much as though this were a great reception and Paul were the host. Just as the musicians came out to take their places, his English teacher arrived with checks for the seats which a prominent manufacturer had taken for the season. She betrayed some embarrassment when she handed Paul the tickets, and a *hauteur* which subsequently made her feel very foolish. Paul was startled for a moment, and had the feeling of wanting to put her out; what business had she here among all these fine people and gay colours? He looked her over and decided that she was not appropriately dressed and must be a fool to sit downstairs in such togs. The tickets had probably been sent her out of kindness, he reflected, as he put down a seat for her, and she had about as much right to sit there as he had.

When the symphony began Paul sank into one of the rear seats with a long sigh of relief, and lost himself as he had done before the Rico. It was not that symphonies, as such, meant anything in particular to Paul, but the first sigh of the instruments seemed to free some hilarious spirit within him; something that struggled there like the Genius in the bottle found by the Arab fisherman. He felt a sudden zest of life; the lights danced before his eyes and the concert hall blazed into unimaginable splendor. When the soprano soloist came on, Paul forgot even the nastiness of his teacher's being there, and gave himself up to the peculiar intoxication such personages always had for him. The soloist chanced to be a German woman, by no means in her first youth, and the mother of many children; but she wore a satin gown and a tiara, and she had that indefinable air of achievement, that world-shine upon her, which always blinded Paul to any possible defects.

After a concert was over, Paul was often irritable and wretched until he got to sleep,—and tonight he was even more than usually restless. He had the feeling of not being able to let down; of its being impossible to give up this delicious excitement which was the only thing that could be called living at all. During the last number he withdrew and, after hastily changing his clothes in the dressing-room, slipped out to the side door where the singer's carriage stood. Here he began pacing rapidly up and down the walk, waiting to see her come out.

Over yonder the Schenley, in its vacant stretch, loomed big and square through the fine rain, the windows of its twelve stories glowing like those of a lighted cardboard house under a Christmas tree. All the actors and singers of any importance stayed there when they were in the city, and a number of the big manufacturers of the place lived there in the winter. Paul had often hung about the hotel, watching the people go in and out, longing to enter and leave school-masters and dull care behind him forever.

At last the singer came out, accompanied by the conductor, who helped her into her carriage and closed the door with a cordial *"Auf Wiedersehen"*— which set Paul to wondering whether she were not an old sweetheart of his. Paul followed the carriage over to the hotel, walking so rapidly as not to be far from the entrance when the singer alighted and disappeared behind the swinging glass doors which were opened by a negro in a tall hat and a long coat. In the moment that the door was ajar, it seemed to Paul that he, too, entered. He seemed to feel himself go after her up the steps, into the warm, lighted building, into an exotic, a tropical world of shiny, glistening surfaces and basking ease. He reflected upon the mysterious dishes that were brought into the dining-room, the green bottles in buckets of ice, as he had seen them in the supper party pictures of the Sunday supplement. A quick gust of wind brought the rain down with sudden vehemence, and Paul was startled to find that he was still outside in the slush of the gravel driveway; that his boots were letting in the water and his scanty overcoat was clinging wet about him; that the lights in front of the concert hall were out, and that the rain was driving in sheets between him and the orange glow of the windows above him. There it was, what he wanted—tangibly before him like the fairy world of a Christmas pantomime; as the rain beat in his face, Paul wondered whether he were destined always to shiver in the black night outside, looking up at it.

He turned and walked reluctantly toward the car tracks. The end had to come some time; his father in his night-clothes at the top of the stairs, explanations that did not explain, hastily improvised fictions that were forever tripping him up, his upstairs room and its horrible yellow wall-paper, the creaking bureau with the greasy plush collar-box, and over his painted wooden bed the pictures of George Washington and John Calvin, and the framed motto, "Feed my Lambs," which had been worked in red worsted by his mother, whom Paul could not remember.

Half an hour later Paul alighted from the Negley Avenue car and went slowly down one of the side streets off the main thoroughfare. It was a highly respectable street, where all the houses were exactly alike, and where business men of moderate means begot and reared large families of children, all of whom went to Sabbath-school and learned the shorter catechism, and were interested in arithmetic; all of whom were as exactly alike as their homes, and of a piece with the monotony in which they lived. Paul never went up Cordelia Street without a shudder of loathing. His home was next the house of the Cumberland minister. He approached it tonight with the nerveless sense of defeat, the hopeless feeling of sinking back forever into ugliness and commonness that he had always had when he came home. The moment he turned into Cordelia Street he felt the waters close above his head. After each of these orgies of living, he experienced all the physical depression which follows a debauch; the loathing of respectable beds, of common food, of a house permeated by kitchen odors; a shuddering repulsion for the flavorless, colorless mass of everyday existence; a morbid desire for cool things and soft lights and fresh flowers.

The nearer he approached the house, the more absolutely unequal Paul felt to the sight of it all; his ugly sleeping chamber; the cold bath-room with the grimy zinc tub, the cracked mirror, the dripping spigots; his father, at the top of the stairs, his hairy legs sticking out from his night-shirt, his feet thrust into carpet slippers. He was so much later than usual that there would certainly be inquiries and reproaches. Paul stopped short before the door. He felt that he could not be accosted by his father tonight; that he could not toss again on that miserable bed. He would not go in. He would tell his father that he had no car-fare, and it was raining so hard he had gone home with one of the boys and stayed all night.

Meanwhile, he was wet and cold. He went around to the back of the house and tried one of the basement windows, found it open, raised it cautiously, and scrambled down the cellar wall to the floor. There he stood, holding his breath, terrified by the noise he had made; but the floor above him was silent, and there was no creak on the stairs. He found a soap-box, and carried it over to the soft ring of light that streamed from the furnace door, and sat down. He was horribly afraid of rats, so he did not try to sleep, but sat looking distrustfully at the dark, still terrified lest he might have awakened his father. In such reactions, after one of the experiences which made days and nights out of the dreary blanks of the calendar, when his senses were deadened, Paul's head was always singularly clear. Suppose his father had heard him getting in at the window and had come down and shot him for a burglar? Then, again, suppose his father had come down, pistol in hand, and he had cried out in time to save himself, and his father had been horrified to think how nearly he had killed him? Then, again, suppose a day should come when his father would remember that night, and wish there had been no warning cry to stay his hand? With this last supposition Paul entertained himself until daybreak.

The following Sunday was fine; the sodden November chill was broken by the last flash of autumnal summer. In the morning Paul had to go to church and Sabbath-school, as always. On seasonable Sunday afternoons the burghers of Cordelia Street usually sat out on their front "stoops," and talked to their neighbors on the next stoop, or called to those across the street in neighborly fashion. The men sat placidly on gay cushions placed upon the steps that led down to the sidewalk, while the women, in their Sunday "waists," sat in rockers on the cramped porches, pretending to be greatly at their ease. The children played in the streets; there were so many of them that the place resembled the recreation grounds of a kindergarten. The men on the steps—all in their shirt sleeves, their vests unbuttoned—sat with their legs well apart, their stomachs comfortably protruding, and talked of the prices of things, or told anecdotes of the sagacity of their various chiefs and overlords. They occasionally looked over the multitude of squabbling children, listened affectionately to their high-pitched, nasal voices, smiling to see their own proclivities reproduced in their offspring, and interspersed their legends of the iron kings with remarks about their sons' progress at school, their grades in arithmetic, and the amounts they had saved in their toy banks.

On this last Sunday of November, Paul sat all the afternoon on the lowest step of his "stoop," staring into the street, while his sisters, in their rockers, were talking to the minister's daughters next door about how many shirt-waists they had made in the last week, and how many waffles some one had eaten at the last church supper. When the weather was warm, and his father was in a particularly jovial frame of mind, the girls made lemonade, which was always brought out in a red-glass pitcher, ornamented with forget-me-nots in blue enamel. This the girls thought very fine, and the neighbors joked about the suspicious color of the pitcher.

Today Paul's father, on the top step, was talking to a young man who shifted a restless baby from knee to knee. He happened to be the young man who was daily held up to Paul as a model, and after whom it was his father's dearest hope that he would pattern. This young man was of a ruddy complexion, with a compressed, red mouth, and faded, near-sighted eyes, over which he wore thick spectacles, with gold bows that curved about his ears. He was clerk to one of the magnates of a great steel corporation, and was looked upon in Cordelia Street as a young man with a future. There was a story that, some five years ago—he was now barely twenty-six—he had been a trifle "dissipated," but in order to curb his appetites and save the loss of time and strength that a sowing of wild oats might have entailed, he had taken his chief's advice, oft reiterated to his employés, and at twenty-one had married the first woman whom he could persuade to share his fortunes. She happened to be an angular school-mistress, much older than he, who also wore thick glasses, and who had now borne him four children, all near-sighted, like herself.

The young man was relating how his chief, now cruising in the Mediterranean, kept in touch with all the details of the business, arranging his office hours on his yacht just as though he were at home, and "knocking off work enough to keep two stenographers busy." His father told, in turn, the plan his corporation was considering, of putting in an electric railway plant at Cairo. Paul snapped his teeth; he had an awful apprehension that they might spoil it all before he got there. Yet he rather liked to hear these legends of the iron kings, that were told and retold on Sundays and holidays; these stories of palaces in Venice, yachts on the Mediterranean, and high play at Monte Carlo appealed to his fancy, and he was interested in the triumphs of cash boys who had become famous, though he had no mind for the cash boy stage.

After supper was over, and he had helped to dry the dishes, Paul nervously asked his father whether he could go to George's to get some help in his geometry, and still more nervously asked for car-fare. This latter request he had to repeat, as his father, on principle, did not like to hear requests for money, whether much or little. He asked Paul whether he could not go to some boy who lived nearer, and told him that he ought not to leave his school work until Sunday; but he gave him the dime. He was not a poor man, but he had a worthy ambition to come up in the world. His only reason for allowing Paul to usher was that he thought a boy ought to be earning a little.

Paul bounded upstairs, scrubbed the greasy odor of dish-water from his hands with the ill-smelling soap he hated, and then shook over his fingers a few drops of violet water from the bottle he kept hidden in his drawer. He left the house with his geometry conspicuously under his arm, and the moment he got out of Cordelia Street and boarded a downtown car, he shook off the lethargy of two deadening days, and began to live again.

The leading juvenile of the permanent stock company which played at one of the downtown theaters was an acquaintance of Paul's, and the boy had been invited to drop in at the Sunday-night rehearsals whenever he could. For more than a year Paul had spent every available moment loitering about Charley Edwards' dressing-room. He had won a place among Edwards' following not only because the young actor, who could not afford to employ a dresser, often found him useful, but because he recognized in Paul something akin to what churchmen term "vocation."

It was at the theater and at Carnegie Hall that Paul really lived; the rest was but a sleep and a forgetting. This was Paul's fairy tale, and it had for him all the allurement of a secret love. The moment he inhaled the gassy, painty, dusty odor behind the scenes, he breathed like a prisoner set free, and felt within him the possibility of doing or saying splendid, brilliant things. The moment the cracked orchestra beat out the overture from *Martha*, or jerked at the serenade from *Rigoletto*, all stupid and ugly things slid from him, and his senses were deliciously, yet delicately fired.

Perhaps it was because, in Paul's world, the natural nearly always wore the guise of ugliness, that a certain element of artificiality seemed to him necessary in beauty. Perhaps it was because his experience of life elsewhere was so full of Sabbath-school picnics, petty economies, wholesome advice as to how to succeed in life, and the unescapable odors of cooking, that he found this existence so alluring, these smartly clad men and women so attractive, that he was so moved by these starry apple orchards that bloomed perennially under the lime-light.

It would be difficult to put it strongly enough how convincingly the stage entrance of that theater was for Paul the actual portal of Romance. Certainly none of the company ever suspected it, least of all Charley Edwards. It was very like the old stories that used to float about London of fabulously rich Jews, who had subterranean halls, with palms, and fountains, and soft lamps and richly apparelled women who never saw the disenchanting light of London day. So, in the midst of that smoke-palled city, enamored of figures and grimy toil, Paul had his secret temple, his wishing-carpet, his bit of blue-and-white Mediterranean shore bathed in perpetual sunshine.

Several of Paul's teachers had a theory that his imagination had been perverted by garish fiction; but the truth was, he scarcely ever read at all. The books at home were not such as would either tempt or corrupt a youthful mind, and as for reading the novels that some of his friends urged upon him —well, he got what he wanted much more quickly from music; any sort of music, from an orchestra to a barrel organ. He needed only the spark, the indescribable thrill that made his imagination master of his senses, and he could make plots and pictures enough of his own. It was equally true that he was not stage-struck—not, at any rate, in the usual acceptation of that expression. He had no desire to become an actor, any more than he had to become a musician. He felt no necessity to do any of these things; what he wanted was to see, to be in the atmosphere, float on the wave of it, to be carried out, blue league after blue league, away from everything.

After a night behind the scenes, Paul found his school-room more than ever repulsive; the hard floors and naked walls; the prosy men who never wore frock coats, or violets in their button-holes; the women with their dull gowns, shrill voices, and pitiful seriousness about prepositions that govern the dative. He could not bear to have the other pupils think, for a moment, that he took these people seriously; he must convey to them that he considered it all trivial, and was there only by way of a joke, anyway. He had autograph pictures of all the members of the stock company which he showed his classmates, telling them the most incredible stories of his familiarity with these people, of his acquaintance with the soloists who came to Carnegie Hall, his suppers with them and the flowers he sent them. When these stories lost their effect, and his audience grew listless, he would bid all the boys good-bye, announcing that he was going to travel for a while; going to Naples, to California, to Egypt. Then, next Monday, he would slip back, conscious and nervously smiling; his sister was ill, and he would have to defer his voyage until spring.

Matters went steadily worse with Paul at school. In the itch to let his instructors know how heartily he despised them, and how thoroughly he was appreciated elsewhere, he mentioned once or twice that he had no time to fool with theorems; adding—with a twitch of the eyebrows and a touch of that nervous bravado which so perplexed them—that he was helping the people down at the stock company; they were old friends of his.

The upshot of the matter was, that the Principal went to Paul's father, and Paul was taken out of school and put to work. The manager at Carnegie Hall was told to get another usher in his stead; the doorkeeper at the theater was warned not to admit him to the house; and Charley Edwards remorsefully promised the boy's father not to see him again.

The members of the stock company were vastly amused when some of Paul's stories reached them—especially the women. They were hard-working women, most of them supporting indolent husbands or brothers, and they laughed rather bitterly at having stirred the boy to such fervid and florid inventions. They agreed with the faculty and with his father, that Paul's was a bad case.

The east-bound train was plowing through a January snow-storm; the dull dawn was beginning to show gray when the engine whistled a mile out of Newark. Paul started up from the seat where he had lain curled in uneasy slumber, rubbed the breath-misted window glass with his hand, and peered out. The snow was whirling in curling eddies above the white bottom lands, and the drifts lay already deep in the fields and along the fences, while here and there the long dead grass and dried weed stalks protruded black above it. Lights shone from the scattered houses, and a gang of laborers who stood beside the track waved their lanterns.

Paul had slept very little, and he felt grimy and uncomfortable. He had made the all-night journey in a day coach because he was afraid if he took a Pullman he might be seen by some Pittsburgh business man who had noticed him in Denny & Carson's office. When the whistle woke him, he clutched quickly at his breast pocket, glancing about him with an uncertain smile. But the little, clay-bespattered Italians were still sleeping, the slatternly women across the aisle were in open-mouthed oblivion, and even the crumby, crying babies were for the nonce stilled. Paul settled back to struggle with his impatience as best he could.

When he arrived at the Jersey City Station, he hurried through his breakfast, manifestly ill at ease and keeping a sharp eye about him. After he reached the Twenty-third Street Station, he consulted a cabman, and had himself driven to a men's furnishing establishment which was just opening for the day. He spent upward of two hours there, buying with endless reconsidering and great care. His new street suit he put on in the fitting-room; the frock coat and dress clothes he had bundled into the cab with his new shirts. Then he drove to a hatter's and a shoe house. His next errand was at Tiffany's, where he selected silver-mounted brushes and a scarf-pin. He would not wait to have his silver marked, he said. Lastly, he stopped at a trunk shop on Broadway, and had his purchases packed into various traveling bags.

It was a little after one o'clock when he drove up to the Waldorf, and, after settling with the cabman, went into the office. He registered from Washington; said his mother and father had been abroad, and that he had come down to await the arrival of their steamer. He told his story plausibly and had no trouble, since he offered to pay for them in advance, in engaging his rooms; a sleeping-room, sitting-room and bath.

Not once, but a hundred times Paul had planned this entry into New York. He had gone over every detail of it with Charley Edwards, and in his scrap book at home there were pages of description about New York hotels, cut from the Sunday papers.

When he was shown to his sitting-room on the eighth floor, he saw at a glance that everything was as it should be; there was but one detail in his mental picture that the place did not realize, so he rang for the bell boy and sent him down for flowers. He moved about nervously until the boy returned, putting away his new linen and fingering it delightedly as he did so. When the flowers came, he put them hastily into water, and then tumbled into a hot bath. Presently he came out of his white bath-room, resplendent in his new silk underwear, and playing with the tassels of his red robe. The snow was whirling so fiercely outside his windows that he could scarcely see across the street; but within, the air was deliciously soft and fragrant. He put the violets and jonquils on the tabouret beside the couch, and threw himself down with a long sigh, covering himself with a Roman blanket. He was thoroughly tired; he had been in such haste, he had stood up to such a strain, covered so much ground in the last twenty-four hours, that he wanted to think how it had all come about. Lulled by the sound of the wind, the warm air and the cool fragrance of the flowers, he sank into deep, drowsy restrospection.

It had been wonderfully simple; when they had shut him out of the theater and concert hall, when they had taken away his bone, the whole thing was virtually determined. The rest was a mere matter of opportunity. The only thing that at all surprised him was his own courage—for he realized well enough that he had always been tormented by fear, a sort of apprehensive dread that, of late years, as the meshes of the lies he had told closed about him, had been pulling the muscles of his body tighter and tighter. Until now. he could not remember a time when he had not been dreading something. Even when he was a little boy, it was always there—behind him, or before, or on either side. There had always been the shadowed corner, the dark place into which he dared not look, but from which something seemed always to be watching him—and Paul had done things that were not pretty to watch, he knew.

But now he had a curious sense of relief, as though he had at last thrown the gauntlet to the thing in the corner.

Yet it was but a day since he had been sulking in the traces; but yesterday afternoon that he had been sent to the bank with Denny & Carson's deposit as usual—but this time he was instructed to leave the book to be balanced. There was above two thousand dollars in checks, and nearly a thousand in the bank notes which he had taken from the book and quietly transferred to his pocket. At the bank he had made out a new deposit slip. His nerves had been steady enough to permit of his returning to the office, where he had finished his work and asked for a full day's holiday tomorrow, Saturday, giving a perfectly reasonable pretext. The bank book, he knew, would not be returned before Monday or Tuesday, and his father would be out of town for the next week. From the time he slipped the bank notes into his pocket until he boarded the night train for New York, he had not known a moment's hesitation.

How astonishingly easy it had all been; here he was, the thing done; and this time there would be no awakening, no figure at the top of the stairs. He watched the snowflakes whirling by his window until he fell asleep.

When he awoke, it was four o'clock in the afternoon. He bounded up with a start; one of his precious days gone already! He spent nearly an hour in dressing, watching every stage of his toilet carefully in the mirror. Everything was quite perfect; he was exactly the kind of boy he had always wanted to be.

When he went downstairs, Paul took a carriage and drove up Fifth Avenue toward the Park. The snow had somewhat abated; carriages and tradesmen's wagons were hurrying soundlessly to and fro in the winter twilight; boys in woolen mufflers were shoveling off the doorsteps; the avenue stages made fine spots of color against the white street. Here and there on the corners were stands, with whole flower gardens blooming behind glass windows, against which the snowflakes stuck and melted; violets, roses, carnations, lilies of the valley—somehow vastly more lovely and alluring that they blossomed thus unnaturally in the snow. The Park itself was a wonderful stage winter piece.

When he returned, the pause of the twilight had ceased, and the tune of the streets had changed. The snow was falling faster, lights streamed from the hotels that reared their many stories fearlessly up into the storm, defying the raging Atlantic winds. A long, black stream of carriages poured down the avenue, intersected here and there by other streams, tending horizontally. There were a score of cabs about the entrance of his hotel, and his driver had to wait. Boys in livery were running up and down the red velvet carpet laid from the door to the street. Above, about, within it all, was the rumble and roar, the hurry and toss of thousands of human beings as hot for pleasure as himself, and on every side of him towered the glaring affirmation of the omnipotence of wealth.

The boy set his teeth and drew his shoulders together in a spasm of realization; the plot of all dramas, the text of all romances, the nerve-stuff of all sensations was whirling about him like the snowflakes. He burnt like a faggot in a tempest.

When Paul came down to dinner, the music of the orchestra floated up the elevator shaft to greet him. As he stepped into the thronged corridor, he sank back into one of the chairs against the wall to get his breath. The lights, the chatter, the perfumes, the bewildering medley of color—he had, for a moment, the feeling of not being able to stand it. But only for a moment; these were his own people, he told himself. He went slowly about the corridors, through the writing-rooms, smoking-rooms, reception-rooms, as though he were exploring the chambers of an enchanted palace, built and peopled for him alone.

When he reached the dining-room he sat down at a table near a window. The flowers, the white linen, the many-colored wine glasses, the gay toilettes of the women, the low popping of corks, the undulating repetitions of the *Blue Danube* from the orchestra, all flooded Paul's dream with bewildering radiance. When the roseate tinge of his champagne was added—that cold, precious bubbling stuff that creamed and foamed in his glass—Paul wondered that there were honest men in the world at all. This was what all the world was fighting for, he reflected; this was what all the struggle was about. He doubted the reality of his past. Had he ever known a place called Cordelia Street, a place where fagged-looking business men boarded the early car? Mere rivets in a machine they seemed to Paul,—sickening men, with combings of children's hair always hanging to their coats, and the smell of cooking in their clothes. Cordelia Street—ah, that belonged to another time and country! Had he not always been thus, had he not sat here night after night, from as far back as he could remember, looking pensively over just such shimmering textures, and slowly twirling the stem of a glass like this one between his thumb and middle finger? He rather thought he had.

He was not in the least abashed or lonely. He had no especial desire to meet or to know any of these people; all he demanded was the right to look on and conjecture, to watch the pageant. The mere stage properties were all he contended for. Nor was he lonely later in the evening, in his loge at the Opera. He was entirely rid of his nervous misgivings, of his forced aggressiveness, of the imperative desire to show himself different from his surroundings. He felt now that his surroundings explained him. Nobody questioned his purple; he had only to wear it passively. He had only to glance down at his dress coat to reassure himself that here it would be impossible for any one to humiliate him.

He found it hard to leave his beautiful sitting-room to go to bed that night, and sat long watching the raging storm from his turret window. When he went to sleep, it was with the lights turned on in his bedroom; partly because of his old timidity, and partly so that, if he should wake in the night, there would be no wretched moment of doubt, no horrible suspicion of yellow wall-paper, or of Washington and Calvin above his bed.

On Sunday morning the city was practically snowbound. Paul breakfasted late, and in the afternoon he fell in with a wild San Francisco boy, a freshman at Yale, who said he had run down for a "little flyer" over Sunday. The young man offered to show Paul the night side of the town, and the two boys went off together after dinner, not returning to the hotel until seven o'clock the next morning. They had started out in the confiding warmth of a champagne friendship, but their parting in the elevator was singularly cool. The freshman pulled himself together to make his train, and Paul went to bed. He awoke at two o'clock in the afternoon, very thirsty and dizzy, and rang for ice-water, coffee, and the Pittsburgh paper.

On the part of the hotel management, Paul excited no suspicion. There was this to be said for him, that he wore his spoils with dignity and in no way made himself conspicuous. His chief greediness lay in his ears and eyes, and his excesses were not offensive ones. His dearest pleasures were the gray winter twilights in his sitting-room; his quiet enjoyment of his flowers, his clothes, his wide divan, his cigarette and his sense of power. He could not remember a time when he had felt so at peace with himself. The mere release from the necessity of petty lying, lying every day and every day, restored his self-respect. He had never lied for pleasure, even at school; but to make himself noticed and admired, to assert his difference from other Cordelia Street boys; and he felt a good deal more manly, more honest, even, now that he had no need for boastful pretensions, now that he could, as his actor friends used to say, "dress the part." It was characteristic that remorse did not occur to him. His golden days went by without a shadow, and he made each as perfect as he could.

On the eighth day after his arrival in New York, he found the whole affair exploited in the Pittsburgh papers, exploited with a wealth of detail which indicated that local news of a sensational nature was at a low ebb. The firm of Denny & Carson announced that the boy's father had refunded the full amount of his theft, and that they had no intention of prosecuting. The Cumberland minister had been interviewed, and expressed his hope of yet reclaiming the motherless lad, and Paul's Sabbath-school teacher declared that she would spare no effort to that end. The rumor had reached Pittsburgh that the boy had been seen in a New York hotel, and his father had gone East to find him and bring him home.

Paul had just come in to dress for dinner; he sank into a chair, weak in the knees, and clasped his head in his hands. It was to be worse than jail, even; the tepid waters of Cordelia Street were to close over him finally and forever. The gray monotony stretched before him in hopeless, unrelieved years; Sabbath-school, Young People's Meeting, the yellow-papered room, the damp dish-towels; it all rushed back upon him with sickening vividness. He had the old feeling that the orchestra had suddenly stopped, the sinking sensation that the play was over. The sweat broke out on his face, and he sprang to his feet, looked about him with his white, conscious smile, and winked at himself in the mirror. With something of the childish belief in miracles with which he had so often gone to class, all his lessons unlearned, Paul dressed and dashed whistling down the corridor to the elevator.

He had no sooner entered the dining-room and caught the measure of the music, than his remembrance was lightened by his old elastic power of claiming the moment, mounting with it, and finding it all-sufficient. The glare and glitter about him, the mere scenic accessories had again, and for the last time, their old potency. He would show himself that he was game, he would finish the thing splendidly. He doubted, more than ever, the existence of Cordelia Street, and for the first time he drank his wine recklessly. Was he not, after all, one of these fortunate beings? Was he not still himself, and in his own place? He drummed a nervous accompaniment to the music and looked about him, telling himself over and over that it had paid.

He reflected drowsily, to the swell of the violin and the chill sweetness of his wine, that he might have done it more wisely. He might have caught an outbound steamer and been well out of their clutches before now. But the other side of the world had seemed too far away and too uncertain then; he could not have waited for it; his need had been too sharp. If he had to choose over again, he would do the same thing tomorrow. He looked affectionately about the dining-room, now gilded with a soft mist. Ah, it had paid indeed!

Paul was awakened next morning by a painful throbbing in his head and feet. He had thrown himself across the bed without undressing, and had slept with his shoes on. His limbs and hands were lead-heavy, and his tongue and throat were parched. There came upon him one of those fateful attacks of clear-headedness that never occurred except when he was physically exhausted and his nerves hung loose. He lay still and closed his eyes and let the tide of his realities wash over him.

His father was in New York; "stopping at some joint or other," he told himself. The memory of successive summers on the front stoop fell upon him like a weight of black water. He had not a hundred dollars left; and he knew now, more than ever, that money was everything, the wall that stood between all he loathed and all he wanted. The thing was winding itself up; he had thought of that on his first glorious day in New York, and had even provided a way to snap the thread. It lay on his dressing-table now; he had got it out last night when he came blindly up from dinner,—but the shiny metal hurt his eyes, and he disliked the look of it, anyway.

He rose and moved about with a painful effort, succumbing now and again to attacks of nausea. It was the old depression exaggerated; all the world had become Cordelia Street. Yet somehow he was not afraid of anything, was absolutely calm; perhaps because he had looked into the dark corner at last, and knew. It was bad enough, what he saw there; but somehow not so bad as his long fear of it had been. He saw everything clearly now. He had a feeling that he had made the best of it, that he had lived the sort of life he was meant to live, and for half an hour he sat staring at the revolver. But he told himself that was not the way, so he went downstairs and took a cab to the ferry.

When Paul arrived at Newark, he got off the train and took another cab, directing the driver to follow the Pennsylvania tracks out of the town. The snow lay heavy on the roadways and had drifted deep in the open fields. Only here and there the dead grass or dried weed stalks projected, singularly black, above it. Once well into the country, Paul dismissed the carriage and walked, floundering along the tracks, his mind a medley of irrelevant things. He seemed to hold in his brain an actual picture of everything he had seen that morning. He remembered every feature of both his drivers, the toothless old woman from whom he had bought the red flowers in his coat, the agent from whom he had got his ticket, and all of his fellow-passengers on the ferry. His mind, unable to cope with vital matters near at hand, worked feverishly and deftly at sorting and grouping these images. They made for him a part of the ugliness of the world, of the ache in his head, and the bitter burning on his tongue. He stooped and put a handful of snow into his mouth as he walked, but that, too, seemed hot. When he reached a little hillside, where the tracks ran through a cut some twenty feet below him, he stopped and sat down.

The carnations in his coat were drooping with the cold, he noticed; all their red glory over. It occurred to him that all the flowers he had seen in· the show windows that first night must have gone the same way, long before this. It was only one splendid breath they had, in spite of their brave mockery at the winter outside the glass. It was a losing game in the end, it seemed, this revolt against the homilies by which the world is run. Paul took one of the blossoms carefully from his coat and scooped a little hole in the snow, where he covered it up. Then he dozed a while.

The sound of an approaching train woke him, and he started to his feet, remembering only his resolution, and afraid lest he should be too late. He stood watching the approaching locomotive, his teeth chattering, his lips drawn away from them in a frightened smile; once or twice he glanced nervously sidewise, as though he were being watched. When the right moment came, he jumped. As he fell, the folly of his haste occurred to him with merciless clearness, the vastness of what he had left undone. There flashed through his brain, clearer than ever before, the blue of Adriatic water, the yellow of Algerian sands.

He felt something strike his chest,—his body was being thrown swiftly through the air, on and on, immeasurably far and fast, while his limbs gently relaxed. Then, because the picture-making mechanism was crushed, the disturbing visions flashed into black, and Paul dropped back into the immense design of things.

"Ichabod": Whittier.

The Devil and Daniel Webster[1]
by STEPHEN VINCENT BENÉT

I T'S A story they tell in the border country, where Massachusetts joins Vermont and New Hampshire.

Yes, Dan'l Webster's dead—or, at least, they buried him. But every time there's a thunderstorm around Marshfield, they say you can hear his rolling voice in the hollows of the sky. And they say that if you go to his grave and speak loud and clear, "Dan'l Webster—Dan'l Webster!" the ground'll begin to shiver and the trees begin to shake. And after a while you'll hear a deep voice saying, "Neighbor, how stands the Union?" Then you better answer the Union stands as she stood, rock-bottomed and copper-sheathed, one and indivisible, or he's liable to rear right out of the ground. At least, that's what I was told when I was a youngster.

You see, for a while, he was the biggest man in the country. He never got to be President, but he was the biggest man. There were thousands that trusted in him right next to God Almighty, and they told stories about him and all the things that belonged to him that were like the stories of patriarchs and such. They said, when he stood up to speak, stars and stripes came right out in the sky, and once he spoke against a river and made it sink into the ground. They said, when he walked the woods with his fishing rod, Killall, the trout would jump out of the streams right into his pockets, for they knew it was no use putting up a fight against him; and, when he argued a case, he could turn on the harps of the blessed and the shaking of the earth underground. That was the kind of man he was, and his big farm up at Marshfield was suitable to him. The chickens he raised were all white meat down through the drumsticks, the cows were tended like children, and the big ram he called Goliath had horns with a curl like a morning-glory vine and could butt through an iron door. But Dan'l wasn't one of your gentlemen farmers; he knew all the ways of the land, and he'd be up by candlelight to see that the chores got done. A man with a mouth like a mastiff, a brow like a mountain and eyes like burning anthracite—that was Dan'l Webster in his prime. And the biggest case he argued never got written down in the books, for he argued it against the devil, nip and tuck, and no holds barred. And this is the way I used to hear it told.

There was a man named Jabez Stone, lived at Cross Corners, New Hampshire. He wasn't a bad man to start with, but he was an unlucky man. If he planted corn, he got borers; if he planted potatoes, he got blight. He had

---

[1] Copyright, 1937, by Stephen Vincent Benét. Published by Rinehart & Company, Inc.

good-enough land, but it didn't prosper him; he had a decent wife and children, but the more children he had, the less there was to feed them. If stones cropped up in his neighbor's field, boulders boiled up in his; if he had a horse with the spavins, he'd trade it for one with the staggers and give something extra. There's some folks bound to be like that, apparently. But one day Jabez Stone got sick of the whole business.

He'd been plowing that morning and he'd just broke the plowshare on a rock that he could have sworn hadn't been there yesterday. And, as he stood looking at the plowshare, the off horse began to cough—that ropy kind of cough that means sickness and horse doctors. There were two children down with the measles, his wife was ailing, and he had a whitlow on his thumb. It was about the last straw for Jabez Stone. "I vow," he said, and he looked around him kind of desperate—"I vow it's enough to make a man want to sell his soul to the devil! And I would, too, for two cents!"

Then he felt a kind of queerness come over him at having said what he'd said; though, naturally, being a New Hampshireman, he wouldn't take it back. But, all the same, when it got to be evening and, as far as he could see, no notice had been taken, he felt relieved in his mind, for he was a religious man. But notice is always taken, sooner or later, just like the Good Book says. And, sure enough, next day, about suppertime, a soft-spoken, dark-dressed stranger drove up in a handsome buggy and asked for Jabez Stone.

Well, Jabez told his family it was a lawyer, come to see him about a legacy. But he knew who it was. He didn't like the looks of the stranger, nor the way he smiled with his teeth. They were white teeth, and plentiful—some say they were filed to a point, but I wouldn't vouch for that. And he didn't like it when the dog took one look at the stranger and ran away howling, with his tail between his legs. But having passed his word, more or less, he stuck to it, and they went out behind the barn and made their bargain. Jabez Stone had to prick his finger to sign, and the stranger lent him a silver pin. The wound healed clean, but it left a little white scar.

After that, all of a sudden, things began to pick up and prosper for Jabez Stone. His cows got fat and his horses sleek, his crops were the envy of the neighborhood, and lightning might strike all over the valley, but it wouldn't strike his barn. Pretty soon, he was one of the prosperous people of the country; they asked him to stand for selectman, and he stood for it; there began to be talk of running him for state senate. All in all, you might say the Stone family was as happy and contented as cats in a dairy. And so they were, except for Jabez Stone.

He'd been contented enough, the first few years. It's a great thing when bad luck turns; it drives most other things out of your head. True, every now and then, especially in rainy weather, the little white scar on his finger would give him a twinge. And once a year, punctual as clockwork, the stranger with the handsome buggy would come driving by. But the sixth year, the stranger lighted, and, after that, his peace was over for Jabez Stone.

The stranger came up through the lower field, switching his boots with a cane—they were handsome black boots, but Jabez Stone never liked the look of them, particularly the toes. And, after he'd passed the time of day, he said, "Well, Mr. Stone, you're a hummer! It's a very pretty property you've got here, Mr. Stone."

"Well, some might favor it and others might not," said Jabez Stone, for he was a New Hampshireman.

"Oh, no need to decry your industry!" said the stranger, very easy, showing his teeth in a smile. "After all, we know what's been done, and it's been according to contract and specifications. So when—ahem—the mortgage falls due next year, you shouldn't have any regrets."

"Speaking of that mortgage, mister," said Jabez Stone, and he looked around for help to the earth and the sky, "I'm beginning to have one or two doubts about it."

"Doubts?" said the stranger, not quite so pleasantly.

"Why, yes," said Jabez Stone. "This being the U. S. A. and me always having been a religious man." He cleared his throat and got bolder. "Yes, sir," he said, "I'm beginning to have considerable doubts as to that mortgage holding in court."

"There's courts and courts," said the stranger, clicking his teeth. "Still, we might as well have a look at the original document." And he hauled out a big black pocketbook, full of papers. "Sherman, Slater, Stevens, Stone," he muttered. "I, Jabez Stone, for a term of seven years— Oh, it's quite in order, I think."

But Jabez Stone wasn't listening, for he saw something else flutter out of the black pocketbook. It was something that looked like a moth, but it wasn't a moth. And as Jabez Stone stared at it, it seemed to speak to him in a small sort of piping voice, terrible small and thin, but terrible human. "Neighbor Stone!" it squeaked. "Neighbor Stone! Help me! For God's sake, help me!"

But before Jabez Stone could stir hand or foot, the stranger whipped out a big bandanna handkerchief, caught the creature in it, just like a butterfly, and started tying up the ends of the bandanna.

"Sorry for the interruption," he said. "As I was saying—"

But Jabez Stone was shaking all over like a scared horse.

"That's Miser Stevens' voice!" he said, in a croak. "And you've got him in your handkerchief!"

The stranger looked a little embarrassed.

"Yes, I really should have transferred him to the collecting box," he said with a simper, "but there were some rather unusual specimens there and I didn't want them crowded. Well, well, these little contretemps will occur."

"I don't know what you mean by contertan," said Jabez Stone, "but that was Miser Stevens' voice! And he ain't dead! You can't tell me he is! He was just as spry and mean as a woodchuck, Tuesday!"

"In the midst of life—" said the stranger, kind of pious. "Listen!" Then a bell began to toll in the valley and Jabez Stone listened, with the sweat running down his face. For he knew it was tolled for Miser Stevens and that he was dead.

"These long-standing accounts," said the stranger with a sigh; "one really hates to close them. But business is business."

He still had the bandanna in his hand, and Jabez Stone felt sick as he saw the cloth struggle and flutter.

"Are they all as small as that?" he asked hoarsely.

"Small?" said the stranger. "Oh, I see what you mean. Why, they vary." He measured Jabez Stone with his eyes, and his teeth showed. "Don't worry, Mr. Stone," he said. "You'll go with a very good grade. I wouldn't trust you outside the collecting box. Now, a man like Dan'l Webster, of course—well, we'd have to build a special box for him, and even at that, I imagine the wing spread would astonish you. He'd certainly be a prize. I wish we could see our way clear to him. But, in your case, as I was saying—"

"Put that handkerchief away!" said Jabez Stone, and he began to beg and to pray. But the best he could get at the end was a three years' extension, with conditions.

But till you make a bargain like that, you've got no idea of how fast four years can run. By the last months of these years, Jabez Stone's known all over the state and there's talk of running him for governor—and it's dust and ashes in his mouth. For every day, when he gets up, he thinks, "There's one more night gone," and every night when he lies down, he thinks of the black pocketbook and the soul of Miser Stevens, and it makes him sick at heart. Till, finally, he can't bear it any longer, and, in the last days of the last year, he hitches up his horse and drives off to seek Dan'l Webster. For Dan'l was born in New Hampshire, only a few miles from Cross Corners, and it's well known that he has a particular soft spot for old neighbors.

It was early in the morning when he got to Marshfield, but Dan'l was up already, talking Latin to the farm hands and wrestling with the ram, Goliath, and trying out a new trotter and working up speeches to make against John C. Calhoun. But when he heard a New Hampshireman had come to see him, he dropped everything else he was doing, for that was Dan'l's way. He gave Jabez Stone a breakfast that five men couldn't eat, went into the living history of every man and woman in Cross Corners, and finally asked him how he could serve him.

Jabez Stone allowed that it was a kind of mortgage case.

"Well, I haven't pleaded a mortgage case in a long time, and I don't generally plead now, except before the Supreme Court," said Dan'l, "but if I can, I'll help you."

"Then I've got hope for the first time in ten years," said Jabez Stone, and told him the details.

Dan'l walked up and down as he listened, hands behind his back, now and then asking a question, now and then plunging his eyes at the floor, as if they'd bore through it like gimlets. When Jabez Stone had finished, Dan'l puffed out his cheeks and blew. Then he turned to Jabez Stone and a smile broke over his face like the sunrise over Monadnock.

"You've certainly given yourself the devil's own row to hoe, Neighbor Stone," he said, "but I'll take your case."

"You'll take it?" said Jabez Stone, hardly daring to believe.

"Yes," said Dan'l Webster. "I've got about seventy-five other things to do and the Missouri Compromise to straighten out, but I'll take your case. For if two New Hampshiremen aren't a match for the devil, we might as well give the country back to the Indians."

Then he shook Jabez Stone by the hand and said, "Did you come down here in a hurry?"

"Well, I admit I made time," said Jabez Stone.

"You'll go back faster," said Dan'l Webster, and he told 'em to hitch up Constitution and Constellation to the carriage. They were matched grays with one white forefoot, and they stepped like greased lightning.

Well, I won't describe how excited and pleased the whole Stone family was to have the great Dan'l Webster for a guest, when they finally got there. Jabez Stone had lost his hat on the way, blown off when they overtook a wind, but he didn't take much account of that. But after supper he sent the family off to bed, for he had most particular business with Mr. Webster. Mrs. Stone wanted them to sit in the front parlor, but Dan'l Webster knew front parlors and said he preferred the kitchen. So it was there they sat, waiting for the stranger, with a jug on the table between them and a bright fire on the hearth—the stranger being scheduled to show up on the stroke of midnight, according to specification.

Well, most men wouldn't have asked for better company than Dan'l Webster and a jug. But with every tick of the clock Jabez Stone got sadder and sadder. His eyes roved round, and though he sampled the jug, you could see he couldn't taste it. Finally, on the stroke of 11:30, he reached over and grabbed Dan'l Webster by the arm.

"Mr. Webster, Mr. Webster!" he said, and his voice was shaking with fear and a desperate courage. "For God's sake, Mr. Webster, harness your horses and get away from this place while you can!"

"You've brought me a long way, neighbor, to tell me you don't like my company," said Dan'l Webster, quite peaceable, pulling at the jug.

"Miserable wretch that I am!" groaned Jabez Stone. "I've brought you a devilish way, and now I see my folly. Let him take me if he wills. I don't hanker after it, I must say, but I can stand it. But you're the Union's stay and New Hampshire's pride! He mustn't get you, Mr. Webster! He mustn't get you!"

Dan'l Webster looked at the distracted man, all gray and shaking in the firelight, and laid a hand on his shoulder.

"I'm obliged to you, Neighbor Stone," he said gently. "It's kindly thought of. But there's a jug on the table and a case in hand. And I never left a jug or a case half finished in my life."

And just at that moment there was a sharp rap on the door.

"Ah," said Dan'l Webster, very coolly, "I thought your clock was a trifle slow, Neighbor Stone." He stepped to the door and opened it. "Come in!" he said.

The stranger came in—very dark and tall he looked in the firelight. He was carrying a box under his arm—a black, japanned box with little air holes in the lid.

At the sight of the box, Jabez Stone gave a low cry and shrank into a corner of the room.

"Mr. Webster, I presume," said the stranger, very polite, but with his eyes glowing like a fox's deep in the woods.

"Attorney of record for Jabez Stone," said Dan'l Webster, but his eyes were glowing too. "Might I ask your name?"

"I've gone by a good many," said the stranger carelessly. "Perhaps Scratch will do for the evening. I'm often called that in these regions."

Then he sat down at the table and poured himself a drink from the jug. The liquor was cold in the jug, but it came steaming into the glass.

"And now," said the stranger, smiling and showing his teeth, "I shall call upon you, as a law-abiding citizen, to assist me in taking possession of my property."

Well, with that the argument began—and it went hot and heavy. At first, Jabez Stone had a flicker of hope, but when he saw Dan'l Webster being forced back at point after point, he just sat scrunched in his corner, with his eyes on that japanned box. For there wasn't any doubt as to the deed or the signature—that was the worst of it. Dan'l Webster twisted and turned and thumped his fist on the table, but he couldn't get away from that. He offered to compromise the case; the stranger wouldn't hear of it. He pointed out the property had increased in value, and state senators ought to be worth more; the stranger stuck to the letter of the law. He was a great lawyer, Dan'l Webster, but we know who's the King of Lawyers, as the Good Book tells us, and it seemed as if, for the first time, Dan'l Webster had met his match.

Finally, the stranger yawned a little. "Your spirited efforts on behalf of your client do you credit, Mr. Webster," he said, "but if you have no more arguments to adduce, I'm rather pressed for time—" and Jabez Stone shuddered.

Dan'l Webster's brow looked dark as a thundercloud.

"Pressed or not, you shall not have this man!" he thundered. "Mr. Stone is an American citizen, and no American citizen may be forced into the service of a foreign prince. We fought England for that in 12 and we'll fight all hell for it again!"

"Foreign?" said the stranger. "And who calls me a foreigner?"

"Well, I never yet heard of the dev—of your claiming American citizenship," said Dan'l Webster, with surprise.

"And who with better right?" said the stranger, with one of his terrible smiles. "When the first wrong was done to the first Indian, I was there. When the first slaver put out for the Congo, I stood on her deck. Am I not in your books and stories and beliefs, from the first settlements on? Am I not spoken of, still, in every church in New England? 'Tis true the North claims me for a Southerner and the South for a Northerner, but I am neither. I am merely an honest American like yourself—and of the best descent—for, to tell the truth, Mr. Webster, though I don't like to boast of it, my name is older in this country than yours."

"Aha!" said Dan'l Webster, with the veins standing out in his forehead. "Then I stand on the Constitution! I demand a trial for my client!"

"The case is hardly one for an ordinary court," said the stranger, his eyes flickering. "And, indeed, the lateness of the hour—"

"Let it be any court you choose, so it is an American judge and an American jury!" said Dan'l Webster in his pride. "Let it be the quick or the dead; I'll abide the issue!"

"You have said it," said the stranger, and pointed his finger at the door. And with that, and all of a sudden, there was a rushing of wind outside and a noise of footsteps. They came, clear and distinct, through the night. And yet, they were not like the footsteps of living men.

"In God's name, who comes by so late?" cried Jabez Stone, in an ague of fear.

"The jury Mr. Webster demands," said the stranger, sipping at his boiling glass. "You must pardon the rough appearance of one or two; they will have come a long way."

And with that the fire burned blue and the door blew open and twelve men entered, one by one.

If Jabez Stone had been sick with terror before, he was blind with terror now. For there was Walter Butler, the loyalist, who spread fire and horror through the Mohawk Valley in the times of the Revolution; and there was Simon Girty, the renegade, who saw white men burned at the stake and whooped with the Indians to see them burn. His eyes were green, like a catamount's, and the stains on his hunting shirt did not come from the blood of the deer. King Philip was there, wild and proud as he had been in life, with the great gash in his head that gave him his death wound, and cruel Governor Dale, who broke men on the wheel. There was Morton of Merry Mount, who so vexed the Plymouth Colony, with his flushed, loose, handsome face and his hate of the godly. There was Teach, the bloody pirate, with his black beard curling on his breast. The Reverend John Smeet, with his strangler's hands and his Geneva gown, walked as daintily as he had to the gallows. The red print of the rope was still around his neck, but he carried a perfumed handkerchief in one hand. One and all, they came into the room with the fires of hell still upon them, and the stranger named their names and their deeds as they came, till the tale of twelve was told. Yet the stranger had told the truth—they had all played a part in America.

"Are you satisfied with the jury, Mr. Webster?" said the stranger mockingly, when they had taken their places.

The sweat stood upon Dan'l Webster's brow, but his voice was clear.

"Quite satisfied," he said. "Though I miss General Arnold from the company."

"Benedict Arnold is engaged upon other business," said the stranger, with a glower. "Ah, you asked for a justice, I believe."

He pointed his finger once more, and a tall man, soberly clad in Puritan garb, with the burning gaze of the fanatic, stalked into the room and took his judge's place.

"Justice Hathorne is a jurist of experience," said the stranger. "He presided at certain witch trials once held in Salem. There were others who repented of the business later, but not he."

"Repent of such notable wonders and undertakings?" said the stern old justice. "Nay, hang them—hang them all!" And he muttered to himself in a way that struck ice into the soul of Jabez Stone.

Then the trial began, and, as you might expect, it didn't look anyways good for the defense. And Jabez Stone didn't make much of a witness in his own behalf. He took one look at Simon Girty and screeched, and they had to put him back in his corner in a kind of swoon.

It didn't halt the trial, though; the trial went on, as trials do. Dan'l Webster had faced some hard juries and hanging judges in his time, but this was the hardest he'd ever faced, and he knew it. They sat there with a kind of glitter in their eyes, and the stranger's smooth voice went on and on. Every time he'd raise an objection, it'd be "Objection sustained," but whenever Dan'l objected, it'd be "Objection denied." Well, you couldn't expect fair play from a fellow like this Mr. Scratch.

It got to Dan'l in the end, and he began to heat, like iron in the forge. When he got up to speak, he was going to flay that stranger with every trick known to the law, and the judge and jury too. He didn't care if it was contempt of court or what would happen to him for it. He didn't care any more what happened to Jabez Stone. He just got madder and madder, thinking of what he'd say. And yet, curiously enough, the more he thought about it, the less he was able to arrange his speech in his mind.

Till, finally, it was time for him to get up on his feet, and he did so, all ready to bust out with lightnings and denunciations. But before he started he looked over the judge and jury for a moment, such being his custom. And he noticed the glitter in their eyes was twice as strong as before, and they all leaned forward. Like hounds just before they get the fox, they looked, and the blue mist of evil in the room thickened as he watched them. Then he saw what he'd been about to do, and he wiped his forehead, as a man might who's just escaped falling into a pit in the dark.

For it was him they'd come for, not only Jabez Stone. He read it in the glitter of their eyes and in the way the stranger hid his mouth with one hand. And if he fought them with their own weapons, he'd fall into their power;

he knew that, though he couldn't have told you how. It was his own anger and horror that burned in their eyes; and he'd have to wipe that out or the case was lost. He stood there for a moment, his black eyes burning like anthracite. And then he began to speak.

He started off in a low voice, though you could hear every word. They say he could call on the harps of the blessed when he chose. And this was just as simple and easy as a man could talk. But he didn't start out by condemning or reviling. He was talking about the things that make a country a country, and a man a man.

And he began with the simple things that everybody's known and felt— the freshness of a fine morning when you're young, and the taste of food when you're hungry, and the new day that's every day when you're a child. He took them up and he turned them in his hands. They were good things for any man. But without freedom, they sickened. And when he talked of those enslaved, and the sorrows of slavery, his voice got like a big bell. He talked of the early days of America and the men who had made those days. It wasn't a spread-eagle speech, but he made you see it. He admitted all the wrong that had ever been done. But he showed how, out of the wrong and the right, the suffering and the starvations, something new had come. And everybody had played a part in it, even the traitors.

Then he turned to Jabez Stone, and showed him as he was—an ordinary man who'd had hard luck and wanted to change it. And, because he'd wanted to change it, now he was going to be punished for all eternity. And yet there was good in Jabez Stone, and he showed that good. He was hard and mean, in some ways, but he was a man. There was sadness in being a man, but it was a proud thing too. And he showed what the pride of it was till you couldn't help feeling it. Yes, even in hell, if a man was a man, you'd know it. And he wasn't pleading for any one person any more, though his voice rang like an organ. He was telling the story and the failures and the endless journey of mankind. They got tricked and trapped and bamboozled, but it was a great journey. And no demon that was ever foaled could know the inwardness of it—it took a man to do that.

The fire began to die on the hearth and the wind before morning to blow. The light was getting gray in the room when Dan'l Webster finished. And his words came back at the end to New Hampshire ground, and the one spot of land that each man loves and clings to. He painted a picture of that, and to each one of that jury he spoke of things long forgotten. For his voice could search the heart, and that was his gift and his strength. And to one, his voice was like the forest and its secrecy, and to another like the sea and the storms of the sea; and one heard the cry of his lost nation in it, and another saw a little harmless scene he hadn't remembered for years. But each saw something. And when Dan'l Webster finished, he didn't know whether or not he'd saved Jabez Stone. But he knew he'd done a miracle. For the glitter was gone from the eyes of judge and jury, and, for the moment, they were men again, and knew they were men.

"The defense rests," said Dan'l Webster, and stood there like a mountain. His ears were still ringing with his speech, and he didn't hear anything else till he heard Judge Hathorne say, "The jury will retire to consider its verdict."

Walter Butler rose in his place and his face had a dark, gay pride on it.

"The jury has considered its verdict," he said, and looked the stranger full in the eye. "We find for the defendant, Jabez Stone."

With that, the smile left the stranger's face, but Walter Butler did not flinch.

"Perhaps 'tis not strictly in accordance with the evidence," he said, "but even the damned may salute the eloquence of Mr. Webster."

With that, the long crow of a rooster split the gray morning sky, and judge and jury were gone from the room like a puff of smoke and as if they had never been there. The stranger turned to Dan'l Webster, smiling wryly.

"Major Butler was always a bold man," he said. "I had not thought him quite so bold. Nevertheless, my congratulations, as between two gentlemen."

"I'll have that paper first, if you please," said Dan'l Webster, and he took it and tore it into four pieces. It was queerly warm to the touch. "And now," he said, "I'll have you!" and his hand came down like a bear trap on the stranger's arm. For he knew that once you bested anybody like Mr. Scratch in fair fight, his power on you was gone. And he could see that Mr. Scratch knew it too.

The stranger twisted and wriggled, but he couldn't get out of that grip. "Come, come, Mr. Webster," he said, smiling palely. "This sort of thing is ridic—ouch!—is ridiculous. If you're worried about the costs of the case, naturally, I'd be glad to pay—"

"And so you shall!" said Dan'l Webster, shaking him till his teeth rattled. "For you'll sit right down at that table and draw up a document, promising never to bother Jabez Stone nor his heirs or assigns nor any other New Hampshireman till doomsday! For any hades we want to raise in this state, we can raise ourselves, without assistance from strangers."

"Ouch!" said the stranger. "Ouch! Well, they never did run very big to the barrel, but—ouch!—I agree!"

So he sat down and drew up the document. But Dan'l Webster kept his hand on his coat collar all the time.

"And, now, may I go?" said the stranger, quite humble, when Dan'l'd seen the document's in proper and legal form.

"Go?" said Dan'l, giving him another shake. "I'm still trying to figure out what I'll do with you. For you've settled the costs of the case, but you haven't settled with me. I think I'll take you back to Marshfield," he said, kind of reflective. "I've got a ram there named Goliath that can butt through an iron door. I'd kind of like to turn you loose in his field and see what he'd do."

Well, with that the stranger began to beg and to plead. And he begged and he pled so humbly that, finally, Dan'l, who was naturally kindhearted, agreed to let him go. The stranger seemed terrible grateful for that and said, just to show they were friends, he'd tell Dan'l's fortune before leaving. So

Dan'l agreed to that, though he didn't take much stock in fortune-tellers ordinarily. But, naturally, the stranger was a little different.

Well, he pried and he peered at the lines in Dan'l's hands. And he told him one thing and another that was quite remarkable. But they were all in the past.

"Yes, all that's true, and it happened," said Dan'l Webster. "But what's to come in the future?"

The stranger grinned, kind of happily, and shook his head.

"The future's not as you think it," he said. "It's dark. You have a great ambition, Mr. Webster."

"I have," said Dan'l firmly, for everybody knew he wanted to be President.

"It seems almost within your grasp," said the stranger, "but you will not attain it. Lesser men will be made President and you will be passed over."

"And, if I am, I'll still be Daniel Webster," said Dan'l. "Say on."

"You have two strong sons," said the stranger, shaking his head. "You look to found a line. But each will die in war and neither reach greatness."

"Live or die, they are still my sons," said Dan'l Webster. "Say on."

"You have made great speeches," said the stranger. "You will make more."

"Ah," said Dan'l Webster.

"But the last great speech you make will turn many of your own against you," said the stranger. "They will call you Ichabod; they will call you by other names. Even in New England, some will say you have turned your coat and sold your country, and their voices will be loud against you till you die."

"So it is an honest speech, it does not matter what men say," said Dan'l Webster. Then he looked at the stranger and their glances locked.

"One question," he said. "I have fought for the Union all my life. Will I see that fight won against those who would tear it apart?"

"Not while you live," said the stranger, grimly, "but it will be won. And after you are dead, there are thousands who will fight for your cause, because of words that you spoke."

"Why, then, you long-barreled, slab-sided, lantern-jawed, fortune-telling note shaver!" said Dan'l Webster, with a great roar of laughter, "be off with you to your own place before I put my mark on you! For, by the thirteen original colonies, I'd go to the Pit itself to save the Union!"

And with that he drew back his foot for a kick that would have stunned a horse. It was only the tip of his shoe that caught the stranger, but he went flying out of the door with his collecting box under his arm.

"And now," said Dan'l Webster, seeing Jabez Stone beginning to rouse from his swoon, "let's see what's left in the jug, for it's dry work talking all night. I hope there's pie for breakfast, Neighbor Stone."

But they say that whenever the devil comes near Marshfield, even now, he gives it a wide berth. And he hasn't been seen in the state of New Hampshire from that day to this. I'm not talking about Massachusetts or Vermont.

The Garden Party [1]

by KATHERINE MANSFIELD

AND after all the weather was ideal. They could not have had a more perfect day for a garden-party if they had ordered it. Windless, warm, the sky without a cloud. Only the blue was veiled with a haze of light gold, as it is sometimes in early summer. The gardener had been up since dawn, mowing the lawns and sweeping them, until the grass and the dark flat rosettes where the daisy plants had been seemed to shine. As for the roses, you could not help feeling they understood that roses are the only flowers that impress people at garden-parties; the only flowers that everybody is certain of knowing. Hundreds, yes, literally hundreds, had come out in a single night; the green bushes bowed down as though they had been visited by archangels.

Breakfast was not yet over before the men came to put up the marquee.

"Where do you want the marquee put, mother?"

"My dear child, it's no use asking me. I'm determined to leave everything to you children this year. Forget I am your mother. Treat me as an honoured guest."

But Meg could not possibly go and supervise the men. She had washed her hair before breakfast, and she sat drinking her coffee in a green turban, with a dark wet curl stamped on each check. Jose, the butterfly, always came down in a silk petticoat and a kimono jacket.

"You'll have to go, Laura; you're the artistic one."

Away Laura flew, still holding her piece of bread-and-butter. It's so delicious to have an excuse for eating out of doors, and besides, she loved having to arrange things; she always felt she could do it so much better than anybody else.

Four men in their shirt-sleeves stood grouped together on the garden path. They carried staves covered with rolls of canvas, and they had big tool-bags slung on their backs. They looked impressive. Laura wished now that she had not got the bread-and-butter, but there was nowhere to put it, and she couldn't possibly throw it away. She blushed and tried to look severe and even a little bit short-sighted as she came up to them.

"Good morning," she said, copying her mother's voice. But that sounded so fearfully affected that she was ashamed, and stammered like a little girl, "Oh—er—have you come—is it about the marquee?"

"That's right, miss," said the tallest of the men, a lanky freckled fellow, and he shifted his tool-bag, knocked back his straw hat and smiled down at her.

"That's about it."

His smile was so easy, so friendly that Laura recovered. What nice eyes he had, small, but such a dark blue! And now she looked at the others, they were smiling too. "Cheer up, we won't bite," their smile seemed to say. How very nice workmen were! And what a beautiful morning! She mustn't mention the morning; she must be business-like. The marquee.

"Well, what about the lily-lawn? Would that do?"

And she pointed to the lily-lawn with the hand that didn't hold the bread-and-butter. They turned, they stared in the direction. A little fat chap thrust out his under-lip, and the tall fellow frowned.

"I don't fancy it," said he. "Not conspicuous enough. You see, with a thing like a marquee," and he turned to Laura in his easy way, "you want to put it somewhere where it'll give you a bang slap in the eye, if you follow me."

Laura's upbringing made her wonder for a moment whether it was quite respectful of a workman to talk to her of bangs slap in the eye. But she did quite follow him.

"A corner of the tennis-court," she suggested. "But the band's going to be in one corner."

"H'm, going to have a band, are you?" said another of the workmen. He was pale. He had a haggard look as his dark eyes scanned the tennis-court. What was he thinking?

"Only a very small band," said Laura gently. Perhaps he wouldn't mind so much if the band was quite small. But the tall fellow interrupted.

"Look here, miss, that's the place. Against those trees. Over there. That'll do fine."

Against the karakas. Then the karaka-trees would be hidden. And they were so lovely, with their broad, gleaming leaves, and their clusters of yellow fruit. They were like trees you imagined growing on a desert island, proud, solitary, lifting their leaves and fruits to the sun in a kind of silent splendour. Must they be hidden by a marquee?

They must. Already the men had shouldered their staves and were making for the place. Only the tall fellow was left. He bent down, pinched a sprig of lavender, put his thumb and forefinger to his nose and snuffed up the smell. When Laura saw that gesture she forgot all about the karakas in her wonder at him caring for things like that—caring for the smell of lavender. How many men that she knew would have done such a thing? Oh, how extraordinarily nice workmen were, she thought. Why couldn't she have workmen for friends rather than the silly boys she danced with and who came to Sunday night supper? She would get on much better with men like these.

It's all the fault, she decided, as the tall fellow drew something on the back of an envelope, something that was to be looped up or left to hang, of these absurd class distinctions. Well, for her part, she didn't feel them. Not a bit, not an atom. . . . And now there came the chock-chock of wooden hammers. Some one whistled, some one sang out, "Are you right there, matey?" "Matey!" The friendliness of it, the—the— Just to prove how happy she was, just to show the tall fellow how at home she felt, and how she despised stupid conventions, Laura took a big bite of her bread-and-butter as she stared at the little drawing. She felt just like a work-girl.

"Laura, Laura, where are you? Telephone, Laura!" a voice cried from the house.

"Coming!" Away she skimmed, over the lawn, up the path, up the steps, across the veranda, and into the porch. In the hall her father and Laurie were brushing their hats ready to go to the office.

"I say, Laura," said Laurie very fast, "you might just give a squiz at my coat before this afternoon. See if it wants pressing."

"I will," said she. Suddenly she couldn't stop herself. She ran at Laurie and gave him a small, quick squeeze. "Oh, I do love parties, don't you?" gasped Laura.

"Ra-ther," said Laurie's warm, boyish voice, and he squeezed his sister too, and gave her a gentle push. "Dash off to the telephone, old girl."

The telephone. "Yes, yes; oh, yes. Kitty? Good morning, dear. Come to lunch? Do, dear. Delighted of course. It will only be a very scratch meal—just the sandwich crusts and broken meringue-shells and what's left over. Yes, isn't it a perfect morning? Your white? Oh, I certainly should. One moment—hold the line. Mother's calling." And Laura sat back. "What, mother? Can't hear."

Mrs. Sheridan's voice floated down the stairs. "Tell her to wear that sweet hat she had on last Sunday."

"Mother says you're to wear that *sweet* hat you had on last Sunday. Good. One o'clock. Bye-bye."

Laura put back the receiver, flung her arms over her head, took a deep breath, stretched and let them fall. "Huh," she sighed, and the moment after the sigh she sat up quickly. She was still, listening. All the doors in the house seemed to be open. The house was alive with soft, quick steps and running voices. The green baize door that led to the kitchen regions swung open and shut with a muffled thud. And now there came a long, chuckling absurd sound. It was the heavy piano being moved on its stiff castors. But the air! If you stopped to notice, was the air always like this? Little faint winds were playing chase, in at the tops of the windows, out at the doors. And there were two tiny spots of sun, one on the inkpot, one on a silver photograph frame, playing too. Darling little spots. Especially the one on the inkpot lid. It was quite warm. A warm little silver star. She could have kissed it.

The front door bell pealed, and there sounded the rustle of Sadie's print skirt on the stairs. A man's voice murmured; Sadie answered, careless, "I'm sure I don't know. Wait. I'll ask Mrs. Sheridan."

"What is it, Sadie?" Laura came into the hall.

"It's the florist, Miss Laura."

It was, indeed. There, just inside the door, stood a wide, shallow tray full of pots of pink lilies. No other kind. Nothing but lilies—canna lilies, big pink flowers, wide open, radiant, almost frighteningly alive on bright crimson stems.

"O-oh, Sadie!" said Laura, and the sound was like a little moan. She crouched down as if to warm herself at that blaze of lilies; she felt they were in her fingers, on her lips, growing in her breast.

"It's some mistake," she said faintly. "Nobody ever ordered so many. Sadie, go and find mother."

But at that moment Mrs. Sheridan joined them.

"It's quite right," she said calmly. "Yes, I ordered them. Aren't they lovely?" She pressed Laura's arm. "I was passing the shop yesterday, and I saw them in the window. And I suddenly thought for once in my life I shall have enough canna lilies. The garden-party will be a good excuse."

"But I thought you said you didn't mean to interfere," said Laura. Sadie had gone. The florist's man was still outside at his van. She put her arm round her mother's neck and gently, very gently, she bit her mother's ear.

"My darling child, you wouldn't like a logical mother, would you? Don't do that. Here's the man."

He carried more lilies still, another whole tray.

"Bank them up, just inside the door, on both sides of the porch, please," said Mrs. Sheridan. "Don't you agree, Laura?"

"Oh, I *do,* mother."

In the drawing-room Meg, Jose and good little Hans had at last succeeded in moving the piano.

"Now, if we put this chesterfield against the wall and move everything out of the room except the chairs, don't you think?"

"Quite."

"Hans, move these tables into the smoking-room, and bring a sweeper to take these marks off the carpet and—one moment, Hans—" Jose loved giving orders to the servants, and they loved obeying her. She always made them feel they were taking part in some drama. "Tell mother and Miss Laura to come here at once."

"Very good, Miss Jose."

She turned to Meg. "I want to hear what the piano sounds like, just in case I'm asked to sing this afternoon. Let's try over 'This Life is Weary.'"

Pom! Ta-ta-ta *Tee*-ta! The piano burst out so passionately that Jose's face changed. She clasped her hands. She looked mournfully and enigmatically at her mother and Laura as they came in.

> This Life is *Wee*-ary,
> A Tear—a Sigh.
> A Love that *Chan*-ges,
> This Life is *Wee*-ary,

> A Tear—a Sigh.
> A Love that *Chan*-ges,
> And then . . . Good-bye!

But at the word "Good-bye," and although the piano sounded more desperate than ever, her face broke into a brilliant, dreadfully unsympathetic
smile.

"Aren't I in good voice, mummy?" she beamed.

> This Life is *Wee*-ary,
> Hope comes to Die.
> A Dream—a *Wa*-kening.

But now Sadie interrupted them. "What is it, Sadie?"

"If you please, m'm, cook says have you got the flags for the sandwiches?"

"The flags for the sandwiches, Sadie?" echoed Mrs. Sheridan dreamily.
And the children knew by her face that she hadn't got them. "Let me see."
And she said to Sadie firmly, "Tell cook I'll let her have them in ten minutes."
Sadie went.

"Now, Laura," said her mother quickly. "Come with me into the smoking-
room. I've got the names somewhere on the back of an envelope. You'll
have to write them out for me. Meg, go upstairs this minute and take that
wet thing off your head. Jose, run and finish dressing this instant. Do you
hear me, children, or shall I have to tell your father when he comes home
to-night? And—and, Jose, pacify cook if you do go into the kitchen, will
you? I'm terrified of her this morning."

The envelope was found at last behind the dining-room clock, though how
it had got there Mrs. Sheridan could not imagine.

"One of you children must have stolen it out of my bag, because I remember vividly—cream cheese and lemon-curd. Have you done that?"

"Yes."

"Egg and—" Mrs. Sheridan held the envelope away from her. "It looks
like mice. It can't be mice, can it?"

"Olive, pet," said Laura, looking over her shoulder.

"Yes, of course, olive. What a horrible combination it sounds. Egg and
olive."

They were finished at last, and Laura took them off to the kitchen. She
found Jose there pacifying the cook, who did not look at all terrifying.

"I have never seen such exquisite sandwiches," said Jose's rapturous voice.
"How many kinds did you say there were, cook? Fifteen?"

"Fifteen, Miss Jose."

"Well, cook, I congratulate you."

Cook swept up crusts with the long sandwich knife, and smiled broadly.

"Godber's has come," announced Sadie, issuing out of the pantry. She
had seen the man pass the window.

That meant the cream puffs had come. Godber's were famous for their
cream puffs. Nobody ever thought of making them at home.

"Bring them in and put them on the table, my girl," ordered cook.

Sadie brought them in and went back to the door. Of course Laura and Jose were far too grown-up to really care about such things. All the same, they couldn't help agreeing that the puffs looked very attractive. Very. Cook began arranging them, shaking off the extra icing sugar.

"Don't they carry one back to all one's parties?" said Laura.

"I suppose they do," said practical Jose, who never liked to be carried back. "They look beautifully light and feathery, I must say."

"Have one each, my dears," said cook in her comfortable voice. "Yer ma won't know."

Oh, impossible. Fancy cream puffs so soon after breakfast. The very idea made one shudder. All the same, two minutes later Jose and Laura were licking their fingers with that absorbed inward look that only comes from whipped cream.

"Let's go into the garden, out by the back way," suggested Laura. "I want to see how the men are getting on with the marquee. They're such awfully nice men."

But the back door was blocked by cook, Sadie, Godber's man and Hans. Something had happened.

"Tuk-tuk-tuk," clucked cook like an agitated hen. Sadie had her hand clapped to her cheek as though she had toothache. Hans's face was screwed up in the effort to understand. Only Godber's man seemed to be enjoying himself; it was his story.

"What's the matter? What's happened?"

"There's been a horrible accident," said cook. "A man killed."

"A man killed! Where? How? When?"

But Godber's man wasn't going to have his story snatched from under his very nose.

"Know those little cottages just below here, miss?" Know them? Of course, she knew them. "Well, there's a young chap living there, name of Scott, a carter. His horse shied at a traction-engine, corner of Hawke Street this morning, and he was thrown out on the back of his head. Killed."

"Dead!" Laura stared at Godber's man.

"Dead when they picked him up," said Godber's man with relish. "They were taking the body home as I come up here." And he said to the cook, "He's left a wife and five little ones."

"Jose, come here." Laura caught hold of her sister's sleeve and dragged her through the kitchen to the other side of the green baize door. There she paused and leaned against it. "Jose!" she said, horrified, "however are we going to stop everything?"

"Stop everything, Laura!" cried Jose in astonishment. "What do you mean?"

"Stop the garden-party, of course." Why did Jose pretend?

But Jose was still more amazed. "Stop the garden-party? My dear Laura, don't be so absurd. Of course we can't do anything of the kind. Nobody expects us to. Don't be so extravagant."

"But we can't possibly have a garden-party with a man dead just outside the front gate."

That really was extravagant, for the little cottages were in a lane to themselves at the very bottom of a steep rise that led up to the house. A broad road ran between. True, they were far too near. They were the greatest possible eyesore, and they had no right to be in that neighbourhood at all. They were little mean dwellings painted a chocolate brown. In the garden patches there was nothing but cabbage stalks, sick hens and tomato cans. The very smoke coming out of their chimneys was poverty-stricken. Little rags and shreds of smoke, so unlike the great silvery plumes that uncurled from the Sheridans' chimneys. Washer-women lived in the lane and sweeps and a cobbler, and a man whose house-front was studded all over with minute bird-cages. Children swarmed. When the Sheridans were little they were forbidden to set foot there because of the revolting language and of what they might catch. But since they were grown up, Laura and Laurie on their prowls sometimes walked through. It was disgusting and sordid. They came out with a shudder. But still one must go everywhere; one must see everything. So through they went.

"And just think of what the band would sound like to that poor woman," said Laura.

"Oh, Laura!" Jose began to be seriously annoyed. "If you're going to stop a band playing every time some one has an accident, you'll lead a very strenuous life. I'm every bit as sorry about it as you. I feel just as sympathetic." Her eyes hardened. She looked at her sister just as she used to when they were little and fighting together. "You won't bring a drunken workman back to life by being sentimental," she said softly.

"Drunk! Who said he was drunk?" Laura turned furiously on Jose. She said, just as they had used to say on those occasions, "I'm going straight up to tell mother."

"Do, dear," cooed Jose.

"Mother, can I come into your room?" Laura turned the big glass door-knob.

"Of course, child. Why, what's the matter? What's given you such a colour?" And Mrs. Sheridan turned round from her dressing-table. She was trying on a new hat.

"Mother, a man's been killed," began Laura.

"*Not* in the garden?" interrupted her mother.

"No, no!"

"Oh, what a fright you gave me!" Mrs. Sheridan sighed with relief, and took off the big hat and held it on her knees.

"But listen, mother," said Laura. Breathless, half-choking, she told the dreadful story. "Of course, we can't have our party, can we?" she pleaded,

"The band and everybody arriving. They'd hear us, mother; they're nearly neighbours!"

To Laura's astonishment her mother behaved just like Jose; it was harder to bear because she seemed amused. She refused to take Laura seriously.

"But, my dear child, use your common sense. It's only by accident we've heard of it. If some one had died there normally—and I can't understand how they keep alive in those poky little holes—we should still be having our party, shouldn't we?"

Laura had to say "yes" to that, but she felt it was all wrong. She sat down on her mother's sofa and pinched the cushion frill.

"Mother, isn't it really terribly heartless of us?" she asked.

"Darling!" Mrs. Sheridan got up and came over to her, carrying the hat. Before Laura could stop her she had popped it on. "My child!" said her mother, "the hat is yours. It's made for you. It's much too young for me. I have never seen you look such a picture. Look at yourself!" And she held up her hand-mirror.

"But, mother," Laura began again. She couldn't look at herself; she turned aside.

This time Mrs. Sheridan lost patience just as Jose had done.

"You are being very absurd, Laura," she said coldly. "People like that don't expect sacrifices from us. And it's not very sympathetic to spoil everybody's enjoyment as you're doing now."

"I don't understand," said Laura, and she walked quickly out of the room into her own bedroom. There, quite by chance, the first thing she saw was this charming girl in the mirror, in her black hat trimmed with gold daisies, and a long black velvet ribbon. Never had she imagined she could look like that. Is mother right? she thought. And now she hoped her mother was right. Am I being extravagant? Perhaps it was extravagant. Just for a moment she had another glimpse of that poor woman and those little children, and the body being carried into the house. But it all seemed blurred, unreal, like a picture in the newspaper. I'll remember it again after the party's over, she decided. And somehow that seemed quite the best plan. . . .

Lunch was over by half-past one. By half-past two they were all ready for the fray. The green-coated band had arrived and was established in a corner of the tennis-court.

"My dear!" trilled Kitty Maitland, "aren't they too like frogs for words? You ought to have arranged them round the pond with the conductor in the middle on a leaf."

Laurie arrived and hailed them on his way to dress. At the sight of him Laura remembered the accident again. She wanted to tell him. If Laurie agreed with the others, then it was bound to be all right. And she followed him into the hall.

"Laurie!"

"Hallo!" He was half-way upstairs, but when he turned round and saw Laura he suddenly puffed out his cheeks and goggled his eyes at her. "My word, Laura! You do look stunning," said Laurie. "What an absolutely topping hat!"

Laura said faintly "Is it?" and smiled up at Laurie, and didn't tell him after all.

Soon after that people began coming in streams. The band struck up; the hired waiters ran from the house to the marquee. Wherever you looked there were couples strolling, bending to the flowers, greeting, moving on over the lawn. They were like bright birds that had alighted in the Sheridans' garden for this one afternoon, on their way to—where? Ah, what happiness it is to be with people who all are happy, to press hands, press cheeks, smile into eyes.

"Darling Laura, how well you look!"

"What a becoming hat, child!"

"Laura, you look quite Spanish. I've never seen you look so striking."

And Laura, glowing, answered softly, "Have you had tea? Won't you have an ice? The passion-fruit ices really are rather special." She ran to her father and begged him. "Daddy darling, can't the band have something to drink?"

And the perfect afternoon slowly ripened, slowly faded, slowly its petals closed.

"Never a more delightful garden party . . ." "The greatest success . . ." "Quite the most . . ."

Laura helped her mother with good-byes. They stood side by side in the porch till it was all over.

"All over, all over, thank heaven," said Mrs. Sheridan. "Round up the others, Laura. Let's go and have some fresh coffee. I'm exhausted. Yes, it's been very successful. But oh, these parties, these parties! Why will you children insist on giving parties!" And they all of them sat down in the deserted marquee.

"Have a sandwich, daddy dear. I wrote the flag."

"Thanks." Mr. Sheridan took a bite and the sandwich was gone. He took another. "I suppose you didn't hear of a beastly accident that happened to-day?" he said.

"My dear," said Mrs. Sheridan, holding up her hand, "we did. It nearly ruined the party. Laura insisted we should put it off."

"Oh, mother!" Laura didn't want to be teased about it.

"It was a horrible affair all the same," said Mr. Sheridan. "The chap was married too. Lived just below in the lane, and leaves a wife and half a dozen kiddies, so they say."

An awkward little silence fell. Mrs. Sheridan fidgeted with her cup. Really, it was very tactless of father . . .

Suddenly she looked up. There on the table were all those sandwiches, cakes, puffs, all uneaten, all going to be wasted. She had one of her brilliant ideas.

"I know," she said. "Let's make up a basket. Let's send that poor creature some of this perfectly good food. At any rate, it will be the greatest treat for the children. Don't you agree? And she's sure to have neighbours calling in and so on. What a point to have it all ready prepared. Laura!" She jumped up. "Get me the big basket out of the stairs cupboard."

"But, mother, do you really think it's a good idea?" said Laura.

Again, how curious, she seemed to be different from them all. To take scraps from their party. Would the poor woman really like that?

"Of course! What's the matter with you to-day? An hour or two ago you were insisting on us being sympathetic, and now—"

Oh, well! Laura ran for the basket. It was filled, it was heaped by her mother.

"Take it yourself, darling," said she. "Run down just as you are. No, wait, take the arum lilies too. People of that class are so impressed by arum lilies."

"The stems will ruin her lace frock," said practical Jose.

So they would. Just in time. "Only the basket, then. And, Laura!"— her mother followed her out of the marquee—"don't on any account—"

"What, mother?"

No, better not put such ideas into the child's head! "Nothing! Run along."

It was just growing dusky as Laura shut their garden gates. A big dog ran by like a shadow. The road gleamed white, and down below in the hollow the little cottages were in deep shade. How quiet it seemed after the afternoon. Here she was going down the hill to somewhere where a man lay dead, and she couldn't realize it. Why couldn't she? She stopped a minute. And it seemed to her that kisses, voices, tinkling spoons, laughter, the smell of crushed grass were somehow inside her. She had no room for anything else. How strange! She looked up at the pale sky, and all she thought was, "Yes, it was the most successful party."

Now the broad road was crossed. The lane began, smoky and dark. Women in shawls and men's tweed caps hurried by. Men hung over the palings; the children played in the doorways. A low hum came from the mean little cottages. In some of them there was a flicker of light, and a shadow, crab-like, moved across the window. Laura bent her head and hurried on. She wished now she had put on a coat. How her frock shone! And the big hat with the velvet streamer—if only it was another hat! Were the people looking at her? They must be. It was a mistake to have come; she knew all along it was a mistake. Should she go back even now?

No, too late. This was the house. It must be. A dark knot of people stood outside. Beside the gate an old, old woman with a crutch sat in a chair, watching. She had her feet on a newspaper. The voices stopped as Laura drew near. The group parted. It was as though she was expected, as though they had known she was coming here.

Laura was terribly nervous. Tossing the velvet ribbon over her shoulder, she said to a woman standing by, "Is this Mrs. Scott's house?" and the woman, smiling queerly, said, "It is, my lass."

Oh, to be away from this! She actually said, "Help me, God," as she walked up the tiny path and knocked. To be away from those staring eyes, or to be covered up in anything, one of those women's shawls even. I'll just leave the basket and go, she decided. I shan't even wait for it to be emptied.

Then the door opened. A little woman in black showed in the gloom.

Laura said, "Are you Mrs. Scott?" But to her horror the woman answered, "Walk in please, miss," and she was shut in the passage.

"No," said Laura, "I don't want to come in. I only want to leave this basket. Mother sent—"

The little woman in the gloomy passage seemed not to have heard her. "Step this way, please, miss," she said in an oily voice, and Laura followed her.

She found herself in a wretched little low kitchen, lighted by a smoky lamp. There was a woman sitting before the fire.

"Em," said the little creature who had led her in. "Em! It's a young lady." She turned to Laura. She said meaningly, "I'm 'er sister, miss. You'll excuse 'er, won't you?"

"Oh, but of course!" said Laura. "Please, please don't disturb her. I—I only want to leave—"

But at that moment the woman at the fire turned round. Her face, puffed up, red, with swollen eyes and swollen lips, looked terrible. She seemed as though she couldn't understand why Laura was there. What did it mean? Why was this stranger standing in the kitchen with a basket? What was it all about? And the poor face puckered up again.

"All right, my dear," said the other. "I'll thenk the young lady."

And again she began, "You'll excuse her, miss, I'm sure," and her face, swollen too, tried an oily smile.

Laura only wanted to get out, to get away. She was back in the passage. The door opened. She walked straight through into the bedroom, where the dead man was lying.

"You'd like a look at 'im, wouldn't you?" said Em's sister, and she brushed past Laura over to the bed. "Don't be afraid, my lass,—" and now her voice sounded fond and sly, and fondly she drew down the sheet—" 'e looks a picture. There's nothing to show. Come along, my dear."

Laura came.

There lay a young man, fast asleep—sleeping so soundly, so deeply, that he was far, far away from them both. Oh, so remote, so peaceful. He was dreaming. Never wake him up again. His head was sunk in the pillow, his eyes were closed; they were blind under the closed eyelids. He was given up to his dream. What did garden-parties and baskets and lace frocks matter to him? He was far from all those things. He was wonderful, beautiful. While they were laughing and while the band was playing, this marvel had come to the lane. Happy . . . happy. . . . All is well, said that sleeping face. This is just as it should be. I am content.

But all the same you had to cry, and she couldn't go out of the room without saying something to him. Laura gave a loud childish sob.

"Forgive my hat," she said.

And this time she didn't wait for Em's sister. She found her way out of the door, down the path, past all those dark people. At the corner of the lane she met Laurie.

He stepped out of the shadow. "Is that you, Laura?"

"Yes."

"Mother was getting anxious. Was it all right?"

"Yes, quite. Oh, Laurie!" She took his arm, she pressed up against him.

"I say, you're not crying, are you?" asked her brother.

Laura shook her head. She was.

Laurie put his arm round her shoulder. "Don't cry," he said in his warm, loving voice. "Was it awful?"

"No," sobbed Laura. "It was simply marvellous. But, Laurie—" She stopped, she looked at her brother. "Isn't life," she stammered, "isn't life—" But what life was she couldn't explain. No matter. He quite understood.

"*Isn't* it, darling?" said Laurie.

I Can't Breathe [1]

by RING LARDNER

July 12

I AM staying here at the Inn for two weeks with my Uncle Nat and Aunt Jule and I think I will keep a kind of a diary while I am here to help pass the time and so I can have a record of things that happen though goodness knows there isn't likely to anything happen, that is anything exciting with Uncle Nat and Aunt Jule making the plans as they are both at least 35 years old and maybe older.

Dad and mother are abroad to be gone a month and me coming here is supposed to be a recompence for them not taking me with them. A fine recompence to be left with old people that come to a place like this to rest. Still it would be a heavenly place under different conditions, for instance if Walter were here, too. It would be heavenly if he were here, the very thought of it makes my heart stop.

I can't stand it. I won't think about it.

This is our first seperation since we have been engaged, nearly 17 days. It will be 17 days tomorrow. And the hotel orchestra at dinner this evening played that old thing "Oh how I miss you tonight" and it seemed as if they

[1] From *Roundup*, copyright, 1924, Charles Scribner's Sons, by permission.

must be playing it for my benefit though of course the person in that song is talking about how they miss their mother though of course I miss mother too, but a person gets used to missing their mother and it isn't like Walter or the person you are engaged to.

But there won't be any more seperations much longer, we are going to be married in December even if mother does laugh when I talk to her about it because she says I am crazy to even think of getting married at 18.

She got married herself when she was 18, but of course that was "different," she wasn't crazy like I am, she knew whom she was marrying. As if Walter were a policeman or a foreigner or something. And she says she was only engaged once while I have been engaged at least five times a year since I was 14, of course it really isn't as bad as that and I have really only been really what I call engaged six times altogether, but is getting engaged my fault when they keep insisting and hammering at you and if you didn't say yes they would never go home.

But it is different with Walter. I honestly believe if he had not asked me I would have asked him. Of course I wouldn't have, but I would have died. And this is the first time I have ever been engaged to be really married. The other times when they talked about when should we get married I just laughed at them, but I hadn't been engaged to Walter ten minutes when he brought up the subject of marriage and I didn't laugh. I wouldn't be engaged to him unless it was to be married. I couldn't stand it.

Anyway mother may as well get used to the idea because it is "No Foolin'" this time and we have got our plans all made and I am going to be married at home and go out to California and Hollywood on our honeymoon. December, five months away. I can't stand it. I can't wait.

There were a couple of awfully nice looking boys sitting together alone in the dining-room tonight. One of them wasn't so much, but the other was cute. And he——

There's the dance orchestra playing "Always," what they played at the Biltmore the day I met Walter. "Not for just an hour not for just a day." I can't live. I can't breathe.

July 13

This has been a much more exciting day than I expected under the circumstances. In the first place I got two long night letters, one from Walter and one from Gordon Flint. I don't see how Walter ever had the nerve to send his, there was everything in it and it must have been horribly embarrassing for him while the telegraph operator was reading it over and counting the words to say nothing of embarrassing for the operator.

But the one from Gordon was a kind of a shock. He just got back from a trip around the world, left last December to go on it and got back yesterday and called up our house and Helga gave him my address, and his telegram. well it was nearly as bad as Walter's. The trouble is that Gordon and I were engaged when he went away, or at least he thought so and he wrote to me right along all the time he was away and sent cables and things and for a while I answered his letters, but then I lost track of his itinery and couldn't write to him any more and when I got really engaged to Walter I couldn't let Gordon know because I had no idea where he was besides not wanting to spoil his trip.

And now he still thinks we are engaged and he is going to call me up tomorrow from Chicago and how in the world can I explain things and get him to understand because he is really serious and I like him ever and ever so much and in lots of ways he is nicer than Walter, not really nicer but better looking and there is no comparison between their dancing. Walter simply can't learn to dance, that is really dance. He says it is because he is flat footed, he says that as a joke, but it is true and I wish to heavens it wasn't.

All forenoon I thought and thought and thought about what to say to Gordon when he calls up and finally I couldn't stand thinking about it any more and just made up my mind I wouldn't think about it any more. But I will tell the truth though it will kill me to hurt him.

I went down to lunch with Uncle Nat and Aunt Jule and they were going out to play golf this afternoon and were insisting that I go with them, but I told them I had a headache and then I had a terrible time getting them to go without me. I didn't have a headache at all and just wanted to be alone to think about Walter and besides when you play with Uncle Nat he is always correcting your stance or your swing or something and always puts his hands on my arms or shoulders to show me the right way and I can't stand it to have old men touch me, even if they are your uncle.

I finally got rid of them and I was sitting watching the tennis when that boy that I saw last night, the cute one, came and sat right next to me and of course I didn't look at him and I was going to smoke a cigarette and found I had left my lighter upstairs and I started to get up and go after it when all of a sudden he was offering me his lighter and I couldn't very well refuse it without being rude. So we got to talking and he is even cuter than he looks, the most original and wittiest person I believe I ever met and I haven't laughed so much in I don't know how long.

. For one thing he asked me if I had heard Rockefeller's song and I said no and he began singing "Oil alone." Then he asked me if I knew the orange juice song and I told him no again and he said it was "Orange juice sorry you made me cry." .I was in hysterics before we had been together ten minutes.

His name is Frank Caswell and he has been out of Darthmouth a year and is 24 years old. That isn't so terribly old, only two years older than Walter and three years older than Gordon. I hate the name Frank, but Caswell is all right and he is so cute.

He was out in California last winter and visited Hollywood and met everybody in the world and it is fascinating to listen to him. He met Norma Shearer and he said he thought she was the prettiest thing he had ever seen. What he said was, "I did think she was the prettiest girl in the world, till today." I was going to pretend I didn't get it, but I finally told him to be sensible or I would never be able to believe anything he said.

Well, he wanted me to dance with him tonight after dinner and the next question was how to explain how we had met each other to Uncle Nat and Aunt Jule. Frank said he would fix that all right and sure enough he got himself introduced to Uncle Nat when Uncle Nat came in from golf and after dinner Uncle Nat introduced him to me and Aunt Jule too and we danced together all evening, that is not Aunt Jule. They went to bed, thank heavens.

He is a heavenly dancer, as good as Gordon. One dance we were dancing and for one of the encores the orchestra played "In a cottage small by a waterfall" and I simply couldn't dance to it. I just stopped still and said "Listen, I can't bear it, I can't breathe" and poor Frank thought I was sick or something and I had to explain that that was the tune the orchestra played the night I sat at the next table to Jack Barrymore at Barney Gallant's.

I made him sit out that encore and wouldn't let him talk till they got through playing it. Then they played something else and I was all right again and Frank told me about meeting Jack Barrymore. Imagine meeting him I couldn't live.

I promised Aunt Jule I would go to bed at eleven and it is way past that now, but I am all ready for bed and have just been writing this. Tomorrow Gordon is going to call up and what will I say to him? I just won't think about it.

July 14

Gordon called up this morning from Chicago and it was wonderful to hear his voice again though the connection was terrible. He asked me if I still loved him and I tried to tell him no, but I knew that would mean an explanation and the connection was so bad that I never could make him understand so I said yes, but I almost whispered it purposely, thinking he wouldn't hear me, but he heard me all right and he said that made everything all right with the world. He said he thought I had stopped loving him because I had stopped writing.

I wish the connection had been decent and I could have told him how things were, but now it is terrible because he is planning to get to New York the day I get there and heaven knows what I will do because Walter will be there, too. I just won't think about it.

Aunt Jule came in my room just after I was through talking to Gordon, thank heavens. The room was full of flowers. Walter had sent me some and so had Frank. I got another long night letter from Walter, just as silly at the first one. I wish he would say those things in letters instead of night letters so everybody in the world wouldn't see them. Aunt Jule wanted me to read it aloud to her. I would have died.

While she was still in the room, Frank called up and asked me to play golf with him and I said all right and Aunt Jule said she was glad my head-ache was gone. She was trying to be funny.

I played golf with Frank this afternoon. He is a beautiful golfer and it is thrilling to watch him drive, his swing is so much more graceful than Walter's. I asked him to watch me swing and tell me what was the matter with me, but he said he couldn't look at anything but my face and there wasn't anything the matter with that.

He told me the boy who was here with him had been called home and he was glad of it because I might have liked him, the other boy, better than himself. I told him that couldn't be possible and he asked me if I really meant that and I said of course, but I smiled when I said it so he wouldn't take it too seriously.

We danced again tonight and Uncle Nat and Aunt Jule sat with us a while and danced a couple of dances themselves, but they were really there to get better acquainted with Frank and see if he was all right for me to be with. I know they certainly couldn't have enjoyed their own dancing, no old people really can enjoy it because they can't really *do* anything.

They were favorably impressed with Frank I think, at least Aunt Jule didn't say I must be in bed at eleven, but just not to stay up too late. I guess it is a big surprise to a girl's parents and aunts and uncles to find out that the boys you go around with are all right, they always seem to think that if I seem to like somebody and the person pays a little attention to me, why he must be a convict or a policeman or a drunkard or something queer.

Frank had some more songs for me tonight. He asked me if I knew the asthma song and I said I didn't and he said "Oh, you must know that. It goes yes, sir, asthma baby." Then he told me about the underwear song, "I underwear my baby is tonight." He keeps you in hysterics and yet he has his serious side, in fact he was awfully serious when he said good night to me and his eyes simply shown. I wish Walter were more like him in some ways, but I mustn't think about that.

July 15

I simply can't live and I know I'll never sleep tonight. I am in a terrible predicament or rather I won't know whether I really am or not till tomorrow and that is what makes it so terrible.

After we had danced two or three dances, Frank asked me to go for a ride with him and we went for a ride in his car and he had had some cock-tails and during the ride he had some drinks out of a flask and finally he told me he loved me and I said not to be silly, but he said he was perfectly serious and he certainly acted that way. He asked me if I loved anybody else and I said yes and he asked if I didn't love him more than anybody else and I said yes, but only because I thought he had probably had too much to drink and wouldn't remember it anyway and the best thing to do was humor him under the circumstances.

Then all of a sudden he asked me when I could marry him and I said, just as a joke, that I couldn't possibly marry him before December. He said that was a long time to wait, but I was certainly worth waiting for and he said a lot of other things and maybe I humored him a little too much, but that is just the trouble, I don't know.

I was absolutely sure he was tight and would forget the whole thing, but that was early in the evening, and when we said good night he was a whole lot more sober than he had been and now I am not sure how it stands. If he doesn't remember anything about it, of course I am all right. But if he does remember and if he took me seriously, I will simply have to tell him about Walter and maybe about Gordon, too. And it isn't going to be easy. The suspense is what is maddening and I know I'll never live through this night.

July 16

I can't stand it, I can't breathe, life is impossible. Frank remembered everything about last night and firmly believes we are engaged and going to be married in December. His people live in New York and he says he is going back when I do and have them meet me.

Of course it can't go on and tomorrow I will tell him about Walter or Gordon or both of them. I know it is going to hurt him terribly, perhaps spoil his life and I would give anything in the world not to have had it happen. I hate so to hurt him because he is so nice besides being so cute and attractive.

He sent me the loveliest flowers this morning and called up at ten and wanted to know how soon he could see me and I hope the girl wasn't listening in because the things he said were, well, like Walter's night letters.

And that is another terrible thing, today I didn't get a night letter from Walter, but there was a regular letter instead and I carried it around in my purse all this afternoon and evening and never remembered to read it till ten minutes ago when I came up in the room. Walter is worried because I have only sent him two telegrams and written him one letter since I have been here, he would be a lot more worried if he knew what has happened now, though of course it can't make any difference because he is the one I am really engaged to be married to and the one I told mother I was going to marry in December and I wouldn't dare tell her it was somebody else.

I met Frank for lunch and we went for a ride this afternoon and he was so much in love and so lovely to me that I simply did not have the heart to tell him the truth, I am surely going to tell him tomorrow and telling him today would have just meant one more day of unhappiness for both of us.

He said his people had plenty of money and his father had offered to take him into partnership and he might accept, but he thinks his true vocation is journalism with a view to eventually writing novels and if I was willing to undergo a few hardships just at first we would probably both be happier later on if he was doing something he really liked. I didn't know what to say, but finally I said I wanted him to suit himself and money wasn't everything.

He asked me where I would like to go on my honeymoon and I suppose I ought to have told him my honeymoon was all planned, that I was going to

California, with Walter, but all I said was that I had always wanted to go to California and he was enthusiastic and said that is where we would surely go and he would take me to Hollywood and introduce me to all those wonderful people he met there last winter. It nearly takes my breath away to think of it, going there with someone who really knows people and has the entrée.

We danced again tonight, just two or three dances, and then went out and sat in the tennis-court, but I came upstairs early because Aunt Jule had acted kind of funny at dinner. And I wanted to be alone, too, and think, but the more I think the worse it gets.

Sometimes I wish I were dead, maybe that is the only solution and it would be best for everyone concerned. I *will* die if things keep on the way they have been. But of course tomorrow it will be all over, with Frank I mean, for I must tell him the truth no matter how much it hurts us both. Though I don't care how much it hurts me. The thought of hurting him is what is driving me mad. I can't bear it.

July 18

I have skipped a day. I was busy every minute of yesterday and so exhausted when I came upstairs that I was tempted to fall into bed with all my clothes on. First Gordon called me up from Chicago to remind me that he would be in New York the day I got there and that when he comes he wants me all to himself all the time and we can make plans for our wedding. The connection was bad again and I just couldn't explain to him about Walter.

I had an engagement with Frank for lunch and just as we were going in another long distance call came, from Walter this time. He wanted to know why I haven't written more letters and sent him more telegrams and asked me if I still loved him and of course I told him yes because I really do. Then he asked if I had met any men here and I told him I had met one, a friend of Uncle Nat's. After all it was Uncle Nat who introduced me to Frank. He reminded me that he would be in New York on the 25th which is the day I expect to get home, and said he would have theater tickets for that night and we would go somewhere afterwards and dance.

Frank insisted on knowing who had kept me talking so long and I told him it was a boy I had known a long while, a very dear friend of mine and a friend of my family's. Frank was jealous and kept asking questions till I thought I would go mad. He was so serious and kind of cross and gruff that I gave up the plan of telling him the truth till some time when he is in better spirits.

I played golf with Frank in the afternoon and we took a ride last night and I wanted to get in early because I had promised both Walter and Gordon that I would write them long letters, but Frank wouldn't bring me back to the Inn till I had named a definite date in December. I finally told him the 10th and he said all right if I was sure that wasn't a Sunday. I said I would have to look it up, but as a matter of fact I know the 10th falls on a Friday because the date Walter and I have agreed on for our wedding is Saturday the 11th.

Today has just been the same thing over again, two more night letters, a long distance call from Chicago, golf and a ride with Frank, and the room full of flowers. But tomorrow I am going to tell Frank and I am going to write Gordon a long letter and tell him, too, because this simply can't go on any longer. I can't breathe. I can't live.

July 21

I wrote to Gordon yesterday, but I didn't say anything about Walter because I don't think it is a thing a person ought to do by letter. I can tell him when he gets to New York and then I will be sure that he doesn't take it too hard and I can promise him that I will be friends with him always and make him promise not to do anything silly, while if I told it to him in a letter there is no telling what he would do, there all alone.

And I haven't told Frank because he hasn't been feeling well, he is terribly sunburned and it hurts him terribly so he can hardly play golf or dance, and I want him to be feeling his best when I do tell him, but whether he is all right or not I simply must tell him tomorrow because he is actually planning to leave here on the same train with us Saturday night and I can't let him do that.

Life is so hopeless and it could be so wonderful. For instance how heavenly it would be if I could marry Frank first and stay married to him five years and he would be the one who would take me to Hollywood and maybe we could go on parties with Norman Kerry and Jack Barrymore and Buster Collier and Marion Davies and Lois Moran.

And at the end of five years Frank could go into journalism and write novels and I would only be 23 and I could marry Gordon and he would be ready for another trip around the world and he could show me things better than someone who had never seen them before.

Gordon and I would separate at the end of five years and I would be 28 and I know of lots of women that never even got married the first time till they were 28 though I don't suppose that was their fault, but I would marry Walter then, for after all he is the one I really love and want to spend most of my life with and I wouldn't care whether he could dance or not when I was that old. Before long we would be as old as Uncle Nat and Aunt Jule and I certainly wouldn't want to dance at their age when all you can do is just hobble around the floor. But Walter is so wonderful as a companion and we would enjoy the same things and be pals and maybe we would begin to have children.

But that is all impossible though it wouldn't be if older people just had sense and would look at things the right way.

It is only half past ten, the earliest I have gone to bed in weeks, but I am worn out and Frank went to bed early so he could put cold cream on his sunburn.

Listen, diary, the orchestra is playing "Limehouse Blues." The first tune I danced to with Merle Oliver, two years ago. I can't stand it. And how funny that they should play that old tune tonight of all nights, when I have been thinking of Merle off and on all day, and I hadn't thought of him before in weeks and weeks. I wonder where he is, I wonder if it is just an accident or if it means I am going to see him again. I simply mustn't think about it or I'll die.

July 22

I knew it wasn't an accident. I knew it must mean something, and it did.

Merle is coming here today, here to this Inn, and just to see me. And there can only be one reason. And only one answer. I knew that when I heard his voice calling from Boston. How could I ever had thought I loved anyone else? How could he ever have thought I meant it when I told him I was engaged to George Morse?

A whole year and he still cares and I still care. That shows we were always intended for each other and for no one else. I won't make *him* wait till December. I doubt if we even wait till dad and mother get home. And as for a honeymoon I will go with him to Long Beach or the Bronx Zoo, wherever he wants to take me.

After all this is the best way out of it, the only way. I won't have to say anything to Frank, he will guess when he sees me with Merle. And when I get home Sunday and Walter and Gordon call me up, I will invite them both to dinner and Merle can tell them himself, with two of them there it will only hurt each one half as much as if they were alone.

The train is due at 2:40, almost three hours from now. I can't wait. And what if it should be late? I can't stand it.

⌇⌇⌇⌇⌇⌇⌇⌇⌇⌇⌇⌇⌇⌇⌇⌇⌇⌇⌇⌇⌇⌇⌇⌇⌇⌇⌇⌇⌇⌇⌇⌇⌇⌇⌇

But It's O! in My Heart[1]

by JOAN VATSEK

HIS home, thought Kathleen, putting her overnight bag down on the stone step and looking up at the red brick building. It was a three-story private house, very like its neighbors to the left and right, and like dozens that she had passed trudging through the streets of Edinburgh from the station, while the gloom of the gathering twilight seemed to close upon her.

His parents are inside, she thought. She could hardly believe, that after all these months, she could be that near to him. He lived here, she thought wonderingly. He pounded on this door when he was a little boy.

[1] By permission of the author. From the magazine *Story*, Nov.—Dec., 1941.

The door was dark green, badly weathered, with splinters of paint coming off. She touched it, and her palm pressed against the rough surface involuntarily, so that she could feel the unevenness digging into her skin. She took away her hand.

I must be careful, she thought. I mustn't give myself away. After all, his parents are conservative, they have to get used to people. Why, they may not like me. This had not occurred to her before, she had been too eager to see them, to talk with them—but now, standing in front of the closed door, she was afraid.

She glanced down at herself, in an absent-minded way, and straightened the jacket of her uniform and her soft khaki tie. Then she took out a compact from her black purse and brought it close to her face so that she could still see, vaguely, the fine line of her mouth, and the deep, questioning eyes that looked back at her anxiously. She snapped away the image.

I can still go back, she thought. She glanced down the empty street, and automatically up into the sky, darkening and empty, too. I can go back to the station, and wait until the next train goes, she thought. I can write another polite little letter, saying that I couldn't come. Or I can breeze in and say, well, here I am, after all it's only a hop from London to Edinburgh, and traveling, in these times, is so simple. Or I can ring the bell and run away.

But I don't even know where he is, she thought, where he is zooming, over what city, or mountain, or desert. I want to see someone of flesh and blood, someone real, who belongs to him, if only for a day—I want to see his mother, she thought.

She straightened and rang the bell.

The shrill, unalterable sound tingling through the unknown halls and crevices of the house was like an electric shock.

What does one say to strangers? she thought frantically, standing stiffly, as if impaled. How do you do. I am here. It is evening. I have come for the night. You asked me you know.

In this quiet, anything can happen, she thought. Perhaps a bomb will drop on the doorstep, and then I will not have to explain why I came.

The door opened. She felt defenseless without a door, staring into the darkness of a hall at a man's lean, shadowy figure, plunged into sudden acquaintance.

"How do you do," said Kathleen.

"How do you do, Miss Neilson," he answered warmly, with a strong Scotch inflection. "We didn't know when you'd be arriving, or I'd have met you. I'll take your bag."

He drew her in, holding her by the hand—friendly, welcoming. My dear, she thought, so this is your father!

It's going to be all right, she thought, it's going to be all right. She wished she could express her gratitude, the sweet taste of relief in her mouth.

As they came out of the hall, the light fell upon his profile, stripped a little, thirty years older, but, the same! She nearly cried out with the joy of it.

She thought, you will be something like your father when you are older. If you have a chance to grow old. If I have a chance to see you grow old. If we ever meet again.

His mother was standing in the doorway of the living room, heavy-set, broad-shouldered, dominating.

Kathleen went toward her.

"How do you do, Mrs. Macdonald. It was so good of you to ask me."

"Good of you to come." She had keen eyes, reserving judgment. She pressed Kathleen's hand, and let her go.

So, thought Kathleen. I am instantly released.

And now they were in the room, with its large fireplace, worn carpet, dark walls, great shabby sofa. They sat down. Room that holds his presence, she thought—dearest room I know—I must stop this, I must pull myself together, I must stop glowing like this, giving myself away without a word. Why, there's his picture on the wall!

Mr. Macdonald was talking.

"We're very glad you're giving us this chance of knowing you." Deliberate, gracious words.

"I meant to come long before," said Kathleen, "ever since I came back to England. But it's rather difficult to get away from the A.T.S. once you are in it."

She began to chatter about the A.T.S. Everything seemed strange at first, she said, especially after Egypt.

"My father is in the army you know," she explained. "It was quite gay in Cairo before the war. Well, it's rather like going back to boarding school now, but it's probably good for me. I share a room with two other girls."

This is better, she thought. Now I'm natural. How long, before I can ask? How long, how long? Have you heard from him lately? Is he well? Where is he?

Where and O where, has your Highland laddie gone?

That's an old song, an old, old song. It's a sad song. I mustn't finish it.

He's gone to fight for England, and to save the English King.

"Yes," she said, "these two girls are quite different. Sally used to work in a hat shop, and Barbara's father is a rear admiral in the Navy."

"In a hat shop?" asked Mrs. Macdonald.

"Yes," said Kathleen. "She's very young."

She thought, That's an excuse for having worked in a hat shop, don't you agree? I'm very young, too. We're all very young—good old war. Brings us all together. No distinctions left, you know. No class prejudice. *Gone to fight for England* . . .

"I'm doing clerical work right now, typing, writing letters, and reports."

Good thing, to have metal under one's fingers, when there's no blown curly hair.

". . . Egypt? Oh, depressing, you know, toward the end. Blackout. Had to be in by nine. But nothing like London."

"Edinburgh's had her raids too," said Mrs. Macdonald.

"Yes, I know."

Where, and O where?

"We heard from Richard, indirectly, a few weeks ago," said Mr. Macdonald.

Bless you, she thought. At last. Without my asking. Because you know —as he always knows—what I want to hear.

"How is he?" she asked.

"He's very well. Flying somewhere over Libya, I understand. At least, he was when this friend got the message."

He might have sent me a message. He might have sent me a—hush.

"I'm sure," said Mr. Macdonald, "that as soon as he can he will write to us, and to you. If it is at all possible."

But this man, she thought, is a man better than any other I have met. Kinder, more sensitive.

"Libya," she repeated. "Very like Egypt, of course." As though, being familiar, it was safe.

"I've never had a clear impression of Egypt," said Mrs. Macdonald. "It's very flat, so Richard writes—none of our mountains. He used to miss them."

"Yes. It's all flat desert, except for a few jagged sand hills. The Delta and the Fayum are green, but flat, too. And nothing grows in the desert."

Except in the spring when the brilliant, wild anemone spring up from the sand, and the slim barley of the Beduin, sown here and there, make sparse miraculous green.

"Yes, there is nothing in the desert," she said.

Except at night, when the stars are turned upside down over it, and it is full of long, reaching wind.

"It is a strange land," she said.

"Richard seems to love it now," said Mrs. Macdonald, shrugging at his vagrancies, possessing him surely, carelessly—her son.

"Yes," said Kathleen, and could not talk of him.

How could she not talk, yet contrive that they keep on talking, so that she could hear his name, over and over? Mr. Macdonald, won't you talk of Richard? Mrs. Macdonald, won't you show me pictures of him? An album? Haven't you an album, Mrs. Macdonald? Don't lock it away from me. Don't lock him away from me.

And it's O! in my heart, that I wish him safe at home!

Mrs. Macdonald got up, heavily. Again Kathleen felt the passive force of this woman, his mother.

"Would you like to go upstairs and wash up a bit before supper?"

"Yes, thank you." She probably looked dirty and tired from the train. But she couldn't have torn herself away, just at first, from these two people she had never seen before.

She went upstairs. His father came with her, carrying her bag, talking of ordinary things like trains and schedules and the difficulty of getting around.

"How glad I am you came," he repeated, in earnest assurance, before he left her.

Kathleen gave a long sigh of peace. She sat down on the edge of the chintz-covered bed, and looked at the drawn white curtains and the black shade nailed across the windows. There was an old-fashioned bureau and a rocking chair, and in one corner of the room, shelves of books.

Walking over, Kathleen touched them lingeringly. He must have read these, she thought. This is his room. It was good of her to give me his room. Robinson Crusoe, Moby Dick. She opened Moby Dick, and there was his signature, and a date, in a round, childish hand.

She held the open page against her tightly for a moment, and it seemed as if the ache that had been there for months now melted a little. After a while she closed the book and put it back in its place.

She shook out her things and opened the cupboard door. On one of the nails hung a tarboosh, the kind of tarboosh that tourists buy, to wear in Cairo for an evening, in jest.

He must have brought it home when he was on leave, Kathleen thought. Two years ago, when I did not know him.

But she left it there. He seemed farther away from her then than when he was a child. That's curious, she thought.

She began to brush her hair, standing in front of the mirror—unseeingly, remembering—brushing and brushing, until it stood out around her face, glinting, full of sparks. She put down the brush and smoothed it down. Hush, she thought, hush.

Will there be a time again, she wondered, glancing at the window, when the bars are taken down? When the wind blows in and out and the lights shine brilliantly, all over the world again? When there is no need to be hushed, to be secret, to wait? When I can walk with my love again?

Darkly the next line of the song that she could not forget, came back to her.

O how and O how, if your Highland laddie die?

She turned, and fled down the stairs.

"Mrs. Macdonald," she called, "Mrs. Macdonald, can I help you?"

There was a short pause. Then Mrs. Macdonald came solidly out of the dining room.

"Thank you," she said, and smiled a little at Kathleen, standing there poised and trembling. "It's all ready," she said, leading the way. "We're having haggis. I hope you like it. It's Richard's favorite dish."

Mr. Macdonald drew out Kathleen's chair.

"Well if you don't like it, don't eat it," he admonished.

"Of course I like it," said Kathleen, after barely finishing the first bite. "It's very good."

If it were wormwood, she thought, wormwood and dust, and Richard liked it, and you gave it to me, I would eat it.

The two older people looked at her and then their glances crossed swiftly. They both laughed a little.

"You've hardly tasted it," remarked Mrs. Macdonald.

Kathleen blushed. "But I do like it, all the same," she said.

"Well, I'm sure he'd be glad to see you downing your haggis so valiantly," said Mr. Macdonald.

"Would he?" asked Kathleen. The question lingered in the air, clear, low, betraying.

After a pause, his mother said in a matter of fact way, "Richard wrote what good friends you were."

"Yes," said his father, "he wrote of you very often, Miss Neilson."

"Please," she said, "call me Kathleen."

"Well," he said. "We've always thought of you as Kathleen."

His eyes went swiftly, unconsciously, to his wife's face. But his wife's face, Kathleen noticed, was closed against him, too. She had a curiously remote expression, even when looking at a person, as though she were gazing at something beyond. But nothing escaped her notice.

What did your son write to you, Mr. Macdonald, she thought, to make your voice so gentle, when you speak to me? I will remember your voice, in all the months to come. I will remember, when there is nothing in the mail.

"You must make me a little map of the R.A.F. camp after supper," said Mr. Macdonald.

Kathleen tried, drawing awkwardly on a piece of note paper.

They were sitting on the big, shabby couch, while Mrs. Macdonald sat in her armchair, remote, as was her habit it seemed, although once or twice her husband glanced at her, frowning a little.

"This," said Kathleen, "is the Nile," drawing a wavery line.

Flat-banked river, cool, flashing in the sun, choked along the edge with bulrushes, or flowing widely, cleaving Cairo, or spreading, spreading, flooding future harvest fields, almost to the desert's edge.

"And this," she said, "is the road to Maadi."

With heavy-headed trees on either side, and he and I, driving slowly, breathing in the smell of the earth, or speeding through the balmy, heady night.

"And here this road turns to Maadi, and this one goes on to Helwan. The camp is here." She made a round spot where the parties were, the crowds and crowds of girls in evening dresses, boys in uniform. In the daytime it was different. Bleak, barren, open to the sun. But at night there were lanterns strung gaily, and little tables, and music.

"I see," said Mr. Macdonald.

And it was as though he really saw all that, with her.

So she drew other little roads, and said, "We used to drive here and here.

And here there was a fort that Napoleon built, and a mosque that we visited, and here, outside of Cairo, the old stone quarries from which they took stones for the pyramids, and here was Memphis."

And Babylon and Nineveh, she thought. And London and Berlin.

"He showed me so many things, Mr. Macdonald, that I had not seen before."

He gave me new eyes, is what I mean, she thought, new eyes for the mist on the river, and the sunset, and the palm trees, that seemed, when I was with him, to be whispering hallelujahs.

"I was very happy with him," she said, in a low voice.

"And so was he with you, Kathleen," said her friend, his father.

Mrs. Macdonald stirred a little, and turned on the radio.

". . . Evacuating. According to authoritative sources, there has been very little loss of life."

We'll play the bagpipes o'er him, thought Kathleen.
We'll play the bagpipes o'er him, and I'll lay me down and cry—
But it's O! in my heart, that my laddie will not die!

You see, she thought, even when that song was written, she could not believe that hers would be among the lost, among the battered and the wounded and the dead.

". . . the General was congratulated, for his excellent leadership. . . . Only two air raids last night, over London, beaten off successfully after the first attacks."

Windows smashed and children crying, or buildings crashed and people dying, what is less or more, in an avalanche of flame? Tall were the towers of Sidon and of Tyre.

"They'll find it's not so easy to conquer England," said Mrs. Macdonald. She sat with her strong hands clasped in her lap, and her face was livelier than Kathleen had yet seen it. She was completely absorbed by the news.

"My wife," said Mr. Macdonald, "goes through every battle. I am not so strong." He smiled a little.

Every time he smiled he brought up a vivid image of Richard in Kathleen's mind. It was as though the parts of his face, that lay dismembered in her memory, so that sometimes she saw his broad, high forehead, sometimes his firm, proud chin with the scar upon it, sometimes his eyes looking at her with an indescribable, whimsically tender expression, sometimes his mouth— as though all these, that had been shattered by their parting, were caught together by the magnet of his father's smile, so like his.

"How long," she asked, "how long do you think the war will last?"

That is the question, she thought, that we ask of one another, uselessly, in Dutch, French, Polish, Finnish, Greek—the question that multiplies and multiplies, until the sum of it must reach the sky—how long, O Lord?

". . . must be destroyed, if we are to survive."

And O, but the long, long time the world will last, drifted through her head from the Rubaiyat—which of our coming and our going heeds, as the sea's self should heed a pebble cast.

The words rippled through her tension, and left her quiet.

"Long," said Richard's father.

He will forget me, she thought, in a year, in two years—he will marry someone else, on leave when he wishes to quench, at least for a while, the loneliness of searchlights in the sky, searching out his heart, his moment of eternity.

I will forget, she thought, because I must.

And she looked at the fireplace, in which there was no fire.

"If only," said his mother suddenly, pettishly, turning off the radio. "Richard could have leave. He hasn't been home for two years."

"It's hardly likely now, my dear," said his father. "Does he look well?" he asked, turning to Kathleen.

"He's sunburnt and strong," she answered. "He flies well. One day we drove out to the field where the Egyptian cadets learn to fly. You can hire planes there, and he took me up."

His mother was listening now.

"We flew low over the wheat fields—so low we could smell the wheat. There was an Egyptian woman standing in the grain and she waved her scarf at us. Then he climbed high, and turned the plane over—it was like being under the sea, with a great pressure all around, and then he twisted and dove—I called to him then, through the megaphone, to stop."

But when it can't be stopped, that dive down, that zooming, that eagerness to be buried in the earth?

We'll play the bagpipes o'er him . . . if we can find him, if we can find him. Was he lost on land, or at sea, officer? Thank you.

But they will not even let me know, she thought despairingly. I am nothing to him, on paper. I cannot read every list of the missing.

"You will let me know, Mr. Macdonald, if—when you hear from Richard again?"

"Of course," he replied, turning his head a little away from her, looking at the darkened windows. Their only son, thought Kathleen. Richard had once said, "Father always wanted a daughter. That's why—that's one of the reasons why," he amended, "he will love you."

Mrs. Macdonald was asking about the Egyptian paintings. Had Kathleen gone to that place, that Sakkara, that Richard wrote about?

"Yes," said Kathleen, "some of the wall paintings on the tombs are very lovely."

Once they were standing before a picture of a young Pharaoh and his wife, painted stiffly side by side, with arms linked, and the same enigmatic, smiling expression on their calm faces.

"The colors," said Kathleen, "are fresh and brilliant, more brilliant than ours."

Richard had taken her hand, and said, "You see, it was always the same."

They had stood before the painting unconsciously falling into the same attitude, side by side. She recalled how moved she had been, by the careful geometry and the tenderness of the crossed arms.

"It is difficult to describe their art," she said.

She talked on. She talked all that evening, and, it seemed to her, all the next day, while the two older people sat, listening to her. She told them anything she thought would interest them, and always, like a drumbeat, came the sound of Richard's name, through everything she said.

A night and a day go quickly.

Kathleen lingered, putting off the time to go. What did it matter if she were tired the next day? Sally would pull her out of bed somehow. Sally. Sally would listen patiently, to her account of the visit. She would say, in her direct, matter-of-fact way, "Well, how was it, Kathy? What are they like?"

And she would try to answer, using adjectives, struggling with words, as she often did, until finally Sally would stop her and say, tolerantly, "All right, I get you. They're wonderful. They'd have to be, of course, to be your Richard's parents."

She would laugh, and Kathleen would laugh, and they would sit like schoolgirls on their cots, in brief relaxation before the next whistle blew. And the days would march briskly by.

Kathleen stood in the hall, ready to leave. Mrs. Macdonald had packed her a little parcel of food, to take on the train.

Mr. Macdonald had wanted to go with her, but she said, in a low voice intended only for him, "Please don't come. I would like to remember you both, here."

So now there was nothing left, but to say good-bye.

"Thank you—" said Kathleen.

"Thank you for coming," said his father quickly.

"Yes," said his mother, "that long journey."

They waited.

"Good-bye," said Kathleen. To leave his house, she thought, to die again. Good-bye, little ghost upon the stairs . . .

His mother stepped forward, took her by the shoulders, and kissed her briefly.

One more smile, Mr. Macdonald, so that I can see his face, for a moment? He took her hand warmly, as he had when she came.

"Good-bye, Kathleen," he said gently. "I hope we will see you soon, in happier times."

"Yes," she said. She tried not to ask, but the words sprang from her lips. "You will let me know?"

You will let me know about the bagpipes? You will—good-bye, good-bye. It is only a step to be over a threshold, and standing outside again.

Kathleen stared at the door, closing her out of his home.

She touched it, hesitantly, in hope and farewell, before she started down the empty street.

The Day of Victory [1]

by HOWARD FAST

WHEN he awoke on the cool brisk morning of the twenty-fifth of November, in that gray time between the dawn and the sunrise, it was with the partly conscious realization that today was different from other days.

Today was a part of November in the year 1783, yet today was marked indelibly. At first he didn't know how that should be, or why, sensing only vaguely that he was here in his headquarters on Manhattan Island, half asleep, half awake, trying to find himself. He was tired, as he had been so often of late; a man grows tired as the years bind him and add up. He would have liked to lie in bed for a few hours more but he knew that to be quite impossible.

He had been dreaming and had awakened from the dream, and he knew it was quite wrong—what so many people said, that you couldn't dream the same thing twice; he knew you could, not twice but a hundred times, and the dream was always the same.

In the dream he came home. In the morning he came home, riding up through the fields while they were still wet with dew. He would go through a field of rye so that the dew would put a polish on his boot tops, and the horse would stamp and dance, the way they do in a field of wet grass. The smells would be sweet, the magnolia blossoms like a thousand lanterns; and he rode right up to the house.

He rode up and old Jackson took his horse. He kissed Martha and it was as if he hadn't been away at all, except perhaps down the road to see a neighbor about selling a newly weaned colt. That was the way in the dream.

Jackson said, "Good morning, sir, Mr. Washington," and Martha scolded about his boots. The dogs frolicked about him eagerly and Jackson was smiling broadly as he said over and over, "Mighty good to see you, sir, Mr. Washington, mighty good to see you."

And, awake now, he knew that it was eight years—no, more than that, and he knew how this day was different.

Dressing, he thought of all the times through the years that he had anticipated this day. Some things stood out more than others; he remembered the time in '76—or was it '77—when he met a mother who had lost her son, and wanting to say something—anything—yet able to think of nothing,

[1] From *Patrick Henry and the Frigate's Keel* (1945). Reprinted with the permission of Duell, Sloan & Pearce.

blundering as a man does, blurted out, "What he died for—I think it will be worth the price."

"What did he die for?"

Trying to explain, he found himself incoherent and she said, "Will this ever be over? Or will it go on and on? And how many more must die?"

And now it was over. He remembered a man who had lost everything, house and family, a man in the ranks who said, "The devil is that you can't think of an end—there is no end. It goes on and a man forgets about peace."

And now it was the end.

He remembered the defeats, the endless hammering defeats, when they all screamed, "Give up! Give up!" When they pleaded, "Peace at any price." When they begged him, "Make us terms." Freedom was a dream. He remembered '76, '77, '78, '79, running away always, hacked, bleeding, leaving brown clots in the summer dust, scarlet splashes in the winter snow, the beggars' army, the winter encampments where they lay and starved and died, the logic with which wise men reasoned that they couldn't win, temperate men that they couldn't exist, judicious men that they couldn't even retreat.

He remembered the plots, the pettiness, the traitors, the defeatists, the weak and the brave, the shoddy and the glorious.

He remembered the women and then it was better. He was a man who had loved women, many women. There was a time when he could dance twelve hours, with a woman on either arm and a quart of wine under his belt. He remembered the women who had carried the wounded into their houses, the women who had fed the beggars, the women who had taken his hand and said they trusted him.

Thinking of the women made him look in his mirror, stare at the long bony face, the tight mouth, the pale gray eyes and the thin red hair. An old man and yet when it started he had been young.

When Washington came out of his room General Knox was waiting for him. Knox was a fine combination of sedateness and excitement, hugely fat, his pudgy hands folded across his stomach, his eyes deep in wrinkles of flesh.

The commander-in-chief said, "Today it is, Harry."

And Knox nodded his big head as casually as he could.

That was the way it was.

"A good day," Knox remarked. "I think we'll have sunshine."

"That would be nice."

"Cool, but not cold."

And why not speak of the weather, he thought, the weather being one of the few things always present. He looked at Knox with new interest, the way you look at men condemned, the way you look at anyone before parting —Knox the faithful, the loyal, the one man beyond suspicion, the one other man who had never lost faith. Knox was fat and paunchy and haggard, the way a fat man can be haggard, and he looked old. Things made men old. Knox was only thirty-three now; when it began, he had been a boy of twenty-five.

"Think of Knox as a boy," he said to himself.

It was quite impossible. How did one take up where one left off? Then Knox had been a bookseller, a chubby talkative boy with a wife and children, but that was eight years ago and more. And Knox spoke about the weather —and it was natural, he thought, quite natural.

And Knox, in turn, staring at the very tall, well-dressed thin man who had come from the bedroom, a Virginia farmer once—but that too forgotten —found more words impossible.

"We will go down to the city slowly," the tall man said and added, "the first time in all these years, Harry. How do you suppose it will look?"

Knox shrugged and somehow managed to say, "And then?"

"And then I'll go home," the Virginia farmer smiled.

Going home was something that had never been out of his mind, never for a day, hardly ever for an hour. Eight years had not turned him into a military man and now he realized that he had never really been a soldier, but rather a private citizen whose life had been temporarily disturbed, who had found that he could not live with certain things as they were and had set out to change them. He had put on a uniform and he was going away for a little while.

His wife had known better; holding both his hands then, she stared at him as if she had seen him for the last time, tall, pock-marked, skinny, a man she knew so well, all his little foibles and faults, and knowing that when he went all the props would go from under her life.

"We'll manage," she said and agreed smilingly that it would just be a short time.

He knew she was lying; they both knew, and stared at each other.

"Well, it has to be done," he had said. "You can't live with a thing hanging over your head."

"You can't," she agreed.

They were reluctant to discuss basic causes and the words *freedom* and *liberty* never were spoken. She reminded him about his woolen underwear.

"I know you don't like to wear it," she complained fretfully.

"But I will."

"And change out of damp clothes."

He nodded, reminding her which fields he planned to plow and seed for the coming year. "I mean, if I am not back," he explained.

"Don't drink too much."

He said he wouldn't and she knew he would. "It will be only a little while," he said, "and then I'll be back."

They were camped in Harlem now and New York City was ten miles to the south.

"That is why I thought we would start early," General McKay said, "and march slowly."

"Yes—" He was called back to reality by the expression on McKay's face.

"You won't be going home, sir?" McKay said softly.

"Yes, I'm going home."

They were alone in the drawing-room of the house he had made his head-quarters. Speaking quickly, almost desperately, McKay said, "You know, sir, this is only the beginning—this must be only the beginning!"

He was a tall heavy-set man, dark-eyed, with deep hollows in his cheeks; brave enough in battle, the Virginian recalled, but fighting with a fury that had no other purpose than the easing of some burning resentment within him. For eight years McKay had lived for no real end; peace seemed to bewilder him. Now he clenched and unclenched his hands as he spoke: "What have we got, sir? What have we got, now that it's over?"

"A great deal, I think," the Virginian said slowly, watching General McKay through narrowing eyes.

"Do you? I think we have nothing, sir. For eight years we've fought and bled out our guts—and for what? For the rest of them to live on the fat of the land. I tell you, sir, there's something better than being a half-pay broken veteran, swilling in taverns—you see—"

The Virginian was watching him with a face as cold as ice but he couldn't stop now; McKay had begun and he must go on.

"You could do it," McKay said. "We have the army, the power, and best of all, the victory. We've won the war and whatever is left now is ours by right. A single coup, a march on Philadelphia—Congress will run like rabbits and then it's ours—"

"Have you spoken to anyone else about this?" The tall man's voice was curiously controlled.

"Several, sir."

The Virginian reached out, took McKay's lapel in his big fist, drew the other close to him and said softly, "I ought to kill you—I am still your commander-in-chief, you know, and I ought to kill you. Who are the others?"

McKay shook his head and the Virginian flung him away so violently that he stumbled and fell.

"Get out! Get out!"

And he was going home, quietly, as he had planned. How his head ached! Was there no peace for him, no rest?

"I could stay," he told himself. "But for how long?"

If it couldn't go on without him it was no good. It had to go on without him, otherwise all their eight years of fighting were for nothing at all. It was better that he didn't know the men McKay had taken into his confidence. This was no longer war, that you could fight with guns and force. A nation, a republic, was no more than the men who made it.

Somehow in the next few days he would have to fight as he had never fought before, but without weapons and alone. He had to go home; all the eight years had been for this, that he should become a private citizen, lay down his arms and go home.

More immediate things pressed upon his attention: the occupation of the last city the enemy held. They were coming back to a New York they had lost a long time ago, so long that it was difficult to remember all the details.

He thought of the men who had been with him when the Continental Army lost New York, in '76. There was old Israel Putnam, dragged away from his farm and his fields. He would never forget old Israel's constant complaint of rheumatism. He was more loyal than most, braver than men half his age.

He thought of Mifflin, who was now President of the Continental Congress —Mifflin who stood by so calmly while Lee and Reed plotted against him, seven years past. And what would Mifflin say to this new nightmarish plot? What would old Tom Paine say, who had pleaded with the troops all the way on that lonely retreat from Hackensack to Trenton?

And what of Nathanael Greene, who had started the thing as a rosy-cheeked Quaker boy and was now a seasoned and veteran commander? Thinking of Greene, he remembered the handsome blade who could not keep his eyes from the ladies; Greene had danced and flirted into this war, but it had done something to him, changed him as it had changed so many others. But through all of it Greene had stood fast—along with Harry Knox, who was chief of artillery.

Knox lasted; nothing had changed him, nothing could. And then the tall man, thinking of what McKay had said, wondered whether Knox had been one of those spoken to about a frightened Congress fleeing from Philadelphia, a military dictatorship—and if so, why had Knox said nothing to him?

The Virginian tensed, telling himself that this thing must be fought calmly and expertly. If he lost his own head, what then?

Knox entered the room, saluted, laid an affectionate hand on the other's arm and said, "Sir, you will lead the troops, won't you?"

"You lead them, Harry."

"If you wish, sir. It's a great honor."

"Of course it's an honor, Harry"—and then Knox looked at him, not quite certain whether he was being gently laughed at or not. The tall, thin man paced along the drawn-up ranks, struck with the thought, once he was outside, that he was reviewing them for the last time, holding on to that thought, yet unable completely to realize it this November morning of 1783.

These were his men, these tattered weary ill-dressed veterans. He sought for the strength in them and found it—not plots and not a march on the Congress, but a strength that comes out of years of fighting shoulder to shoulder.

There was Miles Crock, with him eight full years; George Ross who had enlisted at fifteen; Jacob Fusterbee, close on seventy, tough as leather; Adam Wheelright, Fuller Jackson, Moses Dane, Jeremiah Danbury, Isaac Watson,

Isaac Crane, so many Isaacs, so many Jacobs and Jeremiahs. He said to one, "Going home?"

"Yes, sir—home."

And asked him for the first time, "Are you married?"

"Yes, married."

"And all this, eight years, what have you got out of it?"

"I reckon we've won, sir. Things go on. We're a stiffnecked breed and we went in because we like our own ways. I figure the time ain't wasted—"

For all of them it was much the same—at least, he hoped so, pleaded so to himself, looking into their faces. Once he could not have named ten of these men and now he knew a thousand names. Once he had curled inwardly at the sight of their dirty shirts, patched breeches and rusty muskets; but since then something had happened to him as well as to them. Leaving them he felt lonely and desolate; he sought for the one thing he wanted to take with him, a knowledge of their strength.

As he walked on, the men's faces turned after him. Eight years had made them soldiers, tough, lasting, well trained—the best soldiers in the world, he often thought, in spite of the fact that they wore no uniforms, that their feet were wrapped in rags and sacking. The world's first citizen army, they had done their job, and unlike the professional fighters of other nations, they would become householders once more. But did they realize that?

Stopping in front of one of them, a face that had been at Brooklyn, White Plains, Trenton, Brandywine, Valley Forge, Yorktown, he offered his hand. The other took it shyly.

He would have liked to say something that mattered, like "Good-by, old comrade—believe in what we've fought for, believe!" but he could say nothing and the man who took his hand began to weep, the tears rolling unashamed down his face.

Good soldiers though they were, that was more than they could stand. They roared and clustered around him, hundreds and hundreds of them, reaching for his hands, his arms, just to touch a bit of his clothes, roaring at the top of their lungs.

And in that moment a wave of awful fear passed through him; he saw how what McKay had suggested was possible, if he were just to say the word.

He said nothing, just stood motionless.

General Henry Knox led the troops, walking his horse in silence and watching the tall Virginian who rode with the dignitaries, Governor Clinton, Pierre Van Cortlandt and others. And once the Virginian caught his eye and could have sworn that Knox's glance said, "What will you do? How will you manage it? Or will all the years we fought be for nothing?"

Someone was saying to the tall man in buff and blue, "Really, sir, it's a shame they can't make a better show."

"Better show?" His thoughts were miles away.

"I mean, sir, even in triumph it would be better if they had uniforms instead of rags, I mean if only to produce—"

"They are citizen soldiers," the tall man said coldly. "That's hard to understand, isn't it?"

The other mumbled something and the Virginian's mood changed. Watching the marching men, he said, "I think they understand—look at the way they march."

"Sir?"

He was trying to think it out. The war had been won; the men would go home and try to put things together where they had left off. Some would succeed and some would fail; that was the price and he realized it was a larger price than had been paid for the victory. Did the men know? Were they strong enough?

People forget, he told himself. Here was a new country and a new world and everyone would be too busy living to remember the few thousand poor devils who gave it to them. Things were that way and gratitude was a short-lived virtue.

Someone was saying to him, "But the enemy will see them, and that won't make the best impression, will it?"

"Why, I don't know," the Virginia farmer said, more lightly than he felt. "Why, I really don't know."

As the troops approached New York City the weather turned colder and the men licked up their pace. They marched smartly and with precision, and the thud, thud, thud of their feet echoed over the fields and woods.

A brisk November wind, blowing from over the Palisades, sent dead leaves swirling among the ranks, and occasionally, when they came to an open space on a bluff, they could see the little whitecaps dancing on the Hudson. A single small boat scudded along, its white sail dipping again and again as in salute.

Someone picked up a song. They sang The Green Hills of Pennsylvania, The Pretty Lady of My Heart, The World Turned Upside Down and last of all, their own mocking doggerel, Yankee Doodle. In fine spirits they roared it out, swaggering as they marched along, tilting their long muskets from side to side.

And everywhere along the line of march people had gathered to applaud and gape, boys swaying on fences, clusters of townsfolk who had walked up to welcome them, cheering the way cheers are given for the victors.

The Virginia farmer no longer listened to the chattering of the great men who rode with him. He was living over the time eight years ago when his army fled like rabbits from these same fields and woods of lower Manhattan.

Frightened and defeated and beyond hope: that was what everyone had said. They said that it was all over then, eight years ago, when it had scarcely begun. The faint of heart came out of their holes and pleaded with him to understand that it was all over. And he had been too stolid, too stubborn, too insensate.

He had gone on with the lost fight against impossible odds. Now it was all very far away; eight years dims everything, including suffering; and as he rode along he tried to reach back and understand why the cause had never been lost.

He remembered a letter he had written to his wife, in which he had said, "For me, there is no way back until this is over. You know how I love my home, yet if this last for twenty years, I must stay by it until it is over."

Governor Clinton was saying, "We hear rumors—that the men are dissatisfied, even that they would mutiny and march on Philadelphia."

"And that they would set me up as a dictator? You need not be afraid to say it."

"I've heard that. I trust you, sir—believe me, everyone trusts you—if you could stay?"

"It would accomplish nothing. Who am I? I fought a war with them. I am going home. They would go home too."

"But will they?"

"We aren't soldiers, we are men who took up guns for a little while, do you understand? And now we will put our guns away. We are not a people who live by guns." He could quiet Clinton, but in himself there was an aching doubt.

They were in the city now. Two redcoat files had been drawn up and the Continentals were to march between. The redcoats, disarmed, stood at attention, so stiff and straight and precise that they reminded the Virginian of wooden dolls. Anxiously he looked at his own men; they were not precise; they walked with a swagger, slouched, rolled their shoulders.

There was a difference.

The drums played and the Americans marched between, and now, somehow, no one cheered, no one spoke—because this was so finally, so completely the end.

He had planned, some time before, to slip away quietly; but now he was relieved when word came to him that they would all be gathered in Fraunces' Tavern, where they would expect him to say something before he went.

He made it clear and they knew that he was going away, that he would become a private citizen, just a man, just a farmer. They wanted him for a little while more as he had been for eight years and he in turn knew that in Fraunces' Tavern he would find the answer to the question that perplexed him.

He wore his buff and blue uniform, the uniform he had always worn and which his fellow officers had copied as a symbol of their esteem. He would continue to wear it until he arrived home and then Martha would put it away. She would reseam it and lay it, full of camphor, in a cedar box.

Now at the end, when it seemed that the going home he had planned for so long might be put off indefinitely, the details of the life he had left eight years ago became clearer than ever. Long, long past, it had been something that he accepted, the broad fields, the houses, the trees and fences, the horses and dogs, all his, the property of a very rich man. Martha was a wife who could annoy a man, she had a long tongue, she could scold with the best, as when he lost at cards as he so often did.

"Of course you lost."

"I sometimes win," he would protest.

"Do you? Either way, it seems a childish fashion of finding pleasure."

Having no children of his own, sometimes a realization of loneliness would strike him in the face like a wet cloth and then the emptiness would grow and grow. Then, in those days when everything had been his by right, he had no defense against the dark moods; when they seized him it would seem as if there was little enough reason for him to live.

And suddenly it was gone, his security, his wealth, his broad acres, not taken from him, but at the same time not his by right. Nothing was his by right, not the house, not the life he lived, nothing.

All of it had to be won, to be paid for; the simple right to exist had to be won and wealth was nothing. The right to walk as a free man on his own soil had to be paid for in blood and suffering. Even eight years was not too high a price; when there is only one way, the price is not measured.

Now he looked forward to seeing them in Fraunces' Tavern. How could it be any different for those who had served alongside him?

He recalled the time Martha had come to the terrible winter encampment at Valley Forge, to live there with him for a while, and the way she had said, "Has it always been as bad as this?"—softly, almost fearfully.

"Sometimes better, sometimes worse."

He wasn't wearing his woolsey and suddenly she began to scold but this time there was a difference in her scolding; she too had realized that the good things have their price. Holding her in his arms then, he saw clearly how all his values had changed.

"Will there ever be peace again?" she asked him.

"I think so."

He felt that there would be peace and war and peace for many, many years. Men would have things and those things would be theirs by right and then suddenly it would all be nothing unless it was paid for.

In Fraunces' Tavern, which still stands on Broad Street, they were waiting for him. They had been speaking about many things, the little knot of officers who commanded the army of the United States of America, recalling this and that. Knox had just finished telling how in '76, when they had lost the city, he had tried to make a stand on a little hill just to the north. And apologetically, "You know, I was just a boy, twenty-six then. I thought it was all over—how many times did we think that? He never thought so. Now it seems incredible that he's going away. To go back—well, he was able to do the rest. I suppose it's right to go back."

"If you have something to go back for—"

Copley, a colonel of cavalry, said, "If he goes back, I go back; and if he says, 'Follow me to hell,' I follow him there."

"You could see him saying that? I tell you, he goes home. Haven't I lived and eaten and frozen and starved with him for eight years—and do you think for nothing, for some cheap revolt after all those who have died to make a place where people can live? Then I tell you, you don't know him."

"We know him—"

Knox said huskily, "There is only one way—" feeling a terrible aching fear that perhaps he had been cheated, that perhaps all this had been for nothing, and then added, "It's the only way; you trust him; it has to be that way."

"There might be another way," Alexander Hamilton said thoughtfully. "We'll know when we see him."

They looked at Hamilton, who had loved the Virginian, hated him, been willing to die for him, turned against him and then for him; they knew Hamilton's ambition.

"It's in what he says and does, isn't it?" someone said softly as if in that phrase summing the whole matter up.

"Yes, in what he does."

Then the Virginian came in and there was a sudden hush. Watching them he stood at the door and then he smiled, and still no one said anything.

"I've known you when you were more talkative," he said.

"Sir?"

"Sit down," he nodded. "Haven't we been on our own feet long enough, gentlemen? We've earned the right to be comfortable, to sit in chairs and stretch our feet at the fire."

"You're leaving today?" Hamilton asked. Everything hung on his words and they watched him anxiously.

He refused to think of plots and schemes and said quietly, "I'm going to resign my commission and go home. It's a right I have earned, I think. I am a farmer, gentlemen, not a soldier. The war is over but I'm afraid the peace is just beginning. It will be a good feeling to take off our uniforms after all this time, won't it, gentlemen?"

They stared at him.

The only sign he gave was when he poured a glass of wine. Then his hand trembled slightly and a few drops spilled over the edge.

"To our good health—and to a long, long peace!"

They drank with him. Then he bit his lip and turned away for a moment. On almost every face there was an expression of realization combined with relief.

McKay said, "Sir, will you take my hand?"—stared at Washington and added, pleading, "What is one to know, sir? I'm human; if I wanted too much, I'm empty of that now—"

He remembered McKay in battle; it didn't matter whether he liked McKay or hated him; it mattered what the others thought and now all of them were watching. The war was over; men go home because they believe in what they fought for.

He took McKay's hand and when McKay murmured something about being forgiven, the tall Virginian pretended not to hear. He drank another toast and said, "I wish you all that's good, health and happiness. Go home and live quietly but remember that things come high. We've paid the price, we know."

They poured another toast all around and drank to one another. Knox shattered his glass in the hearth.

The tall man said, "Come to me, each of you."

Knox came first; they grasped hands, the tears running down their faces.

To Whitehall Ferry they all walked together, with their own ragged troops lining each side of the street. The sky was overcast and there was promise of an early snowfall. The troops held their cloaks tight about them and the drums took up a marching beat. The Virginian kept looking at his men; he was no longer afraid; somehow the issue had been decided; a democracy had been made and for many years it would go on. And so nebulous was the whole thing that he was not quite sure now how he managed to turn it so.

"Perhaps I was a fool to be afraid," he thought. Now he could think of nothing but that he was going home.

At the ferry a barge was waiting to take him over to the Jersey shore. The boatmen had already cast off and now held the craft to the docks with their hooks. The boatmen were cold and impatient.

Turning at the last to his friends, the Virginian found nothing he could say; the surge of happiness and gratitude inside him could not be put into words. Awkwardly he stepped into the barge.

"Ready, General Washington?" the mate of the crew demanded.

He nodded. The boatmen pushed off; the oars bit at the water.

At the dock, men and officers stood in a close silent group. Their eyes were on their commander and now as never before they knew him and understood him. They were bereft, yet at the same time strangely happy. Almost to a man there were tears on their cheeks, yet looking at each other they were not ashamed. Knox bit his heavy lips, shook his head like a shaggy bear. Hamilton was like a boy, crying without effort to halt the flow of tears, and McKay was looking at something he had never seen before, smiling curiously. Copley clenched and unclenched his hand, and Mercer stood mute, head bowed.

Just before the boat rounded the point of the Battery, the tall man took off his three-cornered hat and dipped it in salute.

They returned the salute and then the boat was gone.

The Three Swimmers and the Grocer from Yale[1]

by WILLIAM SAROYAN

THE ditches were dry most of the year, but when they weren't dry, they were roaring. As the snows melted in the hills the ditches began to roar and from somewhere, God knows where, arrived frogs and turtles, water snakes and fish. In the spring of the year the water hurried, and with it the heart, but as the fields changed from green to brown, the blossoms to fruit, the shy warmth to arrogant heat, the ditches slowed down and the heart grew lazy. The first water from the hills was cold, swift, and frightening. It was too cold and busy to invite the naked body of a boy.

Alone, or in a group, a boy would stand on the bank of a ditch and watch the water for many minutes, and then, terribly challenged, fling off his clothes, make a running dive, come up gasping, and swim across to the other side. If the boy was the first of a group to dive, the others would soon follow, in order not to walk home in shame. It wasn't simply that the water was cold. It was more that it had no time for boys. The springtime water was as unfriendly as anything could be.

One day in April I set out for Thompson Ditch with my cousin Mourad and a pal of his named Joe Bettencourt, a Portuguese who loved nothing more than to be free and out-of-doors. A school-room made Joe stupid. It embarrassed him. But once out of school, once off the school-grounds, he was as intelligent, as good-natured, casual, sincere, and friendly as anyone could possibly be. As my cousin Mourad said, Joe ain't dumb—he just doesn't want an education.

It was a bright Saturday morning. We had two baloney sandwiches each, and ten cents between the three of us. We decided to walk to the ditch so that we would get there around noon, when the day would be warm. We walked along the railroad tracks to Calwa. Along the state highway to Malaga. And then east through the vineyard country to the ditch. When we said Thompson Ditch, we meant a specific place. It was an intersection of country roads, with a wooden bridge and a headgate. The swimming was south of the bridge. West of the ditch was a big fenced-in pasture, with cows and horses grazing in it. East of the ditch was the country road. The road and the ditch traveled together many miles. The flow was south, and the next bridge was two miles away. In the summertime a day of swimming was incomplete until a boy had gone downstream to the other bridge, rested a

[1] From *My Name Is Aram* (1940), by William Saroyan. By permission of Harcourt, Brace & Company.

moment in the pasture land, and then came back up, against the stream, which was a good workout.

By the time we got out to Thompson Ditch the brightness of morning had changed to a gloom that was unmistakably wintry; in fact, the beginning of a storm. The water was roaring, the sky was gray, growing black, the air was cold and unfriendly, and the landscape seemed lonely and desolate.

Joe Bettencourt said, I came all this way to swim and rain or no rain I'm going to swim.

So am I, I said.

You wait, my cousin Mourad said. Me and Joe will see how it is. If it's all right, you can come in. Can you really swim?

Aw shut up, I said.

This is what I always said when it seemed to me that somebody had unwittingly insulted me.

Well, Joe said, *can* you?

Sure I can swim, I said.

If you ask *him,* my cousin Mourad said, he can do anything. Better than anybody in the world.

Neither of them knew how uncertain I was as to whether or not I could swim well enough to negotiate a dive and a swim across that body of cold roaring water. If the truth were known, when I saw the dark water roaring I was scared, challenged, and insulted.

Aw shut up, I said to the water.

I brought out my lunch and bit into one of the sandwiches. My cousin Mourad whacked my hand and almost knocked the sandwich into the water.

We eat after we swim, he said. Do you want to have cramps?

I had plumb forgotten. It was because I was so challenged and scared.

One sandwich won't give anybody cramps, I said.

It'll taste better after we swim, Joe said.

He was a very kind boy. He knew I was scared and he knew I was bluffing. I knew *he* was scared, but I knew he was figuring everything out a little more wisely than I was.

Let's see, he said. We'll swim across, rest, swim back, get dressed, eat, and unless the storm passes, start for home. Otherwise we'll swim some more.

This storm isn't going to pass, my cousin Mourad said. If we're going to swim, we're going to have to do it in a hurry and start for home.

By this time Joe was taking off his clothes. My cousin Mourad was taking off his, and I was taking off mine. We stood together naked on the bank of the ditch looking at the unfriendly water. It certainly didn't invite a dive, but there was no other honorable way to enter a body of water. If you tried to walk in, you were just naturally not a swimmer. If you jumped in feet first it wasn't exactly a disgrace, it was just bad style. On the other hand, the water was utterly without charm, altogether unfriendly, uninviting, and sinister. It was certainly challenging, though. The swiftness of the water made the distance to the opposite bank seem greater than it was.

Without a word Joe dived in. Without a word my cousin Mourad dived in. The second or two between splashes seemed like long days dreamed in a winter dream because I was not only scared but very cold. With a bookful of unspoken words on my troubled mind, I dived in.

The next thing I knew—and it wasn't more than three seconds later—I was listening to Joe yelling, my cousin Mourad yelling, and myself yelling. What had happened was that we had all dived into mud up to our elbows, had gotten free only with great effort, and had each come up worrying about what had happened to the other two. We were all standing in the cold roaring water, up to our knees in soft mud.

The dives had been standing dives. If they had been running dives we would have stuck in the mud up to our ankles, head first, and remained there until summer, or later.

This scared us a little on the one hand and on the other hand made us feel very lucky to be alive.

The storm broke while we stood in the mud of the ditch.

Well, Joe said, we're going to get caught in the rain anyhow. We might as well stay in a little while anyway.

We were all shivering, but it seemed sensible that we should try our best to make a swim of it. The water wasn't three feet deep; nevertheless, Joe managed to leap out of the mud and swim across, and then back.

We swam for what seemed like a long time, but was probably no more than ten minutes. Then we got out of the water and mud and dressed and, standing under a tree, ate our sandwiches.

Instead of stopping, the rain increased, so we decided to set out for home right away.

We may get a ride, Joe said.

All the way to Malaga the country road was deserted. In Malaga we went into the general store and warmed ourselves at the stove and chipped in and bought a can of beans and a loaf of French bread. The proprietor of the store was a man named Darcous who wasn't a foreigner. He opened the can for us, divided the beans into three parts on three paper plates, gave us each a wooden fork, and sliced the bread for us. He was an old man who seemed funny and young.

Where you been, boys? he said.

Swimming, Joe said.

Swimming? he said.

Sure, Joe said. We showed that river.

Well, I'll be harrowed, the grocer said. How was it?

Not three feet deep, Joe said.

Cold?

Ice-cold.

Well, I'll be cultivated, the grocer said. Did you have fun?

Did we? Joe asked my cousin Mourad.

Joe didn't know whether it had been fun or something else.

I don't know, my cousin Mourad said. When we dived in we got stuck in the mud up to our elbows.

It wasn't easy to get loose from the mud, I said.

Well, I'll be pruned, the grocer said.

He opened a second can of beans, pitched an enormous forkful into his mouth, and then divided the rest onto the three paper plates.

We haven't got any more money, I said.

Now, tell me, boys, the grocer said, what made you do it?

Nothing, Joe said with the finality of a boy who has too many reasons to enumerate at a moment's notice, and his mouth full of beans and French bread.

Well, I'll be gathered into a pile and burned, the grocer said. Now, boys, he said, tell me—of what race are you? Californians, or foreigners?

We're all Californians, Joe said. I was born on G Street in Fresno. Mourad here was born on Walnut Avenue or someplace on the other side of the Southern Pacific tracks, I guess, and his cousin somewhere around in that neighborhood, too.

Well, I'll be irrigated, the grocer said. Now, tell me, boys, what sort of educations have you got?

We ain't educated, Joe said.

Well, I'll be picked off a tree and thrown into a box, the grocer said. Now, tell me, boys, what foreign languages do you speak?

I speak Portuguese, Joe said.

You ain't educated? the grocer said. I have a degree from Yale, my boy, and I can't speak Portuguese. And you, son, how about you?

I speak, Armenian, my cousin Mourad said.

Well, I'll be cut off a vine and eaten grape by grape by a girl in her teens, the grocer said. I can't speak a word of Armenian and I'm a college graduate, class of 1892. Now, tell me, son, he said. What's *your* name?

Aram Garoghlanian, I said.

I think I can get it, he said. Gar-oghlan-ian. Is that it?

That's it, I said.

Aram, he said.

Yes, sir, I said.

And what strange foreign language do *you* speak? he said.

I speak Armenian, too, I said. That's my cousin. *Mourad* Garoghlanian.

Well, I'll be harrowed, he said, cultivated, pruned, gathered into a pile, burned, picked off a tree, and let me see what else? Thrown into a box, I think it was, cut off a vine and eaten grape by grape by a girl in her teens. Yes, sir. All them things, if this doesn't beat everything. Did you encounter any reptiles?

What's reptiles? Joe said.

Snakes, the grocer said.

We didn't see any, Joe said. The water was black.

Black water, the grocer said. Any fish?

Didn't see any, Joe said.

A Ford stopped in front of the store and an old man got out and came across the wood floor of the porch into the store.

Open me a bottle, Abbott, the man said.

Judge Harmon, the grocer said, I want you to meet three of the most heroic Californians of this great state.

The grocer pointed at Joe, and Joe said, Joseph Bettencourt—I speak Portuguese.

Stephen L. Harmon, the Judge said. I speak a little French.

The grocer pointed at my cousin Mourad and Mourad said, Mourad Garoghlanian.

What do you speak? the Judge said.

Armenian, my cousin Mourad said.

The grocer gave the Judge the opened bottle, the Judge lifted it to his lips, swallowed three swigs, beat his chest, and said, I'm mighty proud to meet a Californian who speaks Armenian.

The grocer pointed at me.

Aram Garoghlanian, I said.

Brothers? the Judge asked.

Cousins, I said.

Same thing, the Judge said. Now, Abbott, if you please, what's the occasion for this banquet and your poetic excitement, if not delirium?

The boys have just come from showing that old river, the grocer said.

The Judge took three more swigs, beat his chest three times slowly and said, Come from *what*?

They've just come from swimming, the grocer said.

Have any of you fevers? the Judge said.

Fever? Joe said. We ain't sick.

The grocer busted out with a roar of laughter.

Sick? he said. Sick? Judge, these boys dived naked into the black water of winter and came up glowing with the warmth of summer.

We finished the beans and the bread. We were thirsty but didn't know if we should intrude with a request for a drink of water. At least *I* didn't know, but Joe apparently didn't stop to consider.

Mr. Abbott, he said, could we have a drink of water?

Water? the grocer said. Water, my boy? Water's for swimming in, not for drinking.

He fetched three paper cups, went to a small barrel with a tap, turned the tap, and filled each cup with a light golden fluid.

Here, boys, he said. Drink. Drink the lovely juice of the golden apple, unfermented.

The Judge poured the grocer a drink out of his bottle, lifted the bottle to his lips, and said, To your health, gentlemen.

Yes, sir, Joe said.

We all drank.

The Judge screwed the top onto the bottle, put the bottle into his back pocket, looked at each of us carefully, as if to remember us for the rest of his life, and said, Good-by, gentlemen. Court opens in a half hour. I must pass sentence on a man who says he *borrowed* the horse, *didn't* steal it. He speaks Mexican. The man who says he *stole* the horse speaks Italian. Good-by.

Good-by, we said.

By this time our clothes were almost dry, but the rain hadn't stopped.

Well, Joe said, thanks very much, Mr. Abbott. We've got to get home.

Not at all, the grocer said. *I* thank you.

The grocer seemed to be in a strange silence for a man who only a moment before had been so noisy with talk.

We left the store quietly and began to walk down the highway. The rain was now so light it didn't seem like rain at all. I don't know what to make of it. Joe was the first to speak.

That Mr. Abbott, he said, he's some man.

The name on the sign is Darcous, I said. Abbott's his first name.

First or last, Joe said, he sure is some man.

That Judge was somebody too, my cousin Mourad said.

Educated, Joe said. I'd learn French myself, but who would I talk to?

We walked along the highway in silence. After a few minutes the black clouds parted, the sun came through, and away over in the east we saw the rainbow over the Sierra Nevadas.

We sure showed that old river, Joe said. Was he crazy?

I don't know, my cousin Mourad said.

It took us another hour to get home. We had all thought about the two men and whether or not the grocer was crazy. Myself, I believed he wasn't, but at the same time it seemed to me he had acted kind of crazy.

So long, Joe said.

So long, we said.

He went down the street. Fifty yards away he turned around and said something almost to himself.

What? my cousin Mourad shouted.

He was, Joe said.

Was what? I shouted.

Crazy, Joe shouted back.

Yeah? I shouted back. How do you know?

How can you be cut off a vine and eaten grape by grape by a girl in her teens? Joe shouted.

Suppose he was crazy? my cousin Mourad said. What of it?

Joe put his hand to his chin and began to consider. The sun was shining for all it was worth now and the world was full of light.

I don't think he was crazy, he shouted.

He went on down the street.

He was pretty crazy, my cousin Mourad said.

Well, I said, maybe he's not always.

We decided to let the matter rest at this point until we went swimming again, at which time we would visit the store again and see what happened.

A month later when, after swimming in the ditch, the three of us went into the store, the man who was in charge was a much younger man than Mr. Abbott Darcous. He wasn't a foreigner either.

What'll it be? he said.

A nickel's worth of baloney, Joe said, and a loaf of French bread.

Where's Mr. Darcous? my cousin Mourad said.

He's gone home, the young man said.

Where's that? I said.

Some place in Connecticut, I think, the young man said.

We made sandwiches of the baloney and French bread and began to eat. At last Joe asked the question.

Was he crazy? Joe said.

Well, the young man said, that's hard to say. I thought he was crazy at first. Then I decided he wasn't. The way he ran this store made you think he was crazy. He gave away more than he sold. To hear him talk you'd think he was crazy. Otherwise he was all right.

Thanks, Joe said.

The store was all in order now, and a very dull place. We walked out, and began walking home.

He's crazy, Joe said.

Who? I said.

That guy in the store now, Joe said.

That young fellow? I said.

Yeah, Joe said. That new fellow in there that ain't got no education.

I think you're right, my cousin Mourad said.

All the way home we remembered the educated grocer.

Well, I'll be cultivated, Joe said when he left us and walked on down the street.

Well, I'll be picked off a tree and thrown in a box, my cousin Mourad said.

Well, I'll be cut off a vine and eaten grape by grape by a girl in her teens, I said.

He sure was some man. Twenty years later, I decided he had been a poet and had run that grocery store in that little run-down village just for the casual poetry in it instead of the paltry cash.

The Veterans Reflect[1]

by IRWIN SHAW

THE BELLS were ringing everywhere and the engineer blew the locomotive whistle over and over as they roared up the springtime valley. The hills rolled back from the blue river, and the frail green of the young leaves made them look as though pale green velvet cloth, thready and worn, had been thrown as drapery over their winter sides.

Peter Wylie sat at the window staring dreamily out at the Hudson Valley rolling sweetly and familiarly past him. He smiled when a little girl in front of a farmhouse gravely waved an American flag at the speeding train, and the engineer gravely saluted her in return with a deep roar of the whistle.

Peter Wylie sat at the window of the speeding train and avoided listening to the booming voice of the gentleman talking to the pretty woman across the aisle. He stretched his legs comfortably and half-closed his eyes as he watched the green, quiet country over which, faintly, between towns, came the pealing of bells, because that morning the war had ended.

'. . . Dead two years,' the gentleman was saying. 'His ship went down off Alaska and that was the last we heard of him. Twenty-one years old. Here's his picture, in uniform.'

'He looks so young,' the woman said.

'He had a blond beard. Hardly had to shave. The ship went down in eighteen minutes . . .'

The bells were ringing, Peter thought, and the graves were full of young men who had hardly had to shave, in uniform. His two cousins on his mother's side, killed in Africa, and Martin, who had been his roommate for three years, killed in India, and all the boys from the squadron . . . The graves on the plains and the mountains, the shallow graves on the hard coral islands, and the long well-kept cemetery of the military dead outside the hospital which you looked at through the tall window of your ward as nurses whispered outside in the corridor, and the doctors hurried fatefully by on their crepe soles. 'Convenient,' you said with a slow, remote wave of your hand and with what you hoped was a smile, to the nurse, who seemed always to have come from behind a screen where she wept continuously when not actually needed at a bedside. 'Modern design.'

'What?' the red-eyed nurse had asked blankly.

You had been too tired to explain and merely closed your eyes with the beautiful rudeness of the dying. But you hadn't died. There was a strange

[1] Reprinted by permission of the author. First published in *Accent*, Winter, 1943.

platter-like excavation in your abdomen and you would never really enjoy your food any more, and you would always have to climb stairs slowly even though you were only twenty-nine now on this day when the bells were ringing, but the cemetery and the military dead were still there, and here you were on a train up the Hudson Valley on your way home to see your wife and child, and the guns were quiet and the airplanes idled in the hangars, and the pilots sat around and played cards and tried to remember the telephone numbers of the girls in their home towns.

You were on your way home to see your wife and child. For three years, alone at night, sleepless in strange rooms on other continents; on leave, at a bar, sleepless drinking and laughing, and the brassy old juke boxes playing songs that cried *far away and long ago, far away and long ago,* and all the women being earnest about the war and patriotically anxious to jump into bed with all the pilots, navigators, bombardiers, flight-sergeants, wing-commanders, meteorologists, radio-operators of the air forces of all the United Nations, including the Russian; for three years on the long droning flights across the hundred-mile ripples of the Pacific; for three years, even sometimes at the moment when the bombardier said, 'OK, I'll take it from here,' as the plane ducked in over the target and the anti-aircraft fire bloomed roughly about you, the faces of your wife and daughter slid through your mind, the woman's firm-boned jaw, the moody blue eyes, the wide, full mouth, familiar, loving, changing, merry, tragic, tenderly and laughingly mocking in the secret wifely female understanding of the beloved weaknesses of the man of the family— and the child's face, small, unformed, known only from photographs sent across the oceans, looking out at him through the night with sober, infant gravity . . . Three years, he thought, and tomorrow morning the train will pull into the dirty old station at Chicago and there they'll be, standing in the soot and clangor, hand in hand, the quick, delightful woman and the fat child, picking his uniform out among the other uniforms, with three years' waiting and loving and hoping showing in the faces as he strode down the platform . . .

'Bong-bong!' shouted a little bald man, who was leading two women drunkenly down the aisle toward the diner. 'Bong-bong! We did it!'

'Ding-a-ling! Ring out the wild bells!' The blonde woman right behind the bald man cried out. 'Welcome to America!'

'We applied the crusher,' the bald man told the crowded car. 'The old steel spring technique. Coil back, coil back, coil back, then . . .'

They disappeared around the bend of the car over which the small sign said modestly, 'Women.'

Across the ocean, in the mountains of another country, a man strode out of a darkened house to the long, armored automobile waiting on the night-deserted road. Two men, bundled in army greatcoats, hurried behind him, their boots sighing softly in the damp earth of the courtyard. The chauffeur had the door open, but the man stopped and turned around before he got in and looked at the dark shapes of the mountains rising behind him against the starry sky. He put his hand uncertainly to his collar and pulled at it and took a deep breath. The two men in the greatcoats waited, without looking up, shadowed by the slowly fluttering young foliage of the oaks that bordered the path. The man turned and slowly got into the car, carefully, like an old man who has fallen recently and remembers that his bones are brittle and mend slowly. The other two men sprang into the front seat, and the chauffeur slammed the rear door and ran around to the front and leaped in and started the motor. The automobile sped quietly down the dark road, the noise of its going making a private and faraway *whoosh* that died on the huge and growing darkness of the mountain-circled spring night.

In the back of the car, the man sat bolt upright, his eyes narrow and unseeing, staring straight ahead of him. Off in the hills a church bell pealed and pealed again and again, musical and lonely in the echoing darkness. The lips of the man in the back seat curled slightly, bitterly, as the sound of the pealing village bell wavered on the wind. Germans! he thought. Five million German dead all over the world and the Russians on the road to Berlin and everything worse than 1918 and their leader skulking through the night on backroads towards the Swiss border with a chauffeur and two frightened first-lieutenants and they ring bells as though this was the day after the Fall of France! Germans! Idiots! Imitation suits, imitation rubber, imitation eggs, finally imitation men . . . What was a man expected to do with material like that? And he'd come so close . . . so close . . . The gates of Moscow. But he sat. The statue sat. Everyone else ran, the diplomats, the newspapermen, the government, and Stalin sat there and the people sat . . . Pleasant. Sitting there in his burning house with his gun and his plow . . . and somehow the house didn't burn. Storm-troopers, assault-guards, blitzkrieg veterans . . . at the gates of Moscow and they died. A little cold and they dropped like hothouse violets. So close . . . so close . . .

The bell rang more strongly and in other villages other bells answered.

They'd hang him if they caught him. He'd cried at the last Armistice, he'd hang at this . . . The British use a silk rope when they hang nobility. They wouldn't use silk on him . . . And the bells ringing all around him . . .

He leaned forward and jabbed the chauffeur fiercely in the back.

'Faster!'

The car spurted forward.

'Production,' the booming gentleman across the aisle was saying to the pretty woman, who was leaning closer to him, prettily attentive. 'It was inevitable. American production won this war.'

Peter thought of the graves, of the English and Chinese and Australians and Russians and Serbs and Greeks and Americans who filled them, who had fought bitterly with rifle and cannon and plane across the torn fields and stripped forests where they now quietly lay, under the illusion that if the war was to be won, it was to be won by them, standing there, hot gun in hand, with the shells dropping around them and the scream of the planes overhead and the tanks roaring at them at fifty miles an hour . . .

'I know,' the gentleman was saying. 'I was in Washington from 1941 right to the finish and I saw. I'm in machine tools and I had my hand on the pulse of production and I know what I'm talking about. We performed miracles.'

'I'm sure,' the pretty woman murmured. 'I'm absolutely sure.' She was not as young as she had looked at first, Peter noticed, and her clothes were much shabbier than he had thought, and she looked pretty and impressed and tired and ready to be invited to dinner.

'. . . Plants in seven states,' the man was saying. 'We expanded four hundred per cent. The war's over now, I can talk freely . . .'

The war's over, Peter thought deliciously, settling deeper into his chair, and letting his head rumble pleasantly with the click of the wheels as he leaned back against the cushion, the war's over and machine-tool manufacturers who expanded four hundred per cent can talk freely to women in Pullman cars and tomorrow I see my wife and child and I never have to climb into an airplane again. From now on I walk down to the station and buy a ticket when I want to go someplace and I sit down with a magazine and a whiskey and soda and the train clicks along on steel and solid gravel and the only enemy activity will be an occasional small boy throwing a rock hopefully at the bright windows of the diner flashing by. Tomorrow afternoon he would be walking slowly along the lake front in the spring wind, hand in hand with his wife and child. 'And that, darling, is Lake Michigan. Do you know the water you took a bath in this morning? It comes right from here, especially for you. When your father was a boy he used to stand here and watch the red Indians sail by in their war canoes at forty miles an hour, reciting Henry Wadsworth Longfellow at the top of their voices . . . I can see by the look in your mother's eye that she doesn't believe me and wants an ice cream soda. I can also see by the look in her eye that she doesn't think you should have an ice cream soda so soon after lunch, but I've been thinking about buying you this ice cream soda for three years and the war's over and I don't think she's going to make too much of a fuss . . .'

And tomorrow night, they would lie, soft on their backs in the soft bed, staring idly up at the dark ceiling, his arm under her head, their voices murmuring and mingling with the distant quiet night sounds of the sleeping city, the clack and rumble from the lakefront railroad yards and the soft whisper of automobiles on the highway . . . 'I slept in the same bed in Cairo, Egypt, with a boy from Texas who weighed two hundred and thirty pounds. He wanted to get in the Navy, but he was six feet six inches tall and they said he wouldn't fit on any ship afloat or building. Also he was in love with a girl he met in New York who sold gloves in Saks and he talked about her all night long. She has a thirty-six inch bust and she lives with four girls from Vassar in Greenwich Village and she has a scar on her right buttock six inches long that she got when she fell down iceskating and a man with racing skates ran over her. This is an improvement over sleeping with a two-hundred-and-thirty-pound Texan in the same bed in Cairo, Egypt. Yes, I'll kiss you if you want . . .'

And her voice, close to his ear, in the gentle, tumbled darkness, alive with the fresh night wind off the lake and the familiar smell of her perfume and the frail dry smell of her hair, remembered all the years deep in his nostrils '. . . And she went to the nursery school in Tucson all day while I was on duty in the hospital and they all liked her very much but she had a habit of hitting the other little boys and girls with her shovel and I had to leave her with my sister. I knew you'd laugh. Stop laughing or I'll stuff a pillow in your mouth, Mr. Veteran. You can afford to laugh, out flying around ten thousand miles away with nothing to worry about but Japs and Germans. Wait till you're a mother and seven young mothers descend upon you to tell you your child has swiped at their children with a wooden shovel every day of the school term . . .' And the kiss to stop the laughter and her head under his chin after that and the slow, diminishing chuckles together for the child sleeping in the next room dreaming of other children and more wooden shovels.

And again, her hand thrown softly and possessively on his chest . . . 'There's a lot more hair here than I remember.'

'War. I always put on a lot of hair on my chest in a war. Any objections?'

'No. I'm well-known as a woman who's partial to hairy men. Or is talk like that too vulgar for young soldiers? Am I too fat? I put on eight pounds since 1942 . . . Have you noticed?'

'I'm noticing now.'

'Too fat?'

'Ummmmmmnnn . . .'

'Tell the truth.'

'Ummnnn.'

'I'm going to diet . . .'

'You just wait here and I'll go down and get you a plate of mashed potatoes . . .'

'Oh, shut up! Oh, darling, darling, I'm glad you're home . . .'

Or perhaps they wouldn't talk at all in the beginning. Perhaps they would just touch each other's hand and weep cheek to cheek for the three years behind them and the years ahead and cling to each other desperately through the long cool night and go to his parents' farm in Wisconsin and walk hand in hand in morning sunlight slowly over the greening fields, their feet sinking into the soft loam, content in the first hours with love and silence, until finally they could sit under the wide peaceful sky, off to themselves, with the rich smell of the newly plowed fields and the watermelon-cucumber smell of the river in their nostrils, and then, finally, the words would come . . . The things he had thought on the long flights, the decisions and doubts of the thousand wartime nights, the deep deep hallelujah of his spirit as the train covered the sweet final miles between the war and home. He would tell her the things he had had to bury deep within him through the noisy, bleeding years . . . The times he had been afraid . . . the first time he had seen an enemy squadron small against the horizon, harmless looking dots, growing nearer and larger with insane speed, and the ridiculous way it made him see, over and over again, for some reason, *Acrobatics,* as it was printed in the March *Field Bulletin.* And at the time he had been shot, six hours away from base, on a rough day, lying bleeding on his parachute while Dennis pushed the bomber toward home, and he had managed to keep quiet for the first four hours, but had wept for the last two hours, almost mechanically, although he had felt very calm. And because he was certain he was going to die, he had for the first time permitted himself to think about whether the whole thing was worth it or not, as the plane bucked in the cold air. He could tell her how he had thought, in those long six hours, of all the boys who had lightly roared off at four hundred miles an hour and lightly and thoughtlessly, or at least silently died . . . He would be able to tell her that he had soberly decided, bullet in his belly and sure of death in the roaring plane, that it was worth it, that if he had it to do again he would leave home, wife, child, father, mother, country, and search the German bullet out of the cloud once more, part of the enormous anguish and enormous courage of all the men on sea and beach and mountain locked with him in final struggle against the general enemy. And, then, weeping, on the edge of death, as he thought, he could let himself go . . . and for the first time, in the mist of pain, break down the barrier of reserve that had kept him, even in his most secret thoughts, from admitting even to himself how much he loved all those men behind guns—his friends, boys from the same schools, coolly diving, cannons and machine guns tearing out of their wings, at enemy bombers; the pleasant Englishmen foolishly and desperately confident of their ships, sailing formally and arrogantly into hopeless battle like Englishmen in books; the quilted Chinese rifleman standing forlornly on the brown China earth against tanks and artillery; and huge, muffled Russians, fighting by day and night and snow and rain, implacably and ingeniously and tirelessly killing, oblivious to agony or doubt, intent only on burning and crippling and starving and murdering the enemy . . . He could tell her how deep inside him he had loved all those bloody, weary, cruel, reliable men, how he had felt borne up on that huge tide of men careless of death, and had felt himself to be a part of that tide, agonized, stricken, familiar with defeat, often falsely and frivolously led, but better than the leaders, dangerous, brawling, indivisible . . . and how he had felt linked with those men for all their lives and his, closer to them even though he could not speak their language nor they his, than to his own mother and father, responsible forever for their comfort and glory as they were for his. And he could tell her of the sober exhilaration of these reflections, this deep dredging to his thoughts, this ultimate examination in the light of pain and exhaustion and terror of himself, who never before this had thought deeply or reflected much beyond the everyday cares of average life in a small town, seated at a desk from nine to five, sleeping comfortably in a quiet room in a warm house, going to the pictures twice a week, playing tennis on Sunday, worrying about whether the car was good for another year or not . . .

The long automobile sped down the winding road among the hills on its way through the night to the Swiss border. The man still sat bolt upright on the back seat, his eyes narrow and unseeing, straight ahead of him.

Victories, he thought, how many victories can a man be expected to win? Paris, Rotterdam, Singapore, Athens, Kiev, Warsaw . . . and still they kept coming . . . There was a certain limit to the number of victories that were humanly possible. Napoleon discovered, too . . . Napoleon . . . Napoleon . . . He was tired of that name. In the last days he had ordered that it was not to be spoken in his presence . . . And now they were all hunting for him, like a world full of bloodhounds . . . Germans, English, Russians, Americans, French, Austrians, Poles, Dutch, Bulgarians, Serbs, Italians . . . Well, they had reason. Fools. For a long time it hadn't been hard. The cities fell like rotten apples. But then America and Russia . . . The timing was not quite exact. In politics everything happened before schedule. In war everything happened behind schedule . . . So close, so close . . . The Russians . . . Everything else being equal, the bells would be ringing for another reason tonight if not for the Russians . . . Just that winter had to be the coldest in fifty years. There has to be a certain element of luck . . . Well, all things considered, he had had a successful career. He had started out as a nobody, with his father always yelling at him that he'd never amount to anything and he never could hold a job . . . Today his name was known in every home on the face of the earth, in every jungle . . . Thirty million people had died earlier than they expected because of him and hundreds of cities were leveled to the ground because of him and the entire wealth of all nations of the earth had been strained by him, mines and factories and farms . . . All things considered, he had had a successful career . . . Even his father would have to admit that. Though, to be fair, if he hadn't grabbed first, someone else would have grabbed . . . The thing would have happened without him. He had to admit that. But he had grabbed first and the name known in every home on the face of the earth was Hitler, not any other name . . . So close, so close . . . A little cold and they died . . . Idiots! And now they wanted to hang him. If he could only get across the border, lie low . . . Until the rest of them got tired of killing the Germans. After all, Napoleon came back off Elba. A hundred days. With a little luck he could have stuck . . . Napoleon . . . the name was not to be mentioned. They were going to start worrying about the Russians very soon . . . The Russians, the Russians . . . the armies had been cut up, they had died by the millions . . . and yet, today they were on the road to Berlin. They were going to need someone to stop the Russians and if he could only lie low for a few months, his name would be mentioned . . . And once he got back, there'd be no more mistakes . . . With a little luck . . .

The man on the rear seat relaxed against the cushions and a little smile played around the raw mouth.

'I was interviewed by the Washington *Post*,' the booming gentleman was saying, his voice cutting into Peter's reverie. 'Right before I left. And I told them straight up and down—production must not stop.' Peter looked absently at the booming gentleman. He was a tall fat man with a bald head, but somehow he reminded Peter of all the teacher's pets who had ever been in his classes in grammar school . . . pink, fat face, small, round, pink, satisfied mouth, always impressing everyone with how much he knew and how much in favor he was. Peter closed his eyes and imagined the tall, fat man in an Eton collar with a bow tie and grinned. 'Stop a machine for a day,' the man was saying, 'and industrial obsolescence comes a month nearer. Whether we like it or not we are geared to wartime production.'

'You're so right,' the pretty woman murmured. Peter looked at her closely for the first time. Her clothes were shabby and she had the same wornout, rundown look that the whole country seemed to have, as though the war had rubbed people and things down to the grain, as though the war had kept the whole continent up too many nights, working too hard . . . Teacher's pet was bright and shining, as though he had stepped out of 1941 into a world many years older . . .

'Nobody ever had too many guns. I told them right to their faces.'

'You're so right,' the pretty woman murmured.

'My son was sunk off Alaska . . .' Peter tightened as he recognized the note of boasting in the voice, as though the man were saying he had been elected to an exclusive club. 'My son was sunk off Alaska and I produced machine tools twenty-four hours a day, seven days a week and I have a right to talk. We got it on our hands, I told them, and we have to face the problem fair and square, what are we going to do with them . . .'

'Yes,' murmured the pretty woman, hoping for dinner, over the rumble of the wheels.

He would walk slowly, Peter thought, in the evening, after dinner in the big farm kitchen, with the smells of cooking rich and fragrant in the warm kitchen air and his mother red-faced and aproned and his father tall and scrubbed and quiet, smoking his nickel cigar . . . He would walk slowly along the rutted wagon road with Laura beside him in the bright twilight, full of the warm knowledge that he was in no hurry to get any place, that he could leisurely regard the small hills, accepting the night, and leisurely listen to the last evening concert of the birds, leisurely scuff his shoes in the light country dust of the road over which armored tread had never passed, which had never known blood . . . He could tell Laura finally that of all the good things that had happened to him in this savage, ecstatic century, the best had happened in the moment when he had walked toward her on a train platform in Chicago the day after the war was over . . . He could tell her finally how tired he was, how tired he had been when bone and blood and nerve had collapsed, when no effort had ever seemed possible again, when his body had given up all knowledge of victory or defeat . . . And when somehow planes had to be flown and guns manned and swift, deadly action taken by that sodden bone and blood and nerve . . . and somehow the action taken because of the feeling deep within him that on other fields and in other skies, wearier and more desperate men were still manning guns for him and flying more dangerous skies . . . And the promise he made to himself that when it was over and he was home, surrounded by care and love, he was never going to hurry again, never knowingly perform a violent act, never even raise his voice except in laughter and song, never argue with anyone about anything . . . He wasn't going back to his job. Nine to five in a bank at a desk was no way to crown a career of bloodshed thirty thousand feet over three continents. Perhaps Laura would be able to suggest something for him to do, something quiet and unhurried and thoughtless . . . But first he was going to do nothing. Just wander around the farm and teach the baby how to spell and listen to his father explain his particular reasons for rotating his crops in his own particular way . . . Maybe two, three, five months, a year of that, as long as it took to drain off the blood and weariness, as long as it took for his crippled spirit to open the door of its wartime hospital and step out firmly . . . as long as it took . . .

'The job's just begun,' the booming gentleman was saying. 'Let them ring the bells. It amuses them. But tomorrow morning . . .'

'Yes,' said the pretty woman, eager to agree with everything.

'We've got to face the facts. A businessman faces the facts. What are the facts? The Russians are near Berlin. Right?'

'Yes,' said the woman, 'of course.'

'Berlin. Fine. Unavoidable. The Russians are sitting on Europe . . .'

Peter tried to close his eyes, close his ears, go back to the dear dream of the twilight country road and his wife's hand in his and the dust that had never known blood. But the man's voice tore through and he couldn't help but listen.

'As a businessman I tell you it's an impossible situation.' The man's voice grew louder. 'Intolerable. And the sooner we realize it, the better. The truth is, maybe it's a good thing this war was fought. Dramatizes the real problem. Makes the American people see what the real danger is. And what's the answer? Production! Guns and more guns! I don't care what those Communists in Washington say, I say the war has just begun.'

Peter stood up wearily and went over to the booming gentleman. 'Get out of here,' he said as quietly as he could. 'Get out of here and keep quiet or I'll kill you.'

The booming gentleman looked up at him, his face still with surprise. His little red mouth opened twice and closed silently. His pale eyes stared harshly and searchingly at Peter's worn, bitter face. Then he shrugged, stood up, put out his arm for the lady.

'Come,' he said, 'we might as well eat.'

The pretty woman stood up and started hesitantly, frightenedly, toward the door.

'If it weren't for your uniform,' the booming man said loudly, 'I'd have you arrested. Armistice or no Armistice.'

'Get out of here,' Peter said.

The booming gentleman turned and walked swiftly after the woman and they disappeared toward the diner. Peter sat down, conscious of every eye in the car on him, regretting that he had found his next years' work placed so soon before him and crying so urgently to be done. Well, he comforted himself, at least I don't have to travel for this one.

The engineer blew his whistle on a ten mile stretch of clear track because the war was over and as the hoarse, triumphant sound floated back, Peter closed his eyes and tried to think of his wife and child waiting in the noisy station in Chicago . . .

Salesmanship [1]

by MARY ELLEN CHASE

M R. HENRY STAPLES felt a new spring in his knees as he descended the apartment-house steps and started downtown. Something of the sprightliness of his dreams the preceding night seemed to have gotten into his feet as well as into his mind. Funny how things worked out, he told himself, if you just gave yourself a chance. And fifteen dollars was little enough to pay for such a chance as he had given himself.

To be sure, the full prophecy of his new course on salesmanship had yet to be realized. He had still to be called within the glass doors of the manager's office, to be met with a firm handclasp and the genial proffer of a doubled salary. But with his Saturday's advance from boys' underwear and stockings to suits, things were well on their way.

He took a new and delighted interest in the sounds that issued from nearly every opened window. In their tight little living-room Nora was at last listening to the morning's radio talk on housekeeping hints and receipes for the day. Extremely satisfying to him was the knowledge that she might enjoy this outward and visible sign of his new discovery of powers latent within himself!

He smiled as he recalled Charley's hurried and unwilling exit to school, his earlier participation with his father in the morning exercises which were to make them both "more manly, more fit for this game of living and of life."

Once in the store, his benevolence diffused itself among his fellow employees. He beamed upon floor-walkers, floor-polishers, and stenographers. He commented on the weather to Mr. Nesbit, still in the underwear; to Mr. Sims, who had sold belts and suspenders for years. It seemed impossible, now that he was so gloriously ready, to wait for his first customers.

These he saw before the white coverings were fully removed from the counters, and with that peculiar divination which his course had promised, he marked them as his own. They stood within the entrance-doors waiting for nine o'clock. There was a difference in their attitudes which Mr. Staples, now that such telling things had been called to his attention, noted at once.

The woman, small and inconspicuously dressed, stood close to the window, staring with a rapt expression upon the boy's apparel displayed there, summer things—blazers, flannels, gay shirts—interspersed with the tennis-rackets and golf-sticks. The man stood near the outer doorway, his hands in his pockets, and stared, sulkily, Mr. Staples declared to himself, into the street.

Obviously the woman was to be the purchaser, a conclusion immensely reassuring to Mr. Staples, since from the careful analysis of temperament pro-

[1] By permission of the author. Published in *The Pictorial Review*, July, 1930.

vided by his course the truth had been borne in upon him that he had been expressly fashioned to deal with women rather than with men.

He was not at all surprised when five minutes later they came down the aisle, the man several paces behind.

And Mr. Staples' cordiality knew no reserves. He gave it full swing, partly because he *felt* cordial, partly because he sensed an air of determination in the somewhat set face of his customer, a determination which he must combat with all the forces of persuasion and gallantry at his command.

"In selling there is no asset like extreme politeness," he quoted to himself. "Keep your reservoir filled to the brim."

Seemingly unimpressed by his welcome, the woman came to the point at once.

"I am looking for a blue suit—for a boy—twelve years old."

"Certainly," said Mr. Staples. "Our stock, I may say, is excellent. Were you thinking of serge or cheviot?"

"I hadn't thought very much of—the material."

"I see. It's color you want. But material's important; take my word for that. There's a lot to be said for both. Serge may be dressier, but cheviot won't take a shine or show spots like serge. And it's newer. It's sure to be worn by boys and men for two seasons straight."

"I see," said the woman.

Mr. Staples felt vaguely troubled as he turned toward the cases. He always liked interest in his customers. It made things go better even if they were fussy and hard to suit. He groped about in his mind for something to liven things up a bit.

"You said twelve years old? Now, that's an age to keep you guessing, isn't it? I've a boy twelve myself. They're alive to everything at twelve."

The woman did not answer. Mr. Staples did not resent her neglect to his allusion to Charley, but he had thought his last remark original. Queer how some folks expect the salesman to do it all, and yet he had been forewarned by his course of just such an attitude. Undaunted, he started on another and more direct course.

"How big a boy is he? Large for his age or small?"

"I think you'd say average," said the woman.

"It's always more satisfactory," said Mr. Staples, "to bring them along. But, of course, there's school."

"Yes," replied the woman.

Funny, thought Mr. Staples, as he spread out four suits for her inspection, funny how little help her husband offered. He stood at the extreme end of the counter, fumbling with the buckles and straps of some knickers piled there. Perhaps he was a professor from the college on the hill. They always behaved in that absent-minded fashion, their heads deep in some crazy notion or another.

"You wouldn't want me to lay these aside now, and bring him in, say, at four to try them on?"

"No," she said. "I think not. I'll choose myself."

"I know just how 'tis," remarked Mr. Staples genially. "Try to catch a twelve-year-old after school and there's something doing. Funny how when they get older—"

"This looks about right to me," interrupted the woman, "this cheviot one.'

"You can't go wrong on that," assured Mr. Staples, "no matter what. That's genuine Scotch cheviot, all wool to a thread. My word on it, Madam, and the store's guaranty. That suit'll wear the toughest youngster in this town a good two years—one year for Sunday-school and the like of that, and one for common. And being cheviot, it's not going to show every spot on earth or take the shine that serge is bound to."

He lifted the suit from the counter, hoping thereby to attract the attention of the man; but he still fumbled at the buckles and straps. The woman fingered the cloth, and then with a sudden impulsive gesture put her hand in one of the pockets of the coat.

Mr. Staples laughed aloud.

"I see," he said knowingly. "A boy does always raise Ned with pockets. But these are tough ones and lined with the best. He won't sag these, no matter what he fills them with!"

For a long time, it seemed to Mr. Staples, she kept her hand in that pocket. He began to feel foolish standing there holding the suit up in one hand.

"It's good and roomy, too," he said at last, a little loudly so that she withdrew her hand. "But there's one drawback. There's only one pair of pants to this suit. Most have knickers and longs, but this has only the longs. Most of the kids now, though, wear longs. You see in a sort of dressy suit like this they don't—"

He stopped, surprised at the sudden movement of the man, who walked quickly from the knickers toward the door. But he paused after a moment and, to Mr. Staples' relief, came nearer his wife. She put her arm in his and drew him closer.

"I believe," she said to Mr. Staples, and as she raised her eyes he was surprised again by the brightness of them, "I believe I'll take this very suit. He's always wanted long trousers, but I've thought them rather silly for small boys."

"They're all the rage, Madam," said Mr. Staples, relieved alike by her decision and by her increased interest, though withal puzzled a bit in that she did not seem to be speaking to him at all. "And once he wears them through, you can just combine the coat with sports knickers or flannels, and presto! he's fixed as good as new."

He was not prepared for the silence which greeted his words. A customer might at least acquiesce, he thought, in such an economical suggestion. For just a fraction of a minute he envied men of lesser state, Mr. Nesbit in the underwear and Mr. Sims in belts and suspenders, the sale of whose wares required less tact.

"Successful salesmen," he quoted to himself, "learn to create the atmosphere in which their customers move."

Vaguely conscious that he was, that he himself was moving, however blindly, in an atmosphere not of his own creating, he strove to readjust himself, to be "master of the situation."

"He'll be some surprised this noon when he comes home and finds his longs," he said with what his book would have termed an attractive chuckle.

"We're in somewhat of a hurry," said the man bruskly, startling Mr. Staples by the first and unexpected sound of his voice. "If you'll do the suit up, please."

"Certainly."

Again he made an attempt at livening matters, at disseminating that quality called "homelike," by his course-book.

"Well, we sure must trust each other. Here, I entirely forgot to tell you the price or you to ask!"

"It doesn't matter," said the man, taking out his purse.

"Cash or charge?" asked Mr. Staples, seemingly unconscious of the pocket-book.

"I'll pay for it," said the man.

Mr. Staples consulted the price-tag.

"Twenty-nine fifty," he announced. "And I know that seems a bit steep for a growing boy. But I'll guarantee your money's worth, and if he outgrows it quick, send him in. Alteration's free. And here's my card."

From an inner pocket he secured and extended a bit of new, fresh pasteboard. The man ignored it, but the woman took it.

"Thank you," she said, and smiled suddenly at him, a strange smile which Mr. Staples was at a loss to interpret. "You've been very kind, I'm sure."

"Not at all," said Mr. Staples, now secure in her thanks and in the consciousness of a good sale. "Not at all. We aim to please. I'll tell you what, Madam. With a sale like this we like to throw in a bit of a gift. This Spring it's a baseball, a good league number, none of your twine-and-sawdust balls. If you'll just show your slip in the sports and my card they'll give you one. Present it to the young man with my compliments."

He felt magnanimous as he began to secure the box with stout twine and wrap it in brown paper.

For a moment only the crackling of the paper broke the silence.

"We're late, Margaret," said the man then, his voice high and tense, his hand pulling at her arm. "Come, darling."

Mr. Staples stared. The word of endearment seemed to him so at variance with the tone and gesture. Little as he was given to calling Nora such loving names, he rarely spoke to her in that tone or treated her to such roughness.

Perhaps the woman had not heard his offer of the baseball. He started to repeat it, and then decided not to. If these queer customers did not want something for nothing—why, the store was the gainer.

He looked after them as they walked hurriedly arm in arm toward the door. It had been a good enough sale, but a queer one, one hard to dominate by his own personality.

Then he suddenly recalled an omission which must be rectified, and he hurried after them, book in hand. As he reached them the man was speaking, still in a tense, almost angry voice.

"I told you, Margaret, 'twas crazy to do it yourself."

"Don't worry, dear," said the woman. "I wanted to. And I'm pleased about the long trousers. He's always wanted them."

"I beg your pardon," said Mr. Staples to her as he intercepted them at the door. "Even with cash sales like this the store asks for names and addresses so we can keep track of our patrons. I hope I may have the pleasure of fitting out that youngster again."

He colored a bit under the resentful gaze of the man, but recovered himself when the woman smiled again at him. The course-book was right. His temperament was made for dealing with women.

"Of course," she said, laying her hand upon her husband's arm quite as though she were curbing a restless child. "Mr. and Mrs. Charles Seymour, 100 Forest Avenue. And thank you again."

That evening Mr. Staples stretched out luxuriously upon the green davenport with his paper under the bridge-lamp. He had had a good day, had earned his relaxation.

Charley was fussing with the dial of the radio. Nora was washing the dishes in the kitchenette. Mr. Staples was a thorough reader of his paper. Immersed in the sports, in the society columns, where he often found the names of his patrons, he was oblivious to Charley's impatience.

"Say, Dad, I wish you'd help a fellow. I keep gettin' this correct English stuff when I want baseball. Don't I get enough English in school? I'll say I do!"

"Henry!" called Nora from the sink. "Henry! What's the use of the new radio if you can't help Charley get what he wants?"

But Mr. Staples's eyes were all at once concentrated on one spot, in the last column, on the next to the last page.

SEYMOUR—On Sunday, Charles, aged twelve, only son of Mr. and Mrs. Charles
     Seymour, 100 Forest Avenue. Funeral Tuesday at two o'clock.

"Dad," called Charley again. "This thing's funny. I can't do nothin' with it."

"Henry!" supplemented Nora, appearing now from the kitchenette and snatching the paper from his hands. "My word! You're reading even the deaths. Don't you hear Charley?"

"Yes," said Mr. Staples.

He got up from the davenport and began fussing with the dial of the radio. Queer, he thought, how you couldn't tell some folks some things even after you'd lived years with them. Funny!

"You don't seem to be doing much better, Dad," complained Charley. "It's funny how we can't get what we want, ain't it?"

"Yes, Charley," said Mr. Staples, passing his left hand in a dazed fashion across his forehead.

He glanced about the room, at its tight security, at the fat pink sofa-cushions, at Nora in her beflowered rubber apron, at Charley in his blue suit, at his course-book on the center-table, awaiting his half-hour of study.

"Yes," he repeated, neither to Nora nor to Charley, "yes, 'tis funny. Most things are kind of—funny, I guess."

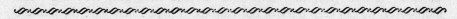

Guidance [1]

by MARGARET WIDDEMER

THE blue limousine checked before the fashionable church on Park Avenue. There was another car, a gray one with a crest on its door, where the chauffeur would have liked to park the limousine.

"Can't you get it any nearer than that?" demanded Mrs. Meriden sharply up the speaking-tube. "Push the other car down."

"What's she doin' here?" murmured her footman to the chauffeur as he lifted a red ear from the hole.

"Askin' for guidance, no doubt," said the chauffeur, with a grin that pointed it out as a good joke.

"Is it guidance?" The handsome young Irish footman snorted softly. "If the young madam got to heaven itself, she'd be telling St. Peter how to handle his job before she'd her halo on straight!" He sprang to open the door, a deferential automaton.

Mrs. Meriden turned a hard, handsome young face to her husband.

"I have to inspect the church furnishing on behalf of the committee," she said. "Fifteen minutes should do it, Allan. We'll get to the Carletons' at exactly the right time."

His tired, gray eyes faced her brilliant black ones with a courteous denial.

"Sorry, Olive. I can just make my own appointment by taking a taxi from here."

"You can't," she said imperiously. "This reception's important."

He smiled a little. "This is more important to me than the reception."

He stepped past her. She heard him speak to a cabby that his upraised cane had summoned.

"Plaza. Fifth Avenue entrance," he said.

[1] Reprinted here by permission of Margaret Widdemer. Published in *Collier's*, February 10, 1934.

She frowned, clicking up the dark aisle. She was too easy with Allan, that was the trouble. She'd have it out with him tonight; once and for all this time. When she had married him six years back he'd been so eager to please, to adjust, to make her happy! And now behaving like this, when everyone knew how much she had forwarded them socially—how good her judgment was.

Her annoyance sharpened to anger when, ending the inspection at her own pew, she found it occupied by a stranger. A slim little girl in a white-collared blue suit, her béreted yellow head bowed on the pew before her, her hands gripping it on either side like a child praying about Santa Claus. Olive touched her on the shoulder, speaking harshly. She had never approved of this high church idea, leaving churches open all day for prayers. It wasn't fair to pew-owners.

"This is my pew. I wish to inspect the cushions. May I ask you to move?"

The girl lifted a soft-blue-eyed face still flushed and intent with prayer. She smiled like a friendly baby.

"Sorry—but—I had to come in and pray for guidance," she said.

"That's nonsense," Olive laid down the law. "What's your problem?" There was a gentleness about the girl that invited dictation. But she rose and moved into the aisle.

"I'd rather not tell you," she said. Then she turned back. "Yes I will! Perhaps you were sent. It's a position I'm offered. An important one. I want it badly. But I have to decide whether it's fair to take it over another girl's head."

Just one of a hundred well-groomed little secretaries, then. Olive had nearly mistaken her for one of her own class. . . . She went on, nevertheless. She felt it was rather fine of her to take time to advise a girl like this.

"Is the other woman giving good service?"

"No. But she thinks so."

"She must be stupid. Are you competent?"

"Yes—oh, yes; I've practically been training for it always!"

"You are weakly sentimental to consider her, then. She'd be sent away anyway. The incompetent must go to the wall."

The girl was not paying attention. Olive felt a sharp contempt for her. . . . Competent! Not likely! She was staring with silly intensity at the pew she had left, at the inconspicuous nameplate.

"Are *you* Mrs. Meriden?" she asked softly.

Olive supposed it was awe in her voice. Perhaps she was trying to make a social contact on the strength of a passing benevolence. Olive called her to account. "Certainly. I told you this was my pew. You asked for advice, listen to it. There is no question of unfairness with incompetents. Take the position before it is given to someone else."

She stood aside, silently dismissing the yellow-haired girl. As she waited, handsome and erect in her furs, she felt regal, complete. . . . Her car waiting without; her ambitions so nearly gained; her handsome, prosperous young husband so nearly broken to her hand, awaiting her shortly at home. . . .

The girl lifted her face, a little strained and pale between the loose golden rings.

"I will do as you advise," she said. She went slowly down the aisle. Mrs. Meriden followed.

From the door of the church she saw the yellow-haired girl speak to the driver of the gray car with the crested panel.

"The Plaza. Fifth Avenue entrance," said the yellow-haired girl in the white-collared blue suit.

Mrs. Packletide's Tiger [1]

by SAKI (H. H. MUNRO)

IT WAS Mrs. Packletide's pleasure and intention that she should shoot a tiger. Not that the lust to kill had suddenly descended on her, or that she felt that she would leave India safer and more wholesome than she had found it, with one fraction less of wild beast per million of inhabitants. The compelling motive for her sudden deviation towards the footsteps of Nimrod was the fact that Loona Bimberton had recently been carried eleven miles in an aeroplane by an Algerian aviator, and talked of nothing else; only a personally procured tiger-skin and a heavy harvest of Press photographs could successfully counter that sort of thing. Mrs. Packletide had already arranged in her mind the lunch she would give at her house in Curzon Street, ostensibly in Loona Bimberton's honour, with a tiger-skin rug occupying most of the foreground and all of the conversation. She had also already designed in her mind the tiger-claw brooch that she was going to give Loona Bimberton on her next birthday. In a world that is supposed to be chiefly swayed by hunger and by love Mrs. Packletide was an exception; her movements and motives were largely governed by dislike of Loona Bimberton.

Circumstances proved propitious. Mrs. Packletide had offered a thousand rupees for the opportunity of shooting a tiger without overmuch risk or exertion, and it so happened that a neighbouring village could boast of being the favoured rendezvous of an animal of respectable antecedents, which had been driven by the increasing infirmities of age to abandon game-killing and confine its appetite to the smaller domestic animals. The prospect of earning the thousand rupees had stimulated the sporting and commercial instinct of the villagers; children were posted night and day on the outskirts

[1] From *The Short Stories of Saki* (H. H. Munro), copyright 1930, by The Viking Press, Inc., by permission of The Viking Press, Inc.

of the local jungle to head the tiger back in the unlikely event of his attempting to roam away to fresh hunting-grounds, and the cheaper kinds of goats
were left about with elaborate carelessness to keep him satisfied with his
present quarters. The one great anxiety was lest he should die of old age
before the date appointed for the memsahib's shoot. Mothers carrying their
babies through the jungle after the day's work in the fields hushed their singing lest they might curtail the restful sleep of the venerable herd-robber.

The great night duly arrived, moonlit and cloudless. A platform had been
constructed in a comfortable and conveniently placed tree, and thereon
crouched Mrs. Packletide and her paid companion, Miss Mebbin. A goat,
gifted with a particularly persistent bleat, such as even a partially deaf tiger
might be reasonably expected to hear on a still night, was tethered at the
correct distance. With an accurately sighted rifle and a thumb-nail pack of
patience cards the sportswoman awaited the coming of the quarry.

"I suppose we are in some danger?" said Miss Mebbin.

She was not actually nervous about the wild beast, but she had a morbid
dread of performing an atom more service than she had been paid for.

"Nonsense," said Mrs. Packletide; "it's a very old tiger. It couldn't spring
up here even if it wanted to."

"If it's an old tiger I think you ought to get it cheaper. A thousand
rupees is a lot of money."

Louisa Mebbin adopted a protective elder-sister attitude towards money
in general, irrespective of nationality or denomination. Her energetic intervention had saved many a rouble from dissipating itself in tips in some
Moscow hotel, and francs and centimes clung to her instinctively under circumstances which would have driven them headlong from less sympathetic
hands. Her speculations as to the market depreciation of tiger remnants
were cut short by the appearance on the scene of the animal itself. As soon
as it caught sight of the tethered goat it lay flat on the earth, seemingly less
from a desire to take advantage of all cover than for the purpose of snatching
a short rest before commencing the grand attack.

"I believe it's ill," said Louisa Mebbin, loudly in Hindustani, for the
benefit of the village head-man, who was in ambush in a neighbouring tree.

"Hush!" said Mrs. Packletide, and at that moment the tiger commenced
ambling towards his victim.

"Now, now!" urged Miss Mebbin with some excitement; "if he doesn't
touch the goat we needn't pay for it." (The bait was an extra.)

The rifle flashed out with a loud report, and the great tawny beast sprang
to one side and then rolled over in the stillness of death. In a moment a
crowd of excited natives had swarmed on to the scene, and their shouting
speedily carried the glad news to the village, where a thumping of tom-toms
took up the chorus of triumph. And their triumph and rejoicing found
a ready echo in the heart of Mrs. Packletide; already that luncheon-party in
Curzon Street seemed immeasurably nearer.

It was Louisa Mebbin who drew attention to the fact that the goat was in death-throes from a mortal bullet-wound, while no trace of the rifle's deadly work could be found on the tiger. Evidently the wrong animal had been hit, and the beast of prey had succumbed to heart-failure, caused by the sudden report of the rifle, accelerated by senile decay. Mrs. Packletide was pardonably annoyed at the discovery; but, at any rate, she was the possessor of a dead tiger, and the villagers, anxious for their thousand rupees, gladly connived at the fiction that she had shot the beast. And Miss Mebbin was a paid companion. Therefore did Mrs. Packletide face the cameras with a light heart, and her pictured fame reached from the pages of the *Texas Weekly Snapshot* to the illustrated Monday supplement of the *Novoe Vremya*. As for Loona Bimberton, she refused to look at an illustrated paper for weeks, and her letter of thanks for the gift of a tiger-claw brooch was a model of repressed emotions. The luncheon-party she declined; there are limits beyond which repressed emotions become dangerous.

From Curzon Street the tiger-skin rug travelled down to the Manor House, and was duly inspected and admired by the county, and it seemed a fitting and appropriate thing when Mrs. Packletide went to the County Costume Ball in the character of Diana. She refused to fall in, however, with Clovis's tempting suggestion of a primeval dance party, at which every one should wear the skins of beasts they had recently slain.

"How amused every one would be if they knew what really happened," said Louisa Mebbin a few days after the ball.

"What do you mean?" asked Mrs. Packletide quickly.

"How you shot the goat and frightened the tiger to death," said Miss Mebbin, with her disagreeably pleasant laugh.

"No one would believe it," said Mrs. Packletide, her face changing colour as rapidly as though it were going through a book of patterns before post-time.

"Loona Bimberton would," said Miss Mebbin. Mrs. Packletide's face settled on an unbecoming shade of greenish white.

"You surely wouldn't give me away?" she asked.

"I've seen a week-end cottage near Dorking that I should rather like to buy," said Miss Mebbin with seeming irrelevance. "Six hundred and eighty, freehold. Quite a bargain, only I don't happen to have the money."

Louisa Mebbin's pretty week-end cottage, christened by her "Les Fauves," and gay in summer-time with its garden borders of tiger-lilies, is the wonder and admiration of her friends.

"It is a marvel how Louisa manages to do it," is the general verdict.

Mrs. Packletide indulges in no more big-game shooting.

"The incidental expenses are so heavy," she confides to inquiring friends.

The End of Something [1]

by ERNEST HEMINGWAY

IN the old days Hortons Bay was a lumbering town. No one who lived in it was out of sound of the big saws in the mill by the lake. Then one year there were no more logs to make lumber. The lumber schooners came into the bay and were loaded with the cut of the mill that stood stacked in the yard. All the piles of lumber were carried away. The big mill building had all its machinery that was removable taken out and hoisted on board one of the schooners by the men who had worked in the mill. The schooner moved out of the bay toward the open lake carrying the two great saws, the traveling carriage that hurled the logs against the revolving, circular saws and all the rollers, wheels, belts and iron piled on a hull-deep load of lumber. Its open hold covered with canvas and lashed tight, the sails of the schooner filled and it moved out into the open lake, carrying with it everything that had made the mill a mill and Hortons Bay, a town.

The one-story bunk houses, the eating-house, the company store, the mill offices, and the big mill itself stood deserted in the acres of sawdust that covered the swampy meadow by the shore of the bay.

Ten years later there was nothing of the mill left except the broken white limestone of its foundations showing through the swampy second growth as Nick and Marjorie rowed along the shore. They were trolling along the edge of the channel-bank where the bottom dropped off suddenly from sandy shallows to twelve feet of dark water. They were trolling on their way to the point to set night lines for rainbow trout.

"There's our old ruin, Nick," Marjorie said.

Nick, rowing, looked at the white stone in the green trees.

"There it is," he said.

"Can you remember when it was a mill?" Marjorie asked.

"I can just remember," Nick said.

"It seems more like a castle," Marjorie said.

Nick said nothing. They rowed on out of sight of the mill, following the shore line. Then Nick cut across the bay.

"They aren't striking," he said.

"No," Marjorie said. She was intent on the rod all the time they trolled, even when she talked. She loved to fish. She loved to fish with Nick.

Close beside the boat a big trout broke the surface of the water. Nick pulled hard on one oar so the boat would turn and the bait spinning far behind would pass where the trout was feeding. As the trout's back came

---

[1] From *In Our Time*, copyright, 1925, Charles Scribner's Sons, by permission.

up out of the water the minnows jumped wildly. They sprinkled the surface like a handful of shot thrown into the water. Another trout broke water, feeding on the other side of the boat.

"They're feeding," Marjorie said.

"But they won't strike," Nick said.

He rowed the boat around to troll past both the feeding fish, then headed it for the point. Marjorie did not reel in until the boat touched the shore.

They pulled the boat up the beach and Nick lifted out a pail of live perch. The perch swam in the water in the pail. Nick caught three of them with his hands and cut their heads off and skinned them while Marjorie chased with her hands in the bucket, finally caught a perch, cut its head off and skinned it. Nick looked at her fish.

"You don't want to take the ventral fin out," he said. "It'll be all right for bait but it's better with the ventral fin in."

He hooked each of the skinned perch through the tail. There were two hooks attached to a leader on each rod. Then Marjorie rowed the boat out over the channel-bank, holding the line in her teeth, and looking toward Nick, who stood on the shore holding the rod and letting the line run out from the reel.

"That's about right," he called.

"Should I let it drop?" Marjorie called back, holding the line in her hand.

"Sure. Let it go." Marjorie dropped the line overboard and watched the baits go down through the water.

She came in with the boat and ran the second line out the same way. Each time Nick set a heavy slab of driftwood across the butt of the rod to hold it solid and propped it up at an angle with a small slab. He reeled in the slack line so the line ran taut out to where the bait rested on the sandy floor of the channel and set the click on the reel. When a trout, feeding on the bottom, took the bait it would run with it, taking line out of the reel in a rush and making the reel sing with the click on.

Marjorie rowed up the point a little way so she would not disturb the line. She pulled hard on the oars and the boat went way up the beach. Little waves came in with it. Marjorie stepped out of the boat and Nick pulled the boat high up on the beach.

"What's the matter, Nick?" Marjorie asked.

"I don't know," Nick said, getting wood for a fire.

They made a fire with driftwood. Marjorie went to the boat and brought a blanket. The evening breeze blew the smoke toward the point, so Marjorie spread the blanket out between the fire and the lake.

Marjorie sat on the blanket with her back to the fire and waited for Nick. He came over and sat down beside her on the blanket. In back of them was the close second-growth timber of the point and in front was the bay with the mouth of Hortons Creek. It was not quite dark. The firelight went as far as the water. They could both see the two steel rods at an angle over the dark water. The fire glinted on the reels.

Marjorie unpacked the basket of supper.

"I don't feel like eating," said Nick.

"Come on and eat, Nick."

"All right."

They ate without talking, and watched the two rods and the fire-light in the water.

"There's going to be a moon tonight," said Nick. He looked across the bay to the hills that were beginning to sharpen against the sky. Beyond the hills he knew the moon was coming up.

"I know it," Marjorie said happily.

"You know everything," Nick said.

"Oh, Nick, please cut it out! Please, please don't be that way!"

"I can't help it," Nick said. "You do. You know everything. That's the trouble. You know you do."

Marjorie did not say anything.

"I've taught you everything. You know you do. What don't you know, anyway?"

"Oh, shut up," Marjorie said. "There comes the moon."

They sat on the blanket without touching each other and watched the moon rise.

"You don't have to talk silly," Marjorie said; "what's really the matter?"

"I don't know."

"Of course you know."

"No I don't."

"Go on and say it."

Nick looked on at the moon, coming up over the hills.

"It isn't fun any more."

He was afraid to look at Marjorie. He looked at Marjorie. She sat there with her back toward him. He looked at her back. "It isn't fun any more. Not any of it."

She didn't say anything. He went on. "I feel as though everything was gone to hell inside of me. I don't know, Marge. I don't know what to say."

He looked on at her back.

"Isn't love any fun?" Marjorie said.

"No," Nick said. Marjorie stood up. Nick sat there, his head in his hands.

"I'm going to take the boat," Marjorie called to him. "You can walk back around the point."

"All right," Nick said. "I'll push the boat off for you."

"You don't need to," she said. She was afloat in the boat on the water with the moonlight on it. Nick went back and lay down with his face in the blanket by the fire. He could hear Marjorie rowing on the water.

He lay there for a long time. He lay there while he heard Bill come into the clearing, walking around through the woods. He felt Bill coming up to the fire. Bill didn't touch him, either.

"Did she go all right?" Bill said.

"Oh, yes." Nick said, lying, his face on the blanket.

"Have a scene?"

"No, there wasn't any scene."

"How do you feel?"

"Oh, go away, Bill! Go away for a while."

Bill selected a sandwich from the lunch basket and walked over to have a look at the rods.

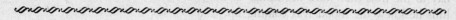

Breakfast[1]

by JOHN STEINBECK

THIS thing fills me with pleasure. I don't know why, I can see it in the smallest detail. I find myself recalling it again and again, each time bringing more detail out of a sunken memory, remembering brings the curious warm pleasure.

It was very early in the morning. The eastern mountains were black-blue, but behind them the light stood up faintly colored at the mountain rims with a washed red, growing colder, greyer and darker as it went up and overhead until, at a place near the west, it merged with pure night.

And it was cold, not painfully so, but cold enough so that I rubbed my hands and shoved them deep into my pockets, and I hunched my shoulders up and scuffled my feet on the ground. Down in the valley where I was, the earth was that lavender grey of dawn. I walked along a country road and ahead of me I saw a tent that was only a little lighter grey than the ground. Beside the tent there was a flash of orange fire seeping out of the cracks of an old rusty iron stove. Grey smoke spurted up out of the stubby stovepipe, spurted up a long way before it spread out and dissipated.

I saw a young woman beside the stove, really a girl. She was dressed in a faded cotton skirt and waist. As I came close I saw that she carried a baby in a crooked arm and the baby was nursing, its head under her waist out of the cold. The mother moved about, poking the fire, shifting the rusty lids of the stove to make a greater draft, opening the oven door; and all the time the baby was nursing, but that didn't interfere with the mother's work, nor with the light quick gracefulness of her movements. There was something very precise and practiced in her movements. The orange fire flicked out of the cracks in the stove and threw dancing reflections on the tent.

I was close now and I could smell frying bacon and baking bread, the warmest, pleasantest odors I know. From the east the light grew swiftly. I came near to the stove and stretched my hands out to it and shivered all over

---

[1] From *The Long Valley*. The Viking Press, 1938.

when the warmth struck me. Then the tent flap jerked up and a young man came out and an older man followed him. They were dressed in new blue dungarees and in new dungaree coats with the brass buttons shining. They were sharp-faced men, and they looked much alike.

The younger had a dark stubble beard and the older had a grey stubble beard. Their heads and faces were wet, their hair dripped with water, and water stood out on their stiff beards and their cheeks shone with water. Together they stood looking quietly at the lightening east; they yawned together and looked at the light on the hill rims. They turned and saw me.

"Morning," said the older man. His face was neither friendly nor unfriendly.

"Morning, sir," I said.

"Morning," said the young man.

The water was slowly drying on their faces. They came to the stove and warmed their hands at it.

The girl kept to her work, her face averted and her eyes on what she was doing. Her hair was tied back out of her eyes with a string and it hung down her back and swayed as she worked. She set tin cups on a big packing box, set tin plates and knives and forks out too. Then she scooped fried bacon out of the deep grease and laid it on a big tin platter, and the bacon cricked and rustled as it grew crisp. She opened the rusty oven door and took out a square pan full of high big biscuits.

When the smell of that hot bread came out, both of the men inhaled deeply. The young man said softly, "Keerist!"

The elder man turned to me, "Had your breakfast?"

"No."

"Well, sit down with us, then."

That was the signal. We went to the packing case and squatted on the ground about it. The young man asked, "Picking cotton?"

"No."

"We had twelve days' work so far," the young man said.

The girl spoke from the stove. "They even got new clothes."

The two men looked down at their new dungarees and they both smiled a little.

The girl set out the platter of bacon, the brown high biscuits, a bowl of bacon gravy and a pot of coffee, and then she squatted down by the box too. The baby was still nursing, its head up under her waist out of the cold. I could hear the sucking noises it made.

We filled our plates, poured bacon gravy over our biscuits and sugared our coffee. The older man filled his mouth full and he chewed and chewed and swallowed. Then he said, "God Almighty, it's good," and he filled his mouth again.

The young man said, "We been eating good for twelve days."

We all ate quickly, frantically, and refilled our plates and ate quickly again until we were full and warm. The hot bitter coffee scalded our throats. We threw the last little bit with the grounds in it on the earth and refilled our cups.

There was color in the light now, a reddish gleam that made the air seem colder. The two men faced the east and their faces were lighted by the dawn, and I looked up for a moment and saw the image of the mountain and the light coming over it reflected in the older man's eyes.

Then the two men threw the grounds from their cups on the earth and they stood up together. "Got to get going," the older man said.

The younger turned to me. "'Fyou want to pick cotton, we could maybe get you on."

"No. I got to go along. Thanks for breakfast."

The older man waved his hand in a negative. "O.K. Glad to have you." They walked away together. The air was blazing with light at the eastern skyline. And I walked away down the country road.

That's all. I know, of course, some of the reasons why it was pleasant. But there was some element of great beauty there that makes the rush of warmth when I think of it.

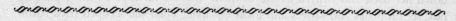

The First Day[1]

by JAMES REID PARKER

W HEN young Dr. Sargent arrived at the college to assume his duties as a member of the faculty, he reversed a lifelong custom. Now that he was well equipped with the suitable degrees, tokens of graduate study, he was about to address a class. Hitherto he had always been among those addressed.

The college had given him an office, with a nice desk and three chairs upholstered in green leather, near his lecture-room. Sitting in one of the green chairs, Sargent nervously fiddled with his notes for the first day. He had the academic equivalent of stagefright. Strange lumps were forming in his throat, and there was a hollow feeling in the pit of his stomach. His watch said five minutes to nine—five minutes before his first college class. The students would be freshmen, as new to the routine as himself.

A warning bell rang. In a moment the corridor was crowded with young men going in and out of lecture-rooms and professors' offices. It was vital and alive, an artery rushing with blood. Sargent opened the door, looked out at the melange of faces and forms, and instantly drew back. For one final minute he enjoyed the delicious security of hiding behind the frosted glass. Then he opened the door again and slipped into the corridor.

[1] From *Academic Procession,* by James Reid Parker. Copyright, 1937, by Harcourt, Brace and Company, Inc.

The crowd was moving more slowly at the entrance to his lecture-room. The men dropped their cigarettes on the floor, and crushed them. Sargent drew rapid, solacing gusts of smoke from his own, and finally relinquished it. Somebody took his arm.

"Who *is* this guy Sargent?" asked a voice. "What do you know about him?"

"Not very much," said Sargent weakly.

The young man had edged forward to exchange confidences in the few brief seconds before Calvary. He was a pleasant-looking chap, with hair cut so close that it stood upright. He must have noticed Sargent's air of help-lessness, because he adopted him at once.

"When we get inside," said the young man, "let's get seats in the last row. That's the best way to do."

"Is it?" responded Sargent.

"Sure," said the young man. "Just do the way I do. Suppose he turns out to be a pain in the neck. We'll be all right if we get in the last row, the first day. Of course, maybe he'll have a special seating arrangement. Some do and some don't. This used to be my brother's college—that's how I know a good deal about the way they do things."

Young Dr. Sargent looked at his friend with the upright hair, and suddenly remembered that his own college life was only three or four years behind him, after all. It had been much like this.

"Suppose he *doesn't* turn out to be a pain in the neck," he offered hopefully. "What do we do then?"

"If he's all right, we might as well move up front after today," said the young man. "You can hear better."

They were inside the lecture-room now. Instructing Sargent to follow, the protector dashed to the last row with a haste born of experience. In any classroom the last row commands a certain popularity. Sargent tried to establish himself as inconspicuously as possible on the platform. This was difficult. He pretended to busy himself with checking over his notes. Presently, without looking up from the lectern, he called the roll. He didn't want to discover who the young man was.

But Sargent was forced to look up when the roll was finished, and the hypnotic power of morbid curiosity drew his eyes to the last row. His guardian's head was buried in a notebook.

"Gentlemen," Sargent began, "this—er—is my first day as a member of the faculty, and—er—if you are in any way nervous about attending a college class for the first time, you can't possibly—um—be as nervous as I am. Er— during the lecture you may smoke if you want to."

Then tension relaxed. He had said the right thing.

PLAYS

All Rights Reserved

PLAYS

NOVELS, stories, and poems are written to be read. But a play is written to be played by actors, on a stage, and before an audience. A radio play is played by actors to the ears of its listeners. Consequently the experience of reading a play is quite different from the experience of reading a story and more difficult. The reader, with the help of the lines and the stage directions, must imaginatively visualize the action on the stage as it would appear if actors were speaking the lines as they move about. But at best a play reader can never completely capture the experience he would have if he were a member of an audience. Both laughter and tears are contagious. The emotional experiences of the theater are more heightened than those of the study.

The plays chosen for inclusion in this volume represent a variety of lengths and types. *Beyond the Horizon* and *Riders to the Sea* involve death and frustration. The outcomes are tragic or pathetic. *The Green Pastures* may be called a chronicle history play. It endeavors to put on the stage episodes from Old Testament story, episodes that run from comedy to tragedy to satire to mysticism. Hence we should not expect it to have close-knit dramatic structure. Like Shakespeare's historical plays it is a loosely constructed pageant. *You Can't Take It with You* is comedy—but like all fine comedy it is a comedy of serious import, satirizing folly and pretense and false standards of living. MacLeish's *Fall of the City* and Norman Corwin's *Good Heavens* represent the newest aspect of drama born of the peculiar necessities of radio presentation to the ear alone. The first of these radio plays demonstrates how poetry comes alive by the magic of the spoken word. The second shows how dramatic technics can vivify the communication of facts and inferences. Will this new radio drama be a permanent addition to dramatic forms? Or will television make it obsolete?

Riders to the Sea[1]

by JOHN MILLINGTON SYNGE

CHARACTERS

MAURYA, *an old woman.*
BARTLEY, *her son.*
CATHLEEN, *her daughter.*
NORA, *a younger daughter.*
MEN AND WOMEN.

SCENE: *An island off the West of Ireland. Cottage kitchen, with nets, oilskins, spinning-wheel, some new boards standing by the wall, etc.* CATHLEEN, *a girl of about twenty, finishes kneading cake, and puts it down in the pot-oven by the fire; then wipes her hands, and begins to spin at the wheel.* NORA, *a young girl, puts her head in at the door.*

NORA [*In a low voice*]. Where is she?

CATHLEEN. She's lying down, God help her, and maybe sleeping, if she's able.

[NORA *comes in softly, and takes a bundle from under her shawl*]

CATHLEEN [*Spinning the wheel rapidly*]. What is it you have?

NORA. The young priest is after bringing them. It's a shirt and a plain stocking were got off a drowned man in Donegal.

[CATHLEEN *stops her wheel with a sudden movement, and leans out to listen*]

NORA. We're to find out if it's Michael's they are; some time herself will be down looking by the sea.

CATHLEEN. How would they be Michael's, Nora? How would he go the length of that way to the far north?

NORA. The young priest says he's known the like of it. "If it's Michael's they are," says he, "you can tell herself he's got a clean burial by the grace of God, and if they're not his, let no one say a word about them, for she'll be getting her death," says he, "with crying and lamenting."

[*The door which* NORA *half closed is blown open by a gust of wind*]

CATHLEEN [*Looking out anxiously*]. Did you ask him would he stop Bartley going this day with the horses to the Galway fair?

[1] Reprinted by permission of Random House, Inc., Inc., New York. First produced in 1904.

663

NORA. "I won't stop him," says he, "but let you not be afraid. Herself does be saying prayers half through the night, and the Almighty God won't leave her destitute," says he, "with no son living."

CATHLEEN. Is the sea bad by the white rocks, Nora?

NORA. Middling bad, God help us. There's a great roaring in the west, and it's worse it'll be getting when the tide's turned to the wind. [*She goes over to the table with the bundle*] Shall I open it now?

CATHLEEN. Maybe she'd wake up on us, and come in before we'd done. [*Coming to the table*] It's a long time we'll be, and the two of us crying.

NORA [*Goes to the inner door and listens*]. She's moving about on the bed. She'll be coming in a minute.

CATHLEEN. Give me the ladder, and I'll put them up in the turf-loft, the way she won't know of them at all, and maybe when the tide turns she'll be going down to see would he be floating from the east.

[*They put the ladder against the gable of the chimney;* CATHLEEN *goes up a few steps and hides the bundle in the turf-loft.* MAURYA *comes from the inner room*]

MAURYA [*Looking up at* CATHLEEN *and speaking querulously*]. Isn't it turf enough you have for this day and evening?

CATHLEEN. There's a cake baking at the fire for a short space [*throwing down the turf*] and Bartley will want it when the tide turns if he goes to Connemara.

[NORA *picks up the turf and puts it round the pot-oven*]

MAURYA [*Sitting down on a stool at the fire*]. He won't go this day with the wind rising from the south and west. He won't go this day, for the young priest will stop him surely.

NORA. He'll not stop him, mother, and I heard Eamon Simon and Stephen Pheety and Colum Shawn saying he would go.

MAURYA. Where is he itself?

NORA. He went down to see would there be another boat sailing in the week, and I'm thinking it won't be long till he's here now, for the tide's turning at the green head, and the hooker's tacking from the east.

CATHLEEN. I hear some one passing the big stones.

NORA [*Looking out*]. He's coming now, and he in a hurry.

BARTLEY [*Comes in and looks round the room; speaking sadly and quietly*]. Where is the bit of new rope, Cathleen, was bought in Connemara?

CATHLEEN [*Coming down*]. Give it to him, Nora; it's on a nail by the white boards. I hung it up this morning, for the pig with the black feet was eating it.

NORA [*Giving him a rope*]. Is that it, Bartley?

MAURYA. You'd do right to leave that rope, Bartley, hanging by the boards. [BARTLEY *takes the rope*] It will be wanting in this place, I'm telling you, if

Michael is washed up tomorrow morning, or the next morning, or any morning in the week, for it's a deep grave we'll make him by the grace of God.

BARTLEY [*Beginning to work with the rope*]. I've no halter the way I can ride down on the mare, and I must go now quickly. This is the one boat going for two weeks or beyond it, and the fair will be a good fair for horses, I heard them saying below.

MAURYA. It's a hard thing they'll be saying below if the body is washed up and there's no man in it to make the coffin, and I after giving a big price for the finest white boards you'd find in Connemara.

[*She looks round at the boards*]

BARTLEY. How would it be washed up, and we after looking each day for nine days, and a strong wind blowing a while back from the west and south?

MAURYA. If it wasn't found itself, that wind is raising the sea, and there was a star up against the moon, and it rising in the night. If it was a hundred horses, or a thousand horses you had itself, what is the price of a thousand horses against a son where there is one son only?

BARTLEY [*Working at the halter, to* CATHLEEN]. Let you go down each day, and see the sheep aren't jumping in on the rye, and if the jobber comes you can sell the pig with the black feet if there is a good price going.

MAURYA. How would the like of her get a good price for a pig?

BARTLEY [*To* CATHLEEN]. If the west wind holds with the last bit of the moon let you and Nora get up weed enough for another cock for the kelp. It's hard set we'll be from this day with no one in it but one man to work.

MAURYA. It's hard set we'll be surely the day you're drownd'd with the rest. What way will I live and the girls with me, and I an old woman looking for the grave?

[BARTLEY *lays down the halter, takes off his old coat, and puts on a newer one of the same flannel*]

BARTLEY [*To* NORA]. Is she coming to the pier?

NORA [*Looking out*]. She's passing the green head and letting fall her sails.

BARTLEY [*Getting his purse and tobacco*]. I'll have half an hour to go down, and you'll see me coming again in two days, or in three days, or maybe in four days if the wind is bad.

MAURYA [*Turning round to the fire, and putting her shawl over her head*]. Isn't it a hard and cruel man won't hear a word from an old woman, and she holding him from the sea?

CATHLEEN. It's the life of a young man to be going on the sea, and who would listen to an old woman with one thing and she saying it over?

BARTLEY [*Taking the halter*]. I must go now quickly. I'll ride down on the red mare, and the gray pony'll run behind me. The blessing of God on you.

[*He goes out*]

MAURYA [*Crying out as he is in the door*]. He's gone now, God spare us,

and we'll not see him again. He's gone now, and when the black night is
falling I'll have no son left me in the world.

CATHLEEN. Why wouldn't you give him your blessing and he looking
round in the door? Isn't it sorrow enough is on every one in this house
without your sending him out with an unlucky word behind him, and a hard
word in his ear?

> [MAURYA *takes up the tongs and begins raking the fire aimlessly with-*
> *out looking round*]

NORA [*Turning towards her*]. You're taking away the turf from the cake.

CATHLEEN [*Crying out*]. The Son of God forgive us, Nora, we're after
forgetting his bit of bread.

> [*She comes over to the fire*]

NORA. And it's destroyed he'll be going till dark night, and he after eating
nothing since the sun went up.

CATHLEEN [*Turning the cake out of the oven*]. It's destroyed he'll be,
surely. There's no sense left on any person in a house where an old woman
will be talking forever.

> [MAURYA *sways herself on her stool*]

CATHLEEN [*Cutting off some of the bread and rolling it in a cloth, to*
MAURYA]. Let you go down now to the spring-well and give him this and he
passing. You'll see him then and the dark word will be broken, and you can
say, "God speed you," the way he'll be easy in his mind.

MAURYA [*Taking the bread*]. Will I be in it as soon as himself?

CATHLEEN. If you go now quickly.

MAURYA [*Standing up unsteadily*]. It's hard set I am to walk.

CATHLEEN [*Looking at her anxiously*]. Give her the stick, Nora, or maybe
she'll slip on the big stones.

NORA. What stick?

CATHLEEN. The stick Michael brought from Connemara.

MAURYA [*Taking a stick* NORA *gives her*]. In the big world the old people
do be leaving things after them for their sons and children, but in this place
it is the young men do be leaving things behind for them that do be old.

> [*She goes out slowly.* NORA *goes over to the ladder*]

CATHLEEN. Wait, Nora, maybe she'd turn back quickly. She's that sorry,
God help her, you wouldn't know the thing she'd do.

NORA. Is she gone round by the bush?

CATHLEEN [*Looking out*]. She's gone now. Throw it down quickly, for
the Lord knows when she'll be out of it again.

NORA [*Getting the bundle from the loft*]. The young priest said he'd be
passing tomorrow, and we might go down and speak to him below if it's
Michael's they are surely.

CATHLEEN [*Taking the bundle*]. Did he say what way they were found?

NORA [*Coming down*]. "There were two men," says he, "and they rowing round with poteen before the cocks crowed, and the oar of one of them caught the body, and they passing the black cliffs of the north."

CATHLEEN [*Trying to open the bundle*]. Give me a knife, Nora; the string's perished with the salt water, and there's a black knot on it you wouldn't loosen in a week.

NORA [*Giving her a knife*]. I've heard tell it was a long way to Donegal.

CATHLEEN [*Cutting the string*]. It is surely. There was a man in here a while ago—the man sold us that knife—and he said if you set off walking from the rocks beyond, it would be seven days you'd be in Donegal.

NORA. And what time would a man take, and he floating?

[CATHLEEN *opens the bundle and takes out a bit of a stocking. They look at them eagerly*]

CATHLEEN [*In a low voice*]. The Lord spare us, Nora! isn't it a queer hard thing to say if it's his they are surely?

NORA. I'll get his shirt off the hook the way we can put the one flannel on the other. [*She looks through some clothes hanging in the corner*] It's not with them, Cathleen, and where will it be?

CATHLEEN. I'm thinking Bartley put it on him in the morning, for his own shirt was heavy with the salt in it. [*Pointing to the corner*] There's a bit of a sleeve was of the same stuff. Give me that and it will do.

[NORA *brings it to her and they compare the flannel*]

CATHLEEN. It's the same stuff, Nora; but if it is itself, aren't there great rolls of it in the shops of Galway, and isn't it many another man may have a shirt of it as well as Michael himself?

NORA [*Who has taken up the stocking and counted the stitches, crying out*]. It's Michael, Cathleen, it's Michael; God spare his soul, and what will herself say when she hears this story, and Bartley on the sea?

CATHLEEN [*Taking the stocking*]. It's a plain stocking.

NORA. It's the second one of the third pair I knitted, and I put up three score stiches, and I dropped four of them.

CATHLEEN [*Counts the stitches*]. It's that number is in it. [*Crying out*] Ah, Nora, isn't it a bitter thing to think of him floating that way to the far north, and no one to keen him but the black hags that do be flying on the sea?

NORA [*Swinging herself round, and throwing out her arms on the clothes*]. And isn't it a pitiful thing when there is nothing left of a man who was a great rower and fisher, but a bit of an old shirt and a plain stocking?

CATHLEEN [*After an instant*]. Tell me is herself coming, Nora? I hear a little sound on the path.

NORA [*Looking out*]. She is, Cathleen. She's coming up to the door.

CATHLEEN. Put these things away before she'll come in. Maybe it's easier she'll be after giving her blessing to Bartley, and we won't let on we've heard anything the time he's on the sea.

NORA [*Helping* CATHLEEN *to close the bundle*]. We'll put them here in the corner.

[*They put them into a hole in the chimney corner.* CATHLEEN *goes back to the spinning-wheel*]

NORA. Will she see it was crying I was?

CATHLEEN. Keep your back to the door the way the light'll not be on you.

[NORA *sits down at the chimney corner, with her back to the door.* MAURYA *comes in very slowly, without looking at the girls, and goes over to the stool at the other side of the fire. The cloth with the bread is still in her hand. The girls look at each other, and* NORA *points to the bundle of bread*]

CATHLEEN [*After spinning for a moment*]. You didn't give him his bit of bread?

[MAURYA *begins to keen softly, without turning round*]

CATHLEEN. Did you see him riding down?

[MAURYA *goes on keening*]

CATHLEEN [*A little impatiently*]. God forgive you; isn't it a better thing to raise your voice and tell what you seen, than to be making lamentation for a thing that's done? Did you see Bartley, I'm saying to you.

MAURYA [*With a weak voice*]. My heart's broken from this day.

CATHLEEN [*As before*]. Did you see Bartley?

MAURYA. I seen the fearfulest thing.

CATHLEEN [*Leaves her wheel and looks out*]. God forgive you; he's riding the mare now over the green head, and the gray pony behind him.

MAURYA [*Starts, so that her shawl falls back from her head and shows her white tossed hair; with a frightened voice*]. The gray pony behind him.

CATHLEEN [*Coming to the fire*]. What is it ails you, at all?

MAURYA [*Speaking very slowly*]. I've seen the fearfulest thing any person has seen, since the day Bride Dara seen the dead man with the child in his arms.

CATHLEEN and NORA. Uah.

[*They crouch down in front of the old woman at the fire*]

NORA. Tell us what it is you seen.

MAURYA. I went down to the spring-well, and I stood there saying a prayer to myself. Then Bartley came along, and he riding on the red mare with the gray pony behind him. [*She puts up her hands, as if to hide something from her eyes*] The Son of God spare us, Nora!

CATHLEEN. What is it you seen?

MAURYA. I seen Michael himself.

CATHLEEN [*Speaking softly*]. You did not, mother; it wasn't Michael you seen, for his body is after being found in the far north, and he's got a clean burial by the grace of God.

MAURYA [*A little defiantly*]. I'm after seeing him this day, and he riding and galloping. Bartley came first on the red mare; and I tried to say "God speed you," but something choked the words in my throat. He went by quickly; and, "The blessing of God on you," says he, and I could say nothing. I looked up then, and I crying, at the gray pony, and there was Michael upon it—with fine clothes on him, and new shoes on his feet.

CATHLEEN [*Begins to keen*]. It's destroyed we are from this day. It's destroyed, surely.

NORA. Didn't the young priest say the Almighty God wouldn't leave her destitute with no son living?

MAURYA [*In a low voice, but clearly*]. It's little the like of him knows of the sea. . . . Bartley will be lost now, and let you call in Eamon and make me a good coffin out of the white boards, for I won't live after them. I've had a husband, and a husband's father, and six sons in this house—six fine men, though it was a hard birth I had with every one of them and they coming to the world—and some of them were found and some of them were not found, but they're gone now, the lot of them. . . . There were Stephen, and Shawn, were lost in the great wind, and found after in the Bay of Gregory of the Golden Mouth, and carried up the two of them on the one plank, and in by that door.

[*She pauses for a moment, the girls start as if they heard something through the door that is half open behind them*]

NORA [*In a whisper*]. Did you hear that, Cathleen? Did you hear a noise in the northeast?

CATHLEEN [*In a whisper*]. There's some one after crying out by the seashore.

MAURYA [*Continues without hearing anything*]. There was Sheamus and his father, and his own father again, were lost in a dark night, and not a stick or sign was seen of them when the sun went up. There was Patch after was drowned out of a curagh that turned over. I was sitting here with Bartley, and he a baby, lying on my two knees, and I seen two women, and three women, and four women coming in, and they crossing themselves, and not saying a word. I looked out then, and there were men coming after them, and they holding a thing in the half of a red sail, and water dripping out of it—it was a dry day, Nora—and leaving a track to the door.

[*She pauses again with her hand stretched out towards the door. It opens softly and old women begin to come in, crossing themselves on the threshold, and kneeling down in front of the stage with red petticoats over their heads*]

MAURYA [*Half in a dream, to* CATHLEEN]. Is it Patch, or Michael, or what is it at all?

CATHLEEN. Michael is after being found in the far north, and when he is found there how could he be here in this place?

MAURYA. There does be a power of young men floating round in the sea, and what way would they know if it was Michael they had, or another man like him, for when a man is nine days in the sea, and the wind blowing, it's hard set his own mother would be to say what man was it.

CATHLEEN. It's Michael, God spare him, for they're after sending us a bit of his clothes from the far north.

[*She reaches out and hands* MAURYA *the clothes that belonged to* MICHAEL. MAURYA *stands up slowly, and takes them in her hands.* NORA *looks out*]

NORA. They're carrying a thing among them and there's water dripping out of it and leaving a track by the big stones.

CATHLEEN [*In a whisper to the women who have come in*]. Is it Bartley it is?

ONE OF THE WOMEN. It is surely, God rest his soul.

[*Two younger women come in and pull out the table. Then men carry in the body of* BARTLEY, *laid on a plank, with a bit of a sail over it, and lay it on the table*]

CATHLEEN [*To the women, as they are doing so*]. What way was he drowned?

ONE OF THE WOMEN. The gray pony knocked him into the sea, and he was washed out where there is a great surf on the white rocks.

[MAURYA *has gone over and knelt down at the head of the table. The women are keening softly and swaying themselves with a slow movement.* CATHLEEN *and* NORA *kneel at the other end of the table. The men kneel near the door*]

MAURYA [*Raising her head and speaking as if she did not see the people around her*]. They're all gone now, and there isn't anything more the sea can do to me. . . . I'll have no call now to be up crying and praying when the wind breaks from the south, and you can hear the surf is in the east, and the surf is in the west, making a great stir with the two noises, and they hitting one on the other. I'll have no call now to be going down and getting Holy Water in the dark nights after Samhain, and I won't care what way the sea is when the other women will be keening. [*To* NORA] Give me the Holy Water, Nora; there's a small cup still on the dresser.

[NORA *gives it to her*]

MAURYA [*Drops* MICHAEL's *clothes across* BARTLEY's *feet, and sprinkles the Holy Water over him*]. It isn't that I haven't prayed for you, Bartley, to the

Almighty God. It isn't that I haven't said prayers in the dark night till you wouldn't know what I'd be saying; but it's a great rest I'll have now, and it's time surely. It's a great rest I'll have now, and great sleeping in the long nights after Samhain, if it's only a bit of wet flour we do have to eat, and maybe a fish that would be stinking.

[*She kneels down again, crossing herself, and saying prayers under her breath*]

CATHLEEN [*To an old man*]. Maybe yourself and Eamon would make a coffin when the sun rises. We have fine white boards herself bought, God help her, thinking Michael would be found, and I have a new cake you can eat while you'll be working.

THE OLD MAN [*Looking at the boards*]. Are there nails with them?

CATHLEEN. There are not, Colum; we didn't think of the nails.

ANOTHER MAN. It's a great wonder she wouldn't think of the nails, and all the coffins she's seen made already.

CATHLEEN. It's getting old she is, and broken.

[MAURYA *stands up again very slowly and spreads out the pieces of* MICHAEL's *clothes beside the body, sprinkling them with the last of the Holy Water*]

NORA [*In a whisper to* CATHLEEN]. She's quiet now and easy; but the day Michael was drowned you could hear her crying out from this to the spring-well. It's fonder she was of Michael, and would any one have thought that?

CATHLEEN [*Slowly and clearly*]. An old woman will be soon tired with anything she will do, and isn't it nine days herself is after crying and keening, and making great sorrow in the house?

MAURYA [*Puts the empty cup mouth downwards on the table, and lays her hands together on* BARTLEY's *feet*]. They're all together this time, and the end is come. May the Almighty God have mercy on Bartley's soul, and on Michael's soul, and on the souls of Sheamus and Patch, and Stephen and Shawn [*bending her head*]; and may He have mercy on my soul, Nora, and on the soul of every one is left living in the world.

[*She pauses, and the keen rises a little more loudly from the women, then sinks away*]

MAURYA [*Continuing*]. Michael has a clean burial in the far north, by the grace of the Almighty God. Bartley will have a fine coffin out of the white boards, and a deep grave surely. What more can we want than that? No man at all can be living forever, and we must be satisfied.

[*She kneels down again, and the curtain falls slowly*]

The Fall of the City [1]

A Verse Play for Radio

by ARCHIBALD MacLEISH

FOREWORD

ANY introduction is a confession of weakness. This one is no exception. It is written because I am anxious to persuade American poets to experiment with verse plays for radio and because I am quite certain the radio verse play I have written will not persuade them of itself.

The argument for radio as a stage for verse is neither long nor sensational. It consists largely in asserting what everyone knows. But such is the character of what everyone knows that no one knows it with enthusiasm. On the basis of the most obvious and elementary facts every poet with a dramatic leaning —and what poet ever lived who was really satisfied with writing the thin little books to lie on the front parlor tables?—should have been storming the studios for years. And yet actually the storming has been thin and infrequent. The British Broadcasting Corporation has presented a few verse plays written expressly for radio and one of them, Geoffrey Bridson's *March of the '45,* is said to have been both interesting and exciting. But the American slate is still approximately clean.

The first fact which everyone knows is that radio is a mechanism which carries to an audience sounds and nothing but sounds. A radio play consists of words and word equivalents and nothing else. There is no visible actor disguised to assume a part. There is no stage-set contrived to resemble a place. There is only the spoken word—an implement which poets have always claimed to use with a special authority. There is only the word-excited imagination—a theater in which poets have always claimed peculiar rights to play. Nothing exists save as the word creates it. The word dresses the stage. The word brings on the actors. The word supplies their look, their clothes, their gestures. The more packed and allusive the word, the more illuminating its rhythms, the more perfectly is the scene prepared, the more convincingly is the play enacted. On the stage, verse is often an obstacle because the artifice of the verse and the physical reality of the scene do not harmonize; it is for this reason that verse is easily accepted on the stage only where the scene is made remote in time and therefore artificial to begin with, or where the verse is blurred out and made to sound as much as possible like prose. But over the radio verse is not an obstacle. Over the radio verse has no visual presence to compete with. Only the ear is engaged and the ear is

[1] Reprinted by permission of Rinehart & Company, Inc. The first performance over the air occurred Sunday evening, April 11, 1937, over the Columbia Broadcasting System Network.

already half poet. It believes at once: creates and believes. It is the eye which is the realist. It is the eye which must fit everything together, must see everything before and behind. It is the eye and not the ear which refuses to believe in the lovely girlhood of the middle-aged soprano who sings Isolde, or the delicate, water-troubling slenderness of the three fat Rhine maidens ridiculously paddling at the ends of three steel ropes. With the eye closed or staring at nothing verse has every power over the ear. The ear accepts, accepts and believes, accepts and creates. The ear is the poet's perfect audience, his only true audience. And it is radio and only radio which can give him public access to this perfect friend.

The second fact which everyone knows and no one observes is the fact that the technique of radio, the ordinary, commercial technique, has developed tools which could not have been more perfectly adapted to the poet's uses had he devised them himself. Writers of prose plays for radio have practically unanimously ignored these tools. They have written for radio precisely as they would write for stage and many, if not most, radio plays have been nothing but stage plays adapted to the microphone. The tools nevertheless exist and the chief of them is the Announcer. The Announcer is the most useful dramatic personage since the Greek Chorus. For years modern poets writing for the stage have felt the necessity of contriving some sort of chorus, some sort of commentator. There is no occasion here to go into the reasons: they are compelling enough. But this chorus, this commentator, has always presented an extremely awkward practical problem. How justify its existence dramatically? How get it on? How get it off again? In radio this difficulty is removed before it occurs. The commentator is an integral part of radio technique. His presence is as natural as it is familiar. And his presence, without more, restores to the poet that obliquity, that perspective, that three-dimensional depth without which great poetic drama cannot exist.

Over and above all this there is the great question of audience. No man who has had the experience of presenting plays first before Broadway audiences and thereafter before such audiences as the radical theaters provide would ever of his own choice return to the Broadway audience. Radio will not of course provide the immediate sense of the live and vigorous audience which the radical theaters give. But radio will reach an infinitely greater number of people and should be capable, in time and with adequate materials, of shaping sections of that greater number into a living audience which the poet and his actors can feel. This consideration alone should deeply move the American poet whose present tragedy is his isolation from any audience vigorous enough to demand his strongest work.

A. MacL.

CHARACTERS

VOICE OF STUDIO DIRECTOR
VOICE OF ANNOUNCER
VOICE OF DEAD WOMAN
VOICE OF 1ST MESSENGER
VOICE OF ORATOR
VOICE OF 2ND MESSENGER
VOICE OF PRIEST
VOICE OF GENERAL
VOICES OF ANTIPHONAL CHORUS
Citizens, dancers, priests, soldiers, etc.

THE FALL OF THE CITY

VOICE OF THE STUDIO DIRECTOR [*orotund and professional*]

Ladies and gentlemen:
This broadcast comes to you from the city.
Listeners over the curving air have heard
From furthest-off frontiers of foreign hours—
Mountain Time: Ocean Time: of the islands:
Of waters after the islands—some of them waking
Where noon here is the night there: some
Where noon is the first few stars they see or the last one.

For three days the world has watched this city—
Not for the common occasions of brutal crime
Or the usual violence of one sort or another
Or coronations of kings or popular festivals:
No: for stranger and disturbing reasons—
The resurrection from death and the tomb of a dead woman.

Each day for three days there has come
To the door of her tomb at noon a woman buried!

The terror that stands at the shoulder of our time
Touches the cheek with this: the flesh winces.
There have been other omens in other cities
But never of this sort and never so credible.
In a time like ours seemings and portents signify.
Ours is a generation when dogs howl and the
Skin crawls on the skull with its beast's foreboding.

All men now alive with us have feared.
We have smelled the wind in the street that changes weather.
We have seen the familiar room grow unfamiliar:
The order of numbers alter: the expectation
Cheat the expectant eye. The appearance defaults with us.

Here in this city the wall of the time cracks.

We take you now to the great square of this city. . . .

[*The shuffle and hum of a vast patient crowd
gradually rises: swells: fills the background.*]

VOICE OF THE ANNOUNCER [*matter-of-fact*]

We are here on the central plaza.
We are well off to the eastward edge.
There is a kind of terrace over the crowd here.
It is precisely four minutes to twelve.
The crowd is enormous: there might be ten thousand:
There might be more: the whole square is faces.
Opposite over the roofs are the mountains.
It is quite clear: there are birds circling.
We think they are kites by the look: they are very high. . . .

The tomb is off to the right somewhere—
We can't see for the great crowd.
Close to us here are the cabinet ministers:
They stand on a raised platform with awnings.
The farmers' wives are squatting on the stones:
Their children have fallen asleep on their shoulders.
The heat is harsh: the light dazzles like metal.
It dazes the air as the clang of a gong does. . . .

News travels in this nation:
There are people here from away off—
Horse-raisers out of the country with brooks in it:
Herders of cattle from up where the snow stays—
The kind that cook for themselves mostly:
They look at the girls with their eyes hard
And a hard grin and their teeth showing. . . .

It is one minute to twelve now:
There is still no sign: they are still waiting:
No one doubts that she will come:

No one doubts that she will speak too:
Three times she has not spoken.

> [*The murmur of the crowd changes—
> not louder but more intense: higher.*]

THE VOICE OF THE ANNOUNCER [*low but with increasing excitement*]

Now it is twelve: now they are rising:
Now the whole plaza is rising:
Fathers are lifting their small children:
The plumed fans on the platform are motionless. . . .

There is no sound but the shuffle of shoe leather . . .

Now even the shoes are still. . . .

We can hear the hawks: it is quiet as that now. . . .

It is strange to see such throngs so silent. . . .

Nothing yet: nothing has happened. . . .

Wait! There's a stir here to the right of us:
They're turning their heads: the crowd turns:
The cabinet ministers lean from their balcony:
There's no sound: only the turning. . . .

> [*A woman's voice comes over the silence of
> the crowd: it is a weak voice but penetrating:
> it speaks slowly and as though with difficulty.*]

THE VOICE OF THE DEAD WOMAN

First the waters rose with no wind. . . .

THE VOICE OF THE ANNOUNCER [*whispering*]

Listen: that is she! She's speaking!

THE VOICE OF THE DEAD WOMAN

Then the stones of the temple kindled
Without flame or tinder of maize-leaves. . . .

THE VOICE OF THE ANNOUNCER [*whispering*]

They see her beyond us: the crowd sees her. . . .

THE VOICE OF THE DEAD WOMAN

Then there were cries in the night haze:
Words in a once-heard tongue: the air
Rustling above us as at dawn with herons.

Now it is I who must bring fear:
I who am four days dead: the tears
Still unshed for me—all of them: I
For whom a child still calls at nightfall.

Death is young in me to fear!
My dress is kept still in the press in my bedchamber:
No one has broken the dish of the dead woman.

Nevertheless I must speak painfully:
I am to stand here in the sun and speak:

[*There is a pause. Then her voice comes
again loud, mechanical, speaking as by rote.*]

The city of masterless men
Will take a master.
There will be shouting then:
Blood after!

[*The crowd stirs. Her voice goes
on weak and slow as before.*]

Do not ask what it means: I do not know:
Only sorrow and no hope for it.

THE VOICE OF THE ANNOUNCER

She has gone. . . . No, they are still looking.

THE VOICE OF THE DEAD WOMAN

It is hard to return from the time past. I have come
In the dream we must learn to dream where the crumbling of
Time like the ash from a burnt string has

Stopped for me. For you the thread still burns:
You take the feathery ash upon your fingers.
You bring yourselves from the time past as it pleases you.

It is hard to return to the old nearness . . .
Harder to go again. . . .

THE VOICE OF THE ANNOUNCER

                              She is gone.
We know because the crowd is closing.
All we can see is the crowd closing.
We hear the releasing of held breath—
The weight shifting: the lifting of shoe leather.
The stillness is broken as surface of water is broken—
The sound circling from in outward.

[*The murmur of the crowd rises.*]

Small wonder they feel fear.
Before the murders of the famous kings—
Before imperial cities burned and fell—
The dead were said to show themselves and speak.
When dead men came disaster came. Presentiments
That let the living on their beds sleep on
Woke dead men out of death and gave them voices.
All ancient men in every nation knew this.

A VOICE OVER THE CROWD

Masterless men . . .

A VOICE OVER THE CROWD

When shall it be . . .

A VOICE OVER THE CROWD

Masterless men
Will take a master . . .

A VOICE OVER THE CROWD

What has she said to us . . .

A VOICE OVER THE CROWD

When shall it be . . .

A VOICE OVER THE CROWD

Masterless men
Will take a master.
Blood after . . .

A VOICE OVER THE CROWD

What has she said to us . . .

VOICES TOGETHER

Blood after!

[*The voices run together into the excited roar of
the crowd. The Announcer's voice is loud over it.*]

THE VOICE OF THE ANNOUNCER

They are milling around us like cattle that smell death.
The whole square is whirling and turning and shouting.
One of the ministers raises his arms on the platform.
No one is listening: now they are sounding drums:
Trying to quiet them likely: No! No!
Something is happening: there in the far corner:
A runner: a messenger: staggering: people are helping him;
People are calling: he comes through the crowd: they are quieter.
Only those on the far edge are still shouting:
Listen! He's here by the ministers now! He is speaking. . . .

THE VOICE OF THE MESSENGER

There has come the conqueror!
I am to tell you.
I have raced over sea land:
I have run over cane land:
I have climbed over cone land
It was laid on my shoulders
By shall and by shan't
That standing by day
And staying by night

Were not for my lot
Till I came to the sight of you.
Now I have come.

Be warned of this conqueror!
This one is dangerous!
Word has out-oared him.
East over sea-cross has
All taken—
Every country.
No men are free there.
Ears overhear them.
Their words are their murderers.
Judged before judgment
Tried after trial
They die as do animals:—
Offer their throats
As the goat to her slaughterer.
Terror has taught them this!

Now he is here!

He was violent in his vessel:
He was steering in her stern:
He was watching in her waist:
He was peering in her prow:
And he dragged her up
Nine lengths
Till her keel lodged
On this nation.

Now he is here
Waylaying and night-lying.
If they hide before dark
He comes before sunup.
Where hunger is eaten
There he sits down:
Where fear sleeps
There he arises.

I tell you beware of him!
All doors are dangers.
The warders of wealth
Will admit him by stealth.
The lovers of men

Will invite him as friend.
The drinkers of blood
Will drum him in suddenly.
Hope will unlatch to him:
Hopelessness open.

I say and say truly
To all men in honesty
Such is this conqueror!
Shame is his people.
Lickers of spittle
Their lives are unspeakable:
Their dying indecent.
Be well warned!
He comes to you slightly
Slanting and sprinting
Hinting and shadowing:
Sly is his hiding:—
A hard lot:
A late rider:

Watch! I have said to you!

THE VOICE OF THE ANNOUNCER

They are leading him out: his legs give:
Now he is gone in the crowd: they are silent:
No one has spoken since his speaking:

They stand still circling the ministers.
No one has spoken or called out:—
There is no stir at all nor movement:
Even the farthest have stood patiently:
They wait trusting the old men:
They wait faithfully trusting the answer.
Now the huddle on the platform opens:
A minister turns to them raising his two arms. . . .

THE VOICE OF THE ORATOR

Freemen of this nation!
The persuasion of your wills against your wisdom is not dreamed of.
We offer themes for your consideration.

What is the surest defender of liberty?
Is it not liberty?

A free people resists by freedom:
Not locks! Not blockhouses!

The future is a mirror where the past
Marches to meet itself. Go armed toward arms!
Peaceful toward peace! Free and with music toward freedom!
Face tomorrow with knives and tomorrow's a knife-blade.
Murder your foe and your foe will be murder!—
Even your friends suspected of false-speaking:
Hands on the door at night and the floor boards squeaking.
Those who win by the spear are the spear-toters.
And what do they win? Spears! What else is there?
If their hands let go they have nothing to hold by.
They are no more free than a paralytic propped against a tree is.

With the armored man the arm is upheld by the weapon:
The man is worn by the knife.

Once depend on iron for your freedom and your
Freedom's iron!
Once overcome your resisters with force and your
Force will resist you!—
You will never be free of force.
Never of arms unarmed
Will the father return home:
The lover to her loved:
The mature man to his fruit orchard
Walking at peace in that beauty—
The years of his trees to assure him.

Force is a greater enemy than this conqueror—
A treacherous weapon.

Nevertheless my friends there *is* a weapon!
Weakness conquers!

Against chainlessness who breaks?
Against wall-lessness who vaults?
Against forcelessness who forces?

Against the feather of the thistle
Is blunted sharpest metal.
No edge cuts seed-fluff.

This conqueror unresisted
Will conquer no longer: a posturer

Beating his blows upon burdocks—
Shifting his guard against shadows.
Snickers will sound among road-menders:
Titters be stifled by laundresses:
Coarse guffaws among chambermaids.
Reddened with rage he will roar.
He will sweat in his uniform foolishly.
He will disappear: no one hear of him!
There *is* a weapon, my friends.
Scorn conquers!

THE VOICE OF THE ANNOUNCER [*the Orator's voice unintelligible under it*]

I wish you could all see this as we do—
The whole plaza full of these people—
Their colorful garments—the harsh sunlight—
The water-sellers swinging enormous gourds—
The orator there on the stone platform—
The temple behind him: the high pyramid—
The hawks overhead in the sky teetering
Slow to the windward: swift to the down-wind—
The houses blind with the blank sun on them. . . .

THE VOICE OF THE ORATOR

There is a weapon.
Reason and truth are that weapon.

Let this conqueror come!
Show him no hindrance!
Suffer his flag and his drum!
Words . . . win!

THE VOICE OF THE ANNOUNCER

There's the shout now: he's done:
He's climbing down: a great speech:
They're all smiling and pressing around him:
The women are squatting in full sunlight:
They're opening packages: bread we'd say by the look—
Yes: bread: bread wrapped between corn leaves:
They're squatting to eat: they're quite contented and happy:
Women are calling their men from the sunny stones:
There are flutes sounding away off:
We can't see for the shifting and moving—

Yes: there are flutes in the cool shadow:
Children are dancing in intricate figures.

[*A drum and flute are
heard under the voice.*]

Even a few old men are dancing.
You'd say they'd never feared to see them dancing.
A great speech! really great!
Men forget these truths in passion:
They oppose the oppressors with blind blows:
They make of their towns tombs: of their roofs burials:
They build memorial ruins to liberty:
But liberty is not built from ruins:
Only in peace is the work excellent. . . .

That's odd! The music has stopped.   There's something—
It's a man there on the far side: he's pointing:
He seems to be pointing back through the farthest street:
The people are twisting and rising: bread in their fists. . . .
We can't see what it is. . . . Wait! . . , it's a messenger.
It must be a messenger. Yes. It's a message—another.
Here he is at the turn of the street trotting:
His neck's back at the nape: he looks tired:
He winds through the crowd with his mouth open: laboring:
People are offering water: he pushes away from them:
Now he has come to the stone steps: to the ministers:
Stand by: we're edging in. . . .

[*There are sounds of people close by: coughs:
murmurs. The Announcer's voice is lowered.*]

Listen: he's leaning on the stone: he's speaking.

THE VOICE OF THE MESSENGER

There has come . . . the Conqueror. . . .

I am to tell you . . .

I have run over corn land:
I have climbed over cone land:
I have crossed over mountains. . . .

It was laid on my shoulders
By shall and by shan't

That standing by day
And staying by night
Were not for my lot
Till I came to the sight of you. . . .

Now I have come.

I bear word:
Beware of this conqueror!
The fame of his story
Like flame in the winter-grass
Widens before him.
Beached on our shore
With the dawn over shoulder
The lawns were still cold
When he came to the sheep meadows:—
Sun could not keep with him
So was he forward.

Fame is his sword.

No man opposing him
Still grows his glory.
He needs neither foeman nor
Thickset of blows to
Gather his victories—
Nor a foe's match
To earn him his battles.

He brings his own enemy!

He baggages with him
His closet antagonist—
His private opposer.
He's setting him up
At every road corner—
A figure of horror
With blood for his color:
Fist for his hand:
Reek where he stands:
Hate for his heat:
Sneers for his mouth:
Clouts for his clothes:
Oaths if he speak:—
And he's knocking him down

In every town square
Till hair's on his blade
And blood's all about
Like dust in a drouth
And the people are shouting
Flowers him flinging
Music him singing
And bringing him gold
And holding his heels
And feeling his thighs
Till their eyes start
And their hearts swell
And they're telling his praises
Like lays of the heroes
And chiefs of antiquity.

Such are his victories!
So does he come:
So he approaches. . . .

    [*A whisper rustles
    through the crowd.*]

No man to conquer
Yet as a conqueror
Marches he forward. . . .

    [*The whisper is louder.*]

Stands in your mountains. . . .

    [*A murmur of voices.*]

Soon to descend on you!

    [*A swelling roar.*]

THE VOICE OF THE ANNOUNCER

That touched them! That frightened them!
Some of them point to the east hills:
Some of them mock at the ministers: 'Freedom!'
'Freedom for what? To die in a rat trap?'
They're frantic with anger and plain fear.
They're sold out they say. You can hear them.

'Down with the government! Down with the orators!
'Down with liberal learned minds!
'Down with the mouths and the loose tongues in them!
'Down with the lazy lot! They've sold us!
'We're sold out! Talking has done for us!' . . .
They're boiling around us like mullet that smell shark.
We can't move for the mob: they're crazy with terror. . . .

A LOUD VOICE [*distant*]

God-lovers!
Think of your gods!

Earth-masters!
Taste your disasters!

Men!
Remember!

THE VOICE OF THE ANNOUNCER

There's a voice over the crowd somewhere.
They hear it: they're quieting down. . . . It's the priests!
We see them now: it's the priests on the pyramid!
There might be ten of them: black with their hair tangled.
The smoke of their fire is flat in the quick wind:
They stand in the thick of the smoke by the stone of the victims:
Their knives catch in the steep sun: they are shouting:
Listen!—

VOICES OF THE PRIESTS

Turn to your gods rememberers!

A SINGLE VOICE

Let the world be saved by surrendering the world:
        Not otherwise shall it be saved.

VOICES OF THE PRIESTS

Turn to your gods rememberers!

A SINGLE VOICE

Let evil be overcome by the coming over of evil:
        Your hearts shall be elsewhere.

VOICES OF THE PRIESTS

Turn to your gods rememberers!

VOICES OF THE PRIESTS [*antiphonally*]

Turn to your gods!
        The conqueror cannot take you!

Turn to your gods!
        The narrow dark will keep you!

Turn to your gods!
        In god's house is no breaking!

Turn to your gods!
        In god's silences sleep is!

Lay up your will with the gods!
        Stones cannot still you!

Lay up your mind with the gods!
        Blade cannot blind you!

Lay up your heart with the gods!
        Danger departs from you!

THE VOICE OF THE ANNOUNCER

It's a wonderful thing to see this crowd responding.
Even the simplest citizens feel the emotion.
There's hardly a sound now in the square. It's wonderful:
Really impressive: the priests there on the pyramid:
The smoke blowing: the bright sun: the faces—

A SINGLE VOICE

In the day of confusion of reason when all is delusion:
In the day of the tyrants of tongues when the truth is for hire:
In the day of deceit when ends meet:
Turn to your gods!

In the day of division of nations when hope is derision:
In the day of the supping of hate when the soul is corrupted:
In the day of despair when the heart's bare:
Turn to your gods!

[*A slow drum beat.*]

THE VOICE OF THE ANNOUNCER

A kind of dance is beginning: a serpent of people:
A current of people coiling and curling through people:
A circling of people through people like water through water. . . .

CHANTING VOICES [*to the drums*]

Out of the stir of the sun
Out of the shout of the thunder
Out of the hush of the star . . .
Withdraw the heart.

THE VOICE OF THE ANNOUNCER [*the chant and drums under*]

A very young girl is leading them:
They have torn the shawl from her bare breast:
They are giving her flowers: her mouth laughs:
Her eyes are not laughing. . . .

CHANTING VOICES

Leave now the lovely air
To the sword and the sword-wearer—
Leave to the marksman the mark—
Withdraw the heart.

THE VOICE OF THE ANNOUNCER [*the chant and drums louder*]

She's coming . . . the drums pound . . . the crowd
Shrieks . . . she's reaching the temple . . . she's climbing it. . . .
Others are following: five: ten . . .
Hundreds are following . . . crowding the stairway. . . .
She's almost there . . . her flowers have fallen . . .
She looks back . . . the priests are surrounding her. . . .

[*The drums suddenly stop: there is an instant's
silence: then an angry shout from the crowd.*]

THE VOICE OF THE ANNOUNCER

Wait! Wait! Something has happened!
One of the ministers: one of the oldest:
The general: the one in the feathered coat:—
He's driving them down with the staff of a banner:
He's climbed after them driving them down:
There's shouting and yelling enough but they're going:
He's telling them off too: you can hear him—

A DEEP VOICE [*chatter of the crowd under it*]

Men! Old men! Listen!
Twist your necks on your nape bones!
The knife will wait in the fist for you.
There is a time for everything—
Time to be thinking of heaven:
Time of your own skins!

Cock your eyes to the windward!

Do you see smoke on those mountains?
The smoke is the smoke of towns.
And who makes it? The conqueror!
And where will he march now? Onward!
The heel of the future descends on you!

THE VOICE OF THE ANNOUNCER

He has them now: even the priests have seen it:
They're all looking away here to the east.
There's smoke too: filling the valleys; like thunderheads! . . .

THE VOICE OF THE GENERAL

You are foolish old men.

You ought to be flogged for your foolishness.
Your grandfathers died to be free
And you—you juggle with freedom!
Do you think you're free by a law
Like the falling of apples in autumn?

You thought you were safe in your liberties!
You thought you could always quibble!

You can't! You take my word for it.
Freedom's the rarest bird!
You risk your neck to snare it—
It's gone while your eyeballs stare!

Those who'd lodge with a tyrant
Thinking to feed at his fire
And leave him again when they're fed are
Plain fools or were bred to it—
Brood of the servile races
Born with the hang-dog face. . . .

THE VOICE OF THE ANNOUNCER

They're all pointing and pushing together:
The women are shouldering baskets: bread: children. . . .
They smell smoke in the air: they smell terror. . . .

THE VOICE OF THE GENERAL [*louder over the increasing sound*]

There's nothing in this world worse—
Empty belly or purse or the ·
Pitiful hunger of children—
Than doing the Strong Man's will!

The free will fight for their freedom.
They're free men first. They feed
Meager or fat but as free men.
Everything else comes after—
Food: roof: craft—
Even the sky and the light of it!

[*The voices of the crowd rise to a
tumult of sounds—drums: shouts: cries.*]

THE VOICE OF THE ANNOUNCER

The sun is yellow with smoke . . . the town's burning. . . .
The war's at the broken bridge.

THE VOICE OF THE GENERAL [*shouting*]

You! Are you free? Will you fight?

There are still inches for fighting!

There is still a niche in the streets!

You can stand on the stairs and meet him!

You can hold in the dark of a hall!

You can die!

    or your children will crawl for it!

THE VOICE OF THE ANNOUNCER [*over the tumult*]

They won't listen. They're shouting and screaming and circling.
The square is full of deserters with more coming.
Every street from the bridge is full of deserters.
They're rolling in with the smoke blowing behind them.
The plaza's choked with the smoke and the struggling of stragglers.
They're climbing the platform: driving the ministers: shouting—
One speaks and another:

THE VOICES OF CITIZENS

The city is doomed!
                There's no holding it!

Let the conqueror have it! It's his!

The age is his! It's his century!

Our institutions are obsolete.
He marches a mile while we sit in a meeting.

Opinions and talk!
Deliberative walks beneath the ivy and the creepers!

The age demands a made-up mind.
The conqueror's mind is decided on everything.

His doubt comes after the deed or never.

He knows what he wants for his want's what he knows.
He's gone before they say he's going.
He's come before you've barred your house.

He's one man: we are but thousands!

Who can defend us from one man?

Bury your arms!   Break your standards!

Give him the town while the town stands!

THE VOICE OF THE ANNOUNCER

They're throwing their arms away: their bows are in bonfires.
The plaza is littered with torn plumes: spear-handles. . . .

THE VOICES OF CITIZENS

Masterless men! . .´.
Masterless men
Must take a master! . . .

Order must master us! . . .

Freedom's for fools:
Force is the certainty!

Freedom has eaten our strength and corrupted our virtues!

Men must be ruled!

Fools must be mastered!

Rigor and fast
Will restore us our dignity!

Chains will be liberty!

THE VOICE OF THE ANNOUNCER

The last defenders are coming: they whirl from the streets like
Wild leaves on a wind: the square scatters them.

Now they are fewer—ten together or five:
They come with their heads turned: their eyes back.

Now there are none. The street's empty—in shadow.
The crowd is retreating—watching the empty street:
The shouts die.

The voices are silent.

They're watching. . . .

They stand in the slant of the sunlight silent and watching.
The silence after the drums echoes the drum beat.

Now there's a sound. They see him. They must see him!
They're shading their eyes from the sun: there's a rustle of whispering:
We can't see for the glare of it. . . . Yes! . . . Yes! . . .
He's there in the end of the street in the shadow. We see him!
He looks huge—a head taller than anyone:
Broad as a brass door; a hard hero:
Heavy of heel on the brick: clanking with metal:
The helm closed on his head: the eyeholes hollow.

He's coming! . . .
                    He's clear of the shadow! . .
                                        The sun takes him.

They cover their faces with fingers. They cower before him.
They fall: they sprawl on the stone. He's alone where he's walking.
He marches with rattle of metal. He tramples his shadow.
He mounts by the pyramid—stamps on the stairway—turns—
His arm rises—his visor is opening. . . .

[*There is an instant's breathless silence: then the
voice of the Announcer low—almost a whisper.*]

                                        There's no one! . . .
There's no one at all! . . .
                    No one! . . .
                                        The helmet is hollow!
The metal is empty! The armor is empty! I tell you
There's no one at all there: there's only the metal:
The barrel of metal: the bundle of armor. It's empty!

The push of a stiff pole at the nipple would topple it.

They don't see! They lie on the paving. They lie in the
Burnt spears: the ashes of arrows. They lie there . . .
They don't see or they won't see. They are silent. . . .

The people invent their oppressors: they wish to believe in them.
They wish to be free of their freedom: released from their liberty:—
The long labor of liberty ended!
                    They lie there!

[*There is a whisper of sound.*
The Announcer's voice is louder.]

Look! It's his arm! It is rising! His arm's rising!
They're watching his arm as it rises. They stir. They cry.
They cry out. They are shouting. They're shouting with happiness.
Listen! They're shouting like troops in a victory. Listen—
'The city of masterless men has found a master!'
You'd say it was they were the conquerors: they that had conquered.

A ROAR OF VOICES

The city of masterless men has found a master!
The city has fallen!
The city has fallen!

THE VOICE OF THE ANNOUNCER [*flat*]

The city has fallen. . . .

Beyond the Horizon[1]
by EUGENE O'NEILL

CHARACTERS

JAMES MAYO, *a farmer*
KATE MAYO, *his wife.*
CAPTAIN DICK SCOTT, *of the bark* "SUNDA," *her brother.*
ANDREW MAYO ⎫
ROBERT MAYO ⎭ *sons of* JAMES MAYO.
RUTH ATKINS.
MRS. ATKINS, *her widowed mother.*
MARY.
· BEN, *a farm hand.*
DOCTOR FAWCETT.

SCENES

Act One

Scene I: The Road. Sunset of a day in Spring.
Scene II: The Farm House. The same night.

Act Two

(Three years later)

Scene I: The Farm House. Noon of a Summer day.
Scene II: The top of a hill on the farm overlooking the sea.
The following day.

Act Three

(Five years later)

Scene I: The Farm House. Dawn of a day in late Fall.
Scene II: The Road. Sunrise.

ACT ONE: SCENE ONE

A SECTION *of country highway. The road runs diagonally from the left, forward, to the right, rear, and can be seen in the distance winding toward the horizon like a pale ribbon between the low, rolling hills with their freshly plowed fields clearly divided from each other, checkerboard fashion, by the lines of stone walls and rough snake fences.*

[1] Reprinted by permission of Random House, Inc. Produced New York, 1920.

The forward triangle cut off by the road is a section of a field, from the dark earth of which myriad bright-green blades of fall-sown rye are sprouting. A straggling line of piled rocks, too low to be called a wall, separates this field from the road.

To the rear of the road is a ditch with a sloping, grassy bank on the far side. From the center of this an old, gnarled apple tree, just budding into leaf, strains its twisted branches heavenwards, black against the pallor of distance. A snake fence sidles from left to right along the top of the bank, passing beneath the apple tree.

The hushed twilight of a day in May is just beginning. The horizon hills are still rimmed by a faint line of flame, and the sky above them glows with the crimson flush of the sunset. This fades gradually as the action of the scene progresses.

At the rise of the curtain, ROBERT MAYO *is discovered sitting on the fence. He is a tall, slender young man of twenty-three. There is a touch of the poet about him expressed in his high forehead and wide, dark eyes. His features are delicate and refined, leaning to weakness in the mouth and chin. He is dressed in gray corduroy trousers pushed into high laced boots, and blue flannel shirt with a bright colored tie. He is reading a book by the fading sunset light. He shuts this, keeping a finger in to mark the place, and turns his head toward the horizon, gazing out over the fields and hills. His lips move as if he were reciting something to himself.*

His brother ANDREW *comes along the road from the right, returning from his work in the fields. He is twenty-seven years old, an opposite type to* ROBERT—*husky, sun-bronzed, handsome in a large-featured, manly fashion—a son of the soil, intelligent in a shrewd way, but with nothing of the intellectual about him. He wears overalls, leather boots, a gray flannel shirt open at the neck, and a soft, mud-stained hat pushed back on his head. He stops to talk to* ROBERT, *leaning on the hoe he carries.*

ANDREW [*Seeing* ROBERT *has not noticed his presence—in a loud shout*]. Hey there! [ROBERT *turns with a start. Seeing who it is, he smiles*] Gosh, you do take the prize for day-dreaming! And I see you've toted one of the old books along with you. [*He crosses the ditch and sits on the fence near his brother*] What is it this time—poetry, I'll bet. [*He reaches for the book*] Let me see.

ROBERT [*Handing it to him rather reluctantly*]. Look out you don't get it full of dirt.

ANDREW [*Glancing at his hands*]. That isn't dirt—it's good clean earth. [*He turns over the pages. His eyes read something and he gives an exclamation of disgust*] Hump! [*With a provoking grin at his brother he reads aloud in a doleful, sing-song voice*] "I have loved wind and light and the bright sea. But holy and most sacred night, not as I love and have loved thee." [*He hands the book back*] Here! Take it and bury it. I suppose it's that year in college gave you a liking for that kind of stuff. I'm darn glad I stopped at high school, or maybe I'd been crazy too. [*He grins and slaps* ROBERT *on the back affectionately*] Imagine me reading poetry and plowing at the same time! The team'd run away, I'll bet.

ROBERT [*Laughing*]. Or picture me plowing.

ANDREW. You should have gone back to college last fall, like I know you wanted to. You're fitted for that sort of thing—just as I ain't.

ROBERT. You know why I didn't go back, Andy. Pa didn't like the idea, even if he didn't say so; and I know he wanted the money to use improving the farm. And besides, I'm not keen on being a student, just because you see me reading books all the time. What I want to do now is keep on moving so that I won't take root in any one place.

ANDREW. Well, the trip you're leaving on tomorrow will keep you moving all right. [*At this mention of the trip they both fall silent. There is a pause. Finally* ANDREW *goes on, awkwardly, attempting to speak casually*] Uncle says you'll be gone three years.

ROBERT. About that, he figures.

ANDREW [*Moodily*]. That's a long time.

ROBERT. Not so long when you come to consider it. You know the *Sunda* sails around the Horn for Yokohama first, and that's a long voyage on a sailing ship; and if we go to any of the other places Uncle Dick mentions— India, or Australia, or South Africa, or South America—they'll be long voyages, too.

ANDREW. You can have all those foreign parts for all of me. [*After a pause*] Ma's going to miss you a lot, Bob.

ROBERT. Yes—and I'll miss her.

ANDREW. And Pa ain't feeling none too happy to have you go—though he's been trying not to show it.

ROBERT. I can see how he feels.

ANDREW. And you can bet that I'm not giving any cheers about it. [*He puts one hand on the fence near* ROBERT]

ROBERT [*Putting one hand on top of* ANDREW's *with a gesture almost of shyness*]. I know that, too, Andy.

ANDREW. I'll miss you as much as anybody, I guess. You see, you and I ain't like most brothers—always fighting and separated a lot of the time, while we've always been together—just the two of us. It's different with us. That's why it hits so hard, I guess.

ROBERT [*With feeling*]. It's just as hard for me, Andy—believe that! I hate to leave you and the old folks—but—I feel I've got to. There's something calling me— [*He points to the horizon*] Oh, I can't just explain it to you, Andy.

ANDREW. No need to, Rob. [*Angry at himself*] Hell! You want to go— that's all there is to it; and I wouldn't have you miss this chance for the world.

ROBERT. It's fine of you to feel that way, Andy.

ANDREW. Huh! I'd be a nice son-of-a-gun if I didn't, wouldn't I? When

I know how you need this sea trip to make a new man of you—in the body, I mean—and give you your full health back.

ROBERT [*A trifle impatiently*]. All of you seem to keep harping on my health. You were so used to seeing me lying around the house in the old days that you never will get over the notion that I'm a chronic invalid. You don't realize how I've bucked up in the past few years. If I had no other excuse for going on Uncle Dick's ship but just my health, I'd stay right here and start in plowing.

ANDREW. Can't be done. Farming ain't your nature. There's all the difference shown in just the way us two feel about the farm. You—well, you like the home part of it, I expect; but as a place to work and grow things, you hate it. Ain't that right?

ROBERT. Yes, I suppose it is. For you it's different. You're a Mayo through and through. You're wedded to the soil. You're as much a product of it as an ear of corn is, or a tree. Father is the same. This farm is his life-work, and he's happy in knowing that another Mayo, inspired by the same love, will take up the work where he leaves off. I can understand your attitude, and Pa's; and I think it's wonderful and sincere. But I—well, I'm not made that way.

ANDREW. No, you ain't; but when it comes to understanding, I guess I realize that you've got your own angle of looking at things.

ROBERT [*Musingly*]. I wonder if you do, really.

ANDREW [*Confidently*]. Sure I do. You've seen a bit of the world, enough to make the farm seem small, and you've got the itch to see it all.

ROBERT. It's more than that, Andy.

ANDREW. Oh, of course. I know you're going to learn navigation, and all about a ship, so's you can be an officer. That's natural, too. There's fair pay in it, I expect, when you consider that you've always got a home and grub thrown in; and if you're set on traveling, you can go anywhere you're a mind to without paying fare.

ROBERT [*With a smile that is half sad*]. It's more than that, Andy.

ANDREW. Sure it is. There's always a chance of a good thing coming your way in some of those foreign ports or other. I've heard there are great opportunities for a young fellow with his eyes open in some of those new countries that are just being opened up. [*Jovially*] I'll bet that's what you've been turning over in your mind under all your quietness! [*He slaps his brother on the back with a laugh*] Well, if you get to be a millionaire all of a sudden, call 'round once in a while and I'll pass the plate to you. We could use a lot of money right here on the farm without hurting it any.

ROBERT [*Forced to laugh*]. I've never considered that practical side of it for a minute, Andy.

ANDREW. Well, you ought to.

ROBERT. No, I oughtn't. [*Pointing to the horizon—dreamily*] Supposing I was to tell you that it's just Beauty that's calling me, the beauty of the far off and unknown, the mystery and spell of the East which lures me in the books I've read, the need of the freedom of great wide spaces, the joy of wandering on and on—in quest of the secret which is hidden over there, beyond the horizon? Suppose I told you that was the one and only reason for my going?

ANDREW. I should say you were nutty.

ROBERT [*Frowning*]. Don't, Andy. I'm serious.

ANDREW. Then you might as well stay here, because we've got all you're looking for right on this farm. There's wide space enough, Lord knows; and you can have all the sea you want by walking a mile down to the beach; and there's plenty of horizon to look at, and beauty enough for anyone, except in the winter. [*He grins*] As for the mystery and spell, I haven't met 'em yet, but they're probably lying around somewheres. I'll have you understand this is a first-class farm with all the fixings. [*He laughs*]

ROBERT [*Joining in the laughter in spite of himself*]. It's no use talking to you, you chump!

ANDREW. You'd better not say anything to Uncle Dick about spells and things when you're on the ship. He'll likely chuck you overboard for a Jonah. [*He jumps down from fence*] I'd better run along. I've got to wash up some as long as Ruth's Ma is coming over for supper.

ROBERT [*Pointedly—almost bitterly*]. And Ruth.

ANDREW [*Confused—looking everywhere except at* ROBERT—*trying to appear unconcerned*]. Yes, Ruth'll be staying too. Well, I better hustle, I guess, and —[*He steps over the ditch to the road while he is talking*]

ROBERT [*Who appears to be fighting some strong inward emotion—impulsively*]. Wait a minute, Andy! [*He jumps down from the fence*] There is something I want to— [*He stops abruptly, biting his lips, his face coloring*]

ANDREW [*Facing him; half-defiantly*]. Yes?

ROBERT [*Confusedly*]. No—never mind—it doesn't matter, it was nothing.

ANDREW [*After a pause, during which he stares fixedly at* ROBERT'S *averted face*]. Maybe I can guess—what you were going to say—but I guess you're right not to talk about it. [*He pulls* ROBERT'S *hand from his side and grips it tensely; the two brothers stand looking into each other's eyes for a minute*] We can't help those things, Rob. [*He turns away, suddenly releasing* ROBERT'S *hand*] You'll be coming along shortly, won't you?

ROBERT [*Dully*]. Yes.

ANDREW. See you later, then.

[*He walks off down the road to the left.* ROBERT *stares after him for a moment; then climbs to the fence rail again, and looks out over the hills, an expression of deep grief on his face. After a moment or so,* RUTH *enters hurriedly from the left. She is a healthy, blonde, out-of-door girl of twenty, with a graceful, slender figure. Her face, though inclined to roundness, is undeniably pretty, its large eyes of a deep blue set off strikingly by the sun-bronzed complexion. Her small, regular features are marked by a certain strength—an underlying stub-*]

*born fixity of purpose hidden in the frankly-appealing charm of her
fresh youthfulness. She wears a simple white dress but no* **hat**]

RUTH [*Seeing him*]. Hello, Rob!

ROBERT [*Startled*]. Hello, Ruth!

RUTH [*Jumps the ditch and perches on the fence beside him*]. I was looking
for you.

ROBERT [*Pointedly*]. Andy just left here.

RUTH. I know. I met him on the road a second ago. He told me you
were here. [*Tenderly playful*] I wasn't looking for Andy, Smarty, if that's
what you mean. I was looking for *you*.

ROBERT. Because I'm going away tomorrow?

RUTH. Because your mother was anxious to have you come home and
asked me to look for you. I just wheeled Ma over to your house.

ROBERT [*Perfunctorily*]. How is your mother?

RUTH [*A shadow coming over her face*]. She's about the same. She never
seems to get any better or any worse. Oh, Rob, I do wish she'd try to make
the best of things that can't be helped.

ROBERT. Has she been nagging at you again?

RUTH [*Nods her head, and then breaks forth rebelliously*]. She never stops
nagging. No matter what I do for her she finds fault. If only Pa was still
living—[*She stops as if ashamed of her outburst*] I suppose I shouldn't complain this way. [*She sighs*] Poor Ma, Lord knows it's hard enough for her.
I suppose it's natural to be cross when you're not able ever to walk a step.
Oh, I'd like to be going away some place—like you!

ROBERT. It's hard to stay—and equally hard to go, sometimes.

RUTH. There! If I'm not the stupid body! I swore I wasn't going to speak
about your trip—until after you'd gone; and there I go, first thing!

ROBERT. Why didn't you want to speak of it?

RUTH. Because I didn't want to spoil this last night you're here. Oh, Rob,
I'm going to—we're all going to miss you so awfully. Your mother is going
around looking as if she'd burst out crying any minute. You ought to know
how I feel. Andy and you and I—why it seems as if we'd always been
together.

ROBERT [*With a wry attempt at a smile*]. You and Andy will still have
each other. It'll be harder for me without anyone.

RUTH. But you'll have new sights and new people to take your mind off;
while we'll be here with the old, familiar place to remind us every minute of
the day. It's a shame you're going—just at this time, in spring, when everything is getting so nice. [*With a sigh*] I oughtn't to talk that way when I
know going's the best thing for you. You're bound to find all sorts of
opportunities to get on, your father says.

ROBERT [*Heatedly*]. I don't give a damn about that! I wouldn't take a
voyage across the road for the best opportunity in the world of the kind Pa
thinks of. [*He smiles at his own irritation*] Excuse me, Ruth, for getting

worked up over it; but Andy gave me an overdose of the practical considerations.

RUTH [*Slowly, puzzled*]. Well, then if it isn't— [*With sudden intensity*] Oh, Rob, why *do* you want to go?

ROBERT [*Turning to her quickly, in surprise—slowly*]. Why do you ask that, Ruth?

RUTH [*Dropping her eyes before his searching glance*]. Because— [*Lamely*] It seems such a shame.

ROBERT [*Insistently*]. Why?

RUTH. Oh, because—everything.

ROBERT. I could hardly back out now, even if I wanted to. And I'll be forgotten before you know it.

RUTH [*Indignantly*]. You won't! I'll never forget— [*She stops and turns away to hide her confusion*]

ROBERT [*Softly*]. Will you promise me that?

RUTH [*Evasively*]. Of course. It's mean of you to think that any of us would forget so easily.

ROBERT [*Disappointedly*]. Oh!

RUTH [*With an attempt at lightness*]. But you haven't told me your reason for leaving yet?

ROBERT [*Moodily*]. I doubt if you'll understand. It's difficult to explain, even to myself. Either you feel it, or you don't. I can remember being conscious of it first when I was only a kid—you haven't forgotten what a sickly specimen I was then, in those days, have you?

RUTH [*With a shudder*]. Let's not think about them.

ROBERT. You'll have to, to understand. Well, in those days, when Ma was fixing meals, she used to get me out of the way by pushing my chair to the west window and telling me to look out and be quiet. That wasn't hard. I guess I was always quiet.

RUTH [*Compassionately*]. Yes, you always were—and you suffering so much, too!

ROBERT [*Musingly*]. So I used to stare out over the fields to the hills, out there— [*He points to the horizon*] and somehow after a time I'd forget any pain I was in, and start dreaming. I knew the sea was over beyond those hills—the folks had told me—and I used to wonder what the sea was like, and try to form a picture of it in my mind. [*With a smile*] There was all the mystery in the world to me then about that—far-off sea—and there still is! It called to me then just as it does now. [*After a slight pause*] And other times my eyes would follow this road, winding off into the distance, toward the hills, as if it, too, was searching for the sea. And I'd promise myself that when I grew up and was strong, I'd follow that road, and it and I would find the sea together. [*With a smile*] You see, my making this trip is only keeping that promise of long ago.

RUTH [*Charmed by his low, musical voice telling the dreams of his childhood*]. Yes, I see.

ROBERT. Those were the only happy moments of my life then, dreaming there at the window. I liked to be all alone—those times. I got to know all the different kinds of sunsets by heart. And all those sunsets took place over there— [*He points*] beyond the horizon. So gradually I came to believe that all the wonders of the world happened on the other side of those hills. There was the home of the good fairies who performed beautiful miracles. I believed in fairies then. [*With a smile*] Perhaps I still do believe in them. Anyway, in those days they were real enough, and sometimes I could actually hear them calling to me to come out and play with them, dance with them down the road in the dusk in a game of hide-and-seek to find out where the sun was hiding himself. They sang their little songs to me, songs that told of all the wonderful things they had in their home on the other side of the hills; and they promised to show me all of them, if I'd only come, come! But I couldn't come then, and I used to cry sometimes and Ma would think I was in pain. [*He breaks off suddenly with a laugh*] That's why I'm going now, I suppose. For I can still hear them calling. But the horizon is as far away and as luring as ever. [*He turns to her—softly*] Do you understand now, Ruth?

RUTH [*Spellbound, in a whisper*]. Yes.

ROBERT. You feel it then?

RUTH. Yes, yes, I do! [*Unconsciously she snuggles close against his side. His arm steals about her as if he were not aware of the action*] Oh, Rob, how could I help feeling it? You tell things so beautifully!

ROBERT [*Suddenly realizing that his arm is around her, and that her head is resting on his shoulder, gently takes his arm away.* RUTH, *brought back to herself, is overcome with confusion*]. So now you know why I'm going. It's for that reason—that and one other.

RUTH. You've another? Then you must tell me that, too.

ROBERT [*Looking at her searchingly. She drops her eyes before his gaze*]. I wonder if I ought to! You'll promise not to be angry—whatever it is?

RUTH [*Softly, her face still averted*]. Yes, I promise.

ROBERT [*Simply*]. I love you. That's the other reason.

RUTH [*Hiding her face in her hands*]. Oh, Rob!

ROBERT. I wasn't going to tell you, but I feel I have to. It can't matter now that I'm going so far away, and for so long—perhaps forever. I've loved you all these years, but the realization never came till I agreed to go away with Uncle Dick. Then I thought of leaving you, and the pain of that thought revealed to me in a flash—that I loved you, had loved you as long as I could remember. [*He gently pulls one of* RUTH's *hands away from her face*] You mustn't mind my telling you this, Ruth. I realize how impossible it all is— and I understand; for the revelation of my own love seemed to open my eyes to the love of others. I saw Andy's love for you—and I knew that you must love him.

RUTH [*Breaking out stormily*]. I don't! I don't love Andy! I don't! [ROBERT *stares at her in stupid astonishment.* RUTH *weeps hysterically*] Whatever—put such a fool notion into—into your head? [*She suddenly throws her arms about his neck and hides her head on his shoulder*] Oh, Rob! Don't go away! Please! You mustn't, now! You can't! I won't let you! It'd break my—my heart!

ROBERT [*The expression of stupid bewilderment giving way to one of overwhelming joy. He presses her close to him—slowly and tenderly*]. Do you mean that—that you love me?

RUTH [*Sobbing*]. Yes, yes—of course I do—what d'you s'pose? [*She lifts up her head and looks into his eyes with a tremulous smile*] You stupid thing! [*He kisses her*] I've loved you right along.

ROBERT [*Mystified*]. But you and Andy were always together!

RUTH. Because you never seemed to want to go any place with me. You were always reading an old book, and not paying any attention to me. I was too proud to let you see I cared because I thought the year you had away to college had made you stuck-up, and you thought yourself too educated to waste any time on me.

ROBERT [*Kissing her*]. And I was thinking— [*With a laugh*] What fools we've both been!

RUTH [*Overcome by a sudden fear*]. You won't go away on the trip, will you, Rob? You'll tell them you can't go on account of me, won't you? You can't go now! You can't!

ROBERT [*Bewildered*]. Perhaps—you can come too.

RUTH. Oh, Rob, don't be so foolish. You know I can't. Who'd take care of Ma? Don't you see I couldn't go—on her account? [*She clings to him imploringly*] Please don't go—not now. Tell them you've decided not to. They won't mind. I know your mother and father'll be glad. They'll all be. They don't want you to go so far away from them. Please, Rob! We'll be so happy here together where it's natural and we know things. Please tell me you won't go!

ROBERT [*Face to face with a definite, final decision, betrays the conflict going on within him*]. But—Ruth—I—Uncle Dick—

RUTH. He won't mind when he knows it's for your happiness to stay. How could he? [*As* ROBERT *remains silent she bursts into sobs again*] Oh, Rob! And you said—you loved me!

ROBERT [*Conquered by this appeal—an irrevocable decision in his voice*]. I won't go, Ruth. I promise you. There! Don't cry! [*He presses her to him, stroking her hair tenderly. After a pause he speaks with happy hopefulness*] Perhaps after all Andy was right—righter than he knew—when he said I could find all the things I was seeking for here, at home on the farm. I think love must have been the secret—the secret that called to me from over the world's rim—the secret beyond every horizon; and when I did not come, it came to me. [*He clasps* RUTH *to him fiercely*] Oh, Ruth, our love is sweeter than any distant dream! [*He kisses her passionately and steps to the ground, lifting* RUTH *in his arms and carrying her to the road where he puts her down*]

RUTH [*With a happy laugh*]. My, but you're strong!

ROBERT. Come! We'll go and tell them at once.

RUTH [*Dismayed*]. Oh, no, don't, Rob, not till after I've gone. There'd be bound to be such a scene with them all together.

ROBERT [*Kissing her—gayly*]. As you like—little Miss Common Sense!

RUTH. Let's go, then. [*She takes his hand, and they start to go off left. ROBERT suddenly stops and turns as though for a last look at the hills and the dying sunset flush*]

ROBERT [*Looking upward and pointing*]. See! The first star. [*He bends down and kisses her tenderly*] Our star!

RUTH [*In a soft murmur*]. Yes. Our very own star. [*They stand for a moment looking up at it, their arms around each other. Then RUTH takes his hand again and starts to lead him away.*] Come, Rob, let's go. [*His eyes are fixed again on the horizon as he half turns to follow her. RUTH urges*] We'll be late for supper, Rob.

ROBERT [*Shakes his head impatiently, as though he were throwing off some disturbing thought—with a laugh*]. All right. We'll run then. Come on! [*They run off laughing as the curtain falls*]

ACT ONE: SCENE TWO

THE *sitting room of the Mayo farm house about nine o'clock the same night. On the left, two windows looking out on the fields. Against the wall between the windows, an old-fashioned walnut desk. In the left corner, rear, a sideboard with a mirror. In the rear wall to the right of the sideboard, a window looking out on the road. Next to the window a door leading out into the yard. Farther right, a black horse-hair sofa, and another door opening on a bedroom. In the corner, a straight-backed chair. In the right wall, near the middle, an open doorway leading to the kitchen. Farther forward a double-heater stove with coal scuttle, etc. In the center of the newly carpeted floor, an oak dining-room table with a red cover. In the center of the table, a large oil reading lamp. Four chairs, three rockers with crocheted tidies on their backs, and one straight-backed, are placed about the table. The walls are papered a dark red with a scrolly-figured pattern.*

Everything in the room is clean, well-kept, and in its exact place, yet there is no suggestion of primness about the whole. Rather the atmosphere is one of the orderly comfort of a simple, hard-earned prosperity, enjoyed and maintained by the family as a unit.

JAMES MAYO, *his wife, her brother,* CAPTAIN DICK SCOTT, *and* ANDREW *are discovered.* MAYO *is his son* ANDREW *over again in body and face—an* ANDREW *sixty-five years old with a short, square, white beard.* MRS. MAYO *is a slight, round-faced, rather prim-looking woman of fifty-five who had once been a school teacher. The labors of a farmer's wife have bent but not broken her, and she retains a certain refinement of movement and expression foreign to the*

MAYO *part of the family. Whatever of resemblance* ROBERT *has to his parents may be traced to her. Her brother, the* CAPTAIN, *is short and stocky, with a weather-beaten, jovial face and a white mustache—a typical old salt, loud of voice and given to gesture. He is fifty-eight years old.*

JAMES MAYO *sits in front of the table. He wears spectacles, and a farm journal which he has been reading lies in his lap. The* CAPTAIN *leans forward from a chair in the rear, his hands on the table in front of him.* ANDREW *is tilted back on the straight-backed chair to the left, his chin sunk forward on his chest, staring at the carpet, preoccupied and frowning.*

As the curtain rises the CAPTAIN *is just finishing the relation of some sea episode. The others are pretending an interest which is belied by the absentminded expressions on their faces.*

THE CAPTAIN [*Chuckling*]. And that mission woman, she hails me on the dock as I was acomin' ashore, and she says—with her silly face all screwed up serious as judgment—"Captain," she says, "would you be so kind as to tell me where the sea-gulls sleeps at nights?" Blow me if them warn't her exact words! [*He slaps the table with the palm of his hands and laughs loudly. The others force smiles*] Ain't that just like a fool woman's question? And I looks at her serious as I could, "Ma'm," says I, "I couldn't rightly answer that question. I ain't never seed a sea-gull in his bunk yet. The next time I hears one snorin'," I says, "I'll make a note of where he's turned in, and write you a letter 'bout it." And then she calls me a fool real spiteful and tacks away from me quick. [*He laughs again uproariously*] So I got rid of her that way. [*The others smile but immediately relapse into expressions of gloom again*]

MRS. MAYO [*Absent-mindedly—feeling that she has to say something*]. But when it comes to that, where *do* sea-gulls sleep, Dick?

SCOTT [*Slapping the table*]. Ho! Ho! Listen to her, James. 'Nother one! Well, if that don't beat all hell—'scuse me for cussin', Kate.

MAYO [*With a twinkle in his eyes*]. They unhitch their wings, Katey, and spreads 'em out on a wave for a bed.

SCOTT. And then they tells the fish to whistle to 'em when it's time to turn out. Ho! Ho!

MRS. MAYO [*With a forced smile*]. You men folks are too smart to live, aren't you? [*She resumes her knitting.* MAYO *pretends to read his paper;* ANDREW *stares at the floor*]

SCOTT [*Looks from one to the other of them with a puzzled air. Finally he is unable to bear the thick silence a minute longer, and blurts out*]. You folks look as if you was settin' up with a corpse. [*With exaggerated concern*] God A'mighty, there ain't anyone dead, be there?

MAYO [*Sharply*] Don't play the dunce, Dick! You know as well as we do there ain't no great cause to be feelin' chipper.

SCOTT [*Argumentatively*]. And there ain't no cause to be wearin' mourning, either, I can make out.

MRS. MAYO [*Indignantly*]. How can you talk that way, Dick Scott, when you're taking our Robbie away from us, in the middle of the night, you might say, just to get on that old boat of yours on time! I think you might wait until morning when he's had his breakfast.

SCOTT [*Appealing to the others hopelessly*]. Ain't that a woman's way o' seein' things for you? God A'mighty, Kate, I can't give orders to the tide that it's got to be high just when it suits me to have it. I ain't gettin' no fun out o' missin' sleep and leavin' here at six bells myself. [*Protestingly*] And the *Sunda* ain't an old ship—leastways, not very old—and she's good's she ever was.

MRS. MAYO [*Her lips trembling*]. I wish Robbie weren't going.

MAYO [*Looking at her over his glasses—consolingly*]. There, Katey!

MRS. MAYO [*Rebelliously*]. Well, I *do* wish he wasn't!

SCOTT. You shouldn't be taking it so hard, 's far as I kin see. This vige'll make a man of him. I'll see to it he learns how to navigate, 'n' study for a mate's c'tificate right off—and it'll give him a trade for the rest of his life, if he wants to travel.

MRS. MAYO. But I don't want him to travel all his life. You've got to see he comes home when this trip is over. Then he'll be all well, and he'll want to—to marry— [ANDREW *sits forward in his chair with an abrupt movement*] —and settle down right here. [*She stares down at the knitting in her lap— after a pause*] I never realized how hard it was going to be for me to have Robbie go—or I wouldn't have considered it a minute.

SCOTT. It ain't no good goin' on that way, Kate, now it's all settled.

MRS. MAYO [*On the verge of tears*]. It's all right for *you* to talk. You've never had any children. You don't know what it means to be parted from them—and Robbie my youngest, too. [ANDREW *frowns and fidgets in his chair*]

ANDREW [*Suddenly turning to them*]. There's one thing none of you seem to take into consideration—that Rob wants to go. He's dead set on it. He's been dreaming over this trip ever since it was first talked about. It wouldn't be fair to him not to have him go. [*A sudden uneasiness seems to strike him*] At least, not if he still feels the same way about it he did when he was talking to me this evening.

MAYO [*With an air of decision*]. Andy's right, Katey. That ends all argyment, you can see that. [*Looking at his big silver watch*] Wonder what's happened to Robert? He's been gone long enough to wheel the widder to home, certain. He can't be out dreamin' at the stars his last night.

MRS. MAYO [*A bit reproachfully*]. Why didn't you wheel Mrs. Atkins back tonight, Andy? You usually do when she and Ruth come over.

ANDREW [*Avoiding her eyes*]. I thought maybe Robert wanted to tonight. He offered to go right away when they were leaving.

MRS. MAYO. He only wanted to be polite.

ANDREW [*Gets to his feet*]. Well, he'll be right back, I guess. [*He turns to his father*] Guess I'll go take a look at the black cow, Pa—see if she's ailing any.

MAYO. Yes—better had, son. [ANDREW *goes into the kitchen on the right*]

SCOTT [*As he goes out—in a low tone*]. There's the boy that would make a good, strong sea-farin' man—if he'd a mind to.

MAYO [*Sharply*]. Don't you put no such fool notions in Andy's head, Dick —or you 'n' me's goin' to fall out. [*Then he smiles*] You couldn't tempt him, no ways. Andy's a Mayo bred in the bone, and he's a born farmer, and a damn good one, too. He'll live and die right here on this farm, like I expect to. [*With proud confidence*] And he'll make this one of the slickest, best-payin' farms in the state, too, afore he gits through!

SCOTT. Seems to me it's a pretty slick place right now.

MAYO [*Shaking his head*]. It's too small. We need more land to make it amount to much, and we ain't got the capital to buy it.

[ANDREW *enters from the kitchen. His hat is on, and he carries a lighted lantern in his hand. He goes to the door in the rear leading out*]

ANDREW [*Opens the door and pauses*]. Anything else you can think of to be done, Pa?

MAYO. No, nothin' I know of. [ANDREW *goes out, shutting the door*]

MRS. MAYO [*After a pause*]. What's come over Andy tonight, I wonder? He acts so strange.

MAYO. He does seem sort o' glum and out of sorts. It's 'count o' Robert leavin', I s'pose. [*To* SCOTT] Dick, you wouldn't believe how them boys o' mine sticks together. They ain't like most brothers. They've been thick as thieves all their lives, with nary a quarrel I kin remember.

SCOTT. No need to tell me that. I can see how they take to each other.

MRS. MAYO [*Pursuing her train of thought*]. Did you notice, James, how queer everyone was at supper? Robert seemed stirred up about something; and Ruth was so flustered and giggly; and Andy sat there dumb, looking as if he'd lost his best friend; and all of them only nibbled at their food.

MAYO. Guess they was all thinkin' about tomorrow, same as us.

MRS. MAYO [*Shaking her head*]. No. I'm afraid somethin's happened— somethin' else.

MAYO. You mean—'bout Ruth?

MRS. MAYO. Yes.

MAYO [*After a pause—frowning*]. I hope her and Andy ain't had a serious fallin'-out. I always sorter hoped the'd hitch up together sooner or later. What d'you say, Dick? Don't you think them two'd pair up well?

SCOTT [*Nodding his head approvingly*]. A sweet, wholesome couple they'd make.

MAYO. It'd be a good thing for Andy in more ways than one. I ain't what you'd call calculatin' generally, and I b'lieve in lettin' young folks run their affairs to suit themselves; but there's advantages for both o' them in this match you can't overlook in reason. The Atkins farm is right next to ourn.

Jined together they'd make a jim-dandy of a place, with plenty o' room to work in. And bein' a widder with only a daughter, and laid up all the time to boot, Mrs. Atkins can't do nothin' with the place as it ought to be done. She needs a man, a first-class farmer, to take hold o' things; and Andy's just the one.

MRS. MAYO [*Abruptly*]. I don't think Ruth loves Andy.

MAYO. You don't? Well, maybe a woman's eyes is sharper in such things, but—they're always together. And if she don't love him now, she'll likely come around to it in time. [*As* MRS. MAYO *shakes her head*] You seem mighty fixed in your opinion, Katey. How d'you know?

MRS. MAYO. It's just—what I feel.

MAYO [*A light breaking over him*]. You don't mean to say—[MRS. MAYO *nods.* MAYO *chuckles scornfully*] Shucks! I'm losin' my respect for your eyesight, Katey. Why, Robert ain't got no time for Ruth, 'cept as a friend!

MRS. MAYO [*Warningly*]. Sss-h-h! [*The door from the yard opens, and* ROBERT *enters. He is smiling happily, and humming a song to himself, but as he comes into the room an undercurrent of nervous uneasiness manifests itself in his bearing*]

MAYO. So here you be at last! [ROBERT *comes forward and sits on* ANDY'S *chair.* MAYO *smiles slyly at his wife*] What have you been doin' all this time —countin' the stars to see if they all come out right and proper?

ROBERT. There's only one I'll ever look for any more, Pa.

MAYO [*Reproachfully*]. You might've even not wasted time lookin' for that one—your last night.

MRS. MAYO [*As if she were speaking to a child*]. You ought to have worn your coat a sharp night like this, Robbie.

SCOTT [*Disgustedly*]. God A'mighty, Kate, you treat Robert as if he was one year old!

MRS. MAYO [*Notices* ROBERT'S *nervous uneasiness*]. You look all worked up over something, Robbie. What is it?

ROBERT [*Swallowing hard, looks quickly from one to the other of them— then begins determinedly*]. Yes, there *is* something—something I must tell you—all of you. [*As he begins to talk* ANDREW *enters quietly from the rear, closing the door behind him, and setting the lighted lantern on the floor. He remains standing by the door, his arms folded, listening to* ROBERT *with a repressed expression of pain on his face.* ROBERT *is so much taken up with what he is going to say that he does not notice* ANDREW'S *presence*] Something I discovered only this evening—very beautiful and wonderful—something I did not take into consideration previously because I hadn't dared to hope that such happiness could ever come to me. [*Appealingly*] You must all remember that fact, won't you?

MAYO [*Frowning*]. Let's get to the point, son.

ROBERT [*With a trace of defiance*]. Well, the point is this, Pa: I'm not going—I mean—I can't go tomorrow with Uncle Dick—or at any future time, either.

MRS. MAYO [*With a sharp sigh of joyful relief*]. Oh, Robbie, I'm so glad!

MAYO [*Astounded*]. You ain't serious, be you, Robert? [*Severely*] Seems to me it's a pretty late hour in the day for you to be upsettin' all your plans so sudden!

ROBERT. I asked you to remember that until this evening I didn't know myself. I had never dared to dream—

MAYO [*Irritably*]. What is this foolishness you're talkin' of?

ROBERT [*Flushing*]. Ruth told me this evening that—she loved me. It was after I'd confessed I loved her. I told her I hadn't been conscious of my love until after the trip had been arranged, and I realized it would mean—leaving her. That was the truth. I *didn't* know until then. [*As if justifying himself to the others*] I hadn't intended telling her anything but—suddenly—I felt I must. I didn't think it would matter, because I was going away. And I thought she loved—someone else. [*Slowly—his eyes shining*] And then she cried and said it was I she'd loved all the time, but I hadn't seen it.

MRS. MAYO [*Rushes over and throws her arms about him*]. I knew it! I was just telling your father when you came in—and, oh, Robbie, I'm so happy you're not going!

ROBERT [*Kissing her*]. I knew you'd be glad, Ma.

MAYO [*Bewilderedly*]. Well, I'll be damned! You do beat all for gettin' folks' mind all tangled up, Robert. And Ruth too! Whatever got into her of a sudden? Why, I was thinkin'—

MRS. MAYO [*Hurriedly—in a tone of warning*]. Never mind what you were thinking, James. It wouldn't be any use telling us that now. [*Meaningly*] And what you were hoping for turns out just the same almost, doesn't it?

MAYO [*Thoughtfully—beginning to see this side of the argument*]. Yes; I suppose you're right, Katey. [*Scratching his head in puzzlement*] But how it ever come about! It do beat anything ever I heard. [*Finally he gets up with a sheepish grin and walks over to* ROBERT] We're glad you ain't goin', your Ma and I, for we'd have missed you terrible, that's certain and sure; and we're glad you've found happiness. Ruth's a fine girl and'll make a good wife to you.

ROBERT [*Much moved*]. Thank you, Pa. [*He grips his father's hand in his*]

ANDREW [*His face tense and drawn comes forward and holds out his hand, forcing a smile*]. I guess it's my turn to offer congratulations, isn't it?

ROBERT [*With a startled cry when his brother appears before him so suddenly*]. Andy! [*Confused*] Why—I—I didn't see you. Were you here when—

ANDREW. I heard everything you said; and here's wishing you every happiness, you and Ruth. You both deserve the best there is.

ROBERT [*Taking his hand*]. Thanks, Andy, it's fine of you to—[*His voice dies away as he sees the pain in* ANDREW'S *eyes*]

ANDREW [*Giving his brother's hand a final grip*]. Good luck to you both! [*He turns away and goes back to the rear where he bends over the lantern, fumbling with it to hide his emotion from the others*]

MRS. MAYO [*To the* CAPTAIN, *who has been too flabbergasted by* ROBERT'S *decision to say a word*]. What's the matter, Dick? Aren't you going to congratulate Robbie?

SCOTT [*Embarrassed*]. Of course I be! [*He gets to his feet and shakes* ROBERT'S *hand, muttering a vague*] Luck to you, boy. [*He stands beside* ROBERT *as if he wanted to say something more but doesn't know how to go about it*]

ROBERT. Thanks, Uncle Dick.

SCOTT. So you're not acomin' on the *Sunda* with me? [*His voice indicates disbelief*]

ROBERT. I can't, Uncle—not now. I wouldn't miss it for anything else in the world under any other circumstances. [*He sighs unconsciously*] But you see I've found—a bigger dream. [*Then with joyous high spirits*] I want you all to understand one thing—I'm not going to be a loafer on your hands any longer. This means the beginning of a new life for me in every way. I'm going to settle right down and take a real interest in the farm, and do my share. I'll prove to you, Pa, that I'm as good a Mayo as you are—or Andy, when I want to be.

MAYO [*Kindly but skeptically*]. That's the right spirit, Robert. Ain't none of us doubts you willin'ness, but you ain't never learned—

ROBERT. Then I'm going to start learning right away, and you'll teach me, won't you?

MAYO [*Mollifyingly*]. Of course I will, boy, and be glad to, only you'd best go easy at first.

SCOTT [*Who has listened to this conversation in mingled consternation and amazement*]. You don't mean to tell me you're goin' to let him stay, do you, James?

MAYO. Why, things bein' as they be, Robert's free to do as he's a mind to.

MRS. MAYO. *Let him!* The very idea!

SCOTT [*More and more ruffled*]. Then all I got to say is, you's a soft, weak-willed critter to be permittin' a boy—and women, too—to be layin' your course for you wherever they damn pleases.

MAYO [*Slyly amused*]. It's just the same with me as 'twas with you, Dick. You can't order the tides on the seas to suit you, and I ain't pretendin' I can reg'late love for young folks.

SCOTT [*Scornfully*]. Love! They ain't old enough to know love when they sight it! Love! I'm ashamed of you, Robert, to go lettin' a little huggin' and kissin' in the dark spoil your chances to make a man out o' yourself. It ain't common sense—no siree, it ain't—not by a hell of a sight! [*He pounds the table with his fists in exasperation*]

MRS. MAYO [*Laughing provokingly at her brother*]. A fine one you are to be talking about love, Dick—an old cranky bachelor like you. Goodness sakes!

SCOTT [*Exasperated by their joking*]. I've never been a damn fool like most, if that's what you're steerin' at.

MRS. MAYO [*Tauntingly*]. Sour grapes, aren't they, Dick? [*She laughs.*
ROBERT *and his father chuckle.* SCOTT *sputters with annoyance*] Good gracious,
Dick, you do act silly, flying into a temper over nothing.

SCOTT [*Indignantly*]. Nothin'! You talk as if I wasn't concerned nohow
in this here business. Seems to me I've got a right to have my say. Ain't I
made all arrangements with the owners and stocked up with some special
grub all on Robert's account?

ROBERT. You've been fine, Uncle Dick; and I appreciate it. Truly.

MAYO. 'Course; we all does, Dick.

SCOTT [*Unplacated*]. I've been countin' sure on havin' Robert for company
on this vige—to sorta talk to and show things to, and teach, kinda, and I got
my mind so set on havin' him I'm goin' to be double lonesome this vige.
[*He pounds on the table, attempting to cover up this confession of weakness*]
Darn all this silly lovin' business, anyway. [*Irritably*] But all this talk ain't
tellin' me what I'm to do with that sta'b'd cabin I fixed up. It's all painted
white, an' a bran' new mattress on the bunk, 'n' new sheets 'n' blankets 'n'
things. And Chips built in a book-case so's Robert could take his books along
—with a slidin' bar fixed across't it, mind, so's they couldn't fall out no matter
how she rolled. [*With excited consternation*] What d'you suppose my officers
is goin' to think when there's no one comes aboard to occupy that sta'b'd
cabin? And the men what did the work on it—what'll *they* think? [*He
shakes his finger indignantly*] They're liable as not to suspicion it was a
woman I'd planned to ship along, and that she gave me the go-by at the last
moment! [*He wipes his perspiring brow in anguish at this thought*] Gawd
A'mighty! They're only lookin' to have the laugh on me for something like
that. They're liable to b'lieve anything, those fellers is!

MAYO [*With a wink*]. Then there's nothing to it but for you to get right
out and hunt up a wife somewheres for that spick 'n' span cabin. She'll have
to be a pretty one, too, to match it. [*He looks at his watch with exaggerated
concern*] You ain't got much time to find her, Dick.

SCOTT [*As the others smile—sulkily*]. You kin go to thunder, Jim Mayo!

ANDREW [*Comes forward from where he has been standing by the door,
rear, brooding. His face is set in a look of grim determination*] You needn't
worry about that spare cabin, Uncle Dick, if you've a mind to take me in
Robert's place.

ROBERT [*Turning to him quickly*]. Andy! [*He sees at once the fixed
resolve in his brother's eyes, and realizes immediately the reason for it—in
consternation*] Andy, you mustn't!

ANDREW. You've made your decision, Rob, and now I've made mine.
You're out of this, remember.

ROBERT [*Hurt by his brother's tone*]. But Andy—

ANDREW. Don't interfere, Rob—that's all I ask. [*Turning to his uncle*]
You haven't answered my question, Uncle Dick.

SCOTT [*Clearing his throat, with an uneasy side glance at* JAMES MAYO *who*

is staring at his elder son as if he thought he had suddenly gone mad] O'
course, I'd be glad to have you, Andy.

ANDREW. It's settled then. I can pack the little I want to take in a few
minutes.

MRS. MAYO. Don't be a fool, Dick. Andy's only joking you.

SCOTT [*Disgruntledly*]. It's hard to tell who's jokin' and who's not in
this house.

ANDREW [*Firmly*]. I'm not joking, Uncle Dick. [*As* SCOTT *looks at him
uncertainly*] You needn't be afraid I'll go back on my word.

ROBERT [*Hurt by the insinuation he feels in* ANDREW's *tone*]. Andy! That
isn't fair!

MAYO [*Frowning*]. Seems to me this ain't no subject to joke over—not
for Andy.

ANDREW [*Facing his father*]. I agree with you, Pa, and I tell you again,
once and for all, that I've made up my mind to go.

MAYO [*Dumbfounded—unable to doubt the determination in* ANDREW's
voice—helplessly]. But why, son? Why?

ANDREW [*Evasively*]. I've always wanted to go.

ROBERT. Andy!

ANDREW [*Half angrily*]. You shut up, Rob! [*Turning to his father again*]
I didn't ever mention it because as long as Rob was going I knew it was no
use; but now Rob's staying on here, there isn't any reason for me not to go.

MAYO [*Breathing hard*]. No reason? Can you stand there and say that
to me, Andrew?

MRS. MAYO [*Hastily—seeing the gathering storm*]. He doesn't mean a
word of it, James.

MAYO [*Making a gesture to her to keep silence*]. Let me talk, Katey.
[*In a more kindly tone*] What's come over you so sudden, Andy? You
know's well as I do that it wouldn't be fair o' you to run off at a moment's
notice right now when we're up to our necks in hard work.

ANDREW [*Avoiding his eyes*]. Rob'll hold his end up as soon as he learns.

MAYO. Robert was never cut out for a farmer, and you was.

ANDREW. You can easily get a man to do my work.

MAYO [*Restraining his anger with an effort*]. It sounds strange to hear
you, Andy, that I always thought had good sense, talkin' crazy like that.
[*Scornfully*] Get a man to take your place! You ain't been workin' here
for no hire, Andy, that you kin give me your notice to quit like you've done.
The farm is yourn as well as mine. You've always worked on it with that
understanding; and what you're sayin' you intend doin' is just skulkin' out
o' your rightful responsibility.

ANDREW [*Looking at the floor—simply*]. I'm sorry, Pa. [*After a slight
pause*] It's no use talking any more about it.

MRS. MAYO [*In relief*]. There! I knew Andy'd come to his senses!

ANDREW. Don't get the wrong idea, Ma. I'm not backing out.

MAYO. You mean you're goin' in spite of—everythin'?

ANDREW. Yes. I'm going. I've got to. [*He looks at his father defiantly*] I feel I oughtn't to miss this chance to go out into the world and see things, and—I want to go.

MAYO [*With bitter scorn*]. So—you want to go out into the world and see thin's! [*His voice raised and quivering with anger*] I never thought I'd live to see the day when a son o' mine 'd look me in the face and tell a bare-faced lie! [*Bursting out*] You're a liar, Andy Mayo, and a mean one to boot!

MRS. MAYO. James!

ROBERT. Pa!

SCOTT. Steady there, Jim!

MAYO [*Waving their protests aside*]. He is and he knows it.

ANDREW [*His face flushed*]. I won't argue with you, Pa. You can think as badly of me as you like.

MAYO [*Shaking his finger at* ANDY, *in a cold rage*]. You know I'm speakin' truth—that's why you're afraid to argy! You lie when you say you want to go 'way—and see thin's! You ain't got no likin' in the world to go. I've watched you grow up, and I know your ways, and they're my ways. You're runnin' against your own nature, and you're goin' to be a'mighty sorry for it if you do. 'S if I didn't know your real reason for runnin' away! And runnin' away's the only words to fit it. You're runnin' away 'cause you're put out and riled 'cause your own brother's got Ruth 'stead o' you, and—

ANDREW [*His face crimson—tensely*]. Stop, Pa! I won't stand hearing that—not even from you!

MRS. MAYO [*Rushing to* ANDY *and putting her arms about him protectingly*]. Don't mind him, Andy dear. He don't mean a word he's saying! [ROBERT *stands rigidly, his hands clenched, his face contracted by pain.* SCOTT *sits dumbfounded and open-mouthed.* ANDREW *soothes his mother who is on the verge of tears*]

MAYO [*In angry triumph*]. It's the truth, Andy Mayo! And you ought to be bowed in shame to think of it!

ROBERT [*Protestingly*]. Pa!

MRS. MAYO [*Coming from* ANDREW *to his father; puts her hands on his shoulders as though to try and push him back in the chair from which he has risen*]. Won't you be still, James? Please won't you?

MAYO [*Looking at* ANDREW *over his wife's shoulder—stubbornly*]. The truth—God's truth!

MRS. MAYO. Sh-h-h! [*She tries to put a finger across his lips, but he twists his head away*]

ANDREW [*Who has regained control over himself*]. You're wrong, Pa, it isn't truth. [*With defiant assertiveness*] I don't love Ruth. I never loved her, and the thought of such a thing never entered my head.

MAYO [*With an angry snort of disbelief*]. Hump! You're pilin' lie on lie!

ANDREW [*Losing his temper—bitterly*]. I suppose it'd be hard for you to explain anyone's wanting to leave this blessed farm except for some outside reason like that. But I'm sick and tired of it—whether you want to believe me or not—and that's why I'm glad to get a chance to move on.

ROBERT. Andy! Don't! You're only making it worse.

ANDREW [*Sulkily*]. I don't care. I've done my share of work here. I've earned my right to quit when I want to. [*Suddenly overcome with anger and grief; with rising intensity*] I'm sick and tired of the whole damn business. I hate the farm and every inch of ground in it. I'm sick of digging in the dirt and sweating in the sun like a slave without getting a word of thanks for it. [*Tears of rage starting to his eyes—hoarsely*] I'm through, through for good and all; and if Uncle Dick won't take me on his ship, I'll find another. I'll get away somewhere, somehow.

MRS. MAYO [*In a frightened voice*]. Don't you answer him, James. He doesn't know what he's saying. Don't say a word to him 'til he's in his right senses again. Please James, don't—

MAYO [*Pushes her away from him; his face is drawn and pale with the violence of his passion. He glares at* ANDREW *as if he hated him*]. You dare to—you dare to speak like that to me? You talk like that 'bout this farm— the Mayo farm—where you was born—you—you [*He clenches his fist above his head and advances threateningly on* ANDREW] You damned whelp!

MRS. MAYO [*With a shriek*]. James! [*She covers her face with her hands and sinks weakly into* MAYO'S *chair.* ANDREW *remains standing motionless, his face pale and set*]

SCOTT [*Starting to his feet and stretching his arms across the table toward* MAYO]. Easy there, Jim!

ROBERT [*Throwing himself between father and brother*]. Stop! Are you mad?

MAYO [*Grabs* ROBERT'S *arm and pushes him aside—then stands for a moment gasping for breath before* ANDREW. *He points to the door with a shaking finger*]. Yes—go!—go!—You're no son o' mine—no son o' mine! You can go to hell if you want to! Don't let me find you here—in the mornin'— or—or—I'll *throw* you out!

ROBERT. Pa! For God's sake! [MRS. MAYO *bursts into noisy sobbing*]

MAYO [*Gulps convulsively and glares at* ANDREW]. You go—tomorrow mornin'—and by God—don't come back—don't dare come back—by God, not while I'm livin'—or I'll—I'll—[*He shakes over his muttered threat and strides toward the door rear, right*]

MRS. MAYO [*Rising and throwing her arms around him—hysterically*]. James! James! Where are you going?

MAYO [*Incoherently*]. I'm goin'—to bed, Katey. It's late, Katey—it's late. [*He goes out*]

MRS. MAYO [*Following him, pleading hysterically*]. James! Take back what you've said to Andy. James! [*She follows him out.* ROBERT *and the* CAPTAIN *stare after them with horrified eyes.* ANDREW *stands rigidly looking straight in front of him, his fists clenched at his sides*]

SCOTT [*The first to find his voice—with an explosive sigh*]. Well, if he ain't the devil himself when he's roused! You oughtn't to have talked to him that way, Andy 'bout the damn farm, knowin' how touchy he is about it. [*With another sigh*] Well, you won't mind what he's said in anger. He'll be sorry for it when he's calmed down a bit.

ANDREW [*In a dead voice*]. You don't know him. [*Defiantly*] What's said is said and can't be unsaid; and I've chosen.

ROBERT [*With violent protest*]. Andy! You can't go! This is all so stupid —and terrible!

ANDREW [*Coldly*]. I'll talk to you in a minute, Rob. [*Crushed by his brother's attitude* ROBERT *sinks down into a chair, holding his head in his hands*]

SCOTT [*Comes and slaps* ANDREW *on the back*]. I'm damned glad you're shippin' on, Andy. I like your spirit, and the way you spoke up to him. [*Lowering his voice to a cautious whisper*] The sea's the place for a young feller like you that isn't half dead 'n' alive. [*He gives* ANDY *a final approving slap*] You 'n' me'll get along like twins, see if we don't. I'm goin' aloft to turn in. Don't forget to pack your dunnage. And git some sleep, if you kin. We'll want to sneak out extra early b'fore they're up. It'll do away with more argyments. Robert can drive us down to the town, and bring back the team. [*He goes to the door in the rear, left*] Well, good night.

ANDREW. Good night. [SCOTT *goes out. The two brothers remain silent for a moment. Then* ANDREW *comes over to his brother and puts a hand on his back. He speaks in a low voice, full of feeling*] Buck up, Rob. It ain't any use crying over spilt milk; and it'll all turn out for the best—let's hope. It couldn't be helped—what's happened.

ROBERT [*Wildly*]. But it's a lie, Andy, a lie!

ANDREW. Of course it's a lie. You know it and I know it,—but that's all ought to know it.

ROBERT. Pa'll never forgive you. Oh, the whole affair is so senseless— tragic. Why did you think you must go away?

ANDREW. You know better than to ask that. You know why. [*Fiercely*] I can wish you and Ruth all the good luck in the world, and I do, and I mean it; but you can't expect me to stay around here and watch you two together, day after day—and me alone. I couldn't stand it—not after all the plans I'd made to happen on this place thinking—[*his voice breaks*] thinking she cared for me.

ROBERT [*Putting a hand on his brother's arm*]. God! It's horrible! I feel so guilty—to think that I should be the cause of your suffering, after we've been such pals all our lives. If I could have foreseen what'd happen, I swear to you I'd have never said a word to Ruth. I swear I wouldn't have, Andy!

ANDREW. I know you wouldn't; and that would've been worse, for Ruth would've suffered then. [*He pats his brother's shoulder*] It's best as it is. It had to be, and I've got to stand the gaff, that's all. Pa'll see how I felt— after a time. [*As* ROBERT *shakes his head*]—and if he don't—well, it can't be helped.

ROBERT. But think of Ma! God, Andy, you can't go! You can't!

ANDREW [*Fiercely*]. I've got to go—to get away! I've got to, I tell you. I'd go crazy here, bein' reminded every second of the day what a fool I'd made of myself. I've got to get away and try and forget, if I can. And I'd hate the farm if I stayed, hate it for bringin' things back. I couldn't take interest in the work any more, work with no purpose in sight. Can't you see what a hell it'd be? You love her too, Rob. Put yourself in my place, and remember, I haven't stopped loving her, and couldn't if I was to stay. Would that be fair to you or to her? Put yourself in my place. [*He shakes his brother fiercely by the shoulder*] What'd you do then? Tell me the truth! You love her. What'd you do?

ROBERT [*Chokingly*]. I'd—I'd go, Andy! [*He buries his face in his hands with a shuddering sob*] God!

ANDREW [*Seeming to relax suddenly all over his body—in a low, steady voice*]. Then you know why I got to go; and there's nothing more to be said.

ROBERT [*In a frenzy of rebellion*]. Why did this have to happen to us? It's damnable! [*He looks about him wildly, as if his vengeance were seeking the responsible fate*].

ANDREW [*Soothingly—again putting his hands on his brother's shoulder*]. It's no use fussing any more, Rob. It's done. [*Forcing a smile*] I guess Ruth's got a right to have who she likes. She made a good choice—and God bless her for it!

ROBERT. Andy! Oh, I wish I could tell you half I feel of how fine you are!

ANDREW [*Interrupting him quickly*]. Shut up! Let's go to bed. I've got to be up long before sun-up. You, too, if you're going to drive us down.

ROBERT. Yes. Yes.

ANDREW [*Turning down the lamp*]. And I've got to pack yet. [*He yawns with utter weariness*] I'm as tired as if I'd been plowing twenty-four hours at a stretch. [*Dully*] I feel—dead. [ROBERT *covers his face again with his hands*. ANDREW *shakes his head as if to get rid of his thoughts, and continues with a poor attempt at cheery briskness*] I'm going to douse the light. Come on. [*He slaps his brother on the back*. ROBERT *does not move*. ANDREW *bends over and blows out the lamp. His voice comes from the darkness*] Don't sit there mourning, Rob. It'll all come out in the wash. Come on and get some sleep. Everything'll turn out all right in the end. [ROBERT *can be heard stumbling to his feet, and the dark figures of the two brothers can be seen groping their way toward the doorway in the rear as*

The Curtain Falls.]

ACT TWO: SCENE ONE

SAME *as Act One, Scene Two. Sitting room of the farm house about half past twelve in the afternoon of a hot, sun-baked day in midsummer, three years later. All the windows are open, but no breeze stirs the soiled white curtains. A patched screen door is in the rear. Through it the yard can be seen, its small stretch of lawn divided by the dirt path leading to the door from the gate in the white picket fence which borders the road.*

The room has changed, not so much in its outward appearance as in its general atmosphere. Little significant details give evidence of carelessness, of inefficiency, of an industry gone to seed. The chairs appear shabby from lack of paint; the table cover is spotted and askew; holes show in the curtains; a child's doll, with one arm gone, lies under the table; a hoe stands in a corner; a man's coat is flung on the couch in the rear; the desk is cluttered up with odds and ends; a number of books are piled carelessly on the sideboard. The noon enervation of the sultry, scorching day seems to have penetrated indoors, causing even inanimate objects to wear an aspect of despondent exhaustion.

A place is set at the end of the table, left, for someone's dinner. Through the open door to the kitchen comes the clatter of dishes being washed, interrupted at intervals by a woman's irritated voice and the peevish whining' of a child.

At the rise of the curtain MRS. MAYO *and* MRS. ATKINS *are discovered sitting facing each other,* MRS. MAYO *to the rear,* MRS. ATKINS *to the right of the table.* MRS. MAYO'S *face has lost all character, disintegrated, become a weak mask wearing a helpless, doleful expression of being constantly on the verge of comfortless tears. She speaks in an uncertain voice, without assertiveness, as if all power of willing had deserted her.* MRS. ATKINS *is in her wheel chair. She is a thin, pale-faced, unintelligent-looking woman of about forty-eight, with hard, bright eyes. A victim of partial paralysis for many years, condemned to be pushed from day to day of her life in a wheel chair, she has developed the selfish, irritable nature of the chronic invalid. Both women are dressed in black.* MRS. ATKINS *knits nervously as she talks. A ball of unused yarn, with needles stuck through it, lies on the table before* MRS. MAYO.

MRS. ATKINS [*With a disapproving glance at the place set on the table*]. Robert's late for his dinner again, as usual. I don't see why Ruth puts up with it, and I've told her so. Many's the time I've said to her "It's about time you put a stop to his nonsense. Does he suppose you're runnin' a hotel—with no one to help with things?" But she don't pay no attention. She's as bad as he is, a'most—thinks she knows better than an old, sick body like me.

MRS. MAYO [*Dully*]. Robbie's always late for things. He can't help it, Sarah.

MRS. ATKINS [*With a snort*]. Can't help it! How you do go on, Kate, findin' excuses for him! Anybody can help anything they've a mind to—as long as they've got health, and ain't rendered helpless like me—[*She adds as a pious afterthought*]—through the will of God.

MRS. MAYO. Robbie can't.

MRS. ATKINS. Can't! It do make me mad, Kate Mayo, to see folks that God gave all the use of their limbs to potterin' round and wastin' time doin' everything the wrong way—and me powerless to help and at their mercy, you might say. And it ain't that I haven't pointed the right way to 'em. I've talked to Robert thousands of times and told him how things ought to be done. You know that, Kate Mayo. But d'you s'pose he takes any notice of what I say? Or Ruth, either—my own daughter? No, they think I'm a crazy, cranky old woman, half dead a'ready, and the sooner I'm in the grave and out o' the way the better it'd suit them.

MRS. MAYO. You mustn't talk that way, Sarah. They're not as wicked as that. And you've got years and years before you.

MRS. ATKINS. You're like the rest, Kate. You don't know how near the end I am. Well, at least I can go to my eternal rest with a clear conscience. I've done all a body could do to avert ruin from this house. On their heads be it!

MRS. MAYO [*With hopeless indifference*]. Things might be worse. Robert never had any experience in farming. You can't expect him to learn in a day.

MRS. ATKINS [*Snappily*]. He's had three years to learn, and he's gettin' worse 'stead of better. Not on'y your place but mine too is driftin' to rack and ruin, and I can't do nothin' to prevent.

MRS. MAYO [*With a spark of assertiveness*]. You can't say but Robbie works hard, Sarah.

MRS. ATKINS. What good's workin' hard if it don't accomplish anythin', I'd like to know?

MRS. MAYO. Robbie's had bad luck against him.

MRS. ATKINS. Say what you've a mind to, Kate, the proof of the puddin's in the eatin'; and you can't deny that things have been goin' from bad to worse ever since your husband died two years back.

MRS. MAYO [*Wiping tears from her eyes with her handkerchief*]. It was God's will that he should be taken.

MRS. ATKINS [*Triumphantly*]. It was God's punishment on James Mayo for the blasphemin' and denyin' of God he done all his sinful life! [MRS. MAYO *begins to weep softly*] There, Kate, I shouldn't be remindin' you, I know. He's at peace, poor man, and forgiven, let's pray.

MRS. MAYO [*Wiping her eyes—simply*]. James was a good man.

MRS. ATKINS [*Ignoring this remark*]. What I was sayin' was that since Robert's been in charge things've been goin' down hill steady. You don't know *how* bad they are. Robert don't let on to you what's happenin'; and you'd never see it yourself if 'twas under your nose. But, thank the Lord, Ruth still comes to me once in a while for advice when she's worried near out of her senses by his goin's-on. Do you know what she told me last night?

But I forgot, she said not to tell you—still I think you've got a right to know, and it's my duty not to let such things go on behind your back.

MRS. MAYO [*Wearily*]. You can tell me if you want to.

MRS. ATKINS [*Bending over toward her—in a low voice*]. Ruth was almost crazy about it. Robert told her he'd have to mortgage the farm—said he didn't know how he'd pull through till harvest without it, and he can't get money any other way. [*She straightens up—indignantly*] Now what do you think of your Robert?

MRS. MAYO [*Resignedly*]. If it has to be—

MRS. ATKINS. You don't mean to say you're goin to sign away your farm, Kate Mayo—after me warnin' you?

MRS. MAYO. I'll do what Robbie says is needful.

MRS. ATKINS [*Holding up her hands*]. Well, of all the foolishness!—well, it's your farm, not mine, and I've nothin' more to say.

MRS. MAYO. Maybe Robbie'll manage till Andy gets back and sees to things. It can't be long now.

MRS. ATKINS [*With keen interest*]. Ruth says Andy ought to turn up any day. When does Robert figger he'll get here?

MRS. MAYO. He says he can't calculate exactly on account o' the *Sunda* being a sail boat. Last letter he got was from England, the day they were sailing for home. That was over a month ago, and Robbie thinks they're overdue now.

MRS. ATKINS. We can give praise to God then that he'll be back in the nick o' time. He ought to be tired of travelin' and anxious to get home and settle down to work again.

MRS. MAYO. Andy has been working. He's head officer on Dick's boat, he wrote Robbie. You know that.

MRS. ATKINS. That foolin' on ships is all right for a spell, but he must be right sick of it by this.

MRS. MAYO [*Musingly*]. I wonder if he's changed much. He used to be so fine-looking and strong. [*With a sigh*] Three years! It seems more like three hundred. [*Her eyes filling—piteously*] Oh, if James could only have lived till he came back—and forgiven him!

MRS. ATKINS. He never would have—not James Mayo! Didn't he keep his heart hardened against him till the last in spite of all you and Robert did to soften him?

MRS. MAYO [*With a feeble flush of anger*]. Don't you dare say that! [*Brokenly*] Oh, I know deep down in his heart he forgave Andy, though he was too stubborn ever to own up to it. It was that brought on his death—breaking his heart just on account of his stubborn pride. [*She wipes her eyes with her handkerchief and sobs*].

MRS. ATKINS [*Piously*]. It was the will of God. [*The whining crying of the child sounds from the kitchen.* MRS. ATKINS *frowns irritably*] Drat that young one! Seems as if she cries all the time on purpose to set a body's nerves on edge.

MRS. MAYO [*Wiping her eyes*]. It's the heat upsets her. Mary doesn't feel any too well these days, poor little child!

MRS. ATKINS. She gets it right from her Pa—bein' sickly all the time. You can't deny Robert was always ailin' as a child. [*She sighs heavily*] It was a crazy mistake for them two to get married. I argyed against it at the time, but Ruth was so spelled with Robert's wild poetry notions she wouldn't listen to sense. Andy was the one would have been the match for her.

MRS. MAYO. I've often thought since it might have been better the other way. But Ruth and Robbie seem happy enough together.

MRS. ATKINS. At any rate it was God's work—and His will be done. [*The two women sit in silence for a moment.* RUTH *enters from the kitchen, carrying in her arms her two-year-old daughter,* MARY, *a pretty but sickly and anæmic-looking child with a tear-stained face.* RUTH *has aged appreciably. Her face has lost its youth and freshness. There is a trace in her expression of something hard and spiteful. She sits in the rocker in front of the table and sighs wearily. She wears a gingham dress with a soiled apron tied around her waist*]

RUTH. Land sakes, if this isn't a scorcher! That kitchen's like a furnace. Phew! [*She pushes the damp hair back from her forehead*]

MRS. MAYO. Why didn't you call me to help with the dishes?

RUTH [*Shortly*]. No. The heat in there'd kill you.

MARY [*Sees the doll under the table and struggles on her mother's lap*]. Dolly, Mama! Dolly!

RUTH [*Pulling her back*]. It's time for your nap. You can't play with Dolly now.

MARY [*Commencing to cry whiningly*]. Dolly!

MRS. ATKINS [*Irritably*]. Can't you keep that child still? Her racket's enough to split a body's ears. Put her down and let her play with the doll if it'll quiet her.

RUTH [*Lifting* MARY *to the floor*]. There! I hope you'll be satisfied and keep still. [MARY *sits down on the floor before the table and plays with the doll in silence.* RUTH *glances at the place set on the table*]. It's a wonder Rob wouldn't try to get to meals on time once in a while.

MRS. MAYO [*Dully*]. Something must have gone wrong again.

RUTH [*Wearily*]. I s'pose so. Something's always goin wrong these days, it looks like.

MRS. ATKINS [*Snappily*]. It wouldn't if you possessed a bit of spunk. The idea of you permittin' him to come in to meals at all hours—and you doin' the work! I never heard of such a thin'. You're too easy goin', that's the trouble.

RUTH. Do stop your nagging at me, Ma! I'm sick of hearing you. I'll do as I please about it; and thank you for not interfering. [*She wipes her moist forehead—wearily*] Phew! It's too hot to argue. Let's talk of something pleasant. [*Curiously*] Didn't I hear you speaking about Andy a while ago?

MRS. MAYO. We were wondering when he'd get home.

RUTH [*Brightening*]. Rob says any day now he's liable to drop in and surprise us—him and the Captain. It'll certainly look natural to see him around the farm again.

MRS. ATKINS. Let's hope the farm'll look more natural, too, when he's had a hand at it. The way thin's are now!

RUTH [*Irritably*]. Will you stop harping on that, Ma? We all know things aren't as they might be. What's the good of your complaining all the time?

MRS. ATKINS. There, Kate Mayo! Ain't that just what I told you? I can't say a word of advice to my own daughter even, she's that stubborn and self-willed.

RUTH [*Putting her hands over her ears—in exasperation*]. For goodness sakes, Ma!

MRS. MAYO [*Dully*]. Never mind. Andy'll fix everything when he comes.

RUTH [*Hopefully*]. Oh, yes, I know he will. He always did know just the right thing ought to be done. [*With weary vexation*] It's a shame for him to come home and have to start in with things in such a topsy-turvy.

MRS. MAYO. Andy'll manage.

RUTH [*Sighing*]. I s'pose it isn't Rob's fault things go wrong with him.

MRS. ATKINS [*Scornfully*]. Hump! [*She fans herself nervously*] Land o' Goshen, but it's bakin' in here! Let's go out in under the trees in back where there's a breath of fresh air. Come, Kate. [MRS. MAYO *gets up obediently and starts to wheel the invalid's chair toward the screen door*] You better come too, Ruth. It'll do you good. Learn him a lesson and let him get his own dinner. Don't be such a fool.

RUTH [*Going and holding the screen door open for them—listlessly*]. He wouldn't mind. He doesn't eat much. But I can't go anyway. I've got to put baby to bed.

MRS. ATKINS. Let's go, Kate. I'm boilin' in here. [MRS. MAYO *wheels her out and off left.* RUTH *comes back and sits down in her chair*]

RUTH [*Mechanically*]. Come and let me take off your shoes and stockings, Mary, that's a good girl. You've got to take your nap now. [*The child continues to play as if she hadn't heard, absorbed in her doll. An eager expression comes over* RUTH's *tired face. She glances toward the door furtively —then gets up and goes to the desk. Her movements indicate a guilty fear of discovery. She takes a letter from a pigeon-hole and retreats swiftly to her chair with it. She opens the envelope and reads the letter with great interest, a flush of excitement coming to her cheeks.* ROBERT *walks up the path and opens the screen door quietly and comes into the room. He, too, has aged. His shoulders are stooped as if under too great a burden. His eyes are dull and lifeless, his face burned by the sun and unshaven for days. Streaks of sweat have smudged the layer of dust on his cheeks. His lips drawn down at the corners, give him a hopeless, resigned expression. The three years have accentuated the weakness of his mouth and chin. He is dressed in overalls, laced boots, and a flannel shirt open at the neck*]

ROBERT [*Throwing his hat over on the sofa—with a great sigh of exhaustion*]. Phew! The sun's hot today! [RUTH *is startled. At first she makes an instinctive motion as if to hide the letter in her bosom. She immediately thinks better of this and sits with the letter in her hands looking at him with defiant eyes. He bends down and kisses her*]

RUTH [*Feeling of her cheek—irritably*]. Why don't you shave? You look awful.

ROBERT [*Indifferently*]. I forgot—and it's too much trouble this weather.

MARY [*Throwing aside her doll, runs to him with a happy cry*]. Dada! Dada!

ROBERT [*Swinging her up above his head—lovingly*]. And how's this little girl of mine this hot day, eh?

MARY [*Screeching happily*]. Dada! Dada!

RUTH [*In annoyance*]. Don't do that to her! You know it's time for her nap and you'll get her all waked up; then I'll be the one that'll have to sit beside her till she falls asleep.

ROBERT [*Sitting down in the chair on the left of table and cuddling* MARY *on his lap*]. You needn't bother. I'll put her to bed.

RUTH [*Shortly*]. You've got to get back to your work, I s'pose.

ROBERT [*With a sigh*]. Yes, I was forgetting. [*He glances at the open letter on* RUTH's *lap*] Reading Andy's letter again? I should think you'd know it by heart by this time.

RUTH [*Coloring as if she's been accused of something—defiantly*]. I've got a right to read it, haven't I? He says it's meant for all of us.

ROBERT [*With a trace of irritation*]. Right? Don't be so silly. There's no question of right. I was only saying that you must know all that's in it after so many readings.

RUTH. Well, I don't. [*She puts the letter on the table and gets wearily to her feet*] I s'pose you'll be wanting your dinner now.

ROBERT [*Listlessly*]. I don't care. I'm not hungry.

RUTH. And here I been keeping it hot for you!

ROBERT [*Irritably*]. Oh, all right then. Bring it in and I'll try to eat.

RUTH. I've got to get her to bed first. [*She goes to lift* MARY *off his lap*. Come, dear. It's after time and you can hardly keep your eyes open now.

MARY [*Crying*]. No, no! [*Appealing to her father*] Dada! No!

RUTH [*Accusingly to* ROBERT]. There! Now see what you've done! I told you not to—

ROBERT [*Shortly*]. Let her alone, then. She's all right where she is. She'll fall asleep on my lap in a minute if you'll stop bothering her.

RUTH [*Hotly*]. She'll not do any such thing! She's got to learn to mind me! [*Shaking her finger at* MARY] You naughty child! Will you come with Mama when she tells you for your own good?

MARY [*Clinging to her father*]. No, Dada!

RUTH [*Losing her temper*]. A good spanking's what you need, my young lady—and you'll get one from me if you don't mind better, d'you hear? [MARY *starts to whimper frightenedly*]

ROBERT [*With sudden anger*]. Leave her alone! How often have I told you not to threaten her with whipping? I won't have it. [*Soothing the wailing* MARY] There! There, little girl! Baby mustn't cry. Dada won't like you if you do. Dada'll hold you and you must promise to go to sleep like a good little girl. Will you when Dada asks you?

MARY [*Cuddling up to him*]. Yes, Dada.

RUTH [*Looking at them, her pale face set and drawn*]. A fine one you are to be telling folks how to do things! [*She bites her lips. Husband and wife look into each other's eyes with something akin to hatred in their expression; then* RUTH *turns away with a shrug of affected indifference*] All right, take care of her then, if you think it's so easy. [*She walks away into the kitchen*]

ROBERT [*Smoothing* MARY's *hair—tenderly*]. We'll show Mama you're a good little girl, won't we?

MARY [*Crooning drowsily*]. Dada, Dada.

ROBERT. Let's see: Does your mother take off your shoes and stockings before your nap?

MARY [*Nodding with half-shut eyes*]. Yes, Dada.

ROBERT [*Taking off her shoes and stockings*]. We'll show Mama we know how to do those things, won't we? There's one old shoe off—and there's the other old shoe—and here's one old stocking—and there's the other old stocking. There we are, all nice and cool and comfy. [*He bends down and kisses her*] And now will you promise to go right to sleep if Dada takes you to bed? [MARY *nods sleepily*] That's the good little girl.

> [*He gathers her up in his arms carefully and carries her into the bedroom. His voice can be heard faintly as he lulls the child to sleep.* RUTH *comes out of the kitchen and gets the plate from the table. She hears the voice from the room and tiptoes to the door to look in. Then she starts for the kitchen but stands for a moment thinking, a look of ill-concealed jealousy on her face. At a noise from inside she hurriedly disappears into the kitchen. A moment later* ROBERT *re-enters. He comes forward and picks up the shoes and stockings which he shoves carelessly under the table. Then, seeing no one about, he goes to the sideboard and selects a book. Coming back to his chair, he sits down and immediately becomes absorbed in reading.* RUTH *returns from the kitchen bringing his plate heaped with food, and a cup of tea. She sets those before him and sits down in her former place.* ROBERT *continues to read, oblivious to the food on the table*]

RUTH [*After watching him irritably for a moment*]. For heaven's sakes, put down that old book! Don't you see your dinner's getting cold?

ROBERT [*Closing his book*]. Excuse me, Ruth. I didn't notice. [*He picks up his knife and fork and begins to eat gingerly, without appetite*]

RUTH. I should think you might have some feeling for me, Rob, and not always be late for meals. If you think it's fun sweltering in that oven of a kitchen to keep things warm for you, you're mistaken.

ROBERT. I'm sorry, Ruth, really I am. Something crops up every day to delay me. I mean to be here on time.

RUTH [*With a sigh*]. Mean-tos don't count.

ROBERT [*With a conciliating smile*]. Then punish me, Ruth. Let the food get cold and don't bother about me.

RUTH. I'd have to wait the same to wash up after you.

ROBERT. But I can wash up.

RUTH. A nice mess there'd be then!

ROBERT [*With an attempt at lightness*]. The food is lucky to be able to get cold this weather. [*As* RUTH *doesn't answer or smile he opens his book and resumes his reading, forcing himself to take a mouthful of food every now and then.* RUTH *stares at him in annoyance*]

RUTH. And besides, you've got your own work that's got to be done.

ROBERT [*Absent-mindedly, without taking his eyes from the book*]. Yes, of course.

RUTH [*Spitefully*]. Work you'll never get done by reading books all the time.

ROBERT [*Shutting the book with a snap*]. Why do you persist in nagging at me for getting pleasure out of reading? Is it because— [*He checks himself abruptly*]

RUTH [*Coloring*]. Because I'm too stupid to understand them, I s'pose you were going to say.

ROBERT [*Shamefacedly*]. No—no. [*In exasperation*] Why do you goad me into saying things I don't mean? Haven't I got my share of troubles trying to work this cursed farm without you adding to them? You know how hard I've tried to keep things going in spite of bad luck—

RUTH [*Scornfully*]. Bad luck!

ROBERT. And my own very apparent unfitness for the job, I was going to add; but you can't deny there's been bad luck to it, too. Why don't you take things into consideration? Why can't we pull together? We used to. I know it's hard on you also. Then why can't we help each other instead of hindering?

RUTH [*Sullenly*]. I do the best I know how.

ROBERT [*Gets up and puts his hand on her shoulder*]. I know you do. But let's both of us try to do better. We can both improve. Say a word of encouragement once in a while when things go wrong, even if it is my fault. You know the odds I've been up against since Pa died. I'm not a farmer. I've never claimed to be one. But there's nothing else I can do under the circumstances, and I've got to pull things through somehow. With your help, I can do it. With you against me— [*He shrugs his shoulders. There is a pause. Then he bends down and kisses her hair—with an attempt at cheerfulness*] So you promise that; and I'll promise to be here when the clock strikes—and anything else you tell me to. Is it a bargain?

RUTH [*Dully*]. I s'pose so. [*They are interrupted by the sound of a loud knock at the kitchen door*] There's someone at the kitchen door. [*She hurries out. A moment later she reappears*] It's Ben.

ROBERT [*Frowning*]. What's the trouble now, I wonder? [*In a loud voice*] Come on in here, Ben. [BEN *slouches in from the kitchen. He is a hulking, awkward young fellow with a heavy, stupid face and shifty, cunning eyes. He is dressed in overalls, boots, etc., and wears a broad-brimmed hat of coarse straw pushed back on his head*] Well, Ben, what's the matter?

BEN [*Drawlingly*]. The mowin' machine's bust.

ROBERT. Why, that can't be. The man fixed it only last week.

BEN. It's bust just the same.

ROBERT. And can't you fix it?

BEN. No. Don't know what's the matter with the goll-darned thing. 'Twon't work, anyhow.

ROBERT [*Getting up and going for his hat*]. Wait a minute and I'll go look it over. There can't be much the matter with it.

BEN [*Impudently*]. Don't make no diff'rence t' me whether there be or not. I'm quittin'.

ROBERT [*Anxiously*]. You don't mean you're throwing up your job here?

BEN. That's what! My month's up today and I want what's owin' t' me.

ROBERT. But why are you quitting now, Ben, when you know I've so much work on hand? I'll have a hard time getting another man at such short notice.

BEN. That's for you to figger. I'm quittin'.

ROBERT. But what's your reason? You haven't any complaint to make about the way you've been treated, have you?

BEN. No. 'Tain't that. [*Shaking his finger*] Look-a-here. I'm sick o' being made fun at, that's what; an' I got a job up to Timms' place; an' I'm quittin' here.

ROBERT. Being made fun of? I don't understand you. Who's making fun of you?

BEN. They all do. When I drive down with the milk in the mornin' they all laughs and jokes at me—that boy up to Harris' and the new feller up to Slocum's, and Bill Evans down to Meade's, and all the rest on 'em.

ROBERT. That's a queer reason for leaving me flat. Won't they laugh at you just the same when you're working for Timms?

BEN. They wouldn't dare to. Timms is the best farm hereabouts. They was laughin' at me for workin' for *you*, that's what! "How're things up to the Mayo place?" they hollers every mornin'. "What's Robert doin' now—pasturin' the cattle in the cornlot? Is he seasonin' his hay with rain this year, same as last?" they shouts. "Or is he inventin' some 'lectrical milkin' engine to fool them dry cows o' his into givin' hard cider?" [*Very much ruffled*]

That's like they talks; and I ain't goin' to put up with it no longer. Everyone's always knowed me as a first-class hand hereabouts, and I ain't wantin'
'em to get no different notion. So I'm quittin' you. And I wants what's
comin' to me.

ROBERT [*Coldly*]. Oh, if that's the case, you can go to the devil. You'll get
your money tomorrow when I get back from town—not before!

BEN [*Turning to doorway to kitchen*]. That suits me. [*As he goes out
he speaks back over his shoulder*] And see that I do get it, or there'll be
trouble. [*He disappears and the slamming of the kitchen door is heard*]

ROBERT [*As* RUTH *comes from where she has been standing by the doorway
and sits down dejectedly in her old place*]. The stupid damn fool! And
now what about the haying? That's an example of what I'm up against.
No one can say I'm responsible for that.

RUTH. He wouldn't dare act that way with anyone else! [*Spitefully, with
a glance at* ANDREW's *letter on the table*] It's lucky Andy's coming back.

ROBERT [*Without resentment*]. Yes, Andy'll see the right thing to do in a
jiffy. [*With an affectionate smile*] I wonder if the old chump's changed
much? He doesn't seem to from his letters, does he? [*Shaking his head*]
But just the same I doubt if he'll want to settle down to a humdrum farm
life, after all he's been through.

RUTH [*Resentfully*]. Andy's not like you. He likes the farm.

ROBERT [*Immersed in his own thoughts—enthusiastically*]. Gad, the things
he's seen and experienced! Think of the places he's been! All the wonderful
far places I used to dream about! God, how I envy him! What a trip!
[*He springs to his feet and instinctively goes to the window and stares out
at the horizon*]

RUTH [*Bitterly*]. I s'pose you're sorry now you didn't go?

ROBERT [*Too occupied with his own thoughts to hear her—vindictively*].
Oh, those cursed hills out there that I used to think promised me so much!
How I've grown to hate the sight of them! They're like the walls of a
narrow prison yard shutting me in from all the freedom and wonder of life!
[*He turns back to the room with a gesture of loathing*] Sometimes I think
if it wasn't for you, Ruth, and— [*His voice softening*] —little Mary, I'd chuck
everything up and walk down the road with just one desire in my heart—
to put the whole rim of the world between me and those hills, and be able
to breathe freely once more! [*He sinks down into his chair and smiles with
bitter self-scorn*] There I go dreaming again—my old fool dreams.

RUTH [*In a low, repressed voice—her eyes smoldering*]. You're not the
only one!

ROBERT [*Buried in his own thoughts—bitterly*]. And Andy, who's had the
chance—what has he got out of it? His letters read like the diary of a—of a
farmer! "We're in Singapore now. It's a dirty hole of a place and hotter
than hell. Two of the crew are down with fever and we're short-handed on
the work. I'll be damn glad when we sail again, although tacking back and

forth in these blistering seas is a rotten job too!" [*Scornfully*] That's about the way he summed up his impressions of the East.

RUTH [*Her repressed voice trembling*]. You needn't make fun of Andy.

ROBERT. When I think—but what's the use? You know I wasn't making fun of Andy personally, but his attitude toward things is—

RUTH. [*Her eyes flashing—bursting into uncontrollable rage*]. You was too making fun of him! And I ain't going to stand for it! You ought to be ashamed of yourself! [ROBERT *stares at her in amazement. She continues furiously*] A fine one to talk about anyone else—after the way you've ruined everything with your lazy loafing!—and the stupid way you do things!

ROBERT [*Angrily*]. Stop that kind of talk, do you hear?

RUTH. You findin' fault—with your own brother who's ten times the man you ever was or ever will be! You're jealous, that's what! Jealous because he's made a man of himself, while you're nothing but a—but a— [*She stutters incoherently, overcome by rage*]

ROBERT. Ruth! Ruth! You'll be sorry for talking like that.

RUTH. I won't! I won't never be sorry! I'm only saying what I've been thinking for years.

ROBERT [*Aghast*]. Ruth! You can't mean that!

RUTH. What do you think—living with a man like you—having to suffer all the time because you've never been man enough to work and do things like other people. But no! You never own up to that. You think you're so much better than other folks, with your college education, where you never learned a thing, and always reading your stupid books instead of working. I s'pose you think I ought to be *proud* to be your wife—a poor, ignorant thing like me! [*Fiercely*] But I'm not. I hate it! I hate the sight of you. Oh, if I'd only known! If I hadn't been such a fool to listen to your cheap, silly, poetry talk that you learned out of books! If I could have seen how you were in your true self—like you are now—I'd have killed myself before I'd have married you! I was sorry for it before we'd been together a month. I knew what you were really like—when it was too late.

ROBERT [*His voice raised loudly*]. And now—I'm finding out what you're really like—what a—a creature I've been living with. [*With a harsh laugh*] God! It wasn't that I haven't guessed how mean and small you are—but I've kept on telling myself that I must be wrong—like a fool!—like a damned fool!

RUTH. You were saying you'd go out on the road if it wasn't for me. Well, you can go, and the sooner the better! I don't care! I'll be glad to get rid of you! The farm'll be better off too. There's been a curse on it ever since you took hold. So go! Go and be a tramp like you've always wanted. It's all you're good for. I can get along without you, don't you worry. [*Exulting fiercely*] Andy's coming back, don't forget that! He'll attend to things like they should be. He'll show what a man can do! I don't need you. Andy's coming!

ROBERT [*They are both standing.* ROBERT *grabs her by the shoulders and glares into her eyes*]. What do you mean? [*He shakes her violently*] What are you thinking of? What's in your evil mind, you—you— [*His voice is a harsh shout*]

RUTH [*In a defiant scream*]. Yes I do mean it! I'd say it if you was to kill me! I do love Andy. I do! I do! I always loved him. [*Exultantly*] And he loves me! He loves me! I know he does. He always did! And you know he did, too! So go! Go if you want to!

ROBERT [*Throwing her away from him. She staggers back against the table —thickly*] You—you slut!

[*He stands glaring at her as she leans back, supporting herself by the table, gasping for breath. A loud frightened whimper sounds from the awakened child in the bedroom. It continues. The man and woman stand looking at one another in horror, the extent of their terrible quarrel brought home to them. A pause. The noise of a horse and carriage comes from the road before the house. The two, suddenly struck by the same premonition, listen to it breathlessly, as to a sound heard in a dream. It stops. They hear* ANDY'S *voice from the road shouting a long hail—"Ahoy there!"*]

RUTH [*With a strangled cry of joy*]. Andy! Andy! [*She rushes and grabs the knob of the screen door, about to fling it open*]

ROBERT [*In a voice of command that forces obedience*]. Stop! [*He goes to the door and gently pushes the trembling* RUTH *away from it. The child's crying rises to a louder pitch*] I'll meet Andy. You better go in to Mary, Ruth. [*She looks at him defiantly for a moment, but there is something in his eyes that makes her turn and walk slowly into the bedroom*]

ANDY'S VOICE [*In a louder shout*]. Ahoy there, Rob!

ROBERT [*In an answering shout of forced cheeriness*]. Hello, Andy! [*He opens the door and walks out as*

The Curtain Falls.]

ACT TWO: SCENE TWO

THE *top of a hill on the farm. It is about eleven o'clock the next morning. The day is hot and cloudless. In the distance the sea can be seen. The top of the hill slopes downward slightly toward the left. A big boulder stands in the center toward the rear. Further right, a large oak tree. The faint trace of a path leading upward to it from the left foreground can be detected through the bleached, sun-scorched grass.*

ROBERT *is discovered sitting on the boulder, his chin resting on his hands, staring out toward the horizon seaward. His face is pale and haggard, his expression one of utter despondency.* MARY *is sitting on the grass near him in the shade, playing with her doll, singing happily to herself. Presently she casts a curious glance at her father, and, propping her doll up against the tree, comes over and clambers to his side.*

MARY [*Pulling at his hand—solicitously*]. Dada sick?

ROBERT [*Looking at her with a forced smile*]. No, dear.· Why?

MARY. Play wif Mary.

ROBERT [*Gently*]. No, dear, not today. Dada doesn't feel like playing today.

MARY [*Protestingly*]. Yes, Dada!

ROBERT. No, dear. Dada does feel sick—a little. He's got a bad headache.

MARY. Mary see. [*He bends his head. She pats his hair*] Bad head.

ROBERT [*Kissing her—with a smile*]. There! It's better now, dear, thank you. [*She cuddles up close against him. There is a pause during which each of them looks out seaward. Finally* ROBERT *turns to her tenderly*]. Would you like Dada to go away?—far, far away?

MARY [*Tearfully*]. No! No! No, Dada, no!

ROBERT. Don't you like Uncle Andy—the man that came yesterday—not the old man with the white mustache—the other?

MARY. Mary loves Dada.

ROBERT [*With fierce determination*]. He won't go away, baby. He was only joking. He couldn't leave his little Mary. [*He presses the child in his arms*]

MARY [*With an exclamation of pain*]. Oh! Hurt!

ROBERT. I'm sorry, little girl. [*He lifts her down to the grass*] Go play with Dolly, that's a good girl; and be careful to keep in the shade. [*She reluctantly leaves him and takes up her doll again. A moment later she points down the hill to the left*]

MARY. Mans, Dada.

ROBERT [*Looking that way*]. It's your Uncle Andy.

[*A moment later* ANDREW *comes up from the left, whistling cheerfully. He has changed but little in appearance, except for the fact that his face has been deeply bronzed by his years in the tropics; but there is a decided change in his manner. The old easy-going good-nature seems to have been partly lost in a breezy, business-like briskness of voice and gesture. There is an authoritative note in his speech as though he were accustomed to give orders and have them obeyed as a matter of course. He is dressed in the simple blue uniform and cap of a merchant ship's officer*]

ANDREW. Here you are, eh?

ROBERT. Hello, Andy.

ANDREW [*Going over to* MARY]. And who's this young lady I find you all alone with, eh? Who's this pretty young lady? [*He tickles the laughing, squirming* MARY, *then lifts her up at arm's length over his head*] Upsy—daisy! [*He sets her down on the ground again*] And there you are! [*He walks over and sits down on the boulder beside* ROBERT *who moves to one side to make room for him*] Ruth told me I'd probably find you up top-side here; but I'd have guessed it, anyway. [*He digs his brother in the ribs affectionately*] Still up to your old tricks, you old beggar! I can remember how you used to come up here to mope and dream in the old days.

ROBERT [*With a smile*]. I come up here now because it's the coolest place on the farm. I've given up dreaming.

ANDREW [*Grinning*]. I don't believe it. You can't have changed that much. [*After a pause—with boyish enthusiasm*] Say, it sure brings back old times to be up here with you having a chin all by our lonesomes again. I feel great being back home.

ROBERT. It's great for us to have you back.

ANDREW [*After a pause—meaningly*]. I've been looking over the old place with Ruth. Things don't seem to be—

ROBERT [*His face flushing—interrupts his brother shortly*]. Never mind the damn farm! Let's talk about something interesting. This is the first chance I've had to have a word with you alone. Tell me about your trip.

ANDREW. Why, I thought I told you everything in my letters.

ROBERT [*Smiling*]. Your letters were—sketchy, to say the least.

ANDREW. Oh, I know I'm no author. You needn't be afraid of hurting my feelings. I'd rather go through a typhoon again than write a letter.

ROBERT [*With eager interest*]. Then you were through a typhoon?

ANDREW. Yes—in the China sea. Had to run before it under bare poles for two days. I thought we were bound down for Davy Jones, sure. Never dreamed waves could get so big or the wind blow so hard. If it hadn't been for Uncle Dick being such a good skipper we'd have gone to the sharks, all of us. As it was we came out minus a main top-mast and had to beat back to Hong-Kong for repairs. But I must have written you all this.

ROBERT. You never mentioned it.

ANDREW. Well, there was so much dirty work getting things ship-shape again I must have forgotten about it.

ROBERT [*Looking at* ANDREW—*marveling*]. Forget a typhoon? [*With a trace of scorn*] You're a strange combination, Andy. And is what you've told me all you remember about it?

ANDREW. Oh, I could give you your bellyful of details if I wanted to turn loose on you. It was all-wool-and-a-yard-wide-Hell, I'll tell you. You ought to have been there. I remember thinking about you at the worst of it, and saying to myself: "This'd cure Rob of them ideas of his about the beautiful sea, if he could see it." And it would have too, you bet! [*He nods emphatically*]

ROBERT [*Dryly*]. The sea doesn't seem to have impressed you very favorably.

ANDREW. I should say it didn't! I'll never set foot on a ship again if I can help it—except to carry me some place I can't get to by train.

ROBERT. But you studied to become an officer!

ANDREW. Had to do something or I'd gone mad. The days were like years. [*He laughs*] And as for the East you used to rave about—well, you ought to see it, and *smell* it! One walk down one of their filthy narrow streets with the tropic sun beating on it would sicken you for life with the "wonder and mystery" you used to dream of.

ROBERT [*Shrinking from his brother with a glance of aversion*]. So all you found in the East was a stench?

ANDREW. *A* stench! Ten thousand of them!

ROBERT. But you did like some of the places, judging from your letters— Sydney, Buenos Aires—

ANDREW. Yes, Sydney's a good town. [*Enthusiastically*] But Buenos Aires —there's the place for you. Argentine's a country where a fellow has a chance to make good. You're right I like it. And I'll tell you, Rob, that's right where I'm going just as soon as I've seen you folks a while and can get a ship. I can get a berth as second officer, and I'll jump the ship when I get there. I'll need every cent of the wages Uncle's paid me to get a start at something in B. A.

ROBERT [*Staring at his brother—slowly*]. So you're not going to stay on the farm?

ANDREW. Why sure not! Did you think I was? There wouldn't be any sense. One of us is enough to run this little place.

ROBERT. I suppose it does seem small to you now.

ANDREW [*Not noticing the sarcasm in* ROBERT's *tone*]. You've no idea, Rob, what a splendid place Argentine is. I had a letter from a marine insurance chap that I'd made friends with in Hong-Kong to his brother, who's in the grain business in Buenos Aires. He took quite a fancy to me, and what's more important, he offered me a job if I'd come back there. I'd have taken it on the spot, only I couldn't leave Uncle Dick in the lurch, and I'd promised you folks to come home. But I'm going back there, you bet, and then you watch me get on! [*He slaps* ROBERT *on the back*] But don't you think it's a big chance, Rob?

ROBERT. It's fine—for you, Andy.

ANDREW. We call this a farm—but you ought to hear about the farms down there—ten square miles where we've got an acre. It's a new country where big things are opening up—and I want to get in on something big before I die. I'm no fool when it comes to farming, and I know something about grain. I've been reading up a lot on it, too, lately. [*He notices* ROBERT's *absent minded expression and laughs*] Wake up, you old poetry book worm, you! I know my talking about business makes you want to choke me, doesn't it?

ROBERT [*With an embarrassed smile*]. No, Andy, I—I just happened to think of something else. [*Frowning*] There've been lots of times lately that I've wished I had some of your faculty for business.

ANDREW [*Soberly*]. There's something I want to talk about, Rob,—the farm. You don't mind, do you?

ROBERT. No.

ANDREW. I walked over it this morning with Ruth—and she told me about things— [*Evasively*] I could see the place had run down; but you mustn't blame yourself. When luck's against anyone—

ROBERT. Don't Andy! It *is* my fault. You know it as well as I do. The best I've ever done was to make ends meet.

ANDREW [*After a pause*]. I've got over a thousand saved, and you can have that.

ROBERT [*Firmly*]. No. You need that for your start in Buenos Aires.

ANDREW. I don't. I can—

ROBERT [*Determinedly*]. No, Andy! Once and for all, no! I won't hear of it!

ANDREW [*Protestingly*]. You obstinate old son of a gun!

ROBERT. Oh, everything'll be on a sound footing after harvest. Don't worry about it.

ANDREW [*Doubtfully*]. Maybe. [*After a pause*] It's too bad Pa couldn't have lived to see things through. [*With feeling*] It cut me up a lot—hearing he was dead. He never—softened up, did he—about me, I mean?

ROBERT. He never understood, that's a kinder way of putting it. He does now.

ANDREW [*After a pause*]. You've forgotten all about what—caused me to go, haven't you, Rob? [ROBERT *nods but keeps his face averted*] I was a slushier damn fool in those days than you were. But it was an act of Providence I did go. It opened my eyes to how I'd been fooling myself. Why, I'd forgotten all about—that—before I'd been at sea six months.

ROBERT [*Turns and looks into* ANDREW's *eyes searchingly*]. You're speaking of—Ruth?

ANDREW [*Confused*]. Yes. I didn't want you to get false notions in your head, or I wouldn't say anything. [*Looking* ROBERT *squarely in the eyes*] I'm telling you the truth when I say I'd forgotten long ago. It don't sound well for me, getting over things so easy, but I guess it never really amounted to more than a kid idea I was letting rule me. I'm certain now I never was in love—I was getting fun out of thinking I was—and being a hero to myself. [*He heaves a great sigh of relief*] There! Gosh, I'm glad that's off my chest. I've been feeling sort of awkward ever since I've been home, thinking of what you two might think. [*A trace of appeal in his voice*] You've got it all straight now, haven't you, Rob?

ROBERT [*In a low voice*]. Yes, Andy.

ANDREW. And I'll tell Ruth, too, if I can get up the nerve. She must feel kind of funny having me round—after what used to be—and not knowing how I feel about it.

ROBERT [*Slowly*]. Perhaps—for her sake—you'd better not tell her.

ANDREW. For her sake? Oh, you mean she wouldn't want to be reminded of my foolishness? Still, I think it'd be worse if—

ROBERT [*Breaking out—in an agonized voice*]. Do as you please, Andy;

but for God's sake, let's not talk about it! [*There is a pause.* ANDREW *stares at* ROBERT *in hurt stupefaction.* ROBERT *continues after a moment in a voice which he vainly attempts to keep calm*] Excuse me, Andy. This rotten headache has my nerves shot to pieces.

ANDREW [*Mumbling*]. It's all right, Rob—long as you're not sore at me.

ROBERT. Where did Uncle Dick disappear to this morning?

ANDREW. He went down to the port to see to things on the *Sunda*. He said he didn't know exactly when he'd be back. I'll have to go down and tend to the ship when he comes. That's why I dressed up in these togs.

MARY [*Pointing down the hill to the left*]. See! Mama! Mama! [*She struggles to her feet.* RUTH *appears at left. She is dressed in white, shows she has been fixing up. She looks pretty, flushed and full of life*]

MARY [*Running to her mother*]. Mama!

RUTH [*Kissing her*]. Hello, dear! [*She walks toward the rock and addresses* ROBERT *coldly*] Jake wants to see you about something. He finished working where he was. He's waiting for you at the road.

ROBERT [*Getting up—wearily*]. I'll go down right away. [*As he looks at* RUTH, *noting her changed appearance, his face darkens with pain*]

RUTH. And take Mary with you, please. [*To* MARY] Go with Dada, that's a good girl. Grandma has your dinner most ready for you.

ROBERT [*Shortly*]. Come, Mary!

MARY [*Taking his hand and dancing happily beside him*]. Dada! Dada! [*They go down the hill to the left.* RUTH *looks after them for a moment, frowning—then turns to* ANDY *with a smile*] I'm going to sit down. Come on, Andy. It'll be like old times. [*She jumps lightly to the top of the rock and sits down*] It's so fine and cool up here after the house.

ANDREW [*Half-sitting on the side of the boulder*]. Yes. It's great.

RUTH. I've taken a holiday in honor of your arrival. [*Laughing excitedly*] I feel so free I'd like to have wings and fly over the sea. You're a man. You can't know how awful and stupid it is—cooking and washing dishes all the time.

ANDREW [*Making a wry face*]. I can guess.

RUTH. Besides, your mother just insisted on getting your first dinner to home, she's that happy at having you back. You'd think I was planning to poison you the flurried way she shooed me out of the kitchen.

ANDREW. That's just like Ma, bless her!

RUTH. She's missed you terribly. We all have. And you can't deny the farm has, after what I showed you and told you when we was looking over the place this morning.

ANDREW [*With a frown*]. Things are run down, that's a fact! It's too darn hard on poor old Rob.

RUTH [*Scornfully*]. It's his own fault. He never takes any interest in things.

ANDREW [*Reprovingly*]. You can't blame him. He wasn't born for it; but I know he's done his best for your sake and the old folks and the little girl.

RUTH [*Indifferently*]. Yes, I suppose he has. [*Gayly*] But thank the Lord, all those days are over now. The "hard luck" Rob's always blaming won't last long when you take hold, Andy. All the farm's ever needed was someone with the knack of looking ahead and preparing for what's going to happen.

ANDREW. Yes, Rob hasn't got that. He's frank to own up to that himself. I'm going to try and hire a good man for him—an experienced farmer—to work the place on a salary and percentage. That'll take it off of Rob's hands, and he needn't be worrying himself to death any more. He looks all worn out, Ruth. He ought to be careful.

RUTH [*Absent-mindedly*]. Yes, I s'pose. [*Her mind is filled with premonitions by the first part of this statement*] Why do you want to hire a man to oversee things? Seems as if now that you're back it wouldn't be needful.

ANDREW. Oh, of course I'll attend to everything while I'm here. I mean after I'm gone.

RUTH [*As if she couldn't believe her ears*]. Gone!

ANDREW. Yes. When I leave for the Argentine again.

RUTH [*Aghast*]. You're going away to sea!

ANDREW. Not to sea, no; I'm through with the sea for good as a job. I'm going down to Buenos Aires to get in the grain business.

RUTH. But—that's far off—isn't it?

ANDREW [*Easily*]. Six thousand miles more or less. It's quite a trip. [*With enthusiasm*] I've got a peach of a chance down there, Ruth. Ask Rob if I haven't. I've just been telling him all about it.

RUTH [*A flush of anger coming over her face*]. And didn't he try to stop you from going?

ANDREW [*In surprise*]. No, of course not. Why?

RUTH [*Slowly and vindictively*]. That's just like him—not to.

ANDREW [*Resentfully*]. Rob's too good a chum to try and stop me when he knows I'm set on a thing. And he could see just as soon's I told him what a good chance it was.

RUTH [*Dazedly*]. And you're bound on going?

ANDREW. Sure thing. Oh, I don't mean right off. I'll have to wait for a ship sailing there for quite a while, likely. Anyway, I want to stay to home and visit with you folks a spell before I go.

RUTH [*Dumbly*]. I s'pose. [*With sudden anguish*] Oh, Andy, you can't go! You can't. Why we've all thought—we've all been hoping and praying you was coming home to stay, to settle down on the farm and see to things. You mustn't go! Think of how your Ma'll take on if you go—and how the farm'll be ruined if you leave it to Rob to look after. You can see that.

ANDREW [*Frowning*]. Rob hasn't done so bad. When I get a man to direct things the farm'll be safe enough.

RUTH [*Insistently*]. But your Ma—think of her.

ANDREW. She's used to me being away. She won't object when she knows it's best for her and all of us for me to go. You ask Rob. In a couple of years down there I'll make my pile, see if I don't; and then I'll come back and settle down and turn this farm into the crackiest place in the whole state. In the meantime, I can help you both from down there. [*Earnestly*] I tell you, Ruth, I'm going to make good right from the minute I land, if working hard and a determination to get on can do it; and I *know* they can! [*Excitedly—in a rather boastful tone*] I tell you, I feel ripe for bigger things than settling down here. The trip did that for me, anyway. It showed me the world is a larger proposition than ever I thought it was in the old days. I couldn't be content any more stuck here like a fly in molasses. It all seems trifling, somehow. You ought to be able to understand what I feel.

RUTH [*Dully*]. Yes—I s'pose I ought. [*After a pause—a sudden suspicion forming in her mind*] What did Rob tell you—about me?

ANDREW. Tell? About you? Why, nothing.

RUTH [*Staring at him intensely*]. Are you telling me the truth, Andy Mayo? Didn't he say—I— [*She stops confusedly*]

ANDREW [*Surprised*]. No, he didn't mention you, I can remember. Why? What made you think he did?

RUTH [*Wringing her hands*]. Oh, I wish I could tell if you're lying or not!

ANDREW [*Indignantly*]. What're you talking about? I didn't used to lie to you, did I? And what in the name of God is there to lie for?

RUTH [*Still unconvinced*]. Are you sure—will you swear—it isn't the reason— [*She lowers her eyes and half turns away from him*] The same reason that made you go last time that's driving you away again? 'Cause if it is—I was going to say—you mustn't go—on that account. [*Her voice sinks to a tremulous, tender whisper as she finishes*]

ANDREW [*Confused—forces a laugh*]. Oh, is *that* what you're driving at? Well, you needn't worry about that no more— [*Soberly*] I don't blame you, Ruth, feeling embarrassed having me around again, after the way I played the dumb fool about going away last time.

RUTH [*Her hope crushed—with a gasp of pain*]. Oh, Andy!

ANDREW [*Misunderstanding*]. I know I oughtn't to talk about such foolishness to you. Still I figure it's better to get it out of my system so's we three can be together same's years ago, and not be worried thinking one of us might have the wrong notion.

RUTH. Andy! Please! Don't!

ANDREW. Let me finish now that I've started. It'll help clear things up. I don't want you to think once a fool always a fool, and be upset all the time I'm here on my fool account. I want you to believe I put all that silly nonsense back of me a long time ago—and now—it seems—well—as if you'd always been my sister, that's what, Ruth.

RUTH [*At the end of her endurance—laughing hysterically*]. For God's sake, Andy—won't you please stop talking! [*She again hides her face in her hands, her bowed shoulders trembling*]

ANDREW [*Ruefully*]. Seem's if I put my foot in it whenever I open my mouth today. Rob shut me up with almost the same words when I tried speaking to him about it.

RUTH [*Fiercely*]. You told him—what you've told me?

ANDREW [*Astounded*]. Why sure! Why not?

RUTH [*Shuddering*]. Oh, my God!

ANDREW [*Alarmed*]. Why? Shouldn't I have?

RUTH [*Hysterically*]. Oh, I don't care what you do! I don't care! Leave me alone! [ANDREW *gets up and walks down the hill to the left, embarrassed, hurt, and greatly puzzled by her behavior*]

ANDREW [*After a pause—pointing down the hill*]. Hello! Here they come back—and the Captain's with them. How'd he come to get back so soon, I wonder? That means I've got to hustle down to the port and get on board. Rob's got the baby with him. [*He comes back to the boulder.* RUTH *keeps her face averted from him*] Gosh, I never saw a father so tied up in a kid as Rob is! He just watches every move she makes. And I don't blame him. You both got a right to feel proud of her. She's surely a little winner. [*He glances at* RUTH *to see if this very obvious attempt to get back in her good graces is having any effect*] I can see the likeness to Rob standing out all over her, can't you? But there's no denying she's your young one, either. There's something about her eyes—

RUTH [*Piteously*]. Oh, Andy, I've a headache! I don't want to talk! Leave me alone, won't you please?

ANDREW [*Stands staring at her for a moment—then walks away saying in a hurt tone*]: Everybody hereabouts seems to be on edge today. I begin to feel as if I'm not wanted around.

[*He stands near the path, left, kicking at the grass with the toe of his shoe. A moment later* CAPTAIN DICK SCOTT *enters, followed by* ROBERT *carrying* MARY. *The* CAPTAIN *seems scarcely to have changed at all from the jovial, booming person he was three years before. He wears a uniform similar to* ANDREW's. *He is puffing and breathless from his climb and mops wildly at his perspiring countenance.* ROBERT *casts a quick glance at* ANDREW, *noticing the latter's discomfited look, and then turns his eyes on* RUTH *who, at their approach, has moved so her back is toward them, her chin resting on her hands as she stares out seaward*]

MARY. Mama! Mama!

[ROBERT *puts her down and she runs to her mother.* RUTH *turns and grabs her up in her arms with a sudden fierce tenderness, quickly turning away again from the others. During the following scene she keeps* MARY *in her arms*]

SCOTT [*Wheezily*]. Phew! I got great news for you, Andy. Let me get my wind first. Phew! God A'mighty, mountin' this damned hill is worser'n goin' aloft to the skys'l yard in a blow. I got to lay to a while. [*He sits down on the grass, mopping his face*]

ANDREW. I didn't look for you this soon, Uncle.

SCOTT. I didn't figger it, neither; but I run across a bit o' news down to the Seamen's Home made me 'bout ship and set all sail back here to find you.

ANDREW [*Eagerly*]. What is it, Uncle?

SCOTT. Passin' by the Home I thought I'd drop in an' let 'em know I'd be lackin' a mate next trip count o' your leavin'. Their man in charge o' the shippin' asked after you 'special curious. "Do you think he'd consider a berth as Second on a steamer, Captain?" he asks. I was goin' to say no when I thinks o' your wantin' to get back down south to the Plate agen; so I asks him: "What is she and where's she bound?" "She's the *El Paso,* a brand new tramp," he says, "and she's bound for Buenos Aires."

ANDREW [*His eyes lighting up—excitedly*]. Gosh, that is luck! When does she sail?

SCOTT. Tomorrow mornin'. I didn't know if you'd want to ship away agen so quick an' I told him so. "Tell him I'll hold the berth open for him until late this afternoon," he says. So there you be, an' you can make your own choice.

ANDREW. I'd like to take it. There may not be another ship for Buenos Aires with a vacancy in months. [*His eyes roving from* ROBERT *to* RUTH *and back again—uncertainly*] Still—damn it all—tomorrow morning *is* soon. I wish she wasn't leaving for a week or so. That'd give me a chance—it seems hard to go right away again when I've just got home. And yet it's a chance in a thousand— [*Appealing to* ROBERT] What do you think, Rob? What would you do?

ROBERT [*Forcing a smile*]. He who hesitates, you know. [*Frowning*] It's a piece of good luck thrown in your way—and—I think you owe it to yourself to jump at it. But don't ask me to decide for you.

RUTH [*Turning to look at* ANDREW—*in a tone of fierce resentment*]. Yes, go, Andy! [*She turns quickly away again. There is a moment of embarrassed silence*]

ANDREW [*Thoughtfully*]. Yes, I guess I will. It'll be the best thing for all of us in the end, don't you think so, Rob? [ROBERT *nods but remains silent*]

SCOTT [*Getting to his feet*]. Then's that's settled.

ANDREW [*Now that he has definitely made a decision his voice rings with hopeful strength and energy*]. Yes, I'll take the berth. The sooner I go the sooner I'll be back, that's a certainty; and I won't come back with empty hands next time. You bet I won't!

SCOTT. You ain't got so much time, Andy. To make sure you'd best leave here soon's you kin. I got to get right back aboard. You'd best come with me.

ANDREW. I'll go to the house and repack my bag right away.

ROBERT [*Quietly*]. You'll both be here for dinner, won't you?

ANDREW [*Worriedly*]. I don't know. Will there be time? What time is it now, I wonder?

ROBERT [*Reproachfully*]. Ma's been getting dinner especially for you, Andy.

ANDREW [*Flushing—shamefacedly*]. Hell! And I was forgetting! Of course I'll stay for dinner if I missed every damned ship in the world. [*He turns to the* CAPTAIN—*briskly*] Come on, Uncle. Walk down with me to the house and you can tell me more about this berth on the way. I've got to pack before dinner. [*He and the* CAPTAIN *start down to the left.* ANDREW *calls back over his shoulder*] You're coming soon, aren't you, Rob?

ROBERT. Yes. I'll be right down.

> [ANDREW *and the* CAPTAIN *leave.* RUTH *puts* MARY *on the ground and hides her face in her hands. Her shoulders shake as if she were sobbing.* ROBERT *stares at her with a grim, sombre expression.* MARY *walks backward toward* ROBERT, *her wondering eyes fixed on her mother*]

MARY [*Her voice vaguely frightened, taking her father's hand*]. Dada, Mama's cryin', Dada.

ROBERT [*Bending down and stroking her hair—in a voice he endeavors to keep from being harsh*]. No, she isn't, little girl. The sun hurts her eyes, that's all. Aren't you beginning to feel hungry, Mary?

MARY [*Decidedly*]. Yes, Dada.

ROBERT [*Meaningly*]. It must be your dinner time now.

RUTH [*In a muffled voice*]. I'm coming, Mary. [*She wipes her eyes quickly and, without looking at* ROBERT, *comes and takes* MARY'S *hand—in a dead voice*] Come on and I'll get your dinner for you.

> [*She walks out left, her eyes fixed on the ground, the skipping* MARY *tugging at her hand.* ROBERT *waits a moment for them to get ahead and then slowly follows as*

The Curtain Falls.]

ACT THREE: SCENE ONE

SAME *as Act Two, Scene One—The sitting room of the farm house about six o'clock in the morning of a day toward the end of October five years later. It is not yet dawn, but as the action progresses the darkness outside the windows gradually fades to gray.*

The room, seen by the light of the shadeless oil lamp with a smoky chimney which stands on the table, presents an appearance of decay, of dissolution. The curtains at the windows are torn and dirty and one of them is missing. The closed desk is gray with accumulated dust as if it had not been used in years. Blotches of dampness disfigure the wall paper. Threadbare trails, leading to the kitchen and outer doors, show in the faded carpet. The top of the coverless table is stained with the imprints of hot dishes and spilt food. The rung of one rocker has been clumsily mended with a piece of plain board. A brown coating of rust covers the unblacked stove. A pile of wood is stacked up carelessly against the wall by the stove.

The whole atmosphere of the room, contrasted with that of former years, is one of an habitual poverty too hopelessly resigned to be any longer ashamed or even conscious of itself.

At the rise of the curtain RUTH *is discovered sitting by the stove, with hands outstretched to the warmth as if the air in the room were damp and cold. A heavy shawl is wrapped about her shoulders, half-concealing her dress of deep mourning. She has aged horribly. Her pale, deeply lined face has the stony lack of expression of one to whom nothing more can ever happen, whose capacity for emotion has been exhausted. When she speaks her voice is without timbre, low and monotonous. The negligent disorder of her dress, the slovenly arrangement of her hair, now streaked with gray, her muddied shoes run down at the heel, give full evidence of the apathy in which she lives.*

Her mother is asleep in her wheel chair beside the stove toward the rear, wrapped up in a blanket.

There is a sound from the open bedroom door in the rear as if someone were getting out of bed. RUTH *turns in that direction with a look of dull annoyance. A moment later* ROBERT *appears in the doorway, leaning weakly against it for support. His hair is long and unkempt, his face and body emaciated. There are bright patches of crimson over his cheek bones and his eyes are burning with fever. He is dressed in corduroy pants, a flannel shirt, and wears worn carpet slippers on his bare feet.*

RUTH [*Dully*]. S-s-s-h! Ma's asleep.

ROBERT [*Speaking with an effort*]. I won't wake her. [*He walks weakly to a rocker by the side of the table and sinks down in it exhausted*]

RUTH [*Staring at the stove*]. You better come near the fire where it's warm.

ROBERT. No. I'm burning up now.

RUTH. That's the fever. You know the doctor told you not to get up and move round.

ROBERT [*Irritably*]. That old fossil! He doesn't know anything. Go to bed and stay there—that's his only prescription.

RUTH [*Indifferently*]. How are you feeling now?

ROBERT [*Buoyantly*]. Better! Much better than I've felt in ages. Really I'm fine now—only very weak. It's the turning point, I guess. From now on I'll pick up so quick I'll surprise you—and no thanks to that old fool of a country quack, either.

RUTH. He's always tended to us.

ROBERT. Always helped us to die, you mean! He "tended" to Pa and Ma and— [*His voice breaks*] and to—Mary.

RUTH [*Dully*] He did the best he knew, I 'pose. [*After a pause*] Well Andy's bringing a specialist with him when he comes. That ought to suit you.

ROBERT [*Bitterly*]. Is that why you're waiting up all night?

RUTH. Yes.

ROBERT. For Andy?

RUTH [*Without a trace of feeling*]. Somebody had got to. It's only right for someone to meet him after he's been gone five years.

ROBERT [*With bitter mockery*]. Five years! It's a long time.

RUTH. Yes.

ROBERT [*Meaningly*]. To *wait*!

RUTH [*Indifferently*]. It's past now.

ROBERT. Yes, it's past. [*After a pause*] Have you got his two telegrams with you? [RUTH *nods*] Let me see them, will you? My head was so full of fever when they came I couldn't make head or tail to them. [*Hastily*] But I'm feeling fine now. Let me read them again. [RUTH *takes them from the bosom of her dress and hands them to him*]

RUTH. Here. The first one's on top.

ROBERT [*Opening it*]. New York. "Just landed from steamer. Have important business to wind up here. Will be home as soon as deal is completed." [*He smiles bitterly*] Business first was always Andy's motto. [*He reads*] "Hope you are all well. Andy." [*He repeats ironically*] "Hope you are all well!"

RUTH [*Dully*]. He couldn't know you'd been took sick till I answered that and told him.

ROBERT [*Contritely*]. Of course he couldn't. I'm a fool. I'm touchy about nothing lately. Just what did you say in your reply?

RUTH [*Inconsequentially*]. I had to send it collect.

ROBERT [*Irritably*]. What did you say was the matter with me?

RUTH. I wrote you had lung trouble.

ROBERT [*Flying into a petty temper*]. You *are* a fool! How often have I explained to you that it's *pleurisy* is the matter with me. You can't seem to get it in your head that the pleura is outside the lungs, not in them!

RUTH [*Callously*]. I only wrote what Doctor Smith told me.

ROBERT [*Angrily*]. He's a damned ignoramus!

RUTH [*Dully*]. Makes no difference. I had to tell Andy something, didn't I?

ROBERT [*After a pause, opening the other telegram*]. He sent this last evening. Let's see. [*He reads*] "Leave for home on midnight train. Just received your wire. Am bringing specialist to see Rob. Will motor to farm from port." [*He calculates*] What time is it now?

RUTH. Round six, must be.

ROBERT. He ought to be here soon. I'm glad he's bringing a doctor who knows something. A specialist will tell you in a second that there's nothing the matter with my lungs.

RUTH [*Stolidly*]. You've been coughing an awful lot lately.

ROBERT [*Irritably*]. What nonsense! For God's sake, haven't you ever had a bad cold yourself? [RUTH *stares at the stove in silence*. ROBERT *fidgets in his chair. There is a pause. Finally* ROBERT's *eyes are fixed on the sleeping* MRS. ATKINS] Your mother is lucky to be able to sleep so soundly.

RUTH. Ma's tired. She's been sitting up with me most of the night.

ROBERT [*Mockingly*]. Is she waiting for Andy, too? [*There is a pause.* ROBERT *sighs*] I couldn't get to sleep to save my soul. I counted ten million sheep if I counted one. No use! I gave up trying finally and just lay there in the dark thinking. [*He pauses, then continues in a tone of tender sympathy*] I was thinking about you, Ruth—of how hard these last years must have been for you. [*Appealingly*] I'm sorry, Ruth.

RUTH [*In a dead voice*]. I don't know. They're past now. They were hard on all of us.

ROBERT. Yes; on all of us but Andy. [*With a flash of sick jealousy*] Andy's made a big success of himself—the kind he wanted. [*Mockingly*] And now he's coming home to let us admire his greatness. [*Frowning— irritably*] What am I talking about? My brain must be sick, too. [*After a pause*] Yes, these years have been terrible for both of us. [*His voice is lowered to a trembling whisper*] Especially the last eight months since Mary —died. [*He forces back a sob with a convulsive shudder—then breaks out in a passionate agony*] Our last hope of happiness! I could curse God from the bottom of my soul—if there was a God! [*He is racked by a violent fit of coughing and hurriedly puts his handkerchief to his lips*]

RUTH [*Without looking at him*]. Mary's better off—being dead.

ROBERT [*Gloomily*]. We'd all be better off for that matter. [*With a sudden exasperation*] You tell that mother of yours she's got to stop saying that Mary's death was due to a weak constitution inherited from me. [*On the verge of tears of weakness*] It's got to stop, I tell you!

RUTH [*Sharply*]. S-h-h! You'll wake her; and then she'll nag at me— not you.

ROBERT [*Coughs and lies back in his chair weakly—a pause*]. It's all because your mother's down on me for not begging Andy for help.

RUTH [*Resentfully*]. You might have. He's got plenty.

ROBERT. How can *you* of all people think of taking money from *him*?

RUTH [*Dully*]. I don't see the harm. He's your own brother.

ROBERT [*Shrugging his shoulders*]. What's the use of talking to you? Well, *I* couldn't. [*Proudly*] And I've managed to keep things going, thank God. You can't deny that without help I've succeeded in— [*He breaks off with a bitter laugh*] My God, what am I boasting of? Debts to this one and that, taxes, interest unpaid! I'm a fool! [*He lies back in his chair closing his eyes for a moment, then speaks in a low voice*] I'll be frank, Ruth. I've been an utter failure, and I've dragged you with me. I couldn't blame you in all justice—for hating me.

RUTH [*Without feeling*]. I don't hate you. It's been my fault too, I s'pose.

ROBERT. No. You couldn't help loving—Andy.

RUTH [*Dully*]. I don't love anyone.

ROBERT [*Waving her remark aside*]. You needn't deny it. It doesn't matter. [*After a pause—with a tender smile*] Do you know Ruth, what I've been dreaming back there in the dark? [*With a short laugh*] I was planning our future when I get well. [*He looks at her with appealing eyes as if afraid she will sneer at him. Her expression does not change. She stares at the stove. His voice takes on a note of eagerness]* After all, why shouldn't we have a future? We're young yet. If we can only shake off the curse of this farm! It's the farm that's ruined our lives, damn it! And now that Andy's coming back—I'm going to sink my foolish pride, Ruth! I'll borrow the money from him to give us a good start in the city. We'll go where people live instead of stagnating, and start all over again. *[Confidently]* I won't be the failure there that I've been here, Ruth. You won't need to be ashamed of me there. I'll prove to you the reading I've done can be put to some use. *[Vaguely]* I'll write, or something of that sort. I've always wanted to write. *[Pleadingly]* You'll want to do that, won't you, Ruth?

RUTH *[Dully]*. There's Ma.

ROBERT. She can come with us.

RUTH. She wouldn't.

ROBERT *[Angrily]*. So that's your answer! *[He trembles with violent passion. His voice is so strange that* RUTH *turns to look at him in alarm]* You're lying, Ruth! Your mother's just an excuse. You want to stay here. You think that because Andy's coming back that— *[He chokes and has an attack of coughing]*

RUTH *[Getting up—in a frightened voice]*. What's the matter? *[She goes to him]* I'll go with you, Rob. Stop that coughing for goodness' sake! It's awful bad for you. *[She soothes him in dull tones]* I'll go with you to the city—soon's you're well again. Honest I will, Rob, I promise! *[*ROB *lies back and closes his eyes. She stands looking down at him anxiously]* Do you feel better now?

ROBERT. Yes. *[*RUTH *goes back to her chair. After a pause he opens his eyes and sits up in his chair. His face is flushed and happy]* Then you *will* go, Ruth?

RUTH. Yes.

ROBERT *[Excitedly]*. We'll make a new start, Ruth—just you and I. Life owes us some happiness after what we've been through. *[Vehemently]* It must! Otherwise our suffering would be meaningless—and that is unthinkable.

RUTH *[Worried by his excitement]*. Yes, yes, of course, Bob, but you mustn't—

ROBERT. Oh, don't be afraid. I feel completely well, really I do—now that I can hope again. Oh, if you knew how glorious it feels to have something to look forward to! Can't you feel the thrill of it, too—the vision of a new life opening up after all the horrible years?

RUTH. Yes, yes, but do be—

ROBERT. Nonsense! I won't be careful. I'm getting back all my strength. *[He gets lightly to his feet]* See! I feel light as a feather. *[He walks to her chair and bends down to kiss her smilingly]* One kiss—the first in years, isn't it?—to greet the dawn of a new life together.

RUTH [*Submitting to his kiss—worriedly*]. Sit down, Rob, for goodness' sake!

ROBERT [*With tender obstinacy—stroking her hair*]. I won't sit down. You're silly to worry. [*He rests one hand on the back of her chair*] Listen. All our suffering has been a test through which we had to pass to prove ourselves worthy of a finer realization. [*Exultingly*] And we did pass through it! It hasn't broken us! And now the dream is to come true! Don't you see?

RUTH [*Looking at him with frightened eyes as if she thought he had gone mad*]. Yes, Rob, I see; but won't you go back to bed now and rest?

ROBERT. No. I'm going to see the sun rise. It's an augury of good fortune. [*He goes quickly to the window in the rear left, and pushing the curtains aside, stands looking out.* RUTH *springs to her feet and comes quickly to the table, left, where she remains watching* ROBERT *in a tense, expectant attitude. As he peers out his body seems gradually to sag, to grow limp and tired. His voice is mournful as he speaks*] No sun yet. It isn't time. All I can see is the black rim of the damned hills outlined against a creeping grayness. [*He turns around; letting the curtains fall back, stretching a hand out to the wall to support himself. His false strength of a moment has evaporated, leaving his face drawn and hollow-eyed. He makes a pitiful attempt to smile*] That's not a very happy augury, is it? But the sun'll come—soon. [*He sways weakly*]

RUTH [*Hurrying to his side and supporting him*]. Please go to bed, won't you, Rob? You don't want to be all wore out when the specialist comes, do you?

ROBERT [*Quickly*]. No. That's right. He mustn't think I'm sicker than I am. And I feel as if I could sleep now— [*Cheerfully*] —a good, sound, restful sleep.

RUTH [*Helping him to the bedroom door*]. That's what you need most. [*They go inside. A moment later she reappears calling back*] I'll shut this door so's you'll be quiet. [*She closes the door and goes quickly to her mother and shakes her by the shoulder*] Ma! Ma! Wake up!

MRS. ATKINS [*Coming out of her sleep with a start*]. Glory be! What's the matter with you?

RUTH. It was Rob. He's just been talking to me out here. I put him back to bed. [*Now that she is sure her mother is awake her fear passes and she relapses into dull indifference. She sits down in her chair and stares at the stove—dully*] He acted—funny; and his eyes looked so—so wild like.

MRS. ATKINS [*With asperity*]. And is that all you woke me out of a sound sleep for, and scared me near out of my wits?

RUTH. I was afraid. He talked so crazy. I couldn't quiet him. I didn't want to be alone with him that way. Lord knows what he might do.

MRS. ATKINS [*Scornfully*]. Humph! A help I'd be to you and me not able to move a step! Why didn't you run and get Jake?

RUTH [*Dully*]. Jake isn't here. He quit last night. He hasn't been paid in three months.

MRS. ATKINS [*Indignantly*]. I can't blame him. What decent person'd want to work on a place like this? [*With sudden exasperation*] Oh, I wish you'd never married that man!

RUTH [*Wearily*]. You oughtn't to talk about him now when he's sick in his bed.

MRS. ATKINS [*Working herself into a fit of rage*]. You know very well, Ruth Mayo, if it wasn't for me helpin' you on the sly out of my savin's, you'd both been in the poor house—and all 'count of his pigheaded pride in not lettin' Andy know the state thin's were in. A nice thin' for me to have to support him out of what I'd saved for my last days—and me an invalid with no one to look to!

RUTH. Andy'll pay you back, Ma. I can tell him so's Rob'll never know.

MRS. ATKINS [*With a snort*]. What'd Rob think you and him was livin' on, I'd like to know?

RUTH [*Dully*]. He didn't think about it, I s'pose. [*After a slight pause*] He said he'd made up his mind to ask Andy for help when he comes. [*As a clock in the kitchen strikes six*] Six o'clock. Andy ought to get here directly.

MRS. ATKINS. D'you think this special doctor'll do Rob any good?

RUTH [*Hopelessly*]. I don't know.

[*The two women remain silent for a time staring dejectedly at the stove*]

MRS. ATKINS [*Shivering irritably*]. For goodness' sake put some wood on that fire. I'm most freezin'!

RUTH [*Pointing to the door in the rear*]. Don't talk so loud. Let him sleep if he can. [*She gets wearily from the chair and puts a few pieces of wood in the stove*] This is the last of the wood. I don't know who'll cut more now that Jake's left. [*She sighs and walks to the window in the rear, left, pulls the curtains aside, and looks out*] It's getting gray out. [*She comes back to the stove*] Looks like it'd be a nice day. [*She stretches out her hands to warm them*] Must've been a heavy frost last night. We're paying for the spell of warm weather we've been having. [*The throbbing whine of a motor sounds from the distance outside*]

MRS. ATKINS [*Sharply*]. S-h-h! Listen! Ain't that an auto I hear?

RUTH [*Without interest*]. Yes. It's Andy, I s'pose.

MRS. ATKINS [*With nervous irritation*]. Don't sit there like a silly goose. Look at the state of this room! What'll this strange doctor think of us? Look at the lamp chimney all smoke! Gracious sakes, Ruth—

RUTH [*Indifferently*]. I've got a lamp all cleaned up in the kitchen.

MRS. ATKINS [*Peremptorily*]. Wheel me in there this minute. I don't want him to see me looking a sight. I'll lay down in the room the other side. You don't need me now and I'm dead for sleep.

[RUTH *wheels her mother off right. The noise of the motor grows louder and finally ceases as the car stops on the road before the farm-*

house. RUTH *returns from the kitchen with a lighted lamp in her hand which she sets on the table beside the other. The sound of footsteps on the path is heard—then a sharp rap on the door.* RUTH *goes and opens it.* ANDREW *enters, followed by* DOCTOR FAWCETT *carrying a small black bag.* ANDREW *has changed greatly. His face seems to have grown highstrung, hardened by the look of decisiveness which comes from being constantly under a strain where judgments on the spur of the moment are compelled to be accurate. His eyes are keener and more alert. There is even a suggestion of ruthless cunning about them. At present, however, his expression is one of tense anxiety.* DOCTOR FAWCETT *is a short, dark, middle-aged man with a Vandyke beard. He wears glasses*]

RUTH. Hello, Andy! I've been waiting—

ANDREW [*Kissing her hastily*]. I got here as soon as I could. [*He throws off his cap and heavy overcoat on the table, introducing* RUTH *and the* DOCTOR *as he does so. He is dressed in an expensive business suit and appears stouter*] My sister-in-law, Mrs. Mayo—Doctor Fawcett. [*They bow to each other silently.* ANDREW *casts a quick glance about the room*] Where's Bob?

RUTH [*Pointing*]. In there.

ANDREW. I'll take your coat and hat, Doctor. [*As he helps the* DOCTOR *with his things*] Is he very bad, Ruth?

RUTH [*Dully*]. He's been getting weaker.

ANDREW. Damn! This way, Doctor. Bring the lamp, Ruth.

[*He goes into the bedroom, followed by the* DOCTOR *and* RUTH *carrying the clean lamp.* RUTH *reappears almost immediately, closing the door behind her, and goes slowly to the outside door, which she opens, and stands in the doorway looking out. The sound of* ANDREW'S *and* ROBERT'S *voices comes from the bedroom. A moment later* ANDREW *re-enters, closing the door softly. He comes forward and sinks down in the rocker on the right of table, leaning his head on his hands. His face is drawn in a shocked expression of great grief. He sighs heavily, staring mournfully in front of him.* RUTH *turns and stands watching him. Then she shuts the door and returns to her chair by the stove, turning it so she can face him*]

ANDREW [*Glancing up quickly—in a harsh voice*]. How long has this been going on?

RUTH. You mean—how long has he been sick?

ANDREW [*Shortly*]. Of course! What else?

RUTH. It was last summer he had a bad spell first, but he's been ailin' ever since Mary died—eight months ago.

ANDREW [*Harshly*]. Why didn't you let me know—cable me? Do you want him to die, all of you? I'm damned if it doesn't look that way! [*His voice breaking*] Poor old chap! To be sick in this out-of-the-way hole without anyone to attend to him but a country quack! It's a damned shame!

RUTH [*Dully*]. I wanted to send you word once, but he only got mad when I told him. He was too proud to ask anything, he said.

ANDREW. Proud? To ask *me?* [*He jumps to his feet and paces nervously back and forth*] I can't understand the way you've acted. Didn't you see how sick he was getting? Couldn't you realize—why, I nearly dropped in my tracks when I saw him! He looks— [*He shudders*]—terrible! [*With fierce scorn*] I suppose you're so used to the idea of his being delicate that you took his sickness as a matter of course. God, if I'd only known!

RUTH [*Without emotion*]. A letter takes so long to get where you were— and we couldn't afford to telegraph. We owed everyone already, and I couldn't ask Ma. She'd been giving me money out of her savings till she hadn't much left. Don't say anything to Rob about it. I never told him. He'd only be mad at me if he knew. But I had to, because—God knows how we'd have got on if I hadn't.

ANDREW. You mean to say— [*His eyes seem to take in the poverty-stricken appearance of the room for the first time*] You sent that telegram to me collect. Was it because— [RUTH *nods silently.* ANDREW *pounds on the table with his fist*] Good God! And all this time I've been—why I've had everything! [*He sits down in his chair and pulls it close to* RUTH's—*impulsively*] But—I can't get it through my head. Why? Why? What has happened? How did it ever come about? Tell me!

RUTH [*Dully*]. There's nothing much to tell. Things kept getting worse, that's all—and Rob didn't seem to care. He never took any interest since way back when your Ma died. After that he got men to take charge, and they nearly all cheated him—he couldn't tell—and left one after another. Then after Mary died he didn't pay no heed to anything any more—just stayed indoors and took to reading books again. So I had to ask Ma if she wouldn't help us some.

ANDREW [*Surprised and horrified*]. Why, damn it, this is frightful! Rob must be mad not to have let me know. Too proud to ask help of *me!* What's the matter with him, in God's name? [*A sudden, horrible suspicion entering his mind*] Ruth! Tell me the truth. His mind hasn't gone back on him, has it?

RUTH [*Dully*]. I don't know. Mary's dying broke him up terrible—but he's used to her being gone by this, I s'pose.

ANDREW [*Looking at her queerly*]. Do you mean to say *you're* used to it?

RUTH [*In a dead voice*]. There's a time comes—when you don't mind any more—anything.

ANDREW [*Looks at her fixedly for a moment—with great pity*]. I'm sorry, Ruth—if I seemed to blame you. I didn't realize— The sight of Rob lying in bed there, so gone to pieces—it made me furious at everyone. Forgive me, Ruth.

RUTH. There's nothing to forgive. It doesn't matter.

ANDREW [*Springing to his feet again and pacing up and down*]. Thank God I came back before it was too late. This doctor will know exactly what to do. That's the first thing to think of. When Rob's back on his feet again we can get the farm working on a sound basis once more. I'll see to that—before I leave.

RUTH. You're going away again?

ANDREW. I've got to.

RUTH. You wrote Rob you was coming back to stay this time.

ANDREW. I expected to—until I got to New York. Then I learned certain facts that make it necessary. [*With a short laugh*] To be candid, Ruth, I'm not the rich man you've probably been led to believe by my letters—not now. I was when I wrote them. I made money hand over fist as long as I stuck to legitimate trading; but I wasn't content with that. I wanted it to come easier, so like all the rest of the idiots, I tried speculation. Oh, I won all right! Several times I've been almost a millionaire—on paper—and then come down to earth again with a bump. Finally the strain was too much. I got disgusted with myself and made up my mind to get out and come home and forget it and really live again. [*He gives a harsh laugh*] And now comes the funny part. The day before the steamer sailed I saw what I thought was a chance to become a millionaire again. [*He snaps his fingers*] That easy! I plunged. Then, before things broke, I left—I was so confident I couldn't be wrong. But when I landed in New York—I wired you I had business to wind up, didn't I? Well, it was the business that wound me up! [*He smiles grimly, pacing up and down, his hands in his pockets*]

RUTH [*Dully*]. You found—you'd lost everything?

ANDREW [*Sitting down again*]. Practically. [*He takes a cigar from his pocket, bites the end off, and lights it*] Oh, I don't mean I'm dead broke. I've saved ten thousand from the wreckage, maybe twenty. But that's a poor showing for five years' hard work. That's why I'll have to go back. [*Confidently*] I can make it up in a year or so down there—and I don't need but a shoestring to start with. [*A weary expression comes over his face and he sighs heavily*] I wish I didn't have to. I'm sick of it all.

RUTH. It's too bad—things seem to go wrong so.

ANDREW [*Shaking off his depression—briskly*]. They might be much worse. There's enough left to fix the farm O. K. before I go. I won't leave till Rob's on his feet again. In the meantime I'll make things fly around here. [*With satisfaction*] I need a rest, and the kind of rest I need is hard work in the open—just like I used to do in the old days. [*Stopping abruptly and lowering his voice cautiously*] Not a word to Rob about my losing money! Remember that, Ruth! You can see why. If he's grown so touchy he'd never accept a cent if he thought I was hard up; see?

RUTH. Yes, Andy.

[*After a pause, during which* ANDREW *puffs at his cigar abstractedly, his mind evidently busy with plans for the future, the bedroom door is opened and* DOCTOR FAWCETT *enters, carrying a bag. He closes the door quietly behind him and comes forward, a grave expression on his face.* ANDREW *springs out of his chair*]

ANDREW. Ah, Doctor! [*He pushes a chair between his own and* RUTH's] Won't you have a chair?

FAWCETT [*Glancing at his watch*]. I must catch the nine o'clock back to the city. It's imperative. I have only a moment. [*Sitting down and clearing his throat—in a perfunctory, impersonal voice*] The case of your brother, Mr. Mayo, is— [*He stops and glances at* RUTH *and says meaningly to* ANDREW] Perhaps it would be better if you and I—

RUTH [*With dogged resentment*]. I know what you mean, Doctor. [*Dully*] Don't be afraid I can't stand it. I'm used to bearing trouble by this; and I can guess what you've found out. [*She hesitates for a moment— then continues in a monotonous voice*] Rob's going to die.

ANDREW [*Angrily*]. Ruth!

FAWCETT [*Raising his hand as if to command silence*]. I am afraid my diagnosis of your brother's condition forces me to the same conclusion as Mrs. Mayo's.

ANDREW [*Groaning*]. But, Doctor, surely—

FAWCETT [*Calmly*]. Your brother hasn't long to live—perhaps a few days, perhaps only a few hours. It's a marvel that he's alive at this moment. My examination revealed that both of his lungs are terribly affected.

ANDREW [*Brokenly*]. Good God!

[RUTH *keeps her eyes fixed on her lap in a trancelike stare*]

FAWCETT. I am sorry I have to tell you this. If there was anything that could be done—

ANDREW. There isn't anything?

FAWCETT [*Shaking his head*]. It's too late. Six months ago there might have—

ANDREW [*In anguish*]. But if we were to take him to the mountains— or to Arizona—or—

FAWCETT. That might have prolonged his life six months ago. [ANDREW *groans*] But now— [*He shrugs his shoulders significantly*]

ANDREW [*Appalled by a sudden thought*]. Good heavens, you haven't told him this, have you, Doctor?

FAWCETT. No. I lied to him. I said a change of climate— [*He looks at his watch again nervously*] I must leave you. [*He gets up*]

ANDREW [*Getting to his feet—insistently*]. But there must still be some chance—

FAWCETT [*As if he were reassuring a child*]. There is always that last chance—the miracle. [*He puts on his hat and coat—bowing to* RUTH] Good-by, Mrs. Mayo.

RUTH [*Without raising her eyes—dully*]. Good-by.

ANDREW [*Mechanically*]. I'll walk to the car with you, Doctor. [*They go out of the door.* RUTH *sits motionless. The motor is heard starting and the noise gradually recedes into the distance.* ANDREW *re-enters and sits down in his chair, holding his head in his hands*] Ruth! [*She lifts her eyes to his*] Hadn't we better go in and see him? God! I'm afraid to! I know he'll read it in my face. [*The bedroom door is noiselessly opened and* ROBERT *appears in the doorway. His cheeks are flushed with fever, and his eyes appear unusually large and brilliant.* ANDREW *continues with a groan*] It can't be, Ruth. It can't be as as hopeless as he said. There's always a fighting chance. We'll take Rob to Arizona. He's got to get well. There *must* be a chance!

ROBERT [*In a gentle tone*]. Why must there, Andy?

[RUTH *turns and stares at him with terrified eyes*]

ANDREW [*Whirling around*]. Rob! [*Scoldingly*] What are you doing out of bed? [*He gets up and goes to him*] Get right back now and obey the Doc, or you're going to get a licking from me!

ROBERT [*Ignoring these remarks*]. Help me over to the chair, please, Andy.

ANDREW. Like hell I will! You're going right back to bed, that's where you're going, and stay there! [*He takes hold of* ROBERT'S *arm*]

ROBERT [*Mockingly*]. Stay there till I die, eh, Andy? [*Coldly*] Don't behave like a child. I'm sick of lying down. I'll be more rested sitting up. [*As* ANDREW *hesitates—violently*] I swear I'll get out of bed every time you put me there. You'll have to sit on my chest, and that wouldn't help my health any. Come on, Andy. Don't play the fool. I want to talk to you, and I'm going to. [*With a grim smile*] A dying man has some rights, hasn't he?

ANDREW [*With a shudder*]. Don't talk that way, for God's sake! I'll only let you sit down if you'll promise that. Remember. [*He helps* ROBERT *to the chair between his own and Ruth's*] Easy now! There you are! Wait, and I'll get a pillow for you. [*He goes into the bedroom.* ROBERT *looks at* RUTH *who shrinks away from him in terror.* ROBERT *smiles bitterly.* ANDREW *comes back with the pillow which he places behind* ROBERT'S *back*] How's that?

ROBERT [*With an affectionate smile*]. Fine! Thank you! [*As* ANDREW *sits down*] Listen, Andy. You've asked me not to talk—and I won't after I've made my position clear. [*Slowly*] In the first place I know I'm dying.

[RUTH *bows her head and covers her face with her hands. She remains like this all during the scene between the two brothers*]

ANDREW. Rob! That isn't so!

ROBERT [*Wearily*]. It *is* so! Don't lie to me. After Ruth put me to bed before you came, I saw it clearly for the first time. [*Bitterly*] I'd been making plans for our future—Ruth's and mine—so it came hard at first— the realization. Then when the doctor examined me, I knew—although he tried to lie about it. And then to make sure I listened at the door to what he told you. So don't mock me with fairy tales about Arizona, or any such rot as that. Because I'm dying is no reason you should treat me as an imbecile or a coward. Now that I'm sure what's happening I can say Kismet to it with all my heart. It was only the silly uncertainty that hurt. [*There is a pause.* ANDREW *looks around in impotent anguish, not knowing what to say.* ROBERT *regards him with an affectionate smile*]

ANDREW [*Finally blurts out*]. It isn't foolish. You *have* got a chance. If you heard all the Doctor said that ought to prove it to you.

ROBERT. Oh, you mean when he spoke of the miracle? [*Dryly*] I don't believe in miracles—in my case. Besides, I know more than any doctor on earth *could* know—because I *feel* what's coming. [*Dismissing the subject*] But we've agreed not to talk of it. Tell me about yourself, Andy. That's what I'm interested in. Your letters were too brief and far apart to be illuminating.

ANDREW. I meant to write oftener.

ROBERT [*With a trace of irony*]. I judge from them you've accomplished all you set out to do five years ago?

ANDREW. That isn't much to boast of.

ROBERT [*Surprised*]. Have you really, honestly reached that conclusion?

ANDREW. Well, it doesn't seem to amount to much now.

ROBERT. But you're rich, aren't you?

ANDREW [*With a quick glance at* RUTH]. Yes, I s'pose so.

ROBERT. I'm glad. You can do to the farm all I've undone. But what did you do down there? Tell me. You went into the grain business with that friend of yours?

ANDREW. Yes. After two years I had a share in it. I sold out last year. [*He is answering* ROBERT'S *questions with great reluctance*]

ROBERT. And then?

ANDREW. I went in on my own.

ROBERT. Still in grain?

ANDREW. Yes.

ROBERT. What's the matter? You look as if I were accusing you of something.

ANDREW. I'm proud enough of the first four years. It's after that I'm not boasting of. I took to speculating.

ROBERT. In wheat?

ANDREW. Yes.

ROBERT. And you made money—gambling?

ANDREW. Yes.

ROBERT [*Thoughtfully*]. I've been wondering what the great change was in you. [*After a pause*] You—a farmer—to gamble in a wheat pit with scraps of paper. There's a spiritual significance in that picture, Andy. [*He smiles bitterly*] I'm a failure, and Ruth's another—but we can both justly lay some of the blame for our stumbling on God. But you're the deepest-dyed failure of the three, Andy. You've spent eight years running away from yourself. Do you see what I mean? You used to be a creator when you loved the farm. You and life were in harmonious partnership. And now— [*He stops as if seeking vainly for words*] My brain is muddled. But part of what I mean is that your gambling with the things you used to love to create proves how far astray— So you'll be punished. You'll have to suffer to win back— [*His voice grows weaker and he sighs wearily*] It's no use. I can't say it. [*He lies back and closes his eyes, breathing pantingly*]

ANDREW [*Slowly*]. I think I know what you're driving at, Rob—and it's true, I guess. [ROBERT *smiles gratefully and stretches out his hand, which* ANDREW *takes in his*]

ROBERT. I want you to promise me to do one thing, Andy, after—

ANDREW. I'll promise anything, as God is my Judge!

ROBERT. Remember, Andy, Ruth has suffered double her share. [*His voice faltering with weakness*] Only through contact with suffering, Andy, will you—awaken. Listen. You must marry Ruth—afterwards.

RUTH [*With a cry*]. Rob! [ROBERT *lies back, his eyes closed, gasping heavily for breath*]

ANDREW [*Making signs to her to humor him—gently*]. You're tired out, Rob. You better lie down and rest a while, don't you think? We can talk later on.

ROBERT [*With a mocking smile*]. Later on! You always were an optimist, Andy! [*He sighs with exhaustion*] Yes, I'll go and rest a while. [*As* ANDREW *comes to help him*] It must be near sunrise, isn't it?

ANDREW. It's after six.

ROBERT [*As* ANDREW *helps him into the bedroom*]. Shut the door, Andy. I want to be alone.

[ANDREW *reappears and shuts the door softly. He comes and sits down on his chair again, supporting his head on his hands. His face is drawn with the intensity of his dry-eyed anguish*]

RUTH [*Glancing at him—fearfully*]. He's out of his mind now, isn't he?

ANDREW. He may be a little delirious. The fever would do that. [*With impotent rage*] God, what a shame! And there's nothing we can do but sit and—wait! [*He springs from his chair and walks to the stove*]

RUTH [*Dully*]. He was talking—wild—like he used to—only this time it sounded—unnatural, don't you think?

ANDREW. I don't know. The things he said to me had truth in them— even if he did talk them way up in the air, like he always sees things. Still— [*He glances down at* RUTH *keenly*] Why do you suppose he wanted us to promise we'd— [*Confusedly*] You know what he said.

RUTH [*Dully*]. His mind was wandering, I s'pose.

ANDREW [*With conviction*]. No—there was something back of it.

RUTH. He wanted to make sure I'd be all right—after he'd gone, I expect.

ANDREW. No, it wasn't that. He knows very well I'd naturally look after you without—anything like that.

RUTH. He might be thinking of—something happened five years back, the time you came home from the trip.

ANDREW. What happened? What do you mean?

RUTH [*Dully*]. We had a fight.

ANDREW. A fight? What has that to do with me?

RUTH. It was about you—in a way.

ANDREW [*Amazed*]. About *me?*

RUTH. Yes, mostly. You see I'd found out I'd made a mistake about Rob soon after we were married—when it was too late.

ANDREW. Mistake? [*Slowly*] You mean—you found out you didn't love Rob?

RUTH. Yes.

ANDREW. Good God!

RUTH. And then I thought that when Mary came it'd be different, and I'd love him; but it didn't happen that way. And I couldn't bear with his blundering and book-reading—and I grew to hate him, almost.

ANDREW. Ruth!

RUTH. I couldn't help it. No woman could. It had to be because I loved someone else, I'd found out. [*She sighs wearily*] It can't do no harm to tell you now—when it's all past and gone—and dead. *You* were the one I really loved—only I didn't come to the knowledge of it till too late.

ANDREW [*Stunned*]. Ruth! Do you know what you're saying?

RUTH. It was true—then. [*With sudden fierceness*] How could I help it? No woman could.

ANDREW. Then—you loved me—that time I came home?

RUTH [*Doggedly*]. I'd known your real reason for leaving home the first time—everybody knew it—and for three years I'd been thinking—

ANDREW. That I loved you?

RUTH. Yes. Then that day on the hill you laughed about what a fool you'd been for loving me once—and I knew it was all over.

ANDREW. Good God, but I never thought— [*He stops, shuddering at his remembrance*] And did Rob—

RUTH. That was what I'd started to tell. We'd had a fight just before you came and I got crazy mad—and I told him all I've told you.

ANDREW [*Gaping at her speechlessly for a moment*]. You told Rob—you loved me?

RUTH. Yes.

ANDREW [*Shrinking away from her in horror*]. You—you—you mad fool, you! How could you do such a thing?

RUTH. I couldn't help it. I'd got to the end of bearing things—without talking.

ANDREW. Then Rob must have known every moment I stayed here! And yet he never said or showed—God, how he must have suffered! Didn't you know how much he loved you?

RUTH [*Dully*]. Yes. I knew he liked me.

ANDREW. Liked you! What kind of a woman are you? Couldn't you have kept silent? Did you have to torture him? No wonder he's dying! And you've lived together for five years with this between you?

RUTH. We've lived in the same house.

ANDREW. Does he still think—

RUTH. I don't know. We've never spoke a word about it since that day. Maybe, from the way he went on, he s'poses I care for you yet.

ANDREW. But you don't. It's outrageous. It's stupid! You don't love me!

RUTH [*Slowly*]. I wouldn't know how to feel love, even if I tried, any more.

ANDREW [*Brutally*]. And I don't love you, that's sure! [*He sinks into his chair, his head between his hands*] It's damnable such a thing should be between Rob and me. Why, I love Rob better'n anybody in the world and always did. There isn't a thing on God's green earth I wouldn't have done to keep trouble away from him. And I have to be the very one—it's damnable! How am I going to face him again? What can I say to him now? [*He groans with anguished rage. After a pause*] He asked me to promise— what am I going to do?

RUTH. You can promise—so's it'll ease his mind—and not mean anything.

ANDREW. What? Lie to him now—when he's dying? [*Determinedly*] No! It's *you* who'll have to do the lying, since it must be done. You've got a chance now to undo some of all the suffering you've brought on Rob. Go in to him! Tell him you never loved me—it was all a mistake. Tell him you only said so because you were mad and didn't know what you were saying! Tell him something, anything, that'll bring him peace!

RUTH [*Dully*]. He wouldn't believe me.

ANDREW [*Furiously*]. You've got to make him believe you, do you hear? You've got to—now—hurry—you never know when it may be too late. [*As she hesitates—imploringly*] For God's sake, Ruth! Don't you see you owe it to him? You'll never forgive yourself if you don't.

RUTH [*Dully*]. I'll go. [*She gets wearily to her feet and walks slowly toward the bedroom*] But it won't do any good. [ANDREW's *eyes are fixed on her anxiously. She opens the door and steps inside the room. She remains standing there for a minute. Then she calls in a frightened voice*] Rob! Where are you? [*Then she hurries back, trembling with fright*] Andy! Andy! He's gone!

ANDREW [*Misunderstanding her—his face pale with dread*]. He's not—

RUTH [*Interrupting him—hysterically*]. He's gone! The bed's empty. The window's wide open. He must have crawled out into the yard!

ANDREW [*Springing to his feet. He rushes into the bedroom and returns immediately with an expression of alarmed amazement on his face*]. Come! He can't have gone far! [*Grabbing his hat he takes* RUTH's *arm and shoves her toward the door*] Come on! [*Opening the door*] Let's hope to God— [*The door closes behind them, cutting off his words as*

The Curtain Falls.]

ACT THREE: SCENE TWO

SAME *as Act One, Scene One—A section of country highway. The sky to the east is already alight with bright color and a thin, quivering line flame is spreading slowly along the horizon rim of the dark hills. The roadside, however, is still steeped in the grayness of the dawn, shadowy and vague. The field in the foreground has a wild uncultivated appearance, as if it had been allowed to remain fallow the preceding summer. Parts of the snake-fence in the rear have broken down. The apple tree is leafless and seems dead.*

ROBERT *staggers weakly in from the left. He stumbles into the ditch and lies there for a moment; then crawls with a great effort to the top of the bank where he can see the sun rise, and collapses weakly.* RUTH *and* ANDREW *come hurriedly along the road from the left.*

ANDREW [*Stopping and looking about him*]. There he is! I knew it! I knew we'd find him here.

ROBERT [*Trying to raise himself to a sitting position as they hasten to his side—with a wan smile*]. I thought I'd given you the slip.

ANDREW [*With kindly bullying*]. Well, you didn't, you old scoundrel, and we're going to take you right back where you belong—in bed. [*He makes a motion to lift* ROBERT]

ROBERT. Don't, Andy. Don't, I tell you!

ANDREW. You're in pain?

ROBERT [*Simply*]. No. I'm dying. [*He falls back weakly.* RUTH *sinks down beside him with a sob and pillows his head on her lap.* ANDREW *stands looking down at him helplessly.* ROBERT *moves his head restlessly on* RUTH's *lap*] I couldn't stand it back there in the room. It seems as if all my life—I'd been cooped in a room. So I thought I'd try to end as I might have—if I'd had the courage—alone—in a ditch by the open road—watching the sun rise.

ANDREW. Rob! Don't talk. You're wasting your strength. Rest a while and then we'll carry you—

ROBERT. Still hoping, Andy? Don't. I know. [*There is a pause during which he breathes heavily, straining his eyes toward the horizon*] The sun comes so slowly. [*With an ironical smile*] The doctor told me to go to the far-off places—and I'd be cured. He was right. That was always the cure for me. It's too late—for this life—but— [*He has a fit of coughing which racks his body*]

ANDREW [*With a hoarse sob*]. Rob! [*He clenches his fists in an impotent rage against Fate*] God! God! [RUTH *sobs brokenly and wipes* ROBERT's *lips with her handkerchief*]

ROBERT [*In a voice which is suddenly ringing with the happiness of hope*]. You mustn't feel sorry for me. Don't you see I'm happy at last—free—free!—freed from the farm—free to wander on and on—eternally! [*He raises himself on his elbow, his face radiant, and points to the horizon]* Look! Isn't it beautiful beyond the hills? I can hear the old voices calling me to come— *[Exultantly]* And this time I'm going! It isn't the end. It's a free beginning —the start of my voyage! I've won to my trip—the right of release—beyond the horizon! Oh, you ought to be glad—glad—for my sake! *[He collapses weakly]* Andy! *[ANDREW bends down to him]* Remember Ruth—

ANDREW. I'll take care of her, I swear to you, Rob!

ROBERT. Ruth has suffered—remember, Andy—only through sacrifice—the secret beyond there— *[He suddenly raises himself with his last remaining strength and points to the horizon where the edge of the sun's disc is rising from the rim of the hills]* The sun! *[He remains with his eyes fixed on it for a moment. A rattling noise throbs from his throat. He mumbles]* Remember! *[And falls back and is still.* RUTH *gives a cry of horror and springs to her feet, shuddering, her hands over her eyes.* ANDREW *bends on one knee beside the body, placing a hand over* ROBERT'S *heart, then he kisses his brother reverently on the forehead and stands up]*

ANDREW *[Facing* RUTH, *the body between them—in a dead voice]* He's' dead. *[With a sudden burst of fury]* God damn you, you never told him!

RUTH *[Piteously]*. He was so happy without my lying to him.

ANDREW *[Pointing to the body—trembling with the violence of his rage]*. This is your doing, you damn woman, you coward, your murderess!

RUTH *[Sobbing]*. Don't, Andy! I couldn't help it—and he knew how I'd suffered, too. He told you—to remember.

ANDREW *[Stares at her for a moment, his rage ebbing away, an expression of deep pity gradually coming over his face. Then he glances down at his brother and speaks brokenly in a compassionate voice]*. Forgive me, Ruth— for his sake—and I'll remember— *[RUTH lets her hands fall from her face and looks at him uncomprehendingly. He lifts his eyes to hers and forces out falteringly]* I—you—we've both made a mess of things! We must try to help each other—and—in time—we'll come to know what's right— *[Desperately]* And perhaps we— *[But RUTH, if she is aware of his words, gives no sign. She remains silent, gazing at him dully with the sad humility of exhaustion, her mind already sinking back into that spent calm beyond the further troubling of any hope as*

The Curtain Falls.]

The Green Pastures [1]

by MARC CONNELLY

CHARACTERS

Mr. Deshee, the Preacher

Myrtle

First Boy

Second Boy

First Cook

A Voice

Second Cook

First Man Angel

First Mammy Angel

A Stout Angel

A Slender Angel

Archangel

Gabriel

God

Choir Leader

Custard Maker

Adam

Eve

Cain

Cain's Girl

Zeba

Cain the Sixth

Boy Gambler

General

Head Magician

First Wizard

Second Wizard

Joshua

First Scout

Master of Ceremonies

First Gambler

Second Gambler

Voice in Shanty

Noah

Noah's Wife

Shem

First Woman

Second Woman

Third Woman

First Man

Flatfoot

Ham

Japheth

First Cleaner

Second Cleaner

Abraham

Isaac

Jacob

Moses

Zipporah

Aaron

A Candidate Magician

Pharaoh

King of Babylon

Prophet

High Priest

Corporal

Hezdrel

Second Officer

[1] Reprinted by permission of the author.   First produced February 26, 1930.

SCENES

PART ONE: SCENE ONE

A CORNER *in a Negro church.*
Ten children and an elderly preacher.
The costumes are those that might be seen in any lower Louisiana town at Sunday-School time. As the curtain rises, MR. DESHEE, *the preacher, is reading from a Bible. The* CHILDREN *are listening with varied degrees of interest. Three or four are wide-eyed in their attention. Two or three are obviously puzzled, but interested, and the smallest ones are engaged in more physical concerns. One is playing with a little doll, and another runs his finger on all the angles of his chair.*

DESHEE. "An' Adam lived a hundred and thirty years, an' begat a son in his own likeness, after his image; an' called his name Seth. An' de days of Adam, after he had begotten Seth, were eight hundred years; an' he begat sons an' daughters; an' all de days dat Adam lived were nine hundred an' thirty years; an' he died. An' Seth lived a hundred an' five years an' begat Enos; an' Seth lived after he begat Enos eight hundred an' seven years and begat sons and daughters. An' all de days of Seth were nine hundred and twelve years; an' he died." An' it go on like dat till we come to Enoch an' de book say: "An' Enoch lived sixty an' five years and begat Methuselah." Den it say: "An' all de days of Methuselah were nine hund'ed an' sixty an' nine years an' he died." An' dat was de oldest man dat ever was. Dat's why we call ol' Mr. Gurney's mammy ol' Mrs. Methuselah, caize she's so ol'. Den a little later it tell about another member of de fam'ly. His name was Noah. Maybe some of you know about him already. I'm gonter tell you all about him next Sunday. Anyway dat's de meat an' substance of de first five chapters of Genesis. Now, how you think you gonter like de Bible?

MYRTLE. I think it's jest wonderful, Mr. Deshee. I cain't understand any of it.

FIRST BOY. Why did dey live so long, Mr. Deshee?

DESHEE. Why? Caize dat was de way God felt.

SECOND BOY. Dat made Adam a way back.

DESHEE. Yes, he certainly 'way back by de time Noah came along. Want to ask me any mo' questions?

SECOND BOY. What de worl' look like when de Lawd begin, Mr. Deshee?

DESHEE. How yo' mean what it look like?

MYRTLE. Carlisle mean who was in N'Orleans den.

DESHEE. Dey wasn't nobody in N'Orleans on 'count dey wasn't any N'Orleans. Dat's de whole idea I tol' you at de end of de first Chapter. Yo' got to git yo' minds fixed. Dey wasn't any Rampart Street. Dey wasn't any Canal Street. Dey wasn't any Louisiana. Dey wasn't nothin' on de earth at all caize fo' de reason dey wasn't any earth.

MYRTLE. Yes, but what Carlisle wanter know is—

DESHEE [Interrupting and addressing little boy who has been playing with his chair and paying no attention]. Now Randolph, if you don't listen, how yo' gonter grow up and be a good man? Yo' wanter grow up an' be a transgressor?

LITTLE BOY [Frightened]. No.

DESHEE. You tell yo' mammy yo' sister got to come wid you next time. She kin git de things done in time to bring you to de school. You content yo'self.

[The little boy straightens up in his chair]

Now, what do Carlisle want to know?

CARLISLE. How he decide he want de worl' to be right yere and how he git de idea he wanted it?

MYRTLE. Caize de Book say, don't it, Mr. Deshee?

DESHEE. De Book say, but at de same time dat's a good question. I remember when I was a little boy de same thing recurred to me. An' ol' Mr. Dubois, he was a wonderful preacher at New Hope Chapel over in East Gretna, he said: "De answer is dat de Book ain't got time to go into all de details." And he was right. You know sometimes I think de Lawd expects us to figure out a few things for ourselves. We know that at one time dey wasn't anything except Heaven, we don't know jest where it was but we know it was dere. Maybe it was everywhere. Den one day de Lawd got the idea he'd like to make some places. He made de sun and de moon, de stars. An' he made de earth.

MYRTLE. Who was aroun' den, nothin' but angels?

DESHEE. I suppose so.

FIRST BOY. What was de angels doin' up dere?

DESHEE. I suppose dey jest flew aroun' and had a good time. Dey wasn't no sin, so dey musta had a good time.

FIRST BOY. Did dey have picnics?

DESHEE. Sho, dey had the nicest kind of picnics. Dey probably had fish frys, wid b'led custard and ten cent seegars for de adults. God gives us humans lotsa ideas about havin' good times. Maybe dey were things he'd seen de angels do. Yes, sir, I bet dey had a fish fry every week.

MYRTLE. Did dey have Sunday School, too?

DESHEE. Yes, dey musta had Sunday School for de cherubs.

MYRTLE. What did God look like, Mr. Deshee?

DESHEE. Well, nobody knows exactly what God looked like. But when I was a little boy I used to imagine dat he looked like de Reverend Dubois. He was de finest looking ol' man I ever knew. Yes, I used to bet de Lawd looked exactly like Mr. Dubois in de days when he walked de earth in de shape of a natchel man.

MYRTLE. When was dat, Mr. Deshee?

DESHEE. Why, when he was gettin' things started down heah. When He talked to Adam and Eve and Noah and Moses and all dem. He made mighty men in dem days. But aldo they was awful mighty dey always knew dat He was beyond dem all. Pretty near one o'clock, time fo' you chillun to go home to dinner, but before I let you go I wan' you to go over wid me de main facts of de first lesson. What's de name of de book?

CHILDREN. Genesis.

DESHEE. Dat's right. And what's de other name?

CHILDREN. First Book of Moses.

DESHEE. Dat's right. And dis yere's Chapter One. [*The lights begin to dim*] "In de beginnin' God created de heaven an' de earth. An' de earth was widout form an' void. An' de darkness was upon de face of de deep."

SCENE TWO

IN THE *darkness many voices are heard singing "Rise, Shine, Give God The Glory." They sing it gayly and rapidly. The lights go up as the second verse ends. The chorus is being sung diminuendo by a mixed company of angels. That is they are angels in that they wear brightly colored robes and have wings protruding from their backs. Otherwise they look and act like a company of happy negroes at a fish fry. The scene itself is a pre-Creation Heaven with compromises. In the distance is an unbroken stretch of blue sky. Companionable varicolored clouds billow down to the floor of the stage and roll overhead to the branches of a live oak tree which is up left. The tree is leafy and dripping with Spanish moss, and with the clouds makes a frame for the scene. In the cool shade of the tree are the usual appurtenances of a fish fry; a large kettle of hot fat set on two small parallel logs, with a fire going underneath, and a large rustic table formed by driving four stakes into the ground and placing planks on top of the small connecting boards. On the table are piles of biscuits and corn bread and the crooked fish in dish pans. There are one or two fairly large cedar or crock "churns" containing boiled custard, which looks like milk. There is a gourd dipper beside the churns and several glasses and cups of various sizes and shapes from which the custard is drunk.*

The principal singers are marching two by two in a small area at the right of the stage. Two MAMMY ANGELS *are attending to the frying beside the kettle. Behind the table, a* MAN ANGEL *is skinning fish and passing them to the cooks. Another is ladling out the custard. A* MAMMY ANGEL *is putting fish on bread for a brood of cherubs, and during the first scene they seat themselves on a grassy bank upstage. Another* MAMMY ANGEL *is clapping her hands disapprovingly and beckoning a laughing* BOY CHERUB *down from a cloud a little out of her reach. Another* MAMMY ANGEL *is solicitously slapping the back of a girl cherub who has a large fish sandwich in her hand and a bone in her throat. There is much movement about the table, and during the first few minutes several individuals go up to the table to help themselves to the food and drink. Many of the women angels wear hats and a few of the men are smoking cigars. A large boxful is on the table. There is much laughter and chatter as the music softens, but continues, during the early part of the action. The following short scenes are played almost simultaneously.*

FIRST COOK [*At Kettle. Calling off*]. Hurry up, Cajey. Dis yere fat's cryin' fo' mo' feesh.

A VOICE [*Off stage*]. We comin', fas' we kin. Dey got to be ketched, ain't dey? We cain't say, "C'm'on little fish. C'm'on an' git fried," kin we?

SECOND COOK [*At Table*]. De trouble is de mens is all worm fishin'.

FIRST MAN ANGEL [*At Table*]. Whut dif'runce do it make? Yo' all de time got to make out like somebody's doin' somethin' de wrong way.

SECOND COOK [*Near Table*]. I s'pose you got de per'fec' way fo' makin' bait.

FIRST MAN ANGEL. I aint sayin' dat. I is sayin' whut's wrong wid worm fishin'.

SECOND COOK. Whut's wrong wid worm fishin'? Ever'thing, dat's all. Dey's only one good way fo' catfishin', an' dat's minny fishin'. Anybody know dat.

FIRST MAN ANGEL. Well, it jest so happen dat minny fishin' is de doggondest fool way of fishin' dey is. You kin try minny fishin' to de cows come home an' all you catch'll be de backache. De trouble wid you, sister, is you jest got minny fishin' on de brain.

SECOND COOK. Go right on, loud mouf. You tell me de news. My, my! You jest de wisest person in de worl'. First you, den de Lawd God.

FIRST MAN ANGEL [*To the custard ladler*]. You cain't tell dem nothin'. [*Walks away to the custard churn*] Does you try to 'splain some simple fac' dey git man-deaf.

FIRST MAMMY ANGEL [*To* CHERUB *on the cloud*]. Now, you heerd me. [*The* CHERUB *assumes several mocking poses, as she speaks*] You fly down yere. You wanter be put down in de sin book? [*She goes to the table, gets a drink for herself and points out the cherub to one of the men behind the table*] Dat baby must got imp blood in him he so vexin'. [*She returns to her position under the cloud*] You want me to fly up dere an' slap you down? Now, I tol' you. [*The* CHERUB *starts to come down*]

STOUT ANGEL [*To the* CHERUB *with a bone in her throat*]. I tol' you you was too little fo' cat fish. What you wanter git a bone in yo' froat fo'? [*She slaps the* CHERUB'S *back*]

SLENDER ANGEL [*Leisurely eating a sandwich as she watches the back-slapping*]. What de trouble wid Leonetta?

STOUT ANGEL. She got a catfish bone down her froat. [*To the* CHERUB] Doggone, I tol' you to eat grinnel instead.

SLENDER ANGEL. Ef'n she do git all dat et, she gonter have de bellyache.

STOUT ANGEL. Ain't I tol' her dat? [*To* CHERUB] Come on now; let go dat bone. [*She slaps* CHERUB'S *back again. The bone is dislodged and the* CHERUB *grins her relief*] Dat's good.

SLENDER ANGEL [*Comfortingly*]. Now she all right.

STOUT ANGEL. Go on an' play wid yo' cousins. [*The* CHERUB *joins the Cherubs sitting on the embankment. The concurrency of scenes ends here*] I ain't see you lately, Lily. How you been?

SLENDER ANGEL. Me, I'm fine. I been visitin' my mammy. She waitin' on de welcome table over by de throne of grace.

STOUT ANGEL. She always was pretty holy.

SLENDER ANGEL. Yes, ma'am. She like it dere. I guess de Lawd's took quite a fancy to her.

STOUT ANGEL. Well, dat's natural. I declare yo' mammy one of de finest lady angels I know.

SLENDER ANGEL. She claim you de best one she know.

STOUT ANGEL. Well, when you come right down to it, I suppose we is all pretty near perfec'.

SLENDER ANGEL. Yes, ma'am. Why is dat, Mis' Jenny?

STOUT ANGEL. I s'pose it's caize de Lawd he don' 'low us 'sociatin' wid de devil any mo' so dat dey cain' be no mo' sinnin'.

SLENDER ANGEL. Po' ol' Satan. Whutevah become of him?

STOUT ANGEL. De Lawd put him some place I s'pose.

SLENDER ANGEL. But dey ain't any place but Heaven, is dey?

STOUT ANGEL. De Lawd could make a place, couldn't he?

SLENDER ANGEL. Dat's de truth. Dey's one thing confuses me though.

STOUT ANGEL. What's dat?

SLENDER ANGEL. I do a great deal of travelin' an' I ain't never come across any place but Heaven anywhere. So if de Lawd kick Satan out of Heaven jest whereat did he go? Dat's my question.

STOUT ANGEL. You bettah let de Lawd keep his own secrets, Lily. De way things is goin' now dey ain't been no sinnin' since dey give dat scamp a kick in de pants. Nowadays Heaven's free of sin an' if a lady wants a little constitutional she kin fly 'til she wing-weary widout gittin' insulted.

SLENDER ANGEL. I was jest a baby when Satan lef'. I don't even 'member what he look like.

STOUT ANGEL. He was jest right fo' a devil. [*An* ARCHANGEL *enters. He is older than the others and wears a white beard. His clothing is much darker than that of the others and his wings a trifle more imposing*] Good mo'nin', Archangel.

[*Others say good morning*]

ARCHANGEL. Good mo'nin', folks. I wonder kin I interrup' de fish fry an' give out de Sunday school cyards? [*Cries of "Suttingly!" "Mah goodness, yes"—etc. The marching* CHOIR *stops*] You kin keep singin' if you want to. Why don' you sing "When de Saints Come Marchin' In"? Seem to me I ain' heard dat lately. [*The* CHOIR *begins "When the Saints Come Marching In," rather softly, but does not resume marching. The* ARCHANGEL *looks off left*] All right, bring 'em yere. [*A prim looking* WOMAN TEACHER-ANGEL *enters, shepherding ten* BOY *and* GIRL CHERUBS. *The* TEACHER *carries ten beribboned diplomas, which she gives to the* ARCHANGEL. *The* CHERUBS *are dressed in stiffly starched white suits and dresses, the little girls having enormous ribbons at the backs of their dresses and smaller ones in their hair and on the tips of their wings. They line up in front of the* ARCHANGEL *and receive the attention of the rest of the company. The* CHOIR *sings through the ceremony*] Now den cherubs, why is you yere?

CHILDREN. Because we so good.

ARCHANGEL. Dat's right. Now who de big boss?

CHILDREN. Our dear Lawd.

ARCHANGEL. Dat's right. When you all grow up what you gonter be?

CHILDREN. Holy angels at de throne of grace.

ARCHANGEL. Dat's right. Now, you passed yo' 'xaminations and it gives me great pleasure to hand out de cyards for de whole class. Gineeva Chaproe. [*The* FIRST GIRL CHERUB *goes to him and gets her diploma. The* CHOIR *sings loudly and resumes marching, as the* ARCHANGEL *calls out another name—and presents diplomas*] Corey Moulter. [SECOND GIRL CHERUB *gets her diploma*] Nootzie Winebush. [THIRD GIRL CHERUB] Harriet Prancy. [FOURTH GIRL CHERUB] I guess you is Brozain Stew't. [*He gives the* FIFTH GIRL CHERUB *the paper. Each of the presentations has been accompanied by hand-clapping from the bystanders*] Now you boys know yo' own names. Suppose you come yere and help me git dese 'sorted right?

[BOY CHERUBS *gather about him and receive their diplomas. The little* GIRLS *have scattered about the stage, joining groups of the adult angels. The angel* GABRIEL *enters. He is bigger and more elaborately winged than even the* ARCHANGEL, *but he is also much younger and beardless. His costume is less conventional than that of the other men, resembling more the Gabriel of the Doré drawings. His appearance causes a flutter among the others. They stop their chattering with the children. The* CHOIR *stops as three or four audible whispers of "Gabriel!" are heard. In a moment the heavenly company is all attention*]

GABRIEL [*Lifting his hand*]. Gangway! Gangway for de Lawd God Jehovah!

[*There is a reverent hush and* GOD *enters. He is the tallest and biggest of them all. He wears a white shirt with a white bow tie, a long Prince Albert coat of black alpaca, black trousers and congress gaiters. He looks at the assemblage. There is a pause. He speaks in a rich, bass voice*]

GOD. Is you been baptized?

OTHERS [*Chanting*]. Certainly, Lawd.

GOD. Is you been baptized?

OTHERS. Certainly, Lawd.

GOD [*With the beginning of musical notation*]. Is you been baptized?

OTHERS [*Now half-singing*]. Certainly, Lawd. Certainly, certainly, certainly, Lawd.

[*They sing the last two verses with equivalent part division*]

> Is you been redeemed?
>   Certainly, Lawd.
> Is you been redeemed?
>   Certainly, Lawd.
> Is you been redeemed?
>   Certainly, Lawd. Certainly, certainly,
>   certainly, Lawd.
>
> Do you bow mighty low?
>   Certainly, Lawd.
> Do you bow mighty low?
>   Certainly, Lawd.
> Do you bow mighty low?
>   Certainly, Lawd. Certainly, certainly,
>   certainly, Lawd.

[*As the last response ends all heads are bowed.* GOD *looks at them for a moment; then lifts His hand*]

GOD. Let de fish fry proceed.

[EVERYONE *rises. The* ANGELS *relax and resume their inaudible conversations. The activity behind the table and about the cauldron is resumed. Some of the choir members cross to the table and get sandwiches and cups of the boiled custard. Three or four of the children in the Sunday School class and the little girl who had the bone in her throat affectionately group themselves about* GOD *as he speaks with the* ARCHANGEL. *He pats their heads, they hang to his coat-tails, etc.*]

ARCHANGEL. Good mo'nin', Lawd.

GOD. Good mo'nin', Deacon. You lookin' pretty spry.

ARCHANGEL. I cain' complain. We just been givin' our cyards to de chillun.

GOD. Dat's good.

[*A small* CHERUB, *his feet braced against one of* GOD's *shoes is using* GOD's *coat tail as a trapeze. One of the* COOKS *offers a fish sandwich which* GOD *politely declines*]

FIRST MAMMY ANGEL. Now, you leave go de Lawd's coat, Herman. You heah me?

GOD. Dat's all right, sister. He jest playin'.

FIRST MAMMY ANGEL. He playin' too rough.

[GOD *picks up the* CHERUB *and spanks him good-naturedly. The* CHERUB *squeals with delight and runs to his mother.* GABRIEL *advances to* GOD *with a glass of the custard*]

GABRIEL. Little b'iled custud, Lawd?

GOD. Thank you very kindly. Dis looks nice.

CUSTARD MAKER [*Offering a box*]. Ten cent seegar, Lawd?

GOD [*Taking it*]. Thank you, thank you. How de fish fry goin'? [*Ad lib. cries of "O. K. Lawd," "Fine an' dandy, Lawd," "De best one yit, Lawd," etc. To the choir*] How you shouters gittin' on?

CHOIR LEADER. We been marchin' and singin' de whole mo'nin'.

GOD. I heerd you. You gittin' better all de time. You gittin' as good as de one at de throne. Why don' you give us one dem ol' time jump-ups?

CHOIR LEADER. Anythin' you say, Lawd. [*To the others*] "So High!"

[*The* CHOIR *begins to sing "So High You Can't Get Over It." They sing softly, but do not march. An* ANGEL *offers his cigar to* GOD *from which* HE *can light* HIS *own*]

GOD. No, thanks. I'm gonter save dis a bit.

[*He puts the cigar in his pocket and listens to the singers a moment. Then he sips his custard. After a second sip, a look of displeasure comes on his face*]

GABRIEL. What's de matter, Lawd?

GOD [*Sipping again*]. I ain't jest sure, yit. Dey's something 'bout dis custahd. [*Takes another sip*]

CUSTARD MAKER. Ain't it all right, Lawd?

GOD. It don't seem seasoned jest right. You make it?

CUSTARD MAKER. Yes, Lawd. I put everythin' in it like I allus do. It's supposed to be perfec'.

GOD. Yeah. I kin taste de eggs and de cream and de sugar. [*Suddenly*] I know what it is. It needs jest a little bit mo' firmament.

CUSTARD MAKER. Dey's firmament in it, Lawd.

GOD. Maybe, but it ain' enough.

CUSTARD MAKER. It's all we had, Lawd. Dey ain't a drap in de jug.

GOD. Dat's all right. I'll jest r'ar back an' pass a miracle. [CHOIR *stops singing*] Let it be some firmament! An' when I say let it be some firmament, I don't want jest a little bitty dab o' firmament caize I'm sick an' tired of runnin' out of it when we need it. Let it be a whole mess of firmament! [*The stage has become misty until* GOD *and the heavenly company are obscured. As he finishes the speech there is a burst of thunder. As the stage grows darker*] Dat's de way I like it.

[*Murmurs from the others; "Dat's a lot of firmament." "My, dat is firmament!" "Look to me like He's created rain," etc.*]

FIRST MAMMY ANGEL [*When the stage is dark*]. Now, look Lawd, dat's too much firmament. De Cherubs is gettin' all wet.

SECOND MAMMY ANGEL. Look at my Carlotta, Lawd. She's soaked to de skin. Dat's *plenty* too much firmament.

GOD. Well, 'co'se we don't want de chillun to ketch cold. Can't you dreen it off?

GABRIEL. Dey's no place to dreen it, Lawd.

FIRST MAMMY ANGEL. Why don't we jest take de babies home, Lawd?

GOD. No, I don' wanta bust up de fish fry. You angels keep quiet an' I'll pass another miracle. Dat's always de trouble wid miracles. When you pass one you always gotta r'ar back an' pass another. [*There is a hush*] Let dere be a place to dreen off dis firmament. Let dere be mountains and valleys an' let dere be oceans an' lakes. An' let dere be rivers and bayous to dreen it off in, too. As a matter of fac' let dere be de earth. An' when dat's done let dere be de sun, an' let it come out and dry my Cherubs' wings.

[*The lights go up until the stage is bathed in sunlight. On the embankment upstage there is now a waist-high wrought iron railing such as one sees on the galleries of houses in the French quarter of New Orleans. The* CHERUBS *are being examined by their parents and there is an ad lib. murmur of, "You all right, honey?" "You feel better now, Albert?" "Now you all dry, Vangy?" until the* ARCHANGEL, *who has been gazing in awe at the railing, drowns them out*]

ARCHANGEL. Look yere!

[*There is a rush to the embankment accompanied by exclamations, "My goodness!" "What's dis?" "I declah!" etc.* GABRIEL *towers above the group on the middle of the embankment.* GOD *is wrapped in thought, facing the audience. The* CHOIR *resumes singing "So High You Can't Get Over It" softly. The babbling at the balustrade dies away as the people lean over the railing.* GABRIEL *turns and faces* GOD *indicating the earth below the railing with his left hand*]

GABRIEL. Do you see it, Lawd?

GOD [*Quietly, without turning his head upstage*]. Yes, Gabriel.

GABRIEL. Looks mighty nice, Lawd.

GOD. Yes.

[GABRIEL *turns and looks over the railing*]

GABRIEL [*Gazing down*]. Yes, suh. Dat'd make mighty nice farming country. Jest look at dat South forty over dere. You ain't going to let dat go to waste is you, Lawd? Dat would be a pity an' a shame.

GOD [*Not turning*]. It's a good earth. [GOD *turns, room is made for him beside* GABRIEL *on the embankment*] Yes. I ought to have somebody to enjoy it. [*He turns, facing the audience. The others, save for the choir who are lined up in two rows of six on an angle up right, continue to look over the embankment*] Gabriel! [GOD *steps down from the embankment two paces*]

GABRIEL [*Joining him*]. Yes, Lawd.

GOD. Gabriel, I'm goin' down dere.

GABRIEL. Yes, Lawd.

GOD. I want you to be my working boss yere while I'm gone.

GABRIEL. Yes, Lawd.

GOD. You know dat matter of dem two stars?

GABRIEL. Yes, Lawd.

GOD. Git dat fixed up! You know dat sparrow dat fell a little while ago? 'Tend to dat, too.

GABRIEL. Yes, Lawd.

GOD. I guess dat's about all. I'll be back Saddy. [*To the* CHOIR] Quiet, angels. [*The* CHOIR *stops singing. Those on the embankment circle down stage.* GOD *goes to embankment. Turns and faces the company*] I'm gonter pass one more miracle. You all gonter help me an' not make a soun' caize it's one of de most impo'tant miracles of all. [*Nobody moves.* GOD *turns, facing the sky and raises his arms above his head*] Let there be man.

[*There is growing roll of thunder as stage grows dark. The* CHOIR *bursts into "Hallelujah," and continues until the lights go up on the next scene*]

SCENE THREE

ENCLOSING *the stage is a heterogeneous cluster of cottonwood, camphor, live oak and sycamore trees, youpon and turkey berry bushes, with their purple and red berries, sprays of fern-like indigo fiera and splashes of various Louisiana flowers. In the middle of the stage, disclosed when the mistiness at rise grows into warm sunlight, stands* ADAM. *He is a puzzled man of 30, of medium height, dressed in the clothing of the average field hand. He is bare-headed. In the distance can be heard the choir continuing "Bright Mansions Above." A bird begins to sing.* ADAM *smiles and turns to look at the source of this novel sound. He senses his strength and raises his forearms, his fists clenched. With his left hand he carefully touches the muscles of his upper right arm. He smiles again, realizing his power. He looks at his feet which are stretched wide apart. He stamps once or twice and now almost laughs in his enjoyment. Other birds begin trilling and* ADAM *glances up joyfully toward the foliage.* GOD *enters.*

GOD. Good mo'nin', Son.

ADAM [*With a little awe*]. Good mo'nin', Lawd.

GOD. What's yo' name, Son?

ADAM. Adam.

GOD. Adam which?

ADAM [*Frankly, after a moment's puzzled groping*]. Jest Adam, Lawd.

GOD. Well, Adam, how dey treatin' you? How things goin'?

ADAM. Well, Lawd, you know it's kind of a new line of wukk.

GOD. You'll soon get de hang of it. You know yo' kind of a new style with me.

ADAM. Oh, I guess I'm gonter make out all right soon as I learn de ropes.

GOD. Yes, I guess you will. Yo' a nice job.

ADAM. Yes, Lawd.

GOD. Dey's jest one little thing de matter with you. Did you notice it?

ADAM. Well, now you mentioned it, Lawd, I kind of thought dey was somethin' wrong.

GOD. Yes suh, you ain't quite right. Adam, you need a family. De reason for dat is in yo' heart you is a family man. [*Flicking the ash off his cigar*] I'd say dat was de main trouble at de moment.

ADAM [*Smiling*]. Yes sir. [*His smile fades and he is puzzled again*] At de same time—dey's one thing puzzlin' me, Lawd. Could I ask you a question?

GOD. Why, certainly, Adam.

ADAM. Lawd, jest what *is* a family?

GOD. I'm gonter show you. [*Indicates a spot*] Jest lie down dere, Adam. Make out like you was goin' to slumber.

ADAM [*Gently*]. Yes, Lawd.

[*He lies down.* GOD *stands beside him and as he raises his arms above his head the lights go down. In the darkness* GOD *speaks*]

GOD. Eve. [*Lights go up.* EVE *is standing beside* ADAM. *She is about twenty-six, and quite pretty. She is dressed like a country girl. Her gingham dress is quite new and clean.* GOD *is now at the other side of the stage, looking at them critically.* EVE *looks at* ADAM *in timid wonder and slowly turns her head until she meets the glance of* GOD. ADAM *stands beside* EVE. *They gaze at each other for a moment.* GOD *smiles*] Now you all right, Eve. [ADAM *and* EVE *face him*] Now I'll tell you what I'm gonter do. I'm gonter put you in charge here. I'm gonter give you de run of his whole garden. Eve, you take care of dis man an' Adam you take care of dis woman. You belong to each other. I don' want you to try to do too much caize yo' both kind of experiment wid me an' I ain't sho' whether you could make it. You two jest enjoy yo'self. Drink de water from de little brooks an' de wine from de grapes an' de berries, an' eat de food dat's hangin' for you in de trees. [*He pauses, startled by a painful thought*] Dat is, in all but one tree. [*He pauses. Then, not looking at them*] You know what I mean, my children?

ADAM AND EVE. Yes, Lawd. [*They slowly turn their heads left, toward the branches of an offstage tree. Then they look back at* GOD]

ADAM. Thank you, Lawd.

EVE. Thank you, Lawd.

GOD. I gotter be gittin' along now. I got a hund'ed thousan' things to do fo' you take yo' nex' breath. Enjoy yo'selves—

[GOD *exits*]

[ADAM *and* EVE *stand looking after Him for a moment, then each looks down and watches their hands meet and clasp*]

[*After a moment they lift their heads slowly until they are again gazing at the tree*]

EVE. Adam.

ADAM [*Looking at the tree, almost in terror*]. What?

EVE [*Softly as she too continues to look at the tree*]. Adam.

[*The* CHOIR *begins singing "Turn You Round" and as the lights go down the* CHOIR *continues until there is blackness. The* CHOIR *suddenly stops. The following scene is played in the darkness*]

MR. DESHEE'S VOICE. Now, I s'pose you chillun know what happened after God made Adam 'n' Eve. Do you?

FIRST GIRL'S VOICE. I know, Mr. Deshee.

MR. DESHEE'S VOICE. Jest a minute Randolph. Didn't I tell you you gotta tell yo' mammy let yo' sister bring you. Carlisle, take way dat truck he's eatin'. You sit by him, see kin you keep him quiet. Now, den, Myrtle what happened?

FIRST GIRL'S VOICE. Why, den dey ate de fo'bidden fruit and den dey got driv' out de garden.

MR. DESHEE'S VOICE. An' den what happened?

FIRST GIRL'S VOICE. Den dey felt ver bad.

MR. DESHEE'S VOICE. I don' mean how dey feel, I mean how dey do. Do dey have any children or anything like dat?

FIRST GIRL'S VOICE. Oh, yes, suh, dey have Cain 'n' Abel.

MR. DESHEE'S VOICE. Dat's right, dey have Cain an' Abel.

BOY'S VOICE. Dat was a long time after they got married, wasn't it, Mr. Deshee? My mammy say it was a hund'ed years.

MR. DESHEE'S VOICE. Well, nobody kin be so sure. As I tol' you befo' dey was jest beginnin' to be able to tell de time an' nobody was any too sure 'bout anythin' even den. So de bes' thing to do is jest realize dat de thing happened an' don't bother 'bout how many years it was. Jest remember what I told you about it gittin' dark when you go to sleep an' it bein' light when you wake up. Dat's de way time went by in dem days. One thing we do know an' dat was dis boy Cain was a mean rascal.

[*The lights go up on the next scene*]

SCENE FOUR

A ROADSIDE. CAIN, *a husky young Negro, stands over the body of the dead* ABEL. *Both are dressed as laborers.* CAIN *is looking at the body in awe, a rock in his right hand.* GOD *enters.*

GOD. Cain, look what you done to Abel.

CAIN. Lawd, I was min'in' my own business and he come monkeyin' aroun' wit' me. I was wukkin' in de fiel' an' he was sittin' in de shade of de tree. He say "Me, I'd be skeered to git out in dis hot sun. I be 'fraid my brains git cooked. Co'se you ain't got no brains so you ain' in no danger."

An' so I up and flang de rock. If it miss 'im all right, an' if it hit 'im, all right. Dat's de way I feel.

GOD. All right, but I'm yere to tell you dat's called a crime. When de new Judge is done talkin' to you you'll be draggin' a ball and chain de rest of yo' life.

CAIN. Well, what'd he want to come monkeyin' aroun' me fo' den? I was jest plowin', min'in' my own business, and not payin' him no min', and yere he come makin' me de fool. I'd bust anybody what make me de fool.

GOD. Well, I ain't sayin' you right an' I ain't sayin' you wrong. But I do say was I you I'd jest git myself down de road 'til I was clean out of de county. An' you better take an' git married an' settle down an' raise some chillun. Dey ain't nothin' to make a man fo'git his troubles like raisin' a family. Now, you better git.

CAIN. Yessuh.

[CAIN *walks off*]

[GOD *watches him from the forestage and as the lights begin to dim looks off. The* CHOIR *begins "Run, Sinner, Run."*]

GOD. Adam an' Eve you better try again. You better have Seth an' a lot mo' chillun.

[*There is darkness. The* CHOIR *continues until the lights go up on the next scene*]

SCENE FIVE

C AIN *is discovered walking on an unseen treadmill. A middle distance of trees, hillsides and shrubbery passes him on an upper treadmill. Behind is the blue sky. He stops under the branches of a tree to look at a sign on a fence railing. Only half the tree is visible on the stage. The sign reads,* "NOD PARISH.   COUNTY LINE."

CAIN [*Sitting down with a sigh of relief under the tree*]. At las'! Phew! [*Wipes his forehead with a handkerchief*] Feels like I been walkin' fo'ty years. [*He looks back*] Well, dey cain' git me now. Now I kin raise a fam'ly. [*An idea occurs to him, and suddenly he begins looking right and left*] Well, I'll be hit by a mule! Knock me down for a trustin' baby! Where I gonter git dat fam'ly? Dat preacher fooled me. [*He is quite dejected*] Doggone!

CAIN'S GIRL [*Off stage*]. Hello, Country Boy!

[CAIN *glances up to the offstage branches of the tree*]

CAIN. Hey-ho, Good lookin'! Which way is it to town?

CAIN'S GIRL [*Off stage*]. What you tryin' to do? You tryin' to mash me? I be doggone if it ain't gittin so a gal cain't hardly leave de house 'out some of dese fast men ain' passin' remarks at her.

CAIN. I ain' passin' remarks.

CAIN'S GIRL [*Off stage*]. If I thought you was tryin' to mash me, I'd call de police an' git you tooken to de first precinct.

CAIN. Look yere, gal, I ast you a question, an' if you don' answer me I'm gonter bend you 'cross my pants an' burn you up.

CAIN'S GIRL [*Off stage*]. I'm comin' down.

[CAIN *takes his eyes from the tree*]

CAIN. Yes, an' you better hurry.

[CAIN'S GIRL *enters. She is as large as* CAIN, *wickedly pretty, and some- what flashily dressed. She smiles at* CAIN]

CAIN'S GIRL. I bet you kin handle a gal mean wid dem big stout arms of your'n. I sho would hate to git you mad at me, Country Boy.

CAIN [*Smiling*]. Come yere. [*She goes a little closer to him*] Don't be 'fraid, I ain' so mean.

CAIN'S GIRL. You got two bad lookin' eyes. I bet yo' hot coffee 'mong de women folks.

CAIN. I ain' never find out. What was you doin' in dat tree?

CAIN'S GIRL. Jest coolin' myself in de element.

CAIN. Is you a Nod Parish gal?

CAIN'S GIRL. Bo'n an' bred.

CAIN. You know yo' kinda pretty.

CAIN'S GIRL. Who tol' you dat?

CAIN. Dese yere two bad eyes of mine.

CAIN'S GIRL. I bet you say dat to everybody all de way down de road.

CAIN. Comin' down dat road I didn't talk to nobody.

CAIN'S GIRL. Where you boun' for, Beautiful?

CAIN. I'm jest seein' de country. I thought I might settle down yere fo' a spell. You live wit' yo' people?

CAIN'S GIRL. Co'se I does.

CAIN. 'Spose dey'd like to take in a boarder?

CAIN'S GIRL. Be nice if dey would, wouldn't it?

CAIN. I think so. You got a beau?

CAIN'S GIRL. Huh-uh!

CAIN [*Smiling*]. You has *now*.

CAIN'S GIRL. I guess—I guess if you wanted to kiss me an' I tried to stop you, you could pretty nearly crush me wit' dem stout arms.

CAIN. You wouldn't try too much, would you?

CAIN'S GIRL. Maybe for a little while.

CAIN. An' den what?

CAIN'S GIRL. Why don' we wait an' see?

CAIN. When would dat be?

CAIN'S GIRL. Tonight. After supper. Think you kin walk a little further now, City Boy?

CAIN. Yeh, I ain't so weary now.

[*She takes his hand*]

CAIN'S GIRL. What yo' name? [*Takes his arm*]

CAIN. Cain. '

CAIN'S GIRL. Then I'm Cain's Gal. Come on, honey, an meet de folks.

[*They exit*]

[*The* CHOIR *is heard singing "You Better Mind," as* GOD *enters.* GOD *watches the vanished* CAIN *and his girl*]

GOD [*After shaking his head*]. Bad business. I don' like de way things is goin' atall.

[*The stage is darkened*]

[*The* CHOIR *continues singing until the lights go up on the next scene*]

SCENE SIX

GOD's *private office in Heaven. It is a small room, framed by tableau curtains. A large window up center looks out on the sky. There is a battered roll-top desk. On the wall next to the window is a framed religious oleograph with a calendar attached to it underneath. A door is at the left. A hat rack is on the wall above the door. There are two or three cheap pine chairs beside the window, and beyond the door. In front of the desk is an old swivel armchair which creaks every time* GOD *leans back in it. The desk is open and various papers are stuck in the pigeonholes. Writing implements, etc. are on the desk. On a shelf above the desk is a row of law books. A cuspidor is near the desk, and a waste basket by it. The general atmosphere is that of the office of a Negro lawyer in a Louisiana town. As the lights go up* GOD *takes a fresh cigar from a box on the desk and begins puffing it without bothering to light it. There is no comment on this minor miracle from* GABRIEL *who is sitting in one of the chairs with a pencil and several papers in his hand. The singing becomes pianissimo.*

GABRIEL [*Looking at the papers*]. Well, I guess dat's about all de impo'tant business this mornin', Lawd.

GOD. How 'bout dat Cherub over to Archangel Montgomery's house?

GABRIEL. Where do dey live, Lawd?

[*The singing stops*]

GOD. Dat little two story gold house, over by de pearly gates.

GABRIEL. Oh, *dat* Montgomery. I thought you was referrin' to de ol' gentleman. Oh, yeh. [*He sorts through the papers and finds one he is looking for*] Yere it 'tis. [*Reads*] "Cherub Christina Montgomery; wings is moltin' out of season an' nobody knows what to do."

GOD. Well, now, take keer of dat. You gotter be more careful, Gabe.

GABRIEL. Yes, Lawd.

[*Folds the papers and puts them in a pocket.* GOD *turns to his desk takes another puff or two of the cigar, and with a pencil, begins checking off items on a sheet of paper before him. His back is turned toward* GABRIEL. GABRIEL *takes his trumpet from the hat rack and burnishes it with his robe. He then wets his lips and puts the mouth piece to his mouth*]

GOD [*Without turning around*]. Now, watch yo'self, Gabriel.

GABRIEL. I wasn't goin' to blow, Lawd. I jest do dat every now an' den so I can keep de feel of it.

[*He leans trumpet against the wall.* GOD *picks up the papers and swings his chair around toward* GABRIEL]

GOD. What's dis yere about de moon?

GABRIEL [*Suddenly remembering*]. Oh! De moon people say it's beginnin' to melt a little, on 'count caize de sun's so hot.

GOD. It's goin' roun' 'cording to schedule, ain't it?

GABRIEL. Yes, Lawd.

GOD. Well, tell 'em to stop groanin'. Dere's nothin' de matter wid dat moon. Trouble is so many angels is flyin' over dere on Saddy night. Dey git to beatin' dere wings when dey dancin' an' dat makes de heat. Tell dem dat from now on dancin' 'roun' de moon is sinnin'. Dey got to stop it. Dat'll cool off de moon. [*He swings back and puts the paper on the desk. He leans back in the chair comfortably, his hands clasped behind his head*] Is dere anythin' else you ought to remin' me of?

GABRIEL. De prayers, Lawd.

GOD [*Puzzled, slowly swinging chair around again*]. De prayers?

GABRIEL. From mankind. You know, down on de earth.

GOD. Oh, yeh, de poor little earth. Bless my soul, I almos' forgot about dat. Mus' be three or four hund'ed years since I been down dere. I wasn't any too pleased wid dat job.

GABRIEL [*Laughing*]. You know you don't make mistakes, Lawd.

GOD [*Soberly, with introspective detachment*]. So dey tell me. [*He looks at* GABRIEL, *then through the window again*] So dey tell me. I fin' I kin be displeased though, an' I was displeased wid de mankind I las' seen. Maybe I ought to go down dere agin—I need a little holiday.

GABRIEL. Might do you good, Lawd.

GOD. I think I will. I'll go down an' walk de earth agin an' see how dem poor humans is makin' out. What time is it, by de sun an' de stars?

GABRIEL [*Glancing out of the window*]. Jest exactly half-past, Lawd.

[GOD *is taking his hat and stick from the hat rack*]

GOD [*Opening the door*]. Well, take keer o' yo'self. I'll be back Saddy. [*He exits*]

[*The stage is darkened. The* CHOIR *begins "Dere's No Hidin' Place," and continues until the lights go up on the next scene*]

SCENE SEVEN

GOD *is walking along a country road. He stops to listen. Church bells are heard in the distance.*

GOD. Dat's nice. Nice an' quiet. Dat's de way I like Sunday to be. [*The sound is broken by a shrill voice of a girl. It is* ZEBA *singing a "blues"*] Now, dat ain't so good. [GOD *resumes his walk and the upper treadmill brings on a tree stump on which* ZEBA *is sitting. She is accompanying her song with a ukulele.* GOD *and the treadmills stop. When the stump reaches the center of the stage, it is seen that* ZEBA *is a rouged and extremely flashily dressed chippy of about eighteen*] Stop dat!

ZEBA. What's de matter wid you, Country Boy? Pull up yo' pants. [*She resumes singing*]

GOD. Stop dat!

ZEBA [*Stops again*]. Say, listen to me, Banjo Eyes. What right you got to stop a lady enjoyin' herself?

GOD. Don't you know dis is de Sabbath? Da's no kin' o' song to sing on de Lawd's day.

ZEBA. Who care 'bout de Lawd's day, anymo'? People jest use Sunday now to git over Saddy.

GOD. You a awful sassy little girl.

ZEBA. I come fum sassy people! We even speak mean of de dead.

GOD. What's yo' name?

ZEBA [*Flirtatiously*]. "What's my name?" Ain't you de ol'-time gal hunter! Fust, "What's my name?" den I s'pose, what would it be like if you tried to kiss me? You preachers is de debbils.

GOD. I ain't aimin' to touch you, daughter. [*A sudden sternness frightens* ZEBA. *She looks at him sharply*] What is yo' name?

ZEBA. Zeba.

GOD. Who's yo' fam'ly?

ZEBA. I'm de great-great gran' daughter of Seth.

GOD. Of Seth? But Seth was a good man.

ZEBA. Yeh, he too good, he die of holiness.

GOD. An' yere's his little gran' daughter reekin' wid cologne. Ain't nobody ever tol' you yo' on de road to Hell?

ZEBA [*Smiling*]. Sho' dat's what de preacher say. Exceptin' of course, I happens to know dat I'm on de road to de picnic groun's, an' at de present time I'm waitin' to keep a engagement wid my sweet papa. He don' like people talkin' to me.

[CAIN THE SIXTH *enters. He is a young buck, wearing a "box" coat and the other flashy garments of a Rampart Street swell*]

CAIN THE SIXTH. Hello, sugah! [*He crosses in front of* GOD *and faces* ZEBA]. Hello, mamma! Sorry I'm late, baby, but de gals in de barrel-house

jest wouldn't let me go. Doggone, one little wirehead swore she'd tear me
down.

    [ZEBA *smiles and takes his hand*]

GOD. What's yo' name, son?

CAIN THE SIXTH [*Contemptuously; without turning*]. Soap 'n' water, Country Boy.

GOD [*Sternly*]. What's yo' name, son?

    [CAIN *slowly turns and for a moment his manner is civil*]

CAIN THE SIXTH. Cain the Sixth.

GOD. I was afraid so.

CAIN THE SIXTH [*His impudence returning*]. You a new preacher?

GOD. Where you live?

CAIN THE SIXTH. Me, I live mos' any place.

GOD. Yes, an' you gonter see dem all. Is de udder young men all like you?

CAIN THE SIXTH [*Smiling*]. De gals don' think so.

    [*He turns toward* ZEBA *again, picks her up and sits on the stump with
the laughing* ZEBA *on his lap*]

ZEBA. Dey ain't nobody in de worl' like my honey-cake.

    [CAIN *kisses her and she resumes her song*]

    [GOD *watches them.* ZEBA *finishes a verse of the song and begins an-
other softly.* CAIN THE SIXTH's *eyes have been closed during the
singing*]

CAIN THE SIXTH [*His eyes closed*]. Is de preacher gone?

    [ZEBA *looks quickly at* GOD *without seeing him, and then looks off.
She stops the song*]

ZEBA. Yeh, I guess he walks fast.

    [CAIN *pushes her off his lap and rises*]

CAIN THE SIXTH [*With acid sweetness*]. Dey tell me las' night you was
talkin' to a creeper man, baby.

ZEBA. Why, you know dey ain't nobody in de world fo' me but you.

CAIN THE SIXTH [*Smiling*]. I know dey ain't. I even got dat guaranteed.
[*Takes a revolver from his pocket*] See dat, baby?

ZEBA. Sho' I see it, honey.

CAIN THE SIXTH. Dat jest makes me positive. [*Puts the gun back*]

ZEBA [*Pushing him back on the stump*] You don' wanter believe dem
stories, papa.

CAIN THE SIXTH [*With sinister lightness*]. No, I didn't believe dem, baby.
Co'se dat big gorilla, Flatfoot, from de other side of de river *is* in town ag'in.

ZEBA. Dat don' mean nothin'. Flatfoot ain't nothin' to me.

CAIN THE SIXTH [*Sitting again*]. Co'se he ain't. Go 'head, sing some mo',
baby.

    [ZEBA *resumes singing*]

GOD. Bad business. [*The treadmills start turning.* GOD *resumes his walk.*
ZEBA, *still singing, and* CAIN THE SIXTH *recede with the landscape.* GOD *is
again alone on the country road. There is a twitter of birds.* GOD *looks up*

and smiles] De birds is goin' 'bout dere business, all right. [*A patch of flowers goes by, black-eyed Susans, conspicuously*] How you flowers makin' out? [*Children's voices answer, "We O.K., Lawd"*] Yes, an' you looks very pretty. [*Children's voices: "Thank you, Lawd." The flowers pass out of sight*] It's only de human bein's makes me downhearted. Yere's as nice a Sunday as dey is turnin' out anywhere, an' nobody makin' de right use of it. [*Something ahead of him attracts his attention. His face brightens*] Well, now dis is mo' like it. Now dat's nice to see people prayin'. It's a wonder dey don' do it in de church. But I fin' I don' min' it if dey do it outdoors.

> [*A group of five adult Negroes and a boy on their knees in a semi-circle, appears. The treadmills stop. The* BOY, *his head bent, swings his hands rhythmically up to his head three or four times. There is a hush*]

GAMBLER. Oh, Lawd, de smoke-house is empty. Oh, Lawd, lemme git dem groceries. Oh, Lawd, lemme see dat little *six*. [*He casts the dice*] Wham! Dere she is, frien's.

> [*Exclamations from the others: "Well damn my eyes!" "Doggone, dat's de eighth pass he make." "For God's sake, can't you ever crap?" etc. The* BOY *is picking up the money*]

GOD. Gamblin'! [*Looks over the group's shoulders*]. An' wid frozen dice!

BOY GAMBLER. Dey's a dolla' 'n' a half talkin' fo' me. How much you want of it, Riney?

FIRST GAMBLER. I take fo' bits. Wait a minute. Mebbe I take a little mo'. [*He counts some money in his hand*]

SECOND GAMBLER [*Glancing up at* GOD]. Hello, Liver Lips. [*To the others*] Looka ol' Liver Lips.

> [*The others look up and laugh good-naturedly, repeating "Liver Lips"*]

FIRST GAMBLER. Ain't his pockets high from de groun'? Ol' High-Pockets.

> [*The others keep saying "Ole Liver Lips." "Ol' Liver Lips don't like to see people dicin'." "Dat's a good name, 'High Pockets'."*]

BOY GAMBLER [*To others*]. Come on, you gonter fade me or not?

> [GOD *seizes the boy's ears and drags him to his feet. The others do not move, but watch, amused*]

GOD. Come yere, son. Why, yo' jest a little boy. Gamblin' an' sinnin'. [GOD *looks at the boy's face*] You been chewin' tobacco, too, like you was yo' daddy. [GOD *sniffs*] An' you been drinkin' sonny-kick-mammy-wine. You oughta be 'shamed. [*To the others*] An' you gamblers oughta be 'shamed, leading' dis boy to sin.

FIRST GAMBLER. He de bes' crap shooter in town, mister.

GOD. I'm gonter tell his mammy. I bet she don' know 'bout dis.

FIRST GAMBLER. No, she don' know. [*The others laugh*] She don' know anythin'.

SECOND GAMBLER. Das de God's truth.

FIRST GAMBLER. See kin you beat 'im, High Pockets. Dey's a dolla' open yere.

GOD. I ain't gonter beat 'im. I'm gonter teach 'im. I may have to teach you all.

[*He starts walking from them. The* BOY *sticks out his tongue the moment* GOD'S *back is turned*]

BOY GAMBLER. If you fin' my mammy you do mo'n I kin. Come on, gamblers, see kin you gimme a little action. Who wants any part of dat dollar?

[*The treadmill carries them off. The* FIRST GAMBLER *is heard saying:* "I'll take anoder two bits," *and the others,* "Gimme a dime's wo'th." "I ain't only got fifteen cents left," *etc., as they disappear*]

GOD [*Walking*]. Where's dat little boy's home? [*The front of a shanty appears and* GOD *stops in front of the door*] Yere's de place. It ain't any too clean, either.

[*Knocks on the door with his cane*]

VOICE IN SHANTY. Who dar?

GOD. Never you min' who's yere. Open de door.

VOICE IN SHANTY. You gotta search warrant?

GOD. I don' need one.

VOICE IN SHANTY. Who you wanter see?

GOD. I wanter see de mammy of de little gamblin' boy.

VOICE IN SHANTY. You mean little Johnny Rucker?

GOD. Dat may be his name.

VOICE IN SHANTY. Well, Mrs. Rucker ain't home.

GOD. Where's she at?

VOICE IN SHANTY. Who, Mrs. Rucker?

GOD. You heerd me.

VOICE IN SHANTY. Oh, she run away las' night wid a railroad man. She's eloped.

GOD. Where's Rucker?

VOICE IN SHANTY. He's flat under de table. He so drunk he cain't move.

GOD. Who are you?

VOICE IN SHANTY. I'se jest a fren' an' neighbor. I come in las' night to de party, an' everybody in yere's dead drunk but me. De only reason I kin talk is I drank some new white mule I made myself, an' it burn my throat so I cain't drink no mo'. You got any mo' questions?

GOD. Not for you.

[*The shanty begins to move off as* GOD *starts walking again*]

VOICE IN SHANTY. Good riddance, I say.

[*Shanty disappears*]

GOD. Dis ain't gittin' me nowheres. All I gotta say dis yere mankind I been peoplin' my earth wid sho' ain't much. [*He stops and looks back*] I got good min' to wipe 'em all off an' people de earth wid angels. No. Angels is all right, singin' an' playin' an' flyin' around, but dey ain't much on workin' de crops and buildin' de levees. No, suh, mankind's jest right for my earth, if he wasn't so doggone sinful. I'd rather have my earth peopled wit' a bunch of channel catfish, dan I would mankin' an' his sin. I jest cain't stan' sin.

[*He is about to resume his walk when* NOAH *enters.* NOAH *is dressed like a country preacher. His coat is of the "hammer-tail" variety. He carries a prayer book under his arm*]

NOAH.   Mo'nin', brother.

GOD.   Mo'nin', brother. I declare you look like a good man.

NOAH.   I try to be, brother. I'm de preacher yere. I don't think I seen you to de meetin'.

[*They resume walking*]

GOD.   I jest come to town a little while ago an' I been pretty busy.

NOAH.   Yeh, mos' everybody say dey's pretty busy dese days. Dey so busy dey cain't come to meetin'. It seem like de mo' I preaches de mo' people ain't got time to come to church. I ain't hardly got enough members to fill up de choir. I gotta do de preachin' an' de bassin too.

GOD.   Is dat a fac'?

NOAH.   Yes, suh, brother. Everybody is mighty busy, gamblin', good-timin', an' goin' on. You jest wait, though. When Gabriel blow de horn you gonter fin' dey got plenty of time to punch chunks down in Hell. Yes, suh.

GOD.   Seems a pity. Dey all perfec'ly healthy?

NOAH.   Oh, dey healthy, all right. Dey jest all lazy, and mean, and full of sin. You look like a preacher, too, brother.

GOD.   Well, I am, in a way.

NOAH.   You jest passin' through de neighborhood?

GOD.   Yes. I wanted to see how things was goin' in yo' part of de country, an' I been feelin' jest 'bout de way you do. It's enough to discourage you.

NOAH.   Yes, but I gotta keep wres'lin wid 'em. Where you boun' for right now, brother?

GOD.   I was jest walkin' along. I thought I might stroll on to de nex' town.

NOAH.   Well, dat's a pretty good distance. I live right yere. [*He stops walking*] Why don' you stop an' give us de pleasure of yo' comp'ny for dinner? I believe my ol' woman has kilt a chicken.

GOD.   Why, dat's mighty nice of you, brother. I don't believe I caught yo' name.

NOAH.   Noah, jest brother Noah. Dis is my home, brother. Come right in.

[GOD *and* NOAH *start walking towards* NOAH's *house which is just coming into view on the treadmill*]

[*The stage darkens, the* CHOIR *sings "Feastin' Table," and when the lights go up again, the next scene is disclosed*]

SCENE EIGHT

INTERIOR of NOAH's *house. The ensemble suggests the combination living-dining room in a fairly prosperous Negro's cabin. Clean white curtains hang at the window. A table and chairs are in the center of the room. There is a cheerful checked tablecloth on the table, and on the wall, a framed, highly colored picture reading "God Bless Our Home."*

[NOAH'S WIFE, *an elderly Negress, simply and neatly dressed,* GOD *and* NOAH *are discovered grouped about the table*]

NOAH. Company, darlin'. [NOAH'S WIFE *takes* NOAH'S *and* GOD'S *hats*] Dis gemman's a preacher, too. He's jest passin' through de country.

GOD. Good mo'nin', sister.

NOAH'S WIFE. Good mo'nin'. You jest ketch me when I'm gittin' dinner ready. You gonter stay with us?

GOD. If I ain't intrudin'. Brother Noah suggested—

NOAH'S WIFE. You set right down yere. I got a chicken in de pot an' it'll be ready in 'bout five minutes. I'll go out de back an' call Shem, Ham 'n' Japheth. [*To* GOD] Dey's our sons. Dey live right acrost de way but always have Sunday dinner wid us. You mens make yo'selves comf'table.

GOD. Thank you, thank you very kindly.

NOAH. You run along, we all right.

[GOD *and* NOAH *seat themselves.* NOAH'S WIFE *exits*]

GOD. You got a fine wife, Brother Noah.

NOAH. She pretty good woman.

GOD. Yes, suh, an' you got a nice little home. Have a ten cent seegar? [GOD *offers him one*]

NOAH. Thank you, much obliged.

[*Both men lean back restfully in their chairs*]

GOD. Jest what seems to be de main trouble 'mong mankind, Noah?

NOAH. Well, it seems to me de main trouble is dat de whol' distric' is wide open. Now you know dat makes fo' loose livin'. Men folks spen's all dere time fightin', loafin' an' gamblin', an' makin' bad likker.

GOD. What about de women?

NOAH. De women is worse dan de men. If dey ain't makin' love powder dey out beg, borrow an' stealin' money for policy tickets. Doggone, I come in de church Sunday 'fo' las' 'bout an' hour befo' de meetin' was to start, and dere was a women stealin' de altar cloth. She was goin' to hock it. Dey ain't got no moral sense. Now you take dat case las' month, over in East Putney. Case of dat young Willy Roback.

GOD. What about him?

NOAH. Dere is a boy sebenteen years old. Doggone, if he didn't elope with his aunt. Now, you know, dat kin' of goin' on is bad fo' a neighborhood.

GOD. Terrible, terrible.

NOAH. Yes, suh. Dis use' to be a nice, decent community. I been doin' my best to preach de Word, but seems like every time I preach de place jest goes a little mo' to de dogs. De good Lawd only knows what's gonter happen.

GOD. Dat is de truth.

[*There is a pause. Each puffs his cigar*]

[*Suddenly* NOAH *grasps his knee, as if it were paining him, and twists his foot*]

NOAH. Huh!

GOD. What's de matter?

NOAH. I jest got a twitch. My buck-aguer I guess. Every now and den I gets a twitch in de knee. Might be a sign of rain.

GOD. That's just what it is. Noah, what's de mos' rain you ever had 'round dese parts?

NOAH. Well, de water come down fo' six days steady last April an' de ribber got so swole it bust down de levee up 'bove Freeport. Raise cain all de way down to de delta.

GOD. What would you say was it to rain for forty days and forty nights?

NOAH. I'd say dat was a *complete* rain!

GOD. Noah, you don't know who I is, do you?

NOAH [*Puzzled*]. Yo' face looks easy, but I don' think I recall de name.

[GOD *rises slowly, and as he reaches his full height there is a crash of lightning, a moment's darkness, and a roll of thunder. It grows light again.* NOAH *is on his knees in front of* GOD]

I should have known you. I should have seen de glory.

GOD. Dat's all right, Noah. You didn't know who I was.

NOAH. I'm jes' 'ol' preacher Noah, Lawd, an' I'm yo' servant. I ain' very much, but I'se all I got.

GOD. Sit down, Noah. Don' let me hear you shamin' yo'se'f, caize yo' a good man. [*Timidly* NOAH *waits until* GOD *is seated, and then sits, himself*] I jest wanted to fin' out if you was good, Noah. Dat's why I'm walkin' de earth in de shape of a natchel man. I wish dey was mo' people like you. But, far as I kin see you and yo' fam'ly is de only respectable people in de worl'.

NOAH. Dey jest all poor sinners, Lawd.

GOD. I know. I am your Lawd. I am a god of wrath and vengeance an' dat's why I'm gonter destroy dis worl'.

NOAH [*Almost in a whisper. Drawing back*]. Jest as you say, Lawd.

GOD. I ain't gonter destroy you, Noah. You and yo' fam'ly, yo' sheep an' cattle, an' all de udder things dat ain't human I'm gonter preserve. But de rest is gotta go. [*Takes a pencil and a sheet of paper from his pocket*] Look yere, Noah. [NOAH *comes over and looks over his shoulder*] I want you to build me a boat. I want you to call it de "Ark," and I want it to look like dis. [*He is drawing on the paper. Continues to write as he speaks*] I want you to take two of every kind of animal and bird dat's in de country. I want you to take seeds an' sprouts an' everythin' like dat an' put dem on dat Ark, because dere is gonter be all dat rain. Dey's gonter to be a deluge, Noah, an' dey's goin' to be a flood. De levees is gonter bust an' everything dat's fastened down is comin' loose, but it ain't gonter float long, caize I'm gonter make a storm dat'll sink everythin' from a hencoop to a barn. Dey ain't a ship on de sea dat'll be able to fight dat tempest. Dey all got to go. Everythin'. Everythin' in dis pretty worl' I made, except one thing, Noah. You an' yo' fam'ly an' de things I said are going to ride dat storm in de Ark. Yere's de way it's to be. [*He hands* NOAH *the paper.* NOAH *takes it and reads*]

NOAH [*Pause. Looks at paper again*]. Yes, suh, dis seems to be complete. Now 'bout the animals, Lawd, you say you want everythin'?

GOD. Two of everythin'.

NOAH. Dat would include jayraffes an' hippopotamusses?

GOD. Everythin' dat is.

NOAH. Dey was a circus in town las' week. I guess I kin fin' dem. Co'se I kin git all de rabbits an' possums an' wil' turkeys easy. I'll sen' de boys out. Hum, I'm jest wonderin'—

GOD. 'Bout what?

NOAH. 'Bout snakes? Think you'd like snakes, too?

GOD. Certainly, I want snakes.

NOAH. Oh, I kin git snakes, lots of 'em. Co'se, some of 'em's a little dangerous. Maybe I better take a kag of likker, too?

GOD. You kin have a kag of likker.

NOAH [*Musingly*]. Yes, suh, dey's a awful lot of differ'nt kin's of snakes, come to think about it. Dey's water moccasins, cotton-moufs, rattlers—mus' be a hund'ed kin's of other snakes down in de swamps. Maybe I better take two kags of likker.

GOD [*Mildly*]. I think de one kag's enough.

NOAH. No. I better take two kags. Besides I kin put one on each side of de boat, an' balance de ship wid dem as well as havin' dem fo' medicinal use.

GOD. You kin put one kag in de middle of de ship.

NOAH [*Buoyantly*]. Jest as easy to take de two kags, Lawd.

GOD. I think one kag's enough.

NOAH. Yes, Lawd, but you see forty days an' forty nights——

[*There is a distant roll of thunder*]

GOD [*Firmly*]. One kag, Noah.

NOAH. Yes, Lawd. One kag.

[*The door in the back opens and* NOAH'S WIFE *enters with a tray of dishes and food*]

NOAH'S WIFE. Now, den, gen'lemen, if you'll jest draw up cheers.

[*The stage is darkened. The* CHOIR *is heard singing "I Want to Be Ready." They continue in the darkness until the lights go up on the next scene*]

SCENE NINE

I N *the middle of the stage is the Ark. On the hillside, below the Ark, a dozen or more men and women, townspeople, are watching* NOAH, SHEM, HAM *and* JAPHETH *on the deck of the Ark. The three sons are busily nailing boards on the cabin.* NOAH *is smoking a pipe. He wears a silk hat, captain's uniform and a "slicker."*

NOAH [*To* SHEM]. You, Shem, tote up some ol' rough lumber, don' bring up any planed up lumber, caize dat ain't fo' de main deck.

SHEM. Pretty near supper time, daddy.

NOAH. Maybe 'tis, but I got de feelin' we ought to keep goin'.

FIRST WOMAN. You gonter work all night, Noah, maybe, huh?

NOAH [*Without looking at her*]. If de sperrit move me.

SECOND WOMAN. Look yere, Noah, whyn't you give up all dis damn foolishness? Don' you know people sayin' yo' crazy? What you think you doin' anyway?

NOAH. I'se buildin' a Ark. [*Other men and women join those in the foreground*] Ham, you better stop for a while 'n see whether dey bringin' de animals up all right. [*He looks at his watch*] Dey ought to be pretty near de foot o' de hill by dis time; if dey ain't you wait fo' dem and bring 'em yo'se'f.

[HAM *goes down a ladder at the side of the ship and exits during the following scene. The newcomers in group have been speaking to some of the early arrivals*]

SECOND WOMAN [*To* THIRD WOMAN, *one of the newcomers*]. No, you don't mean it!

THIRD WOMAN. I do so. Dat's what de talk is in de town.

FIRST MAN. You hear dat, Noah? Dey say yo' ol' lady is tellin' everybody it's gonter rain fo' fo'ty days and fo'ty nights. You know people soon gonter git de idea you *all* crazy.

NOAH. Lot I keer what you think. [*To* JAPHETH]. Straighten up dem boards down dere, Japheth. [*Indicates floor of deck*]

FIRST MAN [*To* THIRD WOMAN]. Was I you, I wouldn't go 'round with Mrs. Noah anymore, lady. Fust thing you know you'll be gittin' a hard name, too.

THIRD WOMAN. Don't I know?

SECOND WOMAN. A lady cain't be too partic'lar dese days.

[ZEBA *and* FLATFOOT, *a tall, black, wicked-looking buck, enter, their arms around each other's waist*]

ZEBA. Dere it is baby. Was I lyin'?

FLATFOOT. Well, I'll be split in two!

FIRST MAN. What you think of it, Flatfoot?

FLATFOOT. I must say! Look like a house wit' a warpin' cellar.

NOAH. Dis yere vessel is a boat.

FLATFOOT. When I was a little boy dey used to build boats down near de ribber, where de water was.

[*The others laugh*]

NOAH. Dis time it's been arranged to have de water come up to de boat. [JAPHETH *looks belligerently over the rail of the Ark at* FLATFOOT. *To* JAPHETH] Keep yo' shirt on, son.

SECOND WOMAN [*To* THIRD WOMAN]. Now, you see de whole fam'ly's crazy.

THIRD WOMAN. Listen, dey ain't gonter 'taminate me. It was me dat started resolvin' dem both out o' de buryin' society.

ZEBA. When all dis water due up yere, Noah?

NOAH. You won't know when it gits yere, daughter.

ZEBA. Is she goin' to be a side-wheeler, like de Bessy-Belle?

FLATFOOT. No! If she was a side-wheeler she'd get her wheels all clogged wid sharks. She gonter have jus' one great big stern wheel, like de Commodore. Den if dey ain't 'nuf water why de big wheel kin stir some up.

[*General laughter. Two or three of the* GAMBLERS *enter and join the group, followed by* CAIN THE SIXTH]

CAIN THE SIXTH. Dere's de fool an' his monument, jest like I said!

[*The* GAMBLERS *and* CAIN THE SIXTH *roar with laughter, slap their legs, etc., the members of the main group talk sotto voce to each other as* CAIN THE SIXTH *catches* ZEBA's *eye.* FLATFOOT *is on her right and is not aware of* CAIN THE SIXTH's *presence*]

NOAH. See how dey makin' out inside, son. [*Stops hammering*]

[JAPHETH *exits into Ark*]

[NOAH *turns and gazes towards the east*]

CAIN THE SIXTH. Hello, honey.

ZEBA [*Frightened but smiling*]. Hello, sugah.

CAIN THE SIXTH [*Pleasantly*]. Ain' dat my ol' frien' Flatfoot wid you?

ZEBA. Why, so 'tis! [FLATFOOT *is now listening. To* FLATFOOT] He's got a gun.

CAIN THE SIXTH. No, I ain't.

[*He lifts his hands over his head.* ZEBA *quickly advances and runs her hands lightly over his pockets*]

ZEBA [*Relieved*]. I guess he ain't.

CAIN THE SIXTH. No, I ain't got no gun for my ol' friend, Flatfoot.

[*He walks up to him*]

FLATFOOT [*Smiling*]. Hi, Cain. How's de boy?

[CAIN *quickly presses his chest against* FLATFOOT's, *his downstage arm sweeps around* FLATFOOT's *body and his hand goes up to the small of* FLATFOOT's *back*]

CAIN THE SIXTH [*Quietly, but triumphantly*]. I got a little knife *fo' him*.

[FLATFOOT *falls dead*]

[*The laughter of the others stops and they look at the scene.* ZEBA *for a moment is terrified, her clenched hand pressed to her mouth. She looks at* CAIN THE SIXTH, *who is smiling at her. He tosses the knife on the ground and holds his hands out to her. She goes to him, smiling*]

ZEBA. You sho' take keer of me, honey.

CAIN THE SIXTH. Dat's caize I think yo' wo'th takin' keer of. [*To the others*] It's all right, folks. I jest had to do a little cleanin' up.

FIRST WOMAN [*Smiling*]. You is de quickes' scoundrel.

FIRST GAMBLER. It was a nice quick killin'. Who was he?

SECOND WOMAN [*Casually*]. Dey called him Flatfoot. From over de river. He wa'nt any good. He owed me for washin' for over a year.

THIRD WOMAN. Used to peddle muggles. Said it had a kick like reg'lar snow. Wasn't no good.

SECOND GAMBLER. Think we ought to bury him?

FIRST MAN. No, just leave him dere. Nobody comes up yere, 'cept ol' Manatee.

[*Indicates* NOAH. *Cries of "Ol' Manatee! Ol' Manatee, dat's good!"*]

NOAH [*Still looking off*]. You bettah pray, you po' chillun.

[*They all laugh*]

FIRST WOMAN. We bettah pray? You bettah pray, Ol' Manatee?

ZEBA. You bettah pray for rain. [*Laughter again*]

NOAH. Dat's what I ain't doin', sinners. Shem! Japheth! [*To others, as he points off. Patter of rain*] Listen!

CAIN THE SIXTH [*Casually*]. Doggone, I believe it *is* gonter shower a little.

FIRST GAMBLER. It do looks like rain.

FIRST WOMAN. I think I'll git on home. I got a new dress on.

ZEBA. Me, too. I wants to keep lookin' nice fo' my sweet papa.

[*She pats* CAIN THE SIXTH's *cheek.* CAIN THE SIXTH *hugs her*]

NOAH [*Almost frantically*]. Ham! Is de animals dere?

HAM [*Off stage*]. Yes, sir, dere yere. We're comin'.

NOAH. Den bring 'em on.

[SHEM *and* JAPHETH *come on deck with their hammers. The stage begins to darken*]

THIRD WOMAN. I guess we all might go home 'til de shower's over. Come on, papa.

SECOND GAMBLER. See you after supper, Noah. [*Crowd starts moving off right*]

NOAH. God's gittin' ready to start, my sons. Let's git dis plankin' done.

ZEBA. Put a bix Texas on it, Noah, an' we'll use it fo' excursions.

[*There is a distant roll of thunder, there are cries of "Good night, Admiral." "See you later." "So long, Manatee," as the crowd goes off. The thunder rumbles again. There is the sound of increasing rain. The hammers of* SHEM *and* JAPHETH *sound louder and are joined by the sounds of other hammerers. There is a flash of lightning. The*

CHOIR *begins "Dey Ol' Ark's a-Movering," the sounds on the Ark become faster and louder. The rush of rain grows heavier*]

NOAH. Hurry! Hurry! Where are you, Ham?

HAM [*Just off stage*]. Yere, I am, father, wid de animals.

NOAH. God's give us his sign. Send 'em up de gangplank.

[*An inclined plane is thrown against the Ark from the side of the stage by* HAM, *who cracks a whip*]

HAM. Get on, dere.

[*The heads of two elephants are seen*]

NOAH. Bring 'em on board! De Lawd is strikin' down de worl'!

[*The singing and the noises reach fortissimo as* HAM *cracks his whip again, and the rain falls on the stage*]

[*The stage is darkened. The* CHOIR *continues singing in the darkness*]

SCENE TEN

WHEN *the lights go up on scene, the Ark is at sea. Stationary waves run in front of it. The hillside has disappeared. The Ark is in the only lighted area.*

SHEM *is smoking a pipe on the deck, leaning on the rail. A steamboat whistle blows three short and one long blast.* SHEM *is surprised. In a moment* HAM *appears, also with a pipe, and joins* SHEM *at the rail.*

SHEM. Who'd you think you was signallin'?

HAM. Dat wasn't me, dat was daddy.

SHEM. He think he gonter git a reply?

HAM. I don't know. He's been gittin' a heap of comfort out of dat likker.

SHEM. De kag's nearly empty, ain't it?

HAM. Pretty nearly almos'. [*They look over the rail. A pause*] Seen anythin'?

SHEM. Dis mornin' I seen somethin' over dere might'a' been a fish.

HAM. Dat's de big news of de week.

SHEM. How long you think dis trip's gonter las'?

HAM. I don't know! Rain fo'ty days 'n' fo'ty nights an' when dat stop' I thought sho' we'd come up ag'inst a san' bar o' somethin'. Looks now like all dat rain was jest a little incident of de trip, [*The whistle blows again*] Doggone! I wish he wouldn't do dat. Fust thing we know he'll wake up dem animals ag'in.

[JAPHETH *appears*]

SHEM. What de matter wit' de ol' man, Jape?

JAPHETH. Doggone, he say he had a dream dat we're nearly dere. Dat's why he pullin' de whistle cord. See kin he git a' answer. [*He looks over the rail*] Look to me like de same ol' territory.

[MRS. NOAH *appears on deck*]

NOAH'S WIFE. You boys go stop yo' paw pullin' dat cord. He so full of likker he think he's in a race.

JAPHETH. He claim he know what he's doin'.

NOAH'S WIFE. I claim he gittin' to be a perfec' nuisance. Me an' yo' wives cain't hardly heah ou'sel'es think. [NOAH *appears, his hat rakishly tilted on his head. He goes to the railing and looks out*] You 'spectin' company?

NOAH. Leave me be, woman. De watah don' look so rough today. De ol' boat's ridin' easier.

NOAH'S WIFE. Ridin' like a ol' mule!

NOAH. Yes, suh, de air don't feel so wet. Shem! 'Spose you sen' out 'nother dove. [SHEM *goes into the Ark*] Ham, go git de sound'n' line. Jape, keep yo' eye on de East.

[JAPHETH *goes to the end of the boat*]

NOAH'S WIFE. As fo' you, I s'pose you'll help things along by takin' a litttle drink.

NOAH. Look yere, who's de pilot of dis vessel?

NOAH'S WIFE. Ol' Mister Dumb Luck.

NOAH. Well, see dat's where you don' know anythin'.

NOAH'S WIFE. I s'pose you ain't drunk as a fool?

NOAH [*Cordially*]. I feel congenial.

NOAH'S WIFE. An' you look it. You look jest wonderful. I wonder if you'd feel so congenial if de Lawd was to show up?

NOAH. De Lawd knows what I'm doin', don' you worry 'bout dat.

NOAH'S WIFE. I wouldn't say anything' ag'inst de Lawd. He suttinly let us know dey'd be a change in de weather. But I bet even de Lawd wonders sometimes why he ever put you in charge.

NOAH. Well, you let de Lawd worry 'bout dat.

[SHEM *appears with the dove*]

SHEM. Will I leave her go, Paw?

NOAH. Leave 'er go.

[*There is a chorus of "Good Luck, Dove," from the group as the dove flies off stage.* HAM *appears with the sounding line*]

Throw 'er over, Boy.

[HAM *proceeds to do so*]

NOAH'S WIFE. An' another thing——

HAM. Hey!

NOAH [*Rushing to his side*]. What is it?

HAM. Only 'bout a inch! Look [*They lean over*]

JAPHETH. It's gettin' light in de East.

[*As* HAM *works the cord up and down,* NOAH *and* NOAH'S WIFE *turn toward* JAPHETH. *The* CHOIR *begins "My Soul Is a Witness for the Lord"*]

NOAH. Praise de Lawd, so it is.

NOAH'S WIFE. Oh, dat's pretty.

NOAH [*To* HAM]. An' de boat's stopped. We've landed. Shem, go down 'n' drag de fires an' dreen de boiler. Yo go help 'im, Ham.

JAPHETH. Look, Paw.

[*The dove wings back to the Ark with an olive branch in its mouth*]

NOAH. 'N' yere's de little dove wid greenery in its mouth! Take 'er down, Jape, so she kin tell de animals. [JAPHETH *exits after* SHEM *and* HAM *carrying the dove. To* MRS. NOAH]. Now, maybe you feel little different.

NOAH's WIFE [*Contritely*]. It was jes' gittin' to be so tiresome. I'm sorry, Noah.

NOAH. Dat's all right, ol' woman. [NOAH's WIFE *exits.* NOAH *looks about him. The lights have changed and the water piece is gone and the ark is again on the hillside. Two mountains can be seen in the distance and a rainbow slowly appears over the Ark. The singing has grown louder*] Thank you, Lawd, thank you very much indeed. Amen.

[*The singing stops with the "Amen."* GOD *appears on the deck*]

GOD. Yo' welcome, Noah.

[NOAH *turns and sees him*]

NOAH. O, Lawd, it's wonderful.

GOD [*Looking about him*]. I sort of like it. I like de way you handled de ship, too, Noah.

NOAH. Was you watchin', Lawd?

GOD. Every minute. [*He smiles*] Didn't de ol' lady light into you?

NOAH [*Apologetically*]. She was kinda restless.

GOD. That's all right. I ain't blamin' nobody. I don' even min' you' cussin' an' drinkin'. I figure a steamboat cap'n on a long trip like you had has a right to a little red eye, jest so he don' go crazy.

NOAH. Thank you, Lawd. What's de orders now?

GOD. All de animals safe?

NOAH. Dey all fin'n' dandy, Lawd.

GOD. Den I want you to open dat starboard door, an' leave 'em all out. Let 'em go down de hill. Den you an' de family take all de seeds 'n' de sprouts an' begin plantin' ag'in. I'm startin' all over, Noah.

[NOAH *exits.* GOD *looks around*]

GOD. Well, now we'll see what happens. [GOD *listens with a smile, as noises accompanying the debarking of the animals are heard. There are the cracks of whips, the voices of the men on the Ark, shouting: "Git along dere." "Whoa, take it easy." "Duck yo' head." "Keep in line dere," etc. Over the Ark there is a burst of centrifugal shadows, and the sound of a myriad of wings.* GOD *smiles at the shadows*] Dat's right, birds, fin' yo' new homes. [*Bird twitters are heard again.* GOD *listens a moment and rests an arm on the railing. He speaks softly*] Gabriel, kin you spare a minute?

[GABRIEL *appears*]

GABRIEL. Yes, Lawd?

[*The sounds from the other side of the Ark are by now almost hushed. The* LORD *indicates the new world with a wave of the hand*]

GOD. Well, it's did.

GABRIEL [*Respectfully, but with no enthusiasm*]. So I take notice.

GOD. Yes, suh, startin' all over again.

GABRIEL. So I see.

GOD [*Looking at him suddenly*]. Don' seem to set you up much.

GABRIEL. Well, Lawd, you see— [*He hesitates*] 'Tain't none of my business.

GOD. What?

GABRIEL. I say, I don't know very much about it.

GOD. I know you don'. I jest wanted you to see it. [*A thought strikes him*] Co'se, it ain' yo' business, Gabe. It's my business. 'Twas my idea. De whole thing was my idea. An' every bit of it's my business 'n' nobody else's. De whole thing rests on my shoulders. I declare, I guess *dat's* why I feel so solemn an' serious, at dis particklar time. You know *dis* thing's turned into quite a proposition.

GABRIEL [*Tenderly*]. But, it's all right, Lawd, as you say, it's did.

GOD. Yes, suh, it's did. [*Sighs deeply. Looks slowly to the right and the left. Then softly*] I only hope it's goin' to work out all right.

PART TWO: SCENE ONE

GOD's *office again.*
    Somewhere the CHOIR *is singing: "A City Called Heaven." In the office are* TWO WOMEN CLEANERS. *One is scrubbing the floor, the other dusting the furniture. The one dusting stops and looks out the window.* *There is a whirr and a distant faint boom. The* CHOIR *stops.*

FIRST CLEANER. Dat was a long way off.

SECOND CLEANER [*At window*]. Yes, ma'am. An' dat must a' been a big one. Doggone, de Lawd mus' be mad fo' sho', dis mo'nin'. Dat's de fo'ty-six' thunde'-bolt since breakfast.

FIRST CLEANER. I wonder where at He's pitchin' dem.

SECOND CLEANER. My goodness, don' you know?

FIRST CLEANER [*A little hurt*]. Did I know I wouldn't ask de question.

SECOND CLEANER. Every one of dem's bound fo' de earth.

FIRST CLEANER. De earth? You mean dat little ol' dreenin' place?

SECOND CLEANER. Dat's de planet. [*Another faint whirr and boom*] Dere goes another.

FIRST CLEANER. Well, bless me. *I* didn't know dey was thunde'bolts.

SECOND CLEANER. Wha'd you think dey was?

FIRST CLEANER [*Above desk*]. I wasn't sho', but I thought maybe He might be whittlin' a new star o' two, an' de noise was jest de chips fallin'.

SECOND CLEANER. Carrie, where you been? Don' you know de earth is de new scandal? Ever'body's talkin' 'bout it.

FIRST CLEANER. Dey kep' it from me.

SECOND CLEANER. Ain't you noticed de Lawd's been unhappy lately?

FIRST CLEANER [*Thoughtfully*]. Yeah, He ain't been his old self.

SECOND CLEANER. What did you think was de matteh? Lumbago?

FIRST CLEANER [*Petulantly*]. I didn't know. I didn't think it was fo' me t'inquieh.

SECOND CLEANER. Well, it jest so happens dat de Lawd is riled as kin be by dat measly little earth. Or I should say de scum dat's on it.

FIRST CLEANER. Dat's mankind down dere.

SECOND CLEANER. Dey mus' be scum, too, to git de Lawd so wukked up.

FIRST CLEANER. I s'pose so. [*Another whirr and boom*] Looks like He's lettin' dem feel de wrath. Ain' dat a shame to plague de Lawd dat way?

SECOND CLEANER. From what I hear dey been beggin' fo' what dey're gittin'. My brother flew down to bring up a saint de other day and he say from what he see mos' of de population down dere has made de debbil king an' dey wukkin' in three shifts fo' him.

FIRST CLEANER. You cain't blame de Lawd.

SECOND CLEANER. Co'se you cain't. Dem human bein's 'd make anybody bile oveh. Ev'rytime de Lawd try to do sompin' fo' dem, doggone if dey don't staht some new ruckus.

FIRST CLEANER. I take notice He's been wukkin' in yere mo' dan usual.

SECOND CLEANER. I wish He'd let us ladies fix it up. Wouldn't take a minute to make dis desk gold-plated.

FIRST CLEANER. I 'spose He likes it dis way. De Lawd's kind o' ol' fashioned in some ways. I s'pose He keeps dis office plain an' simple on purpose.

SECOND CLEANER [*Finishing her work*]. I don't see why.

FIRST CLEANER [*Looking off*]. Well, it's kind of a nice place to come to when He's studyin' somethin' impo'tant. 'Most evahthin' else in heaven's so fin' an' gran', maybe ev'ry now an' den He jest gits sick an' tired of de glory. [*She is also collecting her utensils*]

SECOND CLEANER. Maybe so. Jest de same I'd like to have a free hand wid dis place for a while, so's I could gold it up.

[GOD *appears in the doorway*]

GOD. Good mo'nin', daughters.

FIRST AND SECOND CLEANERS. Good mo'nin', Lawd. We was jest finishin'.

GOD. Go ahead den, daughters. [*Goes to the window*]

FIRST AND SECOND CLEANERS. Yes, Lawd. [*They exeunt. Off stage*] Good mo'nin', Gabriel.

[*Off stage* GABRIEL *says, "Good mo'nin', sisters," and enters immediately. He stands in the doorway for a moment watching* GOD—*a notebook and pencil in his hand*]

GOD. What's de total?

GABRIEL [*Consulting the book*]. Eighteen thousand nine hund'ed an' sixty for de mo'nin'. Dat's includin' de village wid de fo'tune tellers. Dey certainly kin breed fast.

GOD [*Solemnly*]. Dey displease me. Dey displease me greatly.

GABRIEL. Want some more bolts, Lawd?

GOD [*Looking through window*]. Look at 'em dere. Squirmin' an' fightin' an' bearin' false witness. Listen to dat liar, dere. He don' intend to marry dat little gal. He don' even love her. What did you say?

GABRIEL. Should I git mo' bolts?

GOD. Wait a minute. [*He carefully points his finger down through the window*] I'm goin' to git dat wicked man myself. [*From a great distance comes an agonized cry: "Oh, Lawd!"* GOD *turns from the window*] No use gittin' mo' thunde'bolts. Dey don' do de trick. [*He goes to the swivel chair and sits*] It's got to be somethin' else.

GABRIEL. How would it be if you was to doom 'em all ag'in, like dat time you sent down de flood? I bet dat would make dem mind.

GOD. You see how much good de flood did. Dere dey is, jest as bad as ever.

GABRIEL. How about cleanin' up de whole mess of 'em and sta'tin' all over ag'in wid some new kind of animal?

GOD. An' admit I'm licked?

GABRIEL [*Ashamedly*]. No, of co'se not, Lawd.

GOD. No, suh. No, suh. Man is a kind of pet of mine and it ain't right fo' me to give up tryin' to do somethin' wid him. Doggone, mankin' *mus'* be all right at de core or else why did I ever bother wid him in de first place? [*Sits at desk*]

GABRIEL. It's jest dat I hates to see you worryin' about it, Lawd.

GOD. Gabe, dere ain't anythin' worth while anywheres dat didn't cause somebody some worryin'. I ain't never tol' you de trouble I had gittin' things started up yere. Dat's a story in itself. No, suh, de more I keep on bein' de Lawd de more I know I got to keep improvin' things. An' dat takes time and worry. De main trouble wid mankin' is he takes up so much of my time. He ought to be able to help hisself a little. [*He stops suddenly and cogitates*] Hey, dere! I think I got it!

GABRIEL [*Eagerly*]. What's de news?

GOD [*Still cogitating*]. Yes, suh, dat seems like an awful good idea.

GABRIEL. Tell me, Lawd.

GOD. Gabriel, have you noticed dat every now an' den, mankin' turns out some pretty good specimens?

GABRIEL. Dat's de truth.

GOD. Yes, suh. Dey's ol' Abraham and Isaac an' Jacob an' all dat family.

GABRIEL. Dat's so, Lawd.

GOD. An' everyone of dem boys was a hard wukker an' a good citizen. We got to admit dat.

GABRIEL. Dey wouldn't be up yere flyin' with us if dey hadn't been.

GOD. No, suh. An' I don' know but what de answer to de whole trouble is right dere.

GABRIEL. How you mean, Lawd?

GOD. Why, doggone it, de good man is de man dat keeps busy. I mean I been goin' along on de principle dat he was something like you angels— dat you ought to be able to give him somethin' an' den jest let him sit back an' enjoy it. Dat ain't so. Now dat I recollec' I put de first one down dere to take keer o' dat garden an' den I let him go ahead an' do nothin' but git into mischief. [*He rises*] Sure, *dat's* it. He ain't *built* jest to fool 'round' an' not do nothin'. Gabe, I'm gonter try a new scheme.

GABRIEL [*Eagerly*]. What's de scheme, Lawd?

GOD. I'll tell you later. Send in Abraham, Isaac an' Jacob. [*A voice outside calls: "Right away, Lawd"*] You go tell dem to put dem bolts back in de boxes. I ain' gonter use dem ag'in a while.

GABRIEL. O. K., Lawd.

GOD. Was you goin' anywhere near de Big Pit?

GABRIEL. I could go.

GOD. Lean over de brink and tell Satan he's jest a plain fool if he thinks he kin beat anybody as big as me.

GABRIEL. Yes, suh, Lawd. Den I'll spit right in his eye. [GABRIEL *exits*] [GOD *looks down through the window again to the earth below*]

GOD. Dat new polish on de sun makes it powerful hot. [*He "r'ar back"*] Let it be jest a little bit cooler. [*He feels the air*] Dat's nice. [*Goes to his desk. A knock on the door*] Come in.

[ABRAHAM, ISAAC and JACOB *enter. All are very old men, but the beard of* ABRAHAM *is the longest and whitest, and they suggest their three generations. They have wings that are not quite so big as those of the native angels*]

ISAAC. Sorry we so long comin', Lawd. But Pappy and me had to take de boy [*Pointing to* JACOB] over to git him a can of wing ointment.

GOD. What was de matter, son?

JACOB. Dey was chafin' me a little. Dey fine now, thank you, Lawd.

GOD. Dat's good. Sit down an' make yo'selves comf'table. [*The three sit*. MEN: *"Thank you, Lawd"*] Men, I'm goin' to talk about a little scheme I got. It's one dat's goin' to affec' yo' fam'lies an' dat's why I 'cided I'd talk it over wid you, 'fo' it goes into ee-fect. I don't know whether you boys know it or not, but you is about de three best men of one fam'ly dat's come up yere since I made little apples. Now I tell you what I'm gonter do. Seein' dat you human bein's cain't 'preciate anythin' lessen you fust wukk to git it and den keep strugglin' to hold it, why I'm gonter turn over a very valuable piece of property to yo' fam'ly, and den see what kin dey do with it. De rest of de worl' kin go jump in de river fo' all I keer. I'm gonter be lookin' out fo' yo' descendants only. Now den, seein' dat you boys know de country pretty tho'ly, where at does you think is de choice piece of property in de whole worl'? Think it over for a minute. I'm gonter let you make de s'lection.

ABRAHAM. If you was to ask me, Lawd, I don't think dey come any better dan de Land of Canaan.

GOD [*To* ISAAC *and* JACOB]. What's yo' feelin' in de matter?

JACOB [*After a nod from* ISAAC]. Pappy an' me think do we get a pick, dat would be it.

GOD [*Goes to window again; looks out*]. De Land of Canaan. Yes, I guess dat's a likely neighborhood. It's all run over wid Philistines and things right now, but we kin clean dat up. [*He turns from the window and resumes his seat*] All right. Now who do you boys think is de best of yo' men to put in charge down dere? You see I ain't been payin' much attention to anybody in partic'lar lately.

ISAAC. Does you want de brainiest or de holiest, Lawd? [MEN *look up*]

GOD. I want de holiest. I'll make him brainy. [MEN *appreciate the miracle*]

ISAAC [*As* ABRAHAM *and* JACOB *nod to him*]. Well, if you want A Number One, goodness, Lawd, I don't know where you'll git more satisfaction dan in a great-great-great-great grandson of mine.

GOD. Where's he at?

ISAAC. At de moment I b'lieve he's in de sheep business over in Midian County. He got in a little trouble down in Egypt, but t'wan't his doin'. He killed a man dat was abusin' one of our boys in de brick works. Of co'se you know old King Pharoah's got all our people in bondage.

GOD. I heard of it. [*With some ire*] Who did you think put them dere? [*The visitors lower their heads*] It's all right, boys. [*All rise*] I'm gonter take dem out of it. An' I'm gonter turn over de whole Land of Canaan to dem. An' do you know whose gonter lead dem dere? Yo' great, great, great, great, grandson. Moses, ain't it?

ISAAC. Yes, Lawd.

GOD [*Smiling*]. Yes. I been noticin' *him*.

ABRAHAM. It's quite a favor fo' de fam'ly, Lawd.

GOD. Dat's why I tol' you. You see, it so happens I love yo' fam'ly, an' I delight to honor it. Dat's all, gen'lemen. [*The three others rise and cross to the door, murmuring, "Yes, Lawd," "Thank you, Lawd," "Much obliged, Lawd," etc. The* CHOIR *begins, "My Lord's A-Writin' All De Time" pianissimo.* GOD *stands watching the men leave*] Enjoy yo'selves. [*He goes to the window. The singing grows softer. He speaks through the window to the earth*] I'm comin' down to see you, Moses, an' dis time my scheme's *got* to wukk.

> [*The stage is darkened. The singing grows louder and continues until the lights go up on the next scene*]

SCENE TWO

THE *tableau curtains frame the opening of a cave, which is dimly lighted. A large turkey-berry bush is somewhere near the foreground.* MOSES *is seated on the grass eating his lunch from a basket in his lap.* ZIPPORAH, *his wife, stands watching him. He is about forty,* ZIPPORAH *somewhat younger. They are dressed inconspicuously.* MOSES *stutters slightly when he speaks. He looks up to see* ZIPPORAH *smiling.*

MOSES. What you smilin' at, Zipporah?

ZIPPORAH. Caize you enjoyin' yo'self.

MOSES. You is a good wife, Zipporah.

ZIPPORAH. You is a good husband, Moses. [MOSES *wipes his mouth with a handkerchief and begins putting into the basket the various implements of the meal which had been on the ground about him*] Why you suppose it's so dark yere today? Dey's no rain in de air.

MOSES. Seems like it's jest aroun' dis cave. Yo' father's house is got de sun on it. [*He looks in another direction*] Looks all clear down toward Egypt.

ZIPPORAH. Co'se it *would* be fine weather in Egypt. De sky looks all right. Maybe it's gonter rain jest right yere. Why don't you move de sheep over to de other pasture?

MOSES [*A bit puzzled*]. I don' know. It got dark like dis befo' you come along wid de dinner an' I was gonter stop you on de top of de hill. Den somethin' kep' me yere.

ZIPPORAH. S'pose it could be de Lawd warnin' you dat dey's 'Gyptians hangin' 'roun'?

MOSES. Dey may have fo'gotten all about dat killin' by now. Dey got a new Pharaoh down dere.

ZIPPORAH. An' I hear he's jest as mean to yo' people as his pappy was. I wouldn't put it pas' him to send soljahs all the way up yere fo' you.

MOSES. Dat's all right. De Lawd's looked after me so far, I don't 'spect him to fall down on me now. You better be gittin' home.

ZIPPORAH [*Taking the basket*]. I'll be worryin' about you.

MOSES [*Kissing her and then smiling*]. 'Parently de Lawd ain't. He knows I'm safe as kin be. Lemme see you feel dat way.

ZIPPORAH. You is a good man, Moses.

MOSES. I's a lucky man. [ZIPPORAH *exits with the basket.* MOSES *looks up at the sky*] Dat's funny. De sun seems to be shinin' everyplace but right yere. It's shinin' on de sheep. Why ain't dey no cloud dere?

GOD [*Off stage*]. Caize I want it to be like dat, Moses.

MOSES [*Looking about him*]. Who's dat?

GOD [*Off stage again*]. I'm de Lawd, Moses.

MOSES [*Smiling*]. Dat's what you say. Dis yere shadow may be de

Lawd's wukk, but dat voice soun' pretty much to me like my ol' brother Aaron.

GOD [*Off stage*]. Den keep yo' eyes open, son. [*The turkey-berry bush begins to glow and then turns completely red.* MOSES *looks at it fascinated*] Maybe you notice de bush ain't burnin' up.

MOSES. Dat's de truth.

[MOSES *is full of awe but not frightened*]

GOD [*Off stage*]. Now you believe me?

MOSES. Co'se I does. It's wonderful.

[*The light in the bush dies and* GOD *appears from behind it*]

GOD. No, it ain't, Moses. It was jest a trick.

MOSES. 'Scuse me doubtin' you, Lawd. I always had de feelin' you wuz takin' keer of me, but I never 'spected you'd fin' de time to talk with me pussunly. [*He laughs*] Dat was a good trick, Lawd. I'se seen some good ones, but dat was de beatenest.

GOD. Yo' gonter see lots bigger tricks dan dat, Moses. In fac', yo' gonter perfo'm dem.

MOSES [*Incredulously*]. Me? I'm gonter be a tricker?

GOD. Yes, suh.

MOSES. An' do magic? Lawd, my mouth ain't got de quick talk to go wid it.

GOD. It'll come to you now.

MOSES [*Now cured of stuttering*]. Is I goin' wid a circus?

GOD [*Slowly and solemnly*]. Yo' is goin' down into Egypt, Moses, and lead my people out of bondage. To do dat I'm gonter make you de bes' tricker in de worl'.

MOSES [*A little frightened*]. Egypt! You know I killed a man dere, Lawd. Won't dey kill me?

GOD. Not when dey see yo' tricks. You ain't skeered, is you?

MOSES [*Simply and bravely*]. No, suh, Lawd.

GOD. Den yere's what I'm gonter do. Yo' people is my chillun, Moses. I'm sick and tired o' de way ol' King Pharaoh is treatin' dem, so I'se gonter take dem away, and yo' gonter lead dem. You gonter lead 'em out of Egypt an' across de river Jordan. It's gonter take a long time, and you ain't goin' on no excursion train. Yo' gonter wukk awful hard for somethin' yo' goin' to fin' when de trip's over.

MOSES. What's dat, Lawd?

GOD. It's de Land of Canaan. It's de bes' land I got. I've promised it to yo' people, an' I'm gonter give it to dem.

MOSES. Co'se, ol' King Pharaoh will do everything he kin to stop it.

GOD. Yes, an' dat's where de tricks come in. Dey tell me he's awful fond of tricks.

MOSES. I hear dat's *all* he's fon' of. Dey say if you can't take a rabbit out of a hat you cain't even git in to see him.

GOD. Wait'll you see de tricks you an' me's goin' to show him.

MOSES [*Delightedly*]. Doggone! Huh, Lawd?

GOD. Yes, suh. Now de first trick—

[GOD *is lifting a stick which he carries*]

MOSES. Jest a minute, Lawd. [GOD *halts the demonstration*] I'm gonter learn de tricks and do just like you tell me, but I *know* it's gonter take me a little time to learn all dat quick talkin'. Cain't I have my brother Aaron go wid me? He's a good man.

GOD. I was gonter have him help you wid de Exodus. I guess he can watch, too.

MOSES. I'll call 'im. [*He turns as if to shout*]

GOD. Wait. [MOSES *turns and looks at* GOD] I'll bring him. [*Softly*] Aaron!

[AARON *appears between* GOD *and* MOSES *in the mouth of the cave. He is a little taller than* MOSES *and slightly older. He, too, is dressed like a field hand*]

AARON [*Blankly*]. Hey!

[MOSES *goes to him, takes his hand and leads him, bewildered, down to where* MOSES *had been standing alone.* AARON *then sees* GOD]

MOSES [*Almost in a whisper*]. It's all right.

GOD. Don't worry, son, I'm jest showin' some tricks. Bringin' you yere was one of dem. [AARON *stares at* GOD *as if hypnotized*] Now den, you see dis yere rod? Looks like a ordinary walking stick, don' it?

MOSES. Yes, Lawd.

GOD. Well, it ain't no ordinary walkin' stick, caize look. [MOSES *leans forward*] When I lays it down on de groun'——

[*The stage is darkened. The* CHOIR *begins, "Go Down, Moses," and continues until the lights go up on the next scene*]

SCENE THREE

THE *throne room of* PHARAOH. *It suggests a Negro lodge room. The plain board walls are colored by several large parade banners of varying sizes, colors and materials, bordered with gold fringe and tassels on them. Some of the inscriptions on them read:*

SUBLIME ORDER OF PRINCES OF THE HOUSE OF PHARAOH HOME CHAPTER

MYSTIC BROTHERS OF THE EGYPTIAN HOME GUARD LADIES AUXILIARY, No. 1

SUPREME MAGICIANS AND WIZARDS OF THE UNIVERSE

PRIVATE FLAG OF HIS HONOR OLD KING PHARAOH

ROYAL YOUNG PEOPLE'S PLEASURE CLUB

ENCHANTED AND INVISIBLE CADETS OF EGYPT BOYS' BRIGADE

There is one door up right and a window. The throne, an ordinary armchair with a drapery over its back, is on a dais. PHARAOH *is seated on the throne. His crown and garments might be those worn by a high officer in a Negro*

lodge during a ritual. About the throne itself are high officials, several of them with plumed hats, clothing that suggests military uniforms, and rather elaborate sword belts, swords and scabbards. A few soldiers carrying spears are also in his neighborhood and one or two bearded ancients in brightly colored robes with the word "Wizard" on their conical hats. In the general group of men and women scattered elsewhere in the room Sunday finery is noticeable everywhere. Most of the civilians have bright "parade" ribbons and wear medals. In a cleared space immediately before the throne a CANDIDATE MAGICIAN *is performing a sleight-of-hand trick with cards.* PHARAOH *watches him apathetically. He is receiving earnest attention from a few of the others, but the majority of the men and women are talking quietly among themselves. Beside the* CANDIDATE MAGICIAN *are several paraphernalia of previously demonstrated tricks.*

CANDIDATE MAGICIAN [*Holding up some cards*]. Now den, ol' King Pharaoh, watch dis. [*He completes a trick. There is a murmur of "Not Bad." "Pretty Good," etc. from a few of the watchers.* PHARAOH *makes no comment*] Now, I believe de cyard I ast you to keep sittin' on was de trey of diamonds, wasn't it?

PHARAOH. Yeah.

CANDIDATE MAGICIAN. Den kin I trouble you to take a look at it now? [PHARAOH *half rises to pick up a card he has been sitting on, and looks at it*] I believe you'll now notice dat it's de King of Clubs? [PHARAOH *nods and shows the card to those nearest him. The* CANDIDATE MAGICIAN *waits for an audible approval and gets practically none*] An' dat, ol' King Pharaoh, completes de puffohmance.

[*An elderly man in a uniform steps forward*]

GENERAL. On behalf of my nephew I beg Yo' Honor to let him jine de ranks of de royal trickers and magicians.

PHARAOH [*To the two* WIZARDS]. What do de committee think? [*The* WIZARDS *shake their heads*] Dat's what I thought. He ain't good enough. I'd like to help you out, General, but you know a man's got to be a awful good tricker to git in de royal society dese days. You better go back an' steddy some mo', son. [*He lifts his voice and directs two soldiers guarding the door*] Is de head magician reached de royal waitin' room yit? [*One of the soldiers opens the door to look out*] If he is, send him in.

[*The soldier beckons to some one off stage, throws the door open, and announces to the court*]

SOLDIER. De Head Magician of de land of Egypt.

[*A very old and villainous man enters. His costume is covered with cabalistic and zodiacal signs. He advances to the King, the other magician and his uncle making way for him. He bows curtly to* PHARAOH]

HEAD MAGICIAN. Good mo'nin', ol' King Pharaoh.

PHARAOH. Mo'nin', Professor. What's de news?

HEAD MAGICIAN. Evahthing's bein' carried out like you said.

PHARAOH. How's de killin' of de babies 'mongst de Hebrews comin' 'long?

HEAD MAGICIAN. Jes' like you ordered.

PHARAOH [*Genially*]. Dey killed all of 'em, huh?

HEAD MAGICIAN. Do dey see one, dey kill 'im. You teachin' 'em a great lesson. Dey don' like it a-tall.

PHARAOH [*Smiling*]. What do dey say?

HEAD MAGICIAN [*Pawing the air inarticulately*]. I hates to tell in front of de ladies.

PHARAOH. Dey feels pretty bad, huh?

HEAD MAGICIAN. Dat's jest de beginnin' of it. Betwixt de poleece and de soljahs we killed about a thousan' of 'em las' night. Dat's purty good.

PHARAOH [*Thoughtfully*]. Yeh, it's fair. I guess you boys is doin' all you kin. But I fin' I ain't satisfied, though.

HEAD MAGICIAN. How you mean, Yo' Honor?

PHARAOH. I mean I'd like to make dose Hebrew chillun realize dat I kin be even mo' of a pest. I mean I hates dem chillun. An' I'm gonter think of a way of makin' 'em even mo' mizzable.

HEAD MAGICIAN. But dey *ain't* anythin' meaner dan killin' de babies, King.

PHARAOH. Dey must be sump'n. Doggone, you is my head tricker, you put yo' brains on it. [*To the others*] Quiet, whilst de Head Magician go into de silence.

HEAD MAGICIAN [*After turning completely around twice, and a moment's cogitation*]. I tell you what I kin do. All de Hebrews dat ain't out to de buryin' grounds or in de hospitals is laborin' in de brick wukks.

PHARAOH. Yeh?

HEAD MAGICIAN [*After a cackling laugh*]. How would it be to take de straw away from 'em and tell 'em dey's got to turn out jest as many bricks as usual? Ain't dat nasty?

PHARAOH. Purty triflin', but I s'pose it'll have to do for de time bein'. Where's de extreme inner guard? [*One of the military attendants comes forward*] Go on out an' tell de sup'intendent to put dat into ee-ffect. [*The attendant bows and starts for the door. He stops as* PHARAOH *calls to him*] Wait a minute! Tell 'im to chop off de hands of anybody dat say he cain't make de bricks dat way. [*The attendant salutes and exits, the door being opened and closed by one of the soldiers*] Now what's de news in de magic line?

HEAD MAGICIAN. I ain't got very many novelties today, King, I bin wukkin' too hard on de killin's. I'm so tired I don' believe I could lift a wand.

[*There are murmurs of protest from the assemblage*]

PHARAOH. Doggone, you was to 'a been de chief feature o' de meetin' dis mawnin'. Look at de turn-out you got account of me tellin' 'em you was comin'.

HEAD MAGICIAN. Well, dat's de way it is, King. Why don' you git de wizards to do some spell castin'?

PHARAOH. Dey say it's in de cyards dat dey cain't wukk till high noon. [*He glances at the* WIZARDS] Think mebbe you kin cheat a little?

FIRST WIZARD. Oh dat cain't be done, King.

PHARAOH. Well, we might as well adjourn, den. Looks to me like de whole program's shot to pieces. [*He starts to rise, when there is a furious banging on the door*] What's de idea, dere? See who dat is. [*The soldiers open the door.* MOSES *and* AARON *enter, pushing the two soldiers aside and coming down in front of* PHARAOH. *The soldiers are bewildered and* PHARAOH *is angry*] Say, who tol' you two baboons you could come in yere?

MOSES. Is you ol' King Pharaoh?

PHARAOH. Dat's me. Did you heah what I asked you?

MOSES. My name is Moses, and dis is my brother Aaron.

[*Murmur of "Hebrews" spreads through the room*]

PHARAOH [*In a rage*]. Is you Hebrews?

MOSES. Yes, suh.

PHARAOH [*Almost screaming*]. Put 'em to de sword!

[*As the courtiers approach,* AARON *suddenly discloses the rod, which he swings once over his head. The courtiers draw back as if their hands had been stung. Cries of "Hey!" "Lookout," etc.*]

MOSES. Keep outside dat circle.

[*The courtiers nearest* MOSES *and* AARON *look at each other, exclaiming ad lib., "Did you feel dat?" "What is dat?" "What's goin' on, heah?" "My hands is stingin'!" etc.*]

PHARAOH [*Puzzled but threatening*]. What's de idea yere?

MOSES. We is magicians, ol' King Pharaoh.

PHARAOH [*To the* HEAD MAGICIAN]. Put a spell on 'em. [*The* HEAD MAGICIAN *stands looking at them bewildered. To* MOSES] I got some magicians, too. We'll see who's got de bes' magic. [MOSES *and* AARON *laugh. Most of the courtiers are cowering. To the* HEAD MAGICIAN] Go ahead, give 'em gri-gri.

MOSES. Sure, go ahead.

PHARAOH. Hurry up, dey's laughin' at you. What's de matter?

HEAD MAGICIAN. I cain't think of de right spell.

PHARAOH [*Now frightened himself*]. You mean dey got even *you* whupped?

HEAD MAGICIAN. Dey's got a new kind of magic.

PHARAOH [*Gazes at* HEAD MAGICIAN *a moment, bewildered. To the* WIZARDS] I s'pose if de Professor cain't, you cain't.

FIRST WIZARD. Dat's a new trick, King.

HEAD MAGICIAN [*Rubbing his fingers along his palms*]. It's got 'lectricity in it!

PHARAOH. Hm, well dat may make it a little diff'rent. So you boys is magicians, too?

MOSES. Yes, suh.

PHARAOH. Well, we's always glad to see some new trickers in de co't, dat is if dey good. [*He glances about him*] You look like you is O.K.

MOSES. Dat's what we claims, ol' King Pharaoh. We think we's de best in de worl'.

PHARAOH. You certainly kin talk big. Jest what is it you boys would like?

MOSES. We came to show you some tricks. Den we's goin' to ask you to do somethin' for us.

PHARAOH. Well, I s'pose you know I'm a fool for conjurin'. If a man kin show me some tricks I ain't seen, I goes out of my way to do him a favor.

MOSES. Dat's good. Want to see de first trick?

PHARAOH. It ain't goin' to hurt nobody?

MOSES. Dis one won't.

PHARAOH. Go ahead.

MOSES. Dis yere rod my brother has looks jes' like a walkin' stick, don't it?

[*The courtiers now join the King in interest*]

PHARAOH. Uh huh. Le's see.

[AARON *hands him the rod, which* PHARAOH *inspects and returns*]

MOSES. Well, look what happens when he lays it on de groun'.

[AARON *places the rod on the second step of the throne. It turns into a lifelike snake. There are exclamations from the assemblage*]

PHARAOH. Dat's a good trick! Now turn it back into a walkin' stick again. [AARON *picks it up and it is again a rod. Exclamations of "Purty good!" "Dat's all right!" "What do you think of that!" etc.*] Say, you is good trickers!

MOSES. You ain't never seen de beat of us. Now I'm going to ask de favor.

PHARAOH. Sure, what is it?

MOSES [*Solemnly*]. Let de Hebrew chillun go!

PHARAOH [*Rises and stares at them. There is a murmur of "Listen to 'im!" "He's got nerve!" "I never in my life!" "My goodness!" etc.*] What did you say?

MOSES. Let de Hebrew chillun go.

[PHARAOH *seats himself again*]

PHARAOH [*Slowly*]. Don' you know de Hebrews is my slaves?

MOSES. Yes, suh.

PHARAOH. Yes, suh, my slaves. [*There is a distant groaning*] Listen, and you kin hear 'em bein' treated like slaves. [*He calls toward the window*] What was dey doin' den?

MAN NEAR THE WINDOW. Dey's jest gettin' de news down in de brick-yard.

PHARAOH. I won't let them go. [*He snorts contemptuously*] Let's see another trick.

MOSES. Yes, suh, yere's a better one. [*He lowers his head*] Let's have a plague of de flies.

[AARON *raises the rod. The room grows dark and a great buzzing of flies is heard. The courtiers break out in cries of "Get away fum me!"*

*"Take 'em away!" "De place is filled with flies!" "Dis is terrible!"
"Do sump'n, Pharaoh!"*]

PHARAOH [*Topping the others*]. All right—stop de trick!

MOSES. Will you let de Hebrews go?

PHARAOH. Sho' I will. Go ahead stop it!

MOSES [*Also above the others*]. Begone!

[*The buzzing stops and the room is filled with light again, as* AARON
lowers the rod. All except MOSES *and* AARON *are brushing the flies
from their persons*]

PHARAOH [*Laughing*]. Doggone, dat was a good trick! [*The others,
seeing they are uninjured, join in the laughter, with exclamations of "Doggone!" "You all right?" "Sho' I'm all right." "Didn' hurt me," etc.*] You
is good trickers.

MOSES. Will you let de Hebrew chillun go?

PHARAOH [*Sitting down again*]. Well, I'll tell you, boys. I'll tell you
sump'n you didn' know. You take me, *I'm* a pretty good tricker, an' I jest
outtricked you. So, bein' de bes' tricker, I don' think I will let 'em go. You
got any mo' tricks yo'self?

MOSES. Yes, suh. Dis is a little harder one. [AARON *lifts the rod*] Gnats
in de mill pon', gnats in de clover, gnats in de tater patch, stingin' all over.

[*The stage grows dark again. There is the humming of gnats and the
slapping of hands against faces and arms, and the same protests as
were heard with the flies, but with more feeling, "I'm gittin' stung
to death!" "I'm all stung!" "Dey're like hornets!" "Dey's on my
face!" etc.*]

PHARAOH. Take 'em away, Moses!

MOSES [*His voice drowning the others*]. If I do, will you let 'em go?

PHARAOH. Sho' I will, dis time.

MOSES. Do you mean it?

PHARAOH. Co'se I mean it! Doggone, one just stang me on de nose.

MOSES. Begone! [*Lights come up as* AARON *lowers the rod. There is a
moment of general recovery again.* PHARAOH *rubs his nose, looks at his hands,
etc., as do the others*] Now, how about it?

PHARAOH [*Smiling*]. Well, I'll tell you, Moses. Now dat de trick's over—

[MOSES *takes a step toward* PHARAOH]

MOSES. Listen, Pharaoh. You been lyin' to me, and I'm gittin' tired of it.

PHARAOH. I ain't lyin', I'm trickin', too. You been trickin' me and I been
trickin' you.

MOSES. I see. Well, I got one mo' trick up my sleeve which I didn't aim
to wukk unless I had to. Caize when I does it, I cain't undo it.

PHARAOH. Wukk it an' I'll trick you right back. I don' say you ain't a
good tricker, Moses. You is one of de best I ever seen. But I kin outtrick
you. Dat's all.

MOSES. It ain't only me dat's goin' to wukk dis trick. It's me an' de Lawd.

PHARAOH. Who?

MOSES. De Lawd God of Israel.

PHARAOH. I kin outtrick you an' de Lawd too!

MOSES [Angrily]. Now you done it, ol' King Pharaoh. You been mean to de Lawd's people, and de Lawd's been easy on you caize you didn' know no better. You been givin' me a lot of say-so and no do-so, and I didn' min' dat. But now you've got to braggin' dat you's better dan de Lawd, and dat's too many.

PHARAOH. You talk like a preacher, an' I never did like to hear preachers talk.

MOSES. You ain't goin' to like it any better, when I strikes down de oldes' boy in every one of yo' people's houses.

PHARAOH. Now you've given up trickin' and is jest lyin'. [He rises] Listen, I'm Pharaoh. I do de strikin' down yere. I strike down my enemies, and dere's no one in all Egypt kin kill who he wants to, 'ceptin' me.

MOSES. I'm sorry, Pharaoh. Will you let de Hebrews go?

PHARAOH. You heard my word. [AARON is lifting his rod again at a signal from MOSES] Now, no more tricks or I'll—

MOSES. Oh, Lawd, you'll have to do it, I guess. Aaron, lift de rod.

[There is a thunderclap, darkness and screams. The lights go up. Several of the younger men on the stage have fallen to the ground or are being held in the arms of the horrified elders.

PHARAOH. What have you done yere? Where's my boy?

[Through the door came four men bearing a young man's body]

FIRST OF THE FOUR MEN. King Pharaoh.

[PHARAOH drops into his chair, stunned, as the dead boy is brought to the throne]

PHARAOH [Grief-stricken]. Oh, my son, my fine son.

[The courtiers look at him with mute appeal]

MOSES. I'm sorry, Pharaoh, but you cain't fight de Lawd. Will you let his people go?

PHARAOH. Let them go.

[The lights go out. The CHOIR begins, "Mary, Don't You Weep," and continues until it is broken by the strains of "I'm Noways Weary and I'm Noways Tired." The latter is sung by many more voices than the former, and the cacophony ends as the latter grows in volume and the lights go up on the next scene]

SCENE FOUR

THE CHILDREN OF ISRAEL are marching on the treadmill and now singing fortissimo. They are of all ages and most of them are ragged. The men have packs on their shoulders, one or two have hand carts. The line stretches across the stage. It is nearing twilight, and the faces of the assemblage are illumined by the rays of the late afternoon sun. The upper *treadmill carries a gradually rising and falling middle distance past the marchers. The foot of a mountain appears; a trumpet call is heard as the foot of the mountain reaches stage center. The marchers halt. The picture now shows the mountain running up out of sight off right. The singing stops. A babel of "What's de matter?" "Why do we stop?" "Tain't sundown yet!" "What's happened?" "What's goin' on?" "What are they blowin' for?" etc. Those looking ahead begin to murmur. "It's Moses," "Moses." "What's happened to him?" The others take up the repetition of "Moses," and* MOSES *enters, on the arm of* AARON. *He is now an old man, as is his brother, and he totters toward the center of the stage. Cries of "What's de matter, Moses?" "You ain't hurt, is you?" "Ain't that too bad?" etc. He slowly seats himself on the rock at the foot of the mountain.*

AARON. How you feelin' now, brother?

MOSES. I'm so weary, Aaron. Seems like I was took all of a sudden.

AARON. Do we camp yere?

MOSES [*Pathetically*]. No, you got to keep goin'.

AARON. But you cain't go no further tonight, brother.

MOSES. Dis never happened to me befo'.

A YOUNG WOMAN. But you's a ol' man, now, Father Moses. You cain't expect to go as fas' as we kin.

MOSES. But de Lawd said I'd do it. He said I was to show you de Promised Land. Fo'ty years, I bin leadin' you. I led you out o' Egypt. I led you past Sinai, and through de wilderness. Oh, I cain't fall down on you now!

AARON. Le's res' yere fo' de night. Den we'll see how you feel in de mo'nin'.

MOSES. We tol' de scouts we'd meet 'em three miles furder on. I hate fo' 'em to come back all dis way to report. 'Tis gettin' a little dark, ain't it?

AARON. It ain't dark, Brother.

MOSES. No, it's my eyes.

AARON. Maybe it's de dust.

MOSES. No, I jest cain't seem to see. Oh, Lawd, dey cain't have a blind man leadin' em! Where is you, Aaron?

AARON. I'se right yere, Moses.

MOSES. Do you think— [*Pause*] Oh! Do you think it's de time He said?

AARON. How you mean, Moses?

[*Crowd look from one to another in wonder*]

MOSES. He said I could lead 'em to de Jordan, dat I'd *see* de Promised Land, and dat's all de further I could go, on account I broke de laws. Little while back I thought *I* did see a river ahead, and a pretty land on de other side. [*Distant shouts "Hooray!" "Yere dey are!" "Dey travelled quick,"* etc.] Where's de young leader of de troops? Where's Joshua?

[*The call "Joshua" is taken up by those on the right of the stage, followed almost immediately by "Yere he is!" "Moses wants you!" etc.*]

[JOSHUA *enters. He is a fine looking Negro of about thirty.*]

JOSHUA [*Going to* MOSES' *side*]. Yes, suh.

MOSES. What's de shoutin' 'bout, Joshua?

JOSHUA. De scouts is back wid de news. De Jordan is right ahead of us, and Jericho is jest on de other side. Moses, we're dere! [*There are cries of* "Hallelujah!" "De Lawd be praised!" "Hooray!" "De Kingdom's comin'!" *etc. With a considerable stir among the marchers, several new arrivals crowd in from right, shouting,* "Moses, we're dere!" JOSHUA *seeing the newcomers*] Yere's de scouts!

[*Three very ragged and dusty young men advance to* MOSES]

MOSES [*As the shouting dies*]. So it's de River Jordan?

FIRST SCOUT. Yes, suh.

MOSES. All we got to take is de city of Jericho.

FIRST SCOUT. Yes, suh.

MOSES. Joshua, you got to take charge of de fightin' men, an' Aaron's gotta stay by de priests.

JOSHUA. What about you?

MOSES. You are leavin' me behind. Joshua, you gonter get de fightin' men together and take dat city befo' sundown.

JOSHUA. It's a big city, Moses, wid walls all 'round it. We ain't got enough men.

MOSES. You'll take it, Joshua.

JOSHUA. Yes, suh, but how?

MOSES. Move up to de walls wid our people. Tell de priests to go wid you with de rams' horns. You start marchin' 'roun' dem walls, and den——

JOSHUA. Yes, suh.

MOSES. De Lawd'll take charge, jest as he's took charge ev'y time I've led you against a city. He ain't never failed, has he?

SEVERAL VOICES. No, Moses. [*All raise their heads*]

MOSES. And he ain't goin' to fail us now. [*He prays. All bow*] Oh, Lawd, I'm turnin' over our brave young men to you, caize I know you don' want me to lead 'em any further. [*Rises*] Jest like you said, I've got to de Jordan but I cain't git over it. An' yere dey goin' now to take de city of Jericho. In a little while dey'll be marchin' 'roun' it. An' would you please be so good as to tell 'em what to do? Amen. [*To* JOSHUA] Go ahead. Ev'ybody follows Joshua now. Give de signal to move on wid ev'ything. [*A trumpet is heard*] You camp fo' de night in de City of Jericho. [MOSES *seats himself on the rock*]

JOSHUA. Cain't we help you, Moses?

MOSES. You go ahead. De Lawd's got his plans fo' me. Soun' de signal to march. [*Another trumpet call is heard. The company starts marching off.* AARON *lingers a moment*] Take care of de Ark of de Covenant, Aaron.

AARON. Yes, Brother. Good-bye.

MOSES. Good-bye, Aaron. [*The singing is resumed softly and dies away. The last of the marchers has disappeared*] Yere I is, Lawd. De chillun is goin' into de Promised Land. [GOD *enters from behind the hill. He walks to* MOSES, *puts his hands on his shoulders*] You's with me, ain't you, Lawd?

GOD. Co'se I is.

MOSES. Guess I'm through, Lawd. Jest like you said I'd be, when I broke de tablets of de law. De ol' machine's broke down.

GOD. Jest what was it I said to you, Moses? Do you remember?

MOSES. You said I couldn't go into de Promised Land.

GOD. Dat's so. But dat ain't all dey was to it.

MOSES. How you mean, Lawd?

GOD. Moses, you been a good man. You been a good leader of my people. You got me angry once, dat's true. And when you anger me I'm a God of Wrath. But I never meant you wasn't gonter have what was comin' to you. An' I ain't goin' to do you out of it, Moses. It's jest de country acrost de River dat you ain't gonter enter. You gonter have a Promised Land. I been gettin' it ready fo' you, fo' a long time. Kin you stand up?

MOSES [Rising, with GOD's help]. Yes, suh, Lawd.

GOD. Come on, I'm goin' to show it to you. We goin' up dis hill to see it. Moses, it's a million times nicer dan de Land of Canaan. [They start up the hill]

MOSES. I cain't hardly see.

GOD. Don't worry. Dat's jest caize you so old.

[They take a step or two up the hill, when MOSES stops suddenly]

MOSES. Oh!

GOD. What's de matter?

MOSES. We cain't be doin' dis!

GOD. Co'se we kin!

MOSES. But I fo'got! I fo'got about Joshua and de fightin' men!

GOD. How about 'em?

MOSES. Dey're marchin' on Jericho. I tol' 'em to march aroun' de walls and den de Lawd would be dere to tell 'em what to do.

GOD. Dat's all right. He's dere.

MOSES. Den who's dis helpin' me up de hill?

GOD. Yo' faith, yo' God.

MOSES. And is you over dere helpin' them too, Lawd? Is you goin' to tell dem poor chillun what to do?

GOD. Co'se I is. Listen, Moses. I'll show you how I'm helpin' dem.

[From the distance comes the blast of the rams' horns, the sound of crumbling walls, a roar, and a moment's silence. The CHOIR begins "Joshua Fit De Battle of Jericho" and continues through the rest of the scene]

MOSES. You did it, Lawd! You've tooken it! Listen to de chillun'—dey's in de Land of Canaan at last! You's de only God dey ever was, ain't you, Lawd?

GOD [Quietly]. Come on, ol' man. [They continue up the hill]

[The stage is darkened]

MR. DESHEE [In the dark] But even dat scheme didn' work. Caize after dey got into the Land of Canaan dey went to de dogs again. And dey went into bondage again. Only dis time it was in de City of Babylon.

[*The* CHOIR, *which has been singing "Cain't Stay Away," stops as the next scene begins*]

SCENE FIVE

U NDER *a low ceiling is a room vaguely resembling a Negro night club in New Orleans. Two or three long tables run across the room, and on the left is a table on a dais with a gaudy canopy above it. The table bears a card marked "Reserved for King and guests."*

Flashy young men and women are seated at the tables. About a dozen couples are dancing in the foreground to the tune of a jazz orchestra. The costumes are what would be worn at a Negro masquerade to represent the debauchees of Babylon.

FIRST MAN. When did yuh git to Babylon?

SECOND MAN. I jes' got in yesterday.

THIRD MAN [*Dancing*]. How do you like dis baby, Joe?

FOURTH MAN. Hot damn! She could be de King's pet!

A WOMAN. Anybody seen my papa?

THIRD MAN. Don't fo'git de dance at de High Priest's house tomorrow.

[*The dance stops as a bugle call is heard.* Enter MASTER OF CEREMONIES]

MASTER OF CEREMONIES. Stop! Tonight's guest of honor, de King of Babylon an' party of five.

[*Enter the* KING *and five girls. The* KING *has on an imitation ermine cloak over his conventional evening clothes and wears a diamond tiara. All rise as the* KING *enters, and sing, "Hail, de King of Bab— Bab—Babylon"*]

KING. Wait till you see de swell table I got. [*He crosses the stage to his table. The girls are jabbering*] Remind me to send you a peck of rubies in de mo'nin'.

MASTER OF CEREMONIES. Ev'nin', King!

KING. Good ev'nin'. How's de party goin'?

MASTER OF CEREMONIES. Bes' one we ever had in Babylon, King.

KING. Any Jew boys yere?

MASTER OF CEREMONIES [*indicating some of the others*]. Lot o' dem yere. I kin go git mo' if you want 'em.

KING. I was really referrin' to de High Priest. He's a 'ticlar frien' o' mine an' he might drop in. You know what he look like?

MASTER OF CEREMONIES. No, suh, but I'll be on de look-out fo' him.

KING. O.K. Now le's have a li'l good time.

MASTER OF CEREMONIES. Yes, suh. [*To the orchestra*] Let 'er go, boys.

[*The music begins, waiters appear with food and great urns painted gold and silver, from which they pour out wine for the guests. The*

MASTER OF CEREMONIES *exits. The* KING'S *dancing-girls go to the middle of the floor, and start to dance. The* KING *puts his arms about the waists of two girls and draws them to him*]

KING. Hot damn! Da's de way! Let de Jew boys see our gals kin dance better'n dere's. [*There is an ad lib. babel of "Da's de truth, King!" "I don' know—we got some good gals, too!" etc.*] Dey ain' nobody in de worl' like de Babylon gals.

[*The dancing grows faster, the watchers keep time with hand-claps. The door at the left opens suddenly, and the* PROPHET, *a patriarchal, ragged figure enters. He looks belligerently about the room, and is followed almost immediately by the* MASTER OF CEREMONIES]

PROPHET. Stop! [*The music and the dancers halt*]

KING. What's the idea, bustin' up my party?

MASTER OF CEREMONIES. He said he was expected, King. I thought mebbe he was de—

KING. Did you think he was de High Priest of de Hebrews? Why, he's jest an ol' bum! De High Priest is a fashion plate. T'row dis ole bum out o' yere.

PROPHET. Stop!

[*Those who have been advancing to seize him stop, somewhat amused*]

KING. Wait a minute. Don't throw him out. Let's see what he has to say.

PROPHET. Listen to me, King of Babylon! I've been sent yere by de Lawd God Jehovah. Don't you dare lay a hand on de Prophet!

KING. Oh, you're a prophet, is yuh? Well, you know we don' keer much fo' prophets in dis part of de country.

PROPHET. Listen to me, sons and daughters of Babylon! Listen, you children of Israel dat's given yo'selves over to de evil ways of yo' oppressors! You're all wallowin' like hogs in sin, an' de wrath of Gawd ain' goin' to be held back much longer! I'm tellin' you, repent befo' it's too late. Repent befo' Jehovah casts down de same fire dat burned up Sodom and Gomorrah. Repent befo' de— [*During this scene yells increase as the* PROPHET *continues*]

[*The* HIGH PRIEST *enters Left. He is a fat voluptuary, elaborately clothed in brightly colored robes. He walks in hand in hand with a gaudily dressed "chippy"*]

HIGH PRIEST [*Noise stops*]. Whoa, dere! What you botherin' the King fo'?

PROPHET [*Wheeling*]. And you, de High Priest of all Israel, walkin' de town wid a dirty li'l tramp.

KING. Seems to be a frien' o' yours, Jake.

HIGH PRIEST [*Crossing to the* KING *with his girl*]. Aw, he's one of dem wild men, like Jeremiah and Isaiah. Don' let him bother you none. [*Pushes* PROPHET *aside goes to* KING'S *table*]

PROPHET. You consort with harlots, an' yo' pollution in the sight of de

Lawd. De Lawd God's goin' to smite you down, jest as he's goin' to smite down all dis wicked world! [*Grabs* HIGH PRIEST *and turns him around*]

KING [*Angrily against the last part of the preceding speech*] Wait a minute. I'm getting tired of this. Don' throw him out. Jest kill him! [*There is the sound of a shot. The* PROPHET *falls*]

PROPHET. Smite 'em down, Lawd, like you said. Dey ain't a decent person left in de whole world.

[*He dies.* MASTER OF CEREMONIES, *revolver in hand, looks down at the* PROPHET]

MASTER OF CEREMONIES. He's dead, King.

KING. Some of you boys take him out.

[*A couple of young men come from the background and walk off with the body*]

HIGH PRIEST. Don' know whether you should'a done that, King.

KING. Why not?

HIGH PRIEST. I don' know whether de Lawd would like it.

KING. Now, listen, Jake. You know yo' Lawd ain't payin' much attention to dis man's town. Except fo' you boys, it's tho'ly protected by de Gods o' Babylon.

HIGH PRIEST. I know, but jest de same—

KING. Look yere, s'pose I give you a couple hund'ed pieces of silver. Don' you s'pose you kin arrange to persuade yo' Gawd to keep his hands off?

HIGH PRIEST [*Oilily*]. Well of co'se we could try. I dunno how well it would work.

[*As the* HIGH PRIEST *speaks, the* KING *claps his hands.* MASTER OF CERE-MONIES *enters with bag of money*]

KING. Yere it is.

HIGH PRIEST [*Smiling*]. I guess we kin square things up. [*He prays—whiningly*] Oh Lawd, please forgive my po' frien' de King o' Babylon. He didn't know what he was doin' an'—

[*There is a clap of thunder, darkness for a second. The lights go up and* GOD *is standing in the center of the room*]

GOD [*In a voice of doom*]. Dat's about enough. [*The guests are horri-fied*] I's stood all I kin from you. I tried to make dis a good earth. I helped Adam, I helped Noah, I helped Moses, an' I helped David. What's de grain dat grew out of de seed? Sin! Nothin' but sin throughout de whole world. I've given you ev'y chance. I sent you warriors and prophets. I've given you laws and commandments, an' you betrayed my trust. Ev'ything I've given you, you've defiled. Ev'y time I've fo'given you, you've mocked me. An' now de High Priest of Israel tries to trifle wid my name. Listen, you chillun of darkness, yo' Lawd is tried. I'm tired of de struggle to make you worthy of de breath I gave you. I put you in bondage ag'in to cure you an' yo' worse dan you was amongst de flesh pots of Egypt. So I renounce you. Listen to the words of yo' Lawd God Jehovah, for dey is de last words yo' ever hear from me. I repent of dese people dat I have made and I will deliver dem no more.

[*There is darkness and cries of "Mercy!" "Have pity, Lawd!" "We didn' mean it, Lawd!" "Forgive us, Lawd!" etc. The* CHOIR *sings "Death's Gwinter Lay His Cold Icy Hands on Me" until the lights go up on the next scene*]

SCENE SIX

GOD *is writing at his desk. Outside, past the door, goes* HOSEA, *a digni-fied old man, with wings like* JACOB's. GOD, *sensing his presence, looks up from the paper he is examining, and follows him out of the corner of his eye. Angrily he resumes his work as soon as* HOSEA *is out of sight. There is a knock on the door.*

GOD. Who is it?

[GABRIEL *enters*]

GABRIEL. It's de delegation, Lawd.

GOD [*Wearily*]. Tell 'em to come in.

[ABRAHAM, ISAAC, JACOB, *and* MOSES *enter*] Good mo'nin', gen'lemen.

THE VISITORS. Good mo'nin', Lawd.

GOD. What kin I do for you?

MOSES. You know, Lawd. Go back to our people.

GOD [*Shaking his head*]. Ev'ry day fo' hund'eds of years you boys have come in to ask dat same thing. De answer is still de same. I repented of de people I made. I said I would deliver dem no more. Good mo'nin', gen'le-men. [*The four visitors rise and exeunt.* GABRIEL *remains*] Gabe, why do dey do it?

GABRIEL. I 'spect dey think you gonter change yo' mind.

GOD [*Sadly*]. Dey don' know me. [HOSEA *again passes the door. His shadow shows on wall.* GABRIEL *is perplexed, as he watches.* GOD *again looks surreptitiously over His shoulder at the passing figure*] I don' like dat, either.

GABRIEL. What, Lawd?

GOD. Dat man.

GABRIEL. He's jest a prophet, Lawd. Dat's jest old Hosea. He jest come up the other day.

GOD. I know. He's one of de few dat's come up yere since I was on de earth last time.

GABRIEL. Ain' been annoyin' you, has he?

GOD. I don' like him walkin' past de door.

GABRIEL. All you got to do is tell him to stop, Lawd.

GOD. Yes, I know. I don' want to tell him. He's got a right up yere or he wouldn't be yere.

GABRIEL. You needn' be bothered by him hangin' aroun' de office all de time. I'll tell 'im. Who's he think he——

GOD. No, Gabe. I find it ain't in me to stop him. I sometimes jest wonder why he don' come in and say hello.

GABRIEL. You want him to do dat?

[*He moves as if to go to the door*]

GOD. He never has spoke to me, and if he don' wanta come in, I ain't gonter make him. But dat ain't de worst of it, Gabriel.

GABRIEL. What is, Lawd?

GOD. Ev'y time he goes past de door I hears a voice.

GABRIEL. One of de angels?

GOD [*Shaking his head*]. It's from de earth. It's a man.

GABRIEL. You mean he's prayin'?

GOD. No, he ain't exactly prayin'. He's jest talkin' in such a way dat I got to lissen. His name is Hezdrel.

GABRIEL. Is he on de books?

GOD. No, not yet. But ev'y time dat Hosea goes past I hear dat voice.

GABRIEL. Den tell *it* to stop.

GOD. I find I don' want to do that, either. Dey's gettin' ready to take Jerusalem down dere. Dat was my big fine city. Dis Hezdrel, he's jest one of de defenders. [*Suddenly and passionately, almost wildly*] I ain't comin' down. You hear me? I ain't comin' down. [*He looks at* GABRIEL] Go ahead, Gabriel. 'Tend to yo' chores. I'm gonter keep wukkin' yere.

GABRIEL. I hates to see you feelin' like dis, Lawd.

GOD. Dat's all right. Even bein' Gawd ain't a bed of roses. [GABRIEL *exits.* HOSEA's *shadow is on the wall. For a second* HOSEA *hesitates.* GOD *looks at the wall. Goes to window*] I hear you. I know yo' fightin' bravely, but I ain't comin' down. Oh, why don' you leave me alone? You know you ain't talkin' to me. *Is* you talkin' to me? I cain't stand yo' talkin' dat way. I kin only hear part of what yo' sayin', and it puzzles me. Don' you know you cain't puzzle God? [*A pause. Then tenderly*] Do you want me to come down dere ve'y much? You know I said I wouldn't come down? [*Fiercely*] Why don' he answer me a little? [*With clenched fists, looks down through the window*] Listen! I'll tell you what I'll do. I ain't goin' to promise you anythin', and I ain't goin' to do nothin' to help you. I'm jest feelin' a little low, an' I'm only comin' down to make myself feel a little better, dat's all.

[*The stage is darkened.* CHOIR *begins "A Blind Man Stood In De Middle of De Road," and continues until the lights go up on the next scene*]

SCENE SEVEN

IT *is a shadowed corner beside the walls of the temple in Jerusalem. The light of camp fires flickers on the figure of* HEZDREL, *who was* ADAM *in Part I. He stands in the same position* ADAM *held when first discovered but in his right hand is a sword, and his left is in a sling. Around him are several prostrate bodies. Pistol and cannon shots, then a trumpet call. Six young men enter from left in command of a* CORPORAL. *They are all armed.*

CORPORAL. De fightin' stopped fo' de night, Hezdrel.

HEZDREL. Yes?

CORPORAL. Dey're goin' to begin ag'in at cockcrow. [*Man enters, crosses the stage and exits*] Herod say he's goin' to take de temple tomorrow, burn de books and de Ark of de Covenant, and put us all to de sword.

HEZDREL. Yo' ready, ain't you?

EVERYBODY. Yes, Hezdrel.

HEZDREL. Did de food get in through de hole in de city wall?

[*Two soldiers enter, cross the stage and exit*]

CORPORAL. Yessuh, we's goin' back to pass it out now.

HEZDREL. Good. Any mo' of our people escape today?

CORPORAL. Ol' Herod's got de ol' hole covered up now, but fifteen of our people got out a new one we made.

[*Other soldiers enter, cross the stage and exit*]

HEZDREL. Good. Take dese yere wounded men back and git 'em took care of.

CORPORAL. Yes, suh.

[*They pick up the bodies on the ground and carry them offstage as* HEZDREL *speaks*]

HEZDREL. So dey gonter take de temple in de mo'nin'? We'll be waitin' for 'em. Jest remember, boys, when dey kill us we leap out of our skins, right into de lap of God.

[*The men disappear with the wounded; from the deep shadow upstage comes* GOD]

GOD. Hello, Hezdrel—Adam.

HEZDREL [*Rubbing his forehead*]. Who is you?

GOD. Me? I'm jest an ol' preacher, from back in de hills.

HEZDREL. What you doin' yere?

GOD. I heard you boys was fightin'. I jest wanted to see how it was goin'.

HEZDREL. Well, it ain't goin' so well.

GOD. Dey got you skeered, huh?

HEZDREL. Look yere, who is you, a spy in my brain?

GOD. Cain't you see I's one of yo' people?

HEZDREL. Listen, Preacher, we ain't skeered. We's gonter be killed, but we ain't skeered.

GOD. I's glad to hear dat. Kin I ask you a question, Hezdrel?

HEZDREL. What is it?

GOD. How is it you is so brave?

HEZDREL. Caize we got faith, dat's why!

GOD. Faith? In who?

HEZDREL. In our dear Lawd God.

GOD. But God say he abandoned ev' one down yere.

HEZDREL. Who say dat? Who dare say dat of de Lawd God of Hosea?

GOD. De God of Hosea?

HEZDREL. You heard me. Look yere, you *is* a spy in my brain!

GOD. No, I ain't, Hezdrel. I'm jest puzzled. You ought to know dat.

HEZDREL. How come you so puzzled 'bout de God of Hosea?

GOD. I don' know. Maybe I jest don' hear things. You see, I live 'way back in de hills.

HEZDREL. What you wanter find out?

GOD. Ain't de God of Hosea de same Jehovah dat was de God of Moses?

HEZDREL [*Contemptuously*]. No. Dat ol' God of wrath and vengeance? We have de God dat Hosea preached to us. He's de one God.

GOD. Who's he?

HEZDREL [*Reverently*]. De God of mercy.

GOD. Hezdrel, don' you think dey must be de same God?

HEZDREL. I don' know. I ain't bothered to think much about it. Maybe dey is. Maybe our God is de same ol' God. I guess we jest got tired of his appearance dat ol' way.

GOD. What you mean, Hezdrel?

HEZDREL. Oh, dat ol' God dat walked de earth in de shape of a man. I guess he lived wid man so much dat all he seen was de sins in man. Dat's what made him de God of wrath and vengeance. Co'se he made Hosea. An' Hosea never would a found what mercy was unless dere was a little of it in God, too. Anyway, he ain't a fearsome God no mo'. Hosea showed us dat.

GOD. How you s'pose Hosea found dat mercy?

HEZDREL. De only way he could find it. De only way I found it. De only way anyone kin find it.

GOD. How's dat?

HEZDREL. Through sufferin'.

GOD [*After a pause*]. What if dey kill you in de mo'nin', Hezdrel.

HEZDREL. If dey do, dey do. Dat's all.

GOD. Herod say he's goin' to burn de temple—

HEZDREL. So he say.

GOD. And burn de Ark an' de books. Den dat's de end of de books, ain't it?

HEZDREL [*Buoyantly*]. What you mean? If he burns dem things in dere? Naw. Dem's jest copies.

GOD. Where is de others?

HEZDREL [*Tapping his head*]. Dey's a set in yere. Fifteen got out through de hole in the city wall today. A hundred and fifty got out durin' de week.

Each of em is a set of de books. Dey's scattered safe all over de countryside now, jest waitin' to git pen and paper fo' to put 'em down agin.

GOD [*Proudly*]. Dey cain't lick you, kin dey Hezdrel?

HEZDREL [*Smiling*]. I know dey cain't. [*Trumpet*] You better get out o' yere, Preacher, if you wanter carry de news to yo' people. It'll soon be daylight.

GOD. I'm goin'. [*He takes a step upstage and stops*] Want me to take any message?

HEZDREL. Tell de people in de hills dey ain't nobody like de Lawd God of Hosea.

GOD. I will. If dey kill you tomorrow I'll bet dat God of Hosea'll be waitin' for you.

HEZDREL. I *know* he will.

GOD [*Quietly*]. Thank you, Hezdrel.

HEZDREL. Fo' what?

GOD. Fo' tellin' me so much. You see I been so far away, I guess I was jest way behin' de times.

[*He exits. Pause, then trumpet sounds*]

[HEZDREL *paces back and forth once or twice. Another young soldier appears. Other men enter and stand grouped about* HEZDREL]

SECOND OFFICER [*Excitedly*]. De cock's jest crowed, Hezdrel. Dey started de fightin' ag'in.

HEZDREL. We's ready for 'em. Come on, boys. [*From the darkness upstage comes another group of soldiers*] Dis is de day dey say dey'll git us. Le's fight till de last man goes. What d'you say?

CORPORAL. Le's go, Hezdrel!

HEZDREL [*Calling left*]. Give 'em ev'ything, boys!

[*There is a movement toward the left, a bugle call and the sound of distant battle. The lights go out. The* CHOIR *is heard singing, "March on," triumphantly. They continue to sing after the lights go up on the next scene*]

SCENE EIGHT

I T *is the same setting as the Fish Fry Scene in Part I. The same angels are present but the* CHOIR, *instead of marching, is standing in a double row on an angle upstage right.* GOD *is seated in an armchair near center. He faces the audience. As the* CHOIR *continues to sing,* GABRIEL *enters, unnoticed by the chattering angels. He looks at* GOD *who is staring thoughtfully toward the audience.*

GABRIEL. You look a little pensive, Lawd. [GOD *nods his head*] Have a seegar, Lawd?

GOD. No thanks, Gabriel.

[GABRIEL *goes to the table, accepts a cup of custard; chats with the angel behind the table for a moment as he sips, puts the cup down and returns to the side of* GOD]

GABRIEL. You look awful pensive, Lawd. You been sittin' yere, lookin' dis way, an awful long time. Is it somethin' serious, Lawd?

GOD. Very serious, Gabriel.

GABRIEL [*Awed by his tone*]. Lawd, is de time come for me to blow?

GOD. Not yet, Gabriel. I'm just thinkin'.

GABRIEL. What about, Lawd? [*Puts up hand. Singing stops.*]

GOD. 'Bout somethin' de boy tol' me. Somethin' 'bout Hosea, and himself. How dey foun' somethin'.

GABRIEL. What, Lawd?

GOD. Mercy. [*A pause*] Through *sufferin'*, he said.

GABRIEL. Yes, Lawd.

GOD. I'm tryin' to find it, too. It's awful impo'tant. It's awful impo'tant to all de people on my earth. Did he mean dat even God must suffer?

[GOD *continues to look out over the audience for a moment and then a look of surprise comes into his face. He sighs. In the distance a voice cries*]

THE VOICE. Oh, look at him! Oh, look, dey goin' to make him carry it up dat high hill! Dey goin' to nail him to it! Oh, dat's a terrible burden for one man to carry!

[GOD *rises and murmurs "Yes!" as if in recognition. The heavenly beings have been watching him closely, and now, seeing him smile gently, draw back, relieved. All the angels burst into "Hallelujah, King Jesus." * GOD *continues to smile as the lights fade away. The singing becomes fortissimo*]

You Can't Take It with You [1]

by MOSS HART AND GEORGE S. KAUFMAN

CHARACTERS

PENELOPE SYCAMORE	HENDERSON
ESSIE	TONY KIRBY
RHEBA	BORIS KOLENKHOV
PAUL SYCAMORE	GAY WELLINGTON
MR. DE PINNA	MR. KIRBY
ED	MRS. KIRBY
DONALD	THREE MEN
MARTIN VANDERHOF	OLGA
ALICE	

The Scene Is the Home of Martin Vanderhof,
New York

Act One

A Wednesday Evening.

During this act the curtain is lowered to
denote the passing of several hours.

Act Two

A Week Later.

Act Three

The Next Day.

ACT ONE: SCENE ONE

THE *home of* MARTIN VANDERHOF—*just around the corner from Columbia University, but don't go looking for it. The room we see is what
is customarily described as a living room, but in this house the term
is something of an understatement. The every-man-for-himself room would
be more like it. For here meals are eaten, plays are written, snakes collected,
ballet steps practiced, xylophones played, printing presses operated—if there*

[1] Reprinted by permission of Rinehart & Company, Inc. Produced December 14, 1936.

were room enough there would probably be ice skating. In short, the brood presided over by MARTIN VANDERHOF *goes on about the business of living in the fullest sense of the word. This is a house where you do as you like, and no questions asked.*

At the moment, GRANDPA VANDERHOF'S *daughter,* MRS. PENELOPE SYCAMORE, *is doing what she likes more than anything else in the world. She is writing a play—her eleventh. Comfortably ensconced in what is affectionately known as Mother's Corner, she is pounding away on a typewriter perched precariously on a rickety card table. Also on the table is one of those plaster-paris skulls ordinarily used as an ash tray, but which serves* PENELOPE *as a candy jar. And, because* PENNY *likes companionship, there are two kittens on the table, busily lapping at a saucer of milk.*

PENELOPE VANDERHOF SYCAMORE *is a round little woman in her early fifties, comfortable looking, gentle, homey. One would not suspect that under that placid exterior there surges the Divine Urge—but it does, it does.*

After a moment her fingers lag on the keys; a thoughtful expression comes over her face. Abstractedly she takes a piece of candy out of the skull, pops it into her mouth. As always, it furnishes the needed inspiration—with a furious burst of speed she finishes a page and whips it out of the machine. Quite mechanically, she picks up one of the kittens, adds the sheet of paper to the pile underneath, replaces the kitten.

As she goes back to work, ESSIE CARMICHAEL, MRS. SYCAMORE'S *eldest daughter, comes in from the kitchen. A girl of about twenty-nine, very slight, a curious air of the pixie about her. She is wearing ballet slippers—in fact, she wears them throughout the play.*

ESSIE [*Fanning herself*]. My, that kitchen's hot.

PENNY [*Finishing a bit of typing*]. What, Essie?

ESSIE. I say the kitchen's awful hot. That new candy I'm making—it just won't ever get cool.

PENNY. Do you have to make candy today, Essie? It's such a hot day.

ESSIE. Well, I got all those new orders. Ed went out and got a bunch of new orders.

PENNY. My, if it keeps on I suppose you'll be opening up a store.

ESSIE. That's what Ed was saying last night, but I said No, I want to be a dancer.

[*Bracing herself against the table, she manipulates her legs, ballet fashion*]

PENNY. The only trouble with dancing is, it takes so long. You've been studying such a long time.

ESSIE [*Slowly drawing a leg up behind her as she talks*]. Only—eight —years. After all, mother, you've been writing plays for eight years. We started about the same time, didn't we?

PENNY. Yes, but you shouldn't count my first two years, because I was learning to type.

[*From the kitchen comes a colored maid named* RHEBA—*a very black girl somewhere in her thirties. She carries a white tablecloth, and presently starts to spread it over the table*]

RHEBA [*As she enters*]. I think the candy's hardening up now, Miss Essie.

ESSIE. Oh, thanks, Rheba. I'll bring some in, mother—I want you to try it.

[*She goes into the kitchen*]

[PENNY *returns to her work as* RHEBA *busies herself with the table*]

RHEBA. Finish the second act, Mrs. Sycamore?

PENNY. Oh, no, Rheba. I've just got Cynthia entering the monastery.

RHEBA. Monastery? How'd she get there? She was at the El Morocco, wasn't she?

PENNY. Well, she gets tired of the El Morocco, and there's this monastery, so she goes there.

RHEBA. Do they let her in?

PENNY. Yes, I made it Visitors' Day, so of course anybody can come.

RHEBA. Oh.

PENNY. So she arrives on Visitors' Day and—just stays.

RHEBA. All night?

PENNY. Oh, yes. She stays six years.

RHEBA [*As she goes into the kitchen*]. Six years? My, I bet she busts that monastery wide open.

PENNY [*Half to herself, as she types*]. "Six Years Later." . . .

[PAUL SYCAMORE *comes up from the cellar. Mid-fifties, but with a kind of youthful air. His quiet charm and mild manner are distinctly engaging*]

PAUL [*Turning back as he comes through the door*]. Mr. De Pinna! [*A voice from below. "Yah?"*] Mr. De Pinna, will you bring up one of those new sky rockets, please? I want to show them to Mrs. Sycamore. [*An answering monosyllable from the cellar as he turns toward* PENNY] Look, Penny —what do you think of these little fire crackers? Ten strings for a nickel. Listen. [*He puts one down on the center table and lights it. It goes off with a good bang*] Nice, huh?

PENNY. Paul, dear, were you ever in a monastery?

PAUL [*Quite calmly*]. No, I wasn't. . . . Wait till you see the new rockets. Gold stars, then blue stars, then some bombs, and then a balloon. Mr. De Pinna thought of the balloon.

PENNY. Sounds lovely. Did you do all that today?

PAUL. Sure. We made up—oh, here we are. [MR. DE PINNA *comes up from the cellar. A bald-headed little man with a serious manner, and carrying two good-sized skyrockets*] Look, Penny. Cost us eighteen cents to make and we sell 'em for fifty. How many do you figure we can make before the Fourth, Mr. De Pinna?

DE PINNA. Well, we've got two weeks yet—what day you going to take the stuff up to Mount Vernon?

PAUL. Oh, I don't know—about a week. You know, we're going to need a larger booth this year—got a lot of stuff made up.

DE PINNA [*Examining the rocket in his hand*]. Look, Mr. Sycamore, the only thing that bothers me is, I'm afraid the powder chamber is just a little bit close to the balloon.

PAUL. Well, we've got the stars and the bombs in between.

DE PINNA. But that don't give the balloon time enough. A balloon needs plenty of time.

PAUL. Want to go down in the cellar and try it?

DE PINNA. All right.

PAUL [*As he disappears through the cellar door*]. That's the only way you'll really tell.

PENNY [*Halting* DE PINNA *in the cellar doorway*]. Mr. De Pinna, if a girl you loved entered a monastery, what would you do?

DE PINNA [*He wasn't expecting that one*]. Oh, I don't know, Mrs. Sycamore—it's been so long. [*He goes*]

[RHEBA *returns from the kitchen, bringing a pile of plates*]

RHEBA. Miss Alice going to be home to dinner tonight, Mrs. Sycamore?

PENNY [*Deep in her thinking*]. What? I don't know, Rheba. Maybe.

RHEBA. Well, I'll set a place for her, but she's only been home one night this week. [*She puts down a plate or two*] Miss Essie's making some mighty good candy today. She's doing something new with cocoanuts. [*More plates*] Let's see—six, and Mr. De Pinna, and if Mr. Kolenkhov comes that makes eight, don't it? [*At which point a muffled sound, reminiscent of the Battle of the Marne, comes up from the cellar. It is the sky rocket, of course. The great preliminary hiss, followed by a series of explosions.* PENNY *and* RHEBA, *however, don't even notice it.* RHEBA *goes right on*] Yes, I'd better set for eight.

PENNY. I think I'll put this play away for a while, Rheba, and go back to the war play.

RHEBA. Oh, I always liked that one—the war play.

[ESSIE *returns from the kitchen, carrying a plate of freshly made candy*]

ESSIE. They'll be better when they're harder, mother, but try one—I want to know what you think.

PENNY. Oh, they look awfully good. [*She takes one*] What do you call them?

ESSIE. I think I'll call 'em Love Dreams.

PENNY. Oh, that's nice. . . . I'm going back to my war play, Essie. What do you think?

ESSIE. Oh, are you, mother?

PENNY. Yes, I sort of got myself into a monastery and I can't get out.

ESSIE. Oh, well, it'll come to you, mother. Remember how you got out of that brothel. . . . Hello, boys. [*This little greeting is idly tossed toward the snake solarium, a glass structure looking something like a goldfish aqua-*

rium, but containing, believe it or not, snakes] The snakes look hungry. Did Rheba feed them?

PENNY [*As* RHEBA *re-enters*]. I don't know. Rheba, did you feed the snakes yet?

RHEBA. No, Donald's coming and he always brings flies with him.

PENNY. Well, try to feed them before Grandpa gets home. You know how fussy he is about them.

RHEBA. Yes'm.

PENNY [*Handing her the kittens*]. And take Groucho and Harpo into the kitchen with you. . . . I think I'll have another Love Dream.

[MR. SYCAMORE *emerges from the cellar again*]

PAUL. Mr. De Pinna was right about the balloon. It was too close to the powder.

ESSIE [*Practicing a dance step*]. Want a Love Dream, father? They're on the table.

PAUL. No, thanks. I gotta wash.

PENNY. I'm going back to the war play, Paul.

PAUL. Oh, that's nice. We're putting some red stars after the blue stars, then come the bombs and *then* the balloon. That ought to do it. [*He goes up the stairs*]

ESSIE [*Another dance step*]. Mr. Kolenkhov says I'm his most promising pupil.

PENNY [*Absorbed in her own troubles*]. You know, with forty monks and one girl, something ought to happen.

[ED CARMICHAEL *comes down the stairs. A nondescript young man in his mid-thirties. In shirtsleeves at the moment*]

ED. Listen! [*He hums a snatch of melody as he heads for the far corner of the room—the xylophone corner. Arriving there, he picks up the sticks and continues the melody on the xylophone. Immediately* ESSIE *is up on her toes, performing intricate ballets steps to* ED's *accompaniment*]

ESSIE [*Dancing*]. I like that, Ed. Yours?

ED [*Shakes his head*]. Beethoven.

ESSIE [*Never coming down off her toes*]. Lovely. Got a lot of *you* in it. . . . I made those new candies this afternoon, Ed.

ED [*Playing away*]. Yah?

ESSIE. You can take 'em around tonight.

ED. All right. . . . Now, here's the finish. This is me. [*He works up to an elaborate crescendo, but* ESSIE *keeps pace with him right to the finish*]

ESSIE. That's fine. Remember it when Kolenkhov comes, will you?

PENNY [*Who has been busy with her papers*]. Ed, dear, why don't you and Essie have a baby? I was thinking about it just the other day.

ED. I don't know—we could have one if you wanted us to. What about it, Essie? Do you want to have a baby?

ESSIE. Oh, I don't care. I'm willing if Grandpa is.

ED. Let's ask him.

[ESSIE *goes into the kitchen as* PENNY *goes back to her manuscripts*]

PENNY [*Running through the pile*]. Labor play . . . religious play . . . sex play. I know it's here some place.

[ED, *meanwhile, has transferred his attention from the xylophone to a printing press that stands handily by, and now gives it a preliminary workout*]

[MR. DE PINNA *comes out of the cellar, bound for the kitchen to wash up*]

DE PINNA. I was right about the balloon. It was too close to the powder.

ED. Anything you want printed, Mr. De Pinna? How about some more calling cards?

DE PINNA [*As he passes into the kitchen*]. No, thanks. I've still got the *first* thousand.

ED [*Calling after him*]. Well, call on somebody, will you? [*He then gives his attention to* RHEBA, *who is busy with the table again*]. What have we got for dinner, Rheba? I'm ready to print the menu.

RHEBA. Cornflakes, watermelon, some of those candies Miss Essie made, and some kind of meat—I forget.

ED. I think I'll set it up in boldface Cheltenham tonight. [*He starts to pick out the letters*] If I'm going to take those new candies around I'd better print up some descriptive matter after dinner.

PENNY. Do you think anybody reads those things, Ed—that you put in the candy boxes? . . . Oh, here it is. [*She pulls a manuscript out of a pile*] "Poison Gas." [*The door bell sounds*] I guess that's Donald. [*As* RHEBA *breaks into a broad grin*] Look at Rheba smile.

ED. The boy friend, eh, Rheba?

PENNY [*As* RHEBA *disappears into the hallway*]. Donald and Rheba are awfully cute together. Sort of like Porgy and Bess.

[RHEBA *having opened the door, the gentleman named* DONALD *now looms up in the doorway—darkly. He is a colored man of no uncertain hue*]

DONALD. Good evening, everybody!

ED. Hi, Donald! How've you been?

DONALD. I'm pretty good, Mr. Ed. How you been, Mrs. Sycamore?

PENNY. Very well, thank you. [*She looks at him, appraisingly*] Donald, were you ever in a monastery?

DONALD. No-o. I don't go no place much. I'm on relief.

PENNY. Oh, yes, of course.

DONALD [*Pulling a bottle out of each side pocket*]. Here's the flies, Rheba. Caught a big mess of them today.

RHEBA [*Taking the jars*]. You sure did.

DONALD. I see you've been working, Mrs. Sycamore.

PENNY. Yes, indeed, Donald.

DONALD. How's Grandpa?

PENNY. Just fine. He's over at Columbia this afternoon. The Commencement exercises.

DONALD. My, the years certainly do roll 'round.

ED [*With his typesetting*]. M—E—A—T. . . . What's he go there for all the time, Penny?

PENNY. I don't know. It's so handy—just around the corner.

[PAUL *comes downstairs*]

PAUL. Oh, Donald! Mr. De Pinna and I are going to take the fireworks up to Mount Vernon next week. Do you think you could give us a hand?

DONALD. Yes, sir, only I can't take no money for it this year, because if the Government finds out I'm working they'll get sore.

PAUL. Oh! . . . Ed, I got a wonderful idea in the bathroom just now. I was reading Trotzky. [*He produces a book from under his arm*] It's yours, isn't it?

ED. Yah, I left it there.

PENNY. *Who* is it?

PAUL. *You* know, Trotzky. The Russian Revolution.

PENNY. Oh.

PAUL. Anyhow, it struck me it was a great fireworks idea. Remember "The Last Days of Pompeii"?

PENNY. Oh, yes. Palisades Park. [*With a gesture of her arms she loosely describes a couple of arcs, indicative of the eruption of Mt. Vesuvius*] That's where we met.

PAUL. Well, I'm going to do the Revolution! A full hour display.

DONALD. Say!

PENNY. Paul, that's wonderful!

ED. The red fire is the flag, huh?

PAUL. Sure! And the Czar, and the Cossacks!

DONALD. And the freeing of the slaves?

PAUL. No, no, Donald—

[*The sound of the front door slamming. A second's pause, and then* GRANDPA *enters the living room.* GRANDPA *is about 75, a wiry little man whom the years have treated kindly. His face is youthful, despite the lines that sear it; his eyes are very much alive. He is a man who made his peace with the world long, long ago, and his whole attitude and manner are quietly persuasive of this*]

GRANDPA [*Surveying the group*]. Well, sir, you should have been there. That's all I can say—you should have been there.

PENNY. Was it a nice Commencement, Grandpa?

GRANDPA. Wonderful. They get better every year. [*He peers into the snake solarium*] You don't know how lucky you are you're snakes.

ED. Big class this year, Grandpa? How many were there?

GRANDPA. Oh, must have been two acres. *Everybody* graduated. And much funnier speeches than they had last year.

DONALD. You want to listen to a good speech you go up and hear Father Divine.

GRANDPA. I'll wait—they'll have him at Columbia.

PENNY. Donald, will you tell Rheba Grandpa's home now and we won't wait for Miss Alice.

DONALD. Yes'm. . . . [*As he goes through the kitchen door*] Rheba, Grandpa's home—we can have dinner.

PAUL. Got a new skyrocket today, Grandpa. Wait till you see it. . . . Wonder why they don't have fireworks at Commencements.

GRANDPA. Don't make enough noise. You take a good Commencement orator and he'll drown out a whole carload of fireworks. And say just as much too.

PENNY. Don't the graduates ever say anything?

GRANDPA. No, they just sit there in cap and nightgown, get their diplomas, and then along about forty years from now they suddenly say, "Where am I?"

[*ESSIE comes in from the kitchen, bringing a plate of tomatoes for the evening meal*]

ESSIE. Hello, Grandpa. Have a nice day?

GRANDPA [*Watching ESSIE as she puts the tomatoes on the table*]. Hello-have-a-nice-day. [*Suddenly he roars at the top of his voice*] Don't I even get kissed?

ESSIE [*Kissing him*]. Excuse me, Grandpa.

GRANDPA. I'll take a tomato, too. [*ESSIE passes the plate; grandpa takes one and sits with it in his hand, solemnly weighing it*] You know, I could have used a couple of these this afternoon. . . . Play something, Ed.

[*ED at once obliges on the xylophone—something on the dreamy side. Immediately ESSIE is up on her toes again, drifting through the mazes of a toe dance*]

ESSIE [*After a moment*]. There was a letter came for you, Grandpa. Did you get it?

GRANDPA. Letter for me? I don't know anybody.

ESSIE. It was for you, though. Had your name on it.

GRANDPA. That's funny. Where is it?

ESSIE. I don't know. Where's Grandpa's letter, mother?

PENNY [*Who has been deep in her work*]. What, dear?

ESSIE [*Dancing dreamily away*]. Where's that letter that came for Grandpa last week?

PENNY. I don't know. [*Then, brightly*] I remember seeing the kittens on it.

GRANDPA. Who was it from? Did you notice?

ESSIE. Yes, it was on the outside.

GRANDPA. Well, who was it?

ESSIE [*First finishing the graceful flutterings of the Dying Swan*]. United States Government.

GRANDPA. Really? Wonder what *they* wanted.

ESSIE. There was one before that, too, from the same people. There was a couple of them.

GRANDPA. Well, if any more come I wish you'd give them to me.

ESSIE. Yes, Grandpa.

[*A fresh flurry of dancing; the xylophone grows a little louder*]

GRANDPA. I think I'll go out to Westchester tomorrow and do a little snake-hunting.

PAUL [*Who has settled down with his book some time before this*]. "God is the State; the State is God."

GRANDPA. What's that?

PAUL. "God is the State; the State is God."

GRANDPA. Who says that?

PAUL. Trotzky.

GRANDPA. Well, that's all right— I thought *you* said it.

ED. It's nice for printing, you know. Good and short. [*He reaches into the type case*] G — O — D — space — I — S — space — T — H — E

[*The sound of the outer door closing, and* ALICE SYCAMORE *enters the room. A lovely, fresh young girl of about twenty-two. She is plainly* GRANDPA's *grand-daughter but there is something that sets her apart from the rest of the family. For one thing, she is in daily contact with the world; in addition, she seems to have escaped the tinge of mild insanity that pervades the rest of them. But she is a Sycamore for all that, and her devotion and love for them are plainly apparent. At the moment she is in a small nervous flutter, but she is doing her best to conceal it*]

ALICE [*As she makes the rounds, kissing her grand-father, her father, her mother*]. And so the beautiful princess came into the palace, and kissed her mother, and her father, and her grand-father—hi, Grandpa—and what do you think? They turned into the Sycamore family. Surprised?

ESSIE [*Examining* ALICE's *dress*]. Oh, Alice, I like it. It's new, isn't it?

PENNY. Looks nice and summery.

ESSIE. Where'd you get it?

ALICE. Oh, I took a walk during lunch hour.

GRANDPA. You've been taking a lot of walks lately. That's the second new dress this week.

ALICE. Oh, I just like to brighten up the office once in a while. I'm known as the Kay Francis of Kirby & Co. . . . Well, what's new around here? In the way of plays, snakes, ballet dancing or fireworks. Dad, I'll bet you've been down in that cellar all day.

PAUL. Huh?

PENNY. I'm going back to the war play, Alice.

ESSIE. Ed, play Alice that Beethoven thing you wrote. Listen, Alice.

[*Like a shot* ED *is at the xylophone again,* ESSIE *up on her toes*]

[GRANDPA, *meanwhile, has unearthed his stamp album from under a pile of oddments in the corner, and is now busy with his magnifying glass*]

GRANDPA. Do you know that you can mail a letter all the way from Nicaragua for two pesetos?

PENNY [*Meanwhile dramatically reading one of her own deathless lines*]. "Kenneth, my virginity is a priceless thing to me."

ALICE [*Finding it hard to break through all this*]. Listen, people. . . . Listen. [*A break in the music; she gets a scattered sort of attention.*] I'm not home to dinner. A young gentleman is calling for me.

ESSIE. Really? Who is it?

PENNY. Well, isn't that nice?

ALICE [*With quiet humor*]. I did everything possible to keep him from coming here but he's calling for me.

PENNY. Why don't you both stay to dinner?

ALICE. No, I want him to take you in easy doses. I've tried to prepare him a little, but don't make it any worse than you can help. Don't read him any plays, mother, and don't let a snake bite him, Grandpa, because I like him. And I wouldn't dance for him, Essie, because we're going to the Monte Carlo ballet tonight.

GRANDPA. Can't do *anything*. Who *is* he—President of the United States?

ALICE. No, he's vice-president of Kirby & Co. Mr. Anthony Kirby, Jr.

ESSIE. The Boss' son?

PENNY. Well!

ALICE. The Boss' son. Just like the movies.

ESSIE. That explains the new dresses.

ED. And not being home to dinner for three weeks.

ALICE. Why, you're wonderful!

PENNY [*All aglow*]. Are you going to marry him?

ALICE. Oh, of course. Tonight! Meanwhile I have to go up and put on my wedding dress.

ESSIE. Is he good-looking?

ALICE [*Vainly consulting her watch*]. Yes, in a word. Oh, dear! What time is it?

PENNY. I don't know. Anybody know what time it is?

PAUL. Mr. De Pinna might know.

ED. It was about five o'clock a couple of hours ago.

ALICE. Oh, I ought to know better than to ask you people. . . . Will you let me know the minute he comes, please?

PENNY. Of course, Alice.

ALICE. Yes, I know, but I mean the *minute* he comes.

PENNY. Why, of course. [ALICE *looks apprehensively from one to the other; then disappears up the stairs*] Well, what do you think of that?

GRANDPA. She seems to like him, if you ask me.

ESSIE. I should say so. She's got it bad.

PENNY. Wouldn't it be wonderful if she married him? We could have the wedding right in this room.

PAUL. Now, wait a minute, Penny. This is the first time he's ever called for the girl.

PENNY. You only called for me once.

PAUL. Young people are different nowadays.

ESSIE. Oh, I don't know. Look at Ed and me. He came to dinner *once* and just stayed.

PENNY. Anyhow, I think it's wonderful. I'll bet he's crazy about her. It must be he that's been taking her out every night. [*The door bell rings*] There he is! Never mind, Rheba, I'll answer it. [*She is fluttering to the door*] Now remember what Alice said, and be *very* nice to him.

GRANDPA [*Rising*]. All right—let's take a look at him.

PENNY [*At the front door; milk and honey in her voice*]. Well! Welcome to our little home! I'm Alice's mother. Do come right in! Here we are! [*She reappears in the archway, piloting the stranger*] This is Grandpa, and that's Alice's father, and Alice's sister, and her husband, Ed Carmichael. [*The family all give courteous little nods and smiles as they are introduced*] Well! Now give me your hat and make yourself right at home.

THE MAN. I'm afraid you must be making a mistake.

PENNY. How's that?

THE MAN. My card.

PENNY [*Reading*]. "Wilbur C. Henderson. Internal Revenue Department."

HENDERSON. That's right.

GRANDPA. What can we do for you?

HENDERSON. Does a Mr. Martin Vanderhof live here?

GRANDPA. Yes, sir. That's me.

HENDERSON [*All milk and honey*]. Well, Mr. Vanderhof, the Government wants to talk to you about a little matter of income tax.

PENNY. Income tax?

HENDERSON. Do you mind if I sit down?

GRANDPA. No, no. Just go right ahead.

HENDERSON [*Settling himself*]. Thank you.

[*From above stairs the voice of* ALICE *floats down*]

ALICE. Mother! Is that Mr. Kirby?

PENNY [*Going to the stairs*]. No. No, it isn't, darling. It's—an internal something or other. [*To* MR. HENDERSON] Pardon me.

HENDERSON [*Pulling a sheaf of papers from his pocket*]. We've written you several letters about this, Mr. Vanderhof, but have not had any reply.

GRANDPA. Oh, that's what those letters were.

ESSIE. I told you they were from the Government.

[MR. DE PINNA *comes up from the cellar, bearing a couple of giant fire-crackers. He pauses as he sees a stranger*]

DE PINNA. Oh, pardon me.

PAUL. Yes, Mr. De Pinna?

DE PINNA. These things are not going off, Mr. Sycamore. Look.

[*He prepares to apply a match to one of them, as a startled income tax man nearly has a conniption fit. But* PAUL *is too quick for him*]

PAUL. Ah—not here, Mr. De Pinna. Grandpa's busy.

DE PINNA. Oh.

[MR. DE PINNA *and* PAUL *hurry into the hall with their firecrackers*]

HENDERSON [*Now that order has been restored*]. According to our records, Mr. Vanderhof, you have never paid an income tax.

GRANDPA. That's right.

HENDERSON. Why not?

GRANDPA. I don't believe in it.

HENDERSON. Well—you own property, don't you?

GRANDPA. Yes, sir.

HENDERSON. And you receive a yearly income from it?

GRANDPA. I do.

HENDERSON. Of— [*He consults his records*] —between three and four thousand dollars.

GRANDPA. About that.

HENDERSON. You've been receiving it for years.

GRANDPA. I have. 1901, if you want the exact date.

HENDERSON. Well, the Government is only concerned from 1914 on. That's when the income tax started.

GRANDPA. Well?

HENDERSON. Well—it seems, Mr. Vanderhof, that you owe the Government twenty-two years' back income tax.

ED. Wait a minute! You can't go back that far—that's outlawed.

HENDERSON [*Calmly regarding him*]. What's *your* name?

ED. What difference does that make?

HENDERSON. Ever file an income tax return?

ED. No, sir.

HENDERSON. What was your income last year?

ED. Ah—twenty-eight dollars and fifty cents, wasn't it, Essie?

[ESSIE *gives quick assent; the income tax man dismisses the whole matter with an impatient wave of the hand and returns to bigger game*]

HENDERSON. Now, Mr. Vanderhof, you know there's quite a penalty for not filing an income tax return.

PENNY. Penalty?

GRANDPA. Look, Mr. Henderson, let me ask you something.

HENDERSON. Well?

GRANDPA. Suppose I pay you this money—mind you, I don't say I'm going to do it—but just for the sake of argument—what's the Government going to do with it?

HENDERSON. How do you mean?

GRANDPA. Well, what do I get for my money? If I go into Macy's and buy something, there it *is*—I see it. What's the Government give me?

HENDERSON. Why, the Government gives you everything. It protects you.

GRANDPA. What from?

HENDERSON. Well—invasion. Foreigners that might come over here and take everything you've got.

GRANDPA. Oh, I don't think they're going to do that.

HENDERSON. If you didn't pay an income tax, they would. How do you think the Government keeps up the Army and Navy? All those battle-ships . . .

GRANDPA. Last time we used battleships was in the Spanish-American War, and what did we get out of it? Cuba—and we gave that back. I wouldn't mind paying if it were something sensible.

HENDERSON [*Beginning to get annoyed*]. Well, what about Congress, and the Supreme Court, and the President? We've got to pay *them*, don't we?

GRANDPA [*Ever so calmly*]. Not with my money—no, sir.

HENDERSON [*Furious*]. Now wait a minute! I'm not here to argue with you. All I know is that you haven't paid an income tax and you've got to pay it!

GRANDPA. They've got to show me.

HENDERSON [*Yelling*]. We *don't* have to show you! I just told you! All those buildings down in Washington, and Interstate Commerce, and the Constitution!

GRANDPA. The Constitution was paid for long ago. And Interstate Commerce—what *is* Interstate Commerce, anyhow?

HENDERSON [*With murderous calm*]. There are forty-eight states—see? And if there weren't Interstate Commerce, nothing could go from one state to another. See?

GRANDPA. Why not? They got fences?

HENDERSON. No, they haven't got fences! They've got *laws!* . . . My God, I never came across anything like this before!

GRANDPA. Well, I might pay about seventy-five dollars, but that's all it's worth.

HENDERSON. You'll pay every cent of it, like everybody else!

ED [*Who has lost interest*]. Listen, Essie—listen to this a minute.

[*The xylophone again;* ESSIE *goes into her dance*]

HENDERSON [*Going right ahead, battling against the music*]. And let me tell you something else! You'll go to jail if you don't pay, do you hear that? There's a law, and if you think you're bigger than the law, you've got another think coming! You'll hear from the United States Government, that's all I can say!

[*He is backing out of the room*]

GRANDPA [*Quietly*]. Look out for those snakes.

HENDERSON [*Jumping*]. Jesus!

[*Out in the hall, and not more than a foot or two behind* MR. HENDER-SON, *the firecracker boys are now ready to test that little bomber. It goes off with a terrific detonation, and* MR. HENDERSON *jumps a full foot. He wastes no time at all in getting out of there*]

PAUL [*Coming back into the room*]. How did that sound to you folks?

GRANDPA [*Quite judicially*]. I liked it.

PENNY. My goodness, he was mad, wasn't he?

GRANDPA. Oh, it wasn't his fault. It's just that the whole thing is so silly.

PENNY [*Suddenly finding herself with a perfectly good Panama in her hand*]. He forgot his hat.

GRANDPA. What size is it?

PENNY [*Peering into its insides*]. Seven and an eighth.

GRANDPA. Just right for me.

DE PINNA. Who was that fellow, anyhow?

[*Again the door bell*]

PENNY. This *must* be Mr. Kirby.

PAUL. Better make sure this time.

PENNY. Yes, I will.

[*She disappears*]

ESSIE. I hope he's good-looking.

PENNY [*Heard at the door*]. How do you do?

A MAN'S VOICE. Good evening.

PENNY [*Taking no chances*]. Is this Mr. Anthony Kirby, Jr.?

TONY. Yes.

PENNY [*Giving her all*]. Well, Mr. Kirby, come right in! We've been expecting you. Come right in! [*They come into sight;* PENNY *expansively addresses the family*] This is *really* Mr. Kirby! Now, I'm Alice's mother, and that's *Mr.* Sycamore, and Alice's grandfather, and her sister Essie, and Essie's husband. [*There are a few mumbled greetings*] There! Now you know *all* of us, Mr. Kirby. Give me your hat and make yourself right at home.

> [TONY KIRBY *comes a few steps into the room. He is a personable young man, not long out of Yale, and, as we will presently learn, even more recently out of Cambridge. Although he fits all the physical requirements of a Boss' son, his face has something of the idealist in it. All in all, a very nice young man*]

TONY. How do you do?

[*Again the voice of the vigilant* ALICE *floats down from upstairs.* "Is that Mr. Kirby, mother?"]

PENNY [*Shouting up the stairs*]. Yes, Alice. He's *lovely!*

ALICE [*Aware of storm signals*]. I'll be right down.

PENNY. Do sit down, Mr. Kirby.

TONY. Thank you. [*A glance at the dinner table*] I hope I'm not keeping you from dinner?

GRANDPA. No, no. Have a tomato?

TONY. No, thank you.

PENNY [*Producing the candy-filled skull*]. How about a piece of candy?

TONY [*Eyeing the container*]. Ah—no, thanks.

PENNY. Oh, I forgot to introduce Mr. De Pinna. This is Mr. De Pinna, Mr. Kirby. [*An exchange of "How do you do's?"*]

DE PINNA. Wasn't I reading about your father in the newspaper the other day? Didn't he get indicted or something?

TONY [*Smiling*]. Hardly that. He just testified before the Securities Commission.

DE PINNA. Oh.

PENNY [*Sharply*]. Yes, of course. I'm sure there was nothing crooked about it, Mr. De Pinna. As a matter of fact— [*She is now addressing* TONY] —Alice has often told us what a lovely man your father is.

TONY. Well, I know father couldn't get along without Alice. She knows more about the business than any of us.

ESSIE. You're awful young, Mr. Kirby, aren't you, to be vice-president of a big place like that.

TONY. Well, you know what that means, vice-president. All I have is a desk with my name on it. .

PENNY. Is that all? Don't you get any salary?

TONY [*With a laugh*]. Well, a little. More than I'm worth, I'm afraid.

PENNY. Now you're just being modest.

GRANDPA. Sounds kind of dull to me—Wall Street. Do you like it?

TONY. Well, the hours are short. And I haven't been there very long.

GRANDPA. Just out of college, huh?

TONY. Well, I knocked around for a while first. Just sort of had fun.

GRANDPA. What did you do? Travel?

TONY. For a while. Then I went to Cambridge for a year.

GRANDPA [*Nodding*]. England.

TONY. That's right.

GRANDPA. Say, what's an English commencement like? Did you see any?

TONY. Oh, very impressive.

GRANDPA. They are, huh?

TONY. Anyhow, now the fun's over, and—I'm facing the world.

PENNY. You've certainly got a good start, Mr. Kirby. Vice-president, and a rich father.

TONY. Well, that's hardly my fault.

PENNY [*Brightly*]. So now I suppose you're all ready to settle down and —get married.

PAUL. Come now, Penny, I'm sure Mr. Kirby knows his own mind.

PENNY. I wasn't making up his mind for him—was I, Mr. Kirby?

TONY. That's quite all right, Mrs. Sycamore.

PENNY [*To the others*]. You see?

ESSIE. You mustn't rush him, mother.

PENNY. Well, all I meant was he's bound to get married, and suppose the wrong girl gets him?

[*The descending* ALICE *mercifully comes to* TONY's *rescue at this moment. Her voice is heard from the stairs*]

ALICE. Well, here I am, a vision in white. [*She comes into the room— and very lovely indeed*] Apparently you've had time to get acquainted.

PENNY. Oh, yes, indeed. We were just having a delightful talk about love and marriage.

ALICE. Oh, dear. [*She turns to* TONY] I'm sorry. I came down as fast as I could.

RHEBA [*Bringing a platter of sliced watermelon*]. God damn those flies in the kitchen. . . . Oh, Miss Alice, you look beautiful. Where you going?

ALICE [*Making the best of it*]. I'm going out, Rheba.

RHEBA [*Noticing* TONY]. Stepping, huh?

[*The door bell sounds*]

ESSIE. That must be Kolenkhov.

ALICE [*Uneasily*]. I think we'd better go, Tony.

TONY. All right. [*Before they can escape, however,* DONALD *emerges from the kitchen, bearing a tray*]

DONALD. Grandpa, you take cream on your cornflakes? I forget.

GRANDPA. Half and half, Donald.

[*The voice of* BORIS KOLENKHOV *booms from the outer door*]

KOLENKHOV. Ah, my little Rhebishka!

RHEBA [*With a scream of laughter*]. Yassah, Mr. Kolenkhov!

KOLENKHOV. I am so hungry I could even eat my little Rhebishka! [*He appears in the archway, his great arm completely encircling the delighted* RHEBA. MR. KOLENKHOV *is one of* RHEBA's *pets, and if you like Russians he might be one of yours. He is enormous, hairy, loud, and very, very Russian. His appearance in the archway still further traps* ALICE *and* TONY] Grandpa, what do you think? I have had a letter from Russia! The Second Five Year Plan is a failure! [*He lets out a laugh that shakes the rafters*]

ESSIE. I practiced today, Mr. Kolenkhov!

KOLENKHOV [*With a deep Russian bow*]. My Pavlowa! [*Another bow*] Madame Sycamore! . . . My little Alice! [*He kisses her hand*] Never have I seen you look so magnificent.

ALICE. Thank you, Mr. Kolenkhov. Tony, this is Mr. Kolenkhov, Essie's dancing teacher. Mr. Kirby.

TONY. How do you do? [*A click of the heels and a bow from* KOLENK-HOV]

ALICE [*Determined, this time*]. And now we really *must* go. Excuse us, Mr. Kolenkhov—we're going to the Monte Carlo ballet.

KOLENKHOV [*At the top of his tremendous voice*]. The Monte Carlo ballet! It *stinks!*

ALICE [*Panicky now*]. Yes. . . . Well—goodbye, everybody. Goodbye.

TONY. Goodbye. I'm so glad to have met you all. [*A chorus of answering "Goodbyes" from the family. The young people are gone*]

KOLENKHOV [*Still furious*]. The Monte Carlo ballet!

PENNY. Isn't Mr. Kirby lovely? . . . Come on, everybody! Dinner's ready!

ED [*Pulling up a chair*]. I thought he was a nice fellow, didn't you?

ESSIE. Mm. And so good-looking.

PENNY. And he had such nice manners. Did you notice, Paul? Did you notice his manners?

PAUL. I certainly did. You were getting pretty personal with him.

PENNY. Oh, now, Paul . . . Anyhow, he's a very nice young man.

DE PINNA [*As he seats himself*]. He looks kind of like a cousin of mine.

KOLENKHOV. Bakst! Diaghlieff! *Then* you had the *ballet!*

PENNY. I think if they get married here I'll put the altar right where the snakes are. You wouldn't mind, Grandpa, would you?

ESSIE. Oh, they'll want to get married in a church. His family and everything.

GRANDPA [*Tapping on a plate for silence*]. Quiet, everybody! Quiet! [*They are immediately silent—Grace is about to be pronounced.* GRANDPA *pauses a moment for heads to bow, then raises his eyes heavenward. He clears his throat and proceeds to say Grace*] Well, Sir, we've been getting along pretty good for quite a while now, and we're certainly much obliged. Remember, all we ask is just to go along and be happy in our own sort of way. Of course we want to keep our health, but as far as anything else is concerned, we'll leave it to You. Thank You. [*The heads come up as* RHEBA *comes through the door with a steaming platter*] So the Second Five Year Plan is a failure, eh, Kolenkhov?

KOLENKHOV [*Booming*]. Catastrophic!

[*He reaches across the table and spears a piece of bread. The family, too, is busily plunging in*]

THE CURTAIN IS DOWN

ACT ONE: SCENE TWO

LATE *the same night. The house is in darkness save for a light in the hall. Somewhere in the back regions an accordion is being played. Then quiet. Then the stillness of the night is suddenly broken again by a good loud BANG! from the cellar. Somewhere in the nether regions, one of the Sycamores is still at work.*

Once more all is quiet, then the sound of a key in the outer door. The voices of ALICE *and* TONY *drift through.*

ALICE. I could see them dance every night of the week. I think they're marvelous.

TONY. They are, aren't they? But of course just walking inside *any* theatre gives *me* a thrill.

ALICE [*As they come into sight in the hallway*]. It's been *so* lovely, Tony. I hate to have it over.

TONY. Oh, is it over? Do I have to go right away?

ALICE. Not if you don't want to.

TONY. I don't.

ALICE. Would you like a cold drink?

TONY. Wonderful.

ALICE [*Pausing to switch on the light*]. I'll see what's in the ice-box. Want to come along?

TONY. I'd follow you to the ends of the earth.

ALICE. Oh, just the kitchen is enough. [*They go out. A pause, a ripple of gay laughter from the kitchen, then they return.* ALICE *is carrying a couple of glasses,* TONY *brings two bottles of ginger ale and an opener*] Lucky you're not hungry, Mr. K. An ice-box full of cornflakes. That gives you a rough idea of the Sycamores.

TONY [*Working away with the opener*]. Of course, why they make these bottle openers for Singer midgets I never *was* able to—ah! [*As the bottle opens*] All over my coat.

ALICE. I'll take mine in a glass, if you don't mind.

TONY [*Pouring*]. There you are. A foaming beaker.

ALICE. Anyhow, it's cold.

TONY [*Pouring his own*]. Now if you'll please be seated, I'd like to offer a toast.

ALICE [*Settling herself*]. We are seated.

TONY. Miss Sycamore— [*He raises his glass on high*] —to you.

ALICE. Thank you, Mr. Kirby. [*Lifting her own glass*] To you. [*They both drink*]

TONY [*Happily*]. I wouldn't trade one minute of this evening for—all the rice in China.

ALICE. Really?

TONY. Cross my heart.

ALICE [*A little sigh of contentment. Then shyly*]. Is there much rice in China?

TONY. Terrific. Didn't you read "The Good Earth"? [*She laughs. They are silent for a moment*]. I suppose I ought to go.

ALICE. Is it very late?

TONY [*Looks at his watch*]. Very. [ALICE *gives a little nod. Time doesn't matter*] I don't want to go.

ALICE. I don't want you to.

TONY. All right, I won't. [*Silence again*] When do you get your vacation?

ALICE. Last two weeks in August.

TONY. I might take mine then, too.

ALICE. Really?

TONY. What are you going to do?

ALICE. I don't know. I hadn't thought much about it.

TONY. Going away, do you think?

ALICE. I might not. I like the city in the summer time.

TONY. I do too.

ALICE. But you always go up to Maine, don't you?

TONY. Why—yes, but I'm sure I *would* like the city in the summer time.

That is, I'd like it if—Oh, you know what I mean, Alice. I'd love it if *you* were here.

ALICE. Well—it'd be nice if you were here, Tony.

TONY. You know what you're saying, don't you?

ALICE. What?

TONY. That you'd rather spend the summer with me than anybody else.

ALICE. It looks that way, doesn't it?

TONY. Well, if it's true about the summer, how would you feel about—the winter?

ALICE [*Seeming to weigh the matter*]. Yes. I'd like that too.

TONY [*Tremulous*]. Then comes spring—and autumn. If you could—see your way clear about those, Miss Sycamore. . . .

ALICE [*Again a little pause*]. Yes.

TONY. I guess that's the whole year. We haven't forgotten anything, have we?

ALICE. No.

TONY. Well, then—

[*Another pause; their eyes meet. And at this moment,* PENNY *is heard from the stairway*]

PENNY. Is that you, Alice? What time is it? [*She comes into the room, wrapped in a bathrobe*] Oh! [*In sudden embarrassment*] Excuse me, Mr. Kirby. I had no idea—that is, I— [*She senses the situation*] —I didn't mean to interrupt anything.

TONY. Not at all, Mrs. Sycamore.

ALICE [*Quietly*]. No, mother.

PENNY. I just came down for a manuscript— [*Fumbling at her table*]—then you can go right ahead. Ah, here it is. "Sex Takes a Holiday." Well—good night, Mr. Kirby.

TONY. Good night, Mrs. Sycamore.

PENNY. Oh, I think you can call me Penny, don't you, Alice? At least I hope so.

[*With a little laugh she vanishes up the stairs*]

[*Before* PENNY'S *rippling laughter quite dies, BANG! from the cellar.* TONY *jumps*]

ALICE [*Quietly*]. It's all right, Tony. That's father.

TONY. This time of night?

ALICE [*Ominously*]. *Any* time of night. Any time of *day*.

[*She stands silent. In the pause,* TONY *gazes at her fondly*]

TONY. You're more beautiful, more lovely, more adorable than anyone else in the whole world.

ALICE [*As he starts to embrace her*]. Don't Tony. I can't.

TONY. What?

ALICE. I can't, Tony.

TONY. My dear, just because your mother—all mothers are like that, Alice, and Penny's a darling. You see, I'm even calling her Penny.

ALICE. I don't mean that. [*She faces him squarely*] Look, Tony. This is something I should have said a long time ago, but I didn't have the courage. I let myself be swept away because—because I loved you so.

TONY. Darling!

ALICE. No, wait, Tony. I want to make it clear to you. You're of a different world—a whole different kind of people. Oh, I don't mean money or socially—that's too silly. But your family and mine—it just wouldn't work, Tony. It just wouldn't work.

[*Again an interruption. This time it is* ED *and* ESSIE, *returning from the neighborhood movie. We hear their voices at the door, deep in an argument.* ED: "*All right, have it your way. She* can't *dance. That's why they pay her all that money—because she can't dance.*" *And then* ESSIE: "*Well, I don't call that dancing, what she does*"]

[*They come into sight*]

ESSIE. Oh, hello. [*There is an exchange of greetings, a note of constraint in* ALICE's *voice. But* ESSIE *goes right ahead*] Look! What do *you* think? Ed and I just saw Fred Astaire and Ginger Rogers. Do you think she can dance, Mr. Kirby?

TONY [*Mildly taken aback by this*]. Why, yes—I always thought so.

ESSIE. What does she do, anyhow? Now, look—you're Fred Astaire and I'm Ginger Rogers.

[*She drapes herself against* TONY, *a la Ginger Rogers*]

ALICE. Essie, please.

ESSIE. I just want to use him for a minute. . . . Look, Mr. Kirby—

[*Her arms go around his neck, her cheek against his*]

ALICE [*Feeling that it's time to take action*]. Essie, you're just as good as Ginger Rogers. We all agree.

ESSIE [*Triumphantly*]. You see, Ed?

ED. Yeh. . . . Come on, Essie—we're butting in here.

ESSIE. Oh, they've been together all evening. . . . Good night, Mr. Kirby.

[*An exchange of good nights—it looks as though the* CARMICHAELS *are really going upstairs before the whole thing gets too embarrassing. Then* ED *turns casually to* ESSIE *in the doorway*]

ED. Essie, did you ask Grandpa about us having a baby?

ESSIE [*As they ascend the stairs*]. Yes—he said go right ahead.

ALICE [*When they are gone*]. You see? That's what it would be like, always.

TONY. But I didn't mind that. Besides, darling, we're not going to live with our families. It's just you and I.

ALICE. No, it isn't—it's never quite that. I love them, Tony—I love them deeply. Some people could cut away, but I couldn't. I know they do rather strange things—I never know what to expect next—but they're gay, and they're fun, and—I don't know—there's kind of nobility about them. That may sound silly, but I mean—the way they just don't care about things that other people give their whole lives to. They're—really wonderful, Tony.

TONY. Alice, you talk as though only you could understand them. That's not true. Why, I fell in love with them tonight.

ALICE. But your family, Tony. I'd want *you*, and everything about you, everything about *me*, to be—one. I couldn't start out with a part of me that you didn't share, and part of you that I didn't share. Unless we were all one —you, and *your* mother and father—I'd be miserable. And they never can be, Tony—I know it. They couldn't be.

TONY. Alice, every family has got curious little traits. What of it? My father raises orchids at ten thousand dollars a bulb. Is that sensible? My mother believes in spiritualism. That's just as bad as your mother writing plays, isn't it?

ALICE. It goes deeper, Tony. Your mother believes in spiritualism because it's fashionable. And your father raises orchids because he can afford to. My mother writes plays because eight years ago a typewriter was delivered here by mistake.

TONY. Darling what *of* it?

ALICE. And look at Grandpa. Thirty-five years ago he just quit business one day. He started up to his office in the elevator and came right down again. He just stopped. He could have been a rich man, but he said it took too much time. So for thirty-five years he's just collected snakes and gone to circuses and commencements. It never occurs to any of them—

[*As if to prove her point, they are suddenly interrupted at this moment by the entrance of* DONALD *from the kitchen. It is a* DONALD *who has plainly not expected to encounter midnight visitors, for he is simply dressed in a long white nightgown and a somewhat shorter bathrobe —a costume that permits a generous expanse of white nightshirt down around the legs, and, below that, a couple of very black shins. His appearance, incidentally, explains where all that music had been coming from, for an accordion is slung over his shoulder*]

DONALD [*Surprised, but not taken aback*]. Oh, excuse me. I didn't know you folks was in here.

ALICE [*Resigned*]. It's all right, Donald.

DONALD. Rheba kind of fancied some candy, and— [*His gaze is roaming the room*] oh, there it is. [*He picks up* PENNY's *skull, if you know what we mean*] You-all don't want it, do you?

ALICE. No, Donald. Go right ahead.

DONALD. Thanks. [*He feels that the occasion calls for certain amenities*] Have a nice evening?

ALICE. Yes, Donald.

DONALD. Nice dinner?

ALICE [*Restraining herself*]. Yes, Donald.

DONALD. The ballet nice?

ALICE [*Entirely too quietly*]. Yes, Donald.

DONALD [*Summing it all up*]. That's nice.

[*He goes—and* ALICE *bursts forth*]

ALICE. Now! Now do you see what I mean? Could you explain Donald to your father? Could you explain Grandpa? You couldn't, Tony, you couldn't! I should have known! I did know! I love you, Tony, but I love them too! And it's no use, Tony! It's no use!

[*She is weeping now in spite of herself*]

TONY [*Quietly*]. There's only one thing you've said that matters—that makes any sense at all. You love me.

ALICE. But, Tony, I know so well . . .

TONY. My darling, don't you think other people have had the same problem? Everybody's got a family.

ALICE [*Through her tears*]. But not like mine.

TONY. That doesn't stop people who love each other. . . . Darling! Darling, won't you trust me, and go on loving me, and forget everything else?

ALICE. How can I?

TONY. Because nothing can keep us apart. You know that. You must know it. Just as I know it. [*He takes her in his arms*] They want you to be happy, don't they? They *must*.

ALICE. Of course they do. But they can't change, Tony. I wouldn't want them to change.

TONY. They won't have to change. They're charming, lovable people, just as they are. You're worrying about something that may never come up.

ALICE. Oh, Tony, am I?

TONY. All that matters right now is that we love each other. That's right, isn't it?

ALICE [*Whispering*]. Yes.

TONY. Well, then!

ALICE [*In his arms*]. Tony, Tony!

TONY. Now! I'd like to see a little gayety around here. Young gentleman calling, and getting engaged and everything.

ALICE [*Smiling up into his face*]. What do I say?

TONY. Well, first you thank the young man for getting engaged to you.

ALICE. Thank you, Mr. Kirby, for getting engaged to me.

TONY. And then you tell him what it was about him that first took your girlish heart.

ALICE. The back of your head.

TONY. Huh?

ALICE. Uh-huh. It wasn't your charm, and it wasn't your money—it was the back of your head. I just happened to like it.

TONY. What happened when I turned around?

ALICE. Oh, I got used to it after a while.

TONY. I see . . . Oh, Alice, think of it. We's pretty lucky, aren't we?

ALICE. I know that *I* am. The luckiest girl in the world.

TONY. I'm not exactly unlucky myself.

ALICE. It's wonderful, isn't it?

TONY. Yes . . . Lord, but I'm happy.

ALICE. Are you, Tony?

TONY. Terribly . . . And now—good night, my dear. Until tomorrow.

ALICE. Good night.

TONY. Isn't it wonderful we work in the same office? Otherwise I'd be hanging around *here* all day.

ALICE. Won't it be funny in the office tomorrow—seeing each other and just going on as though nothing had happened?

TONY. Thank God I'm vice-president. I can dictate to you all day. "Dear Miss Sycamore: I love you, I love you, I love you."

ALICE. Oh, darling! You're such a fool.

TONY [*An arm about her as he starts toward the hallway*]. Why don't you meet me in the drugstore in the morning—before you go up to the office? I'll have millions of things to say to you by then.

ALICE. All right.

TONY. And then lunch, and then dinner tomorrow night.

ALICE. Oh, Tony! What will people say?

TONY. It's got to come out some time. In fact, if you know a good housetop, I'd like to do a little shouting.

[*She laughs—a happy little ripple. They are out of sight in the hallway by this time; their voices become inaudible*]

[PAUL, *at this point, decides to call it a day down in the cellar. He comes through the door, followed by* MR. DE PINNA. *He is carrying a small metal container, filled with powder*]

PAUL. Yes, sir, Mr. De Pinna, we did a good day's work.

DE PINNA. That's what. Five hundred Black Panthers, three hundred Willow Trees and eight dozen Junior Kiddie Bombers.

[ALICE *comes back from the hallway, still under the spell of her love*]

PAUL. Why, hello, Alice. You just come in?

ALICE [*Softly*]. No. No, I've been home quite a while.

PAUL. Have a nice evening? Say, I'd like you to take a look at this new red fire we've got.

ALICE [*Almost singing it*]. I had a beautiful evening, father.

PAUL. Will you turn out the lights, Mr. De Pinna? I want Alice to get the full effect.

ALICE [*Who hasn't heard a word*]. What, father?

PAUL. Take a look at this new red fire. It's beautiful. [MR. DE PINNA *switches the lights out;* PAUL *touches a match to the powder. The red fire blazes, shedding a soft glow over the room*] There! What do you think of it? Isn't it beautiful?

ALICE [*Radiant; her face aglow, her voice soft*]. Yes, father. Everything is beautiful. It's the most beautiful red fire in the world!

[*She rushes to him and throws her arms about him, almost unable to bear her own happiness*]

CURTAIN

ACT TWO

A WEEK *later, and the family has just risen from the dinner table. Two or three of them have drifted out of the room, but* GRANDPA *and* PAUL *still sit over their coffee cups.*

[*There is, however, a newcomer in the room. Her name is* GAY WEL-LINGTON, *and, as we will presently guess, she is an actress, a nymphomaniac, and a terrible souse. At the moment she sits with a gin bottle in one hand and glass in the other, and is having a darned good time. Hovering over her, script in hand, is a slightly worried* PENNY. ED *is watching the proceedings from somewhere in the vicinity of the printing press, and* DONALD, *leisurely clearing the table, has paused to see if* MISS WELLINGTON *can really swallow that one more drink of gin that she is about to tackle. She does, and another besides*].

[PENNY *finally decides to make a try*].

PENNY. I'm ready to read the play now, Miss Wellington, if you are.

GAY WELLINGTON. Just a minute, dearie—just a minute.

[*The gin again*]

PENNY. The only thing is—I hope you won't mind my mentioning this, but—you don't drink when you're acting, do you, Miss Wellington? I'm just asking, of course.

GAY. I'm glad you brought it up. Once a play opens, I never touch a drop. Minute I enter a stage door, this bottle gets put away till intermission.

GRANDPA [*Who plainly has his doubts*]. Have you been on the stage a long time, Miss Wellington?

GAY. All my life. I've played everything. Ever see "Peg o' My Heart"?

GRANDPA. Yes, indeed.

GAY [*With that fine logic for which the inebriated brain is celebrated*]. I saw it too. Great show. [*She staggers backwards a bit, but recovers herself just in time*] My! Hot night, ain't it?

DONALD [*Ever helpful*]. Want me to open a window, Miss Wellington?

GAY. No, the hell with the weather. [*She takes a second look at the dusky* DONALD] Say, he's cute.

[RHEBA, *who has entered just in time to overhear this, gives* GAY *a look that tells her in no uncertain terms to keep out of Harlem on dark nights. Then she stalks back into the kitchen,* DONALD *close on her heels*]

DONALD [*Trying to explain it all*]. She's just acting, Rheba. She don't mean anything.

PENNY. Well, any time you're ready, we can go up to my room and start. I thought I'd read the play up in my room.

GAY. All right, dearie, just a minute. [*She starts to pour one more drink, then suddenly her gaze becomes transfixed. She shakes her head as though*

*to dislodge the image, then looks again, receives verification, and starts to pour
the gin back into the bottle*] When I see snakes it's time to lay down.

[*She makes for a couch in the corner, and passes right out—cold*]

PENNY. Oh, but those are real, Miss Wellington. They're Grandpa's.
. . . Oh, dear! I hope she's not going to— [*Shaking her*] Miss Wellington! Miss Wellington!

ED. She's out like a light.

PAUL. Better let her sleep it off.

DONALD [*Carrying the news into the kitchen*]. Rheba, Miss Wellington
just passed out.

[*From the nether recesses we hear* RHEBA's *reaction—an emphatic
"Good!"*]

PENNY. Do you think she'll be all right?

GRANDPA. Yes, but I wouldn't cast her in the religious play.

PENNY. Well, I suppose I'll just have to wait. I wonder if I shouldn't
cover her up.

GRANDPA. Next time you meet an actress on the top of a bus, Penny, I
think I'd *send* her the play, instead of bringing her home to read it.

ESSIE [*As* ED *starts in with the printing press*]. Ed, I wish you'd stop
printing and take those Love Dreams around. They're out in the kitchen.

ED. I will. I just want to finish up these circulars.

ESSIE. Well, do that later, can't you? You've got to get back in time to
play for me when Kolenkhov comes.

GRANDPA. Kolenkhov coming tonight?

ESSIE. Yes, tomorrow night's his night, but I had to change it on account
of Alice.

GRANDPA. Oh! . . . Big doings around here tomorrow night, huh?

PENNY. Isn't it exciting? You know, I'm so nervous—you'd think it was
me he was engaged to, instead of Alice.

ESSIE. What do you think they'll *be* like—his mother and father? . . . Ed,
what are you doing *now?*

ED. Penny, did you see the new mask I made last night? [*He reveals a
new side of his character by suddenly holding a homemade mask before his
face*] Guess who it is.

PENNY. Don't tell me now, Ed. Wait a minute . . . Cleopatra.

ED [*Furious*]. It's Mrs. Roosevelt.

[*He goes into the kitchen*]

[PAUL, *meanwhile, has gone to a table in the corner of the room, from
which he now brings a steel-like boat model, two or three feet high,
puts it down on the floor, and proceeds to sit down beside it. From
a large cardboard box, which he has also brought with him, he proceeds to take out additional pieces of steel and fit them into the
model*]

PAUL. You know, the nice thing about these Erector Sets, you can make so many different things with them. Last week it was the Empire State Building.

GRANDPA. What is it this week?

PAUL. The Queen Mary.

PENNY [*Looking it over*]. Hasn't got the right hat on.

[ED *comes in from the kitchen, bringing a pile of about a dozen candy boxes, neatly wrapped, and tied together for purposes of delivery*]

ED [*As* MR. DE PINNA *comes in from the hall*]. Look. Mr. De Pinna, would you open the door and see if there's a man standing in front of the house?

ESSIE. Why, what for?

ED. Well, the last two days, when I've been out delivering, I think a man's been following me.

ESSIE. Ed, you're crazy.

ED. No, I'm not. He follows me, and he stands and watches the house.

DE PINNA. Really? [*Striding out*]. I'll take a look and see.

GRANDPA. I don't see what anybody would follow *you* for, Ed.

PENNY. Well, there's a lot of kidnapping going on, Grandpa.

GRANDPA. Yes, but not of Ed.

ED [*As* MR. DE PINNA *returns from the hall*]. Well? Did you see him?

DE PINNA. There's nobody out there at all.

ED. You're sure?

DE PINNA. Positive. I just saw him walk away.

ED. You see? I told you.

ESSIE. Oh, it might have been anybody, walking along the street. Ed, will you hurry and get back?

ED [*Picking up his boxes*]. Oh, all right.

DE PINNA. Want to go down now, Mr. Sycamore, and finish packing up the fireworks?

PAUL [*Putting the Queen Mary back on the table*]. Yeh, we've got to take the stuff up to Mt. Vernon in the morning.

[*They go into the cellar. Simultaneously the voice of* ALICE, *happily singing, is heard as she descends the stairs*]

ALICE. Mother, may I borrow some paper? I'm making out a list for Rheba tomorrow night.

PENNY. Yes, dear. Here's some.

ALICE [*As she sights* MISS WELLINGTON]. Why, what happened to your actress friend? Is she giving a performance?

PENNY. No, she's not acting, Alice. She's really drunk.

ALICE. Essie, you're going to give Rheba the kitchen all day tomorrow, aren't you? Because she'll need it.

ESSIE. Of course, Alice. I'm going to start some Love Dreams now, so I'll be 'way ahead.

[*She goes into the kitchen*]

ALICE. Thanks, dear . . . Look, mother, I'm coming home at three o'clock tomorrow. Will you have everything down in the cellar by that time? The typewriter, and the snakes, and the xylophone, and the printing press . . .

GRANDPA. And Miss Wellington.

ALICE. And Miss Wellington. That'll give me time to arrange the table, and fix the flowers.

GRANDPA. The Kirbys are certainly going to get the wrong impression of this house.

ALICE. You'll *do* all that, won't you, mother?

PENNY. Of course, dear.

ALICE. And I think we'd better have cocktails ready by seven-fifteen, in case they happen to come a little early. . . . I wonder if I ought to let Rheba cook the dinner. What do you think, Grandpa?

GRANDPA. Now, Alice, I wouldn't worry. From what I've seen of the boy I'm sure the Kirbys are very nice people, and if everything isn't so elaborate tomorrow night, it's all right too.

ALICE. Darling, I'm not trying to impress them, or pretend we're anything that we aren't. I just want everything to—to go off well.

GRANDPA. No reason why it shouldn't, Alice.

PENNY. We're all going to do everything we can to make it a nice party.

ALICE. Oh, my darlings, I love you. You're the most wonderful family in the world, and I'm the happiest girl in the world. I didn't know anyone could *be* so happy. He's so wonderful, Grandpa. Why, just seeing him—you don't know what it does to me.

GRANDPA. Just seeing him. Just seeing him for lunch, and dinner, and until four o'clock in the morning, and at nine o'clock *next* morning you're at the office again and there he is. You just see him, huh?

ALICE. I don't care! I'm in love! [*She swings open the kitchen door*] Rheba! Rheba!

[*She goes into the kitchen*]

GRANDPA. Nice, isn't it? Nice to see her so happy.

PENNY. I remember when I was engaged to Paul—how happy I was. And you know, I still feel that way.

GRANDPA. I know . . . Nice the way Ed and Essie get along too, isn't it?

PENNY. And Donald and Rheba, even though they're *not* married. . . . Do you suppose Mr. De Pinna will ever marry anyone, Grandpa?

• GRANDPA [*A gesture toward the couch*]. Well, there's Miss Wellington.

PENNY. Oh, dear, I *wish* she'd wake up. If we're going to read the play tonight—

[MR. DE PINNA *comes up from the cellar, bringing along a rather large-sized unframed painting*]

DE PINNA. Mrs. Sycamore, look what I found! [*He turns the canvas around, revealing a portrait of a somewhat lumpy discus thrower, in Roman costume—or was it Greek?*] Remember?

PENNY. Why, of course. It's my painting of you as The Discus Thrower. Look, Grandpa.

GRANDPA. I remember it. Say, you've gotten a little bald, haven't you, Mr. De Pinna?

DE PINNA [*Running a hand over his completely hairless head*]. Is it very noticeable?

PENNY. Well, it was a long time ago—just before I stopped painting. Let me see—that's eight years.

DE PINNA. Too bad you never finished it, Mrs. Sycamore.

PENNY. I always meant to finish it, Mr. De Pinna, but I just started to write a play one day and that was that. I never painted again.

GRANDPA. Just as well, too. *I* was going to have to strip next.

DE PINNA [*Meditatively*]. Who would have thought, that day I came to deliver the ice, that I was going to stay here for eight years?

GRANDPA. The milkman was here for five, just ahead of you.

DE PINNA. Why did he leave, anyhow? I forget.

GRANDPA. He didn't leave. He died.

PENNY. He was such a nice man. Remember the funeral, Grandpa? We never knew his name and it was kind of hard to get a certificate.

GRANDPA. What was the name we finally made up for him?

PENNY. Martin Vanderhof. We gave him *your* name.

GRANDPA. Oh, yes, I remember.

PENNY. It was a lovely thought, because otherwise he never would have got all those flowers.

GRANDPA. Certainly was. And it didn't hurt *me* any. Not bothered with mail any more, and I haven't had a telephone call from that day to this.

[*He catches an unwary fly and drops it casually into the snake solarium*]

PENNY. Yes, it was really a wonderful idea.

DE PINNA [*With the picture*]. I wish you'd finish this sometime, Mrs. Sycamore. I'd kind of like to have it.

PENNY. You know what, Mr. De Pinna? I think I'll do some work on it. Right tonight.

DE PINNA. Say! Will you?

[*The door bell rings*]

PENNY [*Peering at the prostrate* GAY]. I don't think she's going to wake up anyhow. . . . Look, Mr. De Pinna! You go down in the cellar and bring up the easel and get into your costume. Is it still down there?

DE PINNA [*Excited*]. I think so!

[*He darts into the cellar*]

PENNY. Now, where did I put my palette and brushes?

[*She dashes up the stairs as the voice of* KOLENKHOV *is heard at the door, booming, of course*]

KOLENKHOV. Rhebishka! My little Rhebishka!

RHEBA [*Delighted, as usual*]. Yassuh, Mr. Kolenkhov!

PENNY [*As she goes up the stairs*]. Hello, Mr. Kolenkhov. Essie's in the kitchen.

KOLENKHOV. Madame Sycamore, I greet you! [*His great arm again encircling* RHEBA, *he drags her protestingly into the room*] Tell me, Grandpa —what should I do about Rhebishka! I keep telling her she would make a great toe dancer, but she laughs only!

RHEBA [*Breaking away*]. No, suh! I couldn't get up on my toes, Mr. Kolenkhov! I got corns!

[*She goes into the kitchen*]

KOLENKHOV [*Calling after her*]. Rhebishka, you could wear diamonds! [*Suddenly he sights the portrait of* MR. DE PINNA] What is that?

GRANDPA [*Who has taken up his stamp album again*]. It's a picture of Mr. De Pinna. Penny painted it.

KOLENKHOV [*Summing it up*]. It stinks.

GRANDPA. I know. [*He indicates the figure on the couch*]. How do you like that?

KOLENKHOV [*Peering over*]. What is *that*?

GRANDPA. She's an actress. Friend of Penny's.

KOLENKHOV. She is drunk—no?

GRANDPA. She is drunk—yes. . . . How are *you*, Kolenkhov?

KOLENKHOV. Magnificent! Life is chasing around inside of me, like a squirrel.

GRANDPA. 'Tis, huh? . . . What's new in Russia? Any more letters from your friend in Moscow?

KOLENKHOV. I have just heard from him. I saved for you the stamp.

[*He hands it over*]

GRANDPA [*Receiving it with delight*]. Thanks, Kolenkhov.

KOLENKHOV. They have sent him to Siberia.

GRANDPA. That so? How's he like it?

KOLENKHOV. He has escaped. He has escaped and gone back to Moscow. He will get them yet, if they do not get him. The Soviet Government! I could take the whole Soviet Government and—grrah!

[*He crushes Stalin and all in one great paw, just as* ESSIE *comes in from the kitchen*]

ESSIE. I'm sorry I'm late, Mr. Kolenkhov. I'll get into my dancing clothes right away.

KOLENKHOV. Tonight you will really work, Pavlowa. [*As* ESSIE *goes up the stairs*] Tonight we will take something new.

GRANDPA. Essie making any progress, Kolenkhov?

KOLENKHOV [*First making elaborately sure that* ESSIE *is gone*] Confidentially, she stinks.

GRANDPA. Well, as long as she's having fun. . . .

[DONALD *ambles in from the kitchen, chuckling*]

DONALD. You sure do tickle Rheba, Mr. Kolenkhov. She's laughing her head off out there.

KOLENKHOV. She is a great woman. . . . Donald, what do you think of the Soviet Government?

DONALD. The what, Mr. Kolenkhov?

KOLENKHOV. I withdraw the question. What do you think of *this* Government?

DONALD. Oh, I like it fine. I'm on relief, you know.

KOLENKHOV. Oh, yes. And you like it?

DONALD. Yassuh, it's fine. Only thing is you got to go around to the place every week and collect it, and sometimes you got to stand in line pretty near half an hour. Government ought to be run better than that—don't you think, Grandpa?

GRANDPA [*As he fishes an envelope out of his pocket*]. Government ought to stop sending me letters. Want me to be at the United States Marshal's office Tuesday morning at ten o'clock.

KOLENKHOV [*Peering at the letter*]. Ah! Income tax! They have got you, Grandpa.

GRANDPA. Mm. I'm supposed to give 'em a lot of money so as to keep Donald on relief.

DONALD. You don't say, Grandpa? You going to pay it now?

GRANDPA. That's what they want.

DONALD. You mean I can come right *here* and get it instead of standing in that line?

GRANDPA. No, Donald. You will have to waste a full half hour of your time every week.

DONALD. Well, I don't like it. It breaks up my week.

[*He goes into the kitchen*]

KOLENKHOV. He should have been in Russia when the Revolution came. Then he would have stood in line—a bread line. [*He turns to* GRANDPA] Ah, Grandpa, what they have done to Russia. Think of it! The Grand Duchess Olga Katrina, a cousin of the Czar, she is a waitress in Childs' restaurant! I ordered baked beans from her only yesterday. It broke my heart. A crazy world, Grandpa.

GRANDPA. Oh, the world's not so crazy, Kolenkhov. It's the people *in* it. Life's pretty simple if you just relax.

KOLENKHOV. How can you relax in times like these?

GRANDPA. Well, if they'd relaxed there wouldn't *be* times like these. That's just my point. Life is simple and kind of beautiful if you let it come to you. But the trouble is, people forget that. I know I did. I was right in the thick of it—fighting, and scratching, and clawing. Regular jungle. One day is just kind of struck me. I wasn't having any fun.

KOLENKHOV. So you did what?

GRANDPA. Just relaxed. Thirty-five years ago, that was. And I've been a happy man ever since.

[*From somewhere or other* GRANDPA *has brought one of those colored targets that one buys at Schwartz's. He now hangs it up on the cellar door, picks up a handful of feathered darts, and carefully throws one at the target*]

[*At the same time* ALICE *passes through the room, en route from kitchen to the upstairs region*]

ALICE. Good evening, Mr. Kolenkhov.

KOLENKHOV [*Bowing low over her hand*]. Ah, Miss Alice! I have not seen you to present my congratulations. May you be very happy and have many children. That is my prayer for you.

ALICE. Thank you, Mr. Kolenkhov. That's quite a thought.

[*Singing gayly, she goes up the stairs*]

KOLENKHOV [*Looking after her*]. Ah, love! That is all that is left in the world, Grandpa.

GRANDPA. Yes, but there's plenty of that.

KOLENKHOV. And soon Stalin will take that away, too. I tell you, Grandpa—

[*He stops as* PENNY *comes down the stairs—a living example of what the well-dressed artist should wear. She has on an artist's smock over her dress, a flowing black tie, and a large black velvet tam-o'-shanter, worn at a rakish angle. She carries a palette and an assortment of paints and brushes*]

PENNY. Seems so nice to get into my art things again. They still look all right, don't they, Grandpa?

GRANDPA. Yes, indeed.

KOLENKHOV. You are a breath of Paris, Madame Sycamore.

PENNY. Oh, thank you, Mr. Kolenkhov.

DONALD [*Coming in from the kitchen*]. I didn't know you was working for the WPA.

PENNY. Oh, no, Donald. You see, I used to paint all the time, and then one day—

[*The outer door slams and* ED *comes in*]

ED [*In considerable excitement*]. It happened again! There was a fellow following me every place I went!

PENNY. Nonsense, Ed. It's your imagination.

ED. No, it isn't. It happens every time I go out to deliver candy.

GRANDPA. Maybe he wants a piece of candy.

ED. It's all right for you to laugh, Grandpa, but he keeps following me.

KOLENKOV [*Somberly*]. You do not know what following is. In Russia *everybody* is followed. I was followed right out of Russia.

PENNY. Of course. You see, Ed—the whole thing is just imagination. [MR. DE PINNA *comes up from the cellar, ready for posing. He wears the traditional Roman costume, and he certainly cuts a figure. He is carrying* PENNY's *easel, a discus, and a small platform for posing purposes*] Ah, here we are! . . . Right here, Mr. De Pinna.

DONALD [*Suddenly getting it*]. Oh, is that picture supposed to be Mr. De Pinna?

PENNY [*Sharply*]. Of course it is, Donald. What's it look like—me?

DONALD [*Studying the portrait*]. Yes, it does—a little bit.

PENNY. Nonsense! What would I be doing with a discus?

KOLENKHOV. Ed, for tonight's lesson we use the first movement of Scheherazade.

ED. Okay.

DE PINNA [*About to mount the platform*]. I hope I haven't forgotten how to pose.

> [*He takes up the discus and strikes the classic pose of the Discus Thrower. Somehow, it is not quite convincing*]

DONALD. What's he going to do with that thing? Throw it?

PENNY. No, no, Donald. He's just posing. . . . Mr. De Pinna, has something happened to your figure during these eight years?

DE PINNA [*Pulling in his stomach*]. No, I don't think it's any different.

> [*With a sudden snort,* GAY WELLINGTON *comes to*]

PENNY [*Immediately alert*]. Yes, Miss Wellington?

> [*For answer,* GAY *peers first at* PENNY, *then at* MR. DE PINNA. *Then, with a strange snort, she just passes right out again*]

PENNY. Oh, dear.

> [ESSIE *comes tripping down the stairs—very much the ballet dancer. She is in full costume—ballet skirt, tight white satin bodice, a garland of roses in her hair*]

ESSIE. Sorry, Mr. Kolenkhov, I couldn't find my slippers.

KOLENKHOV [*Having previously removed his coat, he now takes off his shirt, displaying an enormous hairy chest beneath his undershirt*]. We have a hot night for it, my Pavlowa, but art is only achieved through perspiration.

PENNY. Why, that's wonderful, Mr. Kolenkhov. Did you hear that, Grandpa—art is only achieved through perspiration.

GRANDPA. Yes, but it helps if you've got a little talent with it. [*He returns to his dart throwing*] Only made two bull's-eyes last night. Got to do better than that. [*He hurls a dart at the board, then his eye travels to* MISS WELLINGTON, *whose posterior offers an even easier target*] Mind if I use Miss Wellington, Penny?

PENNY. What, Grandpa?

GRANDPA [*Shakes his head*]. Never mind. . . . Too easy.

> [GRANDPA *throws another dart at the target*]

KOLENKHOV. You are ready? We begin! [*With a gesture he orders the music started; under* KOLENKHOV'S *critical eye* ESSIE *begins the mazes of the dance*]. Foutte temp el levee. [ESSIE *obliges with her own idea of foutte temp el levee*] Pirouette! . . . Come, come! You can do that! It's eight years now. Pirouette! . . . At last! . . . Entre chat! . . . Entre chat! [ESSIE *leaps into the air, her feet twirling*] No, Grandpa, you cannot relax with Stalin in Russia. The Czar relaxed, and what happened to *him*?

GRANDPA. He was too late.

ESSIE [*Still leaping away*]. Mr. Kolenkhov! Mr. Kolenkhov!

KOLENKHOV. If he had not relaxed the Grand Duchess Olga Katrina would not be selling baked beans today.

ESSIE [*Imploringly*]. Mr. Kolenkhov!

KOLENKHOV. I am sorry. [*The door bell rings*] We go back to the pirouette.

PENNY. Could you pull in your stomach, Mr. De Pinna? . . . That's right.

KOLENKHOV. A little freer. A little freer with the hands. The whole body must work. Ed, help us with the music. The music must be free, too.

[*By way of guiding* ED, KOLENKHOV *hums the music at the pace that it should go. He is even pirouetting a bit himself*]

[*From the front door comes the murmur of voices, not quite audible over the music. Then the stunned figure of* RHEBA *comes into the archway, her eyes popping*]

RHEBA. Mrs. Sycamore. . . . Mrs. Sycamore.

[*With a gesture that has a grim foreboding in it, she motions toward the still invisible reason for her panic*]

[*There is a second's pause, and then the reason is revealed in all its horror. The* KIRBYS, *in full evening dress, stand in the archway. All three of them.* MR. *and* MRS. KIRBY, *and* TONY]

[PENNY *utters a stifled gasp; the others are too stunned even to do that. Their surprise at seeing the* KIRBYS, *however, is no greater than that of the* KIRBYS *at the sight that is spread before them*]

[GRANDPA, *alone of them all, rises to the situation. With a kind of old world grace, he puts away his darts and makes the guests welcome*]

GRANDPA. How do you do?

KIRBY [*Uncertainly*]. How do you do?

[*Not that it helps any, but* MR. DE PINNA *is squirming into his bathrobe,* KOLENKHOV *is thrusting his shirt into his trousers, and* ED *is hastily getting into his coat*]

TONY. Are we too early?

GRANDPA. No, no. It's perfectly all right—we're glad to see you.

PENNY [*Getting rid of the smock and tam*]. Why—yes. Only—we thought it was to be tomorrow night.

MRS. KIRBY. Tomorrow night!

KIRBY. What!

GRANDPA. Now, it's perfectly all right. Please sit right down and make yourselves at home.

[*His eyes still on the* KIRBYS, *he gives* DONALD *a good push toward the kitchen, by way of a hint.* DONALD *goes, promptly, with a quick little stunned whistle that sums up HIS feelings*]

KIRBY. Tony, how could you possibly—

TONY. I—I don't know. I thought—

MRS. KIRBY. Really, Tony! This is most embarrassing.

GRANDPA. Not at all. Why, we weren't doing a thing.

PENNY. Just spending the evening at home.

GRANDPA. That's all. . . . Now don't let it bother you. This is Alice's mother, Mrs. Sycamore . . . Alice's sister, Mrs. Carmichael . . . *Mr. Car-*

michael. . . . Mr. Kolenkhov. . . . [*At this point* MR. DE PINNA *takes an antici-patory step forward, and* GRANDPA *is practically compelled to perform the intro-duction*] And—Mr. De Pinna. Mr. De Pinna, would you tell Mr. Sycamore to come right up? Tell him that Mr. and Mrs. Kirby are here.

PENNY [*Her voice a heavy whisper*]. And be sure to put his pants on.

DE PINNA [*Whispering right back*]. All right. . . . Excuse me.

[*He vanishes—discus and all*]

GRANDPA. Won't you sit down?

PENNY [*First frantically trying to cover the prostrate* GAY WELLINGTON]. I'll tell Alice that you're— [*She is at the foot of the stairs*]. —Alice! Alice, dear! [*The voice of* ALICE *from above, "What is it?"*] Alice, will you come down, dear? We've got a surprise for you [*She comes back into the room, summoning all her charm*]. Well !

GRANDPA. Mrs. Kirby, may I take your wrap?

MRS. KIRBY. Well—thank you. If you're perfectly sure that we're not—

[*Suddenly she sees the snakes and lets out a scream*]

GRANDPA. Oh, don't be alarmed, Mrs. Kirby. They're perfectly harmless.

MRS. KIRBY [*Edging away from the solarium*]. Thank you.

[*She sinks into a chair, weakly*]

GRANDPA. Ed, take 'em into the kitchen.

[ED *at once obeys*]

PENNY. Of course we're so used to them around the house—

MRS. KIRBY. I'm sorry to trouble you, but snakes happen to be the one thing—

KIRBY. I feel very uncomfortable about this. Tony, how could you have done such a thing?

TONY. I'm sorry, Dad. I thought it was tonight.

KIRBY. It was very careless of you. *Very!*

GRANDPA. Now, now, Mr. Kirby—we're delighted.

PENNY. Oh, now, anybody can get mixed up, Mr. Kirby.

GRANDPA. Penny, how about some dinner for these folks? They've come for dinner, you know.

MRS. KIRBY. Oh, please don't bother. We're really not hungry at all.

PENNY. But it's not a bit of bother. Ed!— [*Her voice drops to a loud whisper*] Ed, tell Donald to run down to the A. and P. and get half a dozen bottles of beer, and—ah—some canned salmon— [*Her voice comes up again*] —do you like canned salmon, Mr. Kirby?

KIRBY. Please don't trouble, Mrs. Sycamore. I have a little indigestion, anyway.

PENNY. Oh, I'm sorry . . . How about you, Mrs. Kirby? Do you like canned salmon?

MRS. KIRBY [*You just know that she hates it*]. Oh, I'm very fond of it.

PENNY. You can have frankfurters if you'd rather.

MRS. KIRBY [*Regally*]. Either one will do.

PENNY [*To* ED *again*]. Well, make it frankfurters, and some canned corn, and Campbell's soup.

ED [*Going out the kitchen door*]. Okay!

PENNY [*Calling after him*]. And tell him to hurry! [PENNY *again addresses the* KIRBYS]. The A. and P. is just at the corner, and frankfurters don't take *any* time to boil.

GRANDPA [*As* PAUL *comes through the cellar door*]. And this is Alice's father, *Mr.* Sycamore. Mr. and Mrs. Kirby.

THE KIRBYS. How do you do?

PAUL. I hope you'll forgive my appearance.

PENNY. This is Mr. Sycamore's busiest time of the year. Just before the Fourth of July—

[*And then* ALICE *comes down. She is a step into the room before she realizes what ¹as happened; then she fairly freezes in her tracks*]

ALICE. Oh!

TONY. Darling, will you ever forgive me? I'm the most dull-witted person in the world. I thought it was tonight.

ALICE [*Staggered*]. Why, Tony, I thought you— [*To the* KIRBYS]—I'm so sorry—I can't imagine—why, I wasn't—have you all met each other?

KIRBY. Yes, indeed.

MRS. KIRBY. How do you do, Alice?

ALICE [*Not even yet in control of herself*]. How do you do, Mrs. Kirby? I'm afraid I'm not very—presentable.

TONY. Darling, you look lovely.

KIRBY. Of course she does. Don't let this upset you, my dear—we've all just met each other a night sooner, that's all.

MRS. KIRBY. Of course.

ALICE. But I was planning such a nice party tomorrow night . . .

KIRBY [*Being the good fellow*]. Well, we'll come again tomorrow night.

TONY. There you are, Alice. Am I forgiven?

ALICE. I guess so. It's just that I—we'd better see about getting you some dinner.

PENNY. Oh, that's all done, Alice. That's all been attended to.

[DONALD, *hat in hand, comes through the kitchen door; hurries across the room and out the front way. The* KIRBYS *graciously pretend not to see*]

ALICE. But mother—what are you—what did you send out for? Because Mr. Kirby suffers from indigestion—he can only eat certain things.

KIRBY. Now, it's quite all right.

TONY. Of course it is, darling.

PENNY. I asked him what he wanted, Alice.

ALICE [*Doubtfully*]. Yes, but—

KIRBY. Now, now, it's not as serious as all that. Just because I have a little indigestion.

KOLENKHOV [*Helping things along*]. Perhaps it is not indigestion at all, Mr. Kirby. Perhaps you have stomach ulcers.

ALICE. Don't be absurd, Mr. Kolenkhov!

GRANDPA. You mustn't mind Mr. Kolenkhov, Mr. Kirby. He's a Russian, and Russians are inclined to look on the dark side.

KOLENKHOV. All right, I am a Russian. But a friend of mine, a Russian, *died* from stomach ulcers.

KIRBY. Really, I—

ALICE [*Desperately*]. Please, Mr. Kolenkhov! Mr. Kirby has indigestion and that's all.

KOLENKHOV [*With a Russian shrug of the shoulders*]. All right. Let him wait.

GRANDPA [*Leaping into the breach*]. Tell me, Mr. Kirby, how do you find business conditions? Are we pretty well out of the depression?

KIRBY. What? . . . Yes, yes, I think so. Of course, it all depends.

GRANDPA. But you figure that things are going to keep on improving?

KIRBY. Broadly speaking, yes. As a matter of fact, industry is now operating at sixty-four per cent of full capacity, as against eighty-two per cent in 1925. Of course in 1929, a peak year—

> [*Peak year or no peak year,* GAY WELLINGTON *chooses this moment to come to life. With a series of assorted snorts, she throws the cover back and pulls herself to a sitting position, blinking uncertainly at the assemblage. Then she rises, and weaves unsteadily across the room. The imposing figure of* MR. KIRBY *intrigues her*]

GAY [*Playfully rumpling* MR. KIRBY'S *hair as she passes him*]. Hello, Cutie.

> [*And with that she lunges on her way—up the stairs*]

> [*The* KIRBYS, *of course, are considerably astounded by this exhibition; the* SYCAMORES *have watched it with varying degrees of frozen horror.* ALICE, *in particular, is speechless; it is* GRANDPA *who comes to her rescue*]

GRANDPA. That may seem a little strange to you, but she's not quite accountable for her actions. A friend of Mrs. Sycamore's. She came to dinner and was overcome by the heat.

PENNY. Yes, some people feel it, you know, more than others. Perhaps I'd better see if she's all right. Excuse me, please.

> [*She goes hastily up the stairs*]

ALICE. It *is* awfully hot. [*A fractional pause*] You usually escape all this hot weather, don't you, Mrs. Kirby? Up in Maine?

MRS. KIRBY [*On the frigid side*]. As a rule. I had to come down this week, however, for the Flower Show.

TONY. Mother wouldn't miss that for the world. That blue ribbon is the high spot of her year.

ESSIE. I won a ribbon at a Flower Show once. For raising onions. Remember?

ALICE [*Quickly*]. That was a Garden Show, Essie.

ESSIE. Oh yes.

[PENNY *comes bustling down the stairs again*]

PENNY. I'm so sorry, but I think she'll be all right now. . . . Has Donald come back yet?

ALICE. No, he hasn't.

PENNY. Well, he'll be right back, and it won't take any time at all. I'm afraid you must be starved.

KIRBY. Oh, no. Quite all right. [*Pacing the room, he suddenly comes upon* PAUL's *Erector Set*] Hello! What's this? I didn't know there were little children in the house.

PAUL. Oh, no. That's mine.

KIRBY. Really? Well, I suppose every man has his hobby. Or do you use this as a model of some kind?

PAUL. No, I just play with it.

KIRBY. I see.

TONY. Maybe you'd be better off if *you* had a hobby like that, Dad. Instead of raising orchids.

KIRBY [*Indulgently*]. Yes, I wouldn't be surprised.

ALICE [*Leaping on this as a safe topic*]. Oh, *do* tell us about your orchids, Mr. Kirby. [*She addresses the others*] You know, they take six years before they blossom. Think of that!

KIRBY [*Warming to his subject*]. Oh, some of them take longer than that. I've got one coming along now that I've waited ten years for.

PENNY [*Making a joke*]. Believe it or not, I was waiting for an orchid.

KIRBY. Ah—yes. Of course during that time they require the most scrupulous care. I remember a bulb that I was very fond of—

[DONALD *suddenly bulges through the archway, his arms full. The tops of beer bottles and two or three large cucumbers peep over the edge of the huge paper bags*]

PENNY. Ah, here we are! Did you get everything, Donald?

DONALD. Yes'm. Only the frankfurters didn't look very good, so I got pickled pigs' feet.

[MR. KIRBY *blanches at the very idea*]

ALICE [*Taking command*]. Never mind, Donald—just bring everything into the kitchen. [*She turns at the kitchen door*] Mr. Kirby, please tell them *all* about the orchids—I know they'd love to hear it. And—excuse me.

[*She goes*]

GRANDPA. Kind of an expensive hobby, isn't it, Mr. Kirby—raising orchids?

KIRBY. Yes, it is, but I feel that if a hobby gives one sufficient pleasure, it's never expensive.

GRANDPA. That's very true.

KIRBY. You see, I need something to relieve the daily nerve strain. After a week in Wall Street I'd go crazy if I didn't have something like that. Lot of men I know have yachts—just for that very reason.

GRANDPA [*Mildly*]. Why don't they give up Wall Street?

KIRBY. How's that?

GRANDPA. I was just joking.

MRS. KIRBY. I think it's necessary for everyone to have a hobby. Of course it's more to me than a hobby, but my great solace is—spiritualism.

PENNY. Now, Mrs. Kirby, don't tell me you fell for that. Why, everybody knows it's a fake.

MRS. KIRBY [*Freezing*]. To me, Mrs. Sycamore, spiritualism is—I would rather not discuss it, Mrs. Sycamore.

PAUL. Remember, Penny, you've got one or two hobbies of your own.

PENNY. Yes, but not silly ones.

GRANDPA [*With a little cough*]. I don't think it matters what the hobby is—the important thing is to have one.

KOLENKHOV. To be ideal, a hobby should improve the body as well as the mind. The Romans were a great people! Why! What was their hobby? Wrestling. In wrestling you have to think quick with the mind and act quick with the body.

KIRBY. Yes, but I'm afraid wrestling is not very practical for most of us. [*He gives a deprecating little laugh*] I wouldn't make a very good showing as a wrestler.

KOLENKHOV. You could be a *great* wrestler. You are built for it. Look!

> [*With a startlingly quick movement* KOLENKHOV *grabs* MR. KIRBY's *arms, knocks his legs from under him with a quick movement of a foot, and presto!* MR. KIRBY *is flat on his whatsis. Not only that, but instantaneously* KOLENKHOV *is on top of him*]

> [*Just at this moment* ALICE *re-enters the room—naturally, she stands petrified. Several people, of course, rush immediately to the rescue,* TONY *and* PAUL *arriving at the scene of battle first. Amidst the general confusion they help* MR. KIRBY *to his feet*]

ALICE. Mr. Kirby! Are you—hurt?

TONY. Are you all right, father?

KIRBY [*Pulling himself together*]. I—I—uh— [*He blinks, uncertainly*]— where are my glasses?

ALICE. Here they are, Mr. Kirby. . . . Oh, Mr. Kirby, they're broken.

KOLENKHOV [*Full of apology*]. Oh, I am sorry. But when you wrestle again, Mr. Kirby, you will of course not wear glasses.

KIRBY [*Coldly furious*]. I do not intend to wrestle again, Mr. Kolenkhov.
> [*He draws himself up, stiffly, and in return gets a sharp pain in the back. He gives a little gasp*]

TONY. Better sit down, father.

ALICE. Mr. Kolenkhov, how could you do such a thing? Why didn't somebody stop him?

MRS. KIRBY. I think, if you don't mind, perhaps we had better be going.

TONY. Mother!

ALICE [*Close to tears*]. Oh, Mrs. Kirby—please! Please don't go! Mr.

Kirby—please! I—I've ordered some scrambled eggs for you, and—plain salad—Oh, please don't go!

KOLENKHOV. I am sorry if I did something wrong. And I apologize.

ALICE. I can't tell you how sorry I am, Mr. Kirby. If I'd been here—

KIRBY [*From a great height*]. That's quite all right. ·

TONY. Of course it is. It's all right, Alice. We're not going.

[*The* KIRBYS *reluctantly sit down again*]

[*A moment's silence—no one knows quite what to say*]

PENNY [*Brightly*]. Well! That was exciting for a minute, wasn't it?

GRANDPA [*Quickly*]. You were talking about your orchids, Mr. Kirby. Do you raise many different varieties?

KIRBY [*Still unbending*]. I'm afraid I've quite forgotten about my orchids.

[*More silence, and everyone very uncomfortable*]

ALICE. I'm—awfully sorry, Mr. Kirby.

KOLENKHOV [*Exploding*]. What did I do that was so terrible? I threw him on the floor! Did it kill him?

ALICE. Please, Mr. Kolenkhov.

[*An annoyed gesture from* KOLENKHOV; *another general pause*]

PENNY. I'm sure dinner won't be any time at all now.

[*A pained smile from* MRS. KIRBY]

ESSIE. Would you like some candy while you're waiting? I've got some freshly made.

KIRBY. My doctor does not permit me to eat candy. Thank you.

ESSIE. But these are nothing, Mr. Kirby. Just cocoanut and marshmallow fudge.

ALICE. Don't, Essie.

[RHEBA *appears in the kitchen doorway, beckoning violently to* ALICE]

RHEBA [*In a loud whisper*]. Miss Alice! Miss Alice! [ALICE *quickly flies to* RHEBA's *side*] The eggs fell down the sink.

ALICE [*Desperately*]. Make some more! Quick!

RHEBA. I ain't got any.

ALICE. Send Donald out for some!

RHEBA [*Disappearing*]. All right.

ALICE [*Calling after her*]. Tell him to run! [*She turns back to the* KIRBYS] I'm so sorry. There'll be a little delay, but everything will be ready in just a minute.

[*At this moment* DONALD *fairly shoots out of the kitchen door and across the living room, beating the Olympic record for all time*]

[PENNY *tries to ease the situation with a gay little laugh. It doesn't quite come off, however*]

TONY. I've certainly put you people to a lot of trouble, with my stupidity.

GRANDPA. Not at all, Tony.

PENNY. Look! Why don't we all play a game of some sort while we're waiting?

TONY. Oh, that'd be fine.

ALICE. Mother, I don't think Mr. and Mrs. Kirby—

KOLENKHOV. *I* have an idea. I know a wonderful trick with a glass of water.

[*He reaches for a full glass that stands on the table*]

ALICE [*Quickly*]. No, Mr. Kolenkhov.

GRANDPA [*Shaking his head*]. No-o.

PENNY. But I'm sure Mr. and Mrs. Kirby would love this game. It's perfectly harmless.

ALICE. Please, Mother. . . .

KIRBY. I'm not very good at games, Mrs. Sycamore.

PENNY. Oh, but *any* fool could play this game, Mr. Kirby. [*She is bustling around, getting paper and pencil*] All you do is write your name on a piece of paper—

ALICE. But mother, Mr. Kirby doesn't want—

PENNY. Oh, he'll love it! [*Going right on*] Here you are, Mr. Kirby. Write your name on this piece of paper. And Mrs. Kirby, you do the same on this one.

ALICE. Mother, what *is* this game?

PENNY. I used to play it at school. It's called Forget-Me-Not. Now, I'm going to call out five words—just anything at all—and as I say each word, you're to put down the first thing that comes into your mind. Is that clear? For instance, if I say "grass," you might put down "green"—just whatever you think of, see? Or if I call out "chair," you might put down "table." It shows the reactions people have to different things. You see how simple it is, Mr. Kirby?

TONY. Come on, father! Be a sport!

KIRBY [*Stiffly*]. Very well. I shall be happy to play it.

PENNY. You see, Alice? He *does* want to play.

ALICE [*Uneasily*]. Well—

PENNY. Now, then! Are we ready?

KOLENKHOV. Ready!

PENNY. Now, remember—you must play fair. Put down the first thing that comes into your mind.

KIRBY [*Pencil poised*]. I understand.

PENNY. Everybody ready? . . . The first word is "potatoes." [*She repeats it*] "Potatoes." . . . Ready for the next one? . . . "Bathroom." [ALICE *shifts rather uneasily, but seeing that no one else seems to mind, she relaxes again*] Got that?

KOLENKHOV. Go ahead.

PENNY. All ready? . . . "Lust."

ALICE. Mother, this is not exactly what you—

PENNY. Nonsense, Alice—that word's all right.

ALICE. Mother, it's *not* all right.

MRS. KIRBY [*Unexpectedly*]. Oh, I don't know. It seems to me that's a perfectly fair word.

PENNY [*To* ALICE]. You see? Now, you mustn't interrupt the game.

KIRBY. May I have that last word again, please?

PENNY. "Lust," Mr. Kirby.

KIRBY [*Writing*]. I've got it.

GRANDPA. This is quite a game.

PENNY. Sssh, Grandpa. . . . All ready? . . . "Honeymoon." [ESSIE *snickers a little, which is all it takes to start* PENNY *off. Then she suddenly remembers herself*] Now, Essie! . . . All right. The last word is "sex."

ALICE [*under her breath*]. Mother!

PENNY. Everybody got "sex"? . . . All right—now give me all the papers.

GRANDPA. What happens now?

PENNY. Oh, this is the best part. Now I read out your reactions.

KIRBY. I see. It's really quite an interesting game.

PENNY. I knew you'd like it. I'll read your paper first, Mr. Kirby. [*To the others*] I'm going to read Mr. Kirby's paper first. Listen everybody! This is Mr. Kirby. . . . "Potatoes—steak." That's very good. See how they go together? Steak and potatoes?

KIRBY [*Modestly, but obviously pleased with himself*]. I just happened to think of it.

PENNY. It's *very* good. . . . "Bathroom—toothpaste." Uh-huh. "Lust—unlawful." Isn't that nice? "Honeymoon—trip." Yes. And "sex—male." Yes, of course . . . That's really a wonderful paper, Mr. Kirby.

KIRBY [*Taking a curtain call*]. Thank you . . . It's more than just a game, you know. It's sort of an experiment in psychology, isn't it?

PENNY. Yes, it is—it shows just how your *mind* works. Now we'll see how *Mrs.* Kirby's mind works. . . . Ready? . . . This is *Mrs.* Kirby. . . . "Potatoes—starch." I know just what you mean, Mrs. Kirby. . . . "Bathroom —Mr. Kirby."

KIRBY. What's that?

PENNY. Bathroom—Mr. Kirby."

KIRBY [*Turning to his wife*]. I don't quite follow that, my dear.

MRS. KIRBY. I don't know—I just thought of you in connection with it. After all, you *are* in there a good deal, Anthony. Bathing, and shaving—well, you *do* take a long time.

KIRBY. Indeed? I hadn't realized that I was being selfish in the matter. . . . Go on, Mrs. Sycamore.

ALICE [*Worried*]. I think it's a very silly game and we ought to stop it.

KIRBY. No, no. Please go on, Mrs. Sycamore.

PENNY. Where was I . . . Oh, yes. . . . "Lust—human."

KIRBY. Human? [*Thin-lipped*] Really.

MRS. KIRBY. I just meant, Anthony, that lust is after all a—human emotion.

KIRBY. I don't agree with you, Miriam. Lust is not a human emotion. It is depraved.

MRS. KIRBY. Very well, Anthony. I'm wrong.

ALICE. Really, it's the most pointless game. Suppose we play Twenty Questions?

KIRBY. No, I find this game rather interesting. Will you go on, Mrs. Sycamore? What was the next word?

PENNY [Reluctantly]. Honeymoon.

KIRBY. Oh, yes. And what was Mrs. Kirby's answer.

PENNY. Ah—"Honeymoon—dull."

KIRBY [Murderously calm]. Did you say—dull?

MRS. KIRBY. What I meant, Anthony, was that Hot Springs was not very gay that season. All those old people sitting on the porch all afternoon, and —nothing to do at night.

KIRBY. That was not your reaction at the time, as I recall it.

TONY. Father, this is only a game.

KIRBY. A very illuminating game. Go on, Mrs. Sycamore!

PENNY [Brightly, having taken a look ahead]. This one's all right, Mr. Kirby. "Sex—Wall Street."

KIRBY. Wall Street? What do you mean by that, Miriam?

MRS. KIRBY [Nervously]. I don't know what I mean, Anthony. Nothing.

KIRBY. But you must have meant something, Miriam, or you wouldn't have put it down.

MRS. KIRBY. It was just the first thing that came into my head, that's all.

KIRBY. But what does it mean? Sex—Wall Street.

MRS. KIRBY [Annoyed]. Oh, I don't know what it means, Anthony. It's just that you're always talking about Wall Street, even when—[She catches herself] I don't know what I mean . . . Would you mind terribly, Alice, if we didn't stay for dinner? I'm afraid this game has given me a headache.

ALICE [Quietly]. I understand, Mrs. Kirby.

KIRBY [Clearing his throat]. Yes, possibly we'd better postpone the dinner, if you don't mind.

PENNY. But you're coming tomorrow night, aren't you?

MRS. KIRBY [Quickly]. I'm afraid we have an engagement tomorrow night.

KIRBY. Perhaps we'd better postpone the whole affair a little while. This hot weather, and—ah—

TONY [Smoldering]. I think we're being very ungracious, father. Of course we'll stay to dinner—tonight.

MRS. KIRBY [Unyielding]. I have a very bad headache, Tony.

KIRBY. Come, come, Tony, I'm sure everyone understands.

TONY [Flaring]. Well, I don't. I think we ought to stay to dinner.

ALICE [Very low]. No, Tony.

TONY. What?

ALICE. We were fools, Tony, ever to think it would work. It won't. Mr. Kirby, I won't be at the office tomorrow. I—won't be there at all any more.

TONY. Alice, what are you talking about?

KIRBY [*To* ALICE]. I'm sorry, my dear—very sorry . . . Are you ready, Miriam?

MRS. KIRBY [*With enormous dignity*] Yes, Anthony.

KIRBY. It's been very nice to have met you all. . . . Are you coming, Anthony?

TONY. No, father. I'm not.

KIRBY. I see. . . . Your mother and I will be waiting for you at home. . . . Good night.

[*With* MRS. KIRBY *on his arm, he sweeps toward the outer door*]

[*Before the* KIRBYS *can take more than a step toward the door, however, a new* FIGURE *looms up in the archway. It is a quiet and competent-looking individual with a steely eye, and two more just like him loom up behind him*]

THE MAN [*Very quietly*]. Stay right where you are, everybody. [*There is a little scream from* MRS. KIRBY, *an exclamation from* PENNY] Don't move.

PENNY. Oh, good heavens!

KIRBY. How dare you? Why, what does this mean?

GRANDPA. What *is* all this?

KIRBY. I demand an explanation!

THE MAN. Keep your mouth shut, you! [*He advances slowly into the room, looking the group over. Then he turns to one of his men*] Which one is it?

ANOTHER MAN [*Goes over and puts a hand on* ED's *shoulder*]. This is him.

ESSIE. Ed!

ED [*Terrified*]. Why, what do you mean?

ALICE. Grandpa, what is it?

KIRBY. That is an outrage!

THE MAN. Shut up! [*He turns to* ED] What's your name?

ED. Edward—Carmichael. I haven't done anything.

THE MAN. You haven't, huh?

GRANDPA [*Not at all scared*]. This seems rather high-handed to me. What's it all about?

THE MAN. Department of Justice.

PENNY. Oh, my goodness! J-men!

ESSIE Ed, what have you done?

ED. I haven't done anything.

GRANDPA. What's the boy done, Officer?

ALICE. What is it? What's it all about?

THE MAN [*Taking his time, and surveying the room*]. That door lead to the cellar?

PENNY. Yes, it does.

PAUL. Yes.

THE MAN. [*Ordering a man to investigate*]. Mac . . . [MAC *goes into the cellar*] . . . Jim!

JIM. Yes, sir.

THE MAN. Take a look upstairs and see what you find.

JIM. Okay.

[JIM *goes upstairs*]

ED. [*Panicky*]. I haven't done anything!

THE MAN. Come here, you! [*He takes some slips of paper out of his pocket*] Ever see these before?

ED. [*Gulping*]. They're my—circulars.

THE MAN. You print this stuff, huh?

ED. Yes, sir.

THE MAN. And you put 'em into boxes of candy to get 'em into people's homes.

ESSIE. The Love Dreams!

ED. But I didn't mean anything!

THE MAN. You didn't huh? [*He reads the circulars*] "Dynamite the Capitol!" "Dynamite the White House!" "Dynamite the Supreme Court!" "God is the State; the State is God!"

ED. But I didn't mean that. I just like to print. Don't I, Grandpa?

[DONALD *returns with the eggs at this point, and stands quietly watching the proceedings*]

GRANDPA. Now, Officer, the government's in no danger from Ed. Printing is just his hobby, that's all. He prints anything.

THE MAN. He does, eh?

PENNY. I never heard of such nonsense.

KIRBY. I refuse to stay here and—

[MR. DE PINNA, *at this point is shoved through the cellar door by* MAC, *protesting as he comes*]

DE PINNA. Hey, let me get my pipe, will you? Let me get my pipe!

MAC. Shut up, you! . . . We were right, Chief. They've got enough gunpowder down there to blow up the whole city.

PAUL. But we only use that—

THE MAN. Keep still! . . . Everybody in this house is under arrest.

KIRBY. What's that?

MRS. KIRBY. Oh, good heavens!

GRANDPA. Now look here, Officer—this is all nonsense.

DE PINNA. You'd better let me get my pipe. I left it—

THE MAN. Shut up, all of you!

KOLENKHOV. It seems to me, Officer—

THE MAN. Shut up!

[*From the stairs comes the sound of drunken singing—"There was a young lady," etc.* GAY WELLINGTON, *wrapped in* PENNY'S *negligee, is being carried down the stairway by a somewhat bewildered* G-MAN]

THE G-MAN. Keep still, you! Stop that! Stop it!

THE LEADER [*After* GAY *has been persuaded to quiet down*]. Who's that?

GRANDPA [*Pretty tired of the whole business*]. That—is my mother.

[*And then, suddenly, we hear from the cellar.* MR. DE PINNA *seems to
have been right about his pipe, to judge from the sounds below. It
is a whole year's supply of fireworks—bombs, big crackers, little
crackers, sky rockets, pin wheels, everything. The house is fairly
rocked by the explosion*]

[*In the room, of course, pandemonium reigns.* MRS. KIRBY *screams;
the* G-MAN *drops* GAY *right where he stands and dashes for the cellar,
closely followed by* MR. DE PINNA *and* PAUL; PENNY *dashes for her
manuscripts and* ED *rushes to save his xylophone.* KOLENKHOV *waves
his arms wildly and dashes in all directions at once; everyone is rushing this way and that*]

[*All except one. The exception, of course, is* GRANDPA, *who takes all
things as they come.* GRANDPA *just says "Well, well, well!"—and sits
down. If a lot of people weren't in the way, in fact, you feel he'd
like to throw a few darts*]

CURTAIN

ACT THREE

T HE *following day.*
[RHEBA *is in the midst of setting the table for dinner, pausing occasionally in her labors to listen to the Edwin C. Hill of the moment—*
DONALD. *With intense interest and concentration, he is reading aloud
from a newspaper*]

DONALD. ". . . for appearance in the West Side Court this morning. After
spending the night in jail, the defendants, thirteen in all, were brought before
Judge Callahan and given suspended sentences for manufacturing fireworks
without a permit."

RHEBA. Yah. Kept me in the same cell with a strip teaser from a burlesque show.

DONALD. I was in the cell with Mr. Kirby. My, he was mad!

RHEBA. Mrs. Kirby and the strip teaser—they were fighting all night.

DONALD. Whole lot about *Mr.* Kirby here. [*Reading again*] "Anthony
W. Kirby, head of Kirby & Co., 62 Wall Street, who was among those appre-
hended, declared he was in no way interested in the manufacture of fireworks,
but refused to state why he was on the premises at the time of the raid. Mr.
Kirby is a member of the Union Club, the Racquet Club, the Harvard Club,
and the National Geographic Society." My, he certainly is a joiner!

RHEBA. All those rich men are Elks or something.

DONALD [*Looking up from his paper*]. I suppose, after all this, Mr. Tony
ain't ever going to marry Miss Alice, huh?

RHEBA. No, suh, and it's too bad, too. Miss Alice sure loves that boy.

DONALD. Ever notice how white folks always getting themselves in trouble?

RHEBA. Yassuh, I'm glad I'm colored. [*She sighs, heavily*] I don't know what I'm going to do with all that food out in the kitchen. Ain't going to be no party tonight, that's sure.

DONALD. Ain't we going to eat it anyhow?

RHEBA. Well, I'm cooking it, but I don't think anybody going to have an appetite.

DONALD. *I'm* hungry.

RHEBA. Well, *they* ain't. They're all so broke up about Miss Alice.

DONALD. What's she want to go 'way for? Where's she going?

RHEBA. I don't know—mountains some place. And she's *going,* all right, no matter what they say. I know Miss Alice when she gets that look in her eye.

DONALD. Too bad, ain't it?

RHEBA. Sure is.

[MR. DE PINNA *comes up from the cellar, bearing the earmarks of the previous day's catastrophe. There is a small bandage around his head and over one eye, and another around his right hand. He also limps slightly*]

DE PINNA. Not even a balloon left. [*He exhibits a handful of exploded fire-crackers*] Look.

RHEBA. How's your hand, Mr. De Pinna? Better?

DE PINNA. Yes, it's better. [*A step toward the kitchen*] Is there some more olive oil out there?

RHEBA [*Nods*]. It's in the salad bowl.

DE PINNA. Thanks.

[*He goes out the kitchen door as* PENNY *comes down the stairs. It is a new and rather subdued* PENNY]

PENNY [*With a sigh*]. Well, she's going. Nothing anybody said could change her.

RHEBA. She ain't going to stay away long, is she, Mrs. Sycamore?

PENNY. I don't know, Rheba. She won't say.

RHEBA. My, going to be lonesome around here without her. [*She goes into the kitchen*]

DONALD. How *you* feel, Mrs. Sycamore?

PENNY. Oh, I'm all right, Donald. Just kind of upset. [*She is at her desk*] Perhaps if I do some work maybe I'll feel better.

DONALD. Well, I won't bother you then, Mrs. Sycamore.

[*He goes into the kitchen*]

[PENNY *puts a sheet of paper into the typewriter; stares at it blankly for a moment; types in desultory fashion, gives it up. She leans back and sits staring straight ahead*]

[PAUL *comes slowly down the stairs; stands surveying the room a moment; sighs. He goes over to the Erector Set; absentmindedly pulls out the flag. Then, with another sigh, he drops into a chair*]

PAUL. She's going, Penny.

PENNY. Yes. [*She is quiet for a moment; then she starts to weep, softly*]

PAUL [*Going to her*]. Now, now, Penny.

PENNY. I can't help it, Paul. Somehow I feel it's our fault.

PAUL. It's mine more than yours, Penny. All these years I've just been—going along, enjoying myself, when maybe I should have been thinking more about Alice.

PENNY. Don't say that, Paul. You've been a wonderful father. And husband, too.

PAUL. No, I haven't. Maybe if I'd gone ahead and been an architect—I don't know—something Alice could have been proud of. I felt that all last night, looking at Mr. Kirby.

PENNY. But we've been so happy, Paul.

PAUL. I know, but maybe that's not enough. I used to think it was, but—I'm kind of all mixed up now.

PENNY [*After a pause*]. What time is she going?

PAUL. Pretty soon. Train leaves at half past seven.

PENNY. Oh, if only she'd see Tony. I'm sure he could persuade her.

PAUL. But she won't, Penny. He's been trying all day.

PENNY. Where is he now?

PAUL. I don't know—I suppose walking around the block again. Anyhow, she won't talk to him.

PENNY. Maybe Tony can catch her as she's leaving.

PAUL. It won't help, Penny.

PENNY. No, I don't suppose so. . . . I feel so sorry for Tony, too. [GRANDPA *comes down the stairs—unsmiling, but not too depressed by the situation*] [*Anxiously*] Well?

GRANDPA. Now, Penny, let the girl alone.

PENNY. But, Grandpa—

GRANDPA. Suppose she *goes* to the Adirondacks? She'll be back. You can take just so much Adirondacks, and then you come home.

PENNY. Oh, but it's all so terrible, Grandpa.

GRANDPA. In a way, but it has its bright side, too.

PAUL. How do you mean?

GRANDPA. Well, Mr. Kirby getting into the patrol wagon, for one thing, and the expression on his face when he and Donald had to take a bath together. I'll never forget that if I live to be a hundred, and I warn you people I intend to. If I can have things like that going on.

PENNY. Oh, it was even worse with Mrs. Kirby. When the matron stripped her. There was a burlesque dancer there and she kept singing a strip song while Mrs. Kirby undressed.

GRANDPA. I'll bet you Bar Harbor is going to seem pretty dull to the Kirbys for the rest of the summer.

[*With a determined step,* ALICE *comes swiftly down the stairs. Over her arm she carries a couple of dresses. Looking neither to right nor left, she heads for the kitchen*]

GRANDPA. Need any help, Alice?

ALICE [*In a strained voice*]. No, thanks, Grandpa. Ed is helping with the bags. I'm just going to press these.

PENNY. Alice, dear—

GRANDPA. Now, Penny.

[ED *has appeared in the hallway with a couple of hatboxes,* ESSIE *behind him*]

ED. I'll bring the big bag down as soon as you're ready, Alice.

ESSIE. Do you want to take some candy along for the train, Alice?

ALICE. No, thanks, Essie.

PENNY. Really, Alice, you could be just as alone here as you could in the mountains. You could stay right in your room all the time.

ALICE [*Quietly*]. No, mother, I want to be by myself—away from everybody. I love you all—you know that. But I just have to go away for a while. I'll be all right. . . . Father, did you 'phone for a cab?

PAUL. No, I didn't know you wanted one.

PENNY. Oh, I told Mr. De Pinna to tell you, Paul. Didn't he tell you?

ED. Oh, he told *me,* but I forgot.

ALICE [*The final straw*]. Oh, I wish I lived in a family that didn't always forget *every*thing. That—that behaved the way *other* people's families do. I'm sick of cornflakes, and—Donald, and— [*Unconsciously, in her impatience, she has picked up one of* GRANDPA'S *darts; is surprised to find it suddenly in her hand*] —everything! [*She dashes the dart to the floor*] Why can't we, be like other people? Roast beef, and two green vegetables, and—doilies on the table, and—a place you could bring your friends to—without— [*Unable to control herself further, she bursts out of the room, into the kitchen*]

ESSIE. I'll—see if I can do anything. [*She goes into the kitchen*]

[*The others look at each other for a moment, helplessly.* PENNY, *with a sigh, drops into her chair again.* PAUL *also sits.* GRANDPA *mechanically picks up the dart from the floor; smooths out the feathers.* ED, *with a futile gesture, runs his fingers idly over the xylophone keys. He stops quickly as every head turns to look at him*]

[*The sound of the door opening, and* TONY *appears in the archway. A worried and disheveled* TONY]

PENNY [*Quickly*]. Tony, talk to her! She's in the kitchen!

TONY. Thanks. [*He goes immediately into the kitchen*] [*The family, galvanized, listen intently*] [*Almost immediately,* ALICE *emerges from the kitchen again, followed by* TONY. *She crosses the living room and starts quickly up the stairs*] Alice, won't you listen to me? Please!

ALICE [*Not stopping*]. Tony, it's no use.

TONY [*Following her*]. Alice, you're not being fair. At least let me talk to you.

[*They are both gone—up the stairs*]

PENNY. Perhaps if I went upstairs with them . . .

GRANDPA. Now, Penny. Let them alone.

[ESSIE *comes out of the kitchen*]

ESSIE. Where'd they go? [ED, *with a gesture, indicates the upstairs region*] She walked right out the minute he came in.

[MR. DE PINNA *also emerges from the kitchen*]

DE PINNA. Knocked the olive oil right out of my hand. I'm going to smell kind of fishy.

GRANDPA. How're you feeling, Mr. De Pinna? Hand still hurting you?

DE PINNA. No, it's better.

PAUL. Everything burnt up, huh? Downstairs?

DE PINNA [*Nodding, sadly*]. Everything. And my Roman costume, too.

GRANDPA [*To* PENNY]. I told you there was a bright side to everything. All except my twenty-two years back income tax. [*He pulls an envelope out of his pocket*] I get another letter every day.

DE PINNA. Say, what are you going to do about that, Grandpa?

GRANDPA. Well, I had a kind of idea yesterday. It may not work, but I'm trying it, anyhow.

DE PINNA [*Eagerly*]. What is it?

[*Suddenly* KOLENKHOV *appears in the doorway*]

KOLENKHOV [*Even he is subdued*]. Good evening, everybody!

PENNY. Why, Mr. Kolenkhov!

GRANDPA. Hello, Kolenkhov.

KOLENKHOV. Forgive me. The door was open.

GRANDPA. Come on in.

KOLENKHOV. You will excuse my coming today. I realize you are—upset.

PENNY. That's all right, Mr. Kolenkhov.

ESSIE. I don't think I can take a lesson, Mr. Kolenkhov. I don't feel up to it.

KOLENKHOV [*Uncertainly*]. Well, I—ah—

PENNY. Oh, but do stay to dinner, Mr. Kolenkhov. We've got all that food out there, and somebody's got to eat it.

KOLENKHOV. I will be happy to, Madame Sycamore.

PENNY. Fine.

KOLENKHOV. Thank you. . . . Now, I wonder if I know you well enough to ask of you a great favor.

PENNY. Why, of course, Mr. Kolenkhov. What is it?

KOLENKHOV. You have heard me talk about my friend the Grand Duchess Olga Katrina.

PENNY. Yes?

KOLENKHOV. She is a great woman, the Grand Duchess. Her cousin was the Czar of Russia, and today she is a waitress in Childs' Restaurant. Columbus Circle.

PENNY. Yes, I know. If there's anything at all that we can do, Mr. Kolenkhov . . .

KOLENKHOV. I tell you. The Grand Duchess Olga Katrina has not had a good meal since before the Revolution.

GRANDPA. She must be hungry.

KOLENKHOV. And today the Grand Duchess not only has her day off—Thursday—but it is also the anniversary of Peter the Great. A remarkable man!

PENNY. Mr. Kolenkhov, if you mean you'd like the Grand Duchess to come to dinner, why, we'd be honored.

ESSIE. Oh, yes!

KOLENKHOV [*With a bow*]. In the name of the Grand Duchess, I thank you.

PENNY. I can hardly wait to meet her. When will she be here?

KOLENKHOV. She is outside in the street, waiting. I bring her in. [*And he goes out*]

GRANDPA. You know, if this keeps on I want to live to be a hundred and *fifty*.

PENNY [*Feverishly*]. Ed, straighten your tie. Essie, look at your dress. How do *I* look? All right?

[KOLENKHOV *appears in the hallway and stands at rigid attention*]

KOLENKHOV [*His voice booming*]. The Grand Duchess Olga Katrina! [*And the* GRAND DUCHESS OLGA KATRINA, *wheat cakes and maple syrup out of her life for a few hours, sweeps into the room. She wears a dinner gown that has seen better days, and the whole is surmounted by an extremely tacky-looking evening wrap, trimmed with bits of ancient and moth-eaten fur. But once a Grand Duchess, always a Grand Duchess. She rises above everything —Childs', evening wrap, and all*] Your Highness, permit me to present Madame Sycamore— [PENNY, *having seen a movie or two in her time, knows just what to do. She curtsies right to the floor, and catches hold of a chair just in time*] Madame Carmichael— [ESSIE *does a curtsey that begins where all others leave off. Starting on her toes, she merges the Dying Swan with an extremely elaborate genuflection*] Grandpa—

GRANDPA [*With a little bow*]. Madame.

KOLENKHOV. Mr. Sycamore, Mr. Carmichael, and Mr. De Pinna.

[PAUL *and* ED *content themselves with courteous little bows, but not so the social-minded* MR. DE PINNA. *He bows to the floor—and stays there for a moment*]

GRANDPA. All right now, Mr. De Pinna.

[MR. DE PINNA *gets to his feet again*]

PENNY. Will you be seated, Your Highness?

THE GRAND DUCHESS. Thank you. You are most kind.

PENNY. We are honored to receive you, Your Highness.

THE GRAND DUCHESS. I am most happy to be here. What time is dinner?

PENNY [*A little startled*]. Oh, it'll be quite soon, Your Highness—very soon.

THE GRAND DUCHESS. I do not mean to be rude, but I must be back at the restaurant by eight o'clock. I am substituting for another waitress.

KOLENKHOV. I will make sure you are on time, Your Highness.

DE PINNA. You know, Highness, I think you waited on me in Childs' once. The Seventy-second Street place?

THE GRAND DUCHESS. No, no. That was my sister.

KOLENKHOV. The Grand Duchess Natasha.

THE GRAND DUCHESS. *I* work in Columbus Circle.

GRANDPA. Quite a lot of your family living over here now, aren't there?

THE GRAND DUCHESS. Oh, yes—many. My uncle, the Grand Duke Sergei —he is an elevator man at Macy's. A very nice man. Then there is my cousin, Prince Alexis. He will not speak to the rest of us because he works at Hattie Carnegie's. He has cards printed—Prince Alexis of Hattie Carnegie. Bah!

KOLENKHOV. When he was selling Eskimo Pies at Luna Park he was willing to talk to you.

THE GRAND DUCHESS. Ah, Kolenkhov, our time is coming. My sister Natasha is studying to be a manicure, Uncle Sergei they have promised to make floor-walker, and next month I get transferred to the Fifth Avenue Childs'. From there it is only a step to Schrafft's, and *then* we will see what Prince Alexis says!

GRANDPA [*Nodding*]. I think you've got him.

THE GRAND DUCHESS. You are telling *me*?

[*She laughs a triumphant Russian laugh, in which* KOLENKHOV *joins*]

PENNY. Your Highness—did you know the Czar? Personally, I mean.

THE GRAND DUCHESS. Of course—he was my cousin. It was terrible, what happened, but perhaps it was for the best. Where could he get a job now?

KOLENKHOV. That is true.

THE GRAND DUCHESS [*Philosophically*]. Yes. And poor relations are poor relations. It is the same in every family. My cousin, the King of Sweden— he was very nice to us for about ten years, but then he said, I just cannot go on. I am not doing so well, either. . . . I do not blame him.

PENNY. No, of course not. . . . Would you excuse me for just a moment?

[*She goes to the foot of the stairs and stands peering up anxiously, hoping for news of* ALICE]

DE PINNA [*The historian at heart*]. Tell me, Grand Duchess, is it true what they say about Rasputin?

THE GRAND DUCHESS. Everyone wants to know about Rasputin. . . . Yes, my dear sir, it is true. In spades.

DE PINNA. You don't say?

KOLENKHOV. Your Highness, we have to watch the time.

THE GRAND DUCHESS. Yes, I must not be late. The manager does not like me. He is a Communist.

PENNY. We'll hurry things up. Essie, why don't you go out in the kitchen and give Rheba a hand?

THE GRAND DUCHESS [*Rising*]. I will help, too. I am a very good cook.

PENNY. Oh, but Your Highness! Not on your day off!

THE GRAND DUCHESS. I do not mind. Where is your kitchen?

ESSIE. Right through here, but you're the guest of honor, Your Highness.

THE GRAND DUCHESS. But I love to cook! Come, Kolenkhov! If they have got sour cream and pot cheese I will make you some blintzes!

KOLENKHOV. Ah! Blintzes! . . . Come, Pavlowa! We show you something!

[*With* ESSIE, *he goes into the kitchen*]

DE PINNA. Say! The Duchess is all right, isn't she? Hey, Duchess! Can I help?

[*And into the kitchen*]

PENNY. Really, she's a very nice woman, you know. Considering she's a Grand Duchess.

GRANDPA. Wonderful what people go through, isn't it? And still keep kind of gay, too.

PENNY. Mm. She made me forget about everything for a minute.

[*She returns to the stairs and stands listening*]

PAUL. I'd better call that cab, I suppose.

PENNY. No, wait, Paul. I think I hear them. Maybe Tony has—

[*She stops as* ALICE's *step is heard on the stair. She enters—dressed for traveling.* TONY *looms up behind her*]

ALICE. Ed, will you go up and bring my bag down?

TONY [*Quickly*]. Don't you do it, Ed!

[ED *hesitates, uncertain*]

ALICE. Ed, please!

TONY [*A moment's pause; then he gives up*]. All right, Ed. Bring it down. [ED *goes up the stairs as* TONY *disconsolately stalks across the room. Then he faces the Sycamores*] Do you know that you've got the stubbornest daughter in all forty-eight states?

[*The door bell rings*]

ALICE. That must be the cab. [*She goes to the door*]

GRANDPA. If it is, it's certainly wonderful service.

[*To the considerable surprise of everyone, the voice of* MR. KIRBY *is heard at the front door*]

KIRBY. Is Tony here, Alice?

ALICE. Yes. Yes, he is.

[MR. KIRBY *comes in*]

KIRBY [*Uncomfortably*]. Ah—good afternoon. Forgive my intruding. . . . Tony, I want you to come home with me. Your mother is very upset.

TONY [*He looks at* ALICE]. Very well, father . . . Good-bye, Alice.

ALICE [*Very low*]. Good-bye, Tony.

KIRBY [*Trying to ease the situation*]. I need hardly say that this is as painful to Mrs. Kirby and myself as it is to you people. I—I'm sorry, but I'm sure you understand.

GRANDPA. Well, yes—and in a way, no. Now, I'm not the kind of person tries to run other people's lives, but the fact is, Mr. Kirby, I don't think these two young people have got as much sense as—ah—you and I have.

ALICE [*Tense*]. Grandpa, will you please not do this?

GRANDPA [*Disarmingly*]. I'm just talking to Mr. Kirby. A cat can look at a king, can't he?

[ALICE, *with no further words, takes up the telephone and dials a number. There is finality in her every movement*]

PENNY. You—you want me to do that for you, Alice?

ALICE. No, thanks, mother.

PAUL. You've got quite a while before the train goes, Alice.

ALICE [*Into the phone*]. Will you send a cab to 761 Claremont, right away, please? . . . That's right, thank you.

[*She hangs up*]

KIRBY. And now if you'll excuse us . . . are you ready, Tony?

GRANDPA. Mr. Kirby, I suppose after last night you think this family is crazy, don't you?

KIRBY. No, I would not say that, although I am not accustomed to going out to dinner and spending the night in jail.

GRANDPA. Well, you've got to remember, Mr. Kirby, you came on the wrong night. Now tonight, I'll bet you, nothing'll happen at all. [*There is a great burst of Russian laughter from the kitchen—the mingled voices of* KOLENKHOV *and the* GRAND DUCHESS. GRANDPA *looks off in the direction of the laughter, then decides to play safe*] Maybe.

KIRBY. Mr. Vanderhof, it was not merely last night that convinced Mrs. Kirby and myself that this engagement would be unwise.

TONY. Father, I can handle my own affairs. [*He turns to* ALICE] Alice, for the last time, will you marry me?

ALICE. No, Tony. I know exactly what your father means, and he's right.

TONY. No, he's *not,* Alice.

GRANDPA. Alice, you're in love with this boy, and you're not marrying him because we're the kind of people we are.

ALICE. Grandpa—

GRANDPA. I know. You think the two families wouldn't get along. Well, maybe they wouldn't—but who says they're right and we're wrong?

ALICE. I didn't say that, Grandpa. I only feel—

GRANDPA. Well, what *I* feel is that Tony's too nice a boy to wake up twenty years from now with nothing in his life but stocks and bonds.

KIRBY. How's that?

GRANDPA [*Turning to* MR. KIRBY]. Yes. Mixed up and unhappy, the way you are.

KIRBY [*Outraged*]. I beg your pardon, Mr. Vanderhof, I am a very happy man.

GRANDPA. Are you?

KIRBY. Certainly I am.

GRANDPA. I don't think so. What do you think you get your indigestion from? Happiness? No, sir. You get it because most of your time is spent in doing things you don't want to do.

KIRBY. I don't do anything I don't want to do.

GRANDPA. Yes, you do. You said last night that at the end of a week in Wall Street you're pretty near crazy. Why do you keep on doing it?

KIRBY. Why do I keep on—why, that's my *business*. A man can't give up his business.

GRANDPA. Why not? You've got all the money you need. You can't take it with you.

KIRBY. That's a very easy thing to say, Mr. Vanderhof. But I have spent my entire life building up my business.

GRANDPA. And what's it got you? Same kind of mail every morning, same kind of deals, same kind of meetings, same dinners at night, same indigestion. Where does the fun come in? Don't you think there ought to be something *more*, Mr. Kirby? You must have wanted more than that when you started out. We haven't got too much time, you know—any of us.

KIRBY. What do you expect me to do? Live the way *you* do? Do nothing?

GRANDPA. Well, I have a lot of fun. Time enough for everything—read, talk, visit the zoo now and then, practice my darts, even have time to notice when spring comes around. Don't see anybody I don't want to, don't have six hours of things I *have* to do every day before I get *one* hour to do what I like in—and I haven't taken bicarbonate of soda in thirty-five years. What's the matter with that?

KIRBY. The matter with that? But suppose we *all* did it? A fine world we'd have, everybody going to zoos. Don't be ridiculous, Mr. Vanderhof. Who would do the work?

GRANDPA. There's always people that like to work—you can't *stop* them. Inventions, and they fly the ocean. There's always people to go down to Wall Street, too—because they *like* it. But from what I've seen of you, I don't think you're one of them. I think you're missing something.

KIRBY. I am not aware of missing anything.

GRANDPA. I wasn't either, till I quit. I used to get down to that office nine o'clock sharp, no matter how I felt. Lay awake nights for fear I wouldn't get that contract. Used to worry about the world, too. Got *all* worked up about whether Cleveland or Blaine was going to be elected President—seemed awful important at the time, but who cares now? What I'm trying to say, Mr. Kirby, is that I've had thirty-five years that nobody can take away from me, no matter what they do to the world. See?

KIRBY. Yes, I do see. And it's a very dangerous philosophy, Mr. Vanderhof. It's—it's un-American. And it's exactly why I'm opposed to this marriage. I don't want Tony to come under its influence.

TONY [*A gleam in his eye*]. What's the matter with it, father?

KIRBY. Matter with it? Why, it's—it's downright Communism, that's what it is.

TONY. You didn't always think so.

KIRBY. I most certainly did. What are you talking about?

TONY. I'll tell you what I'm talking about. You didn't always think so, because there was a time when you wanted to be a trapeze artist.

KIRBY. Why—why, don't be an idiot, Tony.

TONY. Oh, yes, you did. I came across those letters you wrote to grandfather. Do you remember those?

KIRBY. NO! . . . How dared you read those letters? How dared you?

PENNY. Why, isn't that wonderful? Did you wear tights, Mr. Kirby?

KIRBY. Certainly not! The whole thing is absurd. I was fourteen years old at the time. ·

TONY. Yes, but at *eighteen* you wanted to be a saxophone player, didn't you?

KIRBY. Tony!

TONY. And at twenty-one you ran away from home because grandfather wanted you to go into the business. It's all down there in black and white. You didn't *always* think so.

GRANDPA. Well, well, well!

KIRBY. I may have had silly notions in my youth, but thank God my father knocked them out of me. I went into the business and forgot about them.

TONY. Not altogether, father. There's still a saxophone in the back of your clothes closet.

GRANDPA. There is?

KIRBY [*Quietly*]. That's enough, Tony. We'll discuss this later.

TONY. No, I want to talk about it *now*. I think Mr. Vanderhof is right —dead right. I'm never going back to that office. I've always hated it, and I'm not going on with it. And I'll tell you something else. I didn't make a mistake last night. I knew it was the wrong night. I brought you here on purpose.

ALICE. Tony!

PENNY. Well, for heaven's—

TONY. Because I wanted to wake you up. I wanted you to see a real family—as they really *were*. A family that loved and understood each other. You don't understand *me*. You're never had time. Well, I'm not going to make *your* mistake. I'm clearing out.

KIRBY. Clearing out? What do you mean?

TONY. I mean I'm not going to be pushed into the business just because I'm your son. I'm getting out while there's still time.

KIRBY [*Stunned*]. Tony, what are you going to do?

TONY. I don't know. Maybe I'll be a bricklayer, but at least I'll be doing something I want to do.

[*Whereupon the door bell rings*]

PENNY. That must be the cab.

GRANDPA. Ask him to wait a minute, Ed.

ALICE. Grandpa!

GRANDPA. Do you mind, Alice? . . . You know, Mr. Kirby, Tony is going through just what you and I did when we were his age. I think, if you listen hard enough, you can hear yourself saying the same things to *your* father twenty-five years ago. We all did it. And we were right. How many of us would be willing to settle when we're young for what we eventually get? All those plans we make . . . what happens to them? It's only a handful of the lucky ones that can look back and say that they even came close. [GRANDPA *has hit home.* MR. KIRBY *turns slowly and looks at his son, as though seeing him for the first time.* GRANDPA *continues*] So . . . before they clean out that closet, Mr. Kirby, I think I'd get in a few good hours on that saxophone.

[*A slight pause, then* THE GRAND DUCHESS, *an apron over her evening dress, comes in from the kitchen*]

THE GRAND DUCHESS. I beg your pardon, but before I make the blintzes, how many will there be for dinner?

PENNY. Why, I don't know—ah—

GRANDPA. Your Highness, may I present Mr. Anthony Kirby, and Mr. Kirby, Junior? The Grand Duchess Olga Katrina.

KIRBY. How's that?

THE GRAND DUCHESS. How do you do? Before I make the blintzes, how many will there be to dinner?

GRANDPA. Oh, I'd make quite a stack of them, Your Highness. Can't ever tell.

THE GRAND DUCHESS. Good! The Czar always said to me, Olga, do not be stingy with the blintzes.

[*She returns to the kitchen, leaving a somewhat stunned* MR. KIRBY *behind her*]

KIRBY. Ah—who did you say that was, Mr. Vanderhof?

GRANDPA [*Very offhand*]. The Grand Duchess Olga Katrina, of Russia. She's cooking the dinner.

KIRBY. Oh!

GRANDPA. And speaking of dinner, Mr. Kirby, why don't you and Tony both stay?

PENNY. Oh, please do, Mr. Kirby. We've got all that stuff we were going to have last night. I mean tonight.

GRANDPA. Looks like a pretty good dinner, Mr. Kirby, and'll kind of give us a chance to get acquainted. Why not stay?

KIRBY. Why—I'd like to very much. [*He turns to* TONY, *with some trepidation*] What do you say, Tony. Shall we stay to dinner?

TONY. Yes, father. I think that would be fine. If— [*His eyes go to* ALICE] —if Alice will send away that cab.

GRANDPA. How about it, Alice? Going to be a nice crowd. Don't you think you ought to stay for dinner?

ALICE. Mr. Kirby—Tony—oh, Tony!

[*And she is in his arms*]

TONY. Darling!

ALICE. Grandpa, you're wonderful!

GRANDPA. I've been telling you that for years.

[*He kisses her*]

[ESSIE *enters from the kitchen, laden with dishes*]

ESSIE. Grandpa, here's a letter for you. It was in the ice-box.

GRANDPA [*Looks at the envelope*]. The Government again.

TONY [*Happily*]. Won't you step into the office, Miss Sycamore? I'd like to do a little dictating.

GRANDPA [*With his letter*]. Well, well, well!

PENNY. What is it, Grandpa?

GRANDPA. The United States Government apologizes. I don't owe 'em a nickel. It seems I died eight years ago.

ESSIE. Why, what do they mean, Grandpa?

GRANDPA. Remember Charlie, the milkman? Buried under my name?

PENNY. Yes.

GRANDPA. Well, I just told them they made a mistake and I was Martin Vanderhof, Jr. So they're very sorry and I may even get a refund.

ALICE. Why, Grandpa, you're an old crook.

GRANDPA. Sure!

KIRBY [*Interested*]. Pardon me, how did you say you escaped the income tax, Mr. Vanderhof?

KOLENKHOV [*Bursting through the kitchen door, bringing a chair with him*]. Tonight, my friends, you are going to eat. . . .

[*He stops short as he catches sight of* KIRBY]

KIRBY [*Heartily*]. Hello, there!

KOLENKHOV [*Stunned*]. How do you do?

KIRBY. Fine! Fine! Never was better.

KOLENKHOV [*To* GRANDPA]. What has happened?

GRANDPA. He's relaxing. [ED *strikes the keys of the xylophone*] That's right. Play something, Ed.

[*He starts to play.* ESSIE *is immediately up on her toes*]

THE GRAND DUCHESS [*Entering from the kitchen*]. Everything will be ready in a minute. You can sit down.

PENNY. Come on, everybody. Dinner! [*They start to pull up chairs*] Come on, Mr. Kirby!

KIRBY [*Still interested in the xylophone*]. Yes, yes, I'm coming.

PENNY. Essie, stop dancing and come to dinner.

KOLENKHOV. You will like Russian food, Mr. Kirby.

PENNY. But you must be careful of your indigestion.

KIRBY. Nonsense! I haven't any indigestion.

TONY. Well, Miss Sycamore, how was your trip to the Adirondacks?

ALICE. Shut your face, Mr. Kirby!

KOLENKHOV. In Russia, when they sit down to dinner . . .

GRANDPA [*Tapping on his plate*]. Quiet! Everybody! Quiet! [*Immediately the talk ceases. All heads are lowered as* GRANDPA *starts to say Grace*]

Well, Sir, here we are again. We want to say thanks once more for everything You've done for us. Things seem to be going along fine. Alice is going to marry Tony, and it looks as if they're going to be very happy. Of course the fireworks blew up, but that was Mr. De Pinna's fault, not Yours. We've all got our health and as far as anything else is concerned, we'll leave it to You. Thank You.

> [*The heads come up again.* RHEBA *and* DONALD *come through the kitchen door with stacks and stacks of blintzes. Even the Czar would have thought there were enough*]

CURTAIN

Good Heavens [1]

by NORMAN CORWIN

VOICE [*Misterioso*]. Schwassmann-Wachmann . . . one . . . comet . . . Thomas . . . 18 . . . 11 . . . 0 . . . September . . . 03355 . . . 21465 . . . 11141 . . . motion 10023 . . . 10001 . . . 74095 . . . suddenly brighter . . . spectra desirable!

[*Music: Suspense chord*]

NARRATOR. That was code—and you're quite right, you're listening to a spy story. This is about men who want to get hold of the secret plans of the super nova. This is about the riddle of the White Dwarf. . . . Interested?

[*Music: Introductory cue*]

SECOND NARRATOR. This show concerns astronomy. That code you heard a minute back is no gag. It's the actual wording of a telegram sent out by the head astronomer of Harvard to all observatories in America. What it means would take tall explaining.[1] First, however, we must clear up for you the matter of what kind of life goes on at astronomical observatories.

Now there are a number of common misconceptions about the way serious astronomers spend their time. The interstellar comic strips and pseudo-scientific shocker magazines have encouraged most of us to believe that on a clear night in a telescopic observatory, this sort of thing goes on. . . .

[*Deep power hum as of a generator, in background*]

HOTCHKISS. All right, Billingsgate, you've been looking long enough. Now give me a crack at it.

BILLINGSGATE [*Excited*]. Wait a minute, Hotchkiss, I think I see some-thing moving!

HOTCHKISS. You do? [*To still another astronomer, across the room*] Oh, I say, Dr. Dumke, Billingsgate has detected life on Mars!

BILLINGSGATE. Now, just a moment, Hotchkiss, I didn't say that at all. I merely said I thought I saw something moving.

DUMKE [*Coming on*]. Lemme see, lemme see.

HOTCHKISS. Me first. Lemme see, Billingsgate.

BILLINGSGATE. Here you are, Hotchkiss.

HOTCHKISS. Mm. [*Up*] Increase the magnification two magnitudes.

[*A deep motor sound, cross-cut by the effect of a spark gap*]

[1] From *More by Corwin*, by permission of Henry Holt and Company. Written at the invita-tion of the University of Chicago as part of its fiftieth anniversary celebration and produced on September 28, 1941. The broadcast was dedicated to the Yerkes Observatory. The numbered notes will be found on pp. 1035–1037.

HOTCHKISS. Enough!

BILLINGSGATE AND DUMKE. What do you see?

HOTCHKISS. Nothing. Billingsgate, you were seeing things.

BILLINGSGATE. I resent that, Professor. I was only—

ADDINGTON [*The director, making an entrance*]. Ah, good evening, gentlemen. What's up?

ALL. Good evening, Director. Good evening, Dr. Addington.

DUMKE. Nothing new. Still searching.

ADDINGTON. Very good. Keep your eye glued to Mars. And while you're at it, be on the lookout for exploding stars and new comets. We want to be the first to see them if there are any around.

HOTCHKISS. Right, sir.

ADDINGTON. Also, check a couple of constellations for weather predictions before it gets light.

BILLINGSGATE. Yes, sir.

ADDINGTON. I'm going back to the laboratory to continue work on the rocket ship; but in the meantime, Dumke, will you give Jupiter and Venus the once-over just in case there might be signs of life on them? [*Fading*] Never can tell when something might show up.

DUMKE. Righto, Dr. Addington. [*Up*] Swing 'er six degrees to the west!

VOICE [*Off*]. Swing 'er six degrees to the west.

[*Buzzer; then a bell; then a blast of compressed air; finally a tremendous sound of whirring. When it stops*]

DUMKE. Hold it! Ah! Wonderful sharp focus!

HOTCHKISS. Yeah? What do you see?

DUMKE. Just a moment, now.

HOTCHKISS. Lemme see, lemme see.

BILLINGSGATE. Me first. I was first. . . . [*The squabbling fades under*]

[*Music: A daft cue*]

NARRATOR. No, that is not what goes on in an observatory of a clear night. Astronomers don't keep their eyes glued to their telescopes. They spend very little time gazing at the fancy showpieces of the skies. They hardly ever look at the rings of Saturn or the craters of the moon—they're not at all concerned with watching the planet Mars for signals to be flashed to earth, nor do they ever make weather predictions or have a desire to travel through space on rocket ships.

Do you want to know what really is typical of a night at a big observatory like Yerkes?

Music, please, for atmosphere.

[*Music: A night theme, fading under*]

NARRATOR. It is night in the country. A dark observatory broods under the northern constellations. Off on the horizon there's a faint glow from a town in the valley. But here it is dark—and quiet, except for the scattered small talk of insects in the fields.

[*Night noises in*]

[*We hear steps on stone; they advance up stone stairs. When they stop we hear the sound of a key in a lock*]

NARRATOR. This man is an astronomer. He's alone. He's opening the door of the observatory. Observatories have doors with locks in them, like your house.

[*A door opens, closes; as it does so, the night sounds go out. Slowly the steps advance along a stone floor and upstairs. Then a metal door opens and closes*]

NARRATOR. Now he enters the dome—a great vault full of echoes, dark and cold and draughty. It is solemn, like the inquisition chambers of comic-strip characters who commute between stars.

[*Echo chamber in for steps on metal stairs, then across a wooden hollow floor. We hear the flick of an electric switch; then more steps*]

NARRATOR. A small light goes on now—enough to make out the great hulk of a telescope mounted on a massive pier, bigger-girthed and longer than the fiercest cannon.

Now he pulls a cord which moves a shutter in the dome.

[*Shutter effect—a big Venetian-blind sound, off perspective, and with echo*]

NARRATOR. And now the roof is slit, the heavens shining through.

[*Steps on a wooden floor*]

NARRATOR. This done, he walks to a control board and pulls a lever.

[*A slight high-pitched skidding sound, as of a transmission belt being shifted*]

NARRATOR. And the floor rises. . . .

[*A heavy motor sound—grinding—almost like a subway train at low speed. It stops*]

NARRATOR. The floor has risen beneath his feet, risen three times his height. And now he pulls another lever, and the great refractor swings around to meet the open sector of the dome.

[*Another skidding sound and a slower grinding mesh of heavy gears; motor noises also. At length it stops*]

NARRATOR. This telescope weighs twenty tons, and yet it can be moved by hand. Our friend now reaches up and pulls the eyepiece closer to his eye. Then, having found his field . . .

ASTRONOMER. Right ascension, three hours fifty-five minutes; declination, minus thirteen degrees forty-one seconds. . . .

NARRATOR. He trains it on the star 40 Eridani—40 for its order in the ascension, Eridani for the constellation in which it appears. . . . [This ascension and declination and parallax business is over our heads in more ways than one.] . . . But what is our astronomer doing now? He's twiddling screws to move cross-wires—reading a micrometer, to set the glass steady on its objective. Meanwhile a silent mechanism keeps turning the telescope westward exactly at the rate of the earth's rotation eastward. In this way the poised and balanced superspyglass follows automatically the pinpoint in the sky which the astronomer has singled out.

And now, for a moment, the image of the star is studied. . . .

[*Music: Star theme in*]

40 Eridani! It burns like some forgotten signal lantern at a junction of two skies. The naked eye is clothed now, and it senses something of the unimaginable force that throbs so many, many billions of miles away. It gathers in the long, pulsating rays; it feels the grave and mystic splendor of this numbered sphere whose light for more than sixty years has been traveling through space to keep this rendezvous.

[*Music: Out*]

NARRATOR. He's noted all he needs to note, and now he disengages the eyepiece . . .

[*Small sound of metallic attachment*]

NARRATOR. . . . and substitutes for it a camera plateholder. He's going to take a photograph which later will be studied under microscopes. Exposure? Say ten seconds, for dramatic license; it might well be closer to an hour. He sets an astronomical alarm-clock for the length of the exposure:

[*Clean, quiet ticking. After ten seconds, an ordinary alarm-clock rings*]

NARRATOR. We'll leave the doctor now, while he takes his plate and goes inside a portable dark room to develop it. When he comes out he'll enter in a date book a log of observations concerning 40 Eridani. He will fill in right ascension, declination, date, observatory weather, the outside temperature, the temperature of the telescope tube, the barometric pressure. He will go home at two A.M. Another member of the observatory staff will come in at two and use the telescope till dawn. And when the dawn comes? . . .

A little dawn music, please.

[*Music: A dawn theme*]

NARRATOR. Do practical-minded listeners want to know what good there is in all this? After the stars have been charted, weighed, their distances determined, their elements found out—so what, do you want to know? Well, in the first place, since when does the pursuit of a pure science have to apologize to practical men?

SCIENTIST [*Very apologetically*]. I say, Mr. Pennypacker, do you mind if I pursue my study of spectroheliography? It may take me a lifetime, and it may yield no commercially important results, but—er—uh—

NARRATOR. What does Pennypacker know about the possible practical results of spectroheliography? Pennypacker's busy packing pennies, and let him stick to it. Even if astronomy never meant a hoot toward the improvement of human existence, that would be no reason why its work should not persist, why it should require any statement of defense.

But consider some of astronomy's more practical applications—everyday ones:

ANNOUNCER. When you hear the musical note, the time will be exactly— minutes [2] and — seconds past — o'clock, Eastern Time.

[*Chime*]

WOMAN. It will be high tide at Sandy Hook at — A.M. tomorrow.

NAVIGATOR. Our ship's position is latitude 56 degrees 9 minutes south, longitude 77 degrees 4 minutes west.

TECHNICIAN. The War Department has just ordered forty thousand more tanks of helium.

NARRATOR [*Summarizing*]. Time? The special province of astronomy. Tide? The pull of sun and moon upon the earth. Navigation? Largely a system of solar and lunar measurement. Helium? An element discovered on the sun before it was discovered in the earth. And moreover, Mr. Pennypacker—

ASTRONOMER. The sun and stars hold within them the secret of releasing tremendous quantities of energy from matter. We don't yet know the answer to the riddle of the sun's renewal. If we find out, the earth will never have to worry about exhausting fuel supplies, for the energy taken from an old tin can might move a ship around the world.

NARRATOR. Matter into energy? Here are some facts which may well raise a Pennypacker's hair:

QUESTIONER. Question: How much of the sun's total energy does the earth intercept? Do you think you can guess within 20 per cent?

[*A pause after each of these questions to give it time to sink in and to allow the listener a chance to guess*]

ANSWERER. Answer: One twenty-millionth of 1 per cent.

QUESTIONER. Question: Within a thousand degrees, what is the temperature of the sun's interior?

ANSWERER. Answer: Ten million degrees centigrade.

QUESTIONER. Question: According to Einstein's formula, the sun is losing four million tons of mass each second. At this rate, how soon will it be before it decreases by one-half of 1 per cent? See if you can guess within six months.

ANSWERER. Answer: Seventy-five thousand million years.

NARRATOR. Time for our time motif, orchestra.

[*Music: Time motif*]

NARRATOR. Think you know a lot about time? Do you know the time of day? Do you know what year it is? You think it's 1943? That all depends on where you are. If you asked a citizen of Tokyo,[3] he'd say—

JAPANESE. It's the year 2603.[4]

NARRATOR. Note, please, that in our literal translation from the Japanese our actor doesn't say—

JAPANESE [*Thick singsong*]. It's the year 2603.

NARRATOR. Why do all foreign people in radio dramas speak broken English in their own countries? Oh, well . . . [*Gives up the line of inquiry*] A Mohammedan would tell you—

MOHAMMEDAN. This is the year 1362 of the era of the Hegira.

NARRATOR. An orthodox Jew counts farther back than an orthodox gentile—

JEW. The new year, which commenced last week,[5] is, according to our calendar, 5704.

NARRATOR. And an ancient Byzantine, returned to earth today, would calculate—

BYZANTINE. Why, this is the year 7452.

NARRATOR. Whereas an ancient Greek would figure it—

GREEK [*With a very phony Greek accent*]. Year 2719 of the Olympiads or the third year of the six hundred eightieth Olympiad.

NARRATOR [*With disgust; he's against radio accents*]. Et tu, Workshop. . . . That's all, brother.

NARRATOR [*Withheld cue* [6]]. Now then—let's talk about time: that which is so much a part of us, shaping our lives before we're born; that which we have so much of, yet so little. Time can be measured more easily than it can be defined. This thing, so common in our lives, defies description. For example, now, I'll ask at random two actors in the studio—they are not prepared for this. [*Addressing actor by name*]. ——, how would you define time?

ACTOR. [*Answers*]

NARRATOR. [*Asks another actor*]

SECOND ACTOR. [*Answers*]

NARRATOR. See what I mean? Even measurement is difficult. We count off seconds easily enough, but when it comes to aggregates of seconds, then we have trouble. The year is a big unit to us here on earth, and there's been considerable disagreement as to how to clock it. Between the Gregorian year, which we now employ, and the astronomical year, which astronomers use, there is a difference of twenty-six seconds—and this adds up to a full day every 3323 years.

Did you think our calendar just grew up by itself? Did you think Adam invented it? Why, once a famous pope suppressed ten days in order to straighten out our measurement of time. That's just what he did, and that's what made him famous. Three hundred sixty-one years ago, Pope Gregory the Thirteenth reformed a calendar which had been in service over fifteen hundred years, and which, because of errors in it, had begun to lag behind the solar year. So in order to make things come out even, Gregory suppressed ten days. . . .

GREGORY. Let it be ordained that the fifth day of October of this year of our Lord 1582 be designated as the fifteenth day of October.

NARRATOR. And that's the way it was suppressed.

We go around talking very loosely about time, as though there were only one kind of it.

VOICES. Good morning . . . good afternoon . . . good evening . . . good night . . . yesterday . . . tomorrow . . . when? . . . now . . . early? . . . late . . . soon . . . after . . . before . . . during . . . always . . . never . . .

NARRATOR You'd think, by the commonness of these words, that time was absolutely uniform to our senses and our lives. But of course it's not. To each of us time's a sensation of a special sort, according to what occupies our consciousness at any given moment—

GIRL. Ooh my, the way the time's flown by—it seems like it was only yesterday we started on our honeymoon.

NARRATOR. Or else this sort of measurement—

MAN. You have no idea what a boring time we had! I thought they would never go home. Seemed like a thousand years to me.

NARRATOR. Outside our isolated solar system, time is relative in still another way—it's not what we think it is; no, not even the astronomers are sure of it. They argue theories with such impressive names as—

ASTRONOMER. The relativity of simultaneity.

NARRATOR. Time? That's a program by itself some night. It should have an all-star cast including—

VOICES. Greenwich mean time . . . nautical time . . . absolute time . . . mathematical time . . . empirical time . . . psychological time . . . sidereal time . . . Standard time . . . solar time . . . time-and-a-half . . . three-quarters time . . . time immemorial . . . time out of mind . . . time loan . . . time bomb . . . leisure time . . . hard times . . . time at bat . . . *Time* magazine . . . any old time . . .

NARRATOR. And, of course, time for the time motif.

[*Music: Time motif*]

PROSECUTOR. Is there a doctor of philosophy in the house? Is there anybody listening who thinks he knows all the answers? If so, then let him take the stand.

VOLUNTEER [*Off*]. I'm no Ph.D. or genius, and there may be some answers I don't know, but I've had a decent education.

PROSECUTOR. Good. Would you care to come to the microphone, please?

[*Steps across the floor*]

PROSECUTOR. Be seated, sir. Now tell me: Do parallel lines ever meet?

VOLUNTEER. No, of course not.

PROSECUTOR. Wrong. They do.

VOLUNTEER. I was taught they don't.

PROSECUTOR. Well, I was taught they do.

VOLUNTEER. By whom?

PROSECUTOR. By Einstein. . . . Question Number Two: Can a straight line be extended indefinitely?

VOLUNTEER. How's that again?

PROSECUTOR. If you draw a perfectly straight line, and if it runs off your paper and out of your window and into space—infinitely far—will it keep on going straight forever?

VOLUNTEER. Why, sure.

PROSECUTOR. Wrong. It would finally return to itself.

VOLUNTEER. Why?

PROSECUTOR. Because space is curved.

VOLUNTEER. Now, wait a minute—

PROSECUTOR. Does the sum of the angles of a triangle equal two right angles?

VOLUNTEER. Why, everybody knows that. I was taught that in high school. I suppose that's wrong too, is it?

PROSECUTOR. You're right, you're wrong.

VOLUNTEER [*Hurt*]. Wrong?

PROSECUTOR. Wrong, according to the laws of astronomy—the laws of the heavens—the laws of time and space.

VOLUNTEER. But we're not in space, mister, we're on solid earth.

PROSECUTOR. Wrong again. Not so very solid, sir. Why, every structure in the world—the granite mountain and the shapeless air—the very steel beams of this building are aquiver with atomic life, atremble with great systems of submicroscopic motion.

And what is light and color, what is sound, but more vibration?

VOLUNTEER. Look—you keep your atoms and molecules. I still say the earth is solid. It doesn't wiggle under my feet. It doesn't slip around. It turns smoothly on its axis, it minds its own business, it doesn't get carried away by every new theory that comes along.

PROSECUTOR. You don't have to get reactionary about it.

VOLUNTEER. I'm not getting reactionary.

PROSECUTOR. You are so.

VOLUNTEER. What authority have you got for what you're giving out here?

PROSECUTOR. Authority? Ha!—Will Astronomers Brown, Jones, Smith, and Doe take the stand, please?

[*Four pairs of footsteps*]

PROSECUTOR [*Sotto voce over sound of steps*]. It's not for nothing that the Columbia Workshop [7] hired me as prosecuting attorney. [*Up*] Now, Professor Brown, tell the court: Does the earth wiggle under your feet?

BROWN. Yes, indeed, sir. The crust of the earth apparently slips relative to the terrestrial core. There are on the average of three hundred seventy earthquakes throughout the globe every year.

PROSECUTOR. Thank you. Dr. Jones—does the earth turn smoothly on its axis?

JONES. The axis of the planet does not hold fast, no. Its unsteadiness—

PROSECUTOR. Just a moment. [*Projecting*] No photographs, please, until the hearing is over. . . . All right, go on, Dr. Jones.

JONES. In fact, the crust of the earth slips all the time. It produces complicated vibrations of latitude which bother us sometimes when we are trying to determine position of stars accurately.

PROSECUTOR. Would you bear that out, Mr. Smith?

SMITH. Yes, sir. Moreover the rotation of the earth is not perfectly even, because the sun and moon drag on our equator, giving rise to certain intricate, though minor, motions. And also, the earth itself is changing its form.

PROSECUTOR. Now, Mr. Doe, your colleague speaks of the intricate motions of the earth. Can you name, offhand, the various directions in which our earth is gyrating or drifting?

DOE. Why, yes, sir, that's quite simple. There are six. First there's the daily rotation of the earth. The eastward rotation—night and day.

PROSECUTOR. Speed?

DOE. Oh, about a thousand miles an hour at the equator, seven hundred fifty miles an hour in the latitude of New York.

PROSECUTOR. Yes, Next?

DOE. Second, there's—

VOLUNTEER. All right, all right, the earth is moving in six directions at once. Okay. Now, can I cross-examine *you?*

PROSECUTOR. What was that?

VOLUNTEER. Can I cross-examine you?

PROSECUTOR. I don't get the name?

VOLUNTEER. Just change places with me here.

PROSECUTOR. Well—er—isn't that kind of irregular?

VOLUNTEER. So's our orbit, wise guy.

PROSECUTOR. Who's a wise guy?

VOLUNTEER. You.

PROSECUTOR. Me?

VOLUNTEER. Yes, you.

PROSECUTOR. You wouldn't like a pop on the nose, would you, quiz kid?

VOLUNTEER. Is that a dignified question to ask on a program dedicated to the Yerkes Observatory?

PROSECUTOR [*Contritely*]. No—I guess not. They won't think well of me at Yerkes, will they?

VOLUNTEER. Hardly.

PROSECUTOR. They'll think I'm a yerk!

VOLUNTEER. Step down, brother.

PROSECUTOR. I apologize. You may proceed to cross-examine me.

VOLUNTEER. Now, in the biblical book of Job, there is an allusion to the morning stars singing together.

PROSECUTOR. Morning stars singing together?

VOLUNTEER. Yes. Now, since you are full of astronomical lore, perhaps you can tell me what that sounded like.

PROSECUTOR. I can tell you what it didn't sound like.

VOLUNTEER. All right, what didn't it sound like?

PROSECUTOR. Like this—

[*Music: A quartet of girls singing "Daddy" * in close harmony*]

VOLUNTEER. I move that be stricken from the record.

PROSECUTOR. All right, strick it.

VOLUNTEER. Very well. Now you have attempted in this hearing to demonstrate that the average man entertains several misconceptions regarding the laws of time and space.

PROSECUTOR. Precisely.

VOLUNTEER. Did it ever occur to you that the ordinary man wishes to understand only those forces of nature which he encounters in his daily life?

PROSECUTOR. It occurred to me only yesterday, while I was shaving.

VOLUNTEER. And that he wishes to understand these only so far as it's necessary for him to keep alive and well?

PROSECUTOR. Well?

VOLUNTEER. Then let there be no easy assumption that the man in the street is naïve. It happens that the astronomer has access to far-reaching sources of information, and so *his* naïveté becomes relative—it's simply ignorance on a much higher plane.

PROSECUTOR. This is degenerating into a bull session.

VOLUNTEER. The astronomer knows things which stagger us—but the things he knows he *doesn't* know stagger *him!*

PROSECUTOR. Such as what? Name two.

VOLUNTEER. Such as the White Dwarfs.

PROSECUTOR. Snow White and the White Dwarfs?

VOLUNTEER. No. Dwarfed stars which, while smaller than the earth, have volumes greater than our sun. Their density is so great and their gravity so strong that a cigarette on their surface would weigh about two hundred thousand tons.

PROSECUTOR. What makes White Dwarfs, Daddy?

VOLUNTEER. Astronomers don't know.

PROSECUTOR. What else don't they know?

* Permission to use this song in any production must be obtained directly from the Republic Music Corporation, New York City.

VOLUNTEER. They don't know the limits of the universe. They don't know why some stars flare up suddenly and die down again; they don't know what will happen when galaxies which are now rushing away from us at a rate of forty thousand miles a second accelerate their speed until they reach the speed of light, which is the greatest known speed. [*Fading*]. They don't know about the disintegration of matter. They don't know what happens to all the energy that has been radiated into space. [*He continues under Narrator*] They don't know whether, when they are seeing two stars in a telescope, they are actually seeing two images of the same star, the light from which may have reached us by varying routes through the great curved voids of interstellar space. [*He is faded*]

NARRATOR. He's speaking now of mysteries no earthbound Sherlock Holmes, no Moto, no Fu-Man-Chu can help to solve. These are the spiraled questions, the enigmas hung up in the purple sky. [*Music: Moon motif behind*] They gaze down on the tortured face of our most pitiable planet, gaze down on us with the patience of a long and loping universe. These are the mysteries which our distant children in their clean and honorable and benign societies will still attempt to fathom, looking through the brighter glasses of a happier millennium. These are the passions of the good and goodly heavens—the fierce and holy matters of remoteness beyond the farthest tendrils of the outstretched mind.

[*Music: Out*]

NARRATOR. O men who fish the luminescent and star-strewn seas of galaxy and nebula, of cluster and of constellation—men who silently, alone, patrol the shores of night, who track sidereal wanderers down and weigh and measure them and take their temperatures, you men who've traveled farther standing still than twenty billion Marco Polos, tell us:

Are we not brave and meaning animals? Do we not make a kind of plaintive music of our intermission here? Do we not clock War's baleful equinoxes by the rhythmic dripping of our blood? Are we not hopeful seekers after nebulae of Truth and patient watchers for the ray of Hope?

Tell us, astronomers of all the world's observatories: What is the magnitude of Man?

[*Music: Finale*]

POETRY

POETRY

NOT all people like or understand poetry instinctively. For most people the enjoyment of poetry, like a taste for olives, is an acquired characteristic. Some readers are first attracted by the charm of musical sounds and colorful images and later acquire an interest in the meanings poets endeavor to communicate. Others are attracted first by the meanings and only later learn to enjoy poetical expression. At any rate we must admit that obstacles stand between the untrained reader and his enjoyment and understanding of the experience of reading poems.

In his *Practical Criticism* Mr. I. A. Richards studies some of these obstacles and points out how the realization of them may lead to their removal. The first difficulty is the difficulty of making out the plain sense of poetry. The meaning is likely to be more compactly stated than in prose, or the meaning may be suggested and not explicitly stated at all. The way to overcome this difficulty is to read poetry more attentively and more slowly than one usually reads stories, to reread oftener, and to read each poem aloud at least once.

Similar to the difficulty of making out the plain sense of a poem is the difficulty of apprehending the feeling, tone, and intention of the poem. In simple terms this means that it is frequently by no means easy to be sure that the poet is deadly serious, ironical, satirical, or playful. To help the student over this difficulty the editors have classified the poems printed in this volume, not according to poets or to nationalities or to periods of history, but according to certain broad classifications of poetical forms or intentions. Narrative poems, in which the poet tells a story, are separated from lyric poems in which he expresses his personal thoughts and feelings. The lyrics, in turn, are classified in groups of similar intention—meditative, loving, descriptive, playful, satirical.

Another difficulty is supplied by the tendency nearly all readers have to make stock responses to emotional stimuli. A reference to home and mother may press a button and call up all the reader's own pathetic emotions so that he actually writes his own poem but thinks he is experiencing the poem which pushed the button. Thus even the most tawdry mammy song on the radio may produce the effect. Or a reader of poetry may have become so sick of tawdry mammy songs that he makes a stock response of dislike to the most authentic and honest treatment of the theme. If the reader were a horse we might say that he should be guided by the intentions of the poem instead of taking the bit in his teeth and bolting for home.

Another difficulty is supplied by our doctrinal adhesions. Because we adhere to political conservatism, for instance, we may prevent ourselves from understanding and enjoying poems of social change. Or if we uphold democratic forms of government we may fail to understand and enjoy cavalier tunes. What the reader needs to cultivate is what Coleridge called a "willing suspension of disbelief." We need not give up our doctrines, only keep quiet about them while we courteously listen to the poet singing about his.

If, in spite of all these difficulties, we persevere and finally learn to understand poems, we are sure to attain to new resources of enjoyment, new fields of adventure, and richer and deeper emotional experience.

THOMAS HARDY

The Sacrilege [1]

Part I

I HAVE a Love I love too well
  Where a Dunkery frowns on
    Exon Moor;

I have a Love I love too well,
  To whom, ere she was mine,
'Such is my love for you,' I said,   5
'That you shall have to hood your
    head
A silken kerchief crimson-red,
  Wove finest of the fine.'

"And since this Love, for one mad
    moon,
On Exon Wild by Dunkery Tor,   10
Since this my Love for one mad
    moon
  Did clasp me as her king,
I snatched a silk-piece red and rare
From off a stall at Priddy Fair,
For handkerchief to hood her hair 15
  When we went gallanting.

"Full soon the four weeks neared
    their end
Where Dunkery frowns on Exon
    Moor;
And when the four weeks neared
    their end,
  And their swift sweets outwore, 20
I said, 'What shall I do to own
Those beauties bright as tulips blown,
And keep you here with me alone
  As mine for evermore?'

"And as she drowsed within my van
On Exon Wild by Dunkery Tor— 26
And as she drowsed within my van,
  And dawning turned to day,
She heavily raised her sloe-black eyes
And murmured back in softest wise,
'One more thing, and the charms you
    prize   31
  Are yours henceforth for aye.

"'And swear I will I'll never go
While Dunkery frowns on Exon
    Moor
To meet the Cornish Wrestler Joe 35
  For dance and dallyings.
If you'll to yon cathedral shrine,
And finger from the chest divine
Treasure to buy me ear-drops fine,
  And richly jewelled rings.'   40

"I said: 'I am one who has gathered
    gear
From Marlbury Downs to Dunkery
    Tor,
Who has gathered gear for many a
    year
  From mansion, mart and fair;
But at God's house I've stayed my
    hand,   45
Hearing within me some command—
Curbed by a law not of the land
  From doing damage there!'

"Whereat she pouts, this Love of
    mine,
As Dunkery pouts to Exon Moor,   50
And still she pouts, this Love of
    mine,
  So cityward I go.
But ere I start to do the thing,
And speed my soul's imperilling
For one who is my ravishing   55
  And all the joy I know,

[1] From *Collected Poems*. By permission of
The Macmillan Company, publishers.

"I come to lay this charge on thee—
On Exon Wild by Dunkery Tor—
I come to lay this charge on thee
   With solemn speech and sign: 60
Should things go ill, and my life pay
For botchery in this rash assay,
You are to take hers likewise—yea,
   The month the law takes mine.

"For should my rival, Wrestler Joe,
Where Dunkery frowns on Exon
   Moor—   66
My reckless rival, Wrestler Joe,
   My Love's bedwinner be,
My rafted spirit would not rest,
But wander weary and distrest   70
Throughout the world in wild pro-
   test:
   The thought nigh maddens me!"

Part II

Thus did he speak—this brother of
   mine—
On Exon Wild by Dunkery Tor,
Born at my birth of mother of mine,
   And forthwith went his way   76
To dare the deed some coming
   night . . .
I kept the watch with shaking sight,
The moon at moments breaking
   bright,
   At others glooming gray.   80

For three full days I heard no sound
Where Dunkery frowns on Exon
   Moor,
I heard no sound at all around
   Whether his fay prevailed,
Or one more foul the master were,
Till some afoot did tidings bear   86
How that, for all his practised care,
   He had been caught and jailed.

They had heard a crash when twelve
   had chimed
By Mendip east of Dunkery Tor,   90
When twelve had chimed and moon-
   light climbed;
   They watched, and he was tracked
By arch and aisle and saint and
   night
Of sculptured stonework sheeted
   white
In the cathedral's ghostly light,   95
   And captured in the act.

Yes; for this Love he loved too well
Where Dunkery sights the Severn
   shore,
All for this Love he loved too well
   He burst the holy bars,   100
Seized golden vessels from the chest
To buy her ornaments of the best,
At her ill-witchery's request
   And lure of eyes like stars . . .

When blustering March confused the
   sky   105
In Toneborough Town by Exon
   Moor,
When blustering March confused the
   sky
   They stretched him; and he died.
Down in the crowd where I, to see
The end of him, stood silently,   110
With a set face he lipped to me—
   "Remember." "Ay!" I cried.

By night and day I shadowed her
From Toneborough Deane to Dun-
   kery Tor,
I shadowed her asleep, astir,   115
   And yet I could not bear—
Till Wrestler Joe anon began
To figure as her chosen man,
And took her to his shining van—
   To doom a form so fair!   120

He made it handsome for her sake—
And Dunkery smiled to Exon
    Moor—
He made it handsome for her sake,
  Painting it out and in;
And on the door of apple-green   125
A bright brass knocker soon was seen
And window-curtains white and
    clean
  For her to sit within.

And all could see she clave to him
As cleaves a cloud to Dunkery Tor,
Yea, all could see she clave to him,
  And every day I said,   132
"A pity it seems to part those two
That hourly grow to love more true:
Yet she's the wanton woman who
  Sent one to swing till dead!"   136

That blew to blazing all my hate,
While Dunkery frowned on Exon
    Moor,
And when the river swelled, her fate
  Came to her pitilessly . . .   140
I dogged her, crying: "Across that
  plank

They use as bridge to reach yon bank
A coat and hat lie limp and dank;
  Your goodman's, can they be?"

She paled, and went, I close be-
    hind—   145
And Exon frowned to Dunkery Tor,
She went, and I came up behind
  And tipped the plank that bore
Her, fleetly flitting across to eye
What such might bode. She slid
  awry;   150
And from the current came a cry,
  A gurgle; and no more.

How that befell no mortal knew
From Marlbury Downs to Exon
    Moor;
No mortal knew that deed undue 155
  But he who schemed the crime,
Which night still covers . . . But in
    dream
Those ropes of hair upon the stream
He sees, and he will hear that scream
  Until his judgment-time.   160

RUDYARD KIPLING

The Ballad of East and West [1]

OH, *East is East, and West is West, and never the twain shall meet,*
    Till Earth and Sky stand presently at God's great Judgment Seat;
    But there is neither East nor West, Border, nor Breed, nor Birth,
When two strong men stand face to face, tho' they come from the ends of the
    earth!
Kamal is out with twenty men to raise the Borderside,   5
And he has lifted the Colonel's mare that is the Colonel's pride:
He has lifted her out of the stable-door between the dawn and the day,

[1] From *Departmental Ditties and Barrack Room Ballads,* by Rudyard Kipling, copyright, 1892, 1920, reprinted with permission from Doubleday & Company, Inc.

And turned the calkins upon her feet, and ridden her far away.
Then up and spoke the Colonel's son that led a troop of the Guides:
'Is there never a man of all my men can say where Kamal hides?'   10
Then up and spoke Mahommed Khan, the son of the Ressaldar,
'If ye know the track of the morning-mist, ye know where his pickets are.
'At dusk he harries the Abazai—at dawn he is into Bonair,
'But he must go by Fort Bukloh to his own place to fare,
'So if ye gallop to Fort Bukloh as fast as a bird can fly,   15
'By the favour of God ye may cut him off ere he win to the Tongue of Jagai,
'But if he be passed the Tongue of Jagai, right swiftly turn ye then,
'For the length and the breadth of that grisly plain is sown with Kamal's men.
'There is rock to the left, and rock to the right, and low lean thorn between,
'And ye may hear a breech-bolt snick where never a man is seen.'   20
The Colonel's son has taken a horse, and a raw rough dun was he,
With the mouth of a bell and the heart of Hell, and the head of the gallows-
    tree.
The Colonel's son to the Fort has won, they bid him stay to eat—
Who rides at the tail of a Border thief, he sits not long at his meat.
He's up and away from Fort Bukloh as fast as he can fly,   25
Till he was aware of his father's mare in the gut of the Tongue of Jagai,
Till he was aware of his father's mare with Kamal upon her back,
And when he could spy the white of her eye, he made the pistol crack.
He has fired once, he has fired twice, but the whistling ball went wide.
'Ye shoot like a soldier,' Kamal said. 'Show now if ye can ride.'   30
It's up and over the Tongue of Jagai, as blown dust-devils go,
The dun he fled like a stag of ten, but the mare like a barren doe.
The dun he leaned against the bit and slugged his head above,
But the red mare played with the snaffle-bars, as a maiden plays with a glove.
There was a rock to the left and rock to the right, and low lean thorn between,
And thrice he heard a breech-bolt snick tho' never a man was seen.   36
They have ridden the low moon out of the sky, their hoofs drum up the dawn,
The dun he went like a wounded bull, but the mare like a new-roused fawn.
The dun he fell at a water-course—in a woeful heap fell he,
And Kamal has turned the red mare back, and pulled the rider free.   40
He has knocked the pistol out of his hand—small room was there to strive
' 'Twas only by favour of mine,' quoth he, 'ye rode so long alive:
'There was not a rock for twenty mile, there was not a clump of tree,
'But covered a man of my own men with his rifle cocked on his knee.
'If I had raised my bridle-hand, as I have held it low.   45
'The little jackals that flee so fast, were feasting all in a row:
'If I had bowed my head on my breast, as I have held it high,
'The kite that whistles above us now were gorged till she could not fly.
Lightly answered the Colonel's son:—'Do good to bird and beast,
'But count who come for the broken meats before thou makest a feast.   50
'If there should follow a thousand swords to carry my bones away,

'Belike the price of a jackal's meal were more than a thief could pay.
'They will feed their horse on the standing crop, their men on the garnered
  grain,
'The thatch of the byres will serve their fires when all the cattle are slain.
'But if thou thinkest the price be fair,—thy brethren wait to sup,   55
'The hound is kin to the jackal-spawn,—howl, dog, and call them up!
'And if thou thinkest the price be high, in steer and gear and stack,
'Give me my father's mare again, and I'll fight my own way back!'
Kamal has gripped him by the hand and set him upon his feet.
'No talk shall be of dogs,' said he, 'when wolf and gray wolf meet.   60
'May I eat dirt if thou hast hurt of me in deed or breath:
'What dam of lances brought thee forth to jest at the dawn with Death?'
Lightly answered the Colonel's son, 'I hold by the blood of my clan:
'Take up the mare for my father's gift—by God, she has carried a man!'
The red mare ran to the Colonel's son, and nuzzled against his breast,   65
'We be two strong men,' said Kamal then, 'but she loveth the younger best.
'So she shall go with a lifter's dower, my turquoise-studded rein,
'My broidered saddle and saddle-cloth, and silver stirrups twain.'
The Colonel's son a pistol drew and held it muzzle-end,
'Ye have taken the one from a foe,' said he; 'will ye take the mate from a
  friend?'   70
'A gift for a gift,' said Kamal straight; 'a limb for the risk of a limb.
'Thy father has sent his son to me, I'll send my son to him!'
With that he whistled his only son, that dropped from a mountain-crest—
He trod the ling like a buck in spring, and he looked like a lance in rest.
'Now here is thy master,' Kamal said, 'who leads a troop of the Guides,   75
'And thou must ride at his left side as shield on shoulder rides.
'Till Death or I cut loose the tie, at camp and board and bed,
'Thy life is his—thy fate it is to guard him with thy head.
'So thou must eat the White Queen's meat, and all her foes are thine,
'And thou must harry thy father's hold for the peace of the Border-line,   80
'And thou must make a trooper tough and hack thy way to power—
'Belike they will raise thee to Ressaldar when I am hanged in Peshawur.'

They have looked each other between the eyes, and there they have found no
  fault,
They have taken the Oath of the Brother-in-Blood on leavened bread and salt:
They have taken the Oath of the Brother-in-Blood on fire and fresh-cut sod,
On the hilt and the haft of the Khyber knife, and the Wondrous Names of
  God.   86
The Colonel's son he rides the mare and Kamal's boy the dun,
And two have come back to Fort Bukloh where there went forth but one.
And when they drew to the Quarter-Guard, full twenty swords flew clear—
There was not a man but carried his feud with the blood of the mountaineer.

'Ha' done! ha' done!' said the Colonel's son. 'Put up the steel at your
   sides!   92
'Last night ye had struck at a Border thief—to-night 'tis a man of the Guides!'

Oh, East is East, and West is West, and never the twain shall meet,
Till Earth and Sky stand presently at God's great Judgment Seat;
But there is neither East nor West, Border, nor Breed, nor Birth,   96
When two strong men stand face to face, tho' they come from the ends of
   the earth.

A. E. HOUSMAN

Farewell to Barn and Stack and Tree [1]

FAREWELL to barn and stack and
      tree,
      Farewell to Severn shore.
Terence, look your last at me,
   For I come home no more.

"The sun burns on the half-mown
      hill,   5
   By now the blood is dried;
And Maurice amongst the hay lies
      still
   And my knife is in his side.

"My mother thinks us long away;
   'Tis time the field were mown.   10
She had two sons at rising day,
   To-night she'll be alone.

"And here's a bloody hand to shake,
   And oh, man, here's good-bye;
We'll sweat no more on scythe and
      rake,   15
   My bloody hands and I.

[1] From *A Shropshire Lad* (1896).

"I wish you strength to bring you
      pride,
   And a love to keep you clean,
And I wish you luck, come Lammas-
      tide,
   At racing on the green.   20

"Long for me the rick will wait,
   And long will wait the fold,
And long will stand the empty plate,
   And dinner will be cold."

STEPHEN VINCENT BENÉT

Abraham Lincoln [2]

1809-1865

LINCOLN was a long man.
   He liked out of doors.
   He liked the wind blowing
And the talk in country stores.

He liked telling stories,   5
He liked telling jokes.
"Abe's quite a character,"
Said quite a lot of folks.

[2] From "A Book of Americans," by Rosemary and Stephen Vincent Benét. Copyright,
1933. Rinehart & Company, Inc.

Lots of folks in Springfield
Saw him every day,   10
Walking down the street
In his gaunt, long way.

Shawl around his shoulders,
Letters in his hat.
"That's Abe Lincoln."   15
They thought no more than that.

Knew that he was honest
Guessed that he was odd,
Knew he had a cross wife
Though she was a Todd.   20

Knew he had three little boys
Who liked to shout and play,
Knew he had a lot of debts
It took him years to pay.

Knew his clothes and knew his house.
"That's his office, here.   26
Blame good lawyer, on the whole,
Though he's sort of queer."

Sure, he went to Congress, once.
But he didn't stay.   30
Can't expect us all to be
Smart as Henry Clay.

"Need a man for troubled times?
Well, I guess we do:
Wonder who we'll ever find?   35
Yes—I wonder who."

That is how they met and talked,
Knowing and unknowing.
Lincoln was the green pine.
Lincoln kept on growing.   40

PADRAIC COLUM

A Ballad Maker [1]

ONCE I loved a maiden fair,
    Over the hills and far away,
    Lands she had and lovers to
spare,
    Over the hills and far away.
And I was stooped and troubled sore,
And my face was pale, and the coat I
    wore   6
Was thin as my supper the night be-
    fore.
    Over the hills and far away.

Once I passed in the autumn late,
    Over the hills and far away,   10
Her bawn and byre and painted gate,
    Over the hills and far away.
She was leaning there in the twilight
    space,
Sweet sorrow was on her fair young
    face,
And her wistful eyes were away from
    the place—   15
    Over the hills and far away.

Maybe she thought as she watched
    me come,
    Over the hills and far away,
With my awkward stride, and my
    face so glum,
    Over the hills and far away,   20
"Spite of his stoop, he still is young;
They says he goes the Shee among,
Ballads he makes, I've heard them
    sung
    Over the hills and far away."

[1] From *Poems* (1932). By permission of
The Macmillan Company, publishers.

She gave me good-night in gentle
　　wise,　　　　　　　　　　25
　Over the hills and far away,
Shyly lifting to mine, dark eyes,
　Over the hills and far away.
What could I do but stop and speak,
And she no longer proud but meek?
She plucked me a rose like her wild
　　rose cheek—　　　　　　　31
　Over the hills and far away.

Tomorrow, Mavourneen a sleeveen
　　weds,
　Over the hills and far away,
With corn in haggard and cattle in
　　sheds,　　　　　　　　　35
　Over the hills and far away.
And I who have lost her—the dear,
　the rare—
Well, I got me this ballad to sing at
　the fair,
'Twill bring enough money to drown
　my care.
　　Over the hills and far away.　40

~~~~~~~~~~~~~~~~~~~

WILLIAM ROSE BENÉT

Jesse James [1]

————————————

JESSE JAMES was a two-gun man,
　　(*Roll on, Missouri!*)
　Strong-arm chief of an outlaw
　clan.
　　(*From Kansas to Illinois!*)
He twirled an old Colt forty-five,　5
　　(*Roll on, Missouri!*)
They never took Jesse James alive.
　　(*Roll, Missouri, roll!*)
Jesse James was King of the Wes';
　　(*Cataracks in the Missouri!*) 10

[1] Used by permission of Dodd, Mead & Company, Inc. Copyright, 1935, by Dodd, Mead & Company.

He'd a di'mon' heart in his lef' breas';
　　(*Brown Missouri rolls!*)
He'd a fire in his heart no hurt could
　　stifle;
　　(*Thunder, Missouri!*)
Lion eyes an' a Winchester rifle.　15
　　(*Missouri, roll down!*)

Jesse James rode a pinto hawse;
Come at night to a water-cawse;
Tetched with the rowel that pinto's
　flank;
She sprung the torrent from bank to
　bank.　　　　　　　　　　20

Jesse rode through a sleepin' town;
Looked the moonlit street both up
　an' down;
Crack-crack-crack, the street ran
　flames
An' a great voice cried, "I'm Jesse
　James!"
Hawse an' afoot they're after Jess!　25
　　(*Roll on, Missouri!*)
Spurrin' an' spurrin'—but he's gone
　Wes'.
　　(*Brown Missouri rolls!*)
He was ten foot tall when he stood in
　his boots;
　　(*Lightnin' light the Mis-
　　souri!*)　　　　　　　　30
More'n a match fer sich galoots.
　　(*Roll, Missouri, roll!*)

Jesse James rode outa the sage;
Roun' the rocks come the swayin'
　stage;
Straddlin' the road a giant stan's　35
An' a great voice bellers, "Throw up
　yer han's!"

Jesse raked in the di'mon' rings,
The big gold watches an' the yuther
　things;

Jesse divvied 'em then an' thar   39
With a cryin' child had lost her mar.

The U. S. Troopers is after Jess;
    (*Roll on, Missouri!*)
Their hawses sweat foam, but he's
    gone Wes';
    (*Hear Missouri roar!*)

He was broad as a b'ar, he'd a ches'
    like a drum,   45
    (*Wind an' rain through Missouri!*)
An' his red hair flamed like Kingdom
    Come.
    (*Missouri down to the sea!*)

Jesse James all alone in the rain
Stopped an' stuck up the Eas'-boun'
    train;   50
Swayed through the coaches with
    horns an' a tail,
Lit out with the bullion an' the regis-
    tered mail.

Jess made 'em all turn green with
    fright,
Quakin' in the aisles in the pitch-
    black night;
An' he give all the bullion to a pore
    ole tramp   55
Campin' nigh the cuttin' in the dirt
    an' damp.

The whole U. S. is after Jess;
    (*Roll on, Missouri!*)
The son-of-a-gun, if he ain't gone
    Wes';
    (*Missouri to the sea!*)   60
He could chaw cold iron an' spit blue
    flame;
    (*Cataracks down the Missouri!*)

He rode on a catamount he'd larned
    to tame.
    (*Hear that Missouri roll!*)

Jesse James rode into a bank;   65
Give his pinto a tetch on the flank;
Jumped the teller's window with an
    awful crash;
Heaved up the safe an' twirled his
    mustache;

He said, "So long, boys!" He yelped,
    "So long!
Feelin' poorly to-day—I ain't feelin'
    strong!"   70
Rode right through the wall agoin'
    crack-crack-crack,—
Took the safe home to Mother in a
    gunny-sack.

They're creepin', they're crawlin',
    they're stalkin' Jess;
    (*Roll on, Missouri!*)
They's a rumor he's gone much
    further Wes';   75
    (*Roll, Missouri, roll!*)
They's word of a cayuse hitched to
    the bars
    (*Ruddy clouds on Missouri!*)
Of a golden sunset that busts into
    stars.
    (*Missouri, roll down!*)   80

Jesse James rode hell fer leather;
He was a hawse an' a man together:
In a cave in a mountain high up in
    air
He lived with a rattlesnake, a wolf,
    an' a bear.   84

Jesse's heart was as sof' as a woman;
Fer guts an' stren'th he was sooper-
    human;

He could put six shots through a
        woodpecker's eye
And take in one swaller a gallon o'
        rye.

They sought him here an' they sought
        him there,
        (*Roll on, Missouri!*)   90
But he strides by night through the
        ways of the air,
        (*Brown Missouri rolls!*)
They say he was took an' they say he
        is dead;
        (*Thunder, Missouri!*)
But he ain't—he's a sunset overhead!
        (*Missouri down to the sea!*) 96

Jesse James was a Hercules.
When he went through the woods he
        tore up the trees.
When he went on the plains he
        smoked the groun'
An' the hull lan' shuddered fer miles
        aroun'.   100

Jesse James wore a red bandanner
That waved on the breeze like the
        Star Spangled Banner;
In seven states he cut up dadoes.
He's gone with the buffler an' the
        desperadoes.   104

Yes, Jesse James was a two-gun man
        (*Roll on, Missouri!*)
The same as when this song began;
        (*From Kansas to Illinois!*)
An' when you see a sunset burst into
        flames   109
        (*Lightnin' light the Missouri!*)
Or a thunderstorm blaze—that's Jesse
        James!
        (*Hear that Missouri roll!*)

ANONYMOUS

*Robin Hood Rescuing the Widow's
Three Sons*

THERE are twelve months in all
        the year
        As I hear many men say,
But the merriest month in all the
        year
Is the merry month of May.

Now Robin Hood is to Nottingham
        gone,   5
With a link a down and a day,
And there he met a silly old woman,
Was weeping on the way.

"What news? what news, thou silly
        old woman?
What news hast thou for me?"   10
Said she, "There's three squires in
        Nottingham town
To-day is condemned to die."

"O have they parishes burnt?" he
        said,
        "Or have they ministers slain?
Or have they robbed any virgin,   15
        Or with other men's wives have
        lain?"

"They have no parishes burnt, good
        sir,
        Nor yet have ministers slain,
Nor have they robbed any virgin,
        Nor with other men's wives have
        lain."   20

"O what have they done?" said bold
        Robin Hood,
        "I pray thee tell to me";

"It's for slaying of the king's fallow
    deer,
    Bearing their long bows with thee."

"Dost thou not mind, old woman,"
    he said,   25
    "Since thou made me sup and
    dine?
By the truth of my body," quoth bold
    Robin Hood,
    "You could not tell it in better
    time."

Now Robin Hood is to Nottingham
    gone,
    With a link a down and a day,   30
And there he met with a silly old
    palmer,
    Was walking along the highway.

"What news? what news, thou silly
    old man?
    What news, I do thee pray?"
Said he, "Three squires in Notting-
    ham town   35
    Are condemned to die this day."

"Come change thy apparel with me,
    old man,
    Come change thy apparel for mine;
Here is forty shillings in good silver,
    Go drink it in beer or wine."   40

"O thine apparel is good," he said,
    "And mine is ragged and torn;
Wherever you go, wherever you ride,
    Laugh neer an old man to scorn."

"Come change thy apparel with me,
    old churl,   45
    Come change thy apparel with
    mine;
Here are twenty pieces of good broad
    gold,
    Go feast thy brethren with wine."

Then he put on the old man's hat,
    It stood full high on the crown; 50
"The first bold bargain that I come
    at,
    It shall make thee come down."

Then he put on the old man's cloak,
    Was patched black, blew, and red;
He thought no shame all the day
    long   55
    To wear the bags of bread.

Then put on the old man's breeks,
    Was patched from ballup to side;
"By the truth of my body," bold
    Robin can say,
    "This man loved little pride."   60

Then he put on the old man's hose,
    Were patched from knee to wrist;
"By the truth of my body," said bold
    Robin Hood,
    "I'd laugh if I had any list."

Then he put on the old man's
    shoes,   65
    Were patched both beneath and
    aboon;
Then Robin Hood swore a solemn
    oath,
    "It's good habit that makes a man."

Now Robin Hood is to Nottingham
    gone,
    With a link a down and a down, 70
And there he met with the proud
    sheriff,
    Was walking along the town.

"O save, O save, O sheriff," he said,
    "O save, and you may see!
And what will you give to a silly old
    man   75
    To-day will your hangman be?"

"Some suits, some suits," the sheriff
   he said,
  "Some suits I'll give to thee;
Some suits, some suits, and pence thir-
   teen
   To-day's a hangman's fee."   80

Then Robin he turns him round
   about,
  And jumps from stock to stone;
"By the truth of my body," the sheriff
   he said,
  "That's well jumpt, thou nimble old
   man."

"I was neer a hangman in all my
   life,   85
  Nor yet intends to trade;
But curst be he," said bold Robin,
  "That first a hangman was made.

"I've a bag for meal, and a bag for
   malt,
  And a bag for barley and corn;   90
A bag for bread, and a bag for beef,
  And a bag for my little small horn.

"I have a horn in my pocket,
  I got it from Robin Hood,
And still when I set it to my mouth,   95
  For thee it blows little good."

"O wind thy horn, thou proud fellow,
  Of thee I have no doubt;
I wish that thou give such a blast
  Till both thy eyes fall out."   100

The first loud blast that he did blow,
  He blew both loud and shrill;
A hundred and fifty of Robin Hood's
   men
  Came riding over the hill.

The next loud blast that he did
   give,   105
  He blew both loud and amain,

And quickly sixty of Robin Hood's
   men
  Came shining over the plain.

"O who are yon," the sheriff he said,
  "Come tripping over the lee?"   110
"The're my attendants," brave Robin
   did say,
  "They'll pay a visit to thee."

They took the gallows from the slack,
  They set it in the glen,
They hanged the proud sheriff on
   that,   115
  Released their own three men.

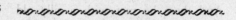

ANONYMOUS

Jesse James [1]

JESSE JAMES was a lad that killed
   a-many a man;
  He robbed the Danville train.
But that dirty little coward that shot
   Mr. Howard
Has laid poor Jesse in his grave.

Poor Jesse had a wife to mourn for
   his life,   5
Three children, they were brave.
But that dirty little coward that shot
   Mr. Howard
Has laid poor Jesse in his grave.

It was Robert Ford, that dirty little
   coward,
I wonder how he does feel,   10
For he ate of Jesse's bread and he
   slept in Jesse's bed,
Then laid poor Jesse in his grave.

[1] From John A. Lomax and Alan Lomax, *American Ballads and Folk Songs.*

Jesse was a man, a friend to the poor,
He never could see a man suffer pain:
And with his brother Frank he robbed the Chicago bank,   15
And stopped the Glendale train.

It was his brother Frank that robbed the Gallatin bank,
And carried the money from the town;
It was in this very place that they had a little race,
For they shot Captain Sheets to the ground.   20

They went to the crossing not very far from there,
And there they did the same;
With the agent on his knees, he delivered up the keys
To the outlaws, Frank and Jesse James.

It was on Wednesday night, the moon was shining bright,   25
They robbed the Glendale train;
The people they did say, for many miles away,
It was robbed by Frank and Jesse James.

It was on Saturday night, Jesse was at home
Talking with his family brave,   30
Robert Ford came along like a thief in the night
And laid poor Jesse in his grave.

The people held their breath when they heard of Jesse's death,
And wondered how he ever came to die.
It was one of the gang called little Robert Ford,   35
He shot poor Jesse on the sly.

Jesse went to his rest with his hand on his breast;
The devil will be upon his knee.
He was born one day in the county of Clay
And came from a solitary race.   40

This song was made by Billy Gashade,
As soon as the news did arrive;
He said there was no man with the law in his hand
Who could take Jesse James when alive.

∿∿∿∿∿∿∿∿∿∿∿∿∿∿∿

JOHN HAY

Jim Bludso of the Prairie Belle [1]

WALL, no! I can't tell whar he lives,
    Because he don't live, you see;
Leastways, he's got out of the habit
Of livin' like you and me.
Whar have you been for the last three year   5
    That you haven't heard folks tell
How Jimmy Bludso passed in his checks
    The night of the Prairie Belle?

He weren't no saint,—them engineers
    Is all pretty much alike,—   10
One wife in Natchez-under-the-Hill
    And another one here, in Pike;
A keerless man in his talk was Jim,
    And an awkward hand in a row,
But he never flunked, and he never lied,—   15
    I reckon he never knowed how.

[1] From *Pike County Ballads*, 1871.

And this was all the religion he
    had,—
  To treat his engine well;
Never be passed on the river;
  To mind the pilot's bell;   20
And if ever the Prairie Belle took
    fire,—
  A thousand times he swore,
He'd hold her nozzle agin the bank
  Till the last soul got ashore.

All boats has their days on the Missi-
    sip,   25
  And her day come at last,—
The Movastar was a better boat,
  But the Belle she *wouldn't* be
    passed.
And so she come tearin' along that
    night—
  The oldest craft on the line—   30
With a niggar squat on her safety-
    valve,
  And her furnace crammed, rosin
    and pine.

The fire burst out as she cleared the
    bar,
  And burnt a hole in the night,
And quick as a flash she turned, and
    made   35
  For that willer-bank on the right.
There was runnin' and cursin', but
    Jim yelled out,
  Over all the infernal roar,
"I'll hold her nozzle agin the bank
  Till the last galoot's ashore."   40

Through the hot, black breath of the
    burnin' boat
  Jim Bludso's voice was heard,
And they all had trust in his cussed-
    ness,
  And knowed he would keep his
    word.

And, sure's you're born, they all got
    off   45
  Afore the smokestacks fell,—
And Bludso's ghost went up alone
  In the smoke of the Prairie Belle.

He weren't no saint,—but at jedgment
  I'd run my chance with Jim,   50
'Longside of some pious gentlemen
  That wouldn't shook hands with
    him.
He seen his duty, a dead-sure thing,—
  And went for it thar and then;
And Christ ain't a-going to be too
    hard   55
  On a man that died for men.

JOHN GREENLEAF WHITTIER

Skipper Ireson's Ride

OF ALL the rides since the birth
    of time,
    Told in story or sung in
rhyme,—
On Apuleius's Golden Ass,
Or one-eyed Calender's horse of brass,
Witch astride of a human back,   5
Islam's prophet on Al-Borak,—
The strangest ride that ever was sped
Was Ireson's out from Marblehead!
  Old Floyd Ireson, for his hard heart,
  Tarred and feathered and carried
    in a cart   10
    By the women of Marblehead!

Body of turkey, head of owl,
Wings a-droop like a rained-on fowl,
Feathered and ruffled in every part,
Skipper Ireson stood in the cart.   15

Scores of women, old and young,
Strong of muscle, and glib of tongue,
Pushed and pulled up the rocky lane,
Shouting and singing the shrill re-
    frain:
    "Here's Flud Oirson, fur his horrd
        hoort,   20
    Torr'd and futherr'd and corr'd in a
        corrt
            By the women o' Morble'ead!"

Wrinkled scolds with hands on hips,
Girls in bloom of cheek and lips,
Wild-eyed, free-limbed, such as
    chase   25
Bacchus round some antique vase,
Brief of skirt, with ankles bare,
Loose of kerchief and loose of hair,
With conch-shells blowing and fish-
    horns' twang,
Over and over the Maenads sang: 30
    "Here's Flud Oirson, fur his horrd
        horrt,
    Torr'd an' futherr'd an' corr'd in a
        corrt
            By the women o' Morble'ead!"

Small pity for him!—He sailed away
From a leaking ship in Chaleur
    Bay,—   35
Sailed away from a sinking wreck,
With his own town's-people on her
    deck.
"Lay by! lay by!" they called to him.
Back he answered, "Sink or swim!
Brag of your catch of fish again!" 40
And off he sailed through the fog and
    rain!
    Old Floyd Ireson, for his hard heart,
    Tarred and feathered and carried in
        a cart
            By the women of Marblehead!

Fathoms deep in dark Chaleur   45
That wreck shall lie forevermore.

Mother and sister, wife and maid,
Looked from the rocks of Marblehead
Over the moaning and rainy sea,—
Looked for the coming that might
    not be!   50
What did the winds and the sea-birds
    say
Of the cruel captain who sailed
    away?—
    Old Floyd Ireson, for his hard
        heart,
    Tarred and feathered and carried
        in a cart
            By the women of Marble-
                head!   55

Through the street, on either side,
Up flew windows, doors swung wide;
Sharp-tongued spinsters, old wives
    gray,
Treble lent the fish-horn's bray.
Sea-worn grandsires, cripple-bound, 60
Hulks of old sailors run aground,
Shook head, and fist, and hat, and
    cane,
And cracked with curses the hoarse
    refrain:
    "Here's Flud Oirson, fur his horrd
        horrt,
    Torr'd an' futherr'd an' corr'd in a
        corrt   65
            By the women o' Morble'ead!"

Sweetly along the Salem road
Bloom of orchard and lilac showed.
Little the wicked skipper knew
Of the fields so green and the sky so
    blue.   70
Riding there in his sorry trim,
Like an Indian idol glum and grim,
Scarcely he seemed the sound to hear
Of voices shouting, far and near:
    "Here's Flud Oirson, fur his horrd
        horrt,   75

Torr'd an' futherr'd an' corr'd in a
     corrt
          By the women o' Morble'eåd!"

"Hear me, neighbors!" at last he
     cried,—
"What to me is this noisy ride?
What is the shame that clothes the
     skin   80
To the nameless horror that lives
     within?
Waking or sleeping, I see a wreck,
And hear a cry from a reeling deck!
Hate me and curse me,—I only dread
The hand of God and the face of the
     dead!"   85
Said old Floyd Ireson, for his hard
     heart
Tarred and feathered and carried
     in a cart
          By the women of Marblehead!

Then the wife of the skipper lost at
     sea
Said, "God has touched him! why
     should we!"   90
Said an old wife mourning an only
     son,
"Cut the rogue's tether and let him
     run!"
So with soft relentings and rude
     excuse,
Half scorn, half pity, they cut him
     loose,
And gave him a cloak to hide him
     in   95
And left him alone with his shame
     and sin.
Poor Floyd Ireson, for his hard
     heart,
Tarred and feathered and carried
     in a cart
          By the women of Marble-
          head!

LEONORA SPEYER

Ballad of Old Doc Higgins [1]

OLD DOC HIGGINS shot a mermaid.
     Vowed he'd catch her, fish or woman, fiend or human;
          Carryin' on along the river, catterwaulin' up the river.
Scarin' fish where they lay hid!
Oh he'd seen her and he'd heard her,   5
Swore before the day was over
There'd be some surprisin' doin's
On the river—maybe murder—
(And what old Higgins swore, he did.)

Old Doc Higgins cleaned his gun.   10
The proper fishin'-hook, he'd swan, for mermaid's gills!

    [1] Reprinted from *Slow Wall*, by Leonora Speyer, by permission of Alfred A. Knopf, Inc.
Copyright 1926 by Leonora Speyer.

The slickest tackle! (Leaning on the pasture-wall old Doc Higgins gave a
    cackle;)
Watch him get her, pesky critter,
Tail and all!

No one knew but old Doc Higgins.   15
No, and none was goin' to know. 'Twarn't no need for folks to know.
He saw Sister Mame's boy go swimmin' to her—natteral fool!
All uncovered was her breast, hair all streamin', shiny's gold;
And the rest—a fish's tail, gormin' up his troutin' pool!

Higgins saw and never told.   20
Have the whole town call him crazy?   Sister Mame's boy, loony, lazy, heard
    him shoutin';
Turned and laughed as they went under; started kissin'—let them wonder,
Knowin' how the boy could swim!
They'd make no laughin'-stock of him.

But here's the thing that riled him so: 25
Just as he was settlin' down to a peaceful mornin's fishin'
(How his baited line would hum up the stream to some swift eddy),
Settin' there enjoyin' things while the fish got good and ready—he could feel
    their noses pushin'—
Just as they was bitin' some, up she'd come!

Naked to the waist, and sassy!   Wavin' to him, swimmin' by, shameless
    hussy;   30
Or just singin' as she floated, kind of high,
No tune at all (and he noted how her tail would flash and swish),
Gorry, how she scared the fish!   Old Doc Higgins on the shore,
Yelled and swore.

And he'd watch her at the turning of the river, see her sink   35
Where the willow near the brink dipped to touch the mermaid's locks;
"Shucks," said old Doc Higgins, "Shucks!"
His ears didn't need no wax (thinking of the deafened crew,
And Odysseus, fettered fast), oh he knew a thing or two,

All the Higginses had learnin', needn't tie *him* to no mast'.   40
Smilin' at him as she passed!   Any lunk-head could see through her,
Like to take a cow-hide to her;
Poor old Mame—her only son—(yes, but listen as you hasten,
Listen to the lonely singing, old man with a gun.)

Ah who will seek Muirish,   45
The lost one, the sea-swan?
Ah ripples, ah road
Where the foolish, the frolicsome
Strayed to her sorrow.
Muirish is gone   50
From the waters of Kerry.
Ah tarry not, sisters,
But speedily come!

Beneath a strange willow
She sits with her sorrow,   55
And all the bright sea-shells
Are spilled from her hair.
Ah sisters, my friends,
Where the ancient tide ends,
Will you fare, will you follow   60
The track of the tears
To Muirish, the lost one,
The sea swan of Kerry?
Ah tarry not, sisters,
My loves and my dears!   65

Ah . . . ah . . . ah . . .

Heathen singin', fit for Satan!—Creeping close as she rose
From beneath her willow-bough, old Doc Higgins held his breath . . .
Now!
And a singing turns to sighing, and a sighing pales to dying,   70
And a dying lifts to death.

Ripples reddening as they float, rippling from a tender throat,
Reddening from a cry of pain.
Old Doc Higgins stood there blinking and his thoughts were not all pretty
As he watched a whiteness sinking. Wished he'd had a good look at her,   75
Never'd get that chance again.

Gosh, it was a first-rate shot! Kissin' Mame's boy as she drowned him,
Lips all pursed up when they found him,
Died of kissin' like as not.
Well, there warn't no use in wishin';   80
And tomorrow he'd go fishin'.

Mist can do strange things to rivers, make a ghost of any river;
Such a day is good for fishing. Old Doc Higgins vowed he'd never

Seen the like, it did beat all, the way the pike
And pickerel came a-crowdin' round; cat-fish too, and Lord, the trout   85
Jumpin' out.

Peter was a fisherman; guessed he'd have to let him pass—
There was bass over there, lyin' low! Always thought he'd like to go,
His time come to meet his God, with fishin'-rod and basket spillin';
He'd be willin'. (Say you so?   90
Old Doc Higgins, say you so?)

Mist that reaches thick and sallow up the ledges of the land,
Up to where a tired old man sits awhile beneath a willow;
(Willow-tree, you remember! But does he?)
And his pipe slips from his hand . . . What's that creeping through the
     sedges?   95
Have a care, old Doc Higgins, sleeping there!

Mist that swirls . . . mist . . . mist . . .
Something holds him by the wrist. (White and wet and cool and strong,
Fish or woman, fiend or human!)
Oh the shoal of leaping girls all about him, all about him,   100
Beautiful and baleful throng—and their song:

Muirish, Muirish, white sea-swan!
Sister slain, sister slain!—And an answering crimson stain
Rises rippling where she sank.
On the whimpering little man, fighting, frightened, on the bank   105
As he wakes—

Sees a face, pale, pale,
Sees a tail,
Snatches at a bough that breaks,
(Vengeful little willow-tree!)   110
"God-a-mighty! Leave me be! *Leave me be!*

Thus they drowned him, old Doc Higgins,
With their arms like wreaths around him, heavy silver wreaths around him,
Struggling, strangling, tightly pressed to a soft, ironic breast;
Thus he lies—   115
In a grave of running water, who had slain a deep-sea daughter.

Old Doc Higgins, old Doc Higgins, wishing to die, a-fishing;
Thus he lies till all things rise; if there still be aught to rise.

WILLIAM MORRIS

The Haystack in the Floods

———————————

HAD she come all the way for this,
　　To part at last without a kiss?
Yea, had she borne the dirt and rain
That her own eyes might see him slain
Beside the haystack in the floods?　5
Along the dripping leafless woods,
The stirrup touching either shoe,
She rode astride as troopers do;
With kirtle kilted to her knee,
To which the mud splashed wretchedly.　10
And the wet dripped from every tree
Upon her head and heavy hair,
And on her eyelids broad and fair;
The tears and rain ran down her face.
By fits and starts they rode apace,　15
And very often was his place
Far off from her: he had to ride
Ahead, to see what might betide
When the roads crossed; and sometimes, when
There rose a murmuring from his men,　20
Had to turn back with promises.
Ah me! she had but little ease;
And often for pure doubt and dread
She sobbed, made giddy in the head
By the swift riding; while, for cold,　25
Her slender fingers scarce could hold
The wet reins; yea, and scarcely, too,
She felt the foot within her shoe
Against the stirrup. All for this:
To part at last without a kiss　30
Beside the haystack in the floods.

For when they neared that old soaked hay,
They saw, across the only way,
That Judas, Godmar; and the three
Red running lions dismally　35
Grinned from his pennon, under which
In one straight line along the ditch,
They counted thirty heads.

　　　　　　　　So then,
While Robert turned round to his men,
She saw at once the wretched end,　40
And, stooping down, tried hard to rend
Her coif the wrong way from her head,
And hid her eyes; while Robert said:
"Nay, love, 'tis scarcely two to one;
At Poictiers where we made them run　45
So fast—Why, sweet my love, good cheer,
The Gascon frontier is so near,
Nought after this."

　　　　　　　But, "O," she said,
"My God! my God! I have to tread
The long way back without you;
　　then　50
The court at Paris; those six men;
The gratings of the Chatelet,
The swift Seine on some rainy day
Like this, and people standing by
And laughing, while my weak hands try　55
To recollect how strong men swim.
All this, or else a life with him,
For which I should be damned at last:
Would God that this next hour were past!"

He answered not, but cried his cry, 60
"St. George for Marny!" cheerily;
And laid his hand upon her rein.
Alas! no man of all his train
Gave back that cheery cry again;
And, while for rage his thumb beat
    fast 65
Upon his sword-hilt, some one cast
About his neck a kerchief long,
And bound him.

        Then they went along
To Godmar; who said: "Now, Je-
    hane,
Your lover's life is on the wane 70
So fast that, if this very hour
You yield not as my paramour,
He will not see the rain leave off—
Nay, keep your tongue from gibe and
    scoff.
Sir Robert, or I slay you now." 75

She laid her hand upon her brow,
Then gazed upon the palm, as though
She thought her forehead bled, and—
    "No!"
She said, and turned her head away,
As there were nothing else to say, 80
And everything were settled. Red
Grew Godmar's face from chin to
    head:
"Jehane, on yonder hill there stands
My castle, guarding well my lands:
What hinders me from taking you, 85
And doing that I list to do
To your fair willful body, while
Your knight lies dead?

        A wicked smile
Wrinkled her face, her lips grew thin,
A long way out she thrust her chin: 90
"You know that I should strangle you
While you were sleeping; or bite
    through

Your throat, by God's help—ah!" she
    said,
"Lord Jesus, pity your poor maid!
For in such wise they hem me in, 95
I cannot choose but sin and sin,
Whatever happens: yet I think
They could not make me eat or drink,
And so should I just reach my rest."
"Nay, if you do not my behest, 100
O Jehane! though I love you well,"
Said Godmar, "would I fail to tell
All that I know?" "Foul lies," she
    said.

"Eh! lies, my Jehane? by God's head,
At Paris folks would deem them
    true! 105
Do you know, Jehane, they cry for
    you:
'Jehane the brown! Jehane the brown!
Give us Jehane to burn or drown!'
Eh—gag me, Robert!—sweet my
    friend,
This were indeed a piteous end 110
For those long fingers, and long feet,
And long neck, and smooth shoulders
    sweet;
An end that few men would forget
That saw it—So, an hour yet:
Consider, Jehane, which to take 115
Of life or death!"

        So, scarce awake,
Dismounting, did she leave that place,
And totter some yards: with her face
Turned upward to the sky she lay,
Her head on a wet heap of hay, 120
And fell asleep. And while she slept,
And did not dream, the minutes crept
Round to the twelve again; but she,
Being waked at last, sighed quietly,
And strangely childlike came, and
    said: 125
"I will not." Straightway Godmar's
    head,

As though it hung on strong wires, turned
Most sharply round, and his face burned.

For Robert—both his eyes were dry,
He could not weep, but gloomily 130
He seemed to watch the rain; yea, too,
His lips were firm. He tried once more
To touch her lips; she reached out, sore
And vain desire so tortured them,
The poor gray lips, and now the hem 135
Of his sleeve brushed them.

       With a start
Up Godmar rose, thrust them apart;
From Robert's throat he loosed the bands
Of silk and mail. With empty hands
Held out, she stood and gazed, and saw 140

The long bright blade without a flaw
Glide out from Godmar's sheath, his hand
In Robert's hair; she saw him bend
Back Robert's head; she saw him send
The thin steel down. The blow told well: 145
Right backward the knight Robert fell,
And moaned as dogs do, being half dead,
Unwitting, as I deem. So then
Godmar turned grinning to his men,
Who ran, some five or six, and beat 150
His head to pieces at their feet.

Then Godmar turned again and said:
"So, Jehane, the first fitte is read!
Take note, my lady, that your way
Lies backward to the Chatelet!" 155
She shook her head and gazed awhile
At her cold hands with a rueful smile,
As though this thing had made her mad.
This was the parting that they had
Beside the haystack in the floods. 160

STEPHEN VINCENT BENÉT

The Raid on Harper's Ferry[1]

THEY reached the Maryland bridge of Harper's Ferry
   That Sunday night. There were twenty-two in all,
   Nineteen were under thirty, three not twenty-one,
Kagi, the self-taught scholar, quiet and cool,
Stevens, the cashiered soldier, Puritan-fathered,   5
A singing giant, gunpowder-tempered and rash.
Dauphin Thompson, the pippin-cheeked country-boy,
More like a girl than a warrior; Oliver Brown,
Married last year when he was barely nineteen;

[1] From *John Brown's Body*, by Stephen Vincent Benét. Copyright, 1928. Rinehart & Company, Inc.

Dangerfield Newby, colored and born a slave,   10
Freeman now, but married to one not free
Who, with their seven children, waited him South,
The youngest baby just beginning to crawl;
Watson Brown, the steady lieutenant, who wrote
Back to his wife,   15
                "Oh, Bell, I want to see you
And the little fellow very much but must wait.
There was a slave near here whose wife was sold South.
They found him hanging in Kennedy's orchard next morning.
I cannot come home as long as such things are done here.   20
I sometimes think that we shall not meet again."

These were some of the band. For better or worse
They were all strong men.
                      The bearded faces look strange
In the old daguerreotypes: they should be the faces   25
Of prosperous, small-town people, good sons and fathers,
Good horse-shoe pitchers, good at plowing a field,
Good at swapping stories and good at praying,
American wheat, firm-rooted, good in the ear.
There is only one whose air seems out of the common,   30
Oliver Brown. That face has a masculine beauty
Somewhat like the face of Keats.
                      They were all strong men.

They tied up the watchmen and took the rifle-works.
Then John Brown sent a raiding party away   35
To fetch in Colonel Washington from his farm.
The Colonel was George Washington's great-grand-nephew,
Slave-owner, gentleman-farmer, but, more than these,
Possessor of a certain fabulous sword
Given to Washington by Frederick the Great.   40
They captured him and his sword and brought them along
Processionally.
              The act has a touch of drama,
Half costume-romance, half unmerited farce.
On the way, they told the Washington slaves they were free,   45
Or free to fight for their freedom.
                      The slaves heard the news
With the dazed, scared eyes of cattle before a storm.
A few came back with the band and were given pikes,
And, when John Brown was watching, pretended to mount   50
A slipshod guard over the prisoners.
But, when he had walked away, they put down their pikes

And huddled together, talking in mourning voices.
It didn't seem right to play at guarding the Colonel
But they were afraid of the bearded patriarch   55
With the Old Testament eyes.
                              A little later
It was Patrick Higgins' turn. He was the night-watchman
Of the Maryland bridge, a tough little Irishman
With a canny, humorous face, and a twist in his speech.   60
He came humming his way to his job.
                              "Halt!" ordered a voice.
He stopped a minute, perplexed. As he told men later,
"Now I didn't know what 'Halt!' mint, any more
Than a hog knows about a holiday."   65
                              There was a scuffle.
He got away with a bullet-crease in his scalp
And warned the incoming train. It was half-past one.
A moment later, a man named Shepherd Heyward,
Free negro, baggage-master of the small station,   70
Well-known in the town, hardworking, thrifty and fated,
Came looking for Higgins.
                              "Halt!" called the voice again,
But he kept on, not hearing or understanding,
Whichever it may have been.   75
                              A rifle cracked.
He fell by the station-platform, gripping his belly,
And lay for twelve hours of torment, asking for water
Until he was able to die.
                              There is no stone,   80
No image of bronze or marble green with the rain
To Shepherd Heyward, free negro of Harper's Ferry,
And even the books, the careful, ponderous histories,
That turn live men into dummies with smiles of wax
Thoughtfully posed against a photographer's background   85
In the act of signing a treaty or drawing a sword,
Tell little of what he was.
                              And yet his face
Grey with pain and puzzled at sudden death
Stares out at us through the bookworm-dust of the years   90
With an uncomprehending wonder, a blind surprise.
"I was getting along," it says, "I was doing well.
I had six thousand dollars saved in the bank.
It was a good town, a nice town, I liked the folks
And they liked me. I had a good job there, too.   95
On Sundays I used to dress myself up slick enough
To pass the plate in church, but I wasn't proud

Not even when the trashy niggers called me Mister
Though I could hear the old grannies over their snuff
Mumbling along, 'Look chile, there goes Shepherd Heyward.   100
Ain't him fine in he Sunday clo'es—ain't him sassy and fine?
You grow up decent and don't play ball in the street,
And maybe you'll get like him, with a gold watch and chain.'
And then, suddenly—and what was it all about?
Why should anyone want to kill me? Why was it done?"   105
So the grey lips. And so the hurt in the eyes.
A hurt like a child's, at punishment unexplained
That makes the whole child-universe fall to pieces.
At the time of death, most men turn back toward the child.

Brown did not know at first that the first man dead   110
By the sword he thought of so often as Gideon's sword
Was one of the race he had drawn that sword to free.
It had been dark on the bridge. A man had come
And had not halted when ordered. Then the shot
And the scrape of the hurt man dragging himself away.   115
That was all. The next man ordered to halt would halt.
His mind was too full of the burning judgments of God
To wonder who it had been. He was cool and at peace.
He dreamt of a lamb, lying down by a rushing stream.

So the night wore away, indecisive and strange.   120
The raiders stuck by the arsenal, waiting perhaps
For a great bell of jubilation to toll in the sky,
And the slaves to rush from the hills with pikes in their hands,
A host redeemed, black rescue-armies of God.
It did not happen.   125
           Meanwhile, there was casual firing.
A townsman named Boerley was killed. Meanwhile, the train
Passed over the bridge to carry its wild news
Of abolition-devils sprung from the ground
A hundred and fifty, three hundred, a thousand strong   130
To pillage Harper's Ferry, with fire and sword.
Meanwhile the whole countryside was springing to arms.
The alarm-bell in Charlestown clanged "Nat Turner has come!
Nat Turner has come again, all smoky from Hell,
Setting the slave to murder and massacre!"   135
The Jefferson Guards fell in. There were boys and men.
They had no uniforms but they had weapons.
Old squirrel-rifles, taken down from the wall,
Shot guns loaded with spikes and scraps of iron.
A boy dragged a blunderbuss as big as himself.   140

They started for the Ferry.
                              In a dozen
A score of other sleepy, neighboring towns
The same bell clanged, the same militia assembled.

The Ferry itself was roused and stirring with dawn.   145
And the firing began again.
                              A queer, harsh sound
In the ordinary streets of that clean, small town,
A desultory, vapid, meaningless sound.

God knows why John Brown lingered! Kagi, the scholar,   150
Who, with two others, held the rifle-works,
All morning sent him messages urging retreat.
They had the inexorable weight of common sense
Behind them, but John Brown neither replied   155
Nor heeded, brooding in the patriarch-calm
Of a lean, solitary pine that hangs
On the cliff's edge, and sees the world below
A tiny pattern of toy fields and trees,
And only feels its roots gripping the rock
And the almighty wind that shakes its boughs,   160
Blowing from eagle-heaven to eagle-heaven.

Of course they were cut off. The whole attempt
Was fated from the first.
                              Just about noon
The Jefferson Guards took the Potomac Bridge   165
And drove away the men Brown posted there.

There were three doors of possible escape
Open to Brown. With this the first slammed shut.
The second followed it a little later
With the recapture of the other bridge   170
That cut Brown off from Kagi and the arsenal
And penned the larger body of the raiders
In the armory.
                 Again the firing rolled,
And now the first of the raiders fell and died,   175
Dangerfield Newby, the freed Scotch-mulatto
Whose wife and seven children, slaves in Virginia,
Waited for him to bring them incredible freedom.
They were sold South instead, after the raid.
His body lay where the townspeople could reach it.   180
They cut off his ears for trophies.

                    If there are souls,
As many think that there are or wish that there might be,
Crystalline things that rise on light wings exulting
Out of the spoilt and broken cocoon of the body,   185
Knowing no sorrow or pain but only deliverance,
And yet with the flame of speech, the patterns of memory,
One wonders what the soul of Dangerfield Newby
Said, in what terms, to the soul of Shepherd Heyward,
Both born slave, both freed, both dead the same day.   190
What do the souls that bleed from the corpse of battle
Say to the tattered night?
                    Perhaps it is better
We have no power to visage what they might say.

The firing now was constant, like the heavy   195
And drumming rains of summer. Twice Brown sent
Asking a truce. The second time there went
Stevens and Watson Brown with a white flag.
But things had gone beyond the symbol of flags.
Stevens, shot from a window, fell in the gutter   200
Horribly wounded. Watson Brown crawled back
To the engine house that was the final fort
Of Brown's last stand, torn through and through with slugs.

A Mr. Brua, one of Brown's prisoners,
Strolled out from the unguarded prison-room   205
Into the bullets, lifted Stevens up,
Carried him over to the old hotel
They called the Wager House, got a doctor for him,
And then strolled back to take his prisoner's place
With Colonel Washington and the scared rest.   210
I know no more than this of Mr. Brua
But he seems curiously American,
And I imagine him a tall, stooped man
A little yellow with the Southern sun,
With slow, brown eyes and a slow way of talking,   215
Shifting the quid of tobacco in his cheek
Mechanically, as he lifted up
The dirty, bloody body of the man
Who stood for everything he most detested
And slowly carrying him through casual wasps   220
Of death to the flyspecked but sunny room
In the old hotel, wiping the blood and grime
Mechanically from his Sunday coat,
Settling his black string-tie with big, tanned hands.

And, then, incredibly, going back to jail.   225
He did not think much about what he'd done
But sat himself as comfortably as might be
On the cold bricks of that dejected guard-room
And slowly started cutting another quid
With a worn knife that had a brown bone-handle.   230

He lived all through the war and died long after,
This Mr. Brua I see. His last advice
To numerous nephews was "Keep out of trouble,
But if you're in it, chew and don't be hasty,
Just do whatever's likeliest at hand."   235

I like your way of talking, Mr. Brua,
And if there still are people interested
In cutting literary clothes for heroes
They might do worse than mention your string-tie.

There were other killings that day. On the one side, this,   240
Leeman, a boy of eighteen and the youngest raider,
Trying to flee from the death-trap of the engine-house
And caught and killed on an islet in the Potomac.
The body lay on a tiny shelf of rocks
For hours, a sack of clothes still stung by bullets.   245

On the other side—Fontaine Beckham, mayor of the town,
Went to look at Heyward's body with Patrick Higgins.
The slow tears crept to his eyes. He was getting old.
He had thought a lot of Heyward. He had no gun
But he had been mayor of the town for a dozen years,   250
A peaceful, orderly place full of decent people,
And now they were killing people, here in his town,
He had to do something to stop it, somehow or other.

He wandered out on the railroad, half-distraught
And peeped from behind a water-tank at the raiders.   255
"Squire, don't go any farther," said Higgins, "It ain't safe."
He hardly heard him, he had to look out again.
Who were these devils with horns who were shooting his people?
They didn't look like devils. One was a boy
Smooth-cheeked, with a bright half-dreamy face, a little   260
Like Sally's eldest.
                    Suddenly, the air struck him
A stiff, breath-taking blow. "Oh," he said, astonished.
Took a step and fell on his face, shot through the heart.

Higgins watched him for twenty minutes, wanting to lift him   265
But not quite daring. Then he turned away
And went back to the town.
The bars had been open all day,
Never to better business.
When the news of Beckham's death spread from bar to bar.   270
It was like putting loco-weed in the whiskey,
The mob came together at once, the American mob,
They mightn't be able to take Brown's last little fort
But there were two prisoners penned in the Wager House.
One was hurt already, Stevens, no fun killing him.   275
But the other was William Thompson, whole and unwounded,
Caught when Brown tried to send his first flag of truce.

They stormed the hotel and dragged him out to the bridge,
Where two men shot him, unarmed, then threw the body
Over the trestle. It splashed in the shallow water,   280
But the slayers kept on firing at the dead face.
The carcass was there for days, a riven target,
Barbarously misused.
Meanwhile the armory yard
Was taken by a new band of Beckham's avengers,   285
The most of Brown's prisoners freed and his last escape cut off.

What need to tell of the killing of Kagi the scholar,
The wounding of Oliver Brown and the other deaths?
Only this remains to be told. When the drunken day
Reeled into night, there were left in the engine-house   290
Five men, alive and unwounded, of all the raiders.
Watson and Oliver Brown
Both of them hurt to the death, were stretched on the floor
Beside the corpse of Taylor, the young Canadian.
There was no light, there. It was bitterly cold.   295
A cold chain of lightless hours that slowly fell
In leaden beads between two fingers of stone.
Outside, the fools and the drunkards yelled in the streets,
And, now and then, there were shots. The prisoners talked
And tried to sleep.   300
John Brown did not try to sleep,
The live coals of his eyes severed the darkness;
Now and then he heard his young son Oliver calling
In the thirsty agony of his wounds, "Oh, kill me!
Kill me and put me out of this suffering!"   305
John Brown's jaw tightened. "If you must die," he said,
"Die like a man." Toward morning the crying ceased.

John Brown called out to the boy but he did not answer.
"I guess he's dead," said John Brown.
If his soul wept   310
They were the incredible tears of the squeezed stone.
He had not slept for two days, but he would not sleep.
The night was a chained, black leopard that he stared down,
Erect, on his feet. One wonders what sights he saw
In the cloudy mirror of his most cloudy heart,   315
Perhaps God clothed in a glory, perhaps himself
The little boy who had stolen three brass pins
And been well whipped for it.
When he was six years old
An Indian boy had given him a great wonder,   320
A yellow marble, the first he had even seen.
He treasured it for months but lost it at last,
Boylike. The hurt of the loss took years to heal.
He never quite forgot.
He could see it now,   325
Smooth, hard and lovely, a yellow, glistening ball,
But it kept rolling away through cracks of darkness
Whenever he tried to catch it and hold it fast.
If he could only touch it, he would be safe,
But it trickled away and away, just out of reach,   330
There by the wall . . .
Outside the blackened East
Began to tarnish with a faint, grey stain
That caught on the fixed bayonets of the marines.
Lee of Virginia, Light Horse Harry's son,   335
Observed it broaden, thinking of many things,
But chiefly wanting to get his business done,
A curious, wry, distasteful piece of work
For regular soldiers.
Therefore to be finished   340
As swiftly and summarily as possible
Before this yelling mob of drunk civilians
And green militia once got out of hand.
His mouth set. Once already he had offered
The honor of the attack to the militia,   345
Such honor as it was.
Their Colonel had
Declined with a bright nervousness of haste.
"Your men are paid for doing this kind of work.
Mine have their wives and children." Lee smiled briefly,   350
Remembering that. The smile had a sharp edge.
Well, it was time.

        The whooping crowd fell silent
And scattered, as a single man walked out
Toward the engine-house, a letter in his hand.   355
Lee watched him musingly. A good man, Stuart.
Now he was by the door and calling out.
The door opened a crack.
               Brown's eyes were there
Over the cold muzzle of a cocked carbine.   360
The parleying began, went on and on,
While the crowd shivered and Lee watched it all
With the strict commonsense of a Greek sword
And with the same sure readiness.
                  Unperceived,   365
The dawn ran down the valleys of the wind,
Coral-footed dove, tracking the sky with coral . . .
Then, sudden as powder flashing in a pan,
The parleying was done.
              The door slammed shut.   370
The little figure of Stuart jumped aside
Waving its cap.
         And the marines came on.
Brown watched them come. One hand was on his carbine.
The other felt the pulse of his dying son.   375
"Sell your lives dear," he said. The rifle-shots
Rattled within the bricked-in engine-room
Like firecrackers set off in a stone jug,
And there was a harsh stink of sweat and powder.
There was a moment when the door held firm.   380
Then it was cracked with sun.
              Brown fired and missed.
A shadow with a sword leaped through the sun.
"That's Ossawattomie," said the tired voice
Of Colonel Washington.   385
            The shadow lunged
And Brown fell to his knees.
            The sword bent double,
A light sword, better for parades than fighting,
The shadow had to take it in both hands   390
And fairly rain his blows with it on Brown
Before he sank.
        Now two marines were down.
The rest rushed in over their comrades' bodies,
Pinning one man of Brown's against the wall   395
With bayonets, another to the floor.

Lee, on his rise of ground, shut up his watch.
It had been just a quarter of an hour
Since Stuart gave the signal for the storm,
And now it was over.　　　　　　　　　　　　400
　　　　　　All but the long dying.

* * *

HERVEY ALLEN
The Blindman [1]

A T Nogent, on the river Marne,
　　　　I passed a burning house and
　　　　　　barn.
I went into the public square
Where pigeons fluttered in the air
And empty windows gaped a-stare.　　5

There crouched a Blindman by the
　　　wall
A-shivering in a ragged shawl,
Who gave a hopeless parrot screech
And felt the wall with halting reach.
He went around as in a trap,　　　　10
He had a stick to feel and rap,
A-rap-a-tap, a-rap-a-tap.

I strode across the public square,
I stopped and spoke him full and fair,
I asked him what he searched for
　　　there.　　　　　　　　　　　　15
Then came a look upon his face
That made me want to leave the
　　　place.
He could not answer for a space,
He moved his trembling hands about
And in-and-out, and in-and-out.　　20

"Kind sir," he said, "I scarcely know—
A week ago there fell a blow—
I think it was a week ago,

I sent my little girl to school,
With kisses and her book and rule,　25
A week ago she went to school."
The pigeons all began to coo.
"A-cock-a-loo, a-cock-a-loo."

"O God! to be a blinded fool:
I cannot find the children's school—
The gate, the court about the pool—
But sir, if you will guide my feet　　32
Across the square and down the
　　　street,
I think I'll know then where it lies.
O Jesu! Give me back my eyes!　　35
O Jesu! Give me back my eyes!"

I led him down the littered street,
He seemed to know it with his feet,
For suddenly he turned aside
And entered through a gateway wide.
It was the court about the pool.　　41
Long shadows slept deep and cool.
No sound was there of beast or bird;
It was the silence that we heard.

"And this," he said, "might be the
　　　place,"　　　　　　　　　　　45
An eager look came on his face.
He raised his voice and gave a call;
An echo mewed along the wall,
And then it rose and then it fell,　　49
Like children talking down a well.
"Go in," he said, "see what you see,
And then come back again for me."

Like one who bears a weight of sin
And walks with fear, I entered in—

A turn—and halfway up the stair   55
There was a sight to raise your hair;
A dusty litter, books and toys,
Three bundles that were little boys,
White faces like an ivory gem;
A statue stood and looked at them.   60

So thick the silence where I stood,
I thought I wore a wooden hood;
The blood went whispering through
    my ears,
Like secrets that one overhears
I looked upon the dead awhile,   65
I saw the gleaming statue smile.
The children slept so sweetly there,
I scarce believed the tainted air.

And then I heard the Blindman's
    stick,
As rhythmic as a watch's tick,   70
A step—a click, a step—a click—
As slow as days grow to a year,
So long it seemed while he drew near,
But sure and blind as death and fate,
He came and said, "I dared not wait,
It was too silent at the gate.   76

"And tell me now, sir, what you see
That keeps you here so silently."
"Three harmless things," I said, "I
    fear,   79
Three things I see but cannot hear,
Three shadows of what was before,
Cast by no light are on the floor."
"Sir," said the Blindman, "lead me
    round,
Lest I should tread on holy ground."

Like men they lead at dawn to
    doom,   85
We slowly climbed the stairway's
    gloom
And came into a sunlit room.
The ceiling lay upon the floor,

And slates, and books, and something
    more—
The master with a glassy stare,   90
Sat gory in his shivered chair
And gazed upon his pupils there.

The Blindman grasped me eagerly.
"And tell me now, sir, what you see?
This is the place where she should
    be—   95
My Eleanor, who used to wear
Short socks that left her brown legs
    bare.
She had a crown of golden hair."
I saw his blind eyes peer and stare,
*Now there and here, now here and
    there.*   100

"Blindman," I cried, "these things I
    see:
Time here has turned eternity.
The clock hands point but only mock,
For it is always three o'clock.
I see the shadows on the wall;   105
I see the crumbling plaster fall."
"Oh! sir," he said, "I crave your
    eyes—
Be not so kindly with your lies."

I drew the Blindman to my side;
I told the truth I wished to hide.   110
I said, "I see your Eleanor
And she is dead upon the floor.
And something fumbles with her hair,
I guess the wind is playing there.
And I see the gray rats sleek and
    stout   115
That dart about and dart about."

"Now, sir," he said, "I love your lies
And Christ be thanked that took my
    eyes!
But lead me, lead me to my dead!
And let me touch her once," he said.
I placed his hand upon her head.   121

And when we left the charnel place
I dared not look upon his face;
For suddenly upon the street
Arose the sound of trampling feet, 125
And wheels that rumbled on the
    ground,
*And ground around and ground
    around.*

The din of them that go to slay,
The shout of men and horses' neigh,
And men and beasts swept on to war
A dreadful drumming on before. 131

It sobbed and throbbed through No-
    gent Town,
Till desolation settled down.
The Blindman leaned against the
    door;
"And tell me, sir, about the war, 135
What is it they are fighting for?"
"Blindman," I cried, "can you not
    see?
It is to set the whole world free!
It is for sweet democracy—"

"I do not know her, sir," he said, 140
"My little Eleanor is dead."

~~~~~~~~~~~~~~~~~~~~~~~~~

JOHN MASEFIELD

Saul Kane's Fight

From "The Everlasting Mercy"[1]

—————————

O N Wood Top Field the peewits
      go
      Mewing and wheeling ever
so;
And like the shaking of a timbrel
Cackles the laughter of the whimbrel.

[1] From *Poems*. By permission of The Macmillan Company, publishers. First published
1911.

In the old quarry-pit they say   5
Head-keeper Pike was made away.
He walks, head-keeper Pike, for harm,
He taps the windows of the farm;
The blood drips from his broken chin,
He taps and begs to be let in.   10
On Wood Top, nights, I've shaked to
    hark
The peewits wambling in the dark
Lest in the dark the old man might
Creep up to me to beg a light.

But Wood Top grass is short and
    sweet   15
And springy to a boxer's feet;
At harvest hum the moon so bright
Did shine on Wood Top for the fight.

When Bill was stripped down to his
    bends
I thought how long we two'd been
    friends,   20
And in my mind, about that wire,
I thought "He's right, I am a liar.
As sure as skilly's made in prison
The right to poach that copse is his'n.
I'll have no luck to-night," thinks I.   25
"I'm fighting to defend a lie.
And this moonshiny evening's fun
Is worse than aught I've ever done."
And thinking that way my heart bled
    so
I almost stept to Bill and said so.   30
And now Bill's dead I would be glad
If I could only think I had.
But no. I put the thought away
For fear of what my friends would
    say.
They'd backed me, see? O Lord, the
    sin   35
Done for the things there's money in.

The stakes were drove, the ropes were
    hitched,
Into the ring my hat I pitched.

My corner faced the Squire's park
Just where the fir trees make it
   dark;   40
The place where I begun poor Nell
Upon the woman's road to hell.
I thought of't, sitting in my corner
After the time-keep struck his warner
(Two brandy flasks, for fear of
   noise,   45
Clinked out the time to us two boys).
And while my seconds chafed and
   gloved me
I thought of Nell's eyes when she
   loved me,
And wondered how my tot would
   end,
First Nell cast off and now my
   friend;   50

And in the moonlight dim and wan
I knew quite well my luck was gone;
And looking round I felt a spite
At all who'd come to see me fight;
The five and forty human faces   55
Inflamed by drink and going to races,
Faces of men who'd never been
Merry or true or live or clean;
Who'd never felt the boxer's trim
Of brain divinely knit to limb,   60
Nor felt the whole live body go
One tingling health from top to toe;
Nor took a punch nor given a swing,
But just soaked deady round the ring
Until their brains and bloods were
   foul   70
Enough to make their throttles howl,
While we whom Jesus died to teach
Fought round on round, three min
   utes each.

And thinking that, you'll understand
I thought, "I'll go and take Bill's
   hand.   75
I'll up and say the fault was mine,

He shan't make play for these here
   swine."
And then I thought that that was silly,
They'd think I was afraid of Billy;
They'd think (I thought it, God for-
   give me)   80
I funked the hiding Bill could give
   me.
And that thought made me mad and
   hot.
"Think that, will they? Well, they
   shall not.
They shan't think that. I will not. I'm
   Damned if I will. I will not."   85
Time!
From the beginning of the bout
My luck was gone, my hand was out.
Right from the start Bill called the
   play,
But I was quick and kept away
Till the fourth round, when work got
   mixed,   90
And then I knew Bill had me fixed.
My hand was out, why, Heaven
   knows;
Bill punched me when and where he
   chose.
Through two more rounds we quar-
   tered wide,
And all the time my hands seemed
   tied;   95
Bill punched me when and where he
   pleased.
The cheering from my backers eased,
But every punch I heard a yell
Of "That's the style, Bill, give him
   hell."
No one for me, but Jimmy's light   100
"Straight left! Straight left!" and
   "Watch his right."

I don't know how a boxer goes
When all his body hums from blows;
I know I seemed to rock and spin,

I don't know how I saved my
   chin;   105
I know I thought my only friend
Was that clinked flask at each round's
   end
When my two seconds, Ed and
   Jimmy,
Had sixty seconds help to gimme.
But in the ninth, with pain and
   knocks   110
I stopped: I couldn't fight nor box
Bill missed his swing, the light was
   tricky,
But I went down, and stayed down,
   dicky.
"Get up," cried Jim. I said, "I will."
Then all the gang yelled, "Out him,
   Bill.   115
Out him." Bill rushed . . . and Clink,
   Clink, Clink
Time! and Jim's knee, and rum to
   drink.
And round the ring there ran a titter:
"Saved by the call, the bloody quitter."

They drove (a dodge that never
   fails)   120
A pin beneath my finger nails.
They poured what seemed a running
   beck
Of cold spring water down my neck;
Jim with a lancet quick as flies
Lowered the swellings round my
   eyes.   125
They sluiced my legs and fanned my
   face
Through all that blessed minute's
   grace;
They gave my calves a thorough
   kneading,
They salved my cuts and stopped the
   bleeding.
A gulp of liquor dulled the pain,   130
And then the two flasks clinked again.

Time!
   There was Bill as grim as death,
He rushed, I clinched, to get more
   breath,
And breath I got, though Billy bats
Some stinging short-arms in my
   slats.   135
And when he broke, as I foresaw,
He swung his right in for the jaw.
I stopped it on my shoulder bone,
And at the shock I heard Bill groan—
A little groan or moan or grunt   140
As though I'd hit his wind a bunt.
At that, I clinched, and while we
   clinched,
His old time right arm dig was
   flinched,
And when we broke he hit me light
As though he didn't trust his
   right,   145
He flapped me somehow with his
   wrist
As though he couldn't use his fist,
And when he hit he winced with pain.
I thought, "Your sprained thumb's
   cracked again."
So I got strength and Bill gave
   ground,   150
And that round was an easy round.

During the wait my Jimmy said,
"What's making Billy fight so dead?
He's all to pieces. Is he blown?"
"His thumb's out."   155
"No? Then it's your own.
It's all your own, but don't be rash—
He's got the goods if you've got cash,
And what one hand can do he'll do.
Be careful this next round or two."   160

Time. There was Bill, and I felt sick
That luck should play so mean a trick
And give me leave to knock him out
After he'd plainly won the bout.

But by the way the man came at
   me   165
He made it plain he meant to bat
   me;
If you'd a seen the way he come
You wouldn't think he'd crocked a
   thumb.
With all his skill and all his might
He clipped me dizzy left and
   right;   170
The Lord knows what the effort
   cost,
But he was mad to think he'd lost,
And knowing nothing else could save
   him
He didn't care what pain it gave him.
He called the music and the dance 175
For five rounds more and gave no
   chance.

Try to imagine if you can
The kind of manhood in the man,
And if you'd like to feel his pain
You sprain your thumb and hit the
   sprain.   180
And hit it hard, with all your power
On something hard for half-an-hour,
While someone thumps you black and
   blue,
And then you'll know what Billy
   knew.
Bill took that pain without a sound 185
Till halfway through the eighteenth
   round,
And then I sent him down and out,
And Silas said, "Kane wins the bout."

When Bill came to, you understand,
I ripped the mitten from my hand 190
And went across to ask Bill shake.
My limbs were all one pain and ache,
I was so weary and so sore
I don't think I'd a stood much more.
Bill in his corner bathed his
   thumb,   195
Buttoned his shirt and glowered glum.
"I'll never shake your hand," he said.
"I'd rather see my children dead.
I've been about and had some fun
   with you,
But you're a liar and I've done with
   you.   200
You've knocked me out, you didn't
   beat me;
Look out the next time that you meet
   me,
There'll be no friend to watch the
   clock for you
And no convenient thumb to crock
   for you,
And I'll take care, with much de-
   light,   205
You'll get what you'd a got to-night;
That puts my meaning clear, I guess,
Now get to hell; I want to dress."

I dressed. My backers one and all
Said, "Well done you," or "Good old
   Saul."   210
"Saul is a wonder and a fly 'un,
What'll you have, Saul, at the Lion?"
With merry oaths they helped me
   down
The stony wood path to the town.

ALFRED, LORD TENNYSON

Ulysses

It little profits that an idle king,
By this still hearth, among these
   barren crags,
Matched with an agéd wife, I mete
   and dole
Unequal laws unto a savage race,
That hoard, and sleep, and feed, and
   know not me.   5
I cannot rest from travel; I will
   drink
Life to the lees.   All times I have
   enjoyed
Greatly, have suffered greatly, both
   with those
That loved me, and alone; on shore,
   and when
Through scudding drifts the rainy
   Hyades   10
Vexed the dim sea. I am become a
   name;
For always roaming with a hungry
   heart
Much have I seen and known,—cities
   of men
And manners, climates, councils, gov-
   ernments,
Myself not least, but honored of them
   all,—   15
And drunk delight of battle with my
   peers,
Far on the ringing plains of windy
   Troy.
I am a part of all that I have met;
Yet all experience is an arch where
   through
Gleams that untraveled world whose
   margin fades   20

For ever and for ever when I move.
How dull it is to pause, to make an
   end,
To rust unburnished, not to shine in
   use!
As though to breathe were life! Life
   piled on life
Were all too little, and of one to me   25
Little remains; but every hour is
   saved
From that eternal silence, something
   more,
A bringer of new things; and vile it
   were
For some three suns to store and
   hoard myself,
And this gray spirit yearning in de-
   sire   30
To follow knowledge like a sinking
   star,
Beyond the utmost bound of human
   thought.
   This is my son, mine own Telema-
   chus,
To whom I leave the scepter and the
   isle,—
Well-loved of me, discerning to fulfil
This labor, by slow prudence to make
   mild   36
A rugged people, and through soft
   degrees
Subdue them to the useful and the
   good.
Most blameless is he, centered in the
   sphere
Of common duties, decent not to fail
In offices of tenderness, and pay   41
Meet adoration to my household gods,
When I am gone. He works his
   work, I mine.
   There lies the port; the vessel puffs
   her sail;

There gloom the dark, broad seas. My mariners,   45
Souls that have toiled, and wrought, and thought with me,—
That ever with a frolic welcome took
The thunder and the sunshine, and opposed
Free hearts, free foreheads,—you and I are old;
Old age hath yet his honor and his toil.   50
Death closes all; but something ere the end,
Some work of noble note, may yet be done,
Not unbecoming men that strove with Gods.
The lights begin to twinkle from the rocks;
The long day wanes; the slow moon climbs; the deep   55
Moans round with many voices. Come, my friends.
'Tis not too late to seek a newer world.
Push off, and sitting well in order smite
The sounding furrows; for my purpose holds
To sail beyond the sunset, and the baths   60
Of all the western stars, until I die.
It may be that the gulfs will wash us down;
It may be we shall touch the Happy Isles,
And see the great Achilles, whom we knew.
Though much is taken, much abides; and though   65
We are not now that strength which in old days
Moved earth and heaven, that which we are, we are,—
One equal temper of heroic hearts,

Made weak by time and fate, but strong in will
To strive, to seek, to find, and not to yield.   70

ROBERT BROWNING

My Last Duchess

FERRARA

THAT'S my last Duchess painted on the wall,
      Looking as if she were alive. I call
That piece a wonder, now: Fra Pandolf's hands
Worked busily a day, and there she stands.
Will't please you sit and look at her? I said   5
"Fra Pandolf" by design, for never read
Strangers like you that pictured countenance,
The depth and passion of its earnest glance,
But to myself they turned (since none puts by
The curtain I have drawn for you, but I)   10
And seemed as they would ask me, if they durst,
How such a glance came there; so, not the first
Are you to turn and ask thus. Sir, 'twas not
Her husband's presence only, called that spot
Of joy into the Duchess' cheek: perhaps   15
Fra Pandolf chanced to say, "Her mantle laps

Over my lady's wrist too much," or
   "Paint
Must never hope to reproduce the
   faint
Half-flush that dies along her throat":
   such stuff
Was courtesy, she thought, and cause
   enough   20
For calling up that spot of joy. She
   had
A heart—how shall I say?—too soon
   made glad,
Too easily impressed: she liked what-
   e'er
She looked on, and her looks went
   everywhere.
Sir, 'twas all one! My favor at her
   breast,   25
The dropping of the daylight in the
   West,
The bough of cherries some officious
   fool
Broke in the orchard for her, the
   white mule
She rode with round the terrace—all
   and each
Would draw from her alike the ap-
   proving speech,   30
Or blush, at least. She thanked men,
   —good! but thanked
Somehow—I know not how—as if she
   ranked
My gift of a nine-hundred-year-old
   name
With anybody's gift. Who'd stoop to
   blame
This sort of trifling? Even had you
   skill   35

In speech—(which I have not)—to
   make your will
Quite clear to such an one, and say,
   "Just this
Or that in you disgusts me; here you
   miss,
Or there exceed the mark"—and if
   she let
Herself be lessoned so, nor plainly set
Her wits to yours, forsooth, and made
   excuse,   41
—E'en then would be some stooping;
   and I choose
Never to stoop. Oh sir, she smiled,
   no doubt,
Whene'er I passed her; but who
   passed without
Much the same smile? This grew; I
   gave commands;   45
Then all smiles stopped together.
   There she stands
As if alive. Will 't please you rise?
   We'll meet
The company below, then. I repeat
The Count your master's known
   munificence
Is ample warrant that no just pretense
Of mine for dowry will be disal-
   lowed;   51
Though his fair daughter's self, as I
   avowed
At starting, is my object. Nay, we'll
   go
Together down, sir. Notice Neptune,
   though,
Taming a sea-horse, thought a rarity,
Which Claus of Innsbruck cast in
   bronze for me!   56

ROBERT FROST

The Death of the Hired Man [1]

MARY sat musing on the lamp-
flame at the table
Waiting for Warren. When
she heard his step,
She ran on tip-toe down the darkened
passage
To meet him in the doorway with
the news
And put him on his guard. "Silas is
back." 5
She pushed him outward with her
through the door
And shut it after her. "Be kind," she
said.
She took the market things from
Warren's arms
And set them on the porch, then
drew him down
To sit beside her on the wooden
steps. 10

"When was I ever anything but kind
to him?
But I'll not have the fellow back," he
said.
"I told him so last haying, didn't I?
'If he left then,' I said, 'that ended it.'
What good is he? Who else will
harbor him 15
At his age for the little he can do?
What help he is there's no depending
on.
Off he goes always when I need him
most.

'He thinks he ought to earn a little
pay,
Enough at least to buy tobacco with,
So he won't have to beg and be be-
holden.' 21
'All right,' I say, 'I can't afford to pay
Any fixed wages, though I wish I
could.'
'Some one else can.' 'Then some one
else will have to.'
I shouldn't mind his bettering him-
self 25
If that was what it was. You can be
certain,
When he begins like that, there's
some one at him
Trying to coax him off with pocket-
money,—
In haying time, when any help is
scarce.
In winter he comes back to us. I'm
done." 30

"Sh! not so loud: he'll hear you,"
Mary said.

"I want him to: he'll have to soon or
late."

"He's worn out. He's asleep beside
the stove.
When I came up from Rowe's I
found him here,
Huddled against the barn-door fast
asleep, 35
A miserable sight, and frightening,
too—
You needn't smile—I didn't recognize
him—
I wasn't looking for him—and he's
changed.
Wait till you see."
                    "Where did you say
he'd been?"

"He didn't say. I dragged him to the
   house,   40
And gave him tea and tried to make
   him smoke.
I tried to make him talk about his
   travels.
Nothing would do: he just kept nodding off."

"What did he say? Did he say anything?"

"But little."
          "Anything? Mary, con-
   fess   45
He said he'd come to ditch the
   meadow for me."

"Warren!"

         "But did he? I just want
to know."

"Of course he did. What would you
   have him say?
Surely you wouldn't grudge the poor
   old man
Some humble way to save his self-
   respect.   50
He added, if you really care to know,
He meant to clear the upper pasture,
   too.
That sounds like something you have
   heard before?
Warren, I wish you could have heard
   the way
He jumbled everything. I stopped to
   look   55
Two or three times—he made me feel
   so queer—
To see if he was talking in his sleep.
He ran on Harold Wilson—you re-
   member—
The boy you had in haying four years
   since.

He's finished school, and teaching in
   his college.   60
Silas declares you'll have to get him
   back.
He says they two will make a team
   for work:
Between them they will lay this farm
   as smooth!
The way he mixed that in with other
   things.
He thinks young Wilson a likely lad,
   though daft   65
On education—you know how they
   fought
All through July under the blazing
   sun,
Silas up on the cart to build the load,
Harold along beside to pitch it on."

"Yes, I took care to keep well out of
   earshot."   70

"Well, those days trouble Silas like a
   dream.
You wouldn't think they would. How
   some things linger!
Harold's young college boy's assur-
   ance piqued him.
After so many years he still keeps
   finding
Good arguments he sees he might
   have used.   75
I sympathize. I know just how it
   feels
To think of the right thing to say too
   late.
Harold's associated in his mind with
   Latin.
He asked me what I thought of
   Harold's saying
He studied Latin like the violin   80
Because he liked it—that an argu-
   ment!
He said he couldn't make the boy
   believe

He could find water with a hazel
    prong—
Which showed how much good
    school had ever done him.
He wanted to go over that. But most
    of all   85
He thinks if he could have another
    chance
To teach him how to build a load of
    hay—"
"I know, that's Silas' one accomplish-
    ment.
He bundles every forkful in its place,
And tags and numbers it for future
    reference,   90
So he can find and easily dislodge it
In the unloading. Silas does that
    well.
He takes it out in bunches like big
    birds' nests.
You never see him standing on the
    hay
He's trying to lift, straining to lift
    himself."   95

"He thinks if he could teach him that,
    he'd be
Some good perhaps to some one in
    the world.
He hates to see a boy the fool of
    books.
Poor Silas, so concerned for other
    folk,
And nothing to look backward to
    with pride,   100
And nothing to look forward to with
    hope,
So now and never any different."

Part of a moon was falling down the
    west,
Dragging the whole sky with it to
    the hills.
Its light poured softly in her lap. She
    saw   105

And spread her apron to it. She put
    out her hand
Among the harp-like morning-glory
    strings,
Taut with the dew from garden bed
    to eaves,
As if she played unheard the tender-
    ness
That wrought on him beside her in
    the night.   110
"Warren," she said, "he has come
    home to die:
You needn't be afraid he'll leave you
    this time."

"Home," he mocked gently.

          "Yes, what else but home?
It all depends on what you mean by
    home.
Of course he's nothing to us, any
    more   115
Than was the hound that came a
    stranger to us
Out of the woods, worn out upon the
    trail."

"Home is the place where, when you
    have to go there,
They have to take you in."
          "I should have called it
Something you somehow haven't to
    deserve."   120

Warren leaned out and took a step or
    two,
Picked up a little stick and brought it
    back
And broke it in his hand and tossed
    it by.
"Silas has better claim on us you
    think
Than on his brother? Thirteen little
    miles   125

As the road winds would bring him
to his door.
Silas has walked that far no doubt
today.
Why didn't he go there? His brother's rich,
A somebody—director in the bank."

"He never told us that."
"We know it though."

"I think his brother ought to help, of
course. 131
I'll see to that if there is need. He
ought of right
To take him in, and might be will-
ing to—
He may be better than appearances.
But have some pity on Silas. Do you
think 135
If he'd had any pride in claiming kin
Or anything he looked for from his
brother,
He'd keep so still about him all this
time?"

"I wonder what's between them."

"I can tell you.
Silas is what he is—we wouldn't
mind him— 140
But just the kind that kinsfolk can't
abide.
He never did a thing so very bad.
He don't know why he isn't quite as
good
As any one. He won't be made
ashamed
To please his brother, worthless
though he is." 145
"I can't think Si ever hurt any one."

"No, but he hurt my heart the way
he lay

And rolled his old head on that
sharp-edged chair-back.
He wouldn't let me put him on the
lounge.
You must go in and see what you can
do. 150
I made the bed up for him there tonight.
You'll be surprised at him—how
much he's broken.
His working days are done; I'm sure
of it."

"I'd not be in a hurry to say that."

"I haven't been. Go, look, see for
yourself. 155
But, Warren, please remember how it
is:
He's come to help you ditch the
meadow.
He has a plan. You mustn't laugh at
him.
He may not speak of it, and then he
may.
I'll sit and see if that small sailing
cloud 160
Will hit or miss the moon."

It hit the moon.
Then there were three there, making
a dim row,
The moon, the little silver cloud, and
she.
Warren returned—too soon, it seemed
to her,
Slipped to her side, caught up her
hand and waited. 165

"Warren," she questioned.

"Dead," was all he answered.

WALTER DE LA MARE

The Listeners [1]

Is there anybody there?" said the
   Traveller,
   Knocking on the moonlit door;
And his horse in the silence champed
   the grasses
Of the forest's ferny floor:
And a bird flew up out of the turret, 5
   Above the Traveller's head:
And he smote upon the door again a
   second time;
'Is there anybody there?" he said.

But no one descended to the Trav-
   eller;
No head from the leaf-fringed sill
Leaned over and looked into his grey
   eyes, 11
Where he stood perplexed and still.
But only a host of phantom listeners
   That dwelt in the lone house then
Stood listening in the quiet of the
   moonlight 15

To that voice from the world of
   men:
Stood thronging the faint moonbeams
   on the dark stair,
That goes down to the empty hall,
Hearkening in an air stirred and
   shaken
By the lonely Traveller's call. 20
And he felt in his heart their strange-
   ness,
   Their stillness answering his cry,
While his horse moved, cropping the
   dark turf,
   'Neath the starred and leafy sky;
For he suddenly smote on the door,
   even 25
   Louder, and lifted his head:—
"Tell them I came, and no one an-
   swered,
   That I kept my word," he said.
Never the least stir made the listeners,
   Though every word he spake 30
Fell echoing through the shadowiness
   of the still house
From the one man left awake:
Ay, they heard his foot upon the
   stirrup,
   And the sound of iron on stone,
And how the silence surged softly
   backward, 35
When the plunging hoofs were
   gone.

[1] From *Collected Poems*. By permission of
Henry Holt and Company, publishers.

VACHEL LINDSAY [1]

The Santa-Fé Trail

(*A Humoresque*)

(I asked the old negro: "What is that bird that sings so well?" He answered: "That is the Rachel-Jane." "Hasn't it another name—lark, or thrush, or the like?" "No. Jus' Rachel-Jane.")

I. IN WHICH A RACING AUTO COMES FROM THE EAST

THIS is the order of the music of the morning:—   *To be sung deli-*
  First, from the far East comes but a crooning.   *cately, to an im-*
          The crooning turns to a sunrise singing.   *provised tune.*
Hark to the *calm*-horn, *balm*-horn, *psalm*-horn.
Hark to the *faint*-horn, *quaint*-horn, *saint*-horn. . .   5
Hark to the *pace*-horn, *chase*-horn, *race*-horn.   *To be sung or*
And the holy veil of the dawn has gone.   *read with great*
Swiftly the brazen car comes on.   *speed.*
It burns in the East as the sunrise burns.
I see great flashes where the far trail turns.   10
Its eyes are lamps like the eyes of dragons.
It drinks gasoline from big red flagons.
Butting through the delicate mists of the morning,
It comes like lightning, goes past roaring.
It will hail all the windmills, taunting, ringing.   15
Dodge the cyclones,
Count the milestones,
On through the ranges the prairie-dog tills—
Scooting past the cattle on the thousand hills. . . .
Ho for the *tear*-horn, *scare*-horn, *dare*-horn,   20   *To be read or*
Ho for the *gay*-horn, *bark*-horn, *bay*-horn.   *sung in a rolling*
Ho for Kansas, land that restores us   *bass, with some*
When houses choke us, and great books bore us!   *deliberation.*
Sunrise Kansas, harvesters' Kansas,
A million men have found you before us.   25
A million men have found you before us.

II. IN WHICH MANY AUTOS PASS WESTWARD

I want live things in their pride to remain.   *In an even, delib-*
I will not kill one grasshopper vain   *erate,   narrative*
Though he eats a hole in my shirt like a door.   *manner.*

[1] From *Collected Poems.* By permission of The Macmillan Company, publishers.

I let him out, give him one chance more.   30
Perhaps, while he gnaws my hat in his whim,
Grasshopper lyrics occur to him.
I am a tramp by the long trail's border,
Given to squalor, rags and disorder.
I nap and amble and yawn and look,   35
Write fool-thoughts in my grubby book,
Recite to the children, explore at my ease,
Work when I work, beg when I please,
Give crank-drawings, that make folks stare
To the half-grown boys in the sunset glare,   40
And get me a place to sleep in the hay
At the end of a live-and-let-live day.

I find in the stubble of the new-cut weeds
A whisper and a feasting, all one needs:
The whisper of the strawberries, white and red   45
Here where the new-cut weeds lie dead.
But I would not walk all alone till I die
Without some life-drunk horns going by.
And up round this apple-earth they come
Blasting the whispers of the morning dumb:—   50
Cars in a plain realistic row.
And fair dreams fade
When the raw horns blow.

On each snapping pennant
A big black name:—   55
The careering city
Whence each car came.
They tour from Memphis, Atlanta, Savannah,
Tallahassee and Texarkana.
They tour from St. Louis, Columbus, Manistee,   60   *Like a train-caller*
They tour from Peoria, Davenport, Kankakee.   *in a Union Depot.*
Cars from Concord, Niagara, Boston,
Cars from Topeka, Emporia, and Austin.
Cars from Chicago, Hannibal, Cairo.
Cars from Alton, Oswego, Toledo.   65
Cars from Buffalo, Kokomo, Delphi,
Cars from Lodi, Carmi, Loami.
Ho for Kansas, land that restores us
When houses choke us, and great books bore us!
While I watch the highroad   70
And look at the sky,
While I watch the clouds in amazing grandeur

Roll their legions without rain
Over the blistering Kansas plain—
While I sit by the milestone 75
And watch the sky,
The United States
Goes by.
Listen to the iron-horns, ripping, racking. *To be given very*
Listen to the quack-horns, slack and clacking. 80 *harshly, with a*
Way down the road, trilling like a toad, *snapping, explo-*
Here comes the *dice*-horn, here comes the *vice*-horn, *siveness.*
Here comes the *snarl*-horn, *brawl*-horn, *lewd*-horn,
Followed by the *prude*-horn, bleak and squeaking:—
(Some of them from Kansas, some of them from Kansas.) 85
Here comes the *hod*-horn, *plod*-horn, *sod*-horn,
Nevermore-to-*roam*-horn, *loam*-horn, *home*-horn.
(Some of them from Kansas, some of them from Kansas.) *To be read or*
    Far away the Rachel-Jane *sung, well-nigh in*
    Not defeated by the horns 90 *a whisper.*
    Sings amid a hedge of thorns:—
    "Love and life,
    Eternal youth—
    Sweet, sweet, sweet, sweet,
    Dew and glory, 95
    Love and truth,
    Sweet, sweet, sweet, sweet."
WHILE SMOKE-BLACK FREIGHTS ON THE DOUBLE-TRACKED RAILROAD *Louder and loud-*
DRIVEN AS THOUGH BY THE FOUL FIEND'S OX-GOAD, *er, faster and*
SCREAMING TO THE WEST COAST, SCREAMING TO THE EAST, 100 *faster.*
CARRY OFF A HARVEST, BRING BACK A FEAST,
AND HARVESTING MACHINERY AND HARNESS FOR THE BEAST,
THE HAND-CARS WHIZ, AND RATTLE ON THE RAILS,
THE SUNLIGHT FLASHES ON THE TIN DINNER-PAILS.
And then, in an instant, ye modern men, 105 *In a rolling bass,*
Behold the procession once again, *with increasing*
The United States goes by! *deliberation.*
Listen to the iron-horns, ripping, racking, *With a snapping*
Listen to the *wise*-horn, desperate-to-*advise* horn, *explosiveness.*
Listen to the *fast*-horn, *kill*-horn, *blast*-horn. . . 110
    Far away the Rachel-Jane *To be sung or*
    Not defeated by the horns *read well-nigh in*
    Sings amid a hedge of thorns:— *a whisper.*
    "Love and life,
    Eternal youth, 115
    Sweet, sweet, sweet, sweet,
    Dew and glory,

Love and truth.
Sweet, sweet, sweet, sweet."

The mufflers open on a score of cars   120 *To be bawled in*
With wonderful thunder,   *the   beginning*
CRACK, CRACK, CRACK,   *with a snapping*
                                                            explosiveness, end-
CRACK-CRACK, CRACK-CRACK,   *ing in a languor-*
CRACK, CRACK, CRACK,   *ous chant.*
Listen to the gold-horn . . .   125
Old horn . . .
Cold horn . . .
And all of the tunes, till the night comes down
On hay-stack, and ant-hill, and wind-bitten town.
Then far in the west, as in the beginning,   130 *To be sung to*
Dim in the distance, sweet in retreating,   *exactly the same*
Hark to the faint-horn, quaint-horn, saint-horn,   *whispered tune as*
Hark to the calm-horn, balm-horn, psalm-horn. . . .   *the first five lines.*

They are hunting the goals that they understand:—   *This section be-*
San Francisco and the brown sea-sand.   135 *ginning sonorous-*
My goal is the mystery that beggars win.   *ly, ending in a*
I am caught in the web the night-winds spin,   *languorous whis-*
The edge of the wheat-ridge speaks to me.   *per.*
I talk with the leaves of the mulberry tree.
And now I hear, as I sit all alone   140
In the dusk, by another big Santa-Fé stone,
The souls of the tall corn gathering round
And the gay little souls of the grass in the ground.
Listen to the tale the cottonwood tells.
Listen to the windmills, singing o'er the wells.   145
Listen to the whistling flutes without price
Of myriad prophets out of paradise.
Harken to the wonder
That the night-air carries. . . .
Listen . . . to . . . the . . . whisper . . .   150
Of . . . the . . . prairie . . . fairies
    Singing o'er the fairy plain:—
    "Sweet, sweet, sweet, sweet.   *To the same whis-*
    Love and glory,   *pered tune as the*
                                                            Rachel-Jane song
    Stars and rain,   155 *—but very slowly.*
    Sweet, sweet, sweet, sweet. . . ."

ODES

PERCY BYSSHE SHELLEY
Ode to the West Wind

I

O WILD West Wind, thou breath
    of Autumn's being,
    Thou, from whose unseen
presence the leaves dead
Are driven, like ghosts from an en-
    chanter fleeing,

Yellow, and black, and pale, and
    hectic red
Pestilence-stricken   multitudes: O
    thou,   5
Who chariotest to their dark wintry
    bed

The wingéd seeds, where they lie cold
    and low,
Each like a corpse within its grave,
    until
Thine azure sister of the Spring shall
    blow

Her clarion o'er the dreaming earth,
    and fill   10
(Driving sweet buds like flocks to
    feed in air)
With living hues and odors plain and
    hill:

Wild Spirit, which art moving every-
    where;
Destroyer and preserver; hear, oh,
    hear!

II

Thou on whose stream, 'mid the steep
    sky's commotion,   15

Loose clouds like earth's decaying
    leaves are shed,
Shook from the tangled boughs of
    Heaven and Ocean.

Angels of rain and lightning: there
    are spread
On the blue surface of thine aëry
    surge,
Like the bright hair uplifted from the
    head   20

Of some fierce Mænad, even from the
    dim verge
Of the horizon to the zenith's height,
The locks of the approaching storm.
    Thou dirge

Of the dying year, to which this clos-
    ing night   24
Will be the dome of a vast sepulcher,
Vaulted with all thy congregated
    might

Of vapors, from whose solid atmos-
    phere
Black rain, and fire, and hail will
    burst: oh, hear!

III

Thou who didst waken from his sum-
    mer dreams
The blue Mediterranean, where he
    lay,   30
Lulled by the coil of his crystálline
    streams,

Beside a pumice isle in Baiæ's bay,
And saw in sleep old palaces and
    towers
Quivering within the wave's intenser
    day,

All overgrown with azure moss and
   flowers   35
So sweet, the sense faints picturing
   them! Thou
For whose path the Atlantic's level
   powers

Cleave themselves into chasms, while
   far below
The sea-blooms and the oozy woods
   which wear
The sapless foliage of the ocean,
   know   40

Thy voice, and suddenly grow gray
   with fear,
And tremble and despoil themselves:
   oh, hear!

IV

If I were a dead leaf thou mightest
   bear;
If I were a swift cloud to fly with
   thee;
A wave to pant beneath thy power,
   and share   45

The impulse of thy strength, only less
   free
Than thou, O uncontrollable! If even
I were as in my boyhood, and could
   be

The comrade of thy wanderings over
   Heaven,
As then, when to outstrip thy skyey
   speed   50
Scarce seemed a vision; I would ne'er
   have striven

As thus with thee in prayer in my
   sore need.
Oh, lift me as a wave, a leaf, a cloud!
I fall upon the thorns of life! I bleed!

A heavy weight of hours has chained
   and bowed   55
One too like thee: tameless, and swift
   and proud.

V

Make me thy lyre, even as the forest
   is:
What if my leaves are falling like its
   own!
The tumult of thy mighty harmonies

Will take from both a deep, autumnal
   tone,   60
Sweet though in sadness. Be thou,
   Spirit fierce,
My spirit! Be thou me, impetuous
   one!

Drive my dead thoughts over the
   universe
Like withered leaves to quicken a
   new birth!   64
And, by the incantation of this verse,

Scatter, as from an unextinguished
   hearth
Ashes and sparks, my words among
   mankind!
Be through my lips to unawakened
   earth

The trumpet of a prophecy! O,
   Wind,
If Winter comes, can Spring be far
   behind?   70

JOHN KEATS

Ode on a Grecian Urn

Thou still unravished bride of
    quietness,
    Thou foster-child of silence
      and slow time,
Sylvan historian, who canst thus ex-
    press
A flowery tale more sweetly than
    our rime:
What leaf-fringed legend haunts
    about thy shape   5
Of deities or mortals, or of both,
    In Tempe or the dales of Arcady?
What men or gods are these? What
    maidens loath?
What mad pursuit? What struggle
    to escape?
    What pipes and timbrels? What
      wild ecstasy?   10

Heard melodies are sweet, but those
    unheard
    Are sweeter; therefore, ye soft pipes,
      play on;
Not to the sensual ear, but, more en-
    deared,
    Pipe to the spirit ditties of no tone:
Fair youth, beneath the trees, thou
    canst not leave   15
    Thy song, nor ever can those trees
      be bare;
    Bold Lover, never, never canst
      thou kiss,
Though winning near the goal—yet,
    do not grieve;
    She cannot fade, though thou
      hast not thy bliss,
    For ever wilt thou love, and she be
      fair!   20

Ah, happy, happy boughs! that can-
    not shed
    Your leaves, nor ever bid the Spring
      adieu;
And, happy melodist, unweariéd,
    For ever piping songs for ever new;
More happy love! more happy, happy
    love!   25
    For ever warm and still to be en-
    joyed,
    For ever panting and for ever
    young;
All breathing human passion far
    above,
    That leaves a heart high-sorrowful
    and cloyed,
    A burning forehead, and a parch-
    ing tongue.   30

Who are these coming to the sacri-
    fice?
To what green altar, O mysterious
    priest,
Lead'st thou that heifer lowing at the
    skies,
    And all her silken flanks with gar-
    lands dressed?
What little town by river or sea-
    shore,
Or mountain-built with peaceful
    citadel,   36
    Is emptied of this folk, this pious
    morn?
And, little town, thy street for ever-
    more
    Will silent be; and not a soul to tell
    Why thou are desolate, can e'er
    return.   40

O Attic shape! Fair attitude! with
    brede
    Of marble men and maidens over-
    wrought,

With forest branches and the trodden
    weed;
Thou, silent form, dost tease us out
    of thought
As doth eternity: Cold Pastoral!   45
When old age shall this generation
    waste,

Thou shalt remain, in midst of
    other woe
Than ours, a friend to man, to whom
    thou say'st,
"Beauty is truth, truth beauty,"—
    that is all
Ye know on earth, and all ye
    need to know.   50

WALT WHITMAN

Pioneers! O Pioneers!

COME, my tan-faced children,
    Follow well in order, get your weapons ready,
    Have you your pistols? have you your sharp-edged axes?
    Pioneers! O pioneers!

For we cannot tarry here,   5
We must march my darlings, we must bear the brunt of danger,
We the youthful sinewy races, all the rest on us depend,
    Pioneers! O pioneers!

O you youths, Western youths,
So impatient, full of action, full of manly pride and friendship,   10
Plain I see you Western youths, see you trampling with the foremost,
    Pioneers! O pioneers!

Have the elder races halted?
Do they droop and end their lesson, wearied over there beyond the seas?
We take up the task eternal, and the burden and the lesson,   15
    Pioneers! O pioneers!

All the past we leave behind,
We debouch upon a newer mightier world, varied world,
Fresh and strong the world we seize, world of labor and the march,
    Pioneers! O pioneers!   20

We detachments steady throwing,
Down the edges, through the passes, up the mountains steep,
Conquering, holding, daring, venturing as we go the unknown ways,
    Pioneers! O pioneers!

We primeval forests felling,   25
We the rivers stemming, vexing we and piercing deep the mines within,

We the surface broad surveying, we the virgin soil upheaving,
    Pioneers! O pioneers!

    Colorado men are we,
From the peaks gigantic, from the great sierras and the high plateaus,   30
From the mine and from the gully, from the hunting trail we come,
    Pioneers! O pioneers!

    From Nebraska, from Arkansas,
Central inland race are we, from Missouri, with the continental blood inter-
    vein',
All the hands of comrades clasping, all the Southern, all the Northern,   35
    Pioneers! O pioneers!

    O resistless restless race!
O beloved race in all! O my breast aches with tender love for all!
O I mourn and yet exult, I am rapt with love for all,
    Pioneers! O pioneers!   40

    Raise the mighty mother mistress,
Waving high the delicate mistress, over all the starry mistress (bend your
    heads all),
Raise the fang'd and warlike mistress, stern, impassive, weapon'd mistress,
    Pioneers! O pioneers!

    See my children, resolute children,   45
By those swarms upon our ear we must never yield or falter,
Ages back in ghostly millions frowning there behind us urging,
    Pioneers! O pioneers!

    On and on the compact ranks,
With accessions ever waiting, with the places of the dead quickly fill'd,   50
Through the battle, through defeat, moving yet and never stopping,
    Pioneers! O pioneers!

    O to die advancing on!
Are there some of us to droop and die? has the hour come?
Then upon the march we fittest die, soon and sure the gap is fill'd,   55
    Pioneers! O pioneers!

    All the pulses of the world,
Falling in they beat for us, with the Western movement beat,
Holding single or together, steady moving to the front, all for us,
    Pioneers! O pioneers!   60

    Life's involv'd and varied pageants,
All the forms and shows, all the workmen at their work,
All the seamen and the landsmen, all the masters with their slaves,
    Pioneers! O pioneers!

All the hapless silent lovers,   65
All the prisoners in the prisons, all the righteous and the wicked,
All the joyous, all the sorrowing, all the living, all the dying,
  Pioneers! O pioneers!

  I too with my soul and body,
We, a curious trio, picking, wandering on our way,   70
Through these shores amid the shadows, with the apparitions pressing,
  Pioneers! O pioneers!

  Lo, the darting bowling orb!
Lo, the brother orbs around, all the clustering suns and planets,
All the dazzling days, all the mystic nights with dreams,   75
  Pioneers! O pioneers!

  There are of us, they are with us,
All for primal needed work, while the followers there in embryo wait behind,
We to-day's procession heading, we the route for travel clearing,
  Pioneers! O pioneers!   80

  O you daughters of the West!
O you young and elder daughters! O you mothers and you wives!
Never must you be divided, in our ranks you move united,
  Pioneers! O pioneers!

  Minstrels latent on the prairies!   85
(Shrouded bards of other lands, you may rest, you have done your work,)
Soon I hear you coming warbling, soon you rise and tramp amid us,
  Pioneers! O pioneers!

  Not for delectations sweet,
Not the cushion and the slipper, not the peaceful and the studious,   90
Not the riches safe and palling, not for us the tame enjoyment,
  Pioneers! O pioneers!

  Do the feasters gluttonous feast?
Do the corpulent sleepers sleep? have they lock'd and bolted doors?
Still be ours the diet hard, and the blanket on the ground,   95
  Pioneers! O pioneers!

  Has the night descended?
Was the road of late so toilsome? did we stop discouraged nodding on our
  way?
Yet a passing hour I yield you in your tracks to pause oblivious,
  Pioneers! O pioneers!   100

Till with sound of trumpet,
Far, far off the daybreak call—hark! how loud and clear I hear it wind,
Swift! to the head of the army!—swift! spring to your places,
Pioneers! O pioneers!

CARL SANDBURG

Chicago [1]

Hog Butcher for the World,
Tool Maker, Stacker of Wheat,
Player with Railroads and the Nation's
Freight Handler;
Stormy, husky, brawling,
City of the Big Shoulders: 5

They tell me you are wicked and I believe them, for I have seen your painted
women under the gas lamps luring the farm boys.
And they tell me you are crooked and I answer: Yes, it is true I have seen the
gunmen kill and go free to kill again.
And they tell me you are brutal and my reply is: On the faces of women and
children I have seen the marks of wanton hunger.
And having answered so I turn once more to those who sneer at this my city,
and I give them back the sneer and say to them:
Come and show me another city with lifted head singing so proud to be alive
and coarse and strong and cunning. 10
Flinging magnetic curses amid the toil of piling job on job, here is a tall bold
slugger set vivid against the little soft cities;
Fierce as a dog with tongue lapping for action, cunning as a savage pitted
against the wilderness,
   Bareheaded,
   Shoveling,
   Wrecking, 15
   Planning,
   Building, breaking, rebuilding,

Under the smoke, dust all over his mouth, laughing with white teeth,
Under the terrible burden of destiny laughing as a young man laughs,
Laughing even as an ignorant fighter laughs who has never lost a battle, 20

Bragging and laughing that under his wrist is the pulse, and under his ribs
    the heart of the people,
                Laughing!
Laughing the stormy, husky, brawling laughter of Youth, half-naked, sweat-
    ing, proud to be Hog Butcher, Tool Maker, Stacker of Wheat, Player with
    Railroads and Freight Handler to the Nation.

ALLEN TATE

Ode to the Confederate Dead [1]

Row after row with strict impu-
    nity
    The headstones yield their
names to the element,
The wind whirrs without recollection;
In the riven troughs the splayed
    leaves
Pile up, of nature the casual sacra-
    ment   5
To the seasonal eternity of death,
Then driven by the fierce scrutiny
Of heaven to their business in the vast
    breath,
They sough the rumor of mortality.

Autumn is desolation in the plot   10
Of a thousand acres, where these
    memories grow
From the inexhaustible bodies that
    are not
Dead, but feed the grass row after
    rich row:
Remember now the autumns that
    have gone—
Ambitious November with the hu-
    mors of the year,   15
With a particular zeal for every slab,
Staining the uncomfortable angels
    that rot

[1] From *Poems, 1928-1931*, by Allen Tate. By permission of the publishers, Charles Scribner's Sons, New York.

On the slabs, a wing chipped here, an
    arm there:
The brute curiosity of an angel's stare
Turns you like them to stone,   20
Transforms the heaving air,
Till plunged to a heavier world below
You shift your sea-space blindly,
Heaving, turning like the blind crab.

Dazed by the wind, only the wind
    The leaves flying, plunge   26

You know who have waited by the
    wall
The twilit certainty of an animal;
Those midnight restitutions of the
    blood
You know—the immitigable pines,
    the smoky frieze   30
Of the sky, the sudden call; you know
    the rage—
The cold pool left by the mounting
    flood—
The rage of Zeno and Parmenides.
You who have waited for the angry
    resolution
Of those desires that should be yours
    tomorrow,   35
You know the unimportant shift of
    death
And praise the vision
And praise the arrogant circumstance
Of those who fall
Rank upon rank, hurried beyond de-
    cision—   40
Here by the sagging gate, stopped by
    the wall.

Seeing, seeing only the leaves
Flying, plunge and expire

Turn your eyes to the immoderate
  past
Turn to the inscrutable infantry ris-
  ing   45
Demons out of the earth—they will
  not last.
Stonewall, Stonewall—and the sunken
  fields of hemp
Shiloh, Antietam, Malvern Hill, Bull
  Run.
Lost in that orient of the thick and
  fast
You will curse the setting sun   50

  Cursing only the leaves crying
  Like an old man in a storm

You hear the shout—the crazy hem-
  locks point
With troubled fingers to the silence
  which
Smothers you, a mummy, in time.
  The hound bitch   55
Toothless and dying, in a musty cel-
  lar
Hears the wind only.

  Now that the salt of their blood
Stiffens the saltier oblivion of the sea,
Seals the malignant purity of the
  flood,   60
What shall we, who count our days
  and bow
Our heads with a commemorial woe,
In the ribboned coats of grim felicity,
What shall we say of the bones, un-
  clean
Their verdurous anonymity will
  grow—   65
The ragged arms, the ragged heads
  and eyes

Lost in these acres of the insane
  green?
The grey lean spiders come; they
  come and go;
In a tangle of willows without light
The singular screech-owl's bright   70
Invisible lyric seeds the mind
With the furious murmur of their
  chivalry.

  We shall say only, the leaves
  Flying, plunge and expire

We shall say only, the leaves whisper-
  ing   75
In the improbable mist of nightfall
That flies on multiple wing:
Night is the beginning and the end,
And in between the ends of distrac-
  tion
Waits mute speculation, the patient
  curse   80
That stones the eyes, or like the jag-
  uar leaps
For his own image in a jungle pool,
  his victim.

What shall we say who have knowledge
Carried to the heart? Shall we take
  the act
To the grave? Shall we, more hopeful, set up the grave   85
In the house? The ravenous grave?

                            Leave now
The turnstile and the old stone wall:
The gentle serpent, green in the mul-
  berry bush,
Riots with his tongue through the
  hush—   90
Sentinel of the grave who counts us
  all!

ROBERT BURNS

Willie Brewed a Peck o' Maut

O WILLIE brewed a peck o' maut,
　And Rob and Allan cam to see;
Three blither hearts, that lee-lang night,
　Ye wad na found in Christendie.

Chorus

We are na fou, we're no that fou, 5
　But just a drappie in our ee;
The cock may craw, the day may daw,
　And aye we'll taste the barley bree.

Here are we met, three merry boys.
　Three merry boys, I trow, are we; 10
And mony a night we've merry been,
　And mony mae we hope to be!

It is the moon, I ken her horn,
　That's blinkin' in the lift sae hie;
She shines sae bright to wyle us hame,
　But, by my sooth! she'll wait a wee.

Wha first shall rise to gang awa,
　A cuckold, coward loun is he!
Wha first beside his chair shall fa',
　He is the king among us three! 20

Sweet Afton

FLOW gently, sweet Afton, among thy green braes,
　Flow gently, I'll sing thee a song in thy praise;
My Mary's asleep by thy murmuring stream,
Flow gently, sweet Afton, disturb not her dream.

Thou stock-dove whose echo resounds through the glen, 5
Ye wild whistling blackbirds in yon thorny den,
Thou green-crested lapwing, thy screaming forbear,
I charge you disturb not my slumbering fair.

How lofty, sweet Afton, thy neighboring hills,
Far marked with the courses of clear winding rills; 10
There daily I wander as noon rises high,
My flocks and my Mary's sweet cot in my eye.

How pleasant thy banks and green valleys below,
Where wild in the woodlands the primroses blow;
There oft as mild ev'ning weeps over the lea, 15
The sweet-scented birk shades my Mary and me.

Thy crystal stream, Afton, how lovely it glides,
And winds by the cot where my Mary resides;
How wanton thy waters her snowy feet lave,
As gathering sweet flow'rets she stems thy clear wave. 20

Flow gently, sweet Afton, among thy
    green braes,
Flow gently, sweet river, the theme of
    my lays;
My Mary's asleep by thy murmuring
    stream,
Flow gently, sweet Afton, disturb not
    her dream.

Auld Lang Syne

SHOULD auld acquaintance be for-
    got,
    And never brought to min'?
Should auld acquaintance be forgot,
    And auld lang syne?

Chorus

For auld lang syne, my dear,   5
    For auld lang syne,
We'll tak a cup o' kindness yet,
    For auld lang syne.

And surely ye'll be your pint-stowp,
    And surely I'll be mine;   10
And we'll tak a cup o' kindness yet
    For auld lang syne.

We twa hae run about the braes,
    And pu'd the gowans fine;
But we've wandered mony a weary
    foot   15
    Sin' auld lang syne.

We twa hae paidled i' the burn,
    From morning sun till dine;
But seas between us braid hae roared
    Sin' auld lang syne.   20

And there's hand, my trusty fiere,
    And gie's a hand o' thine;
And we'll tak a right guid-willie
    waught,
    For auld lang syne.

ALFRED, LORD TENNYSON

Break, Break, Break

BREAK, break, break,
    On thy cold gray stones, O Sea!
    And I would that my tongue
could utter
    The thoughts that arise in me.

O well for the fisherman's boy,   5
    That he shouts with his sister at
        play!
O well for the sailor lad,
    That he sings in his boat on the
        bay!

And the stately ships go on
    To their haven under the hill;   10
But O for the touch of a vanished
        hand,
    And the sound of a voice that is
        still!

Break, break, break,
    At the foot of thy crags, O Sea!
But the tender grace of a day that is
        dead   15
    Will never come back to me.

The Splendor Falls

THE splendor falls on castle walls
    And snowy summits old in
        story;
The long light shakes across the
        lakes,
    And the wild cataract leaps in
        glory.
Blow, bugle, blow, set the wild echoes
        flying,   5
Blow, bugle; answer, echoes, dying,
        dying, dying.

O hark, O hear! how thin and clear,
  And thinner, clearer, farther go-
    ing!
O sweet and far from cliff and scar
The horns of Elfland faintly blow-
    ing! 10
Blow, let us hear the purple glens re-
    plying,
Blow, bugle; answer, echoes, dying,
    dying, dying.

O love, they die in yon rich sky,
  They faint on hill or field or river
Our echoes roll from soul to soul, 15
  And grow for ever and for ever.
Blow, bugle, blow, set the wild echoes
    flying,
And answer, echoes, answer, dying,
    dying, dying.

⌇⌇⌇⌇⌇⌇⌇⌇⌇⌇⌇⌇⌇⌇⌇⌇

ROBERT BROWNING

Marching Along

K ENTISH Sir Byng stood for his
    King,
    Bidding the crop-headed Par-
liament swing:
And, pressing a troop unable to stoop
And see the rogues flourish and hon-
    est folk droop,
Marched them along, fifty-score
    strong, 5
Great-hearted gentlemen, singing this
    song.

God for King Charles! Pym and
    such carles
To the Devil that prompts 'em their
    treasonous parles!
Cavaliers, up! Lips from the cup,

Hands from the pasty, nor bite take
    nor sup 10
Till you're—

  CHO.—Marching along, fifty-score
      strong,
    Great-hearted gentlemen,
      singing this song.

Hampden to hell, and his obsequies'
    knell.
Serve Hazelrig, Fiennes, and young
    Harry as well!
England, good cheer! Rupert is near!
Kentish and loyalists, keep we not
    here, 16

  CHO.—Marching along, fifty-score
      strong,
    Great-hearted gentlemen,
      singing this song?

Then, God for King Charles! Pym
    and his snarls
To the Devil that pricks on such pes-
    tilent carles! 20
Hold by the right, you double your
    might;
So, onward to Nottingham, fresh for
    the fight,

  CHO.—Marching along, fifty-score
      strong,
    Great-hearted gentlemen,
      singing this song!

⌇⌇⌇⌇⌇⌇⌇⌇⌇⌇⌇⌇⌇⌇⌇⌇

CHRISTINA ROSSETTI

When I Am Dead, My Dearest

W HEN I am dead, my dearest,
    Sing no sad songs for me;
    Plant thou no roses at my
head,

Nor shady cypress tree:
Be the green grass above me 5
With showers and dewdrops wet:
And if thou wilt, remember,
And if thou wilt, forget.

I shall not see the shadows,
I shall not see the rain; 10
I shall not hear the nightingale
Sing on as if in pain:
And dreaming through the twilight
That doth not rise nor set,
Haply I may remember, 15
And haply may forget.

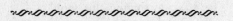

F. W. BOURDILLON

The Night Has a Thousand Eyes

THE night has a thousand eyes,
And the day but one;
Yet the light of the bright
world dies
With the dying sun.

The mind has a thousand eyes, 5
And the heart but one;
Yet the light of a whole life dies
When love is done.

JOHN ADDINGTON SYMONDS

Gaudeamus Igitur [1]

LET us live, then, and be glad
While young life's before us!
After youthful pastime had,
After old age hard and sad,
Earth will slumber o'er us. 5

[1] From a medieval Latin student's song.

Where are they who in this world,
Ere we kept, were keeping?
Go ye to the gods above;
Go to hell; inquire thereof.
They are not; they're sleeping. 10

Brief is life, and brevity
Briefly shall be ended.
Death comes like a whirlwind
strong,
Bears us with his blast along;
None shall be defended. 15

Live this university,
Men that learning nourish;
Live each member of the same,
Long live all that bear its name;
Let them ever flourish! 20

Live the commonwealth also,
And the men that guide it!
Live our town in strength and
health,
Founders, patrons, by whose
wealth
We are here provided! 25

Live all girls! A health to you
Melting maids and beauteous!
Live the wives and women too,
Gentle, loving, tender, true,
Good, industrious, duteous! 30

Perish cares that pule and pine!
Perish envious blamers!
Die the Devil, thine and mine!
Die the starch-necked Philis-
tine!
Scoffers and defamers! 35

ELEGIES

MATTHEW ARNOLD

Rugby Chapel

November, 1857

COLDLY, sadly descends
    The autumn - evening.   The
    field
Strewn with its dank yellow drifts
Of withered leaves, and the elms,
Fade into dimness apace,   5
Silent;—hardly a shout
From a few boys late at their play!
The lights come out in the street,
In the school-room windows;—but
    cold,
Solemn, unlighted, austere,   10
Through the gathering darkness, arise
The chapel-walls, in whose bound
Thou, my father! art laid.

There thou dost lie, in the gloom
Of the autumn evening. But ah!   15
That word, *gloom,* to my mind
Brings thee back, in the light
Of thy radiant vigor, again;
In the gloom of November we passed
Days not dark at thy side;   20
Seasons impaired not the ray
Of thy buoyant cheerfulness clear.
Such thou wast! and I stand
In the autumn evening, and think
Of bygone autumns with thee.   25

Fifteen years have gone round
Since thou arosest to tread,
In the summer-morning, the road
Of death, at a call unforeseen,
Sudden. For fifteen years,   30
We who till then in thy shade
Rested as under the boughs

Of a mighty oak, have endured
Sunshine and rain as we might,
Bare, unshaded, alone,   35
Lacking the shelter of thee.

O strong soul, by what shore
Tarriest thou now? For that force,
Surely, has not been left vain!
Somewhere, surely, afar,   40
In the sounding labor-house vast
Of being, is practiced that strength,
Zealous, beneficent, firm!

Yes, in some far-shining sphere,
Conscious or not of the past,   45
Still thou performest the word
Of the Spirit in whom thou dost
    live—
Prompt, unwearied, as here!
Still thou upraisest with zeal
The humble good from the ground,
Sternly repressest the bad!   51
Still, like a trumpet, dost rouse
Those who with half-open eyes
Tread the border-land dim
'Twixt vice and virtue; reviv'st,   55
Succorest!—this was thy work,
This was thy life upon earth.

What is the course of the life
Of mortal men on the earth?—
Most men eddy about   60
Here and there—eat and drink,
Chatter and love and hate,
Gather and squander, are raised
Aloft, are hurled in the dust,
Striving, blindly, achieving   65
Nothing; and then they die—
Perish;—and no one asks
Who or what they have been,
More than he asks what waves,
In the moonlit solitudes mild   70

Of the midmost Ocean, have swelled,
Foamed for a moment, and gone.

And there are some, whom a thirst
Ardent, unquenchable, fires,
Not with the crowd to be spent,　75
Not without aim to go round
In an eddy of purposeless dust,
Effort unmeaning and vain.
Ah yes! some of us strive
Not without action to die　80
Fruitless, but something to snatch
From dull oblivion, nor all
Glut the devouring grave!
We, we have chosen our path—
Path to a clear-purposed goal,　85
Path of advance!—but it leads
A long, steep journey, through sunk
Gorges, o'er mountains in snow.
Cheerful, with friends, we set forth—
Then, on the height, comes the storm.
Thunder crashes from rock　91
To rock, the cataracts reply,
Lightnings dazzle our eyes.
Roaring torrents have breached
The track, the stream-bed descends　95
In the place where the wayfarer once
Planted his footstep—the spray
Boils o'er its borders! aloft
The unseen snow-beds dislodge
Their hanging ruin; alas,　100
Havoc is made in our train!
Friends, who set forth at our side,
Falter, are lost in the storm.
We, we only are left!　104
With frowning foreheads, with lips
Sternly compressed, we strain on,
On—and at nightfall at last
Come to the end of our way,
To the lonely inn 'mid the rocks;
Where the gaunt and taciturn host　110
Stands on the threshold, the wind
Shaking his thin white hairs—
Holds his lantern to scan
Our storm-beat figures, and asks:

Whom in our party we bring?　115
Whom we have left in the snow?

Sadly we answer: We bring
Only ,ourselves! we lost
Sight of the rest in the storm.　119
Hardly ourselves we fought through,
Stripped, without friends, as we are.
Friends, companions, and train,
The avalanche swept from our side.

But thou wouldst not *alone*
Be saved, my father! *alone*　125
Conquer and come to thy goal,
Leaving the rest in the wild.
We were weary, and we
Fearful, and we in our march
Fain to drop down and to die.　130
Still thou turnedst, and still
Beckonedst the trembler, and still
Gavest the weary thy hand.

If, in the paths of the world,
Stones might have wounded thy feet,
Toil or dejection have tried　136
Thy spirit, of that we saw
Nothing—to us thou wast still
Cheerful, and helpful, and firm!
Therefore to thee it was given　140
Many to save with thyself;
And, at the end of thy day,
O faithful shepherd; to come,
Bringing thy sheep in thy hand.

And through thee I believe　145
In the noble and great who are gone;
Pure souls honored and blest
By former ages, who else—
Such, so soulless, so poor,
Is the race of men whom I see—　150
Seemed but a dream of the heart,
Seemed but a cry of desire.
Yes! I believe that there lived
Others like thee in the past,
Not like the men of the crowd　155

Who all round me to-day
Bluster or cringe, and make life
Hideous, and arid, and vile;
But souls tempered with fire,
Fervent, heroic, and good   160
Helpers and friends of mankind.

Servants of God!—or sons
Shall I not call you? because
Not as servants ye knew
Your Father's innermost mind,   165
His, who unwillingly sees
One of his little ones lost—
Yours is the praise, if mankind
Hath not as yet in its march
Fainted, and fallen, and died!   170

See! In the rocks of the world
Marches the host of mankind,
A feeble, wavering line.
Where are they tending?—A God
Marshaled them, gave them their
    goal.   175
Ah, but the way is so long!
Years they have been in the wild!
Sore thirst plagues them; the rocks,
Rising all round, overawe;
Factions divide them, their host   180
Threatens to break, to dissolve.
—Ah! keep, keep them combined!
Else, of the myriads who fill
That army, not one shall arrive;
Sole they shall stray; in the rocks 185
Stagger for ever in vain,
Die one by one in the waste.

Then, in such hour of need
Of your fainting, dispirited race,
Ye, like angels, appear,   190
Radiant with ardor divine!
Beacons of hope, ye appear!
Languor is not in your heart,
Weakness is not in your word,

Weariness not on your brow.   195
Ye alight in our van! at your voice,
Panic, despair, flee away.
Ye move through the ranks, recall
The stragglers, refresh the outworn,
Praise, re-inspire the brave!   200
Order, courage, return.
Eyes rekindling, and prayers,
Follow your steps as ye go.
Ye fill up the gaps in our files,
Strengthen the wavering line,   205
Stablish, continue our march,
On, to the bound of the waste,
On, to the City of God.

DANTE GABRIEL ROSSETTI
My Sister's Sleep

SHE fell asleep on Christmas Eve.
    At length the long-ungranted
        shade
Of weary eyelids overweighed
The pain nought else might yet re-
    lieve.

Our mother, who had leaned all day 5
    Over the bed from chime to chime,
    Then raised herself for the first
        time,
And as she sat her down, did pray.

Her little work-table was spread
    With work to finish. For the glare
    Made by her candle, she had care 11
To work some distance from the bed.

Without, there was a cold moon up,
    Of winter radiance sheer and thin;
    The hollow halo it was in   15
Was like an icy crystal cup.

Through the small room, with subtle
    sound
  Of flame, by vents the fireshine
    drove
  And reddened. In its dim alcove
The mirror shed a clearness round. 20

I had been sitting up some nights,
  And my tired mind felt weak and
    blank;
  Like a sharp strengthening wine it
    drank
The stillness and the broken lights.

Twelve struck. That sound, by
  dwindling years   25
  Heard in each hour, crept off; and
    then
  The ruffled silence spread again,
Like water that a pebble stirs.

Our mother rose from where she sat:
  Her needles, as she laid them down,
  Met lightly, and her silken gown 31
Settled: no other noise than that.

"Glory unto the Newly Born!"
  So, as said angels, she did say;
  Because we were in Christmas Day,
Though it would still be long till
    morn.   36

Just then in the room over us
  There was a pushing back of chairs,

As some who had sat unawares
So late, now heard the hour, and rose.

With anxious softly-stepping haste 41
  Our mother went where Margaret
    lay,
  Fearing the sounds o'erhead—
    should they
Have broken her long watched-for
    rest!

She stooped an instant, calm, and
    turned;   45
  But suddenly turned back again;
  And all her features seemed in pain
With woe, and her eyes gazed and
    yearned.

For my part, I but hid my face,
  And held my breath, and spoke no
    word: 50
  There was none spoken; but I heard
The silence for a little space.

Our mother bowed herself and wept:
  And both my arms fell, and I said,
  "God knows I knew that she was
    dead."   55
And there, all white, my sister slept.

Then kneeling, upon Christmas morn
  A little after twelve o'clock,
  We said, ere the first quarter struck,
"Christ's blessing on the newly
    born!"   60

VACHEL LINDSAY

The Eagle That Is Forgotten [1]

(John P. Altgeld. Born December 30, 1847; died March 12, 1902)

Sleep softly . . . eagle forgotten . . . under the stone.
Time has its way with you there, and the clay has its own.

"We have buried him now," thought your foes, and in secret rejoiced.
They made a brave show of their mourning, their hatred unvoiced.
They had snarled at you, barked at you, foamed at you day after day,   5
Now you were ended. They praised you, . . . and laid you away.

The others that mourned you in silence and terror and truth,
The widow bereft of her crust, and the boy without youth,
The mocked and the scorned and the wounded, the lame and the poor
That should have remembered forever, . . . remember no more.   10

Where are those lovers of yours, on what name do they call
The lost, that in armies wept over your funeral pall?
They call on the names of a hundred high-valiant ones,
A hundred white eagles have risen the sons of your sons,
The zeal in their wings is a zeal that your dreaming began   15
The valor that wore out your soul in the service of man.

Sleep softly, . . . eagle forgotten, . . . under the stone,
Time has its way with you there and the clay has its own.
Sleep on, O brave-hearted, O wise man, that kindled the flame—
To live in mankind is far more than to live in a name,   20
To live in mankind, far, far more . . . than to live in a name.

[1] From *Collected Poems* by Vachel Lindsay. By permission of The Macmillan Company, publishers.

JAMES STEPHENS
Deirdre [1]

D<small>O</small> not let any woman read this
verse!
　　It is for men, and after them
their sons,
And their sons' sons!

The time comes when our hearts
sink utterly;
When we remember Deirdre and her
tale,　　　　　　　　　　5
And that her lips are dust.

Once she did tread the earth: men
took her hand;
They looked into her eyes and said
their say,
And she replied to them.

More than two thousand years it is
since she　　　　　　　　10
Was beautiful: she trod the waving
grass;
She saw the clouds.

Two thousand years! The grass is
still the same;
The clouds as lovely as they were that
time
When Deirdre was alive.　　　　15

But there has been again no woman
born
Who was so beautiful; not one so
beautiful
Of all the women born.

---

[1] From *Collected Poems* (1930). By permission of The Macmillan Company, publishers.

Let all men go apart and mourn together!
No man can ever love her! Not a
man　　　　　　　　　　20
Can dream to be her lover!

No man can bend before her! No
man say—
What could one say to her? There
are no words
That one could say to her!

Now she is but a story that is
told　　　　　　　　　　25
Beside the fire! No man can ever be
The friend of that poor queen!

A. E. HOUSMAN
To an Athlete Dying Young

T<small>HE</small> time you won your town the
race
　　We chaired you through the
market-place;
Man and boy stood cheering by,
And home we brought you shoulder-
high.

Today, the road all runners come,　5
Shoulder-high we bring you home,
And set you at your threshold down,
Townsman of a stiller town.

Smart lad, to slip betimes away
From fields where glory does not
    stay,   10
And early though the laurel grows
It withers quicker than the rose.

Eyes the shady night has shut
Cannot see the record cut,
And silence sounds no worse than
    cheers   15
After earth has stopped the ears:

Now you will not swell the rout
Of lads that wore their honors out,
Runners whom renown outran
And the name died before the
    man.   20

So set, before its echoes fade,
The fleet foot on the sill of shade,
And hold to the low lintel up
The still-defended challenge-cup.

And round that early-laureled head 25
Will flock to gaze the strengthless
    dead,
And find unwithered on its curls
The garland briefer than a girl's.

ROBERT FROST

A Soldier [1]

HE IS that fallen lance that lies as
    hurled,
    That lies unlifted now, come
    dew, come rust,
But still lies pointed as it plowed the
    dust.
If we who sight along it round the
    world,
See nothing worthy to have been its
    mark,   5
It is because like men we look too
    near,
Forgetting that as fitted to the sphere,
Our missiles always make too short an
    arc.
They fall, they rip the grass, they in-
    tersect
The curve of earth, and striking,
    break their own;   10
They make us cringe for metal-point
    on stone.
But this we know, the obstacle that
    checked
And tripped the body, shot the spirit
    on
Further than target ever showed or
    shone.

[1] From Robert Frost's *Collected Poems*
(1939). Henry Holt and Company.

LIGHTER LYRICS

THOMAS MOORE
The Time I've Lost in Wooing

THE time I've lost in wooing,
 In watching and pursuing
 The light that lies
In woman's eyes,
Has been my heart's undoing.   5

Tho' wisdom oft has sought me,
I scorn'd the lore she brought me,
 My only books
 Were women's looks,
And folly's all they taught me.   10

Her smile when Beauty granted,
I hung with gaze enchanted,
 Like him the sprite
 Whom maids by night
Oft meet in glen that's haunted.   15

Like him, too, Beauty won me;
But when the spell was on me,
 If once their ray
 Was turn'd away,
O! winds could not outrun me.   20

And are those follies going?
And is my proud heart growing
 Too cold or wise
 For brilliant eyes
Again to set it glowing?   25

No—vain, alas! th'endeavor
From bonds so sweet to sever;—
 Poor Wisdom's chance
 Against a glance
Is now as weak as ever.   30

LEIGH HUNT
Rondeau

JENNY kissed me when we met,
 Jumping from the chair she sat
 in;
Time, you thief, who love to get
Sweets into your list, put that in:
Say I'm weary, say I'm sad,   5
 Say that health and wealth have
 missed me,
Say I'm growing old, but add,
 Jenny kissed me!

NATHANIEL PARKER WILLIS
Love in a Cottage

THEY may talk of love in a cot-
 tage,
 And bowers of trellised vine,—
Of nature bewitchingly simple,
 And milkmaids half divine;
They may talk of the pleasure of
 sleeping   5
In the shade of a spreading tree,
And a walk in the fields at morning
 By the side of a footstep free.

But give me a sly flirtation
 By the light of a chandelier,   1c
With music to play in the pauses,
 And nobody very near:
Or a seat on a silken sofa,
 With a glass of pure old wine,
And mamma too blind to discover 15
 The small white hand in mine.

Your love in a cottage is hungry,
　Your vine is a nest for flies,
Your milkmaid shocks the Graces,
　And simplicity talks of pies.　20
You lie down to your shady slumber
　And awake with a bug in your ear,
And your damsel that walks in the
　　morning
　Is shod like a mountaineer.

True love is at home on a carpet,　25
　And mightily likes his ease,
And true love has an eye for a dinner,
　And starves beneath shady trees.
His wing is the fan of a lady,
　His foot's an invisible thing,　30
And his arrow is tipped with a jewel
　And shot from a silver string.

THOMAS HOOD, JR.

A Letter of Advice

Close to being a double Ballade.

WHEN you love—as all men
　　will—
　　Sing the theme of your de-
votion,
Sue—and vow—and worship still—
　Overflow with deep emotion,
Bow to Cupid's sweet decrees,　5
　Lightly wear the happy fetter,
Bend the knee and plead! But please,
　Do not write your love a letter!

Ah! most tempting it may be:　9
　Ink flows free—and pens will write,
And your passion fain you'd see
　Plainly mapped in black and white.
Yet refrain from shedding ink,
　If you can:—'tis wiser—better.
Ere you pen a sentence, think!　15
　Do not write your love a letter.

Hearts may cool and views may
　　change—
　Other scenes may seem inviting,
But a heart can't safely range
　If committed 'tis to writing.　20
What you've written is a writ,
　Holds you closely as a debtor.
Will she spare you? Not a bit!
　Do not write your love a letter!

Think of Breach of Promise cause,　25
　Think of barristers provoking,
Leading you to slips and flaws,
　Turning all your love to joking.
If you've written aught, they'll be
　Safe to find it as a setter—　30
Then you'll wish you'd hearkened
　　me—
　Do not write your love a letter!

Oh, those letters read in Court!
　How the tender things seem stupid!
How deep feeling seems but sport!　35
　How young Momus trips up Cu-
　　pid!
Take my warning then—or soon,
　O'er your folly you'll be fretter,
Saying, "Why, poor, foolish spoon,
　Did I write my love a letter?"　40

FREDERICK
LOCKER-LAMPSON

A Terrible Infant

I RECOLLECT a nurse call'd Ann
　Who carried me about the grass,
　And one fine day a fine young
man
　Came up and kiss'd the pretty lass

She did not make the least objection!
　Thinks I, "Aha!　　　　　　6
　When I can talk I'll tell Mamma!"—
And that's my earliest recollection.

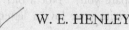

W. E. HENLEY

Ballade Made in the Hot Weather

OUNTAINS that frisk and
　　　sprinkle
　The moss they overspill;
Grass that the breezes crinkle;
　The wheel beside the mill,
　With its wet, weedy frill;　　5
Wind-shadows in the wheat;
A water-cart in the street;
　The fringe of foam that girds
An islet's ferneries;
　A green sky's minor thirds—　10
To live, I think of these!

Of ice and glass the tinkle,
　Pellucid, silver-shrill;
Peaches without a wrinkle;
　Cherries and snow, at will　　15
　From china bowls that fill
The senses with a sweet
Incuriousness of heat;
　A melon's dripping sherds;
Cream-clotted strawberries;　　20
　Dusk dairies set with curds—
To live, I think of these!

Vale-lily and periwinkle;
　Wet stone-crop on the sill;
The look of leaves a-twinkle　　25
　With windlets clear and still;
　The feel of a forest rill
That wimples fresh and fleet

About one's naked feet;
　The muzzles of drinking herds;　30
Lush flags and bulrushes;
　The chirp of rain-bound birds—
To live, I think of these!

Envoy

Dark aisles, new packs of cards,
Mermaidens' tails, cool swards,　　35
　Dawn dews and starlit seas,
White marbles, whiter words—
　To live, I think of these!

The Villanelle　

A dainty thing's the Villanelle.
　Sly, musical, a jewel in rime,
It serves its purpose passing well.

A double-clappered silver bell
　That must be made to clink in
　　chime,　　5
A dainty thing's the Villanelle;

And if you wish to flute a spell,
　Or ask a meeting 'neath the lime,
It serves its purpose passing well.

You must not ask of it the swell　10
　Of organs grandiose and sublime—
A dainty thing's the Villanelle;

And, filled with sweetness as a shell
　Is filled with sound, and launched
　　in time,
It serves its purpose passing well.　15

Still fair to see and good to smell
　As in the quaintness of its prime,
A dainty thing's the Villanelle,
It serves its purpose passing well.

AUSTIN DOBSON

The Ballade of Prose and Rhyme

Double refrain

WHEN the ways are heavy with
    mire and rut,
    In November fogs, in De-
cember snows,
When the North Wind howls, and
    the doors are shut,—
    There is place and enough for the
    pains of prose;
    But whenever a scent from the
    whitethorn blows,   5
And the jasmine-stars at the casement
    climb,
    And a Rosalind-face at the lattice
    shows,
Then hey!—for the ripple of laughing
    rhyme!

When the brain gets dry as an empty
    nut,
    When the reason stands on its
    squarest toes,   10
When the mind (like a beard) has a
    "formal cut,"—
    There is place and enough for the
    pains of prose;
    But whenever the May-blood stirs
    and glows,
And the young year draws to the
    "golden prime,"
    And Sir Romeo sticks in his ear a
    rose,   15
Then hey!—for the ripple of laughing
    rhyme!

In a theme where the thoughts have
    a pedant strut,
    In a changing quarrel of "Ayes"
    and "Noes,"

In a starched procession of "If" and
    "But,"—
    There is place and enough for the
    pains of prose;   20
    But wherever a soft glance softer
    grows,
And the light hours dance to the
    trysting-time,
    And the secret is told "that no one
    knows,"
Then hey!—for the ripple of laughing
    rhyme!

Envoy

In the work-a-day world, for its needs
    and woes,   25
There is place and enough for the
    pains of prose;
But whenever the May-bells clash and
    chime,
Then hey!—for the ripple of laughing
    rhyme!

DANTE GABRIEL ROSSETTI

The Ballad of Dead Ladies

From François Villon

TELL me now in what hidden
    way is
    Lady Flora tne lovely Ro-
man?
Where's Hipparchia, and where is
    Thaïs,
    Neither of them the fairer woman?
    Where is Echo, beheld of no
    man,   5

Only heard on river and mere,—
  She whose beauty was more than
    human? . . .
But where are the snows of yester-
    year?

Where's Héloïse, the learned nun,
  For whose sake Abeillard, I
    ween,   10
Lost manhood and put priesthood on?
  (From Love he won such dule and
    teen!)
  And where, I pray you, is the
    Queen
Who willed that Buridan should steer
  Sewed in a sack's mouth down the
    Seine? . . .   15
But where are the snows of yester-
    year?

White Queen Blanche, like a queen
    of lilies,
  With a voice like any mermaiden,—
Bertha Broadfoot, Beatrice, Alice,
  And Ermengarde the lady of
    Maine,—   20
  And that good Joan whom English-
    men
At Rouen doomed and burned her
    there,—
  Mother of God, where are they
    then? . . .
But where are the snows of yester-
    year?

Nay, never ask this week, fair lord, 25
  Where they are gone, nor yet this
    year,
Except with this for an overword.—
  "But where are the snows of yester-
    year?"

E. B. WHITE

The Twentieth Century Gets Through [1]

The Twentieth Century Limited, First Time
It Has Reached City This Winter Covered with
Icicles. It Forged Its Way Through the Bliz-
zards Upstate and in the West. Mae Murray is
Pictured Standing Beside the Train.—*Caption
of photograph in The World* (New York City).

THE storm king whistled from
    out the North
    As the crack old Limited train
set forth,
With a hey nonny nonny.

The snow blew strong through the
    long, long night,
And settled on objects left and
    right,   5
But the Twentieth Century ploughed
    on through
As a limited train is supposed to do,
With Buffalo, Syracuse, Canastota,
Beneath more snow than their usual
    quota,
  And a hey nonny nonny.   10

From the chilly blast and the raging
    gale,
The Century gathered a coat of mail,
And through the blizzard it plunged
    and reared
With ice for whiskers, snow for a
    beard,
Through miles of sleet and hours of
    snowing   15
There was one bright thought that
    kept it going:

[1] From *The Fox of Peapack and Other Poems.* Harper & Brothers, 1938, by permission.

"If I get to New York in a great big
    hurry
"They'll take my picture with sweet
    Mae Murray,
  "With a hey nonny nonny,
  And a mae murray murray."   20

That was the trend of the Century's
    thought
As on through the fearful night it
    fought:
"I couldn't keep on through the Mo-
    hawk Valley
"For Lillian Gish or Marion Talley, .
"But a blizzard to me is the veriest
    flurry   25
"If it leads to a photo with Mistress
    Murray,
  "With a mae murray murray."

So the Century train, with a sob and
    a shiver,
Continued its course down the Hud-
    son River,
And weary from battling in storm
    and stress,   30
Pulled in and was met by the daily
    press,
And there, sure enough, looking
    warm and furry,
Was the dear little figure of Mistress
    Murray
Who, laying a hand on the Century's
    ice,
Appeared in all papers in less than a
    trice.   35
  With a mae murray murray.

Now here is a thing that I'm anxious
    to know
In the matter of pictures of ice and
    snow:
Assuming that turn-about *is* fair play,
Would photographs work in the
    opposite way?   40
Suppose Mae Murray came out of the
    West
With snow in her hair and ice on her
    chest,
With frost on her eyelid, sleet on her
    nose,
Could she make the Twentieth Cen-
    tury pose?

Would they take a picture of just
    those two,   45
Miss Murray's face all chapped and
    blue?
With the caption: "Girl Comes
    Grimly Through"?
Would the New York Central be
    quick to send
The cream of its trains to the side of
    a friend
Arriving in town all cold and
    shaken   50
And ready to have her picture taken?
  With a hey nonny nonny?

And unless they would, which I
    gravely doubt,
Why, what are these pictures all
    about?
  With a mae murray murray?   55

FRANKLIN P. ADAMS

Ad Leuconoen [1]

IT is not right for you to know, so
do not ask, Leuconoë,
How long a life the gods may
give or ever we are gone away;

[1] From *Tobogganing on Parnassus,* by Franklin P. Adams, copyright 1911, by Doubleday & Company, Inc. Trans. from Horace.

Try not to read the Final Page, the
ending colophonian,
Trust not the gypsy's tea-leaves, nor
the prophets Babylonian,
Better to have what is to come enshrouded in obscurity   5
Than to be certain of the sort and
length of our futurity.
Why, even as I monologue on wisdom and longevity
How Time has flown! Spear some
of it!
The longest life is brevity.

SATIRE

ARTHUR HUGH CLOUGH

The Latest Decalogue

Thou shalt have one God only; who
  Would be at the expense of
  two?
No graven images may be
Worshiped, except the currency:
Swear not at all; for, for thy curse 5
Thine enemy is none the worse:
At church on Sunday to attend
Will serve to keep the world thy
  friend:
Honor thy parents: that is, all
From whom advancement may be-
  fall;   10
Thou shalt not kill; but need'st not
  strive
Officiously to keep alive:
Do not adultery commit;
Advantage rarely comes of it:
Thou shalt not steal; an empty feat, 15
When it's so lucrative to cheat:
Bear not false witness; let the lie
Have time on its own wings to fly:
Thou shalt not covet, but tradition
Approves all forms of competition. 20

EDWIN ARLINGTON ROBINSON

Miniver Cheevy [1]

Miniver Cheevy, child of scorn,
  Grew lean while he assailed
  the seasons;
He wept that he was ever born,
  And he had reasons.

[1] Copyright, Charles Scribner's Sons. By permission of the publishers.

Miniver loved the days of old   5
  When swords were bright and
  steeds were prancing;
The vision of a warrior bold
  Would set him dancing.

Miniver sighed for what was not,
  And dreamed, and rested from his
  labors;   10
He dreamed of Thebes and Camelot,
  And Priam's neighbors.

Miniver mourned the ripe renown
  That made so many a name so
  fragrant;
He mourned Romance, now on the
  town,   15
  And Art, a vagrant.

Miniver loved the Medici,
  Albeit he had never seen one;
He would have sinned incessantly
  Could he have been one.   20

Miniver cursed the commonplace
  And eyed a khaki suit with loath-
  ing;
He missed the mediæval grace
  Of iron clothing.

Miniver scorned the gold he sought,
  But sore annoyed was he without
  it;   26
Miniver thought, and thought, and
  thought,
  And thought about it.

Miniver Cheevy, born too late,
  Scratched his head and kept on
  thinking;   30
Miniver coughed, and called it fate,
  And kept on drinking.

~~~~~~~~~~~~~~~~~~~~~~~~

ROBERT BURNS

From *Lines to John Lapraik*

I AM nae poet, in a sense,
　　But just a rimer, like, by chance,
　　An' hae to learning nae pretense,
　　Yet what the matter?
Whene'er my Muse does on me
　　glance,   5
　　　　I jingle at her.

Your critic-folk may cock their nose,
And say "How can you e'er propose,
You wha ken hardly verse frae prose,
　　To mak a sang?"   10
But, by your leaves, my learnéd foes,
　　Ye're maybe wrang.

What's a' your jargon o' your schools,
Your Latin names for horns an'
　　stools;
If honest nature made you fools,   15
　　What sairs [1] your grammars?
Ye'd better ta'en up spades and
　　shools,[2]
　　Or knappin'-hammers.[3]

A set o' dull conceited hashes [4]
Confuse their brains in college
　　classes!   20
They gang in stirks,[5] and come out
　　asses,
　　　　Plain truth to speak;

[1] Serves.
[2] Shovels.
[3] Hammers for breaking stone.
[4] Fools.
[5] Young bullocks.

An' syne [6] they think to climb Parnassus
　　By dint o' Greek!

Gie me ae spark o' nature's fire,   25
That's a' the learning I desire;
Then tho' I drudge thro' dub an' mire
　　At pleugh or cart,
My Muse, though hamely in attire,
　　May touch the heart.   30

~~~~~~~~~~~~~~~~~~~~~~~~

BERT LESTON TAYLOR

Reform in Our Town [7]

THERE was a man in Our Town
　　And Jimson was his name,
　　Who cried, "Our civic government
Is honeycombed with shame."
He called us neighbors in and said, 5
　　"By Graft we're overrun.
Let's have a general cleaning up,
　　As other towns have done."

The citizens of Our Town
　　Responded to the call;   10
Beneath the banner of Reform
　　We gathered one and all.
We sent away for men expert
　　In hunting civic sin,
To ask these practised gentlemen   15
　　Just how we should begin.

The experts came to Our Town
　　And told us how 'twas done.

[6] Then.
[7] From *A Line o' Verse or Two*, by Bert Leston Taylor. Reprinted here by permission of the author's literary executors.

"Begin with Gas and Traction,
  And half your fight is won.   20
Begin with Gas and Traction;
  The rest will follow soon."
We looked at one another
  And hummed a different tune.

Said Smith, "Saloons in Our Town
* Are palaces of shame."   26
Said Jones, "Police corruption
  Has hurt the town's fair name."
Said Brown, "Our lawless children
  Pitch pennies as they please."   30
Now would it not be wiser
  To start Reform with these?

The men who came to Our Town
  Replied, "No haste with these;
Begin with Gas—or Water—   35
  The roots of the disease."
We looked at one another
  And hemmed and hawed a bit;
Enthusiasm faded then
  From every single cit.   40

The men who came to Our Town
  Expressed a mild surprise,
Then they too at each other
  Looked "with a wild surmise."
Jimson had stock in Traction,   45
  And Jones had stock in Gas,
And Smith and Brown in this and
    that,
  So—nothing came to pass.

The prodigals of Our Town
  Pitch pennies as of yore;   50
Police corruption flourishes
  As rankly as before,
Still are our gilded ginmills
  Foul palaces of shame.
Reform is just as distant   55
  As when the wise men came.

LEE WILSON DODD

Publicity [1]

(An Epistle to Alexander Pope, Esq.,
on Rereading His Satires and
Moral Essays)

AWAKE, my Alexander! where you
      lie
      Snug in Elysium; put your
poppies by;
Shake off Eternity's soft indolence.
But O! inspire me with your infinite
  sense.
The times are out of joint, they always
  are;   5
Rages, as in your day it raged, the
  Star:
Named of the Dog, it maddens! past
  a doubt
Hell's Psychiatric Clinic is let out.
Our Wits now swarm from Bedlam,
  and our Wise
Stare on each other with a wild sur-
  mise,   10
While furious Propaganda, with her
  brand,
Fires the dry prairies of our wide
  Waste Land;
Making the Earth, Man's temporal
  station, be
One stinking altar to Publicity.
Touts from the house-tops bawl their
  wares abroad,   15
From Sex to Service, Cigarettes to
  God;
These bang the drum and those the
  cymbals clash
For Righteousness and Comfort,
  Christ and Cash;

[1] From *The Great Enlightenment*, Harper &
Brothers, 1928, by permission.

While, crowding through dull booths
   for trade designed,
All lead to Shame, and moribund to
   Mind,   20
Science and Art turn mountebanks
   and shriek
"This way for Beauty! Truth is cheap
   this week!"

Quick, then! your rapier-quill, your
   fencer's wrist,
Your magic ink, vitriol and amethyst!
And lend me, last, one-tenth your art
   to mend   25
My cloudy verse, clear guide, phi-
   losopher, and friend.
We have lost much for satire that
   you knew,
Kings, courtiers, fatuous patrons, and
   their crew;
The gilded circles of the Great,
Born into power and eminent by
   Fate.   30
A capful of aristocrats in lace
No longer hide the keys of Fame and
   Place:
Now, faith! we are ruled by men who
   feign to be
The loyal lackeys of Democracy;
Who execute the Will of All (they
   say),   35
But mulct and manage us the same
   old way.
For cold and avaricious men are still
The People's masters, and we do their
   will:
While, oft, th' elected Figureheads of
   State
Serve but as clowns and mummers
   till, too late,   40
Turning our eyes a moment from the
   Show,
We see our wallets and our watches
   go

(Whither no watch or wallet e'er
   returns)
Into some Bandit-Banker's smoking
   urns.
There, mixed with Oil and Brass, our
   scrapings fall   45
Into a magic fund, named Capital,
Controlled by few, and those not
   always known,
The Master-Guardians of Lord Mam-
   mon's Throne.

Nor Scholarship, nor Science, may I
   spare.
Time was, the dedicated Scholar's
   care   50
Was to be faultless in his sensitive
   task;
Nor Fame did he pursue, nor Comfort ask;

There all the honor lies, but not th'
   acclaim
Of ignorant multitudes, which men
   call Fame.
There all the honor lies, but profits
   lurk   55
Rather in self-laudation than good
   work.
The Scholar, now, the Scientist, both
   vie
With Sheiks and Vampires for the
   public eye,
With Pugilists and Columnists, 'tis
   clear,
For the monop'ly of the public ear. 60
Once timid in dim corners, like the
   mouse,
Professors now, like actors, "count the
   house,"
"Take stage," demand a "spot," inspire a "clack,"
And, to "get laughs," will sit upon a
   tack,

Or do a "prat fall" with the veriest
    clown   65
To gain th' attention of our Planet-
    Town.
For Dr. Blah a bold hypothesis,
Proclaimed abroad, is Apotheosis:
To startle, or to thrill, is all his care.
Wherefore he keeps and grooms a
    nesting mare,   70
Forth from whose addled eggs great
    Marvels, sure,
Burst into Print! Hoop la! a Cancer
    cure!
Proves Ectoplasm an Etheric Wave!
Finds a live Pterodactyl in a Cave!
Communicates with Saturn! Changes
    Rat   75
From Male to Female! Educates a
    Cat!
Perfects Atomic Motor! Turns pure
    Silk
To Radium! Conquers Death with
    Turtles' Milk!
Or, in another vein: Psychologist
Says Paranoiacs never have been
    kiss'd!   80

Such are the grave pronouncements of
    our Wise,
And in such verbiage all their honor—
    lies.

Nor do our *Literati* lag behind
In Loud Laryngeal fits of mindless
    Mind.
Seizing on wind-pipe speculations,
    they   85
Collect Thought's tatters to trick out
    a play,
To crazy-patch a novel, or rehearse
Asylum-eccentricities in verse.
Lo, the poor Indian, Gertrude Stein!
    whose brain
Tangled in echolalia writhes in
    vain;   90

Meanwhile, our Critics and our High-
    brows vie
In proving Life is worthless, Love a
    lie,
All Aspiration a mechanic thrust
Toward power, an eddy of the soul-
    less dust;
All Goodness but desire inhibited,   95
And Death a meaningless satire on
    the dead.
Man's a contraption, they assert, who
    came
To consciousness by accident, whose
    flame
Is but a spark struck from the flinty
    breast
Of Nature by the friction of un-
    rest: 100
A spark, 'tis true, that knows itself
    to be
A spark—yet quails before mortality;
A silly spark, whose self-awareness
    gains
It nothing but illusion, passing pains,
More transient pleasures, throe or
    throb or trance,   105
Amid th' electrons, unintentioned
    dance.
Thus is the Mind by its own maggots
    soiled,
Whose only virtue now's to be "hard-
    boiled,"
Tough-fibred, fatuous, cynically pert,
Unwarm'd by sunshine, undismay'd
    by dirt,   110
Stolid toward beauty and anaesthe-
    tized
To all that Socrates or Plato prized,
To all Isaiah dreamed of, Jesus knew,
To all th' ineffable bloom of life, the
    dew
Upon hope's rose, the lustre, the pure
    gleam   115
Of spirit caught from Spirit, streams
    from Stream.

No, no, my Alexander, do not wake!
Drowse on untroubled for Elysium's
    sake!
'Twould mar your rest, and others
    rest, to gain
A bird's-eye prospect of our World's
    sick brain.   120
Nay, do not cloud one dream of
    Lamb's nor fret Montaigne!
Let not our aberrations jog Voltaire,
Or rouse deep Rabelais from his easy
    chair;
Shock from long slumber Lucian, or
    perchance
Spoil the first naps of Butler or of
    France: 125
All mockers of false gods, who loved
    the True,
As all who labor for perfection do:
Yea, mocking, they revered the mys-
    tery
Of Mind, its ardor and integrity,
Its fine discriminations and far
    sweep,   130
As Atom thrills to Atom, Deep to
    Deep.

SIEGFRIED SASSOON

Base Details [1]

I F I were fierce and bald and short
    of breath,
    I'd live with scarlet Majors at the
    Base,
And speed glum heroes up the line to
    death.
    You'd see me with my puffy petu-
    lant face,

[1] From *Counter-Attack* (1918). By permission of the author.

Guzzling and gulping in the best
    hotel,   5
    Reading the Roll of Honor. "Poor
    young chap,"
I'd say—"I used to know his father
    well.
    Yes, we've lost heavily in this last
    scrap."
And when the war is done and youth
    stone dead,
I'd toddle safely home and die—in
    bed.   10

E. E. CUMMINGS

Next to of Course God [2]

"next to of course god america i
love you land of the pilgrims' and so
    forth oh
say can·you see by the dawn's early
    my
country 'tis of centuries come and go
and are no more what of it we should
    worry
in every language even deafanddumb
thy sons acclaim your glorious name
    by gorry
by jingo by gee by gosh by gum
why talk of beauty what could be
    more beauti-
ful than these heroic happy dead
who rushed like lions to the roaring
    slaughter
they did not stop to think they died
    instead
then shall the voices of liberty be
    mute?"

He spoke. And drank rapidly a glass
    of water.

[2] From "is 5," published by Boni & Liveright. Copyright, 1926, by Boni & Liveright.

ROBERT BRIDGES
London Snow

WHEN men were all asleep the
    snow came flying,
  In large white flakes falling
on the city brown,
Stealthily and perpetually settling and
  loosely lying,
  Hushing the latest traffic of the
  drowsy town;
Deadening, muffling, stifling its murmurs failing;   5
Lazily and incessantly floating down
  and down:
  Silently sifting and veiling road,
  roof and railing;
Hiding difference, making uneven-
  ness even,
Into angles and crevices softly drifting
  and sailing.
  All night it fell, and when full
  inches seven   10
It lay in the depth of its uncompacted
  lightness,
The clouds blew off from a high and
  frosty heaven;
  And all woke earlier for the unac-
  customed brightness
Of the winter dawning, the strange
  unheavenly glare:
The eye marveled—marveled at the
  dazzling whiteness;   15
  The ear hearkened to the stillness
  of the solemn air;
No sound of wheel rumbling nor of
  foot falling,
And the busy morning cries came
  thin and spare.

Then boys I heard, as they went to
  school, calling,
They gathered up the crystal manna
  to freeze   20
Their tongues with tasting, their
  hands with snowballing;
  Or rioted in a drift, plunging up to
  the knees;
Or peering up from under the white-
  mossed wonder,
"O look at the trees!" they cried, "O
  look at the trees!"
  With lessened load a few carts
  creak and blunder,   25
Following along the white deserted
  way,
A country company long dispersed
  asunder:
  When now already the sun, in pale
  display
Standing by Paul's high dome, spread
  forth below
His sparkling beams, and awoke the
  stir of the day.   30
  For now doors open, and war is
  waged with the snow;
And trains of somber men, past tale
  of number,
Tread long brown paths, as toward
  their toil they go:
  But even for them awhile no cares
  encumber
Their minds diverted; the daily word
  is unspoken,   35
The daily thoughts of labor and sorrow slumber
At the sight of the beauty that greets
  them, for the charm they have
  broken.

ALGERNON CHARLES SWINBURNE

Autumn in Cornwall

THE year lies fallen and faded
  On cliffs by clouds invaded,
    With tongues of storms up-
    braided,
  With wrath of waves bedinned;
And inland, wild with warning,   5
As in deaf ears or scorning,
The clarion even and morning
  Rings of the south-west wind.

The wild bents wane and wither
In blasts whose breath bows hither 10
Their grey-grown heads and thither,
  Unblest of rain or sun;
The pale fierce heavens are crowded
With shapes like dreams beclouded,
As though the old year enshrouded 15
  Lay, long ere life were done.

Full charged with oldworld wonders,
From dusk Tintagel thunders
A note that smites and sunders
  The hard frore fields of air;   20
A trumpet stormier-sounded
Than once from lists rebounded
When strong men sense-confounded
  Fell thick in tourney there.

From scarce a duskier dwelling   25
Such notes of wail rose welling
Through the outer darkness, telling
  In the awful singer's ears
What souls the darkness covers,
What love-lost souls of lovers,   30
Whose cry still hangs and hovers
  In each man's born that hears.

For there by Hector's brother
And yet some thousand other
He that had grief to mother,   35
  Passed pale from Dante's sight;
With one fast linked as fearless,
Perchance, there only tearless;
Iseult and Tristram, peerless
  And perfect queen and knight. 40

A shrill-winged sound comes flying
North, as of wild souls crying
The cry of things undying,
  That know what life must be;
Or as the old year's heart, stricken 45
Too sore for hope to quicken
By thoughts like thorns that thicken,
  Broke, breaking with the sea.

ROBERT FROST

Stopping by Woods on a Snowy Evening [1]

WHOSE woods these are I think
  I know.
    His house is in the village
    though;
He will not see me stopping here
To watch his woods fill up with snow.

My little horse must think it queer 5
To stop without a farmhouse near
Between the woods and frozen lake
The darkest evening of the year.

[1] From *New Hampshire*, copyright, 1923, Henry Holt and Company. By permission of the publishers.

He gives his harness bells a shake
To ask if there is some mistake.   10
The only other sound's the sweep
Of easy wind and downy flake.

The woods are lovely, dark and deep.
But I have promises to keep,
And miles to go before I sleep,   15
And miles to go before I sleep.

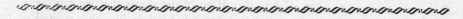

JOHN MASEFIELD

Sea-Fever [1]

I must go down to the seas again, to the lonely sea and the sky,
  And all I ask is a tall ship and a star to steer her by;
  And the wheel's kick and the wind's song and the white sail's
    shaking,
And a gray mist on the sea's face, and a gray dawn breaking.

I must go down to the seas again, for the call of the running tide   5
Is a wild call and a clear call that may not be denied;
And all I ask is a windy day with the white clouds flying,
And the flung spray and the blown spume, and the sea-gulls crying.

I must go down to the seas again, to the vagrant gipsy life,
To the gull's way and the whale's way, where the wind's like a whetted
    knife;   10
And all I ask is a merry yarn from a laughing fellow-rover,
And quiet sleep and a sweet dream when the long trick's over.

[1] From John Masefield, *Collected Poems*. By permission of The Macmillan Company, publishers.

ROBERT P. TRISTRAM COFFIN

Strange Holiness [2]

There is strange holiness around
  Our common days on common
    ground.
I have heard it in the birds

[2] Copyright, 1933, by Harper & Brothers. Reprinted from Harper's Magazine. By permission of the author.

Whose voices reach above all words,
Going upward, bars on bars,   5
Until they sound as high as stars.
I have seen it in the snake,
A flowing jewel in the brake.
It has sparkled in my eyes
In luminous breath of fireflies.   10
I have come upon its track
Where trilliums curled their petals
    back.
I have seen it flash in under
The towers of the midnight thunder.
Once, I met it face to face   15

In a fox pressed by the chase.
He came down the road on feet,
Quiet and fragile, light as heat.
He had a fish still wet and bright
In his slender jaws held tight.   20
His ears were conscious whetted darts,
His eyes had small flames in their
    hearts.
The preciousness of life and breath
Glowed through him as he outran
    death.
Strangeness and secrecy and pride   25
Ran rippling down his golden hide
His beauty was not meant for me,
With my dull eyes, so close to see.
Unconscious of me, rapt, alone,
He came, and then stopped still as
    stone.   30
His eyes went out as in a gust,
His beauty crumbled into dust.
There was but a ruin there,
A hunted creature, stripped and bare.
Then he faded at one stroke,   35
Like a dingy, melting smoke.
But there his fish lay like a key
To the bright lost mystery.

MARK VAN DOREN

After Dry Weather [1]

IF the people under that portico
  Are happy, and point at the pat-
    tering drops;
If barehead boys are parading below
Musical eaves of tall house-tops;

If you lean out of the window here, 5
Contented so with the pavement's
    shine,

[1] From 7 P.M. and Other Poems, A. & C.
Boni. By permission of the author.

And laugh as the covers of cabs appear
With passengers in them dressed to
  dine;

If all of the stones that we can see
Are licking their lips, that waited so
  long—   10
A meadow I know to the north of me
By a hundred miles has caught the
  song.

I am certain the clover has lifted its
  head
For dark, intemperate draughts of
  rain . . .
Once even I thought I had heard the
  tread   15
Of a plunging horse with a sodden
  mane.

A. E. HOUSMAN

Loveliest of Trees [2]

LOVELIEST of trees, the cherry now
    Is hung with bloom along the
      bough,
And stands about the woodland ride
Wearing white for Eastertide.

Now, of my threescore years and ten,
Twenty will not come again,   6
And take from seventy springs a
  score,
It only leaves me fifty more.

And since to look at things in bloom
Fifty springs are little room,   10
About the woodlands I will go
To see the cherry hung with snow.

[2] From A Shropshire Lad.

ARCHIBALD MacLEISH

Poem for the Time of Change [1]

THERE were over me three hawks
This was the season when the
flies will walk
The chimney stones: the kitchen
ceilings:

Three hawks wheeled in the
Ragged and rushing sky: 5
Head to the wind's violence

This was the season when the dopey
flies
In house-room groping where the
vapor rises
Cling and live a little till the wry
Cold   10
Kills them with their numb wings
weakly folded

Three hawks soared in the
Rushing sky: before them
Winter and its snow—
Sleet—the wind blowing: 15
Three hawks soared.

[1] From *Public Speech*. Copyright, Rinehart
& Company, Inc.

EZRA POUND

The Study in Æsthetics [2]

THE very small children in patched clothing,
Being smitten with an unusual wisdom,
Stopped in their play as she passed them
And cried up from their cobbles:
Guarda! Ahi, guarda! ch' è be'a! [3]

5

But three years after this
I heard the young Dante, whose last name I do not know—
For there are, in Sirmione, twenty-eight young Dantes and thirty-four Catulli;
And there had been a great catch of sardines,

And his elders   10
Were packing them in the great wooden boxes
For the market in Brescia, and he
Leapt about, snatching at the bright fish
And getting in both of their ways;
And in vain they commanded him to *sta fermo!*   15

[2] From *Personae*, copyright, Liveright Publishing Corporation, publishers.
[3] "Look! How beautiful!"

And when they would not let him arrange
The fish in the boxes
He stroked those which were already arranged,
Murmuring for his own satisfaction
This identical phrase: 20
    Ch' è be'a.

And at this I was mildly abashed.

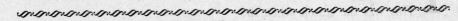

WALT WHITMAN

To a Locomotive in Winter

Thee for my recitative,
Thee in the driving storm even as now, the snow, the winter-day declining,
Thee in thy panoply, thy measur'd dual throbbing and thy beat convulsive,
Thy black cylindric body, golden brass and silvery steel,
Thy ponderous side-bars, parallel and connecting rods, gyrating, shuttling at
    thy sides,
Thy metrical, now swelling pant and roar, now tapering in the distance,
Thy great protruding head-light fix'd in front,
Thy long, pale, floating vapor-pennants, tinged with delicate purple,
The dense and murky clouds out-belching from thy smoke-stack,
Thy knitted frame, thy springs and valves, the tremulous twinkle of thy
    wheels,
Thy train of cars behind, obedient, merrily following,
Through gale or calm, now swift, now slack, yet steadily careering,
Type of the modern—emblem of motion and power—pulse of the continent,
For once come serve the Muse and merge in verse, even as here I see thee,
With storm and buffeting gusts of wind and falling snow,
By day thy warning ringing bell to sound its notes,
By night thy silent signal lamps to swing.
Fierce-throated beauty!
Roll through my chant with all thy lawless music, thy swinging lamps at night,
Thy madly-whistled laughter, echoing, rumbling like an earthquake, rousing
    all,
Law of thyself complete, thine own track firmly holding,
(No sweetness debonair of tearful harp or glib piano thine,)
Thy trills of shrieks by rocks and hills return'd,
Launch'd o'er the prairies wide, across the lakes,
To the free skies unpent and glad and strong.

STEPHEN SPENDER

The Express [1]

A FTER the first powerful plain manifesto
The black statement of pistons, without more fuss
But gliding like a queen, she leaves the station.
Without bowing and with restrained unconcern
She passes the houses which humbly crowd outside,   5
The gasworks and at last the heavy page
Of death, printed by gravestones in the cemetery.
Beyond the town there lies the open country
Where, gathering speed, she acquires mystery,
The luminous self-possession of ships on ocean.   10
It is now she begins to sing—at first quite low
Then loud, and at last with a jazzy madness—
The song of her whistle screaming at curves,
Of deafening tunnels, brakes, innumerable bolts.   14
And always light, aerial, underneath
Goes the elate metre of her wheels.
Streaming through metal landscape on her lines
She plunges new eras of wild happiness
Where speed throws up strange shapes, broad curves
And parallels clean like the steel of guns.   20
At last, further than Edinburgh or Rome,
Beyond the crest of the world, she reaches night
Where only a low streamline brightness
Of phosphorus on the tossing hills is white.
Ah, like a comet through flame she moves entranced   25
Wrapt in her music no bird song, no, nor bough
Breaking with honey buds, shall ever equal.

THOMAS S. JONES, JR.

October Hills [2]

A PRICOT, amber, smouldering rose, and rust:
These hills have drunk the day-spring's purple wine—
Bastions of bronze, turrets of tarnished pine,
And ledges where the yellow corn lies trussed.
Above this burning beauty skyward thrust,   5
Paling to frosty turquoise, faintly shine
Dove-coloured domes in undulating line,
Aerial headlands veiled with silver dust.

These peaks are ghostly when the
    sun's last glow
Recedes from hill to hill in waves
    of gold;   10
    An unseen world their changing
    mists enwall.

Hark! while the winged migrations
    southward go,
From far-off cloudy pinnacles is
    rolled
The thunder of earth's great re-
    cessional.

LOVE LYRICS

PERCY BYSSHE SHELLEY
Love's Philosophy

I

THE fountains mingle with the
    river
    And the rivers with the Ocean,
The winds of Heaven mix for ever
  With a sweet emotion;
Nothing in the world is single;   5
  All things by a law divine
In one spirit meet and mingle.
  Why not I with thine?—

II

See the mountains kiss high Heaven
  And the waves clasp one another; 10
No sister-flower would be forgiven
  If it disdained its brother;
And the sunlight clasps the earth
  And the moonbeams kiss the sea:
What is all this sweet work worth 15
  If thou kiss not me?

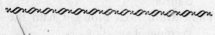

JOHN KEATS
Sonnet

BRIGHT star! would I were stead-
    fast as thou art—
    Not in lone splendor hung aloft
  the night,
And watching, with eternal lids apart,
  Like Nature's patient, sleepless
  Eremite,

The moving waters at their priestlike
  task   5
Of pure ablution round earth's hu-
  man shores,
Or gazing on the new soft fallen
  mask
Of snow upon the mountains and
  the moors—
No—yet still steadfast, still unchange-
  able,
Pillowed upon my fair love's ripen-
  ing breast,   10
To feel for ever its soft fall and swell,
  Awake for ever in a sweet unrest,
Still, still to hear her tender-taken
  breath,
And so live ever—or else swoon to
  death.

LORD BYRON
When We Two Parted

WHEN we two parted
    In silence and tears,
    Half broken-hearted
To sever for years,
Pale grew thy cheek and cold, 5
  Colder thy kiss;
Truly that hour foretold
  Sorrow to this.

The dew of the morning
  Sunk chill on my brow— 10
It felt like the warning
  Of what I feel now.
Thy vows are all broken,
  And light is thy fame:
I hear thy name spoken,   15
  And share in its shame.

They name thee before me,
  A knell to mine ear;
A shudder comes o'er me—
  Why wert thou so dear?   20
They know not I knew thee,
  Who knew thee too well:—
Long, long shall I rue thee,
  Too deeply to tell.

In secret we met—   25
  In silence I grieve,
That thy heart could forget,
  Thy spirit deceive.
If I should meet thee
  After long years,   30
How should I greet thee?—
  With silence and tears.

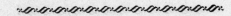

DANTE GABRIEL ROSSETTI

Lovesight

WHEN do I see thee most, be-
    lovèd one?
  When in the light the spirits
of mine eyes
Before thy face, their altar, solemn-
  ize
The worship of that Love through
  thee made known?
Or when in the dusk hours (we two
  alone),   5
  Close-kissed and eloquent of still
  replies
  Thy twilight-hidden glimmering
  visage lies,
And my soul only sees thy soul its
  own?

O love, my love! if I no more should
  see
Thyself, nor on the earth the shadow
  of thee,   10
  Nor image of thine eyes in any
  spring,—
How then should sound upon Life's
  darkening slope
The ground-whirl of the perished
  leaves of Hope,
  The wind of Death's imperishable
  wing?

Mid Rapture

THOU lovely and belovèd, thou
    my love;
  Whose kiss seems still the
first; whose summoning eyes,
Even now, as for our love-world's
  new sunrise,
Shed very dawn; whose voice, at-
  tuned above
All modulation of the deep-bowered
  dove,   5
  Is like a hand laid softly on the
  soul;
  Whose hand is like a sweet voice to
  control
Those worn tired brows it hath the
  keeping of:—

What word can answer to thy word,
  —what gaze
  To thine, which now absorbs within its sphere   10
  My worshiping face, till I am mir-
  rored there
Light-circled in a heaven of deep-
  drawn rays?
What clasp, what kiss mine inmost
  heart can prove,
O lovely and belovèd, O my love?

CHRISTINA ROSSETTI

A Birthday

My heart is like a singing bird
　Whose nest is in a watered
　　shoot;
My heart is like an apple-tree
　Whose boughs are bent with thick-
　　set fruit;
My heart is like a rainbow shell 　5
　That paddles in a halcyon sea;
My heart is gladder than all these
　Because my love is come to me.
Raise me a dais of silk and down; 　9
　Hang it with vair and purple dyes;
Carve it in doves and pomegranates,
　And peacocks with a hundred eyes;
Work it in gold and silver grapes,
　In leaves and silver fleurs-de-lys;
Because the birthday of my life 　15
　Is come, my love is come to me.

ELIZABETH BARRETT BROWNING

If Thou Must Love Me

If thou must love me, let it be for
　nought
Except for love's sake only. Do
　not say
'I love her for her smile . . . her look
　. . . her way
Of speaking gently, . . . for a trick
　of thought
That falls in well with mine, and
　certes brought 　5

A sense of pleasant ease on such a
　day'—
For these things in themselves, Be-
　lovèd, may
Be changed, or change for thee,—and
　love, so wrought
May be unwrought so. Neither love
　me for
Thine own dear pity's wiping my
　cheeks dry,— 　10
A creature might forget to weep, who
　bore
Thy comfort long, and lose thy love
　thereby!
But love me for love's sake, that ever-
　more
Thou mayst love on, through love's
　eternity.

JOSEPH AUSLANDER

Sonnet for Svanhild [1]

Come, let us march seven times
　Death's dark walls round,
　　And sing our songs and step
　with quick sharp tread,
And with our bright breath blow
　them to the ground,
And shout and crown Love king and
　cry Death dead!
O let us twist a wreath for his dear
　head, 　5
And drench it in his dew, and with
　the sound
Of doves and flutes O wipe the gash
　that bled,

[1] Dedication for *The Sonnets of Petrarch*, Longmans, Green & Co., 1931. By permission of the author.

And press wet cloth and pour balm
    on the wound!
For it is Spring, and Love is once
    more lord,
And from the dust of death the white
    brief bud   10
Breaks through, and from the red hilt
    of his sword
A rose will flash out like a drop of
    blood!
What walls can stand, though Death
    builds deep and strong,
When Love strides seven times round
    with storms of song!

EDNA ST. VINCENT MILLAY

Oh, Think Not I Am Faithful to a Vow! [1]

OH, think not I am faithful to a
    vow!
    Faithless am I save to Love's
self alone.
Were you not lovely I would leave
    you now—
After the feet of Beauty fly my own.
Were you not still my hunger's rarest
    food,   5
And water ever to my wildest thirst,
I would desert you—think not but I
    would!—
And seek another, as I sought you
    first.
But you are mobile as the veering air,
And all your charms more changeful
    than the tide,   10
Wherefore to be inconstant is no
    care—

[1] From *A Few Figs from Thistles,* published by Harper & Brothers (copyright, 1922, by Edna St. Vincent Millay).

I have but to continue at your side.
So wanton, light and false, my love,
    are you,
I am most faithless when I most am
    true.

RICHARD ALDINGTON

Prelude [2]

HOW could I love you more?
    I would give up
    Even that beauty I have
loved too well
That I might love you better.
Alas, how poor the gifts that lovers
    give—   5
I can but give you of my flesh and
    strength,
I can but give you these few passing
    days
And passionate words that since our
    speech began
All lovers whisper in all women's
    ears.
I try to think of some one gift   10
No lover yet in all the world has
    found;
I think: If the cold sombre gods
Were hot with love as I am
Could they not endow you with a star
And fix bright youth for ever in your
    limbs?   15
Could they not give you all things
    that I lack?

You should have loved a god; I am
    but dust.
Yet no god loved as loves this poor
    frail dust.

[2] From *The Poems of Richard Aldington,* copyright 1928, 1934. Reprinted by permission from Doubleday & Company, Inc.

An Interlude

THERE is a momentary pause in
  love
  When all the birth-pangs of desire are lulled.

I wait,
And glide upon the crested surge of
  days
Like some sea-god, with tangled,
  dripping beard   5
And smooth hard skin, who glimpses
  from the sea
An earth-girl naked by the long foam
  fringe,
And, utterly forgetting all his life,
Hurries toward her, glad with sudden
  love.

Even in that pause of speed I live; 10
And though the great wave curl in
  spikes of foam
And crash me bleeding at her cool
  small feet
All breathless with the water's sudden
  swirl,
I shall be glad of every stabbing
  wound
If she will hold my tired limbs to hers
And breathe wild love into my mouth
  and thrill   16
Even the blood I shed with that de-
  sire
Which throbs all through me at her
  lightest touch.

Epilogue

HAVE I spoken too much or not
  enough of love?
  Who can tell?

But we who do not drug ourselves
  with lies
Know, with how deep a pathos, that
  we have

Only the warmth and beauty of this
  life   5
Before the blankness of the unending
  gloom.
Here for a little while we see the sun
And smell the grape-vines on the ter-
  raced hills,
And sing and weep, fight, starve and
  feast, and love
Lips and soft breasts too sweet for
  innocence.   10

And in this little glow of mortal life—
Faint as one candle in a large cold
  room—
We know the clearest light is shed by
  love,
That when we kiss with life-blood in
  our lips,
Then we are nearest to the dreamed-
  of gods.   15

๛๛๛๛๛๛๛๛๛๛๛๛๛

JOSÉ GARCIA VILLA

I Can No More Hear Love's Voice [1]

I CAN no more hear Love's
  Voice. No more moves
  The mouth of her. Birds
No more sing. Words
I speak return lonely.   5
Flowers I pick turn ghostly.
Fire that I burn glows
Pale. No more blows
The wind. Time tells
No more truth. Bells   10
Ring no more in me.
I am all alone singly.
Lonely rests my head.
—O my God! I am dead.

[1] From *Have Come, Am Here.* Copyright
1941, 1942, by José Garcia Villa. Reprinted by
permission of The Viking Press, Inc.

ALFRED, LORD TENNYSON

From *In Memoriam*

LIV

O YET we trust that somehow good
　　Will be the final goal of ill,
　　To pangs of nature, sins of will,
Defects of doubt, and taints of blood;

That nothing walks with aimless
　　feet;　　　　　　　　　　5
　　That not one life shall be destroyed,
　　Or cast as rubbish to the void,
When God hath made the pile complete;

That not a worm is cloven in vain;
　　That not a moth with vain desire
　　Is shriveled in a fruitless fire,　11
Or but subserves another's gain.

Behold, we know not anything;
　　I can but trust that good shall fall
　　At last—far off—at last, to all,　15
And every winter change to spring.

So runs my dream; but what am I?
　　An infant crying in the night;
　　An infant crying for the light,
And with no language but a cry.　　20

LV

The wish, that of the living whole
　　No life may fail beyond the grave,
　　Derives it not from what we have
The likest God within the soul?

Are God and Nature then at strife,　5
　　That Nature lends such evil
　　dreams?
　　So careful of the type she seems,
So careless of the single life,

That I, considering everywhere
　　Her secret meaning in her deeds.　10
　　And finding that of fifty seeds
She often brings but one to bear,

I falter where I firmly trod,
　　And falling with my weight of
　　cares
　　Upon the great world's altar-stairs　15
That slope through darkness up to
　　God,

I stretch lame hands of faith, and
　　grope,
　　And gather dust and chaff, and call
　　To what I feel is Lord of all,
And faintly trust the larger hope.　　20

XCVI

You say, but with no touch of scorn,
　　Sweet-hearted, you, whose light-blue
　　eyes
　　Are tender over drowning flies,
You tell me, doubt is Devil-born.

I know not: one indeed I knew　　5
　　In many a subtle question versed,
　　Who touched a jarring lyre at first,
But ever strove to make it true;

Perplexed in faith, but pure in deeds,
　　At last he beat his music out.　　10
　　There lives more faith in honest
　　doubt,
Believe me, than in half the creeds.

He fought his doubts and gathered strength,
He would not make his judgment blind,
He faced the specters of the mind 15
And laid them; thus he came at length

To find a stronger faith his own,
And Power was with him in the night,
Which makes the darkness and the light,
And dwells not in the light alone, 20

But in the darkness and the cloud,
As over Sinaï's peaks of old,
While Israel made their gods of gold,
Although the trumpet blew so loud.

CXVIII

Contemplate all this work of Time,
The giant laboring in his youth;
Nor dream of human love and truth,
As dying Nature's earth and lime;

But trust that those we call the dead 5
Are breathers of an ampler day
For ever nobler ends. They say,
The solid earth whereon we tread

In tracts of fluent heat began,
And grew to seeming-random forms, 10
The seeming prey of cyclic storms,
Till at the last arose the man;

Who throve and branched from clime to clime,
The herald of a higher race,
And of himself in higher place, 15
If so he type this work of time

Within himself, from more to more;
Or, crowned with attributes of woe
Like glories, move his course, and show
That life is not as idle ore, 20

But iron dug from central gloom,
And heated hot with burning fears,
And dipped in baths of hissing tears,
And battered with the shocks of doom

To shape and use. Arise and fly 25
The reeling Faun, the sensual feast;
Move upward, working out the beast,
And let the ape and tiger die.

* * * * *

Strong Son of God, immortal Love,
Whom we, that have not seen thy face,
By faith, and faith alone, embrace
Believing where we cannot prove;

Thine are these orbs of light and shade; 5
Thou madest Life in man and brute;
Thou madest Death; and lo, thy foot
Is on the skull which thou hast made.

Thou wilt not leave us in the dust:
Thou madest man, he knows not why, 10
He thinks he was not made to die;
And thou hast made him; thou art just.

Thou seemest human and divine,
The highest, holiest, manhood, thou
Our wills are ours, we know not how; 15
Our wills are ours, to make them thine.

Our little systems have had their day;
  They have their day and cease to
    be;
  They are but broken lights of thee,
And thou, O Lord, art more than
    they.   20

We have but faith: we cannot know,
  For knowledge is of things we see;
  And yet we trust it comes from
    thee,
A beam in darkness: let it grow.

Let knowledge grow from more to
    more,   25
  But more of reverence in us dwell;
  That mind and soul, according well,
May make one music as before,

But vaster. We are fools and slight;
  We mock thee when we do not
    fear: 30
  But help thy foolish ones to bear;
Help thy vain worlds to bear thy
    light.

Forgive what seemed my sin in me,
  What seemed my worth since I
    began;
  For merit lives from man to man, 35
And not from man, O Lord, to thee.

Forgive my grief for one removed,
  Thy creature, whom I found so fair.
  I trust he lives in thee, and there
I find him worthier to be loved.   40

Forgive these wild and wandering
    cries,
  Confusions of a wasted youth;
  Forgive them where they fail in
    truth,
And in thy wisdom make me wise.

ROBERT BROWNING
Prospice

FEAR death?—to feel the fog in
  my throat,
    The mist in my face,
When the snows begin, and the blasts
    denote
    I am nearing the place,
The power of the night, the press of
    the storm,   5
    The post of the foe;
Where he stands, the Arch Fear in a
    visible form,
    Yet the strong man must go:
For the journey is done and the sum-
    mit attained,
    And the barriers fall,   10
Though a battle's to fight ere the
    guerdon be gained,
    The reward of it all.
I was ever a fighter, so—one fight
    more,
    The best and the last!
I would hate that death bandaged my
    eyes, and forebore,   15
    And bade me creep past.
No! let me taste the whole of it, fare
    like my peers
    The heroes of old,
Bear the brunt, in a minute pay glad
    life's arrears
    Of pain, darkness and cold.   20
For sudden the worst turns the best
    to the brave,
    The black minute's at end,
And the elements' rage, the fiend-
    voices that rave,
    Shall dwindle, shall blend,

Shall change, shall become first a
    peace out of pain,   25
Then a light, then thy breast,
O thou soul of my soul! I shall clasp
    thee again,
And with God be the rest!

MATTHEW ARNOLD

Dover Beach

———————————

THE sea is calm to-night.
    The tide is full, the moon lies
      fair ,
Upon the straits;—on the French
    coast the light
Gleams and is gone; the cliffs of Eng-
    land stand,
Glimmering and vast, out in the tran-
    quil bay.   5
Come to the window, sweet is the
    night-air!
Only, from the long line of spray
Where the sea meets the moon-
    blanched land,
Listen! you hear the grating roar
Of pebbles which the waves draw
    back, and fling,   10
At their return, up the high strand,
Begin, and cease, and then again be-
    gin,
With tremulous cadence slow, and
    bring
The eternal note of sadness in.

Sophocles long ago   15
Heard it on the Ægean, and it
    brought
Into his mind the turbid ebb and flow
Of human misery; we
Find also in the sound a thought,

Hearing it by this distant northern
    sea.   20
The Sea of Faith
Was once, too, at the full, and round
    earth's shore
Lay like the folds of a bright girdle
    furled.
But now I only hear
Its melancholy, long, withdrawing
    roar,   25
Retreating, to the breath
Of the night-wind, down the vast
    edges drear
And naked shingles of the world.

Ah, love, let us be true
To one another! for the world, which
    seems   30
To lie before us like a land of dreams,
So various, so beautiful, so new,
Hath really neither joy, nor love, nor
    light,
Nor certitude, nor peace, nor help for
    pain;
And we are here as on a darkling
    plain   35
Swept with confused alarms of strug-
    gle and flight,
Where ignorant armies clash by night.

WILLIAM ERNEST HENLEY

Invictus

———————————

OUT of the night that covers me,
    Black as the Pit from pole to
      pole,
I thank whatever gods may be
    For my unconquerable soul.

In the fell clutch of circumstance   5
   I have not winced nor cried aloud.
Under the bludgeonings of chance
   My head is bloody, but unbowed.

Beyond this place of wrath and tears
   Looms but the horror of the shade,
And yet the menace of the years   11
   Finds, and shall find me, unafraid.

It matters not how strait the gate,
   How charged with punishments
     the scroll,
I am the master of my fate;   15
   I am the captain of my soul.

EMILY DICKINSON

To Fight Aloud Is Very Brave [1]

To fight aloud is very brave,
   But gallanter, I know,
   Who charge within the bosom,
The cavalry of woe.

Who win, and nations do not see,   5
Who fall, and none observe,
Whose dying eyes no country
Regards with patriot love.

[1] From *The Poems of Emily Dickinson,*
Centenary Edition, edited by Martha Dickinson
Bianchi and Alfred Leet Hampson. Reprinted
by permission of Little, Brown & Company.

We trust, in plumed procession,
   For such the angels go,   10
Rank after rank, with even feet
   And uniforms of snow.

ROBINSON JEFFERS

Fire on the Hills [2]

THE deer were bounding like
    blown leaves
   Under the smoke in front of the
    roaring wave of the brush-fire;
I thought of the smaller lives that
    were caught.
Beauty is not always lovely; the fire
    was beautiful, the terror
Of the deer was beautiful; and when
    I returned   5
Down the black slopes after the fire
    had gone by, an eagle
Was perched on the jag of a burnt
    pine,
Insolent and gorged, cloaked in the
    folded storms of his shoulders.
He had come from far off for the
    good hunting
With fire for his beater to drive the
    game; the sky was merciless   10
Blue, and the hills merciless black,
The sombre-feathered great bird
    sleepily merciless between them.
I thought, painfully, but the whole
    mind,
The destruction that brings an eagle
    from heaven is better than mercy.

[2] Reprinted by permission of Random
House, New York.

HELENE MAGARET

Impiety[1]

LORD, I have not time to pray
  Before the asters blow,
  And should I enter in Thy
church
Perchance I miss the glow
Of branches bright with glint of
  snow.   5

Ah, Lord, Thou shouldst not ask of
  me
One hour spent in prayer
For fear some quiet rain let fall
Its shining hair,
And I, who longed for rain, might
  not be there.   10

I do not want, my Lord, to give
One breath of life to Thee.
I have so little time to live . . .
Thou hast eternity.

THOMAS S. JONES, JR.

The Pyre[2]

WITH solemn sound the bells of
  Rouen peal,
  And in the square the Maid
unarmed, alone,
Lily of France, defender of the
throne,

[1] From Columbia Poetry, 1932, by permission of the author.
[2] From Shadow of the Perfect Rose, Rinehart & Company, Inc., 1937. By permission of John L. Foley, executor of the author's estate.

Faces a death more terrible than steel:
Not thus the wondering armies
  watched her kneel,   5
Still as the warrior angel carved in
  stone,
About her helm Saint Michael's
  banner blown,
The Dragon's head beneath his burnished heel.

And shall the ashes of earth's fairest
  rose
  Be scattered, and the blinding
    sparks consume   10
  This heart which burns more
    fiercely than its pyre?
"Jesus!" On that great cry her spirit
  goes
  Where angels gleam, where April
    gardens bloom,
  Flame over flame, and fire transcending fire.

CONRAD AIKEN

Morning Song, from Senlin[3]

IT IS morning, Senlin says, and in
    the morning
  When the light drips through the
    shutters like the dew,
I arise, I face the sunrise,
And do the things my fathers learned
  to do.

Stars in the purple dusk above the
    rooftops   5
Pale in a saffron mist and seem to die,

[3] From Selected Poems. Permission of the publishers, Charles Scribner's Sons, New York.

And I myself on a swiftly tilting
　　planet
Stand before a glass and tie my tie.

Vine leaves tap my window,　　　9
Dew-drops sing to the garden stones,
The robin chirps in the chinaberry
　　tree
Repeating three clear tones.

It is morning. I stand by the mirror
And tie my tie once more.
While waves far off in a pale rose
　　twilight　　　　　　　　15
Crash on a white sand shore.
I stand by a mirror and comb my
　　hair:
How small and white my face!—
The green earth tilts through a sphere
　　of air
And bathes in a flame of space.　20

There are houses hanging above the
　　stars
And stars hung under a sea . . .
And a sun far off in a shell of silence
Dapples my walls for me . . .

It is morning, Senlin says, and in the
　　morning　　　　　　　　25
Should I not pause in the light to re-
　　member god?
Upright and firm I stand on a star
　　unstable,
He is immense and lonely as a cloud.
I will dedicate this moment before
　　my mirror
To him alone, for him I will comb
　　my hair.　　　　　　　　30
Accept these humble offerings, cloud
　　of silence!
I will think of you as I descend the
　　stair.

Vine leaves tap my window,
The snail-track shines on the stones,
Dew-drops flash from the chinaberry
　　tree　　　　　　　　　35
Repeating two clear tones.

It is morning, I awake from a bed of
　　silence,
Shining I rise from the starless waters
　　of sleep.
The walls are about me still as in the
　　evening,
I am the same, and the same name
　　still I keep.　　　　　　40

The earth revolves with me, yet
　　makes no motion,
The stars pale silently in a coral sky.
In a whistling void I stand before my
　　mirror,
Unconcerned, and tie my tie.

There are horses neighing on far-off
　　hills　　　　　　　　　45
Tossing their long white manes,
And mountains flash in the rose-white
　　dusk,
Their shoulders black with rains . . .
It is morning. I stand by the mirror
And surprise my soul once more;　50
The blue air rushes above my ceiling,
There are suns beneath my floor . . .

. . . It is morning, Senlin says, I
　　ascend from darkness
And depart on the winds of space for
　　I know not where,
My watch is wound, a key is in my
　　pocket,　　　　　　　　55
And the sky is darkened as I descend
　　the stair.
There are shadows across the win-
　　dows, clouds in heaven,

And a god among the stars; and I will
go
Thinking of him as I might think of
daybreak
And humming a tune I know . . . 60

Vine leaves tap at the window,
Dew-drops sing to the garden stones,
The robin chirps in the chinaberry
tree
Repeating three clear tones.

GERARD MANLEY HOPKINS

Pied Beauty [1]

GLORY be to God for dappled things—
    For skies of couple-colour as a brindled cow;
      For rose-moles all in stiple upon trout that swim;
Fresh-firecoal chestnut-falls; finches' wings;
  Landscape plotted and pieced—fold, fallow, and plough;   5
    And all trades, their gear and tackle and trim.

All things counter, original, spare, strange;
  Whatever is fickle, freckled (who knows how?)
    With swift, slow; sweet, sour; adazzle, dim;
He fathers-forth whose beauty is past change: 10
    Praise him.

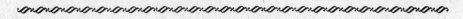

EDITH SITWELL

Still Falls the Rain [2]

The Raids, 1940. Night and Dawn

STILL falls the Rain—
  Dark as the world of man, black as our loss—
  Blind as the nineteen hundred and forty nails
Upon the Cross.

Still falls the Rain   5
With a sound like the pulse of the heart that is changed to the hammer-beat
In the Potter's Field, and the sound of the impious feet

[1] From *Poems* of Gerard Manley Hopkins (1918). By permission of Oxford University Press, New York.
  [2] From *Street Songs,* The Macmillan Company, 1942. Reprinted by permission of the author.

On the Tomb:
>   Still falls the Rain
In the Field of Blood where the small hopes breed and the human brain   10
Nurtures its greed, that worm with the brow of Cain.

Still falls the Rain
At the feet of the Starved Man hung upon the Cross.
Christ that each day, each night, nails there, have mercy on us—
On Dives and on Lazarus: 15
Under the rain the sore and the gold are as one.

Still falls the Rain—
Still falls the blood from the Starved Man's wounded Side:
He bears in His Heart all wounds,—those of the light that died,
The last faint spark   20
In the self-murdered heart, the wounds of the sad uncomprehending dark,

The wounds of the baited bear,—
The blind and weeping bear whom the keepers beat
On his helpless flesh . . . the tears of the hunted hare.

Still falls the Rain—   25
Then—O Ile leape up to my God: who pulles me doune—
See, see where Christ's blood streames in the firmament:
It flows from the Brow we nailed upon the tree
Deep to the dying, to the thirsting heart
That holds the fires of the world,—dark-smirched with pain   30
As Caesar's laurel crown.

Then sounds the voice of One who like the heart of man
Was once a child who among the beasts has lain—
"Still do I love, still shed my innocent light, my Blood, for thee."

ᘒ᙮ᘒ᙮ᘒ᙮ᘒ᙮ᘒ᙮ᘒ᙮ᘒ᙮ᘒ᙮ᘒ᙮ᘒ᙮ᘒ᙮ᘒ᙮ᘒ᙮ᘒ᙮ᘒ᙮ᘒ᙮ᘒ᙮

T. S. ELIOT

Journey of the Magi [1]

> " COLD coming we had of it,
> A   Just the worst time of the year
>   For a journey, and such a long journey:
> The ways deep and the weather sharp,
> The very dead of winter."   5

[1] From *Collected Poems of T. S. Eliot.* Copyright, 1936, by Harcourt, Brace and Company, Inc.

And the camels galled, sore-footed, refractory,
Lying down in the melting snow.
There were times we regretted
The summer palaces on slopes, the terraces,
And the silken girls bringing sherbet.   10
Then the camel men cursing and grumbling
And running away, and wanting their liquor and women,
And the night-fires going out, and the lack of shelters,
And the cities hostile and the towns unfriendly
And the villages dirty and charging high prices: .   15
A hard time we had of it.
At the end we preferred to travel all night,
Sleeping in snatches,
With the voices singing in our ears, saying
That this was all folly.   20

Then at dawn we came down to a temperate valley,
Wet, below the snow line, smelling of vegetation;
With a running stream and a water-mill beating the darkness,
And three trees on the low sky,
And an old white horse galloped away in the meadow.   25
Then we came to a tavern with vine-leaves over the lintel,
Six hands at an open door dicing for pieces of silver,
And feet kicking the empty wine-skins.
But there was no information, and so we continued
And arriving at evening, not a moment too soon   30
Finding the place; it was (you may say) satisfactory.
All this was a long time ago, I remember,
And I would do it again, but set down
This set down
This: were we led all that way for   35
Birth or Death? There was a Birth, certainly,
We had evidence and no doubt. I had seen birth and death,
But had thought they were different; this Birth was
Hard and bitter agony for us, like Death, our death.
We returned to our places, these Kingdoms,   40
But no longer at ease here, in the old dispensation,
With an alien people clutching their gods.
I should be glad of another death."

THOMAS HOOD

The Song of the Shirt [1]

WITH fingers weary and worn,
   With eyelids heavy and red,
   A woman sat, in unwomanly
      rags,
Plying her needle and thread—
Stitch! stitch! stitch!   5
   In poverty, hunger, and dirt,
And still with a voice of dolorous pitch
   She sang the "Song of the Shirt."

"Work! work! work!
   While the cock is crowing aloof!   10
And work—work—work,
   Till the stars shine through the roof!
It's Oh! to be a slave
   Along with the barbarous Turk,
Where woman has never a soul to
      save,   15
   If this is Christian work!

"Work—work—work,
   Till the brain begins to swim;
Work—work—work,
   Till the eyes are heavy and dim! 20
Seam, and gusset, and band,
   Band, and gusset, and seam,
Till over the buttons I fall asleep,
   And sew them on in a dream!

"Oh, men, with sisters dear!   25
   Oh, men, with mothers and wives!
It is not linen you're wearing out
   But human creatures' lives!
Stitch—stitch—stitch,
   In poverty, hunger, and dirt,   30

Sewing at once, with a double thread,
   A Shroud as well as a Shirt.

"But why do I talk of Death?
   That phantom of grisly bone,
I hardly fear its terrible shape,   35
   It seems so like my own—
It seems so like my own,
   Because of the fasts I keep;
Oh, God! that bread should be so dear,
   And flesh and blood so cheap!   40

"Work—work—work!
   My labor never flags;
And what are its wages?   A bed of
      straw,
   A crust of bread—and rags.
That   shattered   roof—this   naked
      floor—   45
   A table—a broken chair—
And a wall so blank, my shadow I
      thank
   For sometimes falling there!

"Work—work—work!
   From weary chime to chime,   50
Work—work—work,
   As prisoners work for crime!
Band, and gusset, and seam,
   Seam, and gusset, and band,
Till the heart is sick, and the brain
      benumbed,   55
   As well as the weary hand.

"Work—work—work,
   In the dull December light,
And work—work—work,
   When the weather is warm and
      bright,   60
While underneath the eaves
   The brooding swallows cling
As if to show me their sunny backs
   And twit me with the spring.

[1] Published in the Christmas number of
Punch, 1843.

"Oh! but to breathe the breath 65
  Of the cowslip and primrose sweet,
With the sky above my head,
  And the grass beneath my feet;
For only one short hour
  To feel as I used to feel, 70
Before I knew the woes of want
  And the walk that costs a meal.

"Oh! but for one short hour!
  A respite however brief!
No blessed leisure for Love or
  Hope, 75
  But only time for Grief!
A little weeping would ease my heart,
  But in their briny bed
My tears must stop, for every drop
  Hinders needle and thread!" 80

With fingers weary and worn,
  With eyelids heavy and red,
A woman sat, in unwomanly rags,
  Plying her needle and thread—
Stitch! stitch! stitch! 85
  In poverty, hunger, and dirt,
And still with a voice of dolorous
  pitch,—
Would that its tone could reach the
  Rich!—
She sang this "Song of the Shirt!"

〜〜〜〜〜〜〜〜〜〜〜〜

C. DAY LEWIS

*Consider These, for We Have
Condemned Them* [1]

_____

CONSIDER these, for we have con-
    demned them;
    Leaders to no sure land,
guides their bearings lost

[1] From *Collected Poems*. Reprinted by permission of Random House, New York.

Or in league with robbers have reversed the signposts,
Disrespectful to ancestors, irresponsible to heirs.
Born barren, a freak growth, root in
  rubble, 5
Fruitlessly blossoming, whose foliage
  suffocates,
Their sap is sluggish, they reject the
  sun.

The man with his tongue in his
  cheek, the woman
With her heart in the wrong place,
  unhandsome, unwholesome;
Have exposed the new-born to worse
  than weather, 10
Exiled the honest and sacked the seer.
These drowned the farms to form a
  pleasure-lake,
In time of drought they drain the
  reservoir
Through private pipes for baths and
  sprinklers.

Getters not begetters; gainers not
  beginners; 15
Whiners, no winners; no triers, be-
  trayers;
Who steer by no star, whose moon
  means nothing.
Daily denying, unable to dig:
At bay in villas from blood relations,
Counters of spoons and content with
  cushions 20
They pray for peace, they hand down
  disaster.

They that take the bribe shall perish
  by the bribe,
Drying of dry rot, ending in asylums,
A curse to children, a charge on the
  state.
But still their fears and frenzies infect
  us; 25

Drug nor isolation will cure this cancer:
It is now or never, the hour of the knife,
The break with the past, the major operation.

~~~~~~~~~~~~~~~~~~~~~~~~~~~~~~

EDWIN MARKHAM

The Man with the Hoe [1]

God made man in his own image in the image of God he made him.
        —*Genesis.*

Bowed by the weight of centuries he leans
    Upon his hoe and gazes on the ground,
The emptiness of ages in his face,
And on his back the burden of the world.
Who made him dead to rapture and despair,   5
A thing that grieves not and that never hopes,
Stolid and stunned, a brother to the ox?
Who loosened and let down this brutal jaw?
Whose was the hand that slanted back this brow?
Whose breath blew out the light within this brain?   10

Is this the Thing the Lord God made and gave
To have dominion over sea and land?
To trace the stars and search the heavens for power;

To feel the passion of Eternity?
Is this the dream He dreamed who shaped the suns   15
And markt their ways upon the ancient deep?
Down all the caverns of Hell to their last gulf
There is no shape more terrible than this—
More tongued with censure of the world's blind greed—
More filled with signs and portents for the soul—   20
More packt with danger to the universe.

What gulfs between him and the seraphim!
Slave of the wheel of labor, what to him
Are Plato and the swing of Pleiades?
What the long reaches of the peaks of song,   25
The rift of dawn, the reddening of the rose?
Through this dread shape the suffering ages look;
Time's tragedy is in that aching stoop;
Through this dread shape humanity betrayed,
Plundered, profaned and disinherited,   30
Cries protest to the Powers that made the world,
A protest that is also prophecy.

O masters, lords and rulers in all lands,
Is this the handiwork you give to God,
This monstrous thing distorted and soul-quencht?   35
How will you ever straighten up this shape;
Touch it again with immortality;

---

[1] Copyrighted by the author and used by his permission.

Give back the upward looking and
  the light;
Rebuild in it the music and the
  dream;
Make right the immemorial in-
  famies,   40
Perfidious   wrongs,   immedicable
  woes?

O masters, lords and rulers in all
  lands,
How will the future reckon with this
  Man?
How answer his brute question in that
  hour
When whirlwinds of rebellion shake
  all shores?   45
How will it be with kingdoms and
  with kings—
With those who shaped him to the
  thing he is—
When this dumb Terror shall rise to
  judge the world,
After the silence of the centuries?

PARE LORENTZ

From *The River* [1]

Soundtrack of the Motion Picture

BLACK spruce and Norway pine,
  Douglas fir and Red cedar,
  Scarlet oak and Shagbark
hickory.
We built a hundred cities and a thou-
  sand towns—
But at what a cost!   5
We cut the top off the Alleghenies and
  sent it down the river.

[1] With permission of Stackpole Sons, publisher.

We cut the top off Minnesota and
  sent it down the river.
We cut the top off Wisconsin and sent
  it down the river.
We left the mountains and the hills
  slashed and burned,
And moved on.   10
We built a hundred cities and a thou-
  sand towns—
But at what a cost!
Poor land makes poor people.
Poor people make poor land.

We got the blacks to plant the cotton
  and they gouged the top off the
  valley.   15
We got the Swedes to cut the forests,
  and they sent them down the
  river.
Then we left a hollow-eyed generation to peck at the worn-out
  valley;
And left the Swedes to shiver in their
  naked North country.
1903, 1907, 1913, 1922, 1927, 1936,
  1937—
For you can't wall out and dam
  two-thirds the water in the country.   20
We built dams but the dams filled
  in.
We built a thousand-mile dyke but it
  didn't hold;
So we built it higher.
We played with a continent for fifty
  years.

Flood control? Of the Mississippi? 25
Control from Denver to Helena;
From Itasca to Paducah;
From Pittsburgh to Cairo—
Control of the wheat, the corn and
  the cotton land;
Control enough to put back a thou-
  sand forests;

Control enough to put the river together again before it is too late
. . . before it has picked up the
heart of a continent and shoved
it into the Gulf of Mexico.

~~~~~~~~~~~~~~~~~~~~~~~~~~~~~

W. H. AUDEN

*Get There If You Can and See the
Land You Once Were Proud
to Own* [1]

GET there if you can and see the
land you once were proud to
own
Though the roads have almost vanished and the expresses never run:

Smokeless chimneys, damaged
bridges, rotting wharves and
choked canals,
Tramlines buckled, smashed trucks
lying on their side across the rails;

Power-stations locked, deserted, since
they drew the boiler fires;   5
Pylons fallen or subsiding, trailing
dead high-tension wires;

Head-gears gaunt on grass-grown pit-
banks, seams abandoned years
ago;
Drop a stone and listen for its splash
in flooded dark below.

Squeeze into the works through
broken windows or through
damp-sprung doors;
See the rotted shafting, see holes gaping in the upper floors;   10

[1] From *Poems.* Reprinted by permission of
Random House, New York.

Where the Sunday lads come talking
motor bicycle and girl,
Smoking cigarettes in chains until
their heads are in a whirl.

Far from there we spent the money,
thinking we could well afford,
While they quietly undersold us with
their cheaper trade abroad;

At the theatre, playing tennis, driving
motor cars we had,   15
In our continental villas, mixing cock-
tails for a cad.

These were boon companions who
devised the legends for our
tombs,
Those who have betrayed us nicely
while we took them to our rooms.

Newman, Ciddy, Plato, Fronny, Pas-
cal, Bowdler, Baudelaire,
Dr. Frommer, Mrs. Allom, Freud, the
Baron, and Flaubert.   20

Lured with their compelling logic,
charmed with beauty of their
verse,
With their loaded sideboards whispered 'Better join us, life is worse.'

Taught us at the annual camps
arranged by the big business men
'Sunbathe, pretty, till you're twenty,
You shall be our servants then.'

Perfect pater. Marvellous mater.
Knock the critic down who
dares—   25
Very well, believe it, copy, till your
hair is white as theirs.

Yours you say were parents to avoid,
avoid then if you please

Do the reverse on all occasion till you
    catch the same disease.

When we asked the way to Heaven,
    these directed us ahead
To the padded room, the clinic and
    the hangman's little shed.   30

Intimate as war-time prisoners in an
    isolation camp,
Living month by month together,
    nervy, famished, lousy, damp.

On the sopping esplanade or from our
    dingy lodgings we
Stare out dully at the rain which falls
    for miles into the sea.

Lawrence, Blake and Homer Lane,
    once healers in our English
    land;   35
These are dead as iron for ever; these
    can never hold our hand.

Lawrence was brought down by
    smuthounds, Blake went dotty as
    he sang,
Homer Lane was killed in action by
    the Twickenham Baptist gang.

Have things gone too far already? Are
    we done for? Must we wait
Hearing doom's approaching foot-
    steps regular down miles of
    straight;   40

Run the whole night through in gum-
    boots, stumble on and gasp for
    breath,
Terrors drawing close and closer,
    winter landscape, fox's death;

Or, in friendly fireside circle, sit and
    listen for the crash
Meaning that the mob has realized
    something's up, and start to
    smash;

Engine-drivers with their oil-cans, fac-
    tory girls in overalls   45
Blowing sky-high monster stores, de-
    stroying intellectuals?

Hope and fear are neck and neck;
    which is it near the course's end
Crashes, having lost his nerve; is over-
    taken on the bend?

Shut up talking, charming in the best
    suits to be had in town,
Lecturing on navigation while the
    ship is going down.   50

Drop those priggish ways for ever,
    stop behaving like a stone:
Throw the bath-chairs right away, and
    learn to leave ourselves alone.

If we really want to live, we'd better
    start at once to try;
If we don't, it doesn't matter, but we'd
    better start to die.

~~~~~~~~~~~~~~~~~~~~~~~~~~~~~~

HELENE MAGARET

Song of the Answerer [1]

(A Reply to Walt Whitman)

———————————————

I

I CELEBRATE America,
    For every atom belonging to
      America belongs to you and
    me,
And is a part of us.
Walt Whitman, come down!

[1] From *The Saturday Review*, December 17,
1938, with permission of the author.

And I will sing your message back to
you.   5
Now, in the fourth month, shoulder
to shoulder let us talk.

I celebrate the shanties of river-rats no
less than the skyscrapers eighty
stories high,
The widow reading, "We regret we
must waive dividends again,"
The Chairman of the Board still
drawing his hundred thousand
twice a year.
I am satisfied with what I see: 10
Sharecroppers starving in the South,
mobs milling in Detroit,
The machine guns down the alleys of
Chicago,
Thieves, murderers, men who traffic
in women,
I give all the same, I receive all the
same.
"And there will never be any more
perfection than there is now."   15

II

I celebrate America,
And beyond America I celebrate the
world.

The new-born babe in its mother's
lap, the father knee-deep in African swamps,
The dead in the gutters of Teruel, and
bodies floating down the Hwang-
Ho River.
"Clear and sweet is my soul, and clear
and sweet is all that is not my
soul."   20
Because we have no God in America,
Does anyone think it is wrong for the
Germans to have a God,
Who commands his people, and feeds
his sheep, and drives the money-
changers out?

Does anyone complain that in Russia
Trotsky had to flee,
And Gorki was murdered, and the
poets sold their souls to breathe
a little longer?   25
"It is well—against such I say not a
word."

All good things are waiting.
I say the deep trenches are being dug
for the happiness of men.
The gas masks being given free, the
big ships growing bigger.
I say we should thank Heaven for
liquid fire, for submarines and
airplanes,   30
And for the new bombs that can destroy a city fifty miles away.
"Has anyone supposed it lucky to be
born?
I hasten to inform him or her it is
just as lucky to die."

~*~*~*~*~*~*~*~*~*~*~*~

FLORENCE CONVERSE

Efficiency Expert [1]

THE conqueror's brow, the conqueror's chin, were his:
    That spacious depth and emi-
nence above
The deepset, steady eyes; that clean,
square angle
Of shaven, sensitive, relentless jaw
With never a reminiscent line of
horse   5
Or rabbit. All his motions were triumphant,
Co-ordinated, effortless, unconscious

[1] From *Efficiency Expert*, The John Day
Company, Inc., by permission.

As undefeated youth; for youth was
 his,—
That young maturity of twenty-seven,
Naïve, intransigent, and so cock-
 sure.   10
Running, he kept the easy conqueror's
 pace—
But at the moment, he was very still.

He had a way of going to the win-
 dow,
Putting the room behind him, shut-
 ting out
The official scenery, those last two
 minutes   15
Before the whistle blew. He had a
 way
Of standing with his hands thrust in
 his pockets,
Eyes on the morrow, tranquilly clair-
 voyant,
Beholding his obedient Plan unfold.
And so he stood there now, but some-
 thing held   20
The eyes from Vision, something
 balked the Plan.
A factor he had hitherto discounted
And turned away from for the sake of
 more
Important calculations and equations
Had failed to disappear. He stood
 bemused,   25
Mulling the problem over (Dammit!
 Why
Should that new Mission House across
 the way
Parade its bread-line past our factory
 windows?).
The whistle boomed; the sharp elec-
 tric gong
Trilled in the corridor; and he, as
 prompt   30
And automatic as a robot, wheeled
Upon the room, upon the model flash-
 ing

Against the western sun.—But robots
 never
Survey their universe through haunted
 eyes.—
He slipped the typed report for the
 directors   35
Into the right-hand top drawer of the
 desk
And pocketed the letter from the
 Soviets,
No motion wasted. But around his
 mouth
A faint aversion curdled when he
 lifted
The model from the desk and carried
 it   40
Gingerly to the safe,—the little model
He had designed to scrap three hun-
 dred men.
(How was it that they didn't cancel
 out?)
The homing river of souls began to
 flow
Along the corridor outside his
 door;   45
He heard the cataract go dashing
 down
The fireproof stairs. It was his daily
 habit,
Integral to the mass psychology
Of his technique, to mingle with that
 flood.   49
His predecessor on the job had failed
Chiefly because of his standoffishness;
A tendency to take the elevator,
To skip before the gong. (And those
 of us,
High-paid, white-collar men, not
 asked to punch
The time-clock, know it's not the
 Management   55
That breaks us, it's the men, if we
 presume
On privilege.) He shivered; but he
 plunged.

And every passing face was turned to meet
His own, at the click of the opening office-door.
And every face was such a friendly face: 60
Tony Vannucci,—yes, he'd have to go.
Four children under ten, another coming;
A darned good fellow, Tony, if he only
Co-ordinated better. Jack Dufour,—
Triplets and twins and seven other kids,   65
And such a pretty French-Canadian wife;
He'd have to go; he'd always be a plodder.
And Archie MacNamara,—Hell! What can you
Do with a man like that? By rights he ought
To be a foreman, but he won't cut out   70
The booze. And Pete, the Swede, another boozer.
And Timmie Corrigan,—so loud, so gay,
So irresponsible, and so good-looking.
They'll miss you at the Company's annual Picnic,
Timmie; they'll miss you on the baseball team   75
In mill sixteen; there's no one else can pitch
Your ball. (Now, there's a possibility!
Professional Baseball? I'll suggest it to him.
So irresponsible?—Still, I'll suggest it.)
And James McConnell,—nothing wrong with him;   80
And Julius Golden, nothing to complain of

In him, except that he's approaching fifty;
And Petersen, and Gammage, and old Jones
The Welshman—every one a steady worker—
They'll go; they'll have to go; three hundred men   85
With families, and next to nothing saved.
Old Jones, with that pure silver voice of his,
Leading the bashful tenors in the glee club
I organized. (O damn my facile genius
For organizing! Jones! my dear old Jones!   90
The devil of it is they're friends of mine,
These men. They trust me.)
        And the word Betrayer,
Emerging suddenly, precipitated
A landslide in his mind that dizzied him.   95
The stair-head took him unaware; he pitched.
It seemed as if a world of kindly hands
Steadied him on the instant. Some-one said
Something about the way we always feel
The first hot day and this was sure a scorcher.   100
But down below him on the clattering stairs,
Faces full of concern kept looking back.
And through the welter of his mind's confusion,
Those opening words he'd scribbled off today
For that address upon the new technique—   105

Two-forty at the Harvard Business
　　School
On Wednesday next—went eddying
　　round and round:
"First catch your men. The Art of
　　Management
Starts with the get-together principle,
Dynamically worded in Rule
　　One: 110
Make yourself solid with the men."

　　　　　　　His gorge
Rose, but he had himself in hand by
　　now,
And eased his hat against the chilly
　　start
Of sweat. And the river pouring
　　down the flume,   115
Bore him along.—
　　　　Thinking, thinking, thinking:
We call it Labor, a collective term
Convenient for mathematical equa-
　　tions,
Dehumanized, but not to be con-
　　fused   120
With Work, or Ergs, or Force, or
　　Energy,
Or Horse Power, or Inertia, or Mo-
　　mentum.
We designate it by a coefficient,
Numerical or other, which must al-
　　ways
Diminish. That's our problem: how
　　to make   125
The human factor vanish. And we
　　do it
On paper, up to ninety-nine percent.
And from the shop, the factory, the
　　mill,
It disappears, almost. That is to
　　say,—

It is displaced. But anything dis-
　　placed   130
Will turn up somewhere else in an
　　equation
As in a universe. Are we confusing
"Displaced" with "vanished" in our
　　computations?
By balance or increase of other terms,
As Time, the Talkies, Mergers, Mo-
　　tion-Study,   135
Shop-Routing, and Machines,—chiefly
　　Machines,—

The term twelve million L has dis-
　　appeared
From Industry; but it persists in Life.
The question is: Need we consider
　　Life
In technological experiment?   140
We haven't thought it necessary, yet.
We don't include it in our formulae.
Or do we? Don't we? There's con-
　　fusion here.
And Life and Labor both begin with
　　L.
Is that our error?—Yes, by God, it
　　clicks!   145
To Hell with mathematical equations!
It's men we're dealing with—(No,
　　Corrigan;
No taxi, thank you. What I need's
　　a walk.
Exercise. Yes; the first hot day; a
　　scorcher.
But cooling off.) It's men we're deal-
　　ing with.   150
It's men. It's men. Twelve million
　　unemployed.
Damnation! Here's that Mission
　　House to pass.

CARL SANDBURG

I Am the People, the Mob[1]

I AM the people—the mob—the
    crowd—the mass.
Do you know that all the great
    work of the world is done
    through me?
I am the workingman, the inventor,
    the maker of the world's food
    and clothes.
I am the audience that witnesses his-
    tory. The Napoleons come from
    me and the Lincolns. They die.
    And then I send forth more Na-
    poleons and Lincolns.
I am the seed ground. I am a prairie
that will stand for much plowing.
    Terrible storms pass over me. I
    forget. The best of me is sucked
    out and wasted. I forget. Every-
    thing but Death comes to me and
    makes me work and give up
    what I have. And I forgot.   5
Sometimes I growl, shake myself and
    spatter a few red drops for His-
    tory of remember. Then—I for-
    get.
When I, the People, learn to remem-
    ber, when I, the People, use the
    lessons of yesterday and no longer
    forget who robbed me last year,
    who played me for a fool—then
    there will be no speaker in all
    the world say the name: "The
    People," with any fleck of a sneer
    in his voice or any far-off smile
    of derision.
The mob—the crowd—the mass—will
    arrive then.

[1] From *Chicago Poems,* Henry Holt and Company, by permission.

ARCHIBALD MacLEISH

Speech to Those Who Say Comrade[2]

THE brotherhood is not by the blood certainly:
But neither are men brothers by speech—by saying so:
Men are brothers by life lived and are hurt for it:

Hunger and hurt are the great begetters of brotherhood:
Humiliation has gotten much love: 5
Danger I say is the nobler father and mother:

Those are as brothers whose bodies have shared fear
Or shared harm or shared hurt or indignity.
Why are the old soldiers brothers and nearest?

[2] From A. MacLeish, *Public Speech.* Copyright, Rinehart & Company, Inc.

For this: with their minds they go over the sea a little   10
And find themselves in their youth again as they were in
Soissons and Meaux and at Ypres and those cities:

A French loaf and the girls with their eyelids painted
Bring back to aging and lonely men
Their twentieth year and the metal odor of danger: 15

It is this in life which of all things is tenderest—
To remember together with unknown men the days
Common also to them and perils ended:

It is this which makes of many a generation—
A wave of men who having the same years   20
Have in common the same dead and the changes.

The solitary and unshared experience
Dies of itself like the violations of love
Or lives on as the dead live eerily:

The unshared and single man must cover his   25
Loneliness as a girl her shame for the way of
Life is neither by one man nor by suffering.

Who are the born brothers in truth? The puddlers
Scorched by the same flame in the same foundries:
Those who have spit on the same boards with the blood in it: 30

Ridden the same rivers with green logs:
Fought the police in the parks of the same cities:
Grinned for the same blows: the same flogging:

Veterans out of the same ships—factories—
Expeditions for fame: the founders of continents: 35
Those that hid in Geneva a time back:

Those that have hidden and hunted and all such—
Fought together: labored together: they carry the
Common look like a card and they pass touching.

Brotherhood! No word said can make you brothers!   40
Brotherhood only the brave earn and by danger or
Harm or by bearing hurt and by no other.

Brotherhood here in the strange world is the rich and
Rarest giving of life and the most valued:
Not to be had for a word or a week's wishing.   45

≈≈≈≈≈≈≈≈≈≈≈≈≈≈≈≈≈≈≈≈≈≈≈≈≈≈≈

STEPHEN SPENDER

*Moving through the Silent
Crowd* [1]

Moving through the silent
crowd
Who stand behind dull
cigarettes
These men who idle in the road,
I have the sense of falling light.

They lounge at corners of the street
And greet friends with a shrug of
shoulder   6

[1] Reprinted by permission of Random
House, New York.

And turn their empty pockets out,
The cynical gestures of the poor.

Now they've no work, like better
men
Who sit at desks and take much
pay   10
They sleep long nights and rise at
ten
To watch the hours that drain away.

I'm jealous of the weeping hours
They stare through with such hungry
eyes.
I'm haunted by these images,   15
I'm haunted by their emptiness.

POEMS ABOUT LIBERTY

JOHN MILTON

From *Areopagitica*

THIS is true Liberty, when free-
born men
Having to advise the public
may speak free,
Which he who can, and will, deserv's
high praise,
Who neither can nor will, may hold
his peace;
What can be juster in a State than
this? 5
⌈Translated from *Euripides*⌉

JOHN DRYDEN

From *The Hind and the Panther*

OF all the tyrannies of human
kind
The worst is that which per-
secutes the mind.
Let us but weigh at what offence we
strike;
'Tis but because we cannot think
alike.
In punishing of this we overthrow 5
The laws of nations and of nature too.
Beasts are the subjects of tyrannic
sway,
Where still the stronger on the
weaker prey;

Man only of a softer mould is made,
Not for his fellows' ruin but their
aid: 10
Created kind, beneficent and free,
The noble image of the Deity.

WILLIAM WORDSWORTH

It Is Not to Be Thought

IT IS not to be thought of that the
Flood
Of British freedom, which, to the
open sea
Of the world's praise from dark an-
tiquity
Hath flowed, "with pomp of waters,
unwithstood,"
Roused though it be full often to a
mood 5
Which spurns the check of salutary
bands
That this most famous Stream in bogs
and sands
Should perish; and to evil and to
good
Be lost for ever. In our halls is hung
Armoury of the invincible Knights of
old: 10
We must be free or die, who speak
the tongue
That Shakespeare spake; the faith
and morals hold
Which Milton held.—In everything
we are sprung
Of Earth's first blood, have titles
manifold.

WALTER SAVAGE LANDOR

A Foreign Ruler

H E SAYS, *My reign is peace,* so
    slays
    A thousand in the dead of
  night.
Are you all happy now? he says,
  And those he leaves behind cry
    quite.
He swears he will have no conten-
  tion,   5
  And sets all nations by the ears;
He shouts aloud, *No intervention!*
  Invades, and drowns them all in
    tears.

ALFRED, LORD TENNYSON

You Ask Me, Why, Though Ill at Ease

Y OU ask me, why, though ill at
    ease,
    Within this region I subsist,
Whose spirits falter in the mist,
And languish for the purple seas.

It is the land that freemen till,   5
  That sober-suited Freedom chose,
  The land where, girt with friends
    or foes,
A man may speak the thing he will;

A land of settled government,
  A land of just and old renown,   10

Where Freedom slowly broadens
  down
From precedent to precedent;

Where faction seldom gathers head,
  But, by degrees to fullness wrought,
  The strength of some diffusive
    thought   15
Hath time and space to work and
  spread.

Should banded unions persecute
  Opinion, and induce a time
  When single thought is civil crime,
And individual freedom mute,   20

Though power should make from
  land to land
  The name of Britain trebly great—
  Though every channel of the State
Should fill and choke with golden
  sand—

Yet waft me from the harbor-mouth,
  Wild wind! I seek a warmer sky   26
  And I will see before I die
The palms and temples of the South.

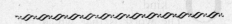

HENRY DAVID THOREAU

Independence

M Y LIFE more civil is and free
    Than any civil polity.

Ye princes, keep your realms
  And circumscribed power,
Not wide as are my dreams,   5
  Nor rich as is this hour.

What can ye give which I have not?
What can ye take which I have got?
  Can ye defend the dangerless?
  Can ye inherit nakedness?   10

To all true wants Time's ear is deaf,
Penurious States lend no relief
    Out of their pelf:
  But a free soul—thank God—
    Can help itself.   15

    Be sure your fate
Doth keep apart its state,—
Not linked with any band,
Even the noblest in the land,—

In tented fields with cloth of gold 20
  No place doth hold,
But is more chivalrous than they are,
  And sigheth for a nobler war;

  A finer strain its trumpet rings,
  A brighter gleam its armor flings. 25

The life that I aspire to live,
  No man proposeth me;
No trade upon the street
  Wears its emblazonry.

SAMUEL FRANCIS SMITH

America

My country,—'tis of thee,
  Sweet land of liberty,
    Of thee I sing;
Land where my fathers died,
Land of the pilgrims' pride,   5
From every mountain side
  Let freedom ring.

My native country,—thee,
Land of the noble, free,
  Thy name I love;   10

I love thy rocks and rills,
Thy woods and templed hills,
My heart with rapture thrills
  Like that above.

Let music swell the breeze,   15
And ring from all the trees
  Sweet freedom's song;
Let mortal tongues awake,
Let all that breathe partake,
Let rocks their silence break,—   20
  The sound prolong.

Our fathers' God,—to Thee,
Author of liberty,
  To Thee we sing;
Long may our land be bright   25
With freedom's holy light,
Protect us by Thy might,
  Great God, our King.

JOHN GREENLEAF WHITTIER

Laus Deo! [1]

It is done!
  Clang of bell and roar of gun
  Send the tidings up and down.
How the belfries rock and reel!
How the great guns, peal on
    peal,   5
Fling the joy from town to town!

  Ring, O bells!
  Every stroke exulting tells
Of the burial hour of crime.
  Loud and long, that all may hear, 10
  Ring for every listening ear
Of Eternity and Time!

[1] On hearing the bells ring on the passage of the Thirteenth Amendment to the Constitution (1865) abolishing slavery.

Let us kneel:
 God's own voice is in that peal,
And this spot is holy ground.   15
 Lord, forgive us! What are we,
 That our eyes this glory see,
That our ears have heard the sound!

 For the Lord
 On the whirlwind is abroad;   20
In the earthquake He has spoken;
 He has smitten with His thunder
 The iron walls asunder,
And the gates of brass are broken!

 Loud and long   25
 Lift the old exulting song;
Sing with Miriam by the sea,
 He has cast the mighty down;
 Horse and rider sink and drown;
"He hath triumphed gloriously!"   30

 Did we dare,
 In our agony of prayer,
Ask for more than He has done?
 When was ever his right hand
 Over any time or land   35
Stretched as now beneath the sun?

 How they pale,
 Ancient myth and song and tale,
In this wonder of our days,
 When the cruel rod of war   40
 Blossoms white with righteous law,
And the wrath of man is praise!

 Blotted out!
 All within and all about
Shall a fresher life begin;   45
 Freer breathe the universe
 As it rolls its heavy curse
On the dead and buried sin!

 It is done!
 In the circuit of the sun   50
Shall the sound thereof go forth,
 It shall bid the sad rejoice,

It shall give the dumb a voice,
It shall belt with joy the earth!

 Ring and swing,   55
 Bells of joy! On morning's wing
Send the song of praise abroad!
 With a sound of broken chains
 Tell the nations that He reigns,
Who alone is Lord and God!   60

ALFRED KREYMBORG

Ballad of the Common Man [1]

For the Jefferson Memorial

To HIM who felt a human sea
 Begin to rise for liberty,
  Build, O men, keep building!

To him who raised the human pen
That freed the first American,   5
 Build, O men, keep building!

For he is in the common star
Of all we live in, all we are
In sons and more sons near and far—
 Build, O men, keep building!   10

And rear your temple all around
Our common feet and common
  ground,
Giving our love a common sound—
 Build, O men, keep building!

And let us feel there is no night   15
Can ever hide the growing light—
The light he saw, the light he
  spread—
And all our sight, though he is dead—
 Build, O men, keep building!

And even though your labor's done 20
And the race may rest in Jefferson,
Rise up again, there's more to be
done!
 Build, O men, keep building!
 Keep on building Men!

~~~~~~~~~~~~~~~~~~~~~~~~~~~~~~~~~~

JOYCE KILMER

The Peacemaker [1]

U PON his will he binds a radiant
  chain,
 For Freedom's sake he is no
longer free.
It is his task, the slave of Liberty,

[1] From *Poems, Essays and Letters,* by Joyce Kilmer, copyright, 1914, 1917, 1918, by Doubleday & Company, Inc.

With his own blood to wipe away a
 stain.
That pain may cease, he yields his
 flesh to pain. 5
 To banish war, he must a warrior
 be.
 He dwells in Night, eternal Dawn
 to see,
And gladly dies, abundant life to
 gain.
What matters Death, if Freedom be
 not dead?
 No flags are fair, if Freedom's flag
 be furled. 10
Who fights for Freedom, goes with
 joyful tread
 To meet the fires of Hell against
 him hurled,
And has for captain Him whose
 thorn-wreathed head
 Smiles from the Cross upon a conquered world.

~~~~~~

LANGSTON HUGHES

Let America Be America Again [2]

L ET America be America again.
 Let it be the dream it used to be.
 Let it be the pioneer on the plain
Seeking a home where he himself is free.

(America never was America to me.) 5

Let America be the dream that dreamers dreamed—
Let it be that great strong land of love
Where never kings connive nor tyrants scheme
That any man be crushed by one above.

(It never was America to me.) 10

[2] Reprinted by permission of Maxim Lieber, authors' representative.

O, let my land be a land where Liberty
Is crowned with no false patriotic wreath,
But opportunity is real, and life is free,
Equality is in the air we breathe.

(There's never been equality for me,   15
Nor freedom in this "homeland of the free.")

Say who are you that mumbles in the dark?
And who are you that draws your veil across the stars?

I am the poor white, fooled and pushed apart,
I am the Negro bearing slavery's scars.   20
I am the red man driven from the land,
I am the immigrant clutching the hope I seek—
And finding only the same old stupid plan.
Of dog eat dog, of mighty crush the weak.

I am the young man, full of strength and hope,   25
Tangled in that ancient endless chain
Of profit, power, gain, of grab the land!
Of grab the gold! Of grab the ways of satisfying need!
Of work the men! Of take the pay!
Of owning everything for one's own greed!   30

I am the farmer, bondsman to the soil.
I am the worker sold to the machine.
I am the Negro, servant to you all.
I am the people, humble, hungry, mean—
Hungry yet today despite the dream.   35
Beaten yet today—O, Pioneers
I am the man who never got ahead,
The poorest worker bartered through the years.

Yet I'm the one who dreamt our basic dream
In that Old World while still a serf of kings,   40
Who dreamt a dream so strong, so brave, so true,
That even yet its mighty daring sings
In every brick and stone, in every furrow turned
That's made America the land it has become.
O, I'm the man who sailed those early seas   45
In search of what I meant to be my home—
For I'm the one who left dark Ireland's shore,
And Poland's plain, and England's grassy lea,

And torn from Black Africa's strand I came
To build a "homeland of the free."   50

The free?

Who said the free? Not me?
Surely not me? The millions on relief today?
The millions shot down when we strike?
The millions who have nothing for our pay?   55
For all the dreams we've dreamed
And all the songs we've sung
And all the hopes we've held
And all the flags we've hung,
The millions who have nothing for our pay—   60
Except the dream that's almost dead today.

O, let America be America again—
The land that never has been yet—
And yet must be—the land where every man is free.
The land that's mine—the poor man's, Indian's, Negro's, ME—   65
Who made America.
Whose sweat and blood, whose faith and pain,
Whose hand at the foundry, whose plow in the rain,
Must bring back our mighty dream again.

Sure, call me any ugly name you choose—   70
The steel of freedom does not stain.
From those who live like leeches on the people's lives,
We must take back our land again,
America!

O, yes,   75
I say it plain,
America never was America to me,
And yet I swear this oath—
America will be!

Out of the rack and ruin of our gangster death,   80
The rape and rot of graft, and stealth, and lives,
We, the people, must redeem
The land, the mines, the plants, the rivers,
The mountains and the endless plain—
All, all the stretch of these great green states—   85
And make America again!

JAMES OPPENHEIM

The Slave [1]

THEY set the slave free, striking off his chains;
  Then he was as much of a slave as ever.

  He was still chained to servility,
  He was still manacled to indolence and sloth,
  He was still bound by fear and superstition,   5
  By ignorance, suspicion, and savagery.
  His slavery was not in the chains,
  But in himself.

  They can only set free men free,
  And there is no need of that: 10
  Free men set themselves free.

GEORGE SANTAYANA

My Heart Rebels against My Generation [2]

MY HEART rebels against my generation,
  That talks of freedom and is slave to riches,
  And, toiling 'neath each day's ignoble burden,
  Boasts of the morrow.

No space for noonday rest or midnight watches,   5
No purest joy of breathing under heaven!
Wretched themselves, they heap, to make them happy,
  Many possessions.

But thou, O silent Mother, wise, immortal,
To whom our toil is laughter,—take, divine one,   10
This vanity away, and to thy lover
  Give what is needful:—

[1] From *Songs for the New Age,* by permission of the author's literary executors.
[2] From *Poems* by George Santayana. Copyright, 1921, by George Santayana, published by Charles Scribner's Sons.

A staunch heart, nobly calm, averse to evil,
The windy sky for breath, the sea, the mountain,
A well-born, gentle friend, his spirit's brother,   15
   Ever beside him.

What would you gain, ye seekers, with your striving,
Or what vast Babel raise you on your shoulders?
You multiply distresses, and your children
   Surely will curse you.   20

O leave them rather friendlier gods, and fairer
Orchards and temples, and a freer bosom!
What better comfort have we, or what other
   Profit in living,

Than to feed, sobered by the truth of Nature,   25
Awhile upon her bounty and her beauty,
And hand her torch of gladness to the ages
   Following after?

She hath not made us, like her other children,
Merely for peopling of her spacious kingdoms,   30
Beasts of the wild, or insects of the summer,
   Breeding and dying,

But also that we might, half knowing, worship
The deathless beauty of her guiding vision,
And learn to love, in all things mortal, only   35
   What is eternal.

BIOGRAPHY

FLORENCE NIGHTINGALE—*Strachey*

Does Florence Nightingale's story rouse your interest? For what reasons? Have you met men or women like her? Do you think it would be a good thing if there were more like her in your home town and in college? Do you feel that the portrait is true? Does Strachey indulge in humor at his heroine's expense? With what effect? How much does Strachey quote, and why? Can you explain the frequent use of question and exclamation? Does the end detract from your admiration of the character? Does it seem to have the same effect as a great tragedy has, purging our minds, as Aristotle declared, through the emotions of pity and terror? Compare its effect with that of the death of Eustacia Vye in *The Return of the Native*.

Possible Themes: 1. A Character Study of a Reformer I Have Known; 2. The Story of a Strong-Willed Woman; 3. Inefficiency in Our Armed Forces; 4. Florence Nightingale Writes a Letter on *The Charge of the Light Brigade* (see Tennyson's poem); 5. Do We Need a Reformer in College?; 6. A Woman's Handicaps Today; 7. The Art of Strachey; 8. Humor and Heroism.

J. E. B. STUART—*Bradford*

Study the arrangement in this biography. How does it differ from that in Strachey's? What is its guiding principle? Note carefully the transitional sentences. What are the characteristics of the ideal officer? Are any of Stuart's ideals or methods out of date? How does the code of honor in modern warfare differ from that maintained in the Civil War?

Possible Themes: The Knight of the Golden Spurs; 2. Chivalry in Modern Warfare; 3. Southern Colonel; 4. A Gentleman of the Old South; 5. Bombing Women and Children; 6. Improvements in Warfare.

ABRAHAM LINCOLN, THE FIRST PRAIRIE YEARS—*Sandburg*

What elements of greatness did Lincoln have to start with? What elements did he acquire by his own efforts? What outside forces or circumstances lent depth and strength to his mind and character? As revealed in this part of his life, does he seem a bigger personality than Florence Nightingale or Stuart, or a smaller? Can you detect anywhere the seeds of the Gettysburg Address? Does Sandburg's familiarity with Illinois and its people appear in these pages? Can you detect passages where Sandburg is revealed as a poet? Do you find any traces of sentimentality in phrasing? After reading Sherman's review of Sandburg's *Lincoln, The Prairie Years,* are there any additions you would like to make?

Possible Themes: 1. How Lincoln Made Himself; 2. The Bigness of Lincoln; 3. If Lincoln Had Gone to College; 4. Lincoln and Stuart—a Contrast; 5. Lincoln and Stuart—a Comparison; 6. The Prairie a Hundred Years Ago; 7. The Meaning of Ann Rutledge; 8. Lincoln Would Have Appreciated Hardy.

FOURS YEARS IN A SHED—*Curie*

What makes scientists, as well as other men, conservative? In what spheres and in what people have you observed similar conservatism? What motives have you discovered for this attitude? If you have read Robinson's *Four Kinds of Thinking* in this book, do you find there a correct diagnosis of the conservative mind? Of the creative mind? Is there any sound argument in favor of conservatism? Should the government endow scientific research or should it be left to the universities and corporations? What valuable researches does our government carry on? What do you know about them? How is the difference between Pierre and Marie Curie brought out? What is the value of a strong emotional nature in science? How does it appear in this narrative? What light does this biography shed on marriage and a career for women? Read Fadiman's review of *Madame Curie* in this book. What does he emphasize?

Possible Themes: 1. Science and Conservatism; 2. The Standpat Mind; 3. The Endowment of Research; 4. Women in Science; 5. The Poetic Side of Science; 6. A Husband, a Home, and a Career; 7. When Should a Married Woman Engage in a Profession?; 8. Dramatic Moments.

ELIZABETH ARDEN—*Harriman*

Compare the careers of Florence Nightingale and Florence Nightingale Graham. Which career seems to have been productive of the greater personal happiness? Does the marriage of Madame Curie or that of "Elizabeth Arden" seem to have been the more successful? Can you offer any explanation? What can be said for the beauty business? What can be said against it? Does the author of this sketch take sides, or is she impartial? What touches, pro and con, do you perceive? What difference in tone from that of the other biographies do you find? How is it produced?

Possible Themes: 1. Two Florence Nightingales; 2. A Recipe for Divorce; 3. The Makings of a Beautician; 4. A Recipe for Beauty; 5. Women Are Fools; 6. Men Like Them That Way; 7. What's Wrong with the Beauty Parlor?; 8. An Ironic Biographic Sketch of a Successful Man.

MY BROTHER STEVE—*Benét*

What difference in attitude do you perceive between Eve Curie's and William Benét's attitudes toward their subjects? How is this accounted for? Read the poems by the two Benét brothers in this book. Do you find any explanation of their congeniality? What factors went into the making of *John Brown's Body?* How important was home environment, reading habits, college training?

Possible Themes: 1. The Story of My Older Brother; 2. The Making of a Poet; 3. The Reading Habit; 4. Brothers and Sisters.

LIFE WITH FATHER—*Day*

Note in these two sketches the introduction of brief explanatory passages. Underline the vigorous verbs. Observe that the diction, though colloquial, is not slangy. Be able to show what each of "Father's" remarks contributes to the realization of his character.

Possible Themes: 1. Father Meets an Emergency; 2. Helpless Male; 3. Tinkering with the Car; 4. Masculine Pride; 5. Housekeeping Crisis; 6. Father and Mother; 7. Who's the Boss?

EARLY IMPRESSIONS—*Adams*

What does Adams mean in the first paragraph by atmosphere or tone? Where and how could one learn to recognize it? What "treasures of sense" were yours in childhood? By what means, by what phrases does Adams convey an impression of his grandmother's personality? What ideas have you been brought up to believe are alone respectable? Is society today approaching a chasm with its eyes turned away? What aspects of American life are neglected by the comfortable classes?

Possible Themes: 1. Sense Impressions of Childhood; 2. Winter versus Summer; 3. She Belonged to Another World; 4. Respectable Beliefs; 5. Religious Stagnation; 6. The Power of Religion.

ROWING—*La Farge*

Into what parts is this autobiographic sketch divided? How are the divisions indicated? Which parts are expository, which descriptive, which narrative? What are the values of athletics? What are its drawbacks?

Possible Themes: 1. How I Trained for . . .; 2. The Way to Handle a Paddle (Tennis Racket, Bazooka, Tommy Gun); 3. The Art of Canoeing (Tackling, Pitching Hay, Broiling a Steak); 4. The Last Lap; 5. The Last Inning; 6. The Last Play; 7. What I Get out of Athletics.

UNIVERSITY DAYS—*Thurber*

Is there a serious aspect to this humorous piece of writing? What devices does the author use to prepare and touch off your sense of humor?

Possible Themes: 1. Laboratory Comedy; 2. Pulling Our Fullback Through; 3. Drill; 4. A Field Trip; 5. And the Class Exploded; 6. Do Instructors Understand?; 7. Is College a Joke?

THE MODERN GOTHIC—*Sheean*

What experience have you had of the seamy side of business? Was Mr. Sheean's experience typical of business in general? Do you prefer "snap" courses? Do you find them valuable? Or are you the victim of your own cleverness? Note the ironic passages regarding the summer students. Does the irony reflect upon them or on the author? Have you begun to find ideas important, exciting? Has the discovery come through contact with some stimulating personality, through classroom discussion, or through books; or did you make the discovery for yourself? Should college mean more than discovering enthusiasms?

Possible Themes: 1. My Experience in Business; 2. My Employer; 3. Ironies of Student Life; 4. Grinds and Collegians; 5. "Getting By"; 6. A Great Teacher; 7. The Thrill of the Library; 8. The Fascination of . . . .

FLYERS ARE INARTICULATE—*Lay*

Read this narrative in conjunction with Eaton's *Daily Theme Eye* in this book. Pick out examples of the writer's eye in Lay's story. What other sense impressions are conveyed? How does the choice of words help? Underscore particularly effective expressions. Is the faculty of fully realizing sensations valuable to those who are not professional writers, and how? What experiences of yours can you recall most completely in sensory detail?

Possible Themes: 1. The Vocabulary of Sensations; 2. What Makes a Story Real?; 3. Sensations on a Plane; 4. The Thrill of Skiing; 5. Is There Poetry in Motoring?; 6. A Country Canter.

BRAVE MEN—*Pyle*

What qualities, in your opinion, made Pyle the most widely read war correspondent? In what ways does he reveal his attitude toward the soldier? How does he produce atmosphere? How does he give a sense of character?

Possible Themes: 1. Ernie Pyle, Brave Man; 2. Ernie Pyle, Writer; 3. GI Joe; 4. The Best Officer I Knew; 5. An Incident of the War; 6. Comradeship among Fighting Men.

THE PERSONAL ESSAY

THE GENTLE GIANTESS—*Lamb*

Look up all unfamiliar words in the dictionary and be ready to give accurate definitions. What does the vocabulary add to the essay? Can you recognize the literary allusions to "the maid's aunt of Brainford," "Atlantean shoulders"? Note the ingenuity of the similes. Note the emphasis on incongruity. How is the essay planned? How does Lamb avoid crudity or cruelty?

Possible Themes: 1. A Native of Brobdingnag; 2. Appearances Are Deceptive; 3. A Midget; 4. A Gentle Soul; 5. Visitors to the Campus.

On Going a Journey—*Hazlitt*

Read what Mr. Maugham has to say in this book about Hazlitt's style. Be able to illustrate each of Maugham's statements by specific sentences or passages. Notice the remarkable range of Hazlitt's enthusiasms; list them. How many of them do you share? Though Hazlitt quarreled with most of his friends, was unfortunate in love and matrimony, and saw most of the political ideals for which he fought crushed by superior force, he was yet able to say with his last breath, "Well, I have had a happy life." Can you account for this?

Possible Themes: 1. Writing with Gusto; 2. Tastes Differ; 3. Adventures of the Road; 4. At a Country Hotel; 5. Faded Hopes; 6. Companions of the Road; 7. Mountain Climbing.

Sounds—*Thoreau*

Try the experiment of excluding other sense impressions for a while and paying attention only to sounds. What memories do they evoke? What thoughts do they provoke? What images of far-off times or places rise? Do you find pleasure in the experience? Can you convey some of it to your readers by choosing those sounds which have called up the most vivid, original, or amusing reflections?

Possible Themes: 1. A Locomotive Whistle; 2. A Bird Call; 3. Traffic Noises; 4. Interrupted Studies; 5. Campus Quietude.

Crabbed Age and Youth—*Stevenson*

What advice have you heard or what proverbs have you read which counsel caution? When is caution wisdom? When is it folly? When is it cowardice? Is Stevenson right in saying that opinions inevitably change with changes in age or circumstances? Is there no possibility of arriving at some fairly solid conclusions early in life? Do college studies offer such a possibility? Does the reading of books? Can you already suggest some ideas which you confidently expect to hold the rest of your life? On what are these ideas based? Study the means by which Stevenson gives vitality and humor to broad generalities.

Possible Themes: 1. On Being Too Cautious; 2. Lying Proverbs; 3. My Generation; 4. When I Am a Grandfather; 5. Boyhood Enthusiasms; 6. Son's Advice to Father; 7. My Permanent Creed.

Hunting the Deceitful Turkey—*Twain*

Here we have a bit of autographic narrative, spiced with humor and random reflections. It would scarcely belong in an autobiography, since it is trivial in subject and probably not too veracious. Can you point to specific passages in which Twain uses exaggeration, understatement, mingling the incongruous, as means to tickle the reader's ribs? Do you remember any passages in Hardy's *Return of the Native* or Huxley's *Evolution and Ethics* which express the same doubt of Nature's benevolence as Twain here sets forth?

Possible Themes: 1. A Wild Goose Chase; 2. Animals Are Human; 3. Outsmarted by a Bird (Dog, Horse); 4. Once When I Was Hunting . . . ; 5. That Fish Got Away from Me; 6. Nature's Little Treacheries.

How Shall I Word It?—*Beerbohm*

Do you consider the first paragraph to be a good introduction to what follows? Is there any novelty in the subject? Note the author's figures of speech, his sudden turns of thought, and his choice of names. What do these things tell you about him? Do you think him malicious? What would happen if we were to tell our real thoughts for even one hour?

Possible Themes: 1. A Letter I Should Like to Write; 2. The Art of Insult; 3. Sweetness and Light in Business Letters; 4. False Courtesy and True; 5. It's Tact That Makes the World Go Round; 6. Are We All Hypocrites?

Mr. Dooley on the Education of the Young—*Dunne*

What faults in American education is Mr. Dooley satirizing? What experience have you had with these faults? What do you think you should have learned in school that you now miss? What do you think Mr. Dooley would say about President Hutchins' ideas on *Gate Receipts and Glory* as presented in this book? Does the dialog form add anything to the naturalness or humor of the essay? What devices does Dunne use to secure his funniest effects?

Possible Themes: 1. A Dialog on School Days; 2. My Parents Discuss My Career; 3. Education for Life; 4. Mr. Dooley on President Hutchins; 5. Some Teachers I Have Known.

Codfish Chowder and Sun—*Coffin*

Do you know a better place to picnic than Pond Island? If so, how would you bring out its fascinations? If not, examine closely how Mr. Coffin brings out the fascinations of his picnic ground.

Possible Themes: 1. The Perfect Picnic; 2. Appetizers; 3. "When We Were Very Young"; 4. Amateur Seamanship; 5. Buried Treasure; 6. The Family on an Outing.

From Spargo to Carver to Speaker—*Broun*

Does this essay illustrate Robinson's distinction between "good reasons" and "real reasons"? (See pp. 354-57.) What feature makes it equally amusing and inoffensive to radical and conservatives? Does it read well? Test the sentences by ear. Note the bookish phrases and the colloquial. Do they harmonize? Why? Is the alliteration effective?

Possible Themes: 1. In the Spring a Young Man's Fancy . . .; 2. Where Are the Notes of Yesteryear?; 3. The Bases Were Full and . . .; 4. Soap-Box Orators; 5. Rugged Individualism in Athletics; 6. I Became a Convert to . . .

A Garland of Ibids—*Sullivan*

Do not forget to read the footnotes. Do not forget that the author's name is Sullivan.

Possible Themes: 1. A Footnote on Frank Sullivan; 2. Cabots and Coughlins; 3. Footnotes on Kittredge's *The Yankee School;* 4. I Like Footnotes; 5. The Irish of It.

Spring Comes to the Farm—*Martin*

How do you like the style of this essay as compared with that of Thoreau's *Sounds* or Coffin's *Codfish Chowder and Sun?* Do you think it fits the subject?

Possible Themes: 1. Spring (or another season) Comes to the Campus; 2. Peace in the Country; 3. Farm Days; 4. The Price of Butter and Eggs; 5. A Woman on the Farm.

Of Goodness—*Jackson*

What differentiates this essay from a sermon? Do the many literary references and quotations add to or detract from its appeal to you? Why? Have you read anything in this book which helps to define goodness, to make it real? What flaws in the American concept of goodness has the war or its aftermath revealed? What can be done about it? Who is the best man or woman you know, and what are his or her essential qualities?

Possible Themes: 1. The Cult of Evil in Germany; 2. The Cult of Evil in America; 3. The Best Man (or Woman) I Know; 4. Sentimental Christianity; 5. Goodness without Brains; 6. Wartime Virtues in Peacetime.

READING, WRITING, AND REVIEWS

OF READING BOOKS—*Lowes*

How many hours a week do you give on the average to the radio? to the moving pictures? to the newspaper? to the picture magazines such as *Life* and *Look?* Add up the total. After careful consideration, estimate how much of that time afforded mere relaxation and entertainment without any sort of intellectual or cultural value. Set down the figure. On the other hand, estimate the number of hours you give weekly to the *voluntary* reading of literature that possesses style, including everything from the best modern weeklies, such as the *New Yorker* and the *New Republic,* to Emerson and *Don Quixote.* Does the comparison afford you satisfaction? Do you ever read for pleasure in your vacations? What? Does the amount and quality of voluntary reading you do bear any relation to your ability to write? What do you consider the ideal conditions for reading?

Possible Themes: 1. The Radio and Illiteracy; 2. Reading Is a Bore; 3. The Time, the Place, and the Book; 4. Buying My Own Books; 5. An Engineer's (or Farmer's, or Business Man's) Reading; 6. Belles Lettres; 7. Shrines for the Soul; 8. My Bible.

THE PURSUIT OF VALUES IN FICTION—*Brewster and Burrell*

What novels or stories have repelled or attracted you most? How did you happen to read them? Can you explain, as the students in this essay have explained, the reasons for your likes and dislikes? Does the explanation lie in your own temperament or environment? Have your tastes in fiction changed? Why? Do you think your chief pleasure in fiction lies in (1) emotional excitement and novelty of experience, or (2) in the sense of human realities seriously faced, or (3) in the suggested solutions of your emotional and intellectual problems? Or do you find all three satisfactions in some books? Does the fact that a novel or story moves you deeply mean that it is great literature? Are there any other tests?

Possible Themes: 1. The Values of a "Thriller"; 2. Why I Hated That Novel; 3. The Fairytales of My Childhood; 4. Required Reading in Fiction; 5. Falling in Love with a Heroine (or Hero); 6. Novels and My Philosophy of Life; 7. The Treatment of Sex in Fiction; 8. Wasting Time on "Westerns"; 9. Re-reading Old Favorites; 10. The Classics Bore Me; 11. Marriage Problems in Fiction; 12. Fiction That Misrepresents Life.

THE NOVELS OF THOMAS HARDY—*Woolf*

What qualities, besides the seeing eye and workmanship, does Mrs. Woolf attribute to Hardy? Do you question any of her statements? So far as your know, is she just to Hardy's style, treatment of fate, characterization, landscape, humor? Can you support your conclusions from *The Return of the Native?* Was it fitting that Hardy's body was buried in Westminster Abbey and his heart in his native village?

Possible Themes: 1. Apply Mrs. Woolf's remarks about another Hardy novel to *The Return of the Native,* and amplify with quotations; 2. Hardy Lies in Westminster Abbey; 3. A Point on Which I Disagree with Mrs. Woolf.

OUTLINE FOR A DEFENSE OF POETRY—*Daniels*

After reading this chapter, can you explain clearly your own feelings about poetry? What misconceptions have you harbored? Has classroom study sharpened or dulled your appreciation? If the proper approach to poetry is hard work, can the experience ever be enjoyable? Are there verses that you enjoy without effort?

What "levels" of poetry (if any) do you thoroughly and spontaneously like? Do you ever read them aloud or memorize them? What kinds of experience or teaching have helped you most to a feeling for poetry?

   Possible Themes: 1. How Poetry Should Not Be Taught; 2. A Poetic Adventure; 3. I'm Incurably Prosaic; 4. On First Looking into . . .; 5. A Great Teacher of Poetry; 6. Nerts for Footnotes; 7. A Defense of Explanatory Notes.

Writing Prose—*Maugham*

Mr. Maugham is the author of many successful stories and plays and of one notable novel, *Of Human Bondage.* Can you criticize the criticisms of the secretary? What did Maugham learn from the "intelligent and charming" don? Is a florid, an ornate prose always affected nonsense? Do you know any passages of such prose which you enjoy? Can you justify them? Is Maugham's attitude explained by his assertion that "life is vulgar"? Is it? Consider the life reflected in some of the biographies, essays, and poems in this book in making your answer? Why is it well for the novice at writing to be content with achieving lucidity, simplicity, and euphony? Can you offer any specific, detailed suggestions as to methods of achieving lucidity in the use of words, sentences, and paragraphs?

   Possible Themes: 1. My Favorite Prose Author and His Style; 2. Learning to Write; 3. English Instructors I Have Known; 4. The Place for Ornate Prose; 5. Practical Hints for the Writer; 6. Hazlitt as a Stylist.

Vocabulary and Success—*O'Connor*

What qualities are indicated by a wide and accurate vocabulary? Why are they called for in successful executives? Does the possession of an excellent vocabulary insure success in practical affairs? What are the best means of securing such a vocabulary? What are the meanings of phenomenon, infer, imply, data, alibi, hectic, masterly, masterful, communist, socialist, deprecate, depreciate, inflammable, junction, juncture, luxuriant, luxurious, precipitate, precipitous, mystic, individual, discomfit, credulous, credible, concrete (adj.), objective, subjective, parody, satire, metaphor, simile?

   Possible Themes: 1. Why Words Count; 2. The Uses of a Dictionary; 3. Why a Business Man (Scientist, Doctor, Sociologist, Lawyer, Banker) Needs a Good Vocabulary; 4. A Few Common Errors in Speech; 5. Latin (French) Helps English.

On Jargon—*Quiller-Couch*

Define jargon. Where have you met with it? What are some familiar examples? Make a list of ten. Consider the word *worth-while,* as in "worth-while oil wells" or "worth-while opera." Why does this word "save trouble"? Give three rules for avoiding jargon.

   Possible Themes: 1. The Psychology of Jargon; 2. Adventures in Jargon; 3. A Defense of "Case" and "Instance"; 4. "Worth-while" Words; 5. Jargon in Textbooks; 6. Say It with Fluff.

The Cliché Expert—*Sullivan*

What is the main point of this skit? Is it merely concerned with the vocabulary of football? How would you distinguish between jargon and the cliché? What can you substitute for the cliché?

   Possible Themes: 1. Baseball Is King; 2. Basketball Is King; 3. Crimes of the Sports Writer; 4. Journalese; 5. The Curse of the Cliché.

Stabilizing the Language through Popular Songs—*Spaeth*

Does Mr. Spaeth mean what he says when he asserts that "*like* becomes a conjunction whether you like it or not," " 'Who do you love?' would lose all its enticing quality if it were made grammatically correct"? If he is not serious, what do you call this kind of jesting? Do you approve of the revolution in grammar illustrated by the last song? Or should this, like other revolutions, be put down by force? On the assumption that you are not a revolutionist, correct every grammatical error in the essay.

Possible Themes: 1. Grammar and Me; 2. The Grammar I Learned in Grammar School; 3. Grammatical Revolution; 4. "C'est Moi" and "It's Me"; 5. The Grammar of College Students; 6. She Don't Talk Like She Was a Lady; 7. Grammar as Logic and Grammar as Manners.

EXCERPTS FROM *A Dictionary—Fowler*

Both Maugham and Fadiman testify that Fowler's *Dictionary of Modern English Usage* is a valuable guide for the professional writer. Fadiman declares: "I refer to Fowler often, but not necessarily to solve a problem in usage, grammar, or pronunciation. I refer to it for spiritual sustenance. It shows me how bad a writer I am and encourages me to do better. . . . If a writer is vulgar in mind, sloppy in thought, and crude in manner, his syntax will find him out. By examining his language with the kind of microscope Fowler supplies, he can spy upon his own defects of character and temperament." What defects in your own mental operations do you discover after reading these excerpts? Be prepared to write out correctly any sentences here given incorrectly. By consulting a grammar or handbook of rhetoric prepare yourself to give the rules covering the mistakes cited under "Illiteracies."

Possible Themes: 1. Slipshod Thinking and Sloppy Writing; 2. Sins of Syntax; 3. Browsing through Fowler; 4. A Menagerie of Metaphors.

THE DAILY THEME EYE—*Eaton*

Do you know anyone who has a sensitive "daily theme eye"? Does he get more "fun out of life" because of it? Is there such a thing as a "daily theme ear or nose"? Did Hardy possess alert senses? Did Keats? Illustrate. Is it possible to cultivate them? How? Read Thoreau's *Sounds* and Lay's *Flyers Are Inarticulate.*

Possible Themes: 1. An Author Who Has the Daily Theme Eye (with quotations); 2. How Can I Learn to See? 3. A Contrast between the Senses of a Man and of a Dog; 4. Cultivation of the Ear; 5. Description of a Person, House, Room, or Animal. (Study the subject closely; describe it in vivid, concise sentences; avoid the obvious and uninteresting; introduce convincing detail); 6. Write two contrasted descriptions of the same person, street, or landscape seen under different conditions, or at different hours, or from different angles; 7. A Study of Sounds (or of Odors).

LETTERS TO THE EDITOR—*Anonymous*

After glancing through the files of a newspaper, can you classify the letters to the editor (1) by the occupation or social standing of the writer; (2) by the motive in writing; (3) by the effectiveness in winning your assent? Buy a few newspapers, classify four or five letters from the correspondence column, and be prepared to read and report on them in class. Which do you consider the most effective letter? Why? What is the social value of correspondence columns?

Possible Themes: 1. Courtesy in the Correspondence Column; 2. What Makes an Effective Letter?; 3. A Fatuous Letter to the Editor; 4. An Answer to an Editorial; 5. A Letter to the College Paper; 6. The Value of the Correspondence Column.

A REVIEW OF *Madame Curie—Fadiman*

Read first Eve Curie's chapter "Four Years in a Shed." What is the main idea conveyed in this review? By what methods is it emphasized? How much space is devoted to the author's and the translator's craftsmanship? How much space to the subject matter? Can you account for these proportions? What touches of irony do you find? What do they add to the review?

Possible Themes: 1. A Review of a Short Biography; 2. A Review of Strachey's *Florence Nightingale.*

A REVIEW OF *The Prairie Years—Sherman*

In conjunction with this review read in this book the selection *Abraham Lincoln, The First Prairie Years.* How does this review differ from Fadiman's in its proportions and arrangement? What are the main points? Be ready to point out vigorous phrases, picturesque images, alliteration, quotation. What common property do Fadiman and Sherman find in the two biographies?

Possible Themes: 1. Addenda to Sherman's Review of *The Prairie Years;* 2. What Makes a Great Biography?

A REVIEW OF *Brave Men—Sheean*

First read the selections from *Brave Men* on pp. 114–122 in this book. What points does Sheean make about Pyle's personality, his appeal to the soldiers and the American public, his literary art? Do you agree? What do you think Sheean means by "the much larger comprehension"? Has *Brave Men* lost any of its power?

Possible Themes: 1. The GI as I Knew Him; 2. Reading War Books; 3. A Review of a War Book.

REVIEWS OF FILMS

What points are considered in these reviews which are identical with points considered in the reviews of books? What additional matters have to be considered? In all three reviews note what is said about the alterations of the story to fit the screen, about the actors, about the photography. What, in your opinion, are the essentials of a great moving picture? What are common defects of Hollywood productions? Be prepared to discuss the merits and demerits of a recent release.

Possible Themes: 1. A Review of a Film; 2. Hollywood Hokum; 3. My Favorite Screen Star; 4. When Is a Screen Production Art?; 5. Would *The Return of the Native* Make a Good Film?

EXPOSITION

RIVETERS—*Editors of "Fortune"*

What is the primary purpose of this exposition? What other purposes may it accomplish? What devices or methods are essential if these purposes are to be attained? Be prepared to show how these methods could be applied to other similar subjects, such as loading a hay wagon, a squeeze play in baseball, organizing a Red Cross unit, a laboratory experiment, a first-aid operation.

Possible Themes: 1. The Essentials of Success in Exposition; 2. Teamwork in . . .; 3. Is Labor Lazy?; 4. Is Labor Overpaid?

THREE KINDS OF HASH—*Rhode*

What principle of organization is employed here? Have you ever had difficulty in following a recipe? What are the main difficulties in writing a useful recipe? Are the introductory remarks of Mr. Rhode necessary? What do they add?

Possible Themes: 1. Mother's Pie; 2. A Perfect Steak; 3. I Can Make Your Mouth Water; 4. Two Kinds of Fudge; 5. A Laboratory Experiment; 6. Making . . .

WHY AN AIRPLANE FLIES—*Langewiesche*

Analyze carefully the many ways in which the author contrives to clarify his exposition. List at least ten. Note the ways in which he stimulates interest, and give examples.

Possible Themes: 1. Why an Airplane Sometimes Flops; 2. Ten Recipes for Clarity; 3. Holding the Reader's Interest; 4. Golf Clubs; 5. How a Rocket-Plane

Works; 6. A Pitcher Explains His Curves; 7. The Essence of Radar; 8. Points in Driving a Car; 9. How to Get More Mileage; 10. You Wouldn't Believe It Possible.

How to Mark a Book—*Adler*

Into what parts is this exposition divided? Is the organization more complicated than that of *Riveters*? What devices does the author use to call attention to the divisions? What examples or illustrations does he use? What do these add to the effectiveness of the exposition? If required by your instructor, mark one of President Hutchins' articles in this book in accordance with Adler's directions.

Possible Themes: 1. Reading as Hard Work; 2. How I Digest a Textbook; 3. Some Questions for Professor Adler; 4. How I Would Mark *How to Mark a Book;* 5. Marking President Hutchins.

The Yankee School—*Kittredge*

What are the topics treated under this title? Note transitions from one topic to another. What purposes do the quotations serve? Study the form of the footnotes. Have you observed instances of expensive school buildings and cheap teachers? Which are more important? What would be the result of paying higher salaries to high-school teachers?

Possible Themes: 1. A Cheap School-Master Makes a Dear School; 2. Life a Hundred Years Ago; 3. Expensive Economy; 4. A research paper, based on firsthand sources, on a specific condition or institution in Colonial or later times; 5. A research paper on the college magazine or on college life fifty or more years ago; 6. A brief biography of a college character based on original sources; 7. A research theme on schools in Shakespeare's day or on medieval schools and schoolboys.

Propaganda Techniques of German Fascism—*Miller*

Study the organization of this article, the form of the footnotes, the reading list with commentary at the end. What value does direct quotation have in this article? Under what conditions does propaganda cease to be a legitimate effort to influence public opinion, as guaranteed by the Bill of Rights, and become a public menace which should be suppressed by law? Do you detect in your reading any of the methods of confusing or misleading the public discussed in this article? If possible, bring to class a newspaper editorial in which you detect a fallacy and point it out.

Possible Themes: 1. When Propaganda Should Be Suppressed; 2. College Propaganda and Its Techniques; 3. It Can Happen Here; 4. Patriotic Societies and Patriotism; 5. I Fell for a Fallacy; 6. Variations in the Gentle Art of Lying.

Marco Polo—*Power*

Note the coherent progress of thought, paragraph by paragraph, till Polo is actually started on his journey. Note the frequent bits of quotation from Matthew Arnold, Browning, Milton, Tennyson, and Coleridge. Why are there no footnotes for these? What kinds of material are supplied with footnotes? Study the precise form and punctuation of each footnote, and be able to explain it. Study the concluding paragraphs and note their force. Why is the bibliography divided into primary and secondary sources?

Possible Themes: 1. A research biography, employing some expository material and attaining a unified effect; 2. The Organization of *Marco Polo;* 3. Reflections on China Today.

Four Kinds of Thinking—*Robinson*

Do Hutchins and Robinson agree substantially as to what we should do with our minds? What defects in the thinking of the past does Robinson emphasize? Can you give examples of these defects from Henry Adams' and Madame Curie's biographies? Are new ideas necessarily sounder than old? Is Robinson right in saying that creative thought must necessarily "change" our minds on all important matters? What does a study of your reveries reveal about yourself? On what subjects do you find yourself wavering from earlier beliefs? Do you attempt to rationalize them? Could you apply creative thought to these problems?

Possible Themes: 1. My Favorite Reveries; 2. Good Reasons and Real Reasons for My Political, Economic, or Religious Creed; 3. The Case for Traditional Beliefs; 4. The Case against Traditional Beliefs; 5. My Father (or Mother) Was Right after All; 6. How I Figured It out for Myself; 7. The World Crisis and Creative Thought.

GATE RECEIPTS AND GLORY—*Hutchins*

Has intercollegiate football given you anything or taught you anything that will be of permanent value? Which statements made by President Hutchins would you, on the basis of your experience or of firsthand, trustworthy information, question? Does the situation call for a radical remedy? If so, do you agree with President Hutchins' suggestions, or do you prefer some other?

Possible Themes: 1. The Inflated Football; 2. Put a Steeple on the Stadium; 3. Who Gets the Gate Receipts?; 4. The Price of Victory; 5. Letter Man vs. Key Man; 6. Alma Mater Ought to Run a Racing Stable; 7. President Hutchins Forgot Something; 8. Reflections of a Philosopher on the Ruins of the Rose Bowl.

THE AMERICAN STUDENT AS I SEE HIM—*Highet*

Have you found Professor Highet's comments on American schools and colleges to be true in your own experience? What do you regard as the chief defects in your own education, particularly in the matter of reading and writing? How much competition in studies as compared with competition in athletics have you found? Does this mean that Americans think less of brains than of brawn? Do you agree that in the future American colleges should make a special effort to train men and women for municipal, state, and federal service? Have some of the failings of American democracy been due to the neglect of this function by the colleges?

Possible Themes: 1. Professor Highet Is Unfair; 2. Professor Highet Is Right; 3. Will the United States Need Specially Trained Men and Women for Government Service?; 4. Is the Study of Literature of Practical Value?; 5. Combining Swine-Raising and Swinburne; 6. What Is the College For?; 7. College Distractions; 8. Working My Way through College.

EDUCATION FOR FREEDOM—*Hutchins*

If medieval boys entered the universities at fourteen, were they cleverer than students of today? Should students enter college two years earlier? What are the basic problems of American life? Can science answer them all? Does President Hutchins define clearly his program of education for citizenship? Would it give clear and final answers to our basic problems? Has your education thus far helped in solving them? How? Can vocational training be given better outside the schools and colleges? On what points do Hutchins and Highet agree, and on what points do they disagree? If you have read in this book the reflections of Henry Adams, Vincent Sheean, and Finley Peter Dunne on education, what light do they shed on the aims and the shortcomings of education?

Possible Themes: 1. The Physical Sciences and Education; 2. The Social Sciences and Education; 3. Literature and Education; 4. An Ideal College Program; 5. I Respectfully Disagree; 6. Does the Success of Democracy Depend on Right Education?; 7. The Value of Writing in Education; 8. The Place and the Age for Vocational Training.

EVEN A.B.'s MUST EAT—*Earnest*

On what points do Hutchins and Earnest agree? On what points do they disagree? What reason have you to think that one or the other is right? Are the instances selected by Earnest to prove that culture is always a by-product of something else sufficient to prove his point? Can you think of instances which refute it? Can you think of ways in which courses in Latin, music, comparative religion, Greek art could be related to your future occupation? If not, should you avoid them? What subjects, apart from those clearly vocational, would be most valuable to you in your vocation, in your personal life, in your functions as a citizen?

Possible Themes: 1. Dean Earnest Has Something; 2. Eating to Live or Living to Eat?; 3. What Music Means to Me; 4. My Educational Menu; 5. Selling Literature; 6. I Want Success and Something More.

ALUMNI AND SOCIAL RESPONSIBILITY—*Pace*

How do you explain the indifference of many alumni to social and political problems? What does inconsistency in attitudes on related problems signify? How can one remedy this defect? What do the figures on magazine subscriptions reveal? If after graduation you were to subscribe to five magazines (not professional or business journals), which would you choose as a good balanced intellectual diet?

Possible Themes: 1. Why Do Alumni Make Sleepy Citizens?; 2. Keeping Posted after College; 3. Civic Responsibilities in a Democracy; 4. The Popular Magazines; 5. I Can't Digest the *Reader's Digest*.

FREE SPEECH IN AMERICA—*Chafee*

What special limitations must be placed on free speech in war time? What limitations are placed by law on free speech and writing in times of peace? Why do these not violate the Bill of Rights? What remedies are there in a democracy for the publication of falsehoods? What can be done about misleading propaganda in regard to racial and international relations, labor and capital, and so forth? How can newspapers, magazines, and the radio be influenced to present controversial questions fairly?

Possible Themes: 1. The Bill of Rights; 2. The English Tradition of Free Speech and Free Press; 3. Nailing a Lie; 4. A Letter to the Editor; 5. Neutralizing Poisonous Propaganda; 6. Publicizing the Truth; 7. The Communist Way; 8. A College Forum.

THE RADIO BOOM AND THE PUBLIC INTEREST—*Smith*

How much time do the radio stations you know best devote to: 1. useful, noncontroversial information, such as weather and crop reports, household hints, and news summaries; 2. popular entertainment, such as soap opera, sporting news, and mystery drama; 3. cultural programs, such as Invitation to Learning, readings from literary classics, and symphonies; 4. discussion and debate on serious problems, such as news commentary and Town Meeting of the Air? What does this situation reveal? Does the responsibility for it lie with the public, the advertisers, the broadcasting companies, or all three? What can the FCC do? What can the individual citizen do to improve matters?

Possible Themes: I. A Visit to a Broadcasting Studio; 2. My Favorite Program; 3. Absurdities of the Radio; 4. Soap Opera; 5. Radio Propaganda; 6. Twirling the Dial; 7. More Government in the Radio Business.

LIBERTY—FOR WHAT?—*Meiklejohn*

Do those who advocate "free enterprise" really wish the removal of all government control of our economic life? Do they wish to end tariffs, taxation, minimum wage and child labor laws, regulation of interstate commerce, and so forth? What is the difference between the New Deal and fascist (or communist) control of the national economy? Do Australia and Sweden furnish examples of a successful middle way between laissez faire and state socialism? How much "fraternity" do we have in the United States? Is it merely sentimental or is it real? Does religion have anything to say on this subject?

Possible Themes: 1. What Did the Revolutionists of '76 Fight For?; 2. Is Laissez-Faire Scientific?; 3. Let Freedom Ring through a Million-Dollar Newspaper Plant; 4. What's Sauce for Business Is Sauce for Labor; 5. What Is "the American Way"?; 6. Fraternity—Colored and White; 7. Christianity and Economics.

AMERICA—*Thompson*

Have you followed Miss Thompson's column in any newspaper? Has she foretold with accuracy the course of international events? Has she earned the right to be regarded as more than a visionary? Do you agree with her definition of what "equality" should mean to Americans? Does it become increasingly clear that the preservation of the democratic ideal at home is tied up with its establishment everywhere?

Possible Themes: 1. The Petty Mind; 2. The American Miracle; 3. The Darker Side of the Picture; 4. The Meaning of Equality; 5. Walt Whitman, American.

THE CITIZEN'S CHARTER—*Crowther*

What factors in this argument contribute to clarity? How does the author create an impression of fairness, of impartiality? What in your experience are the advantages and disadvantages of federal, state, and municipal control and operation? For example, the postal system, price fixing, waging the war, social security? Why did the American people support the New Deal in four elections? Does Crowther offer a just and workable division between the domain of order and the domain of freedom? Can you suggest a better?

Possible Themes: 1. Memories of the Depression; 2. Give Me Freedom—to Sell Apples; 3. What's Wrong with Bureaucracy; 4. Freedom under Big Business; 4. The Citizen's Charter Applied to America; 5. My Ideal State.

THE LESSONS OF TVA—*Lilienthal*

Does this account of TVA suggest other ways, besides that proposed by Crowther, for combining freedom and order? Can you see any objections to this type of federal control? Would it be better to give such control over a region to a private corporation? Can you suggest any other areas where such a plan could be applied? Could it be applied to the slum areas of large cities? How can such projects be kept out of spoils politics?

Possible Themes: 1. Why People Hate the New Deal; 2. My "Ducktown"; 3. The Dust Bowl; 4. Deforestation; 5. Soil Erosion; 6. The Cure for Slums; 7. Boulder Dam (or Columbia Dam).

WHEN CAN THE ATOM BE PUT TO WORK?—*Davis*

What changes in the conditions of living can you expect in the next ten years as a result of the productive use of atomic energy? Is it essential that the government, and not some corporation like General Motors, control this development? Why or why not?

Possible Themes: 1. The Structure of the Atom; 2. The Physics of Atom Smashing; 3. The Age of Superman; 4. Laboratory Miracles; 5. Jules Verne Is Archaic; 6. Controlling Atomic Research.

MODERN MAN IS OBSOLETE—*Cousins*

What is the meaning of national sovereignty? What restrictions have nations placed on themselves in the past? Why did the Hague Conventions and the Kellogg Pact Fail? Why did the United States refuse to join the League of Nations? Why did the League fail? Is isolationism dead? What if the U.N. fails? What can Americans do to strengthen it?

Possible Themes: 1. A Veteran Looks at the Next War; 2. Confessions of an Isolationist; 3. George Washington on Entangling Alliances; 4. The Cost of Isolation; 5. The Chicago *Tribune;* 6. Improving the U.N.; 7. Meditations of the Last Man.

WALT WHITMAN AND THE PEACE—*Hume*

Apart from preserving and strengthening the U.N., what are the chief problems of the postwar world? Can you put in your own words what Whitman believed about democracy? Can his belief be based on experience and reason, or is it a blind faith? In either case, is there any value in reading poetry about democracy? What practical applications have the ideas of Whitman in international affairs?

Possible Themes: 1. Walt Whitman's Creed; 2. Is the Democratic Faith Based on Science or Sentiment?; 3. Are the Germans (the Japanese) Incorrigible?; 4. A Veteran at the Peace Table.

PETTY ANGLO-AMERICAN DIFFERENCES—*Lamont*

What accusations have you most frequently heard against British policies? Which are true, which false, which fail to take into account the other side? Has the United States a clean record in its dealings with Mexico (1846–48), with Spain (1898), with Russia (1919), the League of Nations, the Spanish Republic (1936)? What about our treatment of the American Indian and the Negro? Are we so much holier than the British? From whom did we get the right of *habeas corpus* and trial by jury? Who first abolished slavery—the United States or Britain? Who stood up to Hitler and Mussolini alone for a year, thereby saving us as well as themselves from a fascist tyranny? Who are the exploiters of Anglo-American differences?

Possible Themes: 1. Still Fighting the Revolution of 1776; 2. American Pharisaism; 3. The Anti-British Press; 4. The United States Alone Is Pure; 5. The Two Englands; 6. From Empire to Commonwealth of Nations; 7. Our Debt to Britain.

A TEXAN IN ENGLAND—*Dobie*

What features of American life make for standardization and artificiality? Do Americans pay money to learn "how to make friends and influence people"? Do American women find it necessary to pay millions of dollars to cosmetic manufacturers and "beauticians"? Do these facts support Dobie's contention that we are less natural and unaffected than the British? Do our representatives in Congress tend to be sectionalists and partisans rather than broad-minded patriots? Which of the English novelists, poets, and essayists you have read best express the characteristics defined by Dobie?

Possible Themes: 1. The Cult of Artificiality; 2. The Goose Step in College; 3. A GI's memories of the English; 3. "These Limeys Have Got Guts"; 4. The Professional Briton-Hater; 5. British Poets on Liberty; 6. A Good Word for English Literature; 7. The Englishman (Englishwoman)—Caricature and Reality.

DIALOGUE ON GORKI STREET—*Hersey*

This dialogue does not represent any single actual conversation, but is based on a number of conversations which Hersey, as a war correspondent, held with Russians. What does the typical Russian intellectual want? How does it differ from what the typical American wants? What are the chief obstacles to mutual understanding, tolerance, and cooperation? What do American communists stand for? If you were asked to send three books to Russia to give a true picture of American life and the American spirit, which would you choose?

Possible Themes: 1. The Russian Enigma; 2. Can We Be Friends with Russia?; 3. Three Books for Russia; 4. Dialogue on Main Street; 5. Communists I Have Known.

APOLOGY FOR MAN—*Hooton*

Can we improve mankind without improving the human animal? Are there any ways of improving the breed? Can we encourage the multiplication of the intelligent or discourage the multiplication of the unintelligent? Does war tend to kill off the best men first? Does the Roman Church encourage celibacy for the best minds and encourage large families among the inferior classes? Have the educated classes themselves to blame if human intelligence steadily deteriorates? Can we cure criminals, or are they born vicious? Is Hooton right as to the present intelligence of the people? Does the record of such nations as Switzerland, England, France, and Sweden bear out Hooton's assertion that democracy is a less rational and successful form of government than a dictatorship? What is man's favorite idiocy?

Possible Themes: 1. Breeding Morons; 2. Are We Coddling Criminals?; 3. Practical Eugenics; 4. Do Dictators Make Their Peoples Happy?; 5. Man's Control of Nature; 6. Man Is Half Ape, Half Angel; 7. Why Is Tarzan Popular?; 8. When Kindness Is Unkind; 9. Human Idiocy.

EVOLUTION AND ETHICS—*Huxley*

Thomas Henry Huxley, the famous biologist and champion of the evolutionary theory, delivered this lecture at Oxford in 1893, near the end of his career. He speaks of "taking an immensity of trouble over it." Does the workmanship show? In organization? In tact? Whose sensibilities might have been offended? Look up all unfamiliar words in the dictionary, and be prepared to define them. If your instructor requires, prepare an outline. Which human qualities, once useful or essential to survival, are now becoming less useful or positively dangerous? What is meant by "letting the ape and tiger die"? Has civilized humanity changed essentially; for instance, in regard to torture, slavery, the position of women? Are Huxley's ethics essentially different from those of Christ? What does he think of rugged individualism? Explain how the cosmic process can be thought of as unethical? How do you reconcile the justice and mercy of God with the needless and undeserved suffering in the world?

Possible Themes: 1. Huxley as a Stylist; 2. What Rugged Individualism Has Done to My Family; 3. Does Human Nature Change?; 4. The Ape and Tiger in Man; 5. God Is Just; 6. Men Must Cooperate; 7. The Mosaic Law Gives Place to the Christian; 8. Where Competition Is Still Desirable.

WHY IS GOD SILENT?—*Fosdick*

What do you think Fosdick means by God? Does he prove God's existence? Does he reconcile the sufferings of the innocent and the temporary triumphs of evil with the omnipotence of God? Does he imply that God does not send the thunderstorm, but only silent things? If so, who or what is responsible for thunderstorms, earthquakes, and volcanoes? Is it only the good books which survive? Is Fosdick right in declaring that no international organization can hold together without goodwill? Is he right in maintaining that the triumph of Christianity is proof of God's power? Is there any hope for the betterment of society without an active, organized, inspired Christian church?

Possible Themes: 1. If I Were God; 2. The Mystery of Evil; 3. God Is Silent, but Men Must Speak Out; 4. The Need for the Church; 5. God and the Atomic Bomb; 6. Reading the Bible; 7. The God of *Green Pastures*.

INFALLIBILITY—*Newman*

After reading the selections from Huxley and Hooton, do you think Newman has met the problems of human ignorance and suffering satisfactorily? How does he reconcile the existence of evil with the omnipotence and goodness of God? Does his analogy of "the boy of good make and mind" really support his case? Does he make it clear why reason, correctly exercised, and reason considered actually and historically should lead to opposite conclusions? Do you agree with Newman that an infallible guide in matters of religious faith is desirable? Do you think that the Roman Catholic Church has been successful, wherever and whenever it has prevailed, in fulfilling the functions which Newman assigns to it? What facts of history confirm or contradict his view? Read over what Mr. Maugham says about Newman's style. Be prepared to illustrate his remarks by particular passages.

Possible Themes: 1. Human Misery and God's Goodness; 2. Blame Adam or the Anthropoid Ape?; 3. Catholics in American Politics; 4. Reason, a Giant Evil?

STORIES

THE TELL-TALE HEART—*Poe*

This psychological story, like the famous motion picture *The Cabinet of Dr. Caligari,* explores the workings of a diseased mind. Long before the scientific studies of modern psychology Poe here presents artistically a picture of a psychopathic personality. Did you find the monolog convincing as a betrayal of a diseased mind? Is he a true type of hyperaesthesia? Do you believe he would confess at the end of the story as Poe wishes you to believe he did? If such a mad crime were committed today in your own community, how would your emotional reactions differ from your reactions to this story?

Possible Themes: 1. Compare *The Tell-Tale Heart* with Browning's *My Last Duchess* or with some other example of dramatic monolog; 2. As an exercise of the creative imagination, imagine that you have committed some crime, and write a detailed confession; 3. Sketch the scenario of a motion picture that might be adapted from *The Tell-Tale Heart;* would you want Bela Lugosi or Boris Karloff in the cast?

A LODGING FOR THE NIGHT—*Stevenson*

Did you find this story of 15th Century France an adventure or an experience? (See *The Pursuit of Values in Fiction.*) Where is the emphasis in the story—on action or on character? To what extent do the snow, the wind, the cold contribute to the effect of the story? Would anything have been lost if the story opened inside by the fire instead of outside? Does Stevenson convince you that Villon was a poet as well as a thief? If so, how? Read Rossetti's translation of Villon's *Ballade of Dead Ladies.* Does this authentic poem by a real man sound as if it might have been written by the Villon of Stevenson's historical romance?

Possible Themes: 1. Write the adventures that might have befallen the other ruffians in the story on the night of the murder; 2. Write the scene, with dialog, of the discovery of Thevenin's body by the watch; 3. Discuss in modern terms the question of war and brigandage, hunger and honor which Villon and his noble host debate; 4. After consulting available works of reference, give an account of French costume, architecture, or economic conditions in the 15th Century.

NIGHT CLUB—*Brush*

Miss Brush's story does not develop any single situation or plot to a conclusion. From the separate incidents how many stories do you think might be constructed? Why did the girl take the scissors? What happened to Claire and Sylvia and Amy? Why did the second visitor, the blond girl, change so when Mrs. Brady brought her the glass of water? The artistic problem in *Night Club* was to fuse all these stories into one whole. Has Miss Brush succeeded in doing this? What means does she employ? How does Mrs. Brady's addiction to the true story magazine introduce a note of irony?

Possible Themes: 1. Expand any one of the flashlight incidents in this story. Explain and tell what happened before and after; 2. Narrate similar incidents you have observed in dressing rooms, wash rooms of Pullman cars, lobbies of theaters, or other places where strangers congregate intimately.

PAUL'S CASE—*Cather*

A tragedy may well be defined as a story whose unhappy outcome is the result of a flaw in the hero's character. By this definition is *Paul's Case* a tragedy? Is Paul a victim of his own character or is he a victim of circumstances?

The title of the story, *Paul's Case*, suggests illness, physical or mental. Do you think Paul was a tubercular case? A psychiatric case? Was he insolent because he was full of self-confidence or because he was timid? Could he have overcome his maladjustment by making his daily life more congenial instead of escaping into an unreal world of wish fulfillment?

Possible Themes: 1. Miss Cather compares Paul with a street cat set at bay by a ring of tormentors. From your school days do you recall any girl or boy who was persecuted because he was different from the other children? Tell the story and try to explain why this child was different; 2. The sanest of people at times fail of complete mental poise. They escape for moments into fantastic dream worlds or indulge in orgies of self-pity. Choose some such moment from your own past history—long enough ago so that you are no longer ashamed of it—and tell the story; 3. The action of *Paul's Case* is supposed to have taken place about 1900. If Paul were living the story now what would probably take the place of the symphony and the stock company in his escape from reality? Explain as fully and sympathetically as possible.

The Devil and Daniel Webster—*Benét*

This is a modern and artistic example of a most characteristic American oral form —the "tall story." By the introduction of picturesque exaggerations and impossibilities a celebrity may become fabulous, legendary, and mythical. Folk heroes like Paul Bunyan and Johnnie Appleseed are American favorites. The enjoyment of such stories requires what S. T. Coleridge called "the willing suspension of disbelief for the moment, which constitutes poetic faith." One should read *The Devil and Daniel Webster* in the same spirit as *Christabel* and *The Rime of the Ancient Mariner*. All three are in a sense poems.

Can you point out "tall story" elements in W. R. Benét's *Jesse James? The Odyssey? Beowulf?* By what literary device does Mr. Benét retain the spirit of oral story telling in *The Devil and Daniel Webster?* Does this device help you to suspend your disbelief for the moment? Compare this story with *The Green Pastures* as combinations of the naïve and the heroic. Is Benét just telling a yarn, or is he trying to say something important about men and about America? Defend your answer. Why should this story be chosen as the basis of a libretto for an opera? Did it make a good motion picture?

Possible Themes: 1. Retell a "tall story" or fabulous legend you have heard and give it a local and familiar setting; 2. Try your hand at writing in direct discourse Dan'l Webster's address to the jury of damned souls. This will be very difficult to do well; 3. Write, after visits to appropriate works of reference, a brief biographical sketch of one of the phantom jurors.

The Garden Party—*Mansfield*

The theme of the story is the growing up of a young girl—her emerging from girlhood to womanhood. How does the death of the carter precipitate the process? Observe Laura's reactions and note instances of her girlhood—the scene with the bread and butter at the beginning, the scene of the cream puffs. What episodes indicate her growing maturity? Would the story have been more true or less true if Laura had found death and the dead man horrible instead of beautiful? What are the social implications of Laura's words to the dead man: "Forgive my hat"?

Possible Themes: 1. Laura and the cream puffs. As a child what was one of your favorite foods? Are you still fond of it or have you outgrown your taste? You might write on "my favorite dishes—then and now"; 2. What is your earliest memory of seeing a dead person? Describe the circumstances as you remember them. What effect did the experience have on you? Should children be kept from an early acquaintance with death or not? 3. As you look back over your past what experience seems to mark most clearly the step from your childhood into your present stage of maturity? Narrate it.

I Can't Breathe—*Lardner*

Letters and diaries have long been used as media for telling stories. Could an author characterize this girl any more vividly than she characterizes herself in her diary? Why does Lardner have her use bad grammar, punctuation, and spelling? Were you surprised at the ending? Could you devise a better way for her to extricate herself from her difficulties? Will she really marry Merle Oliver?

In one way story telling by diary resembles story telling by the stream of consciousness method. Both focus on what goes on in the leading character's mind rather than on a succession of events. How do the methods differ in emphasis? Compare the comic effects Lardner gains by his use of bad grammar with those in Spaeth's *Stabilizing the Language through Popular Songs*.

Possible Themes: 1. Rewrite one of the days from the diary in the stream of consciousness method or rewrite Laura's day as diary. Will Laura's use of English resemble the girl's in *I Can't Breathe?*; 2. Here is an actual situation from college history. Three young men gave fraternity pins to the same girl—one in the spring term, one in the mountains in June, one at the shore in August. Write a scene wherein the three men meet and discover the multiple engagement. What is the outcome?

But It's O! in My Heart—*Vatsek*

In the wars of today and in the wars of yesterday, in peace times everywhere and in every age, people fall in love and do or do not get married. But unless you postpone it all till you are fifty you are likely to run into the in-law problem. You will have to meet the parents of your boy friend or girl friend and be looked over with a suspicious and frequently disapproving eye. If you are a young woman, do you know how Kathleen felt before the Macdonald door in Edinburgh? If you are a young man have you ever been through it? Did you like it?

An interesting feature of this fine story is the use of the old Scottish song as title and theme. Have you seen other modern stories where a song has been used in like manner in a story? Such stories exist. Are you interested in the way the story slips into Kathleen's thoughts and out again into the objective world of fact and conversation? Is this or is it not an artistic use of the psychological notions of Robinson in *Four Kinds of Thinking*? Do you know, in this collection or elsewhere, other stories which use this "stream of consciousness" technic?

Possible Themes: 1. Tell the story of the first time you met the parents of the object of your affections. If it was some time ago and you no longer love the boy (or girl), you may treat it humorously (or seriously) if you wish. 2. Does the father or mother usually show more sympathy with the boy or girl who may or may not be added to the family? Write your observations. 3. Should young people marry when the man is going into service or wait till he returns? Write your views or record your experiences.

The Day of Victory—*Fast*

In this story of George Washington at a crisis in his career Howard Fast returns to the material of his historical novel based on the life of Washington, *The Unvanquished*. In the Afterword of this novel Fast says, "All the debunking in the world cannot change the facts of his wonderful simplicity, his complete unselfishness, his humble respect for those who had asked him to leave his home and fight a revolution." Does the short story succeed in demonstrating these qualities of simplicity, unselfishness, and respect? Does Fast's picture of Washington agree with the picture you had formed of him from other sources? Do you feel that Washington

was tempted by McKay's suggestion that he seize power and establish himself as a military dictator? Or does he fear that some of his officers will seize power without him? At what point in the story is the issue decided between dictatorship and democracy? Is there a likelihood that veterans today may endeavor to seize power and establish a dictator after the Fascist or Communist pattern? What governmental weakness or ineptitude might tempt them to do so? What might be their motives: Selfishness? Idealism?

Possible Themes: 1. Retail some other episodes from history from the angle of narration of the leading character; for instance the day of The Gettysburg Address as seen through the eyes and thoughts of Lincoln, or the crossing of the Rubicon through the eyes and thoughts of Caesar; 2. Write a narrative of your leave-taking from your wartime outfit or home town group of intimate friends; 3. Imagine yourself inside McKay instead of inside Washington and rewrite Fast's story, or a scene from it, from that angle.

THE THREE SWIMMERS AND THE GROCER FROM YALE—*Saroyan*

This story, originally appearing in the magazine *Story,* together with many other stories about many of the same characters, became part of the book *My Name Is Aram* (1940). In a prefatory note the author says some wise things about autobiography and fiction. He says that he has returned for his material to Fresno, the town of his boyhood.

"To the ugly little city containing the large comic world, and to the proud and angry Saroyans containing all humanity. While no character in this book is a portrait of any real person living or dead, as the saying is, neither is any person in this book a creation of fiction. No member of my family will be able to find himself in any one person in this book, but at the same time none will be able to find himself wholly absent from any one of them. If this is true of us, it is also probably true of everybody else, which in the opinion of the writer is proper."

Do you find yourself and your family in this story? If you are a man you certainly were a boy once and probably went swimming when the water was still too cold. And girls may meet eccentric and amusing grocers, or newsdealers, or street vendors. Does Saroyan write only about Californians and Americans, or are any of his characters foreigners? Can the consistent avoidance of quotation marks to set off dialog distract you or not?

Possible Themes: 1. Does your childhood harbor memories of escapades, adventures, mishaps and surprises? Write an episode from your early childhood. As Elliot Paul said in an interview: "The whole thing is to have something that you want to say, and if it is based on a life that you've lived some time before, so that your memory has had a chance to go through it and slough off what is not important, what doesn't fit—then much of the work is done. All that remains is to put it down as naturally as you can." 2. Write an essay on Americans who speak foreign languages.

THE VETERANS REFLECT—*Shaw*

This story is an interesting example of modernistic technic in narrative. The author tells the story on three separated but related levels. The first is the level of what happened on the train as it raced up the Hudson River Valley. The second level is contained in Peter's stream of consciousness: going forward in anticipation of his home-coming; going backward in memory of his battle experiences. The third level is that of the imagined Hitler trying to escape into Switzerland, himself engaged in a stream of consciousness. This third level is not a part of Peter's personal experience or memory. It might be omitted without leaving a gap in the story of Peter. Would you prefer the story without the two Hitler scenes? Or do they serve a useful artistic purpose like that of choral background in a radio play or a montage in modernistic art? Defend your answer.

Structurally all the forces in the story converge on the explosion at the very end, when Peter tells the industrialist, "Get out of here and keep quiet or I'll kill you." How do you interpret this explosion? As a release of Peter's overwrought nervous tensions? As a deliberate statement of political allegiance? What adversary does Peter have in mind in the last paragraph but one? Who will be his allies in a fight against this adversary?

Possible Themes: 1. Describe a home-coming after a long separation, either when you came home or when someone came home to you. Compare and contrast this home-coming with your anticipations; 2. Record as revery or stream of consciousness some past experience against a background of subsequent experience. For instance as you sit in a college class room you are at once aware of other students and of the professor's lecture and also of memories of the past and anticipations of the future. 3. Write a letter to the editor of a newspaper pointing out what group or groups you consider hostile to your peace and security and suggesting what should be done about it; 4. Tell the story of the train of circumstances which on one occasion led up to an explosion of your own anger.

SHORT SHORT STORIES

The typical short short stories which are now to be found in a number of magazines are built pretty much on a standard formula of a surprise ending and great economy of timing. They are not so easy to devise and to write as some beginners fancy them to be. This formula is illustrated by *Salesmanship, Guidance, Mrs. Packletide's Tiger,* and *The First Day.* Each of these stories could be expanded with more scenes, dialog, and action. In each instance how far back in the story did you see the surprise coming? Is the surprise in each instance artistically prepared for?

Another type of very short fiction is illustrated by *Breakfast* and *The End of Something.* In these stories there is no snapper at the end. In fact there is little change of direction or of pace and no attempt at trickery or what most people think of as plot. Hemingway and Steinbeck gave sharply etched scenes and with artistic economy throw revealing light on mood and on character. Steinbeck later wove *Breakfast* into the texture of *Grapes of Wrath.* Could *The End of Something* have been incorporated into a novel?

Possible Themes: 1. Try cutting, as for *Reader's Digest,* Miss Chase's story *Salesmanship.* Try to cut it to the length of *Guidance.* Do you lose the nuance of the characterization of Mr. Staples? Do you weaken the irony of "salesman-ship"? 2. *Guidance* is cut to the bone as it stands. Try rewriting it, or part of it, to a larger scale. Write the scene, perhaps, between Mr. Meriden and the yellow-haired girl when they meet at the Plaza. Or a scene btween them before the girl went to the church to pray for guidance. Or a scene between Mr. and Mrs. Meriden which will illustrate more fully her arrogant need to dominate. 3. Write a satiric story or scene from a story or an anecdote in which you will expose the empty pretense of some one to artistic or athletic prowess. Pride will come before a fall. 4. Tell the story of how your own first love affair ended. Instead of saying "I" and "she" or "he," you may use fictitious names, such as "Nick" and "Marjory." That is one way fiction is written. 5. In a scene imitative of *Breakfast* try to capture a mood of elation, courage, and confidence; or a mood of lassitude, discour-agement, and defeat. 6. Write a scene from your first day at college.

PLAYS

RIDERS TO THE SEA—*Synge*

The tragedy of death does not involve those who die but the living who survive. Maurya has already lost four sons to the sea. The play opens with her bitter lamen-

tation for another son drowned and ends in peace with the death of her last. What is the source of Maurya's peace? Is it the comforts of religion? the exhaustion of her spirit? the fact that there is nothing more to lose?

If the story of *Riders to the Sea* were told in three acts as a full length play what would be gained and what lost? A logical playwright starts with the climax of his play in mind and then works back to find the beginning in a situation which introduces the conflict from which the climax arises. In *Riders to the Sea* the climax comes in Maurya's peace after the death of six sons. Where shall the play begin? After the death of the first son? the second? Or as it does begin, with the death of the fifth son? Think over carefully the various steps in the story and consider each step in turn as a possible beginning for the play.

How much of the effect of *Riders to the Sea* comes from its setting? Try thinking of the play in a different setting. What would happen if you made the mother an American woman who loses six sons in a mine or in war?

Possible Themes: 1. Rewrite any brief episode in *Riders to the Sea* with an American setting; 2. If you have lost by death anyone dear to you, you might write the story of your emotional adjustment to the loss. Poets record that such writing helps the mourner to find peace.

The Fall of the City—*MacLeish*

In this allegory for radio the poet is dramatizing the conflict between democracy and totalitarianism. It is a call to arms. A battle cry of freedom. Would the message be more urgent or telling if the setting were of our own day and age instead of something remotely resembling that of Cortez' conquest of Mexico? Would prose be a more appropriate vehicle than poetry for this dramatic story? What does the poet consider the most effective weapon against the conqueror— pacifism, religion, arms?

In his introduction MacLeish speaks of the Announcer in radio as a Greek Chorus. What does he mean? Read Thornton Wilder's play *Our Town*. (It's in Burns Mantle's *Best Plays of 1938*.) How effective is the "Stage Manager" as announcer or Greek Chorus. Observe the radio dramas you hear and read radio plays by Oboler and Corwin. Which use announcers or commentators on the action? Which do not? Study the role of the announcer in Corwin's *Good Heavens*. Is the announcer an artistic advantage? Does MacLeish agree with the authors of *Propaganda Techniques of German Fascism* as to the conditions favorable to a Fascist revolution?

Possible Themes: 1. Make a prose paraphrase of one of the longer speeches. This will test your understanding of the poetry. It will also enable you to test the relative effectiveness of prose and verse as a medium of expression in such a radio play; 2. Write an expository piece making clear your own views on freedom and the proper relationship of the individual and the state.

Beyond the Horizon—*O'Neill*

In this play is Robert's death the tragic climax or is it merely a convenient device for dropping the curtain? Would the play have been more or less tragic if Robert had lived? Robert and Ruth certainly made a failure of their marriage. Whose fault was it? But in the last act Robert calls Andrew "the deepest dyed failure of the three." Was he merely angry or was the accusation true? Is it probable that Ruth and Andrew would have been happy if they had married? Is it probable that Robert would have been happy if he had sailed with Captain Scott? Why were the original plans abandoned? Could any one have prevented the change of plans?

If the climax of the play resides in the demonstration that Robert, Andrew, and Ruth had failed, how far back did the playwright have to go to uncover the motivating causes? Could he successfully have made a one act play of his material by expanding the last act with dialog which would have uncovered the antecedent action of the story?

How important is the setting of the play? Might it just as well have taken place on a southern plantation, a midwestern farm, or a western mine? Why did Mr. O'Neill set it near the seacoast of New England?

Possible Themes: 1. What do you look forward to as a happy and successful life? Money, the right girl (or boy), fame, doing what you are fitted for? What are you planning to do to attain that happy and successful life? Give the question careful thought and write your conclusions; 2. Suppose Robert had gone to sea and Andrew had married Ruth. Write a scene of reunion when Robert returns; 3. Is the outcome of the play the result of external circumstances or the characters of the leading persons? Explain your opinion in an essay.

The Green Pastures—*Connelly*

This play is notable as a skillful handling of difficult material. How has the author managed to maintain a spirit of devoutness in spite of the ludicrous situations and lines? How important is the prolog of the Sunday School teacher and the children in preparing the audience to receive the play in the right spirit? How does the singing of spirituals by the Choir maintain this spirit? What disadvantages would there be in turning up the lights in the house between one scene and the next? Of having no singing between scenes? What would the play lack dramatically if Hosea and Hezdrel did not forecast the Incarnation? Note the symbolism of the identity of Adam-Hezdrel—the old Adam who lost and the new Adam who won. Milton, in Paradise Lost, echoes seventeenth-century theologians in calling Christ, "The New Adam." What other stories, plays, or films have you read or seen which deal with Biblical story? How do these others compare with *The Green Pastures?*

Possible Themes: 1. Have you ever known some ignorant but sincerely devout old man or woman? Write a character sketch; 2. As part of your spiritual autobiography, record some childish and distorted religious ideas you had before you were ten years old; 3. Record your first experience of hearing Negro spirituals sung.

You Can't Take It with You—*Hart and Kaufman*

Brander Matthews once said that a comedy is a farce written by some one who is dead. Is *You Can't Take It with You* a comedy or a farce? Before you answer, it might be well to look up "comedy" and "farce" in an unabridged dictionary.

Do you laugh at Grandpa or with him? Irvin Cobb once told our students the following secret about laughter. "If you say 'What big fools you are,' people won't laugh. But if you say with a grin, 'What fools we all are,' your audience will agree and laugh with you." Do you agree that we are all touched at least a bit with the almost divine madness of the Sycamore family?

Would you rather be as funny as the Sycamores or as tragic as the leading characters in *Riders to the Sea* and *Beyond the Horizon?* Can you use your intelligence to choose between living your life as comedy and being a bad ham actor in a tragedy?

Do you feel that *You Can't Take It with You* is more devoutly religious than *The Green Pastures* or less? Do you say grace at meals better or worse than Mr. Vanderhof? Or are you so silly as not to say grace?

Whose withers are wrung by the genial satire of this comedy? Speakers at university commencements? Ballet dancers? Snake hunters? Amateur playwrights? Income Tax collectors? Wall Street brokers?

Don't neglect the star crossed lovers. Do you believe more in Tony Kirby and Alice or in Romeo and Juliet? How do you expect to get on with your prospective in-laws?

Possible Themes: 1. At what age do you plan to retire from the business or profession you are preparing to enter? Fifty? Sixty? Seventy? Eighty? What will you do with yourself when that time comes? Write out your plans. It won't hurt you to have in mind what you are building toward. 2. Are you blessed with eccentric relatives? Do they annoy you? Embarrass you? Or do you relax and enjoy them? Write a character sketch of such an eccentric relative or friend. 3. You are having your troubles in a world of war and distress. How are you carrying your load? Cheerfully or with a grouch? With courage and laughter or with apprehension and fear? Write a piece about your troubles and what you are doing about them.

GOOD HEAVENS—*Corwin*

Like *The Fall of the City, Good Heavens* is a radio play written for the radio—not an adaptation of a story, novel, or stage play. Corwin as author, director, and producer all in one has been able to integrate his play as an organic unit directed to the ear of the radio listener. The reader of a radio play should endeavor to read with his ear as attentive as his eye.

Corwin's witty *Studio Notes* to *Good Heavens* follow. They illuminate both his technic and his purpose:

STUDIO NOTES

There are few studies more exciting to the imagination than astronomy, and it is to the shame of pedagogues that the principal conveyers of its excitement should be pulp magazines and comic strips of the Buck Rogers variety. Jules Verne in the nineteenth century recognized its grip on the fancy and wrote entertainingly about the very sort of thing Flash Gordon is now devoting his life to, but educators have never yielded to the theory that one can instruct and thrill a student at the same time. Small wonder Whitman should have walked out on the lecturer as he did in "When I heard the learn'd astronomer."

Even astronomy on the popular level of the planetarium with its staff of lecturers is still far too esoteric for most lay minds. I have listened to lectures in a number of planetariums around the country and have yet to hear one that gave me half the excitement of the occasional quiet talk I have had with a practicing astronomer in his home. It's too bad that the greatest show of all should suffer the poorest showmanship. I have a hunch that a sounder popular understanding of astronomy would do much to weaken the grip of astrological drivel on thousands of people.

The basis for this program was a trip which I made to the Yerkes Observatory at Williams Bay, Wisconsin. In typical radio fashion the whole project was crammed into one day: a plane flight from New York to Chicago, a quick hundred-mile auto ride to the observatory, and one peek at 40 Eridani through the great refracting telescope. And of course as soon as I asked the astronomer if I could please take a squint at the rings of Saturn (something I had been wanting to do all my life) the heavens clouded over and there was no more observing to be done that night. Instead we sat around under the great dome for a couple of hours and had a fine bull session. Much of what was said has crept into this script, although in a form perhaps more frivolous than my friends at Yerkes would approve.

Acting. The demonstration of what does *not* go on in an observatory is essentially burlesque, and you can be gay as you like with Hotchkiss, Billingsgate, Dumke, and Addington. A tongue-in-cheek attitude is okay throughout, except for the occasional solo work of the narrator in the body of the show and at the end. The business between the Prosecutor and the Volunteer is intended to be essentially comic (though all data therein are of course authentic). Henry Morgan as the Prosecutor was appropriately insulting and Martin Wolfson gave the Volunteer a plaintive concern for academic truth, together with a belligerence about personal rights in a studio.

Sound. The directions in the script itself are fairly explicit and involve no special problems beyond careful rehearsal of perspectives.

Music. Lyn Murray's score combined the same elements of horseplay and straight talk that are to be found in the script itself. His time motif and star music have all kinds of atmosphere, and if you are thinking of producing this show I recommend applying to Mr. Murray for use of his score. He can be reached in care of CBS, New York.

Rehearsal Routine. No special problems except for the one discussed under Note 6 below.

Additional Notes. 1. The Harvard Observatory translates its telegram of September 19, 1941, as follows:

"Schwassmann-Wachmann One Comet"—the designation of the comet which was discovered jointly by Schwassmann and Wachmann in 1925—the first comet to be discovered by them, the second comet to appear in the year 1925.

"Thomas"—the name of the man who made the observation being telegraphed.

"18"—the day of observation. "11"—magnitude. "0"—description of comet, in this case "almost stellar."

"September"—month of observation.

"03355"—time (in Greenwich Civil-Universal Time) of observation in h, m, s; that is, $3^h/35^m/5^s$.

"21465"—the right ascension of the comet: $21^h 46^m.5$.

"11141"—the declination of the comet: 1 (south) $11° 41'$.

"Motion"—the daily motion of the comet on the celestial sphere. This is computed from the difference between two positions, expressed in:

"10023"—motion in right ascension: 1 (west) $0^m 23^s$.

"10001"—motion in declination: 1 (south) $0° 1'$.

"74095"—a check number only, the sum of the preceding groups of five figures.

"Suddenly brighter" refers to the fact that between the fifteenth and eighteenth of September the comet brightened from the fifteenth to the eleventh magnitude. Understand?

2. If your announcer is facing the studio clock he can fill in the blanks when he gets there.

3. This was written before Pearl Harbor. We are not speaking to citizens of Tokyo right now.

4. Figures for all these years are based on 1943 in our calendar.

5. This broadcast was produced late in September. The Jewish New Year generally falls around this time. In the years 1939-43 it occurred on September 30 and 14 and October 4 and 12.

6. This part of the script should not be rehearsed or made known to the actors before the show takes air. The idea of withholding the cue is to spring it as a surprise on the actors. You will find that in most cases the particular actor will stammer and sputter and come up with nothing resembling a practical definition. Unless, of course, he is unusually articulate. Bartlett Robinson made the mistake of asking the question of Henry Morgan, and the terrible Morgan spoiled the effect with a smooth and equivocal answer.

7. Your own group.

GLOSSARY OF TERMS

Cue: A sound or word or musical phrase used as a signal for the entrance of another sound or word or musical phrase. Director's cues are generally relayed by hand, although in complicated circumstances, light signals are used. The term "cue" is often used loosely to indicate a speech or a printed direction, and in mimeographed scripts where each speech and effect is separately numbered to facilitate reference in rehearsal, each number is called a cue.

Fade: To diminish or increase (fade in) volume, whether by changing positions relative to a microphone or by electrical means on the control board.

Motif: A thematic phrase or passage of music which is reproduced or varied through the course of a script; often, a short musical figure serving both as means of transition and as an aid to the identification of a character or setting.

Under: Behind another effect.

Up: When applied to speech, a direction to distinguish between a personal, narrative, aside, inward, or contemplative quality, and direct address to another person.

Commenting on the elements of horseplay and straight talk in the script, Clifton Fadiman has said, in his introduction to *More by Corwin,* "The horseplay frequently combines with sound, imaginative instruction as in *Good Heavens,* which should be required hearing in every Astronomy I course in every college in the land." Does your Astronomy professor agree with this assertion? Would the method of this radio play be fruitful in the teaching of other sciences? In any school or college you have attended has the use of motion pictures or radio aided in instruction?

Possible Themes: 1. Write a brief radio play such as might be produced on a college radio station. In your play you may convey instruction or urge to action as well as tell a story. Before you do this, listen attentively to a number of radio plays to observe how transitions from one scene or place are managed by speech and sound alone; 2. Write an editorial or essay on the value of radio or motion pictures in the class room; 3. Do you prefer the radio plays presented on sustaining programs or the plays commercially sponsored? (Omit consideration of variety programs and news.) Record your opinion in a letter to the editor of a local or your college newspaper.

POETRY

Read Daniels' essay on poetry, page 214.

BALLADS

Ballads tell or suggest stories, but they differ from other narrative poems in their swinging rhythms and in their frequent use of a chanted refrain. Both characteristics were established by the earliest ballads, anonymous compositions of the Middle Ages which have been transmitted to us by oral tradition and reduced to writing for the most part only within the past two centuries. *Robin Hood Rescuing the Widow's Three Sons* is an authentic old ballad. These ballads have been called popular because they were sung and enjoyed by the common people whose lack of education denied them the enjoyment of more sophisticated poetry. Mountaineers and cow boys still sing old ballads and even compose and sing new ones. They are frequently crude, but at their best are vigorous and stirring as is the anonymous *Jesse James* in this section.

Our modern ballads reprinted here are literary compositions reflecting many of the traits of the old popular ballads. Like many old ballads, *The Sacrilege* and *Farewell to Barn and Stack and Tree* tell stories of stark tragedy among common people. Like many old ballads *The Ballad of East and West* recounts an actual historical occurrence. Which of the ballads use repetition? Which use refrain? Scan a few lines here and there and point out irregularities in the ballad meters.

Compare and contrast the anonymous *Jesse James* with *Robin Hood* as popular ballads. Read in this connection *Casey Jones* and *Frankie and Johnnie.* (They are printed in Sandburg's *American Songbag*.)   Are the last two popular ballads or literary ballads?

Does *The Ballad of East and West* reflect your own view of the proper relationship between races?   What common traits, indicative of the hand of Hardy, do you find in *The Sacrilege* and in his novel *The Return of the Native*?

Possible Themes: 1. Write in clear and orderly prose the story told allusively in the Housman ballad, the Speyer ballad; 2. Transcribe your favorite ballad, not reprinted here, and explain why you like it; 3. Rewrite one of these ballads as a short story.

NARRATIVE POEMS

In reading and rereading the verse stories in this collection perhaps the first question that might profitably be asked is, Why has the author chosen to tell them as poems instead of as prose stories?

The Haystack in the Floods, like *A Lodging for the Night,* tells a story of the Middle Ages. If you were to rewrite the first few hundred words of the poem in such prose as Stevenson wrote in his story you would realize how the flavor would be altered.

Next consider how well adapted the verse form chosen is to the intention of each of these poems.   Do the short, four-stressed couplets fit the rush of Morris' grim story?

It was not the intention of Morris to deal with moral problems in *The Haystack in the Floods*. Should a poem be judged according to the author's intentions or according to the reader's expectations?   Do *The Raid on Harper's Ferry* and *Saul Kane's Fight* deal with moral problems?

Possible Themes: 1. Rewrite as prose story the first three or four hundred words of any one of the narrative poems.   Carefully avoid the danger of carrying over into your prose any of the rime and meter of the poem; 2. Compare and contrast any two of these poems in material, intention, and expression; 3. Rewrite *The Raid on Harper's Ferry* or *Saul Kane's Fight* as a newspaper account of 300 words.

DRAMATIC LYRICS

In the *Poetics* Aristotle classifies poetry as narrative, dramatic, and lyric. In narrative a poet tells a story with, perhaps, occasional comments. In drama the poet shows men in action without comment. In lyric the poet speaks in his own person. The classification is still valid. The poet turns to lyric to express his attitudes and intentions, to communicate his feelings, to resolve if possible the conflicts of his own heart and mind.

In writing dramatic lyrics a poet works much as a dramatist works except that he does not write a play. Tennyson imagines how Ulysses might have felt after he had spent some time at home with his wife Penelope and his son Telemachus and had become restless. He misses the activity that had been his at Troy and on his journey home. Does it express the restlessness of a veteran today?   The lyric is an expression of what Ulysses might have felt.   Does the poem also express something of Tennyson's own personal feeling?   Does the conclusion deal with some of the same problems treated in *In Memoriam?*

In *My Last Duchess* an Italian despot of the Renaissance speaks to an emissary of his future father-in-law. What happened to the previous duchess?   Why?   Why does the duke tell all this to the emissary?   Is the poem more or less lyric than *Ulysses?*

Why should *The Death of the Hired Man* be classified here instead of among the narrative poems?   What lyric qualities does it possess?   Does it communicate Frost's own feelings on the subject of the land, home, the family?

Possible Themes: 1. Write a character sketch of a hired man, or handy man,

who has worked for your family; 2. Write a comparison of *Ulysses* and *Invictus;*
3. If a veteran, write of your own restlessness.

ODES

Odes are poems of praise addressed to a person, a class of persons, a city, an art
object, a natural force, or a moral abstraction. They usually combine description
with meditation and always express the poet's personal attitude. It has been said
that the theme of Keats' ode is that the permanence of art is a comfort in an im-
permanent world. What evidence do you find in the poem in favor of this view?
Against it?

How well do the rhythmical rather than metrical lines of the Whitman and
Sandburg odes seem adapted to the subjects of the odes?

Possible Themes: 1. Describe the two scenes depicted on the two sides of the
vase Keats addresses; 2. Write on the place for the pioneer, or his lack of a place,
in modern American life.

SONGS

Most lyrics may be sung and many that were not written to be sung have received
musical settings. But a song is a lyric written expressly to be sung. Many of Burns's
songs were written to old tunes.

How many of the songs printed in this collection have you yourself sung or
heard sung? Do songs as a rule have greater or less intellectual content than other
lyric forms? Which of these songs seem to call for group singing? Which for
solo singing? Do your doctrinal adhesions interfere with your appreciation of
Willie Brewed a Peck o' Maut or *Marching Along?* Which of the songs seem
almost to supply their own musical settings?

Possible Themes: 1. Tell the story of some very pleasant experience you have
had in group singing—around a camp fire, perhaps, or a fireplace or in church;
2. Tell of your pleasure, or displeasure, in hearing for the first time some famous
solo singer; 3. Write a brief account of student life in the Middle Ages. (Use
Gaudeamus Igitur, and *A Lodging for the Night* among your sources.)

ELEGIES

The modern elegy celebrates the dead and expresses the personal feelings of the
bereaved poet. Frequently it generalizes and points out significant influences of
the dead.

How long after his father's death did Arnold write *Rugby Chapel?* Could he
have recognized the significance of his father's influence so clearly if he had written
immediately after his death? Do you know any one who might be described in
terms similar to those used by Arnold in praising his father? Compare this poem
with *Dover Beach?* Is a similar note sounded?

Rossetti was a painter as well as a poet. Do you recognize a painter's touch in
My Sister's Sleep? How does Rossetti make you hear the silence? How does he
indicate his belief in immortality?

What immortality does Lindsay promise for Altgeld? What effect does the poet
secure by his use of the long lines? Is the poem more modern in spirit than the
others?

Possible Themes: 1. Write a verse or prose elegy for some one, now dead, whom
you loved or admired; 2. Write a brief narrative of your earliest contact with death.
Express your feelings as you recollect them; 3. Write a brief biographical sketch of
Altgeld. Was he right or wrong?

LIGHTER LYRICS

Poets, like other people, cannot be serious all of the time. In their lighter lyrics
they express their moods of playfulness and gaiety. These lighter lyrics need not

be inferior to the solemn ones any more than smiles are inferior to tears. Observe the frequent use of the artificial French verse forms: the rondeau, the triolet, the villanelle, the ballade. Why should these artificial forms be appropriate to verse in lighter moods? Are they inappropriate for more serious verse? Should E. B. White's poem have been listed among the Satires? Defend your answer. Study the contents of Auden, *Oxford Book of Light Verse*. Which poems treat serious subjects with a light touch?

Possible Themes: 1. Write a prose letter of advice in a jocular mood; 2. Study out the rime scheme and metrical structure of the triolet and write one.

SATIRE

Not all of a poet's possible emotions are gentle or kindly. Even a poet sometimes becomes angry. When he does he may write satire. Satire has been defined as denunciation combined with humor. The humor is used, not to soften the edge of the satire, but to give it edge and point.

What do these satires denounce? Is Clough ridiculing the Ten Commandments or a worldly society? Is Robinson ridiculing romance or emotionally dishonest posers?

Are the other satirists in this section inspired by the same idealism as inspired Lee Wilson Dodd? (See the last section of *Publicity*.) In the library consult Pope's *Epistle to Dr. Arbuthnot* and Dryden's *MacFlecknoe*. Compare these poems with *Publicity* for technique and intention.

Does Cummings denounce patriotism or dishonest political oratory? Is Sassoon's gripe against the brass hats of the first World War still applicable to incompetent leaders of the second?

Do any of these satires probe moral hypocrisies or weaknesses in your own character, or are you able to see flaws only in other people? Do your stock responses render difficult or impossible your appreciation of any of the poems in this collection?

Possible Themes: 1. Write a verse or prose satire on some institution, group of people, or person. Don't forget that humor is a necessary ingredient and that the satirist uses edged tools, not clubs and brick-bats; 2. Which poem in this collection do you least appreciate? To what fault of your own is this lack of appreciation due? 3. Transcribe Cummings' sonnet with conventional punctuation and capitalization. Is he in any way justified in having it all printed in lower case?

DESCRIPTIVE LYRICS

From earliest time men and women have been responsive to weather and natural scenery. Some have responded appreciatively to external nature. Some have passionately participated in it. More recently, man-made objects such as locomotives, automobiles, and airplanes have become part of the external nature to which poets respond. Of the descriptive poems here collected, which record appreciation? Which record participation? Compare and contrast *To a Locomotive in Winter* and *The Express*.

By what change of rhythm does MacLeish mark his transition from flies to hawks? Of what does Housman sing, cherry blossoms or mortality? Compare the Housman poem with Miss Magaret's *Impiety*.

Mr. Coffin says that when as a boy he returned later to where the fox dropped the fish, the fish was still there. He became sorry because the fox had lost his fish. Why is this omitted from the poem?

Possible Themes: 1. Write a prose nature description: the city or country after a snow fall, rain in city or country, an animal you have seen in the woods, the sea or a river; 2. Compare and contrast the snow poems by Bridges and Frost; 3. Write a nature description contrasting the same scene at morning and evening, summer and winter, or wet and sunny. 4. Write a prose or verse description in which you record your lyric appreciation or participation in some man-made object: your canoe, automobile, bicycle, or airplane.

LOVE LYRICS

The love of man for woman and of woman for man has inspired more lyric verse than any other personal emotion that moves the hearts of poets. In the group of love lyrics here collected observe the different colorings given the emotion of love. Which are ecstatic? Which regretful? Which physical? Which spiritualized? Which are written to the loved person? Which are descriptive?

What images of coolness and purity does Keats use in the first part of his sonnet to prepare the reader to understand the conclusion as he wished it understood? Does Villa convince you of his unloved desolation? Does Auslander's use of one syllable words contribute to an effect of simplicity and deep feeling?

Since Petrarch wrote his sonnets to Laura, the sonnet form has been a favorite form for love poems. Why is this? Which poems in this group are sonnets? What technical requirements has a sonnet?

Possible Themes: 1. What is your favorite love lyric not printed in this collection? Transcribe it and explain why you think it is fine; 2. Write an original sonnet of your own. It may not be very poetical, but any college student can write a correct sonnet.

POEMS OF DOUBT AND FAITH

In these poems mental and spiritual struggles predominate. The poets seek solutions for the most important problems of their inner lives. Tennyson, Browning, Arnold, and Henley wrestle with the problems of doubt and faith which result from the conflicts between the assertions of the young sciences of geology and biology on the one hand and those of Genesis on the other. Can one believe in a religion based on the Bible and also believe in science? If one loses faith in religion, what can one have faith in? Each poem offers a different personal solution to the problem. What are these solutions? Endeavor to sum up briefly in writing the solution offered by each of the four to the problem of doubt and faith. What sustained Emily Dickinson in a world of woe? What sustained Jeffers in a world of destruction? Are Aiken and Magaret equally religious, if any? What sustained the faith of G. M. Hopkins? What experiences of man's inhumanity to man brought Edith Sitwell and T. S. Eliot to a realization of faith? What else contributed? Who is the speaker in *Journey of the Magi?*

Possible Themes: 1. Have you, like Tennyson and Browning, lost by death a dear friend or relative? Has your faith suffered from the shock of evolutionary theory? The shock of the bombing of civilians? The shock of Dachau and Buchenwald? In prose or verse write of your personal struggle and state your personal solutions; 2. Read of the birth of Jesus in Luke 1-2, and of the Wise Men in Matthew 1-2. Then write an essay on T. S. Eliot's use of his sources in his *Journey of the Magi;* 3. "There are no atheists in fox holes." On the basis of your experience and observation comment on the statement.

POETRY OF SOCIAL CHANGE

Social change in England and America has tended to grant more power and more comfort to increasingly larger numbers of the population. The French Revolution put an end to the exclusive privileges of a feudal aristocracy and a feudal church. The Industrial Revolution gave power and wealth to those whose vision and enterprise gave them control of industrial production. Social change today seems to be a revolt against the exclusive privileges of these great industrialists and against uncontrolled exploitation of natural resources.

In the 19th Century most people believed that social change was in the direction of a better world. An optimistic age believed in progress and its continuation. Since the war of 1914–1918, however, a reaction has set in. A new group of poets has begun to question progress and to criticize the optimism of their fathers. Do these poets' criticisms seem justified? Have the French Revolution, the Industrial Revolution, the Russian Revolution, left abuses that only another revolution can remove?

Against what was Hood protesting? How was this evil removed? By revolution? What is being done about erosion? Can the land be brought back to productivity by laissez faire or only by governmental interference? How can the problems of technological unemployment best be solved? Is poetry or prose the more effective medium for vivifying these and similar problems growing out of social change?

Possible Themes: 1. In your own experience have you observed instances of soil erosion resulting from deforestation? What was done about it? Tell the story; 2. Would there be less unemployment if lower wages were legalized? Discuss in 500 words; 3. Are you angered by the same things that angered Helene Magaret? Write your own *Song of the Answerer* (in prose if you prefer).

Poems about Liberty

Liberty, like love, is the theme of a great deal of lyric poetry. Our own generation is not the first to be passionately concerned with it. Euripedes, whose verse on liberty Milton translated for the title page of *Areopagitica* (1640), was born 480 B.C. From the great days of Athens to those of England and America, Western cultures which have been fertilized by Greek civilization have been devoted to liberty with an intensity incomprehensible to those who have been habituated to oriental despotisms. But liberty like love may mean many things to many people. Three essays we print among *Discussions of Modern Problems,* as well as the poems we group here, illustrate the diversity of definition: *Education for Freedom, Free Speech in America,* and *Liberty—For What?* There is liberty of thought and discussion. There is religious liberty, personal liberty, national liberty, political liberty, spiritual liberty. Then there is that liberty called freedom from want, for which some willingly give up all other liberties. Indeed, as Benét and Cousins say in the Introduction to their anthology, *The Poetry of Freedom,* "In some respects it might almost be said that one man's freedom is another man's captivity."

How do the poems reprinted in *Modern English Readings* demonstrate different concepts and different definitions of liberty? Study each poem and formulate the definition of liberty implicit in it. Point out how the liberty celebrated in one poem is in conflict with the liberty celebrated in another. What liberty do you yourself prize most highly?

Liberty of the press, guaranteed by the Bill of Rights, is limited by laws against printing libel and obscenity. Are these laws proper restraints on liberty or not? What other restraints on liberty of thought and discussion are established by pressure groups which protest against all publications not favorable to their own color, race, or sect? How do foreign governments restrict liberty of speech in the United States? Would you, if you had the power, grant freedom of speech to organizations whose aims you consider evil or would you deny freedom of speech to such organizations?

Possible Themes: 1. Write an answer, in prose or verse, to whichever of these poems you most actively disagree with; 2. Compare and contrast two or three of these poems which seem to present divergent views on liberty; 3. Write an editorial or letter to the editor protesting some act of censorship of the press, by college authorities, pressure groups, or governmental agencies; 4. Express your agreement or disagreement with the extent that traffic laws interfere with the liberty of a person driving a car.

BIOGRAPHIC NOTES

ADAMS, FRANKLIN PIERCE (F.P.A.) (1881—)

American columnist, author, and radio personality, born in Chicago and educated at the University of Michigan. As a writer of light verse, especially modern versions from Horace, he is in the tradition of Eugene Field and Bert Leston Taylor. His volumes of humorous verse include *Tobogganing on Parnassus* (1910), *By and Large* (1914), *So Much Velvet* (1924), and *Christopher Columbus* (1931).

ADAMS, HENRY BROOKS (1838–1918)

The great-grandson of one president and grandson of another, he was born on Beacon Hill, Boston; studied at Harvard under Lowell and Agassiz; studied and traveled in Europe. Was secretary of the American embassy in London and met Browning and the geologist Lyell. Was professor of history at Harvard 1870 to 1877. Resided in Washington for a few years, traveled extensively. In 1895 he became profoundly influenced by medieval life and thought, and wrote *Mont St. Michel and Chartres*. In 1907 appeared his famous autobiography, *The Education of Henry Adams.*

ADLER, MORTIMER JEROME (1902—)

Born in New York and educated at Columbia University (Ph.D. 1928). He is a college professor and author of works on scholastic philosophy, as well as *Art and Prudence* (1937), *How to Read a Book* (1940), and *A Dialectic of Morals* (1941). He has been one of the leaders of the return to the classics theory of education at the University of Chicago.

AIKEN, CONRAD (1889—)

Born in Savannah, Georgia. A.B. Harvard, 1911. Story writer, novelist, anthologist and poet. His selected poems won the Pulitzer Prize for 1930. Author of short stories collected in *Bring! Bring!* and *Costumes for Eros,* and of the novels, *Blue Voyage, Great Circle,* and *King Coffin.*

ALDINGTON, RICHARD (1892—)

Educated at London University. Served in the War 1916–1918. Poet, translator and novelist. His novels: *Death of a Hero* (1929), *The Colonel's Daughter* (1931), *All Men Are Enemies* (1933), and *Women Must Work* (1934). The first collected edition of his poems in the U. S. appeared in 1934.

ALLEN, HERVEY (1889—)

Born in Pittsburgh, Pennsylvania. Attended U. S. Naval Academy 1910–1911, A.B. University of Pittsburgh 1915. First Lt., World War I; wounded in action. Taught at Columbia University 1924–1925. Author of volumes of poetry: *Wampum and Old Gold* and *New Legends;* the novel, *Anthony Adverse; Israfel,* a biography of Poe; *The Forest and the Fort* (1943) and *Bedford Village* (1944) first two volumes of projected six-volume historical novel.

ARNOLD, MATTHEW (1822–1888)

His father, whose death he mourns in *Rugby Chapel,* was Thomas Arnold, headmaster of Rugby, 1828–1842. He was educated at Balliol College, Oxford. His most significant poems were written before 1867 and his prose after 1860. As inspector of schools and as professor of poetry at Oxford, Arnold exerted a stimulating influence on education and the appreciation of literature.

AUDEN, WYSTAN HUGH (1907—)

English poet, educated at Oxford. Youngest of the group that includes Stephen Spender and C. Day Lewis. Has taught school and served as correspondent with Spanish Loyalists and Chinese. Has edited two anthologies, *The Poet's Tongue* and *Oxford Book of Light Verse*. His *Collected Poetry* includes his most important work to 1945.

AUSLANDER, JOSEPH (1897—)

Born in Philadelphia. Harvard, A.B. Instructor at Harvard and from 1929–1935 taught verse writing in the University Extension at Columbia. Poet, editor, and translator. Author of the following volumes of poetry: *Sunrise Trumpets, Hell in Harness, Letters to Women, No Traveler Returns*.

BEERBOHM, MAX (1872—)

Educated at Oxford, which he has parodied so delightfully in that classic of college life, *Zuleika Dobson*. During the gay nineties he was one of the cleverest of the *Yellow Book* set, which included Oscar Wilde and Arthur Symons. He is something of a cosmopolitan, for his wife is a Tennesseean, and for some years before World War II he lived in Italy.

BENÉT, STEPHEN VINCENT (1898–1943)

Born in Bethlehem, Pennsylvania. A.B. Yale, 1919, M.A. 1920. Short story writer and poet. Author of *Tiger Joy* (1925), *Spanish Bayonet* (1926), *John Brown's Body* (Pulitzer Prize for the best volume of verse, 1928), *Ballads and Poems* (1931). Read *My Brother Steve* for fuller details.

BENÉT, WILLIAM ROSE (1886—)

Born Fort Hamilton, N. Y. harbor. Educated at the Albany Academy and Yale. On staff of *Century Magazine* 1911–1918. Then on staff of *The Saturday Review of Literature* to the present. He is the author of some ten volumes of verse, a novel, a book for children, and is compiler of a number of anthologies of poetry. Has taught verse writing at Columbia University.

BOURDILLON, FRANCIS WILLIAM (1852–1921)

Worcester College, Oxford (Scholar) M.A. From 1876 to 1879, resident tutor to Prince and Princess Christian. Took private pupils for the universities. Author of *Among the Flowers and Other Poems* (1878), and *Ailes d'Alouette* (1890). Did editions and translations of *Aucassin and Nicolette, Roman de la Rose* and other medieval poems and romances.

BRADFORD, GAMALIEL (1863–1932)

Born in Boston. Left Harvard for reasons of health. Lived in retirement at Wellesley Hills, Mass. Author of numerous biographical studies which he called psychographs.

BREWSTER, DOROTHY (1883—)

Born in St. Louis. Graduated from Barnard College in 1906, and took her doctorate at Columbia in 1913. Edited *A Book of Modern Short Stories* (1928). Has written reviews of modern fiction and collaborated with Professor Burrell on *Dead Reckonings in Fiction* (1924), and *Modern Fiction* (1934). Associate Professor of English, Columbia University.

BRIDGES, ROBERT (1844–1930)

Educated at Corpus Christi College, Cambridge. Studied and for a time practiced medicine. He gained his reputation as a poet by his *Shorter Poems,* published from 1873 to 1893. He wrote critical essays as well as poetry. Appointed poet laureate in 1913.

BROUN, HEYWOOD (1888–1939)

Born in Brooklyn, N. Y., student at Harvard. Sports editor; war correspondent with A.E.F.; literary critic; author of syndicated column, *It Seems to Me;* founder of newspaper men's union.

BROWNING, ELIZABETH BARRETT (1806–1861)

Married Robert Browning in 1846. Her best poems are those contained in the volume *Sonnets from the Portuguese.*

BROWNING, ROBERT (1812–1889)

Privately educated. He and his wife, Elizabeth Barrett Browning, lived mainly in Italy from their marriage in 1846 to her death in 1861. Best known for his lyrics and dramatic monologs.

BRUSH, KATHARINE (1902—)

Novelist and short story writer. Born at Middletown, Conn. Educated at Centenary Collegiate Institute. Author of *Night Club,* short stories (1929), *Young Man of Manhattan* (1930), *Don't Ever Leave Me* (1935), *This Is on Me* (1940), *You Go Your Own Way* (1941).

BURNS, ROBERT (1759–1796)

Born in Ayrshire, son of a farmer. Became famous with the publication of the Kilmarnock edition of his early poems. Wrote many songs to old traditional airs. His narrative poems include *Tam o' Shanter,* and his satires, *Holy Willie's Prayer.* His language is the northern variety of English spoken in the lowlands of Scotland.

BURRELL, ANGUS (1890—)

Born in Montana. Graduated from the University of Wisconsin in 1914. Served in the navy during World War I. Is now Associate Professor of English at Columbia University. Has published in collaboration with Miss Brewster *Dead Reckonings in Fiction* (1924), and *Modern Fiction* (1934). Edited *The Bedside Book of Famous American Short Stories* (1936), in collaboration with Bennett A. Cerf.

BYRON, GEORGE GORDON, 6th Baron (1788–1824)

Born in London, and educated at Trinity College, Cambridge. Won fame as a poet with *Childe Harold* (1812). His long, unfinished satirical poem *Don Juan* appeared in installments after 1820. He wrote many poetic dramas. He died of fever while assisting the Greeks in a rebellion against Turkey.

CATHER, WILLA SIBERT (1875—)

Novelist and story writer. Born in Winchester, Va., and educated at the University of Nebraska. She was editor of *McClure's Magazine* 1906–12. *Paul's Case* appeared in *The Troll Garden* (1905), her first volume of stories. Her fame rests on the novels including *O Pioneers* (1913), *My Antonia* (1919), *Death Comes for the Archbishop* (1927), *Shadows on the Rock* (1931), and *Sapphira and the Slave Girl* (1940).

CHAFEE, ZECHARIAH, JR. (1885—)
  Professor of Law at Harvard. Educated at Brown and at Harvard Law School (1913). Author of *Freedom of Speech* (1920), *The Inquiring Mind* (1928), and *Cases on Equitable Remedies* (1939).

CHASE, MARY ELLEN (1887—)
  This short story writer, novelist, and professor of English at Smith College was born at Blue Hill, Maine, and educated at the University of Maine (A.B. 1909) and the University of Minnesota (Ph.D. 1922). In addition to many textbooks and other professional books she has written the novels *A Goodly Heritage* (1932), *Mary Peters* (1934), *Silas Crocker* (1935), *Windswept* (1941), and the autobiography *A Goodly Fellowship* (1939).

CLOUGH, ARTHUR HUGH (1819–1861)
  Son of a Liverpool merchant, he was educated at Oxford. He was a fellow at Oriel College, then principal of University Hall, London, and later an examiner in the Education Office. His poems were, for the most part, narrative.

COFFIN, ROBERT P. TRISTRAM (1892—)
  Is a graduate of Bowdoin College, represented his native state of Maine as a Rhodes Scholar at Oxford. Like James's *Passionate Pilgrim,* he discovered another home in England, to which ancestral strains and a devotion to English literature led him. Received the Pulitzer Prize for Poetry in 1936. Author of an autobiography, *Lost Paradise,* and of many volumes of essays and poems.

COLERIDGE, SAMUEL TAYLOR (1772–1834)
  Educated at Christ's Hospital, where he met Charles Lamb, and at Jesus College, Cambridge. He tried soldiering, communism, and journalism. Associated with Wordsworth in the publication of *Lyrical Ballads.* In later life he turned more and more from poetry to essays in literary criticism and philosophy.

COLUM, PADRAIC (1881—)
  Born at Longford, Ireland. Poet, novelist, story writer, dramatist. Associated with W. B. Yeats and Lady Gregory at the beginning of the Irish Theatre movement. Founder and editor of the *Irish Review.* Now lives in New York.

CONNELLY, MARC (1890—)
  Born in Pennsylvania; reporter on Pittsburgh papers; contributor of verse and articles to magazines. Author of *Beggar on Horseback* and *The Green Pastures;* received the Pulitzer Prize for the latter play in 1930.

CONVERSE, FLORENCE (1871—)
  Born in New Orleans. Educated at Wellesley. On editorial staff of *The Churchman,* 1900–1908, and the *Atlantic Monthly,* 1908–1930. Author of *Diana Victrix,* a novel (1897), *The Burden of Christopher* (1900), *Long Will* (1903), *The Blessed Birthday* (1917), *The Children of Light* (1912), *Garments of Praise* (1921), *The Holy Night* (1922), *The House of Prayer, Into the Void* (1926), and *Collected Poems* (1937). The long poem *Efficiency Expert* was published in 1934.

CORWIN, NORMAN (1910—)
  Born in Boston. After ten years as reporter, columnist, and radio editor, he was engaged by CBS in 1938 as a director-producer. A selection of his radio plays has been published in *Thirteen by Corwin* (1942) and *More by Corwin* (1943). Of this master of the newest of literary forms Carl Van Doren has said, "He is to American radio what Marlowe was to the Elizabethan stage."

COUSINS, NORMAN (1912—)

Graduated from Teachers College, Columbia, 1933. Was editor of *Current History,* now editor of *Saturday Review of Literature.* Lectures and writes on books and world affairs. Is moderator and forum leader of Norwalk Town Hall Association (Conn.). Consultant during war to Overseas Publication branch of the Office of War Information. Author of *The Good Inheritance: The Democratic Chance,* 1942; editor (with W. R. Benét) of *An Anthology of the Poetry of Liberty,* 1943. His *Modern Man Is Obsolete,* late in 1945, is an expansion of his much discussed editorial on the social and political implications of atomic energy.

CROWTHER, GEOFFREY (1907—)

Educated Cambridge, Yale, and Columbia. Editor of *The Economist,* the authoritative financial journal of London, since 1938. Books on economics include: *Economics for Democrats,* 1939, and *An Outline of Money,* 1941. During the war, received leave of absence from *The Economist,* and served on the staff of the Minister of Production.

CUMMINGS, EDWARD ESTLIN (1894—)

Born in Cambridge, Mass. Harvard, A.B., A.M. He served in the Ambulance Corps and later as a private in World War I. He is a painter as well as a poet. *The Enormous Room* (1922) gives in prose his memoirs of the war. His poetry, characterized by obscurity and typographical eccentricities, is contained in volumes entitled *XLI Poems, Is 5, CIOPW, IXI. Collected Poems* appeared in 1938.

CURIE, EVE (1904—)

A musician and playwright. Younger daughter of Pierre Curie and Marie Sklodowska Curie, the discoverers of radium. Born in Paris and educated at Sévigné College. Was a music critic and journalist in Paris for years. Author of *The Price of Freedom* (1940).

DANIELS, EARL RICHARDSON KNAPP (1893—)

Associate Professor of English at Colgate University. A.B. Clark University, A.M. Chicago, Ph.D. Harvard. Author of *The Art of Reading Poetry* (1941).

DAVIS, HARRY M. (1906—)

Joint author of *What You Should Know About the Signal Corps,* 1943, giving civilians insight into the dramatic elements of the Signal Corps branch of the Army; and editor of *This Is It!,* the personal narratives of twelve American fighting men. Recently has written articles for New York *Times* on the implications of atomic energy.

DAY, CLARENCE (1874–1935)

Born in New York City, graduated from Yale in 1896. Was for most of his life an invalid. Writer of humorous sketches and essays and of the autobiographical sketches, *God and My Father,* and *Life with Father.*

DE LA MARE, WALTER (1873—)

English story writer, novelist, and poet. His first volume, *Songs of Childhood,* appeared in 1902; *The Listeners and Other Poems* in 1912. *Memoirs of a Midget,* 1924. He writes much about and for children.

DICKINSON, EMILY (1830–1886)

Born at Amherst, Massachusetts, where she lived a quiet and secluded life. Her poems were published after her death; some are not yet published.

DOBIE, J. FRANK (1888—)

Born on a ranch in Live Oak County, Texas. Educated Southwestern University, University of Chicago, and Columbia University. Research fellow Rockefeller Foundation and Guggenheim Foundation. Served as 1st Lt. in U. S. Army, World War I. 1943 went to Cambridge as Professor of American History. *A Texan in England* was a record of that experience. Returned to England to teach in United States Army University near Oxford. Author of fiction and nonfiction on life and literature of the Southwest. Professor of English at University of Texas since 1933.

DOBSON, AUSTIN (1840–1921)

Educated at Strasbourg. On the English Board of Trade, 1856–1901. Author of four volumes of light verse and of seven volumes of serious biographical studies as well as several volumes of collected essays.

DODD, LEE WILSON (1879–1933)

American poet, novelist, and playwright. Born Franklin, Pa. Educated Yale and N. Y. Law School. Author of *A Modern Alchemist* and *The Middle Miles* (books of poems), *The Return of Eve, Speed, His Majesty Bunker Bean* (plays), and *The Book of Susan, Lilia Chenoworth,* and *The Girl Next Door* (novels). *The Great Enlightenment: A Satire in Verse, and Other Selected Verses* appeared in 1928.

DRYDEN, JOHN (1631–1700)

This great English man of letters is "modern" at least in that he took the lead in developing modern prose style in the direction it has followed to the present. See above, p. 239. He was also modern in his support of King James's policy of religious toleration.

DUNNE, FINLEY PETER (1867–1936)

American humorist, creator of "Mr. Dooley," was born in Chicago and as a journalist was connected with the *Times, Evening Post, Times-Herald,* and *Evening Journal.* The Mr. Dooley pieces were published in book form from *Mr. Dooley in Peace and War* (1898) to *Mr. Dooley on Making a Will and Other Necessary Evils* (1919).

EARNEST, ERNEST P. (1901—)

Educated Lafayette College, Harvard, and Princeton. Taught English at Georgia School of Technology and now teaches at Temple University.

EATON, WALTER PRICHARD (1878—)

Born in Massachusetts, graduated from Harvard in 1900. Dramatic critic for many years in Boston and New York, and author of many books on the theatre and outdoor life. Associate Professor of playwriting at Yale in 1933.

ELIOT, THOMAS STEARNS (1888—)

Born in St. Louis, Mo. Graduate of Harvard. He became an English citizen in 1927. His poems include *The Waste Land* (1922), *Ash Wednesday* (1930), *Sweeney Agonistes* (1932). *Collected Poems, 1909–1935,* appeared in 1936. The most recent of his *Four Quartets* was published in 1943. His critical prose essays were collected in *Selected Essays, 1917–1932.* No modern poet has had a greater influence on the younger poets of our generation.

FADIMAN, CLIFTON (1904—)
A.B. Columbia, 1925. Teacher of English at the Ethical Culture High School, 1925-27. Editorial adviser to publishers. Presiding genius of "Information Please."

FARBER, MANNY (1915—)
California painter, living in New York. Founded Abbot Art School in Washington. Contributes articles on art criticism, painting, music, and movies.

FAST, HOWARD (1914—)
Born in New York City. He published his first novel before he was twenty. Two other novels followed before he began his series of historical novels with *Conceived in Liberty* (1939). Other historical novels which followed were *The Last Frontier, Citizen Tom Paine,* and *Freedom Road. The Day of Victory* was published in a collection of his short stories, *Patrick Henry and the Frigate's Keel* (1945).

FISHER, WILLIS (1894—)
A.B. Ohio Wesleyan, 1916. Ph.D. Princeton, 1922. Teacher of English at Sarah Lawrence College. Co-author with Herbert Agar and Eleanor Chilton of a volume of verse, *Fire, Sleet, and Candlelight.*

FOSDICK, HARRY EMERSON (1878—)
Born Buffalo, N. Y. Educated Colgate University, Columbia University and Union Theological Seminary. Holds honorary degrees from almost a dozen American colleges and universities, and an honorary D.D. from Glasgow University. Ordained Baptist minister, 1903. Pastor Riverside Church, N. Y. C., 1930-1946. A famous preacher and author of books and sermons and practical religious guidance, including *Guide to Understanding the Bible,* and *On Being a Real Person.*

FOWLER, HENRY WATSON (1858-1933)
English scholar and essayist. Educated at Rugby and Oxford. Author of *The King's English* (1906). Editor of *Concise Oxford Dictionary* (1911), as well as *Modern English Usage* (1926).

FROST, ROBERT (1875—)
Born in San Francisco and moved at an early age to New England. Studied at Harvard. From 1912 to 1915 he lived in England. His poetical works include: *A Boy's Will* (1913), *North of Boston* (1914), *Mountain Interval* (1916), *New Hampshire* (1923), which won the Pulitzer Prize in 1924, and *West Running Brook* (1928).

HARDY, THOMAS (1840-1928)
Novelist and poet born near Dorchester, England. After an apprenticeship in architecture, he turned to literature. His better known novels include *The Return of the Native* (1878), *Tess of the D'Urbervilles* (1891), and *Jude the Obscure* (1895). *Tess* and *Jude* shocked the puritans, and Hardy wrote no more novels, turning to poetry with *Wessex Poems* (1898). *The Dynasts* (1904-8) deals at length with England's participation in the Napoleonic wars. *Satires of Circumstance* appeared in 1914.

HARRIMAN, MARGARET CASE
Born in New York. Educated at Gardner School, New York, and abroad. Worked on *Vanity Fair.* Now free lances, writing for *New Yorker, Harper's,* and others. *Take Them up Tenderly,* a collection of "Profiles" from the *New Yorker* (1944).

HART, MOSS (1904—)
 When not collaborating with George S. Kaufman (q.v.), he has done the books
for musical shows with Irving Berlin (*Face the Music,* 1932, and *As Thousands
Cheer,* 1933) and with Cole Porter (*Jubilee,* 1935).

HAY, JOHN (1837–1905)
 American author and statesman, born in Salem, Indiana. Brown University,
A.B. 1858. Was Lincoln's assistant private secretary until the President's assassina-
tion. With J. G. Nicolay he wrote *Abraham Lincoln: a History* (1890). He was
Secretary of State under McKinley and Roosevelt. *Pike County Ballads* was pub-
lished in 1891.

HAZLITT, WILLIAM (1778–1830)
 Though born in England, was of Irish extraction and probably loved a fight
as well as anyone else since the world began. With a vitriolic pen he waged lifelong war on the Tories, quarreled with all his friends, divorced one wife, was
deserted by another, and with his dying breath exclaimed, "Well, I have had a
happy life." Besides his capacity for hatred, he possessed an equal capacity for
enthusiasm, which he expressed in his literary criticism and in his familiar essays.

HEMINGWAY, ERNEST (1898—)
 Born in Illinois. Wounded on the Italian front World War I. Newspaper
correspondent, short story writer, and novelist. *In Our Time* first published in
Paris. *The Sun Also Rises* (1926), *Farewell to Arms* (1929), *Death in the After-
noon* (1932), *Winner Take Nothing* (1933), *The Fifth Column,* a play, (1940),
For Whom the Bell Tolls (1940).

HENLEY, WILLIAM ERNEST (1849–1903)
 Born at Gloucester, England, he was a cripple from boyhood. He was a magazine editor, playwright, and lyric poet. His collected works were published in 1908.

HERSEY, JOHN (1914—)
 Son of American missionaries, born in Tientsin, China. Graduated from Yale
1936. Went to Cambridge for postgraduate work. 1937 became a member of *Time*
staff, after spending the summer as secretary to Sinclair Lewis. In 1939, *Time*
sent him to the Orient. Later became Pacific war correspondent, and wrote *Men on
Bataan.* His *Into the Valley,* story of American fighting men on Guadalcanal, was
chosen as "Imperative" by the Council on Books in Wartime. His best-selling
Bell for Adano was based on experiences in the Mediterranean theater of war. He
was Moscow correspondent in 1944, and is now in China for *New Yorker* and *Life.*

HIGHET, GILBERT (1906—)
 Professor of Greek and Latin, Columbia University. Born in Glasgow, Scot-
land. Educated at Glasgow University and at Balliol College, Oxford; thereafter
Fellow of St. John's College, Oxford, until he came to U.S.A. in 1937. Author of
An Outline of Homer (1935) and of various translations of German scholarly works
and of verse translations in *The Oxford Book of Greek Verse in Translation.*

HOOD, THOMAS (1799–1845)
 Born in London. Friend of Lamb, Hazlitt, and De Quincey. Editor of magazines—*London Magazine, Gem, Comic Annual, New Monthly Magazine,* and
Hood's Magazine. Famous for his comic as well as serious verses. *The Song of
the Shirt* first appeared anonymously in *Punch* in 1843.

HOOD, THOMAS, JR. (pen name of Charles Clark, 1806–1880)
Author of *Epsom Races—a Poem, Comic, Punning, and Racy* (1838), printed at Clark's private press. A collection of his humorous and satiric pieces was edited by W. L. Hanchant, London, 1932.

HOOTON, EARNEST ALBERT (1887–)
Since 1930 Professor of Anthropology at Harvard. Born Clemansville, Wisconsin. Educated at Lawrence College (B.A. 1907) and the University of Wisconsin (Ph.D. 1911). Rhodes Scholar at Oxford, 1910–1913. Author of *Up from the Ape* (1931), *Apes, Men and Morons* (1937), *The American Criminal* (1939), and *Why Men Behave Like Apes and Vice Versa* (1940).

HOPKINS, GERARD MANLEY (1844–1889)
English poet, educated at Oxford, where he embraced the Tractarian Movement. He later followed John Henry Newman into the Church of Rome. He was ordained a Roman Catholic priest in 1877, and became Professor of Greek at Dublin in 1884. His *Poems* were collected and edited by his friend Robert Bridges after his death.

HOUSMAN, A. E. (1854–1936)
Educated at Oxford. Professor of Latin at Cambridge University from 1911 to his death. His poems are published in three volumes—*A Shropshire Lad* (1896), *Last Poems* (1922), and *More Poems* in 1936.

HUGHES, JAMES LANGSTON (1902–)
Born Joplin, Mo. Studied at Columbia and at Lincoln University, of which he is a graduate. He is author of the prose works: *The Ways of White Folks* (1934), and *The Big Sea*, an autobiography (1940); and the important volumes of poems: *The Dream Keeper* (1932), and *Shakespeare in Harlem* (1941). He was a Guggenheim Fellow in creative writing in 1935 and a Rosenwald Fellow in 1941.

HUME, ROBERT A.
A.B., Stanford University, 1929, Ph.D. Cornell, 1940. Has taught at Stanford, University of Idaho, Cornell, Purdue, University of British Columbia, and is now Associate Professor of English at University of Nevada. Contributor to *School and Society, South Atlantic Quarterly,* and *American Scholar.*

HUNT, LEIGH (1784–1859)
Educated at Christ's Hospital. Was editor of many liberal magazines and author of miscellaneous essays and critical works. While editor of *The Examiner* he was sentenced to two years' imprisonment for printing reflections on the Prince Regent. He wrote serious as well as light verse.

HUTCHINS, ROBERT MAYNARD (1899–)
Born in Brooklyn, N. Y. Educated at Oberlin and Yale. In ambulance service during World War I. Dean of Yale Law School, 1928–1929. President of the University of Chicago since 1929. Writer of many articles on education.

HUXLEY, THOMAS HENRY (1825–1895)
Was the son of a schoolmaster at Ealing, outside London. Took his degree in medicine in 1845, and went out as a surgeon for four years on H.M.S. *Rattlesnake*. His biological papers attracted attention. In 1851 he was made a Fellow of the Royal Society, and formed friendships with the leading English scientists, including Darwin. In many stormy controversies he championed the cause of evolution.

The Romanes lecture delivered in 1893 on *Evolution and Ethics* is an attempt to show the relation of morals to a severely scientific view of man.

JACKSON, ELIZABETH (1892—)
Educated Radcliffe College. Now Professor of English at University of Minnesota. Author of *The Faith and Fire within Us,* 1944, an analysis of the connection of literature and ideals in our history.

JEFFERS, ROBINSON (1887—)
Born Pittsburgh, Pennsylvania. A.B. Occidental College, 1905. *Tamar and Other Poems* (1924) first brought him fame as a poet. His reputation has increased with the publication of *Roan Stallion, Thurso's Landing,* and *Give Your Heart to the Hawks.* He lives in Carmel, California.

JONES, THOMAS S., JR. (1882–1932)
Born at Boonville, N. Y. Educated at Cornell. His newspaper experience included work as a critic on the dramatic staff of the New York *Times* and as editor of Reuter's Cable Service. He first secured recognition as a poet of distinction with *The Rose Jar* (1915). This was followed by *Sonnets of the Cross* (1922) and, among others, *The Unicorn and Other Sonnets* (1931). His poems were collected and edited by John L. Foley under the title of *Shadow of the Perfect Rose* (1937).

KAUFMAN, GEORGE S. (1889—)
This great collaborator has written 30 successful plays with various co-workers including Connelly, Ferber, Ryskind, Lardner, Woollcott. His collaboration with Moss Hart began with *Once in a Lifetime* (1930), and includes *Merrily We Roll Along* (1934), *You Can't Take It with You* (1936), *I'd Rather Be Right* (1937), *The American Way* (1939), and *The Man Who Came to Dinner* (1939).

KEATS, JOHN (1795–1821)
Born in London. Educated as a surgeon and passed his examinations, but abandoned surgery for poetry. His fame rests on his lyric and narrative poems, the best of which, including *The Eve of St. Agnes* and the odes, were published in 1820.

KILMER, JOYCE (1886–1918)
American journalist and poet, born in New Jersey and educated at Rutgers and at Columbia. He was killed in the second battle of the Marne. His best known lyric, *Trees,* has been set to music and has been parodied countless times. *Poems, Essays, and Letters,* a memorial volume, appeared after his death.

KIPLING, RUDYARD (1865–1935)
Born in Bombay, India, and educated at the United Services College, England. His early stories and verses won him fame while he was a journalist in India from 1882 to 1889. His memorable books include *Kim, The Jungle Books,* and *Puck of Pook's Hill.*

KITTREDGE, GEORGE LYMAN (1860–1941)
Born in Boston. Beginning as a teacher of the classics, he soon turned his attention to the field of English literature and philology. Until his retirement in 1936 was one of the best known lecturers and most distinguished American scholars. His writings cover such diverse fields as *English Witchcraft and James I* and *The Poetry of Chaucer,* and the books of his students would run into the hundreds.

KREYMBORG, ALFRED (1883—)

This American poet and prose writer was born in New York. His poems appear in the volumes *Mushrooms* (1916), *Less Lonely* (1923), *Last Sail* (1929), and *Manhattan Men* (1929). He has written a number of radio plays in verse, an autobiography, *Troubadour* (1925), and a novel, *I'm No Hero* (1933).

LA FARGE, OLIVER (1901—)

Son of Grant La Farge, architect, and grandson of painter John La Farge. Born New York City. B.A., Harvard, 1924. Taught Tulane, anthropological field work in Arizona and New Mexico. Pulitzer Prize for *Laughing Boy,* 1929. Awarded O. Henry Memorial Prize in 1930 for short story "Haunted Ground." Historical officer of Air Transport command, rank major. Served in South America, Africa, England, France, Italy.

LAMB, CHARLES (1775–1834)

Born in London of poor parents. Educated at Christ's Hospital. For thirty-three years was a clerk in the East India House. A strain of insanity in the family showed itself in his sister Mary, the Bridget of the *Essays of Elia.* These he began contributing to the *London Magazine* in 1820, and they fixed his place as the most fascinating and friendly of English essayists.

LAMONT, THOMAS W. (1870—)

Born Claverack, N. Y. Educated Harvard. Honorary degrees from Harvard, Union College, Rochester University, Columbia University, and New York University. Member of J. P. Morgan firm since 1911, chairman of the executive committee since 1940. Was representative of the U. S. Treasury on the American Committee to Negotiate Peace at Paris in 1919.

LANDOR, WALTER SAVAGE (1775–1864)

English poet and prose writer. Educated at Rugby and Oxford. His principal prose works were his *Imaginary Conversations* (1824–1829). Landor's verse was spread over most of his life, mainly from 1798 to 1847. His hatred of the tyranny of Napoleon (*A Foreign Ruler*) led him to expend much of his private fortune to assist the Spaniards in resisting the invader in 1808.

LANGEWIESCHE, WOLFGANG (1907—)

German-born student of sociology. Came to U. S. from Austria in 1930. Studied at Columbia, was research assistant at University of Chicago. Instructor in sociology at Sarah Lawrence College. Author nontechnical books on the art of flying: *I'll Take the High Road,* 1939; and *Stick and Rudder,* 1944.

LARDNER, RINGGOLD WILMER (1885–1933)

Born Niles, Michigan. He was a sportswriter from 1907 to 1919 in South Bend, Chicago, St. Louis, and Boston. His satiric humor is shown in the short stories collected in *You Know Me, Al* (1916), *How to Write Short Stories* (1924), and *Round Up* (1929).

LAY, BEIRNE, JR. (1909—)

Aviator and author of *I Wanted Wings* (1937). Graduated from Yale in 1931 and received his commission in the Army Air Corps in 1934. One of the army pilots who shortly after flew the mail. He was editor of *The Sportsman Pilot* until he rejoined the Air Corps in 1937.

LEWIS, CECIL DAY (1904—)
Born in Ireland and educated at Oxford. He is important as a critic of modern writing as well as a poet. His major work in poetry and criticism appears in *Collected Poems 1929–1933,* and *A Hope for Poetry,* and in *A Time to Dance* (1936). Under the pen name "Nicholas Blake" he has written a series of detective novels.

LILIENTHAL, DAVID ELI (1899—)
Born Morton, Ill. Educated De Pauw University (Phi Beta Kappa) and Harvard Law School. Practiced law in Chicago. Was called by La Follette to reorganize and direct the Wisconsin Public Service Commission. One of the three appointed to the original TVA board in 1933. In 1941 made chairman of the Board of Directors of TVA. Has contributed to *Nation, New Outlook,* and various legal journals. His *TVA—Democracy on the March* was selected by the Scientific Book Club for April, 1944.

LINDSAY, NICHOLAS VACHEL (1879–1931)
Born in Springfield, Illinois. Studied at Hiram College, Chicago Art Institute, New York School of Art. He lectured and recited his poems in many schools and colleges, wrote many volumes of poetry, including *General Booth Enters Heaven and Other Poems* (1913), *The Congo and Other Poems* (1914), *Collected Poems* (1925).

LOCKER-LAMPSON, FREDERICK (1821–1895)
Was a clerk in Somerset House and later in the British Admiralty. A volume of his light verse, *London Lyrics,* appeared in 1857.

LORENTZ, PARE (1905—)
Born West Virginia. Educated West Virginia Wesleyan. Served as motion picture critic on *Judge, Vanity Fair,* and *McCall's.* Wrote and directed the two documentary films, *The Plow that Broke the Plains* and *The River.* The latter has since appeared as a book combining sound track and pictures.

LOWES, JOHN LIVINGSTON (1867—)
Born in Indiana. A.B. Washington and Jefferson, 1886. Studied in Germany and at Harvard. Became Professor of English Literature at Harvard in 1918. Author of many learned articles and some illuminating, delightful books on poets and poetry, particularly *The Road to Xanandu.* Retired from teaching in 1939.

MACLEISH, ARCHIBALD (1892—)
Born in Glencoe, Illinois. A.B. Yale, 1915. LL.B. Harvard, 1919. M.A. Tufts, 1932. Served with the A.E.F. during the World War I. Author of the following volumes of verse: *The Happy Marriage, Streets in the Moon, Frescoes for Mr. Rockefeller's City.* His *Conquistador* won the Pulitzer Prize for Poetry in 1933.

MAGARET, HELENE (1906—)
Born in Omaha, Nebraska. Barnard College A.B. 1932. Van Rensselaer Prize for Poetry, 1932. Author of *The Trumpeting Crane* (1934), a narrative poem, and *Who Walk in Pride* (1945), a novel.

MANSFIELD, KATHERINE, pen name of Katherine Beauchamp (1890–1923)
British short story writer born in New Zealand. Her stories are collected in: *In a German Pension* (1916), *Bliss* (1920), *The Garden Party* (1922), and *The Dove's Nest* (1923). *Poems* appeared in 1923.

MARKHAM, EDWIN (1852–1940)

Poet, lecturer. Born in Oregon City, Ore. Educated San Jose Normal School and western colleges. Was principal and superintendent of schools in California until 1899. Author of *The Man with the Hoe, and Other Poems* (1899), *Lincoln, and Other Poems* (1901), *Gates of Paradise* (1920). His *Children in Bondage* is a collection of articles against child labor.

MARTIN, BETTY FIBLE (1907–)

Born and brought up in the country. Graduated from Barnard (1929) and studied at the Columbia University Law School. She operates a farm in northern Virginia and raises eggs for the Washington market. In 1941 had a short story in *Country Book*.

MASEFIELD, JOHN (1878–)

Born in Herefordshire. Ran away to sea as a boy and served three years on a merchant ship. Became a journalist on the *Manchester Guardian*. His first volume, *Salt Water Ballads* (1902), contained *Sea-Fever*. Since 1911, the date of *The Everlasting Mercy,* he has published many long narrative poems and novels. He was appointed poet laureate in 1930.

MAUGHAM, WILLIAM SOMERSET (1874–)

Born in Paris. Educated at Heidelberg, and trained for medicine at St. Thomas's Hospital, London. Author of novels, stories, and plays. *Of Human Bondage,* an autobiographical novel, published in 1915, is regarded as his greatest achievement.

MEIKLEJOHN, ALEXANDER (1872–)

Born in England, came to the U. S. in 1880. Graduated from Brown University and took his doctorate at Cornell in 1897. Recipient of many honorary degrees. President of Amherst College, 1912–24; Chairman of Experimental College, University of Wisconsin; Director of Center for Social Studies, San Francisco.

MILLAY, EDNA ST. VINCENT (1892–)

Born Rockland, Maine. A.B. Vassar College, 1917. Won first distinction as a poet with *Renascence and Other Poems* (1917). Won the Pulitzer Prize in 1922 for the best volume of verse. Wrote the libretto for *The King's Henchman* (1927), opera by Deems Taylor. Best known for her lyric poetry.

MILLER, CLYDE R. (1888–)

Born in Columbus and educated at Ohio State University. Began as high school teacher and journalist. Professor of Education, Teachers College, and founder of the Institute for Propaganda Analysis.

MILTON, JOHN (1608–1674)

This great poet of liberty was born in London and educated at St. Paul's School and Cambridge. *Areopagitica* (1644) was a plea for freedom of the press from the censorship of the Licensing Act. Its main ideas are written into the First Amendment of the Constitution of the United States. His translation from Euripides on Liberty appears on the title page of the first edition.

MOORE, THOMAS (1779–1852)

Born in Dublin and educated at Trinity College, Dublin. Studied law in London. Won recognition as musician and poet with his *Irish Melodies* (1807–35). He wrote narrative poems, such as *Lalla Rookh,* as well as lyrics. Also wrote a novel, histories, and biographies.

MORRIS, WILLIAM (1834–1895)

Educated at Exeter College, Oxford. Was active as decorator, manufacturer, printer and socialist. His poetry, mostly narrative, reflects his interest in Chaucer and the art and life of the Middle Ages.

MOSHER, JOHN (1892—)

Born at Ogdensburg, New York, and brought up in Albany. Educated at Williams (A.B. 1914). Short story writer and essayist. Has been on the staff of the *New Yorker* from its second year. A selection of his sketches appeared under the title of *Celibate at Midnight* (1940).

NEWMAN, JOHN HENRY (1801–1890)

Born in London. Studied at Oxford, became Fellow of Oriel College. Preacher to the University, 1831–32. Together with Pusey and Keble, inaugurated the Anglo-Catholic or Oxford Movement in the Church of England with the publication of *Tracts for the Times* (1833). Went into retirement at Littlemore. In 1845 was received into the Roman Church. As a reply to Charles Kingsley, wrote *Apologia pro Vita Sua* (1864), an account of his religious development. Created cardinal in 1879.

O'CONNOR, JOHNSON (1891—)

A.B. and A.M., Harvard. After doing astronomical mathematical research, metallurgical research, and electrical engineering research, organized a Human Engineering Laboratory for General Electric Co. to study applicants and employees. Organized and now directs Human Engineering Laboratory at Stevens Institute. Helped to establish other laboratories, including Johnson O'Connor Research Foundation in New York City. Author of books and articles on aptitudes and characteristics in employment groups.

O'NEILL, EUGENE (1888—)

Born on Broadway, the son of an actor, he spent his early childhood with his parents on tour. He attended Catholic schools, and was for a short time at Princeton. He has worked as a sailor and seen Honduras and South America; he has been an actor and a reporter. In 1913 after a physical breakdown, he turned to the study of the drama and to writing plays. He became the chief figure of the Provincetown Group. *Beyond the Horizon* (1920) marks the end of his apprenticeship, and has been followed by *Anna Christie, Emperor Jones, The Hairy Ape,* and *Mourning Becomes Electra.* He won the Pulitzer Prize three times with *Beyond the Horizon, Anna Christie,* and *Strange Interlude.*

OPPENHEIM, JAMES (1882–1939)

American short story writer, novelist, journalist, and poet. Born St. Paul, Minn. Studied at Columbia. From 1909 to 1924 he saw the publication of six volumes of his poetry. The last volume, *The Sea,* is a collection of his poetry.

PACE, C. ROBERT (1912—)

B.A., De Pauw University, 1933. M.A., University of Minnesota, 1935. Director of a study of graduates and students of University of Minnesota (1937–40), having as its purpose the revaluation of general education. Study published as *They Went to College,* 1941.

PARKER, JAMES REID (1909—)
This teacher and story writer was born in Jersey City, N. J. He has an A.B. from Lafayette College and an M.A. from Columbia. He was first an instructor and then a Professor of English at Brooklyn Polytechnic Institute. In 1943 he was commissioned captain in the U. S. Army. His stories have appeared in *Academic Procession* (1937) and *Short Stories from The New Yorker* (1940).

POE, EDGAR ALLAN (1809–1849)
Born in Boston of actor parents, left an orphan at three, brought up by John Allan of Richmond. Attended school in England. One year at University of Virginia and a short time at West Point. Poet, editor, literary critic, story writer. *The Murders in the Rue Morgue* (1841) is said to be the first detective story.

POUND, EZRA (1885—)
Born Hailey, Idaho. A.B., Hamilton College and A.M., University of Pennsylvania. A leader in the modern poetry movement. His first poems, *Personae,* appeared in 1909. Between 1928 and 1934 he published *XXX Cantos* and *Cantos XXXI–XLI.* He has lived much in Italy.

POWER, EILEEN (1889–1940)
Educated at Oxford High School and Girton College, Cambridge. Was director of Studies in History at Girton from 1913 to 1920. In 1931 became professor at the London School of Economics. Author of many studies of the Middle Ages and economic history.

PYLE, ERNIE (ERNEST TAYLOR) (1900–1945)
Born Dana, Ind. Indiana University 1919–23. Reporter and editor on La Porte (Ind.), Washington, and New York papers until 1935, when he began his career as a roving columnist. Wrote daily column from England, North Africa, Europe, and later the Pacific. The human qualities in his writing and his simple, direct, and friendly style made him overwhelmingly America's favorite correspondent in World War II. His books: *Ernie Pyle in England,* 1941; *Here is Your War,* 1943; *Brave Men,* 1944; *Last Chapter,* 1946.

QUILLER-COUCH, SIR ARTHUR (1863—)
Was born in Cornwall and educated at Oxford. He wrote many novels under the pen name of "Q." In 1912 he became Professor of English Literature at Cambridge University. In 1901 he edited *The Oxford Book of English Verse.* His nonfiction books include *The Art of Writing* (1916), *Pages of Prose* (1930), and *The Poet as Citizen* (1934).

RHODE, WILLIAM A. (1904—)
An amateur passion for fine food and fine cookery led him to write the book *Of Cabbages and Kings* (1938). The success of this book led the author to abandon the show business for the food industry. He now owns and operates his own catering company in New York and is author of *This Business of Carving* (1941).

ROBINSON, EDWIN ARLINGTON (1869–1935)
Born in Maine. Studied at Harvard. *The Children of the Night* (1897) was his first important volume of poems. *Collected Poems* won the Pulitzer Prize for 1921. *The Man Who Died Twice* won the prize in 1925, and *Tristram* won the prize in 1927.

ROBINSON, JAMES HARVEY (1863–1936)

Came from Illinois, studied at Harvard and Freiburg, and for many years was Professor of History at Columbia. While teaching he wrote a number of school histories which established new standards in the art of textbook writing. He resigned his position at Columbia to lecture at the New School for Social Research. His *Mind in the Making* is one of those very useful books which bring home to the man in the street the results of scientific thinking.

ROSSETTI, CHRISTINA (1830–1894)

Sister of D. G. Rossetti. Her work included poems of fantasy and verses for the young. The greater number of her poems are religious.

ROSSETTI, DANTE GABRIEL (1828–1882)

Son of an exiled Italian patriot. Educated at King's College, London. A painter of distinction. Made important translations from Italian poetry and wrote a number of lyrics and ballads throughout his life.

SAKI, pen name of Hector Hugh Munro (1870–1916)

Born in Burma, educated in England, served in Burma Military Police. On his return to England he wrote for the periodicals and gained fame for his sharp and witty political and social satires.

SANDBURG, CARL (1878—)

Born in Illinois. Studied at Lombard College. At various times he was soldier, truck-handler, dishwasher, harvest hand, advertising and newspaper writer. *Chicago Poems* (1916) was his first book of poems. Subsequent poems of his have been collected in *Cornhuskers* (1918), *Smoke and Steel* (1920). A great biography is *Abraham Lincoln, The Prairie Years* (1926), *The War Years* (1939).

SANTAYANA, GEORGE (1863—)

This poet, novelist, teacher, and philosopher was born in Spain and educated in Berlin and at Harvard. He taught at Harvard until 1912, when he resigned to write and travel. His important philosophical works, such as *The Life of Reason* (1905–1906), *Realms of Being* (1942), and *The Idea of Christ in the Gospels* (1946) are less well known to the general public than his novel, *The Last Puritan* (1935). His *Poems* appeared in 1923.

SAROYAN, WILLIAM (1908—)

Born in Fresno, California, and educated in the public schools of that city. This original and prolific writer burst on the literary world with *The Daring Young Man on the Flying Trapeze* (1934), a collection of short stories. This was followed by an avalanche of short stories till he turned to the theater and wrote *My Heart's in the Highlands* (1939). He rejected the Pulitzer Prize which was awarded for *The Time of Your Life* (1939). *My Name Is Aram* (1940) is his most mature work to date.

SASSOON, SIEGFRIED (1886—)

Educated at Clare College, Cambridge. He enlisted at the beginning of World War I and won a captaincy and the Military Cross for valor. He won recognition for his poetry with *The Old Huntsman and Other Poems* (1917). *Counter-Attack and Other Poems* (1918) contains many satires against war. He is also the author of the autobiographical prose works: *Memoirs of a Fox Hunting Man, Memoirs of an Infantry Officer,* and *Siegfried's Journey.*

SHAW, IRWIN (1913—)

Born in Brooklyn. He is well known for his plays, *Bury the Dead* (1936) and *The Gentle People* (1939). Many of his short stories about the war have appeared in *The New Yorker*. Two volumes of his stories have been published: *Sailor off the Bremen* (1939) and *Welcome to the City* (1942). During the war he was on the staff of *Stars and Stripes*.

SHEEAN, (JAMES) VINCENT (1899—)

Graduate of the University of Chicago. Foreign correspondent, contributor to the *New Republic, Atlantic Monthly, Asia*. His autobiography, *Personal History*, received high praise.

SHELLEY, PERCY BYSSHE (1792–1822)

Born in Sussex and educated at University College, Oxford, from which he was expelled for circulating a pamphlet on *The Necessity of Atheism*. Poetry inspired by revolutionary idealism. *When the Lamp Is Shattered* written not long before he was drowned while sailing off the Italian coast.

SHERMAN, STUART PRATT (1881–1926)

American critic and educator. For many years Professor of English at the University of Illinois. From 1924 till his death literary editor of the New York *Herald-Tribune*. Author of *Matthew Arnold, The Genius of America, Critical Woodcuts,* and *The Emotional Discovery of America,* the last published after his death.

SITWELL, EDITH (1887—)

This famous English poet and critic is sister to the younger Sitwells, Osbert and Sacheverell. Her poems have been gathered together in Collected Poems (1933). Her critical works include *Poetry and Criticism* (1926) and *Aspects of Modern Poetry* (1934).

SMITH, SAMUEL FRANCIS (1808–1895)

American Baptist clergyman. He wrote the national hymn, *America,* while he was a student at Andover Theological Seminary, in 1832, for a Fourth of July meeting in the Park Street Church, Boston. While pastor in Newton, Mass., he was editor of the *Christian Review*. A collected edition of his poems was published in 1895.

SPAETH, SIGMUND (1885—)

Born at Philadelphia. A.B. Haverford, 1905. Ph.D. Princeton, 1910. Musical critic. Author of numerous books on music, the appreciation of opera, and of magazine articles.

SPENDER, STEPHEN (1909—)

English poet and essayist. Studied at Oxford. *Poems* (1933) and *Vienna* (1934) contain his most notable work to date.

SPEYER, LEONORA (1872—)

Born in Washington, D. C. As a girl she was a professional violinist and appeared as a soloist with the New York and Boston Symphony Orchestras. She began writing verse in 1916 and her first volume of poems, *A Canopic Jar,* was published in 1921. Subsequent volumes of her poetry are *Fiddler's Farewell* (1926), for which she was awarded the Pulitzer Prize, *Naked Heel* (1931), and *Slow Wall* (1939). She teaches a class in the writing of poetry at Columbia University.

STEINBECK, JOHN ERNST (1902—)
Born in California. Educated at Salinas High School and Stanford University. His experience as reporter, bricklayer, watchman, and farm hand is reflected in his fiction. His novels include *The Grapes of Wrath* (1939) and *The Moon is Down* (1942). His short stories are collected in *The Red Pony* (1937), and *The Long Valley* (1938). His play *Of Mice and Men* was a success in 1937.

STEPHENS, JAMES (1882—)
Irish poet and story writer. Famous for his prose fantasy, *The Crock of Gold* (1912). Many of his stories appear in *Etched in Moonlight* (1928). His poems were collected in 1926 and again in 1931.

STEVENSON, ROBERT LOUIS (1850–1894)
The son of a distinguished engineer, he was born in Edinburgh, and educated in the schools and the university of that city. He devoted some years to the law, but his interest in literature diverted him into publishing essays and travel sketches. Ill health forced him to various parts of the world, to France, California, the Adirondacks, Hawaii, and finally to Samoa, where he died of tuberculosis. Besides his essays, he wrote *Dr. Jekyll and Mr. Hyde* and *Treasure Island*.

STRACHEY, LYTTON (1880–1932)
Son of a British general and colonial administrator. Studied at Trinity College, Cambridge. Created a sensation in 1918 with *Eminent Victorians,* a new venture in brief, realistic, and sometimes caustic biography. It was followed by *Queen Victoria* and *Elizabeth and Essex*.

SULLIVAN, FRANK (1892—)
Born at Saratoga Springs, N. Y. A.B. Cornell, 1914. Served in World War I. Journalist and humorist.

SWINBURNE, ALGERNON CHARLES (1837–1909)
Educated at Balliol College, Oxford. First attracted general attention by his *Poems and Ballads* (1866). He wrote voluminously—poetic dramas, lyrics, and prose essays on literary subjects.

SYMONDS, JOHN ADDINGTON (1840–1893)
English author. Educated at Harrow and Balliol College, Oxford. His longest prose work was *The Renaissance in Italy*. He excelled as a translator of the Greek poets, of Michelangelo and Campanella, and of the Latin poems of the Middle Ages. His versions of medieval student verse appear in the volume *Wine, Women and Song*.

SYNGE, JOHN MILLINGTON (1871–1909)
Born in a suburb of Dublin of English Protestant ancestry. Took his degree at Trinity College, Dublin. His passions were nature, music, and languages. He studied music in Germany; lived a poverty-stricken life in Paris, studying French literature and writing. William Butler Yeats persuaded him to return to Ireland, and there he lived on the wild west coast and the Aran Islands. His plays, especially the *Riders to the Sea* and *The Playboy of the Western World,* are regarded as the greatest products of the Irish Renaissance.

TATE, ALLEN (1899—)
Born in Clarke County, Ky. B.A. Vanderbilt University, 1922. Was a Guggenheim fellow for two years. Author of biographies of Stonewall Jackson, Jefferson Davis, Robert E. Lee. He has published two volumes of poems: *Mr. Pope*

and Other Poems and *Poems* (1928–1931). He is one of the leaders of the Agrarian Movement in the South.

TAYLOR, BERT LESTON (1866-1921)

Born at Goshen, Mass. Educated College of the City of New York. Essayist and poet. He conducted a column, "A line-o'-type or two" for years for the Chicago *Tribune*. Verses, which had for the most part appeared in his column, were collected in *A line-o'-verse or two* (1911), *Motley Measures* (1913), and others.

TENNYSON, ALFRED, first Baron Tennyson (1809-1892)

Born in Lincolnshire and educated at Trinity College, Cambridge, where he became acquainted with A. H. Hallam, whose death in 1833 was the occasion of *In Memoriam* (1850). Was appointed poet laureate in 1850 on death of Wordsworth. His poetry deals with many modern problems in religion, politics, and economics.

THOMPSON, DOROTHY (1894—)

Educated at Syracuse University (A.B. 1914) and at Vienna. Newspaper reporter, correspondent, and editorial writer. Author of *Culture under the Nazis* (1936), *Essentials of Democracy* (1938), *Let the Record Speak* (1939), *Christian Ethics and Western Culture* (1940), and of the widely syndicated column *On the Record*.

THOREAU, HENRY DAVID (1817–1862)

American naturalist and individualist philosopher, friend of Emerson and Hawthorne. *Walden, or Life in the Woods* (1854) was based on his two-year solitary residence in a cabin on the shore of Walden Pond, near Concord, Mass. Other books include *The Maine Woods, Cape Cod, Winter,* and his *Journals,* all published after his death.

THURBER, JAMES GROVER (1894—)

Educated at Ohio State University. An editor of *The New Yorker* where many of his humorous and satiric pieces have appeared. Author of *My Life and Hard Times* (1933), *Let Your Mind Alone* (1937), *The Last Flower* (1939), and *Fables for Our Time*. He has also done a play, *Male Animal,* in collaboration with Elliot Nugent.

TWAIN, MARK, pen name of Samuel Langhorne Clemens (1835–1910)

American humorist born in Florida, Missouri, and brought up in Hannibal, Missouri, which gave him the setting for his famous *Tom Sawyer* (1876) and *Huckleberry Finn* (1884). *The Deceitful Turkey,* although not published till 1906, is based on memories of the same period.

VAN DOREN, MARK (1894—)

Born at Hope, Illinois. University of Illinois, A.B., Columbia, M.A., Ph.D. Professor of English at Columbia. Essayist, editor, critic, poet, novelist. Author of the following volumes of poetry: *Spring Thunder and Other Poems, 7 P.M. and Other Poems, Jonathan Gentry*. For *Collected Poems* (1939) he received the Pulitzer Prize.

VATSEK, JOAN (1916—)

New York librarian, daughter of a Hungarian consulate official. She has studied at McGill University and at Columbia, and has taught at a convent in Cairo.

Author of a book of poems, *The Cloak and the Flower*. *But It's O! in My Heart* is her second published story.

VILLA, JOSÉ GARCIA (1918—)
   Born in Manila, P. I., and educated at the University of New Mexico and Columbia. Villa received great critical acclaim for his first volume of poems, *Have Come, Am Here* (1942). "His poetry," says Edman, "reveals an intense and inventive imagery." He received a Guggenheim Fellowship in 1943 and a grant from the American Academy of Arts and Letters. He is in charge of the poetry section at Columbia University Bookstore.

WHITE, ELWYN BROOKS (1899—)
   Born Mount Vernon, N. Y. Educated Cornell. Reporter, free lance writer, and contributor to magazines including *The New Yorker* and *Harpers*. Author of *The Lady Is Cold,* poems (1929), *Is Sex Necessary?* (with J. Thurber) (1929), *Every Day Is Saturday* (1934), *The Fox of Peapack* (1938). Edited *A Subtreasury of American Humor* (1941).

WHITMAN, WALT (1819–1892)
   Born on Long Island, New York. Schoolteacher, editor, journalist, war nurse and poet. His poems were first published in *Leaves of Grass* (1855). Additional poems were added in subsequent editions. His poems on the Civil War were published in *Drum-Taps* (1865).

WHITTIER, JOHN GREENLEAF (1807–1892)
   American poet of Quaker parents. Born and educated at Haverhill, Mass. A leader in the American Anti-Slavery movement. Famous for *Snowbound, The Tent on the Beach,* a cycle of verse tales, and his ballads. J. R. Lowell called *Skipper Ireson's Ride* "by all odds the best of modern ballads."

WIDDEMER, MARGARET (1880—)
   Poet, and fiction writer. Born in Doylestown, Pa., and educated at Drexel Institute Library School. *Old Road to Paradise* (poems) shared with Sandburg the Poetry Society prize for 1919. Her many novels extend from *The Rose Garden Husband* (1915) to *Constancia Herself* (1945).

WILLIS, NATHANIEL PARKER (1806–1867)
   Born at Portland, Maine. Yale, A.B. Established and edited the *American Monthly Magazine*. Author of plays, essays, and poems.

WOOLF, VIRGINIA (1882–1941)
   Born in London. In the home of her father, Leslie Stephen, biographer and literary critic, she met Meredith, Lowell, Stevenson, Ruskin, and Hardy. Married Leonard Woolf in 1912. Author of many novels, including *To the Lighthouse* and *Orlando;* also of the provocative volumes of essays, *A Room of One's Own* and *The Common Reader.*

WORDSWORTH, WILLIAM (1770-1850)
   Born in Cockermouth, England. Educated St. John's College, Cambridge. Attracted by ideals of French Revolution, but repelled later by Reign of Terror. Fame established by *Lyrical Ballads* (1798), containing poems by him and Coleridge. Made poet laureate in 1843.